©Rand McNally & Co., R. L. 84-S-145 Renewal

INTERNATIONAL BUSINESS

Introduction and Essentials

INTERNATIONAL BUSINESS
Introduction and Essentials

Donald A. Ball
California State University, Stanislaus

Wendell H. McCulloch, Jr.
California State University, Long Beach

1989   Third edition

BPI
IRWIN

Homewood, Illinois 60430

To Vicky and Sally
Don, Jr., Dulce, Lianne and Malinda

Editor: John R. Weimeister
Developmental Editor: Rhonda K. Harris
Production Manager: Bette Ittersagen
Production Editor: Ann Cassady
Copy Editing Coordinator: Jean Roberts
Designer: Vargas/Williams Design
Compositor: Carlisle Communications

ISBN 0-256-05825-3

Library of Congress Catalog Card No. 87–72394

Printed in the United States of America

3 4 5 6 7 8 9 0 DO 5 4 3 2 1 0 9

PREFACE

We are extremely pleased that not only users of the first edition adopted the second edition, but that many more of you joined us in using the revised text. It was also gratifying that so many of you took the time to call or write us about new material and improvements that you wished to see in the third edition. As you can imagine, there were numerous and divergent opinions. We gave all of your suggestions serious thought and tried to comply with everyone's wishes to make this a better text. The third edition is truly a team effort.

Scope and Purpose of the Text

As in the previous editions, we begin the text by describing the nature of international business. In Section 2, we examine elements of the international environment and illustrate their effect on management practices. In the final section, we reverse the procedure and deal with the management function, illustrating how management deals with the forces it encounters.

The text continues to be written for the first course in international business, which is generally taken after entry-level courses in the functional areas. Our aim is to provide the student or businessperson with a relatively simple, but accurate, clear introduction to the essentials of international business and the environmental forces that impact on it. When the book is used for an international business course in an MBA program, as a number of you have done, we recommend that the students be required to do supplemental reading. This is common in most graduate courses, and our lists of suggested readings include many diverse, current publications for this purpose.

Changes in This Edition

We had numerous requests for comprehensive cases, and we are pleased that Professor Dave Hunt of the University of Southern Mississippi permitted us to include three of his cases. They include data he gathered while a Fulbright professor in Kenya and are from his recently published book, *Strategic Management: Kenya, A Book of Cases.*

Chapter 3 has an expanded section on present-day thought about economic development and a new section, Contemporary Theories of Foreign Direct Investment. Both additions were in response to numerous requests.

The increased seriousness of the world debt crisis prompted us to discuss this topic in Chapter 4. Those of you who requested a more detailed discussion

v

of the balance of payments will find it in Chapter 5, where there is also a section on the growth in usage of the European currency unit. A number of you felt that "Financial Forces," previously Chapter 10, should follow Chapter 5, "International Monetary System." This change has been made in the third edition.

The Bhopal disaster, the Rhine spill, and their consequences for multinationals are the basis for a new section, Contamination of Resources in the Physical Forces chapter. A case based on the Bhopal accident appears at the end of the chapter.

In our chapter on sociocultural forces, we expanded the section on religion to include additional Far Eastern religions and a short history of Islam. This history discusses the division between the Sunnis and the Shiites, the basis for much that is occurring in the Middle East. This section was requested by several instructors, particularly Professor Jay Vora of St. Cloud State University.

Because of the growth in privatization of government-owned industry, we added this topic to Chapter 9. Material on terrorism, another significant topic for businesspeople, was updated. Chapter 10 has new material on antitrust and restrictive trade practices and more information on protectionism, another "hot topic." Also new to Chapter 10 is a discussion of national differences in the treatment of bribes.

Chapter 12 has been rewritten to incorporate a section on U.S. competitiveness at the macro level, a subject much discussed by scholars, politicians, and businesspeople. In Chapter 17, we discuss the increase in inter-Comecon trade at the expense of East-West trade. A checklist for selling to the Peoples Republic of China is also new.

Material on currency and interest rate swaps as well as on countertrade has been included in Chapter 18. In Chapter 20, we expanded the discussion of quality circles and robotics. The planning section of Chapter 21 has been rewritten to reflect changes in planning by MNEs. Finally, because of many requests, we added a new chapter, 23, on the multinational firm.

New Supplements

In addition to the comprehensive Instructor's Manual available with this text, the test bank is now available in three formats: as a printed manual, on floppy disk for use with IBM and IBM-compatible personal computers, and TeleTest, a customized, phone-in service available from the publisher. The test bank has been improved and expanded in this edition.

For students, the supplemental package includes for the first time a Student Study Guide. Written by Professor Basil Janavaras of Mankato State University, the Student Study Guide includes additional questions for review, outlines, summaries, and other material to enrich the study of international business.

Acknowledgments

To the long list of people to whom we are indebted, we want to add Professors Rufus Barton, Murray State University; James R. Bradshaw, Brigham Young University; Dennis Carter, University of North Carolina—Wilmington; Mark Chadwin, Old Dominion University; Peter DeWitt, University of Central Florida; Galpira Eshigi, Illinois State University; Prem Gandhi, State University of New York—Plattsburgh; Stan Guzell, Youngstown State University; Gary Hannem, Mankato State University; Paul Jenner, Southwest Missouri State University; Michael Kublin, University of New Haven; Eddie Lewis, University of Southern Mississippi; Lois Ann EcElroy Lindell, Wartburg College; Carol Lopilato, California State University, Dominguez Hills; John Setnicky, Mobile College; John Thanopoulos, Akron University; Hsin-Min Tong, Radford University; Dennis Vanden Bloomen, University of Wisconsin—Stout; and George Westacott, State University of New York—Binghamton. We continue to invite your suggestions for making this a more useful text and thank all of you for your interest and input.

Donald A. Ball
Wendell H. McCulloch, Jr.

CONTENTS

INTERNATIONAL BUSINESS

Introduction and Essentials

SECTION 1

THE NATURE OF INTERNATIONAL BUSINESS

Section I describes the nature and scope of international business and introduces the three environments in which international business managers must operate. How well they perform in their undertakings will depend in great measure on their understanding of the domestic, international, and foreign environments.

Chapter 1 presents the concept of the three environments and their forces. From the history of international business, we learn that although the international firm existed before the Civil War, it differed markedly from the present-day multinational enterprise, which is characterized by its explosive growth and closer central control of foreign operations. Managers, realizing that more company personnel must acquire some knowledge of international business, turned to the colleges and universities for assistance in training. From an original base of international trade theory, educators, through intensive research and study, came to include related material from other disciplines, and a new field of study, international business, emerged.

In Chapter 2, information is presented to assist you in comprehending the dynamic growth and the magnitude of both international trade and foreign investment. We discuss why firms go abroad, and we examine the many ways that they do it.

An overview of the theories of international trade and economic development is given in Chapter 3 because a basic understanding of this material will not only help explain the actions already taken by government officials but will frequently provide insight into what they plan to do.

CHAPTER 1

INTRODUCTION TO INTERNATIONAL BUSINESS

"Multinational business is becoming so important that the business school had better prepare all its students for it. The young man who graduates from one of our business schools without the realization of the scope and thrust of multinational business is as unprepared for the reality of our economy as the young man who graduates without a little accounting knowledge."

E. A. Costanzo, vice president, Citibank

4

Learning Objectives

After you study this chapter, you should know:

1. What the distinctions are between firms of the early 1900s and present-day multinational enterprises.
2. The reasons why international business must be a separate field of study.
3. That there are three environments—domestic, foreign, and international—in which the multinational enterprise operates.
4. The forces in these environments that are categorized as controllable and uncontrollable.
5. The many terms used to describe a firm that has substantial operations in more than one country.

Key Words and Concepts

Multinational enterprise (MNE)
Domestic environment
Foreign environment
Self-reference criterion
International environment
Controllable environmental forces
Uncontrollable environmental forces

Business Incident

The magnitude of the impact of international firms on the U.S. economy is not generally appreciated. One should note first of all that total U.S. exports have recently passed $100 billion per year and that total foreign direct investment by U.S. companies has also recently passed the $100 billion mark. Second, a large number of industries have a very significant percentage of their operations overseas. In 1974, the U.S. drug industry, for example, had 31 percent of its operations abroad; farm machinery, 27 percent; construction machinery, 27 percent; tires, 22 percent, office machinery, 20 percent, soaps and detergents, 20 percent; motor vehicles, 18 percent; soft drinks, 18 percent; and so forth.

Of the 500 largest U.S. industrial corporations, at least 25 make more than 50 percent of their profits from their international operations. In 1974, these included International Harvester, 75 percent; Libby, McNeill & Libby, 62 percent; Gillette, 61 percent; Otis Elevator, 60 percent; Pfizer, 60 percent; Coca-Cola, 59 percent; Dow Chemical, 57 percent; Uniroyal, 57 percent; American Standard, 57 percent; IBM, 54 percent; and most of the major oil companies.

It is of overwhelming importance and should therefore be clarified at the outset that, in the context of this report, international business is not confined to doing business within foreign countries. Insofar as the number of business-people is concerned, it is only a small portion of the whole. International business includes all aspects of exporting and importing goods and services in addition to the operation of overseas offices, manufacturing and processing plants, mining operations, and so on. Thus, when one speaks of educating or training people for international business, one refers to all those individuals whose jobs can be better performed if they are familiar with the economy, politics, or culture of one or more foreign countries or if they have an understanding of international politics, economics, finance, or transportation. This includes a wide variety of people who work in various capacities in different types of firms, yet never leave the United States. Their business is affected by competition from imports or utilizes imported parts or services; they correspond with foreign firms; they meet and deal with visiting foreign businessmen or government officials; their work entails an understanding of the foreign sales or foreign operations of their company; they must make decisions that affect, indirectly, the foreign sales or operations of their company; they must fully understand the environment in which their foreign operations are located in order to communicate, in the complete sense of the term, with the company's overseas personnel.

Thus it is seen that the need for international education for the business world is not restricted to the 35,000 businessmen who live overseas, nor to the people who work in the U.S. offices of the 6,000 large companies that have overseas operations, nor to the 20,000 firms that engage in exporting. International business and its indirect effects have become a pervasive factor in the U.S. business scene. It is difficult to point to a firm of any size that is not involved in or affected by some aspect of international business.

From *Business and International Education*
(Washington, D.C.: American Council on Education, 1977), pp. 9–10.

*A*lthough the report from which the business incident was taken was published in 1977, its message is more relevant today than when it was written—*there is an emphatic need for businesspeople to have some knowledge of international business*. Obviously, any firm that derives a sizable portion of its earnings from overseas operations must have among its managers people who are knowledgeable in this area, but as the task force that prepared the report points out, the need for such individuals is not restricted to these firms alone, because "every firm, whether located within the national borders or not, operates in an international environment. . . . International political, economic, and social factors play a growing role in the affairs of American business, and it is only fair to restate that no major area of American business activity today is substantially unaffected by events and conditions occurring outside the United States."[1]

If this is so, and certainly a vice president of one of the most important multinational banks believes it is (see quotation at the beginning of the chapter), then the business school graduate must have some international business training. The agency responsible for accrediting colleges of business, American Assembly of Collegiate Schools of Business (AACSB), agreed with this analysis and in 1974 changed its standards to require that the curriculum of business schools reflect the *worldwide* as well as the domestic aspects of business.

What are the reasons for this emphasis on international business? Are the practices of exporting and establishing operations overseas of recent origin? Let us take a brief look at the history of international business.

History of International Business

International trade and the international firm are not new aspects of business. Even before the time of Christ, merchants were sending representatives abroad to sell their goods. The British East India Company, a trading firm chartered in 1600, established foreign branches, as did a number of American colonial traders in the 1700s. Early examples of American foreign direct investment are the English plants set up by Colt Fire Arms and Ford* (vulcanized rubber), which

*This Ford was no relation to Henry Ford.

were established before the Civil War began. Both operations failed, however, after only a few years.

The first successful American venture into foreign production was the Scotch factory that Singer Sewing Machine built in 1868. By 1880, Singer had become a worldwide organization with an outstanding foreign sales organization and several overseas manufacturing plants. Other firms soon followed, and by 1914 at least 37 American companies had production facilities in two or more overseas locations.[2] Foreign direct investment was no American monopoly, however, as such European concerns as Unilever (Dutch-English), Nestlé (Swiss), Philips (Dutch), and Imperial Chemical (English) were also becoming established in various foreign countries.

This clearly illustrates that multinational firms of a sort existed well before World War I. Why then have they only recently become the object of much discussion and investigation? What differences, if any, are there between the international business firm of the early 1900s and the present-day **multinational enterprise (MNE)**?

Explosive Growth

One important difference is the explosive growth in both the size and the number of U.S. and foreign multinational concerns in the last two decades. Estimates place the total value of foreign direct investment* at about $650 billion, six times the $105 billion for 1967 calculated by the Organization for Economic Cooperation and Development (OECD).[3] During the same period, U.S. foreign direct investment rose from $59 billion to approximately $230 billion. According to a survey by the European Community, approximately 10,000 multinationals are in existence worldwide—4,534 of these are based in the European Community and 2,570 in the United States. However, the sales of the less numerous U.S. multinationals are 43 percent higher than those of the European multinationals.[4]

As a result of this expansion, the subsidiaries of the multinationals have become increasingly important in the industrial and economic life of many nations, both developed and developing, a situation that is in sharp contrast to the one that existed when the dominant economic interests were in the hands of local citizens. The increasing importance of foreign-owned firms in their local economies has caused a number of governments to view this change as a threat to their autonomy. Critics of large multinational firms cite such statistics as the following to "prove" that governments are powerless before them:

1. Only 21 nations have GNPs greater than the total sales of General Motors, the world's largest multinational.

---

*Direct investment is defined in the United States as ownership by an individual or a corporation of 10 percent or more of the voting stock or other means of control over an enterprise. Ownership of less than 10 percent of the voting stock is defined as portfolio investment.

2. The total sales of General Motors surpass the sum of the gross national products of 32 African countries.

As Table 1–1 illustrates, these statements are certainly true. In fact, if nations and industrial firms are ranked by gross national product and total sales, respectively, of the first 100 on the list, 39 are industrial firms. It should be pointed out, however, that regardless of the parent company's size, subsidiaries of these firms operate under the authority of the host nations' governments. MNE affiliates must comply with local laws or be subject to legal action and even expropriation.* Outstanding examples are the loss of the Chilean subsidiaries of Pfizer and ITT and the seizure of Dow Corning's assets in Venezuela by that country's government.[5]

Closer Central Control

A second important difference between the modern multinational firm and the earlier international company is the much closer control now exercised by headquarters.[6] Even though the subsidiaries are scattered over the globe, management in the home office coordinates and integrates their activities. Such control has been made possible by fast air travel and by the ability to rapidly transmit and analyze large amounts of information by means of the telephone, telex, and computers.

In earlier days, overseas travel was by ship, communications were handled primarily by letter, and once information arrived in the home office, several days were required for processing before top management could act on it. Under those conditions, there was little possibility of closely coordinating foreign operations and the local subsidiaries had to be given considerable independence. In addition, poor transportation facilities between countries and the presence of tariff and nontariff trade barriers made it difficult for a firm in one country to market its products in another. This meant that there was less need for close integration, and, thus each subsidiary tended to operate in its own local market.

However, these conditions were changing. The formation of regional marketing groups such as the European Community and the European Free Trade Association and the improvements of transportation facilities made intercountry sales much more feasible. Thus, closer central control became both possible and necessary.

Host Nations' Reaction

As early as the 1950s, host nation governments began to realize that the establishment of an increasing number of businesses controlled by managements out-

---

Expropriation is the seizure of foreign-owned assets by a government. Prompt, adequate, and effective compensation must be made. Expropriation and related subjects are dealt with in Chapters 9 and 10.

Table 1-1

Ranking of MNEs and Nations According to GNP or Total Sales

Rankings	Nation or Firm	GNP or Total Sales for 1985 ($ billions)
21	Sweden	$99.1
22	*General Motors*	96.4
23	South Korea	88.4
24	*Exxon*	86.7
25	Indonesia	86.6
26	Belgium	83.3
27	*Royal Dutch Shell*	81.7
28	Poland	79.0
29	Nigeria	75.9
30	Austria	69.1
31	South Africa	65.3
32	Argentina	65.1
33	Taiwan	63.8
34	Bulgaria	58.1
35	Norway	57.6
36	Denmark	57.3
37	Turkey	56.1
38	*Mobil Oil*	56.0
39	Algeria	55.2
40	Venezuela	53.8
41	Finland	53.5
42	*British Petroleum*	53.1
43	*Ford Motor*	52.8
44	*IBM*	50.1
45	Yugoslavia	47.9
46	*Texaco*	46.3
47	Thailand	42.1
48	*Chevron*	41.7
49	Colombia	37.6
50	Pakistan	36.2
51	Greece	35.3
52	*AT&T*	34.9
53	Hong Kong	33.8
54	Philippines	32.6
55	Egypt	32.2
56	Malaysia	31.9
57	*Du Pont*	29.5
58	*General Electric*	28.3
59	*Standard Oil (Indiana)*	27.2
60	Libya	27.0
61	*IRI (Italy)*	26.8
62	United Arab Emirates	26.4
63	*Toyota*	26.0

Sources: World Bank, *World Bank Atlas 1987,* (Washington, D.C., 1987); and "The World's Largest Industrial Corporations," *Fortune,* August 4 1986, p. 169. Eastern-bloc and Taiwan data from *Handbook of Economic Statistics, 1985,* published by Central Intelligence Agency, September 1985.

side their jurisdiction was resulting in local firms (subsidiaries) that could pursue objectives in conflict with their own. This, they believed, would weaken national sovereignty.

For example, if government leaders believed it necessary to institute a tight monetary policy and thus restrict the amount of capital available for industrial expansion, they feared that foreign-owned subsidiaries might upset their plans by bringing in capital from abroad. If they attempted to raise taxes to reduce purchasing power, absentee owners might shift production elsewhere, and thus sources of employment might be lost.

As governments strove to provide more infrastructure, such as highways, educational facilities, housing, and all the myriad elements of a higher level of living, they required more foreign exchange. These efforts would be weakened by anything that reduced its availability, such as fees paid to outsiders for management services and technological assistance or rules by home offices prohibiting subsidiaries from exporting or buying lower-priced raw materials in the open market rather than from the parent company.

Just how pervasive practices of this kind were was not clear. The multinational enterprise was a new concept, and its operations were not fully understood. To be able to cope with such practices, governments had to know more about the multinationals. By the early 1970s, various organizations, national and supranational, were studying this new kind of business organization. The United Nations established a Commission on Transnational Corporations and an Information and Research Center at UN headquarters to deal on a continuous basis with issues relating to MNE activities. Workshops were set up to train government officials who negotiate with these firms. A U.S. Senate foreign affairs subcommittee conducted an in-depth investigation. All over the world, government technicians, academicians, and business writers were publishing books and studies on the various aspects of the multinational enterprise.[7]

International Business as a Separate Field of Study

The growing importance of foreign markets to international firms plus the fact that thousands of concerns were venturing overseas for the first time made it imperative that managers know something about the intricacies of doing business abroad. International business was becoming too significant to allow managements to continue to train personnel by sending promising but inexperienced persons to the overseas "minor leagues," and so industry turned to the colleges and universities for assistance in training. This put the responsibility on educators who soon realized that the teaching tools, which had come primarily from the study of international trade, were inadequate. To rectify this situation, academicians intensified their study and research from which the new field of international business emerged. It has been much expanded from the initial emphasis on international economics and now includes related material from sociology, anthropology, jurisprudence, political science, geography, and business administration—all of these are fields about which international business managers must have some knowledge.

Adding international aspects as an appendage to the study of a domestic business function does not provide an adequate framework for examining the differences between the domestic and foreign environments in order to understand how these dissimilarities influence management decisions. International business as a separate field of study not only accomplishes this but also provides a means of studying the principal means of conducting international business, the multinational enterprise, whose management requires an expertise in handling situations rarely found in a purely domestic operation.

However, there are those who argue that a separate field of study is unnecessary because the concepts learned in the functional areas of business are universal in nature and can be applied in any part of the world. Our experience leads us to believe that this argument has some foundation. Certain concepts and business practices can be transferred intact, but herein lies a trap—not all of them can. Because of the differences among the foreign environments and the presence of an international environment, some concepts and business practices must be modified, while others cannot be used at all.

Why Is International Business Different?

International business differs from domestic business in that a firm operating across borders must deal with the forces of three kinds of environments—domestic, foreign, and international. In contrast, a firm whose business activities are carried out within the borders of one country needs to be concerned essentially with only the domestic environment. However, no domestic firm is entirely free from the foreign or international environmental forces because the possibility of having to face competition from foreign imports or from foreign competitors that set up operations in its own market is always present. (See Figure 1–1.) Let us first examine these forces and then see how they operate in the three environments.

Forces in the Environments

Environment as used here is the sum total of all the forces surrounding and influencing the life and development of the firm. The forces themselves can be classified as *external* or *internal*. Furthermore, inasmuch as management has

Figure 1-1

THE FOREIGN
FOOTWEAR RACE
FOR THE US MARKET
Page 20

Financial Times of London, World Business Weekly, August 24, 1981

no direct control over them (though it can exert an influence), the external forces are commonly called **uncontrollable environmental forces**. They consist of the following:

1. Competitive
2. Distributive
3. Economic
4. Financial
5. Legal

6. Physical
7. Political
8. Sociocultural
9. Labor
10. Technological

The elements over which management does have some command are the internal forces, such as the factors of production (capital, raw materials, and people) and the activities of the organization (personnel, finance, production, and marketing). These are the **controllable environmental forces** that management must administer in order to adapt to changes in the uncontrollable variables. For instance, when the government decreed that cyclamates could no longer be employed as artificial sweeteners (uncontrollable variable), canners responded by reformulating their products to eliminate them (controllable variable). The process of adaptation does not imply that managers must wait passively for changes to occur, to which they then react. In fact, the most successful administrators are those who are so knowledgeable about the environmental forces that they are not only prepared and waiting but may even contribute to these changes.

The Domestic Environment

The **domestic environment** is composed of the controllable and uncontrollable forces that originate in the home country. Obviously, these are the ones with which managers are most familiar. Being domestic forces does not preclude their affecting foreign operations, however. For example, if the home country is suffering from a shortage of foreign currency, the government may place restrictions on overseas investment to reduce its outflow. As a result, managements of multinationals find that they cannot expand overseas facilities as they would like to do. In another instance from real life, a labor union striking the home-based plants learned that management was supplying parts from its foreign subsidiaries. The strikers contacted the foreign unions, which pledged not to work overtime to supply what the struck plants could not. The impact of this domestic environmental force was felt overseas as well as at home.

Foreign Environments

The forces in the **foreign environments** are the same as those in the domestic environment except that they occur in foreign nations. However, they operate differently for several reasons, including the following.

Different Force Values

Even though the kinds of forces in the two environments are identical, their values often differ widely, and at times they are completely opposed to each other. A good example of diametrically opposed political force values and the bewilderment they create for multinational managers is the case of Dresser Industries and the Soviet pipeline. In June 1982, President Reagan extended the American embargo against shipments of equipment for the pipeline to include foreign companies manufacturing equipment under U.S. license. The Dresser home office instructed the Dresser French subsidiary to stop work on an order for compressors. In August, however, the French government ordered Dresser France to defy the embargo and begin scheduled deliveries under penalty of both civil and criminal sanctions. As the Dresser vice president for finance put it, "The order put Dresser between a rock and a hard place."[8]

Changes Difficult to Assess

Another problem with the foreign forces is that they are frequently difficult to assess, especially their legal and political elements. A highly nationalistic law may be passed to appease a section of the population. To all outward appearances, a government may appear to be against foreign investment, yet pragmatic leaders may actually encourage it. A good example is Mexico. Legislation was enacted that prohibited foreign firms from having wholly owned subsidiaries, but there was a clause permitting exceptions, "if the investment contributes to the welfare of the nation." In 1986, IBM was successful in obtaining permission to establish a wholly owned subsidiary under this clause.

Decision Making More Complex

The multiplicity of the forces in foreign environments makes decision making in those environments more complex than decision making in the domestic environment. Consider managers in the home office who must make decisions affecting subsidiaries in just 10 different countries (many MNEs are in 20 countries or more). They must not only take into account the domestic forces; they must also evaluate the influence of 10 foreign national environments. Instead of having to consider the effects of a single set of 10 forces, as do their domestic counterparts, they have to contend with 10 sets of 10 forces, both individually and collectively, because there may be some interaction.

For example, if management agrees to labor's demands at one foreign subsidiary, the chances are that it will have to offer a similar settlement at another subsidiary because of the tendency of unions to exchange information across borders. Furthermore, as we shall observe throughout the text, not only are there many sets of forces, but there are also extreme differences among them.

Another common cause of the added complexity of foreign environments is managers' unfamiliarity with other cultures. To make matters worse, they will ascribe to others their own preferences and reactions. Thus, the American production manager, facing a backlog of orders, offers his workers extra pay for overtime. When they fail to show up, he is perplexed. "Back home, they always want to make more money." He fails to understand that the workers prefer time off to more money. This *unconscious* reference to the managers' own cultural values, called **self-reference criterion,** is probably the biggest cause of international business blunders. Successful managers are careful to examine a problem in terms of foreign cultural traits as well as their own.

Forces Interrelated

In the chapters that follow, it will be evident that the forces are often interrelated. This in itself is no novelty, because the same situation confronts the domestic manager. What is often different, however, is the types and degrees of interaction that occur. For instance, the combination of high-cost capital and an abundance of unskilled labor in many lesser developed countries may lead to the use of a lower level of technology than would be employed in the more industrialized nations. In other words, given a choice between installing costly, specialized machinery with few workers or less expensive, general-purpose machinery requiring a larger labor force, management will frequently choose the latter when faced with high interest rates and a large pool of available workers. Another example of interaction is that of the physical and sociocultural forces. Barriers to the free movement of a nation's people, such as mountain ranges or deserts, help maintain pockets of very distinct cultures within a country.

International Environment

The **international environment** is essentially the interaction between the environmental forces of the home country and those of the various foreign nations where the company does business. Personnel at the headquarters of a multinational enterprise work in the international environment, whereas personnel in a foreign subsidiary do not unless they too are engaged in international trade through direct exporting or through management of other foreign affiliates. In other words, the sales manager of General Motors–Peru does *not* work in the international environment if he or she sells automobiles only in Peru. Should GM-Peru export to Bolivia, then that person is affected by forces of both the domestic and a foreign environment and is therefore operating in the international environment. Also included in the international environment are the supranational organizations whose actions affect the business community. These are: (1) worldwide bodies such as the World Bank, (2) regional economic groupings of nations (European Community), and (3) organizations of nations bound by industry agreements, of which the Organization of Petroleum Exporting Countries is an example.

International
Business Model

The relationships of the forces in the three environments we have been discussing form the basis for our international business model.

These relationships and their interaction may be likened to a set of gears, as shown in Figure 1–2. The external forces are represented by the gear teeth, which must mesh properly or the system, the multinational enterprise, cannot function. The internal, controllable forces drive the gears and are depicted in our environmental model by the drive shafts at the gears' centers. The interaction of

Japan Air Lines photo by Morris Simoncelli

Tokyo by night.

The Nature
of International
Business

International business today differs vastly from what it was before World War II, a time considered a turning point by many. Although international firms existed well before that time, it was not until the 1950s that international business began its explosive growth. In the last 20 years, international trade has expanded from $200 billion to $2 trillion per year, and foreign investment has risen from $100 billion to $500 billion.

Along with this growth in volume, there has been an increase in the number of countries participating in international business. Japan has become a formidable competitor, and firms from newly industrialized countries such as South Korea, Singapore, Malaysia, India, Brazil, and Taiwan now challenge traditional world leaders. Many other developing nations have international companies as well. A number of factors are responsible for these changes.

To remain competitive both at home and abroad, firms in the United States, Europe, and later Japan, moved production facilities to countries with lower labor costs and began sourcing products and components there. The resultant industrial buildup in the countries with new production facilities created a new group of competitors in the world market. Governments of developing countries also created new competitors when they permitted multinational firms to establish subsidiaries on the condition that part of the firms' outputs would be exported.

Another change is the emergence of global markets and global products. In earlier times, multinational enterprises would develop a process or technology, introduce it in its domestic market, and later market it abroad. Today, the rapid global infusion of technology makes this strategy impossible. Too many world competitors with comparable technical skills exist now to allow one company to maintain a technical monopoly for long. Moreover, research and development costs—plus the initial capital needed to launch a new venture—are so great for technically advanced products that firms must offer them internationally. Because no single market is large enough to support the investment, products must be designed for the global market.

An additional incentive to market globally is the fact that for many products, consumers the world over are becoming similar in education, purchasing power, and lifestyle. Marketers claim that differences among the age groups in Europe, the United States, and Japan are greater than the differences across borders.

The International Environment

The international environment of business is created by the international organizations which write regulations and make recommendations concerning such areas as business practices, labor relations, health standards, measurements, agriculture, and trade. Some of these organizations are the United Nations, the International Monetary Fund, the World Bank, regional development banks, and the European Community.

The monies (currencies) of the major industrial countries are now almost freely interchangeable. The foreign exchange markets for currencies are 24-hour, worldwide operations. Payments can be made electronically, almost instantaneously, and as trades are continuously being made, values of currencies fluctuate rapidly.

European Community

The 12 currencies of European Community member states.

Flags of United Nations members fly in front of U.N. headquarters in New York.

United Nations

Trading at the major stock exchanges, such as those in New York and London, influences business around the world.

The Foreign Environment

The forces that shape the foreign environment are the same as those that influence the domestic environment, but their values can be very different. Concepts or practices that succeed in a home country can be drastic failures in another country where values attributed to these differences are significant. Even so, ideas and customs from one culture can, and often do, gain great acceptance in other cultures. Mexicans, for example, find the same need for 7-Eleven convenience stores as do their northern neighbors even though Mexico and the United States have quite different cultures.

Religion as a cultural force is responsible for many of the attitudes and beliefs affecting human behavior. This, coupled with the fact that leaders of such religions as Buddhism and Islam are also heavily involved in politics, makes it imperative that international business managers understand the basic tenets of the religions practiced in their markets.

Physical forces are important because they set limits on a nation's development. At the same time, as a race we are increasingly circumventing boundaries set by nature. Canada, for example, is replacing its declining petroleum reserves by strip-mining tar sands to extract a high-quality, synthetic crude oil. Likewise, China is constructing 14 tunnels as part of a 400-mile rail line connecting one of the world's largest coal mines to a seaport. Exports from the recently opened mine will provide China with much-needed foreign exchange.

Before venturing into a foreign market, management must consider the customs and practices of the people there. A Coca-Cola billboard is a familiar sight to Tokyo residents. A 7-Eleven store thrives in Mexico.

Figure 1-2

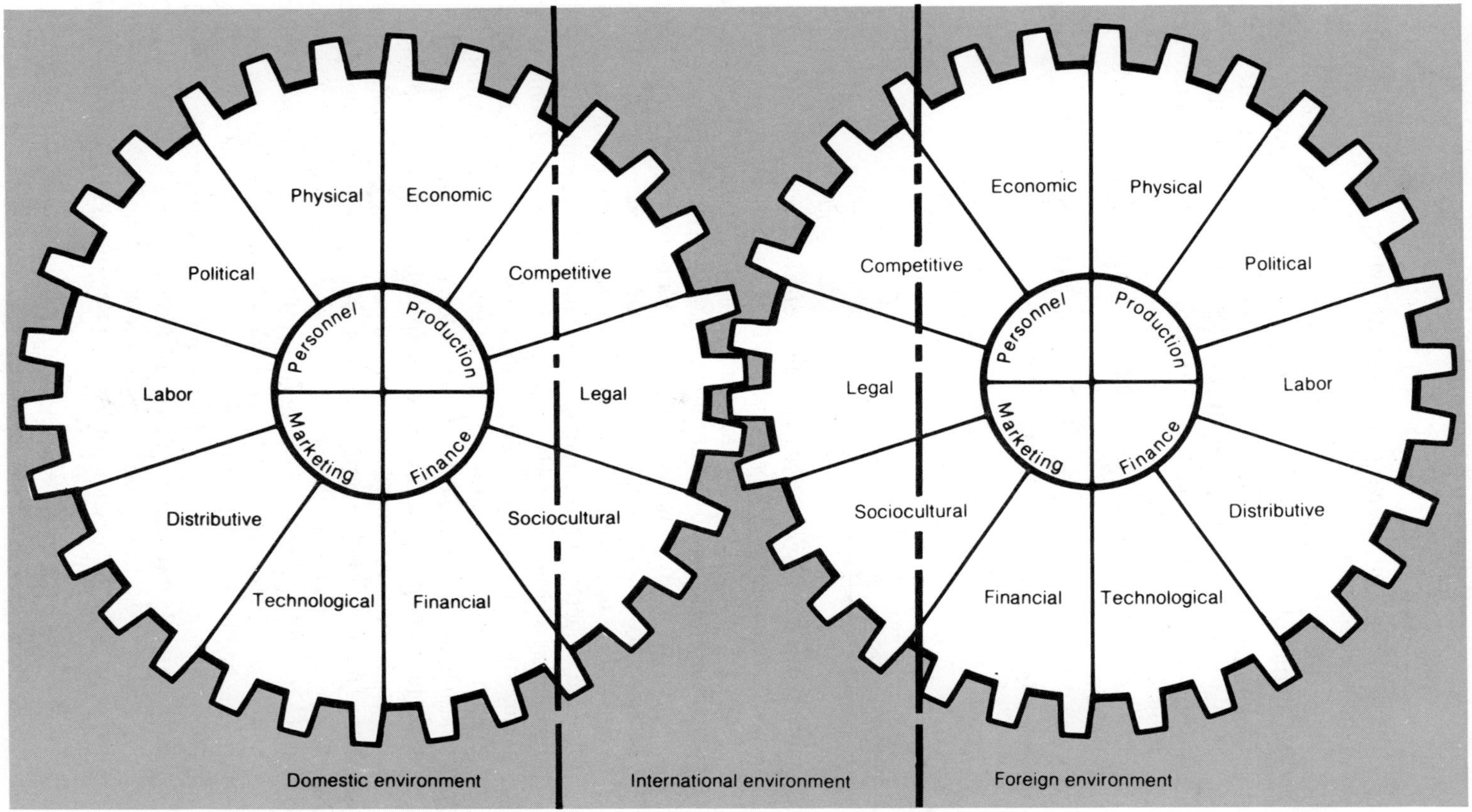

Two interlocking gear diagrams. The first gear (Foreign environment) contains a central hub divided into Production, Finance, Personnel, Marketing, surrounded by segments labeled: Physical, Political, Labor, Distributive, Technological, Financial, Sociocultural, Legal, Competitive, Economic. The second gear (Domestic environment) contains a central hub divided into Production, Finance, Personnel, Marketing, surrounded by segments labeled: Economic, Competitive, Legal, Sociocultural, Financial, Technological, Distributive, Labor, Political, Physical.

Foreign environment

International environment

Domestic environment

the domestic and foreign environments (where the gears mesh) is the international environment.

This is the model we shall be using throughout the book. After describing the nature of international business in Section I, we proceed to examine the supranational organizations and monetary aspects of the international environment in Section II. In Section III, we analyze the uncontrollable forces that make up the foreign and domestic environments and illustrate their effect on management practices. Finally, we reverse the procedure in Section IV and deal with management functions, demonstrating how they are influenced by the uncontrollable forces.

Now that we have introduced a model for studying international business, let us take a moment to clarify some of the terminology.

International
Business Terminology

International business, like every field of study, has its own terminology. To assist you in learning the special vocabulary, an important function of every introductory course, a glossary has been included at the end of the book and the more important terms are listed at the beginning of each chapter.

As with any new discipline, a number of words are employed whose definitions vary among users. *Multinational,* for example, is the most widely accepted term to describe an organization that produces in, markets in, and obtains the factors of production from multiple countries for the purpose of furthering overall enterprise benefits. Yet you will find some persons who use terms such as *transnational, supranational,* and *global* for multinational.* Furthermore, the same word may have two distinct meanings, depending on whether the user is describing *ownership* or the *areas of operation.* For example, multinational as we have used it describes a firm that operates in more than one country; however, government officials in the developing nations commonly use multinational to indicate a joint venture whose owners (governments or groups of stockholders) come from three or more nations.[9] These same officials call a firm operating in two or more countries a *transnational.*[10] This adds to the confusion because for some time transnational has referred to a company whose management and ownership are divided among two or more nations. Shell Oil (Great Britain and the Netherlands) and Unilever (Great Britain and the Netherlands) are called transnationals by Europeans.

Some people use the words *world* and *global* interchangeably with multinational, while others hold that only the first two terms properly describe firms

*In Chapter 23, we draw some distinctions between multinationals and globals.

Figure 1-3

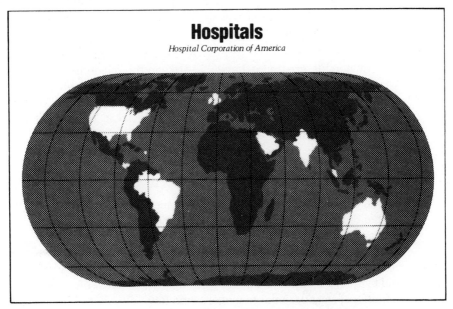

Hospitals

Hospital Corporation of America

Source: Hospital Corporation of America, Annual Report, 1983, p.47

Overseas Locations of a Service MNE, Hospital Corporation of America

that (1) consider the entire world to be their market and (2) allocate their resources without preference for the home country. A United Nations publication described the supranational corporation as one in which *both* the operation and ownership are multinational; yet many reserve this term for a corporate form that does not now exist—one that would be chartered by an international agency such as the United Nations.[11]

In this text, we will employ the following definitions, which are generally accepted by businesspeople:

1. *International business* is business whose activities involve the crossing of national borders. This definition includes not only international trade and foreign manufacturing but also encompasses the growing service industry in areas such as transportation, tourism, banking, advertising, construction, retailing, wholesaling, and mass communications.

2. *Foreign business* denotes the domestic operations within a foreign country. This term is sometimes used interchangeably with international business by some writers.

3. *Multinational enterprise (MNE)* or *multinational corporation (MNC)* is an organization that produces in, markets in, and obtains the factors of production from a number of countries for the purpose of furthering the overall benefit of the organization.

4. *Transnational corporation (TNC)* is a company whose management and ownership are divided evenly between the residents of two nations. Four of the largest transnationals are: (1) Unilever; (2) Shell; (3) Akzo (Enka), a Dutch and German textile manufacturer; and (4) ASEA (Sweden) and Brown Boueri (Switzerland), a new electrical equipment manufacturer formed by the merger of these two firms.

Central Theme of This Book

A solid understanding of the business concepts and techniques employed in the United States and other advanced industrial nations is a requisite for success in international business. However, because transactions take place across national borders, three environments—domestic, foreign, and international—may be involved instead of just one; and thus in international business the concepts and techniques employed in domestic operations must often be adapted to local conditions. International managers who have discovered that there are differences in the environmental forces are better prepared to decide when such adaptations are necessary. To be sure, no one can be an expert on these forces for all nations, but just knowing that there may be differences will cause people to "work with their antennas extended." In other words, they will be aware that when they enter the international business scene, they must be on the lookout for important variations in many of the forces that they take as given in the domestic environment. It is to the study of the three environments that this text is directed.

Summary

Among the most significant business developments in the last 30 years have been the rapid growth of international business and the proliferation of multinational firms. Although a number of companies have been engaged in this area for nearly a century, the explosive growth in the size and the number of international firms is a recent phenomenon, as is the much closer central control exercised by managements. This growth has brought about a need for more managers who can function effectively in the international business environment. To supply this need, industry has turned to colleges and universities for assistance in training. A separate field of study, international business, has evolved from an initial emphasis on international economics, and now includes material from many academic disciplines.

International business differs from its domestic counterpart in that it involves three environments rather than one. An environmental model was introduced to help explain the differences in these environments.

Questions

1. *A firm that markets and produces in multiple countries is called by two different names, depending on whether the user is a resident of an industrialized nation or a government official in a developing nation. What does each person call it? Why might the same name have two different meanings?*
2. *Give examples to show how an international business manager might manipulate one of the controllable forces in answer to a change in the uncontrollable forces.*
3. *Obviously, a nation whose GNP is smaller than the sales volume of a multinational firm is in no position to enforce its wishes on the local subsidiary of that firm. True or false? Please explain.*
4. *We know that a number of firms have been active in international business for nearly a century. Why, then, has the international firm attracted so much attention in the last two decades?*
5. *Business is business, and every firm has to produce and market its goods. Why, then, cannot the managers apply the techniques and concepts they have learned in their own country to other areas of the world?*
6. *What do you believe makes foreign business activities more complex than purely domestic ones?*
7. *Discuss some possible conflicts between host governments and foreign-owned companies.*
8. *International Business is just a new name for the old International Trade course. True or false? Discuss.*
9. *Why, in your opinion, do the authors regard the use of the self-reference criterion as "probably the biggest cause of international business blunders?" Can you think of an example?*

Minicase

1-1 Dansk Manufacturing

(Galawi) Limited

In the developing nation of Galawi,* the president and his cabinet are discussing the results of a meeting with Dick Petersen, managing director of Dansk Manufacturing (Galawi) Limited.

---

*Although Galawi is fictitious, the conditions are not.

The president: Petersen insists that our proposed law to increase company-paid benefits to employees will raise their costs so much they won't be able to compete in the export market anymore. He says that if they can't export, their sales volume will be so low they won't make enough profit to keep the company going. He thinks the home office may order him to close the Galawi operation down. What's your opinion, Mojabum?

Mr. Mojabum, the secretary of labor: Don't forget—we've promised the leaders of the union that we are going to obtain higher benefits for their people. We can't go back on our word.

President: Also, Mojabum, have you considered what the reaction of the workers might be if they don't get the benefits that this law will provide?

Mojabum: That's another concern, Mr. President. This proposed law has received quite a bit of publicity. If it doesn't go into effect, we may face a strike or worse.

President: Such as?

Mojabum: Perhaps some civil unrest, even public demonstrations.

Mr. Akam, the secretary of commerce: That could be serious, I admit, but on the other hand, Galawi needs this company. It provides jobs for over 300 people.

Mr. Bonat, the secretary of the Treasury: Dansk also brought in nearly a million dollars from their exports last year. We need that foreign exchange to help pay for our machinery imports.

Mojabum: I suppose you're right. But why, I wonder, haven't Galawi Manufacturing and Inland Steel Products said much about the proposed law?

President: Probably because they're locally owned and are not able to move like Dansk can. Don't forget, Dansk is a subsidiary of a multinational, and Galawi is just one of their markets. Also, these firms don't export either, so they aren't worrying about keeping costs down to compete in the world market.

That's it, Gentlemen. We can (1) get the law passed to satisfy the union and perhaps lose a company that hires 300 workers and earns some valuable foreign exchange, (2) stop the law from being passed so as not to lose Dansk, or (3) come up with some sort of compromise.

What course of action do you recommend?

Supplementary Readings

Aho, D. Michael. *Bibliography on Foreign Direct Investment*. Boston: Graduate School of Business Administration, Harvard University, 1966.

"AIB Survey." *International Dimension*. Washington, D.C.: AACSB and Academy of International Business, November 1973.

Fayerweather, John. *International Business Management: A Conceptual Framework*. New York: McGraw-Hill, 1969.

Monkiewicz, Jan. *Multinational Production Enterprises*. UNIDO/PC 121, September 10, 1985.

Robinson, Richard D. *International Business Management*. 2nd ed. Hinsdale, Ill.: Dryden Press, 1978.

Robock, Stefan H., and Kenneth Simmonds. *International Business and Multinational Enterprises*. 3rd ed. Homewood, Ill.: Richard D. Irwin, 1983.

Rolfe, Sidney E. *The Multinational Corporation*. New York: Foreign Policy Association, 1969.

Tugendhat, Christopher. *The Multinationals*. New York: Random House, 1972.

Vernon, Raymond. *Sovereignty at Bay*. New York: Basic Books, 1971.

Wilkins, Myra. *The Emergence of Multinational Enterprise*. Cambridge, Mass.: Harvard University Press, 1970.

Endnotes

1. *Business and International Education* (Washington, D.C.: American Council on Education, 1977), p. 1. This report was prepared by individuals from business, government, and education.

2. Mira Wilkins, *The Emergence of Multinational Enterprise: American Business Abroad from the Colonial Era to 1914* (Cambridge, Mass.: Harvard University Press, 1970), pp. 1–212.

3. Sidney E. Rolfe, *The Multinational Corporation* (New York: Foreign Policy Association, 1969), p. 38; and "Direct Investments Abroad," *Selected News Items* (Berlin: Deutsche Bank, March 1980), p. 2. See also Stefan H. Robock and Kenneth Simmonds, *International Business and Multinational Enterprises*, 3rd ed. (Homewood, Ill.: Richard D. Irwin, 1983), p. 23.

4. "More Multinationals in the EEC than in the U.S.," *Business International*, August 6, 1976, p. 254.

5. Richard D. Robinson, *International Business Management*, 2nd ed. (Hinsdale, Ill.: Dryden Press, 1978), p. 424.

6. Christopher Tugendhat, *The Multinationals* (New York: Random House, 1972), p. 11.

7. There are literally dozens of these studies. Among those with heavy impact are Vernon's *Sovereignty at Bay*, Tugendhat's *Multinationals*, the United Nations' *Multinational Corporations in World Development*, and Servan-Schreiber's *American Challenge*.

8. "France Orders Pipeline Deliveries," *Mobile Register*, August 14, 1982, p. 2-A. Later, President Reagan, pressured by Congress, reversed his decision, and the compressors were shipped.

9. A new shipping company, Multinational Shipping of the Caribbean, was formed in 1975 by eight Latin American governments.

10. There has been much discussion in the United Nations over whether to use multinational or transnational. In the first study prepared by the UN Secretariat for the Group of Eminent Persons who were chosen to study multinationals, the term *multinational* was used. However, the report by the Group of Eminent Persons noted that "*transnational* would better convey the notion that these firms operate from home bases across national borders." During discussion of this report, Latin American representatives noted that multinational was already being used in a different context (see endnote 9). The UN Economic and Social Council replaced multinational with transnational in resolutions 1908

and 1913, when it established the Commission on Transnational Corporations. The commission then decided that it should work on the definition of transnational. As yet, no decision has been reached. Other UN-affiliated organizations such as the International Labor Organization still use *multinational enterprise*. From *Multinational Production Enterprises*, UN Industrial Development Organization, September 10, 1985, pp. 1–3.

11. The supranational firm is discussed in *The Development of Management Consultancy* (New York: United Nations, 1973), p. 15.

CHAPTER 2

INTERNATIONAL TRADE AND FOREIGN INVESTMENT

*"M*y friends in nearly every European country tell me that unless Westinghouse can make the equipment locally, we had better forget about submitting a bid."

George Wilcox, vice chairman, Westinghouse

Learning Objectives

After you study this chapter, you should know:

1. The magnitude of international trade and how it has grown.
2. The direction of trade (who trades with whom).
3. The value of analyzing trade statistics.
4. The growth, magnitude, and direction of foreign investment.
5. The defensive and aggressive reasons for going abroad.
6. The weaknesses in using GNP/capita as a basis for comparing economies.
7. The international market entry methods.

Key Words and Concepts

Reverse investment
GNP/capita
Multinational economic unions
Geographic diversification
Management contract
Licensing
Twin factories
Indirect exporting
Direct exporting
Joint venture
Franchising
Contract manufacturing
Competitive alliances

Business Incident

In 1950, when Caterpillar, manufacturer of earthmoving and construction machinery, established its first subsidiary abroad, its export volume was $93 million and comprised 28 percent of its total sales. Since then, the firm has established its own production facilities in Brazil, Canada, France, the United Kingdom, Australia, Belgium, Indonesia, and Mexico. It also has contract manufacturers in France, Norway, South Korea, the United Kingdom, and West Germany and eight major distribution centers outside the United States. By 1981, these facilities were generating $5.2 billion annually in foreign sales, of which $3.5 billion—38 times more than in 1950—resulted from U.S. exports and amounted to 38 percent of Caterpillar's total sales.

From various Caterpillar annual reports.

Caterpillar's experience in augmenting both exports and foreign investment is representative of the performance of many multinational enterprises over the past two decades. However, doing business overseas is not necessarily confined to the Fortune 500 manufacturing firms. Exports of raw materials and services have also grown, as has the participation of smaller firms in world markets. The result has been, as you will see in the following sections, a dramatic escalation of international trade and foreign investment.

International Trade

Volume

By 1980, the volume of international trade in goods and services measured in current dollars had surpassed by over 15 times the amount exported in 1960, just 20 years earlier. Merchandise exports alone amounted to $2 trillion (see Table 2-1). To be sure, a large part of this increase was the result of inflation, but even in constant dollars the volume had nearly quadrupled. One can appreciate its magnitude by noting that this figure is larger than the gross national product of every country in the world except the United States. One fourth of everything grown or made on earth is exported. Interestingly, the year 1981 was a milestone in that for the first time since 1957, international trade measured in current dollars actually declined from the previous year.[1] The reason, of course, was the worldwide recession. By 1984, however, world trade was again increasing.

Table 2-1

World Trade in Merchandise Exports (FOB values; in billions of current U.S. dollars)

	1960	1970	1980	1981	1985	Average Annual Percentage Increase
Total	$128	$313	$1,998	$1,975	$1,939	11.5%
Developed countries	86	225	1,268	1,239	1,265	11.3
United States	20	43	221	234	213	9.9
West Germany[a]	12	35	195	179	183	11.5
France	7	18	111	102	98	11.1
Great Britain	10	19	110	103	101	9.7
Netherlands	4	12	74	69	68	12.0
Japan	4	19	130	152	176	16.3
USSR	6	13	76	79	87	11.3
Developing countries	27	55	558	534	470	12.1
OPEC	n.e.	18	306	285	157	15.5[b]
Centrally planned economies						
Europe and USSR	14	31	157	159	174	10.6
EC	30[c]	88[c]	662[d]	603[e]	639	14.7
EFTA	18[f]	51[g]	117[h]	109[h]	110[h]	6.2
LAIA	7	12	81	87	83	10.4

[a]Includes exports to East Germany.
[b]For 1970–1985.
[c]Original six members only (Belgium, Luxembourg, France, West Germany, Italy, and Netherlands).
[d]Includes original six nations plus Denmark, Ireland, and Great Britain.
[e]Includes Greece.
[f]Original seven members only (Austria, Denmark, Norway, Portugal, Sweden, Switzerland, and Great Britain).
[g]Includes Denmark and Great Britain (members in 1970).
[h]Includes present members only.
n.e. — nonexistent.
EC — European Community.
EFTA — European Free Trade Association.
LAIA — Latin American Integration Association (formerly LAFTA).
Sources: *Statistical Yearbook, 1969* (New York: United Nations), table 142, pp. 369–75; and *Monthly Bulletin of Statistics* (New York: United Nations), June 1982, pp. 106–26, and December 1986, pp 106–27.

How has this increase been distributed? Have some nations fared better than others? You can see from Table 2–1 that the exports of most nations have generally grown at or close to the world average. However, Japan and the developing nations as a unit have exceeded the world average, as has the European Community (EC). An important factor contributing to the EC's high growth rate has been the admission of new member nations. The relatively low rate of growth of the European Free Trade Association (EFTA) in the 1970s reflects the loss of two members (Denmark and Great Britain) to the EC.

The quadrupling of world exports in only two decades is an indication to businesspeople that export opportunities are increasing. However, the export growth of individual nations also portends greater competition from imports in their own markets.

Direction of Trade

What are the destinations of these nearly $2 trillion in exports? If you have never examined trade flows, you may believe that they consist mainly of manufactured goods exported by the industrialized nations to developing countries in return for raw materials. Note, though, that this is not so. Almost 75 percent of the developed nations' trade is with one another. However, it is true that the major part (over 60 percent) of the LDCs' exports also go to the industrialized countries. The main exceptions to this generality are Japan and the centrally planned economies.

Japan—An Exception

Japan, being entirely dependent on foreign sources for raw materials, must import to survive.[2] To pay for its imports, Japanese firms have worked diligently to increase their exports. Many of the developed countries, however, have been unwilling or unable to buy more from Japan because of their balance-of-payment deficits and have imposed import restrictions on the kinds of goods that constitute the bulk of Japan's foreign sales. Because of the opposition to their exports in the industrialized markets, the Japanese have turned to the developing countries. For example, of Japan's total exports in 1985, 59 percent went to developed countries, while 32 percent went to the LDCs. This is in sharp contrast to the 74–20 division experienced by the developed nations as a whole.

Centrally Planned Economies—Another Exception*

In the case of the centrally planned economies, the reasons for their direction of trade are essentially political. These countries as a group have attempted to be as self-sufficient as possible and tend to trade with the West only for goods and services that are unavailable within the Eastern bloc. However, even this trade has been somewhat restricted by their lack of foreign exchange. The Eastern-bloc nations have simply not been able to produce the kinds and quality of goods that the Western nations will pay for. Furthermore, the West, for political and security reasons, has placed restrictions on the kinds of products that it will sell to the East. President Reagan's embargo on material destined for the Soviet pipeline is a recent example.

---

*East-West trade is discussed in Chapter 17.

The Changing Direction of Trade

The percentages in Table 2–2 also indicate that the direction of trade is changing. Western nations have moved from a position of restricting trade with Russia to actively seeking its business. The data clearly indicate that the USSR had shifted its direction of trade in favor of the EC and EFTA nations to the detriment of the East European bloc. However, the 1985 data show that Russia is now shifting back to the communist bloc.

The spectacular growth market of the 1970s was the OPEC countries, especially those in the Middle East. With the huge revenues from greatly increased crude oil prices, these nations became significant markets for just about every region in the world. From slightly more than $4 billion in 1963, imports by the oil-producing nations rose to nearly $130 billion. The Middle Eastern countries were in the market for what the U.S. Department of Commerce called "wholesale quantities of schools and universities, hospitals and clinics, residential and business construction, whole new towns, all types of transportation, power, and communication systems, industrial estates, mills, factories, and processing plants, model farms, fishing facilities, and water supply and purification systems. For the businessman, this translates into a staggering proliferation of marketing opportunities."[3] However, the results of the greatly lower prices of crude oil are apparent in Table 2–2. The OPEC nations, because of reduced earnings, were relatively less important as importers in 1985 than they were in 1980.

Another noteworthy change, only partially observable in Table 2–2, is that two of the most important regional economic groupings, the EC and EFTA, are trading more among themselves and with each other. EFTA's increase is not apparent in the table because two of its members, Denmark and Great Britain, left at the beginning of 1973 to join the EC. An important cause of the increase in EC-EFTA trade is the free trade agreement for manufactured goods reached in 1973. In 1985, 52 percent of the EFTA exports went to the EC.

Major Trading Partners

A still more important analysis for the firm is what is essentially a disaggregation of Table 2–2 to reveal the major trading partners of a particular nation. Management can obtain valuable insights by studying both the home country and the nations where the firm is doing business or is contemplating doing business.

Why Focus on Major Trading Partners?

There are a number of advantages in focusing attention on a nation that is already a sizable purchaser of goods coming from the would-be exporter's country:

1. There are probably no political factors impeding exports from the exporter's country.

Table 2-2

Direction of Trade for Selected Regions and Countries (percentage of region's or country's total merchandise exports to regions or country in columns)

Exports from	Year	Exports to				
		D.C.	U.S.	Can.	Jap.	USSR
Developed countries	1960	70.5%	10.3%	5.7%	2.9%	1.2%
(D.C.)	1970	76.9	12.8	5.1	3.9	5.2
	1980	71.2	9.7	3.4	3.2	1.9
	1986	76.5	16.3	4.6	3.3	1.4
United States (U.S.)	1960	63.8	—	18.3	7.1	0.2
	1970	69.5	—	20.7	10.8	0.3
	1980	59.8	—	15.7	9.5	0.7
	1986	63.3	—	20.8	11.1	0.6
Canada (Can.)	1960	91.7	56.6	—	3.3	0.2
	1970	90.9	65.4	—	4.7	0.6
	1980	85.2	63.4	—	5.7	2.0
	1986	90.1	77.2	—	4.8	1.0
Japan (Jap.)	1960	47.7	27.4	3.0	—	1.5
	1970	54.6	31.1	2.9	—	1.8
	1980	47.5	24.5	1.9	—	2.1
	1986	63.0	38.8	2.6	—	1.5
USSR	1960	19.2	0.4	0.1	1.4	—
	1970	21.2	0.5	0.1	3.0	—
	1980	36.1	0.3	neg.	1.9	—
	1986	25.6	0.4	neg.	1.5	—
European Community	1960	71.9	7.5	1.0	0.7	1.4
(EC)*	1970	80.5	8.1	1.3	1.2	1.2
	1980	77.7	5.6	0.7	1.0	1.6
	1986	81.8	9.3	1.1	1.4	1.2
European Free	1960	71.3	8.7	3.7	0.7	1.2
Trade Association	1970	82.2	6.6	1.3	1.3	2.8
(EFTA)†	1980	79.6	4.9	0.7	1.3	3.4
	1986	81.3	8.2	1.1	1.9	3.5
Less developed	1960	72.3	10.3	1.8	5.1	1.9
countries (LDC)‡	1970	72.4	18.4	1.8	10.8	3.1
	1980	70.1	20.8	1.3	13.9	1.7
	1986	63.4	25.8	1.5	11.1	2.9
Developing Africa	1960	79.2	7.9	0.4	1.5	2.7
(D.A.) (South Africa	1970	81.1	6.7	0.7	4.0	4.1
and Zimbabwe	1980	83.6	31.1	0.2	2.1	0.8
excluded)	1986	73.5	12.3	0.7	1.9	1.8
Developing America	1960	78.9	42.1	1.7	2.8	1.6
(D.Am.) (U.S. and	1970	74.2	32.4	3.4	5.4	3.5
Canada excluded)	1980	64.5	33.6	2.6	4.0	4.7
	1986	65.7	38.4	1.7	4.3	5.9
Organization of	1960	n.e.	n.e.	n.e.	n.e.	n.e.
Petroleum Exporting	1970	75.3	9.7	2.5	12.2	0.9
Countries	1980	75.8	18.4	1.5	17.3	0.3
(OPEC)§	1986	60.6	13.6	0.9	16.9	0.4
Centrally Planned	1960	19.4	0.6	0.1	0.2	17.1
Economies (Eastern	1970	23.0	0.7	0.2	1.5	21.7
Europe and USSR)	1980	31.1	0.9	0.2	1.1	17.4
(CPE)‖	1986	22.1	1.1	0.1	0.9	18.9
Centrally Planned	1960	13.8	0.1	0.3	1.4	48.5
Economies in Asia	1970	31.6	neg.	0.7	12.3	10.2
(CPEA) (excludes	1980	43.8	5.3	0.6	21.5	6.1
intertrade)#	1986	40.8	8.5	1.0	20.0	7.8

* 1980 data include Denmark, Great Britain, and Ireland. Greece added in 1981.
† Excludes Denmark and Great Britain and includes Iceland in 1980 and 1981.
‡ Excludes Zimbabwe exports.
§ OPEC — Algeria, Ecuador, Gabon, Indonesia, Iran, Iraq, Kuwait, Libya, Nigeria, Qatar, Saudi Arabia, United Arab Emirates, and Venezuela.
‖ Includes Albania, Bulgaria, Czechoslovakia, East Germany, Hungary, Poland, Romania, and Russia.
Includes People's Republic of China, Mongolia, North Korea, and North Vietnam.

				Exports to			
EC	EFTA	LDC	D.A	D.Am.	OPEC	CPE	CPEA
24.4%	18.8%	25.5%	6.2%	11.0%	n.e.	2.9%	0.5%
39.5	9.4	18.7	4.1	8.3	3.4%	3.1	0.6
41.1	9.0	23.3	5.2	6.0	7.9	3.6	1.1
42.1	8.1	18.1	3.0	4.3	4.3	2.4	1.6
19.3	11.9	34.7	2.4	17.4	n.e.	1.0	0.0
26.6	4.0	29.6	2.3	15.2	4.8	0.8	0.0
24.8	3.7	36.2	2.9	17.6	8.1	1.8	1.7
24.3	2.7	31.8	2.1	14.5	5.1	1.0	1.5
8.2	19.5	7.6	0.5	3.5	n.e.	0.7	0.2
16.4	1.8	7.4	0.7	4.3	1.1	0.8	0.8
12.8	1.5	10.5	1.4	5.1	2.9	2.7	1.1
6.5	0.7	7.7	0.8	3.8	1.2	1.3	0.9
4.3	5.7	50.6	8.6	6.8	n.e.	1.6	0.2
11.2	3.0	40.0	5.6	5.8	5.1	2.3	3.1
13.2	2.7	45.4	4.6	6.6	14.2	2.8	4.3
14.8	2.9	30.3	1.4	4.2	5.6	1.8	4.9
6.7	6.2	6.6	1.8	1.8	n.e.	56.1	17.3
10.8	4.2	21.0	4.5	5.1	2.9	52.8	5.0
21.9	7.3	18.5	1.8	4.8	2.3	42.1	3.2
12.8	4.2	13.8	1.5	6.3	0.6	53.7	4.2
34.5	21.7	22.4	9.8	5.2	n.e.	4.1	0.8
48.9	16.8	14.0	4.9	3.9	3.4	4.0	0.4
53.6	11.9	17.6	6.5	3.0	7.8	3.5	0.4
56.9	10.9	13.5	4.0	2.2	4.4	2.5	0.8
24.1	21.9	24.6	6.7	4.9	n.e.	3.5	0.7
26.4	26.4	10.8	3.5	3.6	1.8	6.6	0.4
53.1	15.3	13.3	3.6	2.9	5.0	6.6	0.5
53.7	14.6	11.0	2.3	2.5	2.9	5.9	0.8
22.8	16.2	22.3	3.2	3.9	n.e.	3.5	1.0
22.9	3.0	20.2	2.8	6.7	1.9	5.1	0.7
26.9	2.7	24.9	2.3	7.9	3.8	2.9	0.7
21.4	1.7	27.6	2.9	7.0	5.0	4.9	2.6
43.8	21.7	12.8	6.6	0.7	n.e.	5.7	1.4
61.4	4.3	10.7	5.6	2.0	1.2	6.5	1.0
42.8	2.9	12.6	3.1	6.4	1.1	2.6	0.4
53.2	2.6	16.7	6.9	4.7	2.5	6.5	0.5
18.5	11.8	18.0	0.7	7.9	n.e.	3.1	0.5
26.3	3.3	19.1	0.7	17.3	0.9	5.8	0.6
18.1	2.3	26.3	2.2	20.8	3.8	6.3	0.7
18.8	1.7	23.3	2.6	16.7	3.9	8.0	1.5
n.e.	n.e.	n.e.	n.e.	n.e.	n.e.	n.e.	n.e.
43.5	2.0	19.3	2.3	9.1	0.7	1.6	0.1
30.8	3.1	22.2	1.4	8.5	1.3	1.2	0.1
26.6	1.3	34.9	2.3	12.4	3.4	2.6	0.3
7.2	6.8	6.5	1.9	1.8	n.e.	62.3	10.6
12.7	4.6	13.2	3.3	3.1	2.9	60.2	3.4
19.3	6.5	14.9	2.8	3.3	3.2	50.7	2.7
14.4	5.1	11.3	2.0	4.2	2.0	56.7	3.3
6.6	4.6	20.4	2.0	0.5	n.e.	66.0	n.a.
14.2	2.5	47.3	6.5	4.1	5.0	21.1	n.a.
13.0	1.5	43.0	5.6	1.9	6.6	13.1	n.a.
9.4	1.1	45.0	1.8	2.1	2.6	12.5	n.a.

n.a. — not applicable. CPEA data exclude intertrade.
n.e. — nonexistent.
neg. — less than 0.05 percent.
The sum of the percentages of columns D.C., LDC, CPE, and CPEA should total 100 percent. Frequently it does not because of rounding and because the UN data are at times faulty.
Sources: *Monthly Bulletin of Statistics* (New York: United Nations, June 1987), pp. 270–73; and United Nations, *Statistical Yearbook, 1969* (New York: United Nations), pp. 376–83.

2. There should be no strong cultural objections to buying that nation's goods.

3. Satisfactory transportation facilities have already been established.

4. Import channel members (merchants, banks, and customs brokers) are experienced in handling import shipments from the exporter's area.

5. Foreign exchange to pay for the exports is available.

6. The government of a trading partner may be applying pressure on importers to buy from countries that are good customers for that nation's exports. We have seen the efforts of the Japanese, Korean, and Taiwanese governments to persuade their citizens to buy more American goods.

Major Trading Partners of the United States

An example of such an analysis is shown in Table 2–3. We learn from these data that the United States, an industrialized nation, follows generally the tendency we found in Table 2–2; that is, developed nations trade with one another, but there are some exceptions. Two countries, Mexico and Canada, are trading partners because of their geographic proximity. Freight charges are lower, delivery times are shorter, and it is easier and less expensive for buyers and sellers to make contact.

It is interesting to note that in only 20 years the relative importance of many trading partners has changed. The addition of Indonesia to the list of major exporters to the United States is a result of high (compared to 1965) crude oil prices. Taiwan, Hong Kong, and South Korea are sending the United States many of the labor-intensive products that were formerly made here. Taiwan, South Korea, Singapore, Saudi Arabia, and China utilize their export earnings primarily for capital good purchases from the United States to further their industrialization.

Breakdown by Products

The disaggregation of the totals shown in the previous tables into product categories of direct interest to a specific firm is the basis of another important study. Data for this analysis can be obtained from the U.S. Department of Commerce's monthly publication *FT410*. Simply by knowing the Schedule E commodity number of the product in question, the analyst may go directly to the *FT410* and find which countries are the principal importers of U.S. production and what the physical and dollar volumes are. Market growth can be calculated and new markets pinpointed by comparing the annual results appearing in the December issues (see Table 2–4). The same procedure may be used for the preliminary investigation of foreign investment opportunities.[4]

Table 2-3
Major Trading Partners of the United States ($ billion)

	1965 Imports from	Amount	1986 Imports from	Amount	1965 Exports to	Amount	1986 Exports to	Amount
1.	Canada	$4.83	Japan	$85.46	Canada	$5.64	Canada	$45.33
2.	Japan	2.41	Canada	68.66	Japan	2.08	Japan	26.88
3.	UK	1.41	W. Germany	26.13	W. Germany	1.65	Mexico	12.39
4.	W. Germany	1.34	Taiwan	21.25	UK	1.62	UK	11.42
5.	Venezuela	1.02	Mexico	17.56	Mexico	1.11	W. Germany	10.56
6.	Mexico	0.64	UK	16.03	Netherlands	1.09	Netherlands	7.85
7.	Italy	0.62	Korea	13.50	France	0.97	France	7.22
8.	France	0.62	Italy	11.31	India	0.93	Korea	6.36
9.	Brazil	0.51	France	10.59	Italy	0.89	Australia	5.55
10.	Bel. & Lux.	0.49	Hong Kong	9.47	Australia	0.80	Taiwan	5.52
11.	Philippines	0.37	Brazil	7.34	Bel. & Lux.	0.65	Bel. & Lux.	5.40
12.	India	0.35	Venezuela	5.45	Venezuela	0.63	Italy	4.84
13.	Hong Kong	0.34	Switzerland	5.37	Spain	0.47	Brazil	3.89
14.	Neth. Ant.	0.32	China	5.24	S. Africa	0.44	Saudi Arabia	3.45
15.	Australia	0.31	Singapore	4.88	Switzerland	0.37	Singapore	3.38

Notes:
1. Exports are stated on an f.a.s. value basis. Services not included.
2. Imports are stated on CIF value basis. Services not included.
3. UK — United Kingdom.
4. Bel. & Lux. — Belgium and Luxembourg. Their export and import statistics are reported jointly.
5. Neth. Ant. — Netherlands Antilles.

Sources: Bureau of the Census, *Statistical Abstract of the United States* (Washington, D.C., 1979), pp. 862–65; and *Business America*, March 30, 1987, pp. 20–21.

Table 2-4

Comparison of U.S. Exports of Bourbon Whiskey in Containers Holding Not Over One Gallon

	Destination	1978			Destination	1986		
		Quantity (gallons)	Dollar Value ($ millions)	Avg. Price (gallon)		Quantity (gallons)	Dollar Value ($ millions)	Avg. Price (gallon)
1.	W. Germany	254,152	$ 2.485	$ 9.78	1. Japan	719,947	$10.112	$14.05
2.	France	114,759	1.170	10.20	2. Italy	48,412	0.681	14.07
3.	Japan	97,125	1.050	10.81	3. Australia	41,462	0.671	16.18
4.	Gt. Britain	62,452	0.676	10.82	4. France	32,650	0.482	14.76
5.	Italy	68,917	0.653	9.48	5. Netherlands	28,476	0.350	12.29
6.	Australia	22,605	0.420	18.58	6. Mexico	21,359	0.204	9.55
7.	Netherlands	32,402	0.345	10.65	7. Belgium	20,613	0.207	10.04
8.	Canada	30,750	0.300	9.76	8. Panama	18,907	0.227	12.01
9.	Mexico	22,722	0.225	9.90	9. Spain	18,592	0.229	12.32
10.	Switzerland	21,859	0.215	9.84	10. W. Germany	17,847	0.306	17.15
11.	Belgium	19,699	0.203	10.31	11. New Zealand	15,554	0.170	10.93
12.	Sweden	23,477	0.194	8.26	12. Switzerland	13,239	0.162	12.24
13.	Taiwan	14,306	0.184	12.86	13. Singapore	6,795	0.095	13.98
14.	New Zealand	5,219	0.093	17.82	14. Neth. Ant.	6,235	0.076	12.19
15.	Spain	9,143	0.085	9.30	15. Gt. Britain	5,581	0.103	18.46
16.	Iran	8,620	0.082	9.51	16. Thailand	5,430	0.073	13.44
17.	Thailand	8,147	0.073	8.96	17. Haiti	5,149	0.081	15.73
18.	Norway	7,325	0.067	9.15	18. Thailand	4,988	0.075	15.04
19.	Neth. Ant.	6,921	0.066	9.54	19. Hong Kong	4,570	0.072	15.75
20.	Others	90,688	0.871	9.60	20. Others	48,003	0.670	13.96
	Total	921,288	$ 9.458	$10.27		1,084,109	$15.046	$13.88

Sources: U.S. Department of Commerce, *FT410* (Washington, D.C.), December 1978, pp. 2–44, and December 1986, pp. 2–35. Neth. Ant. is Netherlands Antilles.

Summary of the Preliminary Investigation

In summary, these are the preliminary steps that managers can take to get a "feel" for international trade and investment possibilities: (1) a study of the general growth of trade (Table 2-1), (2) an analysis of major trading partners (Tables 2-2 and 2-3), and (3) a breakdown by products (Table 2-4).

International trade, the topic of this section, exists because firms export. However, exporting is only one aspect of international business. The other aspect, overseas production, generally requires foreign investment, the next subject of discussion.

Foreign Investment

Foreign investment may be divided into two components: *portfolio investment*, which is the purchase of stocks and bonds solely for the purpose of obtaining a return on the funds invested, and *direct investment*, by which the investors participate in the management of the firm in addition to receiving a return on their money.

Portfolio Investment

Inasmuch as portfolio investors are not directly concerned with the control of a firm, portfolio investment is of less importance than direct investment to the student of international business. This does not mean that portfolio investments are of negligible size, however. Data from the U.S.Treasury show that persons residing outside the United States hold American stocks and bonds valued at $208 billion ($126 billion in stocks). Although there are stockholders in virtually every country in the world, six countries—Canada, France, the Netherlands, Switzerland, Japan, and the United Kingdom—accounted for over three fourths of the holdings. More than 11 percent of U.S. stocks held abroad were owned by American citizens living abroad. While the ownership of American bonds is evenly divided between private and official* owners, nearly all of the foreign-owned stock is held privately.[5] As you can see, this kind of investment is sizable and should continue to grow as more MNEs sell their parent company shares worldwide.

*Foreign governments.

Table 2-5

Direct Overseas Investment (end of 1985)

	Amount (U.S. $ billions)	Share (percent)
United States	$232.7	36.1%
United Kingdom	116.9	18.1
Netherlands	55.5	8.6
West Germany	52.4	8.1
Japan	44.0	6.8
Canada	33.5	5.2
Other	109.6	17.0
World total	$644.6	100.0%

Source: *Japan 1987: An International Comparison* (Tokyo: Japan Institute for Social and Economic Affairs, 1987), p. 58.

Foreign Direct Investment

Volume

Attempts have been made to estimate the magnitude of foreign direct investment by summing yearly totals of new investments, but this procedure of course understates the present value because of the effects of appreciation and inflation. These factors make an accurate estimate of the book value* impossible to obtain.

In Chapter 1, we stated that the book value of all foreign investments is about $650 billion. The Japanese External Trade Organization in its *White Paper on Overseas Investment, 1987* provides the estimates shown in Table 2-5.

Direction of Foreign Investment

Even though it is impossible to make an accurate determination of the present value of foreign investments, we can get an idea of the rate and amounts of such investments and of the places in which they are being made. This is the kind of information that interests managers and government leaders. It is analogous to what is sought in the analysis of international trade. If a nation is continuing to receive appreciable amounts of foreign investment, its investment climate must be favorable. This means that the political element of the foreign environment is relatively attractive and that the opportunity to earn a profit is greater there than elsewhere. Other reasons for investing exist, to be sure, but if the above are absent, foreign investment is not likely to occur.

---

*Book value—a company's net worth as carried in its financial statements.

In which countries are investments being made, and where do the investments come from? Table 2-6 indicates that the industrialized nations invest primarily in one another just as they trade more with one another.

Actually, foreign investment follows foreign trade. Managements observe that the kinds of products they manufacture are being imported in sizable quantities by a country, and they begin to study the feasibility of setting up production facilities there. They are spurred to action because it is common knowledge that competitors are making similar analyses and may arrive at the same conclusion. Often the local market is not large enough to support local production of all the firms exporting to it, and the situation becomes one of seeing who can become established first. Experienced managers know, too, that governments often limit the number of local firms producing a given product so that those who do set up operations will be assured of having a profitable and continuing business.

U.S. Foreign Investment

The United States is by far the largest investor abroad (over 36 percent of the total; see Table 2-5), and as you can see from Table 2-7, American firms have invested much more in the developed than in the developing countries. Also, as with international trade, the relative importance of regions and countries has been changing. In a period of 25 years, the percentage of American foreign investment in the developed nations has risen from 60.6 percent to 74.9 percent. Europe's share has more than doubled, and of the European countries, Great Britain and West Germany have obtained the greatest dollar increases. Note that although the developing nations as a group have suffered a large percentage decrease, the percentage of investment in the other Asia and Pacific region has doubled.

Foreign Direct Investment in the United States

Foreign direct investment in the United States has risen rapidly, from about $6.9 billion in 1960 to $209 billion in 1986. Of the 67 percent of the total foreign investment accounted for by Europe, MNEs in Great Britain and the Netherlands owned 25 and 20 percent, respectively. Although American investments by German and Japanese firms have been expanding rapidly, their U.S. investment levels of $17.36 and $23.43 billion are still way below the Netherlands' $42.85 billion and Great Britain's $51.49 billion. (See Table 2-8.)

The 15 largest investors in the United States are ranked by revenue in Table 2-9. Although a few firms such as Shell, Nestlé and Bayer have been in this country for many years, most of these investments are recent. You can tell from the names of the American affiliates that their major investment strategy has been to acquire existing firms rather than start from the ground up.

Table 2-6

Direction of Foreign Direct Investment for Selected Regions and Countries (SDR billion)

	1973	1979	1985
Where funds originate			
World	$19.43	$45.33	$57.28[a]
Industrial nations	19.17	45.13	56.31
United States	9.56	19.54	18.00
Great Britain	3.32	9.71	8.10
Japan	1.59	2.24	6.33
West Germany	1.40	3.51	3.89
France	0.78	1.54	2.17
Netherlands	0.77	0.42	1.85
Canada	0.64	2.03	4.44
Sweden	0.25	0.48	1.17
Bel. & Lux.[b]	0.23	1.03	0.27
Australia	0.21	0.29	1.82
Dev. nations (oil export)[c]	0.14	0.37[f]	0.06
Dev. nations (nonoil)[c]	0.12	0.31	0.91
Where funds go			
Industrial nations	$ 9.99	$25.24	$32.47[a]
United States	2.36	9.18	17.69
West Germany	1.71	1.31	0.99
Great Britain	1.50	5.01	3.91
France	0.95	2.00	2.49
Netherlands	0.72	1.51	0.34
Canada	0.69	1.45	2.38[e]
Bel. & Lux.[b]	0.60	0.88	1.02
Italy	0.52	0.28	0.99
Spain	0.33	1.08	1.92
Dev. nations (oil export)[c]	0.23	n.a.	3.05
Dev. nations (nonoil)[c]	3.35	7.85	10.94
Africa	0.26	6.03	9.83
Asia	0.66	1.72	4.78
Singapore	0.33	0.64	1.13
Malaysia	0.14	0.44	0.68
China	n.a.	0.39[g]	1.63
Japan	0.17[d]	0.19	0.62
Western Hemisphere	2.08	4.25	3.99
Argentina	0.01	0.16	0.95
Brazil	1.16	1.87	1.34
Mexico	0.38	0.50	1.03

[a]Amounts do not coincide because of reporting lag.
[b]Bel. & Lux.—Belgium and Luxembourg.
[c]Dev. nations—developing nations.
[d]1974.
[e]1984.
[f]1980.
[g]1982.

Sources: International Monetary Fund, *Balance of Payments Yearbook Supplement to Volumes 31 and 33* (Washington, D.C., December 1980); and *Balance of Payments Statistics Yearbook,* vol. 37, part 2 1986, pp. 64–67.

Table 2-7

U.S. Direct Investment Position Overseas (current U.S. $ billions)

Country or Region	1960		1986							
	Total	Percent of Total	Total	Percent of Total	Manu-facturing	Percent of Manu-facturing	Petroleum	Percent of Petroleum	Other[a]	Percent of Other
Total	$31.87	100.0%	$259.89	100.0%	$107.24	100.0%	$61.15	100.0%	$93.13	100.0%
Developed countries	19.32	60.6	194.71	74.9	87.16	81.3	39.61	64.8	67.94	73.0
Canada	11.18	35.1	50.18	19.3	23.76	22.2	10.94	17.9	15.48	16.6
Europe[b]	6.69	21.0	123.18	47.4	54.13	50.5	24.31	39.8	44.74	48.0
EC[c]	2.65	8.3	96.23	37.0	50.01	46.6	17.78	29.1	28.44	30.5
Bel. & Lux.[d]	0.23	0.7	6.80	2.6	3.31	3.1	S	—	S	—
France	0.74	2.3	9.47	3.6	6.58	6.1	0.51	0.8	2.38	2.6
West Germany	1.01	3.2	20.34	7.8	13.00	12.1	3.21	5.2	4.13	4.4
Italy	0.38	1.2	6.99	2.7	4.87	4.5	0.33	0.5	1.79	1.9
Netherlands	0.28	0.9	11.87	4.6	4.70	4.4	3.42	5.6	3.75	4.0
Great Britain	3.23	10.1	34.99	13.5	13.99	13.0	8.67	14.2	12.33	13.2
Denmark and Ireland	n.a.	—	5.57	2.1	3.51	3.3	S	—	S	—
Greece	n.a.	—	0.19	0.1	0.06	0.1	0.11	0.2	0.02	<0.1
Japan	0.25	0.8	11.33	4.4	5.31	5.0	2.63	4.3	3.39	3.6
Aust. and S.A.[e]	1.20	3.8	10.02	3.9	3.97	3.7	1.74	2.8	4.31	4.6
Developing countries	11.13	34.9	60.61	23.3	20.08	18.7	17.78	29.1	22.75	24.4
Latin America	7.48	23.5	34.97	13.5	15.19	14.2	5.23	8.6	14.55	15.6
Brazil	0.95	3.0	9.14	3.5	7.10	6.6	0.15	0.2	1.89	2.0
Venezuela	2.57	8.1	1.84	0.7	0.93	0.9	0.24	0.4	0.67	0.7
Mexico and Central America	1.54	4.8	9.69	3.7	4.48	4.2	0.60	1.0	4.61	5.0
Other Western Hemisphere	0.88	2.8	6.88	2.6	0.26	0.2	1.84	3.0	4.78	5.1
Africa[f]	0.64	2.0	4.26	1.6	0.29	0.3	3.39	5.5	0.58	0.6
Middle East	1.14	3.6	5.35	2.1	0.25	0.2	2.93	4.8	2.17	2.3
Other Asia and Pacific	0.98	3.1	16.02	6.2	4.35	4.1	6.24	10.2	5.43	5.8
International[g]	1.42	4.5	4.57	1.8	n.a.	—	3.76	6.1	0.81	0.9

[a]Other includes transportation, communications, public utilities, trade, finance, insurance, real estate, mining, banking, and wholesale trade.
[b]No East European investment included.
[c]Great Britain, Ireland, Denmark, and Greece not in EC in 1960. Are included in 1983.
[d]Belgium and Luxembourg.
[e]Australia, New Zealand, and South Africa.
[f]Does not include South Africa.
[g]Shipping companies operating under flags of convenience, primarily those of Panama and Liberia.
n.a. — not applicable.
S — suppressed to avoid disclosure of individual firm.
Sources: *Survey of Current Business* August 1987, p. 29; and *Statistical Abstract of the United States 1977*, p. 755.

Table 2-8
Foreign Direct Investment Position in United States, 1986 ($ billion)

	All Industries	Petroleum	Manufacturing	Trade	Finance	Insurance	Real Estate
All countries	$209.33	$29.63	$68.06	$41.68	$17.29	$13.62	$21.23
Canada	18.31	1.39	5.39	2.48	1.86	1.70	3.18
Europe	141.67	26.14	55.08	22.97	9.52	10.98	9.61
European Community (10)	124.31	25.71	44.55	20.83	8.27	9.15	9.04
Belgium and Luxembourg	2.77	D	0.61	D	0.24	0.0	0.03
France	7.42	D	5.99	0.55	-0.44	0.11	0.06
West Germany	17.36	0.2	7.94	5.68	0.38	1.51	1.14
Italy	1.25	D	0.07	0.21	D	D	D
Netherlands	42.85	D	14.71	5.44	3.56	2.53	2.60
Denmark, Ireland, and Greece	1.28	D	0.23	D	D	D	D
Great Britain	51.40	D	15.00	8.04	3.90	4.97	5.04
Other Europe	17.36	0.44	10.53	2.14	1.23	1.83	0.57
Sweden	3.64	0.34	2.42	0.82	D	0.14	*
Switzerland	12.13	0.05	7.75	0.91	D	1.61	0.45
Other	1.58	0.05	0.36	0.42	0.50	0.08	0.13
Japan	23.43	*	3.02	13.26	3.23	D	2.48
Australia, New Zealand, and South Africa	4.94	D	1.11	D	D	0.01	0.15
Latin America	14.19	0.97	3.01	2.30	1.27	0.79	4.51
Middle East	4.74	D	0.09	D	0.76	0.0	0.89
Other Africa, Asia, and Pacific	2.05	D	0.37	0.46	D	D	0.40

D—suppressed to avoid disclosure of individual companies.
*Less than $10 million.
Source: U.S. Department of Commerce *News Release*, June 24, 1987, pp. 6–7.

Table 2-9

Fifteen Largest Foreign Investments in United States

Foreign Investor	Country	U.S. Company	Industry	Revenue ($ million)	Assets ($ million)
1. Seagram Co., Ltd.	Canada	Joseph Seagrams (100%)	Spirits and wines	$ 2,029	$ 6,301
		E. I. duPont (23%)	Chemicals	27,148	26,773
				29,177	
2. Royal Dutch Shell	Netherlands Great Britain	Shell Oil (100%)	Energy, Chemicals	17,353	26,214
3. British Petroleum	Great Britain	Standard Oil Ohio (95%)	Energy	9,219	15,955
		B P North America (100%)	Energy	4,228	4,224
				13,447	
4. B.A.T.	Great Britain	BATUS (100%)	Paper, tobacco, retailing	5,499	4,242
	Canada	Imasco U.S.A. (100%)	Fast food	1,366	n.a.
		Peoples Drug Stores (100%)	Drug stores	1,206	n.a.
				8,071	
5. Tenglemann Group	Germany	Great A & P Tea (52%)	Supermarkets	7,835	2,080
6. Unilever	Netherlands	Chesebrough-Ponds (100%)	Personal care	2,731	n.a.
		Lever Brothers (100%)	Consumer goods	2,475	837
		Thomas J. Lipton (100%)	Food & beverages	1,303	827
		National Starch (100%)	Adhesives, starch	1,064	743
				7,573	
7. Nestlé	Switzerland	Nestlé Enterprises (100%)	Food, restaurants	3,400E	n.a.
		Carnation (100%)	Food	2,500E	n.a.
		Alcon Laboratories (100%)	Optical products	400E	n.a.
				6,300E	
8. Mitsui & Co.	Japan	Mitsui & Co. USA (100%)	Feed additives, plastics	5,561E	2,990E
9. Petroleos de Venezuela	Venezuela	Citgo Petroleum (50%)	Refining, marketing	4,103	1,209
		Champlin Refining (50%)	Refining	1,200	500
				5,303	
10. Renault	France	American Motors (43%)*	Automotive	3,463	2,225
		Mack Truck (42%)		1,712	1,014
				5,175	
11. Philips	Netherlands	North American Philips (58%)	Electronics	4,532	2,886
		Signetics (100%)	Semiconductors	500E	n.a.
12. Hoechst	Germany	Celanese (100%)	Chemicals	2,891	2,361
		American Hoechst (100%)	Chemicals	1,711	1,308
				4,602	
13. Campeau	Canada	Allied Stores (100%)	Retailing	4,257	5,125
14. Bayer	Germany	Bayer USA (100%)	Chemicals	3,410	2,433
		Agfa-Gevaert (100%)	Photography ⎫		
		Compugraphic (82%)	Typesetting ⎭	765	511
15. Volkswagen	Germany	Volkswagen of America (100%)	Automotive	4,175 4,037	n.a.

*Now property of Chrysler Motors.

Notes: E—Estimated.

n.a.—Not Available.

Source: "The 100 Largest Foreign Investments in the U.S.," *Forbes*, July 27, 1987, pp. 146–50.

Why Go Abroad?

International business firms go abroad for reasons that can be categorized as either aggressive or defensive. However, all of these reasons can be linked in some way to the desire to increase (aggressive) or protect (defensive) profits, sales, and markets.

Fortune states it this way:

> The motivation for all this overseas investment has been endlessly debated and undoubtedly varied greatly from one firm to another. The motivation has also varied over time. During the 50s, most overseas investment was defensive in character, designed to surmount trade barriers that dollar-short nations had erected against U.S. imports. After these barriers began falling in the late 50s, the investment outflow took on a more aggressive cast. Possessed of technological, marketing, and other managerial advantages over foreign companies, U.S. enterprises sought to link these advantages with that of cheap overseas labor. In so doing, the companies could earn more abroad than they could at home and more than local businesses could earn in their own markets.
>
> Beginning in the late 60s, motivations that might once again be described as defensive reasserted themselves. As the dollar became increasingly overvalued, it grew more difficult to export from the United States and more profitable to import. So companies that had never considered going overseas went abroad to manufacture products which five years earlier would have been exported from American plants. Others went overseas to set up export "platforms"—usually in the Third World—to manufacture either for their European subsidiaries or for the U.S. market itself.[6]

The aggressive reasons for going overseas could also conceivably be defensive, depending on the underlying motive. In that sense, the following listing is arbitrary. For example, if the chief executive officer is being hard pressed by the stockholders for greater profits, anything that increases them could have a defensive intent. The reasons for foreign investment that are most often stated *publicly* by company executives are defensive reasons. An example of such reasons is contained in an annual report of Sola Basic, a Wisconsin conglomerate with 10 foreign plants:

> Manufacturing plants are established outside the United States only when necessary to protect sizable markets threatened by local competition, currency restriction, or trade barriers.

Despite such public protestations, we believe that there are some motives for overseas investment that are essentially aggressive.

Aggressive Reasons

Among the reasons for going abroad that are essentially aggressive are to (1) open up new markets, (2) obtain greater profits, (3) acquire products for the home market, and (4) satisfy management's desire for expansion.

Open Up New Markets

Managements are always under pressure for growth, and when they face slow-growth situations at home, they begin to search for new markets outside the home country. They find (1) that a combination of GNP and population growth appears to be creating markets that are reaching the "critical mass" necessary to become viable candidates for their operations and (2) that the economies of many nations where they are not doing business are growing at a considerably faster rate than the economy of their own nation.

New Market Creation. Table 2–10 illustrates the great variety in growth rates among the top and bottom 25 countries ranked by **GNP/capita**. Note the disparity among and between the two groups.

Although nearly everyone looks to GNP/capita as a basis for making comparisons of nations' economies, extreme care must be exercised to avoid drawing unwarranted conclusions. In the first place, because the statistical systems in many developing nations are deficient, the reliability of the data provided by such nations is questionable.

Second, to arrive at a common base of U.S. dollars, the World Bank converts local currencies to dollars. World Bank officials admit that their method of using official exchange rates for the conversion does not accurately reflect the purchasing power of currencies. They say, "The differences in real income between developing and industrialized economies are likely to be exaggerated."[7]

Finally, you must remember that GNP/capita is merely an arithmetic mean obtained by dividing GNP by the total population. However, a nation with a lower GNP but more evenly distributed income may be a more desirable market than one whose GNP is higher. On the other hand, as you will note in the chapter on the economic forces, a skewed distribution of income in a nation with a low GNP/capita may indicate that there is a viable market, especially for luxury goods. People do drive Cadillacs in Bolivia.

The data from Table 2–10 indicate that, from a macro viewpoint, markets around the world are growing, but this does not mean that equally good opportunities exist for all kinds of business. Perhaps surprisingly, economic growth in a nation causes markets for some products to be lost forever while, simultaneously, markets for other products are being created. Take the case of a country in the initial stage of development. With little local manufacturing, it is a good market for exporters of consumer goods. As economic development continues, however, businesspeople see profit-making opportunities in (1) producing locally the kinds of consumer goods that require simple technology or (2) assembling from imported parts products that demand technology of a more advanced nature. Given the tendency of governments to protect local industry, the importation of goods being produced in that country will normally be prohibited. Thus, the exporters of the easy-to-manufacture consumer goods, such as paint, adhesives, toilet articles, clothing, and almost anything made of plastic, will begin to lose this market, which now becomes a new market to producers of the inputs to these "infant industries."

Table 2-10

Population (mid-1985), GNP/Capita (1984), and Average Growth Rates of GNP/capita (1965-1985) and Population (1980-1985) (countries with populations of 1 million or more)*

		1985		Annual Growth Rates (percentage)	
Ranking	Country	GNP/Capita (current $U.S.)	Population (millions)	GNP/ Capita†	Population
1	United Arab Emirates	$19,270	1.4	n.a.	6.2
2	United States	16,690	239.3	1.7	1.0
3	Switzerland	16,370	6.5	1.4	0.2
4	Kuwait	14,480	1.7	−0.3	4.5
5	Norway	14,370	4.2	3.3	0.3
6	Canada	13,680	25.4	2.4	1.1
7	Sweden	11,890	8.4	1.8	0.1
8	Japan	11,300	120.8	4.7	0.7
9	Denmark	11,200	5.1	1.8	0.1
10	West Germany	10,940	61.0	2.7	−0.2
11	Finland	10,890	4.9	3.3	0.5
12	Australia	10,830	15.8	2.0	1.4
13	France	9,540	55.2	2.8	0.6
14	Netherlands	9,290	14.5	2.0	0.4
15	Austria	9,120	7.6	3.5	0.0
16	Saudi Arabia	8,850	11.5	5.3	4.2
17	United Kingdom	8,460	56.5	1.6	0.1
18	Belgium	8,280	9.9	2.8	0.1
19	Singapore	7,420	2.6	7.6	1.2
20	Libya	7,170	3.8	−1.3	3.9
21	New Zealand	7,010	3.3	1.4	0.9
22	Oman	6,730	1.2	5.7	4.8
23	Italy	6,520	57.1	2.6	0.3
24	Hong Kong	6,230	5.4	6.1	1.4
25	Trinidad and Tobago	6,020	1.2	2.3	1.6
86	Haiti	310	5.9	0.7	1.8
86	China	310	1,040.3	4.8	1.2
88	Sudan	300	21.9	n.a.	2.7
89	Tanzania	290	22.2	n.a.	3.5
89	Kenya	290	20.4	1.9	4.1
91	Somalia	280	5.4	−0.7	2.9
91	Rwanda	280	6.0	1.8	3.2
93	India	270	765.1	1.7	2.2
94	Central African Republic	260	2.6	−0.2	2.5
94	Benin	260	4.0	0.2	3.1
96	Niger	250	6.4	−2.1	3.0
97	Madagascar	240	10.2	−1.9	3.2
98	Togo	230	3.0	0.3	3.3
98	Burundi	230	4.7	1.9	2.7
100	Burma	190	36.9	2.4	2.0
101	Zaire	170	30.6	−2.1	3.0

Table 2-10
(concluded)

Ranking	Country	1985		Annual Growth Rates (percentage)	
		GNP/Capita (current $U.S.)	Population (millions)	GNP/Capita†	Population
101	Malawi	170	7.0	1.5	3.1
103	Nepal	160	16.5	0.1	2.4
103	Mozambique	160	13.8	n.a.	2.6
104	Bhutan	160	1.2	n.a.	2.2
106	Mali	150	7.5	1.4	2.3
106	Burkina Faso	150	7.9	1.3	2.6
106	Bangladesh	150	100.6	0.4	2.6
109	Ethiopia	110	43.3	0.2	2.5

All data for overseas departments and territories are excluded. For example, data for Puerto Rico are not included in U.S. data.
*The World Bank does not include GNP/capita estimates for most centrally planned economies, such as the USSR and Poland, because there is a dispute as to the methodology that should be employed.
†GNP/capita growth rates are real.
Source: World Bank, *World Development Report, 1987* (Washington, D.C., 1987).

Typical of the simple production facilities for producing consumer goods is the case of a Mexican firm that manufactures a number of products under licenses from American multinationals, among which are Listerine toothpaste and McCormick spices. The production line that supplies Listerine toothpaste for all of Mexico consists of one 50-gallon mixing tank, into which the imported ingredients are dumped. A mixer looking like an electric outboard motor is clamped to the tank's side. The mixed contents are discharged by gravity to a tube-filling machine, and the whole operation is handled by one man. The McCormick spice production area is made up of a machine that fills small metal cans with ground pepper imported in bulk, plus two girls who sit with 50-pound cardboard drums of imported spices between their legs and fill by hand the familiar paper boxes for whole spices, such as cloves, cinnamon, and pepper. The entire production area is smaller than a basketball court.

Multinational Economic Unions.* The fact that the great majority of nations have experienced population and GNP/capita growth does not necessarily mean that they have attained sufficient size to warrant investment in an organization for either handling exports or producing locally. For many products, many of these nations still lack sufficient market potential. However, when such nations have formed **multinational economic unions** (for example, the European Community and the European Free Trade Association), the new markets have

*Multinational economic unions are groups of nations that have reduced trade and tariff barriers to intragroup trade and are cooperating in economic matters. The forms include free trade areas, customs unions, common markets and required cooperation groups. (see Chapter 4.)

been so much larger that a number of multinationals have bypassed what is often the initial step of exporting and have made their initial market entry by manufacturing locally.

Faster-Growing Foreign Markets. Not only are new markets appearing overseas, but many of these markets are growing at a faster rate than the home market. One outstanding example has been the growth of the Japanese gross national product and GNP/capita, which increased from $43 billion and $458 in 1960 to $1,366 billion and $11,300 in 1985. Table 2–10 shows that Japan's real growth rate averaged 4.7 percent annually, the highest among the large industrial economies. Another group of high-growth markets, the OPEC nations, came into being almost overnight when world crude prices quadrupled. Iran's imports, for example, increased by eight times over the short time span of six years. Interestingly, of the 109 nations in Table 2–10, 57 had average annual GNP/capita growth rates higher than the American growth rate for the period 1965–85.

Faster growth in the markets of developing nations frequently occurs for another reason. When a firm that has supplied the market by exports builds a factory for local production, the host government generally prohibits imports. The firm, which may have had to share the market with 10 or 20 competitors during its exporting days, now has the local market all to itself or shares it with only a small number of other local producers. Before General Tire began manufacturing tires in Chile, probably a dozen exporters, including General Tire, were competing in the market. However, once local production got under way, there was only one supplier for the entire market—General Tire. That is growth.

Obtain Greater Profits

As you know, greater profits may be obtained by either increasing total revenue or decreasing the cost of goods sold, and often conditions are such that a firm can do both.

Greater Revenue. Rarely will all of a firm's domestic competitors be in every foreign market in which it is located. Where there is less competition, the firm may be able to obtain a better price for its goods or services. For example, General Tire had only three competitors in Spain for its V-belt line when dozens of brands were available in the United States.

In addition, firms are sometimes able to introduce new products sooner overseas than in the home country. This is especially true in the pharmaceutical industry. Robert Dean of Smith-Kline Beckman (1985 sales, $3.7 billion) claims that delays by the Food and Drug Administration in approving new products have been responsible for the industry's going abroad. "This industry would not have its international business if not for FDA regulations. We had to have a broader market to pay for the enormous expense of getting a drug on the market." Glenn Utt of Abbott Laboratories ($3.8 billion sales) adds a related reason that appears to be somewhat defensive: "Research costs are getting so high that it requires you to look worldwide."[8]

Lower Cost of Goods Sold. Going abroad, whether by exporting or by producing overseas, can frequently lower the cost of goods sold. Increasing total sales by exporting will not only reduce R&D costs per unit, as Glenn Utt implied, but will also make other economies of scale possible.

Producing in other countries can also be less expensive when labor, raw materials, or energy costs are lower. Moreover, some governments offer special inducements to attract new investment, which greatly lowers the cost of investment and thus the size of the risk. For example, Greece, one of the newest members of the European Community, offers the following: (1) investment grants of up to 50 percent of the investment, (2) interest subsidies to cover up to 50 percent of the interest cost of loans from banks, and (3) reduction of up to 90 percent of a firm's taxable profits. While incentives alone are not considered a sufficient motive for investing overseas, they are certainly a contributing factor. Incentives also exert an influence on where investments will be made. It is obvious, too, that they will positively affect the cost of goods sold.

Improved Communications. This might be considered a supportive reason for opening up new markets overseas, because certainly the ability to communicate with subordinates and customers by telex and telephone has given managers confidence in their ability to control foreign operations if they should undertake them. Managers also know that because of improved transportation, they can either send home-office personnel to help with local problems or be there themselves within a few hours if need be.

> Good communication is so important for multinationals that Barbados has been able to attract industry on the basis of its excellent communications. American Airlines does all of its data processing there, for example.

Shorter traveling time has also been responsible for numerous business opportunities because foreign businesspersons have come to the home country to look for new products to import or new technology to buy.[9] The Department of Commerce, in *Business America*, regularly publishes a list of arrivals who desire to contact suppliers.

Overseas Profits as an Investment Motive. There is no question that greater profits on overseas investments was a strong motive for going abroad in the 1970s. *Business International* reported that 90 percent of 140 Fortune 500 companies surveyed had achieved higher profitability on foreign net assets in 1974. This, of course, was an incentive for firms not yet in foreign markets to go abroad.

However, profits from foreign operations suffered in 1975, when oil prices were quadrupled, European labor was making increased demands, and governments were initiating costly welfare programs.

This situation lasted through 1977, but the ratio of foreign earnings to total earnings (FEBIT/TEBIT) turned up again in 1978 (see Figure 2–1, Part II) and reached a high in 1980. Then foreign profitability dropped in 1981 as the recessionary downturn that began in the United States about mid-1980 appeared overseas. The ratio of foreign earnings to total earnings turned up sharply in 1983, and foreign earnings as a percentage of assets continued to be higher than the U.S. earnings (see Figure 2-1, Part I).[10]

Note that over the period 1978–85 the average growth in foreign earnings outpaced foreign sales growth (5.9 percent versus 4.1 percent), whereas domestic earnings were down an average of 27 percent despite a domestic sales growth of 5.2 percent (Figure 2–1, Part III).

Acquire Products for the Home Market

The relative ease of foreign travel has both created markets for new products and facilitated the search for new products to be introduced in the U.S. market. Americans have traveled abroad in unprecedented numbers during the past decade, and in their travels they have encountered products and customs previously unknown to them. Those who acquired the European habit of drinking wine with their meals, for example, returned home wanting to continue this custom. American marketers, sensitive to this trend, have sent buyers around the world to bring back these new products, and many manufacturers have begun to produce them here. Large retailers such as Sears, Macy's, and J. C. Penney maintain permanent foreign buying offices for the purpose of discovering new products that can be resold in this country.

Satisfy Management's Desire for Expansion

The faster growth mentioned previously helps fulfill management's desire for expansion. Stockholders and financial analysts also expect firms to continue to grow, and those companies operating only in the domestic market have found it increasingly difficult to sustain that expectation. As a result, many firms have expanded into foreign markets. This, of course, is what multinational firms based in small countries, such as Nestle (Switzerland), SKF Bearings (Sweden), and Shell (Great Britain and the Netherlands), discovered decades ago.

These are the reasons for going abroad that are most often cited as being aggressive, although, as you have seen, probably all of these reasons could be viewed as either aggressive or defensive. Let's look now at some reasons that are commonly seen as being defensive.

Defensive Reasons

Protect Domestic Market

Frequently a firm will go abroad to protect its home market. Service companies (accounting, advertising, marketing research, banks, law) will establish foreign oper-

Figure 2-1

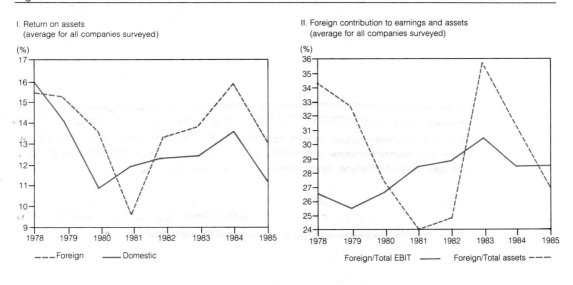

I. Return on assets
(average for all companies surveyed)

II. Foreign contribution to earnings and assets
(average for all companies surveyed)

- - - Foreign   ——— Domestic

Foreign/Total EBIT ———   Foreign/Total assets - - -

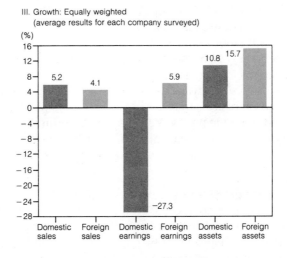

III. Growth: Equally weighted
(average results for each company surveyed)

Domestic sales: 5.2, Foreign sales: 4.1, Domestic earnings: −27.3, Foreign earnings: 5.9, Domestic assets: 10.8, Foreign assets: 15.7

Source: Reprinted from page 309 of the September 29, 1986, issue of *Business International* with the permission of the publisher, Business International Corporation (New York).

ations in markets where their principal accounts are, in order to prevent competitors from gaining access to those accounts. They know that once a competitor has been able to demonstrate to top management what it can do by servicing a foreign subsidiary, it may be able to take over the entire account.[11] Similarly, suppliers to original equipment manufacturers (for example, battery manufacturers to automobile producers) often follow their large customers. These suppliers have an added advantage in that they are moving into new markets with a guaranteed customer base.

A company may also go abroad to protect its domestic market when it faces competition from lower-priced foreign imports. By moving part or all of its production facilities to the countries from which its competition is coming, it can enjoy the same advantages, such as less costly labor, raw materials, or energy. Management may decide to manufacture certain components abroad and assemble them in the home country, or if the product requires considerable labor in the final assembly, it may decide to send components elsewhere for this final operation. A whole new concept, twin factories on the Mexican-American border, came into being because of lower-cost Mexican labor.

Twin Factory Concept. Some American companies whose assembly operations are labor intensive have established **twin factories**—production facilities on each side of the Mexican-American border, a short distance apart. The American plant produces components requiring capital-intensive processes and delivers them to a plant on the Mexican side, which assembles them. Because the Mexican wage, after various devaluations of the peso, is only one sixth of what Americans would receive or one half of the wage paid to workers in Korea, Hong Kong, Singapore, and Taiwan, American firms are competing successfully with the low-cost operators in Asia. General Motors, for example, has 17 plants performing such labor-intensive tasks as cutting and sewing car seats and assembling electrical wire harnesses. Japanese plants that manufacture in the United States, such as Panasonic (TV) and Sanyo (refrigerators), are also taking advantage of Mexico's low wage rates and its proximity to the United States. About 250,000 workers are employed in 800 assembly plants (called *maquiladoras* in Mexico) to assemble products ranging from clothing to computer keyboards. Assembly operations now earn more foreign exchange for Mexico than any other export except petroleum. They surpassed tourism in 1985.[12]

Protect Foreign Markets

Changing the method of going abroad from exporting to overseas production is often necessary to protect foreign markets. The management of a firm supplying a profitable overseas market by exports may begin to note some ominous signs that this market is threatened.

Lack of Foreign Exchange. One of the first signs is a delay in payment by the importers. They have sufficient local currency but are experiencing delays in obtaining foreign exchange from the government's central bank. The credit manager, by checking with the firm's bank and other exporters, learns that this condition is becoming endemic—a reliable sign that the country is facing a lack of foreign exchange. In examining the country's balance of payments, the financial manager may find that its export revenue has declined, while the import volume remains high. Experienced exporters know that import and foreign exchange controls are in the offing and that there is a good chance of losing the market, especially if they sell consumer products. In times of foreign exchange scarcity, governments will invariably give priority to the importation of raw materials and capital goods.

If the advantages of making the investment outweigh the disadvantages, the company may decide to protect this market by producing locally. Managers know that once the company has a plant in the country, the government will do its utmost to provide foreign exchange for raw materials to keep the plant, a source of employment, in operation. Because imports of competing products are prohibited, the only competition, if any, will have to come from other local manufacturers.

Local Production by Competitors. Lack of foreign exchange is not the only reason why a company might change from exporting to manufacturing in a market. Its export business may be growing and payments may be prompt, but still the firm may be forced to set up a plant in the market. The reason for this is that competitors are also enjoying good profits on a volume that may be reaching a point at which it will support local production.

Should a competing firm decide to put up a factory in the market, management must decide rapidly whether to follow suit or risk losing the market forever. Managers know that many governments, especially those in developing nations, will not only prohibit further imports once the product is produced in the country but will also permit only two or three other companies to enter so as to maintain a sufficient market for these local firms. General Motors tried for years to enter Spain, but the Spanish government, believing that there were already enough automobile manufacturers in the country, refused the company entry. Only recently, on the eve of Spain's joining the European Community, was General Motors permitted to enter.

Guarantee Supply of Raw Materials

Few developed nations possess sufficient domestic supplies of raw materials. Japan and Europe are almost totally dependent on foreign sources, and even the United States depends on imports for more than half of its aluminum, chromium, manganese, nickel, tin, and zinc. Furthermore, the Department of the Interior estimates that by the end of the century iron, lead, tungsten, copper, potassium, and sulfur will be added to the critical list.

To assure a continuous supply, manufacturers in the industrialized countries are being forced to invest primarily in the developing nations, where most new deposits are being discovered.[13] Incidentally, even the United States is looked upon as a source of raw materials for some resource-poor nations. Shigeo Muraoka, Japanese deputy general consul, stated the following:

The United States offers an abundance of raw materials. Because Japan has long depended on the United States for various materials such as grain, coking coal, and lumber, it is entirely logical for Japanese firms to establish facilities close to the sources of these essential raw materials.[14]

Acquire Technology and Management Know-How

A reason often cited by foreign firms investing in this country is the acquisition of technology and management know-how. The president of the Korean conglomerate Samsang Group ($15.7 billion in sales), speaking of his expansion plans, said, "When it comes to computers and semiconductors, it would be difficult to bring the technology to our country. If we set up our own plant in the United States, we can more easily gain knowledge."[15] The German chemical giant Bayer ($16 billion in sales) gave this reason for purchasing Miles Laboratories: "to gain access to the company's well-established distribution, marketing, and research and development."[16]

Geographic Diversification

Many managements have chosen to diversify geographically as a means of maintaining stable sales and earnings when the domestic market goes into an economic slump. Such **geographic diversification** has been possible because, historically, foreign economies have lagged behind cyclical changes in the U.S. economy by as much as 12 months. In 1980, the foreign operations of American multinationals were outperforming their domestic counterparts. Sunbeam and Ford, for example, reported that their Mexican business was unusually strong, and Twin-Disc, a transmission manufacturer, said that the slowdown in the European market "wasn't nearly as bad as in the United States."[17] Later, in 1983, the lag was again in evidence when the United States was the first to come out of the recession. Of course, geographic diversification will lose its effectiveness to the extent that European Community governments and the United States succeed in harmonizing their monetary and fiscal policies.

Political Stability

U.S.-based multinationals have not been motivated by political stability to go overseas, although it is often the prime factor in their choice of where to go. However, European and Third World* firms may actually make foreign investments (usually in the United States) for that reason. An owner of a small German firm that opened a plant in Georgia had this to say as he considered the situation in Europe: "I'm uneasy. I like the Americans and want to retire there. America will be the last country to lose its freedom."[18]

---

*Third World countries are those that belong neither to the Eastern bloc dominated by Russian or to the Western industrialized nations.

How to Enter
Foreign Markets

All of the means for becoming involved in overseas business may be subsumed in just two activities: (1) exporting to a foreign market or (2) manufacturing in it.

Exporting

Most firms have begun their involvement in overseas business by exporting—that is, selling some of their regular production overseas. This method requires little in the way of investment and is relatively free of risks. It is an excellent means of getting a feel for international business without committing any great amount of human or financial resources. If management does decide to export, it must choose between *direct* and *indirect* exporting.

Indirect Exporting

Indirect exporting is simpler than direct exporting because it requires neither special expertise nor large cash outlays. Exporters based in their home country will do the work. Management merely follows instructions. Among the exporters available are (1) *manufacturers' export agents*, who sell for the manufacturer; (2) *export commission agents*, who buy for their overseas customers; (3) *export merchants*, who purchase and sell for their own account; and (4) *international firms*, which use the goods overseas (mining, construction, and petroleum companies are examples).

Indirect exporters, however, pay a price for such service: (1) they will pay a commission to the first three kinds of exporters; (2) foreign business can be lost if exporters decide to change their sources of supply; and (3) firms gain little experience from these transactions. This is why many managements that begin in this manner soon change to direct exporting.

Direct Exporting

To engage in **direct exporting**, management must assign the job of handling the export business to someone within the firm. The simplest arrangement is to give someone, usually the sales manager, the responsibility for developing the export business. Domestic employees may handle the billing, credit, and shipping initially, and if the business expands, a separate export department may be set up. A firm that has been exporting to wholesale importers in an area and servicing them by visits from either home office personnel or foreign-based sales representatives frequently finds that sales have grown to a point that will support a complete marketing organization.

Management may then decide to set up a *sales company* in the area. The sales company will import in its own name from the parent and will invoice in local currency. It may employ the same channels of distribution, though the new organization may permit the use of a more profitable arrangement. This type of organization can grow quite large, often invoicing several millions of dollars annually. Before building a plant in Mexico, for many years Eastman Kodak imported and resold cameras and photographic supplies while doing a large business in local film developing. Many firms that began with local repair facilities later expanded to produce simple components. Gradually, they produced more of the product locally until, after a period of time, they produced all of the components in the country.

Foreign business may evolve sequentially over the path just traced (Singer Sewing Machine's experience), or a company may be forced to move directly to local production (nonsequential) for any of the reasons discussed above in the section "Why Go Abroad?"

Foreign Manufacturing

When management does decide to become involved in foreign manufacturing, it generally has five distinct alternatives available, though not all of them may be feasible in a particular country. These are:

1. Wholly owned subsidiary.
2. Joint venture.
3. Licensing agreement.
4. Franchising.
5. Contract manufacturing.

A sixth arrangement, the *management contract*, is utilized by both manufacturing and service companies to earn income by providing management expertise for a fee.

Wholly Owned Subsidiary

The company that wishes to own a foreign subsidiary outright may (1) start from the ground up by building a new plant, (2) acquire a going concern, or (3) purchase its distributor, thus obtaining a distribution network familiar with its products. In this case, of course, production facilities will have to be built. American multinationals certainly prefer wholly owned subsidiaries, but they do not have a marked preference for any of the three means of obtaining them. However, this is not the case for European and Canadian investors. They clearly prefer to acquire a going concern. (See Figure 2–2.)

In recent years, there has been a sizable increase in the number of governments that will not permit wholly owned subsidiaries. Mexico, for example, requires that all Mexican companies have at least 51 percent Mexican ownership except in rare cases. Hewlett-Packard and IBM have been recent exceptions. When they refused to be partners in joint ventures, the government permitted

Figure 2-2

Share of Acquisitions in Total U.S. Investment for Selected Countries, 1986

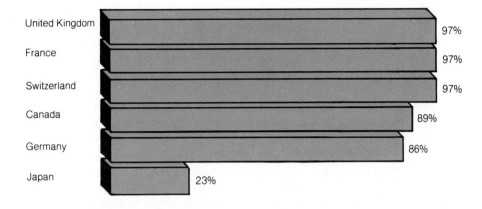

Telephone conversation with office of Foreign Direct Investment, Department of Commerce, June 25, 1987.

the companies to own their Mexican subsidiaries outright because it wanted to stimulate the domestic manufacture of computers.

Joint Venture

A **joint venture** may be (1) a corporate entity between a multinational enterprise (MNE) and local owners, (2) a corporate entity between two or more MNEs that are foreign to the area where the joint venture is located, or (3) a cooperative undertaking between two or more firms of a limited-duration project. Large construction jobs are frequently handled by this last form.

> Ford and Volkswagen have approved a novel plan to form a joint venture, Autolatina, which will oversee both companies' operations in Brazil and Argentina, in an effort to eliminate their Brazilian losses. H. Poling, president of Ford, stated, "The main objectives of the venture would be to ensure continual updating of technology, higher operating efficiencies, and better use of manufacturing facilities." The two firms are expected to share some facilities and some parts. However, each one will retain separate trademarks and their products will be sold and serviced through separate dealer markets. Together, the firms have 15 plants in Brazil and Argentina and employ 75,000 people to produce 900,000 cars and trucks. Their 1985 automotive and credit operations reported sales of $4 billion, making them about the size of American Motors.[19]

When the government of a host country requires that companies have some local participation, foreign firms must engage in a joint venture with local owners in order to do business in that country. In some situations, however, a foreign firm will seek local partners even when there is no local requirement to do so.

Strong Nationalism. Strong nationalistic sentiment may cause the foreign firm to try to lose its identity by joining with local investors. Care must be taken with this strategy, however. Although a large number of people in many LDCs dislike multinationals for "exploiting" them, they still believe, often with good reason, that the products of multinationals are superior to the products of purely national firms. One solution to this ambivalence has been to form a joint venture in which the local partners are highly visible, give it an indigenous name, and then advertise that a foreign firm (actually the partner) is supplying the technology. Even wholly owned subsidiaries have followed this strategy.

> Eastman Kodak has eliminated the word *Kodak* from the names of its 100 percent-owned subsidiaries in Venezuela, Mexico, Chile, Peru, and Colombia. Kodak Venezuela has become Foto Interamericana, and Kodak's large manufacturing company in Mexico is now called Industria Fotografica Interamericana.

Other Joint Venture Benefits. Other factors that influence managements to enter joint ventures are the tax benefits that some nations (Zimbabwe is an example) extend to companies with local partners or a lack of finances, manpower, or local marketing expertise.

> Merck, the largest U.S. maker of ethical drugs, spent $313 million to acquire 50.5 percent of Banyu Pharmaceutical in Japan. Management had been dissatisfied with the performance of Merck's Japanese subsidiary in the world's second-largest ethical drug market. With this acquisition, the 600-person sales force of Merck-Japan was augmented by Banyu's 350 sales representatives. Merck's chairman said, "To bring new products effectively to market in Japan required a larger and more effective marketing organization. With a controlling interest in Banyu, I would hope for a better penetration of the Japanese market."[20]

There are also multinationals that enter into joint ventures as a matter of policy so as to reduce investment risk. Their strategy is to enter into a joint venture with either native partners or another multinational. Still other multinationals such as Ford and Volkswagen have joined together to achieve economies of scale. Incidentally, any division of ownership in a joint venture is possible unless there are specific legal requirements.[21]

Competitive Alliances. Increasingly, multinationals have been establishing **competitive alliances** that may include one or more of the forms we have been discussing. The arrangements of Britain's International Computers Limited (ICL) with Japan's Fujitsu are an example.

ICL felt that it needed assistance in two areas—mainframes and office equipment—in order to share costs, expand access to complementary technologies and markets, and speed product development. It chose Fujitsu for the mainframes, and four distinct agreements were reached:

1. Collaboration with Fujitsu's computer division. ICC provides chip and board design, while Fujitsu contributes chip technology and the expertise in mounting chips in the current boards. Fujitsu assembles and ships the systems to ICL for design and distribution.

2. Cooperation with Fujitsu's semiconductor division to develop dense CMOS technology with 8000 gates. Although this technology did not yet exist, ICL felt that Fujitsu's present technology was more advanced than its own and thus entrusted the design work to Fujitsu.

3. Annual technology meetings to discuss recent developments and search for new areas of cooperation.

4. Commitment to each other as preferential suppliers. When either firm seeks outside sources for components, it gives the other firm the opportunity to bid first.

Although, ICL did not establish any joint ventures with Fujitsu, it did form one with General Electric's information services division to work on office equipment.

There is a danger to Fujitsu's partners inherent in such arrangements, as Professor C. K. Prahalad of the University of Michigan warns: "Fujitsu is soaking up a large number of players in the communications and computer industry." He claims that the Japanese are experts in tunneling into the organizations of other people. "We are amazed when they send 25 people to visit a joint partner here and we take pride in saying that we sent 2 people."

In forming competitive alliances with Mitsubishi, Westinghouse took steps to keep its ally from becoming its competitor in the U.S. market, as you will see.

Since the 1930s, the two firms have had a licensing agreement to exchange technology. After working together for over 50 years, they formed a 50–50 joint venture to produce components for circuit breakers. Headquartered in Japan, the joint venture supplies components only to the two shareholders. Each partner assembles, tests, and markets the final product.

When the expensive dollar destroyed Westinghouse's competitiveness in circuit breakers, the company formed another joint venture with Mitsubishi that took charge of marketing as well as production and development. The joint venture, located in Pittsburgh, sells in the U.S. market products made in Japan, but it plans to build a factory in this country when the demand is sufficient. To protect its market from being taken over by Mitsubishi, Westinghouse has a service agreement with the joint venture, under which the Westinghouse sales staff markets and services the venture's products.[23]

Disadvantages. While the joint venture arrangement offers the advantage of less commitment of financial and managerial resources, and thus less risk, there are some disadvantages for the foreign firm. One, obviously, is the fact that profits must be shared. Furthermore, if the law requires that the foreign investors have no more than a 49 percent participation (common in LDCs), they may not have control. This is because the stock markets in LDCs are either small or nonexistent, so that it is generally impossible to distribute the shares widely enough to permit the foreign firm with its 49 percent to be the largest stockholder.

Lack of control over the joint venture is the reason why many multinationals resist making such arrangements. They feel that they must have tight control of their foreign subsidiaries to obtain an efficient allocation of investments and production and to maintain a coordinated marketing plan worldwide. For example, local partners might wish to export to markets that the MNE serves from its own plants, or they might want to make the complete product locally when the MNE strategy is to produce only certain components there and import the rest from other subsidiaries.[24]

In recent years, numerous LDC governments have passed laws that require local majority ownership for the purpose of giving control of firms within their borders to their own citizens. In spite of these laws, control with a minority ownership is still feasible.

Control with Minority Ownership

There have been occasions when the foreign partner has been able to circumvent the spirit of the law and assure itself control by taking 49 percent of the shares and giving 2 percent to its local law firm or some other trusted national.

Another method is to take in a local majority partner, such as a government agency, an insurance company, or a financial institution, that is content to invest merely for a return while leaving the venture's management to the foreign partner. If neither of these arrangements can be made, the foreign company may still control the joint venture, at least in the areas of major concern, by means of a *management contract*.

Management Contract

The **management contract** is an arrangement under which a company provides managerial know-how in some or all functional areas to another party for a fee that ranges from 2 to 5 percent of sales. Multinationals make such contracts with (1) companies in which they have no ownership (examples: Hospital Corporation of America manages hospitals overseas, and Eastern and Pan American provide management assistance to foreign airlines), (2) joint venture partners, and (3) wholly owned subsidiaries. The last arrangement is made solely for the purpose of allowing the parent to siphon off some of the subsidiary's profits. This becomes extremely important when, as in many foreign exchange–poor nations, the parent firm is limited in the amount of profits that it can repatriate. Moreover, because the fee is an expense, the subsidiary receives a tax benefit.

Used in Joint Ventures. Management contracts can enable the multinational partner to control many aspects of a joint venture even when holding only a minority position. If it supplies key personnel, such as the production and technical managers, the multinational can be assured of product quality with which its name may be associated as well as be able to earn additional income by selling the joint venture inputs manufactured in the home plant. This is possible because the larger multinational is more vertically integrated. A local paint factory, for example, might have to import certain semiprocessed pigments and driers that the foreign partner produces in its home country for domestic operations. If these can be purchased elsewhere at a lower price, the local majority could insist on other sources of supply. This rarely happens, because the production and technical managers can argue that only inputs from their employer will produce a satisfactory product. They are the experts, and they generally have the final word.

Purchasing Commission. There is another source of income that the multinational derives not only from firms with which it has a management contract but also from joint ventures and wholly owned subsidiaries. That source is a commission for acting as purchasing agent of imported raw materials and equipment. This relieves the affiliates of having to establish credit lines with foreign suppliers and assures them that they will receive the same materials used by the foreign partner. The commission received for this service averages about 5 percent of invoice value and is in addition to the management contract fee.

Licensing

Frequently multinationals are called on to furnish technical assistance to firms that have sufficient capital and management strength. By means of a **licensing** agreement, one firm, the licensor, will grant to another firm, the licensee, the right to use any kind of expertise, such as manufacturing processes (patented or unpatented), marketing procedures, and trademarks for one or more of the licensor's products.

> General Tire, for example, has licensed some firms to use its tire technology and others to use its know-how to produce plastic film. At the same time, it has made licensing agreements with V-belt, conveyor belt, and battery manufacturers to use their technology in General Tire subsidiaries.

The licensee generally pays a fixed sum when signing the licensing agreement and then pays a royalty of from 2 to 5 percent of sales over the life of the contract (five to seven years, with option for renewal). The exact amount of the royalty will depend on the amount of assistance given and the relative bargaining power of the two parties.

Of course, the licensor will not share in the profits under the usual agreement, but the royalty it receives is additional income that it can use to support a larger, more capable technical department than it could otherwise have. For most firms, licensing is not a primary source of income, though in the fashion industry it often is. Jacques Roet, chairman of Christian Dior, says,

> Ten years ago, we earned 30 percent of our revenue from our own products and 70 percent from licenses. At present, our own merchandise is yielding only 10 percent, while licenses bring in 90 percent. My objective is to bring direct production up to 15 percent again.[25]

The reason for the last statement is that in 1980, Dior received only $48 million in license fees from overall brand sales (including its own) of $332 million. Although total brand sales rose 25 percent, it collected only a 1 percent increase in revenue. Many managements are reluctant to enter into licensing agreements for this reason and also because they may be creating competitors in other markets (some licensees export) from which the licensor will generally be excluded at least for the product lines covered by the licensing agreement.

Franchising

In recent years, American firms have gone overseas with a new kind of licensing—**franchising**. Franchising permits the franchisee to sell products or services under a highly publicized brand name and a well-proven set of procedures with a carefully developed and controlled marketing strategy. Of the 27,021 overseas outlets operated by 328 American franchising companies, fast-food operations such as McDonald's, Kentucky Fried Chicken and Tastee-Freeze are the most numerous—McDonald's alone has 1929 outlets in 40 countries. As Table 2–11 indicates, Canda is the dominant market for U.S. franchises with 8101 units in operation. Japan is second with 5,659 units and the U.K. is third with 2,456.[26]

Other types of franchisors are hotels (Hilton, Holiday Inn), business services (Muzak, Manpower), soft drinks (Coca-Cola, Orange Crush), home maintenance (Servicemaster, Nationwide Exterminating), and automotive products (Midas).

Contract Manufacturing

International firms employ **contract manufacturing** in two ways. One way is as a means of entering a foreign market without investing in plant facilities. The firm contracts with a local manufacturer to produce products for it according to its specifications. The firm's sales organization markets the products under its own brand, just as Montgomery Ward sells washing machines made by Norge.

The second way is to subcontract assembly work or the production of parts to independent companies overseas. Although the international firm has no equity in the subcontractor, this practice does have some resemblances to foreign direct investment. When the international firm is the largest or only customer of

Table 2-11
Where U.S. Franchisors Operate

Country or Foreign Region	Number of Franchisors
Canada	233
Caribbean	90
Continental Europe	68
Asia (other than Japan and Middle East)	67
Australia	66
Japan	56
United Kingdom	60
Middle East	44
Mexico	35
Africa	29
South America	33
Central America	29
New Zealand	22

Source: *Business America,* March 3, 1986, p. 13.

the subcontractor, it has in effect created in another country a new company that generates employment and foreign exchange for the host nation. Frequently the international firm will lend capital to the foreign contractor in the same way that an MNE will lend funds to its subsidiary. Because of these similarities, this practice has gained the name of "foreign direct investment without investment."

Matsushita's Panasonic division is entering the U.S. major appliance market by buying products made by Canadian and U.S. manufacturers, thus avoiding large capital investment initially. If the appliance line is a success, Panasonic is expected to set up its own factories in the United States.[27]

Paths to Multinationalism

Many large multinational firms with numerous manufacturing subsidiaries all over the world began their foreign operations by exporting. As this stage became successful, they established sales companies overseas to market their exports. Where the sales company was able to develop a sufficiently large market, a plant to assemble imported parts was set up. Finally, the complete product was manufactured locally. However, this sequence should not be construed as the only way to become involved in foreign markets. In some countries, conditions may require that a complete manufacturing plant be the means of initial entry. Multinational firms today are employing all of these methods simultaneously to reach their worldwide markets.[28]

Figure 2-3
International Franchising in 1984

Franchising companies . . .328
Number of franchising outlets . . .27,021

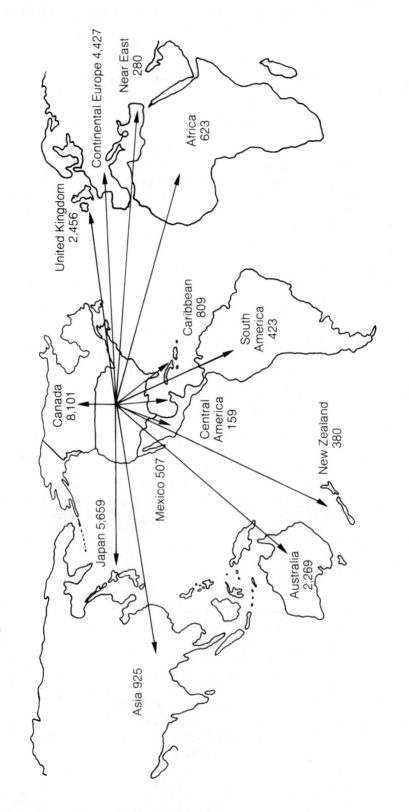

Continental Europe 4,427
Near East 280
Africa 623
United Kingdom 2,456
Caribbean 809
South America 423
Canada 8,101
Central America 159
New Zealand 380
Mexico 507
Japan 5,659
Australia 2,269
Asia 925

Summary

The volume of international trade in goods and services now amounts to nearly $2 trillion dollars, a 15-fold increase in just 20 years. Foreign investment has also grown rapidly and now totals about $640 billion. Although there has been some change in the directions of trade and investment, developed nations still tend to trade with and invest in one another. A noteworthy development in foreign investment has been its rapid increase in the United States ($6.9 billion in 1960 to $209 billion in 1986).

Firms go abroad (exporting and foreign investment) for reasons that are somewhat arbitrarily classified as *aggressive* (open new markets, obtain greater profits, acquire new products, satisfy management's desire for expansion) and *defensive* (protect domestic and foreign markets, guarantee supply of raw materials, acquire technology, geographic diversification).[29]

The two basic means of going overseas are exporting to markets or manufacturing in them. Exporting may be done directly or indirectly. A firm may become involved in foreign manufacturing through various methods: (1) wholly owned subsidiaries, (2) joint ventures, (3) licensing, (4) contract manufacturing, and (5) franchising.

Foreign investment is increasing for the reasons discussed in this chapter. Some firms enter overseas markets by exporting, and as they gain experience, they begin to manufacture in these markets. Others bypass exporting and go directly to foreign production. In this case, they may set up wholly owned subsidiaries, but if the costs are too high or if foreign governments prohibit such investment, firms may still become involved in foreign manufacturing through licensing, joint ventures, contract manufacturing, or franchising.

Questions

1. *The greater part of international trade consists of an exchange of raw materials from the developing nations for the manufactured goods from the developed nations. True or false? Please explain.*
2. *The volume of exports has increased, but the ranking of U.S. trading partners in order of importance remains the same year after year. True or false? Please explain.*
3. *It was suggested in the text that managers can make a preliminary investigation that will give them a "feel" for international trade. Name four publications that they can use for this purpose.*
4. *Although trade between the Eastern-bloc nations and the West is increasing, why do you believe that the volume of such trade is still a small percentage of world trade?*

5. *Nepal, according to Table 2–10, has a GNP/capita 45 percent greater than Ethiopia's. It follows that Nepal is a better market than Ethiopia because its inhabitants are richer. Discuss.*

6. *When international trade specialists in the Department of Commerce district offices are asked by firms or individuals for assistance in exporting, one of their first acts is to check the FT410 to establish market size.*
   a. *What are the advantages of using FT410 data?*
   b. *What are the shortcomings of using FT410 data?*

7. *Why might management decide to bypass indirect exporting and go to direct exporting right from the start?*

8. *A statement is made in the text that the reasons for investing abroad can be linked in some way to a desire to increase profits at an accepted level of risk. What connection is there between this desire and improved communications?*

9. *Suppose the president of your company tells you that its greatest competitor has just announced plans to manufacture in Australia. To protect its market there, he has decided to supply Australia from local production. He asks you to suggest various ways in which this can be accomplished. How would you answer him?*

10. *What is the twin factory concept?*

Minicase

2-1 Method of

Entry for Local

Manufacturing—The

McGrew Company

The McGrew Company, a manufacturer of peanut combines, has for years sold an appreciable number of machines in Brazil. However, a Brazilian firm has begun to manufacture them, and McGrew's local distributor has told Jim Allen, the president, that if McGrew expects to maintain its share of the market, it will also have to manufacture locally. Allen is in a quandary. The market is too good to lose, but McGrew has had no experience with foreign manufacturing operations. Because Brazilian sales and repairs have been handled by the distributor, no one in McGrew has had any firsthand experience in the country.

Allen has made some rough calculations which indicate that the firm can make money by manufacturing in Brazil, but the firm's lack of marketing expertise in the country troubles him. He calls in Joan Beal, the export manager, and asks her to prepare a list of all the options open to McGrew, with their advantages and disadvantages. Allen also asks Beal to indicate her preference.

1. Assume that you are Joan Beal. Prepare a list of all the options, and give the advantages of each.

2. Assuming that the president's calculations are correct and that a factory to produce locally the number of machines that McGrew now exports to Brazil will offer a satisfactory return on the investment, what special information about Brazil will you want to gather?

3. Which of the options would you recommend?

Minicase

2-2 "Quick and Dirty"

Research—Thermo Freezer

Thermo Freezer is a small manufacturer of air conditioners whose sales last year were $16 million. Bob Merchant, the president, is concerned about future growth because sales are increasing at a decreasing rate. He wonders what the possibilities are for exporting. Merchant calls in Henry Adams, the marketing manager, and asks him to do some "quick and dirty" market research. "Henry, I wish you would check U.S. exports of air conditioners for automobiles. Find out the total dollar volume and the countries to which they are being exported. If the figures look good, we can do an in-depth study on the markets that look more promising."

Assume that you are Henry Adams, and obtain the information that Bob Merchant is asking for. (*Hint:* Check the Bureau of the Census *FT410* in the government documents section of your library.)

Supplementary Readings

"Are Foreign Partners Good for U.S. Companies?" *Business Week*, May 28, 1984, pp. 58–60.

"Comparative Alliances: Philips–Du Pont Drive to Win Optical Disc Market," *Business International*, May 19, 1986, pp. 153–55.

Connolly, Seamus G. "Joint Ventures with Third World Multinationals: A New Form of Entry to International Markets." *Columbia Journal of World Business*, Summer 1984, pp. 18–22.

Contractor, Farok J. "Strategies for Structuring Joint Ventures: A Negotiations Planning Paradigm." *Columbia Journal of World Business*, Summer 1984, pp. 30–36.

DeWitt, R. Peter. "Factors Influencing U.S. Investment Abroad," *CSU, Los Angeles Business Forum*, Summer 1986, pp. 12–19.

"Du Pont's Strategy: Finding the Chemistry of Success in Japan." *Business International*, April 5, 1986, pp. 106–08.

"LOF and Nippon Glass Enter Korean Auto Glass Market with Tripartite Venture." *Business International*, December 20, 1985, pp. 401–05.

"Lucky-Goldstar: Using Joint Ventures to Sprint Ahead in the High-Tech Race." *Business Week*, July 9, 1984, pp. 102–03.

Scholl, Russell B. "The International Investment Position of the United States in 1985." *Survey of Current Business*, June 1986.

Stock of Private Direct Investments by DAC Countries in Developing Countries, End 1967. Paris: OECD, 1972.

Endnotes

1. This illustrates an interesting point concerning data provided by supranational organizations and governments. The UN claims that the volume of international trade for 1981 was $1,962 billion, whereas the International Monetary Fund states that it was only $1,832 billion. When queried by telephone, the head of the IMF statistical department explained that because nonmember communist countries did not report to the IMF, he had to use data that came from communist trading partners that were members. Also, when countries are slow in reporting, the IMF and the UN often estimate by extrapolation. Later, when data do arrive, corrections are made. These changes are made continuously and for previous periods. As late as July 1982, the UN made changes in data for the year 1975. Compare the June and July 1982 issues of the *UN Monthly Bulletin of Statistics*, table 52.

2. To produce steel, Japan must import 99.4 percent of the iron ore used, 77 percent of the coal, and 7.5 percent of the scrap steel. In comparison, the United States imports 38 percent, 0.1 percent, and 0.4 percent, respectively. Data from *The United States Steel Industry and Its International Rivals* (Washington, D.C.: Bureau of Economics, Federal Trade Commission, November 1977), p. 31.

3. *The Near East Market* (Washington, D.C.: U.S. Department of Commerce, 1974), p. 2.

4. One of the writers was given the job of searching for countries where production facilities for industrial rubber products might be set up. Included in the preliminary study was an investigation of the amounts of these goods that were currently being imported. It was evident that certain countries could not have local manufacturing facilities because of the magnitude of their imports. This provided an initial list of prospects, which were then investigated according to other criteria established by management.

5. It is believed by the Treasury Department that some of the stock held in other countries is kept by foreign stockbrokers for American residents of the United States. Data were obtained in a telephone conversation with the U.S. Treasury.

6. Sanford Rose, "Why the Multinational Tide is Ebbing." Reprinted from the August 1977 issue of *FORTUNE* magazine by special permission; © 1977, Time, Inc.

7. "Technical Notes," *World Development Report, 1982* (Washington, D.C.: World Bank, 1982), p. 162.

8. "Overhauling the Drug Laws to Promote Competition," *Business Week*, September 4, 1978, p. 65.

9. Of the eight licensing agreements in which one of the writers was involved, five came about as a result of unexpected visits from foreign businessmen. Vernon, a professor of international business, noted in a 1968 study that U.S. foreign investment in developed

nations increased at the same 10 percent rate as did the arrivals and departures of international travelers in North America and Europe from 1953 to 1965. He suggested that there was a direct relationship. From Christopher Tugendhat, *The Multinationals* (New York: Random House, 1972), p. 25.

10. "BI's Profitability Survey," *Business International*, September 29, 1986, pp. 305–11.

11. One of the writers was once offered a job in Peru by an American management consultant who openly admitted that his growth strategy consisted of gaining access to large American accounts by first consulting for one or more of their foreign subsidiaries.

12. "Business Makes a Run for the Border," *Fortune*, August 18, 1986, p.70.

13. It is not only the producers of metals and petroleum products that import a large part of the raw materials they use. Such diverse firms as A&P, Anderson Clayton, and Unilever also maintain large foreign operations to assure a constant supply of coffee (A&P), cotton and coffee (Anderson Clayton), and vegetable oils (Unilever).

14. "Japan's Foreign Direct Investment: Trends and Outlook," *Japan Report* (New York: Japan Information Service, April 16, 1977), p. 2.

15. "Bargain Hunter," *Fortune*, September 6, 1982, p. 11.

16. "Foreigners Grab for Value in the U.S.," *Business Week*, November 14, 1977, pp. 178–79.

17. "As Recession Bites, Many Multinationals Get Lift from Abroad," *The Wall Street Journal*, July 23, 1980, p. 1.

18. "The New Migration—of Money," *Newsweek*, May 3, 1976, p. 65.

19. From "Ford and VW: A Marriage of Convenience," *Business Week*, December 8, 1986; and "Ford, Volkswagen Plan Joint Venture to Oversee Units in Argentina and Brazil," *The Wall Street Journal*, November 25, 1986, p. 25.

20. From "A Japanese Tonic for Merck," *Business Week*, August 22, 1983, p.39.

21. For example, Mexico generally requires 51 percent local ownership, but the percentage rises to 75 percent for insurance companies and financial institutions. For mines, it is 66 percent.

22. "Use a Long Spoon," *Forbes*, December 15, 1986, p. 122.

23. "Westinghouse-Mitsubishi Fuse in Power Market," *Business International*, November 24, 1986, p. 370.

24. One of the writers, who was employed by the Mexican affiliate of an American company, which held 33 percent equity in the affiliate, was asked by the Mexican secretary of commerce why the Mexican plant was not exporting to Guatemala. The reason, which he could not disclose, was that the company served the Guatemalan market from wholly owned plants in the United States and thus kept all the profits. A hurried call to Akron gave him permission to do some exporting to Guatemala to appease the Mexican government, but he was asked, "not to try too hard."

25. "Change of Label at Dior," *Vision*, December 1981, pp. 12–16.

26. U.S. Franchising Industry, *Business America,* March 3, 1986, pp. 11–13.

27. From "Here They Come Again," *Forbes*, June 17, 1985, p. 54.

28. Gillette, in a recent annual report, states that its products are sold in more than 200 countries. It manufactures in 21 countries and markets through agents or distributors elsewhere.

29. For a good analysis of the factors that have influenced U.S. foreign investment, read R. Peter DeWitt's "Factors Influencing U.S. Investment Abroad, "*CSU, Los Angeles Business Forum*, Summer 1986, pp. 12–19.

CHAPTER 3

THEORIES OF INTERNATIONAL TRADE AND ECONOMIC DEVELOPMENT

"Agriculture in the world today is almost universally protected and on a massive scale. The European Community is spending over $20 billion ECUs through the European Community budget, and there is probably as much again spent in the various national budgets. The U.S. is spending $21 billion on agricultural protection of one kind or another. Subsidies to agriculture in Japan amount to some $12 billion, or one third of the total value of Japanese agricultural produce. Expenditures of this sort and this size cannot make sense."

Nigel Lawson, chancellor of the exchequer, OECD ministerial meeting, April 17, 1986

Learning Objectives

After you study this chapter, you should know:

1. Some of the theories that attempt to explain why certain goods are traded internationally.
2. The basic arguments for imposing trade restrictions.
3. What tariff and nontariff trade barriers are.
4. The reasons why GNP/capita alone is insufficient for comparing the rates of economic development among nations.
5. The characteristics that are common to less developed countries.
6. Some of the theories of economic development.
7. Some of the theories of foreign direct investment.

Key Words and Concepts

Mercantilism
Absolute advantage
Comparative advantage
Factor endowment
International Product Life
  Cycle (IPLC)
Tariff barriers
Variable levy
Cross investment

Internalization theory
Underground economy
Voluntary restraint
Technological dualism
Regional dualism
Countertrade
Human needs approach
Monopolistic advantage theory

71

Business Incident

Economists in and out of government have clearly had a major impact on policy. The Employment Act of 1946 created a Council of Economic Advisors to advise the President on the state of the economy and how the goal of full employment could best be achieved. Since 1960 the Council has played a major role in proposing policies. Other economists play major roles in the cabinet, on regulatory commissions and boards, and in many executive departments and administrative agencies. Nor is it necessary to be in government to affect government policy. Dozens of economists have significantly influenced economic policy from the sidelines. Milton Friedman, Paul Samuelson, James Tobin, Lawrence Klein, Arthur Okun, and Paul McCracken are examples of those whose statements are widely reported and help form the opinions of those who make policy decisions.

From R. Lipsey and P. Steiner, *Economics*, 5th ed., p. 14,
reproduced with permission of the publisher, Harper & Row © 1978.

*F*or a number of years now, economists have occupied important positions in governments. In fact, in the 17th and 18th centuries the teachings of the *political economists*, as they were called, had an important influence on the political and economic decisions of the time. Although the name of the profession has changed, economists continue to serve in governments both as advisers and as line personnel. The "tecnicos," economists in the Mexican government, are well known for their influence on the decisions made at high levels, as are the "Chicago boys" in Chile (young Chilean economists trained at the University of Chicago).

What does this signify for international businesspeople? It means that in many of their dealings with governments they will be discussing business with economists and that they must be able to speak the economists' language. When they seek governmental permission to establish new firms, businesspersons must assume that economists will study their proposals, make economic analyses for the decision makers, and may even be responsible for the final decisions. Knowing this, they should see to it that the benefits of their proposals are explained in technically accurate terms and are sound with respect to economic theory. Inasmuch as business decisions and governmental actions are both influenced and explained by many of the concepts of economics, especially in the fields of international trade theory, economic development, and international investment, it is essential that those in international business have a basic understanding of these important disciplines. International trade theory alone cannot fully account for or predict all international business behavior, and economic development theory cannot fully explain all of the actions taken by government officials. Nevertheless, as we shall point out, a number of the concepts of international trade theory and economic development theory do figure importantly in all three environments—domestic, foreign, and international.

International Trade Theory

Why do nations trade? This is the basic question that international trade theory attempts to answer. Historically, economists have looked primarily to price differences as a cause of trade, probably because products were more homogeneous when much of the theory was formulated, and certainly little was known about consumer behavior.

Price differences reflect differences in cost. This and the closely related question of what countries gain by trading were the subject of the classical theory of international trade associated with Ricardo, a famous economist of the 1800s. Before studying his theory of comparative advantage, we should first take a brief look at *mercantilism*, the economic doctrine that preceded it.[1]

Mercantilism

Mercantilism guided government economic policy during the 17th and 18th centuries. The central idea of mercantilism was that more goods were to be exported than imported so that there would be an influx of gold to enrich the nation. Mercantilists were possessed with the notion that a country's wealth comprised only precious metals, and there was little awareness that wealth consists of goods that can be used for production or consumption. Because individuals might trade gold for imports, it was believed that they could not be trusted, and that therefore it was essential for governments to control foreign trade. Domestic industry was encouraged and protected by means of subsidies, import duties, and other controls. After all, when local products were purchased, there was no loss of precious gold to foreigners. Although mercantilism was superseded by classical economic theory, one needs only to listen to present-day arguments for the protection of domestic industry to realize that although mercantilism may be old, it is not dead.

An example of modern-day mercantilism is the new industrial policy based on heavy state intervention that the socialists were creating for France. They nationalized key industries and banks so as to use the power of the state as both (1) stockholder and financier and (2) customer and marketer to revitalize the nation's industrial base. With nearly one third of France's productive capacity and 70 percent of its high-tech electronic capabilities in the hands of the government, its power was approaching the level of state intervention in the 17th century. Some writers were calling this high-tech mercantilism. In 1986, after five years of little growth and high unemployment, the government reversed its policy when Jacques Chiroc, a conservative, won the election for premier against President Mitterand's Socialist candidate. Chiroc proceeded to denationalize $23 billion worth of government holdings in banking, insurance, and industry.

Theory of Absolute Advantage

Increasing dissatisfaction with government control in the era of the mercantilists prompted various writers in the 18th century to advocate a reduction in government protection of local industry and a move toward freer foreign trade. Adam Smith, in his famous work *The Wealth of Nations* (1776), attacked the principles and practices of the mercantilists.[2] He argued that trade for the sake of accumulating gold was foolish when by means of free, unregulated trade a nation could acquire what it did not produce at home. Under free trade conditions, a country could gain most by producing only the goods that it was most efficient at making. Some of the surplus goods could then be traded to obtain those products that could not be produced advantageously at home.

Example

Suppose that in one man-day the following quantities of shoes and wheat can be produced in Countries A and B.

	Output per Man-Day	
Commodity	A	B
Sacks of wheat	2	1
Pairs of shoes	3	4

In the time that it takes someone from A to produce two sacks of wheat, this person can also manufacture three pairs of shoes. In A, therefore, three pairs of shoes should be equal in price to two sacks of wheat. The situation is different in B, because four pairs of shoes are made there in the time that is required to produce one sack of wheat. In this case, one sack of wheat should be as valuable as four pairs of shoes. B has an **absolute advantage** in manufacturing shoes because more shoes can be produced in a man-day there than in A, but more wheat can be obtained in A than in B in one man-day, so A has an absolute advantage in wheat production.

If A can obtain more than three pairs of shoes for two sacks of wheat by trading, then it should trade its wheat for shoes. Similarly, if B can obtain more than one sack of wheat for four pairs of shoes, then it should be willing to trade its shoes for wheat from A. What the exact terms of trade will be is uncertain, but we do know that trade will take place between the limits of two sacks of wheat for three pairs of shoes and two sacks of wheat for eight pairs of shoes.

Terms of Trade

Assume that businesspeople in each country agree on an exchange of one sack of wheat for three pairs of shoes. The person in A will get three pairs of shoes requiring one man-day to produce in A by exporting a sack of wheat, which needs only one-half man-day to produce. The trader from B will receive one sack of wheat requiring one man-day to produce locally by exporting three pairs of shoes, for which only three fourths of a man-day was utilized. Clearly, both countries have gained by trading.

This is easy to understand, but would it still be advantageous to trade when one nation is more efficient than another in the production of *both* products?

Theory of Comparative Advantage

In 1817, the classical economist David Ricardo showed that it would.[3] All that is necessary is that the less efficient country not be *equally* less efficient in the production of *both* goods. Assume that the following quantities can be produced per man-day.

	Output per Man-Day	
Commodity	A	B
Sacks of wheat	2	1
Pairs of shoes	4	3

Note that B is now less efficient than A in the production of both commodities but that *compared* to A, it is more efficient in shoe production than in wheat production. B has, therefore, a **comparative advantage**, or a relative advantage, in shoe production. With no trade between countries, one sack of wheat would be exchanged for two pairs of shoes in A and one sack of wheat for three pairs of shoes in B. If someone in A can get a pair of shoes for anything less than one-half sack of wheat, it would pay to trade. Likewise, if a person in B can obtain more than one sack of wheat for three pairs of shoes, he should trade. In other words, any exchange rate between the limits of one sack of wheat for two pairs of shoes and one sack of wheat for three pairs of shoes will benefit both sides.

Suppose they agree to exchange one sack of wheat for 2 1/2 pairs of shoes. Now a citizen of A with one day's work producing two sacks of wheat can have five pairs of shoes instead of having to work 1 1/4 days for them. A person in B, by working one day to make three pairs of shoes will receive 1.2 (3/2.5) sacks of wheat instead of one. Both have benefited from the exchange because both have received more as a result of their labor. More goods can be produced by specialization, and everyone will have a higher level of consumption. It is this simple concept that is the basis for international trade.

Although economists today commonly talk of three factors of production (land, labor, and capital), in the times of Ricardo and Smith only labor was thought to be important in the calculation of production costs.[4] This is why only the hours of labor were employed in the analysis of absolute and comparative advantage theories. Obviously, too, no consideration was given to the possibility of producing the same goods with different combinations of factors. It was not until 1933 that Ohlin, a Swedish economist, introduced the theory of **factor endowment**, which stated that trade occurs because nations have different relative endowments of production factors.

Heckscher-Ohlin Theory of Factor Endowments

According to the Heckscher-Ohlin theory, trade between regions of a country or between countries is caused by a difference in their factor endowments. If each region concentrates on producing the goods that require a large amount of its relatively abundant factor, those goods ought to have lower production costs and therefore can be sold for less in the international market. Taiwan, having a relative abundance of labor as compared to capital, should concentrate on producing labor-intensive goods. Germany, on the other hand, having relatively more capital than labor, should specialize in capital-intensive products and then trade with Taiwan. When each country makes greater use of the relatively more abundant and thus less expensive factors and then trades internationally, the result should be a higher level of living for all countries.

How does this theory hold up in the real world? Actually, not too badly. Australia, for example, with a relatively large amount of land, does export land-intensive products such as wheat and cattle, while Hong Kong exports goods requiring large inputs of labor. Exceptions to the theory occur for the most part because of some assumptions made by Ohlin that in reality do not exist. Ohlin ignored transportation costs, for example, but if the landed cost (export sales price plus transportation cost to the importing country) is higher than the cost of production in the would-be importing nation, there will probably be little trade. Note, however, that we cannot go so far as to say there will be none, because differences in tastes can still account for trade from the high-cost nation to the low-cost nation. Thus, France sends the United States cosmetics, wine, and clothing (all produced here) and Italy exports automobiles to one of the world's largest car manufacturers. Obviously, a U.S. buyer of a Ferrari sports car did not make the purchase on the basis of price.[5]

The theory also assumes that the same technology is available to all nations, but if this were true, there would be no need for licensing, as discussed in Chapter 2. Quite often, the superiority of a nation's technology permits goods to be produced at a lower price in that nation than in a nation better endowed with the factor most needed. It should be remembered, too, that many goods can be produced by either labor-intensive or capital-intensive methods. One needs only to compare construction methods in most less developed countries with those used in developed nations to appreciate the fact that it is not too difficult at times to substitute people for machines.[6]

Introducing Money

For reasons of simplicity, we have examined the theories of international trade in terms of units of goods—sacks of wheat and pairs of shoes. We could have introduced money earlier, but it would have added nothing to the explanation. However, money can change the direction of trade predicted by the theory. Let us introduce money to see how this may occur.

Example

Suppose that the total cost of land, labor, and capital to produce the daily output of either shoes or wheat is $20 in A and 300 pesos in B. The cost per unit is as follows:

Commodity	Price per Unit	
	A	B
Sack of wheat	$\dfrac{\$20}{2 \text{ sacks}} = \$10/\text{sack}$	300 pesos each
Pair of shoes	$\dfrac{\$20}{4 \text{ pairs}} = \$5/\text{pair}$	$\dfrac{300}{3} = 100$ pesos/pair of shoes

Exchange Rate

The relative prices of the two commodities are different in the two countries, but traders need to know what the absolute prices are in their own currency before trade can take place. To make the conversion from the foreign currency to the domestic currency, they must have the *exchange rate*—the price of one currency stated in units of another. If the current price of B's peso is about four cents in A's currency, someone from B wishing to buy dollars would ask what the dollar costs in pesos. If the peso costs four cents, then the dollar must cost 25 pesos.*

Using the exchange rate $1 = 25 pesos, the prices of the preceding table look like this to a businessperson from A.

---

*Peso = $0.04. To find number of pesos per dollar, divide $1.00 by the price of one peso ($0.04):

$$\frac{\$1.00}{\$0.04/\text{peso}} = \frac{\$1.00 \times \text{peso}}{0.04} = 25 \text{ pesos}$$

	Price per Unit	
Commodity	A	B
Sack of wheat	$10	$12
Pair of shoes	5	4

Wheat producers from A, by exporting wheat to B, can earn $2 more than they would by selling in A, while manufacturers of shoes in B will receive $5 per pair by exporting them rather than selling them in their home market for $4. As long as the exchange rate remains at $1 = 25 pesos, the direction of trade will be as described, but if the value of the peso drops to where the exchange rate becomes $1 = 30 pesos, wheat grown in B will cost the same as wheat from A, and importation from A will cease. Should the peso rise in value so that a dollar will buy only 20 pesos, shoes made in B will now cost the importers in A as much as shoes made in their own country, and they will have no incentive to import. By lowering the price of its currency in terms of other currencies (devaluing), a nation may make its exports more competitive while permitting domestic prices to remain unchanged.

This was the strategy that the Mexican government followed to reduce expenditure by its nationals in the United States and increase the receipts from American tourists in Mexico. After the devaluation, Mexican hotels and goods were much less expensive when the peso prices were converted to dollars. For the Mexican traveler in the United States, however, the same dollar prices cost many more pesos.

The international trade theory we have examined so far is the only explanation of trade that the international businessperson had until the 1960s, when a new concept, the International Product Life Cycle, was offered.[7]

International Product Life Cycle (IPLC)

This more recent approach, which is related to the product life cycle in marketing, can aid in the analysis of a product's export potential as well as predict which products may be in danger from import competition. The concept can be applied to new product introduction by firms in any of the developed nations, such as the United States, Japan, and Germany, but because more new products are introduced in the United States than elsewhere, we shall describe the **International Product Life Cycle** (IPLC) as it applies to this country.

According to the IPLC concept, many products pass through four stages:

1. *United States exports.* The United States possesses the world's largest population of consumers with high per capita income, and in the intense competition for their patronage, manufacturers are forced to search constantly for bet-

ter ways to satisfy their customers' needs. To supply new ideas, these firms maintain large research and development facilities whose personnel are in close contact with the suppliers of inputs that they need for new product development. The sellers of these raw materials are also located here.[8] As we know from studying the product life cycle, design changes are made during the initial stage of production as producers gain experience in the market.[9] By being near their customers, producers are in a position to make these changes rapidly. All of these factors combine to make the United States a leader in new product introduction.

For a period of time, American producers hold a monopoly on the new product's manufacture, and foreigners, as they learn about it, have to place their orders within the United States. American exports grow.

2. *Beginning of foreign production.* Elsewhere, consumers, especially those in other developed nations, have similar needs, and as they become familiar with the new offering, imports may grow large enough to support local manufacture. Overseas subsidiaries may be stimulated to study their markets by the constant stream of new product information supplied by the home office. If the results appear favorable, they may begin local production. Both their risks and their costs are lower because the parent company has "ironed out the bugs" and has already charged them for the technical information in the form of a service charge, which must be paid whether the information is used or not. From areas where the originating firm has no plants, entrepreneurs will come searching for technical information and will be licensed by U.S. manufacturers. Thus, production will begin in a number of the more advanced countries. The original manufacturer will still be exporting to those areas where there is no local production, but its export growth will slow down.

3. *Foreign competition in export markets.* Eventually some of the early foreign producers will become experienced in the marketing and manufacture of the product, and their costs will fall. As their local markets become saturated, they will look for customers elsewhere. If they enjoy lower production costs because of cheaper labor or raw materials, they may be able to undersell American exports. At this stage, foreign firms are competing for export markets with American companies, whose overseas sales will continue to decline.

4. *Import competition in the United States.* The production to satisfy both the home and export markets may be large enough to enable the foreign firm to reach economies of scale similar to those that American producers enjoy. Since it started later, the company possesses a newer plant, which may result in a cost advantage. In this final stage, not only will American exports dwindle but sales to the United States will be stepped up. Such competition may become so severe that American manufacturers will cease production altogether. As the authors of this concept state, the cycle may be repeated as the less developed countries acquire a producing advantage over the more advanced countries.[10]

Although stage 4 has not been substantiated empirically, a number of products appear to be in that stage. Japan, for example, gained the black-and-white TV market from the United States but then lost it to Taiwan. Now Taiwan has turned to the production of color TV from black and white and expects to obtain what has been Japan's market share in the United States.

> M. Matsushita, chairman of Japan's Matsushita Electric, replied when asked what countries have acquired the share of the American market that has been lost by Japan, "Much of our share of the radio market that we had 15 years ago has been taken by companies in Korea, Hong Kong, Singapore, and Taiwan. In color television sets, the countries which have replaced Japan are Taiwan, Mexico, and Korea."[11]

Summary of International Trade Theory

To sum up what we have learned, we can say that the primary reason for international trade seems to be the existence of price differentials among nations. These occur because of differences in production costs, which are, in turn, dependent on relative endowments of production factors and the degree of efficiency with which these factors are employed. However, taste differences, a demand variable, are capable of reversing the direction of trade predicted by the theory.

Trade Restrictions

We have seen that international trade theory provides strong arguments for free, unrestricted commerce. Yet there are "voluntary" quotas on Japanese car exports to the United States, Japanese import duties on aluminum and agricultural products that adversely affect American exports, restrictions of steel imports into the European Community, and so forth. If free trade is so beneficial, why is it that every country in the world is surrounded by trade restrictions?

Arguments for Protection and Their Rebuttal

To understand the arguments for trade restrictions, one must make a distinction between *national* and *individual* interests. At the national level, there is little doubt that a reduction in trade restrictions will benefit the population in general. For example, a Bureau of Economics report to the U.S. Federal Trade Commission notes that the aggregate costs to the U.S. economy of all existing tariffs and quotas on four significant industries—autos, textiles, steel, and sugar—amount to $8.52 billion annually. And a study by a Washington trade group estimates that the public is paying $2.7 billion a year in higher clothing costs because of the 29.3 percent average import duties on clothing products.[12] While an elimination of these duties would benefit the general public, it would be detrimental to American clothing manufacturers and their employees. Naturally, this group would pressure the federal government to place high duties on these products to protect the clothing industry from cheap foreign labor.

Protect Domestic Jobs from Cheap Foreign Labor

There is no question that the lower wage rates paid in some countries *may* result in lower-cost goods, but lower wage rates do not guarantee lower production costs. This is something that newcomers to international business must keep in mind when they see hourly wage comparisons, such as $20 for autoworkers in the United States versus $1.80 for South Korean workers, offered as proof that American firms cannot meet foreign competition.

Wage Rates Are Not Production Costs. A comparison of wages is not the same as a comparison of production costs, because production costs depend on the output per worker. Disparities in worker output in favor of the industrialized nations frequently exist, partly because of differences in attitudes toward work and in the educational levels of the workers, but more important, because the residents of these countries have more capital equipment with which to work.

Another factor to consider is that fringe benefits and government-imposed bonuses are much higher in many nations than they are here. In Mexico, for example, a firm is required by law to distribute a part of its profits to its employees. This can be the equivalent of an extra month's pay. In Chile, companies are required to provide medical and dental services for employees at very nominal fees that in no way cover the actual costs.[13] When fringe benefits are added to hourly wage rates, the wage differential between countries often lessens.

Labor Costs Are Part of Production Costs. We should also remember that the cost of labor is only part of the total production costs. Where wage rates are low, capital costs are usually high, so that total production costs may be greater in a low-wage nation than in a high-wage nation. Why else do manufacturers in lesser developed nations plead for import duties to protect them from the competition of industrialized nations?

Import Protection Can Affect Exports

Those who seek protection from imports use wage-rate comparisons to show that cheaper foreign labor enables products to be produced at less cost and consequently sold at prices lower than those of similar articles manufactured in this country. When American firms cannot meet this price competition, they are forced to lay off workers; in other words, imports take jobs from Americans.

Others answer this argument by pointing out that American exports create jobs and that if an industry threatened by imports obtains tariff protection, the country whose exports are affected may place import duties on our exports. They say that more jobs might be lost because of a cutback on our exports than are gained by reducing U.S. imports.

A study by Wharton Econometric Forecasting Associates seems to confirm this contention. The authors state that the local content laws (which would require imported cars to contain a fixed percentage of American-made parts) would cause 7.3 jobs to be lost in areas of import auto dealers and port and transportation facilities for every new job gained in the American automotive industry.[14]

An increase in import protection by means of higher import duties may affect a nation's exports in still another way. According to one study, if a nation's import duties are increased by 5 percent, for example, the price of the imported product will rise by the same amount.[15] This will contribute to a general rise in prices, which will then contribute to an increase in wages. When production costs rise, manufacturers of domestic products that compete with the imports will increase their prices by 5 percent, and thus profitability will remain the same as it was before the rise in import duties.

The effect on an exporter in that nation is different, however. Even though its costs may go up by 5 percent, the exporter may not be able to increase its prices by the same amount because it has to compete in world markets. The authors of the study conclude that two thirds of the burden of an increase in import duties falls on exporters totally unconnected with the industry receiving import protection.

Scientific Tariff or Fair Competition

In a related argument, the spirit of fair competition is invoked by those who want an import duty equal only to the difference between domestic and foreign production costs. This would eliminate any "unfair" cost advantage that a foreign firm could have because of superior technology, lower capital costs, lower wages, lower taxes from more efficient governmental administration, and so on. The resulting equal prices for domestic and imported goods would permit "fair competition." How fair this competition would be is questionable, because the less efficient producers would be protected from imports while the most efficient exporters to that country would be penalized. In effect, fair competition negates the theory of comparative advantage, which we examined earlier.

Protection of Vital Defense Industries

The argument that import duties are needed to protect vital defense industries is also frequently heard. If competition from lower-priced imports forces domestic firms to close down, these imports might be shut off in the event of a war. Since nearly every product imaginable is consumed by the military, the problem becomes one of deciding which products are truly vital. Opponents of this argument claim that it would be far better to offer subsidies to such firms so that the cost of maintaining these firms in the name of national security would be clearly spelled out.

Infant Industry Argument

Those who advocate import duties to protect infant industries take no issue with the theory of comparative advantage. All they want is protection for a new industry until the labor force is trained, production techniques are mastered, and the operation becomes large enough to enjoy the economies of large-scale production. If there is no such protection during the initial growth period, they argue, lower-priced imports from long-established foreign competitors will make it impossible for the new industry to survive. This implies that the protection is only temporary, but experience has shown that rarely, if ever, will an industry admit voluntarily that it has matured and no longer needs this protection.

Managers will find that this argument is much used today in less developed countries (LDCs). If their company is the first to establish a plant in an LDC, they will normally encounter sympathetic governmental ears to a plea for protection. There is a tendency, however, for some of the less developed countries, such as Chile and Brazil, to lower import duties in order to force their manufacturers to decrease their prices and be more competitive with imported goods. As these manufacturers become able to produce at world prices, it is expected that they will export. The success of this approach is indicated by the fact that Brazil now sells in the world market more than $15 billion annually in goods and services.

Other Arguments

We have examined five of the principal arguments for trade restrictions, but there are others, such as the use of import duties to improve the balance of exports versus imports (high duties will reduce imports) or to restrict the consumption of luxury goods (higher duties are charged for sports cars and yachts than for raw materials and production machinery).

You should have gathered from this discussion that protection from imports generally serves the narrow interests of a special group at the expense of many. While trade barriers can sometimes buy time for the protected industry to modernize and become more competitive in the world market, there is a real danger that a nation's trading partners will retaliate with restrictions that cause injury to industries that have received no protection. Let us examine these restrictions.

Kinds of Restrictions

Import restrictions are commonly classified as *tariff* (import duties) and *nontariff* barriers.[16]

Tariffs

Tariff barriers are the most widely employed trade restrictions, and they may be placed on either exports or imports. Their use as taxes on products coming into a country is generally for the purpose of reducing the volume of imports, although a few small countries still employ them as a source of revenue. Some of the raw material–exporting nations apply tariffs on exports for the same reason. Examples are Chile for copper and Brazil for coffee. Incidentally, the U.S. Constitution forbids export duties of all types.

Ad Valorem, Specific, and Compound. To understand how tariffs are levied, we must distinguish among ad valorem, specific, and compound duties. An *ad valorem* duty is stated as a fixed percentage of the invoice value. For example, the U.S. Tariff Schedule shows that perfumes not containing alcohol pay 7.5 percent ad valorem. When a shipment of this perfume invoiced at $1,000 arrives in the United States, the importer must pay the U.S. Customs Service a fee of $75 in order to take possession of the product. *Specific* duties are fixed sums of money per physical unit of the commodity. An importer of steel pipe must pay a duty of 0.3 cents per pound. Note that the value of the invoice is not considered. However, many commodities are charged both ad valorem and specific duties, which are then called *compound* duties. Returning to our example of perfume, if the perfume contains alcohol, the duty is charged on the basis of eight cents per pound plus 7.5 percent ad valorem. A $1,000 shipment of this perfume weighing 100 pounds would cost $8 specific duty plus $75 ad valorem duty, for a total of $83.

Official Prices. Sometimes foreign prices are so low compared to local prices that even with the import duties added, the landed cost of the imported product is lower than the domestic price. To assure that import duties will be effective in these cases, governments often establish official prices in their tariff schedules, on which the duty is calculated whenever the invoice price is lower. Until 1981, the United States used the American Selling Price for chemical products and footwear. When a pair of tennis shoes arrived in this country with an invoice price of $1, the 20 percent ad valorem duty was *not* calculated on this price. The law required customs appraisers to use the price of a comparable American shoe as the basis for their calculations.

Tariff Factories. Most nations place the highest import duty on a finished good ready for sale to the consumer and charge progressively less as more local input is required. This, of course, is to encourage importers to bring in products in the semifinished state and then use local labor and materials to finish the production process. Such assembly or mixing plants, when they are established to get behind a high tariff wall, are called tariff factories. By studying a nation's import tariff, management can frequently find situations where, with a relatively small investment, an operation can be set up free of import competition from finished products.

Mexico charged about 50 percent ad valorem for a rubber cement imported in one-quart cans. When the same cement was imported in 50-gallon drums, which required buying local cans and labels and hiring a laborer to fill these cans from the drum, the duty dropped to about 25 percent ad valorem. However, the duty was only 10 percent when the rubber compound, ready to be cut up and mixed with locally purchased solvent, was brought in. The only additional equipment required for this last step was a guillotine to cut the rubber compound into small pieces and a man with a strong back and a stick to mix the rubber and solvent.

Variable Levy. The European Community has a novel form of import duty called a **variable levy**, which guarantees that the market prices of imported grains will be the same as those of grains produced locally. Calculated daily, the duty level is set at the difference between world market prices and the support prices for domestic producers.

Nontariff Barriers

When a country is troubled by high inflation, if specific duties are not increased frequently, they may become so low as to be useless as barriers to trade. Furthermore, world prices may drop to such a point that even with import duties, the landed cost of imports may still be competitive with locally priced goods. To be certain that only a limited quantity of a product enters in any given period, many governments resort to **nontariff barriers**, especially quotas.

Quotas. When quantitative trade restrictions, or quotas, are *absolute*, only the amount stipulated by the government may be imported. *Tariff quotas* permit a specified amount to enter the country at low duty rates, but when that quantity has been reached, a much higher duty is charged for all subsequent importations. Quotas are employed either to conserve foreign currency by limiting imports or to protect local manufacturers from foreign competition; and unlike import duties, quotas yield no revenue to the government unless import licenses are sold.

While quotas are usually *global* (that is, a total amount is fixed, with no requirement as to source of supply), they are also at times *discriminatory* (that is, the government designates the supplying countries). The United States has specified for years which nations can ship us sugar and how much each of these nations can send.

To protect American steelmakers from imports of specialty steel, the U.S. government introduced an interesting combination of import duties and quotas in 1983. Additional duties of 10 percent were levied on stainless steel the first year and were reduced by 2 percent per year over the following three years. Global quotas have been placed on other types of steel and will be increased by 3 percent annually.

In 1983, a similar combination of duties and quotas was put on Japanese motorcycles 700 cc or larger to protect Harley-Davidson. The discriminatory

Figure 3-1

Auto Sales and Market Share in the United States

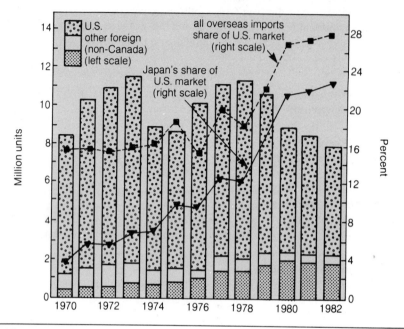

Source: Federal Reserve Bank of Chicago, *International Letter,* February 25, 1983, p. 1.

(only on Japan) five-year sliding duty was first raised from 4.9 percent to 49.4 percent, after which it was to decrease each year until, by 1988, the original value was restored. The restriction was never as effective as expected, because the Japanese quickly shifted to producing 699-cc motorcycles. Nonetheless, the American manufacturer so improved its product and streamlined production that it was able to ask the U.S. International Trade Commission to end import restrictions one year early. This is in sharp contrast to the "temporary" steel import restraints, which have existed with brief gaps since 1968.

Voluntary Restraint. Because there is general agreement among most nations that quotas should not be used except in special circumstances, governments are hesitant to establish them. Instead, exporting nations are asked to use **voluntary restraint**—a euphemism for self-imposed quotas. An example of such a quota is the quota on Japanese car exports to the United States that was instituted in 1981. This caused the U.S. sales of Japanese-made cars to decline from 1.91 million units in 1980 to 1.80 million units in 1982. Note, however, that the Japanese market share increased (see Figure 3–1). This is because there was an even greater sales decline of American-made cars. When the agreement expired in 1986, it was renewed, though the quotas were increased appreciably.

Orderly marketing arrangements also restrict international competition and preserve some of the national market for local manufacturers. They differ from unilaterally imposed quotas and other trade barriers in that they are formal agreements resulting from negotiations between exporting and importing nations. Usually this type of agreement provides for an annual increase in imports.

The largest orderly marketing agreement (OMA) is the Multi-Fiber Arrangement, a pact that includes 54 exporting and importing nations of textiles and garments. About 80 percent of the world's textile and clothing exports to the West are regulated by this agreement. Several more limited OMAs have been arranged by the United States under the Trade Act of 1974. This law gives the president the option of negotiating such agreements instead of imposing tariffs, quotas, or other restrictions recommended by the International Trade Commission.*

Countertrade. Another barrier to free trade is **countertrade**. This is essentially a transaction in which goods are exchanged for goods. The simplest form of countertrade, barter, dates from ancient times, but in recent years various other

Rotarian, September 1985.

"To all department heads: While barter agreements are not opposed per se, caution must—I repeat, must—be observed."

---

*The International Trade Commission, an independent agency of the federal government, advises the president and Congress on matters concerning the commercial and international trade policies of the United States.

kinds of countertrade have been used in East-West trade. Because of shortages of foreign exchange and a lack of markets for their products, many noncommunist nations have also been engaging in countertrade. Iraq obtained warships from Italy in exchange for crude oil, for example. Another example was the purchase by Spain of Colombian coffee in exchange for Spanish buses. Countertrade is a barrier to free trade because the sellers are forced to take goods that they would not otherwise buy, and in doing so, they close off another market from free and open competition. It is estimated that this type of transaction now accounts for about 25 percent of all world trade. We shall examine countertrade in greater depth in later chapters.

Other Nontariff Barriers. Because the general trend around the world is to lower tariffs, governments have been tempted to replace them with less obvious forms of protection. An inventory taken of these barriers revealed that there were over 800 distinct forms.[17] They may be grouped into three major categories: (1) direct government participation in trade, (2) customs and other administrative procedures, and (3) standards.

1. Direct government participation in trade includes *export subsidies* (payments made to manufacturers so that their products are more competitive in the world market) and *countervailing duties*, which are additional import duties levied on imported goods that receive export subsidies. This type of duty is employed to counteract the effect of the subsidy. Also part of this category is the preference that many nations give to national over foreign bidders on government bids. This is best known in the United States as the "buy American" practice. Quotas, OMAs, and countertrade are another part of this category.

2. Customs and other administrative procedures cover customs valuation, classification, and procedures. If government administrators wish to discriminate against a product or a country, they can order the customs inspectors to delay the importation process. The documents are found to be faulty. Weights declared on the invoices do not correspond exactly with actual weights. Customs officials may decide to place the goods in a different classification requiring higher duties.

> Recently the European Community decided that combined alarm clocks and radios were to be classified as radios instead of clocks. The import duty on radios was 14 percent, but on clocks it was only 9 percent. For a while, France relied on customs clearance delays to slow the importation of videotape recorders by decreeing that they would all have to pass through the tiny and relatively inaccessible customs port of Poitiers.

In this second major category of nontariff barriers, much attention has been paid to antidumping measures. *Dumping* is the selling abroad of products at prices lower than those charged in the producing country or in other national markets. The purpose is to force competitors out of business, after which the dumping firm would presumably raise its prices (this is sometimes called *preda-*

tory dumping). Nations into which goods are being dumped usually assess an extra duty to nullify the price differential. Difficulties arise when a lower export price is justified. Sometimes a lower-quality and thus lower-priced model is produced for export, and sometimes the marketing costs for exports are lower. Yet governments, pressured by national firms to stop competition from imports, may still apply antidumping tariffs, which are then truly barriers to trade.

3. All of the rules governing health, security, and packaging constitute standards that can hinder imports. For example, Canada will not permit entry of canned foods unless they are packed in can sizes established by the Canadian government. In Mexico, a product may not be displayed for sale unless all markings are in metric units (discrimination against U.S. products).

Denmark uses a packaging rule to protect its soft-drink industry from foreign competition. All beverages must be sold in returnable bottles. This deters French mineral water producers, because it is too costly to ship the returned bottles back to France for refilling. The European Court of Justice recently ordered Belgium to stop requiring margarine to be packaged as cubes. This rule had been effective in stopping importation from EC countries whose producers used round or rectangular packaging.

Japan ruled some imported canned goods unacceptable under its agricultural standards because the figures of the day, month, and year of canning were spaced too far apart on the labels. "Uniqueness" is another ground that Japan has used to shut out foreign imports. The skin of the Japanese is different, so foreign cosmetics companies must test their products in Japan before selling there. Imports of American tangerines have been limited because the stomachs of the Japanese are small and thus have room only for the local tangerines. Probably the strangest claim that has been advanced is that the snow of Japan is different, and therefore its ski equipment should also be different. A private industry group drafted a new set of standards for ski equipment, including one that increased the thickness of the ski under the binding. It argued that wetter snow and narrower slopes made these standards necessary. Only manufacturers meeting them would be able to use the mark SG, which stood for safety goods. Foreign manufacturers, which have 50 percent of the $440 million Japanese market, argued that the standards set by the International Organization for Standardization were adequate and that the Japanese standards were unnecessary. Only after considerable pressure were the standards canceled.

Denmark, Finland, Norway, and Sweden each apply separate standards for electrical equipment and require individual testing in the country prior to certifying imports.[18] Imagine the plight of the American manufacturer that must make up special products for each of these countries in order to comply with its special standards. The cost of compliance may price the company out of the market. This could be and frequently is the reason why such standards were set up in the first place.

These few examples will give the reader an idea of the complexity involved in trying to eliminate nontariff barriers. Some progress is being made, but it is slow. Meanwhile, the knowledge that such barriers exist should prompt the international businessperson to look for them before attempting to conduct business in a foreign country.

Economic Development

In their search for new markets, managers will find that they are examining the market potential of nations in various stages of development. Since a given stage affects the demand for goods, the state of the distribution system, and even the government's attitude toward foreign enterprise, managers must know enough about economic development to be able to adjust their business strategy to fit the situation. As they study the subject, they will encounter countries described as developed, newly industrializing, developing, less developed, least developed, and underdeveloped.

Developed, Newly Industrializing, Developing, Less Developed, Least Developed, Underdeveloped

The term *developed* refers to the major industrial powers of Europe and to Japan, Australia, New Zealand, the United States, and Canada. The relatively recent term *newly industrializing countries* (NICs) is used to describe the developing nations that have experienced rapid industrial growth over the last 20 years. South Korea, Taiwan, Hong Kong, Singapore, Brazil, and Mexico are considered NICs. Characteristics common to all of these countries are: (1) GNP/capita of $2,000 or more; (2) sizable exports of manufactured goods, including high-technology items; and (3) heavy concentrations of MNE investment. The other terms are employed to describe the state of development of the remaining countries in the world except the communist nations, which are usually placed in a separate nonmarket economy classification.

Although economic development encompasses much more than mere increases in per capita income, nations are usually differentiated by this criterion. Thus, the United Nations has defined the least developed nations as those having an annual gross domestic product per capita of $100 or less (since increased). In addition, the 25 nations so classified have little manufacturing capacity (10 percent or less of gross domestic product) and high illiteracy rates (20 percent or less of the population over age 15 are literate).[19] In this taxonomy, all other nations are called *developed* or *less developed* and occasionally the term *developing* is employed to include both the least and less developed. Businesspeople are cautioned not to use the term *underdeveloped*, as it is now considered pejorative. Clearly, these definitions suit the special purposes of the United Nations and are not necessarily followed by others.

The World Bank,* for example, has virtually ceased to use such terms. In the 1974 *World Bank Atlas*, a distinction was made between developing and industrial nations, but since then the bank has simply grouped nations according to incomes.[20] It now stratefies nations as low-income, middle-income, high-income oil exporters and industrial market economies.[21]

GNP/Capita—An Estimated Average

In spite of the widespread use of the GNP/capita value to classify countries as to their economic development, market analysts must use it with caution. They must remember that GNP/capita is calculated by dividing the market value of all goods and services produced annually in a country by that country's total population. To the uninitiated, a country whose yearly GNP/capita is $500 might be thought to be less developed than one with a yearly GNP/capita of $600. However, before making this assumption, they should realize that even in the United States the value of the GNP is only an estimate. In attempting to include all production in this figure, it is necessary for government economists to impute a dollar value to various goods not sold in the marketplace. A value has to be set on the food a farmer grows for his own consumption, for example.

Probably the most important reason of all for doubting not only the official GNP data but also the number of people said to be employed is the existence of the **underground economy**—the part of the GNP that, because of unreporting or underreporting, is not measured by official statistics. Called the *black economy* in England, the *shadow economy* in Germany, and the *submerged economy* in Italy, the underground economy is estimated to vary from 3.5 percent of GNP in Great Britain to almost 50 percent in India. (See Figure 3-2.)

In addition to reducing the total taxes paid to the government, the underground economy is responsible for all kinds of distortions of economic data. In Italy, for example, there was no record that a single pair of gloves was produced in Naples, yet it is now known that Naples is one of Italy's biggest glovemaking centers—the unreported output is produced by small groups of workers in kitchens and garages. The official government statistical agency estimates that the GDP is at least 15 percent greater than the official figure. The Italians are proud to say that, because of their underground economy, their per capita income has now overtaken that of the British. The *black work* in France is believed to be the reason why 50 percent of all the cement produced vanishes into thin air as far as official records are concerned. Even the USSR has its "second economy." Moonlighting workers form work brigades and rent themselves out at triple the prevailing wage at construction projects that are behind schedule. In one case, they were paid from funds officially recorded as payment for 1,000 spare wrenches![22]

World Bank—an intergovernmental investment institution created in 1945 to make or guarantee loans to member nations for reconstruction and development projects. It is discussed in Chapter 4.

Figure 3-2

Estimates of Underground Economies

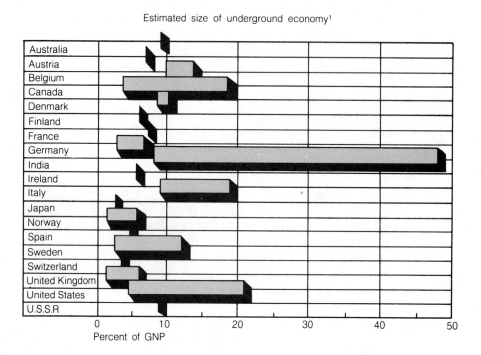

Estimated size of underground economy[1]

Percent of GNP

[1]These data show the ranges of estimates made for each country at different times; they are suggestive and should not be taken to be precise.
Source: "The Underground Economy," *Finance and Development,* December 1983, p. 13.

For these reasons, even the U.S. government, which possesses greater facilities and manpower for producing statistics than any other nation, can only estimate the true value of the goods and services produced. Clearly, other nations, especially the less developed countries, are reporting values that are even more approximate than those of the United States.

Figure 3-2 provides some estimates from studies of the underground economy of 19 countries in various parts of the world and with different social systems. Many of these studies indicate that the underground economy is not only sizable but is also growing faster than the official economy. The figures shown in the chart should be accepted with considerable caution, as they are the result of applying different methodologies and, in some cases, even different concepts. It would not be prudent to make precise cross-country comparisons without first consulting the studies themselves. As research techniques and factual information improve, it will probably become easier to generate estimates that warrant a greater degree of confidence.

The reporting of GNP by these countries is further complicated by the fact that much more of the goods and services produced are consumed outside the money economy (trade by barter) than in this country, and thus a greater amount of imputing must be done.

One other problem with GNP estimates is that official exchange rates are employed to convert foreign currencies to dollars. This procedure tends to underestimate the living levels in developing countries, because prices of comparable items are frequently much lower there. For example, a World Bank study showed that while the 1985 GNP/capita figures for Colombia, Kenya, and India converted to U.S. dollars at official rates were $1,320, $290, and $270, respectively, when they were calculated on the basis of purchasing power equivalents, these values increased to $3,845, $773, and $972.[23] See the table below for other comparisons.

GNP/Capita Alone Is Not Enough

Even if the previously mentioned discrepancies did not exist and we could accept the reported GNP/capita at face value, this alone would not be of much use in comparing the market potential of various countries. When we divided the GNP by the number of inhabitants, we in effect assumed that everyone received an equal share, but we know that this condition does not exist anywhere. In fact, a condition peculiar to the less developed countries is that income is less equally divided in them than in the more developed countries. This is why one will find Cadillacs in Bolivia and yachts in Tanzania. The exporter that dismisses

Per Capita GNP–Purchasing Power Parity versus Official Exchange Rates (1985)

Nation	Purchasing Power Parity	Official Exchange Rates
United States	$16,494	$16,690
Canada	14,959	13,680
Norway	14,098	14,370
Sweden	12,586	11,890
Denmark	12,322	11,200
West Germany	12,158	10,940
Japan	11,666	11,300
France	11,333	9,540
Netherlands	11,332	9,290
United Kingdom	10,882	8,460
Belgium	10,718	8,280
Italy	9,445	6,520

Source: Press release, Organization for Economic Cooperation and Development, February 9, 1987, and *World Development Report 1987* (Washington, D.C.: World Bank, 1987), p. 203.

nations as possible markets solely on the basis of a low GNP/capita will fail to contact some potentially lucrative markets.

It is evident, then, that analysts would prefer something superior to GNP/capita for the purpose of comparing nations' living levels. To this end, various attempts have been made to use indexes composed of nonmonetary indicators. One of these indexes combined the consumption of meat, cement, and steel with the number of vehicles, radios, and telephones, while others included per capita income; electric, cement, and newsprint consumption; caloric intake; and some social factors.[24] But these indexes also have weaknesses, with the result that market analysts often construct their own based on the factors they believe to be pertinent, as we shall see when we discuss the evaluation of markets. Fortunately, there are some characteristics that all LDCs share to some extent.

Common Characteristics of LDCs

Hans Singer, a noted UN economist, taking note of the great diversity of conditions in the less developed countries, once said that an underdeveloped country is like a giraffe: It is difficult to describe, but you always know when you see one. Probably a nation becomes an LDC when it declares itself to be one by applying for foreign aid, and then the developed countries confirm this status by providing assistance. Table 3–1 shows you the size of official government aid (not private) that was given to developing nations in 1986. Although the United States was by far the largest contributor on a dollar volume basis, only Austria provided less assistance as a percentage of GNP than did the United States.

In spite of the fact that there are no precise definitions of a less developed country, most of these countries share the following characteristics:

1. Annual per capita incomes less than $2000, with uneven income distribution among the inhabitants.
2. **Technological dualism**—firms with modern technology alongside firms using very primitive production methods.
3. **Regional dualism**—high income and productivity in some regions and little economic development in others. An eminent example is the undeveloped northeast and the heavily industrialized south of Brazil.
4. Only one in seven families earning its livelihood outside the agricultural sector.
5. Agriculture relatively unproductive.
6. Disguised unemployment or underemployment—using 10 people to do a job that 5 can easily do.
7. Wide range of health problems and much malnutrition.
8. High illiteracy rates and few educational facilities.
9. High population growth. (2.5–4.0 percent annually).

Table 3-1

Official Development Assistance (ODA) in 1985

Country	Volume of ODA ($ billion)	Percent of Total	ODA Percent of GNP
United States	$ 9.78	21.81%	0.23%
Japan	5.63	12.56	0.29
West Germany	3.88	8.65	0.43
Saudi Arabia	3.56	7.94	4.50
France	3.51	7.83	0.49
Italy	2.42	5.40	0.40
United Kingdom	1.75	3.90	0.32
Netherlands	1.74	3.88	1.00
Canada	1.70	3.79	0.48
Sweden	1.09	2.43	0.85
Norway	0.80	1.78	1.20
Australia	0.79	1.76	0.49
Kuwait	0.71	1.58	3.00
Denmark	0.70	1.56	0.89
Belgium	0.54	1.20	0.48
Switzerland	0.43	0.96	0.30
Finland	0.31	0.69	0.45
Austria	0.20	0.45	0.21
United Arab Emirates	0.07	0.16	0.34
New Zealand	0.07	0.16	0.27
Ireland	0.06	0.13	0.28
Rest of OPEC	0.20	0.45	n.a.
Other OECD donors	0.20	0.45	n.a.
(China, India, Israel, Yugoslavia)	0.50	1.12	n.a.
COMECON countries	4.20	9.36	0.27
Total World	$44.84	100.0	

The difference between total world and the sum is due to rounding.
Source: "Financial Resources for Developing Countries," *OECD Press Release* (Paris: OECD), June 19, 1987.

10. Great reliance on one or a few items for export—mainly raw materials and agricultural products.

11. Topography often consisting of deserts, savannas, salt flats, or mountains.

12. Lack of savings and poorly developed banking facilities.

13. Political instability.

How did the less developed countries get into this position, and how can they escape from it? These are the questions that development economists attempt to answer.

Theories of Economic Development

Present-Day Thought

Until the 1970s, economists generally considered economic growth to be synonymous with economic development. However, the realization that economic growth does not necessarily imply development, because such growth has so frequently benefited only a few, has led to the widespread adoption of a new, more comprehensive definition of economic development.

Human Needs Approach

Based on the **human needs approach**, economic development is being defined as the reduction of poverty, unemployment, and inequality in distribution of income. The definition of poverty has also been broadened. Instead of being defined in terms of income, a reduction of poverty has come to mean less illiteracy, less malnutrition, less disease, and a shift from agricultural to industrial production.[25] Note that while economic growth considers only economic change measured by GNP/capita, economic development is also concerned with social changes. To date, there is no one accepted index of economic development, though various attempts are being made to create one.

No One Accepted General Theory

The inclusion of noneconomic variables that differ greatly among the more than 100 developing nations has made it impossible to formulate a generally accepted theory of economic development. Instead, development economists are concentrating on specific problem areas—population growth, income distribution, unemployment, transfer of technology, role of government, investment in human versus physical capital, and so forth.

Relevance for Businesspeople

What is the relevance of a lack of consensus among specialists with respect to development theory? If a particular theory has fallen into disfavor among the experts, does this mean that you can neglect it in dealing with government officials? That depends. It may be that the officials you are contacting still subscribe to the theory. In that case, you will need to emphasize the parts of your proposal that are germane to it. Generally, this is not too difficult, because nearly every proposal will provide not only for physical capital but also for the training of employees, the provision of employment, and the transfer of technology, which are also the goals of most theories. There will even be some redistribution of income through the creation of a middle class composed of managers and highly skilled technicians. As an example, let's look at how you might handle your proposal with respect to the unbalanced growth theory.

Unbalanced Growth Theory

Government officials may subscribe to this theory, which calls for deliberately creating imbalances by investing in an industry, thus requiring further investment in other areas to reduce the imbalance. Will your proposal for an automobile assembly plant create such imbalances? Of course it will. There will be an immediate need for inputs such as tires, batteries, fabric-backed vinyl sheeting for upholstery, and so forth. Suppose a plant for producing the upholstery is built. Then PVC resin must be made locally or imported. If it is made locally, there is a need for the petrochemicals to make the resin. Like the auto assembly plant, many other manufacturing processes will create imbalances—that is, a need for manufactured or semiprocessed inputs not presently available in the host country.

Investment in Human Capital

This recent addition to the theory of economic development recognizes that more than just capital accumulation is needed for growth. There must also be investment in the education of the people so that there are (1) managers to assure that the capital is productive and (2) skilled workers to operate and maintain the capital equipment. If MNE managers know that this view has a strong acceptance in the country where they are seeking permission to establish a plant, they should emphasize this aspect of the investment. It is only rarely that a multinational firm will not have a training program for workers, and nearly all such firms send local managers to the home office to update their skills.

Import Substitution versus Export Promotion

Although developing nations have long considered the exporting of primary products (agricultural and raw materials) to be an important facet of their development strategy, they have not aggressively promoted the exporting of manufactured goods. Instead, they have concentrated on substituting domestically made manufactured products for imports as a way to lessen their dependence on the developed nations.

Unfortunately, import substitution has not reduced their dependence on developed nations as much as it has changed the composition of imports from finished products to capital and semiprocessed inputs. Dependence on the developed nations has increased because now the inability to obtain these inputs due to a lack of foreign exchange or some other reason stops entire industries and throws thousands of people out of work. A recent example was the closing of auto and agricultural machinery plants in Turkey when the Turkish government could not obtain foreign exchange for importing the necessary intermediate products.

Another serious problem with the import substitution strategy stems from the protection to local industry that governments grant by levying high import duties on goods that are also produced domestically. With this umbrella, local manufacturers are under no pressure to lower their costs or improve their quality. Without such pressure, they rarely become competitive in world markets and thus cannot export. Furthermore, other domestic firms that must buy inputs from these high-priced, protected industries cannot export either, because their costs are excessive.

Such problems have caused numerous governments to change from a strategy of import substitution to one of promoting exports of manufactured goods. Spurring this decision has been the rapid export growth of the newly industrializing nations we mentioned earlier. To force companies to become competitive in world markets, some governments have been putting limits on the amount and duration of protection.

The change in strategy affects MNEs in a variety of ways. First, managers of MNE affiliates must be prepared for demands to export by government officials. These affiliates may be given an ultimatum, as were automobile manufacturers in Mexico. "If you need to import parts for your output, you must earn the foreign exchange to pay for them by exporting parts of your production." Now a company asking for permission to set up a plant will certainly be asked what its plans for exporting are. This is a new phenomenon for longtime MNE managers, who have been accustomed to restricting an affiliate to sales in its internal market so as to save the export market for home country production. Second, affiliate managers can no longer count on having permanent protection from competing imports. There are countries where they are likely to be told that after a certain date they will lose their protection and be expected to compete internationally. Lastly, in a situation where two firms are competing for permission to set up a plant, the deciding factor may be that one of them offers its multinational channels of distribution to the affiliate's exports.

The Importance of Keeping Current

These few examples illustrate (1) some of the concepts that underlie the strategies and policies of developing nations and (2) the relationship between the theories of international trade and development. Moreover, they show why experienced international businesspeople keep abreast of developments in both areas.

International Investment Theories

This third set of theories attempts to explain why international investment takes place. The contemporary theory has been expanded considerably from the classical theory, which postulated that differences in interest rates for investments of equal risk are the reason why international capital moves from one nation to another. For this to happen, there had to be perfect competition, but as Kindleberger, a noted economist, stated, "Under perfect competition, foreign direct investment would not occur, nor would it be likely to occur in a world wherein the conditions were even approximately competitive."[26]

Contemporary Theories of Foreign Direct Investment

Monopolistic Advantage Theory

The modern **monopolistic advantage theory** stems from Stephen Hymer's dissertation in 1960, in which he demonstrated that foreign direct investment occurred largely in oligopolistic industries rather than in industries operating under near-perfect competition. This meant that the firms in these industries must possess advantages not available to local firms. Hymer reasoned that the advantages must be economies of scale, superior technology, or superior knowledge in marketing, management, or finance. Foreign direct investment took place because of these product and factor market imperfections.[27]

Product and Factor Market Imperfections

Caves, a Harvard economist, expanded on Hymer's work to show that superior knowledge permitted the investing firm to produce differentiated products that the consumers would prefer to similar locally made goods and thus would give the firm some control over the selling price and an advantage over indigenous firms. To support these contentions, he noted that companies investing overseas were in industries that typically engaged in heavy product research and marketing effort.[28]

International Product Life Cycle (IPLC)

We have already examined this theory to help explain international trade flows, but as we said, there is a close relationship between international trade and international investment. As you saw, the IPLC concept also explains that foreign direct investment is a natural stage in the life of a product. To avoid losing a market that it services by exporting, a company is forced to invest in overseas production facilities when other companies begin to offer similar products. This move overseas will be heightened during the third and fourth stages as the company that introduced the product strives to remain competitive, first in its export markets (stage 3) and later in its home market (stage 4), by locating in countries where the factors of production are less expensive. Twin factories on the Mexican-American border are an example.

Other Theories

Another theory was developed by Knickerbocker, who noted that when one firm, especially the leader in an oligopolistic industry, entered a market, other firms in the industry followed. The follow-the-leader theory is considered defensive because competitors are investing to avoid losing the markets served by exports when the initial investor begins local production. They may also fear that the initiator will achieve some advantage of risk diversification that they will not have unless they also enter the market.[29] In addition, there is always the suspicion that the competitor knows something that they do not and the feeling that it is better to be safe than sorry.

Graham noted that there was a tendency for **cross investment** by European and American firms in certain oligopolistic industries; that is, European firms tended to invest in the United States when American companies had gone to Europe. He postulated that such investments would permit the American subsidiaries of European firms to retaliate in the home market of U.S. companies if the European subsidiaries of these companies initiated some aggressive tactic, such as price cutting, in the European market.[30] Of course, as we noted in Chapter 2, there are a number of other reasons why investment in the United States by foreign multinationals takes place, such as *following the customer* (Japanese parts manufacturers following Japanese auto manufacturers), *seeking knowledge* (Japanese and European investment in the Silicon Valley), and *benefiting from the stability of the American government*.

The **internalization theory** is an extension of the market imperfection theory. The firm has superior knowledge, but it may obtain a higher price for that knowledge by using it than by selling it in the open market. By investing in a foreign subsidiary rather than licensing, the company is able to send the knowledge across borders while maintaining it within the firm, where it presumably yields a better return on the investment made to produce it.[31]

There are other theories that relate to financial factors. Aliber believes that the imperfections in the foreign exchange markets may be responsible for foreign investment. Companies in nations with overvalued currencies are attracted to investment where currencies are undervalued.[32] Although empirical tests are inconclusive, it does seem that a sizable number of U.S. takeovers by European multinationals occurred during the late 1970s, when the dollar was relatively weak. One other financially based theory (portfolio theory) suggests that international operations allow for a diversification of risk and therefore tend to maximize the expected return on investment.[33]

Note that there is one commonality to nearly all of these theories that is supported by empirical tests—the major part of direct foreign investment is made by large, research-intensive firms in oligopolistic industries. Note also that these theories offer reasons why companies find it *profitable* to invest overseas. However, as we stated in Chapter 2, all motives, aggressive and defensive, can be linked in some way to the desire to increase or protect not only profits, but also *sales* and *markets*.[34]

Summary

Why do nations trade? Mercantilist nations did so to build up storehouses of gold. Later, Adam Smith showed that a nation would export goods that it could produce with less labor than other nations. Ricardo proved that even though less efficient than other nations, a nation could still profit by exporting goods. All that was necessary was to hold a comparative advantage in the production of the goods.

The idea that a nation would tend to export products requiring a large amount of a relatively abundant factor was offered by Heckscher and Ohlin in their theory of factor endowment. Finally, the International Product Life Cycle theory states that many products that are first produced in the United States or other developed countries are eventually manufactured in less developed countries and become imports to the very countries where their production began.

Although international trade theory argues for free, unrestricted trade for the benefit of everyone, restrictions on trade still exist because of the pressure of local interest groups. The inability to compete with cheap foreign labor, and the need to protect defense industries and new industries are given as reasons why protection is required. In response to demands for protection, governments impose such restrictions on trade as import duties and quotas and other nontariff barriers.

A useful tool for international managers is an understanding of economic development theory. This will help them realize that in market analysis a comparison of GNP/capita is not enough. They need to investigate the distribution of income and various indexes of consumption as well. Since many government officials are well versed in economic growth theory and are guided by it in their decision making, a knowledge of some of the most popular theories can be advantageous to managers. They must be aware, however, that today development includes not only economic growth but also political and social factors.

International investment theory attempts to explain why foreign direct investment takes place. Product and factor market imperfections provide firms, primarily in oligopolistic industries, with advantages not open to indigenous companies. The International Product Life Cycle theory explains international investment as well as international trade. Some firms follow the industry leader, and the tendency of European firms to invest in the United States, and vice versa, seems to indicate that cross investment is done for defensive reasons. The internalization theory states that MNEs will seek to invest in foreign subsidiaries rather than license their superior knowledge in order to receive a better return on the investment used to develop that knowledge. There are also two financially based explanations of foreign direct investment. The first holds that foreign exchange market imperfections resulting in overvalued and undervalued currencies attract investors from nations with overvalued currencies to nations with undervalued currencies. The second is the portfolio theory, which postulates that foreign direct investment is made to diversify risk. Empirical tests indicate that most foreign direct investment is made by large, research-intensive firms in oligopolistic industries.

Questions

1. Why should international business managers concern themselves with economic development theory? Why not leave that to the economists?
2. Prices in hotels and restaurants in Mexico seem to be too high to most foreign tourists, and the tourist business has been falling off. The Mexican government does not want to try to force local firms to lower prices. What can the government do to make prices more attractive to foreign tourists?
3. The notion that Americans should buy only products manufactured in the United States is a new idea brought about by the flood of cheap Korean imports. True or false? Discuss.
4. The less developed countries complain that they cannot compete in world markets with the developed countries because local capital costs are so high. What is your opinion of this argument?
5. Why do you think the U.S. government introduced the combination of duties and quotas for the importation of motorcycles in the particular form described in the text?
6. Name the four stages of the International Product Life Cycle, and give some examples of products that have gone through these stages.
7. A nation may be less efficient than another in producing certain commodities and still gain from trading them. True or false? Why?
8. In general, how can you distinguish a less developed country from a developed one?
9. What can you learn from the Heckscher-Ohlin theory? Name some countries whose products are what you would expect them to be according to this theory.
10. If countertrade permits nations that lack foreign exchange to trade, how can it be called a barrier to free trade?
11. How does the present definition of economic development differ from the former definition?
12. Why does an export promotion strategy seem preferable to a strategy of import substitution for developing nations?
13. What are the characteristics of most of the firms that invest overseas? What makes it possible for these firms to compete with local companies, according to the monopolistic advantage theory?
14. Describe two theories of foreign direct investment that are related to financial factors.

Minicase

3-1 The Ricardo Case

Suppose that the output per man-day for wine and cloth in Portugal and England are the following:

	Output per Man-Day	
Commodity	Portugal	England
Barrels of wine	2	1
Bolts of cloth	4	3

Suppose also that the total cost of land, labor, and capital to produce the daily output of either wine or cloth is 20 pounds in England or 1,600 escudos in Portugal and that the exchange rate is 1 pound = 50 escudos.

1. What are the prices for the English and Portuguese products in escudos?
2. What are they in English pounds?
3. What will be the direction of trade?
4. What are the upper and lower limits of the terms of trade?
5. The present exchange rate in this example is 1 pound = 50 escudos, but exchange rates do change.
   a. What will the exchange rate have to be to discourage Portuguese traders from importing English products?
   b. What will the exchange rate have to be to discourage English traders from importing Portuguese products?
6. What did you learn about comparative advantage from point 5?

Minicase

3-2 Tarus Manufacturing

John Baker, vice president of Tarus Manufacturing, called in Ed Anderson, the export manager, to discuss the sales results for the new adhesive that Tarus was exporting to its sales subsidiary in Ecuador.

Baker: Ed, how is Tarus Equatoriana doing with the new adhesive we're sending them?

Anderson: Pretty well, John. They've sold 5,000 quarts at 81 sucres or $3 a quart in the last six months.

Baker: Not bad for a small operation. If they keep that up, that product is going to become a best-seller.

Anderson: That's true, and although our profit is good, I think I can improve it.

Baker: Great. How are you going to do that?

Anderson: Well, you know that they have to pay a 40 percent ad valorem import duty on our $1.50 invoice price plus 2.7 sucres per quart specific duty. I've been studying Ecuador's import tariff, and I found that if our subsidiary imports the adhesive in 55-gallon drums, the import duty is only 30 percent ad valorem plus 180 sucres per drum.

Baker: Yes, but they'll have to buy cans and labels and fill them. This adds to their expense.

Anderson: True, but because we won't have to fill the cans or charge them for cans and labels, we will save 20 cents per quart, which we can pass on to them.

Baker: How much will it cost to fill the cans locally?

Anderson: They tell me that the cans, labels, and labor will come to 6.75 sucres, which is 25 cents per can, and the only investment required is a shutoff valve, which they screw in the drum head when the cans are filled.

Baker: I'm not sure I see the advantage, Ed. The cans, labels, and labor are more expensive in Ecuador than they are here. Where is the advantage?

Anderson: Let me show you, John.

Show Ed Anderson's calculations. Disregard any possible freight savings for shipping in bulk.

Supplementary Readings

Buckly, P., and M. Casson. *The Future of the Multinational Enterprise*, London: Macmillan, 1976.

Caves, Richard. "International Corporations: The Industrial Economics of Foreign Investment," *Economica*, February 1971, pp. 5–6.

Doan, Michael. "New Protectionism—A Threat to Trade." *U.S. News & World Report*, February 1, 1982, pp. 51–52.

Guzzardi, Walter, Jr. "How to Foil Protectionism." *Fortune*, March 21, 1983, pp. 76–86.

Heckscher, Eli F. *Mercantilism*. London: Allen & Unwin, 1934.

Hewitt, Garth. "The Growing Perils of Protectionism." *International Management*, May 1980, pp. 16–20.

Higgins, Benjamin. *Economic Development*. New York: W. W. Norton, 1968.

Hymer, Stephen. *The International Operations of International Firms: A Study in Direct Investment*. Cambridge, Mass.: MIT Press, 1976.

Kindleberger, Charles. *American Business Abroad*. New Haven: Yale University Press, 1969.

Kraar, Louis. "Japan Blows Smoke about U.S. Cigarettes." *Fortune*, February 21, 1983, pp. 99–111.

Rogge, Peter G. "Self-Limitation in International Trade—Is It a Last Resort?" *Prospects*, Swiss Bank Corporation, May 1983, p. 9.

Smith, Adam. "An Inquiry into the Nature and Causes of the Wealth of Nations." In *International Trade Theory: Hume to Ohlin*, ed. William R. Allen. New York: Random House, 1965.

Tarr, David G., and Morris E. Morkre. *Aggregate Costs to the United States of Tariffs and Quotas on Imports*. Washington, D.C.: Bureau of Economics, Federal Trade Commission, 1984.

Vernon, Raymond, and Louis Wells, Jr. *Manager in the International Economy*. Englewood Cliffs, N.J.: Prentice-Hall, 1976.

Wells, Louis, Jr. "A Product Life Cycle for International Trade." *Journal of Marketing*, July 1968, pp. 1–6.

Endnotes

1. Eli F. Heckscher, *Mercantilism* (London: Allen & Unwin, 1934).
2. Adam Smith, "An Inquiry into the Nature and Causes of the Wealth of Nations," in *International Trade Theory: Hume to Ohlin*, ed. William R. Allen (New York: Random House, 1965).
3. David Ricardo was one of the great English classical economists who, with Adam Smith, rebelled against heavy government intervention in business—the economic doctrine called mercantilism. Ricardo's theory of comparative advantage is one of the oldest unchallenged economic theories.
4. Economists call this the labor theory of value (only hours of labor determine the prices of goods). However, Ricardo included the cost of capital as "embodied" labor in his labor costs.
5. An executive of a U.S. shirt-manufacturing company once told one of the authors that his firm successfully maintained its market share against imported products because of its ability to change more quickly to the latest fashion and use the latest materials than could foreign competitors. In fact, the firm tried to change what was in fashion in order to make it more difficult and costly for these competitors to meet the U.S. demand.
6. An odd situation occurred in Chile when one of the authors was living there. The government, in an effort to provide work for typists, put high import duties on copying machines to persuade firms to hire more typists to type extra copies instead of making them on the machines. For a long time, it succeeded in its objective.
7. Louis Wells, Jr., "A Product Life Cycle for International Trade," *Journal of Marketing*, July 1968, pp. 1–6.
8. Du Pont, an important supplier to the rubber industry, maintains a laboratory in Akron in order to give rapid service to four of the largest tire manufacturers, which have their main offices and large R&D facilities there.
9. The product life cycle is the history of a product's sales. It is normally divided into four stages: introduction, growth, maturity, and decline. See any Principles of Marketing text.
10. R. Vernon and L. Wells, Jr., *Manager in the International Economy* (Englewood Cliffs, NJ: Prentice-Hall, 1976), p. 186.

11. "Japan Struggles to Keep Its Competitive Edge," *U.S. News & World Report*, August 20, 1979, p. 71.

12. David G. Tarr and Morris E. Morkre, *Aggregate Costs to the United States of Tariffs and Quotas on Imports* (Washington, D.C.: Bureau of Economics, Federal Trade Commission, 1984), p. l; and "A Global Trade War on the Way?" *U.S. News & World Report*, March 1, 1982, pp. 57–58. A vice president of Toyota Motor Sales U.S.A. states that American quotas on Japanese cars have cost American consumers $4 billion in higher prices over a two-year period.

13. One of the authors had very delicate gum surgery performed by the best dental surgeon in Chile at the company dental clinic. It would have cost $1,000 if the work had been done in the United States. The total charge, which covered only the materials used, was $1.92!

14. "The Price of Protection," *Forbes*, August 29, 1983, p. 8.

15. "New Economic Argument Raises Some Questions on Benefits of Protectionism," *Business International*, October 22, 1982, p. 337–38.

16. The word *tariff* has two meanings. Many purists prefer to use the word to describe the table of duties or table of rates (railroads). More commonly, tariffs and import duties are considered synonymous.

17. *Steel Imports—A National Concern* (Washington, D.C.: American Iron and Steel Institute, 1970), p. 87.

18. Department of Commerce, "Foreign Industrial Nontariff Barriers," in *United States International Economic Policy in an Interdependent World* (Washington, D.C.: Commission on International Trade and Investment Policy, 1971), p. 687.

19. "The Plight of the Least Developed Countries—A Call for Special Dispensation," *Survey of International Development*, February 1973, p. 1. Various economic groupings have their own definitions. The Andean Group and the Caribbean Common Market, for example, designate certain members as less developed nations for the purpose of receiving special advantages.

20. *World Development Report 1987* (Washington, D.C.: World Bank, 1987), p. 202.

21. Low income—GNP/capita $400 or less, middle income—$401 to $4,300, industrial market—$4,301 or more. However, 5 nations with more than $4,300 are still classified as middle income economies.

22. " 'Shadow Economy' Translates into Every Language," *Business Week*, April 5, 1982, p. 68.

23. *World Development Report 1987.*

24. Wilfred Beckerman, *International Comparisons of Real Incomes* (Paris: OECD, 1966), p. 29; and Benjamin Higgins, *Economic Development* (New York: W. W. Norton, 1968), pp. 15–17.

25. Charles Kindleberger and Bruce Herrick, *Economic Development*, 3rd ed. (New York: McGraw-Hill, 1977), p. 1.

26. Charles Kindleberger, *American Business Abroad* (New Haven: Yale University Press, 1969).

27. Stephen Hymer, *The International Operations of Internatinal Firms: A Study in Direct Investment*, (Cambridge, Mass.: MIT Press, 1976.)

28. Richard Caves, "International Corporations: The Industrial Economics of Foreign Investment," *Economica*, February 1971, pp. 5–6.

29. F. T. Knickerbocker, *Oligopolistic Reaction and Multinational Enterprise* (Boston: Harvard Business School, 1973).

30. E. M. Graham, "Transatlantic Investments by Multinational Firms: A Rivalistic Phenomenon," *Journal of Post-Keynesian Economics,* Fall 1978, pp. 82–99.

31. P. Buckley and M. Casson, *The Future of Multinational Enterprise* (London: Macmillan, 1976).

32. R. Z. Aliber, "A Theory of Direct Investment," in *The International Corporation* (Cambridge, Mass.: MIT Press, 1970), pp. 17–34.

33. A. Rugman, *International Diversification and the Multinational Enterprise* (Lexington, Mass.: Lexington Books, 1979).

34. A motive not often mentioned is that the investment is sometimes made because the CEO and other top managers want to go to the country to visit. How else can you explain the fact that in pre-Castro Cuba, there were three American tire factories in Havana, with Miami just 90 miles away? Delivery of tires to Cuba could have been made in hours, and at better prices. One of the authors found out why after he spent a winter in Akron working for a tire company. The Cuban subsidiary had financial, marketing, or production problems requiring the presence of the Akron executives only in the wintertime.

SECTION II

THE INTERNATIONAL ENVIRONMENT: ORGANIZATIONS AND MONETARY SYSTEM

The world is becoming increasingly bureaucratized. National governments have grown as new agencies have been formed, and individuals and businesses must deal with bureaucracies for more and more permits, licenses, clearances, and so forth.

This development has spread beyond national borders, and the same phenomenon has been occurring on an international scale. Individuals and businesses may not enjoy the delays and red tape involved in dealing with bureaucracies, but if they are to function successfully, they must learn to do so.

The truth is that dealing with international organizations has some positive features. Some of these organizations, such as the World Bank, the United Nations, the International Monetary Fund, and the Organization for Economic Cooperation and Development, are excellent sources of information for business executives and students. In addition, the World Bank, the regional development banks, and the private development companies are sources of billions of dollars and other currencies to finance government purchases from businesses.

A positive feature of all the bureaucracies from the point of view of students and executives is that they are the sources of thousands of good jobs. Not only do the national governments and international organizations hire thousands of people to be bureaucrats, but businesses must hire thousands more to deal with the bureaucrats.

As a result of huge foreign debt problems, which came to a head in the early 1980s, Poland and other Soviet-bloc countries, Argentina, Brazil, Mexico, and other Latin American countries, and countries elsewhere were unable to meet even interest, much less principal, payments on their debts. The International Monetary Fund was thrust into new prominence as a source of money and as an adviser and enforcer of how it would be spent. The Bank for International Settlements found itself in the unprecedented and unwanted position of making bridge loans.

All of these reasons, we feel, make international organizations an extremely important subject for business executives and students. Therefore, we devote an entire chapter (Chapter 4) to these organizations.

The international monetary system is dealt with in Chapter 5. This system is developing and changing constantly, and the international business student and executive must know where it is and where it has been. The past is important because some influential people and governments want to revive certain practices that are not in use at present.

Whenever you do business or travel internationally, you need different moneys, which are called currencies. Of course, you need U.S. dollars in the United States. But you must have pounds in Britain, francs in France, yen in Japan, and so forth.

Even if you don't travel or do any international business, it can be important to know about the relative values of currencies. Currencies fluctuate in value constantly during one day, and over longer periods their values can change significantly. On the forward, futures, or options markets, you can trade currencies for profit, just as you trade such commodities as wheat and silver. You would buy a currency if you thought its value was going up and sell it if you forecast a drop in its price. If you are in international business, you can use the same currency markets, or banks, to protect yourself against changes in currency values.

Also dealt with in Chapter 5 are the gold standard, the gold exchange standard, nations' balances of payments, and fixed and floating currency exchange regimes.

CHAPTER 4

INTERNATIONAL ORGANIZATIONS

"It has been estimated that every dollar of fund financing in support of adjustment programs has in the recent past generated an additional four dollars of new commercial lending."

J. de Larosière, managing director,
International Monetary Fund,
at the University of Neuchâtel
March 3, 1983

112

Learning Objectives

After you study this chapter, you should know:

1. The United Nations (UN), which has disappointed many of its early supporters as a peacekeeping organization but has become extremely active in the economic and social fields.

2. That the new UN member countries are almost all less developed countries (LDCs). The new member countries are almost all poor, and they are a majority of the UN membership.

3. World Bank loans, which provide borrowing countries with billions of dollars (and other currencies) and are used by these countries to buy goods and services from businesses in member countries.

4. The International Finance Corporation (IFC), which is called the investment banker of the World Bank group because it encourages private investment in LDCs by LDC residents.

5. The International Monetary Fund (IMF), whose size, powers, and activities have been expanding remarkably.

6. The General Agreement on Tariffs and Trade (GATT), which has had considerable success in reducing tariffs and quotas in international trade.

7. The Bank for International Settlements, which got unwanted publicity and activity as a result of the 1982 country debt crises.

8. Standardization of weights and measurements in the metric system, which is being encouraged by the International Organization for Standardization, the UN, and others. This is causing difficulties for American producers.

9. The European Community (EC), which is the most extensive and successful regional economic grouping of nations.

10. The Organization for Economic Cooperation and Development (OECD), which is an excellent source for economic research and statistics.

11. The International Development Association (IDA), which extends credits to the poorest of the poor countries.

Key Words and Concepts

Worldwide organizations
Regional organizations
Contract arbitration
Hard loans
Soft loans
Firm surveillance

Debt default
Debt rescheduling
Tariffs
Quotas
Less developed countries (LDCs)
Common market

Business Incident

The United Nations (UN) has been praised by many as a force for peace because it provides an arena in which potentially hostile countries can negotiate their differences and their misunderstandings. Others have attacked the UN as a very expensive bureaucracy that accomplishes very little of use to the world. Many in Europe and North America claim that the UN has an anti-Western and anti-U.S. bias.

The opinions of those hostile to the UN seem to have been borne out by at least one UN body, the United Nations Educational, Scientific, and Cultural Organization (UNESCO). It is based in Paris, and its longtime director general was Amadou Mahtar M'Bow.

M'Bow was accused of running UNESCO as his personal fiefdom, and the organization was said to hire and fire people and spend money extravagantly without observing its rules. The U.S. was the largest contributor—about 25 percent—to UNESCO's budget.

Member states have the right to audit the books and accounts of UN agencies, and in 1984 the United States informed UNESCO that U.S. Government Accounting Office (GAO) auditors would come to Paris to exercise that right. The week before the GAO people arrived in Paris, a fire of mysterious origin broke out in UNESCO's records archives, but the Paris fire department was able to extinguish the fire before it destroyed all of the records.

The GAO auditors examined the surviving books and accounts, and the following were some of the findings:

Employees were paid without confirmation that they had actually worked.

M'Bow hired 1,400 part-time employees at a cost of about $500,000 without going through the required normal UN job application process.

57 of the 186 UNESCO programs were duplicative.

$1.34 million of 1984 obligations were improperly charged to the 1981–83 budget.

M'Bow had the executive board's meeting room redesigned, using for this purpose $320,000 from a fund to hire professional-level civil servants.

The boardroom redesign contract and other construction contracts were let without competitive bidding

$83,000 was spent for a film on scientific research in M'Bow's native Senegal, and $17,000 was spent for "medals."

Palestine Liberation Organization "students" were paid $188,100.

A number of UNESCO-sponsored conferences featured anti-U.S. speakers.

At one of these conferences, held in 1982 in Mexico, Jack Lang, the French minster of culture, attacked U.S. "cultural imperialism."

It is therefore not surprising that the United States withdrew from UNESCO at the end of 1984. Great Britain withdrew in 1985, and Singapore in 1986. After a bitter electoral battle in 1987, a Spaniard, Frederico Mayor, beat M'Bow and will replace him as director general. The bitterness of the contest indicates UNESCO's problems are not ended.

From various publications.

Given the immense and growing numbers and importance of private and governmental international transactions, it is not surprising that a variety of international organizations have sprung up to facilitate, regulate, measure, or finance them. It behooves the business student, who is increasingly likely to be exposed to international opportunities and problems soon after graduation, to be aware of the existence and functions of a number of these organizations.

Some are **worldwide organizations,** and some are **regional organizations,** with members from only one geographic area. Some are large, some small. Most are groupings of governments, but some are private.

The common element of all the organizations dealt with in this chapter is that they can have importance to businesses. They may be sources of orders or sources of financing. They may be regulatory, or they may aim at standardization of weights and measurements. And, last but not least, they may be sources of jobs for you (see Figure 4–1).

The United Nations

Possibly the best known of the worldwide organizations is the United Nations (UN). Conceived and born amid the idealism and hopes that came with peace following World War II (1939–45), the UN has been a disappointment to many of its original supporters. Others foresaw more accurately what the strengths and weaknesses of the UN would probably be.

During the early UN years, one international law scholar, Professor Edwin Borchard of Yale Law School, cautioned his classes, which contained a number of World War II veterans, not to be too sanguine about enduring peace resulting from the UN. He told them, in effect, to keep their powder dry, and indeed the education or early careers of many of them were interrupted by the Korean War. In fact, one side in that war fought in the name of the UN.

Figure 4-1

The International Monetary Fund

with headquarters in Washington, DC, invites
applications for the position of

ENGLISH TRANSLATOR

Candidates must have English as their mother tongue, a
university degree, preferably in Economics or Law, and
several years of professional experience in translation of
economic texts from both French and Spanish. Proficiency
in other languages would be highly desirable.

Applications should reach the Fund by November 30. A
competitive examination will be held for selected
candidates.

Detailed curriculum vitae should be sent to:

R. M. Broadway
Personnel Officer
Recruitment Division
International Monetary Fund
700 19th Street, N W
Washington DC, 20431

INTERNATIONAL CIVIL AVIATION ORGANIZATION

Economist, Air Carrier Tariffs

Montreal, Canada

Candidates should have appropriate university education and extensive experience in air transport fares and
rates matters. Duties include monitoring of IATA tariff
co-ordination activity and research into other aspects of
international air tariffs.

Command of one of the languages of the Organization
(English, French, Russian, Spanish) and a working
knowledge of one or more of the others desirable.

Salary (assuming dependent family) essentially free of
income tax and including post adjustment, US$35.473
plus generous fringe benefits.

Deadline for applications: 12 November 1985.

Full details and application forms available from **Chief,
Personnel Branch, International Civil Aviation Organization, Suite 400, 1000 Sherbrooke St West, Montreal, Quebec, Canada H3A 2R2.**

Sources: *Economist*, July 20, 1985, p. 84 and November 9, 1985, p. 5.

Of course, there have been many other wars, declared and undeclared, between nations, colonies, provinces, tribes, and ethnic groups throughout the
world since the days of great expectation in the mid-1940s.

Indeed, since the establishment of the UN in 1945, there have been some
140 conflicts in which over 10 million people have died. The UN has done little
to prevent these conflicts or to restore peace, despite peacekeeping expenditures of over $3 billion, of which the United States has paid over $1 billion.

Clearly, the UN has not been a success insofar as its peace-keeping functions are concerned. In its economic and social functions, however, the UN has
made progress, perhaps in part because in its frustrations with peacekeeping it
has devoted more energy and resources to economic and social fields. Those
fields and political activities now absorb the bulk of the UN budget. The results
are of major importance to business.

The UN group is characterized by decentralization, which can be a source
of frustration for the student or businessperson attempting to comprehend or do
business with it. However, the vast amounts of money disbursed by, and the

business available with, members of the group make it worth the time to familiarize oneself with the general organization and with some specifics. Figure 4–2 gives a UN group table of organization.

UN Growth and Change

All UN member nations are members of the General Assembly, in which each nation has one vote regardless of its size, wealth, or power. The number of members has grown rapidly since the UN's establishment in 1945, and new nations continue to join as they gain independence and become sovereign in their territory. To understand recent, current, and probable future developments at the UN, it is necessary to bear in mind one fundamental fact about almost all the new members. They are poor.

Their relative poverty, combined with their numbers (they have far more votes than the wealthier, more developed countries can muster) has radically altered the complexion and operational directions of the UN. These alterations are being expressed in the multiplication of projects aimed at raising the income of the **less developed countries (LDCs).** Such projects include education, irrigation, health, agriculture, raw materials, industrialization, technological transfers from the developed countries (DCs), and many more.

UN Secretariat

Members of the UN have become so deeply concerned with matters of economic development and international trade that despite the growth in the number of and the activities UN specialized agencies and despite the appearance of several new bodies involved with development, the UN itself has expanded its operations into economic fields. Important for business are its preinvestment studies and recommendations for the development of housing, natural resources, and transport and its standardization studies and recommendations concerning measurements and statistics. All these sorts of work are conducted within the Secretariat of the UN by the Department of Economic and Social Affairs (ESA).

Research and Planning

The ESA is active in research and is also operational, with expert personnel available, upon members' requests, to assist in all phases of economic or tax planning, insurance, budgeting, or monetary and fiscal policy-making. The ESA's Resources and Transport Division does much preinvestment study and recommendation that can be of benefit to businesses aware of them.

Purchasing

In connection with its activities, the UN buys equipment through its General Services Office. Much larger quantities of equipment and services are bought by member nations upon the recommendations of ESA's Resources and Transport Division.

Figure 4-2

United Nations organizations

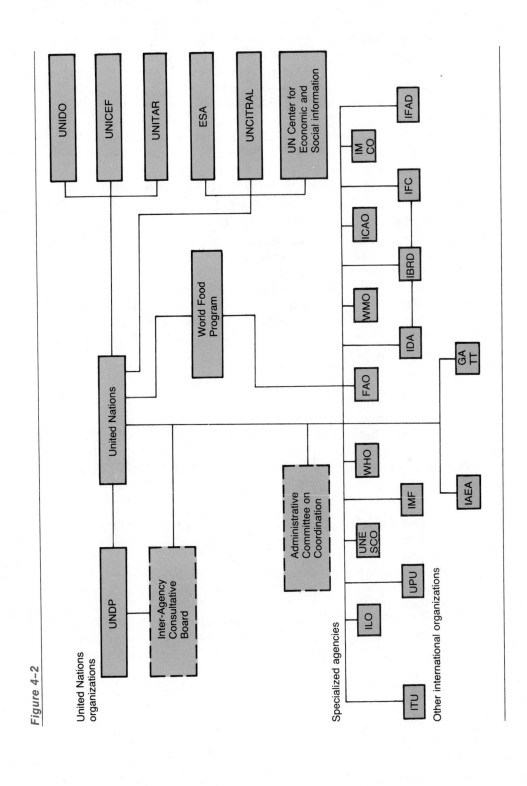

International Trade Law

The UN is increasingly in evidence in the field of international trade law through its Commission on International Trade Law (UNCITRAL). UNCITRAL's purposes are to promote the harmonization and unification of laws dealing with international trade and to identify obstacles to international trade and encourage their elimination.

The Legal Office of the UN had a hand in drafting the Convention on the Recognition and Enforcement of Foreign Arbitral Awards. A number of major trading countries have ratified this convention, which can serve useful purposes for companies dealing in two or more of the ratifying states.

UN Publications

The UN has issued thousands of reports, studies, annual surveys, and yearbooks, and it publishes a number of quarterly or monthly journals. Among the many that can be valuable to international business and its students are. *Yearbook of International Trade Statistics, World Economic Survey, Statistical Yearbook,* and *World Energy Supplies.* Information on the wide range of publications available from the UN can be obtained from the UN in New York or Geneva, either of which will fill orders. Periodically, the UN publishes an edition of the *General Business Guide* (see Figure 4–3).

UN Specialized Agencies

As we have seen, the UN Secretariat is not merely an office management function for UN headquarters. It is active in research and planning for member countries and in international trade law and arbitration. It also publishes material of value to managers and students of business. In addition, there are specialized UN agencies, and we shall look at those of most interest to business.

United Nations Conference on Trade and Development (UNCTAD)

As mentioned above, the newer LDC members of the UN are almost all poor countries, and they constitute a majority of UN membership. They are generally dissatisfied with their economic growth, and UNCTAD is an expression of that dissatisfaction.[1] It was established as a permanent organ of the UN General Assembly* in 1964.[2]

UNCTAD has become a forum and rather effective advocate for the LDCs. It has succeeded in getting countries and international agencies to make low-interest loans or monetary grants to LDCs and to transfer technology to them.

---

*In the General Assembly, the LDC majority is not subject to a veto, as it is in the UN Security Council.

Figure 4-3

UNITED NATIONS DEVELOPMENT PROGRAMME (UNDP)

INTER AGENCY PROCUREMENT SERVICES UNIT (IAPSU)

GENERAL BUSINESS GUIDE

FOR
POTENTIAL SUPPLIERS OF GOODS AND SERVICES
TO
THE UNITED NATIONS SYSTEM

JUNE 1983

3rd Edition

Contents

		Pages
Foreword		iii
United Nations System of Organizations		1
The UN Development System and the Role of UNDP		4
Inter-Agency Procurement Services Unit (IAPSU)		6
Advance Notices on Business Opportunities		7
Origins of Requisitions for Goods and Services		8
Basic Conditions for Potential Suppliers		10
Selection Procedures for Award of Contract		11
Special Conditions of Contract		12
International Competitive Tendering		13
Procurement Activities/Locations and Contacts		14
UN	United Nations Secretariat	15
UN ESCAP	UN Economic Commission for Asia and the Pacific	20
UN ECLA	UN Economic Commission for Latin America	22
UN ECA	UN Economic Commission for Africa	24
UNCTAD	United Nations Conference on Trade and Development	26
UNIDO	United Nations Industrial Development Organization	28
UNEP	United Nations Environment Programme	30
HABITAT	United Nations Centre for Human Settlements	32
UNICEF	United Nations Children's Fund	33
UNDP	United Nations Development Programme	36
WFP	World Food Programme	39
UNHCR	United Nations High Commissioner for Refugees	40
UNRWA	United Nations Relief and Works Agency	41
UNFPA	United Nations Fund for Population Activities	42
UNU	United Nations University	43
ILO	International Labour Organisation	45
FAO	Food and Agriculture Organization of the United Nations	47
UNESCO	United Nations Educational, Scientific and Cultural Organization	49
ICAO	International Civil Aviation Organization	51
WHO	World Health Organization	53
IBRD	World Bank/International Bank for Reconstruction and Development	55
FUND	International Monetary Fund	58
UPU	Universal Postal Union	59
ITU	International Telecommunication Union	60
WMO	World Meteorological Organization	62
IMO	International Maritime Organization	63
WIPO	World Intellectual Property Organization	65
IFAD	International Fund for Agricultural Development	66
IAEA	International Atomic Energy Agency	67
GATT	General Agreement of Tariffs and Trade	69
ITC	International Trade Centre (UNCTAD GATT)	70
WTO	World Tourism Organization	71
AFDB	African Development Bank	72
ASDB	Asian Development Bank	73
IDB	Inter-American Development Bank	75

United Nations Industrial Development Organization (UNIDO)

Here is another agency born of the impatience of the LDCs with the pace of their development. It is the successor to the UN's Center for Industrial Development and an organ of the General Assembly.

UNIDO gives technical assistance, does in-plant training and feasibility studies, compiles and disseminates information on export potentials for LDC industry, and is responsible for coordinating UN activity in industrial development.

United Nations Children's Fund

Created by the General Assembly in 1964 and originally known as the United Nations International Children's Emergency Fund, this organization is still referred to by the initials UNICEF. UNICEF encourages and supports LDCs in their efforts to help their children become healthy, useful citizens. It provides assistance and supplies in many areas, including maternal and child health services, child nutrition, disease control, education, vocational training, and emergency aid.

World Health Organization (WHO)

This organization helps member countries improve health services, works toward the eradication of mass diseases (such as malaria and smallpox), coordinates and stimulates medical research, and runs an international epidemiological intelligence network.

Business Opportunities. The WHO procures millions of dollars worth of laboratory equipment and supplies, pharmaceuticals, vaccines, motor vehicles, insecticides and their dispensers, hospital and medical equipment, and teaching equipment. Worldwide public bidding is the rule.

Food and Agriculture Organization (FAO)

The FAO's activities include promotion and execution of preinvestment surveys and studies in the fields of food and agriculture in the LDCs; operation of cooperative programs (for example with the World Bank or the WHO) to increase agricultural investment in LDCs; and promotion of private and public investments in agriculture and agroindustries. FAO projects include battling against insects and rodents; breeding disease-resistant grains, fruits, and vegetables; improving rangelands and pasturelands; combating animal diseases; training farmers and technical workers; stimulating reforestation and forest management; developing nutrition services; and improving commercial fish farming and the production of fishing fleets.[3]

International Labor Organization (ILO)

This member of the UN group is unique in several regards. For one, it antedates the UN, having been created at the Paris Peace Conference following World War I. The United States became a member of the ILO in 1934.[4]

United States Resigns and Rejoins. Another unique feature of the ILO is that of the four delegates who represent each member country, two represent the government and, in theory, one each represents the employers and the workers. American business and labor leaders have pointed out that such purported divisions are sham or meaningless in communist and other state-run economies in which the government owns the employer companies and controls the labor unions. This consideration plus political maneuvering by the ILO majority caused the United States to resign from the organization in 1977. In 1980, satisfied that the ILO had begun spending more time working for the betterment of world labor conditions and less on politics, the United States rejoined.[5]

Other UN Specialized Agencies

There are other UN agencies, usually highly specialized, that offer opportunities for business and for international business students. We shall name them for you, but we shall not examine them individually. Their names indicate their areas of activities, and if they interest you as potential customers for your company's products or as subjects for study, you can easily find considerable information about them. They include the United Nations Educational, Scientific, and Cultural Organization (UNESCO); the United Nations Development Program (UNDP); the International Civil Aviation Organization (ICAO);* the International Telecommunication Union (ITU); the Universal Postal Union (UPU); the World Meteorological Organization (WMO); the International Atomic Energy Agency (IAEA); and the newest of the UN specialized agencies, which opened for business in December 1977, the International Fund for Agricultural Development (IFAD).

The World Bank

The International Bank for Reconstruction and Development is usually referred to—in its own publications and elsewhere—as the World Bank. The World Bank Group consists of the bank itself, the International Finance Corporation (IFC), and the International Development Association (IDA).

---

*One of the employment opportunity advertisements shown earlier in this chapter is for an economist, air carrier tariffs, for the ICAO.

Applicable to the entire group is the attitudinal preference of most, if not all, governmental borrowers for multinational or international agency loans and assistance rather than bilateral loans or aid. Visions of imperialism, real or imagined, are less likely if the lender/donor is multinational or international.[6] The great majority of group loans or credits* are made to LDCs.

Importance to Business

Here are a few reasons why business should be aware of the World Bank Group's activities: (1) many companies are suppliers to borrowers in group-financed projects, and these borrowers spend billions of dollars each year buying goods and services from businesses; (2) the development finance institutions (discussed below) in LDCs, which are partly financed and assisted technically by the group, are potential capital sources for businesses selling or working in LDCs; (3) the World Bank's center for arbitration may be able to resolve difficulties encountered by business in a foreign country; (4) projects financed by the group tend to be mutually supportive (for example, general benefits result from improved infrastructure and, better economic resource inventories); and (5) the information that the group gathers about a nation's or a project's finances, uses of funds, management abilities, and so forth tends to be more complete and accurate than the information that is likely be available to a private, foreign business.

In June 1986, the United States signed an agreement to become involved with a new international body that would insure investors in foreign countries against loss from war, riot, and other risks. The new body is the Multilateral Investment Guarantee Agency (MIGA), which is affiliated with the World Bank.

MIGA will give advice to investors and try to promote international commercial agreements. Among the risks against which it will insure are breach of contract, expropriation, or a freezing of funds by the host government.

Hard Loans

The World Bank makes **hard loans.** This means that its loans are at prevailing market interest rates and are granted only to sound borrowers for periods not exceeding 25 years. The bank must make relatively safe loans with high assurance of repayment because its own funds are acquired through the sale of securities offerings that must compete with government and private business offerings of all sorts. Investors would not buy World Bank securities at economical interest rates if they felt that the bank's loans were insecure, because the bank must repay the buyers of its securities out of proceeds and profits on its loans.

To date, there have been no defaults on loans made by the World Bank, and its bonds carry the highest quality rating available, that is, AAA. The World

---

*In World Bank terminology, moneys lent by the bank are called *loans*, while those lent by the IDA are referred to as *credits*.

Bank has operated at a profit in every year since 1947, and that profit has been used to make additional loans and to furnish funds for the IDA.[7]

Although no World Bank loans have been officially declared to be in default, some countries have been unable to make payments when called for by the original loan terms. Many of those loans have been rescheduled, giving the debtor countries more time to repay them, but it is quite possible that unless economic conditions improve for debtor LDCs, some World Bank loans will have to be recognized as in default.

Business Opportunities

The billions of dollars and other currencies lent by the World Bank create many opportunities for businesses to sell their products and services to the borrowers. International competitive bidding is a requirement of the bank. However, although the bank announces the signing of each loan, it does not invite bids or tenders from potential suppliers to the financed projects. Such invitations are the responsibility of the government or agency executing the project. Thus, a company desiring to sell to a project must watch for the loan announcements and then contact appropriate officials in the borrowing country or at that country's embassy in its own country.[8]

Information Sources

Quite evidently, that procedure poses difficulties for firms, particularly smaller ones, which would like to sell their products or services to a bank-financed project. In recognition of this, the UN began in 1978 to furnish procurement information. The UN Center for Economic and Social Information in Geneva publishes *Development Forum Business Edition*, a biweekly newspaper that gives details of all major business opportunities opened by the World Bank loans. The newspaper tells what is needed for each project and how to bid for the business.

Among the reports and publications of the World Bank, that can be helpful to business and students are its *Annual Report*, its *Statement of Loans* (quarterly), *Guidelines Relating to Procurement under World Bank Loans and IDA Credits, Uses of Consultants by the World Bank and Its Borrowers*, and *World Bank Atlas of Per Capita Product and Population*. Also available are reports of the World Bank's various General Survey Missions regarding certain countries or areas.

International Finance
Corporation (IFC)

The IFC is the World Bank Group's investment banker. Its sphere is exclusively private risk ventures in the LDCs. The purpose of the IFC is to further economic development by encouraging the growth of productive enterprise in member countries, thus supplementing the activities of the World Bank.[9]

Joint Ventures Favored

The IFC's policy is to favor joint ventures that have some local capital committed at the outset, or at least the probability of local capital involvement in the foreseeable future.[10] This is not to say that the IFC will not cooperate with capital sources outside the host country (the country in which the investment is being made), and there are many examples of such cooperation. Among the industries thus capitalized have been fertilizers, synthetic fibers, tourism, paper, and cotton fabric. The outside capital sources, if in related lines of business, are usually multinational enterprises (MNEs), and a few of those that have cooperated with the IFC have been Phillips Petroleum, AKV Netherlands, ICI, Intercontinental Hotels, and Pechiney-Gobain.

Creation of Local Capital Markets

In return for its investment in a company, the IFC takes securities in the form of stock (equity ownership) or bonds (debt). One objective of the IFC is to sell its securities into a local capital market, and in order to do that, it will help create and nurture such a market. For example, the IFC extended a $5 million credit line to a syndicate of private Brazilian investment banks to provide support for those banks' securities underwriting activities. The banks work with Fondo do Desenvolvimento do Mercado de Capitais, a revolving capital market development fund maintained by the Brazilian central bank. The objectives are (1) to induce the investment banks to assume a greater role in the underwriting of Brazilian securities in Brazil, (2) to improve the access of Brazilian companies to long-term domestic source capital, and (3) to encourage Brazilians to invest in sound domestic securities.[11]

Liaison with Development Finance Companies

The IFC is the liaison within the World Bank Group for the numerous development finance companies (DFCs) (sometimes called development banks, as in Ecuador) that have sprung up, primarily in the LDCs. These DFCs are in many ways local versions of the IFC. Each DFC seeks potentially profitable ventures within its country and assists with feasibility studies. If a venture proceeds, the DFC helps along the way with advice on plant, property, financing, management, or equipment. Finally, the DFC attempts to establish or enlarge a domestic capital market for securities of the venture.[12]

Business Opportunities

On average, each dollar invested or loaned by the IFC attracts $5 from private sources. As of the beginning of 1985, the IFC had $1.5 billion invested for its own account in 74 countries, from Argentina to Zimbabwe, and another $586 million committed but not disbursed.

Like the World Bank, the IFC is reluctant to admit default of a loan or failure of an investment and has rescheduled some loans. Unlike the World Bank however, the IFC has written off a few investments that it judged could not be revived.

Nevertheless, the IFC has continued to grow; its investments were up 55 percent in the 1984–85 fiscal year, to $610 million, and they grew to $700 million in 1985–86. Although IFC investments are in LDCs, the developed countries benefit from them, because the LDCs buy billions of dollars worth of equipment and services from the OECD countries.*

International Development Association (IDA)

The IDA is the "soft" loan (or "credit," as an IDA loan is called) section of the World Bank. Although it shares the bank's administrative staff and grants credits for projects covering the same sorts of projects in the LDCs as the bank's loans, its **soft loans** differ from the "hard" loans of the bank in several important ways. They have 50-year maturities compared to 15- and 25-year maturities of the bank. The IDA may grant 10-year grace periods before repayment of principal or interest must begin, whereas the grace periods of the World Bank usually do not exceed 5 years. The IDA charges only three fourths of 1 percent as a service charge on disbursed loan balances plus one half of 1 percent on undisbursed balances.[13] As is evident from these differences, borrowers from the IDA are the poorest of the poor LDCs, which need credit for development projects but cannot carry the burden on their economies or foreign exchange reserve positions that would result from normal commercial term loans. To the maximum extent possible, the credits are made in the currency of the borrowing member country.[14]

IDA Capital Sources

The IDA cannot raise capital in competitive capital markets, as does the World Bank, and depends instead on subscriptions donated by the DCs and some LDCs. Generally, the DC members make contributions in convertible currencies; the LDC members donate their own currencies.[15]

The resources of the IDA are renewed periodically by a process called "replenishment," whereby 33 supporting nations donate money. The replenishment for 1985–87 was in the amount of $9 billion, but that was increased by about $2 billion when drought and political turmoil caused famine in Africa. That was the seventh replenishment; the IDA is seeking $12 billion in the eighth.

*The Organization for Economic Cooperation and Development is the Paris-based club of the world's richer, industrial nations.

International Monetary Fund (IMF)

Although the IMF deals solely with governments, its policies and actions have profound impact on business worldwide. Its influence and impact may become even greater. Before explaining that statement, we should look briefly at the objectives and activities of the fund as they began and developed. Most of them continue to be important.

The Articles of Agreement of the IMF were adopted at the Bretton Woods Conference in 1944.[16] In general terms, the fund's objectives were, and continue to be, to foster orderly foreign exchange arrangements, convertible currencies, and a shorter duration and lesser degree of balance-of-payments disequilibria. The premise of the fund is that the common interest of all nations in a workable international monetary system far transcends conflicting national interests.[17] One of the fund's original objectives, since abandoned, was the maintenance of fixed exchange rates among member countries' currencies, with par value related to the U.S. dollar, which was valued at $35 per ounce of gold.

Each member country has a quota equal to the amount it subscribes to the IMF. Votes at fund meetings are weighted according to quota size, and the amount a member can draw is related to its quota.[18]

The IMF agreement was entered prior to the founding conference of the United Nations, and when the UN was formed, the fund was brought into relationship with the UN by an agreement. This agreement preserved the fund's independence, which was justified by the need for independent control of monetary management. This need results from the temptations of every government to overspend and cause inflation.[19]

Changes in the IMF

The 1970s and 1980s saw some fundamental changes in the activities and roles of the IMF. As stated above, the IMF abandoned the objective of maintaining the fixed exchange rate system. More accurately stated, the obligation of maintaining such a system remained in the fund's Articles of Agreement, but it was powerless to uphold it in the face of a situation in which all major currencies were floating* rather than fixed in value. In recognition of reality, the articles were amended to legalize the actual current practice, that is, floating exchange rates.

Greater Power for the IMF?

The amended articles also included a new Article IV, which, among other things, empowers the IMF to "exercise **firm surveillance** over the exchange-rate policies" of members.†

---

*Discussion of floating exchange rates as compared to fixed exchange rates will be found in Chapter 5.
†Emphasis added.

There are those who feel that this new surveillance power may permit the fund to move toward the position in the world occupied by central banks nationally.[20] That, of course, would require the surrender of a great deal of sovereignty by the member countries, which many governments will stoutly resist.

New Roles for the IMF
In 1981, the IMF assumed a new role as a lender for development projects in LDCs and a potential new role as a borrower.

A Development Lender. Due in large part to the big increase in the cost of petroleum, the nonoil LDCs' balance-of-payments deficits soared during the late 1970s and into the 1980s. The IMF stepped into this situation, making larger loans for longer periods of time and for purposes other than temporary balance-of-payments corrections. Loans used for long-term development projects will be evaluated by the World Bank, which has been making such loans for years.

A Market Borrower. Prior to 1981, the IMF got all of its capital from member country contributions or from direct borrowing from member countries. The fund's financial resources from member quotas grew from about $65.9 billion in 1980 to approximately $108 billion by the end of 1985. In 1981 the fund was authorized to borrow money in the world's capital markets, but as of autumn 1987 it had not used this authority.[21]

World Debt Crisis and the IMF
Over the years, countries have occasionally been unable or unwilling to pay their debts. When countries were unable to pay debts that came due (**debt default**), the debts were sometimes rescheduled to give them more time to pay (**debt rescheduling**). Debts of Peru, Zaire, and Turkey are among those that were rescheduled.

Usually due to government changes, countries sometimes refuse to pay the debts of previous governments; the new government repudiates the old debt. This occurred when communist governments assumed power in the Soviet Union, the People's Republic of China, and Cuba.

Before 1981, such reschedulings and repudiations were relatively unusual. Suddenly that all changed. First Poland and other Soviet-bloc countries, then Mexico followed by Brazil, Argentina, and other Latin American countries as well as countries in Africa and Asia, found themselves short of money to repay their debts.

Financial and Economic Disaster? Some observers foresaw massive debt repudiations, bank failures, world trade breakdown, and deep depressions with high unemployment. The debts of the non-OPEC developing countries totaled some $520 billion at the end of 1982, and the disaster scenario had all of them defaulting at once—perhaps after forming a debt "OPEC" to coordinate their debt repudiation. (See Figure 4–4.)

Enter the IMF. While Mexico was negotiating its emergency IMF loan in November 1982, it was preparing to inaugurate a new president in December. The outgoing president wanted no part of the austerity programs being insisted on by the IMF, and the incoming president had no official power until December. Jacques de Larosière, the IMF's managing director, prodded both presidents into cooperation.

De Larosiere's problems did not end there. The some 1,400 large and small creditor banks of Mexico wanted no more to do with Mexico, so he called a creditors' meeting in New York, at which he bluntly warned them that unless they came up with $5 billion more for Mexico, the IMF would pull out. They would lose their entire loans if it did that. The creditors went along with the IMF plan.

Such aggressiveness by the IMF was a sharp departure from its previous low-key approach.[22] Add to that the large increases in the IMF lending resources provided by industrial member countries between 1981 and 1986, and the fund had become a major new world force. Lord Harold Lever, an economist and a senior adviser to the British Labor governments of 1974–79, suggested in 1983 that the IMF become the monitor of national export credit agencies to ensure exports of credits as well as exports of goods.[23]

Despite efforts of the IMF, private banks, and debtor and creditor countries and businesses, progress in solving the world debt problem has been slow and spotty. One development was that the United Sates became the world's biggest net debtor in 1986, with foreigners holding $107.4 billion more in American assets than U.S. investors held abroad. Leaving the United States out of the picture, the 15 major debtor countries had external debt of $437.4 billion at the end of 1985 (see Figure 4–5). Into 1987, the debts continued to increase.

IMF Gold Sales Benefit LDCs

One intended effect of enhanced IMF power and the availability of special drawing rights (SDRs are discussed in Chapter 5) was the diminution of the role of gold and the U.S. dollar. A step in that direction was taken in 1976, when the IMF held the first of a series of sales from its gold stock. Those sales continued over a four-year period ending in May 1980, and one sixth of the fund's gold stock was sold. Another sixth was returned to the members.[24]

The money derived from the IMF gold sales was placed in an account called the Special Trust Fund, and that fund used those moneys as another aid to LDCs.[25] The Trust Fund was terminated in 1981, at which time the approximately $400 million of repaid loans and interest were transferred to the fund's supplementary financing facility. Those monies, plus the proceeds of further Trust Fund loan repayments through 1991, were turned over to the Structural Adjustment Facility (SAF) in 1986, to be managed in collaboration with the World Bank, which was contributing its IDA funds to the SAF.

Figure 4-4

How the Bubble Grew (Disbursement Debt of Non-Opec Developing Countries)

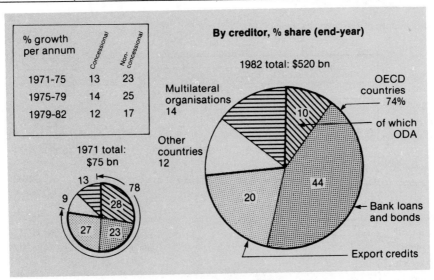

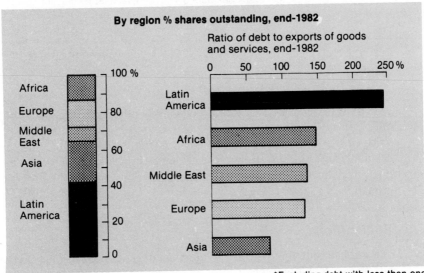

*Excluding debt with less than one-year maturity

Source: *The Economist,* September 24, 1983.

Figure 4–5

External Debt of 15 Debtor Countries, 1985

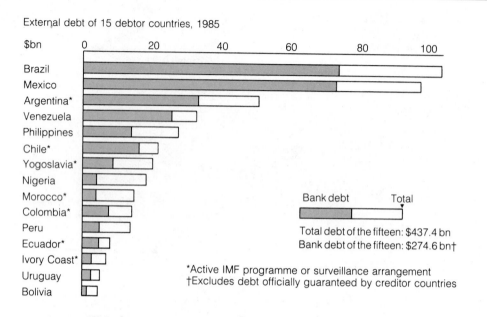

External debt of 15 debtor countries, 1985

Total debt of the fifteen: $437.4 bn
Bank debt of the fifteen: $274.6 bn†

*Active IMF programme or surveillance arrangement
†Excludes debt officially guaranteed by creditor countries

Source: *Euromoney,* December, 1985, p. 126; based on information from Institute of International Finance.

This marked the first formal collaboration between the World Bank and the IMF. Monies of the SAF are not simply lent to the poorer LDCs; the bank and fund work closely with the borrowing governments to develop medium-term macroeconomic and structural adjustment programs that will help correct distortions in their economies, restore viable payment positions, and promote faster economic growth.[26]

Publications

IMF publications that can be of value to international business students and to businesses include *International Financial Statistics, Balance of Payments Yearbook, Direction of Trade, Government Financial Statistics Yearbook, Annual Report of Exchange Restrictions, Annual Reports of the IMF*, and *Summary Proceedings of Annual Meetings*. Mention should also be made of *IMF Staff Papers* on individual countries and of the quarterly publication *Finance & Development*.

INTERNATIONAL MONETAR'

From *The Wall Street Journal*, with permission of Cartoon Features Syndicate.

"OK, I'm sorry we called you a dirty capitalist imperialist swine—now can we have the money?"

Regional Development Banks

Regional development banks are regional versions of the World Bank. There are three major ones: the African Development Bank, the Asian Development Bank and the Inter-American Development Bank.

Their function is to lend money in the less developed countries to build infrastructure, support agriculture and industry, and create jobs. The sources of their funds are several. All get contributions from their member countries, and all except the African Development Bank get money from developed countries that are permitted to be members even though they are not located in the geographic areas. Countries outside Africa are not permitted to be members of that bank, though many of the African countries are in favor of changing this rule. The African Development Bank has raised money in the international capital markets, in the Eurocurrency market, and in the Eurobond market. The Asian Development Bank made a loan to Vietnam in 1977, and the source of those funds was OPEC.

A political controversy arose for the Asian Development Bank in 1983, when the People's Republic of China (PRC) sought to replace the Republic of China (Taiwan) as a member, but after long and intense negotiations a formula was devised to accommodate membership for both. Adding the PRC to membership with India already in has raised fears that the borrowing needs of these large countries will strain the bank's financial resources or crowd out smaller members. However, Masao Fujioka, its president, says, "The bank currently has a lot of resources, and India and China are not expected to make excessive demands."[27] A potentially important strategy switch is under way at the Asian Development Bank—to emphasize more loans to private sector borrowers and fewer to government borrowers.

A part of this strategy switch is the encouragement of securities (stocks and bonds) markets in member countries. Such markets are in varying stages of development in Thailand, the Philippines, Indonesia, and Sri Lanka. Other members, such as Australia, Japan, New Zealand, Hong Kong, Singapore, and Malaysia, already have strong securities markets.

Government subscriptions to the Inter-American Development Bank—its paid-in capital—have declined from 47 percent of the total in 1960 to 7.5 percent in 1980. At the same time, the bank's resources—mostly from private capital markets—have grown from $1 billion to $28 billion. In 1983, the bank raised $200 million through the sale of Eurobonds. Nearly half of its loans have been soft—on easy terms—as it tries to emphasize lending to the poor.

In 1986, the Inter-American Development Bank was midwife to the birth of the Inter-American Investment Corporation as an affiliated organization. The corporation is to support the Latin American private sector with loans, investment, and technical and managerial assistance.

For our purposes, the importance of the regional development bank loans in less developed countries is that the LDC borrowers use much of the borrowed money to purchase goods and services from companies in other countries. The alert business management can earn some of that money.

Private Regional
Development Organizations

Sociéte Internationale Financiere pour les Investissements et Developpement en Afrique S.A. (SIFIDA) is owned by private banks and companies in 19 countries. Two international institutions are shareholders. As indicated by its name, SIFIDA operates in African countries.

Private Investment Company for Asia (PICA) identifies and develops investment opportunities leading to new projects in the Asian LDCs. It tries to encourage local participation in each of the projects. Thirteen turned out to be an unlucky number for PICA, as it lost money for the first time in 1982, its 13th year of operation. It blamed the world recession and the difficulty of getting dividend payouts from closely held companies. Although PICA made a small profit in 1983, this was almost entirely due to property sales, and almost 90 percent of PICA's $65 million capital was invested in the Philippines, which was having financial difficulties in the early and mid-1980s. As a result, PICA was merged into the Australian financial group Elders IXL in May 1984, and a new firm, Elders Pica, was formed to reduce its loan commitments and concentrate on investment management.

Latin American Agribusiness Development Corporation (LAAD) is a private investment and development company whose shareholders are agribusiness and financial companies. Its projects have been in South America, the Caribbean, Mexico, and Central America in production, processing, storage, and marketing in the fields of agriculture, livestock, forestry, and fishing.

The importance of these private investment groups to businesses and students is the same as that of government and international aid and bank organizations. They provide money, technology, and management expertise. Incidentally, the companies named have been able to combine LDC development with profits for themselves in most of their years of operations.

Bank for International Settlements (BIS)

The BIS, located in Basle, Switzerland, has become a second home for central bankers of the world's major industrial countries except for the People's Republic of China, the Soviet Union, and East Germany. It was created in 1930 to handle reparations payments from Germany stemming from World War I. Oddly enough, Hitler's National Socialist government continued to make the agreed reparations payments through World War II.

The BIS is such a convenient meeting place for central banker groups that one needs a program to sort them out. The BIS board of directors consists of the governors of several European central banks. A second group that meets in Basle consists of the central bank governors of the Group of Ten, which has 11 members now that Switzerland has joined but is still called the Group of Ten. The original ten are Belgium, Britain, Canada, France, Holland, Italy, Japan, Sweden, West Germany, and the United States. A third group is that of the European Community (Common Market) countries. Yet another group is the annual general meeting of the governors of the 29 central banks that are BIS shareholders.

In addition to providing a congenial and confidential meeting place for central bankers, the BIS provides secure, anonymous cover for shareholder countries as they transfer large amounts of currency or gold among themselves.

When they do this through the BIS, the currency and gold traders may not be able to figure out the identity of the real buyers and sellers.

The world financial strains in 1982 that enhanced the IMF's role also caused some changes for the BIS. In 1982 and 1983, the BIS made loans to cash-strapped Hungary, Mexico, Argentina, Brazil, and Yugoslavia. These were called "bridge" loans because they were intended to bridge those debtor countries over a period until IMF, government, and private bank loans could be mobilized. The BIS had never made such loans, and by early 1983 its chairman, Fritz Leutwiler, was announcing that it would make no more of them. There were several reasons for his decision. One was that the bridge loans were potentially long term and therefore potentially dangerous due to the short-term nature of deposits at BIS. Another was that the small BIS staff was inadequate to evaluate and administer such loans.[28]

In 1984, Leutwiler was replaced as chairman and president by Jean Godeaux of Belgium. The BIS invests conservatively and regularly reports profits. It announced a profit of 80,171,806 gold francs* for the 1985–86 year, up from 68,366,633 the previous year.[29]

General Agreement on Tariffs and Trade (GATT)

Arising from the optimism among the Western allies following WWII was the ideal of an international organization that would function in the trade areas much as it was hoped that the UN would function in the political and peacekeeping areas. A charter was drawn for an International Trade Organization (ITO) at the Havana Conference in 1948. However, the ITO never came into existence because of the failure of a sufficient number of governments to ratify the charter.

How GATT Was Conceived

At what were thought of as preliminaries to and preparations for an ITO, the American negotiators presented what they envisioned as a step toward an acceptable ITO treaty which was to embody the numerous bilateral trade treaties into one multilateral treaty. They suggested, in the absence of any established international trade rules, that the commercial policy rules of the draft ITO charter be incorporated into a general agreement on tariffs and trade as an interim measure pending ITO ratification. The American suggestions were accepted, and so GATT was born in 1947.[30] Differently stated, the ITO was not ratified as a de jure organization, and GATT became a de facto international trade organization.[31]

*A gold france is worth about $2.

Some observers felt GATT to be a "slender reed" on which to base world progress toward free international trade.[32] Nevertheless, it still exists and it has been extremely successful in some areas of tariff reduction and in other fields.[33]

Benefits for Business

Examples of the other fields in which GATT has been of assistance to international business are quota and import license eradication or relaxation, the introduction of fairer customs evaluation methods, and opposition to discriminatory internal taxes. GATT has also opposed dumping, state subsidies, and other obstructions to free trade.

Of further benefit to business, GATT encourages standardization of import documentation and of rules governing marks of origin, importation of samples, advertising material, and temporary, duty-free import of goods intended for reexport. Also, business is assisted by GATT in its role as a forum for the settlement of disputes. When a firm feels that it has been the victim of discrimination in such matters as taxation or import restrictions, it may complain to its government. If the government cannot find satisfaction through bilateral talks with other governments, it can lodge a formal complaint with GATT.[34]

While the several rounds of GATT negotiations succeeded in reducing many **tariffs** and **quotas,** they did not address other obstacles to trade, such as customs procedures, government procurement restrictions, packaging or language requirements, or product testing. They also failed to deal with obstacles to trade in agricultural products or in services such as banking, insurance, information processing, accounting, or legal services. The latest GATT round, which convened in Uruguay in September 1986, may make progress in reducing those obstacles.

Publications

GATT publications of potential value to international business managers and students include *International Trade* (annual); the *Forum* (quarterly), which features trade promotion topics and examines various countries' commercial policies; *Manual of Export Promotion Techniques*; and *Market Studies*, which deals with area markets for individual products.

Organization of Petroleum
Exporting Countries (OPEC)

Realizing that if the oil-exporting countries were united, they could bargain more effectively with the large oil companies, Iran and Venezuela joined the Arab Petroleum Congress at a Cairo meeting in 1959. Discussions and secret agreements at that meeting became the seeds for OPEC.[35]

The Oil Companies Should Have Listened

Early in 1960, the Venezuelan minister of mines and hydrocarbons and the Saudi oil minister wrote the oil companies that were operating in Venezuela and the Middle East, requesting that they consult with the host governments before making any price changes. In August 1960, the oil companies reduced oil prices, and it is said that the host governments learned of it only when they read it in the newspapers. In any event, they had not been consulted. This made them angry and also increased their anxiety about the control and conservation of their natural resources. In that atmosphere, they called a meeting on September 14, 1960, in Baghdad.

In attendance at the meeting were representatives of Iran, Iraq, Kuwait, Saudi Arabia, and Venezuela. OPEC was formed. The OPEC members took charge of pricing.

The first headquarters of OPEC was in a relatively small apartment in Geneva. There was general skepticism as to the durability of the new organization and hesitancy on the part of some potential employees to take what they feared would be short-term jobs.[36]

Clearly, the skeptics have been proved wrong. OPEC's headquarters have been moved to Vienna, and its members, in addition to the founders named above, include Qatar, Libya, Indonesia, Abu Dhabi, Algeria, Ecuador, and Gabon.

Economic Muscle and Political Strength

OPEC soon began to test its strength, and the price of petroleum began to rise. At the end of 1973 and in early 1974, OPEC demonstrated its potentially devastating strength with the oil embargo by its Arab members against the Netherlands and the United States, accompanied by very large price increases to all customers. Its strength stemmed from the comparative cohesiveness of the members and from the fact that it controlled some 68 percent of the world's known petroleum reserves.[37] OPEC supplied some 84 percent of the European Community's oil needs and over 90 percent of Japan's.[38]

Was OPEC Too Greedy?

Although the cost was recession and unemployment, by 1979 the oil-importing countries had fairly well adjusted to the 1973–74 OPEC price increases. Then, in 1979–80, OPEC hit the world with a new price hike of some 150 percent. Although that brought OPEC a bonanza in the short run, it also sent demand plunging even further than it had during the mid-1970s and created a glut of oil

Figure 4-6

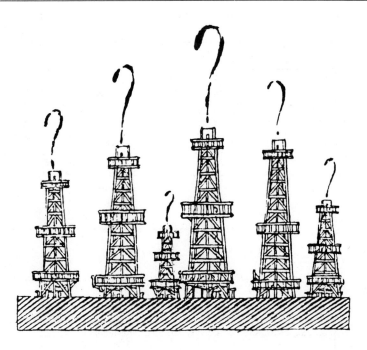

supplies. Prices fell, and although OPEC did not dissolve, its members fell to squabbling among themselves about prices and production shares of a diminished market.

Figure 4–7 is a good illustration of how dramatically oil prices increased between 1972 and 1983, from under $3 per barrel to over $34. Prices then dropped a few dollars.

OPEC had taken control of pricing their product progressively until they had full control by 1974. A spot market for oil developed in Rotterdam during the 1970s, and in 1983 trading of crude oil futures began on both the New York Mercantile Exchange and the Chicago Board of Trade. With an oil surplus, OPEC no longer sets prices but follows where an increasingly free market leads. One author believes that even if supplies tighten again, the strong free markets, now developed, will exert powerful influences on price.[39]

As can be seen in Figure 4–7, oil prices began to descend in 1983, and Figure 4–8 shows how steep the descent was, from $34 per barrel to about $28.50,

Figure 4-7

Light Arab Crude Oil Price 1972-1983

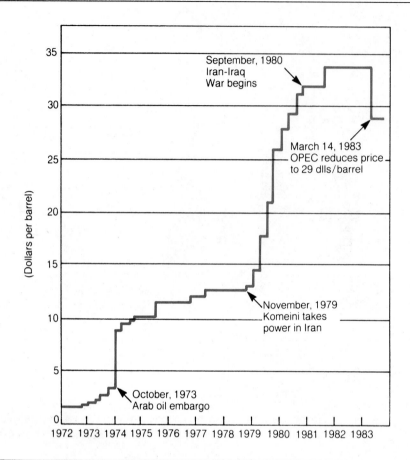

where they stabilized until 1985. At that point, an even more dramatic price drop carried prices to the $12–$15 levels.

OPEC struggled to agree on production cuts in order to end the price slide. While most oil-importing countries rejoiced at the lower energy cost, the price slide caused grave damage to non-OPEC oil producers and exploration for new fields virtually ceased. This led many observers to worry that the world could again become dependent on OPEC.

Figure 4–8

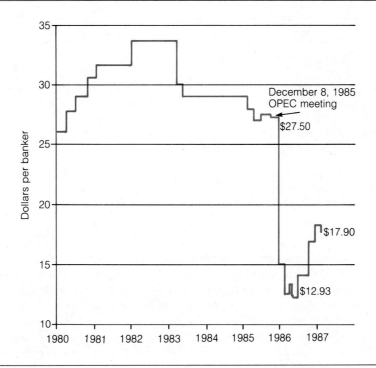

Source: *Energy Information Administration Weekly Petroleum Status Report,* May 2, 1986, and subsequent news items.

International Organization for Standardization (ISO) and International Electrotechnical Commission (IEC)

The work of the International Organization for Standardization (ISO) and the International Electrotechnical Commission (IEC) affects the lives of millions throughout the world and is growing in importance. The IEC promotes standardization of materials and equipment in almost every sphere of electrotechnology. The ISO recommends standards in other fields of technology with a view to facilitating international exchanges of goods and services.

Table 4-1

The EC, U.S., Japan, and USSR (1985)

	EC	U.S.	Japan	USSR
Population (millions)	322	239	121	278
GDP ($ billions)	2,406	3,865	1,308	1,100*
Per capita GDP ($)	7,470	16,190	10,830	3,906*
Imports of goods ($ billions, CIF)	314†	345	131	86*
Exports of goods ($ billions, FOB)	292†	213	177	90*

*Estimates.
†Including intra-EEC trade would more than double these figures.
Source: ABECOR Country Report, European Economic Community, August 1985.

Both organizations are headquartered in Geneva and have national bodies in countries having four fifths of the world's population.[40] The member for the United States is the American National Standards Institute in New York.

All measurement standards are in the metric system, which poses problems for American producers that have not converted to metric. These problems are increasing as the number of products standardized to ISO and IEC specifications are growing rapidly.[41] In many countries, a producer cannot sell to the government unless its products meet these standards.

European Community (EC)

The EC, usually referred to as the Common Market and frequently as the EEC (for European Economic Community), joins most of the economic and industrial might of western Europe and most of its population. The EC is the largest import and export market in the world. It is second only to the United States in the size of its gross domestic product, and it accounts for 21 percent of world trade, compared with 16 percent for the United States and 9 percent for Japan. Table 4-1 gives some comparisons between the EC, the United States, Japan, and the USSR.

Customs Union Stage of Development

Even though the EC is generally called the Common Market, it has not yet reached that stage of development. It has succeeded in abolishing most tariffs and quotas among its members and in establishing a common tariff and quota wall on goods from outside, and is therefore at the customs union stage of development.

When the EC succeeds in abolishing all restrictions on the movement of capital and labor (including management and the professions), it will be a **common market**. It has taken several steps in that process.

The EC has also made some progress toward harmonizing the economic policies and institutions of its member countries. The European Monetary System (EMS),* which commenced operation in 1979, is an example of that. Of course, it has long been a dream of some Europeans that someday there would be a "United States of Europe—" a political union.

Membership Expanding

In 1981, Greece became the 10th EC member, joining Belgium, Denmark, France, Ireland, Italy, Luxembourg, the Netherlands, the United Kingdom, and West Germany. In 1985, Portugal and Spain brought the EC's membership to 12 nations. Turkey has indicated interest in membership, and discussions have begun with the Turkish government. Key indicators and comparisons of the 12 EC member countries can be seen in Table 4–2.

Regional Groupings of Nations Other than EC

The success of the EC has led nations to form a number of other groupings with similar, but usually more limited, objectives. None of those groupings has come as close to being a true common market as the EC; however, some have become customs unions and others free trade areas. A free trade area exists when a group of countries abolishes restrictions on mutual trade but each country keeps its own quotas and tariffs on trade with countries outside the group. An *industrial* free trade area, such as the European Free Trade Association, has free trade in industrial products only.

Some of these groupings and their members are:

Andean Common Market: Bolivia, Colombia, Ecuador, Peru, and Venezuela.

Arab Common Market: Egypt, Iraq, Jordan, Kuwait, Libya, Mauritania, and Syria.

---

*See Chapter 5 for discussion of the EMS.

Table 4-2
Key Indicators of EC Member Countries for 1985

	Population (millions)	GDP ($ billions)	Per Capita GDP ($)	Proportion of Labor Force in Agriculture (%)	Consumer Prices (% change)*	Exports† ($ billions)	Imports† ($ billions)
Total EEC	322.2	2,406.4	7,470	9.4	6.4	644.5	662.9
Belgium	9.9	77.5	7,830	3.0	4.9	53.7‡	56.0‡
Denmark	5.1	56.6	11,100	6.7	4.7	17.0	18.2
France	55.2	503.1	9,110	7.9	5.8	97.0	107.1
Germany	61.0	611.8	10,030	5.6	2.2	183.3	157.6
Greece	10.0	33.1	3,310	29.4	19.3	4.5	10.2
Ireland	3.6	18.2	5,060	16.6	5.4	10.4	10.0
Italy	57.1	354.0	6,200	11.2	9.2	78.4	90.5
Luxembourg	0.4	3.5	9,560	4.4	3.1	n.a.‡	n.a.†
Netherlands	14.5	122.3	8,430	5.0	2.3	68.5	65.4
Portugal	10.2	20.4	2,000	24.5	19.2	6.0	8.1
Spain	38.6	167.5	4,340	16.7	8.8	24.2	29.9
United Kingdom	56.6	438.4	7,750	3.1	6.1	101.5	109.9

*Percentage change year on year.
†Total merchandise trade (exports FOB, imports CIF) with all countries of the world, including EEC.
‡Luxembourg trade included in figures for Belgium.
Source: ABECOR Country Report, European Economic Community, August 1986.

Association of South-East Asian Nations (ASEAN): Indonesia, Malaysia, the Philippines, Singapore, Thailand, and Brunei.

Caribbean Common Market: Belize, Grenada, St. Vincent and the Grenadines, St. Lucia, Dominica, Antigua, St. Kitts/Nevis, Montserrat, Trinidad and Tobago, Jamaica, Guyana, and Barbados.

Caribbean Community: Same membership as in the Caribbean Common Market.

Caribbean Group for Cooperation in Economic Development: Barbados, Belize, Dominican Republic, Guyana, Jamaica, Suriname, Antigua, Dominica, Grenada, Montserrat, St. Kitts/Nevis, St. Lucia, and St. Vincent and the Grenadines.

Central African Customs and Economic Union: Benin, Cape Verde, Gambia, Ghana, Guinea, Guinea-Bissau, Nigeria, and Togo.

Central American Common Market: Costa Rica, Guatemala, Honduras, Nicaragua, and El Salvador.

Club du Sahel: Cape Verde Islands, Chad, Gambia, Mali, Mauritania, Niger, Senegal, and Burkina Faso.

Council for Mutual Economic Assistance (Comecon): Russia, Bulgaria, Mongolia, Czechoslovakia, East Germany, Hungary, Poland, Romania, Cuba, and Vietnam. Finland is an associate member.

Customs and Economic Union of Central Africa: Cameroon, Central African Republic, Congo and Gabon.

Economic Community of West African States (ECOWAS): Benin, Dahomey, Gambia, Guinea, Ivory Coast, Liberia, Mauritania, Niger, Nigeria, Sierra Leone, Togo, Burkina Faso, Mali, Guinea-Bissau, Senegal, and Ghana.

European Free Trade Associations (EFTA): Austria, Finland, Iceland, Norway, Sweden, and Switzerland.

Gulf Cooperation Council: Kuwait, Saudi Arabia, Bahrain, Qatar, United Arab Emirates, and Oman.

Latin American Association for Integration (LAAI): Argentina, Bolivia, Chile, Colombia, Ecuador, Paraguay, Peru, Uruguay, and Venezuela.

Mano River Union: Guinea, Liberia, and Sierra Leone.

New Zealand–Australia Free Trade Agreement (NAFTA).

Regional Cooperation for Development (RCD): Iran, Pakistan, and Turkey.

South Asia Association for Regional Cooperation: Bangladesh, Bhutan, India, Maldives, Nepal, Pakistan, and Sri Lanka.

West African Monetary Union: Benin, Ivory Coast, Niger, Senegal, Burkina Faso, and Togo.

Figure 4-9

Bulletin of Crédit Suisse, Zurich, Spring 1983.

Organization for Economic Cooperation and Development (OECD)

The members of OECD are the noncommunist DCs. The OECD is classified as regional because it originated in Europe and most of its members are European. However, among its members now are Australia, Canada, Japan, New Zealand, and the United States.

You should be familiar with the OECD because it produces and publishes extensive research and statistics on numerous international business and economic subjects. Also, it produced a declaration of guidelines of good business practices for MNEs operating in OECD countries.[42]

Material from and about the OECD may be obtained from OECD Publications and Information Center, 1750 Pennsylvania Avenue, N.W., Washington, DC 20006.

Summary

A striking and pervasive theme which runs through the literature about most of the organizations dealt with here is activity concerning LDCs. Several agencies, such as UNCTAD and UNIDO, were created for the specific benefit of the LDCs.

Others, such as WHO and FAO, have seen their operations turn more and more toward aiding the LDCs. Still others, which were primarily involved in technical and standardization activities, have become to some degree operational with on-the-scene assistance for the LDCs; in this category are the postal, telecommunications, and civil aviation organizations.

All of the OPEC countries are LDCs, and the efforts they are making to become DCs before the oil runs out are presenting huge market opportunities for international business. Their investment policies and activities are causing many opportunities and problems for the international financial sectors, as well as for nonoil government central banks and treasuries.

The growth of concern for LDCs and of activities to aid them should not surprise the reader. The post-World War II era has been one of rapid decolonization by the Western countries, and many new independent nations have emerged. Almost all of them are less developed countries (LDCs), and all except the oil exporters are poor. Previously, they were colonies of some, usually developed and usually European, countries and of little concern to the rest of the world. Now, with independence and power through the UN and its related organizations, they are asserting their aspirations for better levels of living.

We have seen that the severe debt problems of numerous countries have caused the IMF to become richer and more aggressive, while the BIS was pushed into making emergency, country loans for the first time in its history. It is trying to terminate that activity.

Questions

1. *What are some reasons why businesspeople and business students should be aware of the more important international organizations?*
2. *What is the common feature shared by all or almost all new UN member countries?*
3. *When the World Bank makes a loan, how can a business, which would like to sell products or services to the borrower, go about making sales?*
4. *a. Which part of the World Bank Group is referred to as its investment banker?*
   b. Why?
5. *What are development finance companies (DFCs)?*
6. *How do IDA credits differ from World Bank loans?*
7. *The agreement between the IMF and the UN preserves considerable independence for the fund. Why?*
8. *What new authority did the revised Article IV of the IMF Articles of Agreement give the fund?*
9. *What changes have occurred at the IMF as a result of multinational debt repayment problems?*
10. *What are some GATT functions that are of benefit to business?*
11. *a. What group of nations brought about the creation of UNCTAD?*
    b. Why?
12. *What are some of the most notable results flowing from the influx of so many poor, new LDCs into the UN and other organizations?*
13. *What is the EC?*
14. *What is the importance of the OECD for business and students?*
15. *a. Where did the Structural Adjustment Facility get its money?*
    b. Why is the facility a landmark for the IMF and the World Bank?
    c. For whose benefit is the facility, and what will the bank and the fund do with and for the borrowers?
16. *What are the purposes of the World Bank's Multilateral Investment Guarantee Agency?*

Minicase
4-1 Use of International
Organizations—Setting up a
100 Percent-Owned Subsidiary

You are an international business consultant in the United States. Your specialty is exporting to and investing, licensing, or franchising in LDCs.

One of your clients is a hotel company that wants to build, operate, and 100 percent own a hotel in Guatemala. Your client is willing to put up about half of the original capital but wants to be assured that its share of the profits can be converted to U.S. dollars and repatriated as dividends.

To what organizations discussed in Chapter 4 might you look for assistance in raising the rest of the needed capital? To what organizations might you look for information concerning a Guatemalan company's ability to convert profits into U.S. dollars and remit them to the United States?

[handwritten annotations:]
International Finance Corp.
Inter-American Development Bank
ADELA ⇐ best
International Monetary Fund

Minicase
4-2 Use of International
Organizations—Establishing
a Franchise Operation

Suppose this client wanted to put up little or none of the initial capital and wanted no ownership interest in the Guatemalan hotel. Your client will supply plans and knowledge for the design, construction, and furnishing of the hotel. It will publicize the hotel and sell rooms to tourists and conventions.

Your client will provide management and wants to be paid fees to compensate for its know-how, advertising, sales, and management.

Would you proceed any differently than in Minicase 4–1?

[handwritten:] International Monetary Fund IMF

Minicase
4-3 Use of International
Organizations—Securing
Business Leads

Another of your clients is a construction company that has the capability and desire to undertake projects abroad. From what sources discussed in Chapter 4 might you find jobs for this client?

[handwritten:] UNIDO   IDA   World Bank

Minicase

4-4 Use of International Organizations—Finding Overseas Markets

A third client is a manufacturer of small to relatively large pumps and motors. From what sources discussed in Chapter 4 might you find customers for this client?

Supplementary Readings

Adler, John H. "Development Theory and the Bank's Development Strategy." *Finance & Development*, December 1977, pp. 31–34.

Anjaria, S. J. "A New Round of Global Trade Negotiations." *Finance & Development*, June 1986, pp.2–6.

Aufricht, Hans. *The Fund Agreement: Living Law and Emerging Practice*. Princeton, N.J.: Princeton University Press, 1969.

Baker, James C. *The International Finance Corporation: Origins, Operations, and Evaluation*. New York: Praeger Publishers, 1978.

Burki, Shahid Javed, and Norman Hicks. "International Development Associaiton in Retrospect." *Finance & Development*, December 1982, pp. 22–25.

deVries, Margaret Garritsen. *The International Monetary Fund, 1966–1971: The System under Stress*. Washington, D.C.: IMF, 1977.

Diamond, William. *Development Finance Companies: Aspects of Policy and Operations*. Baltimore: Johns Hopkins University Press, 1968.

Elmandjra, Mahdi. *The United Nations System, An Analysis*. Hamden, Conn.: Archon Books, 1973.

The First Ten Years of the World Health Organization. Geneva: World Health Organization, 1958.

Gold, Joseph. *The Standby Arrangements of the International Monetary Fund*. Washington, D.C.: IMF, 1970.

Goodrich, Leland M. *The United Nations in a Changing World*. New York: Columbia University Press, 1976.

"IFC Foreign Portfolio for Development: an IFC Initiative." *Finance & Development*, June 1986, p. 23.

IFC Preliminary Project Information Required. Washington, D.C.: IFC, 1976.

"IMF's Structural Adjustment Facility." *Finance & Development*, June 1986, p. 39.

Jenks, C. W. *Human Rights and International Labor Standards*. London: Stevens, 1960.

Kelly, Margaret. "Fiscal Deficits and Fund-Supported Programs." *Finance & Development*, September 1983, pp. 37–39.

Lorsignol, O., and C. Delevennat. "Pressing for Free Trade for All." *Vision*, November 1977, pp. 29–32.

Lowe, John W. "The IFC and the Agribusiness Sector." *Finance & Development*, September 1973, pp. 25–28.

Morse, David A. *The Origin and Evolution of the I.L.O. and Its Role in the World Community.* Ithaca, N.Y.: Cornell University Press, 1969.

Nakagama, Sam. "The Benefits of OPEC's Misery." *Euromoney*, December 1984, pp. 124–28.

"OECD Economic Outlook." *OECD Observer*, January 1986, pp. 27–33.

Pandit, Shrikrishna A. "IMF Resident Representatives." *Finance & Development*, September 1973, pp. 30–33.

Reichmann, Thomas, and Richard Stillson. "How Successful Are Programs Supported by Standby Arrangements?" *Finance & Development*, March 1977, pp. 22–25.

Russell, Ruth B. *A History of the United Nations Charter.* Washington, D.C.: Brookings Institution, 1958.

Sharp, Walter C. *The United Nations Economic and Social Council.* New York: Columbia University Press, 1969.

Shihata, Ibrahim. "Increasing Private Capital Flows to LDCs." *Finance & Development*, December 1984, pp. 6–9.

Struc, Ernest. "The Trust Fund." *Finance & Development*, December 1976, pp. 30–31.

"World Bank: Soul Searching in Washington." *Euromoney,* December 1985, pp. 122–131.

Yudelman, Montagne. "Integrated Rural Development Projects: The Bank's Experience." *Finance & Development*, March 1977, pp. 15–18.

Endnotes

1. Pierre Lortie, *Economic Integration and the Law of GATT* (New York: Praeger Publishers, 1975), p. X.
2. United Nations General Assembly Resolution 1975 (XIX).
3. Gove Hambridge, *The Story of FAO* (New York:Van Nostrand Reinhold, 1955); and *Let There Be Bread* (Rome: Food and Agriculture Organization, 1951).
4. Alice Cheyney, ed., *The International Labor Organization* (Philadelphia: American Academy of Political and Social Science, 1933).
5. *The Wall Street Journal*, February 14, 1980, p. 22.
6. Alec Cairncross, *The International Bank for Reconstruction and Development*, Princeton University Essays in International Finance, no 33 (March 1949), p. 27.
7. Eugene H. Rotberg, "The World Bank, A Financial Appraisal, I," *Finance & Development*, September 1976, pp. 14–18; *World Bank and I.D.A.: Questions and Answers* (Washington, D.C.: World Bank, 1971); and Charles N. Henning, William Pigott, and Robert Haney Scott, *International Financial Management* (New York: McGraw-Hill, 1978), pp. 307–11.
8. John A. King, "Procurement under World Bank Projects," *Finance & Development*, June 1975, pp. 6–11, 31; and David M. Sassoon, "Monitoring the Procurement Process," *Finance & Development,* June 1975, pp. 11–13.
9. Article I of the Articles of Agreement of the International Finance Corporation (Washington, D.C., June 20, 1956), p. 3.
10. IFC General Policies (Washington, D.C.: IFC, 1970).

11. IFC News, *Finance & Development*, March 1973, p. 2.

12. *Private Development Finance Companies* (Washington, D.C.: IFC 1964).

13. *Finance & Development*, March 1982, pp. 7–8.

14. Eugene H. Rotberg, "The World Bank: A Financial Appraisal, II," *Finance & Development*, December 1976, pp. 36–39.

15. J. Weaver, *The International Development Association: A New Approach to Foreign Aid* (New York: Praeger Publishers, 1965).

16. United Nations Monetary and Finance Conference, Bretton Woods, New Hampshire, July 1 to 22, 1944, Department of State Publication 287, Conference Series 55 (Washington, D.C.: Department of State, 1944).

17. A. Acheson and others, *Bretton Woods Revisited* (Toronto: University of Toronto Press, 1972).

18. Oscar L. Altman, "Quotas in the International Monetary Fund," International Monetary Fund Staff Papers, 5, no. 2 (1956).

19. Leland M. Goodrich and Edward Hambro, *Charter of the United Nations: Commentary and Documents*, rev. ed. (Boston: World Peace Foundation, 1949), p. 349.

20. For a discussion of how surveillance is working, see G. G. Johnson, "Enhancing the Effectiveness of Surveillance," *Finance & Development*, December 1985, pp. 2–5.

21. Margaret Garritsen de Vries, "The IMF: 40 Years of Challenge and Change," *Finance & Development*, September 1985, pp. 7–10.

22. Art Pine, "IMF Becomes Leader," *The Wall Street Journal*, January 11, 1983, p. 56.

23. *Economist*, July 9, 1983, pp. 14–16.

24. J. J. Polak, "The Fund after Jamaica," *Finance & Development*, June 1976, pp. 7–9, 12–13.

25. *Finance & Development*, March 1980, p. 2.

26. *Finance and Development* June 1986, p. 39.

27. Cheah Cheng Hye, "ADB Goes Begging for Borrowers," *The Asian Wall Street Journal*, February 10, 1986, p. 5.

28. Peter Norman, "BIS Backs Off," *The Wall Street Journal*, February 2, 1983, p. 29.

29. *Bank for International Settlements, Fifty-sixth Annual Report, 1st April 1985–31st March 1986*, p. 1.

30. Richard N. Gardner, *Sterling-Dollar Diplomacy* (Oxford: Oxford University Press, 1956).

31. Gerard Curzon, *Multilateral Commercial Diplomacy* (New York: Praeger Publishers, 1965).

32. Gardner, *Sterling-Dollar Diplomacy*, pp. 379–80.

33. Bernard Norwood, "The Kennedy Round: A Try at Linear Trade Negotiations," *Journal of Law and Economics*, October 12, 1966, pp. 297–319; Ernest M. Preeg, *Traders and Diplomats* (Washington, D.C.: Brookings Institution, 1970); John W. Evans, *The Kennedy Round in American Trade Policy: The Twilight of GATT?* (Cambridge, Mass.: Harvard University Press, 1971); Sidney Golt, *The GATT Negotiations, 1973–1974; A Guide to the Issues* (London, Washington, and Ottawa: British-North America Committee, 1974); and B. Balassa and M. E. Dreinin, "Trade Liberalization under the Kennedy Round: The Static Effects," *Review of Economics and Statistics*, May 1967, pp. 125–37.

34. Kenneth W. Dam, *The GATT, Law, and International Economic Organization* (Chicago: University of Chicago Press, 1970); and "GATT, An Analysis and Appraisal of the General Agreement on Tariffs and Trade" (Medford, Mass.: Fletcher School of Law and Diplomacy, 1955).

35. Perez Alfonze, "The Organization of Petroleum Exporting Countries," (Caracas) *Monthly Bulletin*, no. 2 (1966).

36. Wendell H. McCulloch, Jr., notes of interviews and conversations with OPEC employees and others in Geneva.
37. *International Petroleum Encyclopedia*, 1979, pp. 194–95, table 6.
38. Luis Vallenilla, *Oil: The Making of a New Economic Order* (New York: McGraw-Hill, 1975).
39. James Cook, "Comeuppance," *Forbes*, May 9, 1983, pp. 55–56.
40. Brochure published by IEC and ISO, 1, rue de Varembe 1211, Geneva 20, Switzerland.
41. *European Free Trade Area Bulletin*, March 1974, pp. 6–8.
42. OECD, International Investment and Multinational Enterprises, adopted June 21, 1976, OECD Doc. 21 (76) 4/1 (1976).

CHAPTER 5

INTERNATIONAL MONETARY SYSTEM AND BALANCE OF PAYMENTS

"Countries don't go bust."

Walter Wriston, chairman, Citibank

Learning Objectives

After studying this chapter, you should know:

1. That almost every country in the world has its own currency and that wherever you travel or do business, you need some of the local currency.
2. That the currencies of a few of the wealthier countries are convertible relatively freely into other currencies but that most currencies are not freely convertible.
3. That although the price of gold has fluctuated widely, the price trend has been steadily upward.
4. The international monetary system, which was fashioned at Bretton Woods and was based on international cooperation, using such new institutions as the International Monetary Fund (IMF).
5. That the United States has run a BOP deficit in most years since 1958, which resulted in billions of U.S. dollars being held by nonresidents of the United States.
6. That in 1971 the fixed currency exchange rate system established at Bretton Woods began to come apart and currencies began to float in relation to each other.
7. That historically London and New York have been major money markets but that many other money markets have developed around the world—in the Middle East, Asia, and the Caribbean.
8. Special drawing rights, which may become the main reserve asset for nations and possibly even an international currency.
9. The European Monetary System (EMS), which is a step toward the reimposition of fixed currency exchange rates and has established gold as one of its official reserve assets.
10. The European Currency Unit (ECU), a value unit established by the EMS. Many bonds on the Eurobond markets are now denominated in ECUs, and the uses and usefulness of ECUs are increasing.
11. That the current monetary system may be significantly changed as a result of the world credit crisis.
12. The balance-of-payments accounts.

Key Words and Concepts

Convertible currencies
Bretton Woods
Gold standard
Gold window
Gold exchange standard
Central bank
Fiscal policies
Monetary policies
Money markets
Special drawing rights (SDRs)
Market methods (to correct a BOP deficit)
Central reserve assets
Floating exchange rates
Fixed exchange rates
European Monetary System (EMS)
European Currency Unit (ECU)

Business Incident

One of the phone line lights flashed and was quickly answered by a currency dealer. As soon as the caller spoke, the dealer responded quietly, "1010," and replaced his phone on its hook. He then stated in a voice that could be heard around the trading room, "I've got 2 million at 1010."

Another trader was on her phone and said "1000." She then announced, "Got a million at 1000."

In the course of a few seconds, two customers had traded their French francs for 3 million U.S. dollars. The trades were made at exchange rates of 8.1010 and 8.1000 francs per dollar. The action took place in the trading room of a bank in the City, London's financial center, shortly after the news was flashed that a Soviet plane had shot down a Korean passenger jet. The customers felt that the U.S. dollar would appreciate in value if hostilities escalated in the aftermath of the Soviet missiles.

When the U.S. dollar began to drop in value on the foreign exchange markets in early 1985, traders and investors scrambled to make money on the changes. Wall Street brokerage houses came up with ways to play further drops in the dollar's quotes. Some recommended the stocks of companies with large European or Japanese operations. Others touted currency futures or options contracts—for instance, buying deutsche marks or yen for profit if they gained in value against the dollar. A more conservative approach was to buy short-term notes or bonds payable in European Currency Units (ECUs).

Although the American consumer pays U.S. dollars (US$s) for the German car or Scotch woolens purchased in the United States, the car manufacturer in Germany and the wool processor in Scotland must have, respectively, deutsche marks (DM) and sterling (£) in order to meet their local expenses. At some point, the US$s must be exchanged for the necessary DM and £. Underlying the mechanics and rates of exchange (both of which are dealt with in some detail in Chapter 6) is the international monetary system. The currencies mentioned above are **convertible currencies** (that is, they are readily convertible in the market), but many currencies are not. For example, the currencies of most less developed countries (LDCs) and communist countries are not convertible or are legally convertible only at artificial, government-established rates.

The international businessperson or student should have some knowledge

Figure 5–1

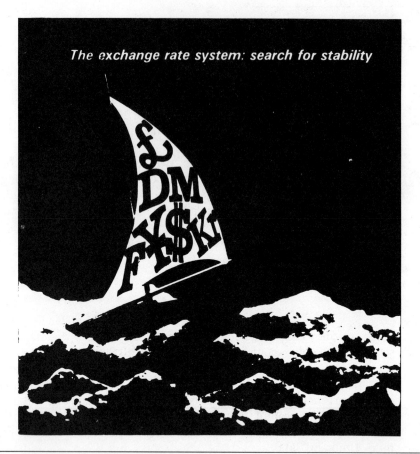

The exchange rate system: search for stability

From *Finance & Development,* a quarterly publication of the International Monetary Fund and the World Bank, March 1979

of the history and current state of the international monetary system. History is important because of its lessons and also because a vocal minority wants to resurrect varieties of it, namely the gold standard and fixed currency exchange rates. Post–gold standard, 20th-century developments should be studied for the same reasons, while current practices are, by definition, what businesspeople, economists, governments, and institutions are doing now. Informed guesses about the future are necessary ingredients of the forecasting and planning in which each of those groups must be involved.

A Brief Gold Standard
History and Comment

From about A.D. 1200 to the present, the direction of the price of gold has been generally up.[1] True, there have been wide fluctuations in that price and an investor in gold should have steady nerves, though law-abiding American investors were for a time spared that source of nervousness because it was illegal for them to own gold bullion between 1933 and 1976. During that period, the price of gold rose from about $21 per ounce to just under $200 in December 1976, when Americans were again legally free to own gold in bullion form. As it developed, Americans did not rush into the market, and the price has fluctuated between a bit over $100 and over $800 per ounce since 1976.

On December 22, 1717, Sir Isaac Newton, master of the mint, established the price of gold at 3 pounds, 17 shillings, 10.5 pence per ounce. England was then on the gold standard and stood willing to convert gold to currency, or vice versa, until World War I (WWI), except during the Napoleonic Wars. During that period, London was the dominant center of international finance. It has been estimated that more than 90 percent of world trade was financed in London.[2]

Most trading or industrial countries adopted the **gold standard**. Each country set a certain number of units of its currency per ounce of gold, and the comparison of the numbers of units per ounce from country to country was the exchange rate between any two currencies on the gold standard.

Countries May Lose Their Gold

Fundamental to the working of the gold standard was the undertaking of each country to exchange gold for its currency at the set rate. Thus, if a country had bought more from abroad than it had sold abroad, foreigners would accumulate its currency, which they could turn in for gold at its central bank. The amount of currency that the country could issue was based on the amount of gold it held, so as it lost gold, the amount of currency in circulation had to be contracted. Less currency in circulation tends to deflate an economy, bringing, among other results, lower prices.

As prices went down, the country's products tended to become more competitive, because they were comparatively less expensive in world markets. The opposite was going on in the surplus countries (the ones that had sold more abroad than they had bought), so the prices of their products tended to go up, making them more expensive and less competitive in the world markets. Then the deficit country would sell more of its products and move into surplus, while the previously surplus country would sell less, thus causing it to fall in deficit, and gold would begin to flow in the opposite direction.

This system, with gold supplemented by sterling (British currency on deposit in London banks), worked until WWI, when gold convertibility was suspended. To meet its war expenses, Britain became a deficit country and had too little gold to cover its net debits. There was a short-lived flirtation with the gold standard between WWI and WWII (dealt with briefly in the next section of this chapter), but it never again performed as well as it had before WWI.

Return to the Gold Standard?

Although the gold standard has not been the international monetary system for many years, it has had some ardent and influential advocates in recent years. One of the staunchest was Jacques Rueff, who until his death in 1978 was a member of the French Academy and an adviser to the French government. The heart of Rueff's argument may be expressed by one word, *discipline*.

Under the gold standard, a government cannot create money that is not backed by gold. Therefore, no matter how great the temptation to create more money for political advantage, without regard for economic results, a government cannot do so without the established amount of gold. This is the discipline that Jacques Rueff argued is the only effective means of avoiding inflation.[3]

One argument for a return to the gold standard, thus making gold the reserve asset of nations, is based on the premise that the current situation, in which the U.S. dollar (US$) is the reserve asset, is unsustainable. As world trade, investment, and economies grow, countries need more reserves. With the US$ as the reserve asset, other countries can increase their reserves only if the United States increases its net reserve indebtedness with a balance-of-payments (BOP) deficit. The United States can increase its liquidity only at the expense of other countries; a U.S. BOP surplus would drain US$ reserves from other countries. Thus, under the present system, the reserves of other countries can increase only if the largest debtor nation in the world—the United States—goes further into debt.

It has been suggested that the five nations with the largest economies should agree to settle their accounts with one another in gold, not US$s.[4] If a gold standard were established, what should be the price of gold? Lewis Lehrman advocates $500 an ounce, based on production costs. Arthur Laffer picks a price in the $200 range, based on the increase in the consumer price level since gold was $35 an ounce. A third school of thought, identified with Robert Mundell, suggests pegging the price where it happens to be on the day that the five nations agree to institute a gold standard.[5]

Gold and Inflation

Roy W. Jastram of the University of California at Berkeley wrote a book in which he constructed a wholesale price index indicating that prices in England doubled between 1585 and 1718.[6] Prices then remained more or less stable until 1930, when Britain gave up its post-WWI attempt to maintain the gold standard. From a 1930 base of 100, the index rose to 162 in 1946, 406 in 1956, 507 in 1966, and 1,248 in 1976.

The US$ was convertible into gold under a regime established after WWII that lasted until 1971. Jastram's index for the United States, with 1930 = 100, moved to 90.8 in 1940, 186 in 1948, 204 in 1951, 247.5 in 1970, and 410.2 in 1976.

Laffer advocates a return to convertibility of the US$ into gold. He points out that in the period 1957–67, when the US$ was convertible into gold, inflation averaged 1.7 percent annually. In March 1968, a two-tier gold market was in effect and convertibility of the US$ was limited. In the next three years, inflation escalated to a 4.9 percent average annual rate. Convertibility was officially scrapped in 1971, and inflation rose to a 7.5 percent annual rate from 1971 through mid-1979. In 1979, inflation was in double figures and the price of gold soared.[7]

Gold is a traditional haven against inflation; its price increases as currency values depreciate. When new fiscal and monetary policies were inaugurated in 1981 and the U.S. inflation rate fell to some 1 to 3 percent per year, gold prices, which had reached over $800 per ounce in 1980, moderated to around $330 in 1984. Inflation remained relatively low into 1986, but as the Federal Reserve System continued an easy money policy, increasing the money supply relatively rapidly to avert a recession, people began to fear a renewal of inflation. During August and September 1986, the price of gold climbed from about $350 per ounce to about $430 per ounce. By September, 1987, it was trading at over $460.

The Period from WWI to WWII

As mentioned above, Britain's gold supply was not sufficient to cover its foreign expenses in waging WWI. Two results were a reduction of confidence in sterling and Britain's departure from the gold standard. In addition, the United States and France became more important in international trade and finance after WWI.

However, London remained a major international financial center and the pound sterling continued to be a widely used currency. The British government wished to return to the gold standard but was delayed by a sharp recession in the United States[8] and by the hyperinflation that struck Germany and ended with the value of the German mark at 4 trillion for one US$ in 1923.[9]

Attempts to Revive the Gold Standard

In 1924 and 1925, Germany and Britain returned to the gold standard, but not for long, and it never operated as smoothly as it had before WWI. Now the French franc and the US$ assumed international payment and finance roles along with sterling, and as relative confidence in those currencies ebbed and flowed and as gold was demanded by countries with a surplus of one of the currencies, the system collapsed in 1931.[10]

Depression

Beginning in 1929 and extending to the outbreak of WWII, the world suffered a major depression. After the 1931 collapse of the gold standard as it had operated since the mid-1920s, governments either instituted exchange controls (dealt with in Chapter 6) or let their currencies float* to whatever values were established by currency market trading. One result was the creation of five currency blocs for international payments purposes.[11] These blocs were:

1. The exchange control area of central and southeastern Europe dominated by Germany.
2. The sterling area, principally the British Commonwealth and Scandinavia.
3. The dollar area, which included the United States and most of Central America and northern South America.
4. The gold bloc countries of Western Europe.
5. The yen area, comprising Japan and its possessions.

The depression and the collapse of a generally accepted monetary system, with the resulting development of separate currency blocs, impeded international trade and investment during the 1930s. WWII broke out in 1939, and then the world's attention was neither on peaceful trade and investment nor on international monetary systems, except for preoccupation with methods for financing the war efforts.

Bretton Woods and the Gold
Exchange Standard

Actually, consideration of how the international monetary system should operate after WWII did not await the firing of the last shot. Before that, in 1944, representatives of the major Allied powers, with the United States and Britain assuming the dominant roles, met at **Bretton Woods**, New Hampshire, to plan for the future.

There was general consensus (1) that stable exchange rates were desirable but that experience might dictate adjustments; (2) that floating or fluctuating

---

*A currency is said to float freely when the governments do nothing to affect its value in the world currency markets. Other varieties of floating are discussed later in this chapter.

exchange rates had proved unsatisfactory, though the reasons for this opinion were little discussed; and (3) that the government controls of trade, exchange, production, and so forth that had developed from 1931 through WWII were wasteful, discriminatory, and detrimental to expansion of world trade and investment. In spite of (3), the conferees recognized that some conditions, for example, reconstruction from war damage or development of less developed countries (LDCs), would require government controls.

To achieve its goals, the Bretton Woods Conference established the International Monetary Fund (IMF). Article I of the IMF Articles of Agreement set forth its purposes, which reflected the consensus referred to above.[12] The IMF Articles of Agreement entered into force in December 1945.

The IMF agreement was the basis for the international monetary system from 1945 until 1971. It is doubtful, however, that the role that would be assumed by, or thrust upon, the US$, which became the major international reserve asset, was fully foreseen.[13]

The US$ was agreed to be the only currency directly convertible into gold for official monetary purposes. An ounce of gold was agreed to be worth US$35, and other currencies were assigned so-called par values in relationship to the US$. For example, the British pound's par value was US$2.40, the French franc's was US$0.18, and the German mark's was US$0.2732.[14]

It was recognized that each member country would be subject to different pressures at different times. The pressures could be caused by political or economic events or trends and could render the par values (currency exchange rates) established at Bretton Woods unrealistic. A major force that affects currency exchange rates is the balance of payments (BOP) of the member countries.

Balance of Payments

One task assumed by the IMF was assistance to member countries having difficulties in keeping their balance of payments (BOP) out of deficit.* A country's BOP is a very important indicator for business management of what may happen to the country's economy, including what the government may cause to happen. If the BOP is in deficit (that is, if more money is going out than is coming in), inflation is often the cause and the company must adjust its pricing, inventory, accounting, and other practices to inflationary conditions. The government may take measures to deal with inflation and the deficit. These may be so-called market measures, such as deflating the economy or devaluing the currency, or nonmarket measures, such as currency controls, tariffs, or quotas.

Even if a company does not consider itself an international company, it will be affected by inflation and by the government's methods of combating infla-

---

*A deficit occurs when the residents of a country are paying nonresidents more than they are earning or otherwise getting from nonresidents. The opposite is a surplus.

tion. All of those methods have the common goals of causing the country's residents to buy fewer foreign goods and services and to sell more to foreigners.

Debits and Credits in International Transactions

International debit transactions are those which involve payments by domestic residents to foreign residents, and international credit transactions are the opposite. Taking America as the domestic economy, a list of debit transactions would include:

A. Dividend, interest, and debt repayment services on foreign-owned capital in America.

B. Merchandise imports.

C. Purchases by Americans traveling abroad.

D. Transportation services bought by Americans on foreign carriers.

E. Foreign investment by Americans.

F. Gifts by Americans to foreign residents.

G. Imports of gold.

The opposite would be examples of credit transactions. For example, dividend, interest, and debt repayment services on American-owned capital abroad are credits on the American ledger.

Double-Entry Accounting

While writers use debit and credit transaction language, each international transaction is an exchange of assets with a debit and credit side. Thus, the BOP is presented as a double-entry accounting statement in which total credits and debits are always equal. The statement of a country's BOP is divided into several accounts, which are illustrated in Table 5–1.

Current Account

Three subaccounts are included in the current account (A) goods or merchandise, (B) services, and (C) unilateral transfers. A and B are sometimes treated together, and they include the real (as opposed to the financial) international transactions, exports and imports.

A. The goods or merchandise account deals with "visibles," such as autos, grain, machinery or equipment, that can be seen and felt as they are exported or imported. The net balance on merchandise transactions is referred to as the country's trade balance.

B. The account services deals with "invisibles" that are exchanged or bought internationally. Examples are (1) dividends or interest on foreign investments, (2) royalties on patents or trademarks held abroad, (3) travel, (4) insurance, and (5) transportation.

Table 5-1

Balance-of-Payments Accounts

	Debits	Credits
1. Current account		
A. Merchandise imports and exports		
B. Services		
Net goods and services balance		
C. Unilateral transfers		
To abroad		
From abroad		
Net current account balance		
2. Capital account		
A. Direct investment		
To abroad		
From abroad		
B. Portfolio investment		
To abroad		
From abroad		
C. Short-term capital		
To abroad		
From abroad		
Net capital account balance		
3. Official reserves account		
A. Gold export or import (net)		
B. Increase or decrease in foreign exchange (net)		
C. Increase or decrease in liabilities to foreign central banks (net)		
Net official reserves		
4. Net statistical discrepancy		

C. Unilateral transfers are transactions with no quid pro quo; some of these transfers are made by private persons or institutions, and some by governments. Some private unilateral transfers are for charitable, educational, or missionary purposes; others are gifts from migrant workers to their families in their home countries and bequests or the transfer of capital by people migrating from one country to another. The largest government unilateral transfers are aid—which may be in money or kind—from developed countries to developing countries. Pension payments to nonresidents and tax receipts from nonresidents are two other government-related unilateral transfers.

Capital Account

The capital account records the net changes in a nation's international financial assets and liabilities over the BOP period, which is usually one year. A capital inflow—a credit entry—occurs when a resident sells stock, bonds, or other financial assets to nonresidents. Money flows in to the resident, while at the same time the resident's long-term international liabilities are increased, as it will pay dividends (profit) on the stock and other assets and interest on the bonds and ultimately it will redeem the bonds.

Subaccounts under the capital account are (A) direct investment, (B) portfolio investment, and (C) international movements of short-term capital.

A. Direct investments are investments in enterprises or properties located in one country that are "effectively controlled" by residents of another country. Effective control is assumed for BOP purposes (1) when residents of one country own 50 percent or more of the voting stock of a company in another country or (2) when one resident or an organized group of residents of one country own 25 percent or more of the voting stock of a company in another country.

B. Portfolio investments include all long-term—more than one year—investments that do not give the investors effective control over the object of the investment. Such transactions typically involve the purchase of stocks or bonds of foreign issuers for investment—not control—purposes, and they also include long-term commercial credits to finance trade.

C. Short-term capital flows involve changes in international assets and liabilities with an original maturity of one year or less. Some of the fastest-growing types of short-term flows are for currency exchange rate and interest rate hedging in the forward, futures, option, and swap markets. (These subjects are dealt with in Chapter 18, "Financial Management.") Among the more traditional sorts of short-term capital flow are payments and receipts for international finance and trade, short-term borrowings from foreign banks, exchanges of foreign notes or coins, and purchases of foreign commercial paper or foreign government bills or notes.

The volatility, private nature, and wide varieties of short-term capital flows make them the most difficult to measure of the BOP items, and therefore the least reliable. The wide fluctuations of currency exchange rates and interest rates during the 1980s has caused the surge in hedging activities mentioned above, with attendant surges in short-term capital movements.

Official Reserves Account

The official reserves account deals with gold imports and exports, increases or decreases of foreign exchange (foreign currencies) held by the government, and decreases or increases in liabilities to foreign central banks. The last item in this account is the errors and omissions entry, which is now called "statistical discrepancy."

Total BOP credits and debits must equal each other because of the double-entry accounting system used to report the BOP. Because some BOP figures are inaccurate and incomplete (this is notably true of the short-term capital flows item), the statistical discrepancy item is plugged in to bring total credits and debits into accounting balance.

Balance-of-Payment Equilibrium and Disequilibrium

While the BOP is always in accounting balance, the odds are astronomical that it would be so without the statistical discrepancy item. There would be a surplus or a deficit in almost every case, but the BOP would nevertheless be considered in equilibrium if over a three- to five-year period the surpluses more or less cancel out the deficits.

Temporary BOP Deficits

In IMF terminology, the deficit years for a country in equilibrium are referred to as temporary. They are corrected by the country's monetary and fiscal policies, and perhaps by short-term IMF loans and advice.

Fundamental BOP Deficits

The fundamental BOP deficit is too severe to be repaired by any **monetary policies** or **fiscal policies** that the country can apply; there are economic, social, and political limits to how much a country can deflate its economy, which causes unemployment, or devalue its currency, which causes higher prices for imports.

In these cases, the IMF rules permitted the countries' currencies to be devalued from the par values per US$ set at Bretton Woods; the amount of the devaluation was agreed by the country and the IMF. Although there were many par value changes between 1946 and 1971, none led to international financial crises of the kind that followed the devaluations of 1931. This was due at least in part to the performance of the IMF; it was able to maintain generally stable exchange rates, and when changes became necessary, it was able to prevent the competitive devaluations that proved so futile and destructive in the 1930s.

The devaluations of the 1946–71 period were in terms of the US$, so its relative value went up in terms of the devalued currencies. This caused the prices of American goods and services to go up in terms of other currencies, since after devaluation, more units of those currencies were required to buy US$s. This, in turn, was one cause of an American BOP deficit that began in 1958.

American BOP Deficit

From the end of WWII until about 1958, there was a shortage of US$s for the development of world trade and investment. Even during that era, many dollars flowed abroad due to government aid, private investment, and tourism; around 1958, the United States began to run a series of BOP deficits, the flow of dollars became a flood, and the US$ shortage ended. The United States could have tried **market methods** (deflate the economy or devalue the US$) to slow or reverse the deficit, but it did not, and its trading partner countries did not urge it to do so.*

---

*Nonmarket methods to deal with a BOP deficit include currency exchange controls, tariffs, and quotas.

Why Market Methods Were Not Attempted

Vivid recollections of the hunger and hardships of the 1930s depression caused U.S. leaders to see deflation as the greater danger, and it was not until the late 1960s that inflation was perceived by the U.S. government as a possible cause of another depression. The US$ had been enshrined at Bretton Woods as the key currency in the gold exchange standard and had become, along with gold, the central reserve asset of most countries. Those countries were understandably reluctant to see a reduction in the value of part of their reserves, and U.S. authorities seemed to feel that this nation's prestige would be tarnished by a devaluation of the US$.[15]

Moreover, foreign competitors of U.S. exports derived a price advantage from the overvaluation of the US$. As pointed out above, almost all of the 1946–71 currency value changes were devaluations in terms of the US$; thus, foreign goods and services became relatively less expensive for holders of US$s, but at the same time U.S. exports were becoming relatively more expensive for holders of other currencies, who bought fewer of those more expensive goods and services. The foreign competitors of U.S. firms did not want to lose that advantage, and their governments discouraged any U.S. inclination to devalue the US$.

Raising the US$ price of gold would amount to a dollar devaluation in terms of other currencies unless they also devalued. It was generally recognized that the US$ was overvalued and that, if permitted to float, its value would fall vis-à-vis the currencies of most of the industrialized countries.

The United States had thousands of troops stationed in Europe and Asia and could have saved billions of dollars in expenditures abroad by bringing them home. But the host countries, for example, Germany, Japan, South Korea, and South Vietnam, brought strong pressures on the U.S. government not to reduce its forces, and the United States felt obliged to maintain them.

Gold Exchange Standard

As the United States failed to even try market methods to end its BOP deficit, and other rather halfhearted attempts had little success, dollars piled up in foreign hands, including those of government **central banks**. At this point, beginning in 1958, the "exchange" part of the **gold exchange standard** began to function.

Gold for Dollars

The exchange feature agreed on at Bretton Woods required the United States to deliver an ounce of gold to any central bank of an IMF member country that presented US$35 to the U.S. Treasury. As dollars accumulated in foreign hands in amounts greater than were needed for trade and investment, the central banks began turning them in to the U.S. Treasury for gold.

Figure 5-2

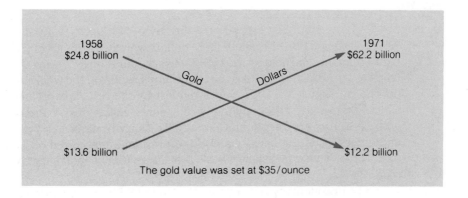

1958
$24.8 billion

1971
$62.2 billion

Gold   Dollars

$13.6 billion $12.2 billion

The gold value was set at $35/ounce

Gold and Dollars Go Abroad

During the years 1958 through 1971, the United States ran up a cumulative deficit of $56 billion. The deficit was financed partly by use of the U.S. gold reserves, which shrank from $24.8 billion to $12.2 billion,[16] and partly by incurring liabilities to foreign central banks. During this period, those liabilities increased from $13.6 billion to $62.2 billion.[17] This is illustrated by Figure 5.2.

The main reason the foreign central banks were willing to accept so many dollars was that those dollars were treated as a central reserve asset. They provided liquidity growth to support growing world trade and finance, but in the late 1960s and into 1971, the central banks became increasingly nervous at the volume of US$ accumulation. A number of them turned in excess dollars for gold, but by the mid-1960s more dollars were held by the banks than there was gold left in the U.S. Treasury. By 1971, the Treasury held only 22 cents worth of gold for each US$ held by those banks.[18]

As indicated, another reason foreigners accepted so many US$s was that these dollars provided liquidity to support world trade and investment, which grew rapidly in the post-WWII era. Of course, this meant that liquidity growth depended on U.S. BOP deficits, but such deficits could not continue indefinitely without deterioration of confidence in the strength of the U.S. economy and of the US$. Here is illustrated the inherent contradiction of the gold exchange standard. Foreigners needed and wanted growing numbers of dollars for many purposes but became nervous when the amounts of dollars they held exceeded the amount of gold held by the United States at the established price of $35 per ounce of gold.[19]

August 15, 1971, and the
Next Two Years

As noted above, by 1971, many more dollars were in the hands of foreign central banks than the gold held by the U.S. Treasury could cover. The event said to have triggered the drastic decisions made at Camp David* on the weekend that began on Friday, August 13, 1971, was a request by the British government that the United States cover US$3 billion of its reserve against loss.[20] President Nixon, with Treasury Secretary John Connally, Treasury Undersecretary Paul Volcker, and others made the decisions that the president announced on Sunday night (the 15th). Those decisions shook the international monetary system to its roots.[21]

The president announced that the United States would no longer exchange gold for the paper dollars held by foreign central banks. He was said to have "closed the **gold window**."

The shock caused currency exchange markets to remain closed for several days, and when they reopened, they began playing a new game for which few rules existed. Currencies were floating, and the stated US$ value of 35 per ounce of gold was now meaningless because the United States would no longer exchange any of its gold for dollars. The gold exchange standard was ended.

The president also imposed and announced a 10-percent surcharge on imports from all industrial countries except Canada. He demanded those countries lower their obstacles to imports from the United States in return for cancelling the surcharges. Agreement on trade obstacles was reached in December 1971 along with new currency exchange rates which devalued the US$. The new rates could not be maintained, and by 1973 currencies were floating.

Politicians versus Speculators

Two attempts were made to agree on durable, new sets of **fixed exchange rates**, one in December 1971 and the other in February 1973. Both times, however, banks, businesses, and individuals (collectively referred to as speculators by unhappy politicians) felt that the central banks had pegged the rates incorrectly, and each time the speculators proved correct. Of course, the speculators' prophecies could be said to have been self-fulfilling in that they put billions of units of the major currencies into the currencies they felt to be strong, for example, the deutsche mark (DM), the Dutch guilder, and the Swiss franc, thereby making them even stronger. The speculators profited, and one writer commented, "It wasn't a holdup. It was more like an invited robbery."[22]

---

*Camp David is a relatively isolated retreat in the Maryland mountains that U.S. presidents frequently use to escape the pressures of Washington.

In March 1973, the major currencies began to float in the foreign exchange markets, and still prevail **floating exchange rates**.[23] However, Western Europe has moved back toward a fixed system, the European Monetary System.

1973 to the Present

There are two kinds of currency floats, and these are referred to by various commentators as free or managed or as clean or dirty. The free (clean) float is one of the world's closest approaches to perfect competition, because there is no government intervention and because billions of the product (units of money) are being traded by thousands of buyers and sellers. Buyers and sellers may change sides on short notice as information, rumors, or moods change or as their clients' needs differ.

In the managed (dirty) float, governments intervene in the currency markets as they perceive their national interests to be served. For example, several nations accused Japan of market intervention during the mid-1970s, selling yen and buying European currencies and the US$ to keep the yen lower in value, and thus make the Japanese exports less expensive and more competitive.[24] Nations usually explain their interventions in the currency market in terms of "smoothing market irregularities" or "assuring orderly markets."

Currency Areas

The U.S. dollar, Canadian dollar, Japanese yen (¥), Swiss franc, British pound (£), and several other currencies are floating in value against one another and against the European Currency Unit (ECU), a grouping of eight Western European currencies. Most currencies of developing countries (LDCs) are pegged (fixed) in value to one of the major currencies or to currency baskets such as the ECU, special drawing rights (SDRs), or some specially chosen currency mix or basket (see Figure 5–3).[25]

Snake

In Europe during the mid-1970s, a currency grouping was created, the so-called snake. The snake comprised several European currencies, led by the German mark (usually referred to by currency traders as the deutsche mark and abbreviated as DM). The member currencies endeavored to keep their values close to one another and to float together against the US$, the yen, and other currencies. The reptile's health was damaged by the departure of several currencies, such as the pound sterling, the Italian lira, and the Swedish krona, and by the in-and-out relationship of the French franc.[26]

The snake was so called because of how it appeared in a graph showing the member currencies floating against nonmember currencies, such as the yen or

Figure 5-3

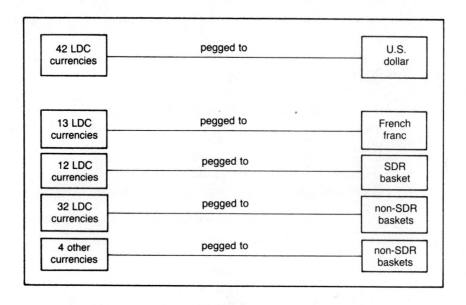

Source: *International Financial Statistics,* September 1985, p. 18.

the Canadian or U.S. dollar. There was an agreed central value, shown by the dotted line, but currencies could fluctuate up or down from the central value to an agreed ceiling or floor value, shown by the solid lines.

When the currency group fluctuated in terms of a nonmember currency, a graph would show the ups and downs thus:

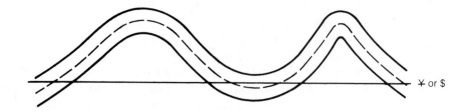

To some this looks like a snake, and that is what the system was called. The snake was the forerunner of the European Monetary System (EMS), discussed below.

Experience with Floating

Such immense amounts of major currencies were being bought and sold each trading day that government efforts to keep their currencies at fixed exchange rates failed. The central banks stopped trying to peg the major currencies' exchange rates in 1973. OPEC hiked the price of petroleum over 400 percent early in 1974, and there were fears that the banking and monetary systems would not be able to handle the resulting changes in the amounts and directions of currency flows.[27]

Fears Not Realized

However, despite occasional flare-ups and occasional sharp changes in the relative values of currencies, the system did not collapse. Indeed, the volatility of exchange rate movements diminished after a period of uncertainty with the new system, in 1973–74. Uncertainty was heightened by the sudden, drastic increase of oil prices by OPEC. In those days, it could be difficult and costly to engage in a foreign exchange transaction. By 1977, the cost of undertaking foreign exchange transactions was about the same as it had been under the Bretton Woods system.[28]

The system has still not collapsed, even though the value of the US$ fluctuated widely between 1977 and 1987. Beginning in June 1977, the US$ fell in value about 28 percent against the Swiss franc, 20 percent against the Japanese yen, and some 15 percent against the deutsche mark within a year. Many laid the blame for the dollar's weakness on inflationary American fiscal and monetary policies, particularly the latter.

In 1979, the American Federal Reserve System (Fed) slowed the rate of monetary growth and the US$ began to move up in value. The new administration that took office in 1981 continued the anti-inflationary policies instituted by Fed Chairman Paul A. Volcker in 1979, and indeed inflation did fall. As it fell, the value of the US$ rose, and by the beginning of 1985 it had risen about 80 percent against a trade-weighted basket of other major currencies.

Then, beginning in March 1985, the dollar exchange rate reversed its climb, and by summer 1986 it had dropped about 33 percent in terms of the deutsche mark and the Swiss franc and 31 percent against the Japanese yen.

Forecasting Float Direction

Such large changes in short time periods prompted efforts by everyone affected to forecast currency value changes. Such changes have many causes, including political events and expectations and government economic policies. A major cause is present and forecast relative inflation from country to country. One means of measuring relative inflation is purchasing power parity (PPP), the theory of which is that an exchange rate between the currencies of two countries is in equilibrium when it equates the prices of a basket of goods and services in both countries.

One product sold world-wide that is—or is supposed to be—the same everywhere is McDonalds's "Big Mac" hamburger. The *Economist* did a PPP study using Big Mac as the basket in 15 countries. The report of that study is in the accompanying reading.

Reading

On the Hamburger Standard

Depressing though it may be to gourmets, the "Big Mac" hamburger sold by McDonald's could well oust the basket of currencies as an international monetary standard. After all, it is sold in 41 countries, with only the most trivial changes of recipe. That ought to say something about comparative prices. Think of the hamburger as a medium-rare guide to whether currencies are trading at the right exchange rates.

Big Mac watchers will rely on the theory of purchasing power parity (PPP) for currencies. This argues that an exchange rate between two currencies is in equilibrium (i.e. at PPP) when it equates the prices of a basket of goods and services in both countries—or, in this case, the rate of exchange that leaves hamburgers costing the same in each country. Comparing actual exchange rates with PPP is one indication of whether a currency is under- or overvalued.

The Economist's *correspondents around the world have been gorging themselves in a bid to test Mac-PPPs. In Washington, a Big Mac costs*

Source: *Economist* September 6, 1986, p. 77.

Currency Dealers Get Younger by the Day

Reading

On the Hamburger Standard (continued)

$1.60; in Tokyo, our Makudonarudo *correspondent had to fork out Y370 ($2.40). Dividing the yen price by the dollar price yields a Mac-PPP of $1 = Y231; but on September 1, the dollar's actual exchange rate stood at Y154. The same method gives a Mac-PPP against the deutsch mark of DM2.66, compared with a current rate of DM2.02. Conclusion: on Mac-PPP grounds, the dollar looks undervalued against the yen and the deutsche mark.*

Sterling is different. The Mac-PPP for the pound is $1.45 (69p to the dollar), within a whisker of the actual rate of around $1.49. But the pound's Mac-PPP against the deutsche mark is DM3.86, suggesting that sterling is undervalued at DM3.02. British industrialists, who squeal about the pound's current "strength," will now like hamburgers even less.

The Australian dollar appears to have been heavily oversold; it is 34 percent below its Mac-PPP rate against the American dollar. Meanwhile, the Irish pound seems to be spot on. However, our correspondent in Ireland has uncovered an opportunity for arbitrage. This month, a Big Mac can be enjoyed in Dublin for just 20 tokens from milk cartons.

The hamburger standard provides the United States with strong evidence for its contention that Asian NICs (newly industrializing coun-

Big MacCurrencies: Hamburger Prices Around the World

Country	Price in Local Currency*	Implied Purchasing Power Parity of the Dollar†	Actual Exchange Rate September 1	Percent over (+) or under (−) Valuation of US$
Australia	A$1.75	1.09	1.64	+ 50
Belgium	BFr90	56	42	− 25
Brazil	Cz$2.5	7.80	13.80	+ 78
Britain	£1.10	0.69	0.67	− 3
Canada	C$1.89	1.18	1.39	+ 18
France	FFr16.4	10.30	6.65	− 35
Hong Kong	HK$7.60	4.75	7.80	+ 64
Ireland	IR£1.18	0.74	0.74	− 1
Japan	Y370	231	154	− 33
Holland	F14.35	2.72	2.28	− 16
Singapore	S$2.80	1.75	2.15	+ 23
Spain	Ptas260	163	133	− 18
Sweden	SKr16.5	10.30	6.87	− 33
United States	$1.60	—	—	—
West Germany	DM4.25	2.66	2.02	− 24

*Prices may vary slightly between branches.
†Foreign price divided by dollar price.
Source: McDonald's.

Reading

On the Hamburger Standard (concluded)

tries) ought to upvalue their currencies; they are more or less tied to the dollar, so their exchange rates have barely budged during the past 18 months. A hamburger costs 64 percent more in Washington than in Hong Kong—i.e., on Mac-PPP grounds the dollar is 64 percent overvalued against the Hong Kong dollar. It is also 23 percent too high against the Singapore dollar.

Caveat Hamburger

The hamburger standard has its limitations. Using purchasing power parities to forecast movements in exchange rates can produce misleading results. For instance, price differences between countries can be distorted by taxes, transport costs, property costs, or such things as the famously high retail markups in Japan and West Germany.

A more serious objection is that a PPP simply indicates where exchange rates should be in the long run if price levels were the only difference between countries. In fact, there are many other differences. So even though PPPs are handy for converting living standards (GDP per person) into a common currency, they are not necessarily the best way to judge the exchange rate needed to bring the current account of the balance of payments into "equilibrium." Confused? Some economics can be hard to digest.

The advocates of floating argued that it would end BOP disequilibria because the value of each currency would float up or down to a point where supply equaled demand. It has not worked that way, at least in part due to the reluctance of governments to permit extreme changes in the value of their currencies. Governments have intervened in the currency markets to moderate or prevent value changes. The American BOP deficit set new records in 1985 and 1986.

Money Markets, Foreign Exchange

The daily volume of foreign exchange trading in the world's three leading **money markets** has grown at a rapid pace. London is in the lead, handling some $90 billion; New York comes second with some $50 billion; and Tokyo is a close third, with some 48 billion. The studies leading to these estimates were conducted in March 1986 by the Bank of England, working with the Federal Reserve Bank of New York and the Bank of Japan.

These studies underscore the pivotal role of London in world currency trading. Because the London market shares trading hours with markets in Asia and the Middle East during its morning session and with the New York market during its afternoon session, it has more transaction opportunities than do the New York or Tokyo markets.

The growth of foreign exchange trading in recent years has greatly outpaced world trade even though trade has also expanded. This has been due to the near explosions in international investment and in hedge and swap transactions. Hedges and swaps are explained in Chapter 18.

Banks, currency brokers, and securities houses are major currency dealers. The Bank of England said that 30 percent of London volume was in sterling (British pounds)–US$ transactions and 28 percent in deutsche mark–US$ transactions. The remainder was between the US$ and other major currencies. The Fed found that in New York the most traded currencies—all with the US$—were deutsche marks, followed by Japanese yen, British pounds, Swiss francs, and Canadian dollars.

London, New York, and Tokyo have the biggest currency markets but by no means the only ones. Other important markets are in Los Angeles and San Francisco, Hong Kong, Singapore, Bahrain, Frankfurt, Zurich, and Paris, and trades can be made 24 hours a day at one or more of these markets.

Billions of US$s are traded around the world in the various currency markets. Smaller—but still large—amounts of the other currencies of major market countries are also traded outside the borders of the issuing countries, and all of these currencies are used as national reserve assets of countries as well as in trade, investments, hedges, and swaps.[29]

Beginning in the 1960s, there was a growing feeling that an asset other than national currencies or gold should be created to replace them at least insofar as they are used as central reserve assets. In 1969, the IMF established special drawing rights (SDRs) for that purpose.

SDRs in the Future

Special drawing rights, SDRs, may be a step toward a truly international currency. The US$ has been the closest thing to such a currency since gold in the pre-WWI gold standard system, but the US$ must also serve as a national currency, and the roles sometimes conflict.

SDRs, bookkeeping entries at the IMF, were created in 1969 by agreement of the IMF members, whose accounts are credited with certain amounts of SDRs from time to time. It is the objective of some to make the SDR the principal reserve asset in the international monetary system.[30]

Value of the SDR

The SDR's value is based on a "basket" of the five following currencies (the percentage of each currency are in parentheses) U.S. dollar (42), German mark (19), the British pound (13), the French franc (13), and the Japanese yen (13). The SDR's value has remained more stable than that of any single currency, and that stability has made the SDR increasingly attractive as a unit for denominating international transactions. Future payment under a contract, for example, may be agreed to be made in a national currency at its rate in terms of the SDR on the payment date, [31] and some Swiss and British banks will now accept accounts denominated in SDRs. [32]

Holders of SDRs

SDRs are held by the IMF, its 151 members, and 16 official institutions, typically regional development or banking institutions; nonmember holders of SDRs must be prescribed by the IMF. All holders can buy and sell SDRs both spot and forward and receive or use SDRs in loans, pledges, swaps, grants, or settlement of financial obligations. Holders receive interest at a rate that is determined weekly by reference to the weighted-average interest rate on short-term obligations in the money markets of the same five countries whose currencies are included in the SDR valuation basket.

SDRs as Central Reserve Assets

A major purpose envisioned for SDRs was to replace currencies and gold as **central reserve assets** of nations. That has not happened. After the first allocation of 9 billion SDRs to members in 1972, they constituted 6.1 percent of the central reserves, while foreign exchange made up 65.3 percent and gold 24.5 percent at $35 per ounce. There was a second SDR allocation in 1979 of 13 billion, but total reserves went up faster, so that by 1983 SDRs constituted only 3.4 percent of the central reserves. Currencies had increased to 78.7 percent, and gold had fallen to 8.2 percent, but that was on the basis of valuing gold at $35 per ounce. In the gold markets, the price of gold had soared to over $800 in 1980 and gold traded between some $300 and $465 per ounce from then into 1987.

European Monetary System (EMS) and the European Currency Unit (ECU)

In 1979, the **European Monetary System** (EMS) came into existence. It is a large step back to fixed currency exchange rates and is an enlarged version of the snake, mentioned previously.

The **European Currency Unit (ECU)** was established as the EMS bookkeeping currency. Its value is determined by reference to a "basket" of European currencies. The weights of each currency in the ECU are shown in Table 5–2.

The ECU is becoming more widely used in the Eurobond market and elsewhere; by 1983, the volume of ECU bonds was surpassed only by that of bonds denominated in US$s and deutsche marks. ECU bond issues increased from ECU 190 million in 1981 to about ECU 9.5 billion in 1985.

One reason the ECU has become more popular than the SDR is that neither the US$ nor the yen are included in the currency basket that determines its value. The exchange rates of the US$ and, to a lesser extent, the yen have fluctuated much more widely than have those of the European currencies in the ECU bas-

Table 5-2

	In Absolute Amounts of Currency	As Percentage Shares
Deutsche mark	0.719	32
French franc	1.31	19
Pound sterling	0.0878	15
Netherlands guilder	0.256	10.1
Italian lira	140	10.2
Belgian franc	3.71	8.2
Danish krone	0.219	2.7
Irish pound	0.00871	1.2
Luxembourg franc	0.14	0.3
Greek drachma	1.15	1.3

Source: *Europe*, January-February 1986.

ket. Both the US$ and the yen are in the SDR basket, so the SDR's value has been less stable than that of the ECU.

Another reason the ECU's use has surpassed that of the SDR is active sponsorship of the ECU by European governments, banks and businesses; the SDR has received no such support. The ECU is being used for various purposes, and support and supplementary networks have been put in place. Bank accounts can be denominated in ECUs, and ECU traveler's checks are available. Between units of some large multinational enterprises, debits and credits are denominated in ECUs as they buy, sell, or borrow from one another.

Countries outside the European Community have begun to utilize ECUs (e.g., the Soviet Union, Cameroon, Romania, Sweden, and New Zealand), and recently American companies have issued bonds denominated in ECUs. ECU futures and options contracts are available at markets in Amsterdam, Chicago, and Philadelphia. And, last but not least, an association of banks together with the European Investment Bank (a unit of the European Community) has begun a multilateral, electronic clearing system for ECU transactions. It will be administered by the Bank for International Settlements, which will perform functions for the ECU similar to the U.S. Federal Reserve clearing of dollar transactions.

The EMS member countries (Britain did not become a full member at the beginning and was still debating membership in 1987) agreed to maintain their currency values within an agreed range in relation to one another. An important feature, not available to the old snake, will be the European Monetary Cooperation Fund (EMCF). It will be composed of dollars, gold, and member country currencies, and it is to be used to support the efforts of member countries to keep their currency values within the agreed relationship to the other currencies. The EMCF can carry considerable clout when it comes into being. It is to have the equivalent of about $32 billion with which to work.[33]

Another difference between the EMS and its ancestor, the snake, is that the exchange rates of the EMS are flexible. If one currency proves weaker than another and the governments cannot or will not take steps to correct the situation, the EMS exchange rates can be changed. There have been several rate rearrangements since 1979. If a snake member country could not keep its currency up to the agreed strength, it dropped out and ceased to be a member.

Summary

Although debate continues about the relative merits of fixed exchange rates compared to the floating (mostly dirty) ones that have been in effect since 1973, many feel that the shocks and strains suffered by the international monetary system since 1971 would have made fixed rates impossible. The inherent contradiction of the gold exchange standard led to the collapse of the fixed or par rates established at Bretton Woods. Then the shocks of the OPEC petroleum price increases, the strains of the BOP gyrations of such countries as the United Kingdom and Italy, and the U.S. deficits combined with the German and Japanese surpluses, would have made impossible the sustained maintenance of fixed exchange rates during the mid- and late 1970s and the 1980s.

So we find ourselves at the present situation of currency areas, US$, £, Ff, or SDR, with the LDCs pegged to a major currency and those currencies in a managed float. But even with the float, persistent BOP imbalances have not been avoided, and the world is seeking methods to bring about better balance among the important economies. In theory, floating currencies should achieve balance, but they have not. The gold standard is in the past, and the gold exchange standard fell of its own weight.

As matters stand, coordination must be on a nation-by-nation basis, and the policies called for in the world's best interests may be extremely unpopular politically within a country. For example, restraint of monetary base growth may be called for, but fears of depression and unemployment may deter national leaders from implementing such a policy.

Developments mentioned in this chapter may hold some promise of making desirable coordination possible. One possibility is greater use of SDRs which could permit the growth of world liquidity to be controlled by the IMF instead of being dependent on the size or existence of the U.S. BOP deficit.

Countries measure their BOP on an annual basis; the BOP measures the flows of money from residents of a country to nonresidents, and vice versa. It is in surplus if more money is coming in than is going out; the opposite is a deficit. The BOP contains a current account, a capital account, and an official reserves account, and it is balanced by the statistical discrepancy account.

Another attempt at coordination, and at fixed currency exchange rates, is the European Monetary System (EMS), inaugurated in 1979. Its members include most of Europe's most important economic powers, and it will have a huge fund of gold, U.S. dollars, and European currencies with which to achieve its goals.

The EMS created a unit of value called the European Currency Unit (ECU), the use of which as a denomination for bonds issued by European and other organizations has surpassed that of the SDR. There are bank accounts and traveler's checks in ECUs, and some multinational companies use ECUs for settlement of accounts between company units. The original purpose of the ECU was that it be used for settlement of accounts among EMS members just as the SDR is used for settlement of accounts among IMF members.

Finally, what about gold? Pulling in one direction have been economists and government officials who want to demonetize gold and substitute for it special drawing rights (SDRs) and national currencies. They point out that SDRs can be controlled in number by the IMF in response to world need for liquidity, while the quantity, not to mention the price, of gold cannot be so controlled. There are other arguments against gold, such as the sources of most newly mined ore—the USSR and South Africa.

Other economists and officials pull in the other direction. They favor keeping gold as a part of reserve assets. The basis of their argument is the discipline that gold imposes on politicians who want to inflate national economies for temporary political advantage.

Now that national governments and central banks can buy gold, it is virtually certain that some of them will. Gold is part of the EMS reserves. It is too soon to write it out of the international monetary system.

Questions

1. *What was Rueff's argument for the gold standard?*
2. a. *Describe the international monetary system devised at Bretton Woods.*
   b. *What were its strengths?*
   c. *Discuss the inherent contradiction of the gold exchange standard.*
3. *How does "dirty" float differ from "clean"?*
4. *What sorts of currency areas have developed in the post-1973 international monetary system?*
5. *What institutions make most of the world's current money markets?*
6. a. *What is a special drawing right?*
   b. *Discuss its current and potential uses.*
7. *Why would fixed exchange rates have been difficult to maintain from 1973 to the present?*
8. *Why might the EMS be able to achieve fixed currency exchange rates among its member countries?*

9. *Why should business managers be aware and wary of the BOP of the country in which their business operates?*
10. *What is the ECU, and why has it become more used than the SDR?*

Minicase

5-1 Use of Special

Drawing Rights

You are the financial executive of an American construction company. Your company is about to contract for a multiphase project in Italy. Progress payments will be made, but most of the money will not be due until near the end of the project, eight or nine years in the future.

Your company wants to be paid in US$s. The Italian customer wants to make payments in Italian lira (Il). You fear devaluation of the Il in terms of the US$ over the term of the contract.

Draft a contract payment clause to be used as a compromise. Use special drawing rights (SDRs) in your clause.

Minicase

5-2 You Need Deutsche

Marks (DM) and Yen (¥)

You are the financial manager of a large American company based in Los Angeles, and you do most of your banking with two banks. One of the banks has its head offices in Los Angeles; the other is a branch of a bank headquartered in San Francisco.

Your management has been negotiating to purchase companies in its business in other countries as the best use of a large amount of dollars that it has received from the sale of assets in the United States. It wants to expand internationally.

One day your CEO calls you, and it is clear that he is extremely excited. You hurry to his office, where he tells you that, by coincidence, two great deals have jelled at the same time; one is in Germany, the other in Japan, and the sellers want prompt cash payment in their own currencies.

You pick up *The Wall Street Journal*, find the foreign exchange column, make quick calculations, and realize that these two purchases will take all the money your company has for acquisitions—$90 million—and maybe a little more. You give that news to the boss, who responds, "I want those companies,

From *The Wall Street Journal*, with permission of Cartoon Features Syndicate.

"May I have my allowance in Deutsche Marks, Dad?"

and it is your job to get them within the acquisition budget and not a penny more. Now go get the deutsche marks and yen we need for cash payment within seven days."

You run back to your office and phone both of your traditional bankers to price DM and (¥). They call back with quotes that are similar but not exactly the same. But even the best combination will cost more than the $90 million, and you know your CEO. He means "not a penny more."

What would you do next? Would you go back to the boss with the bad news and suggest that he choose one of the two acquisitions? Would you try anything else before reporting to him? If so, what?

Supplementary Readings

Aliber, Robert Z. *Monetary Reform and World Inflation*. Beverly Hills, Calif.: Sage Publications, 1973.

Bareau, Paul Louis Jean. *The Disorder in World Money: From Bretton Woods to SDRs*. London: Institute of Economic Affairs for the Wincott Foundation, 1981.

Bergel, Clive. "ECU Plays Growing International Role." *Europe*, January–February, 1986, pp. 28–29.

Bernholz, Peter. "The Introduction of Inflation-Free Monetary Constitutions (Gold Standard)." *Economic and Financial Prospects,* April–May 1986, pp. 1–5.

Black, Stanley W. *Floating Exchange Rates and National Economic Policy.* New Haven: Yale University Press, 1977.

Boyerde La Giroday, Frederic. *Myth and Reality in the Development of International Monetary Affairs.* Essays in International Finance, no. 105. Princeton, N.J.: International Finance Section, Department of Economics, Princeton University, 1974.

Carbaugh, Robert J. *The International Monetary System: History, Institutions, Analysis.* Lawrence: University Press of Kansas, 1976.

Coombs, Charles. *The Arena of International Finance.* New York: John Wiley & Sons, 1976.

Dixon, Joly. "Monetary Reform and the ECU." *Europe,* May 1986, pp. 18–20.

Eiteman, David K., and Arthur I. Stonehill. *Multinational Business Finance.* Reading, Mass.: Addison-Wesley Publishing, 1982, chaps. 2 and 3.

Hansen, Alvin Harvey. *The Dollar and the International Monetary System.* New York: McGraw-Hill, 1965.

Hood, William C. "International Money, Credit and the SDR." *Finance & Development,* September 1983, pp. 6–9.

Ishiyama, Yoshida. "The Theory of Optimum Currency Areas." IMF Staff Papers, 22, no. 2. Washington, D.C.: IMF, July 1975, pp. 344–83.

Kvasnicka, Joseph G. "Why the U.S. Is Trying to Reduce the Dollar's Value." *International Letter,* Federal Reserve Bank of Chicago, September 1985.

Miles, Marc A. *Devaluation, the Trade Balance, and Balance of Payments.* New York: M. Decker, 1978.

Monroe, Wilbur F. *International Monetary Reconstruction: Problems and Issues.* Lexington, Mass.: Lexington Books, 1974.

Mundell, Robert A., and Jacques J. Polak. *The New International Monetary System.* New York: Columbia University Press, 1977.

Pick, Franz. *The U.S. Dollar, 1940–1976: An Advance Obituary.* New York: Pick Publications, 1976.

Root, Franklin R. *International Trade and Investment.* Cincinnati: South-Western Publishing, 1984, chaps. 2, 9, and 10.

Safire, William. *Before the Fall.* New York: Belmont City Books, 1975.

Sarcinelli, Mario. "The EMS and the International Monetary System: Toward Greater Stability." *Quarterly Review,* Banca Nazional del Lavoro, March 1986, pp. 57–84.

Solomon, Robert. *The International Monetary System, 1945–1976: An Insider's View.* New York: Harper & Row, 1977.

Thanassoulas, Constantine. "A Balance of Payments Mystery—The Case of the Growing Discrepancy." *Barclays Review,* August 1985, pp. 59–62.

Wanniski, Jude. *The Way the World Works: How Economies Fail and Succeed.* New York: Basic Books, 1978.

Wihlborg, Clas. *Currency Risks in International Financial Markets.* Princeton Studies in International Finance, no. 44. Princeton, N.J.: International Finance Section, Department of Economics, Princeton University, 1978.

Williamson, John. *The Lending Policies of the International Monetary Fund*. Washington, D.C.: Institute for International Economics, 1982.

Endnotes

1. Charles N. Henning, William Pigott, and Robert Haney Scott, *International Financial Management* (New York: McGraw-Hill, 1978), p. 149.
2. Albert C. Whitaker, *Foreign Exchange*, 2nd ed. (New York: Appleton-Century-Crofts, 1933), p. 157.
3. Jacques Rueff, *The Wall Street Journal*, June 5, 6, and 9, 1969.
4. John Mueller, "The Reserve Currency Curse," *The Wall Street Journal*, September 4, 1986, p. 26.
5. "Sell Some Gold," editorial, *The Wall Street Journal*, September 4, 1986, p. 26.
6. Roy W. Jastram, *The Golden Constant: The English and American Experience, 1560–1976* (New York: John Wiley & Sons, 1977).
7. Arthur B. Laffer, "Making the Dollar as Good as Gold," *Los Angeles Times*, October 30, 1979, part IV, p. 3.
8. Frederick C. Mills, *Economic Tendencies in the United States* (New York: National Bureau of Economic Research, 1932).
9. Costanino Breschiani-Turroni, *The Economics of Inflation* (London: Allen & Unwin, 1937).
10. Henning, Pigott, and Haney, *International Financial Management*, pp. 89–95.
11. League of Nations, *International Currency Experience* (Geneva: League of Nations, 1944), p. 198.
12. *Articles of Agreement, International Monetary Fund* (Washington, D.C.: IMF, 1944), Article I.
13. Robert Z. Aliber, *The Future of the Dollar as an International Currency* (New York: Praeger Publishers, 1966).
14. For a discussion of how the pars were set, see Henning, Pigott, and Haney, *International Financial Management*, pp. 108, 218.
15. Theodore Sorenson, *Kennedy* (New York: Harper & Row, 1965), p. 408. See also *Maintaining the Strength of the United States Dollar in a Strong Free World Economy*, (Washington, D.C.: U.S. Treasury Department, January 1968), p. xi: and *Economic Report of the President*, January 1964, p. 139.
16. *Federal Reserve Bulletin*, September 1969 and January 1974.
17. Ibid., December 1971 and January 1974.
18. Ibid., January 1974, p. A75.
19. This was perceived by the French economist Jacques Rueff, who also forecast the results; see endnote 3. The contradiction is discussed by Franklin R. Root, *International Trade and Investment* (Cincinnati: South-Western Publishing, 1984), pp. 179–80.
20. William Safire, *Before the Fall* (New York: Belmont City Books, 1975), p. 514. The size of the British request has been questioned; see Charles Coombs, *The Arena of International Finance* (New York; John Wiley & Sons, 1976), p. 218, where Coombs says that the Bank of England request was for cover of only US$ 750 million.
21. Wilson E. Schmidt, "The Night We Floated," International Institute for Economic Research, Original Paper 9, October 1977.
22. Ibid., p. 7.

23. For detailed accounts of the international monetary system during the 1971–73 period, see Coombs, *Arena of International Finance*, chap. 12; and Robert Solomon, *The International Monetary System* (New York: Harper & Row, 1977), chaps. 12–15.

24. For discussions of the varieties and methods of clean or dirty floats plus comparisons of float versus peg, see, for example, Weir M. Brown, *World Afloat: National Policies Ruling the Waves*, Essays in International Finance, no. 116 (Princeton, N.J.: International Finance Section, Department of Economics, Princeton University, May 1976); Harry G. Johnson, *Further Essays in Monetary Economics* (London: Allen & Unwin, 1972); Anthony M. Lanyi, *The Case for Floating Exchange Reconsidered*, Essays in International Finance, no. 72 (February 1976); and Raymond F. Mikesell and Henry M. Goldstein, *Rules for a Floating Regime*, Essays in International Finance, no. 109 (March 1975).

25. Root, *International Trade and Investment*, chap. 10.

26. Stanley W. Black, *Floating Exchange Rates and National Economic Policy* (New Haven: Yale University Press, 1977), pp. 23–26, 49–50, 129–30, 149–50, 154–56, and 173–74.

27. Charles N. Stabler, "Banks and Their Foreign Loans," *The Wall Street Journal*, January 29, 1976, p. 16.

28. Geoffrey Bell, "The International Financial System and Capital Shortages," in *The World Capital Shortage*, ed. Alan Heslop (Indianapolis, Ind.: Bobbs-Merrill, 1977), pp. 35–57.

29. Roger Smith, "Dollar Signs: Hectic Trades Set the Values," *Los Angeles Times*, April 11, 1978, part IV, p. 1.

30. Peter Kenen, "Techniques of Central International Reserves," paper presented at the J. Marcus Flemming Memorial Conference, International Monetary Fund, November 12, 1976.

31. John Parke Young, "Can the Dollar Be as Solid as the Rock of SDRs?" *Los Angeles Times*, April 5, 1978, part 4, p. 2.

32. Ibid.

33. *IMF Survey*, March 1979, p. 99.

SECTION III

FOREIGN ENVIRONMENT

In Chapter 1, we stated that many of the business practices followed in the United States can be transferred intact and applied in other countries. However, we also mentioned that because of the differences in environmental forces, some ways of doing business must be adapted to meet local conditions.

In Section III, we shall examine these forces to see how they differ from those American businesspeople are accustomed to encountering in this country. Only by such an investigation can we discover whether (1) we can transfer the business practice as is, (2) we must adapt it to local conditions, or (3) we cannot use it at all.

Having examined the international monetary system in Section II, we begin Section III with a discussion of the uncontrollable financial forces (Chapter 6) with which MNEs must contend. Some of these forces are foreign currency exchange risks, balance of payments, taxation, tariffs, monetary and fiscal policies, inflation, and national accounting rules.

Next we look at the physical forces—location, topography, and climate (Chapter 7). We offer examples to illustrate their influence on both the controllable and uncontrollable forces. The constantly changing situation in natural resources is emphasized not only because of their importance to firms that consume them but also because the income from new discoveries frequently creates new markets. The "Contamination of Resources" section focuses on the Bhopal and Rhine disasters and their consequences for MNEs.

Chapter 8 discusses the significance of the sociocultural forces for international businesspeople. It points out that the wide variety of attitudes and values among cultures affects managers of all the business functions. Although executives normally do not have time to become thoroughly immersed in a nation's culture, they should be familiar at least with those aspects that affect their business relationships.

In Chapter 9, we investigate the political forces which are a powerful factor in the success or failure of a foreign venture. Some of these are nationalism, terrorism, unstable governments, international organizations, government-owned businesses, and various ideological forces.

189

Legal forces, the subject of Chapter 10, reflect a nation's political climate. Managements of international firms must be familiar with the host country's laws because those laws set the constraints within which the managers must operate. In this chapter, we discuss laws concerning taxation, antitrust, imports, price and wage controls, labor, currency, and industrial property.

The composition, skills, attitudes, and union activities of an area's labor pool must be investigated because these labor forces affect productivity and, ultimately, the firm's profitability. Chapter 11 discusses these forces.

Competition is growing in world markets for a number of reasons, including (1) new competition, (2) slowly growing markets, and (3) contracting markets. As Chapter 12 points out, a firm's ability to compete frequently depends on its ability to obtain adequate channels of distribution.

Finally, in Chapter 13, we consider the economic forces. Managements must know how the scarce resources of land, labor, and capital are being allocated to the production and distribution of goods and services and the manner in which they are consumed. We explore important economic and socioeconomic dimensions of the economy.

CHAPTER 6

FINANCIAL FORCES

"We're getting used to volatility; we're getting good at coping with it now."

Citicorp foreign exchange currency trader

"Traders aren't paranoid—there really are people after them."

Virick Martin, currency trader
at Merrill Lynch Capital Markets

Learning Objectives

After you study this chapter, you should know:

1. How to read and understand foreign exchange quotations.
2. The difference between spot and forward rates.
3. Some causes of exchange rate changes.
4. Government intervention in currency exchange markets.
5. How to recognize a currency exchange risk.
6. Government currency controls.
7. Some effects of inflation on business.
8. Monetary and fiscal policies that cause or combat inflation.
9. How accountants in different countries deal with inflation and how various organizations are attempting to harmonize accounting systems internationally.
10. Why business must watch BOP developments, international monetary reserves, exchange rate forecasts, and comparative inflation rates.

Key Words and Concepts

Spot rate
Forward rate
Currency exchange controls
Harmonized Commodity Description
   and Coding System
Export incentives
Quota
Tariff
Income tax
Inflation
Monetary policies
Fiscal policies
Central reserve assets
Vehicle currency
Intervention currency
Trading at a premium or a discount

Business Incident

In 1984, after the U.S. dollar (US$) had increased in value against the Japanese yen (¥) in an almost uninterrupted rise since 1981, many "experts," including currency traders, thought that the US$ had peaked. Expecting the dollar's value to fall, the chief trader of Fuji Bank's New York money-dealing operation arranged to sell (short) large amounts of dollars for future delivery, betting that he would earn a huge profit when he purchased the lower-cost dollars for many fewer ¥ on the delivery date.

He lost the bet. Instead of going down, the US$ continued to go up, and he lost $48 million for Fuji over a four-month period.

*T*he "uncontrollable" financial forces on which we will touch include foreign currency exchange risks, national balances of payment, taxation, tariffs, national monetary and fiscal policies, inflation, and national business accounting rules. "Uncontrollable" means that these forces originate outside the business enterprise. It does not mean that the financial management of companies is helpless to minimize their disadvantages; those disadvantages may even be turned to the company's advantage.

We shall have a look at what causes exchange rates to change and at how governments sometimes intervene in foreign exchange markets. Finally, we shall emphasize the importance for management to remain aware of BOP developments, exchange rate forecasts, inflation forecasts, government fiscal and monetary policies, and other financial forces.

Fluctuating Currency Values

An attempt is being made to bind together the values of most of the major European currencies in the European Monetary System (EMS). Although several currency value realignments have been made by the members of EMS since its inception in 1979, there has been less value fluctuation than was experienced before EMS and less fluctuation than has occurred in the currencies of the major non-EMS countries. The currencies of the other leading trading countries float and fluctuate in value relative to each other and to the EMS. Those countries include Australia, Britain, Canada, Japan, and the United States.

The company financial manager must understand how to protect against losses or optimize gains from such fluctuations. Another level of currency exchange risk is encountered when a nation suspends or limits convertibility of its currency, and the manager must try to foresee and minimize or avoid losses resulting from large holdings of inconvertible and otherwise limitedly useful currency.

When you have a currency that you want to convert into another currency, the first thing you might do is look for the value of the currency you have in terms of the one you want. The international currency exchange quotations that you would look at are found in business publications such as *The Wall Street Journal* or the *Financial Times* and in the business section of most major newspapers.

Foreign Exchange
Quotations

The foreign exchange quotations, the price of one currency expressed in terms of another, can be confusing until you have examined how they are reported. In the world's currency exchange markets, the U.S. dollar (US$) is the common unit being exchanged for other currencies. Even if a holder of Japanese yen (¥) wants British pounds (£), the trade will be to buy US$s with the ¥ and then to buy £s with the US$s. The reasons for this procedure are historical and practical.

Historically, the international monetary system established at Bretton Woods just before the end of World War II set the value of the US$ in terms of gold at $35/ounce. The values of all the other major currencies were then stated in terms of the US$; for example, the yen was worth 0.28 of a U.S. penny, the French franc (Ff) was worth 18 cents, the German mark (DM) was worth 27 cents, and the £ was worth $2.40. In other words, the US$ was established as the keystone currency at the center of the world's monetary system.

The practical reasons for the continuing central position of the US$ are the several functions it has come to perform in the world. It is the main **central reserve asset*** of many countries. It is the most used **vehicle currency**† and **intervention currency**.‡

Among the reasons why the US$ is in great demand worldwide are its so-called safe haven aspect and its universal acceptance. Even if U.S. interest rates and investment opportunities were less attractive, there would still be a feeling that money is safe in American securities or property. Inflation has been brought

---

*Other central reserve assets are gold, SDRs, and other hard currencies.

†A vehicle currency is the money used as a vehicle for trade. The US$ is used as the denomination and payment currency of most world trade. For example, payments by petroleum-importing countries to OPEC are in US$s.

‡An intervention currency is the currency used by a central bank to intervene in the foreign exchange markets. For instance, if Italy wished to strengthen the lira, it would take US$s from its central reserve assets and use them to buy lira, thus strengthening the lira in the exchange markets.

to a low level, and the country is seen as less likely than others to be invaded or to elect a socialist government. It is seen as a safe haven.

As to universal acceptance, if you have traveled internationally with US$s, you have found them welcome everywhere. A dramatic example was the scene in the film *The Killing Fields* in which the Cambodian doctor/prisoner was asked by the Vietnamese officer for whom he worked to take the officer's young son and try to escape with the boy to Thailand. The officer gave the doctor a small emergency kit whose contents included a roll of American $20 bills.

Refer to Figure 6–1 where you see the price for one Swiss franc (Sf) quoted in the first column directly to the right of "Switzerland (Franc)" as .6137. This means that one Sf costs US$ 0.6137. For a less expensive currency, look at the South Korean won which is quoted as .001163, so that each won costs that fraction of an American dollar. Two examples of currencies that cost more than US$1.00 on October 7, 1986, were the British pound at $1.4630 and the Kuwait dinar at $3.4199.

Sf 1.6295 = US$1.00

There is more to be learned from reading the foreign exchange quotes in *The Wall Street Journal* or other financial and business publications. Using Figure 6–1, you will see to the right of the "Switzerland (Franc)".6137 quote the figure .6177. Now look to the tops of the columns in which those numbers appear, and you will find the abbreviations, "Tues." and "Mon." As you probably have surmised, the .6137 quote is the price at the close of trading on Tuesday, October 7, 1986, while .6177 was the quote at the close of the previous trading day. Those two quotes tell you that the US$ strengthened a little vis-à-vis the Swiss france during Tuesday's trading; it cost US$0.6137 to buy one Sf at Tuesday's close, while it had cost fractionally more, US$0.6177 at Monday's close.

There is another way of expressing the value relationships between currencies. Look again at the "Switzerland (franc)" line in Figure 6–1, and move to the right of the number about which we spoke. There you find another "Tues." and another "Mon." column; the quote in the "Tues." column is 1.6295, while it is 1.6190 under "Mon." These quotes inform us how many Swiss francs it took to buy one US$ at the close of trading on each of those days, and they are the mirror images of the two quotes to the left. Observe that about one more Swiss centime was needed to buy one US$ after Tuesday's trading than was needed after Monday's trading; in other words, the Sf had weakened a little vis-à-vis the US$.

Spot rates

The **spot rate** is the exchange rate between two currencies for their immediate trade. The rate on the same line as the name of the country is the spot rate. You will note in Figure 6–1 that the spot rate for Swiss francs was .6137.

Figure 6-1

FOREIGN EXCHANGE

Tuesday, October 7, 1986

The New York foreign exchange selling rates below apply to trading among banks in amounts of $) million and more, as quoted at 3 p.m. Eastern time by Bankers Trust Co. Retail transactions provide fewer units of foreign currency per dollar. *

Country	U.S. $ equiv. Tues.	Mon.	Currency per U.S. $ Tues.	Mon.
Argentina (Austral) ...	.94967	.94967	1.0530	1.0530
Australia (Dollar)	.6340	.6350	1.5773	1.5748
Austria (Schilling)	.07117	.07143	14.05	14.00
Belgium (Franc)				
Commercial rate	.02415	.02424	41 40	41.25
Financial rate	.02398	.02407	41.70	41.55
Brazil (Cruzado)	.07262	.07262	13.77	13.77
Britain (Pound)	1.4340	1.4372	.6974	.6958
30-Day Forward	1.4280	1.4312	.7003	.6987
90-Day Forward	1.4170	1.4200	.7057	.7042
180-Day Forward	1.4010	1.4030	.7138	.7128
Canada (Dollar)	.7212	.7220	1.3865	1.3850
30-Day Forward	.7225	.7233	1.3840	1.3825
90-Day Forward	.7256	.7262	1.3780	1.3770
180-Day Forward	.7307	.7337	1.3685	1.3630
Chile (Official rate) ...	.005127	.005127	195.04	195.04
China (Yuan)	.2707	.2707	3.6943	3.6943
Colombia (Peso)	.004865	.004865	205.56	205.56
Denmark (Krone)	.1325	.1333	7.5450	7.500
Ecuador (Sucre)				
Official rate	.007055	.007055	141.75	141.75
Floating rate	.006645	.006645	150.50	150.50
Finland (Markka)	.2050	.2062	4.8775	4.8500
France (Franc)	.1527	.1533	6.5490	6.5160
30-Day Forward	.1532	.1539	6.5280	6.4950
90-Day Forward	.1539	.1547	6.4990	6.4620
180-Day Forward	.1548	.1556	6.4610	6.4260
Greece (Drachma)	.007448	.007491	134.25	133.50
Hong Kong (Dollar) ...	.1283	.1283	7.7915	7.7915
India (Rupee)	.07867	.07818	12.71	12.79
Indonesia (Rupiah)	.0006112	.0006112	1636.00	1636.00
Ireland (Punt)	1.3525	1.3680	.7394	.7309
Israel (Shekel)	.6711	.6711	1.4900	1.4900
Italy (Lira)	.0007230	.0007267	1383.00	1376.00
Japan (Yen)	.006485	.006491	154.20	154.05
30-Day Forward	.006493	.006501	154.00	153.80
90-Day Forward	.006500	.006510	153.80	153.60
180-Day Forward	.006519	.006525	153.40	153.25
Jordan (Dinar)	3.1240	3.1240	.3201	.3201
Kuwait (Dinar)	3.4199	3.4199	.2924	.2924
Lebanon (Pound)	.02281	.02281	43.85	43.85
Malaysia (Ringgit)	.3815	.3812	2.6210	2.6230
Malta (Lira)	2.6525	2.6525	.3770	.3770
Mexico (Peso)				
Floating rate	.001287	.001287	777.00	777.00
Netherland(Guilder) .	.4423	.4444	2.2610	2.2500
New Zealand (Dollar) .	.5040	.5045	1.9841	1.9821
Norway (Krone)	.1361	.1367	7.3450	7.3150
Pakistan (Rupee)	.0588	.0588	17.00	17.00
Peru (Inti)	.07168	.07168	13.95	13.95
Philippines (Peso)	.04888	.04888	20.46	20.46
Portugal (Escudo)	.006861	.006872	145.75	145.50
Saudi Arabia (Riyal) ..	.2667	.2667	3.7495	3.7495
Singapore (Dollar)	.4615	.4613	2.1670	2.1680
South Africa (Rand)				
Commercial rate	.4490	.4505	2.2272	2.2198
Financial rate	.2155	.2150	4.6404	4.6512
South Korea (Won)	.001163	.001140	860.00	877.00
Spain (Peseta)	.007552	.007587	132.40	131.80
Sweden (Krona)	.1457	.1463	6.8625	6.8350
Switzerland (Franc) ..	.6137	.6177	1.6295	1.6190
30-Day Forward	.6150	.6192	1.6260	1.6150
90-Day Forward	.6167	.6207	1.6215	1.6110
180-Day Forward	.6196	.6234	1.6140	1.6040
Taiwan (Dollar)	.02724	.02724	36.71	36.71
Thailand (Baht)	.03834	.03834	26.08	26.08
Turkey (Lira)	.001416	.001416	706.37	706.37
United Arab(Dirham) .	.2723	.2723	3.673	3.673
Uruguay (New Peso)				
Financial	.006192	.006192	161.50	161.50
Venezuela (Bolivar)				
Official rate	.1333	.1333	7.50	7.50
Floating rate	.04545	.04033	22.00	24.79
W. Germany (Mark) ..	.4995	.5027	2.0020	1.9890
30-Day Forward	.5000	.5035	2.0000	1.9860
90-Day Forward	.5012	.5045	1.9950	1.9820
180-Day Forward	.5025	.5076	1.9900	1.9700
SDR	1.21295	1.21773	0.824440	0.821201
ECU	1.03778	1.04705	....	....

Special Drawing Rights are based on exchange rates for the U.S., West German, British, French and Japanese currencies. Source: International Monetary Fund.

ECU is based on a basket of community currencies. Source: European Community Commission.

z-Not quoted.

* Bankers Trust Company is one of the major New York banks that trades actively in foreign currencies. By long-standing arrangement, its selling rate quoted at 3 P.M., New York time, is the one published by *The Wall Street Journal* and other financial publications.

Source: *The Wall Street Journal,* October 8, 1986.

Forward Rates

The **forward rate** is the cost today for a commitment by one party to deliver to or take from another party an agreed amount of a currency at a fixed, future date. The commitment is a forward contract, and for frequently traded currencies such contracts are usually available on a 30-, 60-, 90-, or 180-day basis. You may be able to negotiate with banks for different time periods or for contracts in other currencies.

Refer to "Switzerland (Franc) 30-Day Forward" quotation in Figure 6–1, and you will see that it is .6150. Compare that with the spot rate of .6137, and you see that it would cost more in US$s to buy Sfs for delivery in 30 days than for delivery today. Looking down at the 90- and 180-day quotes, you see that the premium grows larger. This means that traders in the forward markets believe that the Swiss franc will strengthen in US$ terms for at least six months.

If in the forward markets it cost fewer US$s to buy for 30-, 90-, or 180-day delivery, the other currency would be **trading at a discount** rather than **trading at a premium**. That was the case on most days between 1981 and 1985, while the US$ rose in value almost constantly. Early in 1985, it ceased to rise and lost value on most days; on October 7, 1986, none of the currencies quoted in the "Foreign Exchange" column were trading at a forward discount.

So Many Yen, So Few Pounds

Look again at Figure 6–1, and you will see that it took about 154 yen to buy one US$, whereas less than one pound was enough for a dollar. Glancing up and down the column, you find that an Indonesian rupiah holder would need 1,636 rupiahs for US$1 and that a different number is required by holders of each of the other currencies quoted. It might seem that the fewer units of a currency required to buy a dollar, the harder or "better" that currency is compared to the others, but that is not necessarily correct.

As we have seen, the currencies of the world's major countries were set in value relative to the US$ at the end of World War II. Those exchange rates were the rates in the markets at that time; they were historical accidents. Since then, and particularly since 1973, the relative values of currencies, their convertibility, their hardness or softness, have been set by the supply and demand volumes of the foreign exchange markets. Those volumes are influenced by the policies of the various governments—their monetary and fiscal policies, their trade policies, and so on. Thus, the number of units of a currency per US$ on any given day does not indicate the relative strength of that currency. Many other factors must be examined to determine that.

The cost of a forward contract is the premium or discount required over the spot rate. Whether there is a premium or a discount and its size depend on the expectations of the world financial community, businesses, individuals, and governments about what the future will bring. These expectations factor in such considerations as supply and demand forecasts for the two currencies, relative inflation in the two countries, relative productivity and unit labor cost changes, expected election results or other political developments, and expected government fiscal, monetary, and currency exchange market actions.

Bid and Asked Prices

When travelers or businesses contact a bank or an exchange agency to buy or sell a currency, they find a bid price and an asked price. The bid is the lower. The quotation for the French franc may be .16 bid and .17 asked. If the customer has

Figure 6-2

| February 1 Goods delivery date exchange rate | August 1 Payment date exchange rate |

Suppose: US$1 = Ff6   US$1 = Ff6

Whichever party bore the currency exchange risk, neither gained nor lost.

Suppose: US$1 = Ff6   US$1 = Ff7

Whichever party bore the currency exchange risk lost. It now requires Ff7 to buy the US$1, which could have been bought for Ff6 at the time the goods were delivered.

Suppose: US$1 = Ff6   US$1 = Ff5

Whichever party bore the currency exchange risk gained. It now requires only Ff5 to buy the US$1, which would have cost Ff6 at the time the goods were delivered.

francs to sell, the bank or agency is bidding—offering—16 cents (U.S. pennies) for each franc. If the customer wants to buy francs, the bank or agency is asking 17 cents, a higher price. The difference provides a margin—profit—for the bank or agency.

Commercial, Financial, Official, Floating

In Figure 6–1, you will note two spot reports for Belgium, Ecuador, South Africa, and Venezuela. The Belgian and South African give commercial and financial rates. The commercial rate is for import/export transactions, and the financial rate is for all other transactions. The official Ecuadorian and Venezuelan rates are the exchange control rates, while the floating rates are the free market exchange rates of those currencies in U.S. dollar terms.

Fluctuating Exchange Rates Create Risk

When your activities involve more than one country, you must deal with more than one currency. For example, an American company exporting to France will, in most cases, want to receive US$s. If credit is involved, so that payment is not made when the goods are delivered, one of the parties will have a currency exchange risk. If the French importer agrees to pay French francs, then the American exporter bears a risk that the value of the French franc will fall and thus the French francs will buy fewer US$s when received than they would have at the earlier goods delivery date. On the other hand, if the French importer agrees to pay in US$ at a future time, it is the importer who bears that risk. (See Figure 6–2.)

The MNE financial manager is not without weapons for dealing with this type of risk. These are presented in Chapter 18. More potentially hazardous for the MNE, a country in which the company has assets may institute exchange controls.

Currency Exchange Controls

Currency exchange controls limit or prohibit the legal use of a currency in international transactions. Typically, the value of the currency is arbitrarily fixed at a rate higher than its value in the free market, and it is decreed that all purchases or sales of other currencies be made through a government agency. A black market inevitably springs up, but it is of little use to the finance manager, who usually wants to avoid breaking the laws of a country in which the company is operating. In addition, the black market is rarely able to accommodate transactions of the size involved in MNE business.

Thus, the MNE, along with all other holders of the controlled or blocked currency, must pay more than the free market rate if permission to buy foreign currency is granted by the government. If permission is not granted or if the cost of foreign currency is uneconomically high, the blocked currency can be used only within the country. This usually presents problems of finding suitable products to buy or investments to make within the country.*

People will go to remarkable extremes to get blocked money out of exchange-controlled countries. A few years ago, in the west of France, an employee of a company operating in France strapped on a big money belt packed with large-denomination French franc bank notes. He then put on hang glider wings and glided into Switzerland, where he bought Swiss francs and deposited them in a Swiss bank account.

In New Delhi, the local manager of a major international airline gave a case of Scotch to a government official. Shortly thereafter, the agency for which that official worked granted the airline permission to use blocked rupees to buy almost US$20 million and transfer them to the airline's home country.

Those were extreme methods of converting blocked currencies to convertible currencies; the methods were, of course, also illegal. The great majority of MNE finance managers do not resort to such methods, but there are legal steps that they can take to protect the firm from the adverse effects of currency exchange controls. Those steps are considered in Chapter 18.

Table 6–1, prepared by Ernst & Whinney International, lists countries, their currencies and their dividend remittance rates, and notes whether there are restrictions on the remittance of dividends. Information about currency exchange controls can be obtained from numerous other sources also, such as Business Latin America, Business International and Global Risk Assessments.

*See the business incident at the beginning of Chapter 18.

Table 6–1

United States Dollar Exchange Rates, December 31, 1986

The rate is that prevailing in the respective countries at which a bank or other dealer sells U.S. dollars for the purpose of remitting dividends.

Country	Currency	Symbol	Dividend Remittance Rate	Restrictions
Angola	Kwanza	Kw	0.0330972	Yes
Argentina	Austral	A	0.7942812	Yes
Australia	Dollar	$A	0.6596	No
Austria	Shilling	AS	0.0730193	No
Bahamas	Dollar	$	1.00	No
Bahrain	Dinar	BD	2.6490066	No
Belgium*	Franc	BF	0.02477	No
Bermuda	Dollar	BD$	1.00	No
Brazil	Cruzado	Cr$	0.0669389	Yes
Brunei	Dollar	B$	0.4576659	No
Canada	Dollar	Can$	0.7243752	No
Cayman Islands	Dollar	CI$	1.1976048	No
Channel Islands				
Guernsey	Pound	£	1.4768	No
Jersey	Pound	£	1.4768	No
Chile	Peso	$	0.004878	Yes
China, People's				
Republic of	Renminbi	RmB	0.270879	Yes
Colombia	Peso	Col$	0.0045662	Yes
Costa Rica	Colon	¢	0.017094	No
Cyprus	Pound	CY£	1.9530	Yes
Denmark	Krone	DKr	0.1334045	No
Ecuador	Sucre	S	0.0068027	Yes
Egypt	Pound	£E	0.728014	Yes
El Salvador†	Colon	¢	0.20	Yes
Finland	Finnmark	Fmk	0.2082466	No
France	Franc	F	0.1549187	No
Germany, West	Deutsche mark	DM	0.5141917	No
Greece	Drachma	Dr	0.0072003	Yes
Guatemala	Quetzal	Q	1.00	Yes‡
Hong Kong	Dollar	$	0.1282051	No
India	Rupee	Rs	0.0756504	Yes
Indonesia	Rupiah	Rp	0.0006094	Yes
Iran	Rial	Rls	0.0132363	Yes
Ireland,				
Republic of	Pound	£Ir	1.3925	No
Italy	Lira	Lit	0.0007401	Yes
Japan	Yen	¥	0.0061881	No
Jordan	Dinar	JD	2.8985507	Yes
Kenya	Shilling	KSh	0.0636898	Yes

Table 6-1

(concluded)

Country	Currency	Symbol	Dividend Remittance Rate	Restrictions
Korea, South	Won	W	0.0011557	Yes
Kuwait	Dinar	KD	3.4153005	No
Lebanon	Pound	LL	0.0113636	No
Liberia	U.S. dollar	$	1.00	No
Libya	Dinar	LD	3.1806616	Yes
Luxembourg	Franc	LF	0.0247463	No
Malaysia	Dollar	M$	0.3838771	No
Mexico	Peso	Mex$	0.0010858	Yes
Netherlands	Guilder	DFL	0.4559444	No
Netherlands Antilles	Neth. Antilles guilder	NAf	0.5555555	No
New Zealand	Dollar	$NZ	0.5165	No
Nigeria	Naira	₦	0.3852971	Yes
Norway	Krone	NKr	0.1349345	No
Oman	Rial	RO	2.5974026	No
Panama	Balboa	B	1.00	No
Peru§	Sol	S/	0.0493583	Yes
Philippines	Peso	₱	0.0487258	Yes
Portugal	Escudo	Esc	0.0068955	Yes
Qatar	Riyal	QR	0.2746498	No
Saudi Arabia	Riyal	SR	0.2665956	No
Singapore	Dollar	S$	0.4596644	No
South Africa	Rand	R	0.446	Yes
Spain	Peseta	Pta	0.0074173	Yes
Sri Lanka	Rupee	Rs	0.0350508	Yes
Sweden	Krona	SEK	0.1567398	No
Switzerland	Franc	SwF	0.6134969	No
Taiwan	Dollar	NT$	0.0281294	Yes
Thailand	Baht	B	0.0381971	No
Trinidad and Tobago	Dollar	TT$	0.2777777	Yes
Turkey	Lira	TL	0.0013961	Yes
United Arab Emirates	Dirham	Dh	0.2711497	No
United Kingdom	Pound sterling	£	1.4768	No
Uruguay	New peso	N$	0.0054432	No
Venezuela	Bolivar	Bs	0.0439947	Yes
Zimbabwe	Dollar	Zim$	0.595912	Yes

*Dividends can be remitted at the official rate if certain documentation is present; otherwise, dividends must be remitted at the free market rate.
†The free market rate is shown and is used for remitting dividends and most other transactions. The official rate (0.40) is used for importing equipment and other basic products.
‡Local capital only.
§Transmittal of dividends is forbidden until August 1988.

Balance of Payments

Balance of payments (BOP) was discussed in some detail in Chapter 5, but we would be remiss not to mention it as a major financial force. The state of a nation's BOP will tell observant management much of value. If the BOP is slipping into deficit, the government is probably considering one or more market or nonmarket measures to correct or suppress that deficit. Management should be alert for either currency devaluation or restrictive monetary or fiscal policies to induce deflation.

Another possibility is that currency or trade controls may be coming. With foresight, the MNE management can adjust to or at least soften their impact.

On the export side, the MNE may start shopping for **export incentives**—government incentives to make its exports easier or more profitable. Lower-cost capital may be available if the company can demonstrate that exports will be boosted.

Tariffs or Duties*

The words *tariffs* and *duties* are used interchangeably. These can be high or low, and it is of great importance to business to minimize them.

Classification of Goods

One element in the decision as to how much **tariff** is charged is another decision as to what the item being imported is. This is not as easy as it may sound, because it depends on how the item is classified under one of the two major classification systems.

Brussels Tariff Nomenclature (BTN)

Most of the world uses the BTN, which contains 1,100 headings, each subdivided into many subheadings. Under BTN, articles of import are grouped according to the nature of the materials from which the articles are made. If there is more than one material in an article, it is classified as if it consisted of the material that gives it its "essential character." Which material is chosen can make very large differences in the tariff rate applied, and disagreement is frequent between the customs officials and the importers.

---

*Tariffs are dealt with as part of the "Trade Restrictions" section of Chapter 3 and as one of the legal forces in Chapter 10.

The U.S. Tariff Schedule (USTS)

The United States does not adhere to the BTN but uses the USTS, which is different. For our purposes, it is sufficient to say that the USTS is also a complex system. Of course, the difficulties are compounded by the existence of two major systems.

The Harmonized Commodity Description and Coding System

In 1970, representatives of the Customs Cooperation Council (CCC) discussed the problems caused by the two systems with other international organizations and at a meeting of the Economic Commission for Europe it was agreed that the CCC was the organization best suited to harmonize the BTN and the USTS. The CCC study and work resulted in 1983 in a system capable of meeting the requirements of customs authorities, statisticians, carriers, and producers. The new system, the **Harmonized Commodity Description and Coding System**, will replace the BTN and USTS. Its implementation is scheduled for January 1, 1988.

Customs Unions

The European Community (EC) and other groupings of nations that we discussed in Chapter 4 have lowered or abolished tariffs on trade among member countries. They add another dimension to the decision-making processes of MNE executives. For example, would the expenses, legal problems, and personnel problems necessary to establish production within a customs union be justified by tariff savings?

Taxation

Inasmuch as most international business is conducted by corporations, we are concerned with tariffs paid by and taxes levied on corporations. The point may be made that corporations don't pay taxes; they only collect them. In the end, people pay taxes.[1] The taxes may be collected from customers in higher prices, from employees in lower wages, from stockholders in lower dividends or capital gains, or from suppliers in smaller orders. However, even though corporations act as tax collectors rather than bearing the ultimate burden, it is very much in their best interest to minimize taxes. If a corporation can achieve a lower tax burden than its competitors, it can lower prices to its customers or make higher profits with which to pay higher wages and dividends. The prices of its stock tends to rise, and it can be a better customer for the components and raw materials it buys from others.

All of this is true for all corporations, but for the MNE there are more taxes—more countries—to consider, and therefore more risks. There are also more opportunities to save taxes.

Different Taxes in Different Countries

Some countries have lower taxes than others, and there are countries that levy no tax on certain forms of income. Among major industrial countries, Australia relies most heavily on income and profit taxes, raising some 55 percent of its tax revenue through them. Only about 17 percent of French revenue comes from income and profit taxes, and the U.S. percentage is 42. France levies the highest social security taxes, and along with Canada and Australia, it levies the highest consumption taxes, such as value-added and sales taxes.

In Chapter 18, we shall see how MNE financial managers can sometimes use different tax regimes and other measures to lower their taxes legitimately. Chapter 10 deals with taxes as legal forces.

The amount of taxes paid is affected by inflation. At one time some thought that inflation was a problem limited to the LDCs and that the industrialized countries need not worry about it. Recent experience has shown how erroneous that view was, and so we shall examine inflation.

Inflation

The phenomenon of increasing prices for almost everything over a period of time is familiar. Contagious **inflation** was probably the major cause of the end of the unprecedented world economic boom that lasted from the end of World War II until 1973. As prices of internationally traded goods rose due to a combination of rising demand and increased money supplies in all the DCs, inflation fever spread from one DC to the others.[2]

Inflation's Effects on Interest Rates

Inflation is clearly a financial force from outside the company but one with which finance managers must deal as best they can. As one indication of the effect of inflation on the cost of money when raised by the company, see Figure 6–3.

Every country with a lower interest rate than that of the United States had a lower inflation rate, and vice versa. Argentina's inflation rate was 160 percent. While the prime rate was 84 percent, most businesses paid over 90 percent, and installment loans cost 100 percent or more if would-be borrowers could find lenders. Banks, businesses, and people with money are not eager to lend it at interest rates that are lower than inflation rates.

Figure 6–3 clearly illustrates the connection between inflation and interest rates. Table 6–2 shows more current inflation and interest figures for several industrial countries.

Since 1978, the time illustrated by Figure 6–3, both inflation and interest rates have come down in most industrial countries. Nevertheless, the relationship continues, as can be seen in Table 6–2. Germany and Japan have the lowest inflation and interest rates, and the countries with higher inflation bear higher interest.

Figure 6–3

Prime Interest Rates Charged by Banks at One Point in 1978

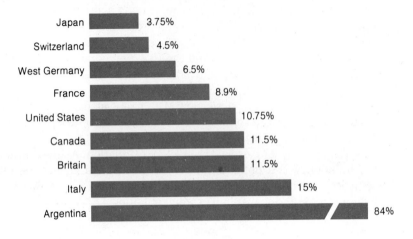

Japan 3.75%
Switzerland 4.5%
West Germany 6.5%
France 8.9%
United States 10.75%
Canada 11.5%
Britain 11.5%
Italy 15%
Argentina 84%

Source: Reprinted from *U.S. News & World Report,* November 20, 1978. Copyright 1978 U.S. News & World Report, Inc.

Table 6–2

1986 Inflation and Interest Rates

	Inflation Rate (percent)	July 3, 1986, Six-Month Euro-currency Interest Rate (percent)
Canada (C$)	4.2	$8-\frac{3}{8}$
France (Ff)	3.7	$7-\frac{5}{16}$
West Germany (DM)	1.0	$4-\frac{9}{16}$
Japan (Y)	1.2	$4-\frac{9}{16}$
United Kingdom (£)	4.0	$9-\frac{11}{16}$
United States (US$)	3.75	$6-\frac{11}{16}$

National Monetary and Fiscal Policies

Monetary policy involves the amount of money in circulation and whether and how fast that amount grows, Money includes cash and various kinds of accounts.

Fiscal policies deal with the collecting and spending of money by governments. What kinds of taxes are levied at what rates? On what and in what amounts does the government spend money?

Since World War II, several countries have been able to stop inflation and in some instances to keep it down. Policies that were adopted in 1948 in West Germany, in 1953 in the United States, and in 1958 in France succeeded in halting inflation. Those policies had two common denominators: (1) they removed artificial economic controls, such as wage and price controls; and (2) they applied fiscal and monetary restraint. The restraint included lower taxes and slower growth in the nation's money supply.[3]

Britain since 1979 and the United States since 1980 are two more recent examples of countries that have succeeded in lowering their inflation rates from around 20 percent per year to the 3–4 percent range. At the other extreme, many believe that the infamous hyperinflation of the German mark in 1923 is the world's record. It is not. That dubious distinction belongs to the Hungarian pengo; inflation in Hungary in 1946 was a thousand times worse than the earlier German inflation. In 1939, one US$ bought 3.38 Hungarian pengos; in July 1946, the same dollar was worth 500,000,000,000,000,000,000 (500 million trillion) pengos. Never before or since has so much still official money been worth so little.

Spending versus Saving

In addition to being affected by the size of the money supply and its rate of growth, inflation is affected by the velocity of its turnover and by the willingness of people to save rather than spend it. Spending drives prices up, while saving

YOUR CHANGE SEÑOR!

Reprinted with special permission from International Management, October 1981. Copyright ©, McGraw-Hill Publications Company. All rights reserved.

Coping with treble-digit inflation

provides funds for investment in more efficient, productive, and job-creating capital equipment or research and development.

Higher Savings, Lower Inflation

Over the period 1977–1982, Switzerland at 4.2 percent had the lowest annual inflation rate of any of the Organization for Economic Cooperation and Development (OECD) nations . The Japanese rate for the period was 4.6 percent. The net national savings ratios as percentages of GDP* for those two countries for the same period were 18.1 percent and 18 percent, respectively. For the United States, the comparable figures were 9.8 percent inflation and 5.6 percent savings.

We do not mean to imply that the percentage of income saved by a country is the only determinant of its inflation rate. Far from it. Savings rates are an important influence, but there are many other influences on inflation. In addition, the causes and uses of savings differ from country to country; savings may be withheld from wages by the government and used for government purposes or they may be induced by favorable tax laws and used for private investment.[4]

Importance of Inflation to Business

Even within a single country, inflation is of concern to management. Should it raise capital at all, and if so, should this be done through equity or debt? High inflation rates encourage borrowing because the loan will be repaid with cheaper money. But high inflation rates bring high interest rates (see Figure 6–3) or may discourage lending. Potential lenders may fear that even with high interest rates the amount repaid plus interest will be worth less than the amount lent. Instead of lending, the money holder may buy something that is expected to increase in value.

High inflation rates make capital expenditure planning more difficult. Management may allocate $1 million for a plant and be forced to pay much more to complete construction.

Inflation and the Multinational

All of this also applies to international business with the complication that inflation rates are different in different countries. For this reason, management of a multinational must try to forecast the rates for each of the countries in which the MNE is active. The comparative inflation rates will affect the comparative currency values as the currencies of high-inflation countries weaken vis-à-vis the currencies of the countries whose inflation rates are lower. Management will try to minimize holdings of the weaker currencies.

---

*The GDP is the gross domestic product, which is the gross national product minus net factor—or property invisible—payments, such as dividends, interest, and royalties.

Higher inflation rates cause the prices of the goods and services produced or offered by a country to rise, and thus the goods and services become less competitive. The company's affiliate in that country finds it more difficult to sell its products in export, as do all other producers there. Such conditions tend to cause balance-of-payments (BOP) deficits, and management must be alert to changes in government policy to correct the deficit. Such changes could include more restrictive fiscal or monetary policies, currency controls, export incentives, and import obstacles.

Relative inflation rates affect where the multinational raises and invests capital. Interest rates tend to be higher where inflation is higher, and high inflation discourages new investment for all of the reasons we have seen.

Nominal and Real Interest Rates

Another important consideration for business, whether borrowing or lending, is the real rate of interest, and the inflation rate is one element in its computation. The nominal interest rate is the rate charged by the lender or the rate that a bond issue carries. From the nominal rate is subtracted the inflation rate, and the result is the real rate. When a lender charges, for example, 10 percent interest on a one-year loan and the inflation rate is 5 percent, the real rate of return for the lender is 5 percent, because the money is worth 5 percent less when it is repaid than it was worth when it was lent.

When money is lent for longer periods of time (5, 10, or 20 years), the lenders and borrowers must forecast—guess—what inflation will do over those longer periods. The longer the time, the more difficult the forecast, but the point here is that it is not only today's inflation rate that matters; it is also the lenders' and borrowers' forecasts that govern interest rates on loans or even whether loans will be made.

Table 6–3 illustrates computations of real interest rates for the US$ from 1970 into early 1984. The "Three-Month Eurodollar Rate" is the nominal interest rate charged. The next column shows the inflation rate in the United States for the year, and subtracting that rate from the nominal rate, the table arrives at the real rate shown in the third column.

You will note that lenders lost money in the real interest rate sense in 1975, 1976, and 1977, when the real rate was negative. Another phenomenon to observe is the high real rate that began in 1981; even though U.S. inflation came down from its 1980 high, nominal interest rates went up. They came down in 1982 and 1983, but not enough to bring real rates below 6 percent, which historically is quite high. Probably the main reason for this is that lenders do not believe inflation will be kept in check; they are protecting themselves against higher future inflation, which they forecast.

Table 6–4 shows real interest rates in the five largest economies in 1985 and 1986. They have remained higher than they were in the 1970s and until 1981.

Table 6–3

Dollar Interest Rates and Inflation

	Three-Month Eurodollar Rate	U.S. Inflation	Real Interest Rate
1970	8.5	5.9	2.6
1971	6.6	4.3	2.3
1972	5.4	3.3	2.1
1973	9.3	6.2	3.1
1974	11.0	11.0	0
1975	7.0	9.1	−2.1
1976	5.6	5.8	−0.2
1977	6.0	6.5	−0.5
1978	8.8	7.6	1.2
1979	12.0	11.3	0.9
1980	14.0	13.5	0.5
1981	16.8	10.4	6.4
1982	12.2	6.2	6.0
1983	9.6	3.2	6.4
March 7, 1984	10.3	4.1	6.2

Source: *Barclays Review*, May 1984, p. 32.

Table 6–4

Real Interest Rates

	June 1985	January 1986	March 1986	July 28, 1986
United States	3.7	3.9	4.9	4.8
Japan	3.6	5.4	4.5	4.2
West Germany	3.4	3.4	4.4	5.1
France	3.8	4.6	5.5	5.1
United Kingdom	5.5	7.3	7.5	7.2

Three-month rates deflated by the annual change in consumer prices.
Source: *Barclays Review*, August 1986, p. 90.

Accounting Practices

Accounting practices to reflect inflation vary from country to country and have been changing. The MNE financial management must be prepared to use host country practices for business there and to translate those figures for home country use. We shall look first at the U.S. practices. Both inflation and currency exchange fluctuations will cause companies' financial and earning statements to differ widely, depending, in part, on accounting practices.

With reference first to inflation, generally accepted accounting principles in the United States are still based on the assumption of price stability in spite of the country's inflation experience during the 1970s and into the 1980s. Correct understanding of the financial results reported for a company operating in an inflationary economy requires a conversion of accounting measures based on historic costs into a more realistic inflation-adjusted system.

Price-Level Accounting

Recently there has been some progress toward price-level accounting in U.S. accounting practices. Price-level accounting uses for depreciation purposes the replacement cost of an item rather than its original or historic cost Thus, if inflation is 20 percent per year and an item costs $1 million, at the end of one year the company could apply its depreciation percentage to $1.2 million rather than only $1 million. The higher depreciation amount will reduce reported earnings, but it will also reduce taxes. Many feel that some sort of inflation-adjusted accounting would give more realistic results.

Some firms have shifted to the last-in, first-out (LIFO) inventory accounting method from first-in, first-out (FIFO). Also, accelerated appreciation methods are frequently used, although the latter are better categorized as investment incentives than price-level accounting devices. Even with accelerated depreciation methods, the American company can still depreciate only the historic cost of the equipment, though its replacement may cost much more.

Securities and Exchange Commission (SEC)

In the United States, the SEC has required the larger American firms to provide current price-related information in their annual filings with the SEC. Such information must include the replacement cost of plant and equipment and of inventories. Annual reports to stockholders must tell them that such information is available from the company on request.

Financial Accounting Standards Board (FASB)*

In 1979, the FASB issued a rule in accordance with which about 1,300 companies reported inflation-adjusted data in their 1979 returns in addition to their usual financial results. The new information includes inflation-adjusted cash dividends for each of the last five years, stock market prices adjusted for inflation, and inflation-adjusted income.[5]

The results of the FASB rule, called FASB 33, were dramatic, though they should not have been surprising. Nonadjusted operating income (using pre–FASB

---

*The FASB is the private (nongovernment) organization that establishes accounting standards for American business.

33 methods) for 500 large nonfinancial firms was overstated, on average, by about $75 million each for 1979. That sounded bad, but worse was to come; for 1981, the gap grew to $100 million. Two examples for 1982 are revealing. Time, Inc. reported a healthy nominal income of $243 million, but when inflation was wrung out, Time's income dropped $149 million, to $94 million. Exxon's figures were worse. Inflation adjustments turned a $4.2 billion income report into a $296 million loss.

The application of FASB 33 is complex; valuations are frequently subjective; and managements have not been enthusiastic, at least in part because inflation-adjusted earnings make them look anywhere from less good to bad. The upshot is that the future of inflation-adjusted accounting in the United States remains uncertain.[6]

Accounting Practices in Other Countries

A French manufacturing company listed in 1985 on the Paris Bourse (stock exchange) appeared to be a promising investment. Its financial statement showed good sales and a healthy profit. A comparable American firm in the same business showed disappointing results and appeared to be a poor investment choice.

But, before buying the stock of the French company or selling that of the American company, an investor should learn something about the different accounting practices used by the two companies in getting to the bottom line. In this instance, they used different foreign currency translation methods during a year of wild exchange rate fluctuations. Because these companies took different paths to the bottom line, the figures there are not a reliable gauge of their respective performance.

Accounting experts warn that such lack of uniformity in financial statements—the absence of a worldwide accounting language—threatens the growing internationalization of trade, investment, and securities markets. If investors and MNE managers can't get understandable financial information about foreign companies and subsidiaries, they are less likely to venture abroad.

There are forces at work to harmonize and clarify accounting practices. In addition to and perhaps more effectively than the international bodies mentioned below, many international companies are themselves amending their systems. As more concerns from outside the United States seek to tap the huge American capital markets, they must adopt U.S. accounting standards to meet government filing requirements and to attract investors.

Countries other than the United States have, in varying degrees, adopted inflation-related accounting methods. The Netherlands and Brazil are two that have done so.[7] So have Mexico, Germany, the United Kingdom, and Australia.[8] However, there are two methods of inflation accounting and many variations on the basic themes.

Inflation Accounting Methods

One method is *general purchasing power–adjusted (GPP)*. Under this system, books are based on historic costs, but current dollars (or other currency) are converted into inflation-adjusted "real" dollars by using a general price index.

The other method is *current value accounting* (generally known as *CCA*, after the British terminology, *current cost accounting*). It requires that individual assets—such as machines, factories, or supplies—be measured in current prices rather than the actual cost at which they were acquired in the past.

The British, however, have been backsliding in this matter of inflation-related accounting. Their Accounting Standard Committee (ASC) rule requiring inflation-adjusted profit figures lapsed at the end of 1985. There were two reasons for this. One was that inflation had retreated to some 5 percent from the 25 percent of 1975 and the 20 percent of 1980. The other was that the rule was fiercely opposed by most British businesses and many accountancy firms.

Commenting on the ASC's abandonment of the inflation accounting rule, the *Economist* stated, "While . . . replacement costs are sometimes irrelevant, historic costs always are . . . . Historic-cost accounts show auditors at their worst; content to be precisely wrong instead of keen to be approximately right; and deaf to people interested more in the future than in the past.[9]

Different Countries, Different Methods

Some countries have adopted the GPP method and others have adopted the CCA method. The result could be added confusion for an MNE that must maintain books under differing systems, but work to harmonize the systems is being done by the International Accounting Standards Committee, a cooperative association of accounting bodies in 65 nations. Other international bodies working explicitly to eliminate the differences among the accounting practices of countries include the International Federation of Accountants, the UN Commission on Transnational Corporations, the OECD, and the EC.

Despite the best efforts of the above-named organizations to harmonize international accounting standards and the efforts of companies that want to raise capital in foreign markets to adapt to the accounting standards of those markets, some are not optimistic that harmonization will occur quickly. Both the OECD secretary-general and the FASB chairman feel that the goal is a long way off, and the FASB chairman points out that even within the United States, harmonization is difficult, so he is a pessimist about global progress. National pride and widely varying national laws are further obstacles to harmonization.

Different Countries, Fluctuating Currency Exchange Rates
FASB 8 and 52

The need to interpret the financial results of the various subsidiaries of an MNE in light of inflation in several countries and differing accounting standards from country to country is separate and distinct from the need to translate foreign currency accounts into their US$ equivalents. Translation is complicated by the fluctuating relative values of currencies, discussed above. In this area, the FASB took a decisive, though generally unpopular, step. It was known as FASB Statement No. 8.

FASB 8 was born because of the desire of financial analysts and accountants for uniformity in companies' reports which include items involving two or more countries whose currencies are fluctuating up and down in value. The 103-page statement required companies to translate balance sheet items, such as debt, at current exchange rates, while other items, such as inventories, were to be translated at historic rates. All assets and liabilities had to be translated even though there had been no sale or other realized gain or loss.

Since FASB 8 was issued, the value of the US$ has fluctuated widely in terms of the currencies of several of its major trading and investment partners. All of this has produced wide and unpredictable swings in reported earnings.

A money making company may have to report lower earnings or a loss due to unrealized currency value changes. Or an economic loser may be able to report a profit because of such changes.

FASB 8 came under heavy attack from business. As a result, the FASB made changes in 1981 that sharply reduced the effect of erratic swings in foreign currency values on most companies' earnings.[10] FASB 52 replaced FASB 8.

Countries Went Bust

During the 1970s lending binge by banks to developing countries (LDCs), the chairman of a major bank was quoted as saying, "Countries don't go bust." He was proved wrong, and a new and ominous financial force is now acting on international business. Contrary to many expectations, a number of developing countries found themselves unable to pay even the interest, much less the principal, on their debts. The crisis for Poland occurred in 1981; for Mexico, Brazil, Argentina and others, it occurred in 1982 and thereafter.

We examined this matter in Chapter 4 from the point of view of the International Monetary Fund (IMF) and the Bank for International Settlements (BIS) because the IMF has been thrust into and has taken the lead role in trying to resolve these crises as they continue to arise, and the BIS has made bridge loans while the IMF was preparing to act.

Because these crises are so important and constitute a present and growing force on international business, we shall discuss some of the background in this chapter. Also, we can suggest some possible solutions.

Causes of Increasing
LDC Indebtedness

The immediate causes of the growing debts were the jumps in oil prices (crude oil represents an average of 16 percent of the merchandise imports of the nonoil LDCs). In 1973–74, oil prices quadrupled; they then doubled in 1979–80, and that increase from a higher base represented an even larger increase in absolute terms than the 1973–74 rise.

Then, because the increased oil prices with their inflationary consequences led to a fall in economic activity in the developed world, another critical element of economic injury to the LDCs was a subsequent drop in the prices of primary nonoil commodities, which account for 45 percent of LDC (excluding Mexico and OPEC LDCs) exports. Mexico and the OPEC LDCs were hurt by the drops in oil prices beginning in 1981 as well as by uneconomic uses of the oil revenue and borrowed monies they received during the 1970s and in the early 1980s.

Third, after the 1979–80 oil price jump, interest rates increased. That affected all new loans and the many existing loans that carried variable* rather than fixed interest rates. Every 1 percent increase in US$ interest rates costs the LDCs some $2½ billion per year more in interest payments.

Fourth, the US$ began to strengthen in value in the foreign exchange markets during 1980. It continued up into 1985 and gained over 80 percent on a trade-weighted basis by March 1985. LDCs borrow mainly in dollars but export in many currencies, so the rise in the value of the US$ created new burdens; they must earn that much more in deutsche marks, yen, francs, and so on to pay the US$ debts.

The US$ peaked in value in terms of the yen and West European currencies in February 1985. At that time it began to move down in terms of those currencies, and by January 1987 it had fallen some 45 percent in terms of the yen and the deutsche mark and 30 percent against the British pound. However, the US$ weakened little or even continued to gain in exchange for currencies of Canada, Asian newly industrializing countries, and Mexico and other Latin American countries, all of which are important trading partners of the United States.

Debt Problem Solutions

The IMF, the BIS, national central banks, and commercial banks have been scrambling for solutions.

---

*A variable interest rate is increased or decreased periodically based on some reference interest rate, such as the U.S. prime rate or the London Interbank Offer Rate (LIBOR).

Table 6-5

Reschedulings as a Percentage of Nonoil LDC Debt

Year	(1) Amount Rescheduled ($ billions)*	(2) Nonoil LDC Debt ($ billions)	Column 1 as Percent of Column 2
1973	0.4	130.1	0.3%
1974	1.5	160.8	0.9
1975	0.5	190.8	0.3
1976	0.5	228.0	0.2
1977	0.4	278.5	0.1
1978	2.3	336.3	0.7
1979	3.9	396.9	1.0
1980	6.1	474.0	1.3
1981	10.1	555.0	1.8
1982	10.6	613.4	1.7
1983	63.0†	664.3	9.5

*Refers to amounts for which formal reschedulings were agreed/signed in that year.
†If amounts for which rescheduling negotiations were initiated but not finalized during 1983 were included, this figure would rise to $104 billion, some 15 percent of total LDC debt.
Sources: *Barclays Review,* May 1984, p. 35; based on Barclays Group Economics Department estimates and information from the IMF.

Short Term

The short-term answers have been rescheduling of debts as they came due and the debtor country was unable to pay.

Table 6-5 shows the growth of the rescheduling process since 1973. As the note at the bottom of Table 6-5 indicates, when negotiations at the end of 1983 are included, $104 billion of LDC debt—some 15 percent of the total—had been renegotiated or were in the process of being renegotiated.

But renegotiations are becoming more and more difficult. The BIS, the commercial banks, and the central banks are reluctant to come up with more money, and the IMF's resources are finite.

The debtor countries are balking at the stringent austerity programs being insisted on by the IMF. The LDCs' economic growth has halted as new money they get from exports or loans must be used to repay debt rather than for productive investments. Social unrest, including rioting, has broken out.

The debtor countries are in desperate straits, but the industrialized countries are also being damaged. As the debtor countries use money to repay debts, they do not buy goods and services from the developed countries. As a result, the developed countries have lost billions of dollars of export business and thousands of jobs.

Table 6-6
Major Debtor Nations

Country	Amount of Foreign Debt (as of December 1985; in $ billions)	Major Export Items
Brazil	99.0	Citrus, soybeans, coffee, manufactured goods (April 1986)
Mexico	97.0	Oil, wheat, rice (March 1986)
Argentina	48.0	Beef, grain, oil, seeds (March 1984)
Venezuela	35.0	Oil (July 1985)
Poland	28.0	Manufactured goods, raw materials (December 1985)
Philippines	27.0	Industrial, agricultural (April 1986)
Chile	21.0	Copper, agricultural (April 1986)
Yugoslavia	19.0	Industrial, minerals, and textiles (October 1983)
Nigeria	20.0	Oil (March 1986)
Peru	14.0	Oil, fisheries, rice (April 1986)
Colombia	13.0	Coffee, cotton, bananas (November 1985)
Ecuador	8.0	Coffee, cocoa
Uruguay	5.0	Beef, wool, rice, fish (December 1985)
Panama	3.8	Sugar, bananas, clothing (October 1985)
Bolivia	4.0	Tin, natural gas (July 1986)

Source: U.S. Department of Commerce.

The LDC debtor countries can reduce their debts only by exporting more than they import and thus running BOP surpluses. Table 6-6 shows some of those countries, the amounts of their debts, and their major export products.

Some of the LDC debtor countries have been able to run BOP surpluses and make debt payments. However, these surpluses have been achieved as much by cutting imports as by expanding exports, and that has slowed or stopped economic development in the debtor countries and also hurt exports from countries that had been suppliers before the imports were curtailed.

Most of the LDC debtor countries have needed more money from private banks and international agencies and have been lent more. This has caused the debt burdens of these countries to increase at the same time that their economic development has been retarded, a process that cannot be sustained.

Longer-Term Solutions

Quite a number of cures have been suggested. We shall list a few.

1. Borrowing countries will have to pursue policies ensuring that new money they obtain is used for economic growth rather than for consumption capital flight, or overambitious government schemes or armaments.

2. Borrowers should build up reserves in good years to enable them to withstand the fluctuations in commodity export prices that are inevitable even if there are no more oil price shocks.

3. The developed countries must strive for their own economic growth and open their markets to LDC exports even though that means competition with some developed country industries.

4. The IMF and other creditors must not try to enforce too stringent austerity measures on debtors. Social unrest and trade contraction must be avoided or at least minimized.

5. The IMF, the World Bank, and other agencies that aid LDCs must be assured of sufficient funding so that they can take long-term views.

6. Parts of the huge LDC external debts—some $660 billion by the fall of 1986—must be changed in form to types of equity. These could be ownership interests in projects being developed or shares of export earnings. Other parts of the debts should be lengthened in maturity, with interest rate ceilings applied.

7. The LDCs must relax their restrictions on foreign investments and on repatriation of profits from existing investments. They must encourage new money from MNEs—nonbank sources—because the banks are now overcommitted with LDC loans and are not likely good prospects for new, economic growth money.

8. Blame for the debt crises belongs to several parties. The LDCs borrowed more than they could productively invest, and much of the borrowed money was wasted at home or corruptly sent abroad for the personal accounts of political leaders. The lending banks were encouraged to lend by the governments of their countries because the governments were thus relieved to that extent of foreign aid demands by the LDCs. But the banks must also bear a share of the blame; they made limited inquiries regarding the uses of the borrowed money or the soundness of the projects in which the money would be invested. They failed to get collateral to secure the loans, and one reason they were so casual was that the loans were almost always to governments or guaranteed by governments. One leading banker said, "Governments don't go bust"; he and his colleagues were proved wrong.

As a contribution to the solution of the debt crises, the banks should establish schedules to write down the loans on their books over a period of several years. Some European banks have already begun to sell off portions of these loans at discounts, and a market now exists for the discounted loans.

In May, 1987, Citicorp added $3 billion to its loan loss reserves for foreign debt. Even though that caused a $2.5 billion second quarter loss and a loss of $1 billion for the year, the move won positive reaction in U.S. financial markets. It was viewed as a realistic appraisal of the bank's chances of being repaid its loans to developing nations, which totaled $14.8 billion at the end of 1986.

SUMMARY

The MNE financial management must be aware of many financial forces that originate outside the company. Some of them, such as inflation, taxation, and fiscal and monetary policies of government, affect domestic as well as international business. But even for such forces, the concerns of the domestic manager are of a different magnitude than the concerns of the international manager because the domestic manager has to cope with only one country, whereas the international manager has to cope with two or more countries. The same may be said of accounting principles, which differ widely from country to country and in their degrees of recognition of inflation.

Fluctuating currency exchange rates, currency controls, and attendant risks are almost uniquely international problems. So are quotas and tariffs.

The balance of payments affects both domestic and international companies. It, of course, is related to inflation, taxation, fiscal and monetary policies, and such other factors as the competitiveness of a country's goods and services in the world markets.

The international debt crises have added new financial forces with which managers must cope. Many debtor countries must struggle to pay debts and have less money to pay for imports of goods or services.

As suggested in the introduction, the MNE financial manager is not without means for protecting and advancing the company. Those means are subjects of Chapter 18.

Questions

1. *In an American financial paper, you see the quotation: "Norway (krone) _____.1361." What does that mean?*
2. *On the same day, you see the quotation: "Norway (krone)_____7.345." What does that mean?*
3. *In the world's currency-trading markets, why is the US$ the central currency through which almost all major trades go?*
4. *What is the difference between spot and forward currency markets?*
5. *When it is said that a currency is trading at a premium to the US$ in the forward market, what does that mean? Why would this happen?*

6. *If you agree to pay a certain amount of foreign currency to someone in six months, which of you bears the currency fluctuation risk? Explain.*
7. *What are currency controls? Why are they imposed?*
8. *What is the importance of the state of the BOP to MNEs?*
9. *What are some ways in which inflation affects business decisions?*
10. *Have countries ever succeeded in stopping inflation? How?*
11. *What is inflation-adjusted accounting? ?*
12. *What two other numbers must you know in order to compute real interest rates?*
13. *What is meant by currency translation?*
14. *In order to surmount the current debt crises, what are some things that must be done by (a) the LDCs, (b) the developed, creditor countries, and (c) the creditor banks?*

Minicase

6-1 Are the Socialists

Coming?

You are the chief financial officer of Moulin S.A., a French manufacturing subsidiary of an American parent MNE. Moulin's product is sold in France and exported to countries within the EC, but the French market has received Moulin's major marketing attention.

The year is 1981, and the French presidential elections will be held in one month. One candidate is the incumbent, Giscard d'Estaing, heading a center/right coalition of political parties that has governed France since World War II. Everyone is familiar with the policies and personalities of this coalition. Opposing it is a socialist/communist coalition headed by the socialist François Mitterrand, and the opinion polls show Mitterrand's group holding a small lead.

Would you expect this situation to have any effect on the value of the French franc (Ff)? What effect, and why? If no effect, why not?

Would the situation cause you to recommend more or less emphasis on export marketing, or no change? Explain.

You have insisted on payment by your export customers in Ffs. Will you make any change in that policy? Explain.

Minicase

6-2 The Socialists

Have Arrived

It is a year later. You are still CFO of Moulin, and Mitterrand's coalition has been in control of the French government for eight months. France has begun to run a BOP deficit, and the government is supporting the value of the Ff within the EMS.

What significance do those developments have for Moulin? What, if anything, different do you recommend for the conduct of Moulin's business because of those developments? Explain.

Supplementary Readings

Exchange Risks

Black, S. *International Money Markets and Flexible Exchange Rates.* Princeton Studies in International Finance, no. 32. Princeton, NJ.: International Finance Section, Department of Economics, Princeton University, 1973.

Culbertson, William P., Jr. "Purchasing Power Parity and Black Market Exchange Rates." *Economic Inquiry,* May 1975, pp. 107–20.

"Currency Parity Clauses Stand for Fairness," *Euromoney*, December 1984, pp. 133–135.

Diebold, J. "The Economic System at Stake." *Foreign Affairs*, May, 1972, p. 167.

Feldman, Robert A. "Foreign Currency Options." *Finance & Development*, December 1985, pp. 38–41.

Kindleberger, Charles P. *International Economics.* Homewood, Ill.: Richard D. Irwin, 1973. Chap. 17.

Mayer, Martin. *The Fate of the Dollar.* New York: Times Books, 1980.

Root, Franklin R. *International Trade and Investment.* 5th ed. Cincinnati: South-Western Publishing, 1984. Chap. 5.

Salemi, Michael K. "The Efficiency of Forward Foreign Exchange Markets." *Economic and Financial Prospects*, August–September 1986, pp. 5–6.

Winder, Robert. "Be Big and Bright." *Euromoney,* May 1986, pp. 184–202.

Taxation

Bartlett, Bruce. "Supply-Side Sparkplug." *Policy Review*, Summer 1986, pp. 42–47.

Hariss, C. Lowell. "Value-Added Taxation." *Columbia Journal of World Business*, July–August 1971, pp. 18–86.

"How Value-Added Tax Works: It May Be Nearer than You Think." *Professional Report*, October 1979, pp. 23–24.

Owens, Jeffrey. "Tax Reform: Some European Ideas." *Europe*, September 1986, pp. 18–20.

Ricks, David A. *International Dimensions of Corporate Finance*. Englewood Cliffs, N.J.: Prentice-Hall, 1978. Chap. 2.

Todd, Jonathan. "Battle Threatens over Tax on Multinationals." *Europe*, November–December 1983, pp. 22–23.

"Value-Added Analysis—Staying Ahead of Costs." *AIIE Transactions*, Fall 1981, pp. 215–21.

"The Value-Added Tax: Fact and Fancies." *Management Review*, February 1980, pp. 8–13.

"VAT—The International Flavor of the Month." *Accountancy*, January 1981, pp. 108–9.

Inflation

DeSaint-Phalle, Thibaut. *Trade, Inflation, and the Dollar*. New York: Oxford University Press, 1981.

Emele, Bruno "The Global Purchasing-Power, Effects of Oil Price Changes." *Economic and Financial Prospects*, August–September 1986, pp. 1–4.

Harvey, Jack L. "Expected Growth in the Industrial Countries Revised Upward." *International Letter*, Federal Reserve Bank, Chicago, June 1986.

Monthly Economic Letter, New York Citibank, October 1977, pp. 8–9, 12–18; and December 1980, pp. 8–11.

Tariffs

Curtiss, George Boughton. *Protection and Prosperity*. New York: Garland Publishing, 1974.

Kleitz, Anthony. "Tariff Preferences for the Developing Countries." *OECD Observer*, March 1983, pp. 38–41.

Kvasnicka, Joseph G. "Restrictions on Imports: An Answer to U.S. Trade Problems?" *International Letter*, Fedral Reserve Bank, Chicago, April 1985.

Michaely, Michael. *Theory of Commercial Policy: Trade and Protection*. Chicago: University of Chicago Press, 1977.

Michalski, Wolfgang; Henry Ergas; and Barrie Stevens. "Costs and Benefits of Protection." *OECD Observer*, May 1985, pp. 18–23.

Ogi, Adolph. "World Freed Trade in Danger." *Bulletin, Credit Suisse Magazine*, September 1985, pp. 14–16.

Monetary and Fiscal Policies

Bingham, T. R. G. "Financial Innovation and Monetary Policy." *OECD Observer*, January 1985, pp. 24–26.

Black, Stanley W. *Floating Exchange Rates and National Economic Policy*. New Haven: Yale University Press, 1977.

Davidson, Paul. *International Money and the Real World*. New York: John Wiley & Sons, 1982.

Friedman, Milton, ed. *Studies in the Quantity Theory of Money.* Chicago: University of Chicago Press, 1956.

Humphrey, Thomas N. *The Monetary Approach to the Balance of Payments, Exchange Rates, and World Inflation.* New York: Praeger Publishers, 1982.

Newman, Nigel. "Fiscal Expansion." *Barclays Review*, November 1985, pp. 69–80.

Robbins, Lionel Charles, and Baron Robbins. *Money, Trade, and International Relations.* New York: St. Martins Press, 1971.

Accounting

Ernst & Whinney publishes a number of international accounting guides.

Nair, R. D. "Empirical Guidelines for Comparing International Accounting Data." *Journal of International Business Studies*, Winter 1982, pp. 85–98.

Price, Waterhouse & Co. publishes a number of international accounting guides.

Endnotes

1. Discussed by Robert Z. Aliber, *The International Money Game*, 2nd. ed. (New York: Basic Books, 1976), pp. 189–90.

2. Samuel I. Katz, " 'Managed Floating' as an Interim International Exchange Rate Regime, 1973–1975," *New York University Bulletin*, 1975–3 (New York: Center for the Study of Financial Institutions, New York University, 1975), pp. 13–14.

3. Vermont Royster, "Thinking Things Over, 'A Thrice Told Tale,' " *The Wall Street Journal*, May 10, 1978, p. 18.

4. "International Perspectives," *OECD Observer*, March 1983, pp. 17–26.

5. Tom Herman, "Your Money Matters," *The Wall Street Journal*, February 4, 1980, p. 40.

6. Susan Lee, "Yawning GAAP: Why Interest in Inflation Accounting Is Flagging," *Barron's*, August 15, 1983, p. 13.

7. Morton Backer, "Valuation Reporting in the Netherlands: A Real-Life Example," *Financial Executive*, January 1973, pp. 40–50.

8. *Business International*, November 3, 1978, pp. 347–50.

9. "Quill-Pen Accounting," *Economist*, February 4, 1986, p. 55.

10. Tom Herman, "Accounting Body Seeks to Change Currencies Rule," *The Wall Street Journal*, April 11, 1980, p. 20.

CHAPTER 7 PHYSICAL FORCES

"Look at a map of the world, as large a map as possible. At first sight it seems a maze of lines, colors, and unfamiliar names. Go on looking and studying until the mere mention of a town, country, or river enables it to be picked out immediately on the map. Those who are concerned with overseas marketing must, as a basis, know their export geography as well as they know the streets around their home."

Henry Deschampsneufs, *Selling Overseas,*
(London: Business Publications, 1960), p. 46

Learning Objectives

After you study this chapter, you should know:

1. The importance of a country's *location* in political and trade relationships.
2. The importance of *topography.*
3. That *climate* exerts a broad influence on business.
4. Why international business managers must be aware of developments in natural resources.
5. What has been the impact of industrial disasters such as Bhopal and the Rhine spill on multinational firms generally.

Key Words and Concepts

Location
Topography
Climate
Tropical forests
Seabed mining

Business Incident

Oshawa, Ontario—What would you do with 12,000 shiny new 1981 Chevrolet Malibus, built for the desert but gathering snow on Canadian parking grounds?

General Motors of Canada, Ltd. hopes it won't have to answer the question. The cars are part of an estimated $200 million (Canadian) deal between GM and Iraq. Since the agreement was signed last spring, the sale has brought GM nothing but trouble. The first cars shipped to Iraq were mechanically unfit for its hot, dusty climate. Iraq has refused to take any more cars until the first 13,500 get fixed. And now, according to Ed Lumley, Canada's minister for international trade, there's some dispute over the validity of the original contract.

When the Malibus hit Baghdad's roads and streets, their air filters choked on the dust and their transmissions labored in the heat and traffic. GM tripled to 36 its full-time engineers and mechanics in Baghdad, where they are installing supplementary air filters and changing clutches. The troubles, insists Ross Scott, vice president of market development for GM of Canada, weren't out of the ordinary. "It's typical that it's being seen as a 'crisis' in the Middle East," Scott complains. "It's sort of like when you bring out a new product in North America. Things show up that you hadn't anticipated."

Two thirds of the cars still in Canada are sitting on acres of rented space at the Dartmouth docks in Nova Scotia. The rest are parked at GM in Oshawa. All the cars have been refitted with new filters and clutches. As to whether GM will still earn a profit, if it does collect for the cars, after its additional expenses, Scott will say only, "We hope so."

Peggy Berkowitz, "GM Runs into A Middle East Crisis: It's Too Hot and Dusty in Baghdad," *The Wall Street Journal*, February 23, 1982, p. 37.

*T*he business incident illustrates how the failure to know some very basic facts about the physical forces in a market can turn what appears to be a lucrative business deal into a loss—in this case, all because the marketing official did not know that it was hot and dusty in Baghdad!

Product modification because of the differences in the physical forces among markets is only one reason for their importance in international business. Their major significance lies in the fact that so many of the other forces—cultural, distributive, political, and economic—are affected by them. In fact, this relationship is so strong that geographers specialize in such fields as political, economic, and cultural geography. Not only are there maps that show political boundaries and typography, but there are also maps that indicate land use, transportation flows, commercial flows, and even race and language use. As one writer stated, the physical character of a country is perhaps the principal and broadest determinant of both the society found there and the means by which that society undertakes to supply its needs.[1]

Clearly, a study in depth of any one of these facets of geography is impossible for all but the specialists, but a basic knowledge of the location, size, topography, climatic conditions, and natural resources of countries is a necessary tool for those expecting to engage in commercial relations with them.

Location

One of the first steps that newcomers to international business should do is to study a good world atlas. They will find it extremely useful to be able to locate a country in the proper continent and to place it there correctly with respect to bordering nations. When someone mentions Bolivia, they should be capable of conjuring up a mental picture of a relatively large (equal to the combined area of California and Texas), landlocked country in South America, bordered by Peru, Chile, Argentina, Paraguay, and Brazil. Furthermore, they should have an idea of the country's shape, how it compares in size with its neighbors, and what its capital and important cities are.

A nation's **location** can explain much of the political environment in which business must operate. For example, Japan is a neighbor to the two largest communist nations, the Soviet Union and China, and it is separated by only a narrow strip of water from the Korean peninsula, where the armies of North and South Korea confront each other. Japan's close geographic proximity to the Soviet Union, China, and North Korea forces it to develop stable relations with them, while the similarity of Japan's political ideas and economic system to those of the United States and Western European countries causes it to maintain close ties with these governments. The result is a careful balancing act that Japan hopes will offend no one.

Finland and Austria are European nations that are essentially Western-style democracies. However, because of their common borders with communist nations, they are forced to be extremely careful not to offend their eastern neighbors by their political actions. This is undoubtedly the principal reason why neither nation has joined the European Community although both are members of the more loosely organized European Free Trade Association.

Location is also a factor in trade relationships. As you saw in Chapter 2, two of the largest trading partners of the United States, Canada and Mexico, lie on its borders. Proximity to these markets makes deliveries faster, freight costs lower, and the servicing of clients less expensive. Proximity to the market is also the reason why Japan's sales to ASEAN, the southeast Asian trading group, are 40 percent higher than U.S. sales and 75 percent greater than the sales of the European Community, a still more distant supplier.

Topography

Topography—the surface features of a region, such as mountains, plains, deserts, and bodies of water—contributes greatly to differences in the economies, cultures, politics, and social structures of countries. These elements not only affect physical distribution but also often require special adaptations of the product or its package. Although marketing analysts are apt to suspect that countries with large areas, such as Russia, India, and Canada, possess marked physical and climatic variations, they may be surprised to learn that such variations exist in smaller countries as well. Therefore, if the effects of topography are not taken into account, some important factors in the market appraisal are certain to be overlooked. In the sections to follow, we shall examine some of the chief surface features to illustrate what the analyst should look for.

Mountains and Plains

Because it is less costly to build roads and railroad beds on flat terrain, we would expect the transportation system to be more developed in a predominantly flat country than in a mountainous country. From this, it follows that there should be less difficulty with physical distribution in such a country than in a country crossed by mountains.

Perhaps it is less apparent, though, that differences in topography can partition an already small market into a number of smaller ones. Colombia is an example. Three distinct ranges of the Andes Mountains divide it from north to south into four separate markets with distinctive industries, climates, and cultures, and even with different dialects. (See Figure 7–1.)

Located close to the equator, Colombia has no seasons, but because of the great differences in altitudes it experiences a wide range of climates (temperature and humidity), from tropical jungles in the lowlands to snow-covered mountains 10,000 feet high.[2] Imagine the production and inventory problems that such differences occasion for the manufacturer that must supply a distinct product and package for each zone.[3]

One should not think that these kinds of temperature and humidity differences are peculiar to Colombia. On the contrary, such conditions are so common that the analyst should assume that they exist (especially in the Tropical Zone) until he has proven to his satisfaction that they do not. A topographical map will indicate which countries in the tropics possess a combination of mountains and lowlands—a combination certain to cause the same kinds of extremes in temperature and humidity as are found in Colombia.

Mountains also create concentrations of population either because the climate is more pleasant at higher altitudes or because they form barriers to population movements. Nearly four fifths of Colombia's population is located in one third of its total area (the western highlands), where the climate is moderate. In Brazil, 80 percent of its 120 million inhabitants live within a narrow 300-mile-wide coastal strip separated from the rest of the country by a mountain chain.

Figure 7-1
Map of Colombia

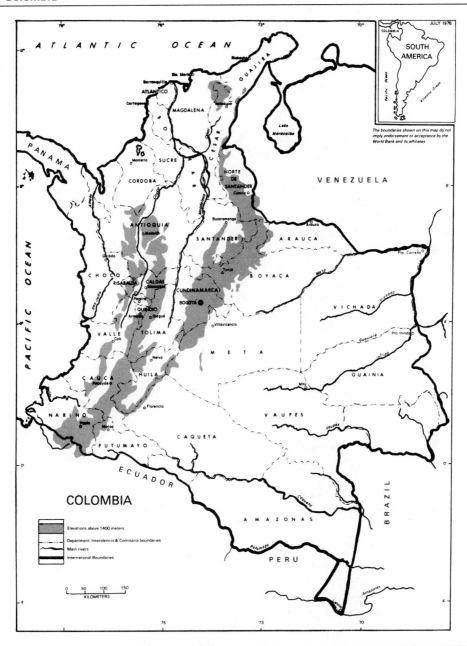

IBRD 3638R, July 1976. Reproduced by permission of the World Bank.

Except in the tropics, the population density generally decreases as the elevation increases. If a population map is placed over a topographical map, the blank areas on the population map generally coincide with the areas of higher elevation. For example, 90 percent of Switzerland's population is located in a narrow belt at the base of the Alps. This is because dense population requires commerce, manufacturing, and agriculture, all of which are dependent on the good transportation and ease of communication afforded by the plains.

Similarly, sizable mountain ranges in Spain are responsible for the formation of five natural and distinct regions, each of which has unique geographic and cultural features. Regional feeling is very strong in the areas of Galicia, Catalonia, and the Basque country. In fact, large separatist movements in Catalonia and the Basque country have long agitated to secede from Spain and form separate nations. In 1979 elections, a majority of the voters chose greater local autonomy but not total separation from Spain. This did not satisfy the Basque separatists who continue to wage attacks against the government.

Although Castilian Spanish is the official language for all of Spain, the areas of Galicia, Catalonia, and the Basque country each have their own language, which is used in commerce and in the home. If a company assigned a Spaniard from Madrid to cover Barcelona, the principal city of Catalonia, market penetration would be extremely difficult.[4]

Switzerland is another country that is separated into distinctive cultural regions by mountains. In a country one half the size of Maine, four different languages are spoken—Italian, French, German, and Romansch (see Figure 7–2). To the consternation of the advertising manager attempting to reach all regions of the country, each of the three major language groups has its own radio and television network, and the fourth, Romansch, is also used by the German stations. For a really confused cultural and political situation caused by mountains, see the reading at the end of this chapter on Kleines Walsertal, Austria.

Deserts, Tropical Forests, and Bodies of Water

Deserts and tropical forests are like mountains in that they, too, separate markets, make transportation more difficult, and create concentrations of population.

Deserts

Australia, the smallest and flattest of the world's continents, is also the world's driest. Most of the central portion is flat, barren, and arid, giving it a close resemblance to the Sahara Desert (see Figure 7–3).

As a result, more than half of the population is concentrated in only one sixth of the total area and two thirds of the inhabitants live in the state capitals, which are also major seaports. This gives Australia one of the highest percentages of urban population in the world (86 percent), surpassed only by Kuwait

Figure 7-2
The Cantons and Major Language Areas of Switzerland

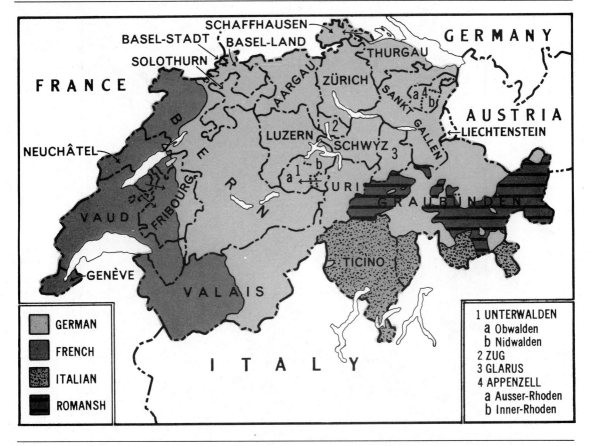

(92 percent), the United Kingdom (91 percent), Israel (90 percent), and Belgium (89 percent).

Since Australia is a vast but thinly populated country, the physical distribution of goods poses some problems. Much of the movement of goods between cities is handled by coastal shipping rather than by rail or road transportation, as is usually the case in developed countries. It is estimated that transportation accounts for as much as 30 percent of the final cost of a commodity, as compared with the more usual 10 percent encountered in the European Community and the United States.[5]

Even though 70 percent of the country is extremely dry, the market analyst should be cautioned that some parts of the north resemble the monsoon

Figure 7-3
Map of Australia

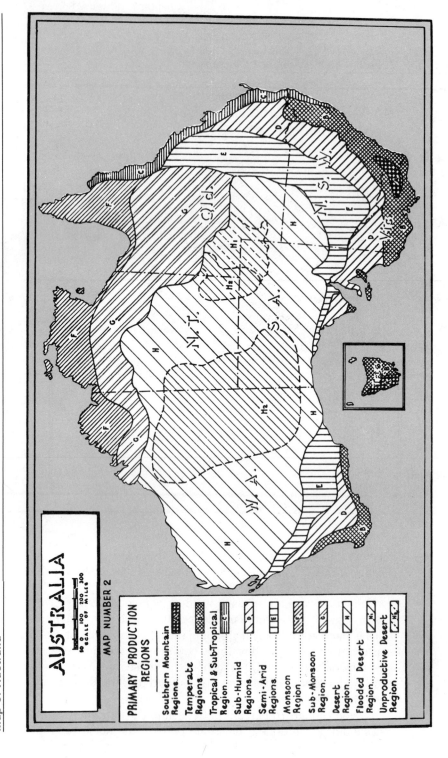

Figure 7-4
Skiways in Iran

areas of India, receiving up to 100 inches of rainfall a year. Thus, the firm planning to enter the Australian market faces the same problem of extreme differences in temperature and humidity as are found in Colombia, though the causes are different.

The temperature differences would be even greater if it were not for the uniform topography of Australia. In countries with large, hot desert areas but with irregular surfaces, the temperature range is more extreme. Summertime temperatures in Iran reach over 130° F. while in the winter, the great altitude of much of the country results in temperatures of $-18°$ F. or lower. From December to March, a 1½-hour drive from Tehran, the capital, will put the skier on the ski slopes of Ab-Ali of Shemshak (see Figure 7-4).

It should be noted that Iran is an excellent example of a nation whose population distribution is strongly influenced by climate and topography. Over 70 percent of the country, consisting mostly of mountains and deserts, is uninhabited.

Tropical Rain Forests

The effect of tropical rain forests on population concentration can be seen in Peru. There, rain forests cover 60 percent of the land but are inhabited by only 10 percent of the population. The greatest tropical forest of them all in the Brazi-

Courtesy of Standard Chartered Bank

Rhine Waterway

lian Amazon Basin includes over 1 million square miles (one fourth the U.S. land area) but is inhabited by only 3 percent of Brazil's population. The population density is so low (one person per square mile) that this region has been called one of the world's greatest "deserts." Few parts of the world other than true deserts have such a low population density.

While it is true that the heavy vegetation of tropical rain forests makes transportation difficult, this factor alone does not stop human settlement. What discourages settlers has been a combination of heavy vegetation, harsh tropical climate, and the generally poor quality of the soil. These conditions exist not only in the tropical rain forests of Peru and Brazil but also in those of equatorial Africa and Southeast Asia.

Bodies of Water

We have seen that mountains, deserts, and tropical forests act as barriers to transportation and dividers of markets. A fourth surface feature, bodies of water, has exactly the opposite effect. Any map of world population clearly shows that bodies of water attract people. Nearly every major river valley has a preponderant share of the area's population not only because of the availability of fertile soil, water for irrigation, and the low level of the surrounding land but also because of the inexpensive transportation afforded by the river.

Inland Waterways. Before the construction of railways, only water transport was economically practical for hauling bulk goods over long distances. Even after railroads were built, the volume of goods on the waterways increased wherever industrialization spread. Now, however, the relative importance of water transport has decreased compared to rail transportation—with one notable exception, the Rhine Waterway.[6]

The Rhine Waterway, the main transportation artery of Europe, still carries a greater volume of traffic than all the railroads that run parallel to it. The Rhine River and its connecting waterways provide a pathway for goods from or to all of West Germany, the French Rhône area, Switzerland, Austria, and even the Czech Danube region. By means of the Rhine, Switzerland, a landlocked country, has through its port of Basel a direct waterway connection to Rotterdam, the world's largest port, some 500 miles distant. (See Figures 7–5 and 7–6.) Although Switzerland has one of the finest railroad systems in Europe, 40 percent of its foreign trade continues to be shipped through Basel.[7]

Extensive use is made of navigable waterways in every continent except Australia, which has no important inland water routes. In Eastern Europe, the interconnected system of the Volga and Don rivers allows watercraft to reach Moscow from the White, Baltic, Black, and Caspian seas. In South America the most frequently used waterways are the Magdalena, Orinoco, Parana, and Amazon rivers, while in Africa the Nile, Congo, and Niger rivers are predominant. Navigation on inland waterways is evident in Asia too, some of the more important navigable waterways being the Ganges in India, the Indus in Pakistan, and

Figure 7–5

Europe's Major Inland Waterways

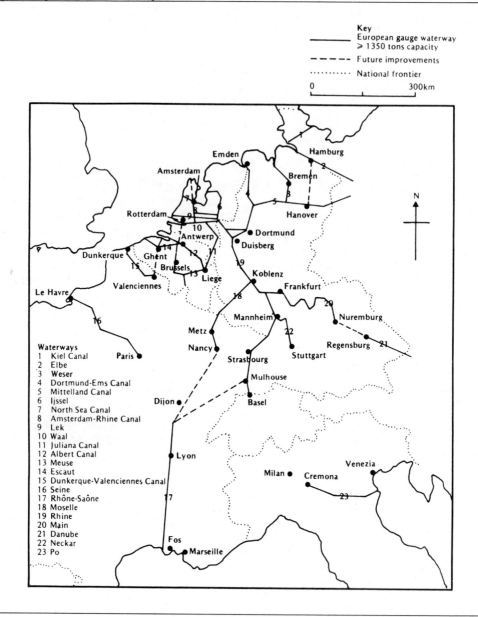

Key
—— European gauge waterway ≥ 1350 tons capacity
– – – Future improvements
········ National frontier

0   300km

Waterways
1 Kiel Canal
2 Elbe
3 Weser
4 Dortmund-Ems Canal
5 Mittelland Canal
6 Ijssel
7 North Sea Canal
8 Amsterdam-Rhine Canal
9 Lek
10 Waal
11 Juliana Canal
12 Albert Canal
13 Meuse
14 Escaut
15 Dunkerque-Valenciennes Canal
16 Seine
17 Rhône-Saône
18 Moselle
19 Rhine
20 Main
21 Danube
22 Neckar
23 Po

Source: John Tripper, *Canals and Waterways in the EEC*, European Studies, no. 21 (London: European Community Information Service, 1975).

Figure 7-6
Major Traffic Flows

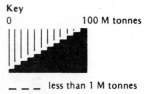

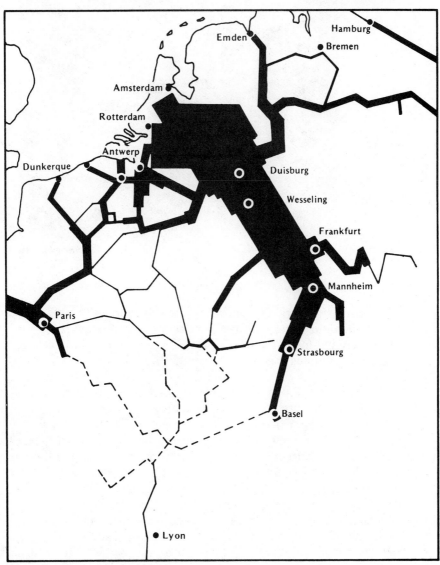

Source: John Tripper, *Canals and Waterways in the EEC,* European Studies, no. 21 (London: European Community Information Service, 1975).

Courtesy of Swiss National Tourist Office

Basel Port

the densest network of waterways in the world (30,000 kilometers)—the Yangtze River in eastern China.[8] Not only have waterways served as centers for settlement and industrial development initially, but they have also acted as a continuing stimulus to economic growth.

Outlets to the Sea. Historically, navigable waterways with connections to the ocean have permitted low-cost transportation of goods and people from the coast to the interior of a country, and even now they are very often the only means of access from the coast of many less developed nations. This has been a particularly troublesome problem for Africa, in which 14 of the world's landlocked developing countries are located. Almost one third of all the sub-Sahara countries are landlocked, and some of these countries are more than 1,000 kilometers from the sea by the shortest land route. The implications for these poor nations are obvious: they must construct costly, long truck routes and extensive feeder networks for relatively low volumes of traffic. Moreover, governments with coastlines through which the exports and imports of the landlocked nations must pass are in a position to exert considerable political influence. Small wonder that struggles for outlets to the sea still exist and are an important factor in the political as well as the economic forces.[9]

One outstanding example is the century-long struggle by Bolivia to regain from Chile an outlet to the Pacific Ocean. These countries have held discussions for decades, but no workable agreement has been reached. In 1976, Chile made what could be an acceptable proposal and Bolivia may finally have a small strip of land on the Pacific Ocean. Until it does, however, tension between these two governments will continue to run high.[10]

Farther south, the two giants of South America, Brazil and Argentina, have used Paraguay's need for an outlet to the Atlantic to promote their ambitions to be the leader of the continent. For years, Paraguay's only connection to the ocean was through the port of Buenos Aires. Brazil, observing that Paraguay was experiencing difficulty over the right to use Argentina's waterways, erected the Friendship Bridge on the Paraguayan-Brazil border and completely paved a highway linking Paraguay with the Brazilian port of Paranagua. To further facilitate the movement of Paraguayan goods, Brazil declared the port a free zone only for Paraguay. This led to numerous cooperative ventures between the two countries, and it appears that Paraguay is now solidly in Brazil's area of influence. Important to international businesspeople is the knowledge that closer political ties bring closer economic ties, which alter traditional trading patterns. That certainly has been the case in this instance.[11]

Climate

Only **climate** (temperature and precipitation) rivals topography in importance as an aspect of the physical environment. Within a broad range, climate can set the limits on what people can do both physically and economically. When the climate is permissive, we generally find large aggregations of population, but when the climate is harsh, population concentrations are scarce. Certainly, nonclimatic factors will help determine people's development, but without a permissive climate, people are severely limited in what they can accomplish.

Similar climates tend to occur in the same latitudes and in the same continental positions. Northwestern Europe and the United States are in similar latitudes, are strongly influenced by the ocean, and have mild, moist climates. Kansas and central Asia are dry, with cold winters and hot summers; both of these areas are at similar latitudes and far from the sea. While latitudes and continental positions are not the only factors affecting climates, they are certainly the most influential.[12]

Tropical versus Temperate Zones

Because the force of climate is so important, numerous experts have tried to show that different climates cause differences in economic development and even in human temperament and ability. Their thesis is that the greatest economic and intellectual development has taken place in the temperate climates of

Figure 7-7

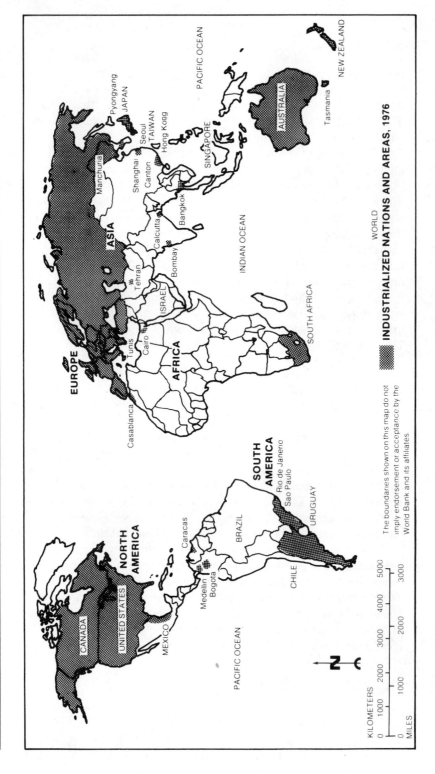

INDUSTRIALIZED NATIONS AND AREAS, 1976

The boundaries shown on this map do not imply endorsement or acceptance by the World Bank and its affiliates.

Source: Andrew M. Kamarack, *The Tropics and Economic Development* (Baltimore: Johns Hopkins University Press, 1976), pp. 6–7. Copyright © 1976 by the International Bank for Reconstruction and Development/The World Bank.

northern Europe and the United States, whereas there has been less development in the tropics because the climate limits human energy and mental power. The map shown in Figure 7–7, illustrates the basis for this argument.

Unfortunately, this simplistic explanation often leads managers to believe that people in the tropics are inherently inferior—a factor that will seriously affect a firm's relationships with the governments and people of tropical nations. What is needed is an investigation in depth of the effects of tropical climates on agriculture, on exploration for mineral resources, and on people themselves.

In *The Tropics and Economic Development*, Andrew Kamarck has shown that many of the factors responsible for the underdeveloped state of most tropical nations are present because of the tropical climate but that there is not a one-to-one relationship between state of development and climate.[13] For example, because temperatures do not drop sufficiently in the cooler months to kill pests and parasites, as occurs in the Temperate Zones, these are free to breed and multiply all year round. Therefore, weevils, locusts, and birds destroy crops; parasites and flies kill cattle; and people are constantly infected with debilitating parasitic and amoebic diseases.

A World Bank study of plantation workers in Indonesia found that 45 percent of the male workers suffered from iron deficiency anemia, which results from parasites. Their output was 20 percent lower than that of nonanemic workers.[14] In Peru, 113 out of 122 men tested in the armed forces harbored a parasitic infection.[15] How can workers perform effectively if, first, they have insufficient food because insects destroy the crops and, second, they lack the strength to work because they are infested with strength-sapping parasites?

Many managers who are aware of these reasons for lower worker productivity have taken steps to remedy the situation. Subsidized lunches coupled with free medical treatment at a company-owned infirmary have resulted in dramatic improvements in worker performance. A 20 percent increase in the anemic workers' output should more than cover the cost of providing these services. What manager would not invest in the workers' welfare if this also benefits the firm? All that is necessary here is to acknowledge that people in the tropics are not inherently lazy but are unable to perform as well as they might because of parasitic diseases and a lack of good nutrition.

Kamarck points out that conditions are changing. Techniques are evolving that will control pests and parasites, and once these are under control, "the characteristics that now hinder the Tropics may then give them advantages over the Temperate Zones." This is especially true of agriculture because of the more rapid plant growth in the tropical areas.[16]

Climatic Implications for International Business

Climatic conditions can greatly affect a firm's product mix. In the warmer parts of the world, we would expect that air conditioners and summer sports equipment will find a ready market, whereas heaters and heavy clothing will not.

However, as we have seen, the high altitudes of some large population centers do create opportunities that may be passed over by the less knowledgeable.

Because summertime in nations north of the equator is wintertime in nations south of the equator, firms operating worldwide are precluded from mounting a global promotional effort if their sales are seasonal. Furthermore, the climatic differences caused by great variations in topography can add considerably to the production and inventory costs of products that cannot withstand wide temperature ranges or extreme conditions of humidity. Such products may require special packaging as in the case of many consumer products, or even distinctive adaptations, as in the case of electrical and mechanical equipment.

Inventory costs may be prohibitively high for some firms if they are required to carry two distinct stocks so as to serve both the cool, dry climate of the mountains and the hot, moist conditions of the lowlands. Such a segmentation of an already small market may cause the entire operation in a country to be unprofitable.

Mineral Resources

Of all the natural resources, it is the supply of exhaustible minerals and mineral fuels that has most concerned governments and businesses. During the Arab-Israeli war in 1973, we saw how Arab exporters of petroleum used an oil embargo on some nations and the threat of an embargo on other nations to obtain political support from Western Europe. The realization by oil-importing nations that not only their industries but also their national defense depended on a substance that other nations could use as a political force initiated a worldwide campaign to conserve minerals and mineral fuels and to search for new energy sources.

Alternative Energy Sources

Oil Sands and Shale

One potential energy source is the tar sands of Athabasca, Canada, which contain bitumen, a tarlike crude. Instead of being pumped from wells, bitumen is strip-mined and sent to a separation plant, where it is converted into a higher-quality synthetic crude oil. Although this crude is more costly to produce than conventional crude, after OPEC quadrupled its prices in 1974, a Sun Oil plant at Athabasca, which began production in 1967, suddenly became profitable.

The subsequent decline in world prices made the future of synthetic oil production uncertain, but the lack of discoveries of conventional crude to replace Canada's depleting reserves motivated the Canadian government to offer new tax incentives to bitumen producers. Various projects are under way to expand the production of synthetic crude. One fourth of Canada's total oil production already comes from this source. It is estimated that Canada has 70 billion barrels of recoverable oil in the form of bitumen, which is sufficient to meet its needs for the next 130 years.[17]

The United States has an equal amount of oil that is known to be recoverable from shale rock in Colorado, Utah, and Wyoming. However, the recovery process is also expensive, which makes the end product unable to compete with today's prices of conventional crude. In addition, there are environmental problems connected with the disposition of huge quantities of waste shale. So far, Union Oil is the only company to have built a recovery plant.

Crude from Coal

A promising source of synthetic oil and gas is coal gasification. South Africa, concerned about being shut off from crude oil imports for political reasons, has built three Sasol plants; these supply a large portion of its oil and gas needs from low-grade coal, which is in plentiful supply. A coal gasification plant built in North Dakota with South Africa's help will produce enough gas to heat a quarter of a million homes. At present, a consortium operates a 1,000-ton-per-day plant in California.[18]

New Finds

Spurred by the high oil prices of the 1970s, which required oil-importing nations to divert huge sums of foreign exchange to pay for their oil imports, many governments opened their countries to oil exploration by foreign firms. In just a few years, new oil finds were made in the Middle East, Africa, Asia, and Latin America. Nations that are either approaching self-sufficiency in oil or have even begun to export it include Egypt, Syria, Oman, Tunisia, Malaysia, Zaire, Angola, Congo, Benin, Cameroon, India, Australia, Argentina, Peru, Brazil, and Colombia.[19] Colombia became an oil exporter in 1986, after Occidental Petroleum discovered a new field with a billion barrels of petroleum, (the amount may reach 2 billion barrels as exploration continues). In 1984, when the field was discovered, oil imports cost Colombia $500 million. Government officials estimate that by 1990 Colombia will earn nearly $2 billion annually from oil exports. Another nation, Pakistan, may join the oil-exporting nations in three or four years. Its oil production already meets one third of its daily needs, and new discoveries are causing its Oil and Gas Development Corporation to claim that it has billions of barrels of untapped reserves.[20] The increased oil production that has been supplanting OPEC imports has caused OPEC's members to lose revenue in two ways: (1) world oil prices have been driven down; and (2) some OPEC nations have reduced their output to try to avoid price erosion.

How has this affected companies that depended heavily on OPEC members for sales in the 1970s? Because they have been obtaining less revenue from their oil sales, OPEC members have had to reduce their purchases. However, firms that keep abreast of this shift in crude oil production are able to compensate somewhat for their loss in sales to OPEC members by opening new markets in the non-OPEC nations that discover oil.

Nonfuel Minerals

Although much of the world's attention has centered on the discovery of new energy sources, Table 7-1 shows that there are also other mineral resources about which governments and industry are apprehensive. Nearly all of the world's chrome, manganese, platinum, and vanadium are produced by South Africa and the Soviet Union. Chrome and manganese are indispensable for hardening steel; platinum is a vital catalytic agent in the oil-refining process and is used in automotive catalytic converters; and vanadium is an ingredient in a steel alloy for metal-cutting tools. From 1980 to 1983, the United States depended on South Africa to supply 49 percent of its platinum, 55 percent of its chromium, 39 percent of its manganese, and 44 percent of its vanadium. Although South Africa has never threatened to stop the export of these strategic metals, government and industry leaders are well aware that should the South African source be lost, the major industrial societies in the West would be heavily dependent on the Soviet Union for their supply, both in wartime and peacetime.

Table 7-1

Major World Sources of Industrial Minerals

Mineral	Distribution of Reserves (percent of world total)	Resources*	Reserves†	Ratio of Reserves to 1983 Demand (years)‡
		(million metric tons)		
Aluminum	Guinea (27), Australia (21), Brazil (11), Jamaica (9), India (5)	48,000	21,000§	268
Chromium	South Africa (78), USSR (12), Zimbabwe (2), Finland (2), Philippines (1)	39,400	290	97
Cobalt	Zaire (38), Cuba (29), Zambia (10), New Caledonia (6), Indonesia (5)	11	3.6	182
Columbium	Brazil (79), USSR (17), Canada (3), Nigeria (2), Zaire (1)	17	4	428
Copper	Chile (23), U.S. (17), Zambia (9), Zaire (8), Mexico (5)	2,087‖	340	42

Table 7-1
(concluded)

Mineral	Distribution of Reserves (percent of world total)	Resources*	Reserves†	Ratio of Reserves to 1983 Demand (years)‡
		(million metric tons)		
Gold	South Africa (59), USSR (16), U.S. (6), Canada (3), Brazil (2)	0.075	0.04	39
Iron	USSR (35), Brazil (15), Australia (14), India (7), Canada (6)	89,000	65,300	154
Lead	U.S. (22), Australia (17), USSR (13), Canada (13), South Africa (4)	1,400	95	32
Manganese	South Africa (41), USSR (36), Gabon (11), Australia (8), Brazil (2)	4,000 +	907	114
Nickel	Cuba (34), Canada (14), USSR (13), Indonesia (7), South Africa (5)	130	53	77
Platinum	South Africa (79), USSR (20)	0.10	0.03	167
Silver	USSR (16), Canada (15), Mexico (14), U.S. (12), Australia (10)	0.78	0.24	33
Tantalum	Thailand (27), USSR (17), Australia (17), Nigeria (12)	0.30	0.03	30
Titanium	Brazil (20), South Africa (14), India (12), Norway (14), Australia (9)	700	170	102
Vanadium	USSR (60), South Africa (20), China (14), U.S. (4)	64	4	150
Zinc	Canada (15), U.S. (13), Australia (11), South Africa (6), USSR (6)	1,800	170	28

*Resources are those supplies whose location, grade, quality, and quantity are known or are estimated from geologic evidence, including economic, marginally economic, and subeconomic components.
†Reserves are the portion of resources that can be economically extracted or produced at the time of determination.
‡For example, aluminum will last 268 years if consumed at the 1983 rate.
§Bauxite; multiply by 0.212 to convert to aluminum.
‖Includes seabed deposits.
Source: *World Almanac* (New York: Newspaper Enterprise Association, 1986), p. 121.

Bleak Situation?

The situation appears bleak, but remember that we are discussing *known reserves*. Do other sources exist? Consider this. Only relatively small areas, mostly in the traditional mining countries, have been adequately explored. For example, it is estimated that only 5 percent of the potential mineral-containing areas in Mexico and only 10 percent of those in Bolivia have been studied extensively.

Furthermore, a relatively new technology, satellite mapping, has enabled geologists to locate new sources. They row know that Brazil, for example, possesses extensive deposits of chrome, nickel, copper, lead, zinc, and manganese.

Seabed Mining—An Untapped Source

The existence of metal deposits on the ocean floor was discovered in 1876, when a British explorer found a number of small, metal-containing nodules. Little attention was paid to them until the 1960s, when tests showed that these nodules were present in practically every sea and in some lakes, such as Lake Michigan. However, the nodules richest in metallic content are nearly all located on the ocean floor, at depths of from 3 to 5 miles. Although geologists are not sure how they are formed, they do know where they are most numerous and what their metallic content is. Analysis shows that all of the nodules contain some 30 metals but have an extremely high copper, nickel, manganese, and cobalt content. This last metal, all of which is now imported in the United States, is especially important, as it is widely used in military and vital civilian technologies. For example, 900 pounds of cobalt are needed to produce just one engine for the F16 fighter plane.[21] Table 7–2 compares the metal content of seabed sources with that of land sources.

Metal deposits are also found in the crust of chimneylike structures up to 100 feet in height that were formed when hot water rushed up from active volcano vents in the sea floor. The polymetallic deposits contain significant quantities of cobalt, manganese, nickel, and other metals.

Table 7–2
Average Metal Content (percent)

	Copper	Cobalt	Nickel	Manganese
North Pacific	1.16	0.23	1.28	24.6
North Atlantic	0.15	0.34	0.30	14.2
South Atlantic	0.15	0.31	0.48	18.0
Indian Ocean	0.19	0.28	0.50	14.7
Continental reserves				
Minimum	0.50	0.07	0.40	40.0
Maximum	0.50	0.10	1.00	50.0

Source: "In Search of Metals on the Seabed," *Kredietbank Weekly Bulletin* (Brussels), June 13, 1980, p.1.

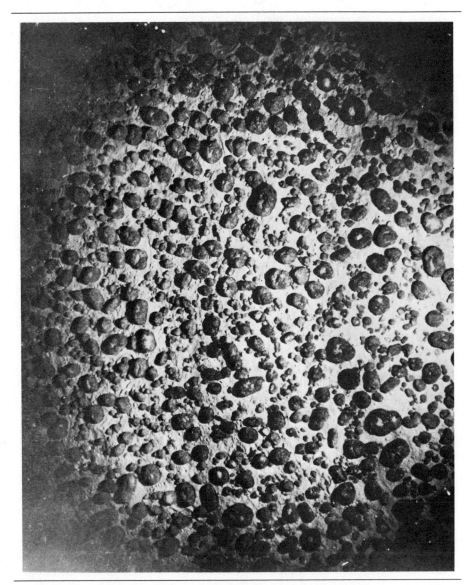

Potato-sized manganese nodules on the sea floor of the Central Pacific

Since 1974, 140 nations have been negotiating an agreement to put seabed mining under the control of the International Seabed Authority, a UN affiliate. In July 1982, the United States announced that it would not sign the Law of the Sea Convention because it objected to the seabed mining provisions. Instead, President Reagan proclaimed a U.S. Exclusive Economic Zone, which extends the jurisdiction of the United States to include all mineral resources within 200 nautical miles of the U.S. coast and the coast of U.S. island territories. Six international consortia, which include American companies, have already spent millions of dollars perfecting technologies to mine the seabed nodules. However, the combination of low mineral prices and the uncertainty of mining rights have kept the firms from proceeding on a commercial scale.

Changes Make Monitoring Necessary

Mineral Resources

You saw how crude oil prices spurred the discovery of oil by non-OPEC members as they sought to lessen their dependence on imported oil. New land-based sources of strategic nonfuel minerals have also been discovered, and we have learned that the seabeds contain vast amounts of these minerals in the form of nodules and seafloor crusts.

Concomitantly, important discoveries are being made that could lessen our need for these minerals. For example, in 1984 the U.S. Air Force in conjunction with Pratt and Whitney announced the development of two new *cobalt-free* superalloys for possible application in a new generation of fighter jet engines.[22] Probably the most fascinating discovery of all is a solar-powered technique to produce hydrogen from *water*. Instead of using gasoline for fuel, aircraft and automobiles might use hydrogen. Already, Lockheed is working on a NASA-sponsored study of a hydrogen-fueled airplane and engineering students from South Africa have built the first car to run on hydrogen fed into a conventional gasoline engine.[23]

What is the significance to businesspeople of these new discoveries? Obviously, sellers of commodities and products that are being threatened by the discoveries must monitor them and prepare for new competition. More important, *all* firms supplying goods and services to nations that depend on the traditional minerals for foreign exchange to pay for those goods and services must be aware of developments that can destroy old markets and create new ones. Imagine the loss of purchasing power in the Middle Eastern countries if lower-cost hydrogen available from water takes the place of gasoline! We have already seen the cutbacks in the purchases of these countries because of lower crude oil prices, but what if petroleum were needed only by the petrochemical industry and not for transportation?

Other Changing Physical Forces

Mineral resources are not the only physical forces that change. Modifications of infrastructure, most of which are of great significance to businesspeople, are being made constantly. For example, new settlements and new industries are attracted to areas in which dams have been built to control flooding, and provide power and irrigation water. New highways and new railways reduce delivery

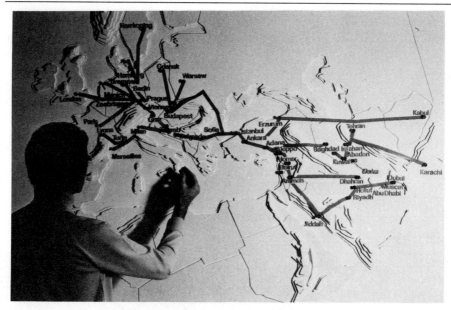

Courtesy of *Aramco World Magazine*

times to present markets and thus enable firms to cut their distribution costs by reducing their inventories.

In 1964, two Englishmen left London for Kabul, Afghanistan, in a tractor-trailer loaded with Linotype letterpresses. They had convinced their customer that direct door-to-door delivery was better than the usual method of sending freight to Afghanistan: a ship to Karachi; a train to Peshawar, and a truck to Kabul. Twenty-five days later, they delivered their merchandise to the delighted importer, who told them that the delivery would have taken at least three months over the normal route and that there would have been cargo damage because of the frequent rehandling. This was the beginning of a new business that increased dramatically in the 1970s, when the volume of exports was too great for port facilities to handle. The port congestion was so great that ships were waiting up to 120 days to unload cargo. Road improvements continue to be made, and it is now possible to go from London to Saudi Arabia (5,600 miles) in 17 to 21 days. One of the fastest deliveries to the Middle East was made when a construction company in Qatar urgently needed some heavy equipment. A Volvo tractor-trailer hauled 12 pieces of machinery, each of which was 8 feet high and 4 feet wide, from Sweden to Qatar (4,800 miles) in just nine days. Had the machinery gone by ship, the delivery would have taken a month or more.[24]

Those of us who live where there are various alternative routes to reach an area cannot comprehend the power of a newly completed all-weather highway to bring life to a heretofore inaccessible region

Until recently, the Chaco, which comprises 60 percent of Paraguay's land area, was virtually deserted due to a lack of roads to connect it with the eastern part of the country, where Asuncion, the capital, and the main consumption centers are located. Completion of the Trans-Chaco Highway has enabled an increasing volume of Chaco-grown products to reach these centers, to which farmers and cattlemen are traveling to spend their new incomes on modern machinery and equipment. The government plans to settle thousands of farm families from eastern Paraguay along this new roadway.

Even without government intervention, settlements follow new road construction. For example, the Brasilia-Belem highway, although only a few years old, already has 38 cities with over 2 million people along its length.

Figure 7-10

Courtesy of Inter-American Development Bank

The Trans-Andean Highway

Contamination of Resources

Historically, nations have paid relatively little attention to the contamination and destruction of the world's natural resources. Entire forests have been destroyed by people wanting to get firewood or to clear land and by contaminated air and water. Pollution control of air and water was considered a luxury that governments, anxious to attract new industry and to keep the industry they had, could ill afford to impose. As the secretary of mines and energy for the state of Bahia, Brazil, stated, "Brazil can't afford pollution control like Japan or the U.S. It's cultural imperialism."[25]

However, such tragedies as the Bhopal disaster and the horrendous Sandoz spill into the Rhine have forced officials to realize that the price for such negligence is too high.

The Bhopal Disaster

What is described as the world's worst man-made industrial disaster killed some 2,800 people and injured another 270,000. On December 3, 1984, the deadly gas methyl isocyanate, used in the production of pesticides, leaked from storage tanks at the Bhopal plant of Union Carbide (India), a joint venture of Union Carbide (50.9 percent) and Indian capital. Since the leak, Union Carbide–U.S. has provided $20 million, including relief, severance pay for workers fired when the Bhopal plant was closed, and funds for treatment and job-training centers. In the summer of 1985, Union Carbide reportedly offered to pay out $300 million over 30 years, but India, attempting to hold the company to American compensation standards, rejected the offer. A key issue—whether the more than 100 lawsuits seeking billions of dollars from Union Carbide should be tried in American or Indian courts—was decided by an American court which ruled that the case should be heard in India. Union Carbide then agreed to pay $500 million in compensation to survivors.[26]

The Rhine Spill

On November 1, 1986, a fire broke out in the Sandoz warehouse in Basel, Switzerland, where pesticides were stored. The building had neither automatic alarms nor a sprinkler system. By the time fire brigades arrived, the fire had spread throughout the building. The drainage system could not handle all of the water that was pumped into the flames, and soon chemicals mixed with water flowed into the Rhine nearby.

No one was harmed, and it was not until two days later that the first dead fish appeared. Soon, cities on the river turned off their river supplies of drinking water and closed floodgates to protect tributaries from contamination. In one part of the Upper Rhine, between Karlsruhe and Basel, almost every creature died. Experts claimed that a 120-mile section from Basel to Dusseldorf would be biologically dead for at least two years.

Days later there was yet another spill when a containment system broke, allowing the equivalent of two tons of mercury to enter the river. Then Ciba-Geigy, Switzerland's largest chemical manufacturer, announced that on October 31 more than 100 gallons of herbicide had leaked into the river.

Sandoz said that it would accept claims for which it was liable by law, but governments, individuals and businesses in five countries will try to make Sandoz, Ciba-Geigy, and the Swiss government pay for the damages they inflicted. Critics were comparing the Swiss government's 24-hour delay in advising other governments to the Russian delay in informing the West about the Chernobyl disaster.[27]

Consequences for Multinationals

These and other accidents, such as the Seveso disaster in Italy, are raising questions about the operating practices of multinational firms and about the adequacy of environmental legislation in many countries. Even before the Rhine spill, this river had become one of the most polluted waterways in the world, but the Sandoz accident has moved West European governments to strengthen their laws, controls, and inspection.

Multinationals in hazardous industries will resist the minority positions in joint ventures mandated by numerous governments when such positions cause them to lose control to the local majority on questions of equipment, plant safety, and environmental controls. An international law specialist claims that if the Bhopal litigation removes the protection that multinationals now have from the liabilities of their foreign subsidiaries, "it would be a major obstacle to international trade and investment as we know it.[28]

SUMMARY

The importance of a good knowledge of geography has perhaps not been given the emphasis it deserves. Because of the changes that have occurred, what was learned in grammar school geography will not suffice today. Businesspeople should be familiar with the locations of countries, their significant landforms, and their climates. These elements of the physical forces exert a powerful influence on the cultural and political forces. Mountain ranges, deserts, and tropical forests act as barriers to the movement of people, goods, and ideas, whereas bodies of water facilitate such movements.

Businesspeople must not be misled into believing that because the major industrialized nations are located in temperate climates, it follows that natives of the tropics are inherently inferior. It is parasitic diseases and poor nutrition that are responsible for their lower productivity.

Because of the rapid depletion of the known sources of natural resources, firms dependent on them for production have been forced to search for new supplies in previously unexplored regions. New discoveries are important to all firms, however, because they frequently create new markets. If substitutes are found that will decrease the need for a natural resource, a number of currently strong markets may diminish in importance.

Industrial accidents such as the Bhopal disaster and the Rhine River spill have caused both the industrialized and the developing nations to be more concerned about the protection of national resources. Multinational firms are being questioned about their operating practices worldwide. They, in turn, are examining their foreign involvements to see which of them would be extremely risky if the Bhopal litigation in the United States removes the protection from the liabilities of foreign subsidiaries that they now have.

Questions

1. *Go to the chalkboard and draw a map of South America. How many countries can you locate? Do you know their capitals?*
2. *Of the 25 nations listed by the United Nations as the least developed among the developed nations, 14 are landlocked. Is this a coincidence, or is the lack of a seacoast a contributing factor to their slower development?*
3. *Analyze the potential of oil shale and oil sands as future energy sources. What problems are involved in using these natural resources?*
4. *Assume that you are a member of your company's long-range planning committee. You have heard that experiments have been successful in separating hydrogen from water and that the hydrogen is then combined with carbon to form hydrocarbons. It is said that the product may cost 20 percent less than crude oil obtained from wells. Discuss with your colleagues how this development may affect your marketing plans in the Middle East and in the oil-poor developing countries.*
5. *The manager of your Chilean manufacturing subsidiary in Antofagasta reports that it is now possible to ship goods by train from Antofagasta to São Paulo, Brazil, via Santa Cruz, Bolivia, in about seven days. Check a map of South America, and speculate on what this means in terms of new business for the subsidiary.*
6. *The director of personnel in your firm's home office tells you, the plant manager home on leave from the Indonesian subsidiary, "The only reason we have an infirmary in our American plants is to take care of workers injured on the job. Why do you want to staff our infirmary in Indonesia with nutritionists and experts in parasitic diseases?" How would you answer that?*
7. *Your firm is planning to enter the markets in northern South America with electric motors. The vice president of marketing, who has had no experience in selling to this region, announces, "Our inventory requirements will be simple. Since the climate is moist and humid in these countries, we'll have*

to supply the higher-priced models that we market along the U.S. Gulf Coast and we can forget about the less expensive motors we sell up North. Fortunately, our competitors will have to do the same thing because of the climate, so we won't have to worry much about price competition." You are the export manager. What is your reaction?

8. *Explain how the physical forces of a country influence its sociocultural forces.*

9. *International businesspeople, unless they are in the business of refining minerals or petroleum, have no need to concern themselves with world developments in natural resources. True or false? Explain.*

10. *There are many critics of the U.S. policy of friendship with South Africa. Do you believe that the physical forces influence our policy? (Hint: Analyze Table 7–1, and check South Africa's location on a world map.)*

11. *What will be the consequences for multinational firms of such disasters as the Rhine spill and the Bhopal accident?*

Reading

Kleines Walsertal*

Far removed in language and culture from Gurro, but still in the mountain paradise class, is Kleines Walsertal, the most eccentric valley in all Europe. This one is in Austria. Or is it? **Legally, Kleines Walsertal is part of Austria, but you cannot enter it from there, since the region is shut off from the homeland by a U-shaped headwall of impenetrable mountains.** *Thus, you have to make a round-the-mulberry-bush trip into West Germany and enter through the town of Oberstdorf.*

The valley is also easily accessible from the shore of Lake Constance in Germany and from Munich, about 100 miles to the southwest. Visitors (mostly skiers) are welcome in Walsertal's three villages—Riezlern, Hirschegg, and Mittelberg-Baad—and can easily find lodgings in a farmhouse for as little as $1.50 a day (German marks, please!).

Surprisingly enough, in Kleines Walsertal Austrian goods are subject to import duties, while German goods move in free. Yet the people who live there are ruled by Austrian laws, vote in Austrian elections, and pay Austrian taxes. **They are, moreover, of Swiss origin, but the language they speak is virtually incomprehensible to the Swiss and resembles neither Austrian nor German.** *And add to these curiosities the fact that the postal trucks serving the valley are German, but the stamps on the letters are Austrian, payable in German marks! This comic opera situation is a puzzler to most visitors, but not to the Austrians. Wryly, they refer to it as "Austria's only colony," and when they pay a call there, they realize, to their chagrin, that Austrian shillings are not accepted. Though this is still Austrian soil, Ger-*

*Permission to reprint granted by *Travel Magazine, Inc.*, Floral Park, NY 11001.

Reading
Kleines Walsertal* (concluded)

man marks are the only legal tender. And pleas from Austrian authorities to Walsertal's 4,000 inhabitants to accept the motherland's money have gone unheeded. The Walsertalians prefer to trade with German money, since it has "always been done that way—so why bother changing over and complicating things even more?"

Most of these curious circumstances and the resulting split personality of the valley have come about as a result of an agreement concluded in 1891 by German and Austrian statesmen. Because the valley could only be entered via Germany, one of the things decided was that German customs officers should have the responsibility of controlling the frontier. But across the border, law and order are maintained by the Austrians.

To put an end to this land without a country, Austrian authorities are now considering building a road so that the 38 square miles of isolated never-never land can be tied umbilically to the homeland. Just recently, an antenna was installed on a nearby peak, and for the first time the inhabitants can watch Austrian television. Pleased with the new TV setup, the proud people who have been living here for centuries nevertheless say they do not want a new state highway leading to the other side of the mountain.

Undersea Ore Find in Pacific OceanSaid to Be Worth Millions

Scientists of the National Oceanic and Atmospheric Administration (NOAA) have discovered an immense undersea ore deposit worth billions of dollars in the eastern Pacific about 350 miles west of Ecuador. The rich lodes can be easily mined because they are on the surface around old volcanic vents. Although they are 8,500 feet below the ocean surface, the technology to get them already exists. Because of the depth and coldness, there is no life and no current. The area could be mined with virtually no damaging ecological effects. Using a deep-diving submersible, the scientists found a wide band of metallic sulfide deposits almost three fourths of a mile long. The ore body is 650 feet wide and 130 feet thick and is estimated to weigh 25 million tons.

The deposit is approximately 10 percent copper, worth $2 billion, and 10 percent iron. Other minerals include molybdenum, vanadium, zinc, cadmium, tin, and lead. The richness of the copper deposit (10 times that found in land mines) illustrates how the hot water shooting from the volcanic vents for 1,000 years has concentrated the minerals.

Similar volcanic areas have been found off the coast of Mexico and the coasts of Washington and Oregon.

Source: "Undersea Ore Find in Eastern Pacific Said Worth Billions," *Mobile Press-Register*, October 7, 1981, p. 5A.

Minicase

7-1 Planning for Mineral Shortages*

The long-range planning committee of the James Metal Products Company is meeting to discuss the firm's dependence on imported raw minerals.
The president, John Ashe, speaks:

Ashe: Gentlemen, as you know, we are here to discuss what we can do to protect ourselves in case of a mineral shortage. You all remember that when rebel soldiers invaded Zaire, the price of cobalt shot up from $12 to $100 per kilo. No one knew how long supplies would be interrupted, and so everyone bid up the stocks that were available. We need a plan to reduce our vulnerability in the event of other shortages.

Stan Williams, the technical manager: John, wasn't the Zaire affair an oddity? That won't happen again, will it?

Ashe: Well, Stan, the experts foresee the increasing use of strategic materials as political weapons to reach social, economic, or even ideological objectives. Don't forget that some 20 countries control the most important materials and that the top three producers often account for 50–90 percent of worldwide production.

Don Olsen, executive vice president: Furthermore, Stan, the situation for some minerals is extremely delicate because most of these producers are Third World countries that have little domestic use for the materials they produce.

Roy Jackson, the production manager: Can someone tell me exactly what minerals we are talking about? I know what we use, but I don't know which ones are critical. Can you tell us, Pete?

Pete Jones, purchasing agent: I am in about the same position you are, Roy. I found out that cobalt was critical when the price suddenly skyrocketed, but we haven't experienced serious problems with the others. We have been able to get what we want in the open market.

Don Olsen: I read somewhere that the production of strategic materials in the Third World is often supervised by a single ministry or a state-owned company. That makes it pretty easy to use minerals as a bargaining tool for political favors or military support. You remember how some of the European governments acquiesced to political pressure from OPEC members during the oil shortage.

*Source: "How Dependent Are You on Strategic Minerals? Firms Should Take Stock," *Business International*, April 24, 1981, pp. 132–33; and "A Strategy for Coping with Mineral Shortages," *International Management*, April 1981, pp. 53–54.

Ashe: I don't believe, Don, that nonoil cartels are as threatening as OPEC has been, because there are more chances for substitution and recycling for minerals than there are for oil. Of course, if the African producers of chromium, nickel, or cobalt decided to join forces in a cartel, that could be serious.

Jackson: John, I can see some substitution possibilities. Just the other day, a design engineer told me that instead of making a part from stainless steel, he was going to use plain carbon steel and then give it a coat of paint to protect it.

Olsen: John, don't you think that it's up to governments to act to protect us against shortages? They can relax environmental laws and institute tax incentives to encourage domestic production. They might even extend the NATO concept to include protection of Japan, Brazil, Argentina, South Africa, Indonesia, and the Gulf states. They could have an international military force to occupy and operate important mineral fields when necessary. What I don't see is what we as a company can do.

Ashe: Don, we've already touched on four major areas where we can take action to make us less vulnerable to supply disruptions. Let's review them. What are the steps that James Metal Products can take?

Minicase

7-2 The Mendoca Disaster

The president of the Universal Chemical Company has just been awakened at his home by a telephone call from his general manager in Mendoca, Republic of Northern Africa. Very excited, and at times incoherent, the manager blurts out to the president that a leaky valve has permitted a deadly gas to escape into the atmosphere. It has already killed or injured dozens of slum dwellers living next to the factory, and the gas cloud is drifting toward Mendoca, which is 10 miles to the north. The company maintenance crew, fitted with masks and protective clothing, is trying to stop the leak. The plant has been shut down, and all the employees have been evacuated. The manager asks the president for help. The president tells him to follow through with what he has started and orders him to call the president's office day or night as often as is necessary to report new developments. He requests that the manager's phone be manned around the clock by members of the local management team.

1. What must the president do immediately?

2. What must he do in the immediate future?

Supplementary Readings

Bartels, Robert. *Comparative Marketing: Wholesaling in Fifteen Countries*. Homewood, Ill.: Richard D. Irwin, 1963.

Basta, S. S., and A. Churchill. "Iron Deficiency Anemia and the Productivity of Adult Males in Indonesia." Staff Working Paper no. 175. Washington, D.C.: World Bank, 1974.

"The Blotch on the Rhine." *Newsweek,* November 24, 1986, pp. 58–60.

Brewer, G. Daniel. "Hydrogen-Powered Aircraft." *ICAO Bulletin*, October 1980.

"The Economic Aspects of the Law of the Sea." *The Morgan Guaranty Survey* (New York: Morgan Guaranty Trust Company), February 1976.

Gladwin, Thomas M., and Ingo Walter. "Bhopal and the Multinational." *The Wall Street Journal,* January 16, 1985, p. 16.

"India's Bhopal Suit Could Change the Rules." *Business Week,* April 22, 1985, p. 38.

Kamarck, Andrew M. *The Tropics and Economic Development*. Washington, D.C.: World Bank, 1976.

Murphey, Rhoads. *An Introduction to Geography*. Skokie, Ill.: Rand McNally, 1966.

"Our Growing Dependence on Others for Key Resources." *U.S. News & World Report,* November 12, 1979.

"Polymetal Sulphides: More Riches from the Sea?" *DESI Facts 82/2.* (New York: United Nations), March 1982.

"The Road to the Sea Continues Full of Obstructions." *Comercio Exterior de Mexico* (Mexico City: Banco de Comercio Exterior), March 1977, pp. 87–94.

"Suddenly, a Deathwatch on the Rhine." *Business Week,* November 24, 1986, p. 52.

Endnotes

1. Robert Bartels, ed., *Comparative Marketing: Wholesaling in Fifteen Countries* (Homewood, Ill.: Richard D. Irwin, 1963), p. 4.

2. The mean annual temperature for Barranquilla and Cartagena is 82° F, while in Bogota, it is only 57° F.

3. A product with adequate cooling and lubrication for the Temperate Zone would function well in Bogota but might be woefully deficient in Barranquilla.

4. When a sales engineer from Madrid and one of the writers went to Barcelona, the Detroit of Spain, on a business trip, we were accompanied on our visits to customers by our salesman from Barcelona. Our meetings with customers always followed the same pattern. The Barcelona salesman would begin the meeting by telling the customer we were from Madrid and did not speak Catalan, the local language. The meeting would proceed in Spanish until either the customer or our local salesman, in searching for a word in Spanish, would use the more familiar (to him) in Catalan word. This would trigger the other to begin speaking in Catalan (completely unintelligible to anyone speaking only Spanish), and the sales engineer and the writer would be completely in the dark as to what was being discussed. After a moment, the local salesman and the customer would realize what they were doing and apologize. The discussions in Spanish would be resumed, and then the switch to Catalan would be repeated. If our local salesman had not been present to smooth over these lapses and provide the necessary empathy with the customer, these meetings would have been disastrous.

5. *Australia* (New York: Chemical Bank, 1972), p. 15.

6. Rhoads Murphey, *An Introduction to Geography* (Skokie, Ill.: Rand McNally, 1966), p. 128.

7. *The Netherlands* (New York: First National City Bank, 1979), p. 26; and Charles C. Colby, *North Atlantic Arena* (Carbondale: Southern Illinois University Press, 1966), pp. 12–32.

8. Joseph E. Van Riper, *Man's Physical World* (New York: McGraw-Hill, 1962), p. 525.

9. "News from Latin America," *Comercio Exterior de Mexico* (Mexico City: Banco di Comercio Exterior), March 1977, pp. 87–94.

10. Until 1866, Bolivia possessed a 160-mile coastline, but a treaty with Chile that year reduced it by 60 miles. As a result of a war in 1879, primarily between Bolivia and Chile, though Peru also intervened, Bolivia lost this coastline to Chile. Peru also lost 160 miles of coastline, but in 1929 it was able to regain 35 miles. Bolivia has been holding discussions with Chile ever since in an effort to obtain its outlet to the sea. In 1975, Chile proposed ceding a narrow strip to Bolivia but demanded what Bolivia considered excessive compensation. Peru offered an alternative solution in 1976, by which all three countries would share in the sovereignty of a port of northern Chile. Rumors were then strong that there might be an armed confrontation between Peru and Chile. This crisis passed without a serious incident and it looked as though Bolivia and Chile might reach an agreement as a result of a new Bolivian proposal made in 1987. However, the Chilean government rejected it.

    This dispute affects business transactions between the two countries. In 1968, one of the writers, representing a Chilean subsidiary of an American multinational firm, called on a large government-owned mine in Bolivia to sell Chilean-made products. The purchasing agent asked how anyone could expect her, a Bolivian, to buy goods made in Chile. She appreciated the fact that the parent company was American, but as she said, "the products are still made in Chile."

11. For an informative description of how Brazil, in the author's opinion, is using the construction of highways, railroads, and bridges to connect its borders with those of its neighbors for the purpose of bringing them under Brazil's political and economic influence, see "Brazil: Potencia Emergente" (Emerging Power), *Vision*, August 1, 1976. The author claims that the 3,000-mile-long Transamazon Highway, which starts at Recife and arrives at the Peruvian border, could provide a route all the way to Lima if the Peruvian government would only complete a short 100-mile stretch. For some reason, Peru seems reluctant to do so.

12. Murphey, *Introduction to Geography*, p. 72.

13. Andrew M. Kamarck, *The Tropics and Economic Development* (Washington, D.C.: World Bank, 1976), p. 5.

14. S. S. Basta and A. Churchill, "Iron Deficiency Anemia and the Productivity of Adult Males in Indonesia," Staff Working Paper no. 175 (Washington, D.C.: World Bank, 1974), p. 49.

15. Kamarck, *Tropics and Economic Development*, p. 60.

16. Ibid., pp. 90–91.

17. "Canadian Oil Boom Is Seen in Unwieldy Crude," *The Wall Street Journal*, December 30, 1985, p. 6.

18. *1985 Annual Report,* (Washington D.C.: U.S. Synthetic Fuels Corporation).

19. "Discovery in Colombia Points Up Big Change in World Oil Picture," *The Wall Street Journal*, May 13, 1985, p. 1.

20. "Exploring for Oil in Pakistan," *U.S. News & World Report*, July 15, 1985, p. 48.

21. "Ocean Mining: Boom or Bust?" *Technology Review*, April 1984, pp. 55–56.

22. William S. Kirk, "Cobalt," *Minerals Handbook*, vol. 1, (Washington, D.C.: U.S. Department of the Interior, 1985), pp. 269–77.

23. The engine output is altered by varying the amount of hydrogen, not the air, as in a conventional carburetor. From "Students Develop Unique Gas Car," *SA Digest*, April 27, 1984, p. 10. Mitsubishi, working with the Japanese government, is also trying to develop a hydrogen-powered car.

24. "The Long Route East," *Aramco World Magazine*, November–December, 1977.

25. "The War on Pollution Spreads Worldwide," *Business Week*, September 27, 1986, pp. 82–83.

26. "Bhopal Settlement Reported," *Modesto Bee*, November 17, 1987, p. 1.

27. "The Blotch on the Rhine" *Newsweek*, November 24, 1986, pp. 58–60; and "Suddenly, a Deathwatch on the Rhine," *Business Week*, November 24, 1986, p. 52.

28. "India's Bhopal Suit Could Change the Rules," *Business Week*, April 22, 1985, p. 38; and Thomas M. Gladwin and Ingo Walter, "Bhopal and the Multinational," *The Wall Street Journal*, January 16, 1985, p. 16.

CHAPTER 8

SOCIOCULTURAL FORCES

"**O**ur culture is our routine of sleeping, bathing, dressing, eating, and getting to work. It is our household chores and actions we perform on the job, the way we buy goods and services. . . . It is the way we greet friends or address a stranger . . . and even to a large extent what we consider right or wrong."[1]

Ina C. Brown, professor of anthropology,
Scarritt College

Learning Objectives

After you study this chapter, you should know:

1. That there are significant differences among cultures.
2. That cultural differences exert a pervasive influence on all business functions.
3. The major sociocultural components: *(a)* aesthetics, *(b)* attitudes and beliefs, *(c)* religion, *(d)* material culture, *(e)* education, *(f)* language, *(g)* societal organization, *(h)* legal characteristics, *(i)* political structure.
4. The manner in which these components affect business relationships.

Key Words and Concepts

Protestant ethic
Caste system
Islam
Animism
Triangle of domination
Brain drain
Kinship
Extended family
Technological dualism
Unspoken language
Lingua franca

Business Incident

The Marlboro man. Jut-jawed and grizzled, he tirelessly rides the plain or pauses contemplatively atop his steed to survey the terrain. It sells a lot of cigarettes.

In the United States, that is. In Hong Kong, it bombed. Or didn't do well enough to satisfy Philip Morris, Inc., the manufacturer. It turned out that the Hong Kong Chinese, an increasingly affluent and a totally urban people, didn't see the charm of riding around alone in the hot sun all day.

Philip Morris swiftly threw together a Hong Kong–style Marlboro man. He is still a cowboy and satisfactorily virile, but younger than the American version and better dressed. He owns a truck as well as a horse. And the ads suggest that he, unlike his American counterpart, owns a piece of Marlboro country.

It does the job. "Marlboro's running faster than any of us," laments a competitor here.

This community, with almost 5 million people, fast is becoming one of the more attractive markets in Asia. In the past 18 months, some half a dozen big, international ad agencies have opened offices here or linked up with local agencies—mindful, among other things, that Hong Kong sits on the doorstep of the potentially vast China market.

Often enough, the approach that works elsewhere works here. Ronald McDonald, the hamburger clown, looks about the same in Hong Kong as he does in Illinois. So does that bull that is the worldwide trademark for Merrill Lynch, Pierce, Fenner & Smith. But most advertisers coming here must tailor their campaigns to suit local customs, superstitions, and tastes—or risk a fiasco.

For instance, an American cleansing product manufacturer worked up some commercials that showed people tossing hats around in jest. One had a green hat landing on a male model's head. And that was the end of that creative strategy; it was pointed out to the advertiser that among Chinese a green hat signifies that the male in question is a cuckold. The commercial was dropped.

Similarly, the Singer Company, maker of sewing machines, proposed an outdoor ad campaign using bright Prussian blue. Singer's local distributor hastily pointed out that blue of that particular shade is known here as the death color. That campaign was halted, too. On the other hand, red and gold represent just about everything good to Hong Kong Chinese, and products packaged in those colors have an immediate edge.

"Be Sure Not to Wear a White Hat if You Visit Hong Kong." Reprinted with permission from *The Wall Street Journal*, April 10, 1979 © Dow Jones & Company, Inc., 1979. All rights reserved.

*A*s the business incident indicates, one of the difficulties businesspeople face when they cross national borders is the necessity to work in societies and cultures that are different from their own. The problems they encounter in dealing with a single culture and language in their own country are multiplied by the number of cultures and subcultures they find in each of their foreign markets. No matter whether they are in marketing, finance, production, or personnel management, the more sensitive they are to the attitudes, feelings, and opinions of others, the more competent they will be.

All too often, unfortunately, people who are familiar with only one cultural pattern may believe that they have an awareness of cultural differences elsewhere, when in reality they do not. Unless they have had occasion to make comparisons with other cultures, they are probably not even aware of the important features of their own. They are probably also oblivious to the fact that each society considers its culture superior to all others (ethnocentricity) and that their attempts to introduce the "German way" or the "American way" may be met with stubborn resistance.

How do international businesspeople learn to live with other cultures? The first step is a realization that there are cultures different from their own. Then they must go on to learn the characteristics of those cultures so that they may adapt to them. E. T. Hall, a famous anthropologist, claims that this can be accomplished in only two ways: (1) spend a lifetime in a country, or (2) undergo an extensive, highly sophisticated training program that covers the main characteristics of culture, including the language. The program he mentions is more than an area orientation in which participants are briefed on a country's customs. What Hall refers to is a study of what culture is and what it does and the acquisition of some knowledge of the various ways in which human behavior has been institutionalized.[2]

What Is Culture?

Although there are as many definitions of culture as there are anthropologists, most anthropologists view culture as being the *sum total of the beliefs, rules, techniques, institutions, and artifacts that characterize human populations.*[3] In other words, culture consists of the learned patterns of behavior common to members of a given society—the unique lifestyle of a particular group of people.[4] Most anthropologists also agree that (1) culture is *learned,* not innate, (2) the various aspects of culture are *interrelated,* (3) culture is *shared,* and (4) culture *defines the boundaries* of different groups.[5]

Because society is composed of people and their culture, it is virtually impossible to speak of one without relating to the other. Anthropologists often use the terms interchangeably or combine them into one word—*sociocultural.*[6] This is the term we shall use, because the variables in which businesspeople are interested are both social and cultural.

Significance of Culture for
International Business

The study of foreign cultures is of primary importance to those engaged in international business because cultural differences exert a pervasive influence on all of the business functions. In marketing, for example, the wide variation in attitudes and values prevents many firms from using the same promotional appeals in all markets.

> Renault created a fun car image for its Renault 5 in France, which was shown in advertisements with eyes in the headlights and a mouth in the bumper talking to the reader. This humorous image was not deemed suitable in Germany, where the purchase of an automobile is viewed as a serious undertaking. There, the car's safety features and modern engineering were emphasized. In Italy, where drivers are concerned with road performance, acceleration and road-handling ability were stressed.[7]

Differences among these cultures required dissimilar promotional approaches.

Personnel problems can result from differences in attitudes toward authority, another sociocultural variable. Latin Americans have traditionally regarded the manager as the *patron* (master), an authoritarian figure responsible for their welfare. When American managers, accustomed to a participative leadership style are transferred to Latin America, they must become more authoritarian, or their employees will consider them weak and incompetent and they will encounter serious difficulties in having their orders carried out.

> A production manager who had been sent to Peru from the United States was convinced that he could motivate the workers to higher productivity by instituting a more democratic decision-making style. He brought in trainers from the home office to teach the supervisors how to solicit suggestions and feedback from the workers.
>
> Shortly after the new management style was introduced, the workers began quitting their jobs. When asked why, they replied that the new production manager and his supervisors apparently didn't know what to do and were therefore asking the workers for advice. Obviously, the company wouldn't last long with that kind of management, and they wanted to quit before the collapse, because then everyone would be hunting for a job at the same time.

Production managers have found that attitudes toward change can seriously influence the acceptance of new production methods, and even treasurers come to realize the strength of the sociocultural forces when, armed with excellent balance sheets, they approach local banks, only to find that the banks attach far more importance to who they are than to how strong their companies are.[8] These are just a few examples to show that sociocultural differences do affect all of the business functions. As we examine the components of the sociocultural forces, we shall mention others.

Figure 8-1

Courtesy of Regie Nationale des Usines Renault

In France, it's the supercar.

Sociocultural Components

From the foregoing, it should be apparent that to be successful in their relationships with people in other countries, international businesspeople must be students of culture. They must have factual knowledge, which is relatively easy to obtain, but they must also become sensitive to cultural differences, and this is more difficult. Hall, as we saw, recommended spending a lifetime in a country or, in lieu of this, undergoing an extensive program to study what the culture is and what it does. But most newcomers to international business do not even have the opportunity for area orientation. They can, however, take the important first step of realizing that there are other cultures. In this short chapter, we cannot do more than point out some of the important sociocultural differences as they concern businesspeople, in the hope that the readers will become more aware of the need to be culturally sensitive—to know that there are cultural differences for which they must be on the lookout.

The concept of culture is so broad that even the ethnologists (cultural anthropologists) have to break it down into topics to facilitate its study. A listing of such topics will give us a better understanding of what culture is and may also

Figure 8-2

il viaggio
è lungo

Renault 5
è comoda.

RENAULT

Renault 5 la 'cittadina del mondo.

. . . but in Italy, it's the citizen of the world.

serve as a guide to the international manager when he or she is analyzing a particular problem from the sociocultural viewpoint.

As you can imagine, experts vary considerably as to the components of culture, but the following list is representative of their thinking and of manageable length: (1) aesthetics, (2) attitudes and beliefs, (3) religion, (4) material culture, (5) education, (6) language, (7) societal organization, (8) legal characteristics, and (9) political structures.[9] We shall examine the first seven components in this chapter and leave the legal characteristics and political structures for later chapters.

Aesthetics

Aesthetics pertains to a culture's sense of beauty and good taste and is expressed in the arts, drama, music, folklore, and dances.

Art

Of particular interest to international businesspeople are the formal aspects of art, color, and form, because of the symbolic meanings they convey. Colors, especially, can be deceptive because they mean different things to different cultures. The color of mourning is black in the United States, white in the Far East.[10] Green is a restful color to us, but it is repugnant to people in Asian countries, where it connotes the illness and death of the jungle. While in the United States mints are packaged in blue or green paper, in Africa the wrapper is red. These examples illustrate that marketers must be careful to check if colors have any special meanings before using them for products, packages, or advertisements.

Be careful of symbols too. Seven signifies good luck in the United States but just the opposite in Singapore, Ghana, and Kenya. In Japan, the number 4 is unlucky. In general, the marketer should avoid using a nation's flag or any symbols connected with religion.[11]

It is also important to learn whether there are local aesthetic preferences for form that could affect the design of the product, the package, or even the building in which the firm is located. The American style of steel and glass in the midst of oriental architecture will be a constant reminder to the local population of the outsider's presence.

Music and Folklore

Musical commercials are generally popular worldwide, but the marketer must know what kind of music each market prefers, because tastes vary. Thus, the commercial that used a ballad in the United States might be better received to the tune of a bolero in Mexico or a samba in Brazil. However, if the advertiser is looking to the youth market with a product patently American, then American music will help reinforce its image.

Those who wish to steep themselves in a culture find it useful to study its folklore, which can disclose much about a society's way of life. However, this is usually more than the foreign businessperson has time for, though the incorrect use of folklore can sometimes cost the firm a share of the market. For example, associating a product with the cowboy would not obtain the same results in Chile or Argentina as it does in the United States, because in these countries the cowboy is a far less romantic figure—it's just a job. In another instance, a U.S. company may be paying handsome royalties to use American cartoon characters in its promotion, only to find they are considerably less important in foreign markets. In Mexico, songs of the "Singing Cricket" are known to all youngsters and their mothers, and a commercial tie-in with that character would be as advantageous to the firm as its use of Peanuts or Mickey Mouse. In many areas, especially where nationalistic feeling is strong, local firms have been able to compete successfully with foreign affiliates by making use of indigenous folklore in the form of slogans and proverbs. As Herskovits states, tales of folklore are valuable in maintaining a sense of group unity.[12] Knowing them is an indication that one belongs to the group, which recognizes that the outsider is unfamiliar with its folklore.

Attitudes and Beliefs

Every culture has a set of attitudes and beliefs that influence nearly all aspects of human behavior and help bring order to a society and its individuals. The more managers can learn about certain key attitudes, the better prepared they will be to understand why people behave as they do, especially when their reactions are different from those that the managers have learned to expect in dealing with their own people.

Among the wide variety of subjects covered by attitudes and beliefs, some are of prime importance to the businessperson. These include attitudes toward time, toward achievement and work, and toward change.

Attitudes toward Time

This cultural characteristic probably presents more adaptation problems for Americans overseas than any other. Time is important in the United States, and much emphasis is placed on it. If we must wait past the appointed hour to see an individual, we feel insulted. This person is not giving our meeting the importance it deserves. Yet the wait could mean just the opposite elsewhere. Latin American or Middle Eastern executives may be taking care of the minor details of their business so that they can attend their important visitor without interruption.

Mañana. Probably one of the most vexing problems for the newcomer to Latin America is the *mañana* attitude. Ask the maintenance man when the machine will be ready, and he responds *mañana*. The American assumes that this means "tomorrow," the literal translation, but the maintenance man means "some time in the near future," and if he is reprimanded for not having the machine ready the next day, he is angry and bewildered. He reasons that everyone knows *mañana* means "in the next few days." If Americans do not know it, they had better learn.

Americans, Be Prompt. Few cultures give the same importance to time that Americans and Europeans do. If any appointment is made with a group of Germans to see them at 12 noon, we can be sure they will be there, but to get the same response from a Brazilian, we must say noon English hour. If not, the Brazilian may show up anytime between noon and 2 o'clock. Since the American penchant for punctuality is well known in the Middle East, Americans are expected to arrive on time and lateness from Americans is considered impolite. The Arabian executives, however, will usually not arrive at the appointed hour. After all, why should they change their lifetime habits just for a stranger?[13]

Directness and Drive. The American pride in directness and drive is interpreted by many foreigners as being brash and rude. Although we believe it expedient to get to the point in a discussion, this attitude often irritates others. Time-honored formalities are a vital part of doing business, and any attempt to move the negotiations along by ignoring some of the accepted courtesies invites disaster.

Deadlines. Our emphasis on speed and deadlines is often used against us in business dealings abroad. In Far Eastern countries such as Japan, the American may be asked how long he or she plans to stay at the first meeting. Then negotiations are purposely not finalized until a few hours before the American's departure, when the Japanese know they can wring extra concessions from the foreigner because of his or her haste to finish and return home on schedule. Russian negotiators reportedly employ a similar strategy.[14]

Attitudes toward Achievement and Work

There is a saying in Mexico, "Americans live to work, but we work to live." This is an example of the extreme contrasts among cultures in their attitudes toward work. Where work is considered necessary to obtain the essentials for survival, once these have been obtained, people may stop working. They do not make the accomplishment of a task an end in itself. This attitude is in sharp contrast to the belief in many industrial societies that work is a moral, and even a religious, virtue.

To the consternation of the production manager with a huge back order, the promise of overtime often fails to keep the workers on the job. In fact, raising employees' salaries frequently results in their working less (economists call this effect the backward-bending labor supply curve).

It is important, however, to note that an attitudinal change has occurred repeatedly in many less developed countries as more consumer goods have become available. The *demonstration effect* (seeing others with these goods) and improvements in infrastructure (roads to bring the products to them and electric power to operate them) cause workers to realize they can have greater prestige and pleasure by owning more goods. Thus, their attitude toward work changes, not because of any alteration of their moral or religious values, but because they now want what only money can buy.

> A Mexican distributor came to one of the writers to complain that a number of his salesmen were producing well for the first week or two of the month but were then slacking off. Investigation showed that the commissions plus salary earned during the periods of high production were about the same each time. It was apparent that the salesmen had earned what they required to live so that they could loaf the rest of the month. By instituting contests and informing the salesmen's wives about the prizes to be won, considerable improvement was obtained.

In the industrialized nations, the opposite trend is being observed. There is a tendency toward longer vacations and shorter workweeks with greater emphasis on leisure activities. One-month vacations are now common in Europe.

Religion and Achievement. Researchers have found that there are differences among cultures with respect to achievement motivation, and attempts have been made to explain these differences on the basis of religion, as we will see in the next section. Although religion is not the only explanatory variable and may not be the principal explanatory variable, the correlation between the predominant religion and a nation's per capita income is too high to disregard altogether the influence of religion on past economic growth.[15]

Prestigious Jobs. Another aspect of the attitude toward work is the prestige associated with certain kinds of employment. In this country, some types of work are considered more prestigious than others, but there is nowhere near the disdain for physical labor here that there is in many less developed countries. The result is an overabundance of attorneys and economists and a lack of toolmakers and welders even when the wages are higher for the latter. The distinction between blue-collar workers and office employees is especially great, as typified by the use of two words in Spanish for worker—*obrero* (one who labors) signifies a blue-collar worker, whereas *empleado* (employee) signifies an office worker.[16]

Source of Recruits. The lesson to be learned from this discussion is that there are generally sharper differences in the attitudes toward work and achievement among other cultures than American managers find in their own culture. When these managers go abroad, their problem is to recruit subordinates with a need to progress, whatever the underlying motive. Many firms have been successful

Figure 8-3

Courtesy: McDonald's Corporation

The new idea

in locating such persons among relatively well-educated members of the lower social class who view work as a route to the prestige and social acceptance that have been denied them because of their birth.

Attitudes toward Change

The American firm, accustomed to the rapid acceptance by Americans of something new, is frequently surprised to find that new does not carry that kind of magic in markets where something tried and proven is preferred to the unknown. Europeans are fond of reminding Americans that they are a young nation lacking traditions. The near reverence for traditional methods makes it more difficult for the production manager to install a new process, for the marketer to introduce a new product, or for the treasurer to change the accounting system.

The New Idea. Yet, undeniably, international firms are agents of change, and their personnel must be able to counter resistance to it. The new idea will be more readily acceptable the closer it can be related to the traditional one while at the same time being made to show its relative advantage. In other words, the more consistent a new idea is with a society's attitudes and experiences, the more quickly it will be adopted.

Economic Motivation. In these times of worldwide inflation and rising expectations, economic motives can be a strong influence for accepting change. Thus, if factory workers can be shown that their income will increase with the new machine or housewives can be convinced that the new frozen food will enable them to work and still provide satisfactory meals for their families, they can be persuaded by the gain in their economic welfare to accept ideas that they would otherwise oppose.

Religion

Religion, an important component of culture, is responsible for many of the attitudes and beliefs affecting human behavior. A knowledge of the basic tenets of some of the more popular religions will contribute to a better understanding of why people's attitudes vary so greatly from country to country.

Protestant Ethic

We have already mentioned the marked differences in the attitudes toward work and achievement. Europeans and Americans generally view work as a moral virtue and look unfavorably on the idle. This view stems in part from the **Protestant work ethic** as expressed by Luther and Calvin, who believed it was the duty of Christians to glorify God by hard work and the practice of thrift.*

*In Asia, similar attitudes are being called the Confucian work ethic.

From *The Wall Street Journal*, with permission of Cartoon Features Syndicate.

"The Protestant work ethic isn't cutting it, so we're switching to Shinto."

Asian Religions

People from the Western world will encounter some very different notions about God, man and reality in Asian religions. In the Judeo-Christian tradition, this world is real and significant because it was created by God. Human beings are likewise significant, and so is time, because it began with God's creation and will end when his will has been fulfilled. Each human being has only one lifetime to heed God's word and achieve everlasting life.

In Asian religions, especially in the religions of India, the ideas of reality are different. There is a notion that this world is an illusion because nothing is permanent. Time is cyclical, so all living things, including humans, are in a constant process of birth, death, and reincarnation. The goal of salvation is to escape from the cycle and move into a state of eternal bliss (*nirvana*). The notion of *karma* (moral retribution) holds that evil committed in one lifetime will be punished in the next. Thus, *karma* is a powerful impetus to do good so as to achieve a higher spiritual status in the next life. Asians who hold these views cannot imagine that they have not had past lives when they may have been plants, animals, or human beings. Of the seven best-known religions that originated in Asia, four came from India (Hinduism, Buddhism, Jainism, and Sikhism), two from China (Confucianism and Taoism), and one from Japan (Shinto).[17]

Hinduism. This is a conglomeration of religions, without a single founder or a central authority, that are practiced by more than 80 percent of India's population. Although there is great diversity among regions and social classes, Hinduism has certain characteristic features. Most Hindus believe that everything in the world is subject to an eternal process of death and rebirth (*samsura*) and that individual souls (*atmans*) migrate from one body to another. They believe that one can be liberated from the *samsura* cycle and achieve the state of eternal bliss (*nirvana*) by (1) yoga (purification of mind and body), (2) devout worship of the gods, or (3) good works and obedience to the laws and customs (dharmas) of one's caste.

A knowledge of the **caste system** is important to managers because the castes are the basis of the social division of labor. The highest caste, the Brahmins or priesthood, is followed by the warriors (politicians, landowners), the merchant caste, the peasants, and the untouchables. An individual's position in a caste is inherited, as is that person's job within the caste, and movement to a higher caste can be made only in subsequent lives. If the gods choose to punish a person, his or her next life will be at a lower caste level. Although the government of India has officially outlawed discrimination based on the caste system, and in fact has worked to improve the situation of those in the lower castes, such discrimination still exists. The manager who places a member of a lower caste in charge of a group from a higher one does so at a considerable risk of employee dissatisfaction.[18]

Buddhism. This religion began in India as a reform movement of Hinduism. At the age of 29, Prince Gautama rejected his wife, son, and wealth and set out to solve the mysteries of misery, old age, and death. After six years of experimenting with yoga, which brought no enlightenment, he suddenly understood how to break the laws of *karma* and the endless cycle of rebirth (*samsura*). Gautama emerged as the Buddha (the Enlightened One).

He renounced the austere self-discipline of the Hindus as well as the extremes of self-indulgence, both of which depended on a craving that locked people into the endless cycle of rebirth. Gautama taught that by extinguishing desire, his followers could attain enlightenment and escape the cycle of existence into *nirvana*. By opening his teaching to everyone, he opposed the caste system.

Because Buddhist monks are involved in politics in the areas where their religion is prevalent and because they are a mobilizing force for political and social action, managers working in these areas need to be aware of what these religious leaders are doing. Even American public opinion was influenced by pictures of Buddhist monks who had set themselves on fire to protest American participation in the Vietnam War.

The Buddhist teaching that if the followers of Buddha have no desires, they will not suffer is also important, because if they have no desires, Buddhists and Hindus have little motive for achievement and for the acquisition of material goods.

Jainism. This religion was founded by Mahavira, a contemporary of Buddha. The Jain doctrine teaches that there is no creator, no god, and no absolute principle. Through right faith, correct conduct, and right knowledge of the soul, Jains can purify themselves, become free of *samsura*, and achieve *nirvana*. Although relatively few in number, Jains are influential leaders in commerce and scholarship. Their greatest impact on Indian culture is manifested in the widespread acceptance of their nonviolence doctrine, which prohibits animal slaughter, war, and even violent thoughts.

Sikhism. This is the religion of an Indian ethnic group, a military brotherhood, and a political movement that was founded by Nanek, who sought a bridge between Hinduism and Islam. Sikhs believe that there is a single god, but they also accept the Hindu concepts of *samsura, karma* and spiritual liberation. The Sikhs' holiest temple was partly destroyed in 1984 by Indian troops that suppressed their movement for self-government. More than 80 percent of all Sikhs live in the Indian state of Punjab, which they hope to make an autonomous state.

Confucianism. This is not so much a religion as a public philosophy embodying the Chinese norms of social and personal morality. Confucius refused to speculate on the existence of the Chinese deities or on whether there was life after death. He taught that all people have the principle of unselfish love for others within themselves, the cultivation of which is its own reward. Confucius also prescribed a gentle decorum, which accounts for the Chinese emphasis on politeness, deference to elders, and such courtesies as bowing.

Taoism. This is a mystical philosophy founded by Lao-tzu, a contemporary of Confucius. Taoism, which means "philosophy of the way," holds that each of us mirrors the same forces, the male and the female energies (yin and yang) that govern the cosmos. The aim of Taoist meditation and rituals is to free the self from distractions and become empty so as to allow the cosmic forces to act. There should be a unity of the person with nature, so that good acts become spontaneous.

Shintoism. This is the indigenous religion of Japan. It has no founder or bible. Shinto legends define the founding of the Japanese empire as a cosmic act, and the emperor was believed to have divine status. As a part of the World War II settlement, he was forced to renounce such a claim. Shintoism has no elaborate theology or even an organized weekly worship. Its followers come to the thousands of Shinto shrines when they feel moved to do so.

Islam

About 750 million followers make this youngest universal faith the second largest after Christianity (which has 1.4 billion adherents). **Islam** means "to submit" in Arabic, and Muslim, meaning "submitting," is the present participle of the same verb. This faith accepts the Koran, a collection of Allah's (God's) revelations to Muhammad, the founder of Islam, as God's eternal word. Unlike the founders of the other major religions, the prophet Muhammad was not only the spokesman of Allah but also the founder of what became a vast temporal and ecclesiastical empire; in other words, he was a head of state as well as a prophet of God. In Muslim nations, there is no separation of church and state.

The basic spiritual duties of all Muslims consist of the five pillars of faith: (1) accepting the confession of faith ("There is no God but God, and Muhammad is the Messenger of God"); (2) making the five daily prayers while facing Mecca (Muhammad's birthplace, where he was inspired to preach God's word in the year A.D. 610); (3) giving charity; (4) fasting during the daylight hours of Ramadan, a 29- or 30-day month in Islam's lunar calendar; and (5) making a pilgrimage to Mecca at least once in their lifetime. Some Muslims claim that there is a sixth duty, *jihad*, which refers to the various forms of striving for the faith, such as the inner struggle for purification. However, this term is often translated as "the holy war."

As important as the division that opened in Christendom with the Reformation is the split that occurred between the Sunnis and the Shiites over the succession to Muhammad's authority. His survivors decided that his successors (called caliphs) should be elected by members of the Islamic community, and they were—four times—but after the fourth successor, Ali (Muhammad's cousin), was murdered, the caliphate passed to the monarchical house of Ummaya. Ali's son, Hussayn, claimed that the caliphate was his, as Muhammad's heir, and he started a rebellion to confirm his claim. Hussayn was killed in a battle by a Sunni caliph.

This split the Muslim world between the Sunnis (followers of the Prophet's Path) and the Shiites (Party of Ali). After their defeat, the Shiites, feeling that they had been wronged, became dissenters within the Arab empire who were given to violence against authority. Although the Shiites and the Sunnis agree on the fundamentals of Islam, they differ in other respects. The Sunnis are an austere sect that is less authoritarian and more rational than the Shiites. In their view, as long as Muslims accept Allah, they are free to interpret their religion as they like. The Shiites, on the other hand, insist that those claiming to be Muslim must put themselves under the authority of a holy man (*ayatollah*). This has created a clergy that wields enormous temporal and spiritual power. It was the Iranian Shiite clergy who brought down the shah of Iran.[19]

Businesspeople doing business with Muslim countries should understand the Sunni-Shiite conflict, because much of what occurs in these countries is the result of this conflict. Although most Muslim countries are Sunni-governed, many of them, such as Kuwait, the emirates, Bahrein, and other small states in the Gulf, have substantial Shiite populations. Furthermore, small Shiite minorities can cause trouble for the government. For example, Saudi Arabia's Shiite population is very small—only 250,000—but it is concentrated in the eastern oil fields. Iran's Shiite government continually broadcasts appeals to the Saudi Shiites to overthrow the regime. In Iraq, 52 percent of the population is Shiite, and as you can imagine, this division has given rise to violent clashes between religious dissidents and the government's all-Sunni army. Syria, on the other hand, is predominantly Sunni, but its government is controlled by secular, pro-Soviet Baathist socialists who belong to a Shiite sect (Alawi).[20]

Even where the Sunni-Shiite conflict is not a problem, two of the five pillars of faith can be bothersome to Western managers. The dawn-to-dusk fasting during the month of Ramadan causes workers' output to drop sharply, and the requirement to pray five times daily also affects output, because when they hear the call to prayer, Muslim workers stop whatever they are doing to pray where they are.

An American manager in Pakistan for the purpose of getting a new factory into production came to the plant the first day, saw that production had started as it should, and went to his office to do some work. Suddenly, all of the machinery stopped. He rushed out, expecting to find a power failure. Instead, he found workers on their prayer rugs. The manager returned to his office and lowered his production estimates.

Animism

In a number of African and Latin American countries, **animism,** a kind of spirit worship that includes magic and witchcraft, is a major religion. It is often combined with Catholicism to present a strange mixture of mysticism, taboos, and fatalism. Animists believe that their dead relatives are ever present and will be pleased if the living act in the same way as their ancestors. The resultant strong tendency to perpetuate traditions makes it extremely difficult for marketers and production managers to initiate changes. To be accepted, these changes must relate to the animists' beliefs. The foreign manager must also be cognizant of the proper religious protocols in situations such as factory and store dedications. Note the aircraft dedication by the High Lama in Bhutan (see Figure 8–4). If the evil spirits are not properly exorcised, they will remain to cause all sorts of problems, such as worker injuries, machinery breakdowns, and defective products.

Evil spirits wreaked havoc in an American-owned semiconductor factory in Kuala Lumpur, Malaysia. The plant consists of an enormous room filled with hundreds of women looking into microscopes and television monitors.

One afternoon, a girl claimed she saw an ugly old woman in her microscope. The operator was pulled screaming to the first-aid room. The manager admitted that was a mistake. "Before I knew it, we had girls all over being held down by supervisors. It was like a battlefield."

The factory was evacuated, but when the night crew arrived, the spirit returned. "Word had gone out that evil spirits were loose in the factory because of a dance we had the previous weekend. At night, it was worse. All we could do was hold them down, carry them out to the buses, and send them home."

The next morning, a licensed healer was brought in. His recommendation—sacrifice a goat. That afternoon, a goat was killed and its blood was sprinkled on the factory floor. It was cooked in the cafeteria and eaten by the workers.

"Next morning, we started up, and everything was fine."[21]

Figure 8–4

Courtesy ICAO Bulletin and Rolf Christ

After this airplane landed at Paro on January 14 as directed by the Neten (High Lama), religious ceremonies for its consecration were performed by the Neten and 40 other Buddhist Lamas, seen here in the background of the photograph.

The International Motivator

We have seen that religion is a major influence for shaping the attitudes, beliefs, motivations, and values of a culture. The international manager, accustomed to the Protestant ethic, which extols the virtues of industriousness and thrift, is often frustrated to find that in areas where other religions predominate, buyers and workers do not react to incentives as they do in his or her own country. Fortunately, aspirations for material goods are emerging as an international motivator that is overcoming many religious prejudices.

Material Culture

Material culture refers to all man-made objects, and its study is concerned with *how* man makes things (technology) and *who* makes *what* and *why* (economics). Material culture is the cultural component for which the most hard data are available and the aspect of culture with which international firms are most familiar. The market study, essential for any foreign investment decision, investigates the state of a nation's material culture—the products that people own or would like to own and the economic variables, such as level of income and its distribution, that determine whether the market can afford those products.

Technology

Technological superiority is frequently the prime motive for overseas investment, but before committing resources, managements will assess the general level of technology. This provides them with information about a number of variables that can affect their investment, such as the availability of raw materials and energy, the types of workers they can hire, and the state of the transportation system.

Technology Requires Change. Technology not only covers the basic sciences and their application to production but also includes skills in marketing, finance, and management. Its cultural aspects are important to international managers because new products and production methods often require people to change their beliefs and ways of living. The self-employed farmer frequently finds the discipline required to become a factory worker excessively demanding. If workers have been accustomed to the production conditions of cottage industries in which each individual performs all of the production operations, they find it difficult to adjust to the monotony of tightening a single bolt. The "throw away instead of repair" philosophy behind the design of so many new products necessitates a change in the use habits of people who have been accustomed to repairing something to keep it operating until it is thoroughly worn out. *Generally, the greater the difference between the old and new method or product, the more difficult it is for the firm to institute a change.*

High GNP—High Level of Technology. The differences in levels of technology among nations are used as a basis for judging whether nations are advanced or retarded. Generally, a nation with a higher GNP/capita utilizes a higher level of technology than one whose per capita income is smaller. Because of technological dualism, however, analysts must be wary of assuming that just because the general technological level is low, the particular industry they are examining is employing a simple technology.

Technological Dualism. Technological dualism is a prominent feature of many LDCs. In the same country, one sector may be technologically advanced, with high productivity, while the production techniques of another sector may be old and labor intensive. This condition may be the result of the host government's insistence that foreign investors import only the most modern machinery rather than used but serviceable equipment that would be less costly and could create more employment.

Sometimes the preferences are reversed, with the host government beset by high unemployment arguing for labor-intensive processes, while the foreign firm prefers automated production, both because it is the kind with which the home office is most familiar and because its use lessens the need for skilled labor, which is usually in short supply. To understand which policy the host government is following, management must study its laws and regulations and talk with host country officials.

Government Controls. The influence of technology is very great because the level of technology used affects the size of the foreign investment, the quality and number of workers employed, and even what a particular country can produce.[22] For these reasons, plus what many LDC governments consider abuses in the sale of technology by the multinationals, many LDCs have enacted strong laws controlling the purchase of technical assistance. The Andean Group nations, Mexico, India, South Korea, and, to a lesser extent, Argentina and Brazil now have investment laws that limit the the amount of royalties paid and prohibit many of the restrictions regularly used by the multinationals, such as those that oblige licensees to purchase raw materials from the licensor, prohibit licensees from exporting, and require licensees to transfer to licensors any improvements they have made in the technology. This worldwide trend among developing nations toward a severe limitation on the after-sale control that an MNE has over its own technology has caused many MNEs not only to cut back on licensing but also to reduce new foreign investments.[23]

Cultural Aspects of Technology. Another factor that multinational managements must now consider when selling technology to the less developed countries is its cultural aspects. Will the new technology require massive cultural changes that the public is not yet prepared to make? Increasingly, LDC government leaders are realizing that immaterial basic needs must be considered along with the desire for material goods. In other words, *what* is produced is no longer the sole consideration; people are also looking critically at *how* it is produced.

The LDCs' Reaction. Because of complaints from developing nations that technology from the industrialized countries was excessively capital intensive as well as expensive, the United Nations Industrial Development Organization (UNIDO) established an Industrial and Technological Bank (INTIB) in 1977 to facilitate the exchange of technologies that are simpler, less expensive, or more appropriate than those obtainable from developed nations. In addition, a Technological Information Exchange System was created to permit the exchange of information concerning the terms and conditions of the technology contracts approved by government technology regulatory agencies. Another INTIB activity is a Joint Patents Program with the World Intellectual Property Organization. Valuable information is obtained from patent documents, cataloged, and made available to firms in developing nations.

Figure 8-5
Triangle of Domination

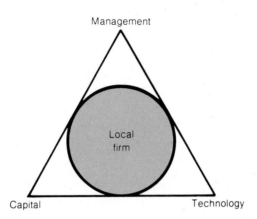

Apparently, the activities of INTIB will reduce the profitability in sales of technology by the MNEs. Since all governments will have access to the terms of licensing contracts, charging one client more than another for the same technology will be difficult. The inclusion of technology as part of a package deal will be less lucrative because information furnished by INTIB will improve the ability of an LDC regulatory body to separate the cost of know-how from that of hardware and engineering. Finally, some technology that firms in LDCs would have heretofore had to purchase from multinationals will be available free of charge.

This will aid a number of LDC governments that, by insisting that the foreign supplier of technology should not also furnish capital and management, are attempting to prevent MNEs from gaining control of local firms. These governments believe that requiring separate sources for these three factors will help local industry avoid being enclosed in a **triangle of domination,** a name given to a theory purporting to explain the multinationals' investment strategy in developing countries. According to this theory, when a single multinational firm supplies technology, capital, and management (vertices of the triangle) to a local company, it can close the triangle around the local firm and completely dominate it (see Figure 8-5). To avoid such control by multinationals, the triangle must be kept open by acquiring these factors from separate sources. Japan is an example held up to the developing nations as one country that kept the triangle open and was thus able to industrialize without foreign "domination."[24]

Economics
The decision the MNE headquarters makes as to the kind of technology to be used by a subsidiary will, within any constraints imposed by the host govern-

ment, depend on various measurements of the material culture. Economic yardsticks such as power generated/capita, number of high school graduates, and so on can uncover possible problems in the distribution and promotion of the product, help determine market size, and provide information on the availability of such resources as raw materials, skilled and unskilled labor, capital equipment, economic infrastructure (communications, financial system), and management talent. These and other aspects of the economic forces will be discussed in greater depth in Chapter 13.

Education

Although education in its widest sense can be thought of as any part of the learning process that equips an individual to take his or her place in the adult society, nearly everyone in the Euroamerican culture equates education with formal schooling.

Education Yardsticks

The firm contemplating foreign investment has no indicators of the educational level of a country's inhabitants except the usual yardsticks of formal education: literacy rate, kinds of schools, quantity of schools and their enrollments, and possibly the amount per capita spent on education. Such data underestimate the size of the vocationally trained group in the many developing countries where people learn a trade through apprenticeships starting at a very early age (12–13 years). Like other international statistics, the published literacy rate must be suspect. The literacy census often consists of asking respondents whether they can read and write, and the signing of their names is taken as proof of their literacy. Nonetheless, these data do provide some assistance. Marketers are interested in the literacy rate because it helps them decide what type of media to employ and at what level they should prepare advertisements, labels, point-of-purchase displays, and owner's manuals. The personnel manager will use the literacy rate as a guide in estimating what kinds of people will be available for staffing the operation.

As with most kinds of data, the trends in education should be studied. It is important to realize that the general level of education is rising throughout the world. In the last 20 years, the percentage of the population aged 20–24 that is enrolled in higher education has doubled in the industrialized nations and tripled in the developing countries.[25] The implication for marketers is that they must prepare to meet the needs of more sophisticated and wiser consumers.

While these data are indicative of the general level of education, unfortunately they tell us nothing about the quality of education, nor do they indicate how well the supply of graduates meets the demand.

Educational Mix

Until the 1970s, management education in Europe lagged far behind what was available in the United States. There was a feeling that managers were born, not made, and that they could be trained only on the job. Thus, there was little demand for formal business education.

However, a combination of factors has caused a proliferation of European business schools patterned on the American model:

1. Increased competition in the European Community, resulting in a demand for better-trained managers.
2. The return to Europe of American business school graduates.
3. The establishment of American-type schools with American faculty and frequently with the assistance of American universities.

This trend has been much slower to develop in the LDCs, where, historically, higher education has emphasized the study of the humanities, law, and medicine. Engineering has not been popular because, with the exception of architecture and civil engineering, there have been few engineering job opportunities in these preindustrial societies. Business education has not prospered because a business career lacked prestige.[26]

As the LDCs industrialize, there is greater competition in the marketplace and the job opportunities for engineers and business school graduates increase. Not only do the multinationals recruit such personnel, but the local firms do too when they find that the new competition forces them to improve the efficiency of their operations.

Brain Drain

Most developing nations are convinced that economic development is impossible without the development of human resources, and for the last two decades especially, governments have probably overinvested in higher education in relation to the demand for students. The result has been rising unemployment among the educated, which has led to a **brain drain**—the emigration of professionals to the industrialized nations. An UNCTAD study showed that from 1960 to 1972 over 300,000 scientists, engineers, and physicians left the developing countries. The United States, Great Britain, and Canada received 75 percent of the total. Fifty percent of the professionals came from Asia, particularly India and the Philippines.[27] The International Labor Organization estimates that each emigrant signifies a loss of $20,000 to the country; on that basis, the cost of the brain drain to the LDCs would be over $6 billion.[28]

Brain drain facts:
1. Each year, 6,000 Taiwanese come to study in the United States, but only 20 percent return home.
2. There are 8,000 Israeli engineers in the United States, which Israel says has created a severe bottleneck in its own development of sophisticated industry.

3. About one half of the 1,000 students who graduate anually from the 27 Philippine medical schools go abroad.

The prime minister of Jamaica made an interesting observation. During the period 1977–80, over 8,000 top professionals, 50 percent of the country's most highly trained citizens, emigrated, primarily to the United States. He estimated that the education of these people cost his nation $168.5 million. During that same period, U.S. aid to Jamaica totaled only $116.3 million.[29]

Developing countries are now demanding that the industrial nations pay compensation for the loss of revenue due to the outflow of skilled people. In rebuttal, a U.S. State Department economist told a UN conference that "the proposal tends to ignore the fact that people are people. They aren't commodities, and they aren't traded."[30] Obviously, he knew nothing about professional baseball.

Government authorities are deeply concerned about the loss of skills and have come to realize that there must be faster new job creation, not only to stop the costly loss but also to avoid serious political repercussions. To provide more jobs, they are adopting developmental plans that encourage labor-intensive exports and discourage the introduction of laborsaving processes. The pressure of the unemployed educated is also forcing officials in many areas to soften the terms for foreign investment.

Adult Literacy

Many governments are also questioning the wisdom of spending funds to highly educate a few and are now giving priority to primary education as a means of achieving universal *literacy*. The success of these programs and of the programs to reduce adult illiteracy is evidenced by the fact that from 1960 to 1980 world adult illiteracy was reduced from 42 percent of the adult population to 31 percent. Table 8–1 illustrates the improvements that have been made.

Inasmuch as the results of an adult literacy program are immediate, whereas it takes 10 to 20 years for the primary school generation to be productive, more attention is being given to adult education, an important trend for MNE managements to note. For example, in only four years, Brazil was able to reduce the illiteracy rate for adult Brazilians by one third, and the cost, allowing for dropouts, was only $11 per student. The program's annual budget was $26 million, which is less than New York City spends just to repair and maintain its school buildings.[31]

Women's Education

Another important trend, especially for marketers, is the fall in the illiteracy rate for women. The literacy differences between older and younger female age groups is striking. In Africa, which has the world's highest illiteracy rate, the percentage of women who could read and write grew from 18 to 27 percent between 1970 and 1980, and it is expected to rise to 40 percent by 1990.

Table 8-1
Adult Population and Literacy

	Adult Population (millions)		Adult Literacy (percent)	
	1960	1980*	1960	1980
Low-income economies	883	1,262	34	52
Middle-income economies	409	663	48	65
High-income oil exporters (Libya, Saudi Arabia, Kuwait, the emirates)	4	8	9	32
Industrial market economies	438	523	96	99
East European nonmarket economies	218	261	97	99

*After 1983, the World Bank ceased to publish adult illiteracy rates.
Source: *World Development Report, 1983* (New York: Oxford University Press), p. 196–97.

Nearly every government now has a goal, if not an actual policy, of providing free and compulsory primary education for both sexes. In many LDCs, the number of female university students has risen quickly. In Libya the percentage of female students rose from 2 percent in 1960 to 11 percent in 1970, and in some African nations university enrollments of women have multiplied from 7 to 16 times.

In Latin America, the enrollment of women in universities rose from 24.6 percent of the student population in 1960 to 41 percent in the 1970s. The number of Latin American women entering the work force, according to an Inter-American Development Bank study, is doubling every 20 years. In almost every country, educated women have fewer, healthier, and better-educated children than do uneducated women. They achieve higher labor force participation rates and higher earnings. Undoubtedly, this is leading to an increased share of women in the family's decision making, which will require marketers to redo their promotional programs in order to take advantage of this consequential trend.[32]

Language

Probably the most apparent cultural distinction that the newcomer to international business perceives is in the means of communication. Differences in the spoken language are readily discernible, and after a short period in the new culture it becomes apparent that there are variations in the unspoken language (manners and customs) as well.

Spoken Language

Language is the key to culture, and without it, people find themselves locked out of all but a culture's perimeter. At the same time, there is no way to learn a language so that the nuances, double meanings of words, and slang are understood

Figure 8-6

Europe, March–April 1984, p. 35

Evidence of the language division. Where to go? North or south?

unless one also learns the other aspects of the culture. Fortunately, the learning of both goes hand in hand; a certain feel for a people and their attitudes naturally develops with a growing mastery of their language.

Languages Delineate Cultures. Spoken languages demarcate cultures, just as physical barriers do. In fact, there is nothing equal to the spoken language for distinguishing one culture from another.[33] If two languages are spoken in a country, there will be two separate cultures (Belgium); if four languages are spoken, there will be four cultures (Switzerland); and so forth.[34] What is occurring in Canada because of the sharp divisions between the English- and French-speaking regions is ample evidence of the force of languages in delineating cultures. The differences among the Basques, Catalonians, and Spaniards and the differences between the French and Flemish of Belgium are other notable examples illustrating that there are sharp cultural and often political differences between language groups. (see Figures 8–6 and 8–7) However, it does *not* follow from this

Figure 8–7

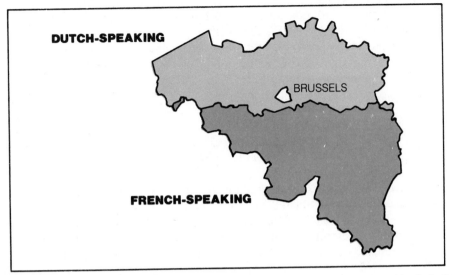

Europe, March–April 1984, p. 34

Belgium Divided

generalization that cultures are the same wherever the same language is spoken. As a result of Spain's colonization, Spanish is the principal language of 21 Latin American nations, but no one should believe that Chile and Mexico are culturally similar. Many words in both the written and spoken languages of these countries are completely different. Even within a country, words vary from one region to another.

Foreign Language. Where many spoken languages exist in a single country (India and many African nations), one foreign language usually serves as the principal vehicle for communication across cultures. Nations that were formerly colonies generally use the language of their ex-rulers; thus French is the **lingua franca** or "link" language of former French and Belgium colonies in Africa, English in India, and Portuguese in Angola.[35] Although they serve as a national language, these foreign substitutes are not the first language of anyone and, consequently, are less effective for reaching mass markets or for day-to-day conversations between managers and workers than are the native tongues. Even in countries with only one principal language, such as Germany and France, there are problems of communication because of the large numbers of Greeks, Turks, Spaniards, and others who were recruited to ease labor shortages. A German supervisor may have workers from three or four countries and be unable to speak directly with any of them. To ameliorate this situation, managements try to separate the work force according to origin; that is, all Turks are placed in the paint shop, all Greeks on the assembly line, and so on, but the preferred solution is to teach managers the language of their workers. Invariably, such training has resulted in an increase in production, fewer product defects, and higher worker morale.

> General Tire-Chile sponsored a reverse language training program in which every employee could take free English courses given on the premises after work. Not only managers but also supervisors and even workers attended classes. The program was an excellent morale builder.

Must Speak the Language. It goes without saying that marketers must be able to speak the language if they are to attain any reasonable measure of success. Even when customers speak the sales representative's language, they will accept as a compliment the visitor's efforts to converse in their tongue. In many countries, it is a social blunder to begin a business conversation by talking business. Most foreigners expect to establish a social relationship before doing business, and the casual, exploratory conversation that precedes business talks may take from 15 minutes to several meetings, depending on the importance of the transaction. Obviously, a better rapport can be established in a one-on-one conversation than through an interpreter.

Translation. The marketer's ability to speak the language well does not eliminate the need for translators. The smallest of markets requires technical manuals, catalogs, and good advertising ideas, and a lack of local talent to do the work does not mean that the organization must do without these valuable sales aids. The solution, even when the parent firm does not insist on international standardization, is to obtain this material from headquarters and have it translated if the costs are not prohibitive and suitable reproduction facilities are available locally. If the catalog or manual cannot be reproduced locally the translation can be made and sent to the home office for reproduction. The home office already has the artwork, so the only additional cost is setting the type for the translation.

Allowing headquarters to translate can be extremely risky because words from the same language frequently vary in meaning from one country to another or even from one region to another, as was mentioned earlier. A famous example that illustrates how only a single word incorrectly translated can ruin an otherwise good translation occurred in Mexico. The American headquarters of a deodorant manufacturer sent a Spanish translation of the manufacturer's international theme, "If you use our deodorant, you won't be embarrassed in public." Unfortunately, the translator used the word *embarazada* for embarrassed, which in Mexican Spanish means pregnant. Imagine the time that the Mexican subsidiary had with that one.[36]

Use Two Translations. To avoid translation errors, the experienced marketer will prefer what are really two translations. The first will be made by a bilingual native, whose work will then be translated back by a bilingual foreigner to see how it compares with the original. This work should be done preferably in the market where the material is to be used. No method is foolproof, but the double-translation approach is the safest way that has been devised so far.

Some problems with translations:
1. "Hydraulic ram" was translated from English to Italian as "wet sheep."
2. An Indonesian exchange student translated "software" for an instruction book accompanying a computer being shipped to Indonesia as "underwear tissue" and "computer junk."
3. A Paris clothing store had this sign in the window: "Come inside for a fit."
4. A notice in a Moscow hotel lobby: "Ladies are requested not to have children in the bar."
5. Probably the best translation was found on an elevator door of a Romanian hotel: "The lift is being fixed for the next few days. During that time, we regret that you will be unbearable."

Technical Words. The usual run of translators have a problem with technical terms that do not exist in a language and with common words that have a special meaning for a certain industry. Portuguese, for example, is rich in fishing and marine terms, a reflection of Portugal's material culture, but unlike English, it is exceedingly limited with respect to technical terms for the newer industries. The only solution is to employ the English word or fabricate a new word in Portuguese. Unless translators have a special knowledge of the industry, they will go to the dictionary for a literal translation that frequently makes no sense or is erroneous.

Resolving such problems by using English words may not be a satisfactory solution even if the public understands them, especially in France or Spain, which have national academies to keep the language "pure." The French have gone so far as to ban by law over 300 anglicisms, and Belgium is considering doing the same. An example of this purification move is the change from *le hot dog* to *le saucisson de francfort* (the sausage of Frankfurt). Although the French government has admitted defeat in its efforts to get rid of the old standbys such as *le weekend, le parking*, and *le jogging*, it has drawn the line on the scientific use of such American computer terms as *le hardware* and *le databank*. The French Academy has been asked to create French substitutes.[37]

At first thought this may seem to be another bureaucratic boondoggle akin to studying the love life of a gnat, but on further reflection one comprehends that these countries have good economic reasons for keeping their languages pure as part of their global campaign to teach it to foreigners.[38] Those learning French are not only potential tourists but also become more empathetic toward anything French. The Argentine engineer who reads French and not English will

Pearson, *Knickerbocker News*, Albany, New York

"First, le coca cola. Now peanut butter. Who will save La Belle Langue Française?"

turn to French technical manuals and catalogs before specifying the supplier for the new power plant he is designing. However, if he constantly finds English technical terms in the French text, which forces him to go to his Spanish-English dictionary, he may decide to learn English and read American manuals and catalogs.

In Japan, the reverse situation exists, probably because for decades the country coveted foreign products while it struggled to overtake the more advanced West. Even now, most Japanese apparently like to see English written on their products. For example, Japanese cars sold in the domestic market have almost nothing but English on them. A Nissan official explains that English is thought to be more attractive to the eye. Perhaps this is why people quench their thirst with a best-selling soft drink called "Pocari Sweat" and order from menus announcing "sand witches" and "miss Gorilla" (mixed grill). They also puff away on a cigarette called Hope.[39]

No Unpleasantness. One last aspect of the spoken language worthy of mention is the reluctance in many areas to say anything disagreeable to the listener. The politeness of the Japanese and their consideration for others make no a little-used word even when there are disagreements. The American executive, pleased that her Japanese counterpart is nodding and saying yes to all of her proposals may be shaken later to learn that all the time the listener was saying

Politeness at a Japanese department store

yes (I hear you) and not yes (I agree). Western managers who ask their Brazilian assistants whether something can be done may receive the answer *meio difícil* (somewhat difficult). If managers take this answer literally, they will probably tell the assistants to do it anyway. The assistants will then elaborate on the difficulties until, hopefully, it will finally dawn on the executives that what they ask is impossible, but the Brazilians just don't want to give them the bad news.

Unspoken Language

Nonverbal communication or the **unspoken language** can often tell business people something that the spoken language does not if they understand it. Unfortunately, the differences in customs among cultures may cause misinterpretations of the communication.

Closed Doors. Americans know that one of the perquisites of an important executive is a large office with a door that can be closed. Normally, the door is open as a signal that the occupant is ready to receive others, but when it is closed, something of importance is going on. Contrary to the American open-door policy, Germans regularly keep their doors closed. Hall says that the closed door does not mean that the person behind it wants no visitors but only that he or she considers open doors sloppy and disorderly.[40]

Office Size. Although office size is an indicator of a person's importance, it means different things to different cultures. In the U.S., the higher the executive, the larger and more secluded is the office, but in the Arab world the president may be in what for us is a small, crowded office. In Japan, the top floor of a department store is reserved for the "bargain basement" (bargain penthouse?) and not for top managment. The French prefer to locate important department heads in the center of activities, with their assistants located outward on radii from this center. To be safe, never gauge people's importance by the size and location of their offices.

Conversational Distance. Anthropologists report that conversational distances are smaller in the Middle East and Latin America, though our personal experience in Latin America has not shown this to be the case.[41] Whether or not this generality is true, we must remember that generalities are like arithmetic means; perhaps more people do than do not act in a certain way in a culture, but the businessperson will be dealing with just a few nationals at a time. Luck may have it that he or she will meet exceptions to the stereotype.

The Language of Gift Giving

Gift giving is an important aspect of every businessperson's life both here and overseas. Entertainment outside office hours and the exchange of gifts are part of the process of getting better acquainted. However, the etiquette or language of gift giving varies among cultures, just as the spoken language does, and although foreigners will usually be forgiven for not knowing the language, certainly they and their gifts will be better received if they follow local customs.

Acceptable Gifts. In Japan, for example, one never gives an unwrapped gift or visits a Japanese home empty handed. A gift is presented with the comment

© Behrendt, *Het Parool.* Amsterdam

". . . And these people did not accept any bribes . . ."

that it is only a trifle, which implies that the humble social position of the giver does not permit giving a gift in keeping with the high status of the recipient. He in turn will not open the gift in front of the giver because he knows better than to embarrass him by exposing the trifle in the giver's presence.

Japanese use gift giving to convey one's thoughtfulness and consideration for the receiver, who over time builds up trust and confidence in the giver. Japanese never give four of anything or an item with four in the name because the word sounds like the one for death. White and yellow flowers are not good choices for gifts because in many areas they connote death. In Germany, red roses to a woman indicate strong feelings for her, and if you give cutlery, always ask for a coin in payment so that the gift will not cut your friendship. Cutlery is a friendship cutter for the Russians and French also. Traditions vary greatly throughout the world, but generally safe gifts everywhere are chocolates, red roses, and good Scotch whisky (not in the Arab world, however—instead, bring a good book or something useful for the office).[42]

Bribes. The bribery scandals of the 1970s exposed the practice of giving very expensive items and money to well-placed government officials in return for special favors or large orders.

When the Securities and Exchange Commission, the U.S. government regulatory agency that administers the securities laws, discovered that managements were not disclosing to the public that they were making large foreign payments, it began a program of voluntary disclosure that has uncovered "questionable" payments made in the United States and abroad by over 400 companies.

Although the exposure is recent, it has been common knowledge in the international business community that gifts or money payments are necessary to obtain favorable action from government officials, whether to obtain a large order, receive faster service from customs agents, or procure a permit to erect a plant. Its pervasiveness worldwide is illustrated by the variety of names for bribes—*mordida* (bite in Latin America), *dash* (West Africa), *pot de vin* (jug of wine—France), *la bustarella* (envelope left on Italian bureaucrat's desk), or *grease* (United States). Even the Russians are not exempt according to a *Business International* study of MNE managers, who declared that representatives of the Russian state trading organization permit gifts to be deposited in their Swiss bank accounts.

According to Radio Moscow, one man who was arrested for taking bribes had in his possession 12 cars, 47 tape recorders and color TVs, 79 suits, and 149 pairs of shoes. Another had 735,000 roubles ($970,000 in cash), 450 gold coins, and 398 gold watches.[43]

Questionable Payments. Bribes come in all forms and sizes from the petty "expediting" payments that have been necessary to get poorly paid government officials to do their normal duties to huge sums to win large orders.[44] Included by the Securities and Exchange Commission (SEC) as questionable payments are contributions to foreign political parties and the payment of agents' commissions even when these actions are not illegal in the country where they are made.[45] The United States, in effect, is requiring American firms to operate elsewhere according to this country's laws, which frequently places these firms at a competitive disadvantage.* Many managements have responded by issuing strict orders not to make any questionable payments, legal or illegal, and some have been surprised to find that their business has not fallen off as they expected. Their action has been reinforced by a number of governments that have either passed stricter laws or begun to enforce those they already have. Given the combination of low salaries of foreign officials and the intense competition for business, one should not be too sanguine about the prospects for completely eliminating this practice.[46]

Societal Organization

Every society has a structure or an organization that is the patterned arrangement of relationships defining and regulating the manner by which its members interface with one another. Anthropologists generally study this important aspect of culture by breaking down its parts into two classes of institutions—those based on *kinship* and those based on the *free association* of individuals.

Kinship
The family is the basic unit of institutions based on **kinship.** Unlike the American family, which is generally composed of the parents and their children, families in many nations—especially in the developing ones—are extended to include all relatives by blood and by marriage.

Extended Family. The impact of the **extended family** on the foreign firm derives from the fact that it is a source of employees and business connections. The trust that people place in their relatives, however distant, may motivate them to buy from a supplier owned by their cousin's cousin even though the price is higher. Local personnel managers are prone to fill the best jobs with family members, regardless of their qualifications.

Member's Responsibility. Although the extended family is large, each member's feeling of responsibility to it is strong. An individual's initiative to work is discouraged when he or she may be asked to share personal earnings with unemployed extended family members, no matter what the kinship is. Responsibility to the family is frequently a cause of high absenteeism in developing countries where the worker is called home to help with the harvest. Managements have spent large sums to provide comfortable housing for workers and their immediate families only to find them living in crowded conditions when members of the extended family have moved in.

*This subject is discussed further in Chapter 10.

Pedro Diaz Marin. In Latin America, where the extended family form is common, individuals use the maternal surname (Marin) as well as the paternal (Diaz) to indicate both branches of the family. It is a common sight to find two businesspeople or a businessperson and a government official, when meeting for the first time, exploring each other's family tree to see whether they have common relatives. If they find any kinship at all, the meeting goes much more smoothly—after all, they're relatives.

Associations

Social units not based on kinship, known as associations by the anthropologists, may be formed by age, sex, or common interest.[47]

Age. Manufacturers of consumer goods are well aware of the importance of segmenting a market by age groups, which often cut across cultures. This fact has enabled marketers to succeed in selling such products as clothing and records to the youth market in both developed and developing nations. However, international marketers may go too far if they assume that young people everywhere exert the same buying influence on their parents as they do here. Kellogg's attempt to sell cereals in Great Britain through children was not successful because English mothers are less influenced by their children with respect to product choice than are American mothers. The senior citizen segment is an important separate group in the United States, where older people live apart from their children, but where the extended family concept is prevalent, older people continue to live with and exert a powerful influence on younger members of the family.

Sex. Generally, the less developed the country, the less equal are the sexes with respect to job opportunities and education. As nations industrialize, more women enter the job market and thus assume greater importance in the economy. This trend is receiving greater impetus as the women's movement for equality of the sexes spreads to the traditionally male-dominated societies of less developed countries.

A word of caution, however, must be given to those who, noting the apparently sequestered life of women in some areas, conclude that they have little voice in what the family buys or how it acts. Despite the outward appearance of male domination, women exert a far more powerful influence behind closed doors than the unknowing outsider might suspect.

Common Interest. The common interest groups are composed of people who are joined together by a common bond, which can be political, occupational, recreational, or religious.[48] Even before entering a country, management should identify such groups and assess their political and economic power. As we will see in later chapters, consumer organizations have forced firms to change their product, promotion, and prices, and investments have been supported or opposed by labor unions, which are often a powerful political force.

Class Mobility

In most countries the ease of moving from one social class to another lies on a continuum from the rigid caste system of India to the relatively flexible social structure of the United States. Less developed countries tend to be located nearer the position of India, whereas the industrial nations are closer to the U.S. position. As industrialization progresses, barriers to mobility become weaker. Mobility between classes must be assessed by management because interclass rigidity, especially when it is accompanied by low social status for business, can make it extremely difficult for the firm to obtain good management personnel locally.

Summary

Culture, the sum total of the beliefs, rules, techniques, institutions, and artifacts that characterize the human population, is of interest to anyone who does business in other countries because of its pervasive influence on all the functions of the firm. To be successful in their relationships overseas, international business people must be students of culture. They must not only obtain factual knowledge; they must also become culturally sensitive. Because society is composed of people and their cultures, we have followed the practice of many anthropologists in calling the variables *sociocultural*. Although the experts differ considerably as to the relevant components of culture, the following list is representative of their thinking: (1) aesthetics, (2) attitudes and beliefs, (3) religion, (4) material culture, (5) education, (6) language, (7) societal organization, (8) legal characteristics, and (9) political structure.

Aesthetics is concerned with a culture's sense of beauty and good taste and is expressed in the arts, drama, music, folklore, and dances. Examples have been given to illustrate their importance in business. Attitudes and beliefs, especially those concerned with time, achievement, work, and change, can be radically different from those to which the businessperson is accustomed. Being aware of the differences can often decide the outcome of a business venture. A knowledge of the basic tenets of other religions will contribute to a better understanding of their followers' attitudes.

Material culture, especially technology, is of great importance to managements contemplating overseas investments. Foreign governments are becoming increasingly involved in the sale and control of technical assistance. The educational level will not only determine the kinds of people available to staff foreign operations but will also exert an important influence on the affiliate's marketing mix.

Language is the key to culture and must be learned if a person is to understand the people of a culture. Generally, there will be as many cultures in a country as there are languages. Students of culture should learn both the spoken and unspoken language. A knowledge of how a society is organized is useful because it is the societal organization that defines and regulates the manner in which its members interface with one another. The extended family and the responsibility of each member to it are especially significant.

The nine cultural components mentioned in this chapter will serve as a helpful checklist to managers who must make cultural assessments.

Questions

1. *How do attitudes toward time, attitudes toward change, and attitudes toward achievement and work affect the various functional areas of international business (personnel, marketing, and so forth)?*
2. *Why are international firms called agents of change? Give some examples.*
3. *John Adams, with 20 years' experience as a general foreman in an American firm, is sent as production superintendent to the company's new plant in Cali, Colombia. He was chosen because of his outstanding success in handling workers. Adams uses the participative leadership style. Can you foresee his having any problems in this new job?*
4. *Americans are accustomed to arriving at noon if the appointment is set for noon. What can American businesspeople do to cure the Brazilians of arriving late?*
5. *How can the international firm get people to accept a new idea?*
6. *Is there any relationship between religion and the attitude toward achievement?*
7. *What is the relationship between religion and business in the Middle East?*
8. *What is occurring in the LDCs that makes licensing agreements less attractive for the international firm?* the govt is a partner in that they approve on disprove. They are
9. *What is probably the most foolproof way of avoiding translation errors?*
10. *Gift giving in other countries seems to be very involved. How can traveling business executives keep track of all the rules?*
11. *The competition is giving bribes—shouldn't we? Discuss.*
12. *What is the significance of the extended family for the international manager?*

Reading
Be Attuned to Business Etiquette

The proverb "When in Rome, do as the Romans do" applies do the business representative as well as the tourist. Being attuned to a country's business etiquette can make or break a sale, particularly in countries where thousand-year-old traditions can dictate the rules for proper behavior.

Source: *Foreign Agriculture*, U.S. Department of Agriculture, February 1987, pp. 18–19.

Some of the considerations anyone interested in being a successful marketer should be aware of include:

Local customs, etiquette, and protocol. (An exporter's behavior in a foreign country can reflect favorably or unfavorably on the exporter, the company, and even the sales potential for the product.)

Body language and facial expressions. (Often, actions do speak louder than words.)

Expressions of appreciation. (Giving and receiving gifts can be a touchy subject in many countries. Doing it badly may be worse than not doing it at all.)

Choices of words. (Knowing when and if to use slang, tell a joke, or just keep silent is important.)

The following informal test will help exporters rate their business etiquette. See how many of the following you can answer correctly. (Answers follow the last question.)

1. *You are in a business meeting in an Arabian Gulf country. You are offered a small cup of bitter cardamom coffee. After your cup has been refilled several times, you decide you would rather not have any more. How do you decline the next cup offered to you?*
   a. *Place you palm over the top of the cup when the coffee pot is passed.*
   b. *Turn your empty cup upside down on the table.*
   c. *Hold the cup and twist your wrist from side to side.*

2. *In which of the following countries are you expected to be punctual for business meetings?*
   a. *Peru*
   b. *Hong Kong*
   c. *Japan*
   d. *China*
   e. *Morocco*

3. *Gift giving is prevalent in Japanese society. A business acquaintance presents you with a small wrapped package. Do you:*
   a. *Open the present immediately and thank the giver?*
   b. *Thank the giver and open the present later?*
   c. *Suggest that the giver open the present for you?*

4. *In which of the following countries is tipping considered an insult?*
   a. *Great Britain*
   b. *Iceland*
   c. *Canada*

5. *What is the normal workweek in Saudi Arabia?*
   a. *Monday through Friday*
   b. *Friday through Tuesday*
   c. *Saturday through Wednesday*

6. *You are in a business meeting in Seoul. Your Korean business associate hands you his calling card, which states his name in the traditional Korean order: Park Chul Su. How do you address him?*
   a. *Mr. Park*
   b. *Mr. Chul*
   c. *Mr. Su*

7. *In general, which of the following would be good topics of conversation in Latin American countries?*
   a. *Sports*
   b. *Religion*
   c. *Local politics*
   d. *The weather*
   e. *Travel*

8. *In many countries, visitors often are entertained in the homes of clients. Taking flowers as a gift to the hostess is usually a safe way to express thanks for the hospitality. However, both the type and color of the flower can have amorous, negative, or even ominous implications. Match the country where presenting them would be a social* faux pas.
   a. *Brazil*   1. *Red roses*
   b. *France*   2. *Purple flowers*
   c. *Switzerland*   3. *Chrysanthemums*

9. *In Middle Eastern countries, which hand does one use to accept or pass food?*
   a. *Right hand*
   b. *Left hand*
   c. *Either hand*

10. *Body language is just as important as the spoken word in many countries. For example, in most countries, the thumbs-up sign means "OK." But in which of the following countries is the sign considered a rude gesture?*
    a. *Germany*
    b. *Italy*
    c. *Australia*

Reading

Be Attuned to Business Etiquette (concluded)

Anwers:1—c. *It is also appropriate to leave the cup full. 2*—a, b, c, d, *and* e. Even in countries where local custom does not stress promptness, overseas visitors should be prompt. *3*—b. *4*—b. *5*—c. *6*—a. *The traditional Korean pattern is surname, followed by two given names. 7*—a, d, *and* e. *8*—a *and 2. Purple flowers are a sign of death in Brazil, as are chrysanthemums in France (*b *and 3). In Switzerland (*c *and 1), as well as in many other north European countries, red roses suggest romantic intentions. 9*—a. *Using the left hand would be a social gaffe. 10*—c.

How's Your Business Etiquette?

8–10 Congratulations—you have obviously done you homework when it comes to doing business overseas.
5–7 While you have some sensitivity to the nuances of other cultures, you still might make some social errors that could cost you sales abroad.
1–4 Look out—you could be headed for trouble if you leave home without consulting the experts.

Where to Turn for Help

Whether you struck out completely in the business etiquette department or just want to polish your skills, there are several sources you can turn to for help.
Books. *While 20 years ago business etiquette information may have been difficult to locate, most good bookstores today carry a variety of resource materials to help the traveling business representative.*
Workshops and seminars. *Many private business organizations and universities sponsor training sessions for the exporter interested in unraveling the mysteries of doing business abroad.*
State marketing specialists. *In some states, your first contact should be your state agriculture department, where international specialists there can pass on their expertise or put you in touch with someone who can.*

Minicase

8–1 Is It a Bribe?

Nick Brown, the sales manager of the Johnson Rubber subsidiary in El Pais, has been selling about a half million dollars a year in industrial rubber products (rotary drilling hose, oil suction and discharge hose) to the government-owned oil monopoly. He faces stiff competition from the local subsidiary of another multinational rubber manufacturer, which is trying to increase its share of the business. The principal reason for his success is his personal friendship with Captain Corona, the buyer. Brown has never bought anything for Corona except an occasional lunch and a reasonably priced ($50) Christmas gift.

One day in December, he received a call from Captain Corona, who said that just as he was leaving the house, his wife complained that she needed a new refrigerator. Corona was calling Brown because he knew that the marketing manager of a refrigerator manufacturer was Brown's close friend and he wondered whether Brown could arrange for a discount through his friend. Brown told Captain Corona that he would call his friend to see whether the friend could get Corona the discount.

After the call, Brown began thinking about his conversation with Corona. The man was responsible for his receiving a half million dollars in orders every year. This was three times the business his competitor was obtaining, even though the product quality and prices were similar. Every year, he gave the captain a Christmas present worth about $50. The refrigerator would cost $250. Never had the captain asked him for anything. Johnson Rubber had no rules restricting the value of gifts, but employees were expected to exercise good judgment. Could this be the beginning of a series of requests for expensive gifts, or was Captain Corona only interested in getting the best price possible?

What would you do if you were Nick Brown?

Minicase

8–2 Evans Machinery–France*

Evans Machinery–France is the French subsidiary of Evans Machinery, headquartered in Chicago. The firm specializes in the production of highly sophisticated materials-handling equipment, most of which must be specially designed for the job. There are few competitors in France or in any other part of the European Community.

Business has been excellent, though recently the company lost two sizable orders to a French competitor. One customer was the government-owned automobile factory, Renault, and the other was a French-owned textile factory. Both customers had made various purchases from Evans Machinery in the past.

Frank Bowen, the subsidiary's managing director, sat in his office reviewing the two lost sales. He knew that the French competitor did not have Evans' technical capability, and he was confident that the competitor's price could not

*This case is based on "French Buyers' Reply to Foreign Suppliers: A Not-So-Subtle 'Non,' " *Business Europe*, August 26, 1977, pp. 256–66.

have been significantly lower. Bowen walked to the window overlooking the front of the building. He was proud of that plant. The lawn was well kept. There was a flagpole with the American flag flying, just as in Chicago. Bowen was thinking that he had a good chance for the executive vice president's job that was coming up soon back at headquarters if Evans Machinery–France continued to do as well as it had done for the last three years under his management. The loss of two sizable orders wouldn't help his record, though. What was the reason? An idea came to him. He would call his friend Henri in Renault's technical department. Bowen liked Henri, who had been educated in the United States and spoke English like an American. He explained to Henri that he was concerned about having lost Renault's order. Did Henri know why this had happened? After a pause, Henri spoke, "Frank, my friend, the boom years in France are over, and the government is concerned. The order was earmarked for a French company."

What can Frank Bowen do to stop this loss of orders?

Supplementary Readings

Ball, D. "The Triangle of Domination, The LDCs' Answer to the Multinationals." *Journal of Business Administration*, Fall 1975, pp. 180–81.

Barnouw, V. *An Introduction to Anthropology.* Chicago: Dorsey Press, 1975.

Brady, I., and B. Isaac. *A Reader in Cultural Change.* Vol. 1. Cambridge, Mass.: Schenkman Publishing, 1975.

"Bribes vs. Gifts: Soviet Interpretation Unclear." *Business Eastern Europe*, February 10, 1986, p. 45.

Douglas, S., and B. DuBois. "Looking at the Cultural Environment for International Marketing Opportunities." *Columbia Journal of World Business*, Winter 1977.

Hall, E. T. *The Hidden Dimension.* Garden City, N.Y.: Doubleday, 1969.

Harvis, P. R., and R. T. Moran. *Managing Cultural Differences.* Houston: Gulf Publishing, 1979.

Herskovits, M. J. *Man and His Works.* New York: Alfred A. Knopf, 1952.

"A Linguistic Problem," *Europe* (Washington, D.C.: European Community), September 1986, pp. 3–4.

McGrath, P. "Women: Education Is the Key." *Development Forum*, December 1976.

"Mind in the Middle." *Japan Update* (Tokyo: Keizai Koko Center), Autumn 1986, p. 29.

"On Saving the Language." *Europe* (Washington, D.C.: European Community), March 3, 1986, p. 3.

Ricks, David. *Big Business Blunders.* (Homewood, Ill.: Dow Jones-Irwin), 1983.

"Sunnis? Shiites? What's That Got to Do with Oil Prices?" *Forbes*, April 12, 1982, pp. 88–89.

Terpstra, V., and K. David. *The Cultural Environment of International Business.* 2nd ed, Cincinnati: South-Western Publishing, 1985

Woodward, K. L. "Religions of Asia." *Modern Maturity*, December 1984, pp. 72–74.

Endnotes

1. I. C. Brown, *Understanding Other Cultures* (Englewood Cliffs, N.J.: Prentice-Hall, 1963), p. 4.
2. E. T. Hall, *Beyond Culture* (Garden City, N.Y.: Anchor Press/Doubleday, 1977), p. 54.
3. I. Brady and B. Isaac, *A Reader in Cultural Change*, vol.1 (Cambridge, Mass.: Schenkman Publishing, 1975), p. x.
4. V. Barnouw, *An Introduction to Anthropology* (Chicago: Dorsey Press, 1975), p. 5.
5. Hall, *Beyond Culture*, p. 16.
6. G. Foster, *Traditional Societies and Technological Change* (New York: Harper & Row, 1973), p. 11.
7. S. Douglas and B. DuBois, "Looking at the Cultural Environment for International Marketing Opportunities," *Columbia Journal of World Business*, Winter 1977, pp. 106–7.
8. One of the writers installed in a Spanish factory new production equipment that was to replace old but still serviceable machinery. Before leaving for a week's work in Madrid, he tested the equipment, trained some workers to use it, and advised the supervisor that it was ready. On his return, he was surprised to find that the new equipment was not being utilized. The supervisor explained that the old machinery was working well and he didn't want to "disrupt production." Actually, the new equipment was easier to use and would greatly increase output. Realizing that drastic action was called for, the writer grabbed a sledge hammer and made a token effort to destroy the old equipment. Only then did the supervisor get the message. Admittedly, the action was unorthodox, but it did bring immediate results. Not wanting to replace a still serviceable object with a new object, even when the new object is superior, is a quite common attitude in many countries.
9. This classification depends in part on M. J. Herskovits, *Man and His Works* (New York: Alfred A. Knopf, 1952), p. 634. It was embellished by anthropologists at the University of South Alabama.
10. In Brazil, it's purple, and in Mexico, it's yellow.
11. Saudi religious leaders were enraged when a Taiwanese firm sold "blasphemous" shoes in their country. How could they walk on the sacred name, Allah, which was molded into the sole? From L. Copeland and Lewis Griggs, *Going International* (New York: Random House, 1985), pp. 63–64.
12. Herskovits, *Man and His Works*, p. 414.
13. "Bridging That Other Gulf," *Vision*, May 1975, p. 50.
14. "You Can Do Business in Russia," *U.S. News & World Report*, July 7, 1975, p. 56.
15. For a detailed critique of McClelland's Achievement Theory, see Benjamin Higgins' discussion in *Economic Development* (New York: W. W. Norton, 1968), pp. 241–44.
16. It is impossible to transmit adequately the connotations of the two words. No one proudly says that he is an *obrero* even if he earns more than the *empleado* who is a file clerk.
17. Kenneth L. Woodward, "Religions of Asia," *Modern Maturity*, December 1984–January 1985, pp. 72–74.
18. V. Terpstra and K. David, *The Cultural Environment of International Business*, 2nd ed. (Cincinnati: South-Western Publishing, 1985), p. 89.
19. Woodward, "Religions of Asia," pp. 75–78.
20. "Sunnis? Shiites? What's That Got to Do with Oil Prices?" *Forbes*, April 12, 1982, pp. 88–99.
21. From an interview with the general manager in "Malaysian Malady: When the Spirit Hits, a Scapegoat Suffers," *The Wall Street Journal*, March 3, 1980, p. 1.

22. Exports and foreign exchange earnings can be affected if the product cannot compete in the world market because of excessive manufacturing costs, inferior quality, or an obsolete design.

23. The reason is that the MNEs will generally make licensing agreements even with wholly owned foreign subsidiaries in order to establish a legal basis for requiring royalty payments and service fees.

24. See D. Ball, "The Triangle of Domination, the LDCs' Answer to the Multinationals," *Journal of Business Administration*, Fall 1975, pp. 180–81.

25. World Bank, *World Development Report, 1983* (New York: World Bank, 1983), pp. 196–97.

26. In Chile, one of the writers was given an engineer to train as a V-belt technician. When he began using engineering terms, he noticed that the engineer could not comprehend him, and so he asked the man what kind of engineer he was. To his surprise, the answer was *commercial engineer.* In a land of professional titles, apparently the government thought that this was the best way to give professional recognition to business graduates. In Latin America, a person is commonly addressed by his professional title—*Ingeniero* Garcia (engineer) or *Licenciado* Lopez (economist or attorney). A similar practice is followed in Germany.

27. UNCTAD, "Economic Effects of the Outflow of Trained Personnel from Developing Countries," in *The Reverse Transfer of Technology* (New York: United Nations, 1975), p. 1.

28. "Migracion de Professionales," *Comercio Exterior* (Mexico City: Banco Nacional de Comercio Exterior), May 1978, p. 581. An occasional paper published by the Vienna Institute for Development states that the estimated investment or capital value of the brains that emigrated from the developing countries to the United States, Canada, and the United Kingdom amounted to about $50 billion during the period 1961–72. See *Problems of Technology Transfer,* Vienna Institute for Development, November 23, 1978, p. 9.

29. "Costly Brain Drain," *Development Forum* (Geneva: United Nations), March 1982, p. 12.

30. "Developing Countries Demand Compensation for Loss of Skilled People to Industrial Nations," *The Wall Street Journal*, September 3, 1982, p. 30.

31. E. McDowell, "Brazil's Amazing Literacy Plan, " *The Wall Street Journal*, December 3, 1974, p. 28.

32. P. McGrath, "Women: Education is the Key," *Development Forum* (Geneva: United Nations), December 1976, p. 8.

33. Herskovits, *Man and His Works*, p. 440.

34. Africa has an unparalleled mixture of cultures and languages. For example, Kenya has 22 distinct languages and Nigeria has 125.

35. To avoid using English as the link language, Hindi was declared to be the official language. As late as 1986, Tamil-speaking students from the south were rioting against the imposition of Hindi, which was spoken by 30 percent of the population, mainly in the north. The students wanted English to be the link language.

36. This mistake was caught before it was published locally, but an incident happened to one of the writers, newly arrived in Brazil, that did go all over the country. The ad manager, a Brazilian, brought him a campaign emphasizing that car owners should maintain 24 pounds per square inch in their tires to get maximum wear. To really get the point across, life-size figures of a tire company salesman were made up, with the name of the company and a large 24 printed across his chest. Care was taken to get these figures out to the dealers, who were to set them up on a "D day." The writer, sitting in his São Paulo office, proud of the unusually good coordination of the campaign, began receiving calls from

competitors asking what type of people worked in his company. Over the laughter came the message—24 in Brazilian Portuguese means homosexual!

37. "Paris," *Europe*, March–April 1983, p. 40.

38. The French are especially strong, having more than 1,000 French "cultural centers" worldwide where a native can learn the language for a very modest sum. The close link between a language and the other cultural components assures the French that the language students will become familiar with all the aspects of French culture. The United States, by the way, has a similar program, as does Russia to a lesser extent.

39. "In Japan, They Demand English—Even if It's Bad," *Modesto Bee*, July 10, 1983, p. E-6.

40. E. T. Hall, *The Hidden Dimension* (Garden City, N.Y.: Doubleday, 1969), pp. 134–35.

41. One of the writers, who lived in Latin America for 15 years, was surprised to read this statement in *The Silent Language in Overseas Business* by E. T. Hall. His Mexican wife, who had lived on both sides of the border, absolutely refuted it, so when he went to Ecuador recently as a consultant, he was careful to observe conversational distances. In no instance did he note any appreciable difference.

42. "Personal Business," *Business Week*, December 6, 1976, pp.91–92.

43. "On the Take," *Parade Magazine*, p. 8, in *Mobile Press Register*, March 6, 1977; and *Financial Times*, July 1986, p. 10.

44. One of the writers was able to reduce by one half the average age of receivables from a major governmental customer by the payment of $4 a month to a clerk whose sole job was to arrange suppliers' invoices according to their dates, so that the oldest were on top and would be paid first. His company's invoices were placed on top regardless of their date and were paid promptly.

45. Interestingly, the Foreign Corrupt Practices Act of 1977 *permits* "grease" to be paid when its sole purpose is expediting nondiscretionary official actions.

46. A British businessman in Hong Kong put it this way: "Of course, everybody does it. The difference between the rest of us and you Americans is that you kiss and tell. I don't see much point in giving somebody a $5 million bribe and then telling the whole world about it." From *Mobile Register*, February 27, 1976, p. 5B.

47. Herskovits, *Man and His Works*, p. 303.

48. V. Terpstra, *International Marketing* (Hinsdale, Ill.: Dryden Press, 1986), p. 106.

CHAPTER 9

POLITICAL FORCES

"Politics have no relation to morals."

Niccolo Machiavelli

"By the twentieth century the middle class will no longer exist. It will have been overcome as a direct result of the class struggle."

Karl Marx and Friedrich Engels in *The Communist Manifesto*

Learning Objectives

After you study this chapter, you should know:

1. The ideological forces that affect business and how they affect it.
2. The importance of government-owned business even in countries that refer to themselves as capitalist.
3. Nationalism as a powerful emotional force with political repercussions on business and some of the impacts that it can have on business.
4. The necessity of adequate government protection of business and its personnel from terrorism and invasion.
5. The impact of business of government instability and of sudden changes in government policy.
6. The effects on business of traditional hostilities between peoples and nations.
7. The growth of international organizations and their political powers.
8. Labor as a political force.
9. The strengths that most MNEs can utilize to influence political decisions.

Key Words and Concepts

Ideology
Expropriation
Capitalism
Right wing
Conservative
Nationalism
Stability
Traditional hostilities

Communism
Confiscation
Socialism
Left wing
Liberal
Terrorism
Instability
Privatization

Business Incident

Governments frequently take over privately owned businesses, expropriate them, and pay the previous owners some compensation. Sometimes it goes the other direction, and governments sell businesses to private buyers.

In 1982, the British government sold National Freight Consortium, Britain's largest freight handler, to its 12,000 workers. They paid the equivalent of $1.50 per share, and by August 1983 the shares were valued at about $5.10.

The worker-owners say they now turn off unnecessary lights and take better care of trucks and other equipment than they did before. Sales and profits are rising, in part because of the boost in workers' drive and motivation.

As a private company, National has a freedom to invest that it did not have as a state-owned firm. It has bought an Australian moving company in a move to internationalize its business. The finance director says National probably could not have got British government approval for such an investment and that the Australian government would probably not have welcomed investment by a nationalized company.

John Marcom, Jr., The Wall Street Journal, August 30, 1983, p. 30.

*C*hapter 10 deals with the legal forces affecting international business. Of course, laws and their interpretation and enforcement reflect political ideologies and outlooks as well as government stability and continuity. Therefore, this chapter is intended as background for and companion to Chapter 10.

In a number of ways, the political climate of the country in which a business operates is as important as the country's topography, its natural resources, and its climate in the sense of weather. Indeed, we shall see examples in which a hospitable, stable government can encourage business investment and growth in spite of geographic or weather obstacles and scarcity of natural resources. The opposite is equally true. Some areas of the world which are relatively blessed with natural resources and with not too difficult topography and weather have been very little developed because of government instability. Occasionally, the government of a country is hostile to investment in its territory by MNEs even though they might provide capital, technology, and training for development of the country's resources and people.

Many of the political forces with which business must cope have ideological sources, but there are a large number of other sources. These include nationalism, terrorism, traditional hostilities, unstable governments, international organizations, and government-owned business.

It should be pointed out that the MNE itself can be a political force. There are MNEs with budgets or sales larger than the GNP of some of the countries with which they negotiate. Although budgets and GNPs do not translate directly or necessarily into power, it should be clear that companies with bigger budgets and countries with bigger GNPs possess more assets and facilities with which to negotiate. Refer to Table 1–1 for some examples.

This chapter will provide an indication of the types of risks to private business posed by political forces. As we shall see, some of the risks can stem from more than one political force.

As with the other forces facing international business, management is usually not helpless to deal with the political forces. We shall examine some tools and measures available to MNE executives dealing with political risk in Chapter 21.

Ideological Forces

Such names as communism, socialism, capitalism, liberal, conservative, left wing, and right wing are used to describe governments, political parties, and people. These names indicate ideological beliefs.

Communism

In communist countries, the government owns all the major factors of production. With minor exceptions, all production in these countries is by state-owned factories and farms. Labor unions are government controlled.

Communism as conceived by Karl Marx was a theory of social change directed to the ideal of a classless society. As developed by Lenin and others, communism advocates the seizure of power by a conspiratorial political party, the maintenance of power by stern suppression of internal opposition, and commitment to the ultimate goal of a worldwide communist state.

Although private companies from noncommunist countries usually cannot own plants in a communist country, they can do business with it. We shall discuss how this is done in Chapter 17. But before we get there, we should point out that recent developments in the People's Republic of China are opening opportunities for foreign investment.

Communist Government Takeover of a Previously Noncommunist Country

This business risk is not dealt with in Chapter 17. Given one of communism's basic tenets, state ownership of all the productive factors, private business will be taken over by the government. This occurred in Russia after the 1917 Bolshevik Revolution, and it has been repeated after each communist takeover of a country.

Compensation for Expropriated Property. To date, none of the new communist governments have compensated the foreign former owners directly. A few of the owners have gotten some reimbursement indirectly out of assets of the communist government seized abroad after the communist government confiscated foreign private property within its country. For example, the U.S. government seized assets of the Soviet Union in the United States after American property in the USSR was confiscated. American firms or individuals whose property had been confiscated in the USSR could file claims with a U.S. government agency, and if they could substantiate their loss, a percentage of it was paid.

Expropriation and Confiscation. The rules of traditional international law recognize a country's right to expropriate the property of foreigners within its jurisdiction. But those rules require the country to compensate* the foreign owners, and *in the absence of compensation,* **expropriation** *becomes* **confiscation**.

Capitalism

The capitalist, free enterprise ideal is that all the factors of production should be privately owned. Under an ideal **capitalism**, government would be restricted to only those functions that the private sector cannot perform—national defense; police, fire, and other public services; and government-to-government international relations. No such government exists.

Reality in so-called capitalist countries is quite complex. The governments of such countries typically regulate privately owned businesses quite closely, and frequently these governments own businesses.

Regulations and Red Tape

All businesses are subject to countless government laws, regulations, and red tape in their activities in the United States and all other capitalist countries. Special government approval is required to practice the professions, such as law or medicine. Tailored sets of laws and regulations govern banking, insurance, transportation, and utilities. States and local governments require business licenses and impose use restrictions on buildings and areas.

Complying with all the laws and regulations and coping with the red tape require expertise, time, and, of course, expense. Risk is always present that a business may be found in noncompliance, and that can result in fines or even in the imprisonment of its management.

---

*"Prompt, adequate, and effective compensation" is the statement of the traditional international law requirement for legal expropriation.

Socialism

The **socialism** doctrine advocates government ownership or control of the basic means of production, distribution, and exchange. Profit is not an aim.

In practice, so-called socialist governments frequently have performed in ways not consistent with the doctrine. One of the most startling examples of this is Singapore, which professes to be a socialist state but which in reality is aggressively capitalistic.[1]

European Socialism

In Europe, socialist parties have been in power in several countries, including Great Britain, France, Spain, Greece, and West Germany. In Britain, the Labour party—as the socialists there call their political party—has nationalized some basic industries, such as steel, shipbuilding, coal mining, and the railroads, but has not gone much further in that direction. There is a vocal left wing* of the Labour party which would nationalize all major British business, banks, and insurance companies. At the 1984 Labour Party Conference, a member of the left wing was selected to head the party.

Social Democrats is the name the West Germans use for their socialist political party. During the several years that this party was in power before it lost to the Christian Democrats in 1982, it nationalized nothing and, in action and word, seemed more capitalist than socialist. The socialist governments of France and Spain have embarked on programs to privatize government-owned businesses; such programs do not conform to pure socialist doctrine.

LDC Socialism

The less developed countries (LDCs) very often profess and practice some degree of socialism. The government typically owns and controls most of the factors of production. Among the characteristics of an LDC are shortages of capital, technology, and skilled management and labor. Aid from DCs or from international organizations usually comes to (and hopefully through) the LDC government. Many of the educated citizens tend to be in or connected with the LDC government. It follows that the major factories and farms would be owned or controlled by the government.

Unless the LDC government is communist, it will make occasional exceptions and permit capital investment. This happens when the LDC perceives advantages which would not be possible without the private capital. The advantages could be more jobs for its people, new technology, skilled managers or technicians, and export opportunities.

---

*The term *left wing* connotes a group that advocates more government ownership and involvement, while the term *right wing* refers to a group that wants less government interference with business and individuals.

Risks for Businesses Dealing with Socialist Countries

As you can see, there is an extremely wide range of practice among the countries that profess socialism. At the extreme illustrated by Singapore, one must be careful to comply with all the applicable laws and regulations, as in a capitalist country. At the other extreme, such as an LDC where most or all of the major production factors are government owned, one must do business much as it is done in a communist country.

Conservative or Liberal

We should not leave the subject of ideology without mention of these words as they have come to be used in the mid- and late 20th century. Politically, the word **conservative** is used to connote a person, group, or party that wishes to minimize government activity and to maximize the activities of private businesses and individuals. Conservative is used to mean something similar to **right wing,** but in the United States and the United Kingdom, the latter is more extreme. For instance, the Conservative party, one of the major political parties in the United Kingdom, is said to have a right-wing minority.

Politically, in the United States in the 20th century, the word **liberal** has come to mean the opposite of what it meant in the 19th century. It has come to connote a person, group, or party that urges greater government participation in the economy and regulation or ownership of business. Liberal and **left wing** are similar, but the latter is generally used to indicate more extreme positions closer to socialism or communism.

Unique to the United States

This usage has not spread outside the United States.

> A conversation one of the authors had with an Italian lawyer at lunch in Rome turned to politics. The Italian identified himself as a liberal, and the author understood it in the American meaning. As the conversation proceeded, the author learned that he had been wrong. The lawyer meant it in the Italian sense; he was a member of the Liberal party, a political party near the right end of the Italian political spectrum.

There are also other Liberal parties in Europe. They are not liberal in the American sense.

We do not want to overemphasize the importance of the labels *conservative*, *liberal*, *right wing*, and *left wing*. For one thing, individuals and organizations may change over time or may change as they perceive shifts in the moods of voters. Some feel that these labels are too simplistic or even naive and that reality is more complex. Nevertheless, we wanted to bring them to your attention because they are much used in media and other discussions of international events and because different political forces flow from, for example, a right-wing government than from a left-wing one.

Reading
Right and Left—What Do These Terms Mean?

A former member of the British Parliament made some interesting points on this subject. He found the Far Left similar to the Far Right.

"The terms 'Right' and 'Left' are losing their purchase. Under conventions established earlier in our century, people on the Far Right are seen as 'Fascists' and people on the Far Left as 'Communists,' so that on the Left-Right axis, the two are supposed to be opposites, or at least at opposite extremes as far away from each other as it is possible to get. But a majority of observers seem to agree that the kinds of society they establish when they get into power have fundamental features of a striking nature in common— and are a good deal more like each other than either of them is like Liberal Democracy, which is supposed to separate them in the middle, halfway between them."

Government Ownership
of Business

One might reasonably assume that government ownership of the factors of production is found only in communist or socialist countries, but that assumption is not correct. Very large segments of business are owned by the governments of numerous countries which do not consider themselves either communist or socialist. From country to country, there are wide differences in the industries that are government owned and in the extent of government ownership (see Figure 9–1).

Why Firms Are Nationalized

There are a number of reasons, sometimes overlapping, why governments put their hands on firms. Some of them are: (1) to extract more money from the firms—the government suspects that the firms are concealing profits; (2) an extension of (1)—the government feels that it could run the firms more efficiently and make more money; (3) ideological—when left-wing governments are elected, they sometimes nationalize industries, as has occurred in Britain, France, and Canada; (4) to catch votes as politicians save jobs by putting dying industries on life-support systems which can be disconnected after the election; (5) because the government has pumped money into a firm or an industry, and control usually follows money; and (6) happenstance, as with the nationalization after WWII of German-owned firms in Europe.

Figure 9–1

Who owns how much?

Privately owned: ○ all or nearly all

Publicly owned: 25% 50% 75% ● all or nearly all

	Posts	Telecommunications	Electricity	Gas	Oil production	Coal	Railways	Airlines	Motor industry	Steel	Shipbuilding	
Australia	●	●	●	●	○	○	●	75%	○	○	na	Australia
Austria	●	●	●	●	●	●	●	●	●	●	na	Austria
Belgium	●	●	25%	25%	na	○	●	●	○	50%	○	Belgium
Brazil	●	●	●	●	●	●	●	25%	○	75%	○	Brazil
Britain	●	●	●	●	25%	●	●	75%	50%	75%	●	Britain
Canada	●	25%	●	○	○	○	75%	75%	○	○	○	Canada
France	●	●	●	●	na	●	●	75%	50%	75%	○	France
West Germany	●	●	75%	50%	25%	50%	●	●	25%	○	25%	West Germany
Holland	●	●	75%	75%	na	na	●	75%	50%	25%	○	Holland
India	●	●	●	●	●	●	●	●	○	75%	●	India
Italy	●	●	75%	●	na	na	●	●	25%	75%	75%	Italy
Japan	●	●	○	○	na	○	75%	25%	○	○	○	Japan
Mexico	●	●	●	●	●	●	●	50%	25%	75%	●	Mexico
South Korea	●	●	75%	○	na	25%	●	○	○	75%	○	South Korea
Spain	●	50%	○	75%	na	50%	●	●	○	50%	75%	Spain
Sweden	●	●	50%	●	na	na	●	50%	○	75%	75%	Sweden
Switzerland	●	●	●	●	na	na	●	25%	○	○	na	Switzerland
United States	●	○	25%	○	○	○	25%*	○	○	○	○	United States

na - not applicable or negligible production

* including Conrail

Source: *Economist* (December 30, 1978); p. 39. According to the *Economist* of December 21, 1985, the percentages stated in Figure 9–1 were unchanged.

Everybody's Doing It

All governments are in business to some degree, but outside the communist or LDC areas, none is so far into business as Italy.[2]

Italy

The Italian government-owned Institute for Industrial Reconstruction (IRI) has been called an "industrial octopus."[3] In 1978, IRI was a leader in one category: it lost more money—$970 million—than any other company. (The number 2 loser was another state-owned company, British Steel, which lost $798 million.) The Italian government owns companies in many industries, including salt, tobacco, matches, mining, railways, airlines, auto manufacturing, steel, telephone, power plants, banking, restaurants, chocolate and ice cream production, radio and television stations, and refineries.

The losses of IRI continued, and by the end of 1986 its accumulated losses since 1979 were about $12 billion. In late 1984, however, a new chairman took over and began the gigantic job of turning IRI around. He is Ramano Prodi, a highly respected industrial economist whose strategy is to get IRI out of doing things that the private sector can do better. Prodi may have some difficulty selling off parts of IRI because the socialist premier, Bettino Craxi, was opposed to doing so. In 1987, Craxi was succeeded by a Christian Democrat as premier but the socialists remained a part of the ruling coalition.

IRI's losses fell in 1985 and 1986, and cash flow increased as some of the managers brought in by Prodi to run IRI companies turned losers to winners. Nevertheless, it is too early to say whether Prodi and his team can turn the world's champion loser into a winner.

The United States

Historically, the United States has been opposed to nationalizing industries, but it took a large step in that direction when it set up the Consolidated Rail Corporation (Conrail) in 1976. Conrail took over six bankrupt railroads in the U.S. Northeast. Ten years later the U.S. government was taking steps to sell Conrail; one proposal was to sell it to a private rail company, but this evoked opposition from Conrail's managers and employees as well as from competing railroads. Instead, its stock was sold publicly to private buyers who included many Conrail workers and managers.

France

The French government has been in business for centuries. When Louis XIV began building the magnificent Versailles Palace, the plans included thousands of mirrors and crystal chandeliers. The Venetians were the dominant glassmakers of the world at that time, and Louis's finance minister, Colbert, did not like the thought of paying them for all of those mirrors and chandeliers. Colbert set up the company now known as Saint-Gobain, and Louis insisted on owning the company himself, rather than allowing noble and idle courtiers to own it. Louis feared that if they owned the company, they would become rich and powerful and possible rivals to his rule.

Likewise, socialists did not nationalize the Renault automobile company. Charles de Gaulle's post-WWII government did so to avenge its founder's collaboration with the occupying Germans. Renault has drawn money from the French government for investments and has made some profits in the years since.

In 1981, the socialists under François Mitterrand won French elections and promptly nationalized six big industrial groups and 36 private banks and bought controlling stakes in three other companies. That has proved to be expensive.

Only one of the companies taken over, Compagnie Générale d'Electricité, was profitable in 1982, and several were nearly broke when the Mitterrand government seized them. A French banker remarked, "Perhaps that is why we have not seen a single case of shareholders contesting their compensation," when the government paid for the seized shares. In 1983, it cost over 60 billion French francs (about $7.5 billion) for the French government to keep its nationalized industries in business. This was nearly double their 1980 cost.

Between 1981 and 1986, the French government invested over $5 billion in the industries it nationalized—20 times more than private shareholders had invested over a 20-year period. At least partly as a result of that investment, many nationalized firms have been brought back to profit (exceptions are the steelmakers Sacilor and Usinor and the automaker Renault).

Unfair Competition?

Where government-owned companies compete with privately owned companies, the complaint is sometimes made by the private companies that the government companies have unfair advantages. Some of the complaints are: (1) government-owned companies can cut prices unfairly since they do not have to make profits; (2) they get cheaper financing; (3) they get government contracts; (4) they get export assistance; and (5) they can hold down wages with government assistance.[4]

Government-Private Collaboration Difficult

The objectives of private firms and those of government agencies and operations are usually different. Figure 9–2 illustrates some of the differences.

Privatization

The tide turned during the early 1980s, and by 1986 the selling of state assets—from airlines to telephone companies—had captivated politicians everywhere, even in socialist Spain and communist China. Given the American devotion to

Figure 9–2

Planners and Business Investors—Why Can't They Collaborate?

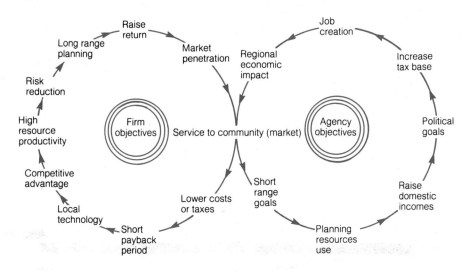

Source: Robert P. Vichas and Kimon Constas, "Public Planners and Business Investors—Why Can't They Collaborate?" *Long Range Planning,* no. 3 (Pergamon Press, Ltd., 1981), p. 83.

private enterprise, it is odd but accurate to report that the United States is lagging behind other countries in selling its assets.

Among countries involved in the **privatization** movement are Canada, the United States, Mexico, Chile, Brazil, Britain, France, Spain, Italy, Holland, West Germany, Turkey, Thailand, Singapore, Japan, the Philippines, and Malaysia. Britain, under Margaret Thatcher, is the acknowledged leader of the movement.

Perhaps surprisingly, among the services and assets being privatized are social security, public housing, highways, and bus service.

Private Sector More Efficient than State?

Proof beyond all doubt may be impossible to obtain. Academics nonetheless try. One study found that it cost the New York Department of Sanitation $40 (of which $32 was for labor) to deal with a ton of rubbish. It cost private collectors only $17 (of which $10 was for labor).

Research in Australia found the private airline, Ansett, considerably more productive than the public sector's Trans Australian Airline. Interviews with managers moving from the public to the private system show a large majority who say that privatization has improved their performance. They cite the demoralizing effects of political interference and bureaucratic delay when their companies were government owned.

Italy Too?

Italy was singled out above as the Western government that was perhaps most involved in business ownership. However, it too has joined the move toward privatization, and IRI realized some $4 billion between 1983 and 1986 by selling shares of some of its companies. Another state-owned giant, Ente Nazionale Idrocarburi (ENI), has also sold companies to the private sector, and one of them is Montedison. Before its sale in 1981, Montedison's losses were running at more than a half billion dollars annually. Today the Milan-based diversified chemicals company has been turned around; it earned about $170 million in 1986, and it is expanding internationally.

Nationalism

Nationalism has been called the "secular religion of our time." In most of the older countries, loyalty to one's country and pride in it were based on such shared common features as race, language, religion, or ideology. Many of the newer countries, notably in Africa, have accidental boundaries resulting from their colonial past, and within these countries, there are several tribes and languages. That has resulted in civil wars, as in Nigeria and Angola, but it has not prevented these new countries from developing instant and fierce nationalism.

Nationalism is an emotion which can cloud or even prevent rational dealings with foreigners. The ills of a society can be blamed on foreign companies, which is what the chief of the joint staffs oi the Peruvian military did when the military forces took charge in Peru.

Some of the effects of nationalism on MNEs are: (1) requirements for minimum local ownership or local product assembly or manufacture; (2) reservation of certain industries for local companies; (3) preference of local suppliers for government contracts; (4) limitations on the number and types of foreign employees; (5) protectionism, using tariffs, quotas, or other devices; (6) seeking a "French solution"* instead of a foreign takeover of a local firm;[5] and in the most extreme cases, (7) expropriation or confiscation.[6]

Government Protection

A historic function of government, of whatever ideology, has been the protection of the economic activities—farming, mining, manufacturing, or whatever—within its geographic area of control. These must be protected from attack and

---

*The French solution is to make every effort to find a French company rather than a foreign one to take over the French firm.

destruction or robbery by terrorists, bandits, revolutionaries, and foreign invaders. The mines of Shaba were not so protected.

Economically Targeted Invasion

The mineral production of the Shaba Province of Zaire accounts for some 75 percent of Zaire's total export earnings.[7] Military forces, apparently armed and trained in Angola, invaded Shaba twice during the 1970s, and Zaire's military was unable to protect Shaba.

The output of the Shaban mines was virtually halted, at least temporarily, and that seems to have been the intent of the invaders. They retreated without attempting to establish control over the area as soon as rescue forces arrived from France and Belgium, but before retreating, they massacred several hundred Europeans who played a major role in the production of Zaire's wealth. The invaders also killed many of the native workers, but not indiscriminately as with the Europeans. The natives were murdered selectively, and those chosen were, in large part, the skilled workers, technicians, and executives of the mines.[8]

Terrorism

Since the 1970s, the world has been plagued by various groups that have hijacked airplanes, shot and kidnapped people, and bombed people and objects. A common denominator of these terrorist groups has been hatred of the social, economic, and political orders that they find in the world. Another characteristic is their confusion as to what sort of order they would substitute if they had the chance.

Acts of **terrorism** have occurred worldwide outside the communist countries. We shall look at the Italian experience to observe some results of terrorism and of the countermeasures taken against it. Italy was chosen because it has been so hard hit.

Terrorism against Politicians

There have been many politically inspired shootings of politicians, judges, and police. A typical method is to shoot at the knees, but some are killed, as was Aldo Moro in 1978. Moro had been premier of Italy, and at the time of his kidnapping and murder he was the leader of a political party.

Violence against Business, Too

Politicians are not the only targets of terrorist violence. Fiat S.P.A., Italy's largest private enterprise, says that acts of insubordination and violence cut its output more than 12 percent in 1979 and sharply increased costs.

In addition to the more commonly known costs of terrorist activity (property damage, ransom payments, and expenditures for security), terrorism has

Figure 9-3

Permission granted by CIGNA Corporation. Copyright 1984, Carl Fischer. All rights reserved.

Not all corporate takeovers are the result of a winning proxy fight.

detrimental effects on the productivity of companies. U.S. manufacturers in El Salvador offer prime examples. With travel of trained technicians to plants in the country largely embargoed, machinery that breaks down remains idle, distribution of products comes to a standstill, and some firms are forced to ship machinery back to the United States for overhauls.

Labor-intensive operations can respond more flexibly to terrorism. They can suspend operations temporarily or pull out permanently—with little or no loss of investment in equipment.

Kidnapping for Ransom

Kidnapping is another weapon used by terrorists. The victims are held for ransom, frequently very large amounts, which provides an important source of funds for the terrorists. Italian industry is not alone in being subjected to terrorism and kidnapping for ransom. For example, it is said that industry in Argentina has paid ransom of several hundred million dollars for the release of kidnapped business executives.[9]

By 1986 Colombia and Peru had become the most dangerous places for American executives, and a long stay by a high-ranking American executive in either country is risky. Brief visits are usually fairly safe because kidnappings take a while to plan, so top executives from the United States practice what is called commando management. They arrive in Bogota or Lima as secretly as possible, meet for a few days with local employees, and fly off before kidnappers learn of their presence.[10]

Countermeasures by the Government

The Italian government issued a series of antiterrorist decrees in December 1979. A special antiterrorist squad, some 25,000 strong, was created in 1979, giving the police new powers to arrest and question suspects.[11]

Between 1975 and 1982, terrorist groups almost shattered Italy's faith in its ability to govern itself without resorting to a communist- or fascist-style police state. Over 3,000 suspected or convicted terrorists had been jailed or sentenced to prison, and in January 1983, 32 people were sentenced to life imprisonment for Moro's kidnapping and murder. Among the encouraging signs were the increase in the numbers of penitents and defectors and the fact that the terrorists were having more difficulty in recruiting as their charisma among Italian youth faded.

Remaining Terrorists Find New Allies. As their original source of recruits—educated, idealistic young Italians—became disenchanted, the remaining terrorist leaders turned to crime. They cooperated with Mafia groups in kidnapping for ransom. They cooperated with the Soviet, Libyan, and Syrian secret services in running heroin and guns from Turkey and Eastern Europe to the West, and although they call themselves communist revolutionaries, much of the money and guns they got was supplied to neofascist terrorists.[12]

Government-Sponsored Terrorism; Acts of War. During the 1980s, evidence began to mount that many terrorists were trained, financed, and directed by governments—for example, the Soviet Union, Iran, Syria, and Libya. The U.S. Navy and Air Force bombed Tripoli, the Libyan capital, in spring 1986 because the U.S. government was convinced that the Libyan government had sponsored terrorism that had cost American lives. In fall 1986, a British court convicted a Palestinian of trying to smuggle explosives aboard an El Al Israel 747 aircraft, concealed in the baggage of his pregnant girlfriend. The flight from London to Tel Aviv would have been blown up over Austria. It was developed at the trial that the material for the explosives had been brought into London in Syrian diplomatic pouches aboard the Syrian government airline and that the Syrian ambassador had sanctioned or even directed the operation. In international law, government action to damage or kill in another country is an act of war.

More Female Terrorists. A Rand study found a high percentage of female terrorists. Profiles of German and Italian female terrorists show that they have generally proved more ruthless and dangerous than their male counterparts. They are tougher and crueler, and men in groups dominated by women are more brutal and competitive than men in other groups.[13]

Countermeasures by Industry

Beginning in November 1979, Fiat fired several hundred workers for insubordination and violence. An Italian labor court upheld Fiat when the workers sued to retrieve their jobs. Perhaps more surprising, an important part of Italy's Communist party leadership agreed with Fiat management that the firings were reasonable and proper.

As kidnapping and extortion directed against businesses and governments have become common fund-raising and political techniques for terrorists, insurance against such acts has grown into a multimillion-dollar business. The world's largest kidnapping and extortion underwriting firm is located in London. The firm is Cassidy and Davis, which underwrites for Lloyd's of London and says that it covers some 9,000 companies. Cassidy and Davis does not sit back and wait for claims to be filed. It runs antiterrorism training courses for executives, in which the subjects covered range from defensive driving techniques—escape tactics and battering through blockades—to crisis management. Country-by-country risk analyses are instantly available on international computer hookups.

Cassidy and Davis works closely with Control Risk, Ltd., a London-based security service company. Control Risk works behind the scenes to advise companies or families in negotiations with kidnappers.

Cassidy and Davis encourages its clients to use Control Risk services. The premiums for the insurance underwritten by Cassidy and Davis range from some $3,000 a year for $1.5 million of coverage in low-risk England to $60,000 a year for the same coverage in high-risk Peru.[14]

Government Stability

Government **stability** can be approached from two directions. One can speak of either a government's simple ability to maintain itself in power or the stability or permanence of a government's policies. It is safe to generalize that business (indeed almost all agricultural, commercial, and financial activities) prospers most when there is a stable government with permanent—or at most, gradually changing—policies.

Stability and Instability: Examples and Results

Instability in Lebanon

Here is a classic example of the impact of a change from order to chaos—from stability to **instability**—on the business and finance of a prosperous country. Until 1974, Lebanon prospered as the trading, banking, MNE regional headquarters, business services (that is, accounting, legal, and financial services), transportation, and tourist center of the Middle East. The country achieved this prosperity with virtually no natural resources. Its land is mostly arid desert or mountains. Its prosperity was the work of an industrious people given political stability.

Then civil war broke out in Lebanon. The details of that civil war are beyond the scope of this book, but its reasons included ideological and religious differences. The results were catastrophic.

Homes, offices, banks, stores, transportation, communications, and sanitary facilities were destroyed. The people fled the country or fought and survived as best they could. Almost all of the previous commercial activities ended.

Stability in Bolivia

In 152 years of independence from Spain, Bolivia had 187 governments. Then, in 1972, a government seized power that by 1976 had established the durability record for any government in the 20th century. The economic results were startling and encouraging.

Bolivia's GNP grew by 7.3 percent in 1975 and 7 percent in 1976, and its inflation rate was about 12 percent. At the same time, such neighbors as Argentina, Chile, and Peru were experiencing varying types of political unrest, were growing more slowly or not at all, and were suffering much higher rates of inflation.

Hector Ormachea, the Bolivian government official in charge of negotiating development loans abroad, spoke of "projects, not politics." And projects resulted—more than 300 of them by 1977. They ranged from roads into areas previously accessible only by air to oil exploration, mining ventures, and agricultural and industrial development.

Unused Wealth. Bolivia is potentially a very rich country. Its resources include tin, zinc, antimony, copper, gold, tungsten, and bismuth, and it is more than self-sufficient in oil despite very little recent exploration or drilling.

The country's resources have scarcely been touched, at least in part because of Bolivia's previous political instability. Past governments had been quick to nationalize foreign mines. Given the mid-1970s stability, European, Japanese, and U.S. firms negotiated to explore for and extract the resources.[15]

Renewed Foreign Confidence. Another sign of renewed foreign confidence in Bolivia was given in 1977. Underwriters led by the Arab Finance Corporation and Merrill Lynch International handled the sale in Europe of Bolivian debt securities. While the amount was a relatively small $15 million, it was the first offering to foreign investors in about 50 years. Until Bolivia had achieved political stability, it would have been fruitless to try to borrow money abroad; no one would have lent it.[16]

Perils of Pauline. By 1979 there was further political turmoil in Bolivia, and between then and 1985 there were 12 Bolivian governments—most of them military. Inflation soared to about 25,000 percent in 1985, and in that year over half of Bolivia's export earnings—some $600 million—came from sales of cocaine; less than $500 million came from sales of minerals, oil, gas, and agricultural products. While the few cocaine traffickers got rich, the great bulk of the Bolivian population—growing at 2.6 percent a year—sank more deeply into poverty. Domestic investment declined and production collapsed.

Miracle of La Paz?* In 1985, a new Bolivian president, Victor Paz Estenssero, was democratically elected. Estenssero immediately froze salaries in the state sector (which accounted for roughly 40 percent of the economy), removed price controls, stopped subsidies, slashed many import tariffs, floated the peso, and liberalized labor laws to allow easy firing and hiring. He told state enterprises to cover their costs or close, put new taxes on cars and houses, and offered a back tax amnesty.

Inflation plunged to near zero, foreign development aid is being restored, local investments have been starting up, and an attack has been begun on the big drug traffickers. Both the World Bank and the International Monetary Fund have provided millions to finance Bolivia's agricultural and industrial recovery and to compensate it for the collapse of international tin prices (tin was once Bolivia's main export).[17]

It remains to be seen whether the dramatic turn of events in 1985–86 will be sustained and the country returned to its mid-1970s run of good performance. Formidable political pressures are being exerted against the present government; the disgruntled government employees, tin workers, cocaine producers and smugglers, and potentially the army could throw the country back into turmoil.

Permanence or Continuity of Government Policy toward Business

While government policy toward business is usually in a state of gradual change, managements expect and can adapt to that. It is sudden, radical change that cre-

*La Paz is the capital of Bolivia.

ates uncertainty and concern. This has been defined as a form of government instability.[18]

An example of an abrupt change in policy was the Indian government's promulgation of the Foreign Exchange Regulation Act. Under that act, the Indian government ordered International Business Machines (IBM) to sell 60 percent of its Indian business to Indian citizens. Rather than comply, IBM pulled out of India, closing its 800-employee operation.[19]

In 1978, IBM decided to withdraw from Nigeria also. The reason was a law similar to the Indian law.[20] It should be pointed out that IBM's pullouts were not due solely to the prospect of losing majority ownership of its subsidiaries. They also involved IBM policies about worldwide integration and trade secrets.

In both India and Nigeria, IBM tried to negotiate a mutually agreeable compromise but did not succeed. However, it was successful under a similar law in Indonesia and remains in business there.[21]

Traditional Hostilities

One need mention only a few of the **traditional hostilities** to illustrate their powerful impact on business and trade.

Arab-Israel

Israel is surrounded on three sides by Arab countries, but until the peace efforts initiated by the Egyptian Anwar Sadat, the Arab countries would not trade or have other peaceful dealings with it. Indeed, they boycott companies that trade with Israel, and because some of the Arab countries are extremely rich OPEC members, the boycott can be financially painful.*

Zimbabwe-Rhodesia and South Africa

This is black-white racial hostility. When Zimbabwe (then Rhodesia) declared unilateral independence from Britain rather than accept a black majority government, the UN, led by Britain, imposed wide-ranging trade embargoes on Rhodesia. South Africa, the Soviet Union, and, reportedly, a number of other countries ignored or evaded the embargo, but normal patterns of trade and investment were disrupted.[22]

In 1986, South Africa became the target of embargoes by the U.S. and West European countries opposed to South Africa's apartheid practices.

*See Chapter 10 for discussion of U.S. law dealing with this boycott.

North Atlantic Treaty Organization (NATO)–Warsaw Pact

For years after WWII, during the so-called Cold War, the NATO nations (Canada, the United States, and Western Europe plus Greece and Turkey) embargoed goods considered to have strategic military value to the Warsaw Pact (most of the communist countries led by the Soviet Union). As ideas of détente pervaded NATO, the embargo was considerably relaxed. Then, with Soviet- backed Cuban troops marching about Africa and Soviet troops invading Afghanistan, the embargo was stiffened. But stiff or relaxed, the NATO embargo has been in effect for years and is a political force acting on international trade.

International Organizations

As discussed above, nationalism is a powerful political force which has grown greatly during the mid- and late 20th century. There are also international political forces with which business must contend. Here we shall cover briefly the political impact of some of the international organizations that we introduced in Chapter 4.

The United Nations (UN)

The UN is highly politicized. The member countries vote as blocs formed because of ideology or perceived similar objectives. There are the communist and noncommunist groupings and the developed countries versus the less developed countries.

United Nations personnel advise UN members on such matters as tax, monetary, and fiscal policies. The UN is active in the harmonization of laws affecting international trade. It had a hand in drafting an international commercial arbitration convention. It has drafted a code of conduct for MNEs. Any of the political ideologies we have discussed can be reflected in the content and spirit of tax, trade, and arbitration laws; conduct codes; and of fiscal or monetary policies.

UNCTAD is credited with having influenced the IMF to ease its restrictions on loans to LDCs. This is important to banks lending to and suppliers selling to LDCs.

Virtually all of the specialized UN agencies are now actively advising LDCs what to buy for their agriculture, industry, airlines, health programs, weather stations, and so forth. These are huge markets for business.

The World Bank Group

One or another member of the World Bank Group finances large parts of the purchases made by LDCs. Although the bank's charter bans political activity by its officers and employees, it is reported that its president was involved in campaign-planning strategy for one of the U.S. presidential candidates in 1980.[23]

IMF, GATT, and OPEC

The IMF can have great influence on the fiscal and monetary policies of the nations that it assists, and as reported in Chapter 4, there are many who feel that its power is growing.

Although GATT has in general striven to lower barriers to trade, it has condoned their erection by LDCs in some cases. Import barriers are of course an important political force affecting multinational business operations.

The political power of OPEC was discussed in Chapter 4. We mention it here again to remind you that petroleum is now as much a political force as it is a commodity.

The EC

Slowly but surely, the member nations of the EC are surrendering parts of their sovereign powers to the Brussels headquarters. One need mention only a few areas to realize the extent of the EC's influence on business. Among other things, the EC is working to harmonize laws dealing with taxes, patents, labor conditions, competition, insurance, banking, and capital markets.

Harmonization of differing national laws is one matter, but the EC has now gone a step beyond that—to lawmaking. This is occurring in such fields as company law, antitrust, and consumer and environmental protection.[24]

In May 1983, the EC finance ministers adopted the so-called Seventh Directive, which is an accounting rule under which MNEs will have to submit consolidated accounts for their entire enterprise, worldwide. It is thought that some American MNEs might welcome the Seventh Directive, as it could lay open the financial condition of some of their European competitors much more than present practice.[25]

The Organization for Economic Cooperation and Development (OECD)

This 24-member organization of industrialized countries has issued "Guidelines for Multinational Enterprises." One writer states that rather than being a stifling set of legal dos and don'ts, the guidelines create a voluntary set of principles upon which to build sound international economic relations.[26] Nevertheless, these ostensibly voluntary guidelines can have a significant impact.

> When Badger, Raytheon's subsidiary in Belgium, closed shop, it did not have enough money to meet its labor termination obligations. The Belgian government and labor unions used the pressure of the OECD "voluntary" guidelines to require Raytheon to pay Badger's obligations.[27]

Labor

Workers and labor unions are the subject of Chapter 11, but we would be remiss if we did not mention them in connection with the political forces bearing on business. The European labor unions are ideologically oriented, usually toward the left. The American unions are said to be more pragmatic, but in practice they are extremely active politically. They supply large amounts of money and political workers to support the political candidates they favor.

In Europe, the United States, and, increasingly, in Japan, labor makes its political force felt not only at the polls but also in the legislatures. The unions lobby for or against laws as these are perceived to be for or against the interests of labor.

Multinational Enterprises (MNEs)

International business is not merely a passive victim of political forces. It can be a powerful force in the world political arena.[28]

Forty Percent of World's Top Economic Units Are Firms, Not Nations

The MNE negotiating with a country may be bigger than the country. According to rankings in 1984, General Motors' sales of $83.9 billion made it the 28th largest economic unit. Its sales were larger than the $80.4 billion GNP of Iran. Exxon's sales of $90.9 billion made it the 23rd largest economic unit, surpassing Indonesia. Of course, the GNP of the great majority of other countries is still smaller.[29]

Such financial size carries power. However, the MNE's power need not rest solely on size. It can come from the possession of scarce capital, technology, and management plus the capability to deploy those resources around the world. The MNE may have the processing, productive, distributive, and marketing abilities necessary for the successful exploitation of raw materials or for the manufacture, distribution, and marketing of certain products. Those abilities are frequently not available in LDCs. Overall, the role of MNEs has been growing, not declining.[30]

MNE Goals and Means to Achieve Them

An MNE can choose a number of means to bring pressure on a government. The MNE may be considering an investment in a country or may be seeking licenses or permits in countries where it has invested. Or it may be trying to mitigate adverse effects of the country's laws as they change. The means are dealt with here; the elements for management decisions about which means to apply are discussed in Chapter 22.

Host Government Competition

Almost all countries welcome new investments in chosen industries and areas. An MNE in a position to make investments can look for countries where the economic and political environments are favorable, and if there is more than one such country, the MNE's bargaining position is enhanced. The same would apply to a first-time investment or to the enlargement of an existing investment.

Home Government Pressure

From time to time, the MNE can get its home government to intercede with the host government. This has occurred most often when extreme circumstances such as the confiscation of the MNE's assets by the host country have been involved. A different sort of reason for requesting government help involved Japan. MNEs dissatisfied with the Japanese government's reluctance to permit foreign ownership of firms in Japan have obtained the assistance of European and American governments in pressuring that government to relax this policy.

Protective Local Coloration

Earlier in this chapter we had a look at nationalism, which, you will remember, causes foreigners to be disliked at one time or another in most countries. A foreign MNE can utilize a number of devices to conceal or diminish its foreignness. It can use a local-sounding name—Spanish in Spanish-speaking countries, German in German-speaking ones, and so forth. It can use local persons in local company management. It can assist local entrepreneurs to set up farms and factories to supply its raw materials or components needs. It can work in partnership with local companies and individuals. And it can even change nationality.

The MNE can also change the products it markets. In response to an export drive of the Mexican government, Coca-Cola de Mexico strayed far from the traditional Coca-Cola drink. It exported oregano to Los Angeles, coffee to Houston, ceramics and sweaters to Germany, and baskets to New York.[31]

R&D, Management, Distribution, Capital Sources

Among the strengths usually available to MNEs are research and development capability, management expertise, marketing ability, and a variety of capital sources. Some or all of these strengths may be available to a host country only through the multinational firm.

The MNE can use such of its strengths as may be required to gain favorable conditions from the host country. In addition, it can use the threat of withholding technology, capital, distribution, or whatever may deter a host country from expropriating MNE assets within its borders.

Country Risk Assessment (CRA)

It is arbitrary to place this subject in a chapter on political forces because CRA involves many risks other than political risks. It is probably important enough to warrant a separate chapter, but one of our objectives is to avoid an overlong book. We will introduce our readers to CRA here; there is a growing literature about it, and those who are interested can find much material.[32]

Although it is arbitrary to put CRA in this chapter, it is not unreasonable, because the political events of recent years have concentrated much more attention on the subject. Firms that had already done CRA updated and strengthened the function, and many other companies began CRA.

Types of Country Risks

Country risks are increasingly political in nature, caused or influenced by political developments. There are wars, revolutions, and coups. Less dramatic, but nevertheless important for businesses, are government changes by election of a socialist or nationalist government which may be hostile to private business and particularly to foreign-owned business.

The risks may be economic or financial. There may be persistent balance-of-payment deficits or high inflation rates. Repayment of loans may be questionable.

Labor conditions may cause investors to pause. Labor productivity may be low, or labor unions may be militant.

Laws may be changed about such subjects as taxes, currency convertibility, tariffs, quotas, or labor permits. The chances for a fair trial in local courts must be assessed.

Terrorism may be present. If it is, can the company protect its personnel and property?

Information Content for CRA

The types of information that a firm will need to judge country risks will vary according to the nature of its business and the length of time required for the investment, loan, or other involvement to yield a satisfactory return.

Nature of Business

Consider, for example, the needs of a hotel company compared with those of heavy-equipment manufacturers or manufacturers of personal hygiene products or mining companies. Banks have their own sets of problems and information needs. Sometimes there are variations between firms in the same industry or on a project-to-project basis. The nationality—home country—of the company may be a factor; does the host country bear a particular animus, or friendly attitude, toward the home country?

Length of Time Required

Export financing usually involves the shortest time period of exposure. Typically, payments are made within 180 days—usually less—and exporters can get insurance or bank protection.

Bank loans can be short, medium, or long term. However, when the business includes host country assembly, mixing, manufacture, or extraction (oil or minerals), long-term commitments are necessary.

With long-term investment or loan commitments, there are inherent problems with risk analysis that cannot be resolved. Most such investment opportunities require 5, 10, or more years to pay off. But the utility of risk analyses of social, political, and economic factors decreases precipitously over longer time spans.

Who Does Country Risk Assessing?

General or specific analysis, macro or micro analysis, and political, social, and economic analysis have been conducted—perhaps under different names—for years. The Conference Board located bits and pieces of CRA being performed in various company departments—for example, the international division and the public affairs, finance, legal, economics, planning, as well as product-producing departments. Sometimes the efforts were duplicative, and the people in one department were unaware that others in the company were similarly involved.

Efforts are now being made to concentrate CRA and to maximize its effectiveness for the company. Part of this involves guidelines about the participation of top management.

Another source of country risk analysis is the outside consulting and publishing firm. As CRA has mushroomed in perceived importance, a number of such firms have been formed or have expanded.

Instead of or in addition to the outside consultants, a number of firms have buttressed their internal risk analysis staffs by hiring such experts as international business or political science professors or retired State Department, CIA, or military people.

CRA Procedure

There are a multitude of possible approaches to CRA. One set of steps, suggested by the Swiss bank Credit Suisse, is illustrated in Table 9–1.

One of the steps suggested in Table 9–1 is arrow diagrams, and Figure 9–4 provides an illustrative arrow diagram of the domestic stability of Saudi Arabia. Note that this diagram starts with the world economy; it does not include consideration of the Iran-Iraq war and other Middle East unrest.

Table 9-1

Major Methodological Steps Used in Political Risk Analysis

Determining the situation: Where do we stand?

1. Collecting information on countries and events
2. Compiling data
3. Creating and running a documentation service
4. Setting up a data base
5. Evaluation of periodical information services
6. Application of simple indicators
7. Composite indicators (indices)
8. Scaling
9. Construction of typologies
10. Classification
11. Multidimensional scaling

Explanation: Why are things as they are?

12. Arrow diagrams
13. Cognitive mapping: analysis of motives and intentions
14. Utilization of theoretical findings
15. Systematic evaluation of the professional literature
16. Systems analysis
17. Correlations analysis
18. Regression analysis
19. Analysis of nonlinear relationships
20. Partial and multiple correlations analysis
21. Multiple regression analysis
22. Path analysis

Preview: What's ahead?

23. Historical analogies
24. General analogies
25. Systematic expert judgment
26. Delphi analysis
27. Bayesian inference
28. Cross-impact analysis
29. Early warning indicators
30. Extrapolation with moving averages
31. Trend analysis
32. Time series analysis
33. Spectral analysis
34. Combined time series and trend analysis
35. Analysis of changing trends

Preparing decisions: What can we do?

36. Decision tree in problem analysis
37. Game theory approach to problem analysis
38. Scenario writing
39. Application of morphological approaches
40. Gaming
41. Computer simulation
42. Econometric models
43. Global models

Deciding: What will we do?

44. Decision tree
45. Decision matrix
46. Decision tree with incomplete information (linear partial information analysis)

Source: *Bulletin*, Crédit Suisse, Autumn 1983, p. 6.

Figure 9-4

Domestic Political Stability in Saudi Arabia (example of an arrow diagram)

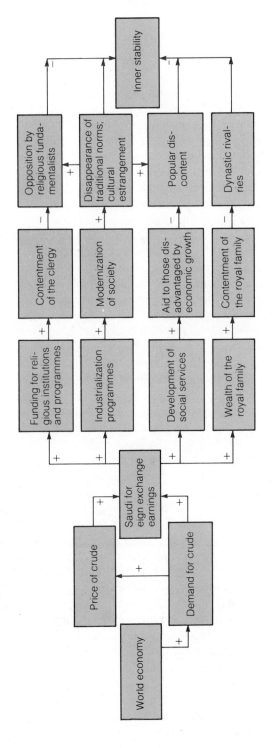

Source: *Bulletin*, Crédit Suisse, Autumn 1983, p. 6.

Summary

Ideologies are defined in dictionaries and textbooks. Countries and political parties use names with ideological meanings to describe themselves, but you must view these names cautiously because the political and economic actions of countries and parties may not be what you would expect from their names.

This is not true for the communist countries, whose political and economic actions have followed form, though, as we shall discuss in Chapter 17, some surprising changes are occurring in the People's Republic of China. Among other things, they confiscate all important privately owned factors of production.

The problem in capitalist countries is to abide by the many laws and regulations that affect business. In addition, several governments of capitalist countries own varieties of companies which operate both domestically and internationally, sometimes in competition with privately owned companies. As in the case of Great Britain, countries sometimes denationalize or privatize government-owned companies by selling them to private investors who are, in some instances, the company's employees.

Nationalism is an emotional force with political effects. If foreign companies wish to operate in a country, they must deal with nationalism, and there are quite a few ways for them to do so.

Some governments are unable, to a greater or lesser degree, to protect business and its managers from terrorism or other forms of attack. Countermeasures are being taken against terrorism which promise to reduce its frequency and success. Terrorism seems to be becoming less idealistic and more brutal as it turns to collaboration with the Mafia and the Soviet and other secret services as well as with fascist groups and profits from sales of guns and drugs.

Another new development in the terrorist tale is the emergence of more and more evidence that nations are training and financing terrorists and directing terrorist attacks in other countries. Evidence has implicated Syria, the Soviet Union, Iran, and Libya. In international law, such state activities are acts of war.

Gradual changes of government policies toward business are expected by business and can be coped with. However, sudden changes of such government policies or sudden changes of government are unsettling or alarming to business. When confronted by such changes, it tends to go away or stay away.

Traditional hostilities between world groups cause problems for business. One of these groups may boycott a company if it deals with the other. The UN or other groups of nations may embargo trade with some country or other group.

International organizations such as the UN and the EC are becoming more politicized and are gaining more political powers. Their influence on international business is growing.

Labor is a major political force. Even where it does not control important political parties, it can dispose of large amounts of money and personnel to affect elections and influence governments.

The MNE has political power. Some MNEs have more resources than the nations with which they deal. In addition, MNEs can use technology, distribution, management, capital sources, and other strengths in their negotiations with host countries.

Increasing world unrest, which stems from many causes, has made systematic country risk assessment necessary for banks and businesses operating internationally. They can seek help for such assessments from a number of sources, internal and external.

Questions

1. a. *What is ideology?*
   b. *Why is it important to international business?*
2. a. *What is the capitalist, free enterprise ideal?*
   b. *What is the actual situation in capitalist countries?*
3. *How and why do socialist LDCs and privately owned MNEs cooperate to their mutual profit?*
4. *What are some reasons why "capitalist" governments nationalize private businesses?*
5. a. *What is nationalism?*
   b. *What are some effects it can have on foreign business?*
6. *What impact can terrorism have on business?*
7. *Why does business fear sudden changes of government policies?*
8. *How can traditional hostilities affect business?*
9. *Give some examples of activities of international organizations which affect business.*
10. *Why do labor organizations have political power?*
11. *How can MNEs use their strengths to influence government policies?*
12. *What is country risk assessment as practiced by MNEs, and why is it a growing practice?*
13. *Is country risk assessment an exact science? Explain.*
14. a. *In terms of exposure to political risk (for example, expropriation), which of the following businesses would you consider the most and least vulnerable?*

Banks	*cosmetics manufacturers*
mines	*manufacturers personal hygiene*
oil fields	*products*
oil refineries	*Hotels*
heavy equipment manufacturers	*Automobile manufacturers*

   b. *Are the most vulnerable businesses high profile or low profile, and what are some ways to change the profile of a company in a foreign country?*

Minicase

9-1 Company Privatization

You are the chief executive officer of a company which the government has just denationalized by selling the company's stock to the company's employees. In the past, any major decision about company policy required approval by a government agency, which was time consuming. Wages and salaries had been established by reference to civil service "equivalents," and incentive payments were unheard of. Maintenance of the plant and equipment was lax, breakdowns were frequent and expensive, and utility expenses were high.

You want the newly privatized company to be a success. Suggest some programs that you would institute to improve its chances of success.

Minicase

9-2 Country Risk

Assessment

You are a management consultant who specializes in international business. One of your clients is considering investing in a manufacturing facility in South America and requests your advice about what risks it should look out for and what measures it can take to protect the company and its personnel.

Research a South American country to learn what risks a foreign investor will face there, not including commercial or private competition risks. Advise your client.

Supplementary Readings

Aitken, Thomas. "Assessing the Political Environment: An Emerging Function in International Companies." New York: Conference Board, 1980.

Ball, Donald A., and Wendell H. McCulloch, Jr. "Country Risk Analysis: Fad or Business Investment?" *Collegiate Forum*, Spring 1982, p. 12.

Barnet, Richard J., and Ronald E. Muller. *Global Reach: The Power of the Multinational Corporations.* New York: Simon & Schuster, 1974.

Beever, R. Colin. *Trade Unions and Free Labour Movement in the EEC.* London: Chatham House, 1969.

Behrman, Jack N. *Conflicting Constraints on the Multinational Enterprise: Potential for Resolution.* New York: Council of the Americas, 1974.

_____. *Decision Criteria for Foreign Direct Investment in Latin America.* New York: Council of the Americas, 1974.

_____. *International Business—Government Communications: U.S. Structures, Actors, and Issues.* Lexington, Mass.: Lexington Books, 1975.

Black, Robert. *Multinationals in Contention: Responses at Governmental and International Levels:* A Research Report from the Conference Board's Public Affairs Research Division. New York: The Conference Board, 1978.

Brookstone, Jeffrey M. *The Multinational Businessman and Foreign Policy: Entrepreneurial Politics in East-West Trade and Investment.* New York: Praeger Publishers, 1976.

Combes, David L. *Politics and Bureaucracy in the European Community: A Portrait of the Commission of the EEC.* Beverly Hills, Calif.: Sage Publications, 1970.

Fayerweather, John. *World Business: Promise and Problems.* New York: Macmillan, 1970.

Gabriel, Peter P. "MNCs in the Third World: Is Conflict Unavoidable?" *Harvard Business Review,* July–August 1972, pp. 17–24.

Green, Robert T. *Political Instability as a Determinant of U.S. Foreign Investment.* Austin: Bureau of Business Research, University of Texas at Austin, 1972.

"Growing Impact of Government." *U.S. News & World Report,* May 1, 1978, pp. 52–54.

Haendel, Dan. *Foreign Investments and the Management of Political Risk.* Boulder, Colo.: Westview Press, 1979.

Hedlund, Gunnar. *The Multinational Corporation, the Nation State, and the Trade Unions: An European Perspective.* Kent, Ohio: Kent University Press, 1977.

Hodges, Michael. *Multinational Corporations and National Government: A Case Study of the United Kingdom's Experience, 1964–1970.* Lexington, Mass.: Lexington Books, 1974.

"How the Multinationals Are Reined In." *Business Week,* March 12, 1979, p. 76.

Kapoor, Ashok. *International Business-Government Relations: U.S. Corporate Experience in Asia and Western Europe.* New York: AMACOM, 1973.

Kobrin, Stephen Jay. *Foreign Direct Investment, Industrialization, and Social Change.* Greenwich, Conn.: JAI Press, 1977.

Parry, Thomas G. *The Multinational Enterprise: International Investment and Host-Country Impacts.* Greenwich, Conn.: JAI Press, 1980.

Pirie, Madsen. *Dismantling the State: The Theory and Practice of Privatization.* Dallas: National Center for Policy Analysis, 1985.

"Public Sector Enterprise." *Economist,* December 30, 1978, pp. 37–58.

Rogers, Jerry, ed. *Global Risk Assessments: Issues, Concepts, and Applications.* Riverside, Calif.: Global Risk Assessments, 1986.

Solomon, Lewis D. *Multinational Corporations and the Emerging World Order.* Port Washington, N.Y.: Kennikat Press, 1978.

Stauffer, Robert Burton. *Nation-Building in a Global Economy: The Role of the Multinational Corporation.* Beverly Hills, Calif.: Sage Publications, 1973.

Stephenson, Hugh. *The Coming Clash: The Impact of Multinational Corporations on National States.* New York: Saturday Review Press, 1973.

Streeten, Paul. *Development Perspectives.* New York: St. Martin's Press, 1981.

Turner, Louis. *Invisible Empires: Multinational Companies and the Modern World.* London: Hamilton, 1970.

Vernon, Raymond. *Storm over the Multinationals: The Real Issues.* Cambridge, Mass.: Harvard University Press, 1977.

Wengert, Norman I. *The Political Allocation of Benefits and Burdens: Economic Externalities and Due Process in Environmental Protection*. Berkeley: Institute of Governmental Studies, University of California, 1976.

Endnotes

1. Keyes Beech, "Singapore Reeks with Riches and the Good Life," *Los Angeles Times*, April 21, 1980, part 4, p. 1.
2. For a good survey of public sector enterprise, see "The State in the Market," *Economist*, December 30, 1978, pp. 37–58.
3. Murray Seeger, "Italy Takes Prize for Its Corporate Octopus," *Los Angeles Times*, November 1, 1979, part 1, p. 12.
4. Charles C. Tillinghast, Jr., "Competing against State-Owned Companies," paper presented at the Academy of International Business Annual Meeting, 1979.
5. Felix Kessler, "France's Erratic Policies on Investment by Foreigners Confuse Many U.S. Firms," *The Wall Street Journal*, April 7, 1980, p. 24.
6. For a good discussion of nationalism, see Richard N. Farmer and Barry M. Richman, "Behavioral Problems in International Business," *International Business*, 3rd ed. (Bloomington, Ind.: Cedarwood Press, 1980), chap. 5, pp. 165–81.
7. *Economist*, May 27, 1978, p. 61.
8. Ibid.
9. David. G. Hubbard, "Lilliput Revisited: A Data-Based Critique of Corporate Captivity in Connection with Kidnapping and Terrorist Threat," in *The International Essays for Business Decision Makers*, ed. Mark B. Winchester, vol. 4 (Dallas: Center for International Business, 1979), pp. 19–31.
10. Brian O'Reilly, "Business Copes with Terrorism," *Fortune*, January 6, 1986, pp. 47–55.
11. *Economist*, December 22, 1979, pp. 31–32.
12. Claire Sterling, "The Red Brigades Have Strange Partners in Crime," *The Wall Street Journal*, August 18, 1982, p. 27.
13. "Terrorism and Beyond: An International Conference on Terrorism and Low-Level Conflict," Brian M. Jenkins, conference director, R—2714-DOE/DOJ/DOS/RC, December 1982.
14. Peter Almond with Bill Whalen, "Insurance against Terrorists an Emerging Growth Industry," *Insight*, March 17, 1986, pp. 52–54.
15. Everett G. Martin, "Playing It Cool in Bolivia," *The Wall Street Journal*, June 3, 1976, p. 14.
16. *The Wall Street Journal*, April 11, 1977, p. 12.
17. *Economist*, May 24, 1986, p. 76; and Eric Morgenhaler, "Clamping Down," *The Wall Street Journal*, August 13, 1986, p. 1.
18. Philip R. Cateora, *International Marketing*, 5th ed. (Homewood, Ill.: Richard D. Irwin, 1983), p. 154.
19. *Los Angeles Times*, November 29, 1977, part 4, p. 1.
20. *The Wall Street Journal*, June 27, 1978, p. 8.
21. *The Wall Street Journal*, December 20, 1977, p. 9.
22. For an interesting treatment of U.S. relations with South Africa, see Chester A. Crocker, "The United States and South Africa: Coping with Complexity," in *The International Essays for Business Decision Makers*, ed. Mark B. Winchester, vol. 4 (Dallas: Center for International Business, 1979), pp. 189–99.

23. Shirley Hobbs Scheibla, "McNamara's Band Sour," *Barron's*, December 3, 1979, pp. 9, 26, 27.
24. *Business International*, January 21, 1983, pp. 17–19.
25. H. Peter Dreyer, "EC Adopts Company Accounting Rule," *Europe*, July–August 1983, p. 33.
26. Lee L. Morgan, "Opportunities for Mutual Action by Government and Business Leaders in 1977," in *Contemporary Perspectives in International Business*, ed. Harold W. Berkman and Ivan R. Vernon (Skokie, Ill.: Rand McNally, 1979), p. 284.
27. William J. Barton, "International Government Relations: A Required Management Function for International Business," in *The International Essays for Business Decision Makers*, ed. Mark B. Winchester, vol. 3 (New York: AMACOM, 1978), pp. 218–19.
28. For a good discussion of the powers that an MNE can use, see Stefan H. Robock, Kenneth Simmonds, and Jack Zwick, *International Business and Multinational Enterprises* (Homewood, Ill.: Richard D. Irwin, 1983), chap. 12.
29. See Table 1–1.
30. Raymond Vernon, "Storm over the Multinationals: Problems and Prospects," in *Contemporary Perspectives in International Business*, ed. Harold W. Berkman and Ivan R. Vernon (Skokie, Ill.: Rand McNally, 1979), pp. 237–53; adapted from Raymond Vernon, *Storm over the Multinationals: The Real Issues* (Cambridge, Mass.: Harvard University Press, 1977).
31. *Business Latin America*, June 9, 1976, pp. 3–4.
32. For several good discussions of various aspects of CRA, see Jerry Rogers, ed., *Global Risk Assessments: Issues, Concepts, and Applications*, book 2 (Riverside, Calif.: Global Risk Assessments, 1986).

CHAPTER 10

LEGAL FORCES

"**A**fter 35 years, I have finished a comprehensive study of European comparative law. In Germany, under the law, everything is prohibited, except that which is permitted. In France, under the law, everything is permitted, except that which is prohibited. In the Soviet Union, under the law, everything is prohibited, including that which is permitted. And in Italy, under the law, everything is permitted, especially that which is prohibited."

Newton Minow, former chairman of the U.S. Federal Communications Commission, in a speech to the Association of American Law Schools

Learning Objectives

After you study this chapter, you should know:

1. The complexity, due to their many sources (such as national laws, treaties, international organizations, and private international law), of the legal forces which may confront you.
2. That taxes frequently have purposes other than the raising of revenue.
3. That U.S. antitrust laws and their enforcement are the world's strictest.
4. That in some countries industrial espionage is a crime for which the penalties include fines or imprisonment.
5. The concept of sovereign immunity, which can protect a government from being sued or prevent a court from having jurisdiction over it.
6. That there are contract devices and institutions to assist in the interpretation or arbitration of international contracts.
7. The need to examine the law of each country where you do business to assure protection of your patents, trademarks, trade names, copyrights, and trade secrets.
8. The need to study the tariff, quota, and other trade obstacles of each country into which you wish to import a product.
9. The possibility that your property in a foreign country may be seized by the government or that you may be forced to give up control of it.
10. The danger of money damages or imprisonment if your company manufactures or sells a faulty or dangerous product or if an employee fails to observe host country law or falls afoul of corrupt police or army units.
11. The need to comply with wage and price controls and with currency exchange controls.
12. The numerous difficulties and burdens placed by U.S. laws and practices on American MNEs, which no other industrialized country imposes on its MNEs. This puts the American MNEs at a competitive disadvantage in the international market.

Key Words and Concepts

Nonrevenue tax purposes
Direct taxes
Indirect taxes
National tax jurisdiction
Territorial tax jurisdiction
Tax treaties
Foreign tax credit
Antitrust laws
Restrictive trade practices
  legislation
Extraterritorial application
  of laws

Sovereign immunity
Industrial espionage
Arbitration
Tariffs
Quotas
Domestication
Product liability
Price and wage controls
Currency-exchange controls
Treaty of Rome
Questionable or dubious payments

Business Incident

Kenny International Corporation is a stamp-distributing company owned by two New Yorkers, Finbar B. Kenny and his wife, Marianne. Kenny had the exclusive rights to distribute the stamps of the Cook Islands. Most of the stamps are sold to collectors, and such sales totaled $1.5 million in 1978. Domestic sales, for actual postage, were only about $20,000 in 1978. Kenny split the $1.5 million with the Cook Islands.

In March 1978, there was a general election in the Cook Islands. According to the U.S. Justice Department, in an effort to protect its valuable franchise, Kenny agreed to help reelect the then premier, Sir Albert Henry, and his political party. To that end, Kenny used $337,000 out of the Cook Island account to charter jet passenger planes. The planes flew some 450 Cook Islanders in from New Zealand, and their votes provided the margin of victory that secured Sir Albert's reelection. In July 1978, however, the Cook Islands High Court disallowed those votes as "tainted by bribery" and threw Sir Albert out of office.

Kenny pleaded guilty to breaking Cook Island law and repaid the $337,000. But American law? It was also broken, said the U.S. Justice Department, and the Kennys pleaded guilty in a U.S. federal district court in Washington. Their company was fined $50,000.

The U.S. law that was broken was the Foreign Corrupt Practices Act of 1977. The Kenny case was the first criminal action brought under it.

From *The Wall Street Journal*, August 3, 1979, p. 29. Reprinted with permission. © Dow Jones & Company, Inc. 1979. All rights reserved.

*A*ny attempt to teach a course on "The Legal Forces That Affect International Business" would be overwhelmed or bogged down by the immensity and variety of those forces. International business is affected by countless thousands of laws and regulations on hundreds of subjects that have been issued by states, nations, and international organizations.

Nevertheless, this text, which is an introduction to international business, would be incomplete if it did not inform students or businesspersons that many legal forces do affect international business and if it did not give them an idea of what some of the most important are. We shall examine first several national legal forces, with brief comments, and then we shall discuss some international legal forces.

Although many U.S. laws and regulations affect the activities of multinational firms, there has been no successful effort to coordinate them. Some of them are at cross-purposes, and some diminish the competitiveness of American business as it attempts to compete with foreign companies. We shall close this chapter with a brief examination of some of these laws and regulations. The business incident about Kenny International's legal difficulties illustrates the application of one such law.

We shall now proceed to deal with specific legal forces. (They are not presented in any particular order.) Some of them, such as taxation, concern every business and businessperson, whereas others, such as antitrust, involve fewer firms.

Some Specific National Legal Forces

Taxation

Purposes

The primary purpose of certain taxes is not necessarily to raise revenue for the government. That fact may surprise the reader who has not had occasion to study taxation. Some of the many **nonrevenue tax purposes** are: to redistribute income, to discourage consumption of such products as alcohol or tobacco, to encourage consumption of domestic rather than imported goods, to discourage investment abroad, to achieve equality of the tax amounts paid by taxpayers earning comparable amounts, and to grant reciprocity to resident foreigners under a tax treaty.

Even this short list of purposes (there are many more) suggests the economic and political pressures brought to bear on government officials who are responsible for tax legislation and collection. Powerful groups in every country push for tax policies that favor their interests. These groups and interests differ from country to country and frequently conflict, which accounts, in part, for the complexity of the tax practices that affect MNEs.

National Differences of Approach

Among the many nations of the world, there are numerous differences in tax systems.

Tax Levels. For one thing, tax levels range from relatively high (up to 100 percent in some instances) in some West European countries to zero in tax havens.* Some countries have capital gains taxes,† and some do not. Those that have them tax capital gains at different levels. Incidentally, the United States levies the highest capital gains tax.

---

*A tax haven is a country in which income of defined types incurs no tax liability.
†Capital gain is realized when an asset is sold for an amount greater than its cost.

Table 10-1

Value-Added Tax on a Loaf of Bread

Stage of Production	Selling Price	Value Added	VAT at 10 percent	Cumulative VAT
Farmer	30¢	30¢	3¢	3¢
Miller	50¢	20¢	2¢	5¢
Wholesaler	70¢	20¢	2¢	7¢
Retailer	$1.10	40¢	4¢	11¢

Tax Types. There are different types of taxes. We have just introduced one, the capital gains tax. Although the United States levies a relatively high capital gains tax, it relies for most of its revenue on the income tax. As indicated by the name, this tax is levied on the income of individuals and businesses. A generality, subject to exceptions, is that the higher the income, the higher the income tax. In the 1970s and 1980s, much discontent developed among Americans over the impact of the income and other taxes. Possibly as a result of that, there has been growing support for a *value-added tax (VAT)* in the U.S. Congress and Treasury.

Suggestions are that the U.S. VAT be similar to the VATs in effect in all European Community countries, for which the VAT is a main source of revenue. A simplified example of how the VAT works on a loaf of bread can be seen in Table 10–1. We shall assume a VAT of 10 percent. The wheat farmer sells to the miller for 30 cents the part of the wheat that eventually becomes the loaf. So far, the farmer has added 30 cents of value by planting, growing, and harvesting the wheat. The farmer sets aside 3 cents (10 percent of 30 cents) to pay VAT. The miller makes loaves of bread out of the wheat and sells them to the wholesaler for 50 cents each. Thus, the miller has added 20 cents of value (50 cents − 30 cents) and must pay a VAT of 2 cents (10 percent of 20 cents). The wholesaler now advertises and distributes the loaves selling them to retailers at 70 cents. The wholesaler has added 20 cents of value and owes 2 cents VAT. Finally, the retailer adds 40 cents by its display, advertising, and sales efforts and owes 4 cents of VAT. The loaf of bread is sold for $1.10 retail and has borne a cumulative VAT of 11 cents, 10 percent of $1.10.

The VAT has proponents and opponents.[1] You can read the footnote and other material for details, but in general they are as follows: The proponents say the VAT is relatively simple and can be raised or lowered easily to balance desired income with the burden. The opponents argue that it is a consumption-type tax that bears most heavily on the poor.

Another argument of VAT proponents in the United States is that the present situation, in which the major European countries rely heavily on the value-added tax, is unfair to the United States because of GATT* regulations. GATT

*See Chapter 4 for discussion of the General Agreement on Tariffs and Trade.

permits the rebate of VAT when a product is exported from a country but does not permit rebate of income taxes. The rebates permit lower-priced, more competitive goods, and VAT proponents want the United States to inaugurate the VAT and lower income taxes in order to take advantage of those GATT rules.

Complexity of Tax Laws and Regulations. From country to country, the complexity of tax systems differs. Many consider that of the United States to be the most complex; the Internal Revenue Code runs over 5,000 pages, and official interpretations add more than 10,000 to that number. In addition to the code and Treasury interpretations, there are countless thousands of pages of judicial rulings.

Who Obeys the Law? Compliance with tax laws and their enforcement vary widely. Some countries, such as Germany and the United States, are strict. Others, such as Italy and Spain, are relatively lax, the Italian practice being for the taxpayer to declare a very low taxable income amount to which the government counters with a very high amount. They then negotiate to a compromise figure.

> One of the authors remembers the shock and horror which greeted his suggestion to Italian tax advisers that a new Italian subsidiary of an American MNE declare its true income to the Italian authorities. As the advisers forcefully pointed out, no one would believe us.

Sources of Taxed Income Differ. The United States taxes income of U.S. citizens and residents worldwide, regardless of its source, even though they live and work abroad. Most other countries do not tax the foreign income of their citizens if they live and work abroad.

Other Differences. There are many other differences, too numerous even to list here, but a few are: tax incentives to invest in certain areas, exemptions, costs, depreciation allowances, foreign tax credits, timing, and double corporate taxation—that is, taxation of the profits of a corporation and then of the dividends paid to its stockholders.

Tax Conventions (Treaties)

Because of the innumerable differences among the tax practices of the nations many of them have signed tax treaties with each other. Typically, a tax treaty defines such terms as income, source, residency, and what constitutes taxable activities in each country. It also reduces taxation by each country of income going to residents who are nationals of the other and deals with taxation by each country of nationals of the other living or working in the country. All of these treaties contain provisions for the exchange of information between the tax authorities of the two countries.

Antitrust and Restrictive Trade Practices Legislation

In the tax area, it is the taxpayers (we are dealing with international business taxpayers) against the tax collectors (the governments). In antitrust, it is business versus government and, increasingly, government versus government.

U.S. Laws and Attitudes Are Different

The U.S. **antitrust laws** are stricter and more vigorously enforced than those of any other country. However, other countries, as well as the EC, are becoming more active in the antitrust field.

The West German antitrust laws are the toughest after those of the United States, and during 1986 the German Federal Cartel Office was tightening its grip, literally in some cases. Wolfgang Kartte, president of the Cartel Office, tells the story of a raid his investigators made on the office of a heating equipment supplier. One of the supplier's managers stuffed a memo into his mouth and tried to swallow it, but a quick-thinking investigator grabbed the man by the throat and forced him to spit out the memo. Half-chewed but still legible, it provided valuable evidence of illegal price-fixing.

The EC Commission was also stepping up its trust-busting activities. In December 1985, it levied the highest fine yet for breaking restrictive trade practices rules. The Dutch chemical company Akzo Chemie was fined 10 million ECU (about $8.8 million). Four months later, in April 1986, the Commission broke its own record again with an ECU 57.8 million (about $56.2 million) fine on 15 members of a European chemical cartel.

A number of important differences in antitrust laws, regulations, and practices exist between the United States, other nations, and the EC. One difference is the effort of the United States to apply its laws extraterritorially (outside the United States). We deal with that later in this chapter. Another difference is the per se concept of the U.S. law.

Under U.S. laws, certain activities, such as price-fixing, are said to be illegal per se. This means that they are illegal even though no injury or damage results from them.

The **Treaty of Rome,** which established the EC, has sections dealing with antitrust or restrictive trade practices.[2] You do not find in those sections the per se illegality concept of U.S. antitrust law. For example, a cartel that allows consumers a fair share of the benefits is legally acceptable in the EC. Also, the treaty is not violated by market dominance—only by misuse of that dominance to damage competitors or consumers.

The EC versus Hoffman-La Roche

As indicated above, EC antitrust enforcement is not toothless. In 1979, the EC Court of Justice upheld the EC Commission decision that the giant Swiss drug

MNE Hoffman-La Roche was guilty of abusing its dominant position. Hoffman was fined DM732,000.[3]

There was at least one bizarre element in the Hoffman case. Stanley Adams, a British subject, was an employee at the company's head office in Basle, Switzerland. He took some confidential documents about Hoffman's pricing and marketing practices and made them available to the EC antitrust regulators, who were already investigating the company. The company and the Swiss government reacted furiously, and when Adams, who was in Italy when the loss of the documents was discovered, returned to Switzerland, he was arrested and convicted under Swiss laws against industrial espionage. He was sent to prison, and his wife committed suicide upon being told that he would be in prison at least 20 years. Finally, the EC bailed him out of the Swiss prison and he left the country.

Although Adams had his freedom, his troubles were not over. He was unable to get credit or employment, and he lost a farm he tried to operate in Italy. He then moved to England and sued the EC Commission for £500,000 damages for revealing his identity to Hoffman and for not warning him of the dangers he faced if he returned to Switzerland. In 1985, Adams won his case in the European Court of Justice.

The Swiss Government versus the EC

The Hoffman-La Roche case caused government-versus-government friction. The EC complained to the Swiss that Adams should not be prosecuted under Swiss law, because all he had done was to cooperate with the EC Commission's efforts to enforce the law. The Swiss prosecuted and convicted him, notwithstanding the EC's complaints, because he had violated Swiss law in Switzerland.

The U.S. Government versus Other Governments

A more common example of government-versus-government conflict is pitting the U.S. government against various other governments as the United States attempts to enforce its antitrust laws outside U.S. borders. In 1979, a grand jury in Washington, D.C., indicted three foreign-owned ocean-shipping groups on charges of fixing prices without getting approval from the U.S. Federal Maritime Commission. The other governments, European and Japanese, protested bitterly, arguing (1) that shipping is international by definition, so that the United States has no right to act unilaterally, and (2) that the alleged offenses were both legal and ethical practices outside the United States.[5]

Sir Freddie Laker's airline, a low-price transatlantic service, ceased operations on February 5, 1982. Shortly thereafter, its liquidators commenced a private antitrust suit in an American court, alleging that some other airlines had conspired to put Laker out of business. They asked over $1 billion in damages, and two other British airlines were among the defendants.

The private suits irked the British government, but what disturbed it most was the U.S. Justice Department's move in spring 1983 to begin a criminal grand jury investigation of essentially the same allegations. It was another example of the U.S. government's efforts to apply its law extraterritorially.

Other Governments versus the U.S. Government

In 1977, the United States tried to force seven executives of the British company Rio Tinto-Zinc to testify in connection with an antitrust action in the United States. In that instance, Britain's highest court, the House of Lords, turned down the U.S. demands on the grounds that they were an infringement of British jurisdiction and sovereignty and that the United States was trying to investigate the activities of companies not subject to U.S. jurisdiction.[6]

A number of countries have passed statutes to prevent persons within their territories from cooperating with the United States and have established criminal sanctions for those that comply with U.S. law in violation of those statutes. Among these countries are Australia, Canada, Britain, the Netherlands, and West Germany. Thus, persons or companies can find themselves in the position of being forced to break the law of either the United States or of a country with this type of statute.

U.S. Labor versus OPEC

One of the oddest attempts to use U.S. antitrust laws to achieve results internationally was the lawsuit filed in December 1978 by the International Association of Machinists and Aerospace Workers (IAM) against OPEC. The IAM charged price-fixing which had caused severe damage to the U.S. economy.

OPEC, as a group of nations, claims sovereign immunity, which would prevent its being sued in the courts of a non-OPEC nation. In 1976, however, the United States adopted the Foreign Sovereign Immunities Act, which strips immunity from a government when it engages in commercial activities. The IAM argued that producing and selling petroleum was a commercial activity—OPEC had nationalized and was operating assets previously owned and operated by private oil companies in OPEC territories. The IAM's position was that because those private American oil companies would clearly be subject to U.S. antitrust prosecution for price-fixing, the new OPEC owners should also be liable and should not be permitted to rely on sovereign immunity.

West Germany, the country second to the United States in aggressive antitrust policy, decided not to take on the oil cartel. "They were just too big for us," said one Berlin* official, and he was talking about the oil companies, not OPEC.[7] It remains to be seen what will flow (more or less oil?) from the IAM action, though the issue was probably settled in 1981, when a federal court of appeals ruled that it had no jurisdiction over OPEC oil pricing. The IAM has not appealed that ruling.

---

*Berlin is the site of the West German cartel office.

Tariffs, Quotas, and Other Trade Obstacles

Every country has laws on one or more of these subjects. The purposes of **tariffs** are to raise revenue for the government and to protect domestic producers. Tariffs are either ad valorem, which means that they are a percentage of the value of the imports, or they are specific. The specific tariff is based on the weight or number of items imported. **Quotas,** which limit the number or amount of imports, are for protection.

There are many other forms of protection or obstacles to trade in national laws. Some are health or packaging requirements. Others deal with language, such as the mandatory use of French on labels and in advertising, manuals, warranties, and so forth for goods sold in France.

The following list is a sampling of U.S. export products, export destinations, and the trade barriers encountered at the destinations.

Product	Destination	Barrier
Carbon steel	EC	Imports limited to 8 percent of market
Pesticides	Canada	Residue standards bar some U.S. chemicals
Machine tools	Japan	Government subsidizes domestic industry
Machine tools	Argentina	Money from sales must remain in Argentina for months
Paperboard	Japan	Specifications require smoother board than is produced in the United States

In other countries, U.S. exports may encounter weak patent or trademark protection, very high tariffs, zero quotas, quarantine periods, or a variety of other obstacles.

Of course, the United States imposes barriers against the import of a number of products from abroad and it even has laws restricting the export of some of its own products. Examples of the latter are oil from the Alaska North Slope, timber from federal lands, and high-technology products on which export license requirements have been imposed in an effort to keep them out of hostile hands, such as the Soviet Union or terrorists.

Only in the late 1970s did Japanese government-owned companies open a crack in their "Buy Japan" policy. Before that, they would buy only from Japanese suppliers. Under heavy pressures from the United States and the EC, the Japanese prime minister ordered Nippon Telephone and Telegraph to open its procurement to bids by foreign suppliers.

By early 1983, however, William E. Brock, the U.S. trade representative, was complaining that the prime minister's order and a U.S.-Japanese agreement

Reprinted by permission: Tribune Media Services.

"Okay, guys, now let's go over the rules one more time . . ."

Copyright 1985 by Tom Meyer/San Francisco Chronicle

to implement the order had had "little value as it had worked to date." Brock threatened to terminate the agreement unless more orders were forthcoming from Nippon Telephone and Telegraph to American suppliers.[9]

In 1982, the French came up with a novel protectionist device. Japanese videotape recorders were one of the French imports causing a large balance-of-payments deficit with Japan. The recorders normally entered France through the major port of Le Havre, which had a large detachment of customs officers to process imports. Then the French government issued a decree which required all of the recorders to enter France through Poitiers, which had a tiny customs post. The result was long delays that reduced the number of recorders entering France.

Expropriation or Confiscation

Governments frequently pass laws under which they expropriate or confiscate foreign-owned property. OPEC members have seized foreign-owned assets within their borders, particularly natural resource assets.

Domestication

Domestication is a less drastic takeover of foreign assets. Here the host government uses various forms of pressure to "persuade" foreign owners to sell some significant percentage, usually enough to enable the host government or local shareholders to gain control of the foreign-owned company.[10] A number of countries, including the Andean Pact nations, Brazil, India, Mexico, and Nigeria, have enacted laws or enforced policies to require or encourage foreign-owned companies to sell part ownership to the host government or to local shareholders. This is referred to as "Mexicanization" if it occurs in Mexico, "Brazilianization" if it occurs in Brazil, and so forth.

Product Liability, Civil and Criminal*

Manufacturers' liability for faulty or dangerous products was a boom growth area for the American legal profession in the 1960s and 70s. Liability insurance premiums have soared, and there are concerns that smaller, weaker manufacturing companies cannot survive.

Now that boom is spreading in Europe, where the EC Commission and the Council of Europe are pushing new **product liability** laws. Those laws would standardize and toughen the present tangle of national laws.[11]

Another new development in Europe is causing what the president of one U.S.-controlled company in France called a "fear psychosis." This development

---

*Civil liability calls for payment of money damages. Criminal liability results in fines or imprisonment.

THE WALL STREET JOURNAL

From *The Wall Street Journal*, with permission of Cartoon Features Syndicate.

"He's in jail. May I take a message?"

is criminal liability of management for workers' death or injuries. In France, managers have been found guilty of involuntary homicide* and criminal responsibility after accidents caused workers' deaths.

In Britain, a 1976 Health and Safety Act gave inspectors the right to haul accused managers into courts which have the power to impose prison terms.[12]

Pressures which could result in stiffer product safety standards are coming from numerous directions. One of them is the UN Economic and Social Council, and another is the International Organization of Consumers Unions.[13]

The European Parliament and many other groups have expressed concern that too sweeping government involvement in product safety and too heavy liability burdens on industry will stifle product innovation and hit small producers, which would be less able to either afford higher insurance premiums or pass on higher self-insurance costs. The British government has also expressed that point of view.

The British dissented from a July 1985 EC Council of Ministers directive to the effect that plaintiffs could seek redress for damages without having to prove negligence on the part of the manufacturers. The British position is that manufacturers should not be liable for product defects which—given the state of scientific and technical knowledge—could not have been detected when the product was made. This is called a "state-of-the-art" or "development risks" defense.

Nevertheless, the costs of liability insurance have risen and the availability of liability insurance has shrunk in all European countries. Product liability laws varied among EC countries in 1987, but an EC directive required all countries to introduce new legislation by July 1988. One important difference be-

---

*This means causing the death of some person or persons, and it is a crime even though it was "involuntary"—that is, you did not intend it to happen.

tween European and American law in this field is that punitive damages,*
which have played a large part in high U.S. awards, are not permitted in EC
countries. Another difference is that European lawyers cannot take cases on a
contingency fee† basis; American lawyers commonly do so.[14]

Price and Wage Controls

Some countries that have price and wage control laws call them "voluntary,"
but the governments can bring pressures to bear on companies or labor unions
that raise prices or demand wage increases above established percentages. The
U.S. government, for example, has withheld government business from companies which violate its guidelines. This has resulted in lawsuits by labor unions
challenging the legality of such punishment by the government because wage
increases exceeded "voluntary" guidelines.

Communist countries, of course, just set prices and wages. There are no
significant free markets and no effective labor unions which are not government
agencies. Most noncommunist countries also have some price and wage control
laws.[15] As inflation spreads and grows in the world, **price and wage controls**
can be expected to become more widespread and more restrictive.

Labor Laws

Virtually every country has laws governing working conditions and wages for its
labor force. Even though hourly wages may be low in a country, the employers
must beware, because fringe benefits can greatly increase labor costs. Fringe
benefits can include profit sharing, health or dental benefits, retirement funds,
and more. Some labor laws make the firing of a worker almost impossible or at
least very expensive.

Currency Exchange Controls

Almost every country has **currency exchange controls**—laws dealing with the
purchase and sale of foreign currencies. Most countries, including the LDCs and
the communist countries, have too little hard foreign currency.‡ There is the
rare case, such as Switzerland, which sometimes feels it has too much.

Exchange Control Generalities

The law of each country must be examined, but some generalities can be made.
In those countries where hard foreign currency is scarce, it is allocated by a government agency. Typically, an importer of productive capital equipment would
be given priority over an importer of luxury goods.

---

*Punitive damages are in addition to the actual damages proven and are awarded to punish the man-
ufacturer of a faulty product.
†Contingency fees are lawyers' fees paid only if the plaintiff's case is won or settled by agreement of
the defendant to make a payment.
‡A hard currency is one that is readily exchangeable for any other currency in the world.

People entering such a country must declare how much currency of any kind they are bringing in. Upon departure, they must declare how much they are taking out. One side of the intent is to discourage bringing in the national currency that the traveler may have bought abroad at a better exchange rate than the traveler can get inside the country. The other side is to encourage the bringing in of hard foreign currency.

Switzerland—A Special Case

Switzerland is a special case because its government has imposed controls to keep foreign currencies out rather than in. Switzerland enjoyed relatively low inflation during the 1970s and into the 1980s, and its Swiss franc has remained one of the hardest of the hard currencies. As a result, people from all over the world have wanted to get their money into Switzerland, and the Swiss have felt the need to defend against being inundated by too much currency, which would cause their inflation to escalate. They have used several devices to discourage the inflow of foreign money. Among these devices are low interest rates and even a negative interest rate on some kinds of deposits. Limitations have been placed on the sale to foreigners of bonds denominated in Swiss francs.

Miscellaneous Laws

Individuals working abroad must be alert to avoid falling afoul of local laws and of corrupt police, army, or government officials. Some examples may serve to make the point.

A Plessey employee, a British subject, is serving a life sentence in Libya for "jeopardizing the revolution by giving information to a foreign company." In the summer of 1986, two Australians were executed in Malaysia for possession of 15 grams or more of hard drugs. Saudi Arabia and other Muslim countries strictly enforce sanctions against importing or drinking alcohol or wearing revealing clothing. Foreigners in Japan who walk out of their homes without their alien registration card can be arrested, as was one man caught without his card while he was carrying out the garbage. In Thailand, you can be jailed for mutilating paper money or for damaging coins that bear the picture or image of the royal prince, as was one foreigner who stopped a rolling coin with his foot. Neither *Playboy* nor *Penthouse* can be brought into Singapore. In Italian insurance law, a fire is defined differently (see advertisement on page 358).

International Forces

Contract Enforcement

Increasingly, businesses find themselves contracting with governments or government-owned companies. This is a common occurrence now; in communist countries, all commercial activities of any importance are conducted by govern-

IN ITALY THIS ISN'T A FIRE.

A pile of oily rags bursts into flame.

And a profitable operation of an American company is reduced to a pile of ashes.

The real disaster, however, occurs when the home office discovers that their standard Italian fire insurance doesn't cover damage from spontaneous combustion.

How could this happen?

Easily. They bought insurance written in another language. From another country. With different standards for coverage.

The fact is, buying insurance outside the U.S. is complicated.

Which is why so many corporations are turning to a single policy from CIGNA Worldwide's international specialists.

They know, for instance, that in Japan standard fire protection doesn't include damage from lightning. And in Pakistan, nearly all fire coverage must be specified by endorsements.

With the industry's largest network of local representatives, spanning some 160 countries, we can offer you the kind of service that ensures loss control support just about anywhere: Service that simplifies claims adjustment. And policy administration.

A program from CIGNA Worldwide provides uniform coverage that eliminates gaps in protection and costly overlapping policies. What's more, it offers the kind of economy you can't get buying insurance piecemeal.

If your business is international, you should be buying insurance on an international scale.

To learn how you can do just that, write CIGNA Corporation, Department RH, One Logan Square, Philadelphia, PA 19103.

After all, something's wrong when you're not covered for a fire because of the way it started.

CIGNA Worldwide. Another example of CIGNA's personalized service to business around the world.

ment agencies. To buy from or sell to such countries, one must contract with those agencies only. The same is true of many LDCs, and there are numerous government-owned companies in Western Europe. Contract enforcement problems of different natures can arise when one of the contract parties is a government.

A Communist Government

An example involving a communist country arose in 1977, when Rolimpex, the Polish state export agency, reneged on a contract it had made in 1974 to sell and deliver sugar to a British company. By 1977, sugar prices were much higher than they had been in 1974 and Poland faced a sugar shortage due to bad harvests. The British company sued Rolimpex in an English court, where Rolimpex lawyers argued that the Polish government had forbidden Rolimpex to perform the contract, which constituted "government intervention beyond seller's control." The lawyers of the British company countered that in a communist country the government is the sole seller of goods, so Rolimpex and the Polish state should be considered identical. They argued that to forbid yourself to perform a contract is not a legal defense when you breach it by nonperformance.

The British trial court found for Rolimpex. There has been considerable discussion of the possible long-term damage that the court's decision may do Poland if potential foreign contract parties refuse to do business with Polish agencies or charge higher prices because of the risk that the Polish contract party, always a government agency, can breach the contract with impunity.[16]

An LDC Government

An LDC that has used the sovereign immunity* defense is Nigeria. In 1975, Nigeria ordered far too much cement from international suppliers and then tried to cancel as many contracts as possible.[17] When Nigeria was sued by the suppliers, it argued that as a government it could not be sued. The lawsuits were settled before a court decided the legality of Nigeria's argument.

Other International Contract Problems

Even if governments are not parties to international contracts, problems of jurisdiction, interpretation, and enforcement arise. When the two contracting parties are in one country, the courts of that country have jurisdiction, interpretation is under that country's laws, and a court judgment can be enforced through the procedures of that country. When residents of two or more countries contract, those easy answers are not available.

---

*A government is said to be sovereign over the area and people under its control. It has complete power. An extension of that power is the government's immunity to being sued unless it consents to be sued.

It is to the credit of international business, including government agencies doing business, that world trade goes smoothly as a rule and has grown tremendously in volume.

World trade grew at an average annual rate of 8.5 percent from 1963 to 1973 and 4.25 percent from 1973 to 1979. In 1980, the dollar value of world trade reached a peak of $2 trillion.[18] World trade fell more than 11 percent during the recession-hit years between 1980 and 1983 and was down to about $1.666 trillion in 1983. Trade activity then began to expand again, reaching $1.763 trillion in 1984 and $1.785 trillion in 1985, for a two-year gain exceeding 7 percent, and the growth continued in 1986.

The point we mean to make is that although recession may temporarily depress trade, the growth of trade over many years and the resumption of that growth after recession give evidence that most international contracts are performed fairly satisfactorily in spite of legal uncertainties.

Solutions to Jurisdiction, Interpretation, and Enforcement Problems

Devices used in attempts to solve the jurisdiction, interpretation, and enforcement problems in international contracts include contractual clauses agreeing, for example, (1) what law shall be applicable (for example, the law of France or the law of New York) in the interpretation of such contracts; (2) which language (where two or more are involved) shall govern ambiguities or contradictions of translations; (3) to submit to the jurisdiction of a specified court (for example, that of the Canton of Geneva or that of the Argentine court in Buenos Aires); and, increasingly popular, (4) to submit to arbitration (for example, by the International Chamber of Commerce in Paris or by an arbitration panel in London, where many international grain contract disputes are settled).[19]

Among the advantages of **arbitration** as compared to court proceedings are speed and informality. The courts in many countries have backlogs of cases, and it can be months or years between the time a lawsuit is filed and the time it comes to trial. In business, such delays and their accompanying uncertainties are expensive. The courts of all countries have numerous formalities and procedures that have been built up over the years, and these can make it slow, difficult, or impossible to introduce evidence that the parties feel is relevant and important.

Arbitration can solve both problems. The parties can choose their arbitrators and get into arbitration immediately. In addition, arbitrators are not bound by court procedures. They can admit and consider any evidence they believe relevant and important. A further advantage of arbitration is that the parties can waive any right to appeal from the arbitrators' award, whereas in court the loser in the first court to hear the case can almost always appeal to a higher court. Appellate procedures can consume further months or years, thus extending the uncertainties as to final results. As we have said, uncertainties are costly to business.

Arbitration by the International Chamber of Commerce was mentioned. It should be added that the American Arbitration Association and arbitral groups in Switzerland are frequently used to arbitrate international contract disputes.

Enforcement of foreign arbitration awards can pose problems. An attempted solution is the UN Convention on the Recognition and Enforcement of Foreign Arbitral Awards. The United States has adhered to this convention, and adherence binds a nation to compel arbitration when the parties have so agreed and to enforce awards.[20]

In instances where the contract in dispute involves investment in a country from abroad, another arbitration tribunal is available. This is the International Center for Settlement of Investment Disputes, sponsored by the World Bank. Investors were encouraged in 1986 when Indonesia proved willing to abide by a decision of the center even though an adverse opinion could have cost the country several million dollars.

Patents, Trademarks, Trade Names, Copyrights, and Trade Secrets

A *patent* is a government grant to the inventor of a product or process of the exclusive right of manufacturing, exploiting, using, and selling the invention or process. Trademarks and trade names are designs and names, often officially registered, by which merchants or manufacturers designate and differentiate their products. Copyrights are exclusive legal rights of authors, composers, playwrights, artists, and publishers to publish and dispose of their works. Trade secrets are any information that a business wishes to hold confidential.

Trade secrets can be of great value, but each country deals with and protects them in its own fashion. The duration of protection differs, as do the products that may or may not be protected. Some countries permit the production process but not the product to be protected. Therefore, international business must study and comply with the laws of each country where it might want to manufacture, create, or sell a product.

Patents

In the field of patents, some degree of standardization is provided by the International Convention for the Protection of Industrial Property, sometimes referred to as the Paris Union.[21] Some 90 countries, including the major industrial nations, have adhered to this convention.

Most Latin American nations and the United States are members of the Inter-American Convention. The protection it provides is similar to that afforded by the Paris Union.

A major step toward the harmonization of patent treatment is the European Patent Organization (EPO). Members are the EC countries plus Austria,

Sweden, and Switzerland. Through EPO, an applicant for a patent need file only one application in English, French, or German in order to be granted patent protection in all member countries. Prior to EPO, an applicant had to file in each country in the language of that country. That is still necessary in every country that is not a member of EPO.

At the UN, representatives of the developing nations have been mounting attacks on the exclusivity and length of patent protection. They want to shorten the protection periods from the current 15 to 20 years down to 5 years or even 30 months. The companies in the industrialized countries, which are responsible for the new technology eligible for patents, are resisting the changes. They point out that the only incentives they have to spend the huge amounts required to develop the technology are periods of patent protection long enough to recoup their costs and make profits.[22]

Trademarks

Trademark protection varies from country to country, as does its duration, which may last from 10 to 20 years. Such protection is covered by the Madrid Agreement of 1891 for most of the world, though there is also the General American Convention for Trademark and Commercial Protection for the Western Hemisphere. In addition, protection may be provided on a bilateral basis in friendship, commerce, and navigation treaties.

Trade Names

Trade names are protected in all countries adhering to the Industrial Property Convention which was mentioned above in connection with patents. Goods bearing illegal trademarks, or trade names or false statements on their origin are subject to seizure at importation into those countries.

> Two thirds of Kenya's 1979 coffee crop was lost after treatment with a worthless powder packaged to look like an effective, popular fungicide. More than 357 heart pumps were recalled from U.S. hospitals in 1978 because it was feared that some of the $20,000 devices contained bogus parts imported at $8 each.

Goods counterfeiting was once confined to such items as designer jeans, jewelry, tape recordings, and sporting goods. As the above examples indicate, commercial counterfeiting has now reached a point where it jeopardizes the health and safety of consumers, not just their pocketbooks.[23]

Copyrights

Copyrights get protection under the Berne Convention of 1886, which is adhered to by 55 countries, not including the United States. However, the United States adheres to the Universal Copyright Convention of 1954, which has been adopted by some 50 countries.

Figure 10-1

Courtesy Larry Besselp/*Los Angeles Times*

Cheap copies of Cartier Vermeil watch—more than 4,000 of them—are destroyed by 12-ton roller.

Trade Secrets

Trade secrets are protected by laws in most nations. Employers everywhere use employee secrecy agreements, which in some countries are rigorously enforced.*

---

*Remember the unfortunate Mr. Adams, who was imprisoned by the Swiss for giving Hoffman-La Roche secrets to the EC, and the even more unfortunate Mrs. Adams, who committed suicide after being told that her husband would be in prison 20 years.

In 1980, the U.S. Justice Department got the first conviction for industrial espionage—stealing trade secrets—under a 1970 law. Early in the 1970s, the Japanese company Mitsubishi tried to buy technology from the American company, Celanese Corporation. Celanese would not sell, but one of its employees would.

The manager of a Celanese plant was paid $130,000 for Celanese secrets worth an estimated $6 million. Action under the 1970 law was brought by the Justice Department against the manager and a Mitsubishi subsidiary in the United States. The Mitsubishi subsidiary pleaded guilty and was fined $300,000. The manager got four years in prison, and Mitsubishi got a bargain.[24]

Industrial espionage among companies which develop and use high technology is not unusual, but 1983 saw the end of an extraordinary example of corporate warfare between two of the world's mightiest and most technologically advanced corporations. Hitachi tried to obtain trade secrets of IBM, and in June 1982, two Hitachi employees were arrested by the FBI. IBM and the FBI had cooperated in what *Fortune* called a "superbly executed sting." In February 1983, Hitachi and two of its employees pleaded guilty to an indictment of conspiring to transport stolen IBM property from the United States to Japan.

International
Standardizing Forces

Several international standardizing forces have already been discussed. In the tax area, there are tax conventions (treaties) among nations. Each country tries to make each such treaty as nearly as possible like the others, so that patterns and common provisions may be found among them.

In antitrust, the EC member countries operate under Articles 85 and 86 of the Treaty of Rome. In an unusual bilateral move, West Germany and the United States signed an executive agreement on antitrust cooperation. This was the first attempt by national governments to cooperate on antitrust matters concerning MNEs operating in both countries.[25]

In the field of commercial contract arbitration, we mentioned the UN Convention. If the disputed contract involves investment from one country into another, it can be submitted for arbitration by the International Center for Settlement of Investment Disputes at the World Bank.

Several international patent and other agreements were pointed out. Chapter 4 covered a number of UN-related organizations and other worldwide associations. Each of them has some harmonizing or standardizing effect. The same can be said of the regional international groupings and organizations dealt with in Chapter 4.

A Few U.S. Laws That Affect
the International
Business of U.S. Firms

Although every law relating to business arguably has some effect on international activities, some laws warrant special notice. We will look briefly at U.S. antitrust and taxation laws, the Foreign Corrupt Practices Act, and the Antiboycott act.

Antitrust

Earlier in this chapter, we mentioned the hostility aroused among foreign governments by the aggressive enforcement abroad of U.S. antitrust laws.

The Laws Impede U.S. Exports

An aspect of U.S. antitrust that impedes exports is the rules which prevent American companies from teaming up to bid on major projects abroad. For example, General Electric and Westinghouse had to compete against each other for pieces of the $450 million Brazilian Itaipu Dam generator and turbine contracts. The contracts went to a huge European group led by Siemens of Germany and Brown Boveri of Switzerland. The European governments actively supported their companies. The U.S. government, however, would not let GE and Westinghouse cooperate and did nothing to support their efforts.[26]

Such restrictions on cooperation abroad were cited as the worst obstacle to exports caused by the U.S. antitrust regulations and enforcement procedures in a study by the National Association of Manufacturers (NAM). About 70 percent of the over 100 companies which responded to the NAM questionnaire said that U.S. antitrust laws and practices caused a decline in their international competitiveness.

Export Trading Companies (ETCs)

In October 1982, the Export Trading Company Act of 1982 was signed into law by President Reagan. The centerpiece of the ETC Act is its limitation of the applicability of antitrust law to foreign trade. There are many ambiguities in the act, but it does make some important changes in antitrust law.

Companies wishing to establish ETCs apply to the U.S. government for a certificate of antitrust immunity. The certificate safeguards the ETC from government prosecution—assuming that the ETC performs as indicated in the certificate application—but does not immunize the ETC against private party antitrust suits. However, any damages awarded in such suits are limited to actual damages rather than the treble damages awarded in other such private actions.*

The ETC Act also permits American banks to own shares of ETCs. Some of the larger banks are moving aggressively into the ETC field, offering financing and even countertrade† services to ETC shareholders. Smaller banks are feeling competitive pressures to get involved in ETCs for fear that larger banks will take their export company customers.[27]

Despite passage of the ETC act, there is strong feeling both in and out of government that the antitrust laws constitute severe burdens on the ability of American companies to compete at home or abroad with foreign competitors. The late Malcolm Baldrige, secretary of commerce in the Reagan administration, made several points. The U.S. antitrust laws were largely written in the early 1900s, and they followed the economic theory of that time: "Big is bad; small is good." That theory was proper when other countries could not compete with us and U.S. companies did not need to export to grow. But now, more than 70 years later, U.S. goods face severe competition at every turn. More than 70 percent of U.S. products face some kind of import competition, and the range and variety of that competition are increasing. The world economy has changed, trade patterns have changed, but the antitrust laws have not.

Baldrige and others would like Congress to repeal Section 7 of the Clayton Act, which prohibits mergers and acquisitions that *may* reduce competition or *tend to* create a monopoly. Baldrige made this comment on the italicized words: "No one can live in an environment where the antitrust enforcers try to read your mind and then can arrest you for their idea of what you might be thinking."[28]

Taxation

As we have remarked, the U.S. tax system is considered by many to be the world's most complicated. That in itself makes doing business more complicated and, therefore, more expensive for a U.S. MNE than for MNEs based elsewhere. There is, however, one tax incentive for exports worthy of mention.

Export Incentive

In 1971, the U.S. Congress amended the Internal Revenue Code (IRC) to permit the Domestic International Sales Corporation (DISC) as an encouragement for

---

*The possibility of treble damages against British Airways is one of the worries of the UK government because of the private antitrust action being brought against BA and other airlines by the Laker Airways liquidator.

†Countertrade is a generic term for the many methods of trading when the customer does not have enough hard currency to buy what it wants from other countries. This subject is discussed in Chapter 17.

American companies to export. This gave a tax break to companies that manufactured in the United States with American labor and exported the product.

It worked. The U.S. Treasury estimated that in the fiscal year ended June 30,1976, DISC operations boosted U.S. exports to an amount some $2.9 billion higher than they would have been without DISCs.[29] In spite of that and in the face of continuing and growing U.S. BOP deficits, the Carter administration recommended that the DISC be abolished.[30] U.S. labor unions favor its abolition on the basis that it favors big business, even though exports mean jobs. Congress did not abolish the DISC, but it did cut back the tax benefits originally provided.

The Tax Reform Act of 1984 largely replaced the DISC with the new Foreign Sales Corporation (FSC). From the point of view of exporters, a major advantage of the FSC over the DISC is that the tax exemption is permanent—there is no recapture of the benefit in future years if dividends are paid or if the FSC no longer satisfies qualification requirements. Another break given exporters by the 1984 law is permanent forgiveness of taxes deferred under DISC provisions.

Taxing Americans Who Work Abroad

The United States is almost alone among countries in taxing its people according to nationality rather than on the basis of where they live and work. As a result, Americans living or working in another country must pay taxes there and to the United States. In addition to higher tax payments, this requires the time and expense of completing two sets of complicated tax returns. In 1981, the sections of the IRC dealing with this subject were again amended. Although the burden of completing two tax returns was not lifted, the new law gave relief, starting in 1982, in the amount of American taxes to be paid.

The 1981 IRC change increased the exemption of foreign-earned income from American income taxes in 1982 to a maximum of $75,000, and that was to increase $5,000 per year until 1986, when the exclusion maximum would be $95,000. The new law also permitted exclusion of housing allowances* in excess of $6,059, a figure tied to treatment of government employees. Tax legislation in 1984 froze the maximum foreign earned income exclusion at $80,000 per year through 1987, with $5,000 increases in 1988, 1989, and 1990, at which time the $95,000 limit would be reached; under the previous law, the limit would have been reached in 1986. Congress changed matters again in 1986. In the major tax act of that year, one change was to reduce the maximum exemption from $95,000 to $85,000.

Foreign Corrupt Practices Act (FCPA)

During the 1970s, revelations of "**questionable**" or "**dubious**" **payments** by American companies to foreign officials rocked governments in the Netherlands and Japan. Congress considered corporate bribery "bad business" and "unnec-

---

*See Chapter 22 for treatment of compensation packages for expatriate employees.

essary," and President Carter found it "ethically repugnant." As a result, the Foreign Corrupt Practices Act (FCPA) was passed and signed.

Uncertainties

There were a number of uncertainties about terms used in the FCPA. An interesting one involves *grease*. According to the FCPA's drafters, the act does not outlaw grease* or facilitating payments made solely to expedite nondiscretionary official actions. Such actions as customs clearance or transatlantic telephone calls have been cited. There is no clear distinction between supposedly legal grease payments and illegal bribes. To confuse matters further, U.S. Justice Department officials have suggested that they may prosecute some grease payments anyway under earlier antibribery laws which were written to get at corruption in the United States.[31]

Other doubts raised by the FCPA concerned the accounting standards it requires for compliance. That matter is connected to questions about how far management must go to learn whether any employees, subsidiaries, or agents may have violated the act; even if management were unaware of an illegal payment, it could be in violation if it "had reason to know" that some portion of a payment abroad might be used as a bribe.[32]

Other Countries' Reactions to Bribes

Attitudes of business and government officials in Europe toward the FCPA range from amusement to incredulity, and no other government has taken a position similar to that represented by the FCPA—quite the opposite.[33] West German tax collectors, for example, permit resident companies to deduct foreign bribes, which are called *sonderpesen* or special expenses. In Britain, corrupt payments, even to British government officials, qualify for tax deductions. Even the government-owned British Leyland (BL) was found to have been paying bribes overseas to obtain orders for its Range Rovers.

> One comical aspect of the BL story was that its factories were unable to produce enough Rover vehicles to meet the very large demand for them in the export market. The bribes for new orders were being paid at a time when BL already had more orders than it could fill.

Another interesting, and possibly embarrassing, facet of the BL story is that it was published in British newspapers only two weeks after the British prime minister, James Callaghan, had promised to eliminate "irregular practices and improper conduct" in international business. The promise was made to President Carter, who wanted other countries to cooperate with the United States in stopping such practices and conduct.

---

*Other words with similar connotations are *dash, squeeze, mordida, cumshaw,* and *baksheesh.* Bribes and questionable payments were mentioned in connection with sociological forces in Chapter 7.

Just how pervasive these practices are was disclosed by Lloyd N. Cutler, a Washington attorney who did a study of the subject for the Northrop Corporation. Cutler was quoted as saying, "Almost all European and Japanese export sales of the type that generate corrupt payments are arranged with government export financing or other government support."[34] So far, no other industrialized nation has a law resembling the FCPA, and an anticommercial bribery treaty proposed by the United States is languishing in an inactive committee of the United Nations.

In 1985, Dancare Corporation, a Danish company, got in trouble because of $730,000 in bribes that it had paid to Saudi Arabia. The trouble was not that it had paid the bribes, but that the bribes were not clearly indicated as such in the company's tax records. The Danish tax chief now advises Danish firms to book illicit payments openly under "bribes." Whether the bribes are in the form of cash, sexual favors, or luxury goods doesn't matter, as long as their value is noted on the tax records. Receipts are desirable but not essential.[35]

Bribes paid in Denmark are illegal; bribes paid abroad to secure export business are both legal and a tax-deductible expense. In the contest for the Saudi Arabian business, the Dancare Corporation bid was more than $730,000 above potential American competitors. Of course, they would have been in violation of the FCPA if they paid a bribe to get the contract and certainly would have been unable to deduct the payment from American taxes.

Is America Losing?

Is the FCPA causing American exporters to lose business? Yes, answer a number of companies, several of which are in the construction business. The United States, which in 1976 ranked first in the overseas construction market, dropped to fifth in 1987, falling behind Japan, Korea, West Germany, and Italy.

A White House task force on export disincentives has studied the FCPA, among other disincentives. Its rough, preliminary estimate of exports lost to American business as a result of the FCPA is $1 billion per year.[36]

The view that the FCPA is causing American companies to lose export business is not unanimous. In 1976, the Securities and Exchange Commission (SEC) forecast that cessation of the payment of foreign bribes would not seriously affect the ability of American business to compete in world markets.[37]

A study made by Professor Richman in 1977–78 indicated that it was unwise and unsound, on both ethical and economic grounds, for U.S. corporations to engage in questionable foreign payments and practices. Professor Richman's study covered 65 U.S. corporations and agreed with the SEC conclusions.[38]

Contradicting the SEC and Professor Richman was a study published in 1979. In this study, a questionnaire was sent to 200 corporate controllers randomly selected from Fortune 500 companies. Seventy percent of the respondents felt that prohibiting questionable payments would cause U.S. business to lose foreign contracts.[39]

A poll commissioned by *Business Week* in 1983 about the FCPA found that "executives are surprisingly divided over what changes should be made." Most, however, agreed on three points: (1) that Congress should clarify what it meant by "grease" payments, (2) that the law made it difficult to sell in countries where bribery was a way of life, and (3) that this hurt U.S. exports.[40]

Antiboycott Law

As a part of the hostility and wars between the Arab countries and Israel, several of the Arab countries boycott foreign companies which do business with Israel. They will not buy from such companies. Inasmuch as several Arab countries are extremely rich oil producers, they are very large potential markets from which sellers do not like to be excluded. In 1977, however, the United States passed an act forbidding American companies to comply with any Arab boycott law or regulation.

Contrast American and British Attitudes

As in the case of the FCPA, no other country has any such antiboycott law. A British House of Lords select committee studying similar legislation for Britain found 2.7 billion reasons to bury it in 1978. During 1977, British exports to Arab markets totaled £2.7 billion.[41]

Action under the Antiboycott Law

Some complained that the antiboycott law was laxly enforced in the early years of its existence; fines ran around $500 to $600 for each violation. Then, in 1982, the Department of Commerce, which enforces the law, became more aggressive; more companies were charged with boycott-related offenses, and the fines imposed were in larger amounts.[42] The largest so far is a $323,000 fine levied against Citibank. As the Department of Commerce continued to tighten enforcement, it collected $1.4 million in fines from 53 companies in 1984, up from $520,000 from 48 companies the previous year.

The regulations that implement the antiboycott legislation forbid response to any Arab question or questionnaire which deals with Israel. As a condition of bidding on a contract with an Arab country your company may be asked whether any components to be supplied under the proposed contract will be sourced in Israel. Even though your company has no Israeli suppliers and no intention of using any, it would be a violation of the antiboycott law and regulations to so inform the Arab country.

Are Export Contracts Being Lost?

Is the antiboycott law causing American exporters to lose business? Yes, according to Chase Manhattan Bank, especially in the relatively hard-line Arab countries, such as Iraq, Libya, and Syria. Even in other Arab countries friendlier to the United States, the law causes difficulties and burdens not faced or borne by non-American competitors.[43] Commenting on the law and the government's tough enforcement of it, Philip Hinson, Middle East affairs director of the U.S. Chamber of Commerce, says, "They've had a randomly harmful effect on U.S. exports."

Another complaint by American companies about the law is the cost of compliance. Joseph Komalick, editor of the *Boycott Law Bulletin*, says that some U.S. multinationals have as many as 20 lawyers check the legality of Middle East contracts to make sure they don't violate the law.[44]

One argument against the boycott legislation is that it hurts American business but does no harm to the Arab countries. They can buy whatever they want—or adequate substitutes—from Europe or Japan.[45]

Some Laws and Agencies Aid U.S. Exports and Investment

We do not mean to give the impression that all U.S. laws and government agencies pose obstacles to the international business of U.S. companies. The U.S. Department of Commerce actively encourages exports by American companies. U.S. embassies and consular offices can be helpful with information and introductions for Americans who wish to export to or invest in foreign countries. The FSC provides some tax incentives for U.S. exporters.

Changes in Laws and Regulations Possible

During the Carter administration, a White House task force on export disincentives was established. One of its preliminary findings was mentioned in this chapter. When the Reagan administration assumed office in 1981, moves to lessen disincentives gained momentum. One complaint about the Foreign Corrupt Practices Act was that it was unclear. Bill Brock, U.S. trade representative, recommended legislation to make its provisions clearer and to end its unintended effect of weakening American businesses competing with foreign companies.[46] The U.S. Treasury began studies of tax law and regulation changes to lower U.S. tax burdens on Americans abroad. Committees of Congress began to study these and other disincentives to U.S. exports and investments.

From all of this may come new laws and regulations to encourage American exports and investments abroad. These, of course, will not be made without opposition; the opposition arguments are that bribery weakens competition, distorts markets, and is morally wrong. The opposition to change fears that change will encourage bribery.[47]

European Parliament— U.S. Congress Compared

Palais de l'Europe in Strasbourg

Capitol of the United States

European Parliament	U.S. Congress
Legislative roles. Only advisory, on proposals made by Commission before their consideration by the Council. Must approve budget.	***Legislative roles.*** Exclusive authority to introduce legislation. Two houses consider, amend, and move draft laws to the other for final vote; bills passed proceed to President for action.
Relation to executive. Reacts to specific Commission proposals, but provides public forum for E.C. issues. Can remove entire Commission but not replace it. Can force some changes in budget. Questions Commissioners in plenary.	***Relation to executive.*** Legislative co-responsibility. Consents to treaties and appointments (Senate). Has own investigative and budget arms to check on executive. Committees both authorize and allot funds and oversee expenditure. Questions executive officials in committee.
Election, chambers, sessions. Elected for five-year term by direct vote, but under national electoral laws. Single chamber.meets one week in plenary, two weeks in committee, and one week in political groups each month.	***Election, chambers, sessions.*** Two chambers: House elected for 2 years by equal population districts; Senate elected for 6 years by states; generally equal roles in legislation. House and Senate together set a calendar of sessions which average 180–200 days a year.
Jurisdictions. Community laws, regulation, and budget (in part) which cover areas defined by the Treaty of Rome creating the E.C. Defense excluded.	***Jurisdictions.*** Entire federal structure which, under the Constitution, extends to almost every aspect of country except local and state taxing, police, and education functions.

Source: *Europe Magazine*, Washington, D.C., May–June, 1984.

Staffs. Entrance exam into civil service status for secretariat; free hire for political groups. Very small personal staff.

Committee structure.
Substantive (12): Political Affairs; Agriculture; Economic & Monetary; Energy, Research & Technology; External Economic Relations; Social Affairs & Unemployment; Regional Policy & Planning; Transport; Environment, Public Health & Consumer Protection; Youth, Culture, Education, Information & Sport; Development & Cooperation. *Budgetary:* Budget; Budgetary Control. *Institutional:* Rules of Procedure & Petitions; Verification of Credentials; Institutional Affairs.

Leadership. President and 12 vice presidents represent national and party balance in plenary vote; they form Bureau for general direction of Parliament; 7 political group chairmen are added to form Enlarged Bureau which handles most important matters involving political management. Five questors serve as ombudsmen for many administrative matters. Rapporteurs, selected by committee members, draft and defend reports. Committee chairmen function as non-partisan managers.

Role of parties. Committee assignments, chairmenships and inter-parliamentary delegations determined by relative size of each of 7 political groups. Discipline varies depending on ideological breadth of groups, but generally is much greater than in U.S. Congress. Group chairmen elected for one-half of 5-year term of Parliament but may be re-elected. Parties tried to run Community-wide electoral campaigns in first direct election in 1979 with varying success. Most members elected on party-list system, which requires them to keep active role in national parties.

Staffs. Generally meritocratic entrance to committee staff. Political appointment for some housekeeping jobs. Large personal staffs.

Committee structure.
Substantive (17) (House used as example, but Senate is similar): Agriculture; Armed Services; Banking, Finance & Urban Affairs; Education & Labor; Energy & Commerce; Foreign Affairs, Intelligence; Interior & Insular Affairs; Judiciary; Merchant Marine & Fisheries; Post Office & Civil Service; Public Works & Transportation; Science & Technology; Small Business; Veterans; Ways & Means. *Budgetary:* Appropriations; Budget. *Institutional:* Administration; Rules; Standards of Conduct. *Investigative:* Government Operations.

Leadership. *House:* Speaker elected by majority party and speaks for it, but his function, partly, is to represent House in broad non-partisan way; majority and minority parties each name leader and whip. These five form leadership for the management of 435-member House. *Senate:* Vice president is constitutionally presiding officer, but this is largely a ceremonial function; majority and minority leaders, and their whips, manage 100-member Senate on collegial basis. *Both:* Committee chairmen and (in last decade) subcommittee chairmen play major role in writing legislation and managing it on floor.

Role of parties. Only two major parties. Decisions taken by each house on organization generally follow party votes. Substantive issues bring more diversity although Speaker and President can have effects in organizing party positions. National parties very weak and have almost no effects on Congress which runs own campaign committees, by party, in each house. No effective means of disciplining errant members. Committee assignments and chairmanships depend on party caucus votes. Seniority plays presumptive role in these votes.

Common Law or Civil Law?

Historically, there has been a clear distinction between common law, which developed in England and spread to the English colonies, and civil law, which originated on the continent of Europe. Courts made common law as they decided individual cases; civil law was made by kings, princes, or legislatures issuing decrees or passing bills.

As time has passed, legislatures and government agencies in the United States have made more and more laws and regulations. The courts, in turn, have interpreted these laws and regulations as parties have argued about what they mean. That is the sort of procedure one finds in Europe, but vast differences in practices have developed which have less to do with traditional common–civil law approaches than with historic government-citizen (or subject) relationships and attitudes.

European Practice

Europe has a history of thousands of years of tyranny which recently has been covered with a veneer of democracy. People have greater reason to fear their governments in Europe than in the United States, and government service has more prestige. Before a new law is presented to the legislature (which, unlike legislatures in the United States, is always controlled by the same political party that controls the executive branch), consensus is achieved among most of the people, businesses, and government agencies that will be affected.

In contrast to American practices, European legislation is rarely amended and regulations are rarely revised. Courts are not as often asked to give their interpretations, and if they are, the decisions are rarely appealed. Once a consensus has been reached, it is considered very bad form to open the subject again, and those who do may find themselves left out of the consultations the next time around.

American Practice

In contrast to European custom, Americans have a weaker tradition of obeying their governments and have had very little fear of them. Americans are much more likely than Europeans to challenge laws in the courts, in the streets, or by disobedience. Legislation in America is a product of an ongoing adversary proceeding, not of consensus; law is written by one independent branch of government for implementation by a second and for interpretation by yet a third. Different political parties or people with conflicting philosophies frequently control the three different branches of government.

Laws and regulations are constantly being amended or revised by the legislatures and the agencies. Courts interpret laws in ways that are sometimes surprising, and courts may strike laws down as being unconstitutional.

In the United States, the legislative body is now called Congress, and it convened as representatives of the several English colonies even before the United States became a country. In Europe, the legislative body of the European Community is called the European Parliament. It was brought into being by the Treaty of Rome, which was signed in 1957. The accompanying reading contains an interesting comparison of those two legislatures.

Summary

We have seen that taxes can have many purposes, and raising revenue for the government is only one of them. Other purposes are the encouragement of activities deemed desirable by the government and the discouragement of others. Taxes are used to redistribute income, to protect certain industries, and to accomplish many other goals.

Taxes differ greatly from country to country. Some countries have high taxes, others low or no taxes. Most countries have some sort of income tax, but many rely more on the value-added tax (VAT). Enforcement of tax laws is strict in the United States and some other countries but relatively lax elsewhere.

The United States has the most comprehensive antitrust laws, and it tries to apply and enforce them extraterritorially. Other countries resent what they perceive as intrusion into their sovereignty as the United States attempts to bring their citizens and companies under U.S. law for acts performed outside the United States. Other countries and the European Community have antitrust-type laws, which are frequently called restrictive trade practices laws, but none of them is as vigorously enforced as are the U.S. antitrust laws.

Nations try to protect or favor their own business by putting obstacles in the way of imports. The obstacles can be tariffs, quotas, packaging requirements, health requirements, or any of hundreds of other requirements that foreign goods must satisfy before they are permitted into the country.

Nations sometimes seize foreign-owned property. If they don't take 100 percent of the property, they may "domesticate" it by taking enough—for example, 51 percent ownership—to control it.

Executives of companies in Europe are discovering that their companies and even they personally can be liable to workers or to the public if one of their products causes injury or death. The liability can be civil or criminal.

Price and wage control laws are found in most countries. As inflation continues, these laws can be expected to be expanded.

Labor laws exist everywhere and must be studied. They can greatly increase labor costs above the hourly wages paid to employees.

Although money (currency) flows relatively freely among the industrialized countries, they are the minority. Almost all LDCs and communist countries have currency control laws, and some of them enforce these laws very harshly.

Contracts between parties in different countries can cause problems that are not present when the parties to contracts are citizens of only one country, in situations where one of the parties fails to perform satisfactorily. However, many solutions have been found, such as agreements in the contracts as to applicable law or language or as to arbitrating differences before a named body such as the International Chamber of Commerce.

Industrial property such as patents is protected by a number of multinational conventions (treaties) and by bilateral treaties. The protection of trade secrets took a step forward in 1980, when the United States got the first criminal conviction under an industrial espionage law. Other countries enforce similar laws.

There is a growing complaint by American business that U.S. laws and their enforcement by the government is lessening the competitiveness of U.S. companies as compared to foreign companies. Cited are the antitrust and tax laws, the Foreign Corrupt Practices Act, and the antiboycott law.

Questions

1. *What are some purposes of taxes other than to raise revenue?*
2. *Why do some people feel that a VAT should replace some or all of the U.S. income tax?*
3. *What is a national tax system?*
4. *What objections have other countries to extraterritorial application by the United States of its antitrust laws?*
5. *What was the chief legal argument made on behalf of OPEC in the antitrust suit against it by the IAM?*
6. *What are some advantages that arbitrating contract disputes may have as compared to using the courts?*
7. *Are tariffs the only type of obstacle to international trade? If not, name some others.*
8. *Can product liability be criminal? If so, in what sort of situation?*
9. *Why do most countries impose currency exchange controls?*
10. *How might the ETC Act limit U.S. antitrust activity abroad?*
11. a. *Does the Foreign Corrupt Practices Act forbid all bribes? Explain.*
    b. *Does the antiboycott law permit U.S. exporters to Arab countries to certify that the products are not of Israeli origin if that is true?*
    c. *Do countries such as Britain, France, Germany, and Japan, whose companies compete with American companies, have such laws as the FCPA and the antiboycott statute?*
12. a. *Comparing the United States with Western Europe, what are the differences in practices as to making, amending, and interpreting laws?*
    b. *What are the reasons for those differences?*

Minicase

10-1 American Law

Your company manufactures specialty motors in the United States. Business in the United States has been slack, and you have embarked on an export drive using facilities of the Department of Commerce as well as a private export sales agency.

You know that Saudi Arabia is an excellent potential market for your motors as it rapidly expands factories, ports, hospitals, and many other facilities. Therefore, you are delighted when your sales agency phones you one day to inform you that your motors are perfect for a new Saudi refinery for which procurement is beginning. The agent has the Saudi invitation to bid for the contract and is sending it by express to you today.

The invitation is received the next day. The agent was right. Your motors precisely match the specifications, you know the competition, and you feel confident that you can win this big, market-entry order.

Accompanying the invitation is a questionnaire for new bidders for Saudi business. The questions are about your company—how long in business, the identity of its customers and suppliers, its financial strength, and the identity of its officers, directors, and major shareholders. The company is well established and has many satisfied customers and dependable suppliers, all in the United States. There is no single, dominant stockholder, and all of the directors and officers are experienced, reputable Americans.

Should the above facts alert you to any possible American law problems? Explain.

Minicase

10-2 Italian Law

A California-based company is expanding very well and has just made its first export sale. All of its sales and procurement contracts up to now have contained a clause providing that if any disputes should arise under the contract, they would be settled under California law and that any litigation would be in California courts.

The new foreign customer, which is Italian, objects to these all-California solutions. It says it is buying and paying for your products, so Italian law and courts should govern and handle any disputes.

You are the CEO of the California company, and you very much want this order. You are pleased with the service your law firm has given, but you know it has no international experience. What sort of solutions would you suggest that your lawyers research as possible compromises between your usual all-California clause and the customer's wish to go all-Italian?

Supplementary Readings

Aaron, Henry J., ed. *The Value-Added Tax: Lessons from Europe*. Washington D.C.; Brookings Institution, 1981.

Basche, James R. *Unusual Foreign Payments: A Survey of the Policies and Practices of U.S. Companies*. New York: Conference Board, 1976.

Cateora, Phillip R. *International Marketing*. 5th ed. Homewood, Ill.; Richard D. Irwin, 1983. Chap. 7.

de Jantscher, Milka Casanegra. "Tax Havens Explained." In *Contemporary Perspectives in International Business*, ed. Harold W. Berkman and Ivan R. Vernon. Skokie, Ill.: Rand McNally, 1979, pp. 83–92.

"Foreign Patent Protection for Exporters." *Business America*, August 27, 1979, pp. 3–14.

Greanias, George C. *The FCPA: Anatomy of a Statute*. Lexington, Mass.: Lexington Books, 1982.

Henning, Charles N.; William Pigott; and Robert Haney Scott. *International Financial Management*. New York: McGraw-Hill, 1978. Chap. 17.

Jackson, John H. *Legal Problems of International Economic Relations*. St. Paul, Minn.: West Publishing, 1977.

Jacoby, Neil Herman. *Bribery and Extortion in World Business: A Study of Corporate Political Payments Abroad*. New York: Macmillan, 1977.

Lewis, P. "Taxing Americans Abroad: New U.S. Tax Law May Affect Business in Europe." In *Contemporary Perspectives in International Business*, ed. Harold W. Berkman and Ivan R. Vernon. Skokie, Ill.: Rand McNally, 1979, pp. 77–82.

Ricks, David A. *International Dimensions of Corporate Finance*. Englewood Cliffs, N.J.: Prentice-Hall, 1978. Chap. II.

Robinson, Richard D. *International Business Management*. Hinsdale, Ill.: Dryden Press, 1978. Chap. 7.

Robock, Stefan H., and Kenneth Simmonds. *International Business and Multinational Enterprises*. Homewood, Ill.: Richard D. Irwin, 1983. Chaps. 8, 10, 11.

Rodriguez, Rita M., and E. Eugene Carter. *International Financial Management*. 2nd ed. Englewood Cliffs, N.J.: Prentice-Hall, 1979. Appendix 1.

Root, Franklin R. *International Trade and Investment*. Cincinnati: South-Western Publishing, 1984. Chaps. 8, 15, 23.

Terpstra, Vern. *The Cultural Environment of International Business*. Cincinnati: South-Western Publishing, 1978. Chap. 8.

Weston, J. Fred, and Bart W. Sorge. *Guide to International Financial Management*. New York: McGraw-Hill, 1977. Chap. 7.

———. *International Managerial Finance*. Homewood, Ill.: Richard D. Irwin, 1972, chap. 7.

Endnotes

1. Dan Throop Smith, "Value-Added Tax: The Case for," *Harvard Business Review*, November-December 1970, pp. 77–85; and Stanley S. Surrey, "Value-Added Tax: The Case Against," *Harvard Business Review*, November–December 1970, pp. 86–94.

2. Article 85 of the treaty limits cartels, and Article 86 concerns abuses of an individual company's dominant position where trade between EC member states is affected.

3. *Economist,* February 17, 1979, pp. 58–59.

4. Raymond Hughes, law courts correspondent, "Partial Victory for Adams in Commission Case," *Financial Times of London,* July 12, 1985, p. 2.

5. *Economist,* June 9, 1979, pp. 91–92.

6. *Economist,* December 10, 1977, pp. 77–78.

7. *Economist,* June 30, 1979, p. 80.

8. "France Issues Regulations on Language Requirements," *Commerce America,* June 6, 1977, p. 21.

9. Sam Jameson, "Japan Phone Chief Irked by U.S. Sales Complaint," *Los Angeles Times,* February 23, 1983, p. 1.

10. "Brazil: Even Components Must Be Brazilianized," *Business Week,* January 24, 1977, p. 34.

11. *Economist,* July 30, 1977, pp. 64–65.

12. *Business Week,* March 29, 1976, p. 48.

13. *Business International,* April 22, 1983, pp. 123–24.

14. Michael Skapinker, "Why the Product Liability Plague Is No Longer Just a U.S. Malady," *International Management,* July 1986, pp. 27–34

15. *Business Europe,* December 23, 1977, pp. 404–5.

16. *Business International,* July 22, 1977, pp. 225–26.

17. *Economist,* October 21, 1978, p. 137.

18. *International Letter,* Federal Reserve Bank of Chicago, March 11, 1983.

19. *The Wall Street Journal,* February 28, 1979, p. 14.

20. Cecilia E. Cosca and Joseph J. Zimmerer, "Judicial Interpretations of Foreign Arbitral Awards under the UN Convention," *Law and Policy in International Business,* Summer, 1976, p. 737.

21. For discussion of this convention, see Richard D. Robinson, *International Business Management,* 2nd ed. (Hinsdale, Ill.: Dryden Press, 1978), pp. 583–86.

22. "Pooh-Poohing Patent Protection," *Business International,* July 22, 1983, p. 228; and "At the U.N., a Mounting War on Patents," *Backgrounder,* Heritage Foundation, October 4, 1982.

23. Karen Tumulty, "Witnesses Warn of Commercial Counterfeiting," *Los Angeles Times,* August 3, 1983, part I, p. 1.

24. *Economist,* January 12, 1980, pp. 72–73; and *The Wall Street Journal,* January 21, 1980, pp. 1, 27.

25. *Business International,* July 9, 1976, pp. 217–18.

26. *Business Week,* April 10, 1978, p. 60.

27. "Trading Company Act—I: A Look at What It Does in Antitrust Area," *Business International,* November 12, 1982, pp. 361–63; "Trading Company Act—II: Opening for Bankers Is Wide but Complex," *Business International,* November 26, 1982, pp. 379 and 382; "Trading Company Act—III: Allowable Scope of Action Poses Real Dilemmas for ETCs," *Business International,* December 17, 1982, pp. 401–3; "Trading Company Act—IV: Conflicting Interests and Goals Key Concerns of Banks, MNCs," *Business International,* December 31, 1982, pp. 409–11. For a look at perceived flaws in the ETC Act, see "Export Trading Companies: Current Legislation, Regulation, and Commercial Bank Involvement," *Columbia Journal of World Business,* Winter 1981, pp. 42–47; and "Drawback Seen in Liberal Export Trading Company Regs from FRB," *Peat, Marwick Executive Newsletter,* June 16, 1983, p. 4.

28. Malcolm Baldrige, "Rx for Export Woes: Antitrust Relief," *The Wall Street Journal*, October 15, 1985, p. 32.
29. *The Wall Street Journal*, April 14, 1978, p. 14.
30. Ibid.
31. John S. Estey and David W. Marston, "Pitfalls (and Loopholes) in the Foreign Bribery Law," *Fortune*, October 9, 1978, pp. 182–88.
32. Barbara Crutchfield George and Mary Jane Dundas, "Responsibilities of Domestic Corporate Management under the Foreign Corrupt Practices Act," *Syracuse Law Review*, 31, no. 4, 1980, pp. 866–905; "Some Guidelines on Dealing with Graft," *Business International*, February 25, 1983, p. 62.
33. Interviews conducted by one of the authors in Europe during July and August 1979.
34. Jerry Landauer, "Proposed Treaty against Business Bribes Gets Poor Reception Overseas, U.S. Finds," *The Wall Street Journal*, March 28, 1977, p. 26.
35. *The Wall Street Journal*, October 31, 1985, p. 32.
36. *International Herald Tribune*, August 3, 1979, p. 11.
37. Report of the Securities and Exchange Commission on Questionable and Illegal Corporate Payments and Practices, May 1976.
38. Barry Richman, "Can We Prevent Questionable Foreign Payments?" *Business Horizons*, June 1979, pp. 14–19.
39. James J. Benjamin, Paul E. Dascher, and Robert G. Morgan, "How Corporate Controllers View the Foreign Corrupt Practices Act," *Management Accounting*, June 1979, pp. 43–45, 49.
40. "The Antibribery Act Splits Executives," *Business Week*/Harris Poll, September 19, 1983, p. 11.
41. *Economist*, September 2, 1978, p. 101.
42. Laurie McGinley, "Boycott Law Enforcement Is Toughened," *The Wall Street Journal*, December 9, 1982, p. 33.
43. *Wall Street Journal*, April 3, 1978, p. 6.
44. Eduardo Lochica, "U.S. Law Successfully Blocks Arab Bid to Keep American, Israeli Firms Apart," *The Wall Street Journal*, July 14, 1984, p. 28.
45. David Ignatius, "Catch 22: Trading with Iraq," *The Wall Street Journal*, March 25, 1982, p. 22.
46. Bill Brock, "Foreign Corrupt Practices Act Causes Confusion, Hurts Exports," *Los Angeles Times*, June 7, 1981, part VI, p. 3.
47. William Proxmire, "Integrity Never Hurt a Sale," *Los Angeles Times*, June 7, 1981, part 4, p. 3.

CHAPTER 11

LABOR FORCES

"**M**oves of unions to join a board of directors offer little to American unions. We do not want to blur in any way the distinctions between the respective roles of management and labor in the plant. If unions were to become a partner in management, they would be most likely the junior partner in success and the senior partner in failure."

Thomas R. Donahue, executive assistant to the president, AFL–CIO, in *Los Angeles Times,* April 22, 1979, p. 3

"To stay competitive, U.S. manufacturers must redesign their products to be assembled by robots that act like machines, not humans."

Technology Review, April 1985, p. 59

382

Learning Objectives

After you study this chapter, you should know:

1. Forces beyond management control which affect the availability of labor.
2. Political or economic repression, which causes people to flee. As many leave as can get out, regardless of age, skills, sex, or state of health.
3. That refugees are a source of labor but also a burden for the countries to which they flee.
4. That other workers go to countries to fill specific jobs for which they have the requisite skills. They are called guest workers.
5. The composition of a nation's labor force, which affects productivity.
6. Other forces that affect productivity.
7. That a foreign employer must be aware of the social status, sex, race, traditional society, or minorities attitudes of the host country. Failure to take them into account can be costly.
8. That labor union strengths and philosophies differ mightily from area to area.
9. That in important parts of the industrial world, labor is getting a voice in management.

Key Words and Concepts

Labor quality	Sex
Labor quantity	Race
Labor mobility	Traditional society
Labor migration	Minorities
Labor force composition	Labor market
Labor productivity	Labor unions
Benefit/burden ratios	Multinational labor activity
Social status	Codetermination

Business Incident

"Responsibility follows power" is a law of politics. If it is disregarded—as it was for instance by the union members on the board of Volkswagen, who delayed the company's plan to build a plant in the United States because it would have meant "exporting German workers' jobs"—the result is serious damage. In VW's case, the share of the American automobile market fell from 8 percent in 1969 to less than 1 percent now. As a result, the survival of the whole operation is threatened, including the jobs of many German workers.

From *The Wall Street Journal*, September 22, 1982, p. 28.

*T*he quality, quantity, and composition of the available labor force are considerations of great importance to an employer. This is particularly true if the employer is required to be efficient, competitive, and profitable. As we have indicated, there are government-owned plants whose objectives are to provide employment or essential services, and in these plants profitability and competitiveness are secondary.

Labor quality refers to the attitudes, education, and skills of available employees. **Labor quantity** refers to whether there are enough available employees with the skills and so forth required to meet your business needs. Circumstances can arise in which there are too many available workers, and this can be good or bad for the business.

If there are more qualified people than you can economically employ, your bargaining position as an employer is strengthened; you can choose the best at relatively low wages. On the other hand, high unemployment can cause and precede social and political unrest, which is usually not conducive to profitable business.

Many of the labor conditions in an area are determined by the social, cultural, religious, attitudinal, class distinction, and other forces which we have already discussed. Other determinants of labor conditions are political and legal forces, and here we shall enlarge somewhat on those that were introduced in Chapters 9 and 10. A number of steps that management can take to avoid or minimize labor problems or maximize labor strengths are presented in Chapters 20 and 22, which deal with personnel and staffing.

Here we shall look at such subjects as labor availability, the reasons for its availability or scarcity, the types of labor that are likely to be available or scarce under different circumstances, productivity, and employer-employee relationships. These relationships are affected by employee organizations such as labor unions. One cannot generalize about unions because they differ so greatly from country to country or even within one country.

Management of private business in capitalist societies has been thought of as representing the shareholders/owners and bondholders/lenders who put up the money that enabled the business to start and run. The shareholders and bondholders could call the tunes. Some new and different music is now being heard by management in several countries where labor is getting seats on the boards of directors. Management has been reluctant to see that happen, and one of the reasons for that reluctance is illustrated in the business incident.

Labor Mobility

Classical economists assumed the immobility of labor, one of the factors of production. Undoubtedly, labor is imperfectly mobile; leaving aside political and economic obstacles, more complications are involved in moving people than in moving capital or most goods.

But however imperfect the mobility of labor, **labor mobility** does exist. At least 60 million people left Europe to work and live overseas between 1850 and 1970; since World War II, an estimated 30 million workers—in large part from southern Europe and North Africa—moved into northern European countries, though this movement is slowing or even reversing now;[1] millions of workers from across North Africa and from Pakistan and India are filling all kinds of jobs in the oil-rich OPEC countries of the Middle East. The maps and numbers in Figure 11–1 illustrate the extent and directions of **labor migration** in Europe, North Africa, and the Middle East.

There are probably 8 million Mexicans at work in the United States (most illegally), and the number is growing. In addition, there are also many Cubans, Haitians, Central Americans, Southeast Asians, and others in the U.S. work force. The causes of these migrations were and are combinations of problems, economic or political, at their sources and perceived opportunities at their destinations.

Refugees: Political and Economic

Throughout history, there have been flights of people from oppression. During the decades of the 1960s and 70s, millions fled from East to West Germany, from the People's Republic of China to Hong Kong and elsewhere, from North to South Vietnam and then as "boat people" from Vietnam to wherever they could land and hope to be accepted. In 1980, the flight of people from Cuba resumed. These were and are political refugees. Those going from Mexico to the United States and from southern Europe to northern Europe go for primarily economic reasons: better jobs and pay.

Figure 11–1

Labor Migration

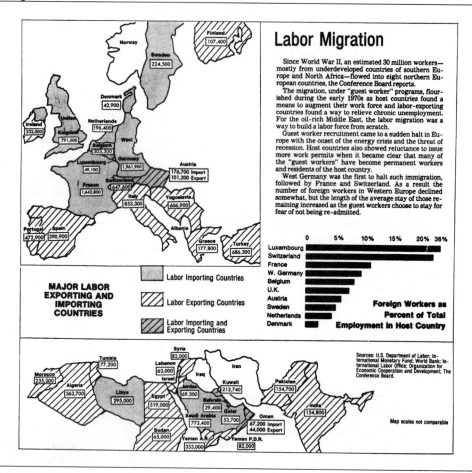

Copyright, 1980 *Los Angeles Times,* Reprinted by permission from October 25, 1980, issue

25 Million Migrants

Around the world, there are estimated to be at least 25 million people who have migrated to another country. Every day, 1,000 or more Afghans come out of their rugged highlands into Pakistan. Colombians move into the Venezuelan oil country, though that slowed as oil prices slid during 1985 and 1986. The drop in oil prices made Nigeria a less attractive destination, and the strong Ivory Coast economy has made it the new magnet country in central Africa. Into South Africa, more than 200,000 men trek each year from black African states to work that country's mines. Oil-producing and industrializing Malaysia is estimated to have more than a million illegal aliens, most of whom are from overcrowded

Indonesia. Because most Argentineans are urbanites, much fertile land is not being farmed, and that draws immigrants from Chile, Bolivia, Paraguay, and Uruguay.

Refugees Welcome?

Refugees are not welcome in most countries. The few countries willing to accept some refugees will take only limited numbers. Their reasons differ. Countries near Vietnam and Cambodia, from which refugees flow, are poor and have difficulty in feeding their own people. Most of the richer countries, such as Japan and the countries of Western Europe, are not racially diverse and are reluctant to bring in large numbers of alien races. European countries with guest workers (see below) are experiencing some race relations problems. Even in a relatively rich and racially diverse country such as the United States, which is accepting—or getting—millions of refugees, there are difficulties. One of them is finding work for all of the new people, and another is educating their children.

Packing Up

When oil prices were high, the Middle East's fastest-growing export was labor. For such countries as Egypt, Jordan, Pakistan, and North and South Yemen, workers' remittances were bigger than total merchandise exports. As tumbling oil prices pushed the area's oil producers into recession, the expatriates who flocked to jobs there in the 1970s and early 1980s were packing their bags and going home. The home countries will sorely miss the income, but on the bright side, the returning workers will bring the skills they learned abroad and the capital they earned there.

Labor Shortages and
Guest Workers

Countries which receive many refugees or which have high birthrates may have too many people for the available jobs, but there are also countries that have too few people. France, Germany, the Scandinavian countries, and Switzerland fall into the latter category. Those countries have few refugees and low birthrates. To them have come the so-called guest workers, who are in the country legally to perform certain types of jobs, usually in service, factory, or construction work.

In 1983, there were 4.3 million immigrants in France who did not qualify for French nationality, including 1.4 million Arabs and 106,000 people from black Africa. West Germany had 4.6 million foreigners, of whom 1.7 million are Turks. England, Switzerland, and the Scandinavian countries also had large numbers of foreign workers and their families. Most of the guest workers are from southern Europe, North Africa, and Turkey.

Figure 11–2

Courtesy *OECD Observer* September 1983, p. 15

Needed: 20 million jobs between 1984 and 1989

Guest Worker Problems

Economic

The guest workers provide the labor needed by the host countries, which is desirable as long as the economies are growing. But when the economies slow, as they did during the mid-1970s and again in the early 1980s, fewer workers are needed and problems appear. Unemployment increases among the native workers, who then want the jobs held by guest workers. It is conveniently forgotten that the guest workers took jobs that the natives would not do when times were good. To appease their citizens, some countries refused to renew the guest workers' permits. In other countries, where the work was seasonal, the guest workers were deported at the end of the season instead of being permitted to stay and take other work. The French, for example, paid surplus foreign workers 10,000 francs (about $2,000) as a "go home" bonus,[2] and in 1983 Germany offered "repatriation assistance" equivalent to about $4,000, plus a lesser amount per child, for certain unemployed foreign workers to leave.[3]

Racial

The introduction of large numbers of foreigners into host countries caused some racial frictions even while the economies were healthy. In France, for instance, Algerian workers claim that 80 countrymen were killed in racial conflicts between 1975 and 1979. French workers often refuse to share low-cost housing projects with outsiders, especially Arabs and Africans.

The Swiss complain about "overforeignization," and a proposal to drastically cut the number of foreigners was only narrowly defeated in a national referendum.

In Germany, there is concern about the foreigners—workers and their families—who show no signs of wanting to leave. The worst relations are with the Turks, who form the largest alien group.

The alien workers and their families are frequently crowded into older, substandard housing. They have created slum neighborhoods in the midst of wealthy Western Europe, and with higher birthrates they are growing in numbers more rapidly than the natives, whose birthrates are among the world's lowest.

A potentially more acute foreign labor problem exists in the Arab Gulf countries. The rapid infrastructural development of the 1970s and early 1980s created huge demands for foreign workers. With lowered oil revenues and infrastructure* largely completed, there is a surplus of foreign workers; many of them are not legally in the host countries but are reluctant to go home.

Some percentages illustrate the gravity of the problems. In the United Arab Emirates (UAE) 80 percent of the workers are foreign (mostly Asian), and in Kuwait, only about 25 percent of the workers are Arab.[4] An even smaller percentage are Kuwaitis, and there is some worry in the area about the large numbers of Egyptians, Lebanese, and Palestinians in important positions.

---

*A nation's infrastructure consists of its social and economic foundations—schools, hospitals, power plants, railroads, highways, ports, communications, airfields, and so forth.

Composition of the

Labor Force

Political or Economic Refugees and Guest Workers

When people flow into a country as refugees, the resulting growth of the labor force includes whatever ages, sexes, and skills are able to get in. They are not coming for specific jobs; they are fleeing oppression or poverty. At the outset, they cause problems for the host country, which must try to feed, clothe, educate, and find work for the newcomers.

Some, for various reasons, remain burdens on the host country or on international refugee relief agencies. So it has been for many of the Palestinians ousted from Israel. This is not to suggest that the Palestinians are less intelligent or industrious than other groups. Their problems and difficulties have been tremendously increased by the wars and political upheavals in the Middle East.

Others find more peaceful surroundings, adapt relatively quickly, and become upwardly mobile in their new society. This holds true for many of the Cuban refugees in the United States. Many believe that the rehabilitation and growth of downtown Miami owes much to the Cubans' influence and work.[5]

Quite different is the type of worker involved in the movement from southern to northern Europe. There, specific types of workers and skills were needed, and only persons who fit the needs were given work permits. They often did not or could not bring their families. They tended to be immediate benefits rather than burdens to the host economy.

The status of the Mexicans in the United States falls between that of the guest worker status and that of the political refugee. For one thing, the great majority of guest workers are legally in the host country; the opposite is true for the Mexicans in the United States. For the most part, the Mexicans are economic, not political, refugees, but they bring their families when possible, thus creating more social burdens than do guest workers. Although the Mexicans usually come to work, they do not necessarily come prepared for specific jobs that are available in the host country.

Labor Force Composition and Comparative Productivity

Another change in **labor force composition** in the United States began in the mid-1970s. The percentage of adult women in the American labor force increased by some 10 percent during the decade of the 1970s.[6] By 1986, 62 percent of all American women aged 18 to 64 worked at least part-time. In that year, 52 percent of all women over the age of 16 were in the labor force, up from 43 percent in 1970 and less than 34 percent in 1950.[7] In addition, women have been making inroads in fields formerly viewed as the exclusive domain of men.

Yet another change was the influx of more young workers. Both the end of the American involvement in the Vietnam War and some questioning about the value of a university education resulted in a smaller proportion of young people continuing school and a large proportion entering the job market. The inexperience of many new workers has been given as a cause of slower productivity growth.

To accommodate these new workers, the United States created more new jobs between 1973 and 1978 than any other industrial country, and that process continued through 1986. This was a great humanitarian and economic achievement, but relative productivity suffered, in part because so many less experienced workers entered the work force at the same time. The newly working women were joined by the refugees from Mexico and elsewhere and by young men and women who were demobilized after the Vietnam War. No other industrialized country was involved in that war to the extent that the United States was.

The comparative growth in total labor forces and the female portion of that growth are illustrated by Table 11–1. The size of the U.S. labor force increased by 24.3 million workers between 1974 and 1986, a gain of over 26 percent. The number of female workers grew by 15.7 million, a growth of almost 44 percent. A unique feature of U.S. labor force growth—female and male—is that many of the new workers are political or economic refugees who speak little if any English in addition to being unskilled.

Table 11–1 demonstrates clearly how much more rapidly the American labor force grew in comparison to those of the other main industrial countries, and the increase in the number of working women was a major part of that growth.

Partly as a result of all the new workers, **labor productivity,** or output per hour, grew more slowly in the United States than in most of the other industrial countries. This is illustrated by the figures in Table 11–2.

While entry into the labor force of large numbers of relatively unskilled laborers is a cause of slow productivity growth, that difficulty can be overcome, and America may be in the process of doing so. Table 11–2 shows improvement in the output per hour of American workers, even though it still trails that of workers in most industrial countries.

Figure 11–3 shows a still brighter competitive picture for the United States. From being the industrial world's laggard in productivity growth during the 1960s, by the 1982–85 period it was very close to other industrial countries in that respect.

Comparative unit labor cost figures also offer some hope that America's decline in competitiveness may be ending. Unit labor cost is the cost in labor to produce one unit of output. Table 11–3 illustrates the improvement of America's comparative position.

Table 11-1

Growth of the Labor Force in Selected Industrial Countries (in millions)

	1974	1975	1976	1977	1978	1979	1983	1984	1985	1986 1st quarter
Italy										
Total labor force	19.6	19.8	20.0	21.7	21.9	22.2	23.1	23.4	23.6	23.8
Female workers	5.4	5.5	5.7	6.9	6.9	7.2	7.8	8.1	8.2	8.5
Japan										
Total labor force	53.1	53.2	n.a.	54.5	55.3	55.9	57.1	59.2	59.6	58.8
Female workers	19.2	19.5	n.a.	20.7	21.2	21.5	22.1	23.5	23.7	24.0
Sweden										
Total labor force	4.0	4.1	4.1	4.1	4.2	4.2	4.3	4.4	4.4	4.3
Female workers	1.6	1.7	1.7	1.7	1.8	1.8	2.0	2.1	2.1	2.1
United Kingdom										
Total labor force	25.6	25.8	26.0	26.2	26.3	26.3	26.1	27.1	27.6	N.A.
Female workers	9.6	9.7	9.8	10.0	10.1	10.3	10.1	10.8	11.1	N.A.
United States										
Total labor force	93.2	94.7	96.9	99.5	102.5	104.9	110.8	115.2	117.1	117.5
Female workers	35.8	36.9	38.4	39.9	41.5	43.5	46.9	49.8	51.2	51.5
West Germany										
Total labor force	26.7	26.4	26.1	26.0	26.2	n.a.	27.4	27.6	27.8	28
Female workers	9.8	9.8	n.a.	9.8	9.8	n.a.	10.4	10.6	10.7	N.A.

Source: Organization for Economic Cooperation and Development, *Labor Force Statistics Yearbook for 1976*. Quarterly Supplement, February 1980; *OECD Observer*, March 1983, pp. 20–21; and *OECD Quarterly Labor Force Statistics*, 1986.

Table 11–2

Growth of Productivity in Selected Industrial Countries (output per hour; 1977 = 100)

	1982	1983	1984	1985
United States	105	112	118	121
Japan	135	142	152	159
West Germany	112	119	124	131
France	123	129	135	140
United Kingdom	112	121	126	129
Canada	101	107	111	115

Figure 11–3

Labor productivity* in Manufacturing Industry (Annual growth rates)

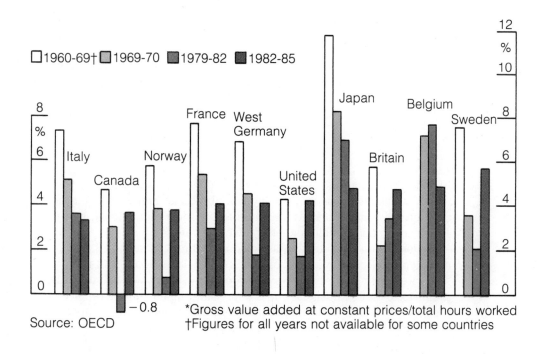

Source: OECD

*Gross value added at constant prices/total hours worked
†Figures for all years not available for some countries

*Not seasonally adjusted. †Average of latest three months compared with average of previous three months, at annual rate.
Source: *Economist,* June 28, 1986, p. 101; based on information obtained from OECD.

Table 11-3
Unit Labor Costs in Selected Industrial Countries (1977 = 100)

	1982	1983	1984	1985	1986 (1st quarter)
United States	115	111	109	111	111
Japan	112	113	108	109	113
France	132	146	158	167	170
West Germany	109	108	107	107	110
United Kingdom	114	116	120	128	134
Canada	126	125	128	130	132

Source: *OECD Main Economic Indicators*, August 1986.

In addition to the relative skill of labor forces, there are other causes of rapidity or slowness of productivity growth. These causes are interlocking, and we shall look briefly at some of them.

Research and Development (R&D)

More efficient tools and machines result from more extensive and effective R&D. The R&D that a company can do depends on its management policies but also on how many after-tax dollars are available and on whether R&D can be deducted as a pretax expense. Governments do a great deal of R&D which can also boost productivity.[8]

Tax Policies

As indicated, a nation's tax policies can influence how much money is available to private business for R&D. They can also make immense differences in the amount available to private business to buy new plant, tools, and machines. They can do this through higher or lower tax rates.

Policies on depreciation are also important. Present U.S. tax policy permits depreciation only of the historic cost of plant, tools, and machines. With high rates of inflation, however, the replacement cost will be much higher than the historic cost. If business could depreciate the current or replacement cost, the result would be lower taxes and more money left to the company for R&D, reinvestment, or other uses. See Chapter 6 for more on this.

Savings Rates

If people save a large percentage of their income (as opposed to spending it on current consumption), there is a larger pool of money available with which to buy company stocks or lend to business. People save for such reasons as creating

Figure 11-4

OECD Countries Net National Savings Ratio, 1983 **(as percent of GDP)**

Focus: Savings—Most figures on a country's savings concentrate on the gross total—what is left over from all its disposable income after deducting private and government consumption. But that ignores the fact that a certain minimum of savings is needed to offset the inevitable depreciation in a country's capital stock; only net savings are available for genuinely new investment. For developed countries, the difference between the two is great. In America, gross savings are 16% of GNP, net savings under 3%. Even thrifty Japan has a net savings ratio (16% of GNP) barely half aits gross ratio (30%). The difference is smaller in poor countries: with less capital, they have less to depreciate.

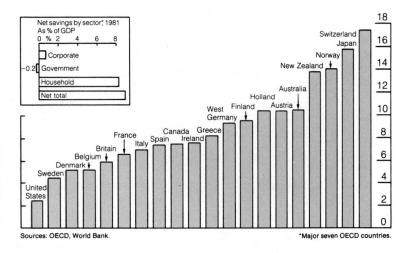

Sources: OECD, World Bank.   *Major seven OECD countries.

*Not seasonally adjusted.
Economist, April 8, 1985, p. 97; based on information from OECD and World Bank.

a nest egg against hard times and because they have confidence in their currencies. A number of countries give tax breaks to interest or dividends earned on savings, and some countries have involuntary savings plans. Most OECD countries have savings rates higher than those of the United States and have higher economic and productivity growth rates.[9]

Figure 11-3 shows the United States to have one of the slowest rates of productivity growth among the countries included. It also demonstrates the relationship of productivity to increases in unit labor costs, both of which, when they are worse than those of the competition, result in bigger trade deficits.

Despite some relative improvement in output per hour by American labor (Table 11-2), productivity growth (Figure 11-3), and unit labor costs (Table 11-3), the U.S. trade deficit has continued to mount. It rose to approximately $105 billion in 1984, $124 billion in 1985, and $160 billion in 1986. Perhaps the improvements have not been sufficient or have not yet been felt in international markets.

One area in which there has been no improvement in U.S. performance is the percentage of income saved by Americans. Figure 11-4 illustrates this, showing the United States to be at the bottom of the list. There is therefore less American capital available to finance business modernization and growth, not to mention the many government needs for capital.

Figure 11-5

Courtesy *OECD Observer* September 1983, p. 24

To reinforce the competitive advantage now provided by lower labor costs, the skills of the labor force must be enhanced.

Other Influences on Productivity

In any economy beyond the most primitive, people use tools and machines to enhance their productive capacities. Clearly, workers with more efficient tools and machines can produce more than those with less efficient ones.

Other data indicate the rate of productivity growth from 1950 through 1985. They show the reasons for the results illustrated in Figure 11-3. U.S. productivity growth was slowest, at 2.6 percent per year, while that of Japan was highest, at 8.7 percent.[10] One study identified 11 reasons for declining productivity growth worldwide. Slowdown in the rates of investment was felt to be the most important reason in the United States and Europe. Relative increase in the cost of capital was listed first in Australia, Canada, and the LDCs. In Japan, the increase in health, security, and pollution controls was named as the worst obstacle. The other eight causes for slower productivity growth discussed by this study were: (1) worker discontent and alienation, (2) growth in public sector and government contracts, (3) government efforts to redistribute wealth, (4) slowdown in technological innovation, (5) changes in the composition and allocation of the work force, (6) slowdown in managerial improvement, (7) shift from labor to raw materials savings, and (8) increased government requests for information and data.[11]

Social Status, Sex, Race, Traditional Society, or Minorities: Considerations in Employment Policies

Social Status

There are societies in which a person's **social status** is established by the caste or social group into which the person is born. India presents an extreme example of the caste system, and intercaste battles which cause fatalities and home burnings still occur between upper-caste Hindus and the untouchables whom Mahatma Gandhi called harijans, the children of God.[12] Obviously, a would-be employer must tread carefully when both upper-caste Hindus and harijans are in the employee pool.

Some say that the class system in Great Britain is eroding, but people there are still classified by the accents they acquire at home and school. When Margaret Thatcher was elected prime minister, commentators saw fit to point out that she was "only" the daughter of a small-store owner even though her accent was "upper class," apparently acquired at Oxford University. Although class differences do not cause riots in Britain, as caste differences do in India, a foreign employer should, nevertheless, be conscious of the possibilities for friction arising from those differences.

In Japan, there remains an odd caste holdover from the 17th century, when the feudal Togugawa regime imposed a rigid social pecking order on the country. The warrior-administrator samurai were at the top. Below them were farmers and artisans, then merchants, and at the very bottom, those with occupations considered dirty and distasteful, such as slaughterers, butchers, and tanners.

As in India where discrimination against untouchables is illegal, all natives of Japan are legally equal. However the descendants of the lowest Japanese class remain trapped in their ghettos, working in small family firms that produce knitted garments, bamboo wares, fur and leather goods, shoes, and sandals. They call themselves burakumin (ghetto people), and they claim that they number about 3 million people living in some 6,000 ghettos. Their average income is far below that of other Japanese.

Sex

Degrees of women's liberation and of women's acceptability in the work force range from fairly advanced in the United States to virtually nil in many countries. Even where women have made some strides out of their traditional roles, their progress is not necessarily secure, as witness the women's marches in Iran when the Islamic government which succeeded the shah ordered women back to their traditional dress and roles.

The employer must consider the sexist attitudes of the host society. In a country such as the United States, which has seen large strides in the status and acceptability of women in business and the professions, the hiring and promotion of women can be a business advantage. It can also be a legal advantage, because it complies with "affirmative action" laws and regulations of the U.S. and state governments. These laws encourage the hiring and promotion of women and minorities. But there are many countries in which customs, attitudes, or religion are hostile to women in the professions or business.

> Think like a man,
> act like a lady,
> work like a dog.
> That is the formula
> for the success of a
> woman working in
> the man's world of
> Japanese business.

One of the quotations at the beginning of Chapter 22 indicates the scarcity of females in Japanese management. Women make up only 6.7 percent of the executive roster of the country, which is far below the American or Swedish rates. One reason is tradition, which is a burden for women executives in most countries.

A second reason is after-hours drinking sessions, which are prevalent in many countries but more prevalent in Japan. Much of Japanese consensus decision making is accomplished during such sessions. Women managers tend to consider these a waste of time and to be somewhat uncomfortable at the freewheeling exchanges among the men as inhibitions fall away. The drinking is often very heavy, and drunkenness is not a disgrace; overimbibers are delivered carefully home.

The discomfort goes both ways. One computer salesman, talking about after-hours drinking sessions with his female section chief, complained, "I don't know what to talk about with her. She's not married, so I must avoid any remarks with sexual connotations. With a man, I could have a drink and talk about anything."

Other Countries Hinder Women

Japan is not the only country where women are encountering problems in making or retaining progress. We spoke of the setback of women in Iran, and women have been having troubles in other Moslem countries also.

One step forward in Pakistan has been accompanied by several steps backward. The forward step was a decision by the federal court that women could serve as judges. Two of the backward steps are: banning women from taking part in public sporting events and changing the law of evidence to make the word of one male witness equal to that of two women. When women in Lahore protested against this devaluation of their legal personalities, they were set upon by the police, who injured 13 of the protestors.

Other backward steps in Pakistan are proposals to deny women the vote, to deny them the right to drive a car (as in Saudi Arabia), to halve the blood money paid for a female victim as compared with a male victim, and to impose the death penalty for prostitution, but only for the woman and not for her customer. Segregated schools for women only are being established. Women cannot attend men's schools in Saudi Arabia, and that country, which gives much financial aid to Pakistan, is thought to be a strong influence on its policies. A pointer to what the segregated female schools may teach is provided by one college, which has banned women from physics and mathematics and channeled them instead into a new course called household accounts.

Women Can Be Burned

Women's hardships in Pakistan are mild by comparison with what's going on next door in India. There, the grisly practice of wife-burning goes on unabated. The women are doused with kerosene and set aflame by in-laws greedy for more dowry. Dowry has been illegal since 1961, but the law is toothless.[13]

Many girls do not live long enough to worry about marriage. There was a tradition of female infanticide in north India, and today, girl children are allowed to die of neglect and starvation. In 1982, a Stanford researcher in China (PRC) lost his grant after he alleged that female infanticide is practiced widely in rural China.

Soviet Women

In 1982, a Soviet feminist was sentenced to four years in jail to be followed by two years of internal exile for the offense of challenging the state doctrine that the female sex has been fully liberated since the 1917 Bolshevik Revolution. Women are equal at law, but life contradicts the law.

In 1980, Julia Voznesenskaya, the daughter of a high-ranking Soviet army officer, was exiled after writing a firsthand account of a women's work camp for *Almanac: Women and Russia,* the USSR's first feminist underground journal. In exile in Munich, Voznesenskaya wrote a book from which the following grim depiction of the current state of Soviet sisterhood is taken.

In Mother Russia, women are still the second sex. Their working hours are spent as all-purpose workhorses, breeders, sex objects, rape victims. Their dreams are modest; not of women's liberation, but merely of a more civilized version of patriarchy and the status quo.[14]

Race

Unfortunately, examples of racial conflicts and discrimination are found worldwide. There have been black versus white conflicts in such places as the United States, South Africa, and Great Britain and Arab, Indian, or Pakistani versus black conflicts in Africa. Earlier in this chapter, we discussed racial friction caused by guest workers in Europe, and there has been bloody conflict in Sri Lanka between Tamils and Sinhalese.

The South African separate-races system, called apartheid, has been denounced in North America and Western Europe as well as in South Africa. Powerful pressures were put on American and European companies to disinvest from—take their money and presences out of— South Africa. Some felt that disinvestment would cause the South African government to end apartheid.

Others disagreed, including some prominent black South Africans and white business and political leaders opposed to apartheid. One black leader, the Zulu* chief Buthelezi, argued that disinvestment would rob blacks of needed jobs. Another, Lucy Mvubelo, head of the black National Union of Clothing Workers, felt that foreign investment offered the best hope of economic progress for South African blacks.[15]

Helen Suzman, a white political opposition leader in the South African Parliament, has been an unrelenting foe of the government's apartheid policies. She had this to say about sanctions by the U.S. government: "But, should the U.S. Congress impose sanctions, the results would be disastrous for those the United States most wants to help." She referred to sanctions as "a moral free lunch."[16]

Congress, nevertheless, enacted sanctions, and American as well as European companies disinvested out of South Africa. In the companies' cases, disinvestment was, by their own statements, motivated at least in part by economic considerations; the South African operations had become unprofitable, and they feared further economic deterioration as well as social and political unrest.

The immediate results of sanctions and disinvestment have included the toughening of apartheid enforcement practices by the government, the loss of jobs held by blacks and anger of blacks and the South African government at U.S. government and companies.

It remains to be seen whether the longer-term results will weaken apartheid and assist the majority black population. From both the business and politi-

---

*The Zulu tribe is the largest in South Africa.

cal points of view, the disinvestments and sanctions are unprecedented or unusual, so that the outcomes are difficult to predict.

In another part of the world, Japan has come under increasing criticism for its laws denying Japanese citizenship to anyone not of the Japanese race. The largest "alien" group affected is the Koreans, many of whom were brought to Japan as workers when it occupied Korea. Now the second- and third-generation descendants of those Koreans, all of whom were born in Japan, with Japanese as their native tongue, are still "aliens" and not granted the rights and privileges of Japanese citizenship. The relatively few Vietnamese refugees permitted into Japan are beginning to feel the same racial discrimination.

Racism seems to be a worldwide phenomenon. In 1987, black students marched in Peking to protest racial discrimination by Chinese students and the People's Republic of China government. The students presented their complaints to the Moroccan ambassador, who was the dean of the African diplomatic corp in the People's Republic of China.

In the interest of balance, it should be pointed out that blacks have been known to discriminate against other races. Probably the best-known instance occurred in Uganda where the black-run government seized the property, shops, and land of people of Indian or Pakistani heritage, drove them out, and turned the seized assets over to black Ugandan citizens.

Traditional Society

A number of LDCs have barely begun to modernize, and many of their people are still relatively primitive. They may be organized in tribal groups with a chief, in feudal organizations with a patron or landowner at the head, or in some other paternalistic arrangement. Here the foreign employer may be forced to assume the paternal position and become the protector and master rather than the employer in the usual sense.[17] Workers sometimes come to the company with personal problems and family problems, and the manager should not turn them away. There may be problems with a wife or husband, with a child's education, or with the family's health.

In the ambience of a **traditional society,** the employer must keep in mind tribal and family loyalties. Nepotism may be the rule rather than the exception.

Minorities

Traditional societies combined with racial attitudes sometimes present opportunities combined with problems for employers. There are societies in which merchants, businesspeople, and bankers are looked down upon, and the people prefer to follow political, religious, military, professional, or agricultural careers. In such societies, outsiders may dominate commercial and banking activities. Some examples are the Indians and Pakistanis in East Africa, the Chinese in Southeast Asia, and the Greeks in Turkey.

An advantage for a foreign employer moving into these societies is that such **minorities** may be immediately available, bringing financial and managerial skills to the employer. They speak the local language and usually one or more others, and they are less nationalistic and more likely to be aggressive.

A disadvantage is that such people are often unpopular with the majority local population. The foreign employers can easily become too dependent on minority employees, thus becoming isolated and insulated from the real world of the majority.[18]

Employer-Employee Relationships

When a foreign employer arrives in a **labor market,** it must take what it finds. Of course, a prudent company will have included the labor market among its measurements when considering whether to invest in a country. One measurement is illustrated in Table 11-4. As indicated below in discussions about union-management relations in the United Kingdom, these sorts of figures change from year to year. The purpose of the table is to illustrate the kinds of measurement results that your research will turn up.

As you see, Table 11-4 gives information about labor strikes, or "work stoppages" as they are termed in the table. There are four series of numbers: the number of work stoppages, the number of workers involved, the number of working days lost, and the number of days lost per thousand employees. The last series, days lost per thousand employees, is the only one giving direct comparisons among the 14 countries reported upon, which vary greatly in size, population, and culture.

Looking at that series and confining ourselves to the 1975–83 period, we find some surprising numbers. For example, even though Australia, Canada, Italy, New Zealand, and the United Kingdom all have populations smaller than that of the United States, each of those countries lost more days per thousand employees to work stoppages than did the United States.

Another feature which might surprise the reader is the occasional great change from year to year. Note the surge in the number of days lost in the United Kingdom in 1979 and in Sweden in 1980.

The prospective employer's first reaction to figures such as those shown in Table 11-4 might be to scratch one or more of those countries from investment plans and put all of its money into West Germany, Japan, the Netherlands, or Switzerland. However, that would give too much importance to the raw numbers—for example, days lost per 1,000 employees—without looking behind them.

Here are some other questions that the planner should look into: (1) Was the period abnormal for any of the countries? (2) Were the strikes peaceful, or were they accompanied by violence, destruction, or death? (3) Were the strikes industrywide, or were they only against selected employers? (4) Were the strikes wildcat (unannounced), or was there usually warning that they were coming? and (5) Do the unions and the workers abide by labor agreements, and if not, what can the employer do?

The company planning investment in the traditional-society LDCs will examine the cultural, religious, tribal, and other factors discussed elsewhere. Of course, religious, racial, and linguistic schisms are not confined to LDCs. Among the developed countries where such problems exist are Belgium, Canada, Ireland, and Spain, and the United States is not free of racial disturbances. In addition to these matters, a would-be employer will study the organizations of laborers.

Labor Unions: European Different from American

European **labor unions** are usually identified with political parties and socialist ideology. A sense of worker identity is common in these unions, probably because European labor gained freedom from feudalism as well as various rights and powers through collective action.

In the United States, on the other hand, many civil rights, including the vote, were already possessed by laborers by the time unions became important. As a result, unionism in the United States has been more pragmatic than political and more concerned with the immediate needs of the workers.[19]

Labor legislation in the United States mostly confined itself to the framework of collective bargaining. In Europe, government's role is more active, with wages and working conditions frequently legislated. Many Latin American governments are very active in employer-employee relationships, frequently because the unions are weak and the union leaders are inexperienced or uneducated.

The system in Great Britain is somewhat unique, being characterized by relative lack of legal restraints. Labor agreements can be breached by either side without risking breach-of-contract types of legal action. Another disadvantage from the point of view of orderly, forecastable labor relations, is the two-headed nature of Britain's labor relations system. Under one head are the industrywide collective agreements, which often conflict with the other head, the factory understandings between management and individual workplace groups. The conflicts result in gaps between contract and effective wages, chaotic grievance procedures, and a high number of "unofficial strikes."[20]

You will note in Table 11-4 that the number of strike days for the United States are greater than the number for Great Britain (UK). One reason is U.S. strikes tend to be longer than those in the UK or, for that matter, in most other countries. Another difference is that U.S. strikes usually occur at the termination date of a labor contract, after negotiations and a strike vote. Thus, although the strike may be lengthy, the employer, the suppliers, and the customers have

Table 11–4

Work Stoppages, Workers Involved, and Work Time Lost, 14 Countries, 1955–1983

Item and Year	United States[1]	Australia[2]	Belgium[3]	Canada[4]	Denmark[5]	France[6]
Work Stoppages						
1955	363	1,532	143	159	13	2,672
1956	287	1,306	148	229	98	2,440
1957	279	1,103	115	245	14	2,623
1958	332	987	43	259	15	954
1959	245	865	57	216	23	1,512
1960	222	1,145	61	274	82	1,494
1961	195	815	38	287	34	1,963
1962	211	1,183	40	311	26	1,884
1963	181	1,250	48	332	19	2,382
1964	246	1,334	41	343	40	2,281
1965	268	1,346	43	501	37	1,674
1966	321	1,273	74	617	22	1,711
1967	381	1,340	58	522	22	1,675
1968	392	1,713	71	582	17	1,103
1969	412	2,014	88	595	48	2,207
1970	381	2,738	151	542	77	2,942
1971	298	2,404	184	569	31	4,318
1972	250	2,298	191	598	35	3,464
1973	317	2,538	172	724	205	3,731
1974	424	2,809	235	1,218	134	3,381
1975	235	2,432	243	1,171	147	3,888
1976	231	2,055	281	1,039	204	4,348
1977	298	2,090	220	803	228	3,281
1978	219	2,277	195	1,058	314	3,195
1979	235	2,042	215	1,050	218	3,121
1980	187	2,429	132	1,028	225	2,118
1981	145	2,915	—	1,048	94	2,442
1982	96	2,060	—	677	180	—
1983[8]	81	—	—	641	—	—
Workers involved (000's)[13]						
1955	2,055	445	119	60	6	792
1956	1,370	428	176	89	66	666
1957	887	337	339	81	3	2,161
1958	1,587	283	63	111	9	858
1959	1,381	237	123	95	6	581
1960	896	603	19	49	20	839

Germany Federal Republic of[7]	Italy[8]	Japan[9]	Netherlands	New Zealand	Sweden	Switzerland	United Kingdom[10]
—	1,864	659	63	65	18	4	2,419
—	1,781	646	80	50	12	5	2,648
—	1,646	827	37	51	17	2	2,859
—	1,756	903	73	49	10	3	2,629
—	1,800	887	48	73	17	4	2,093
—	2,348	1,063	121	60	31	8	2,832
—	3,388	1,401	43	71	12	0	2,686
—	3,532	1,299	24	96	10	2	2,449
—	4,003	1,079	104	60	24	4	2,068
—	3,727	1,234	53	93	14	1	2,524
—	3,061	1,542	60	105	8	2	2,354
—	2,299	1,252	20	145	26	2	1,937
—	2,554	1,214	8	89	7	1	2,116
—	3,272	1,546	11	153	7	1	2,378
—	3,698	1,783	28	169	41	1	3,116
—	4,065	2,260	99	323	134	3	3,906
—	5,482	2,527	15	313	60	11	2,228
—	4,699	2,498	31	266	44	5	2,497
—	3,676	3,326	7	394	48	(^{11})	2,873
—	5,087	5,211	14	380	85	3	2,922
—	3,535	3,391	5	428	^{12}85	6	2,282
—	2,645	2,720	11	487	73	19	2,016
—	3,223	1,712	9	562	35	9	2,703
—	2,415	1,517	11	411	99	10	2,471
—	1,850	1,153	30	523	207	8	2,080
—	2,000	1,133	11	352	212	5	1,330
—	1,964	955	11	289	68	1	1,338
—	1,691	944	12	326	46	1	1,528
—	—	—	—	—	—	—	1,255
598	1,186	1,033	22	20	3.9	0.4	671
52	1,240	1,098	37	14	1.6	0.3	508
45	1,117	1,557	1	16	1.6	0.1	1,359
203	1,147	1,279	5	14	0.1	0.8	524
22	1,464	1,216	8	19	1.2	0.1	646
17	1,754	918	76	14	1.5	0.2	819

Table 11-4

(continued)

Item and Year	United States[1]	Australia[2]	Belgium[3]	Canada[4]	Denmark[5]	France[6]
Workers Involved (000's)						
1961	1,031	300	13	98	153	1,270
1962	793	354	22	74	10	834
1963	512	413	18	83	7	1,148
1964	1,183	546	41	101	8	1,047
1965	999	475	19	172	14	688
1966	1,300	395	42	411	10	1,029
1967	2,192	483	38	252	10	2,824
1968	1,855	720	29	224	29	464
1969	1,576	1,285	25	307	36	1,444
1970	2,468	1,367	108	262	56	1,080
1971	2,516	1,327	87	240	6	3,235
1972	975	1,114	67	706	8	2,721
1973	1,400	803	62	348	337	2,246
1974	1,796	2,005	56	581	142	1,564
1975	965	1,398	86	506	59	1,827
1976	1,519	2,190	107	1,571	87	2,023
1977	1,212	596	66	218	36	1,920
1978	1,006	1,076	91	402	59	705
1979	1,021	1,863	56	463	157	967
1980	795	1,173	27	441	62	501
1981	729	1,252	—	339	53	329
1982	656	723	—	444	53	468
1983[8]	909	—	—	328	—	
Working days lost (000s)[18]						
1955	21,180	1,011	1,002	1,875	10	3,079
1956	26,840	1,121	948	1,246	1,087	1,423
1957	10,340	3,789	630	1,477	7	4,121
1958	17,900	440	294	2,817	9	1,138
1959	60,850	365	983	2,227	18	1,938
1960	13,260	725	334	739	61	1,070
1961	10,140	607	92	1,335	2,308	2,601
1962	11,760	509	271	1,418	15	1,902
1963	10,020	582	247	917	24	5,992
1964	16,220	911	444	1,581	18	2,497

Germany Federal Republic of[7]	Italy[8]	Japan[9]	Netherlands	New Zealand	Sweden	Switzerland	United Kingdom[10]
22	2,408	1,680	9	17	0.1	0.0	779
79	2,652	1,518	2	40	3.5	0.2	4,423
316	3,398	1,183	26	15	2,8	1.1	593
6	3,036	1,050	8	35	1.9	0.4	883
6	2,075	1,682	23	15	0.2	0.0	876
196	1,690	1,132	11	33	29.4	0.0	544
60	1,987	733	2	28	0.1	0.1	734
25	4,414	1,163	5	37	0.4	0.1	2,258
90	6,752	1,412	12	44	9.0	.0	1,665
184	3,520	1,720	52	110	26.7	0.3	1,801
536	3,452	1,896	36	86	62.9	2.3	1,178
23	4,073	1,544	20	60	7.1	0.5	1,734
185	5,763	2,236	58	116	4.3	(^{14})	1,528
250	7,396	3,621	3	71	17.5	0.3	1,626
36	12,920	2,732	(^{15})	75	(^{11})16.6	0.3	809
169	11,002	1,356	15	201	8.7	2.4	668
34	13,072	692	36	159	13.1	1.4	1,166
487	8,299	660	3	158	8.3	1.2	1,041
77	14,914	450	32	158	32.3	0.5	4,608
45	12,260	563	20	108	746.7	3.6	834
253	7,443	247	9	79	99.2	(^{13})	1,513
40	9,761	216	70	119	5.1	(^{13})	2,103
—	—	—	—	—	16.5	—	541
854	3,497	3,467	133	52	158.8	1.0	3,781
1,580	1,937	4,562	213	24	4.0	1.4	2,083
1,072	3,287	5,634	7	28	53.0	0.7	8,412
782	2,606	6,052	37	19	15.0	2.1	3,462
62	7,282	6,020	14	30	23.9	2.0	5,270
38	1,254	4,912	467	36	18.5	1.0	3.024
68	7,880	6,150	25	38	2.1	0.0	3,046
451	19,045	5,400	9	93	5.0	1.4	5,798
1,846	10,075	2,770	38	54	25.0	70.7	1,755
17	11,328	3,165	44	67	34.0	4.6	2,277

Table 11–4

(continued)

Item and Year	United States[1]	Australia[2]	Belgium[3]	Canada[4]	Denmark[5]	France[6]
Working days lost (000s)[18]						
1965	15,140	816	70	2,350	242	980
1966	16,000	732	533	5,178	15	2,524
1967	31,320	705	182	3,975	10	4,204
1968	35,567	1,079	364	5,083	34	423
1969	29,397	1,958	163	7,752	56	2,224
1970	52,761	2,394	1,432	6,540	102	1,742
1971	35,538	3,069	1,240	2,867	21	4,388
1972	16.764	2,010	354	7,754	22	3,755
1973	16,260	2,635	866	5,776	3,901	3,915
1974	31,809	6,293	580	9,222	184	3,380
1975	17,563	3,510	610	10,909	100	3,869
1976	23,962	3,799	896	11,610	210	5,011
1977	21,258	1,655	659	3,308	230	3,666
1978	23,774	2,131	1,002	7,393	129	2,200
1979	20,409	3,964	622	7,834	173	3,657
1980	20,844	3,320	222	8,975	187	1,686
1981	16,908	4,192	—	8,878	652	1,496
1982	9,061	2,158	—	5,795	93	2,328
1983[8]	17,461	—	—	4,464	—	—
Days lost per thousand employees in nonagricultural industries[16]						
1955	429	361	408	466	8	277
1956	526	390	376	291	875	126
1957	201	217	1,471	333	6	353
1958	353	150	116	631	7	96
1959	1,164	121	388	482	14	163
1960	248	232	130	156	44	89
1961	189	194	35	278	1,614	213
1962	214	158	101	285	10	151
1963	178	176	90	178	16	460
1964	280	263	159	295	12	185
1965	252	226	25	416	153	71
1966	257	188	189	863	9	180

Germany Federal Republic of[7]	Italy[8]	Japan[9]	Netherlands	New Zealand	Sweden	Switzerland	United Kingdom[10]
49	5,945	5,669	55	22	4.1	0.2	2,925
27	13,620	2,742	13	99	351.6	0.1	2,398
390	7,294	1,830	6	139	0.4	1.7	2,787
25	8,299	2,841	14	130	1.2	1.8	4,690
249	35,325	3,634	22	139	112.4	0.2	6,846
93	17,861	3,915	263	277	155.7	2.6	980
4,484	10,699	6,029	97	163	839.0	7.5	3.551
66	15,820	5,147	134	135	10.5	2.0	3,909
563	19,749	4,604	584	272	11.8	([11])	7,197
1,051	15,743	9,663	7	184	57.6	2.8	4,750
69	20,603	8,016	([17])	215	[11]44.5	1.8	6,012
534	18,950	3,254	14	488	24.7	19.6	3,284
24	13,364	1,518	236	437	87.2	4.6	142
4,281	8,559	1,357	3	381	37.1	5.3	9,405
483	22,002	930	307	382	28.7	2.3	9,474
128	12,626	1,001	55	360	4,478.5	5.7	1,964
58	8,046	554	24	245	209.1	([17])	4,266
15	15,488	538	215	314	1.8	0.6	5,313
—	—	—	—	—	38.9	—	3,593
52	400	203	48	81	65	1	180
93	216	249	75	37	2	1	98
61	355	287	2	42	21	([18])	394
44	278	293	13	27	6	1	163
3	762	278	5	43	9	1	247
2	427	216	153	50	7	([18])	138
3	766	257	8	51	1	0	137
22	1,800	214	3	122	2	1	258
90	928	106	12	69	8	29	78
1	1,045	117	13	83	11	2	100
2	567	201	16	26	1	([18])	127
1	1,307	93	4	114	112	([18])	103

Table 11–4
(concluded)

Item and Year	United States[1]	Australia[2]	Belgium[3]	Canada[4]	Denmark[5]	France[6]
Days lost per thousand employees in nonagricultural industries[16]						
1967	483	174	65	641	6	295
1968	535	259	130	795	20	29
1969	429	455	57	1,170	32	150
1970	759	535	484	951	58	114
1971	507	666	411	407	12	282
1972	230	432	117	1,058	12	236
1973	215	546	281	743	2,055	240
1974	413	1,279	184	1,138	98	203
1975	230	717	196	1,324	54	234
1976	303	770	291	1,382	110	300
1977	259	336	214	387	120	216
1978	277	433	326	839	64	129
1979	231	800	200	853	85	214
1980	235	653	71	945	93	98
1981	172	802	—	908	330	88
1982	102	413	—	615	47	136
1983	195	—	—	471	—	—

[1]Excludes disputes involving less than 1,000 workers or lasting less than a full day or shift. For international comparisons, data on disputes involving six workers or more should be used. The United States no longer collects work stoppages data at this level of activity. However, they are available to 1981 in the *Handbook of Labor Statistics*, BLS Bulletin 2175 (1983), table 147.
[2]Excludes disputes resulting in less than 10 working days lost.
[3]Excludes workers indirectly affected.
[4]Excludes disputes resulting in less than 10 working days lost. Excludes workers indirectly affected by a dispute in their own establishment.
[5]Includes only disputes involving members of the Employers' Federation in 1956–67. Excludes political disputes and disputes resulting in less than 100 working days lost.
[6]Excludes disputes in agriculture and public administration. For 1968, the period of the national strike in May and June is excluded.
[7]Includes the Saar beginning in 1957 and West Berlin beginning in 1961. Excludes disputes lasting less than 1 day unless a loss of more than 100 working days is involved.
[8]Preliminary.
[9]Excludes strikes in the agricultural sector, political strikes, and workers indirectly affected by a dispute in their own establishment. Data on hours lost are converted into working days by dividing by 8.

Germany Federal Republic of[7]	Italy[8]	Japan[9]	Netherlands	New Zealand	Sweden	Switzerland	United Kingdom[10]
19	683	60	2	159	([18])	1	122
1	763	91	4	148	([18])	1	207
12	3,186	115	6	154	35	([18])	302
4	1,560	120	70	297	48	1	488
205	924	178	26	171	250	3	625
3	1,367	150	36	147	3	1	1,102
25	1,668	128	154	302	3	([11])	324
48	1,285	268	2	179	16	1	659
3	1,649	222	([18])	207	[12]12	1	269
25	1,503	88	4	465	7	8	148
1	1,014	41	62	412	24	2	456
199	647	36	1	359	10	2	420
22	1,630	24	78	360	8	1	1,296
6	921	25	14	340	1,175	2	531
3	583	14	6	241	55	([18])	200
([18])	1,120	13	56	309	([18])	([18])	254
—	—	—	—	—	10	—	175

[10]Excludes disputes lasting less than four hours and workers indirectly affected by a dispute in their own establishment.

[11]Only two strikes occurred, each one lasting not more than a couple of hours.

[12]Excludes one dispute in agriculture involving 7,000 workers and 321,000 working days lost.

[13]Workers are counted more than once if they were involved in more than one stoppage during the year.

[14]Excludes disputes not connected with terms of employment or conditions of labor and disputes involving less than 10 workers or lalsting less than 1 day unless a loss of more than 100 working days is involved. Includes workers indirectly involved in the establishment, but not those in other establishments.

[15]Less than 500 workers involved.

[16]Days lost include all stoppages in effect.

[17]Less than 500 working days lost.

[18]Less than one day per thousand employees.

—Data not available.

Source: *Handbook of Labor Statistics*, (Washington, D.C. Bureau of Labor Statistics, U. S. Department of Labor, June 1985).

had time to prepare. By contrast, the "wildcat" strike (little or no advance notice)—common in Britain—catches everyone unprepared and tends to cause more damage even though it may be brief.

The situation in Britain has improved as to days lost through strikes and labor productivity. In 1979, British industry lost about 9.5 million working days through strikes. In 1983, it lost only 3.6 million working days. Labor productivity has improved sharply.

Many credit the improvement to the policies of Margaret Thatcher's government, which was elected in 1979 and reelected in 1983 and 1987. Her government is building a framework of laws that make union leaders answerable to their members and open union funds to civil lawsuits.

Of course, the British union leaders and the Labour party leaders—much the same people—are protesting bitterly and fighting the changes. They accuse the Thatcher government of being antilabor. She responds that if the unions keep British labor on strike and unproductive, they will destroy the very jobs they claim to defend.[21]

Refer again to Table 11–4 and observe the situations in Japan and the United States. The much higher number of days lost in the United States is one reason why Japanese automobile and other manufacturers hesitated to build factories in the United States.

There has been so much discussion and writing about Japanese labor and labor policies that we should comment at least briefly about them. Already mentioned have been the relatively high productivity of Japanese labor and the low number of days lost to strikes.

The better productivity is probably the result of greater savings being invested in capital equipment and perhaps stems from the loyalty of labor to the employer. Some say that traditional loyalty to the family or the emperor has been transferred to the employer. The practice of lifetime employment by much of Japan's larger industry would reinforce the loyalty and reduce the tendency to strike.[22]

In West Germany and France, the influences of law and government administrative actions are more extensive and evident. Negotiations are conducted on national or at least regional levels, and in France government representatives take part.[23]

Multinational Labor Activities

The internationalization of business has been under way for many years, and the MNE has expanded rapidly since the 1950s. National unions have begun to perceive opportunities for MNEs to escape the organizing reach of unions by the relatively simple step of transferring to or commencing production in another country. The MNEs' opportunities are seen as dangers to the unions.

To combat those dangers, national unions have begun to (1) collect and disseminate information about MNEs, (2) consult with unions in other countries,

(3) coordinate with those unions policies and tactics in dealing with some specific MNEs, and (4) encourage international MNE codes of conduct.[24] Such **multinational labor activity** is likely to increase, although unions are divided by ideological differences and are frequently strongly nationalistic. Vastly more effort and money have been spent on lobbying for protection of national industries than on cooperating with unions in other countries.

Some developments that occurred in 1980 demonstrate, however, that cooperation is possible. The Geneva-based International Union of Food and Allied Workers Association coordinated a boycott of Coca-Cola in Sweden, Spain, Mexico, and Finland. The cause of the boycott was alleged "antilabor practices" by the Coca-Cola franchise holder in Guatemala.

The International Metalworkers Federation asked West European governments to use their economic power against International Telephone & Telegraph Corporation (ITT) because it wanted changes in ITT's "personnel and social policies."

The first important arena in which successful multinational unionism may develop is the European Community (EC). The 12 EC member countries are steadily eliminating or harmonizing their tariffs, taxes, monetary systems, laws, and much more. The resulting atmosphere will be more hospitable for the cooperation of national unions.[25]

In addition, in spite of their variations in method and short-term objectives, national unions have managed to cooperate within three international organizations—the International Confederation of Trade Unions, the International Trade Secretariats, and the International Labor Organization. The last, you will remember, is a UN body.[26]

However, in one highly competitive field—automobiles—the internationalization of the industry is emphasizing differences rather than cooperation among national unions. The managements of car companies have long since stopped being as alarmed by threats of international action as they were when the unions first made them. Natural nationalism is made worse in some countries by multiunion industries, and when political differences are added, unions frequently find themselves competing rather than cooperating with one another.[27]

Codetermination

Europe, particularly West Germany, is in the vanguard of another labor development, which, at first sight, horrified many business managers and owners. Laws were adopted which required that employees be given seats on the employer board of directors.

It Began in Germany

Worker participation in management, frequently called **codetermination,** began in the German coal and steel industries in 1951. The law gave worker and shareholder representatives each 50 percent of the directorships. A neutral board member selected by both sides breaks any deadlocks, but that vote has rarely been needed, as labor and shareholder representatives usually resolve their differences.[28]

The 50–50 system was extended to all large German industry by a 1976 law that was challenged in court by German employers but upheld by the West German high court in March 1979.[29]

It Has Spread

Other European countries and Japan either have or are seriously discussing co-determination-type legislation or practices. In the United States, neither business nor labor showed much enthusiasm for codetermination until the late 1970s. However, things are changing in the United States where the terms *industrial democracy* and *worker participation* are sometimes used.

New Developments in the United States

During the late 1970s and into the 1980s, the concept of industrial democracy spread in America. Both Chrysler Corporation and American Motors have United Automobile Workers (UAW) officers as members of their boards of directors. Workers at General Motors get together in "quality circles" to help make decisions about their jobs and production quality. The Communications Workers of America signed a contract in August 1980 with American Telephone & Telegraph that included worker participation concepts. New labor contracts in the steel, rubber, oil, paper, glass, aerospace, food processing, and electrical products industries contain similar concepts. In addition, hundreds of large and small nonunion employers have adopted their own versions of industrial democracy; among these are IBM and Texas Instruments.[30]

Not everyone in the United States is pleased with worker participation (see the first quotation at the beginning of this chapter). When Douglas Fraser, the UAW president, was elected to Chrysler's board in 1980, there were fears in labor and management that the conflicts between the two jobs were too great. The fears persisted in the mid-80s.

In his efforts to sell a new Chrysler contract to the UAW rank and file, Fraser reversed the typical charge of labor leaders—that management is bargaining in bad faith when it claims that it cannot afford fatter wage and benefit offers. Fraser took just the opposite tack and chided the Chrysler chairman for painting too rosy a picture of Chrysler's finances. He even said that Chrysler's reported profits were based in part on financial "manipulations."

As a result, neither the UAW nor Chrysler management was happy with Fraser. Some union members felt that he had not squeezed the company hard enough; management feared that his talk of financial weakness and manipulation would hurt the company's reputation with its bankers and the investment community.[31]

PRC Returns Power to Management

In an interesting switch, factories in the People's Republic of China have been ending their decades-long experiment in "industrial committees" of workers with important voices in management. China has been turning back to the single executive responsibility and authority system.[32] Production and innovation apparently suffered in the absence of central executive authority, and there was confusion as to organization and responsibilities.

The change in the PRC seems to be away from the political and toward the pragmatic choice of managers. The industrial committee members were chosen because of their political purity, but increasingly managers are being chosen because of their know-how and ability.

Summary

Before investing in a country or an area, a company management will examine the potential employee pool—its composition, skills, and attitudes. These are elements over which management has no control before it invests and which may change for reasons beyond its control after investments have been made. It is the purpose of this chapter to bring at least some of these elements to your attention.

Management may find itself dealing with a labor force that consists of local citizens or foreigners. If the workers are foreign to the host country, they may be guest workers who are legally in the country to perform certain tasks which the natives do not want to do. Foreign workers may also be refugees, legally or illegally in the host country, who came primarily to escape something and not primarily to perform specific work.

Foreign workers sometimes cause problems. When the economy slows, the local citizens want the jobs held by them. Even in prosperity, there are racial conflicts between foreign workers and the natives.

The composition of the labor force affects labor productivity, and when the labor force grows rapidly due to an influx of unskilled workers, productivity suffers. Another influence on productivity is the capital equipment available to the labor force. The amount of capital equipment is affected by (1) research and development and (2) savings rates, both of which can be encouraged or discouraged by tax policies.

Management moving into a different country should also consider, as they affect employment policies, the local attitudes toward social status, sex, race, religion, and minorities. Management would have to perform differently in a traditional society than in a more-developed, industrialized country.

An MNE management weighing investment in a country should study the labor unions and the strike records. Labor laws and government intervention in employer-employee relationships should be examined.

Labor unions have begun to be active internationally and to coordinate studies and labor action. Such coordination has been growing in Europe, and it was in Europe—first in Germany—that codetermination began. Some sort of worker participation in management can now be found in several European countries, Japan, and the United States.

Questions

1. *a. How could an excess of qualified employees be beneficial for an employer?*
   b. How could it be detrimental?
2. *Classical economists assumed the labor factor of production to be immobile. Is this assumption correct in the modern world?*
3. *What are some differences between labor that moves as do the European guest workers and labor that moves as do political or economic refugees?*
4. *What is the effect on productivity of the influx into the work force of inexperienced, unskilled workers?*
5. *How could a caste system affect employment decisions?*
6. *What is a typical response of an American MNE to demands that it close its South African subsidiaries?*
7. *In several Southeast Asian and South Pacific countries, the Chinese minority in those countries is prominent in banking, finance, and business. What are the dangers for a foreign employer staffing the local company primarily with such a minority?*
8. *What is a major difference between European as compared to American unions?*
9. *What are the prospects for effective multinational union collaboration? Discuss.*
10. *a. What is codetermination?*
    b. Has codetermination worked well? Discuss.
11. *What are some arguments against codetermination?*
12. *In Soviet law, women are equal with men. How does Soviet life reflect Soviet law in this respect?*

Minicase
11-1 Codetermination—
Deutsche Stevens*

"Have you been following the problems that Opel has been having because of Mitbestimmung (codetermination)?"† Mat Burns, the president of Deutsche Stevens, a wholly owned subsidiary of Houston-based Stevens Industries, was talking to his management committee. "The worker representatives on the board of directors have become very militant. They are bringing up a lot of issues in board meetings that ought to be settled by labor negotiations."

"What kinds of issues, Mat?" asked Ned Webster, vice president for production.

Burns: Things like the right to name the new personnel director, improve retirement benefits, and even plant ventilation. This militancy is also being felt in the legitimate issues that the board ought to discuss. It used to be that management presented the worker representatives with investment decisions after they were made, but now, I'm told, they want to review them one at a time very carefully. They say that it is as important to use funds to improve working conditions as it is to spend them for increased production capacity and product development.

Jim Perrin, vice president for personnel: Mat, do you know what is the cause of this increased militancy?

Burns: I've been told that there are a number of causes. One is the rapid growth of the work force. Since 1975, it has grown from 33,000 to 43,000 employees. The newest workers are younger and, of course, do not have the loyalty to Opel that the old-time employees have.

Perrin: Do you think that's the only reason?

Burns: No, I've been told that there are others. The plant is running at full capacity and is crowded and uncomfortable. Part of the plant dates from the 1930s. The head of the works council claims that the workers are under pressure to produce every second, as he puts it, and that conditions are very severe.‡

Webster: Sounds bad, Mat, but we don't have these problems; not yet, anyway.

Burns: That's true, but remember, we have less than 2,000 employees, so only a third of our board of directors consists of workers' representatives. However,

---

*"West Germany, the Worker Dissidents in Opel's Boardroom," *Business Week*, July 23, 1979, p. 79.
†Opel is General Motors' German subsidiary.
‡The works council is a body composed of employees elected by all the employees of the plant. It monitors the carrying out of labor agreements and is involved in grievance proceedings.

as you know, we are getting close to that figure. Marketing wants to add a whole new product line, and this will require us to add at least 400 new employees, which will put us over the 2,000 level. That means we shall have an equal representation of labor and management on the board. In the event of a tie, I can still cast the deciding vote for management. However, every time I have to do that, the labor representatives are going to feel frustrated, and it's going to show up on the production line.

Ludwig Schmidt, company attorney: Mat, maybe there's another way to do it.

Burns: How's that, Ludwig?

Schmidt: Well, ITT's subsidiary, Standard Elektrik Lorenz, has changed two of its companies to limited partnerships, which makes them exempt from the law. Other companies are spinning off operations into separate companies so that no one company has more than 2,000 employees. They still must have a one-third worker representation on the board, as we do now, but that's better than a 50–50 split. *

Burns: That seems like a good idea, Ludwig—the forming of another company, I mean. Will you get together with Don here [Don Jones, vice president for marketing] and see if we should form a new company? You'll want to be in on these discussions, too, Ned. Also, Ned, I wish you and Jim would review our working conditions to see if we have any potential problem areas similar to Opel's. Parts of our plant are rather old, and we have been pushing the workers pretty hard to get the production out, haven't we?

1. What would you suggest if you were either the attorney or the marketing manager? Are there any problems involved if a separate company is formed to handle the new product line?

2. What should the vice president for production and the vice president for personnel consider?

3. Do any large American companies have worker representation on their boards of directors?

Minicase

11–2 Racism

Your company, an American MNE, has decided to expand aggressively in Asia. It plans to source much of its raw material and subcontracting there and manufacture and market throughout Asia, from Japan in the north, through New Zealand in the south.

---

* "Companies in Germany Confront Codetermination Practice," _Business Europe_, January 20, 1978, p. 22.

You were appointed to organize and direct this major new effort, and one question was where to locate the regional headquarters for the Asian Division. After considerable study, you selected the island nation of Luau.

Luau's advantages are several. It is about equidistant between New Zealand and Japan. It was a British colony, so the main language is English. It has a relatively efficient telephone and telegraph system and good air service to all the major Asian destinations in which you are interested and to the United States.

Not least important, the Luau government is delighted to have your company locate and invest there. It has made very attractive tax concessions to the company and to its personnel who will move there.

The company moves in, leases one large building, and puts out invitations to bid on the construction of a larger building, which will be its permanent headquarters. Now, as you begin to work much more with the private banking and businesspeople of Luau and less with government officials, you begin to be more aware of a Luau characteristic about which you had not thought much previously. Almost all of the middle- and upper-management personnel in the business and finance sector are of Chinese extraction. The native population of Luau, which is the great majority, is a Micronesian race.

Upon inquiring why the Chinese are dominant in banking and business while the Micronesians stay with farming, fishing, government, and manual labor, you are told that that is the way it has developed historically. The Chinese enjoy and are good at banking and business, while the native Luauans do not like those activities and have stayed with their traditional pastimes. The two groups buy and sell from and to each other, but there are almost no social relations and very little business or professional overlap between the groups. Occasionally, some of the Micronesians study abroad, and some work abroad for periods; when they return, they frequently go to work in a bank or business or take a government position.

You must staff your headquarters with middle- and lower-management people and with clerical help. You find that the only applicants for the jobs are Chinese, and you select the best who are available. They are quite satisfactory, and the operation gets off to a good start.

Then, as the months pass, you notice a gradual change of attitude toward you and the company among the government officials and among the people in general. They have become less friendly, more evasive, and less cooperative. You ask your Chinese staff about it, but they have noticed nothing unusual.

What could be happening? Why might the Chinese staff not notice it? What might you do to improve government and public relations?

Supplementary Readings

Adams, Walter, ed. *The Brain Drain*. New York: Macmillan, 1979.

Banks, Robert, and Jack Stieber, ed. *Multinationals, Unions, and Labor Relations in Industrialized Countries*. Ithaca, N.Y.: New York State School of Industrial and Labor Relations, Cornell University, 1977.

Blanpain, Roger. *The Badger Case and the OECD Guidelines for Multinational Enterprises.* Translated by Michael Jones. Deventer, Netherlands: Kluwer, 1977.

Blum, Alfred, ed. *International Handbook of Industrial Relations: Contemporary Developments and Research.* Westport, Conn.: Greenwood Press, 1981.

Kao, Charles. *Brain Drain.* Hong Kong: Mei Ya China International Specie Bank, 1980.

King, Charles, and Mark van de Vall. *Models of Industrial Democracy: Consultation, Codetermination, and Workers Management.* New York: Mouton, 1978.

Liebhaberg, Bruno. *Industrial Relations and Multinational Corporations in Europe.* New York: Praeger Publishers, 1981.

Lindert, Peter. *International Economics.* Homewood, Ill.: Richard D. Irwin, 1986.

Morgan, Alun, and Roger Blanpain. *The Industrial Relations and Employment Impacts of Multinational Enterprises: An Inquiry into the Issues.* Paris: Organization for Economic Cooperation and Development, 1977.

Northrup, Herbert R., and Richard L. Rowan. "Multinational Collective Bargaining Activity: The Factual Record in Chemicals, Glass, and Rubber Tires." *Columbia Journal of World Business,* Spring 1974, pp. 112–17.

Seham, Martin C. "Transnational Labor Relations: The First Steps Are Being Taken." *Law and Policy in International Business,* Spring 1974, pp. 337–74.

Shaw, Robert d'A. "Foreign Investment and Global Labor." *Columbia Journal of World Business,* July–August 1971, pp. 52–62.

Sirota, David, and J. Michael Greenwood. "Understand Your Overseas Work Force." *Harvard Business Review,* January–February 1971, p. 60.

Thim, Alfred L. "How Far Should German Co-determination Go?" *Challenge* July 1981, p. 13.

Endnotes

1. Barry Newman, "Unwelcome Guests," *The Wall Street Journal,* May 9, 1983, pp. 1, 22.
2. *Economist,* May 21, 1977, pp. 85–86.
3. *Economist,* August 6, 1983, p. 39.
4. *Business International,* August 19, 1983, pp. 257, 261.
5. Anthony Ramirez, "Making It," *The Wall Street Journal,* May 20, 1980, pp. 1, 27.
6. *Economist,* April 14, 1979, p. 80.
7. *Equal Employment Opportunity for Women: U.S. Policies* (Women's Bureau, U.S. Department of Labor, 1982), table 2.
8. Paul W. McCracken, "Congress and the Budget Beanstalk," *The Wall Street Journal,* February 29, 1980, p. 22.
9. June Kronholz, "The Super-Savers: Europe's Saving Rate Far Outstripping U.S., Aids Economic Growth," *The Wall Street Journal,* October 5, 1979, pp. 1, 33.
10. "Unit Labor Costs: A Key to Trade Survival," *Monthly Economic Letter* (New York: Citibank), August 1979, pp. 9–14; and Lester C. Thurow, "Why U.S. Productivity Is So Low," *Los Angeles Times,* January 27, 1981, part 4, p. 3.
11. Michel A. Amsalem, "The Decline in Productivity Growth—Causes, Consequences, and Possible Remedies," *Columbia Journal of World Business,* Winter 1981, pp. 48–56.
12. *Los Angeles Times,* February 27, 1980, part 1, p. 2. See also "The Cost of Caste," The *Economist,* February 16, 1980, pp. 46–47.

13. "India: A Pyre of One's Own," *Economist*, August 27, 1983, pp. 25–26.

14. Julia Voznesenskaya, *The Women's Decameron* (New York: Atlantic Monthly Press, 1986).

15. William Raspberry, "Black South African Pleads for U.S. Investment," *Los Angeles Times*, October 24, 1979, part 2, p. 7.

16. Miles Cunningham, "Government Member, Not Friend, " *Insight*, September 1, 1986, p. 31.

17. Charles H. Savage, "Social Reorganization in a Factory in the Andes," Monograph no. 7 (Ithaca, N.Y.: Society for Applied Anthropology, 1964), pp. 3–4.

18. See discussion of employee attitudes and motivation in Sincha Ronen, *Comparative and Multinational Management* (New York: John Wiley & Sons, 1986), chap. 5.

19. Everett M. Kassalow, *Trade Unions and Industrial Relations: An International Comparison* (New York: Random House, 1969).

20. Adolf Sturmthal, *Comparative Labor Movements: Ideological Roots and Institutional* Development (Belmont, Calif.: Wadsworth Publishing, 1972), pp. 141, 166–67.

21. Rosemary Brady, "Taming the Bullyboy," *Forbes*, August 1, 1983, p. 102.

22. There are countless books and articles about Japanese labor and management practices. A few are: Yoshi Tsurumi, *The Japanese Are Coming* (Cambridge, Mass.: Ballinger Publishing, 1976); Robert H. Hayes, "Why Japanese Factories Work," *McKinsey Quarterly*, Autumn 1982, pp. 32–48; and Hugh Sandeman, "The Best at the Game," The *Economist*, July 18, 1981, a survey of Japanese industry.

23. Michael Z. Brooke and H. Lee Remmers, *International Management and Business Policy* (Boston: Houghton Mifflin, 1978), chap. 13.

24. David W. Blake, "Corporate Structure and International Unionism," *Columbia Journal of World Business*, March-April 1972, pp. 19–26; see also Duane Kujawa, ed., *International Labor and Multinational Enterprise* (New York: Praeger Publishers, 1975).

25. Lloyd Ulman, "The Rise of the International Union?" in *Bargaining without Boundaries*, ed. Flanagan and Weber, p. 66; see, also, discussion in Stefan H. Robock, Kenneth Simmonds, and Jack Zwick, *International Business and Multinational Enterprise*, rev. ed. (Homewood, Ill.: Richard D. Irwin, 1977), pp. 551–56.

26. Adolf Sturmthal, "Union Differences," *Europe*, May-June 1983, pp. 35–36.

27. *Economist*, March 15, 1986, pp. 69–69.

28. James Furlong, *Labor in the Boardroom—the Peaceful Revolution* (Princeton, N.J.: Dow Jones Books, 1977).

29. *The Wall Street Journal*, March 12, 1979, p. 18.

30. Harry Bernstein, "Democracy Moves into Workplace," *Los Angeles Times*, October 23, 1980, part 1, pp. 1, 14–15.

31. "Doug Fraser's Conflicts," *The Wall Street Journal*, September 22, 1982, p. 28.

32. *Los Angeles Times*, March 7, 1978, pp. 9–10.

CHAPTER 12

COMPETITIVE AND DISTRIBUTIVE FORCES

One Definition of National Competitiveness:

" 'International competitiveness' means the ability of a country's producers to compete successfully in world markets and with imports in its own domestic market. Competitiveness is generally measured by results—by the shares which a country attains in its markets, due allowance being made for its size and stage of development. Competitiveness in this very general sense comes close to being synonymous with overall economic performance."

From *Economic Progress Report*
(London: British Treasury, July 1983), p. 1. Published by
the British Treasury

Another Definition:

"We define competitiveness as the ability of a nation to improve its standard of living through current earnings, not borrowing, while investing sufficiently in plant and equipment to ensure sustained growth in the future."

Charles McMillion, director of
Congressional Competitiveness Caucus

But Milton Friedman is not impressed:

"The concept of a 'competitive edge' for a country as a whole is meaningless."

Milton Friedman, Nobel Laureate in Economics

Learning Objectives

After you study this chapter, you should know:

1. The reasons for the increase in international competition.
2. The sources of this competition.
3. The two basic categories of data in the competitive forces analysis.
4. The channel members available to those who export indirectly, export directly, or manufacture overseas.
5. Structural trends in wholesaling and retailing.
6. The differences in wholesaling and retailing agencies among nations.
7. The factors influencing channel selection.
8. The bases on which management compares channel alternatives.

Key Words and Concepts

Generalized System of
  Preferences (GSP)
Lomé Convention
Counterfeiting
Market organization
Competitors' strengths and
  weaknesses
Cooperative exporters
Trading companies

Voluntary retailer chains
Hypermarkets
Superstores
Sogo shosha
Parallel importing
Export trading company (ETC)
National competitiveness
Industrial targeting

Business Incidents

There's a lot of grumbling these days from the people who sell Japanese consumer electronics in the $35 billion U.S. market. Salespeople at Panasonic complain about the little four-cylinder company cars that they get now, quite a comedown from the six-cylinder cars that the Matsushita subsidiary used to furnish. They don't get sympathy from the boss, who now squeezes into economy-class airplane seats.

This is ironic to executives of American consumer electronics companies. Because of an expensive yen, Japan's electronics giants find themselves in a predicament similar to the one their American rivals were in when the dollar was so much stronger. Some of them are already losing heavily because their markets are being invaded by lower-cost Asian manufacturers from Korea, Taiwan, and Singapore. A General Electronics vice president claims that the Japanese are becoming the world's highest-cost producers. As profits disappear, Japanese electronics producers are responding as American manufacturers did—shipping production overseas and increasing foreign sourcing.

Based on "Japan Can't Make a Quick Yen in the U.S. Anymore," *Business Week,* February 23, 1987, pp. 120–21.

In recent years, with total sales of about $200 million, Max Factor has enjoyed a growth rate 15 percent higher than that of the Japanese cosmetics industry in general, in part because of its adaptation of the marketing strategies of the leading Japanese cosmetics firms, with franchise corners in major retail outlets and a completely Japanese distribution system.

"Interdependence—on the Move in Japan," *Forbes,* March 5, 1979, p. 24.

In Japan, General Foods, after an unsuccessful attempt to go it alone, joined forces with Ajinomoto. Now General Foods owns 17 percent of the market. Similarly, Warner Lambert (Schick blades), by tying up with Hattori Watch Company, has outdone archrival Gillette, which followed American practice and attempted to bypass wholesalers. The Ministry of International Trade and Industry stressed that skillful use of existing distribution channels was the key to success in Japan.

"Tie-Ups with Japanese Firms Surest Road to Success," *Liberal Star* (Tokyo), May 10, 1982, p. 6.

*T*hese are just a few examples of the growing competition in world markets, and as the General Foods, Schick, and Max Factor incidents illustrate, success or failure against competitors frequently rests on the ability to obtain adequate channels of distribution, the subject of the second half of this chapter.

Competitive Forces

The quotations at the beginning of this chapter illustrate the new concern for competitiveness at the *national level* (also called *absolute* or *macro level*), which is being shown in the United States, in Europe, and more recently, as the yen has appreciated against the dollar, in Japan. American political consultants predict that the issue of **national competitiveness** will dominate the national agenda for years to come. "The candidate who captures it can control American politics," says one political expert.[1] A Congressional Competitiveness Caucus has been formed to "solve the problem of national competitiveness" (second quotation), although Milton Friedman says that such a concept is "meaningless" (third quotation). Let us examine some of the reasons for the growing intensity of competition.

Reasons for Intensification

What factors are responsible for the intensification of international competition? Two basic reasons stand out: (1) new competition and (2) markets that are growing more slowly than anticipated or are actually contracting.

New Competition

New competition for a firm may come from established producers that are entering its market for the first time or from new entrants in the industry. Competitors from both sources are appearing in the markets of developed and developing nations.

Developed Nations. The data concerning the direction and amounts of trade and investment which we examined in Chapter 2 are indicative of the fact that competition is intensifying in the industrialized nations, such as those of Western Europe, Japan, and the United States.

1. Western Europe. Firms from this region are facing increased competition in both their own markets and in their overseas markets from companies headquartered in Europe, Japan, the United States, and the newly industrializing countries (NICs). The major reason for greater inter-European competition has been the formation of the European Community, which created one market in place of six. Not only did the larger market attract new competitors from outside Europe but it also gave firms that had heretofore been selling in only one member country easy access to five additional markets. The cross-border competition was felt by all companies in the EC, but France's protected industry was particularly hard hit. As one French official put it, "The Common Market is making national monopolies disappear."[2]

New competition within the EC began with the admission of Greece in 1981 and was heightened when Spain and Portugal entered in 1986. In addition, producers of industrial products in the EC and the EFTA are now confronting one another in their own markets as a result of an agreement that created a common free trade area in 1980 (see Figure 12–1).

To strengthen their domestic firms against this new foreign competition, governments have actively encouraged mergers among national firms. Great Britain, for example, persuaded virtually all locally owned automobile companies to become part of British Leyland and was responsible for the creation of a single English computer company, ICI, from various smaller ones. At the instigation of the government, multibillion-dollar companies were formed in the steel and chemical industries, and in Germany various corporate unions were permitted in the computer, steel, and aerospace industries.

Although the bulk of the new competition has come from developed countries, products from the LDCs and communist-bloc countries are also appearing increasingly in Western Europe. This is one of the reasons why the petrochemical industry underwent the worst crisis in its history in the early 1980s. New competition from the Soviet-bloc, oil-rich countries (Saudi Arabia, Norway, Mexico), and newly industrialized countries (South Korea, Singapore) worsened an already bad situation caused by a worldwide recession and high oil prices.

Admittedly, Western producers created their own competition, always a possibility whenever technical assistance is sold or licensed abroad. They built plants in Eastern Europe to be paid for with finished products under buy-back arrangements. As an indication of the gravity of the situation, it has been estimated that during the 1980s as much as 25 percent of the Soviet-bloc production would be sold in world markets.

New plants are on-stream in the OPEC countries, which are determined to increase their income from crude oil by turning it into higher-priced petrochemicals. Saudi Arabia alone has invested billions of dollars in projects with which it aims to capture 5 percent of the world's chemical market by the end of the 1980s.[3] Ten years after that, the Saudis, with the help of partners such as Shell, Dow, Exxon, Mobil, Celanese, and Mitsubishi, expect to have 15 percent of the market. If this comes to pass, the country will be a major industrial power.[4]

Another potential competitor, Mexico, although not a member of OPEC, has gas and oil reserves now thought to be second only to Saudi Arabia's in the free world. Already 80 percent self-sufficient in petrochemicals, Mexico continues to build world-scale plants and is now exporting synthetic resins to the Middle East, the Far East, North America, and South America.

Multinational petrochemical manufacturers in both Europe and the United States have reacted to the new competition by shutting down much of their production of the basic commodity chemicals and switching to higher value-added specialty products, such as pharmaceuticals and pesticides. They have also

Figure 12-1

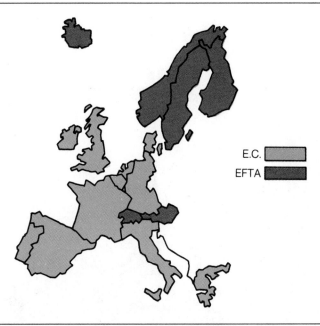

E.C.
EFTA

The newly created European Free Trade Zone takes in some 350 million consumers.

greatly modernized their plants. The average U.S. chemical plant, for example, is less than 10 years old.[5] Although the large petrochemical manufacturers are the world's most efficient producers, they have a problem competing with firms in OPEC countries that buy petroleum feedstock at a fifth of its cost to firms in industrialized countries.[6]

Competition is also being felt in the automotive industry as Soviet-bloc producers move into these markets with Polish and Russian versions of the Fiat, Czech Skodas, and Russian Moscovitches. Their lower prices and sturdier construction have been especially well received in Scandinavia. Fiat's practice of supplying technical assistance to foreign manufacturers without prohibiting exportation has resulted in as many as four brands of Fiat appearing in a single small market.

In Guayaquil, Ecuador, four dealers in what appeared to be the same car were located within blocks of one another. On closer examination, the cars were found to be Fiats (Italy), SEATS (Spain), Polskis (Poland), and Ladas (Russia).

Another competitor, Japan, which in 1970 sold very few automobiles in Europe, now has market shares ranging from 20 to 25 percent in Switzerland,

Figure 12-2

Courtesy Michael Knigin © 1981

Japanese Juggernaut in Europe

Austria, Belgium, and the Netherlands to 35 percent in Denmark, Ireland, and Norway. Even in Great Britain and West Germany, which build small, fuel-efficient vehicles, the Japanese market share is over 10 percent.

Automobiles are only one facet of the Japanese onslaught in Europe. As in the United States, Japanese imports have nearly eliminated the European motorcycle industry. Japanese cameras and watches are market leaders, and every small color TV tube used in Europe is made by Japanese electronic companies with local production facilities.

In just five years, Japanese exports to Europe doubled—from $17 billion in 1982 to over $30 billion in 1986. European firms reacted by initiating a wave of dumping complaints to force the European Community to raise antidumping duties, but even more worrisome to Japanese exporters is the threat to include an "anti-screwdriver" provision in EC import regulations. European and also

American officials complain that Japanese companies are avoiding dumping penalties by importing products in pieces invoiced at lower prices and assembling them with no more capital equipment than a screwdriver. Requiring higher local content would halt this practice, but it would also accelerate local investment by Japanese parts manufacturers, thus reducing the benefits that European firms could expect to receive from this provision. We have seen this occur in the United States in the case of Japanese automobile manufacturers.[7]

But European corporate executives are not blaming their governments for all of their competitive problems. A poll asking 300 executives from 15 European nations what they felt were obstacles to a competitive Europe revealed that their prime concern was the work force's limited flexibility and mobility (54 percent). The lack of a truly "common" market in Europe ranked second (52 percent), high labor costs third (46 percent), and low levels of R&D fourth (40 percent). They began to blame themselves only at the fifth-ranked obstacle, lack of organizational flexibility and adaptability (39 percent), and the seventh, poor commercial and marketing skills (24 percent). Excessive governmental regulations ranked sixth (39 percent).[8]

Since the poll was taken, however, the dollar has dropped sharply against European currencies and has become a greater obstacle. To remain competitive, firms are cutting overhead, strengthening sales forces, and introducing new products at a faster rate. Many are expanding to lower-cost areas outside their borders, just as American firms did when the dollar was at its highest value. In Germany, for example, Nixdorf Computer has moved its production of computerized cash registers for Montgomery Ward to Singapore and a maker of machine tools has made the astounding decision to fill 70 percent of its U.S. orders from a Connecticut factory.[9]

Two preferential arrangements, the **Generalized System of Preferences (GSP)** and the **Lomé Convention,** are worthy of mention because of the additional competition from the LDCs that they cause for developed nations (see Figure 12–3). The GSP, instituted under the auspices of GATT upon the insistence of UNCTAD members, gives preferential treatment to LDC exports of industrial goods and some agricultural products without requiring reciprocity. The Lomé Convention is an association agreement between 66 African, Caribbean, and Pacific states (ACP) and the EC, by means of which 99.2 percent of ACP exports enter the European Community duty free.

2. Japan. The major reason for the increased competition within Japan over the last two decades has been the gradual relaxation by its government of the legal and administrative barriers to imports and foreign investment. The government, under pressure from Japan's trading partners to open its markets to outsiders, has responded with tariff reductions, changes in the law to permit wholly owned foreign subsidiaries, and a general streamlining of government administrative procedures. The private sector has also cooperated by sending missions to the United States and Europe to promote an interest in doing business in Japan.

Figure 12–3

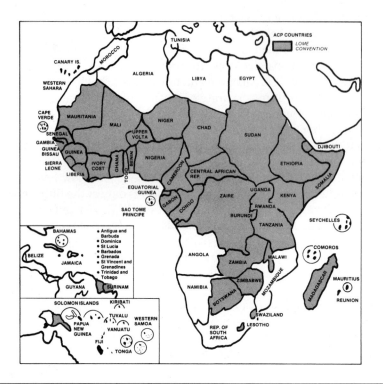

This map shows the countries linked to the EC in the Lomé Convention trade-and-aid treaty.

These activities have resulted in a stepped-up involvement of foreign firms in the Japanese economy. In data processing, for example, six American multinationals compete with Japanese producers for a share of the world's second-largest market. IBM is the largest of these, with a 20.2 percent market share, though it has slipped to the number 2 position behind Fujitsu (22.3 percent) in the overall ranking. However, as a result of its stunning victory in the 1983 espionage suit against fourth-ranked Hitachi (14.9 percent), IBM may soon regain market leadership.

Another area of business in which the American multinationals have achieved significant market penetration is the restaurant industry. Fast-food chains such as McDonald's, Kentucky Fried Chicken, and Denny's have been so successful in what is described as a $34 billion market that they have appreciably altered Japanese dining habits. Such multinationals as Avon, PepsiCo, Exxon, Nestlé, and Coca-Cola have shown that the Japanese market is penetrable when time and money are spent to first investigate the market and then to make a long-term commitment to develop it. Table 12–1 lists various foreign brands with large Japanese market shares.

It is in the export market, however, that Japanese manufacturers are finding their greatest challenge. The appreciation of the yen from 260 per dollar in 1985 to 145 per dollar in 1987 has caused exporters' profits to decrease by more than 60 percent. Export volume has dropped, though the results have been masked by the fact that Japanese trade statistics are reported in dollars. Since the yen has appreciated against the dollar faster than exports valued in yen have fallen, Japan's export performance appears to be better than it really is.

The newly industrializing countries whose currencies have not risen appreciably against the dollar are making serious inroads into Japanese export markets, especially the United States. South Korea has greatly increased its U.S. market share of television sets, steel, VCRs, and, more recently, automobiles.[10]

In response to this competition, Japanese firms have attempted to maintain export market share by passing through only part of the yen's appreciation to foreign customers. For example, Toyota raised its U.S. prices in 1986 just three times, for a total of 10 percent, although the yen appreciated more than 30 percent. In addition, Japanese firms are trying to avoid direct competition from the NICs by hurriedly bringing out sophisticated new products that will justify higher prices, such as luxury automobiles and large-screen TVs. They are also building plants in countries where labor costs are lower, and they are increasing their investments in the United States and Europe to protect themselves from the appreciated yen.

Japan was facing unprecedented rates of unemployment and company failures by 1987, and the government had come to realize that in order to sustain economic growth the country must reduce its current high dependence on exports and enlarge the domestic market. The increase in government spending and the tax-revision plan are indications that it is moving in this direction, though its new tax of the VAT type is a tax on domestic consumption.[11]

3. United States. Over the past two decades, the United States has experienced growing competition from the multinationals, primarily Japanese and European, that have come in great numbers to this country. Such firms as Volkswagen, Volvo, Sony, and Michelin are just a few of the hundreds of foreign competitors that, attracted by the dollar's depreciation, have found it advantageous to serve the American market from within. A growing protectionist sentiment in the United States has provided an additional stimulus for setting up American-based operations. Widespread mergers of large firms have created giants, especially in Europe, that now believe they are sufficiently powerful to compete in the American market against the American multinationals. In addition, the size of the market, the availability of raw materials, the developed capital markets, and the political stability in this country have all contributed to the massive flow of investments into the United States, which are creating new competitors and strengthening old ones.

Imports from the LDCs are competing both with American manufacturers and with exporters from the developed nations. Starting with low-technology

Table 12-1
Foreign Products with Large Market Shares in Japan

Items	Producers (Brands)	Nationalities	Percent
Carbonated beverages	Coca-Cola Co.	United States	60%
	PepsiCo, Inc.	United States	5
Instant coffee	Nestlé Alimentana S.A.	Switzerland	63
	General Foods Corp.	United States	17
Black tea	Unilever, Ltd. (Lipton)	Britain	27
	R. Twining & Co., Ltd.	Britain	23
	Brooke Bond Liebig, Ltd.	Britain	11
Dry soup	CPC International, Inc. (Knorr)	United States	84
	Nestlé Alimentana S.A.	Switzerland	8
Canned soup	CPC International, Inc. (Knorr)	United States	21
	Campbell Soup Co.	United States	39
	Heinz (H.J.) Co.	United States	8
Sportswear	Adidas	West Germany	
	Hauser	France	60
	Lacoste, and so forth	France	
Disposable diapers	Procter & Gamble Co.	United States	50
Plastic foam products	Dow Chemical Co.	United States	30
	BASF A.G.	West Germany	30
Plasticizer (BBP)	Monsanto Chemical Co.	United States	100
Butyl rubber	Esso Eastern Chemicals, Inc.	United States	100
Deodorizers	American Drug	United States	59
Turbochargers	Garrett Corp.	United States	64
Panel heaters	Dimplex	Britain	40
	Koehring	United States	50
	Hosty Corp.	United States	
	Balkan Australia	Australia	3
Large computers	IBM Corp.	United States	40
	Sperry Rand Corp. (Univac)	United States	12
Instant cameras	Eastman Kodak Co.	United States	45
	Polaroid Overseas Corp.	United States	45
Golf balls	Dunlop	Britain	55
	Wilson	United States	
	Top-Flite (Spaulding)	United States	7
	Titleist	United States	
Safety razor blades	Warner-Lambert Co.	United States	70
	Gillette Co.	United States	10
Chemical admixtures for concrete	Martin Marietta Corp.	United States	50
Camping stoves	Application des Gaz	France	67
	EPI Gas, Ltd.	Britain	29
Stem wineglasses	Owens Illinois, Inc.	United States	60
	T. G. Durand	France	20
	Schott Zwiesel	West Germany	

Source: *Liberal Star* (Tokyo), May 10, 1982, p. 6.

products, such as textiles and shoes, imports from the newly industrializing countries now include goods with higher technological content, such as VCRs, TVs, and computers. Subsidiaries of American and European automobile manufacturers have been exporting engines and other automotive parts to the United States for some time, but they are now exporting the finished product. Mercedes-Benz (Brazil), for example, has sold trucks to the United States since 1973, and now Volkswagen and Ford have entered the market.[12] Hyundai, a Korean firm, is selling passenger cars in the United States; Taiwanese and Malaysian firms are expected to begin in 1988.

The rising volume of U.S. imports has so dwarfed U.S. exports that in 1986, the trade deficit of this country had reached $170 billion, thereby raising the concern for national competitiveness that we mentioned earlier.

One problem with the concept of national competitiveness is the lack of agreement as to how it should be measured. Comparisons of labor costs, export growth rates, the average value of the dollar expressed in the currencies of trading partners, and the balance of trade are among the yardsticks that have been suggested, but the experts find fault with all of them. One of these experts is Professor Ralph Edfelt of San Jose State University, who argues that neither the trade balance nor the investment balance is appropriate for making judgments on U.S. competitiveness.[13]

> According to Edfelt, as more U.S. imports come from foreign subsidiaries of American firms, while U.S. exports are increasingly provided by American subsidiaries of foreign firms, the distinction between "we" and "they" is becoming meaningless. Furthermore, any discussion of export performance must include its relationships with international investment flows, which Edfelt likens to import and export transactions. The United States is the world's largest exporter of direct investment, the earnings remittances from which do not appear in the merchandise trade account of the balance of payments. Similarly, portfolio investments in the United States are the exporting of U.S. investment opportunities, and recent U.S. export surpluses of this kind have exceeded the deficits on merchandise trade. We should regard, says Edfelt, the recent annual growth in foreign investment in this country in excess of U.S. investment abroad as a vivid indicator of strength rather than as an indicator of a declining U.S. international competitiveness.[13] Malcolm Forbes, Jr., comments, "Contrary to everyone's impression, the United States is no 97-pound weakling in world markets. The trade deficit is primarily the result of our growing while the rest of the world stagnates. In dollar terms, our exports are no worse than they were several years ago. But our customers can't buy more if they do not have money or credit. Imports have risen because the American economy has expanded. As a proportion of GNP, imports today are slightly lower than they were six years ago."[14]

How can U.S. manufacturers increase exports? By 1985, the dollar was at an all-time high, having appreciated 55 percent against the currencies of 16 other in-

Figure 12-4

U.S. Exchange Rate Indices (1980 Q 1 = 100)

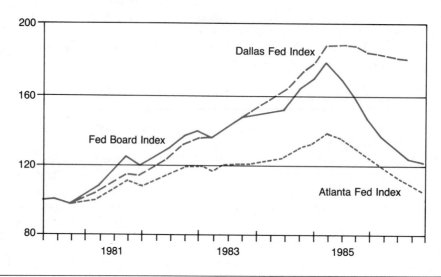

Dallas Fed Index—Covers 13 countries. Fed Board Index—Covers 10 industrialized nations. Atlanta Fed Index—Covers 18 nations, including NICs, but not LDCs with high inflation rates.
Source: Bank of Montreal *Business Review,* January-February, 1987, p. 6.

dustrialized nations.[15] This caused the prices of American exports stated in those currencies to increase by that amount, while exporters to the United States were able to lower their dollar prices and still receive as many marks, yen, and so forth as before.

To compete both at home and abroad, American firms moved production facilities overseas where currencies were cheaper compared to the dollar and also increased their purchases of foreign-made components and finished products. In February 1985, however, the dollar began to decline. Export orders began to increase, and American producers became more price competitive at home as European and Japanese exporters started to raise their prices to obtain the same amount of their currencies as before.

However, the dollar's sharp decline did not reduce the U.S. trade deficit as much or as quickly as many had expected. One reason is that the dollar did not decline against all currencies but actually remained stable or rose against those of some major competitors, such as Canada, Taiwan, Korea, Brazil, and Mexico. Its increase in value against the weaker currencies of such nations occurred mainly because these nations had far higher inflation rates than the United States. Indexes showing this change in U.S. competitiveness are confusing because each index includes different currencies. Figure 12-4 compares just three of the many indexes that have been published, and Table 12-2 shows how little the dollar has depreciated against the currencies of Asian NICs.

Table 12-2

Movement in Value of U.S. Dollar against Asian Currencies (12 months to December 1986)

New Taiwanese dollar	-9.3%
South Korean won	-3.2
Hong Kong dollar	-0.5
Singapore dollar	$+1.8$
People's Republic of China renmimbi	$+16.3$

$+$ = appreciation of US\$; $-$ = depreciation of US\$
Source: *Monthly Summary,* National Australia Bank, March, 1987, p. 4.

Another reason is one we mentioned previously—exporters did not raise their prices to the extent that the dollar depreciated but instead sacrificed part of their profits to preserve market share. Still another reason is that it takes time for buyers to terminate contracts and switch to U.S. suppliers, but probably the most significant reason is that competitiveness is not based solely on price. There are a host of nonprice factors, such as quality, delivery time, after-sales service, reliability of supply, and trade barriers to U.S. exports.

These factors suggest various measures that can be taken to increase American exports. American government officials can maintain pressure on other governments to reduce their trade barriers and stimulate their economies to increase demand for American exports. Germany has lowered its discount rate and Japan has reduced its income tax, for example, as a result of American insistence. The government can also support American companies that face competition from targeted industries.

Industrial targeting, the practice by governments of assisting selected industries to grow by a variety of means, is becoming common in Europe and Japan. France, for example, modernized its railroad industry by modernizing its rail system. Equipment contracts were given only to French suppliers. By building a strong home base first, French suppliers were ready for the export market. Increasingly, the U.S. mass transit market is being dominated by the French and the Japanese, both of whose governments support target industries. Another industry targeted by European nations is the manufacture of aircraft built around the Airbus, which is estimated to have received $6 billion in subsidies since the 1970s. A Boeing official states that the "Airbus was allowed to start a program without a sufficient order base and at production rates that would force a U.S. manufacturer to shut down."[16]

Some economists believe that the most significant action the U.S. government can take to decrease the trade deficit is to lower the federal budget deficit, thereby decreasing the amount of savings consumed by the government.[17] With more savings available for lending, American firms could obtain capital for expansion and equipment renewal at a cost more in line with what foreign companies pay, thereby improving their competitiveness in world markets. However, others claim that the trade deficit exists because the strong U.S. economy has created a demand for imports greater than the volume of American exports that the less robust foreign economies can buy. In fact, it has been estimated that if economic activity outside the U.S. grew by one percent, the U.S. trade balance would improve by $10 billion per year.

At any rate, not all of the responsibility lies with the government; management and labor must also act. Managers must become more aggressive against foreign competition. They must prepare long-range strategic plans and be willing to invest long term, as 3M has done, instead of expecting an immediate return.

In 1970, 3M had 30 percent of the market for magnetic recording tape, which it had developed. Yet in only five years Japanese producers such as Maxell and TDK had taken most of that market.

Now 3M is in another war with the Japanese—videotape. The company believes that the Japanese thought they could drive it out of tapes again by slashing prices, but this time 3M has matched their prices. The company is spending heavily to improve the quality and production efficiency of its tapes and floppy disks—22 percent of its total capital budget. It is also spending heavily on packaging, advertising, and sales promotion. Says the sales director of TDK's American subsidiary, "I have never seen an effort of this magnitude."

The company appears to be winning in its battle, as it is now the leading branded producer in the United States, with 19 percent market share. It has 13 percent of the world market. One dramatic change is 3M's departure from its practice of refusing to fund ventures that do not measure up to its ROI standards. The group vice president in charge of these products insists that 3M will not give in: "We are positioning everything with the long term in mind." An industry analyst adds, "For one of the first times, the company is looking longer than just one quarter."[18]

Tom Peters (*A Passion for Excellence*) asks why American firms don't extend themselves to meet Japan's needs. He cites the example of the American automobile manufacturers. In 1985, Detroit managed to sell only 1,300 cars in Japan, while BMW sold 6,000, a 50 percent increase over 1984. The reason, Peters claims, is that U.S. producers refuse to put steering wheels on the right side and then assume that the Japanese don't buy American cars because they don't like them. According to Peters, it is our closed minds, not the policies of the host country governments, that lead to most of our failures abroad.[19]

Labor must also take the long-term view, and unions have done so in recent years. There has been a marked increase in their willingness to work with management instead of maintaining the traditional adversarial role. Managers' efforts to share profits and to involve workers in decision making by means of quality circles and shop floor meetings have contributed to this change in attitude.

Developing nations. Although the LDCs depend primarily on the developed nations to buy their products, there is a growing desire on their part to lessen this dependence. That desire has been formalized by the creation of regional economic groups in Latin America, Asia, Africa, and the Middle East that have been particularly successful with manufactured goods.

Measured in current dollars, during the period 1965–85, trade in these products among the developing nations, including the NICs, increased 25 times as compared to an increase of 1.9 times in overall trade volume, which consists primarily of commodities. Between 1965 and 1985, in other words, among developing nations the percentage of total trade that was manufactured goods rose from 3 percent to 40 percent. If we remove the percentage of the total manufactured exports of the NICs that went to developing nations, developing nations' exports of manufactured goods to other developing nations increased by 17 times. During the same period, only five industrialized nations—New Zealand, Australia, Norway, Belgium, and Denmark—increased their percentages of manufactured goods exported going to developing countries. Japan, Great Britain, and Ireland had the largest decrease—more than 10 percent each, as compared to 5 percent for the United States.[20]

However, competition for LDC markets is not confined to members of the regional economic groups. In the Middle East, the traditional suppliers and contractors from the developed nations are being challenged by firms from South Korea, India, the Philippines, Pakistan, Turkey, and Brazil. South Korea, especially, has become a power in international construction because its labor, management, and technology have proven to be productive, highly adaptable to local conditions, and inexpensive. In Saudi Arabia, for example, several construction projects have been completed by Korean, Taiwanese, Pakistani, and Indian firms at half the cost estimated by European and American companies. This has caused the U.S. market share to slip from 1st place to 12th.[21] As one Middle Eastern construction ministry official put it, "South Koreans work as hard as Americans used to."

Steelmaking is another industry in which competition from LDC manufacturers is escalating in both developed and developing nations. The traditional steel exporters, Europe and Japan, have to confront competitors from Mexico, Korea, Brazil, and Taiwan not only in their overseas markets but also at home. Korea now supplies three quarters of Japan's imported steel. Interestingly, the financing and the technology for Korea's largest plant were supplied by the Japanese.

One of the steel exporters, Brazil, has an especially diverse export mix, and much of the more than $10 billion in manufactured products that it exports annually goes to developing nations (43 percent). Brazilian exports are especially strong in Africa because of geographic proximity and similarities of race, culture and climate. Brazil sells such products as automobiles, trucks, armored vehicles (it is the largest exporter in the world after the USSR), airplanes, and heavy construction equipment.

Nigerian officials who awarded a $45 million contract to a Brazilian firm to design Nigeria's communication system felt that "the Brazilians were closer to their problem" than the European and American competitors.[22]

The emerging pattern of developing nations doing business with one another is enabling foreign subsidiaries of European and American multinationals to obtain business that their home offices cannot acquire. General Motors, Caterpillar, Volkswagen, and Saab-Scania are examples of firms whose Brazilian affiliates are participating in the $1 billion African-Brazilian trade.

A special kind of competition confronted by multinationals in developing and developed nations is **counterfeiting.** The use of manufacturers' names on products that are copies of the genuine article is estimated to be costing the legitimate owners $60 billion annually and is especially prevalent in Taiwan, South Korea, Thailand, the Philippines, and Hong Kong.

In Taiwan, which is said to be the counterfeit center of Asia, it is possible to buy an Apolo II for between $200 and $500, as compared to the suggested retail price of $1,530 for an Apple II. Everlight and Everoline compete in the market with Eveready, Varseling and Vansyline are mistaken for Vaseline, and Cartier imitations sell for $23.[23]

Easy-to-copy products with high markups, such as luxury goods (Gucci, Vuitton, and Chanel No. 5), have long been counterfeited, but products now routinely copied include pesticides, fertilizers, drugs, toys, car and airplane parts, food, and electronic items.

The copiers are fast too. AT&T showed a brand-new telephone at the Las Vegas Trade Show in 1983. A Taiwanese firm that saw the display copied, produced, and marketed the phone before AT&T could bring it to market. The Taiwanese dropped the product, however, when AT&T protested.[24]

Besides costing legitimate manufacturers sales, these fakes sometimes bring tragedy to users when, as is frequent, they fail to perform as well as the original. Farmers in Zaire and Kenya bought what they thought was Chevron's top-quality pesticide, which turned out to be a fake made of chalk. The two countries lost two thirds of their cash crops for that year. Bell Helicopter found counterfeit parts in 600 helicopters sold to civilians and the military; it said that some of them may have caused crashes. One or more tragedies were avoided when the Food and Drug Administration recalled 350 pumps used to keep people alive during open-heart surgery. It found an $8 counterfeit part in a $20,000 pump that threatened to stall.[25]

Stopping counterfeiters is no simple matter for the rightful owner of a trademark or a patent. This valuable industrial property must be registered and violators must be prosecuted in every country where the firm wants protection. Furthermore, even when the imitators lose, the penalties are often negligible—$20,000 in Hong Kong and $3,750 in Taiwan. However, a new Taiwanese law passed in 1983 as a result of pressure from foreign governments includes a jail

Figure 12–5

Courtesy: les must de Cartier

Vrai (true) and Faux (false)

sentence of up to five years. In addition, arrests in Taiwan have increased by 50 percent.

Levi Strauss has probably gone further than most firms to rid the market of imitations. The company has a corporate security organization with an annual million-dollar budget to stop this unfair competition. Levi Strauss was also instrumental in forming the International Anticounterfeiting Coalition, which now has 60 member firms from 11 countries. Member firms exchange information on problems they are encountering in certain markets and how they are handling them. The coalition lobbies in the United States and other countries to increase the penalties for commercial counterfeiting. Because of these efforts, U.S. Customs is now empowered to seize and destroy counterfeit goods when they are discovered at a point of entry.[26]

Another type of unfair competition may result when a firm copies a patented design and markets a version under its own trademark without paying a royalty to the rightful owner. This can sometimes be accomplished by "reverse engineering" (taking the finished article apart), or when that is not feasible, the copier may obtain blueprints or process information by means of *industrial espionage*.

Figure 12–6

Source: © 1984, Walt Disney Productions

From fake dolls to . . . .

For years, companies have been acquiring information about each other by hiring competitors' employees, talking to competitors' customers, and so forth. More recently, however, intensified competition has motivated corporations to become more sophisticated in this endeavor, even to the point of committing illegal acts. In 1978, for example, the Mitsubishi Corporation was indicted on charges of trying to steal industrial secrets from Celanese. In 1982, the U.S. Department of Justice charged 19 Japanese businessmen from another subsidiary of Mitsubishi and Hitachi with conspiring to steal confidential trade secrets from IBM. Agie, a Swiss manufacturer of sophisticated machine tools, won compensation from Hitachi for copying its technology and filed a suit against Mitsubishi Electric for patent violation.[27]

The Soviet Union has undertaken a massive program to steal technology from American firms, especially those in Silicon Valley. Industrial espionage carried on by firms in this country and by foreign companies and governments is estimated to cost American industry $20 billion annually.[28]

Slowly Growing or Contracting Markets

Whether an industry's markets grow more slowly than anticipated or actually contract, a condition of overcapacity generally follows. Anxious to sell their output, firms then become more aggressive, and competition heightens.

Figure 12-7

Courtesy of Chevron Corp.

Fake fungicides

Market Growth Slower than Anticipated

The petrochemical industry, mentioned earlier as one beset by new competitors, is also suffering from overcapacity. After the 1974 surge in demand, the wave of excessive optimism as to future growth that hit the industry prompted all of the petrochemical producers to expand their facilities simultaneously. Unfortunately, the anticipated demand did not materialize. Various factors were responsible for this: (1) a slackening of economic growth, (2) increased prices of the finished product because of higher crude oil prices and greater investment in pollution control, and (3) a tapering off of product substitution and innovation, which had been major factors in the annual 15 percent market growth of the 1960s.

The increased competition has forced firms to apply all of the familiar remedies such as plant closures, price-cutting, and a search for higher-added-value products to compensate for the loss of volume growth in the basic products. There has also been a greater emphasis on marketing, especially market segmentation. Thus, manufacturers of insecticides have been focusing their technology on making specific chemicals to control specific insects in specific geographic areas instead of producing the single product for a more costly, indiscriminate spraying.

In Europe, the combination of high imports and excess production capacity, not only in petrochemicals but also in steel, shipbuilding, and even automobiles, is bringing forth proposals in the EC for industry cartels that would provide for price setting, import controls, production cutbacks, and market sharing. All of these procedures are a reversal of the EC's efforts to increase rather than limit competition, and not all European firms are enthusiastic about them. Machinery producers, for example, complain that higher steel prices put them at a price disadvantage in world markets. Governments that have built plants in depressed areas to reduce unemployment are reluctant to cut back production. The alternative feared by proponents of the cartelization scheme is voluntary agreements among private firms. These, they believe, would restrict competition even more.

Contracting Market

What happens when a new product lasts longer than the one it replaced? If there is no increase in the rate of new applications, the market contracts. This is precisely what occurred in the European tire market. The replacement demand for tires with the old bias ply construction was 2.5 tires per automobile per year; the replacement demand for the new radial tires is one tire per automobile per year. Admittedly, longer product life is not the only reason why well-known manufacturers such as Trelleborg, Uniroyal, Goodrich, and Metzeler have ceased production in Europe, but it is a major factor. Excess production capacity brought about by overinvestment in the expanding market of the 1960s is another. A third is that East European nations are competing with inexpensive exports produced in factories built with West European technology.

Even if the replacement product were not more durable, we should expect to find many strong competitors in the tire market. Competition is always intense for any mature product and is, as we have seen, one of the motives for investing overseas. Sales in the home country may be topping out because of market saturation, whereas elsewhere the product is virtually unknown. To discover these opportunities, managements require an analysis of the competitive forces.

Competitive Forces Analysis

A thorough understanding of the competitive forces is mandatory for making sound investment decisions. The final choice between two markets, apparently similar in all other aspects, frequently hinges on the relative competitive intensity as revealed by the competitive forces analysis. After the investment decision has been made, the competitive analysis continues to be of interest to the marketing manager inasmuch as the firm's marketing strategy will be strongly influenced by what he or she considers to be the strengths and weaknesses of the competitors' offerings. In recent years, a number of firms have established a competitive information system that provides for a constant monitoring of the competitive forces rather than sporadic investigations. In either case, all of the data gathered can be subsumed in two categories: (1) market organization and (2) competitors' strengths and weaknesses.

Market Organization

This measure of competitive intensity is concerned with the number and size of firms offering similar products or services and the barriers that impede the entrance of new firms.

Number and Size of Competitors. To correctly identify the size and number of competitors, management must first carefully define the firm's line of business. Generally, the firm views any company producing similar or substitutable products as a competitor; in certain industries, however, especially those that compete for the customer's discretionary income, the definition of the business must be broad. Thus, a manufacturer of cement kilns has no problem with competitive identification, but a producer of golf clubs must consider a wide variety of competitive products, ranging from other brands of golf clubs to a vacation in Acapulco.

The importance of knowing which companies are already supplying a market with similar products lies in the fact that oftentimes the firm already has experience in competing with these companies in other countries. The marketing manager who encounters in the country under study a competitor that is known to fight for market share on the basis of price can be reasonably certain that the foreign affiliate follows the same strategy. Should the competing firms be unknown, the marketing manager will want to know whether there are a few competitors of approximately equal size (oligopoly) or many of varying size (monopolistic competition). Competition is usually less intense in the first situation (automobiles compared with small appliances).

Barriers to Entry. The barriers to entry, which are generally political or are related to market size and growth, indicate to management the degree of difficulty that both the firm and future competitors may have in entering a market. Where it is relatively easy to establish a business, competition will usually be greater.

1. Political forces. The political forces, as you have seen, can be a formidable barrier to entry because no firm can operate in a country without governmental approval. Laws barring foreigners from entering specified industries or from acquiring a majority ownership are extremely common. Even when these laws do not exist, governmental assistance through subsidies, grants, tax assistance, or favoritism in purchasing may suffice to deter foreign investment. In Chapter 3, you learned that the prospective exporter faces all sorts of tariff and nontariff barriers erected by governments to protect local business from foreign competition.

2. Market size and growth. Market size is another consideration, because the smaller markets of many countries are incapable of supporting as many suppliers as can those of the larger industrialized nations. This is especially significant for the capital-intensive steel, petroleum, and automotive industries, all of which require a minimum market size to be economically viable.

Research that reveals markets to be stagnant, slow-growing, or dominated by one supplier (especially one that prices low) may also dissuade the firm from entering; though before dismissing them out of hand, management will usually want to analyze thoroughly the prospective competitors' strengths and weaknesses.

Competitors' Strengths and Weaknesses

An analysis of the strengths and weaknesses of foreign competitors will cover the same points as are covered by a domestic analysis: market share, effectiveness of the marketing mix, appropriateness of the promotional mix, and so on. One of the many sources of such information is home country customers with affiliates in the market under study. They are generally well informed about such matters as the kind of service their subsidiaries receive, local product quality, and prices paid.

If the product is imported, data concerning the amount and the supplying countries are a matter of public record and are usually available from the appropriate government department. In addition, the U.S. Department of Commerce, banks, credit agencies, wholesalers, retailers, business periodicals, local chambers of commerce, and the firm's sales representatives are all sources of information that, when collected and analyzed, can provide management with a comprehensive report of its competitors' strengths and weaknesses.

Distributive Forces

The channels of distribution, systems of agencies through which a product and its title pass from the producer to the user, are both a controllable and an uncontrollable variable. They are controllable to the extent that the channel captains are free to choose from the available channels those that will enable them to reach their target markets, perform the functions they require at a reasonable cost, and permit them the amount of control they desire.* If the established channels are considered inadequate, they may assemble different networks.

> Coca-Cola, dissatisfied with the complex Japanese system of distributing through layers of wholesalers, created its own system, by means of which 17 bottlers sell directly to over 1 million retailers. The dramatic reduction in

---

*The *channel captain* is the dominant and controlling member of a channel of distribution.

distributive costs coupled with the fact that each bottler was well versed in its own market enabled Coca-Cola to obtain 60 percent of the Japanese market. Note, however, that although a new system was created, new agencies were not.

The distributive *structure,* the agencies themselves, is generally beyond the marketer's control, so that it must use those that are available. Yet new agencies are occasionally created when the established institutions do not fulfill the channel captain's requirements.

UK automaker Austin Rover, long established in Germany, had lost 60 percent of its dealers because of a low-quality image. Although its new models had achieved European-wide success, its German dealers managed to sell only 0.15 percent of the market. Searching for a novel approach, Austin Rover concluded a deal with Massa, Germany's largest retailer and owner of 27 hypermarkets (huge combination supermarket/discount stores), under which Massa was to build showrooms and service departments at each of its store sites. The enormous advertising power obtained through Massa's newspapers, delivered to 5.5 million households, coupled with Massa's reputation for quality enabled the chain to sell 800 cars the first month. Rover expects Massa to sell more cars than all of its 200 traditional dealers.[29]

International Channel of Distribution Members

The selection of channel of distribution members to link the producer with the foreign user will depend first of all on the method of entry into the market. In Chapter 2, you learned that to do business overseas a firm must either export to a foreign country or manufacture in it. If the decision is to export, the firm may do so *directly* or *indirectly.* Figure 12–8 shows that management has considerable latitude in forming the channels.

Indirect Exporting

For indirect exporting, there are a number of U.S.- based exporters that (1) sell for the manufacturer, (2) buy for their overseas customers, (3) buy and sell for their own account, or (4) purchase on behalf of foreign middlemen or users. Although each type of exporter usually operates in the following manner, any given company may actually perform one or more of these functions.

1. Exporters that sell for the manufacturer.
   a. *Manufacturers' export agents* act as the international representatives for various noncompeting domestic manufacturers. They usually direct promotion, consummate sales, invoice, ship, and handle the financing. They are commonly paid a commission for carrying out these functions in the name of the manufacturer.

Figure 12-8
International Channels of Distribution

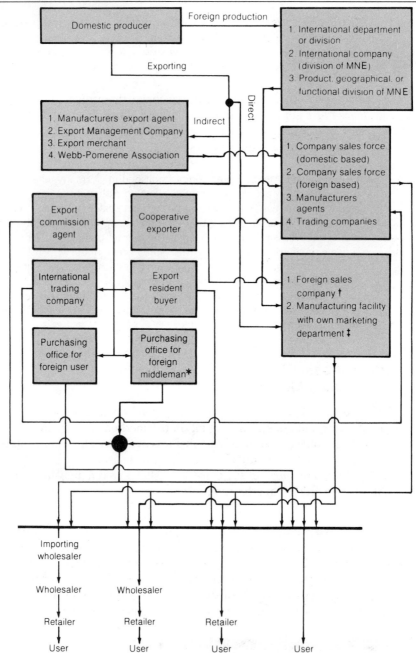

*There should be no direct connection between this category and the user. For simplification, a separate line to eliminate the user is not shown.

†Can be wholly owned or a joint venture. The foreign sales company may sell imports as well as local production from licensee, contract manufacturer, or joint venture.

‡Can be wholly owned, joint venture, or a licensee.

b. *Export management companies (EMCs)*, formerly known as combination export managers (CEMs), act as the export department for several noncompetitive manufacturers. They will also transact business in the name of the manufacturer and handle the routine details of shipping and promotion. When the EMC works on a commission basis, the manufacturer invoices the customer directly and carries any financing required by the foreign buyer. However, most EMCs work on a buy-and-sell arrangement under which they pay the manufacturer, resell the product abroad, and invoice the customer directly. Depending on the arrangement, the EMC may act in the name of the firm it represents or in its own name.

c. *International trading companies* are similar to EMCs in that they also act as agents for some companies and as merchant wholesalers for others. This, however, is only part of their activities. They frequently export as well as import, own their own transportation facilities, and provide financing. W. R. Grace was at one time a major trading company that operated on the Pacific coast of South America. It owned sugar mills, large import houses, various manufacturing plants, a steamship company, and an airline. Although there have been a number of European and American international trading companies in operation for centuries, certainly the most diversified and the largest are the Japanese **sogo shosha** (general trading companies).

The general trading companies were originally established by the *zaibatsu* —centralized, family-dominated economic groups such as Mitsui, Mitsubishi, and Sumitomo—to be the heart of their commercial operations. The head of Mitsui, for example, established a general trading company, Mitsui Bussan, at the same time (1870s) that he created the Mitsui Bank. Both institutions served as the nucleus for the rest of the Mitsui empire. The general trading companies obtained export markets, raw materials, and technical assistance for other companies of the zaibatsu and also imported goods for resale. Included in the zaibatsu in addition to banks and general trading companies were transportation, insurance, and real estate companies and various manufacturing firms. In 1933, 6.2 percent of Japan's social overhead capital belonged to four major zaibatsu— Mitsui, Mitsubishi, Yasuda, and Sumitomo. Although the zaibatsu were forced to dissolve after World War II, the companies that had been their major components survived.

One of the largest general trading companies is Mitsui & Co. In 1986, this sogo sosha had $102 billion in sales and employed 12,000 persons throughout the world. It also had equity investments in more than 400 companies in Japan and 250 overseas. Although Mitsui & Co. is huge, it is only one company in the Mitsui Group (formerly the Mitsui zaibatsu), which consists of several hundred companies whose activities range from steelmaking and shipbuilding to banking and insurance, from paper to electronics, and from petroleum to warehousing, tourism, and nuclear energy. Interestingly, the Mitsui Group is not a legal entity but exists as an informal organization of major enterprises that have related interests and related financial structures. They cooperate in promoting the economic interests of group members. To ensure cooperation, the top executives of the 68 major components of the former Mitsui zaibatsu meet for a weekly luncheon meeting.[30] Total sales for the Mitsui Group amounted to $210 billion in 1985. Interestingly, the American subsidiaries of Mitsubishi and Mitsui together account for 10 percent of *all* U.S. exports.

In 1982, the Reagan administration, impressed by the success of Japanese, Taiwanese, and Korean general trading companies, worked closely with Congress to obtain the passage of the Export Trading Company Act. The measure provides the mechanism for creating a new indirect export channel, the **export trading company (ETC).** For the first time in U.S. history, businesses were permitted to join together to export goods and services or offer export facilitating services without fear of violating antitrust legislation. Bank holding companies may also participate in ETCs. This will not only increase the ability of trading companies to finance export transactions but will also give them access to the banks' extensive international information systems. Furthermore, because ETCs can import as well as export, they can engage in countertrade by selling their customers' products in other markets.[31]

In spite of these advantages, American companies haven't rushed to establish ETCs. A few firms, such as General Electric, Sears, and General Motors, had formed trading companies before passage of the bill. After the bill became law, K mart formed a trading company, as did two banks, Bank of America and Security Pacific. First National of Chicago formed a joint venture with Sears.[32] None of these, however, is as large as a sogo shosha, nor do they form part of large industrial groups, as do the Japanese trading companies. The ETCs of Bank of America and Security Pacific are capitalized at only $20 and $10 million, respectively.[33] Although the ETCs do not have as much freedom to act as do the Japanese trading companies, they will be much more competitive than export management companies were before the act was passed.

2. Exporters that buy for their overseas customers. *Export commission agents* represent overseas purchasers such as import firms and large industrial users. They are paid a commission by the purchasers for acting as resident buyers in industrialized nations.

3. Exporters that buy and sell for their own account.
   a. **Export merchants** purchase products directly from the manufacturer and then sell, invoice, and ship them in their own names so that foreign customers have no direct dealing with the manufacturer, as they do in the case of the export agent. If export merchants have an exclusive right to sell the manufacturer's products in an overseas territory, they are generally called *export distributors*. Some EMCs may actually be export distributors for a number of their clients.

Figure 12-9

Courtesy R. J. Reynolds, 1982 Annual Report

Colonel Sanders in Japan (a joint venture with Mitsubishi, a sogo shosha)

b. **Cooperative exporters,** sometimes called piggyback or mother hen exporters, are established international manufacturers that sell the products of other companies in foreign markets along with their own. Carriers (exporters) may purchase and resell in their own name, or they may work on a commission basis. Carriers, like EMCs, serve as the export departments for the firms they represent. Large companies such as General Electric, Borg-Warner, and Singer have been acting as piggyback exporters for years. A single carrier usually represents between 10 and 20 suppliers, though there is one large manufacturer of industrial machinery that has more than 1,000!

c. *Webb-Pomerene Associations* are organizations of competing firms that have joined together for the sole purpose of export trade. The Export Trade Act of 1918 provides for the formation of such groups and generally exempts them from antitrust laws. They are permitted to buy from the members and sell abroad, set export prices, or simply direct the promotional activities that are destined for overseas markets. At this time, there are only 30 associations, of which those in phosphate rock, wood pulp, movies, and sulfur are the most active. The Webb-Pomerene Associations failed to become an important export channel because (1) the antitrust exemption was very vague and (2) the exporting of services was not included. The intent of the Export Trading Act is to remedy these deficiencies.

4. Those that purchase for foreign users and middlemen.

a. Large foreign users such as mining, petroleum, and international construction companies buy for their own use overseas. The purchasing departments of all the multinational firms are continually buying for their foreign affiliates, and both foreign governments and foreign firms maintain purchasing offices in industrialized countries.

b. *Export resident buyers* perform essentially the same functions as export commission agents. However, they are generally more closely associated with a foreign firm. They may be appointed as the official buying representatives and paid a retainer, or they may even be employees. This is in contrast to the export commission agent, who usually represents a number of overseas buyers and works on a transaction-by-transaction basis.

Direct Exporting

If the firm chooses to do its own exporting, it has four basic types of overseas middlemen from which to choose: (1) manufacturers' agents, (2) distributors, (3) retailers, and (4) trading companies. These may be serviced by sales personnel who either travel to the market or are based in it. If the sales volume is sufficient, a foreign sales company may be established to take the place of the wholesale importer. The manufacturing affiliates of most multinationals also import from home country plants or from other subsidiaries products that they themselves do not produce.

1. **Manufacturers' agents** are residents of the country or region in which they are conducting business for the firm. They represent various non-

competing foreign suppliers, and they take orders in these firms' names. Manufacturers' agents usually work on a commission basis, pay their own expenses, and do not assume any financial responsiblity. They often stock the products of some of their suppliers, thus combining the functions of agent and wholesale distributor.

2. **Distributors** or wholesale importers are independent merchants that buy for their own account. They import and stock for resale. Distributors are usually specialists in a particular field, such as farm equipment or pharmaceuticals. They may be given exclusive representation and, in return, agree not to handle competing brands. Distributors may buy through manufacturers' agents when the exporter employs them, or they may send their orders directly to the exporting firm. Instead of manufacturers' agents, exporters may employ their own salespeople to cover the territory and to assist the distributors. For years, multinational firms such as Caterpillar, Firestone, and Goodrich have utilized field representatives in export territories.

3. **Retailers,** especially of consumer products requiring little after-sales servicing, are frequently direct importers. Contact on behalf of the exporter is maintained either by a manufacturers' agent or by the exporter's sales representative based in the territory or traveling from the home office.

4. **Trading companies** are relatively unknown in the United States but are extremely important importers in other parts of the world. In a number of African nations, trading companies are not only the principal importers of goods ranging from consumer products to capital equipment, but they also export such raw materials as ore, palm oil, and coffee. In addition, they operate department stores, grocery stores, and agencies for automobiles and farm machinery. Although many trading companies are large, they are in no way comparable in either size or diversification (products and functions performed) to the sogo shosha.

Trading companies in Brazil, Korea, Taiwan, and Malaysia are a recent development. They are of little use to exporters to these countries, inasmuch as their primary function is to promote their own country's exports. On the other hand, the English *importer/factor,* which performs some of the functions of a trading company, is of value to exporters. It will, on behalf of foreign manufacturers, warehouse goods, price them for the local market, deliver anywhere in the country, and factor (buy the seller's accounts receivable). The exporter must still develop the sales, however.

Another form of trading company is owned by the state. State trading companies handle all exports and imports in the communist bloc, and in noncommunist nations where an industry is a government monopoly, such as tobacco in Spain or petroleum in Mexico, exporters or their agents must deal with these government-owned entities.

Foreign Production

When the firm is selling products produced in the local market, whether manufactured by a wholly owned subsidiary, a joint venture, or a contract manufacturer, management's concern is with the internal channels. Generally, the same types of middlemen are available although the established channels, and their manner of operating may be appreciably different from those to which management is accustomed. Differences between the foreign and domestic environmental forces are responsible.

Wholesale Institutions

In other developed nations, as in the United States, the marketer will be able to select wholesalers that take title to the goods (merchant wholesalers, rack jobbers, drop shippers, cash-and-carry wholesalers, truck jobbers) and those that do not (agents, brokers). However, also as in the United States, large-scale retailers are bypassing wholesalers to purchase directly from manufacturers, and concomitantly many manufacturers, in an effort to lower distribution expense, are assuming the wholesaling function. Pressure from both their suppliers and their customers is forcing many smaller independent wholesalers out of business, with the result that in many countries wholesalers are becoming greater in size but fewer in number. An example is Austria. Over a recent period of eight years, the number of its wholesalers fell by 14 percent, while the average number of employees rose by 25 percent. In Norway, there were 10 percent fewer wholesalers after a 10-year period, but as in Austria, the number of employees increased 41 percent. Similar trends in wholesaler concentration have been noted not only in Europe and the United States but also in such developing countries as Brazil and Argentina.

The diversity of the wholesaling structure among nations may be seen in Table 12–3. Generally, you will find that the structure varies with the stage of economic development. In the less developed countries that depend on imports to supply the market, the importing wholesalers are large and few in number and the channels are long. Historically, many of the importers were trading companies formed by the multinationals to import the machinery and supplies required by their local operation and to export raw materials for use in the home country plants. To obtain distributor prices, they were required by their suppliers to sell to other customers as well. Some of these operations became extremely diversified, owning automobile and industrial machinery agencies, grocery stores, and department stores. They literally could and did supply a complete city and an industry with all of its requirements.

As colonies became nations, the new governments began applying pressure to convert these trading companies to local ownership. Furthermore, these countries were industrializing, which meant that more goods were being produced locally and less goods were being imported. Many of the local manufacturers were able to take control of the channels from the import jobber. To obtain more extensive market coverage, they canceled the importing wholesaler's ex-

Table 12-3
Wholesaling and Retailing in Selected Countries

Country	Number of Wholesalers	Employees per Wholesaler	Population per Wholesaler	Number of Retailers	Employees per Retailer	Population per Retailer	Population Retailers to Wholesalers
United States (1982)	416,000	12.0	556	1,923,200	7.5	120	4.6
Australia (1982)	39,319	9.2	386	110,500	6.7	136	2.8
Austria (1983)	12,890	11.5	590	37,524	6.0	203	2.9
Brazil (1980)	46,000	9.6	2,630	885,600	3.2	136	19.3
Chile (1983)	561	28.3	20,600	1,125	21.2	10,300	2.0
Ecuador (1980)	3 381	7.1	2,248	79,080	1.9	96	23.4
El Salvador (1982)	384	18.5	132,800	1 435	8.6	33,540	3.7
Finland (1983)	5,400	14.5	888	35,800	5.1	134	6.6
France (1984)	79,700	4.0	689	608,600	2.7	90	7.6
Greece (1983)	24,400	2.0	406	164,400	1.8	60	6.7
Hungary (1982)	17,500	11.4	611	55,400	6.0	193	3.2
Ireland (1981)	2,200	14.4	1 590	32,600	3.5	107	14.8
Japan (1982)	429,000	9.5	276	1,721,000	3.7	69	4.0
Korea (1982)	45,568	3.8	862	542,458	1.7	72	11.9
Norway (1983)	11,900	8.1	344	34,000	3.7	121	2.9
Philippines (1981)	20,642	7.6	2,403	280,000	2.5	177	13.6
Portugal (1981)	6,600	21.0	1,506	14,800	8.2	672	2.2
Singapore (1981)	18,794	5.7	112	16,457	4.0	128	0.9
Sweden (1982)	20,900	8.2	397	55,800	4.8	149	2.7
Swaziland (1983)	79	15.2	9,240	646	7.6	1,130	8.2
USSR (1980)	140,000	16.5	1,900	695,200	6.7	383	5.0

Sources: *Statistical Yearbook, 1983–84* (New York: United Nations, 1986), pp. 866–90; and *Statistical Abstract of the United States, 1986,* pp. 779 and 785. European data are from *European Marketing Data and Statistics, 1986–87* (London: Euromonitor Publications, 1986, p. 229.

Figure 12–10

Passenger Car Distribution Channels in Japan

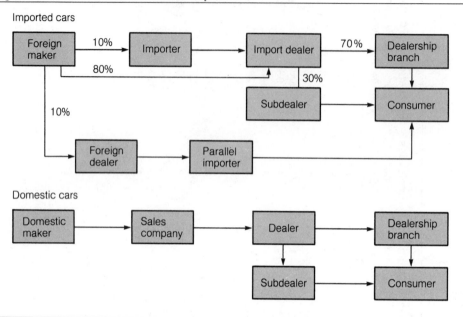

Note: A parallel importer acts independently of the foreign manufacturer and its authorized importer by obtaining the product from another source. It is a competitor of the authorized importer.
Source: *Economic Eye Tokyo,* June 1983, p. 20.

clusivity and gave their product lines to new wholesalers, many of which were formed by ex-employees of the importer. As economic development continued, markets broadened, permitting greater specialization by more and smaller wholesalers. Increased competition at all levels tended to force wholesaler concentration, as we discussed earlier. The small sample in Table 12–3 hints at this cycle. Compare the few large wholesalers in Chile, El Salvador, and Swaziland (employees per wholesaler and population per wholesaler) with the smaller and more numerous wholesalers in the United States and Austria. As always, there are exceptions to any generalization, and the exceptions in this case have occurred because of the legal, economic, physical, and sociocultural forces.

One of the most notable exceptions is the complex distribution system of Japan. Characterized as a formidable trade barrier by foreign firms attempting to enter the market, the maze of wholesalers and retailers employed to reach the consumer in Japan has been severely criticized for its inefficiency. Figure 12–10 illustrates that channels for automobiles are certainly complex, but even simple products such as soap may move through a sales company, three wholesalers, and a retailer in going from the manufacturer to the final customer. Note another difference—the presence of a parallel importer. This intermediary buys from an overseas dealer and competes with the authorized importer, which buys directly from the manufacturer.

Defenders of the multiple-layer wholesale system explain that it arose because of the difficulty of transporting goods over long distances in earlier days and because of the large number and small size of most retail outlets. They claim that values placed on established business and personal relationships have retarded the rationalization of the system. Nevertheless, some very noticeable changes have been occurring. The mom-and-pop stores that dominated retailing are losing out to convenience stores (there are 3,000 7-Elevens in Japan) and to chains of specialty stores. Also, department stores and supermarkets have been increasing their efforts to sell their own brands and manufacturers have been establishing their own retail outlets. "A vast restructuring of the Japanese retailing industry is under way," declares a recent report by Solomon Brothers, U.S. investment bankers.[34]

The Japanese External Trade Organization makes the following statements to explain why the trend toward concentration of wholesaling has developed:

1. As the degree of industrial concentration in production increases, there is a tendency to minimize the number of intermediaries.

2. As retailing concentrates with the development of volume sales outlets, direct ties to makers increase in importance.[35]

These, of course, are the causes of wholesaler concentration everywhere, as we mentioned previously.

Retail Institutions

The variation in size and number is even greater for retailers than for wholesalers. In Table 12–3, compare Chile, Austria, and France, for example. Generally, *the less developed the country, the more numerous, the more specialized, and the smaller are the retailers*. France is an exception because the situation of many small retailers has been maintained by stringent laws that have kept the expansion of supermarkets and mass merchandisers at a much lower rate than that of similarly developed countries. Obviously, Chile's ambulatory peddlers, common in all LDCs, are not included in its retailer count, even though from the manufacturer's standpoint these retailers can be responsible for considerable sales volume. In Africa, the market "mammy" who walks the street selling to passersby from a pan on the top of her head is a major outlet for small-unit goods such as soap, cigarettes, and candy. Although the system seems primitive and ineffective to a Westerner, the market mammy is a powerful force, and associations of these women act as banks, back wholesalers, and even influence politicians.

When retailing methods in the developed and developing nations are compared, the following generalizations are notable: *in going up the scale from LDCs to developed countries, one encounters more mass merchandising; more self-service, large-sized retail units; and a trend toward retailer concentration* (see Figure 12–11.)

Figure 12–11

Food Distribution Methods at Various Levels of Development

a. Route of transactions

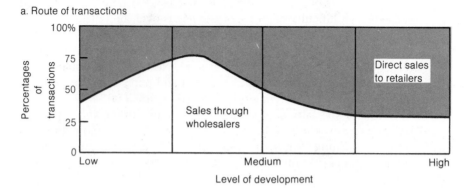

b. Type of retailer

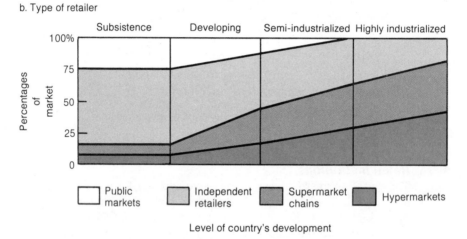

Source: L. Solis and A. Montemayor, "Modernización Comercial y Desarrollo Economico," *Comercio y Desarrollo,* November–December 1977, p. 7.

Typical of this trend is the emergence of the European **hypermarkets**—a huge combination supermarkets/discount house with five or six acres of floor space where both soft goods and hard goods are sold. A similar type of outlet in Japan, the **superstore,** is a recent phenomenon that now accounts for over 10 percent of all retail sales. In Scandinavia and Switzerland, there is also a marked trend toward retailer concentration, but it is occurring for the most part through retailer-controlled voluntary chains and consumer cooperatives rather than through company-owned chains. The growth in Germany of the new types of outlets is typical of what is happening in the developed and the more advanced developing nations (see Figure 12–12).

Figure 12-12

Market Shares of German Retail Outlets

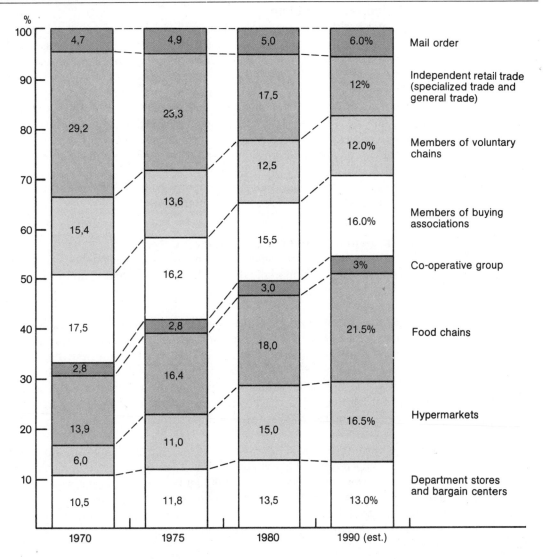

Source: *You in the German Market* (Hamburg: Axel Springer Publishing Group, 1976), p. 40. 1990 projection from *Retail Trade International,* London; Euromonitor 1986, p. 494.

Channel Selection

Direct or Indirect Marketing

The first decision that management must make is whether to use middlemen, because it frequently has the option of marketing directly to the final user. Sales to original equipment manufacturers (OEMs)* and governments are, for the most part, made directly, as are the sales of high-priced industrial products such as turbines and locomotives because the firm is dealing with relatively few customers and transactions but with large dollar volume. Even in these cases, export sales may be consummated by local agents if (1) management believes that this is politically expedient or (2) the country's laws demand it.

Other types of industrial products and consumer goods are marketed indirectly. The channel members are selected on the basis of their market coverage, their cost, and their susceptibility to company control.[36] They must also, of course, perform the functions required by management.

Factors Influencing Channel Selection

The factors that influence the selection of market channels may be classified as the characteristics of the market, the product, the company, and the middlemen.

Market Characteristics. Inasmuch as the reason for using channels is to enable the manufacturer to reach its target markets, the obvious place to start in channel selection is at those markets. Which of the available alternatives offer the most adequate coverage? It is most likely that because of the variance in the target markets, the firm will require multiple channels. Large retailers, governments, and OEMs may be handled by the company sales force or manufacturers' agents, whereas smaller retailers are supplied through wholesalers.

Product Characteristics. A low-cost product sold in small quantities per transaction generally requires long channels, but if the goods are perishable, short channels are preferable. If the product is highly technical in nature, it may be impossible to obtain knowledgeable middlemen and the manufacturer will be forced either to sell directly through company-owned distributors or to train independent middlemen. Caterpillar has enjoyed tremendous success in choosing this second alternative.

Company Characteristics. A firm that has adequate financial and managerial resources is in a much better position to employ its own sales force or agents than one that is lacking in these areas. A financially weak company must use middlemen that take title to and pay for the goods. If management is inexperi-

---

*Original equipment manufacturers buy components that are incorporated into the products they produce (for example, spark plugs to an automobile manufacturer).

enced in selling to certain markets, it must employ middlemen who have that experience.

Middlemen's Characteristics. Most industrial equipment, large household appliances, and automobiles require considerable after-sales servicing, and much of the firm's success in marketing depends on it. If the firm is not prepared to provide this service, it cannot use agents. The same is true for warehousing and promotion to the final user. If the firm is unable to perform these functions or perceives a cost advantage in not performing them, then it must select middlemen that will service, warehouse, and promote its products.

It may be that no channel members are available to reach the firm's target markets and perform the desired functions. If there are none, management must decide to (1) desist from entering the market, (2) select other target markets, or (3) create a new channel. For example, if a frozen-food processor, after studying the available channels, finds that wholesale and retailer cold-storage facilities are nonexistent, it can either abandon the market or persuade middlemen to acquire the facilities. In a number of overseas markets, firms have purchased the equipment and either rented, leased, or sold it on easy terms to distributors and retailers.

> An Italian cheese producer in Brazil not only supplied cold-storage equipment but also established gathering facilities for the dairy farmers. The company provides veterinarians and dairy experts to teach the dairy farmers how to maintain their herds and increase output. Nestlé has similar programs throughout its LDC markets.

Legal Requirements. Because the legal requirements for terminating middlemen vary from country to country, the time to think about how to terminate an agreement is before it is made. While most countries have no special laws that penalize or preclude the termination of an agreement between the manufacturer and middlemen, some do. In Venezuela, for example, unjustly discharged agents may be entitled to the same severance benefits as discharged employees. In other countries, laws specify high termination compensation related to an agent's longevity, past earnings, goodwill, or "investment" in the product line. Countries having laws making it difficult to terminate agreements include Belgium, Costa Rica, the Netherlands, Norway, and Sweden. Evidently, before preparing a contract, management must consult local attorneys or local correspondents of international law firms.[37]

Information Sources

There are various sources that will provide information about channels of distribution. The U.S. Department of Commerce, banks, credit agencies, and American chambers of commerce in foreign cities are all good. If the names of other companies whose products are being handled by prospective channel members are known, these companies should be contacted. We will discuss the information sources at greater length in the chapter on exporting (Chapter 16).

Summary

International competition has intensified for two reasons: (1) new competitors and (2) markets that have grown more slowly than anticipated or that have contracted. A recent development in international competition has been the appearance of LDC-based firms in the markets of other developing nations and the heightening of competition from foreign companies that have moved into the Japanese and American markets. There has been growing concern about national competitiveness in the United States, Europe, and, as the yen appreciated to a new high, in Japan.

Data concerning (1) the marketing organizations and (2) the competitors' strengths and weaknesses will enable management to understand the competitive forces, a requisite for making sound investment decisions and formulating marketing strategies.

The channels of distribution are both a controllable and an uncontrollable variable. Managements are free to choose channels (controllable), but generally they must select channels from those that are available (uncontrollable). When the established channels or agencies do not fulfill the firm's requirements, it will occasionally create new ones.

The wholesaling and retailing structures vary with the stage of economic development. Generally, the less developed the country, the more numerous, the more specialized, and the smaller are the middlemen. There is a worldwide trend among the developed countries and the more advanced LDCs toward a concentration of wholesalers and retailers. In going up the scale from LDCs to the industrialized nations, one encounters more mass merchandising, more self-service, and larger retail units.

When selecting channels of distribution, management must consider the characteristics of the market, the product, the company, and the middlemen.

Questions

1. *Discuss the two reasons given in the text for the intensification of international competition.*
2. *a. What does national competitiveness mean?*
   b. How is it measured?
3. *Many people expected the U.S. trade deficit to drop rapidly with the decline in the value of the dollar. Why hasn't this happened?*

4. *Define counterfeiting in the sense used in the text. Why is counterfeiting a problem for the legitimate trademark owners?*
5. *Discuss the two major categories of data that are gathered for the competitive force analysis.*
6. *Name the sources from which information for the competitive force analysis can be obtained.*
7. *Name the four requirements on which management will compare channel alternatives.*
8. *What are the four kinds of U.S.-based exporters that are available to firms that prefer to export indirectly?*
9. *Name and discuss the four basic types of overseas middlemen for companies that are exporting directly.*
10. *Why are so many small, independent wholesalers being forced out of business?*
11. *Describe the cycle through which a wholesaling structure passes when it goes from a few large wholesalers and returns to this same condition.*
12. *What are the characteristics of the retailing structure as you go up the scale from the LDCs to the developed nations?*
13. *Describe two relatively new retailing units that have appeared in foreign markets.*
14. *Discuss the five factors affecting the selection of middlemen.*
15. *What is a sogo shosha? Discuss the similarities and differences between the sogo shosha and the U.S. answer to it.*

Minicase

12-1 Aikens Malaysia and

the Parallel Importer*

Jim Hutton, managing director of Aikens Malaysia, is discussing the latest competitive threat with Irene Olson, the marketing manager.

Jim Hutton: So you say that product from the home plant in Cleveland is being imported and sold here in competition with our locally made product?

Irene Olson: That's right, Jim. There's a parallel importer that buys in the United States and ships the product here. I wonder how he can compete pricewise when he has to pay those transportation costs. In fact, he and his wholesalers are making more than our wholesalers because they sell to the public at a higher price. My wholesalers tell me that the Malaysians will pay more for the imported product. There isn't any difference in quality, is there, Jim?

*Based on "Parallel Imports Menace Companies in Malaysia," *Business Asia,* September 25, 1981, pp. 306–7.

Jim Hutton: No. On the contrary, we're following Cleveland specs to the letter. The people here can get the same high-quality product made locally, and they're supporting a local industry that hires 500 Malaysian workers. As to the costs, remember, Irene, that our production costs are higher here. Our plant is newer and is being depreciated rather heavily. Furthermore, our production runs are much smaller, and that also makes our costs higher. We just don't have the economies of scale that Cleveland has. The lower wages here just can't compensate for this big difference. There's another angle, though. What about the import duties on the Cleveland product?

Irene Olson: They're rather low, although they're higher than the duties on the raw materials we import.

Jim Hutton: But the difference in duties is not high enough to compensate for our higher production costs, right?

Irene Olson: That's about it, Jim. There's also another aspect to consider.

Jim Hutton: What's that?

Irene Olson: As you know, the Malaysian ringit fluctuates with respect to the dollar. My wholesalers tell me that the importer watches the fluctuations closely, and when the ringit is low, he places a large order. At times, he can gain as much as a 20 percent advantage. Jim, do we take advantage of these currency fluctuations when we buy imported raw materials?

Jim Hutton: We try to, but since we have to order them months in advance, we're not able to respond very quickly to changes in the currency values.

Irene Olson: You know, Jim, the importer has another advantage. He gets a free ride from our advertising. We do all the promoting, and he reaps the benefits. He doesn't need to advertise.

Jim Hutton: Irene, I've just thought of something. How does this guy get our American product in the first place?

Irene Olson: I understand that he just places orders with our export department in Cleveland.

Jim Hutton: Don't those people know what the final destination is?

Irene Olson: Sure they do. He has to tell them when he places the order. By U.S. law, the destination has to be on the U.S. invoice. Cleveland knows he is not an American distributor. In fact, he gets an extra 10 percent because he does buy for export. Cleveland figures that exports should not have to pay any part of the domestic marketing costs.

Jim Hutton: This is a tough one, Irene. I have an idea. Didn't we and not Cleveland register our trademark here in Malaysia?

Irene Olson: Yes, Aikens Malaysia is the owner of the trademark.

Jim Hutton: It seems to me, Irene, that there are a number of things we can do to reduce and possibly eliminate competition from this parallel importer. Will you draw up a plan for us?
Assume that you are Irene Olson. Draw up a plan for Jim Hutton.

Minicase

12-2 Reciprocal Market
Penetration*

Kenichi Ohmae of McKinsey & Co. (a U.S. multinational consulting firm) has put forward the concept of reciprocal market penetration. He calculates that in 1984 Japanese imports from the United States were $25.6 billion, while goods produced in Japan by American subsidiaries totaled $43.9 billion, making the total American penetration in the Japanese market $69.5 billion. In the same year, Americans purchased $56.8 billion of Japanese imports and another $12.8 billion in goods produced and sold in the United States by Japanese firms, for a total penetration of $69.6 billion. Ohmae believes that this reveals an overall parity that is more than a coincidence. Because Japan's population is about one half that of the United States, these figures also suggest that the Japanese spend twice as much per capita on American products as Americans spend on Japanese products.

The vice chairman of Mitsubishi Motors claims that "these figures reflect a fundamental structural difference in the way that the economies o' the U.S. and Japan have developed over the past several decades. For the most part, Japanese companies have stayed home and entered overseas markets through exports, while American companies were much more aggressive about setting up production in overseas markets. Quite a few major American companies have achieved prodigious successes in the Japanese market, but for obvious reasons they have not gone out of their way to tell the world about it."

1. The Mitusbishi executive states that Japan is moving in the right direction to change the mix of exports to the United States and the goods produced by Japanese subsidiaries in the United States. What is his basis for making this statement?

2. Assuming that Ohmae's figures are correct, what will be the impact on jobs, profits, and the economy as a whole in each country as the Japanese mix between exports to and production in the United States approaches the U.S. mix for its exports to and its production in Japan?

3. What does the concept of market penetration do to the U.S. argument that Japanese American trade greatly favors Japan?

Supplementary Readings

Assessing Your Worldwide Competitors. New York: Business International Corp., 1983.

Berney, Karen. "Competing in Japan." *Nation's Business*, October, 1986, pp. 28–30.

"Castle under Siege." *Forbes*, February 9, 1987, pp. 104–5.

*Source: "Toward a True Internationalism," *Speaking of Japan*, January 1987, p. 25.

Edfelt, Ralph. "The U.S. Business in International Competitiveness Perspective." *Issues in International Business*, Winter–Spring 1986, pp. 17–24.

"The Europeans Start to Play a Little Rough." *Business Week*, February 9, 1987, p. 47.

The Export Trading Company Act of 1982. Washington, D.C.: Chamber of Commerce of the United States of America, January 1983.

"Japanese Managers Alarmed in Land of the Rising Sun." *International Management*, December 1986, pp. 58–66.

"Japan's Comeback Plan." *Fortune*, September 29, 1986, pp. 136–42.

"Japan's Three-Tiered Distribution." *Industrial Distribution*, July 1986, pp. 53–57.

"Korea's Big Push Has Just Begun." *Fortune*, March 16, 1987, pp. 72–76.

Lenberg, R. A., and T. H. Becker. "A New International Marketing Era for the U.S. Small and Medium-Sized Business." Paper presented at Western Marketing Educator's Conference, Sacramento, California, April 21–23, 1983.

Mitsui Group: Yesterday, Today, and Tomorrow. Rev. ed. Tokyo: Mainichi Newspapers, 1982.

"Prying Japan's Import Doors Open Another Crack." *International Management*, April 1986, pp. 75–81.

"The Quest for the '88 Issue." *Newsweek*, January 19, 1987, pp. 14–16.

Scouton, William. "Export Trading Companies." *Business America* (Washington, D.C.: U.S. Department of Commerce), October 18, 1982, pp. 3–14.

"Surveying the United Kingdom's Distribution and Sales Channels." *Business America* (Washington, D.C.: U.S. Department of Commerce), December 3, 1979, pp. 12–14.

Takahashi, Senjuro. "Is the Distribution System a Trade Barrier?" *Economic Eye* (Tokyo), June 1983, pp.4–5.

Endnotes

1. "The Quest for the '88 Issue," *Newsweek*, January 19, 1987, pp. 14–16.
2. "Pechiney-Ugine: Merging to Gain Muscle," *Business Week*, January 8, 1972, p. 44.
3. "Saudi Chemicals Buildup Worries West European Firms," *C & EN*, February 4, 1985, pp. 14–18.
4. "Move Over," *Forbes*, April 12, 1982, p. 82.
5. "Rediscovering the Formula for Profits," *Business Week*, January 12, 1987, p. 72.
6. "U.S. Petrochemical Firms Face Big Threat" *The Wall Street Journal*, February 12, 1982, p. 48.
7. "The Europeans Start to Play a Little Rough," *Business Week*, February 9, 1987, p. 47.
8. "A Panel of European Business Executives Sees a Narrowing of Gap with U.S., Japan," *The Wall Street Journal*, June 26, 1985, p. 30.
9. We ask you to pardon the irony. From "The Mark Puts a Stranglehold on Exporters," *Business Week*, February 23, 1987, p. 60.
10. "The Rampaging Yen Is Leaving a Trail of Misery," *Business Week*, February 16, 1987, pp. 46–47.
11. "Japan: Adjusting to the High Yen," *Prospects*, Swiss Bank Corporation, 1986, p. 9; and "Dollar Signs," *The Wall Street Journal*, January 26, 1987, p. 1
12. "A Hefty 42% of Growth," *Brasil*, October 1986, pp. 34–37.

13. Ralph Edfelt, "U.S. Business in International Competitive Perspective," *Issues in International Business*, Winter–Spring, 1986, pp. 17–24.
14. "Facts and Comments, II," *Forbes*, February 9, 1987, p. 25.
15. "Seventeen Industrial Countries," *IMF Survey*, January 12, 1987, p. 7.
16. "America's Hidden Problem," *Business Week*, August 29, 1983, pp. 50–54.
17. "Dollar Signs," *The Wall Street Journal*, January 26, 1987, p. 1.
18. "How 3M Is Trying to Out-Japanese the Japanese," *Business Week*, August 26, 1985, p. 65.
19. Tom Peters, "Closed Minds Can't Open Markets," *U.S. News & World Report*, March 3, 1986, p. 59.
20. "Origin and Destination of Manufactured Exports," *World Development Report 1987* (Washington, D.C.: World Bank 1987), tables 10 and 14.
21. "Asian Companies Grab Bigger Slice of Mideast Markets," *Business Europe*, February 1981, p. 46.
22. "Latin Leader," *The Wall Street Journal*, October 16, 1981, p. 1.
23. "Fighting the Fakes from Taiwan," *Fortune*, May 30, 1983, pp. 114–16.
24. "The Counterfeit Trade," *Business Week*, December 16, 1985, p. 67.
25. "The Counterfeit Trade," *Business Week*, December 16, 1985, pp. 64–72.
26. "Company Lawyers," *Business International*, April 23, 1982, pp. 129–30.
27. "A Machine Toolmaker Defends Its Cutting Edge against Japan," *Business Week*, August 29, 1983, p. 40.
28. "Corporate Cloak and Dagger," *Time*, August 30, 1982, pp. 62–65.
29. "Austin Rover Link with Retailer to Break Open German Market," *Business Europe*, January 18, 1985, pp. 17–18.
30. Actually, major companies within the zaibatsu were split up and made independent organizations. The present Mitsui sogo shosha, Mitsui & Co., was started in 1947. See *Mitsui Group*, rev. ed. (Tokyo: Mainichi Newspapers, 1982), pp. 30–31.
31. *The Export Trading Company Act of 1982* (Washington, D.C.: Chamber of Commerce of the United States of America, January 1983).
32. "ETC Act Update '85," *Business International*, July 7, 1985, pp. 209–10.
33. "Here Come the New Yankee Traders," *Business Week*, May 30, 1983, p. 50.
34. "Mom-and-Pop Stores Lose Favor in Japan," *The Wall Street Journal*, March 16, 1987, p. 26.
35. *Planning for Distribution in Japan* (Tokyo: Jetro, 1982), p. 71.
36. W. J. Stanton, *Fundamentals of Marketing*, 7th ed. (New York: McGraw-Hill, 1984), pp. 382–83.
37. "What the Worst Laws Say," *Business International*, July 12, 1985, p. 218.

CHAPTER 13

ECONOMIC FORCES

Profound thoughts about economic forecasting:

*"F*orecasting is difficult, especially about the future."

Victor Borge

"Economic forecasters have successfully predicted 14 of the last 5 recessions."

Anonymous

Learning Objectives

After you study this chapter, you should know:

1. The purpose of an economic analysis.
2. The kinds of information that economic analyses provide.
3. The important economic and socioeconomic dimensions, their significance, and their relationship with one another.
4. The usefulness of national economic analyses.
5. What is meant by industry dimensions.
6. Where to go to obtain economic information.

Key Words and Concepts

GNP/capita
Income distribution
Disposable income
Discretionary income
Population density
Rural-to-urban shift
National economic plans
Indicative planning

Business Incident

Business Week reports that, "for guidance on economic trends abroad that affect their investments and profits, U.S. multinational corporations are turning increasingly to a handful of economic consulting specialists. Recent upheavals in world currency markets and new doubts about the strength of the economic recovery in Europe and Japan are spurring the movement. Already some 100 companies, including Campbell Soup, G. D. Searle, Union Carbide, and Shell Oil, are using the data-gathering and forecasting services of the builders of the few international econometric models." The same publication also stated that "two prominent model builders in the international field—Data Resources Inc. and Chase Econometrics Associates Inc.—are well known for their domestic econometric models. Now others are beginning to crowd into the global arena, including Forex Research and Economic Models Ltd., both of London, and the Organization for Economic Cooperation and Development, which has gone commercial with its statistical service."

These organizations offer economic data banks and forecast such variables as production, imports and exports, prices, wages, employment, capital flows, currency values, and interest rates for most countries in the industrialized world.

Reprinted from the April 26, 1976, issue of *Business Week* by special permission. ©1976 by McGraw-Hill, New York, NY 10020. All rights reserved.

*O*f all the uncontrollable forces with which businesses must contend, economic forces are undoubtedly the most significant. How the scarce resources of land, labor, and capital are being allocated to the production and distribution of goods and services and the manner in which they are consumed are of paramount importance to managers. To keep abreast of the latest developments and also to plan for the future, firms for many years have been assessing and forecasting the economic conditions at the local, state, and national levels.

The purpose of these analyses is, first, to appraise the overall outlook of the economy and then to assess the impact of economic changes on the firm. To appreciate the extent to which a change in just one factor of the economy can affect all the major functional areas of the firm, let us examine Figure 13–1.

A forecast of an increase in employment would cause most marketing managers to revise upward their sales forecasts, which, in turn, would require production managers to augment production. This might be accomplished by adding another work shift, but if the plant is already operating 24 hours a day, new machinery will be needed. Either situation will require additional workers and raw materials, which will result in an extra workload for the personnel and pur-

Figure 13-1

Impact of Economic Forecast on Firm's Functional Areas

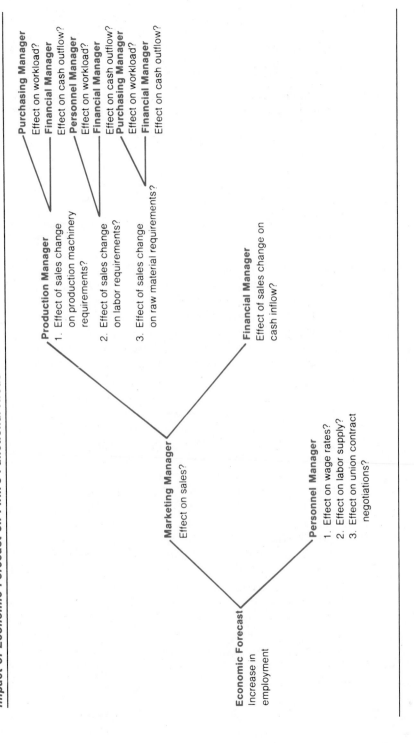

chasing managers. Should both the raw materials and labor markets be tight, the firm will probably have to pay prices and wage rates that are higher than normal. The financial manager may then have to negotiate with the banks for a loan to enable the firm to handle the greater cash outflow until additional revenue is received from increased sales.

Note that all of this occurs because of a change in only one factor. Actually, of course, many economic factors are involved and their relationships are complex. By means of an economic analysis, an attempt is made to isolate and assess the impact of those factors that are believed to affect the firm's operations.

International Economic Analyses

When the firm enters overseas markets, economic analyses become more complex because now managers must operate in two new environments, foreign and international. In the foreign environment, not only are there many economies instead of one, but they are also highly divergent. Because of these differences, policies designed for the economic conditions in one market may be totally unsuitable for the economic conditions in another market. Components of the international environment such as regional groupings (EC, EFTA) and supranational organizations (UN, IMF) can at one time or another have an effect on the firm, and consequently their actions must be monitored continually.[1]

International economic analyses should provide economic data on both actual and prospective markets. In addition, as part of the competitive forces assessment, many multinationals also monitor the economic conditions of nations where their major competitors are located, because changing conditions may strengthen or weaken their competitors' ability to compete in world markets.

Because of the importance of economic information to the control and planning functions at headquarters, the collection of data and the preparation of reports must be the responsibility of the home office. However, foreign-based personnel (subsidiaries and field representatives) will be expected to contribute heavily to studies concerning their markets. Data from areas where the firm has no local representation can usually be somewhat less detailed and are generally available in publications from national and international agencies.[2] An especially good source for economic information on a single country is the reports from central or international banks. A listing of these and other useful publications will be found in the Appendix.[3] Other possible sources are the American chambers of commerce located in most of the world's capitals, the commercial attachés in U.S. embassies, the United Nations, the World Bank, the International Monetary Fund, and the Organization for Economic Cooperation and Development.

Dimensions of the Economy

To estimate market potential as well as to provide input to the other functional areas of the firm, managers require data on the size and the rates of change of a number of economic and socioeconomic factors. For an area to be a potential market, it must have sufficient people with the means to buy a firm's products. Socioeconomic data provide information on the number of people, and the economic factors tell us if they have purchasing power.

Economic Dimensions

Among the more important economic dimensions are GNP, distribution of income, personal consumption expenditures, personal ownership of goods, private investment, and unit labor costs.

GNP. Gross national product, the total of all final goods and services produced, and gross domestic product (GNP less net foreign factor incomes) are the values used to measure an economy's size. GNPs range from nearly $4 trillion for the United States to $5 million for Tuvalu (South Pacific). What is the significance of GNP for the international businessperson? Is India with a GNP of $195 billion a more attractive market than Austria with only $69 billion? A comparison of gross national product does give some idea of the total economic size of markets, but to compare the purchasing power of nations, we need to know among how many people this total income is divided.

GNP/Capita. The not altogether satisfactory method of employing **GNP/capita** to compare purchasing power reveals that Austria is far ahead of India, with $9,150 versus $250. In other words, although India's pie is much larger, there are many more people to eat it. Figure 13–2 illustrates the relationship between population (area), /GNP/capita (height), and GNP (volume).

What can we learn from GNP/capita? As we saw in Chapter 3, we can generally assume that the higher its value, the more advanced is the economy. Exceptions to this generalization are the oil-producing nations, which, although they have high GNP/capita because of their large GNP and small populations, by no means possess advanced economies. Their high GNP growth rates do, nevertheless, mark them as fast-growing markets, for which managers are always searching. Frequently, given the choice between investing in a nation with a higher GNP/capita but a lower growth rate and a nation in which these conditions are reversed, management will choose the latter.

While differences in GNP/capita do tell us something about the relative wealth of a nation's inhabitants, this information is somewhat misleading because few of them have the equal share indicated by this average. This first crude estimate of purchasing power must be refined by incorporating data on how the national income is actually distributed.

Figure 13-2

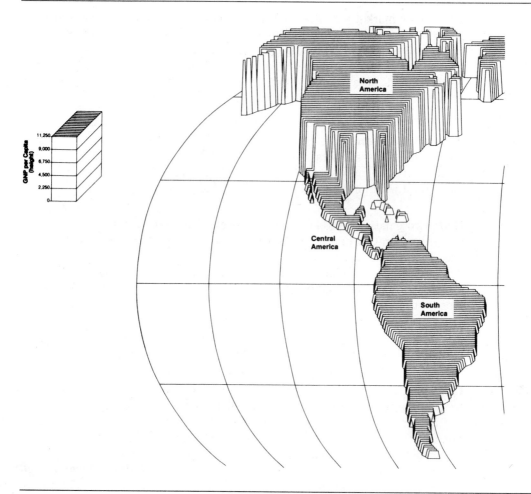

Note: Because of some unresolved methodological issues, the World Bank does not estimate the GNP per capita for nonmember nations with centrally planned economies.
Source: *1983 World Bank Atlas* (Washington, D.C.: World Bank, 1983).

Income Distribution. Data on **income distribution** are more difficult to obtain than data on GNP/capita, but studies can be found. The most comprehensive collection of income distribution studies (81 countries), *Size Distribution of Income*, is published by the World Bank. Unfortunately, not all of the studies used the same population unit, so for some countries cross-country comparisons are difficult.

Of the six population units employed, three seem most comparable. These are *households* (the most useful to market analysts), *economically active popu-*

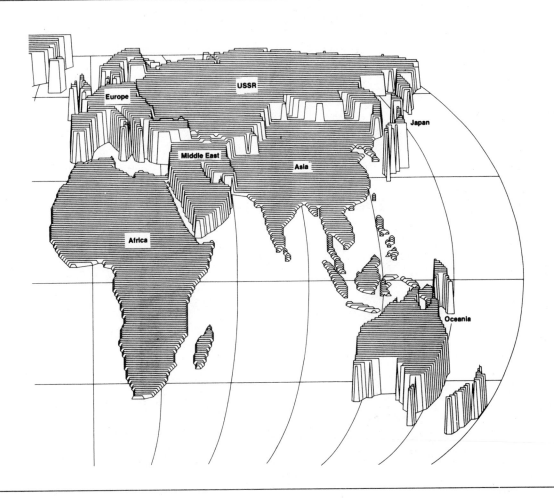

lation, and *income recipient.* Because for some nations, studies have been made based on *both* households and income recipients or households and economically active population, it is possible to calculate the variations in income distribution, which are apparently caused by the use of the different population units. Our comparisons of these studies rarely showed differences greater than 2 percent among the three population units. Inasmuch as there is no pattern to the differences, there is no way to adjust the data for the various population units. Results of the most recent studies based on the three population units we prefer are shown in Table 13–1.

Table 13-1

Income Distribution Estimates (percentage of national income received by population quintiles)

Country	Lowest 20 Percent	20–40 Percent	40–60 Percent	60–80 Percent	Highest 20 Percent
1. Argentina (70)(H)	4.4	9.7	14.1	21.5	50.3
2. Australia (75–76)(H)	5.4	10.0	15.0	22.5	47.1
3. Bahamas (70)(H)	3.4	8.8	14.3	22.9	50.6
4. Bangladesh (81–82)(H)	6.6	10.7	15.3	22.1	45.3
5. Barbados (69–70)(IR)	6.8	11.8	15.8	21.6	44.0
6. Belgium (78–79)(H)	7.9	13.7	18.6	23.8	36.0
7. Brazil (72)(H)	2.0	5.0	9.4	17.0	66.6
8. Canada (81)(H)	5.3	11.8	18.0	24.9	40.0
9. Chile (68)(H)	4.4	9.0	13.8	21.4	51.4
10. Colombia (70)(IR)	2.9	17.1	12.6	18.9	59.5
11. Costa Rica (71)(H)	3.3	8.7	13.3	19.9	54.8
12. Denmark (81)(H)	5.4	12.0	18.4	25.6	38.6
13. Ecuador (70)(EAP)	1.8	3.4	7.3	15.5	72.0
14. El Salvador (76–77)(H)	5.5	10.0	14.8	22.4	47.3
15. Egypt (74)(H)	5.8	10.7	14.7	20.8	48.0
16. Finland (81)(H)	6.3	12.1	18.4	25.5	37.6
17. France (75)(H)	5.3	11.1	16.0	21.8	45.8
18. Gabon (68)(IR)	3.2	5.3	8.8	15.2	67.5
19. Germany, East (70)(H)	10.4	15.9	19.6	23.4	30.7
20. Germany, West (78)(H)	7.9	12.5	17.0	23.1	39.5
21. Honduras (67)(H)	2.3	5.0	8.0	16.9	67.8
22. Hong Kong (80)(H)	5.4	10.8	15.2	21.6	47.0
23. Hungary (82)(H)	6.9	13.6	19.2	24.5	35.8
24. India (75–76)(H)	7.0	9.2	13.9	20.5	49.4

Table 13-1
(continued)

	Country	Lowest 20 Percent	20–40 Percent	40–60 Percent	60–80 Percent	Highest 20 Percent
25.	Indonesia (76)(H)	6.6	7.8	12.6	23.6	49.4
26.	Ireland (73)(H)	7.2	13.1	16.6	23.7	39.4
27.	Israel (79–80)(H)	6.0	12.0	17.7	24.4	39.9
28.	Italy (77)(H)	6.2	11.3	15.9	22.7	43.9
29.	Ivory Coast (85–86)(H)	2.4	6.2	10.9	19.1	61.4
30.	Jamaica (58)(H)	2.2	6.0	10.8	19.8	61.2
31.	Japan (79)(H)	8.7	13.2	17.5	23.1	37.5
32.	Kenya (76)(H)	2.6	6.3	11.5	19.2	60.4
33.	Korea (76)(H)	5.7	11.2	15.4	22.4	45.3
34.	Lebanon (55–60)(H)	5.1	7.2	10.8	17.5	59.4
35.	Malawi (67–68)(H)	10.4	11.1	13.1	14.8	50.6
36.	Malaysia (73)(H)	3.5	7.7	12.4	20.3	56.1
37.	Mauritius (80–81)(H)	4.0	7.5	11.0	17.0	60.5
38.	Mexico (77)(H)	2.9	7.0	12.0	20.4	57.7
39.	Nepal (76–77)(H)	4.6	8.0	11.7	16.5	59.2
40.	Netherlands (81)(H)	8.3	14.1	18.2	23.2	36.2
41.	New Zealand (81–82)(H)	5.1	10.8	16.2	23.2	44.7
42.	Norway (82)(H)	6.0	12.9	18.3	24.6	38.2
43.	Pakistan (70–71)(H)	8.4	12.2	16.0	21.9	41.5
44.	Panama (73)(H)	2.0	5.2	11.0	20.0	61.8
45.	Peru (72)(H)	1.9	5.1	11.0	21.0	61.0
46.	Philippines (85)(H)	5.2	8.9	13.2	20.2	52.5
47.	Portugal (73–74)(H)	5,2	10.0	14.4	21.3	49.1
48.	Sierra Leone (67–69)(H)	5.6	9.5	12.8	19.6	52.5

Table 13–1

(concluded)

Country	Lowest 20 Percent	20–40 Percent	40–60 Percent	60–80 Percent	Highest 20 Percent
49. Spain (80–81)(H)	6.9	12.5	17.3	23.2	40.0
50. Sri Lanka (80–81)(H)	5.8	10.1	14.1	20.3	49.8
51. Surinam (62)(H)	9.3	12.0	15.5	21.2	42.0
52. Sweden (81)(H)	7.4	13.1	16.8	21.0	41.7
53. Switzerland (78)(H)	6.6	13.5	18.5	23.4	38.0
54. Taiwan (72)(H)	8.8	13.5	17.5	23.0	37.2
55. Tanzania (69)(H)	5.8	10.2	13.9	19.7	50.4
56. Thailand (75–76)(H)	5.6	9.6	13.9	21.1	49.8
57. Trinidad and Tobago (75–76)(H)	4.2	9.1	13.9	22.8	50.0
58. Tunisia (70)(IR)	4.2	7.2	12.0	21.1	55.5
59. Turkey (73)(H)	3.5	8.0	12.5	19.5	56.5
60. United Kingdom (79)(H)	7.3	12.4	17.7	23.4	39.2
61. United States (80)(H)	5.3	11.9	17.9	25.0	39.9
62. Uruguay (67)(H)	4.4	9.8	15.2	23.1	47.5
63. Venezuela (70)(H)	3.0	7.3	12.9	22.8	54.0
64. Yugoslavia (78)(H)	6.6	12.1	18.7	23.9	38.7
65. Zambia (76)(H)	3.4	7.4	11.2	16.9	61.1
66. Zimbabwe (76)(H)	3.4	7.4	11.2	16.9	61.1

Notes:
1. Numbers in parentheses—year of study.
2. H—households—includes both single-person and multiperson households.
3. EAP—economically active population—refers to individuals who are able to work, both employed and unemployed. In developing countries EAP usually refers to males 15 years and older, whereas in developed nations EAP includes both males and females. Working ages differ among countries.
4. IR—income recipient—individuals who receive any kind of income, including social security and transfer incomes.

Sources: Shail Jain, "Size Distribution of Income" (Washington, D.C.: World Bank, 1975, and "Income Distribution," *World Development Report, 1987* (Washington, D.C.: World Bank, 1987), table 26, pp. 252–53.

In spite of the difficulties associated with income distribution studies, such as inconsistent measuring practices and wide variations in the representativeness of samples, the data provide some useful insights for businesspeople:

1. They confirm the belief that, generally, income is more evenly distributed in the advanced nations, although there are important variations among *both* developed and developing nations.

2. From comparisons over time (not shown), it appears that income redistribution proceeds very slowly, so that older data are still useful.

3. These same comparisons indicate that income inequality increases in the early stages of development, with a reversal of this tendency in the later stages. This is true for developed, developing, and socialist nations. The fact that the middle quintiles are growing at the expense of the top and bottom 20 percent signifies an increase in middle-income families, which are especially significant to marketers.

Contingent on the type of product and the total population, either situation (relatively even or uneven income distribution) may represent a viable market segment. For example, although Ecuador's total GNP is only $11 billion, the fact that 20 percent of the population receives 72 percent of the income indicates that there is a sizable group of people who are potential customers for low-volume, high-priced luxury items. On the other hand, it is apparent that the market is rather small (9.4 million population) for low-priced, high-volume goods. This simple calculation based on GNP, total population, and income distribution may be all that is required to indicate that a particular country is not a good market; however, if the results look promising, the analyst will proceed to gather data on personal consumption.

Personal Consumption. One area of interest to marketers is the manner in which consumers allocate their **disposable income** (after-tax personal income) between purchases of essential and nonessential goods. Manufacturers of a certain class of essentials—household durables, for instance—will want to know the amounts spent in that category, whereas producers of nonessentials will be interested in the magnitude of **discretionary income** (disposable income less essential purchases), for this is the money available to be spent on their products. Fortunately, disposable incomes and the amounts spent on essential purchases are available from the *UN Statistical Yearbook*, and discretionary income may be obtained by subtracting the total of these items from disposable income. More detailed expenditure patterns can frequently be found in economic publications. Table 13–2, which reproduces data found in *Business International*, is an example.

Although not every type of expenditure is included in this study, the categories shown are of interest to many firms. Note the wide variation among nations at similar levels of development.

Table 13-2

Consumption Patterns for Selected Countries, 1983

Country	Private Consumption Expenditure/ Capita (US$)	Percentage of Private Consumption Expenditures		
		Food Beverages, and Tobacco	Clothing	Household Durables
United States	$9,906	15.3%	6.2%	5.8%
Switzerland	8,708	27.8	4.6	5.3
Norway	6,224	26.3	7.4	8.0
Japan	6,038	23.4	6.2	5.6
France	5,826	21.1	6.4	8.9
Sweden	5,759	24.5	7.1	6.5
Denmark	5,712	24.6	5.9	7.0
West Germany	5,698	24.6	8.5	10.7
Belgium	5,040	25.3	6.1	12.5
Netherlands	4,993	19.6	7.1	7.7
United Kingdom	4,666	25.6	6.6	2.3
Italy	3,825	30.0	8.2	6.7
Hong Kong	3,714	21.9	18.7	11.6
Venezuela	1,669	47.0	4.6	5.4
Mexico	1,556	36.1	11.4	12.9
South Korea	1,210	44.7	6.9	4.3
Colombia	972	36.7	5.9	5.3
Jamaica	609	46.6	3.2	5.9
Sri Lanka	273	58.6	6.1	3.7
India	174	60.9	9.0	4.3

Source: "Indicators of Market Size for 117 Countries," *Business International*, 1986.

World Development Indicators, the first of a new series of World Bank handbooks begun in 1978, publishes both private and public consumption growth rates from 1960 to the present.

Other indicators that add to our knowledge of personal consumption are those concerned with the ownership of goods. In addition, the per capita values for the consumption and production of strategic materials such as steel, cement, and energy serve as measures of a nation's affluence and level of development. As Table 13-3 illustrates, the more industrialized nations have considerably higher values for these indicators than do the LDCs.

Private Investment. The amount of private investment (the part of national income allocated to increasing a nation's productive capacity) is another factor that contributes to the analysis of market size and growth. New investment

Table 13-3

Per Capita Ownership or Consumption of Key Goods and Materials for Selected Countries, 1984

Country	Private Consumption Expenditure ($/capita)	Passenger Cars/000 Population*	Telephones/ Thousand Population†	TV Sets/ Thousand Population	Steel Consumed (kilos/ capita)	Percentage of U.S. Energy Consumption/ Capita*	Cement Production (metric tons/ thousand population)	Electricity (KWH/person)
Europe								
France	$5,826	377	542	315	276	41.5	414	5.5
West Germany	5,698	402	509	362	489	60.5	469	6.4
Italy	3,825	360	385	240	359	32.4	665	3.1
Sweden	5,759	362	859	390	441	50.5	285	14.1
Switzerland	8,708	388	762	331	352	39.3	634	7.3
United Kingdom	4,666	294	513	335	256	50.3	239	0.5
Middle East								
Egypt	n.a.	9	12	84	43	6.2	100	n.a.
Israel	3,372	141	354	144	201	26.0	449	3.0
Kuwait	n.a.	306	152	341	627	58.3	n.a.	1.2
Saudi Arabia	n.a.	116	131	225	752	40.2	n.a.	n.a.
Africa								
Ethopia	109	1	3	1	n.a.	0.2	n.a.	<0.1
Kenya	190	7	12	4	11	1.0	58	0.1
Mauritius	900	29	n.a.	88	n.a.	3.0	n.a.	0.4
South Africa	1,210	88	116	64	175	33.7	248	3.3*
Asia								
India	174	1	5	3	18	2.5	39	0.2
Japan	6,038	221	530	253	622	36.6	660	4.9
Pakistan	250	4	5	10	17	2.5	46	0.2
Philippines	444	7	13	18	32	3.3	77	0.3

Table 13-3
(concluded)

Country	Private Consumption Expenditure ($/capita)	Passenger Cars/000 Population*	Telephones/ Thousand Population†	TV Sets/ Thousand Population	Steel Consumed (kilos/ capita)	Percentage of U.S. Energy Consumption/ Capita*	Cement Production (metric tons/ thousand population)	Electricity (KWH/person)
South America								
Argentina	1,771	120	96	208	107	20.0	185	1.4
Brazil	388	72	73	172	76	7.0	145	n.a.
Chile	1,151	42	53	222	50	9.8	109	1.1
Eastern Europe								
Romania	1,230	11	90	170	501	47.9	568	3.1
East Germany	n.a.	171	200	357	500	77.7	692	6.6
Poland	n.a.	87	101	232	416	47.2	451	3.7
Soviet Union	n.a.	40	88	291	576	63.5	473	5.4
Yugoslavia	n.a.	122	112	202	232	23.6	405	3.2
North America								
Canada	7,388	431	555	537	529	100.0	334	16.1
Mexico	1,556	62	79	97	92	18.5	235	1.0
United States	9,907	535	695	599	479	100.0	298	10.3

*1983.
†1982.
n.a.—not available.
Source: "Indicators of Market Size for 117 Countries," *Business International*, 1986.

From *The Wall Street Journal,* with permission of Cartoon Features Syndicate.

"Here's a leading economic indication—my wallet is empty!"

brings about increases in GNP and the level of employment, which are signals to the analyst of a growing market. A history of continual investment growth signifies, furthermore, that a propitious investment climate exists; that is, there are numerous profitable investment opportunities and the government enjoys the confidence of the business community. Table 13-4 shows that there are wide variations among nations.

Unit Labor Costs. One factor that contributes to a favorable investment opportunity is the ability to obtain unit labor costs (total direct labor costs/units produced) lower than those currently available to the firm. Foreign trends in these costs are closely monitored because each country experiences a different rate of increase.

Countries with slower-rising unit labor costs attract management's attention for two reasons. First, they are investment prospects for companies striving to lower production costs, as discussed in Chapter 2, and second, they may become sources of new competition in world markets if other firms in the same industry are already located there.

Relative changes in wage rates may also cause the multinational firm that obtains products or components from a number of subsidiaries to change its sources of supply.

Table 13-4

Average Annual Growth Rate of Consumption and Investment for Selected Countries (percent)

Country	Public Consumption		Private Consumption		Gross Domestic Investment	
	1965–1980	1980–1985	1965–1980	1980–1985	1965–1980	1980–1985
Low-income countries						
Ethopia	6.4	5.8	3.6	1.0	−0.6	1.6
Burundi	7.3	1.9	3.9	1.4	9.0	5.6
India	6.3	10.7	3.1	4.4	4.8	4.6
Central African Republic	−1.1	−4.6	4.2	−0.7	−5.4	14.3
Lower-middle-income countries						
Zambia	3.4	4.2	3.1	1.9	6.4	−20.0
Indonesia	11.4	5.2	6.3	5.9	16.1	5.6
El Salvador	7.0	0.6	4.1	−2.3	6.6	−2.1
Paraguay	5.1	7.1	6.3	3.1	13.5	−8.8
Upper-middle-income countries						
Korea	6.7	3.4	7.9	5.5	16.5	9.6
Israel	6.5	0,2	9.1	2.2	10.2	−5.5
Mexico	8.5	3.3	5.9	0.1	8.5	−9.1
Singapore	10.1	9.4	7.8	4.5	13.9	7.4
Industrial market economies						
Spain	5.0	4.0	4.9	0.3	4.0	−2.6
Japan	5.1	2.8	6.1	3.0	6.7	2.4
United States	1.9	4.2	3.5	3.0	1.8	5.2
Switzerland	2.7	2.3	2.6	1.1	0.8	0.9

Source: Adapted from *World Development Report, 1987* (Washington, D.C.: World Bank, 1987, pp. 208-9.

General Motors, noting that costs were climbing in Germany, switched the source of supply of Opels sold in the United States to Japan in order to take advantage of the relatively lower Japanese costs. Rollei, a German camera manufacturer, moved part of its production to Singapore for the same reason.

What are the reasons for the relative changes in labor costs? Three factors are responsible: (1) compensation, (2) productivity, and (3) exchange rates. Hourly compensation tends to vary more widely than wages because of the appreciable differences in the size of fringe benefits. Unit labor costs will not rise in unison with compensation rates if the gains in productivity outstrip the increases in hourly compensation. In fact, if productivity increases fast enough, the unit costs of labor will decrease even though the firm is required to pay more to the workers.

Table 13–5 illustrates the rapidity with which labor compensation costs change. In 1975, five nations had higher average hourly rates when expressed in dollars than did the United States. This number had increased to seven by 1980, but then dropped to zero in 1982. The United States had the highest hourly rate until 1986, when it was surpassed by Switzerland, West Germany, and Norway. Note that in 1987 the dollar bought fewer units of all currencies and, as you would expect, the average labor cost expressed in dollars increased in all countries. However, the dollar cost did not increase at the same rate as the exchange rate did. Why? It is because an increase expressed in dollars may be due to one or both of the following: (1) a real increase in labor costs and (2) an appreciation of the local currency with respect to the dollar.

For example, the German average hourly rate in dollars rose from $13.17 to $16.74, a large 27.1 percent increase. But did that increase result from real wage gains, or did it occur because the conversion to dollars in 1987 was made with more expensive German marks? To find out:

1. Convert 1986 hourly rate to marks: $13.44 × 1.9916 = 26.767 marks.
2. Convert 1987 hourly rate to marks: $16.74 × 1.8075 = 30.258 marks.
3. Percentage increase in marks = 30.258/26.767 = 13.0 percent.
4. Therefore, (27.1 − 13.0)/27.1 = 52 percent of the apparent increase in hourly cost was due to a more expensive currency.[4]

Other Economic Dimensions

Only a few of the many economic indicators have been mentioned. Others that may be included in the analysis are the foreign trade balance, the degree of industrialization (sectoral breakdown of GNP), the availability of manpower, and the prices of competitive products, production inputs, and energy.[5] Which of the economic measurements the analyst chooses to consider will depend on the industry and on the purpose of the study. A preinvestment analysis will be much more detailed than one used for screening potential markets, and the require-

Table 13-5

Labor Compensation Rates, 1975-1987

	Average Hourly Rate Including Fringe Benefits (US $)				Relative Index (US = 100)		Average Annual Exchange Rates (Units Local Currency to $1)	
	1987	1986	1980	1975	1987	1986	1987*	1986
West Germany	16.74	13.44	12.33	6.35	124	103	1.8075	1.9916
Switzerland	16.63	13.37	11.04	6.24	123	102	1.4935	1.6647
Norway	16.17	13.17	11.68	6.60	120	101	6.6900	7.5284
Belgium	15.64	12.78	13.15	6.07	116	98	37.200	41.442
Sweden	14.72	12.23	12.51	6.78	109	93	6.2995	6.9143
Netherlands	14.65	11.99	12.06	6.60	108	92	2.0380	2.2502
Denmark	14.04	11.18	10.95	7.18	104	85	6.800	7.529
U.S.	13.52	13.09	9.80	6.33	100	100	—	—
Finland	12.96	10.57	8.27	4.63	96	81	4.3880	4.8986
Austria	12.88	10.30	8.56	4.70	95	79	12.680	14.030
Italy	12.52	10.27	8.00	4.65	93	78	1308.000	1381.80
France	12.40	10.45	9.12	4.33	92	80	6.0425	6.5428
Japan	11.48	9.50	5.61	3.05	85	73	143.10	162.29
Ireland	9.09	7.80	5.88	3.27	67	60	0.6744	0.7322
G. Britain	8.96	7.46	7.38	3.01	66	57	0.6088	0.6960
Spain	7.79	6.35	5.96	2.55	58	49	125.90	134.74
Greece	4.86	4.19	3.73	1.40	36	32	134.75	140.31
Portugal	2.45	2.04	2.06	1.58	18	16	140.20	146.89
Korea	1.80	1.55	1.11	0.37	13	12	845.50	864.49

*1987 rates are as of June 3, 1987.

Source: *Business Europe*, January 28, 1983, p. 26, and June 15, 1987, p. 2.
Dollar Conversions are at average annual exchange rates for 1975, 1980, and 1986, and at current rates (June 3, 1987) for 1987.

ments of a petrochemical manufacturer (industrial products) will differ from those of a food canner (consumer goods). In any event, the analyst will seek data in foreign markets for the same variables that have proven to be related to domestic sales.

Socioeconomic Dimensions

A complete definition of market potential must also include detailed information about the population's physical attributes as measured by the socioeconomic dimensions. Just as we began with GNP in the study of purchasing power, we shall begin this section with an analysis of the total population.

Total Population. Total population, the most general indicator of potential market size, is the first characteristic of the population that the analysts will examine. They readily discover that there are immense differences in population sizes, which range from a billion inhabitants in China to less than 1 million each for 34 countries. The fact that many developed nations have less than 10 million inhabitants makes it apparent that population size alone is a poor indicator of economic strength and market potential. Switzerland, for example, with only 6.4 million people, is far more important economically than Bangladesh, with 101 million. Clearly, more information is needed; only for a few low-priced, mass-consumed products such as soft drinks, cigarettes, and soap does population size alone provide an accurate basis for estimating consumption.

For products not in this category, large populations and populations that are increasing rapidly may not signify an immediate enlargement of the market, but if incomes grow over time, eventually at least a part of the population will become customers. Insight into the rapidity with which this is occurring may be obtained by comparing population and GNP growth rates (Table 2–10 in Chapter 2). Where GNP increases faster than the population, there is probably an expanding market, whereas the converse situation is not only an indication of possible market contraction but may even point out a country as a potential area of political unrest. This possibility is strengthened if an analysis of the educational system discloses an accruement of technical and university graduates. These groups expect to be employed as and receive the wages of professionals, and when sufficient new jobs are not being created to absorb them, the government can be in serious trouble. Various developing nations already face this difficulty: Egypt and India are two notable examples.[6]

Age Distribution. Because few products are purchased by everyone, marketers must identify the segments of the population that are more apt to buy their goods. For some firms, age is a salient determinant of market size, but unfortunately the distribution of age groups within populations varies widely. Generally, because of higher birth and fertility rates, the developing countries have a more youthful population than the industrial countries. Figure 13–3 illustrates the tremendous

Figure 13–3

Population by Age and Sex—1975 and 2000 (millions)

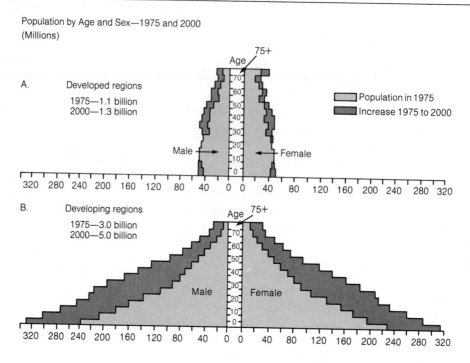

Population by Age and Sex—1975 and 2000 (Millions)

A. Developed regions
1975—1.1 billion
2000—1.3 billion

B. Developing regions
1975—3.0 billion
2000—5.0 billion

Population in 1975
Increase 1975 to 2000

Source: Morgan Guaranty Survey, December 1982, p. 12; based on information from U.S. Bureau of the Census.

difference in population growth between the developed and developing countries.

This situation is far from being static, however, as decreasing birthrates are becoming a worldwide phenomenon. Of the 128 countries listed in *World Development Report*, only 16 experienced increases in their crude birthrates over the period 1965–85. One of these was in the communist bloc (Soviet Union); six were classified as middle-income nations; and the rest were low-income nations.[7]

Many forces are responsible for reductions in birthrates. Governments are supporting family planning programs, to be sure, but there is ample evidence that improved levels in health and education along with an enhanced status for women, a more even distribution of income, and a greater degree of urbanization are all acting to reduce the traditional family size.[8]

While this is welcomed by governments in developing nations, the declining birthrate is causing concern in the governments of the industrialized countries. In Europe, for example, governments are preparing to lay off thousands of high school teachers, cut university subsidies, and extend the period that draftees serve in the NATO and Warsaw Pact armed forces. By the year 2000, when there will be fewer working taxpayers, they expect serious labor shortages and greatly increased retirement and medical costs.

In contrast to LDC governments that are offering incentives to lower birthrates, European governments are searching for ways to increase birthrates. In East Germany, for example, interest-free loans are given to young parents and part of the debt is forgiven each time they have a baby. In France, all parents receive substantial payments and services to help with child rearing. Despite these efforts, the birthrate continues to fall. No one knows why, though many argue that a change in lifestyle is responsible. Many young women want careers to give them a better level of living. They perceive children as an expense rather than as an investment for support in old age.[9]

Company presidents in the developed nations are fearful that the discrepancy between developed and developing nations in the aging rate of the labor force will put their companies at a competitive disadvantage. Morale among younger workers in the developed countries may fall because the slowing of turnover in the higher-paying jobs requiring years of experience will keep them from advancing in their careers.

Also, their hospitalization costs for firms in the developed countries will be higher than those for firms in the LDCs and NICs because of a greater proportion of older workers. Similarly, pension costs are increasing because more employees live to full retirement age and then live longer after retirement. For example, the dependency ratio (workers to pensioners) of General Motors–U.S. fell from 10 to 1 in 1967 to less than 4 to 1 by 1984. *Fortune* economists predict that by the year 2000 the dependency ratio will be 2.78 to 1 for West German companies and 3.33 to 1 for Japanese companies. They expect the U.S. ratio to be 4.17 to 1, which they feel will enhance this country's competitive advantage.[10]

Population Density and Distribution. Other aspects of population that concern management are **population density** and **population distribution.** Densely populated countries tend to make product distribution and communications simpler and less costly, and thus one might expect Pakistan with 120 inhabitants per square kilometer to be an easier market to service than Canada (2.5/square kilometer) or Brazil (15.9/square kilometer). This expectation, though, is another of those that are based on an arithmetic mean. We must learn how these populations are distributed.

One needs only to compare the urban percentages of total population to learn that Canada and Brazil possess population concentrations that facilitate the marketing process. While only 29 percent of Pakistan's population is urban, the percentages for Brazil and Canada are 73 and 77 percent, respectively. The physical forces, as we saw in Chapter 7, contribute heavily to the formation of these concentrations.[11]

An important phenomenon that is changing the population distribution is the **rural-to-urban shift,** which is occurring everywhere, especially in develop-

Figure 13-4

Population by Age **(as a percentage of total population)**

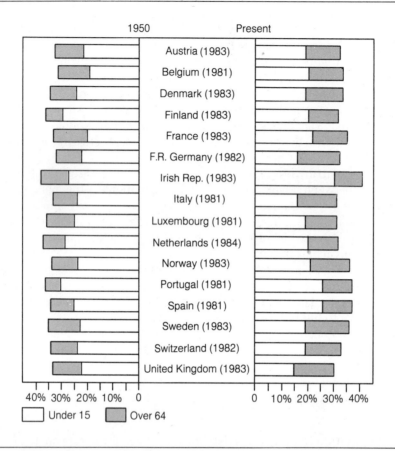

Sources: *Barclays Review,* Barclays Bank, Ltd., November 1978, p. 80; and *Demographic Yearbook, 1984,* (New York: United Nations, 1986), table 7, pp. 188–256.

ing countries, as people move to cities in search of higher wages and more conveniences. This shift is significant to marketers because city dwellers, being less self-sufficient than persons living in rural areas, must enter the market economy. City governments also become customers for equipment that will expand municipal services to handle the population influx.

An indicator of the extent of this movement is the change in the percentages of urban population. As Table 13–6 indicates, the greatest urban shifts are occurring in the low- and middle-income countries. With the exception of Egypt and the Netherlands, in no country anywhere is there a net flow in the other direction. As you would expect, the percentage of the labor force in agriculture is also decreasing.

The Most Populous Cities in the Year 2000 (millions)

1975

1.	New York–Northeastern New Jersey	19.8
2.	Tokyo - Yokohama	17.7
3.	Mexico City	11.9
4.	Shanghai	11.6
5.	Los Angeles–Long Beach	10.8
6.	São Paulo	10.7
7.	London	10.4
8.	Greater Bombay	9.3
9.	Rhine - Ruhr	9.3
10.	Paris	9.2

2000

1.	Mexico City	31.0
2.	São Paulo	25.8
3.	Tokyo - Yokohama	24.2
4.	New York–Northeastern New Jersey	22.8
5.	Shanghai	22.7
6.	Beijing	19.9
7.	Rio de Janeiro	19.0
8.	Greater Bombay	17.1
9.	Calcutta	16.7
10.	Djakarta	16.6

Note that six of the largest urban centers will be in Asia and that none will be in Europe.

Table 13–6

Rural-to-Urban Shift

	Percentages of Population in Urban Areas		Percentage Increase	Percentage of Labor Force in Agriculture		Percentage Increase
	1965	1985		1965	1980	
Low-income countries	17	22	29	77	72	−6.0
Middle-income countries	37	48	30	56	43	−23.0
Industrialized countries	70	75	7	14	7	−50.0
Centrally planned economies	52	65	25	34	22	−35.0

Source: *World Development Report, 1987* (Washington, D.C.: World Bank, 1987), pp. 264–65, 266–67.

Other Socioeconomic Dimensions

There are other socioeconomic dimensions that can provide useful information to management. The increase in the number of working women, for example, is highly significant to marketers since it may result in larger family incomes, a greater market for convenience goods, and a need to alter the promotional mix. Personnel managers are interested in this increase because it results in a larger labor supply. It also signifies that changes may be required in production processes, employee facilities, and personnel management policies.

Data on the country's divorce rate, when available, will alert the marketer to the formation of single-parent families and single-person households, whose product needs and buying habits differ in many respects from those of a two-parent family. In many countries, there are important ethnic groups that require special consideration by both marketing and personnel managers.

> The importance of the Chinese and Indian populations in Malaysia is emphasized by the fact that the Malaysian government has gone so far as to lay down specific targets for Malay representation in employment and ownership of business to enable the Malays to catch up with these groups. In Quebec, numerous policies have been adopted to "Frenchify" business.[12]

Which of these and other socioeconomic indicators are actually used will depend on a number of factors, such as the type of product, the target market, and the marketing strategy.

National Economic Plans

One other source of economic data that may prove useful to the firm, especially for its marketers, is the **national economic plans** that many countries publish. These range from the annual and five-year plans used as production control instruments by the communist countries to the "indicative" plans of some free market economies.

Prior to 1981, the five-year plans of the communist countries, with the exception of Yugoslavia, attempted to control all economic activity, including target quantities for domestic production, importation, and exportation. These were, in effect, marketing plans, and they were used as such by firms doing business with the Eastern-bloc nations. If the plans did not include the suppliers' products, the chances for their sale during the period were generally slim.[13]

The 1981–85 plans, however, introduced a change in the planning concept. Because of the widespread failure to meet the goals of the previous five-year plans, a number of communist-bloc nations have taken a more flexible approach. They now look at the five-year plan as a long-term target that does not have to be attained by means of five one-year increments, as was the case previously. Moreover, the plans are no longer considered fixed and unchangeable.[14]

Does this mean that they are now of no use to Western suppliers? Not at all. The plans and the speeches that accompany them continue to be useful guides for indicating East European priorities and trends. For example, a high target rate for a sector is evidence that a high priority has been placed on it. This means that it will now receive a greater part of the nation's resources, which should result in greater sales opportunities for the sector's suppliers.[15]

Planning as done by the Eastern-bloc nations, especially the German Democratic Republic, Hungary, and Czechoslovakia, is approaching the indicative planning of Western and Third World countries. Instead of setting production goals that are then passed down as orders to production units, under **indicative planning** the government merely establishes basic targets. It then attempts by means of the usual fiscal and monetary tools to create favorable conditions for business so that the targets may be attained. Although indicative plans do not have the same force as the five-year plans of the communist bloc, they do disclose the sectors favored by the government. This favoritism may be manifested in many ways, among which are special tax concessions to investors and foreign exchange allocations (when controlled) to purchase imported capital equipment and raw materials. The case at the end of this chapter describes Pakistan's sixth five-year plan in considerable detail.

Information about national development plans is regularly reported in such publications as *Business International* and *Business America*. Commercial attachés in American embassies and the overseas American chambers of commerce are sources of additional information.

Industry Dimensions

Every firm is concerned about the general economic news because of its impact on consumer purchases, prices of raw materials, and investment decisions, but certain factors are more significant than others to a given industry or to a specific functional area. The size and growth trend of the number of automobiles in a market, for example, is of paramount importance to a battery manufacturer but would be of no interest to a producer of toys. Neither would the quantity of machine operators graduated by technical schools be useful to financial managers, although such data are vital for personnel departments of manufacturing plants. The industry section of the economic analysis will contain information not only about competing firms but also about industries that are either suppliers of inputs or purchasers of the company's products.

In the larger multinationals, staff economists generally do their own industry research, which is supplemented by studies purchased from independent research organizations such as Fantus (New York) or the Economist Intelligence Unit (London) and studies that are published by government agencies, trade associations, chambers of commerce, and business publications. The firm that is too small to employ in-house economists can obtain expert assistance from outside consultants, many of whom are professors of international business in nearby colleges and universities. The names of private consulting firms can be obtained from the district offices of the U.S. Department of Commerce.

Another good source of both economic and financial information is the international departments of most banks, many of which publish reports and forecasts. *International Finance* (Chase Manhattan Bank) and the *Foreign Exchange Review* (Manufacturer's Hanover Trust) are excellent newsletters containing data on inflation, exchange and interest rates, trade balances, and various economic indicators. Additional publications (many are free) are listed in the Appendix.

Summary

To keep abreast of the latest economic developments and also to plan for the future, firms regularly assess and forecast economic conditions at the local, state, and national levels. When they enter international operations, the economic analysis increases in complexity because managers are operating in two new environments, foreign and international. There are more economies to study, and these economies are frequently highly divergent.

The various functions of the firm require data on the size and rates of change of a number of economic and socioeconomic factors. Among the most important economic dimensions are GNP, GNP/capita, distribution of income, personal consumption expenditures, private investment, and unit labor costs. The principal socioeconomic dimensions are total population, age distribution, population density, and population distribution.

Considerable information is available from publications put out by supranational agencies, governments, and banks and from business publications. National economic plans, for which no American counterpart exists, provide an insight as to government expectations. In the communist countries, national plans are often the equivalent of market studies. There is a tendency on the part of some communist governments to take a more flexible approach in their planning, however.

Questions

1. *Explain the difference between indicative planning and the planning done by Eastern-bloc nations.*
2. *Management learns from the economic analysis of Country A that wage rates will increase by 10 percent next year. Which functional areas of the firm might be concerned?*
3. *Use sources in the library to learn which country with over 1 million population in each continent is the leader in the rate of GNP/capita growth over*

the last 10 to 15 years. In each case, is the rate of increase greater than the rate of population growth?

4. What common problem does the use of GNP/capita and population density values present?

5. Why is management interested in the amount and trend of unit labor costs in other countries?

6. According to the table for income distribution (Table 13–1), which six nations, although relatively poor (GNP/capita of $1,200 or less), might constitute viable markets for high-priced luxury goods because of the highly skewed distribution of income? What is the approximate population of this segment? How can you use this information?

7. Declining birthrates appear to be a worldwide phenomenon. Why are they falling?

8. In 1987 and 1986, West Germany and Switzerland had the highest average hourly compensation rates.
   a. What was the percentage increase in dollars for each?
   b. What was the percentage increase in the labor cost of each country when stated in that country's currency?
   c. What percentage of the change in the hourly rate of each country when stated in dollars was due to changes in the franc-dollar and mark-dollar exchange rates?

9. Name the five lower-middle-income countries classified by the World Bank in the latest World Development Report that have experienced the greatest average annual growth rate in urban population (1980–85). Of what significance is this to the multinational marketing manager?

10. Choose a country and a product and estimate the market potential of the product based on the economic and socioeconomic dimensions. What other environmental forces should be investigated?

Minicase

13-1 From Turnaround to Takeoff—Pakistan's Sixth Five-Year Plan

Objective Realism: Deregulation, Economic Liberalization, and Social Justice in Pakistan's Sixth Five-Year Plan

Pakistan's economy has turned around in the past five years. Real growth averaged better than 6 percent despite the world recession. Exports pushed ahead an average 9.2 percent annually in real terms. Manufacturing expanded by 9 percent yearly, again in real terms. Agricultural production increased at a rate a full 50 percent above the rate of population increase, eliminating chronic food shortages. Inflation dropped from 16 percent to 5 percent. Public programs were consolidated, private enterprise encouraged.

This performance signals that Pakistan's economic viability is no longer in doubt. Indeed, if the targets of the nation's sixth five-year plan are met, the economy should enter the takeoff phase.

For most of its history, Pakistan has grappled with the problem of economic development. The results have been mixed. Although sustained, even dramatic, growth has been achieved in some periods, notably during the 1960s, there have also been periods when the momentum slackened, as in the early and mid-1970s. In retrospect, what clearly proved the most successful growth strategy turned on encouragement of private enterprise and improving the agricultural sector. Yet it must also be admitted that even at their apex Pakistan's past development efforts did not do enough to improve the conditions under which the majority of Pakistanis live; the benefits of the trickle-down effect remained weak indeed.

Pakistan's sixth five-year plan, formally presented last month, seeks to combine what generated economic growth in the past with programs addressing the long-neglected problem of social justice and the equitable distribution of the benefits of growth. "The plan," observes Planning Minister Dr. Mahbub-ul-Haq, "is a pragmatic response to the objective realities facing Pakistan today."

"The main aim of the sixth plan," Finance Minister Ghulam Ishaq Khan said in his June budget address, "is to consolidate and institutionalize growth in the economy and to use the potential generated by this growth for the purpose of improving income and employment levels and for providing basic amenities of life to the people."

The sixth plan is based squarely on the achievements of Pakistan's recently completed fifth plan. Adopted in mid-1978, the fifth plan attempted to correct distortions that had entered the structure of the economy during the 1970s.

In contrast to most development plans, therefore, the dominant thrust was less expansion than consolidation. The plan's primary objectives were to trim down the portfolio of public sector development projects, which had expanded beyond Pakistan's resources, and to stimulate growth on a rational basis.

The plan largely succeeded in achieving these objectives. For example:

Ninety percent of the plan targets were achieved. Most of the ongoing development projects were completed.

A start was made on correcting regional economic imbalances, with a manifold increase in development expenditures for the most backward areas.

Despite the world recession, there was a consistent 6 percent rise in real GDP. Exports gained an average 9.2 percent. The overall inflation rate was cut from 16 percent to 5 percent.

The manufacturing sector won a 9 percent average increase, with the government slowly liberalizing the economy. Agro-based industries were denationalized. Private-sector investment doubled, from Rs8.8 billion in 1977–78 to Rs19.5 billion in 1982–83.

The agricultural sector achieved a 4.4 percent average increase, as improved agricultural services, better credit facilities, and higher support prices brought a surge in agricultural output. For the first time ever, Pakistan was able not only to feed its own people but also to export wheat and rice.

The plan was less successful in meeting physical and social infrastructure needs. The world recession and high inflation eventually cut into the money available for development. Despite some significant gains (more villages were electrified in these 5 years than in the previous 30) social and physical infrastructure programs still tended to have the lowest priority and were the first to be cut as the investment shortfall materialized. Finally, in the plan's last year, the government recognized the danger and launched a crash program in these areas to give the next plan a head start on solving the country's persistent infrastructure problems and its rapidly worsening energy problems.

Taken as a whole, however, the fifth plan had two singular achievements. First, it reintroduced growth as a normal feature in Pakistan's economy. Second, it at least suggested that the economy had an underlying real growth rate—that given nominal stability and a reasonable business environment, Pakistan's economy ought to achieve a minimum 5 percent growth, year in, year out.

Pakistan's sixth plan aims at achieving a 6.5 percent average annual real GDP growth rate for 1983–88, a 4.9 percent average increase in the agrarian sector, a 9.3 percent average rise in manufacturing, and over the plan's five-year span, a 20 percent real gain in family income. Exports ought to double; imports will increase 76 percent. Three and a third million new jobs will be created.

Projecting a 6.5 percent annual inflation rate, the plan calls for public sector investment of Rs290 billion. This includes Rs116.5 billion for energy, Rs20.5 billion for industry, Rs15.3 billion for agriculture, Rs57.5 billion for transport and communications, Rs19.8 billion for education, and Rs13 billion for health. In addition, the plan projects private sector investment of Rs200 billion.

Human Resource Development

What sets the sixth plan apart from the rest of Pakistan's economic history is its intense concern for the equitable distribution of the benefits of the country's economic gains. Economic growth cannot be sustained, Dr. Haq stresses, "without human resource development."

Under the sixth plan, allocations for these areas will increase substantially—education and manpower training are up 255 percent over the fifth plan; health, 184 percent; population welfare programs, 283 percent; physical planning and housing, 72 percent. Taken together, this represents a dramatic shift in priorities. Almost 17 percent of total public sector expenditures are for human resource development in the sixth plan, as against 13 percent in the fifth plan.

The sixth plan's targets are just as ambitious. Literacy is to double, with the literacy rate increasing from 23.5 percent to 48 percent. Primary school enrollment is to rise 75 percent. For the rural population, access to clean water will expand from 22 percent to 45 percent and access to sewage facilities will climb from 4 percent to 10 percent. By the end of the plan, 81 percent of the villages in Pakistan will be electrified.

Achieving these objectives will not be easy. The plan calls for a pragmatic approach. Education and training provide good examples. In areas where there are no primary schools and the number of students may be too few to justify a building, mosques are now being used. The basic school curriculum for the first years of primary school will be simplified to make it more relevant for village students. The government will upgrade secondary and vocational education, improving teacher training, facilities, and materials. There is to be a broad-based scholarship program to enable the economically disadvantaged to obtain an education. Higher education will be strengthened. There will be an emphasis on improving the quality of medical and professional training. Expenditures on science and technology under the plan will increase fourfold.

Literacy is essential to social modernization. Indeed, it is difficult to improve many aspects of the lives of the poor to enable them to take full advantage of the benefits of growth without an increase in literacy. Thus, the plan calls for a literacy campaign, targeting 5 million men and, significantly, 10 million women between the ages of 10 and 19. The plan also suggests several nonconventional approaches that have worked elsewhere around the world. These include giving academic credits or scholarships to college students to spread literacy and requiring employers to teach illiterate employees or be penalized.

Deregulation

The sixth plan cannot succeed without full private sector support. The scale of the plan's objectives requires a doubling of total private sector investment, in real terms, between now and 1987–88. The government recognizes this, and the plan calls for the "general advance of private entrepreneurship in all spheres of economic activity."

Under the fifth plan, the government made a start at improving public-private sector relations by beginning the process of deregulating the economy. As a result, private investment rose from 4.1 percent of GNP (at market prices) in 1977–78 to 4.9 percent in 1982–83, with expectations of further increases.

The sixth plan intends to go much further. It hopes to return private sector investment to the 8 percent GNP level last attained at the end of the third plan. At the same time, it calls for a substantial public sector "load shedding" in order to concentrate the government's financial resources on priority energy, infrastructure, and human resource development projects. Hence, the sixth plan aims at gradually reducing public sector involvement in industry, cutting the public sector's proportion of new investment from 47:53 in 1982–83 to 15:85 by 1987–88. Further denationalizations are possible. Some public sector corporations may allow private equity participation to raise additional capital. Many activities once reserved exclusively for the public sector—including highways, airlines, airports, electricity generation, schools, health clinics, oil and gas exploration, and minerals—are now to be opened up to direct or indirect private sector participation.

The sixth plan regards clearing away the tangle of bureaucratic controls choking the economy as a primary motive force behind increasing private sector investment, especially in industry, which contributes 17 percent of GDP and 65 percent of exports. Thus, the government intends to continue deregulation. "This has been an overregulated system," Dr. Haq comments, "and deregulation must be a phased process. But it will come."

Yet the plan also makes clear that in cutting out the red tape that has angered many businessmen in Pakistan for so long, the government seeks to create a more efficient, internationally competitive economy. "There will be no more room for tax breaks," the plan declares, "overprotected markets, and cheap access of scarce investable funds. Those who wish to live by the logic of the market must also be prepared to die by the same logic."

Replacing the old regulatory system will be a new, more realistic industrial policy. The government will issue an industrial investment schedule, specifying priority industries where investment can be made without limit and where no prior government approval is necessary. The government will also ensure that adequate foreign exchange is available for the private sector. Investors in priority industries will be able to obtain foreign exchange up to a liberal ceiling, as well as automatic approval for foreign equity participation, loans, and licensing agreements, under guidelines laid down in the schedule.

Foreign investment will be encouraged. The government has reaffirmed its no-nationalization guarantee and the free repatriation of profits and royalties. A number of double-taxation avoidance agreements have been negotiated. Foreign investors are generally permitted to structure their investments in Pakistan along whatever equity lines they wish. Export processing zones are being developed. Foreign portfolio investors will be allowed to finance private sector business ventures directly.

Agriculture

Pakistan is an agricultural nation. Agriculture contributes 29 percent of GDP and employs 55 percent of the work force. Although Pakistan's gains in manufacturing are—and will continue to be—impressive, its growth potential lies in agriculture.

The fifth plan put Pakistan back on the track toward fulfilling this potential. The aim of the sixth plan is to consolidate these gains and to move from agricultural self-sufficiency into exports. The plan will continue to increase agricultural inputs. Fertilizer consumption is to rise 46 percent. Improved seeds will become available under a World Bank–funded program. The number of farmers eligible for institutional credit will double. Farm mechanization will be encouraged with credit. Small tractors are now being introduced into Pakistan, and by 1987–88 the total number of farm tractors is expected to rise from 137,400 to 337,000.

Extension services will be modernized. New approaches will be taken. New types of experimental and demonstration farms will be established. The primary aim will be to help small- and medium-sized farmers improve their technological level.

The infrastructure of the agrarian sector will be significantly improved. The government will build more rural roads: during the fifth plan, 5,000 kilometers of village roads were constructed, bringing the total to approximately 46,000 kilometers. Under the present plan, 40,000 kilometers more are to be built and some 36,000 kilometers of canal roads, hitherto closed to the public, will be opened.

Similarly, irrigation will be upgraded. Pakistan has the world's most extensive irrigation system, covering 70 percent of all agriculture. This system, unfortunately, is old, poorly maintained, and inefficient. The government will improve technology and maintenance. It will remodel canals and drains and institute the command water management system.

Pakistan's government wants to introduce more high-value crops. Thus, in the sixth plan the emphasis will shift from staples (wheat and rice) to import substitution (oilseeds and protein-based crops). The plan will promote exports. Rice exports are expected to increase by 9 percent a year, while raw cotton is to increase 8.5 percent. Fish and fish preparations will gain 14 percent annually. There is a strong demand for high-value fruits and vegetables in the Middle East, which current production cannot meet.

Regional Development

As with many other developing countries, one of Pakistan's problems has been the uneven rate of growth between different parts of the country. Pakistan began to grapple seriously with the issue during the fifth plan, when the government launched an integrated approach to the problems of backwardness in Baluchistan—the largest province in area, the smallest in population, and the poorest by almost every known indicator. Under the fifth plan, development expenditures rose from Rs402m in 1977–78 to Rs650m in 1982–83. In addition, a special Rs19.5 billion aid package was put together for international funding.

The results were significant. There was a clear impact on the economy and the inhabitants of the province. In particular, farmers proved unexpectedly responsive to modern technology and market forces. Cereal production doubled; output of fruits and vegetables increased 21 percent. The province discovered a strong market in the Middle East. From being an economic nowhere in the 1970s, Baluchistan became Pakistan's new economic frontier—with 15 million acres of virgin soil, undiscovered natural resources, and a substantial flow of migrants seeking a better life. The sixth plan will carry further the province's transformation. With a basic allocation of Rs21.0 billion, the plan aims at pump-priming the provincial economy to stimulate self-sustaining growth of 10–12 percent a year.

The success of the fifth plan in Baluchistan has also led to expansion of regional development to other less developed parts of the nation during the sixth plan, The Frontier and Tribal areas, Azad Kashmir, and Pakistan's Northern Region have many geopolitical, historical, social, and economic similarities with Baluchistan. But in contrast to Baluchistan, these mountainous areas suffer from relative overpopulation and net outward migration. Under the sixth plan, development expenditures will triple in these areas to Rs9.3 billion, with the aim of creating the preconditions for sustained economic growth through improved agriculture and irrigation and through the construction of more roads to open difficult terrain and make natural resources accessible.

Energy

In the sixth plan, Pakistan begins to adjust to the world energy crisis. Until now, the emphasis has been mainly on funding balance-of-payments deficits and cushioning the blow of rising oil prices through direct and indirect subsidies. Even under the fifth plan, the energy development allocation totaled only Rs39 billion, with several key targets left unmet. Consequently, oil imports have continued to drain foreign exchange out of the economy, and, more recently, worsening power shortages have forced load shedding during peak periods. "We have lost valuable time," Dr. Haq admits. "It takes five or six years to build a new power station. Energy now is potentially a serious bottleneck to economic growth."

Thus, in the sixth plan energy holds a dominant position. The allocation for energy development is Rs116.5 billion—38.2 percent of public sector investment. A national energy program is aimed at meeting six basic objectives. First, and most immediate, this program seeks to alleviate present shortages and to expand capacity to accommodate Pakistan's anticipated growth needs over the next five years. Second, it will develop indigenous energy resources to help reduce oil imports. Third, it will provide for the country's long-term needs with a view to attaining energy self-reliance during the seventh plan. Fourth, it calls for increased private sector participation in energy development. Fifth, it will expand rural electrification. Sixth, it will work toward realistic energy prices.

More specifically, the energy program will increase power-generating capacity from 4,809 megawatts to 8,604 megawatts during the sixth-plan period. Shortages will persist until 1986 or 1987, when plants that began late in the previous plan come on-stream. But future energy requirements are anticipated, with work starting on power stations having a total generating capacity of 9,662 megawatts for completion during the seventh plan. These include the 900-megawatt Chashma-1 nuclear power project.

Pakistan's energy program also calls for expanding domestic oil production from 13,000 to 21,000 barrels a day and natural gas average daily consumption from 852 to 1,204 million cubic feet. Oil and gas exploration are to be opened to private sector participation. Overall public sector participation is targeted at Rs15 billion, while private sector participation is expected to provide another Rs15.7 billion. A hydrocracker plant and a new refinery are to be built. Both will be paid for by self-financing and commercial borrowings, not government grants.

The government seeks to increase Pakistan's coal production from the current 1.7 million tons a year to 2.6 million in 1987–88 and 5.4 million in 1988–89. Pakistan has 102 metric tons proven reserves of lignites and another 1,178 metric tons of subbituminous coal. In 1947, coal contributed 59.1 percent of total commercial energy requirements. It dropped in 1982–83, when it supplied only 5.1 percent. Rising output, along with increasing availability of nuclear and hydroelectric power, should begin at last to cut into oil imports during the next plan.

The human side of energy is not neglected: 20,000 villages will be electrified during the next five years. This will bring the number to approximately 36,400, or 81 percent of the villages in Pakistan. Particular attention will be given to clearing obstacles to the use of electricity in villages already connected to the grid so that more villagers can realize the benefits.

Feasibility

Pakistan's economy can enter its takeoff phase if the targets set in the sixth plan are achieved to any reasonable level of success. The level of success attained depends, in turn, on two other considerations—funding and implementation.

Funding is inherently problematic. The government of Pakistan does not have the full resources to carry out this plan. Indeed, the plan makes clear that there has to be, first and foremost, mobilization of the private sector on an unprecedented scale. Total private sector investment is put at Rs200 billion. The extent to which the private sector meets this challenge will depend largely on the ability of government to create a favorable investment climate through deregulation and the development of Pakistan's physical and social infrastructure. The funds are there.

A second necessity, that of financial support for the plan, is foreign resources—pegged at Rs135 billion ($10 billion). Of this sum, Rs98 billion ($7.3 billion) is likely to be gross foreign aid and the rest commercial borrowing, foreign equity, and private investment. Although Pakistan has been fortunate in the treatment it has received from international donors, the plan clearly seeks to reduce such dependence. As the finance minister, who also chairs the planning commission, explained in his budget speech: "The sixth plan will continue our gradual march toward national self-reliance." The financing of the plan through net external flows is projected to go down from 25 percent in 1982–83 to 19 percent in 1987–88.

Implementation

Pakistan's ability to implement the plan is more certain. Although the quality of the bureaucracy varies, the planning commission staff is sophisticated and perceives that the implementation process does have weaknesses. The plan makes allowances for operating problems and administrative lapses. Quips one foreign-trained official: "I'm a government planner. If I can't conceive of difficulties in the field, I'm a fool." Adds a colleague: "We have emphasized the areas of our basic strengths in the plan." Consequently, although some infrastructure bottlenecks, such as energy, could pose a potential problem for the plan's first few years, the production side should respond well, giving the economy the impetus needed for success.

1. What are the basic goals of Pakistan's sixth five-year plan?
2. a. What will be the government's stance toward private industry?
   b. Give some specific examples that led you to answer *2a* as you did.
3. a. Does the plan give any indication as to how the government regards foreign investment?
   b. What are the reasons for your answer?
4. a. International marketing managers and export managers frequently study national plans for sales opportunities. What kinds of firms should benefit from Pakistan's sixth five-year plan?
   b. What kinds of products will be imported?
5. What is the message that may bother companies, foreign and nationally owned, that are already in Pakistan?

Supplementary Readings

Adelman, I., and Cynthia Taft Morris. "An Anatomy of Income Distribution Patterns in Developing Nations." Economic Staff Working Paper no. 116, World Bank, September 23, 1971.

"Europe's Population Bomb." *Newsweek*, December 15, 1986, p. 2.

Heller, P. S., and R. Hemming. "Aging and Social Expenditures in Major Industrial Countries." *Finance & Development*, December 1986, pp. 18–21.

Indicators of Market Size for 117 Countries. New York: Business International, 1986.

Jain, Shail. *Size Distribution of Income.* Washington, D.C.: World Bank, 1975.

Simon, Julian. "Wealth in Numbers." *Development Forum,* (New York: UN Division for Economic and Social Information), July–August, 1986, p. 3.

World Development Report. Washington, D.C.: World Bank, 1987.

"The World Population Heading for 6 Billion." *Weekly Bulletin*. (Brussels: Kredietbank), May 2, 1986, p. 1.

Endnotes

1. Many of these factors, of course, also affect the domestic concern, but the international firm is generally more vulnerable and usually must react more quickly.
2. If management for some reason is already interested in a country as a possible site for investment, the same detailed information will be required as is required for an area where the firm is already involved.
3. An excellent bibliography, *International Bibliography, Information, Documentation* (IBID), is published quarterly by UNIPUB. Abstracts of publications and studies containing economic and demographic data are included.
4. You can make your own table for 34 countries by first getting the average hourly earnings in national currency from the U.S. Department of Labor, Bureau of Statistics, *Handbook of Labor Statistics*. However, the data in this publication lag considerably, so you then go to the latest issue of *International Financial Statistics*, published monthly by the IMF. Here, for each country listed in the *Handbook,* you can find a very recent index of average hourly costs. Multiplying a ratio of the IMF's index values by the latest value in national currency in the *Handbook,* you can derive more recent values in local currency. Then you go back to the IMF publication and select the average exchange rates for the years you are comparing and convert national currencies to dollars. You will find differences between *Business Europe's* figures and the results you obtain by this method. We're not sure why, but obviously *Business Europe* either used different exchange rates or obtained different values expressed in national currency (probably the exchange rates). This illustrates the problem in expressing any national statistic in dollars.
5. A prolonged, unfavorable trade balance could be the forerunner to increased government restrictions on imports, a negative signal to the firm contemplating exporting to that country. If investment is under consideration, this condition could indicate that local leaders would be highly receptive to the proposition and might even offer investment incentives.
6. Developed nations are not immune either. France, the Netherlands, and Belgium have recently been faced with this problem, and some people believe that the United States is heading in that direction (the Department of Education's cutback in grants to medical schools).
7. *World Development Report, 1986* (Washington, D.C.: World Bank, 1987), pp. 256–57.
8. Robert S. McNamara, *Addresses to the Massachusetts Institute of Technology* (Washington, D.C.: World Bank, April 28, 1979), p. 22.
9. "Europe's Population Bomb," *Newsweek*, December 15, 1986, p. 52.
10. "The Economies of the 1990's," *Fortune*, February 2, 1987, p. 24.
11. From "Urbanization," *World Development Report, 1987,* table 31, pp. 266–67.
12. D. L. Horowitz, "Ethnic Demands Abroad," *The Wall Street Journal*, December 18, 1978, p. 27.
13. In reality, the five-year plan is a budget, which in turn is equivalent to a market study for potential exporters to communist countries.
14. "Eastern European Plans: 1981–85 Targets to Be Sober and Flexible," *Business International*, June 26, 1981, pp. 202–3.
15. "Five Year Plans: Guide to EE Sales Strategy?" *Business Eastern Europe*, May 15, 1981, pp. 153–54.

SECTION IV

HOW MANAGEMENT DEALS WITH ENVIRONMENTAL FORCES

Section I introduced you to international business, trade, investment, and economic development. Section II presented the framework of international organizations and the monetary system within which international business functions. Section III discussed a number of the forces which affect international business and with which its management must cope.

Section IV will give you a number of the management responses and solutions to problems caused or magnified by the foreign and international environments. The reader should bear in mind that this book is intended to be only an introduction to international business. The student or businessperson who wishes to delve more deeply into specific areas should look to textbooks specializing in those areas. Fortunately, some business and law schools are offering more internationally oriented courses.

Chapters 14 and 15 deal with assessing and analyzing markets and with international marketing as it differs from domestic marketing. Chapter 16, on export practices and procedures, logically follows international marketing. Chapter 17 covers a unique sort of international trade, that between the communist and noncommunist worlds.

Chapters 18 through 22 present management solutions to or methods of dealing with the environmental forces discussed in Section III. Chapter 18 covers financial management, while Chapter 19 deals with production systems. Chapter 20 presents material on labor relations policies as they relate to nonexecutive, technical, or sales employees. Chapters 21 and 22 are intended to cap the solutions and methods material dealing with planning, organization, political risks, control, and executive personnel policies. The final chapter, Chapter 23, treats the multinational enterprise (MNE) as a distinct entity.

CHAPTER 14

MARKET ASSESSMENT AND ANALYSIS

"Gone are the days of foreign firms wandering into Tokyo expecting Japan to be just another market. A number of promising new opportunities have been seized by foreign-affiliated companies, but all of them have been preceded by intensive market research."

Japan Economic Journal, February 26, 1979, p. 14

Learning Objectives

After you study this chapter, you should know:

1. The market screening process.
2. Some of the sources for U.S. export data, information on political and legal barriers, and sociocultural information.
3. The use of *market indicators* and *market factors*.
4. What is meant by *estimation by analogy*.
5. Some of the problems that the researcher may encounter when conducting a market research study in a foreign market.
6. The meaning and purpose of a marketing information system.

Key Words and Concepts

Market factors
Market indicators
Market screening
Regression analysis
Trend analysis
Estimation by analogy
Marketing information system (MIS)

Business Incident

Business International reports that General Electric planners annually compile reports on approximately 20 key countries. These reports are distributed early in the year to the top 200 or so executives throughout the corporation. Besides containing detailed data on political, economic, and social factors for each country, they give an overview of all current GE activities in each country.

Business International also states, "To further assess foreign business opportunities in important developing countries, a 'flying squad' made up, for example, of the manager of international planning, a corporate planner, an international economist, and an international sales manager will periodically undertake opportunity studies on a targeted 'crash' basis. After thorough advance preparation, the squad conducts an investigation on site through extensive in-depth interviews with prominent local businessmen, law firms, accounting firms, bankers, other MNC local plant managers, government officials, and other principal local contacts."

Reprinted from page 351 of the November 4, 1977, issue of *Business International* with the permission of the publishers, Business International Corporation.

*T*he analysis and assessment of markets as made by General Electric is not—and should not be—undertaken only by the large MNEs. Because a viable market is the basis for every business, managements of all firms must (1) be certain that there is a market for their products or services, (2) estimate its potential, and (3) be apprised of its characteristics. Furthermore, because the return on investment occurs over a period of time, management should be confident that the market will continue to exist long enough for the investment to be fully recovered.

The kinds of data required to make sound decisions concerning foreign ventures are similar to those that the domestic firm uses. In most respects, the requirements for opening a new sales territory in Belgium are the same as the requirements for opening one in Illinois. Similarly, the criteria for building a plant in California will also govern the decision to build one in France. Thus, we see that the analysis and assessment of markets is essentially the same for both domestic and overseas markets. However, the presence of the foreign and international environments provides additional dimensions that increase the complexity of such analysis and assessment for overseas markets.

Market Analysis and Assessment—Where to Market

The analysis and assessment of foreign markets begins after management, for any of the reasons discussed in Chapter 2, has decided that an investment in those markets is warranted. More often than not, the motive for going abroad also dictates where the firm should go.

Suppose a manufacturer of glass jars that is the exclusive supplier of jars to a producer of baby foods in this country learns that its important customer is about to build a plant in Brazil. This firm knows that if it fails to follow its customer to Brazil with a production facility, its American competitor, which already has a plant there, will supply its customer's subsidiary. Once the competitor becomes a supplier even to just the subsidiary, a customer-supplier relationship begins that may eventually lead to business in the United States. To protect its American business, our firm must also build a Brazilian plant. In this case, the firm's management needs information only about Brazil.

There are two occasions, however, when a firm does require a broad study of world markets: (1) management of a firm selling exclusively in the domestic market believes that sales could be increased by expanding into overseas markets; and (2) a firm that is already a multinational wishes to monitor world markets systematically to be certain that changing conditions are not creating potential markets of which its management is unaware. Both situations require an inexpensive, relatively fast method of analyzing and assessing the more than 180 countries in order to pinpoint the most suitable prospects. One such method, in the opinion of many experienced managers, is market screening.

Market Screening

Market screening is a method of market analysis and assessment that permits management to identify a small number of desirable markets by eliminating those judged to be less attractive. This is accomplished by subjecting the countries to a series of screenings based on the environmental forces examined in Section III. Although these forces may be placed in any order, the arrangement suggested in Figure 14–1 is designed to progress from the least to the most difficult analysis based on the accessibility and subjectivity of the data. In this way, the least number of candidates is left for the final, most difficult screening.[1]

Figure 14-1
Selection of Foreign Markets

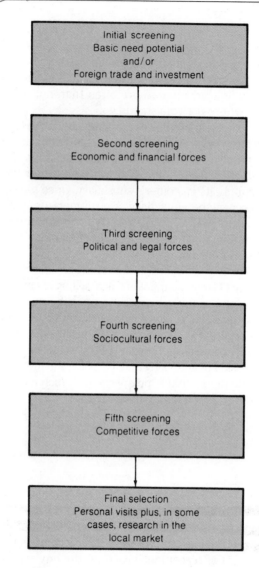

Initial Screening

Basic Need Potential

An initial screening based on the basic need potential is a logical first step, because if the need is lacking, no reasonable expenditure of effort and money will enable the firm to market its goods or services. For example, the basic need potential of certain goods is dependent on various physical forces, such as climate, topography, or natural resources. If the firm produces air conditioners, the analyst will look for countries with warm climates. Manufacturers of large farm tractors would not consider Switzerland a likely prospect, because of the mountainous terrain, and only countries known to possess gold deposits would be potential customers for gold-dredging equipment.

Generally, producers of specialized industrial materials or equipment experience little difficulty, in assessing their basic need potential. The builder of cement kilns, for example, can obtain the names and addresses of cement plants worldwide merely by contacting the Portland Cement Association in Chicago. A list of the firms in an industry, often on a worldwide basis, is available either from the industry association or from specialized trade journals.

This is certainly straightforward, but what about the less specialized products of more widespread consumption?

Foreign Trade and Investment

If the nature of the good or service is such that a definite basic need potential cannot be readily established, analysts can, as we saw in Chapter 2, analyze the flows of foreign trade and investment to see where competitors' products are going now. Even for the situation where a basic need is clearly indicated, most experienced researchers will still investigate the trade flows in order to have an idea of the magnitude of present sales.

Management is aware, of course, that imports alone are rarely a measure of the full market potential. Myriad reasons are responsible, among which are lack of foreign exchange, high prices (duties and high markups), and political pressures (Chile and the duplicating machines mentioned in Chapter 3).

Moreover, import data indicate only that a country has been buying certain products from abroad and are no guarantee that it will continue to do so. Managements know that a competitor may decide to produce locally, which in many markets will cause imports to cease. Change in a country's political structure may stop imports also, as we saw in the case of Iran, where suddenly orders worth billions of dollars were canceled. Nevertheless, when there is no local production, import data do enable the firm to know how much is currently being purchased and provide management with an estimate, though conservative, of the immediate market potential at the going price. If local production is being considered and calculations show that goods produced in the country could be sold at a lower price, even without knowing the price elasticity of demand, the firm can reasonably expect to sell more than the quantity being imported.

When recent import data are unavailable, a useful surrogate is the amounts and destinations of U.S. exports, which are obtainable from the *Foreign Trade Report (FT410)* published by the U.S. Department of Commerce. The analyst will be able to calculate the imports of a number of major U.S. trading partners rather accurately by combining data from the *FT410* with the U.S. market share published in the Department of Commerce annual *Market Share Reports*. Additional information is available from *Economist, Business International*, and other publications listed in the Appendix.

Another possible source of information is data from importing nations. Although frequently incomplete, such data may still be useful because the fact that a given product is imported at all indicates that no insurmountable restraints are imposed by the uncontrollable forces.

Second Screening—The Financial and Economic Forces

After the initial screening, the analyst will have a much smaller list of prospects. This list may be further reduced by a second screening based on the financial and economic forces. Trends in the rates of inflation, of exchange, and of interest are among the major financial points of concern. Credit availability, paying habits of customers, and rates of return on similar investments are still other financial factors that should be considered. It should be noted that this screening is not a complete financial analysis. This will come later if the market analysis and assessment disclose that a country has sufficient potential for capital investment.

Economic data may be employed in a number of ways, but there are two measures of market demand based on them that are especially useful. These are *market indicators* and *market factors*. Other methods for estimating demand that depend on economic data are regression analysis and trend analysis.

Market Indicators — *tell you the size of the market & relative strength*

Market indicators are economic data that serve as yardsticks for measuring the relative market strengths of various geographic areas. A well-known American example is the Buying Power Index published in the annual "Survey of Buying Power" by *Sales and Marketing Management*. The purpose of this index is to enable marketers to compare the relative buying power of counties and cities in the United States.

A somewhat similar index on a worldwide scale is published by *Business International*. This index employs 42 indicators for 117 nations. The indicators include population, GDP, various categories of private consumption expenditures, and the production or consumption of steel, cement, electricity, and energy. These indicators are weighted and combined to form composite indexes of (1) market size, (2) market intensity, and (3) market growth.

1. *Market size* shows the relative size of each market as a percentage of the total world market. The percentages for each market are obtained by averaging data on population (given double weight), urban population, private consumption expenditures, steel consumption, cement and electricity production, and ownership of telephones, cars, and television sets.

2. *Market intensity* measures "the richness of the market" or the degree of concentrated purchasing power as compared to the world intensity of 1.00. The intensity for each market is calculated by averaging per capita consumption of energy and steel, ownership of telephones and TVs, and the production of cement and electricity. Double weight is given to overall private consumption expenditures and to ownership of automobiles. The proportion of urban population is also included and double-weighted.

3. *Market growth* is an average of the percentage growth of the following indicators over the past five years: population, steel consumption, cement and electricity production, and ownership of cars, trucks, buses, television sets, and telephones.

An analysis of these three indexes will show the international sales manager which major regions and major markets were the fastest growing, what their growth rates were, and which have the highest degree of concentrated purchasing power. Table 14–1 presents these indexes which show that from 1973 to 1983 Eastern Europe, the Middle East, Africa, Asia, and Latin America increased their market size measured as a percentage of the world market. However, all of these areas except Eastern Europe have market intensity indexes below the world average. Nevertheless, they and all other markets except North America increased their "richness." Looking at the 10 major markets, you find that the USSR, Brazil, and Spain were the only countries that increased their market size, though the market intensity index rose in Japan, West Germany, and Italy. Regional indexes for other nations are published in the regional newsletters of *Business International*. Minicase 14–2 gives the latest European values, for example. By comparing the values of the indexes with the sales results of the company's subsidiaries, management can quickly judge their performance. Other uses of the indexes are to set sales targets and to serve as a basis for allocating the promotional budget.

Market Factors

Market factors are similar to market indicators, except that they tend to correlate highly with the market demand for a given product. If the analyst of a foreign market has no factor for that market, he or she can usually use one from the domestic market to get a reasonable approximation. Moreover, if they work for a multinational firm, they may be able to obtain market factors developed by comparable subsidiaries. To be able to transfer these relationships to the country under study, the analyst must assume that the underlying conditions affecting demand are similar in that market.

Table 14-1
World Market Intensity Index, 1973 versus 1983

	Market Size (percent of world market)		Market Intensity (world = 1.00)		Five-Year Market Growth (percent)	
	1973	1983	1973	1983	1973–1978	1978–1983
Major regions						
Western Europe	24.51%	22.35%	2.02%	2.04%	13.62%	−7.3%
EC	(18.20)	(16.28)	(2.40)	(2.37)	(10.37)	(4.23)
EFTA	(2.89)	(2.44)	(2.35)	(2.38)	(6.71)	(10.89)
Eastern Europe	15.82	16.96	1.25	1.50	36.65	12.82
Middle East	1.84	2.47	0.41	0.52	82.08	44.19
Africa	4.00	4.73	0.21	0.27	47.52	37.03
Asia (market economies)	19.28	21.31	0.35	0.38	25.49	20.90
Australasia	1.26	1.24	2.71	2.78	19.86	13.17
North America	26.35	22.67	3.91	3.65	15.33	−0.89
Latin America	6.93	8.26	0.65	0.69	46.75	22.23
LAIA	(6.07)	(7.35)	(0.67)	(0.73)	(52.21)	(20.69)
World (total or average)	100.00	100.00	1.00	1.00	21.27	10.38
Major markets						
United States	24.09	20.69	3.96	3.68	14.61	−1.10
USSR	10.77	12.04	1.22	1.50	48.23	15.15
Japan	7.98	7.55	2.29	2.38	14.99	8.48
West Germany	5.01	4.37	2.74	2.86	12.30	6.25
United Kingdom	3.94	3.22	2.33	2.27	−0.12	−1.64
France	3.67	2.95	2.45	2.30	18.35	−2.77
Italy	3.43	3.28	2.07	2.16	10.62	−12.86
Brazil	2.29	2.78	0.61	0.71	77.28	15.20
Canada	2.27	1.98	3.43	3.37	22.99	2.12
Spain	1.74	1.98	1.57	1.86	15.96	23.70

Source: BI/DATA. Reprinted from page 31 of the January 27, 1986, issue of *Business International* with the permission of the publisher, Business International Corporation (New York).

The transfer process, **estimation by analogy,** works like this: If car registration $\times$ 1.6 is used to estimate annual tire purchases in the United States, the forecaster who has no market factor for the country under study can use the same 1.6 for that market. The constant in the country under study may be somewhat different (it usually is), but with this approach the estimates will be in the right ballpark. Many such factors exist, and generally research personnel, either in the domestic operation or in foreign subsidiaries, are familiar with them.

Regression Analysis
In **regression analysis,** instead of one economic variable such as car registration, the domestic division may be utilizing several in a linear regression model of the form $MP = a + bx_1 + \ldots zx_n$, where MP = market potential and the x's are independent economic variables such as GNP, number of telephones, or births. Again, the analyst has the choice of employing the same model or, when sufficient local data are obtainable, constructing a new one by means of regression analysis.[2]

Trend Analysis
When the historic growth rates of either the pertinent economic variables or imports are known, future growth can be forecast by means of **trend analysis.** A time series may be constructed, or the arithmetic mean of past growth rates may be applied to historical data. Caution is advised when using this second method because if the average annual growth rate is applied mechanically, in just a few years the dependent variable may reach an incredible size. For example, a 5 percent growth rate compounded annually will result in a doubling of the original value in only 15 years.

Inasmuch as trend analysis is based on the assumption that past conditions affecting the dependent variable will remain constant, the analyst will generally modify the outcome to take into account any changes that can be foreseen. Often there are obvious constraints that will limit upward growth, one of which is the near certainty that competitors will enter the market if large increases in demand continue for very long.

Periodic Updating
If the estimates are altered appreciably in the periodic updatings that all long-term forecasts undergo, management may change the extent of the firm's involvement to be in line with the new estimates. Fortunately, the alternative forms of participation in a market permit the firm to become progressively more involved, with corresponding increases in investment. Most companies can enter a market in stages, perhaps in this sequence: exporting, establishment of a foreign sales company, local assembly, and finally manufacturing. Even when the decision is whether to produce overseas, management may plan to assemble a combination of imported and domestically produced parts initially and then

progressively to manufacture more components locally as demand rises. Automobile manufacturers have begun a number of foreign operations employing this strategy.

Third Screening—Political and Legal Forces

The elements of the political and legal forces that can eliminate a nation from further consideration are numerous.

Entry Barriers

Import restrictions can be positive or negative, depending on whether management is considering exporting (can the firm's products enter the country?) or setting up a foreign plant (will competitive imports be kept out?). If one of management's objectives is 100 percent ownership, will the nation's laws permit it, or is some local participation required? Will the government accept a minority local ownership, or must a minimum of 51 percent of the subsidiary be in the hands of nationals? Are there laws that reserve certain industries for either the government or its citizens?[3] Depending on management's preferences, any one of these conditions may be sufficient cause for eliminating a nation from further consideration.

Profit Remittance Barriers

When there are no objectionable requisites for entry, a nation may still be excluded if there are what management believes to be undue restrictions on the repatriation of earnings. Limits linked to the amount of foreign investment or other criteria may be set, or the nation may have a history of inability to provide foreign exchange for profit remittances.

> Decision 24 of the Andean Group has for years limited remittances to 14 percent of the foreign investment and automatic reinvestment of profits to 5 percent. Now these restraints have been loosened to 20 and 7 percent, respectively, in an effort to make foreign investment more attractive.

Other Factors

Another factor of serious import is the stability of the government, which is more important than its form. Business can adapt to form and thrive as long as the conditions are stable. Instability creates uncertainty, and this complicates planning. An often heard complaint of businesspeople is that "they've changed the rules again."

Other concerns of management are tax laws, safety standards, price controls, and the many other factors we examined in the chapters on the political and legal forces. No matter how large a nation's potential market is, if its legal and political constraints are unacceptable to management, that nation must be eliminated from further consideration.

Some excellent sources of this kind of information may be found in *Financing Foreign Operations*, published by Business International; *Overseas Business Reports*, obtainable from the U.S. Department of Commerce; the *Ernst and Ernst International Series;* and *Digest of Commercial Laws of the World*, published by Oceana.

Fourth Screening—Sociocultural Forces

A screening of the remaining candidates on the basis of sociocultural factors is arduous because these "facts" are highly subjective. The analyst, unless he or she is a specialist in the country, must rely on the opinions of others. It is possible to hire consultants, but they are expensive. U.S. Department of Commerce specialists can provide some assistance, and frequently professional organizations and universities hold seminars at which the sociocultural aspects of doing business in a particular area or country are explained. Reading *Overseas Business Reports* (U.S. Department of Commerce), international business publications (*Business International* and the *Economist*), and specialized books will augment the analyst's sociocultural knowledge. The use of a checklist of the principal socioeconomic components as explained in Chapter 8 will serve as a reminder of the many factors that must be considered in this screening.

After the fourth screening, the analyst should have a list of countries for which an industry demand appears to exist. However, what management really wants to know is which of these countries seem to be the best prospects for the *firm's* products. A fifth screening based on the competitive forces will assist in providing this information.

Fifth Screening—Competitive Forces

In this screening, markets are examined on the basis of such elements of the competitive forces as:

1. The number, size, and financial strength of the competitors.
2. Their market shares.
3. Their apparent marketing strategies.
4. The apparent effectiveness of their promotional programs.
5. The quality levels of their product lines.
6. The source of their products—imported or locally produced.
7. Their pricing policies.
8. The levels of their after-sales service.

9. Their distribution channels.
10. Their coverage of the market. (Could market segmentation produce niches that are now poorly attended?)

Countries in which management believes that strong competitors make a profitable operation difficult to attain are eliminated.

Final Selection of New Markets

Those countries that still appear to be good prospects should be visited by an executive of the firm. Before leaving, this person will review the data from the various screenings along with any new information that the researcher can supply. Based on this review and on experience in making similar domestic decisions, the executive will prepare a list of points on which information must be obtained upon arrival. Management will want the facts uncovered by the desk study (the five screenings) to be corroborated and will expect a firsthand report on the market, which will include information on competitive activity and appraisal of the suitability of the firm's present marketing mix and the availability of ancillary facilities (warehousing, service agencies, media, credit, and so forth).

Field Trip

The field trip should not be hurried; as much time should be allotted to this part of the study as would be spent on a similar domestic field trip. Often time can be saved if the executive can join a government-sponsored trade mission or visit a trade fair, because such events attract the kinds of people this person will want to interview.

For many situations, the executive's report will be the final input to the information on which the decision is based. However, there will be occasions when the proposed human and financial resource commitments are so great that management will insist on gathering data in the proposed market rather than depending solely on the desk and field reports.[4] This would undoubtedly be the position of a consumer products manufacturer that envisions entering a large competitive market of an industrialized country. It might also be the recommendation of the executive making the field trip if he or she discovered that market conditions were substantially different from those to which the firm was accustomed. In these situations, research in the local market will not only supply information on market definition and projection but will also assist in the formulation of an effective marketing mix.

Research in the Local Market

When the firm's research personnel have had no experience in the country, it is advisable to hire a local research group to do the work unless there is a subsidiary in a neighboring country from which a research team may be borrowed.

Generally, home country research techniques may be used, though they may need to be adapted to local conditions. It is imperative, therefore, that the person in charge of the project have experience either in that country or in one that is culturally similar and preferably in the same geographic area.

Just as at home, the researchers will first try to obtain secondary data, but they frequently find that, except in developed nations, they either cannot find what they need or what they encounter is suspect. Fortunately, international agencies such as the United Nations and the IMF regularly hold seminars to train government officials in data collection, so that the recency and quality of secondary data in some countries are improving.

If secondary data are unavailable, the researchers must collect primary data, and here they face other complications caused by *cultural problems* and *technical difficulties*.

Cultural Problems. If the researchers are not proficient in the country's language, the questionnaire for recording the data must be translated. As we learned in the chapter on the sociocultural forces, a number of languages may be spoken in a country, and even in countries where only one language is used, the meaning of some words changes from one region to another.

Cultural problems continue to plague the researchers as they try to collect data. The low level of literacy in many developing nations makes the use of mail questionnaires virtually impossible. If a housewife is interviewed in a country where the husband makes the buying decisions, the data obtained from her are worthless. Respondents sometimes refuse to answer questions because of their general distrust of strangers. In other instances, however, the custom of politeness toward everyone will cause respondents to give answers calculated to please the interviewer.

Often there is a practical reason for not wanting to be interviewed. In some countries, income taxes are based on the apparent worth of individuals as measured by their tangible assets. In such countries, when an interviewer asks a respondent if there is a stereo or TV in the household, the interviewer is suspected of being a tax assessor and the respondent refuses to answer. To overcome this problem, experienced researchers often hire college students as interviewers because their manner of speech and dress correctly identify them for what they are.

Technical Difficulties. As if the cultural problems were not enough, the researcher may also encounter technical difficulties. First, up-to-date maps are often unavailable. Streets chosen to be sampled may have three or four different names along their length, and the houses may not be numbered. Telephone surveys can be a formidable undertaking, because in many countries only the wealthy have telephones and the telephone directories are frequently out of date. In countries such as Brazil and Mexico, researchers often have problems in using their own phones because overloaded circuits make it next to impossible to get a line.[5] Should they consider using a mail survey, they might change their minds when they learn that mail deliveries within a city may take weeks or are sometimes not even made.

> The postal service in Italy is so slow (two weeks for a letter to go from Rome to Milan) that Italian firms use private couriers to go to Switzerland to dispatch their foreign mail.

Mail questionnaires are not well received in Chile, where the recipient is required to pay the postman for each letter delivered. The response to a mail survey is often low by American standards in countries where the respondent must go to the post office to mail a letter—for example, Brazil. To increase returns, firms often offer such premiums as lottery tickets or product samples to persons who complete a mail questionnaire.

Research as Practiced

The fact that hindrances to marketing research exist does not mean that it is not carried out in foreign markets. As you might surmise from the discussion of the availability of secondary data, marketing research is highly developed in industrialized nations, where markets are large and incorrect decisions are costly.[6] Problems like those we have mentioned are prevalent in the less developed nations, but they are well known to those who live there. It does not take long for the newcomer to become aware of them either, because longtime residents are quick to point them out.

There is a tendency in these nations to do less research and use simpler techniques, because often a firm is in a seller's market, which means that everything produced can be sold with a minimum marketing effort. Bigger headaches, such as a constant lack of foreign exchange for importing raw materials or the necessity of operating in an economy suffering from hyperinflation, require top management to concentrate its efforts in areas other than marketing. Competition is generally less intense because there are fewer competitors and because their managements are grappling with the same problems, which keep them from devoting more time to the marketing function. Although the situation is changing, the most common technique still seems to be a combination of trend analysis and the querying of knowledgeable persons (salespeople, channel members, and customers), whose findings are then adjusted on the basis of the subjective considerations of the researchers.[7]

Recapitulation of the
Screening Process

There is no denying that the screening procedure we have outlined is both difficult and time-consuming, but it does assure management that the principal factors have not been overlooked. Since most market-entry decisions can be implemented in stages, if conditions change or if additional information shows that the initial decision was incorrect, the firm can usually make adjustments in time to avoid losses.

To obtain this additional information in order to update the data obtained during the market-screening process, management must receive a constant flow of information concerning the controllable and uncontrollable variables. This can best be provided by a marketing information system.

Marketing Information System (MIS)

The **marketing information system (MIS)** is simply an organized continuous process of gathering, storing, processing, and disseminating information for the purpose of making marketing decisions. The system's size and complexity can range from a simple filing cabinet in a small firm to a component of an international business information system employing computers to process and store data, such as is found in large MNEs. The means are less important than the end, which is to enable marketing managers to use all the sources of information at their disposal. These are:

1. *Internal sources*—market analyses, special research reports, and data from company sales, production, financial, and accounting records as reported by foreign subsidiaries, sales representatives, and channel of distribution members.

2. *External sources*—reports from governments, trade associations, banks, consultants, and customers.

Both types of sources can provide data concerning the changes and trends in the uncontrollable environmental variables as well as feedback on the performance of the firm's controllable marketing variables. Information from the MIS is used to assist management in deciding *where* and *what* to market (identifying and assessing present and potential markets) and *how* to market (formulating the marketing mix).

Summary

A complete market analysis and assessment as described in this chapter would be made by a firm that either is contemplating entering the foreign market for the first time or is already a multinational but wants to monitor world markets systematically in order to avoid overlooking marketing opportunities. Many of the data requirements for a foreign decision are the same as those required for a similar domestic decision, though it is likely that additional information about some of the international and foreign environmental forces will be needed.

Essentially, the screening process consists of examining the various forces in succession and eliminating countries at each step. The sequence of screening based on (1) market potential, (2) economic and financial forces, (3) political and legal forces, (4) sociocultural forces, (5) competitive forces, and (6) personal visits is ordered so as to have a successively smaller number of prospects to consider at each of the succeedingly more difficult and expensive stages.

When the proposed commitment of the financial and human resources is large, managements may be reluctant to make a decision based solely on the desk study and will require that research be undertaken in the market. If the researchers cannot obtain satisfactory secondary data, they will need to collect primary data.

Cultural problems such as a low level of literacy and distrust of strangers complicate the data-gathering process, as do technical difficulties, such as a lack of maps, telephone directories, and adequate mail service. These hindrances to marketing research do not prevent the work from being done. There is a tendency in many markets, however, to do less research and use simple techniques.

To provide continuing information on changes in the uncontrollable variables as well as feedback on the performance of the firm's marketing mix, many companies have set up a marketing information system to gather, store, and use marketing information in an organized manner.

Questions

1. *Select a product for screening. List the sources of information for each of the first five screenings.*
2. *Select a country and a product that you believe your firm can market in that country. Prepare a study based on the information obtained from the first four screenings for your firm's executive committee, which will decide whether to proceed with your recommendations.*
3. *What is the basis for the order of screenings presented in the text?*
4. *If import data for a country are unobtainable, what readily available data might serve as a substitute?*
5. *What are some barriers related to the political and legal forces that may eliminate a country from further consideration?*
6. *What is the reason for making personal visits to markets that survive the first five screenings?*
7. *What are the two principal kinds of complications that the researchers face when they collect primary data in a foreign market?*

8. *Why is it that often less market research is done in developing countries?*
9. *What market research technique seems to be the most frequently used in the less developed countries?*
10. *What is the purpose of a marketing information system?*

Minicase

14–1 "Quick and Dirty"

Research—Universal Tire

Company

Sam Johnson, president of Universal Tire International, calls June Ashton, head of marketing research:

Johnson: June, you may have heard that I have been talking with Dates Rubber about giving us a license to make fan belts in our Spanish factory.

Ashton: I was surprised to hear that, Sam. We don't make fan belts in any of our factories now. Why are we interested in Spain?

Johnson: It's because one of the large automobile manufacturers there told our Spanish plant that if it can make a belt of American quality for them, they'll give it the major share of their tire business. This company is tired of having fan belt problems.

Ashton: You feel, then, that our plant can make a satisfactory belt with Dates technology. Is it expensive?

Johnson: Who cares? With the size of that OEM business in tires, we could give the belts away. Look, the reason I'm calling you is that the Dates attorney called to say that they've agreed to our conditions for the Spanish contract and are ready to sign. However, he also asked if we want the rights to produce the belts in any of our other overseas plants. The reason he is asking is that one of our competitors has approached them for licenses, but he wants to give us first chance because we began talking with them first. The countries we don't want will be open to our competitor. June, do you have any way to run a quick check to see which, if any, of our other plants we should include in the agreement? It seems, offhand, as though Colombia might be a good prospect, perhaps Venezuela and possibly Ecuador. Mexico is out, I imagine, because Goodrich and Goodyear already have local production.

Ashton: What about our French or German plants?

Johnson: Oh, I wouldn't think so. A number of companies produce belts in France. In fact, somebody is producing belts in every EC country. I'll bet the United States doesn't export a single belt to Europe.

Ashton: What are we talking about with respect to market size? How many belts do we need to make a year for this operation to be viable?

Johnson: The Dates president told me that we won't need much new equipment because the same machinery that prepares the inputs for tires can be used for belts. We can buy some used production machinery, also. He says we shouldn't have to spend more than $200,000 per plant on machinery. Training costs for labor are low because an experienced tire builder can be trained in a matter of days to build belts. According to Dates, if we can sell 150,000 belts a year at about $2 per belt, their average export price for automobile and truck belts, we can make money.

Ashton: We're talking about a minimum of $300,000 gross revenue per country.

Johnson: That's right, and we don't have to start production immediately in all the countries we name in the contract. It's really more of an option that we are getting. What we're doing is staking out the territory in which we want to build belts within the next three to four years.

Ashton: If we don't ask for all the countries where we have tire plants now, can we go back to Dates later for those?

Johnson: Only if our competitor hasn't taken them.

Ashton: Let's ask for all of them now, then.

Johnson: It may be that we won't want to put up belt plants in all the places where we have tire plants. If we ask for the right to produce in a market, Dates will expect us to go through with it—not all at once, because we don't have the supervisors and engineers available to do that. I believe they'll give us three, possibly four years. Anything else I can tell you?

Ashton: Let's see. I don't have time to get import figures from any of the countries, so I'll have to go with the *FT466* or *FT410*. Both reports will show the major markets for U.S. exports, but, of course, they won't give us total imports of any market. I've got the automobile and truck registrations because we use them for forecasting tire sales. Can I call Dates for market help?

Johnson: No, unfortunately. They said specifically that the license excludes their marketing know-how. They won't give that to anyone.

Ashton: Did you by any chance find out how long their belts were lasting?

Johnson: Yes, I remember that when we were talking about product quality, he bragged that their belts had an average life of four years, which he said was good, considering that this included older cars with worn pulleys as well as new cars. He also said that Dates makes fan belts for more kinds of cars and trucks than any other manufacturer anywhere. That's all he'd tell me. I know it's not much to go on, but will you take a look at the markets where our plants are and choose which ones we ought to enter within the next five years? It would be helpful if you would rank them and give me your reasons why you ranked them as you did.

Ashton: One last question. What about the number of fan belts per car? Most European cars don't have air conditioning. Can I safely assume one belt per car?

Johnson: That will probably be a little conservative, but use the one belt per car figure for this study. When we get to the point of designing a plant, we'll get more data on the actual belts per make and model.

Ashton: Let me have a couple of hours, and I'll get back to you.

For which of the countries where Universal now has tire factories do you believe Ashton will recommend fan belt production? How will she rank them? Why will she rank them in this manner? (Note: All of the information that Ashton has on hand is contained in the following table.)

Ashton's Data

Country*	1983 Auto Registration	Percent Annual Increase (over past five years)	1983 Truck Registration	Percent Annual Increase
1. Colombia	820,000	10.8%	200,000	2.4%
2. Venezuela	1,495,000	5.4	857,000	9.2
3. Ecuador	76,000	2.7	172,000	4.6
4. Saudi Arabia	1,202,000	20.2	1,534,000	19.2
5. South Korea	381,000	15.6	404,000	15.2
6. Kuwait	520,000	10.1	179,000	8.6
7. Nigeria	739,000	12.8	621,000	12.6
8. Spain	8,714,000	5.9	1,573,000	5.0
9. France	20,600,000	3.1	3,230,000	5.4
10. Mexico	4,671,000	9.2	1,916,000	9.6

1983 U.S. exports of motor vehicle belts (value in dollars):*

1.	Colombia	$ 541,651
2.	Venezuela	514,322
3.	Ecuador	168,676
4.	Saudi Arabia	264,340
5.	South Korea	723,724
6.	Kuwait	88,508
7.	Nigeria	206,460
8.	Spain	72,092
9.	France	2,074,330
10.	Mexico	543,263

*The countries shown are those where Universal Tire plants are located.

Minicase
14–2 Shafner Products
International

Shafner Products International, the international division of Shafner Products, is responsible for the production and marketing of the company's products (washers, dryers, electric ranges, refrigerators, and dishwashers) outside the United States. Shafner Products International is organized geographically with five headquarters: (1) Western Europe; (2) Middle East; (3) Africa; (4) Asia, including Australia; and (5) Latin America.

Bill Easton, president of Shafner Products International (SPI), is concerned about sales in the West European region. Although they are rising, they are not keeping pace with the sales increases in other regions. He has just finished reading an article about *Business International*'s market indexes and wonders whether they could be helpful. Easton decides to call Jim Allen, SPI vice president for marketing, to his office.

Easton: Jim, do you know anything about the market indicators that *Business International* publishes?

Allen: I've heard of them. They try to do for the world what the Buying Power Index of *Sales and Marketing Management* does for the United States.

Easton: Yes, something like that. You know that I have been concerned for some time now that although our European sales are increasing, they're not keeping pace with sales in the other regions.

Allen: Well, this is due in large part to the fact that Europe is a mature market. Also, the demographics are relatively better for us in the other regions.

Easton: Perhaps. At any rate, I compared the European percentage of our total sales with *BI*'s percentage of world market for Europe. Here's the comparison:

Total Sales (1983)	European Region (1983)	European to Total (percent)	*BI* Market Size
$1,210 million	$251.3 million	20.80%	22.35

You can see that our percentage is only 1½ percent below average. Interestingly, our sales growth has averaged about 2.5 percent annually over the past five years while the growth rate shown in the BI report is negative. [Table 14–1 in text.]

Allen: Wait a minute, Bill. How is *BI* measuring the market size? Is it population, GNP/capita, consumer expenditure, or what?

Easton: They use all of these and more. Here is the way they calculate market size. You can see the variables they use.

$$\text{Size} (\%) = \frac{2(POP) + POPU + PCE + KWH + STL + CEM + TEL + CAR + TV}{2(POPR) + POPUR + PCER + KWHR + STLR + CEMR + TELR + CARR + TVR} \times 100$$

where:

POP = Total population
POPU = Urban population
PCE = Private final consumption in U.S. dollars
KWH = Electricity production
STL = Apparent crude steel consumption
CEM = Cement production
TEL = Telephones in use
CAR = Passenger cars in use
TV   = Television sets in use

A variable ending in R stands for regional total.

Allen: Well, these are not the indicators we use. We look at housing starts, size of households, and marriages, as well as population and private consumer expenditures.

Easton: Do you combine them or weight them in any way?

Allen: Yes, we use a regression equation that includes these variables.

Easton: So, if each market's sales increase is in line with the increases in these variables, you feel that we're doing a decent job in each market?

Allen: At least this indicates that we're holding our own, and of course we're always trying to increase market share. Another calculation we make is sales dollars per household in each market. We divide our sales in Norway, for example, by the number of households in Norway. We do that for each market and compare them. I learned this from our domestic company.

Easton: I didn't know about that one. Tell you what, Jim. I've also got a *BI* report on the West European markets. Since we are in every one of them either with a factory or a sales company, we can use it as is. Why don't you compare the percentages of our sales in each country to our total sales in the European region with the market size in the *BI* report. Let's see if we have any weak spots. Look at the column "Market Intensity" too. It seems to me that we need to concentrate on the richer markets. And check our growth rates with their market growth rates. You might have our research department look at *BI*'s variables. Rather than use their results, you might prefer to use their methodology with your own variables. In other words, study the *BI* report and see if it can help us in any way. Please get back to me when you're finished.

1. According to the *BI* market share index, which Shafner subsidiaries appear to have problems?
2. Which countries are doing well?

Shafner Products International Sales in European Region

Country	1983 Sales ($ millions)	Average Annual Growth, 1978–1983 (percent)
Belgium-Luxembourg	$ 8.41	0.9%
Denmark	4.10	0.8
France	32.82	2.4
Germany	54.74	2.0
Greece	5.39	4.5
Ireland	2.58	3.3
Italy	38.70	2.3
Netherlands	8.42	1.2
United Kingdom	31.02	0.7
Austria	6.23	2.6
Finland	3.18	3.0
Norway	4.78	2.2
Portugal	3.35	3.5
Spain	21.64	3.0
Sweden	8.62	1.5
Switzerland	6.18	2.4
Turkey	11.12	3.9
	$251.30	

Business International's *Market Indicators for Western Europe*

Country	Market Size (percent)	Market Intensity	Annual Market Growth (percent)
Belgium-Luxembourg	3.0%	1.22	1.3%
Denmark	1.5	1.15	−0.1
France	15.6	1.22	1.7
Germany	19.5	1.37	0.6
Greece	2.2	0.84	3.2
Ireland	0.7	0.69	0.2
Italy	14.5	1.04	1.2
Netherlands	3.7	1.05	0.5
United Kingdom	14.1	1.02	−0.3
Portugal	1.5	0.47	2.3
Spain	8.2	0.82	2.3
EC total	84.4	1.08	1.1
Norway	1.7	1.69	1.2
Austria	2.1	1.16	1.3
Finland	1.6	1.28	3.4
Sweden	3.1	1.54	0.9
Switzerland	2.3	1.55	1.4
Turkey	4.8	0.21	5.8
Europe total	100.0%	1.00	1.3

Source: *Business Europe,* February 10, 1986, p. 3.

3. What else can you learn from the data?

4. What do you think of Allen's method of calculating dollars of Shafner sales per household?

5. Can you think of independent variables that might be more useful than those that *BI* employs?

Supplementary Readings

Brasch, John. "Effective Sales Forecasting in a Developing Country? Difficult—Sometimes Impossible." Paper presented at the Rocky Mountain Council for Latin American Studies, Tucson, Arizona, 1977.

"Consumers' Nondurables." *Business International*, June 16, 1986, p. 190.

Decision Making in International Operations—201 Checklists. New York: Business International, 1980.

Gasman, Lawrence D. "7 Rules for International Research." *Marketing News*, September 17, 1982, p. 5.

Kravis, Irving B.; A. Kenessey; A. Heston; and R. Summers. *A System of International Comparisons of Gross Product and Purchasing Power.* Baltimore: Johns Hopkins University Press (publisher for the World Bank), 1975.

"Market Research Wins Fans in India." *Advertising Age*, January 26, 1987, p. 57.

Mitchell, Dawn. "A European Researcher's View of European Business Marketing." *Business Marketing*, April 1984, pp 72–75.

Peebles, Dean M., and John K. Ryans, Jr. "Managing International Advertising Research." *International Advertising.* Newton, Mass.: Allyn & Bacon, 1984.

Pring, David C. "American Firms Rely on Multinational Research Suppliers to Solve Marketing Problems Overseas." *Marketing News*, May 15, 1981, p. 2.

Rabier, Jacques-René. *European Consumers.* Brussels: Commission of the European Communities, 1976.

Ricks, David A. *Big Business Blunders.* Homewood, Ill.: Dow Jones-Irwin, 1983.

Specht, Marina. "Uruguay: Latin America's Favorite Test Market." *Advertising Age*, January 20, 1984, p. 52.

Endnotes

1. Richard D. Robinson recommends a similar methodology, which he calls filtering; see Robinson, in *International Business Management*, 2nd ed. (Hinsdale, Ill.: Dryden Press, 1978), pp. 52–55. Also see F. T. Haner, *Multinational Management* (Columbus, Ohio: Charles E. Merrill Publishing, 1973), pp. 24–25; and R. Wayne Walvoord, "Export Market Research," *American Export Bulletin*, May 1980, pp. 82–91.

2. Regression analysis is a statistical technique employing the least squares criterion to determine the relationship between a dependent variable and one or more independent variables. In the text, MP is the dependent variable and x_1 through x_n are the independent variables. The analyst wants to solve for the constants a through z. For an in-depth explanation of regression analysis, see any statistics text.

3. Commonly, public utilities, mineral extraction, and banking are reserved for either the government or its citizens. However, there is a tendency for many of the LDCs to limit foreign participation to 49 percent generally and to even less in certain industries.
4. Some secondary and even primary data will be gathered on the field trip, but the manager rarely has the time or the ability to conduct a complete research study.
5. While in São Paulo, one of the writers wanted to call Santos (an hour's drive away). The assistant to his secretary, whose principal occupation was to dial for an outside line, had tried to place the call all morning. Finally, at noon, he drove to Santos, completed his business, and returned to find the woman still dialing.
6. An example of the excellent work done in Europe is a study of the interests and aspirations of European consumers, which is conducted by a consortium of research firms for the EC every six months. Over 9,500 residents from all nine countries are interviewed.
7. John Brasch, "Effective Sales Forecasting in a Developing Country? Difficult—Sometimes Impossible," paper presented at the Rocky Mountain Council for Latin American Studies, Tucson, Arizona, 1977.

CHAPTER 15

MARKETING INTERNATIONALLY

"**A**nd because people are basically the same the world over, our experience of person-to-person selling works just as well abroad as it does in the United States. Our Venezuelan representative could serve people in suburban Virginia as readily as she does in her mountain village."

Avon annual report, 1976

Learning Objectives

After you study this chapter, you should know:

1. The reasons for differences between marketing domestically and marketing internationally.
2. The reasons why multinational managers wish to standardize the marketing mix.
3. Why it is often impossible to standardize the marketing mix worldwide.
4. The product strategies that can be formed from three product alternatives and three kinds of promotional messages.
5. How legal forces affect the promotional mix.
6. How cultural forces affect the promotional mix.
7. The intricacies of transfer pricing.

Key Words and Concepts

Standardization of the marketing mix
Programmed-management approach
Total product
Brand piracy
Transfer price

Business Incident

Foremost pinpoints four key elements in its Asian strategy that have helped it surmount the obstacles inherent in an LDC market:

1. *Educating consumers.* In LDCs where living standards are generally low and habits differ considerably from those in industrialized countries, educating consumers about new products is a crucial part of any marketing strategy. In one of its pioneering efforts, Foremost established a school education program to introduce fresh milk to Thai consumers who were accustomed to canned and powdered milk. The grass-roots program included promotional films, pamphlets, talks by registered nurses about nutrition, and free milk.

Foremost admits that this process is slow but believes it is effective, since it is directed not only at end-users but also at a future generation of consumers. To educate the general public, aside from students, the company has hired local well-known nutritionists to create recipes that incorporate its products into local dishes.

Another tool Foremost uses to educate consumers is franchised ice cream parlors. After several years of study, the firm decided in 1976 to branch out into the ice cream parlor business in Bangkok, taking advantage of the improvement in purchasing power of Thai consumers and the presence of a very energetic manager in the country. It soon found out that ice cream parlors became a viable operation on their own merits, as well as an effective educational method. By demonstrating the various ways that ice cream be served, the parlors helped popularize the product.

The parlors have boosted the company's sales of ice cream to other retail operations and to commercial outlets, such as restaurants and coffee shops, which have been inspired to create new ice cream desserts. The modern, clean, well-run parlors have also given the product an upbeat image and help Foremost keep an eye on consumer preferences.

2. *Catering to local tastes.* The corporation believes that the ability to create new flavors that please local palates is one reason for its success. It changes the taste of milk by adding strawberry and banana flavors, and it uses many local fruits and flavors in its ice cream. At present, its Bangkok ice-cream parlors offer 26 flavors.

Taste testing is an important practice carried out at three levels. First, Foremost selects a panel of taste testers carefully from its factory employees to reflect the preferences of typical Thai consumers. The formulas accepted by the group are next tested in a school, where opinions are solicited and choices recorded. That stage helps the firm refine the product before testing it in an isolated market, very often a small rural town. Free samples are distributed, and opinions probed. If the product goes over well, it is formally launched.

3. *Promotion, rather than advertising.* In a developing economy in which many houses lack refrigeration, ice cream is consumed primarily away from home. Thus, sales hinge heavily on availability, and consequently, media advertising is less effective than skillful promotion. Foremost's solution is a widespread network of retailers, attractive point-of-sale displays such as conspicuous logos at retail outlets, and heavy use of such promotional techniques as giveaways, including novel ice cream sticks, bonus offers, and free product samples.

4. *Relations with retailers.* Since small retailers in LDCs are chronically short of credit, marketers often find it necessary to carry some of the financial burden. Foremost supplies some stores with refrigeration equipment and leases it to others at favorable terms. To ensure that its ice cream is stored under the best conditions, the firm often sends its technicians to help local refrigerator manufacturers improve on designs. At the retail level, it dispatches maintenance technicians regularly to its retailers to service their refrigeration equipment, even machines it did not supply.

Reprinted from page 209 of the July 1978 issue of *Business International* with permission of the publisher, Business International Corporation (New York)

*I*f the marketing concepts and techniques that are learned and practiced in the United States can be applied in overseas markets as the business incident illustrates, why distinguish between marketing domestically and marketing internationally? Isn't it true that marketers anywhere must (1) know their markets, (2) develop products or services to satisfy customers' needs, (3) price the products or services so that they are readily acceptable in the market, (4) make them available to the buyers, and (5) inform potential customers and persuade them to buy?

Added Complexities of
International Marketing

Although the basic functions of domestic and international marketing are the same, the distinction lies in the fact that the international markets served differ widely because of the great variations in the uncontrollable environmental forces that we examined in Section III. Moreover, even the forces we think of as being controllable vary among wide limits: distribution channels to which the marketer is accustomed are unavailable, certain aspects of the product may be different, the promotional mixes are often dissimilar, and distinct cost structures may require different prices to be set. The increased complexity of the international marketing managers' task is readily perceived when one realizes that they must plan and control a variety of marketing strategies rather than one and then must coordinate and integrate those strategies into a single multinational marketing program.

International marketers, like their domestic counterparts, must develop marketing strategies by assessing the firm's potential foreign markets and analyzing the many alternative marketing mixes. Their aim is to select target markets that the firm can serve at a profit and to formulate combinations of tactics for product, price, promotion, and distribution channels that will best serve those markets. In the previous chapter, we examined the market assessment and selection process; in this chapter, we shall study the formulation of the marketing mix.

The Marketing Mix (What and How to Sell)

As we indicated above, the marketing mix consists of a set of strategy decisions made in the areas of product, promotion, pricing, and distribution for the purposes of satisfying the customers in a target market. The number of variables included in these four areas is extremely large, making possible hundreds of combinations. Because the domestic operation has already established a successful marketing mix, the temptation to follow the same procedures overseas is strong. Yet, as we have seen, important differences between the domestic and foreign environments may make a wholesale transfer of the mix impossible. The question that the international marketing manager must resolve is, "Can we standardize worldwide, must we make some changes, or must we formulate a completely different marketing mix?"

Standardization, Adaptation, or Completely Different?

Management would prefer **standardization of the marketing mix**—that is, it would prefer to employ the same marketing mix in all of the firm's operations because standardization can produce significant cost savings. If the same product that is sold in the domestic market can be exported, there can be longer production runs that lower manufacturing costs. Even when the standard product is manufactured overseas, production costs will be less because the extra research and design expense of either adapting domestic products or designing new ones for foreign sales will be avoided. Just the task of keeping many sets of specifications current requires additional, highly paid personnel in the home office.[1] For the many products, both consumer and industrial, that require spare parts for after-sales servicing, standardization greatly simplifies logistics and acquisition.

If advertising campaigns, promotional materials (catalogs, point-of purchase displays), and sales training programs can be standardized, the expensive creative work and artwork need be done only once. Standardized pricing strategies for multinational firms that source markets from several different plants avoid the embarrassment of having an important customer receive two distinct quotations for the same product. Although economies of scale are not as readily attainable for standardizing channels of distribution as for the other elements of the marketing mix, there is some gain in efficiency when the international marketing manager can use the same strategy in all markets. In summary, the benefits from standardization of the marketing mix are: (1) lower costs, (2) easier control and coordination from headquarters, and (3) reduction of the time consumed in preparing the marketing plan.

In spite of the advantages of standardization, most firms find it necessary to either modify the present mix or develop a new one. The extent of the changes depends on the type of product (consumer or industrial), the environmental forces, and the degree of market penetration desired by management.

Product Strategies

The product is the central focus of the marketing mix. If it fails to satisfy the needs of consumers, no amount of promotion, price cutting, or distribution will persuade them to buy. The housewife will not repurchase a detergent if the clothes do not come out as clean as the TV commercials say they will. She will not be deceived by advertisements announcing friendly service when her experience demonstrates otherwise.

In formulating product strategies, it is especially important that the international marketing manager never overlook the fact that the product is more than a physical object. The **total product,** which is what the customer buys, also includes the package, the brand name, accessories, after-sales service, the warranty, and instructions for use. The fact that the total product is purchased often makes it less expensive and easier for the multinational firm to adapt the present product or even create a new one without altering its physical characteristics. Different package sizes and promotional messages, for example, can create a new total product for a distinct market. The relative ease of creating a new total product without changing the manufacturing process is an important reason why there is more physical product standardization internationally than one might expect.

Figure 15–1

Continuum of Sensitivity to the Foreign Environment

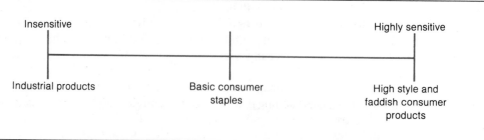

Insensitive   Highly sensitive

Industrial products   Basic consumer   High style and
                              staples   faddish consumer
                                                    products

Type of Product

One important factor that influences the amount of change to be made in a product is its classification as a consumer or industrial product. Generally speaking, consumer products require greater adaptation than industrial products to meet the demands of the world market. If the consumer products are high style or the result of a fad, they are especially likely to require changes. We can think of these product types as being on a continuum ranging from insensitive to highly sensitive to the foreign environment, as shown in Figure 15–1.[2]

Industrial Products. As one would gather from Figure 15–1, many highly technical industrial products can be sold unchanged worldwide. Transistors, for example, are used wherever radios are manufactured. Timken advertises that its bearings are interchangeable no matter where they are produced (see Figure 15–2).

If product changes are required, they may be only cosmetic, such as converting gauges to read in the metric system by pasting a new face on a dial or printing instruction plates in another language. Relatively simple adaptations such as lengthening pedals or changing seat positions are frequently sufficient to compensate for the physical differences of foreign operators.

Somewhat more drastic modifications may be necessary for some products because of two problems that are especially prevalent in the developing countries—a tendency to *overload equipment* and to *slight maintenance*. These problems are comprehensible to anyone familiar with the cultural and economic forces in the foreign environment. Unlike American children, who grow up owning automobiles and working with tools, the mechanics and operators in many foreign countries rarely have such experience until they enter a training program, which is often on the job.[3]

A bulldozer operator learns that if he pulls a lever and steps on a pedal, his machine will push whatever is in front of it. It is not uncommon to see a bulldozer pushing on some immovable object until the engine fails or a part breaks

Figure 15-2

Timken Ad

If you buy the same bearing in a different country, is it really the same bearing?

Timken bearings are made to the same exact standards all over the world. The outer race you buy in Canada fits the inner race you buy in Australia.

The idea of overseas manufacturing loses a lot of its charm if you can't get the right bearings abroad.

It means you have to redesign your equipment or your product to fit whatever bearing is available locally.

But there's an easy solution to the international bearing crisis: Timken® tapered roller bearings.

We have plants in Australia, Brazil, Canada, England, France, South Africa and the U.S.A.

Plus a worldwide network of distributors servicing customers around the world.

And because of master gauge control, our components are uniform and interchangeable—all over the world.

Even in this technological age, that's a pretty uncommon advantage.

Which is why we think it helps make Timken bearings worth more in the long run.

The Timken Company, Canton, Ohio 44706.

Worth more in the long run.

TIMKEN®
REGISTERED TRADEMARK

Courtesy The Timken Company

from the overload. The extraordinary noise coming from the engine makes no impression on the operator. In spite of the careful instructions concerning cleanliness that ball bearing manufacturers include in the package, one can find a mechanic removing the protective oiled paper to leave the bearing exposed to dust and grime before using it (he probably can't read). A very low-paid, uneducated man may be given the responsibility of lubricating equipment worth millions of dollars. He may overgrease or miss half of the fittings, and the equipment is destroyed.

To overcome these difficulties, such manufacturers as Caterpillar and Allis-Chalmers have established very thorough training programs wherever their products are sold. Many manufacturers have prepared simple instructions with plenty of pictures to get their message across to persons with limited reading ability. The other alternative is to modify the equipment, perhaps using a simpler bearing system that requires little maintenance. The machine may make more noise and be less efficient, but it runs longer with less maintenance.

Where the technology of even the adapted product is too advanced for their customers, manufacturers may market an entirely different product to accomplish the same purpose. A firm that produces electric cash registers in the United States, for example, may be able to earn good profits by marketing a hand-operated model in areas where electricity is unavailable. Products considered obsolete in advanced countries are frequently what the developing countries need.[4] Also, foreign subsidiaries sometimes find market opportunities for product lines not manufactured by the parent company.

> Marketing managers in General Tire's affiliates saw the profit possibilities in selling batteries to their tire customers. Although the domestic company does not produce them, management through licensing agreements, obtained the technology for their subsidiaries, so that this totally new product is now manufactured in a number of foreign plants.

Occasionally, adaptations are necessary to meet local legal requirements, such as those that govern noise, safety, or exhaust emissions. To avoid changing the product, some manufacturers follow the practice of designing it to meet the most stringent laws even though this means that it will be overdesigned for the rest of the markets. Renault, for example, produced for the entire U.S. market a model of its R 18 that met the California emission requirements (the most demanding in the United States).

In some instances, governments have passed very strict laws to protect a local manufacturer from imports. When this occurs, it may be preferable to design the product to the next most stringent laws and stay out of the first market. Of course, this is what the government had in mind when it passed the laws. However, a word of caution for the company in this situation—test the local manufacturer's product before giving up on the market. It has happened that the local product also failed to meet the specifications. When confronted with this evidence, the government has had to change the laws.

Consumer Products. While consumer products generally require greater modification to meet local market requirements than do industrial products, some of them can be sold unchanged to certain market segments. Consumer products of this kind include a number of luxury items such as large automobiles, sporting equipment, and expensive kitchen appliances. This is because in every country of the free world there is a market segment that is more similar to the same segment in other free world countries with respect to economic status, buyer behavior, tastes, and preferences than it is to the rest of the segments in the same country. This market segment includes the "jet set," foreign-educated and well-traveled citizens, and expatriates. Many products and services foreign to local tastes and preferences have been successfully introduced by first being marketed to this group. Gradually, members of other market segments have purchased these products and services until consumption has become widespread.[5]

In introducing new products, especially when the goal is immediate market penetration, the marketer must be aware that *generally, as you go down the economic and social strata in each country, you tend to find greater dissimilarities among countries with respect to social and cultural values*. It follows from this that in general, the deeper the immediate market penetration desired, the greater must be the product modification. This does not necessarily mean that the physical product must be changed. Perhaps a modification of one of the other elements of the total product is sufficient—a different size or color of the package, a change in the brand name, or a new positioning if the product is consumed differently.

> Mars faced a drop in Bahrein's imports of candy when it was ready to launch M&Ms. Fortunately, its marketing research discovered that Bahrainis consider the peanut to be a health food, so Mars repositioned its peanut M&Ms. The company was able to turn the hot Gulf climate to its advantage by emphasing its traditional slogan: "M&Ms melt in your mouth, not in your hand." As you will see later in this chapter, Mars followed promotional strategy number 2: same product—different message, although part of the message (slogan) remained the same.[6]

Detergent manufacturers were able to achieve deeper market penetration by offering consumers with limited purchasing power the small packages that we find only in American laundromats. In humid climates, cookies and crackers are packed in metal boxes to preserve both the package and the product.

Foreign Environmental Forces

In Section III, we examined the foreign environmental forces rather extensively, so here we will limit our discussion to a few concrete examples of how some of these forces affect product offerings.

Sociocultural Forces Dissimilar cultural patterns generally necessitate changes in food and consumer goods. Although Coca-Cola appears to be highly standardized internationally, its sweetness varies according to local tastes. Campbell lost heavily in England until it adapted its soup to local palates. The error was compounded by its failure to educate the housewife that its soup was condensed. She compared the Campbell can of ready-to-eat soup with the larger Heinz can and bought the latter. Inexplicably, two years passed before Campbell initiated the necessary educational advertising.[7] Nestlé has learned that there is a variety of taste preferences for coffee, too, so it now offers more than 40 different blends of instant coffee to satisfy them.

While some multinational firms such as Kodak and Campbell have been extremely successful in employing the same brand name, label, and colors worldwide, other firms are sometimes surprised to learn that they must change to other names, labels, or colors because of cultural differences. Green packages are taboo in the Far East because they remind the public of the dangers and illnesses of the jungle, but gold appears frequently on packages in Latin America because Latin Americans view it as a symbol of quality and prestige. In the Netherlands blue is considered warm and feminine, but the Swedes consider it masculine and cold.

Even if the colors can remain the same, instructions on labels, of course, must be translated into the language of the market. Firms selling in areas where two or more languages are spoken, such as Canada or Switzerland, may use multilingual labels. Where instructions are not required, as in the case of some consumer or industrial products whose use is well known, there is an advantage to printing the label in the language of the country best known for the product. French labels on perfumes and English labels on industrial goods help to strengthen the product's image.

> One firm put a label in English on a Mexican-made can of penetrating oil. To comply with the law, a gummed sticker saying "envasado en Mexico" (can filled in Mexico) was placed over part of the label. The Mexican product, unlike most locally made industrial products, had excellent acceptance right from the start.

A perfectly good brand name may have to be scrapped because of its unfavorable connotations in another language. An American product failed to make it in Sweden because its name translated to "enema." In Latin America, a product had to be taken off the market when the manufacturer found that the name meant "jackass oil." Of course, this problem occurs in both directions, as a Finnish brewery found when it was about to introduce "Koff" beer and "Siff" soft drinks to this country. Incidentally, an economic constraint to the international standardization of brand names is the refusal of some multinationals to let a subsidiary put their brand on a locally made product if it fails to meet their quality standards because of the inability to import the necessary raw materials or because the required production equipment is unavailable.

An important difference in the social forces to which American marketers are not accustomed is the housewife's preference in other nations, both developed and developing, for making daily visits to the small neighborhood specialty shops and the large, open markets where she can socialize while shopping. More frequent buying permits smaller packages, which is especially important to the shopper who has no automobile in which to carry her purchases. However, this custom is changing in Europe, where a growing sophistication of consumption patterns is demanding the kinds of assortments that only a large store can offer. Shopping frequency is also slowing as the European housewife, especially if she is employed, is finding that she does not have as much free time as she previously had. One can easily draw a parallel in this situation with that which began in the 1940s in the United States. The same conditions of rising incomes, a growing middle class, and an increasing number of working wives are combining to put a premium on the shopper's time, and just as occurred in the United States, supermarkets, mass merchandising, and catalog selling are moving to fill this need.

Legal Forces. Legal forces can be a formidable constraint in the design of product strategies because if the firm fails to adhere to a country's laws governing the product, it will be unable to do business in that country. Laws concerning pollution, consumer protection, and operator safety are being enacted rapidly in many parts of the world and are severely affecting the marketer's freedom to standardize the product mix internationally. For example, American machinery manufacturers exporting to Sweden have found their operator safety requirements to be even stricter than those required by OSHA, so that if they wish to market in Sweden, they must produce a special model. Similarly, the stricter American emission control laws force producers of foreign automobiles to make significant model changes in order to sell in the United States.

Laws prohibiting certain classes of imports are extremely common everywhere, as potential exporters learn when they research the world for markets. We know that products considered to be luxuries as well as products already being manufactured are among the first to be excluded from importation, but such laws also affect local production. As we saw in the previous section, prohibition of essential raw material imports can require a subsidiary to manufacture a product substantially different from what the parent company produces.

Foods and pharmaceuticals are especially influenced by laws concerning purity and labeling. Food products sold in Canada, whether imported or produced locally, are subject to strict rules that require both English and French on the labels as well as metric and inch-pound units. The law even dictates the space permitted between the number and the unit—16 oz. is correct, but 16oz. is not. The Venezuelan government, in an effort to protect the consumer from being overcharged for pharmaceuticals, has decreed that the manufacturer or the importer must affix to the package the maximum retail price at which the product can be sold.[8] Because of the Saudi Arabians' preoccupation with avoiding food containing pork, the label of any product containing animal fat or meat that is sold in Saudi Arabia must state the kind of animal used or must state that no swine products were used.

Legal forces may also prevent a multinational firm from employing its brand name in all of its overseas markets. Managements accustomed to the American law, which establishes the right to a brand name by priority in use, are surprised to learn that in code law countries a brand belongs to the person registering it first. Thus, the marketer may go into foreign markets expecting to use the company's long-established brand name only to find that someone else owns it. The name may have been registered by someone who is employing it legitimately for his own products or it may have been pirated—that is, registered by someone who hopes to profit by selling the name back to the originating firm.

Both reasons stopped Ford from marketing its automobiles under established names in Mexico and Germany. In the case of Mexico, the reason was brand piracy. Ford refused to pay the high price that the registrant wanted for the name, so that for years the Falcon was known as the Ford 200. The use of the name Mustang by a bicycle manufacturer in Germany was legitimate. The firm was producing under that name when Ford entered the market.

To avoid Ford's predicament, the firm must register its brand names in every country where it wants to use them or where it might use them at a future date. And this must be done rapidly. The Paris Convention grants a firm that has registered a name in one country only six months' priority in registering it elsewhere.

Economic Forces. The great disparity among the world markets with respect to income is an important obstacle to worldwide product standardization. Many products from the industrialized countries are simply too expensive for consumers in the developing countries, so that if the firm wishes to achieve market penetration, it must either simplify the product or produce a different, less costly one.

General Motors developed a light commercial vehicle unlike anything in its usual product line, which was to be produced in the poorer countries. Highly utilitarian, the vehicle has no expensive curved metal parts in the body and can be manufactured by labor-intensive processes requiring little capital investment. Only the engine and drive train are imported from General Motors–England. Similarly, Hoover saw an opportunity to sell a simple washing machine to Mexicans who could not afford the high-priced American-type machine. Although Hoover had no American model to simplify, it was able to copy its inexpensive English washer, which became an overnight success.

Economic forces affect product standardization in still another way. Poor economies signify poor infrastructure—bad roads, lack of sufficient electric power, and so on. Driving conditions in Mexico required Goodrich to design a tire for cut and bruise resistance rather than for high speed as in the United States. The tire was so successful that residents in U.S. border towns preferred it to the U.S. product even though its price was higher.

In North Africa during the 1950s, the high cost of trucks and the failure of their owners to appreciate the damaging effects of overloads resulted in the piling of freight unbelievably high to achieve maximum earnings. The normal rayon carcass, which could not resist the weight and flexing, failed miserably. Because European manufacturers were making inroads on their North African market, Goodyear was forced to produce a steel-wire truck tire in the United States exclusively for that market. Years passed before the tire was available in the American market.

The lack of a constant supply of electricity, another characteristic of many of the poorer countries, has compelled refrigerator manufacturers to supply a gasoline-driven product and office equipment firms to manufacture hand-operated machines. As one would expect, this condition has also provided the producers of small diesel standby generators with a ready market. Any users requiring a steady source of power, such as hospitals and theaters, are potential customers.

Market size influences the product mix, and in the poorer countries, the populations not only are frequently smaller, but they also contain a large number of economic zeros (people who have no means to purchase anything but the bare necessities of life), thereby making the already small market even smaller. This means that normally the foreign subsidiary cannot afford to produce as complete a product mix as does the parent. Most automobile manufacturers assemble only the least expensive line (Chevrolet and Opel for General Motors–Mexico) and broaden the local product mix by importing, when permitted, the luxury cars. This marketing technique is practiced by all multinationals whenever possible because a captive foreign sales organization is available to promote the sales of the home organization's exports and because the revenue derived helps to pay the subsidiary's overhead. Philips, the Dutch electrical products giant, owns a light-bulb plant in Chile that supplements its revenue by importing various small domestic appliances from its parent. Some foreign manufacturing subsidiaries carry this practice one step further by selling imports from other firms when these products are suited to their present distribution channels and marketing expertise.

Physical Forces. Elements of the physical forces such as climate and terrain also mitigate against international product standardization. Where the heat is intense, gasoline-driven machinery and automobiles must be fitted with larger radiators for extra cooling capacity. Gasoline must have a higher flash point to prevent vapor locks and stalling. As we noted in the chapter on the physical forces, insects proliferate when the winters are not cold enough to kill them. The problems this causes the agricultural industry are obvious, but even some consumer products are affected. In Brazil, the combination of intense heat and wooden floors forced the floor wax manufacturers to add a flea killer to their formulations.[9]

The heat and high humidity in many parts of the tropics require electrical equipment to be built with extraheavy insulation. Consumer goods that are affected by moisture must be specially packaged to resist its penetration. Thus, one finds pills wrapped individually in foil and baked goods packaged in tin boxes to prevent their degradation by moisture.

High altitudes frequently require product alteration. Food manufacturers have found that they must change their cooking instructions for people who live at high altitudes because at such altitudes it takes much longer to cook and bake. The thinner atmosphere requires producers of cake mixes to include less yeast. Gasoline and diesel motors generate less power at high altitudes, so that often the manufacturer must supply a larger engine.

Mountainous terrain implies high-cost highways, so that in the poorer countries roads of the quality we know are nonexistent. Trucks traveling poorer quality roads need tires with thicker treads and heavy-duty suspensions. Because of the rough ride, packaging must be stronger than that used in the United States. From these examples, we can appreciate the fact that even though an unchanged product may be culturally and economically acceptable in a market, the effect of the physical forces alone may be strong enough to require some product modification.

Because of space limitations, it is impossible to examine the influence of every one of the environmental forces on foreign product strategies. We believe that sufficient practical examples have been offered so that these, together with the information contained in the chapters on these forces, will give the reader an idea of their pervasiveness not only in the formulation of the product strategies but also in the design of the entire marketing mix. In fact, as we will show at the end of this chapter, a useful guide in the marketing mix preparation is a matrix in which the marketing mix variables are tabulated against the environmental forces.

Promotional Strategies

Promotion, one of the basic elements of the marketing mix, is communication that secures understanding between a firm and its publics for the purpose of bringing about a favorable buying action and achieving a long-lasting confidence in the firm and the product or service it provides. Note that this definition employs the plural, publics, because the seller's promotional efforts must be directed to more than just the ultimate consumers and the channel of distribution members. Far too often, the other publics have been ignored by business not only in the United States but in other markets as well. Managements have awakened to the fact that the old advice of always maintaining a low profile in a foreign country is not necessarily the best course of action. Many multinationals have changed this strategy and are now making the general public and governments aware of their public service activities.

Because promotion both influences and is influenced by the other marketing mix variables, it is possible to formulate six distinct product strategies by combining the three alternatives of: (1) marketing the same product everywhere, (2) adapting the product for foreign markets, and (3) designing a different product with (1) the same, (2) adapted, or (3) different messages.[10]

1. *Same product—same message.* When marketers find that target markets vary little with respect to product use and consumer attitudes, they can of-

Figure 15-3
Advertisements for the Identical Luxury Product

La Impresión Que Causa Va Más Allá De Las Palabras.

El nombre de instrumentos de escritura más respetado en el mundo. Garantía mecánica vitalicia.

CROSS®
SINCE 1846

A. T. Cross Export Company
Lincoln, Rhode Island 02865 U.S.A.

The Impression It Makes Goes Beyond Words.

The world's most respected name in writing instruments. Lifetime mechanical guarantee.

CROSS®
SINCE 1846

A. T. Cross Export Company
Lincoln, Rhode Island 02865 U.S.A.

Source: *Newsweek,* November 25, 1985, and *Visión,* December 1985.

fer the same product and use the same promotional appeals in all markets. Avon, Maidenform, Coca-Cola, and A.T. Cross follow this strategy. See Figure 15–3.

2. *Same product—different message.* The same product may satisfy a different need or be used differently elsewhere. This means that the product may be left unchanged, but a different message is required. Honda's campaign "You meet the nicest people on a Honda" appeals to Americans who use their motorcycles as a pleasure vehicle, but in Brazil, Honda stresses economy as it tries to make its product a means of basic transportation.

3. *Product adaptation—same message.* In cases where the product serves the same function but must be adapted to different conditions, the same message is employed with a changed product. A number of product alterations have been cited in the section on product strategies.

4. *Product adaptation—message adaptation.* When both product use and buying habits are unlike those of the home country, both the message and the product must be modified. In Chile, greeting cards carry no message and are sufficiently general in design so that they may be used for a number of occasions. The Starlight Tissue Company of West Germany is turning out rolls of toilet paper with English lessons printed on them. The course consists of 26 lessons, with each roll bearing one lesson that is repeated on every sixth square of paper. The promotion states that the idea is for Germans who say that they have always wanted to learn English but have never had the time.

5. *Different product—same message.* As we pointed out in our discussion of the economic forces' influence on product strategies, the potential customers in many markets cannot afford the product as manufactured in the firm's home country. The product may also be too technologically advanced to gain widespread acceptance. To overcome these obstacles, multinationals have frequently produced a very distinct product for these markets. The previously mentioned low-cost automobile and inexpensive manually operated washing machine are two examples. The promotional message, however, can be very similar to what is used in the developed countries if the product performs the same functions.

6. *Different product for the same use—different message.* Frequently the different product requires a different message as well. Welding torches rather than automatic welding machines would be sold on the basis of low acquisition cost rather than high output per labor hour. LDC governments faced with high unemployment would be persuaded by a message emphasizing the job-creating possibilities of labor-intensive processes rather than the labor saving of highly automated machinery.

The tools for communicating these messages—the promotional mix—are personal selling, advertising, sales promotion, publicity, and public relations.

No one of these tools is inherently superior to the others, though circumstances in a given situation may dictate that one of them should be emphasized more than the others. Just as in the determination of the product strategies, the composition of the promotional mix will depend on the type of product, the environmental forces, and the amount of market penetration desired.

Advertising

Of all the promotional mix elements, advertising is the one with the greatest similarities worldwide. The reason for this is that most advertising everywhere is based on American practices. U.S. ad agencies have greatly aided the global propagation of American techniques as they have followed their domestic customers overseas. Today the major American agencies are all multinational, with wholly owned subsidiaries, joint ventures, and working agreements with local agencies. As an illustration of how complete U.S. domination is, nearly all of the world's 50 largest agencies are American. Japan is second, with 7.

Undoubtedly, this factor and the economies of scale have prompted many multinational firms to stress the standardization of advertising procedures. Coca-Cola, for example, estimates that it saves more than $8 million annually in the cost of thinking up new imagery by repeating the same theme everywhere. Texas Instruments, which used to have four different creative approaches in Scandinavia (one for each country), now runs similar ads in all four countries at a saving of $30,000 a commercial.

The multinational advertising agencies obviously argue for international standardization because their presence in various world markets gives them a sales advantage over the local agency. This approach often appeals as well to top managements, which want their firms to present a single, unified image and logo in all markets. A good example of a standard logo is General Tire's "Big G," shown in Figure 15–4.

Although the advertising campaign may often be standardized worldwide, international advertisers generally prefer national media to reach mass audiences. One exception to this generalization, however, is the situation in which the advertisements are shown on a European TV station that is also viewed in neighboring countries or are placed in internationally distributed publications such as *Reader's Digest, Time, The Wall Street Journal, Business Week,* and *Fortune.*

The international advertising manager must be prepared to hear arguments against standardization from personnel in the foreign subsidiaries. "Our market is unique," they will argue, "and so we can't use what the home office sends us." The manager's task is to weigh the pros and cons of standardization, taking into consideration the cost of lower morale that it might bring and then choosing the approach that will apparently produce the greatest sales at the least cost. When making this decision, he or she needs to realize that certain factors may at times be decisive, such as the type of product, media availability, and the foreign environmental forces.

Figure 15–4

General Tire Logo

Source: Courtesy General Tire International Company

Type of Product. Buyers of industrial goods and luxury products usually act on the same motives the world over, and thus these products lend themselves to the standardized approach. This enables manufacturers of capital goods such as NCR and Westinghouse to prepare international campaigns that require very little modification in the various markets. Certain consumer goods markets are similar too. When the product is low priced, is consumed in the same way, and is bought for the same reasons, then generally the same appeals and advertising campaigns can be employed. Examples of such products are gasoline, soft drinks, detergents, cosmetics, and airline services.

Firms such as Esso (now Exxon), Coca-Cola, Avon, and Procter & Gamble have for years used the international approach successfully. The only changes they have made are a translation into the local language and the use of natives as models. Figure 15–5 illustrates how Esso's highly successful "tiger in the tank" campaign looked in several languages.

Availability of Media. Even though the message may be standardized, international advertising managers will find that they cannot use the same media mix from country to country because the media are not equally available in all markets. Radio and TV are highly government regulated, and many stations do not accept advertising. In India, only 26 of the 82 government-controlled radio stations carry commercials, and since a maximum of just 10 percent of the broadcast time can be devoted to them, this medium has limited appeal to advertisers. The situation is even more difficult in Denmark, Norway, Sweden, Belgium, Finland, and Switzerland, where there is no commercial radio at all; in the first four of these countries, there is also no commercial TV (see Figure 15–6).

However, the situation in a number of these markets is changing rapidly. Denmark expects to have a commercial TV channel in 1988, and Norway and Sweden should follow a year or two later. Countries that already have commercial TV are adding new channels. France has added three and the Netherlands has added one. Also, more radio stations are obtaining permits to carry advertising.

Most noncommercial stations in Europe, both radio and TV, are owned and operated by each nation's PTT authority (postal, telephone, and telegraph), which collects a license fee from radio and TV owners. Advertisers that want to reach markets with no commercial radio buy time on one of the legal stations located outside the country to which it transmits or on a local illegal station. Well-known legal stations are Radio Luxembourg, Radio Sud (Andorra), Radio Monte Carlo, and Europe 1 (Germany). Illegal stations broadcast from hidden locations until they are caught and their equipment is confiscated. In spite of these difficulties, it is estimated that there are as many as 10,000 pirates on the air, many of which sell advertising.[11]

Nothing similar has existed for television except Radio-Television Luxembourg (RTL), whose programs can be picked up 100 kilometers into eastern France and southern Belgium, and even farther by cable. Incidentally, RTL is a large operation, the second-largest taxpayer (banking is first) in Luxembourg.

Figure 15-5
Esso Tiger Ad

Source: Reproduced with permission of Exxon Corporation

Figure 15-6

Cabling Europe

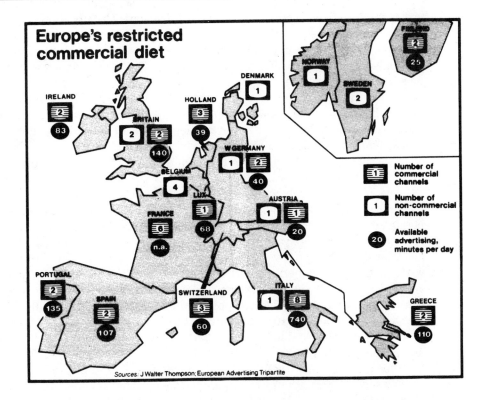

Sources: J Walter Thompson; European Advertising Tripartite

Note: Values shown are for national TV networks only and do not include regional stations in Spain and Italy. They do not include private cable TV networks such as Sky Channel.
Source: Toby Syfret, "Pan-European Problems for Satellite Advertisers, *Marketing Week,* February 6, 1987, p. 46.

As you noted in Figure 15–6, commercial TV in some of the most important industrialized nations in the world (those of Western Europe) is either nonexistent or is highly restricted with respect to available advertising time. This situation began to change, however, in 1982, when a British TV producer realized that the many European cable systems built to improve TV reception in the home could receive programs from a satellite already in orbit. He formed Satellite Television, now called Sky Channel, which distributes a service that reaches more than 7 million households in 11 European nations. Low-cost English-language programs, such as movies, sports, and American TV reruns, interspersed with advertising are broadcast every evening for eight hours.

Compare that with German government-owned television stations, whose commercials are restricted to 20 minutes per evening between 6 P.M. and 8 P.M. and none at all on Sundays and holidays. It is no wonder that multinationals such as Coca-Cola, Wrigley, Kellogg, Polaroid, and Schweppes are customers of Sky Channel or Music Box, a newer English cable system.[12]

Even where commercials are permitted, the scheduling and price setting are generally in the hands of government agencies. Usually there is no such thing as a sponsored program, and often the advertisers cannot even choose the time of day that the commercial will air. In some instances, blocks of time are auctioned off to wholesalers; these then retail spots to advertisers which often must buy them a year ahead of time.

Until the Italian constitutional court ruled that the government had no TV monopoly, Italian advertisers not only had to buy time a year in advance but were also forced to buy space in government publications and time on radio. It was a common practice in Italy as well as other countries to schedule blocks of advertisements that would run for five minutes or more with anywhere from 10 to 20 consecutive commercials.

After the monopoly was broken, Italy became the only country in Europe where private TV advertising was unregulated. This had a major impact on corporate advertising strategies. For the first time, there was as much advertising space as the customers wanted. TV advertising expenditures increased so rapidly that the private networks now capture 30 percent of total expenditures, whereas the state-owned network receives only 16.5 percent. The ban on advertisements of automobiles, liquor, and jewelry was relaxed by the state network when private channels accepted them. Fiat, Renault, Ford, and Alfa Romeo are now among the 10 largest advertisers in Italy.[13].

What has occurred in Italy is spreading to other European markets. Satellites for both cable systems and direct broadcasting are making it extremely difficult for governments to keep out commercial TV. For example, in Belgium, one of the last of the EC nations to maintain the advertising ban on domestic TV networks, 40 cable companies feed 15 channels from six countries into the homes of 87 percent of the nation's 3 million TV owners.[14] Advertising is permitted on Belgian cable TV networks when the programs originate from foreign-based stations such as Sky Channel. In 1984, the Belgian government permitted public sector companies such as the railroads, even foreign-owned ones, to promote themselves but not their products. Advertising agencies believe that before long the rules will be relaxed to permit advertising by commercial companies.[15]

Figure 15–6 illustrates the great variation among markets as to the availability of time for TV advertising, though the advent of privately owned stations is changing this situation. For example, the available advertising minutes per day have increased in Italy from 65 minutes on three commercial networks in 1983 to 740 minutes on five major and three minor networks. There is also little uniformity in pricing. Although the prices in Germany are twice as high as those in the United States, they are only two thirds as high as those in France and Great Britain.

Africa is marked by a scarcity of all media. Only 163 radio stations serve an area twice the size of the United States, and although there are 84 TV stations in all, one third of them are located in just two countries (Nigeria—18 and Ivory

Figure 15-7

R. J. Reynolds Annual Report, 1981, p. 7.

Sales promotion in Spain

Coast—10). Ten countries have no TV. Even these numbers are misleading, because in many countries the stations are government owned and noncommercial. Although there are 168 daily newspapers in the 51 African countries, 86 of them are located in only six countries. Nine countries have no daily paper, and 13 have only one.[16] In this seller's market, an advertiser may find that the newspaper has accepted too many ads for the available space. Some newspapers' solution is a raffle to decide which ads will be published!

In Latin America and the Middle East, the opposite situation exists: there are too many newspapers and magazines. The problem in those regions is choosing the right ones for the firm's target market. In which of the 900 newspapers in Brazil or the 400 in Turkey should the ad be placed? Circulation figures are greatly exaggerated, and the advertisers must also be careful of the publication's political

Figure 15-8

R. J. Reynolds Annual Report, 1981, p. 8.

Innovative promotion of a new brand, Century, on the beaches of Rio de Janeiro

position to avoid associating their firms with the "wrong side"—the one contrary to what the majority of their potential customers believe in.

These problems and the high illiteracy rate in some nations have forced advertisers to go to other media to reach their markets. Cinema advertising is heavily used in many parts of the world, as are billboards. In the Middle East, where media options are limited, videotape ads are rapidly becoming an integral part of the media mix. Advertisers penetrate this lucrative market by buying spots on a popular video. Three or four breaks with six or seven spots each are created at the beginning, middle, and end of the film. Three quarters of the households in the United Arab Emirates, Saudi Arabia, and Kuwait have videocassette recorders, and in the first three months after release a well-received video can draw an audience of 1 million viewers in Saudi Arabia alone.[17] In a number of lesser-developed countries, automobiles equipped with loudspeakers circulate through the cities announcing products, and street signs are furnished by advertisers that hang their messages on them. Homeowners can get a free coat of paint by permitting advertisers to put ads on their walls. Where mail delivery is reliable, direct mail is a powerful medium, as are trade fairs. Probably one of the most ingenious campaigns ever was that of a tea company that gave away thousands of printed prayers with a tea commercial on the other side to pilgrims bound for Mecca. Table 15–1 illustrates how the constraints we have discussed affect the distribution of advertising expenditures.

The point is that media of some kind are available in every country, and the local managers and ad agencies are familiar with the advantages of each kind. Media selection is extremely difficult for international advertising managers who try to standardize their advertising mix from the home office. We have mentioned only some of the problems, but from these the reader can appreciate that the variation in media availability is a strong reason for leaving this part of the advertising program to the local organization.

Foreign Environmental Forces. Like variations in media availability, the foreign environmental forces act as deterrents to the international standardization of advertising, and as you would expect, among the most influential of these forces are the *sociocultural* forces, which we examined in Chapter 8.

A basic cultural decision for the marketer is whether to position the product as foreign or local, and which way to go seems to depend on the country, the product type, and the target market. In Germany, for example, consumers are not at all impressed by the carmaker that announced that it had American know-how. "After all," reason the Germans, "if so many Americans prefer Volkswagen and Mercedes over U.S. cars, why shouldn't we?" At the same time, purely American products such as bourbon, fast-food restaurants, and blue jeans have made tremendous inroads not only in Germany but in the rest of Europe. McDonald's introduced the "Big Mac" in London by advertising: "For 48 pence, the United States of America."

Similarly in Japan, American identity for consumer products enhances their image. The young and the status conscious prefer the casual American look in clothing and seek the American label that identifies the wearer as belonging to the "in group." The influence of the American-style fast-food restaurants on Japanese youth was emphasized in a survey taken by the Japanese Ministry of Agriculture, which found that more than 50 percent of the country's teenagers would rather eat occidental foods than the traditional dishes. These restaurants are now grossing over two billion dollars, with U.S.-based ventures such as McDonald's (already the second-largest Japanese restaurant business), Dairy Queen, Mister Donut, and Kentucky Fried Chicken accounting for over 50 percent of that amount.[18] The experience of the suppliers to the youth market already indicates that this too is essentially an international market segment, much like the market for luxury goods. What this means for marketers is that they can formulate international advertising campaigns for these consumers that will require little more than a translation into the local language. Before mak-

Table 15-1

Advertising Expenditures in Selected Countries, 1985

Rank	Country	Total Expenditures ($ millions)	Percent of Total					Advertising Expenditures per Capita ($)
			Print	Cinema	Radio	TV	Direct Advertising	
1	United States	$94,750	32.0%	n.a.	6.8%	21.9%	16.4%	397.11
2	Japan	12,809	35.3	n.a.	5.2	35.2	n.a.	106.13
3	United Kingdom	6,442	57.2	0.4%	1.7	28.1	9.3	114.22
4	West Germany	5,430	65.2	0.8	3.4	9.4	11.9	89.02
5	Canada	4,465	38.3	n.a.	9.4	17.1	6.7	175.79
6	France	3,292	41.1	1.9	9.1	17.1	12.9	59.86
7	Brazil	2,453	31.9	0.2	4.0	58.7	0.8	17.52
8	Australia	2,318	48.5	1.4	9.2	34.0	n.a.	148.56
9	Netherlands	2,027	48.3	0.2	1.4	4.8	39.1	139.79
10	Italy	1,951	41.1	0.3	4.0	49.2*	n.a.	34.16
20	India	512	80.0	2.0	3.0	10.0	n.a.	0.67
30	Malaysia	182	61.3	0.4	1.6	29.5	0.9	11.75
40	Qatar	45	36.8	n.a.	n.a.	63.2	n.a.	148.81
42	Cyprus	10	27.1	n.a.	13.6	59.3	n.a.	14.05
45	Nepal	1†	48.4	0.5	33.2	m.n.a.	6.5	0.06†

*As an illustration of how commercial TV availability affects promotional expenditures, in 1981, when freedom of TV advertising in Italy was just beginning, only 15.2 percent of total advertising expenditures was spent on TV.
†Lowest value of the 45 nations reporting.
n.a.—data not available.
m.n.a.—medium not available.
Source: *World Advertising Expenditures*, Starch, INRA, Hooper & LAA 1986, pp. 20, 21.

Figure 15-9

Courtesy: McDonald's Corporation

The typical exterior design of McDonald's restaurants in Japan

ing the decision concerning local versus foreign identity, however, management is advised once again to check with local personnel on a country-by-country basis.

Inasmuch as communication, the reason for advertising, is impossible if the language is not understood, translations must be made into the language of the consumers. Unfortunately for the advertiser, almost every language varies from one country to another. The same word may be perfectly apt in one country while signifying something completely different or even vulgar in another, as was illustrated in Chapter 8. To avoid translation errors, the experienced advertising manager will use (1) a double translation and (2) plenty of illustrations with short copy.

Closely allied to the cultural forces, since generally a nation's laws reflect public opinion, are the legal forces, which exert an extremely pervasive influence on advertising. We have seen how laws affect media availability, but they also restrict the kinds of products that can be advertised and even the copy employed in the advertisements.

Goodyear found that it could not use its international campaign claiming that nylon tire cord was stronger than steel in Germany, because doing so would violate a law against comparing products. Coca-Cola thought that Malaysia also had such a ban. Consequently, when Pepsi-Cola mounted a half-million-dollar taste test campaign on TV, Coke's ad agency protested. However, Pepsi had followed the rules in not naming the competitor's products. It merely showed side-by-side taste tests of two different products in unmarked bottles. The government body that regulated advertising stated that it had no objection to the taste tests, and the commercials resumed.

Until 1986, many products were banned from French TV: jewelry, margarine (to protect milk producers), airlines (to protect Air France), publications, films, concerts, records, retailers, and alcoholic drinks. But many changes occurred when La 5, France's first all-commercial network, began operation in 1986. First, the programs are livelier, and even more important for advertisers, commercial breaks during programs are permitted. Also, companies can advertise such products as books, wine, beer, and margarine, all of which are banned from government-owned stations. However, the ban still exists for child models in ads and for the use of non-French words when there is a French equivalent. Announcers cannot get friendly with the audience either—the formal *vous* must always be employed.[19]

Advertisers in the Islamic nations have had to be resourceful to avoid censorship. The use of women's photos in advertisements is forbidden unless the models are clearly Western—preferably blondes or redheads. "Erotic" sound effects are not permitted: a TV soft-drink commercial with a girl licking her lips to show she liked the taste was declared "obscene." In Pakistan, the government decreed that women models could advertise only women's products on TV. They cannot advertise cars or men's cologne, for example. Imagine Ford trying to sell its Mercury with a slinky male posed seductively behind the wheel, or how about an all-male Old Spice commercial?[20]

Just as in the United States, there is a strong tendency for governments elsewhere to control advertising even more as government leaders urged on by consumer groups enact stricter laws. In Sweden, consumer ombudsmen (government officials) can require companies to provide total disclosure in advertising. If they wish, these ombudsmen can force a manufacturer of cameras to state not only the cost of the camera but also what the film and processing will cost the buyer. Products that do not live up to their claims can be forced off the market. Mexico's new law on consumer protection gives major emphasis to advertising. Dealers as well as suppliers are obligated to make good any guarantees or offers announced to the public and must even obtain governmental approval before announcing a sale or a special offer.

In some governments, a strong bias against advertising in general or against certain media is reflected in advertising taxes. The result of variations in the taxation of advertising media is to limit the advertisers' choice among media and to cause them to employ more of the other promotional mix elements than they might normally use. All national governments in Europe except Switzerland apply a value-added tax to advertising, though France, Ireland, the Netherlands, Norway, the United Kingdom, and West Germany exempt foreign-based companies that place advertising from the home country. Some of these countries also place additional taxes on advertising. Greece is notorious for extra taxes that are really punitive—47 percent on TV, 20 percent on newspapers and radio, and 16 percent on magazines. Advertisers using billboards pay as much as 50 percent extra when municipal taxes are included. It is important to know whether local taxes are levied, because they can be very discriminatory. Outdoor advertising is subject to an additional local tax in Italy, as is outdoor and cinema advertising in Portugal. Futhermore, in many countries such taxes vary among municipalities.[21]

Programmed-Management Approach. With so many obstacles to international standardization, what should be the approach of the international advertising manager? The opinion of some experts seems to be that good ideas and good promotions can cross international borders. Robert Trebus of Marsteller International believes that far too often businesspeople ask how the product can be sold in Germany without first asking how the firm did it successfully in Sweden. Trebus states that "rarely will a campaign be a success in Sweden without having registered a like success in Greece." He believes that too many managers are convinced that to be successful in different markets, they must approach each market differently.[22] This school of thought looks for similarities across segments and countries so as to capitalize on them by providing promotional themes with worldwide appeal.

A second school of thought believes that even though human nature is the same everywhere, it is also true that a Spaniard will remain a Spaniard and a Belgian a Belgian. Thus, it is preferable to develop separate appeals to take advantage of the differences among customers in different cultures and countries.

The results of a study made by *International Advertiser* showed that the primary reason (50 percent of the respondents) for global standardization was cost reduction in planning and control. International brand and corporate image was second (38 percent), and simplification of coordination and control was third (31 percent). The primary reasons against standardization were insufficient consideration of local peculiarities (53 percent), the heterogeneous media scene (25 percent), and differences in the stage of the product life cycle (19 percent). The survey indicated that the extent of actual standardization of advertising decisions was generally higher than the judgment on the possibility of standardization. This means that the reasons in favor of standardization influence the basic objective of the international firm more than do the obvious differences among nations.[23]

From the previous discussion, you have probably already gathered that neither the entirely standardized nor the entirely local campaign is the best way to handle international advertising. There is a middle ground, called by some the **programmed-management approach,** in which the home office and the foreign subsidiaries agree on marketing objectives, after which each puts together a tentative advertising campaign. This is submitted to the home office for review and suggestions. The campaign is then market tested locally, and the results are submitted to the home office, which reviews them and offers comments. The subsidiary then submits a complete campaign to the home office for review. When the home office is satisfied, the budget is approved and the subsidiary begins implementing the campaign. The result may be a highly standardized campaign for all markets or one that has been individualized to the extent necessary to cope with local market conditions. The programmed-management approach gives the home office a chance to standardize those parts of the campaign that may be standardized but still permits flexibility in responding to different marketing conditions.[24]

> Instead of having 43 different versions of ads running worldwide, as in the past, Playtex requested its ad agency, Grey, a huge multinational with affiliates in 33 major cities overseas, to develop a global campaign for TV that would work in every market. Grey's main office in New York prepared the boards (a series of still pictures with suggested dialogue depicting the commercial) and sent them to its overseas affiliates with instructions to look for things that would not work in their markets. The agency also showed Playtex foreign managers videotapes of potential models. Dozens were rejected until they all agreed on three that were deemed to have universal appeal (see accompanying photographs).
>
> Although the cross-your-heart message was the same everywhere, there were some local differences that had to be taken into account. One was the brassiere style. The French like lacy bras, whereas Germans and Americans prefer the plainer types. Also, European TV permits live models, whereas South African and U.S. TV do not (two U.S. networks changed this rule in 1987).To accommodate these differences, shots were made both ways and then spliced into the ads for each market. To comply with Australian law, the Australian ads had to be shot locally.
>
> Names for the bras had to be found for different languages because WOW (without wires) could not be translated literally. Traumbugel (dream wire) was used in Germany, Alas (wings) in Spain, and Armagique (contraction for structure and magic) was chosen for France. Interestingly, even the packaging is different. Bras are put on hangers in the UK and the United States but are packaged in boxes elsewhere.
>
> Global advertising permitted Playtex to present one unified message in all markets and also to save money. Grey claims that it was able to produce the WOW ad for a dozen countries at a cost of only $250,000. The average cost of producing a single U.S. ad is $100,000.

Personal Selling

Along with advertising, personal selling constitutes a principal component of the promotional mix. The importance of this promotional tool as compared to advertising depends to a great extent on the relative costs, the funds available, media availability, and the type of product sold.

Just as in the United States, manufacturers of industrial products rely more on personal selling than advertising to communicate with their overseas markets. However, producers of consumer products may also emphasize per-

sonal selling overseas, especially in the developing countries, because salespeople in these countries will often work for less compensation than would be demanded in the home country. A newcomer to marketing must be careful, nonetheless, to consider all of the expenses in maintaining a salesperson, as frequently expense items such as automobiles and their maintenance (rough treatment on bad roads) may be three or four times the U.S. cost. Fringe benefits are commonly stipulated by law, and these too often comprise a higher percentage of the base wage in other countries.

Marketing managers will also give greater emphasis to personal selling where commercial TV and radio are unavailable or where the market is too small to support an advertising campaign.

International Standardization. By and large, the organization of the overseas sales force, sales presentation, and training methods are very similar to those employed in the home country.

Avon follows the same plan of person-to-person selling in Venezuela or the Far East as it does in this country and is extremely successful with it. When Avon entered Mexico, many of the local experts predicted that its plan would fail. The Mexican middle-class housewife would be out of the home shopping and playing bridge. The wall around the house would keep the Avon lady from reaching the front door, and when she rang the bell, the maid, as she did with all peddlers, would not let her in. Other American firms had used this approach and had failed for these reasons. However, Avon made small but important changes. For one thing, it mounted a massive advertising campaign to educate the Mexicans as to what they could expect from the visits before sending its salespeople out. Although the advertisements were the same as those used in the United States, the advertising campaign was more extensive because the Mexican housewife had to be taught a new concept. This was not the common door-to-door salesperson whom she knew but a professional trained to help her look beautiful. Avon recruited educated middle-class women as representatives and trained them well. They were encouraged to visit their friends, much as Tupperware representatives do. What was essentially an American plan, with slight changes for cultural differences, made Avon's entry into the Mexican market an unqualified success.

Other firms also follow their home country approach. Missionary salespeople from pharmaceutical manufacturers such as Pfizer and Upjohn introduce their products to physicians, just as they do in the United States. Sales engineers from General Electric and Westinghouse supply their customers with the same kind of information that is required in this country. Salespeople calling on channel members perform the same tasks of informing middlemen, setting up point-of-purchase displays, and fighting for shelf space as do their American counterparts.

Recruitment. Recruiting salespeople in foreign countries is at times more difficult than recruiting them in the home country because sales managers frequently have to cope with the stigma attached to selling that still exists in some areas (cultural forces). To help overcome this obstacle, salespeople are given titles that are essentially translations of American titles designed for the same purpose (territory or zone manager).

Another instance of the influence of cultural forces on recruiting is the need to hire salespeople who are culturally acceptable to customers and channel members. This can be difficult and costly in an already small market that is further subdivided into several distinct cultures with different customs and even languages, as we saw in the chapter on physical forces. If a cultural pocket will support a salesperson at all, the experienced sales manager will make every effort to recruit a person indigenous to the region.

American firms are aided in recruitment by their reputation for having excellent training programs. These generally come from the home office and are adapted, if necessary, to local conditions. When the product is highly technical, the new employees are often sent to the home office for training. Of course, the opportunity to take such a trip is also an effective recruiting tool.

Sales Promotion

Sales promotion provides the selling aids for the marketing function and includes such activities as the preparation of point-of-purchase displays, contests, premiums, and trade show exhibits. If there is no separate department for these activities, they will be performed in either the advertising or sales department.

The international standardization of the sales promotion function is not difficult, because the experience of the multinationals has shown that what is successful in the United States generally proves effective overseas. There are some cultural and legal constraints to consider, nonetheless, when sales promotion techniques are transferred to other countries.

Legal Constraints. Laws concerning sales promotion tend to be more restrictive in foreign countries than they are in the United States. The kinds of premiums offered are often required to have some relation to the product, or the value of premiums may be limited to a given percentage of the product purchase price. Mexico requires that special offers and cents-off deals be approved by a government agency before they can be put into effect. While these legal restrictions are bothersome, they have not stopped the use of sales promotion.

Sociocultural and Economic Constraints. The cultural and economic constraints are more consequential than the legal constraints and do make some sales promotions difficult to use. If a premium is to fulfill the objective of being a sales aid for the product, it must be meaningful to the purchaser. A gadget to be used in the kitchen will be valued by the American housewife but will not be particularly attractive to a Latin American housewife if she has two maids to do the housework. Firms that attach premiums to the outside of packages in the less developed countries usually do this just once. Less than a week after the packages are on the shelf, the detached premiums are already being sold in the streets. Putting the prize inside the package is also no guarantee that it will be there when the purchaser takes the package home.[25]

Contests, raffles, and games, however, have been extremely successful in countries where people love to play the odds. If Latin Americans or Irishmen will buy a lottery ticket week after week hoping to win the grand prize playing against odds of 500,000 to 1, why shouldn't they participate in a contest that costs them nothing to enter? Point-of-purchase displays are well accepted by retailers, though many establishments are so small that there is simply no place to put all of the displays that are offered them. Sales promotion is generally not as sophisticated overseas as it is in the United States, and our experience indicates that even American subsidiaries do not make sufficient use of the ideas coming from headquarters. The international marketing manager who prepares a well-planned program after studying the constraints of the local markets can expect excellent results from the time and money invested.

Public Relations

Public relations is the firm's communications and relationships with its various publics, including the governments where it operates, or, as one writer has put it, "Public relations is the marketing of the firm."[26] Although American multinationals have had organized public relations programs for many years in the United States, they have paid much less attention to this important function elsewhere.

Ironically, it is on the whole not true that the multinationals have neglected public service activities through their foreign subsidiaries—only that they have failed to inform their publics of what they are doing. Exxon has for years sponsored the study of foreign art students in the United States, and the ITT International Fellowship Program, started in 1973, has already enabled more than 250 students from 41 countries to pursue advanced degrees in the United States and abroad. The foreign subsidiary that does not participate in local charitable and cultural activities is exceedingly rare, but far too often only the recipients know about it.

The rising wave of nationalism and antimultinational feeling in many countries has made it imperative that companies with international operations improve their communications to their nonbusiness publics with more effective public relations programs.

An example of a successful public relations program is the one launched by Nestlé in response to an attack by the International Baby Food Action Network (IBFAN). This consumers' organization accused the company of persuading mothers in LDCs to bottle-feed with formula rather than breast-feed their babies. The IBFAN and various church groups that advocated breast-feeding charged that contaminated water in the formula was contributing to infant mortality. This was the same water, of course, that had always been mixed with homemade baby food. Although 17 multinationals sold infant formula, Nestlé was singled out for attack, according to the boycott director, "because it has the largest market share."[27]

The company responded to the attack by implementing the 1981 World Health Organization's code on the marketing of breast-milk substitutes. It also created a semi-independent review panel to examine its marketing practices and its adherence to the code. This unprecedented action slowed the attack of its critics, who finally called the boycott off. It is predicted that American Home Products will be the next candidate for a boycott.

Other consumer activist groups that appear to be in a position to inflict significant public relations damage on MNEs are (1) Pesticide Action Network, (2) Health Action International for pharmaceuticals, and (3) the World Council of Churches, which is concerned with such issues as the nature of Third World poverty and Western support for "racist, authoritarian" regimes.[28]

One of the most vexing problems that MNEs have is how to deal with such critics. Some try to defuse criticism before it becomes a full-scale attack by holding regularly scheduled meetings at which topics of interest are debated. Others prefer to meet with critics privately, though they may find themselves caught in a never-ending relationship in which the critics continually escalate their demands. This is especially true of single-issue groups, whose existence depends on the continuance of the issue.

A successful strategy employed by some firms has been to address the issue without dealing directly with the critics. Instead, they work with international or governmental agencies. Another alternative is to do nothing. It may be that if the criticism receives no publicity, it will die from lack of interest.

An important tool for communicating corporate citizenship is the corporate balance sheet, which shows in detail the net contribution of the subsidiaries to their countries of residence. The Argentine and Brazilian affiliates of Clark Equipment Company regularly prepare a kind of balance sheet that describes employee benefits; contributions to the local economy in terms of salaries, taxes, and local purchases; and balance-of-payment contributions. Negative items, including payments for technology and remittance of dividends, are spelled out, but the bottom line makes it clear that the operations of the subsidiary constitute an important gain for the host country. It is reported that other firms are now following this example of good public relations.[29]

Pricing Strategies

Pricing, the third element of the marketing mix, is an important and complex consideration in formulating the marketing strategy. Pricing decisions affect other corporate functions, directly determine the firm's gross revenue, and are a major determinant of profits.

Pricing, a Controllable Variable

Marketers, especially Americans, have become increasingly cognizant of the fact that effective price setting consists of something more than mechanically adding a standard markup to a cost. To obtain the maximum benefits from pricing, management must regard it in the same manner as it regards other controllable variables; that is, pricing is one of the marketing mix elements that can be varied in order to achieve the marketing objectives of the firm.

For instance, if the marketer wishes to position a product as a high-quality item, setting a relatively high price will reinforce promotion that emphasizes quality. However, combining a recognizably low price with a promotional emphasis on quality could result in an incongruous pairing that would adversely affect consumer credibility—the low price might be interpreted as the correct price for an inferior product. Pricing can also be a determinant in the choice of middlemen, because if the firm requires a wholesaler to take title, stock, promote, and deliver the merchandise, it must give the wholesaler a much larger trade discount than would be demanded by a broker, whose services are much more limited.

These examples illustrate one of the reasons for the complexity of price setting—the interaction of pricing with the other elements of the marketing mix. In addition, two other sets of forces influence this variable: (1) interaction between marketing and the other functional areas of the firm and (2) environmental forces.[30]

International Standardization

Multinational firms that pursue a policy of unifying corporate pricing procedures know that pricing is acted on by the same forces that militate against the international standardization of the other marketing mix components. Pricing for the overseas markets is more complex because managements must be concerned with two kinds of pricing: (1) *foreign national pricing*, which is domestic pricing in another country, and (2) *international pricing* for exports.

Foreign National Pricing. Many foreign governments in their fight against inflation have instituted price controls, and the range of the products affected varies immensely from country to country. Some governments attempt to fix prices on just about everything, while others are concerned only with essential goods. Unfortunately, there is no agreement on what is essential, so that in one market the prices of gasoline, food products, tires, and even wearing apparel may be controlled, while in another market only the prices of staple foods may be fixed. In nations with laws on unfair competition, it may be the minimum sales price that is controlled rather than the maximum. The German law is so comprehensive that under certain conditions even premiums and cents-off coupons may be prohibited because they are considered to violate the minimum price requirements. The international marketer must be watchful of a recent tendency of many nations, especially EC members, to open up their markets to price competition by weakening and even abolishing retail price maintenance laws.

Prices can vary because of appreciable cost differentials on opposite sides of a border. One government may levy higher import duties on imported raw materials or may subsidize public utilities, while another may not. Differences in labor legislation will cause labor costs to vary. Competition among local suppliers may be intense in one market, permitting the affiliate to buy inputs at better prices than those paid by an affiliate in another market, which must purchase raw materials from a single supplier, possibly a government monopoly.

Competition on the selling side is also diverse. It frequently happens that an affiliate in one market will face heavy local competition and be severely limited in the price it can charge, while in a neighboring market a lack of competitors will allow another affiliate to charge a much higher price. As regional economic groupings reduce trade barriers among members, such opportunities are becoming fewer because firms must then meet regional as well as local competition.

Because the multinational firm, for a number of reasons, does not introduce a new product simultaneously in all markets, the same product will not be in the same stage of the product life cycle everywhere. In markets where it is in the introductory stage, there is an opportunity to charge a high "skimming" price or a low "penetration" price, depending on such factors as market objectives, patent protection, price elasticity of demand, and competition. As the product reaches the maturity or decline stage, the price may be lowered, if doing so permits a satisfactory return. It is apparent that because life cycles vary among markets, prices too will be different.

International Pricing. International pricing involves the setting of prices for goods produced in one country and sold in another. The pricing of exports to unrelated customers falls in this category and will be treated separately in the chapter on exporting. There is a special kind of exporting, *intracorporate sales*, which is exceedingly common among the multinationals as they attempt to rationalize production by requiring subsidiaries to specialize in the manufacture of some products while importing others. Their imports may consist of components that are assembled into the end product, such as engines made in one country that are mounted in car bodies built in another, or they may be finished products imported to complement the product mix of an affiliate. No matter what the end use is, problems exist in setting an intracorporate price (**transfer price**).

Because it is possible for the multinational firm as a whole to gain while both the buying and selling subsidiaries "lose" (receive prices that are lower than would be obtained through an outside transaction), the tendency is for transfer prices to be set at headquarters. The reason for this apparent anomaly is that the multinational obtains a profit from *both* the seller and the buyer.

The selling affiliate would like to charge other subsidiaries the same price that it charges all customers, but when combined with transportation costs and import duties, such a price may make it impossible for the importing subsidiary to compete in its market. If headquarters dictates that a lower-than-market transfer price be charged, the seller will be unhappy because its profit-and-loss statement suffers. This can be a very real headache to personnel whose promotion and bonuses depend on the bottom line. In Chapter 22, we will see how home office management deals with this problem.

Both foreign governments and the U.S. government are also interested in profits and the part transfer prices play in their realization, because of the influence of profits on the amount of taxes paid. Foreign tax agents and the IRS have become very much aware that because of differences in tax structures, a multinational can obtain meaningful profits by ordering a subsidiary in a country with high corporate taxes to sell at cost to a subsidiary in a country where corporate taxes are lower. The profit is earned where less income tax is paid, and the multinational clearly gains.

Transfer prices may also be employed to circumvent currency restrictions. When a country is suffering from a lack of foreign exchange, it may impose controls that totally prohibit, or at least place a low limit on, the amount of profit that can be repatriated. Suppose Country A, lacking dollars, places severe controls on all dollar transactions. There is trade with Country B, which does have dollars or another convertible currency. The home office could order its subsidiary in A to buy from the B affiliate at a price well over cost, which would transfer A's profit to B. Once in B, the profits could be sent home. The same strategy could be followed in any situation where it appeared necessary to either reduce A's profits or take them out of the country, such as:

1. Imminent currency devaluation.
2. Governmental pressure to reduce prices because of excessive profits.
3. Labor's clamor for higher wages based on high profits earned.

The manipulation of transfer prices for the reduction of income taxes and import duties or the avoidance of exchange controls has caused many governments to insist on arm's-length prices—the prices charged to unrelated customers. Under Section 482 of the Internal Revenue Code, U.S. tax authorities are empowered to reconstruct an intracorporate transfer price and tax the calculated profits whenever there is reason to suspect that low prices were set for tax evasion. Customs authorities in a number of European countries have increased the invoice price of imports by as much as 125 percent, forcing the importing subsidiary to pay a much higher than normal duty.

In spite of the advantages of transfer price manipulation, there are apparently sufficient reasons why many multinationals prefer to price at arm's length. A study of 130 American firms revealed that 60 percent of the companies preferred this method. Besides governmental intervention (especially under Section 482), executives stated that only by means of this policy could foreign managements be properly monitored and evaluated. Some who dissented stated that while their underlying policy is based on arm's-length transactions, modifications were made to take advantage of legal tax savings. As for the need to establish a standard transfer pricing policy, most managements agree that it is advantageous to have one, but they add that it must be flexible and subject to frequent review.[31]

Distribution Strategies

The development of distribution strategies is a difficult task in the home country, but it is even more so internationally, where multinational marketing managers must concern themselves with two functions rather than one: (1) getting the products *to* foreign markets (exporting) and (2) distributing the products *within* each market (foreign distribution). In this section, we will examine foreign distribution only, leaving the export channels for the next chapter.

Interdependence of Distribution Decisions

When making decisions on distribution, care must be taken to analyze their interdependence with the other marketing mix variables. For example, if the product requires considerable after-sales servicing, the firm will want to sell through dealers that have the facilities, manpower, and capital to purchase equipment and spare parts and to train servicemen. This will necessitate using a merchant wholesaler, which will demand a larger trade discount than would an agent, since an agent does not perform these functions. Channel decisions are critical because they are *long-term* decisions; once established, they are far less easy to change than those made for price, product, and promotion.

International Standardization

While management would prefer to standardize distribution patterns internationally, there are two fundamental constraints on its doing so: (1) the variation in the availability of channel members among the firm's markets and (2) the inconsistency of the influence of the environmental forces. Because of these constraints, international managers have found it best to establish a basic but flexible overall policy. This policy is then implemented by the subsidiaries, which design channel strategies to meet local conditions.

Availability of Middlemen. As a starting point in their channel design, local managers have the successful distribution system used in the domestic operation. Headquarters support for a policy of employing the same channels worldwide will be especially strong when the entire marketing mix has been built around a particular channel type, such as a direct sales force or franchised operators. Avon, Encyclopaedia Britannica, and McDonald's are examples of firms that consider their distribution systems inviolate, so that locally there is little latitude in planning channel strategies.[32] However, companies utilizing the more common types of middlemen are usually more inclined to grant the local organization greater freedom in channel member selection.

Although a general rule for any firm entering a foreign market is to adapt to the available channels rather than create new ones, a number of multinationals have successfully avoided the traditional channels because of their appalling inefficiencies. Coca-Cola did this in Japan, as we mentioned in Chapter 12.

Experienced marketers know that they cannot get their products to the consumer by the same retail channel in every country, and even in Europe the differences are substantial. What is the best way to sell toys in France? A sure outlet is the hypermarket, which sells 36 percent of all toys purchased in France, whereas in Germany the hypermarket accounts for only 15 percent of toy sales (see Table 15–2). The most important kind of outlet for toys in Germany is independent retailers , which are organized into buying groups. Table 15–2 also indicates that there are differences in the way shoes are sold in these two neighboring countries.

Foreign Environmental Forces. Environmental differences among markets add to the difficulty in standardizing distribution channels. Changes caused by the cultural forces generally occur over time, but those caused by the legal forces can be radical and quick and can slow dramatically trends that are responding to cultural demands.

To illustrate, hypermarkets, which are changing distribution patterns in Europe and particularly in France, a nation of small shopkeepers, numbered only 11 in that country in 1972. The combination of lower prices and one-stop shopping caught on with the French consumer, and 51 hypermarkets were opened in 1973. Manufacturers that saw a quick end to small shopkeepers failed to appreciate their political power. The Royer Law, passed in 1973, gave local urban commissions, often dominated by small merchants, the power to refuse

Table 15-2

Percentage of Total Sales by Type of Outlet

	Percent of Total Sales
Shoes	
Germany	
Organized independents (buying groups)	35%
Major shoe chains	29
Mail	7
Department stores	6
Hypermarkets	6
Discount stores	6
Independent shoe stores	4
Other retailers	7
	100%
France	
Independent shoe stores	56%
Direct sales	14
Clothing stores	2
Department stores	2
Variety stores	1
Other retailers	25
	100%
Toys	
Germany	
Organized independent toy stores (buying groups)	37%
Department stores	27
Hypermarkets	15
Mail	8
Independent toy stores	4
Other retailers	9
	100%
France	
Hypermarkets/supermarkets	36%
Toy stores	22
Department and variety stores	14
Mail	8
Other retailers	20
	100%

Source: *Retail Trade International* (London: Euromonitor, 1986), pp. 162, 171, 480, 489.

construction permits for supermarkets and hypermarkets. After the law took effect, only 40 percent of the large-store applications were approved, with the result that just 14 hypermarkets were opened in 1975.[33]

While the trend toward more giant stores has not been stopped by the law (there were 550 French hypermarkets in 1985), it has certainly been slowed. The president of Carrefour, France's largest hypermarket chain, says, "It is becoming increasingly hard to find a site where we can get a building permit. Opposition of small shopkeepers is the only thing keeping us from growing more rapidly." Similar laws in Italy and Belgium are keeping the concentration of retail trade at less than half of what it is in European nations without such laws (England, Germany, Netherlands).[34]

Manufacturers in the EC that have tried to prevent distributors from selling across national borders have been prohibited from doing so by the Commission through the EC's antitrust laws. Exclusive distributorships have been permitted, but every time that the manufacturer has included a clause prohibiting the distributor from exporting to another EC country, the clause has been stricken from the contract. In effect, the multinational that has two factories in the EC with different costs, and thus distinct prices, is practically powerless to prevent products from the lower-cost affiliate from competing with higher-cost products from the other affiliate.

Economic differences also make international standardization difficult, although marketers can adapt to economic changes. In 1960, very little frozen food was sold in France because of the consumer's preference for fresh food. However, tight economic conditions forced many housewives to seek employment, and with less time to spend preparing meals, they turned to frozen food. An added attraction of frozen food items was the fact that their prices did not rise as fast as those of fresh foods. The result has been sales increases of 10 percent or more a year since 1973. In Japan, high prices have also forced women to find jobs, and they no longer have time to shop for and prepare the traditional Japanese foods. More than 50 chains of convenience stores fill their needs by offering convenience foods. The 7-Eleven chain alone has over 2,000 stores in Japan. To appreciate the growth of this company, consider these facts: Japan's second-largest supermarket chain, Ito-Yokado, which operates the 7-Eleven stores under license from the Southland Corporation in the United States, began in 1972. It had only 15 stores by 1975, but by 1980 this number had increased to 800, and now there are over 2,000.[35]

Worldwide, marketers are seeing cultural barriers fall as economic conditions force housewives to obtain employment to supplement household income. The premium that outside employment places on their time is leading them to prefer one-stop shopping, laborsaving devices, and convenience foods. The result is an upheaval in the way goods are distributed, but American marketers that have U.S. experience as a guide are in a position to make inroads on their foreign competitors, for which this is a new phenomenon.

Table 15-3

Foreign Environment Constraints to International Standardization of Marketing Mix

Factors Limiting Standardization	Product	Price	Distribution	Sales Force	Promotion
1. Physical forces	1. Varying climatic conditions—special packaging, extra insulation, mildew protection, extra cooling capacity, special lubricants, dust protection, special instructions 2. Difficult terrain—stronger parts, larger engines, stronger packing	1. Special product requirements add to costs 2. Difficult terrain—extra transportation costs, higher sales expense (car maintenance, longer travel time)	1. Difficult terrain—less customer mobility, necessitating more outlets, each with larger stock 2. Varied climatic conditions—more stock needed when distinct products are required for different climates	1. Dispersion of customers 2. Difficult terrain—high traveling expense 3. Separate cultures created by barriers—salespeople from each culture necessary.	1. Cultural pockets created by barriers—separate advertisements for different languages, dialects, words, customs 2. Different climates—distinct advertising themes
2. Sociocultural forces	1. Attitudes toward products 2. Colors—varying significance 3. Languages—labels, packaging 4. Religion—consumption patterns 5. Attitudes toward time—differences in acceptance of timesaving products 6. Attitudes toward change—acceptance of new products	1. Cultural objections to product—lower prices for market penetration 2. Lower educational level, lower incomes—lower prices for mass market acceptance 3. Attitudes toward bargaining	1. More, perhaps smaller, firms to handle various subcultures 2. Positive attitudes toward bargaining—small retailers 3. Attitudes toward change—varying acceptance of new kinds of outlets 4. Different shopping habits—different outlets	1. Separate salespeople for subcultures 2. Attitudes toward work, time, achievement, and wealth; vary among cultures—difficult to motivate and control sales force 3. Different buying behavior—different kinds of sales forces	1. Language—special labels, instructions, advertisements: unfavorable connotations 2. Literacy, low—simplelabels, instructions, advertisements with plenty of graphics 3. Symbolism—responses differ 4. Different significances of colors 5. Attitudes toward advertising

7. Educational levels—varying comprehension of instructions, varying ability to use product
8. Tastes and customs
9. Different shopping habits

6. Male or female buying influence
7. Cultural pockets—different promotions
8. Religion—varying taboos and restrictions
9. Attitudes toward foreign products and companies

3. Legal-political forces

1. Some products prohibited
2. Certain features required or prohibited
3. Label and packaging requirements
4. Product standards
5. Patent laws
6. Tax laws
7. Import duties and restrictions
8. Local production required of all or part of product
9. Requirements to use local inputs

1. Retail price maintenance
2. Markups controlled
3. Antitrust laws
4. Import duties
5. Tax laws
6. Transfer pricing controls

1. Some kinds of middlemen outlawed
2. Markups controlled
3. Retail price maintenance
4. Turnover taxes
5. Restrictions on middlemen—number and kinds of lines handled, licenses for each line
6. Ease of changing middlemen

1. Selling practices regulated
2. Employment laws

1. Use of languages
2. Legal limits to expenditures
3. Taxes on advertising
4. Prohibition of promotion for some products
5. Special requirements for promotion of some products (cigarettes, pharmaceuticals)
6. Media availibility
7. Trademark laws

4. Economic forces

1. Purchasing power—package size, product sophistication, quality levels
2. Wages—varying requirements for laborsaving products

1. Different prices

1. Availability of outlets
2. Size of inventory
3. Size of outlets
4. Dispersion of outlets
5. Extent of self-service
6. Length of channels

1. Sales force expense
2. Availability of workers

1. Media availability
2. Funds available
3. Emphasis on saving time
4. Experience with products

Table 15-3
(concluded)

Factors Limiting Standardization	Product	Price	Distribution	Sales Force	Promotion
	3. Condition of infrastructure— heavier products, hand instead of power operated 4. Market size— varying width of product mix				
5. Competitive forces	1. Rate of new product introduction 2. Rate of product improvement 3. Quality levels 4. Package size	1. Competitors' prices 2. Number of competitors 3. Degree of importance of price in marketing mix	1. Competition's control of middlemen 2. Competition's margins to middlemen 3. Competition's choice of middlemen	1. Competitors' sales force— number and ability 2. Competitors' emphasis on personal selling in promotional mix 3. Competitors' rates and methods of compensation	1. Competitors' promotional expenditures 2. Competitors' promotional mix 3. Competitors' choice of media
6. Distributive forces	1. Service requirements 2. Package size 3. Branding— dealers' brands	1. Margins required	1. Availability of middlemen 2. Number of company distribution centers	1. Size of sales force 2. Kind and quality of sales force	1. Kinds of promotion 2. Amounts of promotion

Foreign Environmental Forces and Marketing Mix Matrix

The matrix shown in Table 15–3 summarizes many of the constraints on the internationalization of the marketing mix that have been discussed in this chapter and in Section III. Table 15–3 will serve as a reminder of the many factors that marketing managers should consider when they are contemplating the standardization of one or more of the marketing mix elements.

Summary

Although the basic marketing functions are the same for both domestic and international marketing, the markets served can be very dissimilar because of differences in the environmental forces. The work of the international marketing manager has an added complexity caused by the necessity of planning and controlling marketing strategies in a number of countries instead of just one. Most multinational firms would prefer to standardize the marketing-mix components internationally in order to lower their costs and simplify their control, but market differences caused by varying environmental forces militate against standardization.

Questions

1. *Define and show the relationship of the following with international business:*
   a. *Brand piracy.*
   b. *Programmed management of advertising.*
   c. *Hypermarket.*
   d. *Transfer price.*
   e. *Intermediate technology.*
2. *If the basic functions of domestic and international marketing are the same, why distinguish between the two?*
3. *What are two principal reasons why American research techniques must be modified when they are employed abroad? Give examples.*
4. *Why should multinational managers be interested in standardizing the marketing mix in all of their foreign operations?*
5. *Which of the two classes of products, industrial or consumer, generally requires greater change in order to be sold in the foreign market? Why?*
6. *What change in consumer behavior is occurring in foreign markets that is a repetition of what happened in the United States?*

7. *Which of the foreign environmental forces have been particularly influential as deterrents to the international standardization of the product?*
8. *Discuss the six distinct product strategies that are made possible by combining the three alternatives of selling the same product everywhere, adapting it to foreign markets, or designing a completely different product with the same, adapted, or different message.*
9. *What are some of the problems encountered in foreign advertising?*
10. *At least the job of translating is straightforward. All that is necessary is to give the copy to a bilingual native. True or false? Please explain.*
11. *Of all the elements of the marketing mix, personal selling is the most difficult to standardize internationally. True or false? Please explain.*
12. *Transfer pricing can be a useful tool to multinational managers. What can they accomplish with it?*

Minicase

15-1 U.S. Pharmaceutical

of Korea*

U.S. Pharmaceutical of Korea (USPK) was formed in 1969. Its one manufacturing plant is located just outside Seoul, the capital. Although the company distributes its products throughout South Korea, 40 percent of its total sales of $5 million were made in the capital last year.

There are no governmental restrictions on whom the company can sell to. The only requirement is that the wholesaler, retailer, or end user have a business license and a taxation number. Of the 400 wholesalers in the country, 130 are customers of USPK, accounting for 46 percent of the company's total sales. The company also sells directly to 2,100 of the country's 10,000 retailers; these account for 45 percent of total sales. The remaining sales are made directly to high-volume end users, such as hospitals and clinics.

Tom Sloane, marketing manager of USPK, would prefer to make about 90 percent of the company's sales directly to retailers and the remaining 10 percent directly to high-volume users. He believes however, that this strategy is not possible because there are so many small retailers. Not only is the sales volume per retailer small, but there is also a risk involved in extending them credit. USPK tends to deal directly with large urban retailers and leaves most of the nonurban retailers to the wholesalers.

However, the use of wholesalers bothers Sloane for two reasons: (1) he has to give them larger discounts than he gives retailers that buy directly from the firm; and (2) because of the intense competition (300 pharmaceutical manufac-

*Based on "Distributing Goods to Korean Consumers: One Firm's Problems," *Business Asia*, May 13, 1977, p. 149.

turers in Korea), his wholesalers frequently demand larger discounts as the price for remaining loyal to USPK.

This intense competition affects another aspect of USPK's operations—collecting receivables. USPK has found that many wholesalers collect quickly from retailers but delay paying it. Instead, they invest in ventures that offer high short-term returns. For example, lending to individuals can bring them interest rates of up to 3 percent a month. The company's receivables meanwhile range from 75 to 130 days. Wholesalers are also the cause of another problem. Many are understaffed and have to rely on "drug peddlers" for sales. The drug peddlers (there are perhaps 4,000 just in Seoul) make most of their money either by cutting the wholesaler's margins (selling at lower than recommended prices) or by bartering USPK's products for other pharmaceuticals. They do this by finding retail outlets where products are sold for less than the printed price. They exchange USPK's products at a discount for other drugs, which they sell to other retail outlets at a profit. As a result, USPK's products end up on retailers' shelves at prices lower than those that the company and its reputable wholesalers are selling them for.

The pharmaceutical industry has made some progress in persuading wholesalers and retailers to adhere to company price lists, but nonadherence is still a serious problem. One issue that manufacturers have not been able to resolve as yet is the manner in which demands from hospitals and physicians for gifts should be handled.

Sloane believes that the industry can do much to solve these problems, although intense competition has thus far kept the pharmaceutical manufacturers from joining together to map out a solution.

1. What should Tom Sloane and U.S. Pharmaceutical of Korea do to improve collections from wholesalers?

2. How would you handle the distribution problem?

3. Can anything be done through firms in the industry to improve the situation?

4. How would you handle the demands for gifts?

Minicase

15-2 Marketing a Potentially Harmful Product*

The Swiss pharmaceutical MNE Hoffman-La Roche has made a major breakthrough in the relief of a serious disabling disease that affects 3 percent of the

*Based on "Marketing a Product that Is Potentially Harmful," *Business Europe*, April 8, 1982, pp. 107–8.

world's population. Their new product Tigason, is the first product that effectively controls severe cases of psoriasis and dyskeratoses, skin disorders that cause severe flaking of the skin. Sufferers from this disease frequently retreat from society because of fear of rejection, thus losing their families and their jobs. Tigason does not cure the disease, but it causes the symptoms to disappear. There is one potential problem. Because of the risk of damage to unborn babies, women should not take the drug for one year before conception or during pregnancy. Hoffman-La Roche is well aware of the potential for harm to the company if the product is misused. It has seen the problems of another Swiss firm, Nestlé. After much discussion, the company has decided that the product is too important to keep off the market. It is, after all, the product that gives the greatest relief to sufferers.

The marketing department is asked to formulate a strategy for disseminating product information and controlling Tigason's use.

What do you as marketing manager recommend?

Minicase

15-3 Cigarette Marketing
Strategy in Brazil*

In an effort to take market share from one another in a shrinking market, Brazil's top three cigarette manufacturers are launching inexpensive brands. This is in response to the trading down by Brazil's smokers because of difficult economic conditions. The trend is to buy more low-priced cigarettes, those priced at the bottom of the country's 11-tier cigarette price structure, which is labeled A through K. Prices range from US$0.25 for the A class to US$0.63 for the K class.

The current battle is in the C class, priced at US$0.29 per pack. As an example of the downtrading that has taken place, the C class now holds 21 percent of the market share, whereas its share was 1 percent only a year ago. A new factor that is expected to both accelerate the downtrading and increase the overall drop in consumption, which amounted to over 2 percent last year, is the new government-controlled 50 percent price increase for all brands.

The three major companies and their overall brand shares are British American Tobacco (79 percent), Philip Morris (11 percent), and R. J. Reynolds (nearly 9 percent).

In the intensified competition for market share of the lower-priced cigarettes, British American Tobacco's new C brand, Belmont, has taken 15 percent of Brazil's cigarette market in only seven months. R. J. Reynolds' Mustang (Class B—US$0.27) has become that company's best-selling brand, with a 5 per-

---

*Adapted from "Brazil Cigaret Marketers in Low-End Share Battle," *Advertising Age*, February 6, 1984, p. 34.

cent market share. Incidentally, Belmont was launched in the B class but was moved up to C because BAT was not earning any money at the B prices. Philip Morris now obtains 19 percent of its volume from two resurrected Liggett & Myers brands, Mistura Fina and Master, both in the C category.

The current marketing strategy has two new C brands which are poised to strike at each other from the test market. Four months ago, BAT started testing its Montreal brand, apparently to counter Reynolds' Monaco brand. According to a Reynolds executive, "We put Monaco in test marketing as a warning, saying, 'We're ready to roll another C brand out if you do.' "

As recently as one year ago, cigarette sales were evenly divided between the H–K upper-level brands and the A–G lower-level brands. Then BAT started the downtrading by expensive launches of Plaza in the E class and Cassino in the D. Now the cheaper brands account for 59 percent of the market. The very cheapest brands (A, B, C) increased their market share from 6.5 percent to 26 percent in a year. For example, BAT's best-selling Hollywood brand fell from 30 percent to 25 percent of its total sales as Belmont became its best-selling brand.

Because C brands are just marginally profitable, there is little money to spend on advertising other than a minimal use of radio and billboards. Instead, they are being pushed to cigarette retailers and wholesalers in a fierce giveaway war. The three manufacturers are loading up these middlemen with free gifts ranging from calculators to dominoes.

As a result of the increased popularity of cheaper brands with low margins and a shrinking market, spending for ads in the media dropped about 30 percent last year for all manufacturers. R. J. Reynolds' cut was more severe—its marketing and ad spending were reduced by half.

Says one cigarette marketing executive, "Cooperatively, we've succeeded in screwing up our product mixes."

1. How would you describe the companies' marketing strategies up to this point?

2. Do their American operations follow the same strategy?

3. If the home offices question the Brazilian subsidiaries about the appropriateness of their strategy, what do you believe the marketing managers of the subsidiaries would reply?

4. What do you believe the subsidiaries should do to improve their profitability?

Supplementary Readings

Birnbaum, Phyllis. "Honorable Fussy Customer." *Across the Board*, March 1986, pp. 24–30.

Cateora, Phillip R. *International Marketing.* 5th ed. Homewood, Ill.: Richard D. Irwin, 1983.

"Close-In Pricing System Protects Avon's Margins in Hyperinflationary Nations." *B.I. Money Report*, February 10, 1986, p. 33.

Firoz, Nadeem M.; Harrison McDonald; and Fatemeh F. Bafighadimi. "Easing the Road to Success in International Advertising." *Issues in International Business*, Winter-Spring 1986, pp. 31–35.

Garsombke, Dianne J., and Thomas W. Garsombke. "Cultural Disparity in International Marketing Management: A Framework for the Overseas Agent's Selection and Supervision Process." *Issues in International Business*, Summer–Fall 1986, pp. 19–26.

"Global Advertising: Multinational vs. International: Pros and Cons." *International Advertiser*, February 1986, pp. 34–37.

"The Hazards of Cross-Cultural Advertising." *Business America*, April 2, 1984, pp. 20–23.

"How Companies Are Advertising on Pan-European Television." *Business International Ideas in Action*, June 19, 1986, pp. 13–18.

Jain, Sabhash C. *International Marketing Management*. Belmont, Calif.: Kent Publishing, 1984.

Keegan, W. J. "A Conceptual Framework for Multinational Marketing." *Columbia Journal of World Business*, November 1972, pp. 67–78.

Leontiades, James C. *Multinational Corporate Strategy*. Lexington, Mass.: D.C. Heath, 1985.

"Managing European Public Affairs for Maximum Impact." *Business International Ideas in Action*, August 4, 1986, pp. 5–10.

"More Freedom on French TV." *International Advertiser*, June 1986, pp. 12–48.

Peebles D.; J. Ryans, Jr.; and I. Vernon, "Coordinating International Advertising." *Journal of Marketing*, January 1978, pp. 28–34.

"Print, Outdoor, and Video Lead Arabian Media Mix." *International Advertiser*, February 1986, pp. 24–25.

Retail Trade International, 1986. London: Euromonitor, 1986.

"Revlon Strives for One Look." *International Advertiser*, April 1986, pp. 28–29.

Ricks, D. *Big Business Blunders*. Homewood, Ill.: Richard D. Irwin, 1983.

Terpstra, Vern. *International Marketing*. 3rd ed. Hinsdale, Ill.: Dryden Press, 1983.

"Transfer Prices in Multinational Enterprises." *Weekly Bulletin* Brussels: Kredietbank, January 23, 1981.

"U.S. -Style TV Turns On Europe." *Fortune*, April 13, 1987, pp. 96–97.

Walters, Peter G. P. "International Marketing Policy: A Discussion of the Standardization Construct and Its Relevance for Corporate Policy." *Journal of International Business*, Summer 1986, pp. 55–69.

"Westinghouse Covers the World with One Ad Campaign." *Advertising World*, September 1984, pp. 6–8.

Endnotes

1. R&D is still highly concentrated in the home country, which means that at least the important product changes for the foreign markets must be made there. Foreign and domestic personnel compete for R&D time. Also, a product specification is rarely "frozen" (look at the minor changes in automobiles during a single model year). The job of advising all of

the production facilities of these modifications is difficult enough, but it is much more complex when the product is not internationally standardized.

2. W. J. Keegan, "A Conceptual Framework for Multinational Marketing," *Columbia Journal of World Business*, November 1972, pp. 67–78.

3. One of the writers went to pick up his car in a garage and asked the mechanic whether he had test-driven it after finishing the work. Much to his surprise, the mechanic answered that he had not—he did not know how to drive!

4. At times, the obsolete products may find a market in developed countries. A large American tire manufacturer does a good business in the United States importing tires for antique cars from its foreign subsidiaries where these sizes are in regular production because the old cars are still on the road.

5. A common complaint of Americans living abroad is that "they can't get a good hamburger." A Brazilian-American in Rio de Janeiro built a drive-up similar to Dairy Queen and was successful almost immediately. The first customers were Americans and members of the international segment described in the text, but before long the word got around and Brazilians became customers. Twenty years ago, there was only one A&W Root Beer stand and one Dairy Queen in Mexico City, catering mostly to expatriates. Today there are all kinds of fast-food outlets, and the Mexicans are buying. This scenario has been repeated again and again for hundreds of products and services. The American GI, of course, has also been an important propagator of American products.

6. "Consumer Nondurables," *Business International*, June 16, 1986, p. 190.

7. D. Ricks, *Big Business Blunders* (Homewood, Ill.: Dow Jones-Irwin, 1983), p. 24.

8. Other LDCs follow this practice also. The pharmaceuticals mentioned are those sold in the United States with a prescription. To our knowledge, there is no country other than the United States where prescription drugs are counted or weighed and then packaged and labeled by the pharmacist. Elsewhere, the manufacturers, many of which are American subsidiaries, package the prescription drugs in small packages containing dosages that are commonly prescribed by the physician. The patient takes a prescription written by the physician in the language of the country (no Latin) and hands it to the pharmacist. He or she reaches up on the shelf and gives the customer a package. The pharmacist does not count, does not fill a plastic vial, and does not type labels. Incidentally, each package carries an insert that describes the common dosage, symptoms of overdose, and precautions to take when using the drug. Interestingly, the American Medical Association and owners of pharmacies have striven to block the idea of inserts in the United States. Their reason: the American public, unlike people in other countries, is not well enough educated to understand the insert.

9. We believe but cannot prove that sales of flea powder per capita should be high there. All the Americans we knew used to douse their legs liberally with it before going to the movies. If not, they would be eaten alive.

10. Warren J. Keegan, "Multinational Product Planning: Strategic Alternatives," *Journal of Marketing*, January 1969, pp. 58–62, combines these alternatives to formulate five product strategies.

11. The original pirate stations were located aboard ships off the coast of England and Holland. England passed a law that stopped them from operating, though one of them, Radio Caroline, is reported to be back in business. Land-based pirates number in the thousands. See "Illicit Radio Signals Fell British Airways," *The Wall Street Journal*, August 25, 1983, p. 25.

12. "Europe Braces for Free-Market TV," *Fortune*, February 20, 1984, pp. 74–82; and "Ideas in Action; *Business Europe*, June 13, 1986, p. 13.

13. "Advertising Boom on Italian Private TV Networks," *Business Europe,* October 7, 1983, pp. 315–16; and "European TV Ads," *Advertising World,* July 1986, pp.28–29.

14. "BBC Deal Gets Tepid Response," *Advertising Age,* November 21, 1983, p. 44; and "TV without Frontiers: Dramatically Changing Ad Scene in Europe," *Business International,* March 17, 1986, p. 83.

15. "Belgium Edges toward TV Advertising," *Business Europe,* January 27, 1984, p. 31; and "What's Happening in Germany," *International Advertiser,* September 1985, p. 18..

16. Data from *Africa South of the Sahara* and *The Middle East and North Africa* (London: Europa Publications, 1987).

17. "Videotapes Are Common throughout Middle East," *International Advertiser,* February 1986, p. 31.

18. "Golden Arches on the Ginza," *Speaking of Japan,* June 1986, pp. 24–27; and various annual reports.

19. "More Freedom on French TV." *International Advertiser,* June 1986, p. 12.

20. "Women, Advertising, and Islam," *Chicago Tribune,* August 4, 1982, sec. 3, p. 2.

21. From various articles in *Advertising World* and *Business International.*

22. Robert S. Trebus, "Can a Good Ad Campaign Cross Borders?" *Advertising World,* Spring 1978, pp. 6–8.

23. "Global Advertising: Multinational vs. International: Pros and Cons," *International Advertiser,* February 1986, pp. 34–37.

24. D. Peebles, J. Ryans, and I. Vernon, "Coordinating International Advertising," *Journal of Marketing,* January 1978, pp. 28–34.

25. While living in Mexico, one of the writers bought a product for the plastic toy it contained. When he opened the package at home, there was no toy for the children. Examining the package closely, he found that a small slot had been made in the top. Where labor costs and store revenues are low, the income from the sales of these premiums is extra profit for the retailer.

26. Vern Terpstra, *International Marketing* (New York: Holt, Rinehart, & Winston, 1972), p. 407.

27. "A Boycott over Infant Formula," *Business Week,* April 23, 1979, pp. 137–38; and "New Attack on Nestlé," *Advertising Age,* October 17, 1983, p. 44.

28. "Early Warning for MNCs," *Business International,* January 28, 1983, pp. 28–29.

29. "A Balance Sheet That Shows Host Countries What You Do for Them," *Business International,* June 20, 1975, p. 198.

30. The finance department wants prices that are both profitable and conducive to a steady cash flow, but the plant manager wants prices that will permit large sales volumes and long production runs. The legal department is worried about possible antitrust violations, and the tax expert is concerned with how prices will affect total tax loads. Even the domestic sales manager may be involved, wanting export prices that are high enough to prevent having to compete against exports that are reimported to the United States.

31. J. Greene and M. Duerr, *Intercompany Transactions in the Multinational Firm* (New York: Conference Board, 1970), p. 8. Although this is an old study, more recent articles indicate that most managements still feel the need for a standard transfer pricing policy.

32. For the first time in Avon's history, the company is distributing products outside the usual door-to-door channel. Facial cream is being sold in Chinese department stores. However, an Avon representative declared that the company expects to sell door-to-door in China at some future time. From *Marketing News,* October 15, 1982, p. 1.

33. "Self-Service Store Uptrend Continues in France," *Foreign Agriculture*, U.S. Department of Agriculture, November 15, 1976, pp. 8–10.
34. "The Distribution Sector on the Internationalization Path," *Weekly Bulletin* (Brussels: Kredietbank), April 3, 1981, pp. 1–4.
35. *Retailing Trade International* (London: Euromonitor, 1986), pp. 269-70.

CHAPTER 16

EXPORT PRACTICES AND PROCEDURES

1. In the private sector, 5.8 million jobs, or 6.5 percent of total U.S. employment, are directly or indirectly related to exports.
2. One of every six jobs in manufacturing is due to exports.
3. One of nearly every four acres of U.S. farmland produces for export.
4. In 1986, exports of the rapidly growing services sector amounted to $80 billion—one third of merchandise exports.

But . . .

5. A relatively small number of American companies account for most exports: 5 exporters, for 11 percent, 50 exporters, for 30 percent, and 1,000 exporters for 60 percent of *all* merchandise exports. There are at least 18,000 firms that could export but do not.

"U.S. Trade Facts," *Business America,* May 12, 1986, p. 12; and "Outlook Is Brightening for Service Exports," *Business America,* March 30, 1987, p. 5.

Learning Objectives

After you study this chapter, you should know:

1. The main elements of the export sales assistance programs of the U.S. Department of Commerce.
2. The elements of the export marketing plan.
3. The meaning of the various terms of sale.
4. The kinds of payment terms that are offered.
5. The kinds of export documents that are required.
6. Some sources for export financing.
7. The important innovations in materials handling in sea and air transport.

Key Words and Concepts

Terms of sale
Factoring
Forfaiting
Pro forma invoice
Letter of credit
Documentary drafts
Foreign sales corporation (FSC)
Foreign trade zone (FTZ)
Foreign freight forwarders
Bill of lading (B/L)
Containerization
RO-RO
LASH
Total systems concept
Export licenses

Business Incident

Du Pont, the eighth-largest U.S. exporter, has been able to remain a competitor in the tough chemical export market because it began to pay serious attention to exports back in 1978, when the dollar's value fell sharply. "We recognized that our business was changing from national to regional or global, so you didn't have a lot of options," says P. J. Roessel, Du Pont director of international planning. "If you didn't participate in those foreign markets, your competitors would gradually get stronger and come and eat your lunch in the U.S."

Du Pont's marketing strategy is to promote the sale of U.S. exports by its overseas manufacturing subsidiaries. "We have plotted back for 25 years and have found that as we have invested and built abroad, exports have gone up in complete tandem," says Roessel. "Such subsidiaries are able to 'pull' products from the parent company to achieve real market synergy." A Japanese Du Pont subsidiary, for example, makes engineering plastics for autos and has developed markets for polyester and acetyl products made by Du Pont in the United States.

"Smoother Sailing Overseas," *Business Week*, April 18, 1986, p. 289.

*D*u Pont is typical of the large multinationals that do considerable exporting even though they possess foreign production facilities. Of the 20 largest U.S. exporters listed in Table 16–1, only the aircraft manufacturers have no overseas plants.

Many of these firms, like Du Pont, supply numerous foreign markets from exports because no firm, no matter how large it is, can afford to manufacture in every country where its goods are sold. Markets that are too small to support local production are supplied by exports from either the home country or a foreign affiliate. In markets of sufficient size to justify the manufacturing of some, but not all, of the product mix, it is rather common to supplement the sales of local production with imports. Thus, an automobile plant in an LDC will produce the least expensive cars and, laws permitting, import the luxury models. A notable exception to this generality was Iran, where, because of the wealth generated from high crude oil prices, General Motors began its assembly operations with the Cadillac.

Exporting to markets that were formerly closed to the firm has been made possible by the formation of regional economic groups such as the EC and the EFTA. By setting up a plant in a member country, a firm is free to market its products throughout the region. Firms that supplied each member country from local plants prior to the formation of these regional markets have also increased their exports. The free movement of goods within the EC and similar market groupings has enabled the multinationals to obtain greater economies of scale by dividing the production of components among their subsidiaries rather than

Table 16-1

The 20 Largest U.S. Exporters in 1986

	Company	Products	Exports ($ millions)	Total Sales ($ millions)	Exports as Percent of Sales
1.	General Motors	Autos, locomotives	$8,366	$102,814	8.1
2.	Boeing	Aircraft	7,330	16,341	44.9
3.	Ford	Autos and parts	7,244	62,716	11.6
4.	General Electric	Aircraft engines, locomotives	4,348	35,211	12.4
5.	IBM	Information systems	3,058	51,250	6.0
6.	Du Pont	Chemicals, fibers, plastics	2,960	27,148	10.9
7.	Chrysler	Autos and parts	2,810	22,514	12.5
8.	McDonnell Douglas	Aircraft, missiles	2,805	12,661	22.2
9.	United Technologies	Aircraft engines	2,126	15,669	13.6
10.	Eastman Kodak	Photographic equipment	2,044	11,550	17.7
11.	Caterpillar	Construction equipment	2,016	7,321	27.5
12.	Hewlett-Packard	Computers	1,405	7,102	19.8
13.	Allied-Signal	Aircraft, chemicals	1,358	11,794	11.5
14.	Digital Equipment	Computers	1,354	7,590	17.8
15.	Philip Morris	Tobacco, food	1,300	20,681	6.3
16.	Occidental Petroleum	Agricultural products, coal	1,092	15,344	7.1
17.	Union Carbide	Chemicals, plastics	1,091	7,828	13.9
18.	Westinghouse	Generating equipment	1,079	10,731	10.1
19.	Motorola	Semiconductors	1,061	5,888	18.0
20.	Raytheon	Aircraft, defense systems	1,056	7,308	14.5

Source: America's Leading Exporters," *Fortune,* July 20, 1987, pp. 72–73.

permitting each foreign plant to produce all parts of the finished product. For example, an MNE's plant in Germany may make engines, while its English plant may make transmissions. Each of these plants is required to export and import, so that both plants may assemble the finished automobile.

Increasingly, LDC governments are stipulating that the multinational affiliates must export. Some have gone so far as to insist that sufficient foreign exchange must be earned by the local affiliate to cover the cost of all its imports. Because of this requirement, Volkswagen de Mexico exports so much coffee that the Mexican government is fearful that Volkswagen will disturb the world coffee market. Nissan Mexicana exports not only coffee but also honey, chick-peas, and horsemeat.

One other reason why more foreign affiliates have engaged in exporting is that many multinationals need their exports in order to remain competitive in their home markets. Various firms either import labor-intensive components produced in their foreign affiliates or export the components for assembly in countries where labor is less expensive. The final product is then imported for sale in the home country. The Mexican-American twin plant arrangement discussed in Chapter 2 is based on this concept.

Exporting—An Important Facet of International Business

The strong emphasis on exporting in the multinational firms indicates that exporting is a vital part of international business. Therefore, their managements must have the same degree of expertise in this area that they have in the administration of foreign production facilities. However, the need for personnel with a knowledge of exporting is not limited to large firms. The Department of Commerce estimates that three out of five American firms that export have fewer than 100 employees.

If both large and small American companies find exporting to be profitable, why is it that as a percentage of GNP, U.S. exports of goods and services are minuscule—about 9 percent—compared to an average of over 25 percent for the EC member nations? Why are there an estimated 20,000 firms in this country that sell exportable products but shun foreign markets?

Why Don't They Export?

The two major reasons that U.S. firms give for not exporting are: (1) a preoccupation with the vast American market and (2) a reluctance to become involved in a new and unknown operation. When nonexporting firms are asked why they are not active in international markets, they generally mention the following as problem areas: (1) locating foreign markets, (2) payment and financing procedures, and (3) export procedures.[1] Let us examine these problems.

Locating Foreign Markets

The first step in locating foreign markets, whether for export or foreign manufacturing, is to determine whether a market exists for the firm's products. The initial screening step described in Chapter 14 indicated a procedure to follow that will pose no problem for the experienced market analyst who is well acquainted with the sources of information and assistance that are available. However, newcomers to exporting, especially the smaller firms, may still be at a loss as to where to start, and for them, the U.S. Department of Commerce export assistance program can be especially helpful.

Figure 16-1

"THE TROUBLE WITH FOREIGN TRADE IS IT'S OVER-PRICED, OVER-RATED AND OVER THERE."

Your buyer needs financing, but in the time it takes you to check his credit position, you could lose the contract. His country's import regulations have recently changed. He wants to pay in his own currency. His documents need to be processed rapidly. And when the detailed specification finally arrives, there's no translation.

Why should anybody bother with overseas business?

Because, if the pitfalls can be avoided, the rewards are considerable.

Which is why you should be talking to us before you put a toe in the water.

We have the range of products, the local expertise, the speed and the organization to make every aspect of foreign trade easier and more profitable for our customers.

Why the Barclays network works.

At Barclays, you don't have to talk to layers of people who can't help. You begin with the one who can. And that person is connected to a banking system that spans 83 countries, with assets of $86* billion.

But we're more than a study in world geography.

We're people who talk to each other. Within a working day, your Barclays officer can exchange information and ideas with colleagues in every major financial center around the world. We can provide the speed and accuracy essential to completing any transaction. Most of all, we can offer the peace of mind that comes from knowing you've got experts working for you – at both ends of your deal.

BARCLAYS

Department of Commerce Export Assistance Program

Foreign Market Research

Probably the quickest and least expensive way for the inexperienced firm to begin is to contact the international trade specialist in the nearest Department of Commerce district office.

The specialist will first consult U.S. export statistics compiled by the Bureau of the Census of the U.S. Department of Commerce. These data come in various formats and publications, but the *FT410* is generally the most useful. This monthly publication shows the quantity and/or value of each product exported from the United States and the countries to which it was exported (see Table 2–4 in Chapter 2). Another publication, *Market Share Reports*, compares the exports of U.S. goods with those from other major supplier nations. These reports identify trends in the value of exports from each country and estimate the American share of that value for about 900 manufactured products sold in 100 country markets.

A relatively new service, *Export Statistics Profile*, shows the exports of specific U.S. products to individual countries. Each profile consists of an *Export Market Brief*, which gives a quick picture of the industry's export potential including growth rate, fastest-growing items, leading foreign markets, and foreign competitors; a *Trade Opportunity Frequency Report* which indicates the number of sales leads collected by the Department of Commerce for the last four years; and *Statistical Tables*, which show a five-year flow of exports for the industry.

At this point, the research may have identified a small number of potential markets. For those that are among the 14 countries for which the Department of Commerce has the Comparison Shopping Service, by paying $500 per market, the firm will receive a custom-tailored market research survey on a specific product of its choice. This service provides information on marketability, names of competitors, comparative prices, distribution channels, and names of potential sales representatives. Each study is conducted on-site by a U.S. commercial officer. For markets not included in the service, a Department of Commerce specialist may recommend such publications as *Country Market Surveys*, *Competitive Assessments*, and *Annual Worldwide Industry Reviews*, all of which are available on an industry basis. There are still other helpful publications and services.

Foreign Economic Trends Reports summarize the economic and commercial trends in a country and are a good source of information as to which American products are most in demand. A series of reports, *Overseas Business Reports* (OBR), provide basic background data on specific countries. Each OBR discusses separate topics on a single country, such as basic economic data, foreign trade regulations, market factors, and trade with the United States. The firm may subscribe to *Business America*, a biweekly magazine, whose "International Commerce" section contains announcements about (1) U.S. promotions abroad in which the firm can participate, (2) foreign concerns looking for licensors, joint venture partners, or distributorships; and (3) opportunities to make direct sales.

Direct or Indirect Exporting

When it has been established that there is an existing or potential market for its goods, the firm must choose between exporting indirectly through U.S.-based exporters or exporting directly using its own staff. If it opts for indirect exporting as a way to test the market, the trade specialist can provide assistance in locating one of the types of exporters listed in Chapter 12. However, should the firm prefer to set up its own export operation, then it must obtain overseas distribution. By means of an *Export Mailing List*, a computerized data base of foreign firms indexed by product and type of firm (importers, agents, distributors, and so forth), the exporter can do a broad-based mailing to solicit new representatives and customers. For $90 per market, the Department of Commerce through its Agent-Distributor Search Service will conduct a search for agents (manufacturers' representatives) or distributors (importing wholesalers) and will generally be able to submit the names up to six interested prospects that they have personally interviewed. The exporters may then obtain information covering their commercial activities and competence by requesting the Department of Commerce to supply a *World Traders Data Report*. Credit reporting agencies such as Dun & Bradstreet, FCIB (Finance, Credit, and International Business Association), and the exporter's bank will also supply credit information.

The Foreign Agricultural Service of the U.S. Department of Agriculture offers similar services to potential exporters of agricultural products.

Show and Sell

A part of the Department of Commerce export assistance program that can be extremely helpful in both locating foreign representatives and making sales is called Show and Sell. This consists of various kinds of exhibitions that are recommended by foreign service trade specialists as they discover trade opportunities in their markets. The exhibitions include specific product line shows held in one of the 7 U.S.-owned trade centers throughout the world, commercial exhibits in the American pavilions of international trade fairs, and catalog exhibits in U.S. foreign service posts when the opportunities for participation in product exhibitions are limited. Many American firms take part in these exhibitions because in this way they can meet foreign businesspeople who are attracted by the possibility of seeing various suppliers to their industry in one visit.

Export Marketing Plan

As soon as possible, an export marketing plan must be drawn up. The experienced firm will already have a plan in operation, but newcomers will usually need to wait until they have accumulated at least some of the information from the foreign market research.

Same as Domestic Marketing Plan

Essentially, the export marketing plan is the same as the domestic marketing plan. It should be specific about (1) the markets to be developed, (2) the marketing strategy for serving them, and (3) the tactics required to make the strategy operational. Sales forecasts and budgets, pricing policies, product characteristics, promotional plans, and details on the arrangements with foreign representatives are required. In other words, the export marketing plan will spell out what must be done and when, who should do it, and how much money will be spent.

Marketing Mix

Because the comments in Chapter 15 concerning the marketing mix are valid for exporters, there is no need for a detailed discussion here. Two aspects that do require some explanation, however, are *export pricing* and *sales agreements for foreign representatives*.

Pricing Policies. A recent study of the Export-Import Bank shows that "uncompetitive prices" accounted for 56 percent of the sales lost to foreign competitors and for 50 percent of the export value lost. This indicates that American exporters generally need to pay more attention to export pricing.

One new area of concern for many firms that are beginning to export is the necessity to quote **terms of sale** that are different from those normally used. For domestic sales, the company may be quoting FOB factory, which means that all costs and risks from that point on are borne by the buyer. Foreign customers, however, may insist on one of the following terms of sale:

1. *FAS (free alongside ship), port of exit.* The seller pays all of the transportation and delivery expense up to the ship's side. The buyer is responsible for any loss or damage to the shipment from that point on.

2. *CIF (cost, insurance, freight), foreign port.* The seller quotes a price that includes the cost of the goods, insurance, and all transportation and miscellaneous charges to the named foreign port in the country of final destination. If the buyer requires an on-board bill of lading (the usual case), then it is responsible for any loss or damage to the goods after they are delivered on board the vessel.

3. *C&F (cost, freight), foreign port.* This is similar to CIF except that the buyer purchases the insurance, either because it can obtain the insurance at a lower cost or because its government, to save foreign exchange, insists that it use a local insurance company.[2]

CIF and C&F terms of sale are more convenient for foreign buyers because to establish their cost, they merely have to add the import duties, landing charges, and freight from the port of arrival to their warehouse.

However, these terms can present a problem for new exporters if they forget the miscellaneous costs incurred in making a CIF shipment and simply add freight, insurance, and export packing costs to the domestic selling price.[3] The resulting price may be too low, but more often it will be too high, because the domestic marketing and general administrative costs that are included in the domestic selling price are frequently greater than the actual cost of making the export sale.

The preferred pricing method is the use of the "factory door" cost (production cost without domestic marketing and general administrative costs), to which are added the direct cost of making the export sale and a percentage of the general administrative overhead. This percentage can be derived from managers' estimates of the part of their total time spent on export matters. The minimum FOB price will be the sum of these costs plus the required profit. If research in a market has shown either that there is little competition or that competitive prices are higher, then, of course, the exporter is free to charge a high price in that market (price skim) or to set a low price in order to gain a larger percentage of the market (penetration pricing). The course of action taken will depend on the firm's sales objectives, just as it does in the domestic market.

Sales Agreement. The sales agreement should specify as simply as possible the duties of the representative and the firm. Most of what is contained in the contract for a domestic representative can be used in export also, but special attention must be given to two points: (1) designation of the responsibilities for patent and trademark registration and (2) designation of the country and state, if applicable, whose laws will govern a contractual dispute.[4] U.S. exporters would prefer to stipulate the laws of the United States and their home state, but many nations, especially those of Latin America, will not permit this (Calvo Doctrine). If an American state can be designated, its laws may be followed even though the dispute is adjudicated in a foreign country.[5]

Payment and Financing Procedures

The second major problem area concerns payment and financing procedures.

Export Payment Terms

Payment terms, as every marketer knows, are often a decisive factor in obtaining an order. As a sales official of an international grain exporter put it, "If you give credit to a guy who is broke, he'll pay any price for your product." This is somewhat exaggerated, but it is a fact that customers will often pay higher prices when terms are more lenient. This is especially significant in countries where capital is scarce and interest rates are high. The kinds of payment terms offered by exporters to foreign buyers are: (1) cash in advance, (2) open account, (3) consignment, (4) letters of credit, and (5) documentary drafts.

Cash in Advance

When the credit standing of the buyer is not known or is uncertain, cash in advance is desirable. However, very few buyers will accept these terms, because part of their working capital is tied up until the merchandise has been received and sold. Furthermore, they have no guarantee that they will receive what they ordered. As a result, few customers will pay cash in advance unless the order is either small or for a product of special manufacture.

Open Account

When a sale is made on open account, the seller assumes all of the risk, and therefore these terms should be offered only to reliable customers in economically stable countries. The exporter's capital, of course, is tied up until payment has been received.

Consignment

This follows the procedure well known in the United States by which goods are shipped to the buyer and payment is not made until they have been sold. All of the risk is assumed by the seller, and such terms should not be offered without making the same extensive investigation of the buyer and country that is recommended for open account terms. Multinationals frequently sell goods to their subsidiaries on this basis.

Letters of Credit

Only cash in advance offers more protection to the seller than an export **letter of credit (L/C).** This is a document issued by the buyer's bank, which promises to pay the seller a specified amount when the bank has received certain documents stipulated in the letter of credit by a specified time.

Confirmed and Irrevocable. Generally, the seller will request that the letter of credit be *confirmed* and *irrevocable*. Irrevocable means that once the credit has been accepted by the seller, it cannot be altered or canceled by the customer without the seller's consent. If the irrevocable letter of credit is *not* confirmed, the correspondent bank (Merchants National Bank of Mobile in Figure 16–2) has no obligation to pay the seller, Smith & Co., when it receives the documents listed in the letter of credit. Only the issuing bank, Banco Americano in Bogota, is responsible. If Smith & Co. wishes to be able to collect from an American bank, it will insist that the credit be confirmed by such a bank. This is generally done by the correspondent bank, as it was in Figure 16–2. In this case, when the Merchants National Bank of Mobile confirmed the credit, it undertook an obligation to pay Smith & Co. if all of the documents listed in the letter were presented on or before the stipulated date.

Note that nothing is mentioned about the goods themselves; the buyer has stipulated only that an air waybill issued by the carrier be presented as proof

Figure 16-2

Letter of Credit Specimen

THE MERCHANTS NATIONAL BANK OF MOBILE
MOBILE, ALABAMA

FOREIGN DEPARTMENT

Confirmed Irrevocable Straight Credit   Credit No. 0000

Smith & Company
P. O. Box 000   Mobile, Alabama, April 1, 19___
Towne, Alabama 36000

DEAR SIRS:

WE ARE INSTRUCTED BY Banco Americano, Bogota, Colombia

TO ADVISE YOU THAT THEY HAVE OPENED THEIR IRREVOCABLE CREDIT IN YOUR FAVOR FOR ACCOUNT OF

Compañia Santandereana de Automotores Ltda. "Sanautos", Bucaramanga, Colombia

UNDER THEIR CREDIT NUMBER 111-222   FOR A SUM OR SUMS NOT EXCEEDING A TOTAL OF $40,000.00

(FORTY THOUSAND NO/100 U.S. DOLLARS)

AVAILABLE BY YOUR DRAFTS ON US AT   sight   FOR INVOICE

VALUE OF 100%

TO BE ACCOMPANIED BY
1. Commercial Invoice: five copies signed by the beneficiaries with sworn
    statement regarding price and origin of merchandise.
2. Air Waybill: three non-negotiable copies, consigned to the order of:
    Sanautos, Carrera 15 Calle 29, Bucaramanga, for notification of same.
3. Consular Invoice: three copies.
4. Certificate of Origin: three copies
5. Copy of the airmail letter addressed to: Sanautos, Apartado Aereo No. 936,
    ▨▨▨▨▨▨▨▨▨▨ Bucaramanga, Colombia, remitting original of shipping documents
    requested.
6. Packing List: three copies.
7. Copy of the airmail letter addressed to: Compañia de Seguros Bolivar, Calle 36,
    No. 17-03, Bucaramanga, Colombia, covering details of shipment of merchandise,
    for insurance purposes.
Evidencing shipment of: "Repuestos para vehiculos automotores, registro de importacion
No. 67038 del 21 de Noviembre de 19—." Port of Shipment: any American port.
Destination: Bucaramanga. Partial shipments are permitted.
ALL DRAFTS SO DRAWN MUST BE MARKED "DRAWN UNDER THE MERCHANTS NATIONAL BANK OF MOBILE CREDIT

NO. 0000, Banco Americano No. L/C 111-222

THE ABOVE MENTIONED CORRESPONDENT ENGAGES WITH YOU THAT ALL DRAFTS DRAWN UNDER AND IN COMPLI-
ANCE WITH THE TERMS OF THIS CREDIT WILL BE DULY HONORED ON DELIVERY OF DOCUMENTS AS SPECIFIED IF PRE-
SENTED AT THIS OFFICE ON OR BEFORE June 27, 19___   : WE CONFIRM THE CREDIT
AND THEREBY UNDERTAKE THAT ALL DRAFTS DRAWN AND PRESENTED AS ABOVE SPECIFIED WILL BE DULY HONORED
BY US.

UNLESS OTHERWISE EXPRESSLY STATED, THIS CREDIT IS SUBJECT TO THE UNIFORM CUSTOMS AND PRACTICE FOR
COMMERCIAL DOCUMENTARY CREDITS FIXED BY SEVENTH CONGRESS OF THE INTERNATIONAL CHAMBER OF COMMERCE
AND CERTAIN GUIDING PROVISIONS, ALL AS ADOPTED BY CERTAIN BANKS AND OTHER CONCERNS IN THE U. S. A.

YOURS VERY TRULY,

_____ _____
ASSISTANT MANAGER   VICE PRESIDENT, ASSISTANT CASHIER.
John Doe, Vice President   Allen Jones, Vice President

cc Banco Americano, Bogota, Colombia

Figure 16-3

Letter of Credit Transaction

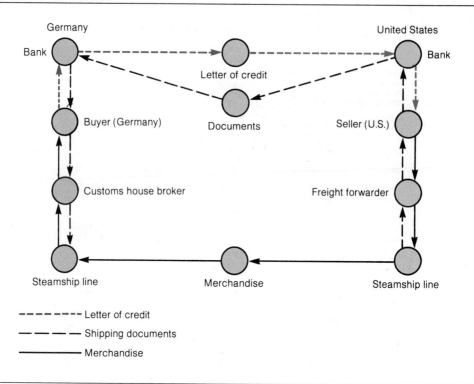

that shipment has been made. Even if bank officials knew that the plane had crashed after the takeoff, they would still have to pay Smith & Co. Banks are concerned with documents, not merchandise.

Prior to opening a letter of credit, a buyer frequently requests a **pro forma invoice.** This is the exporter's formal quotation containing a description of the merchandise, price, delivery time, proposed method of shipment, ports of exit and entry, and terms of sale. It is more than a quotation, however. Generally, the bank will use it when opening a letter of credit, and in countries requiring import licenses or permits to purchase foreign exchange, government officials will insist on receiving copies.

Letter of Credit Transactions. Figure 16-3 illustrates the routes taken by the merchandise, letter of credit, and documents in a letter of credit transaction.

When a German buyer accepts the terms of sale that provide for a confirmed irrevocable letter of credit, it goes to its bank to arrange for opening the required letter. The buyer will furnish the bank with the information contained in the pro forma invoice, specify the documents that the exporter must present to obtain payment, and set the expiration date for the credit.

The German bank then instructs its correspondent bank in the United States to confirm the credit and inform the seller that it has been established. The seller prepares the merchandise for shipment and notifies the freight forwarder, which books space on a ship, prepares the export documents, and arranges to have the merchandise delivered to the port. The documents, together with a sight or time draft drawn by the seller, are presented to the U.S. bank, which pays the seller and forwards the documents for collection to the German bank.

To obtain the documents that give title to the shipment, the buyer must either pay the *sight draft* or accept a *time draft*. Having done so, the buyer receives the documents, which are then given to the customhouse broker. The customhouse broker acts as the buyer's agent in receiving the goods from the steamship line and clearing them through the German customs.

Documentary Drafts

When the exporter believes that the political and commercial risks are not sufficient to require a letter of credit, the exporter may agree to payment on a **documentary draft** basis, which is less costly to the buyer.

An *export draft,* shown in Figure 16–4, is an unconditional order drawn by the seller on the buyer instructing the buyer to pay the amount of the order upon presentation (sight draft) or at an agreed future date (time draft). Generally, the seller will request its bank to send the draft and documents to a bank in the buyer's country, which will proceed with the collection as described in the letter of credit transaction.

Although documentary draft and letter of credit terms are similar, there is one important difference. A confirmed letter of credit guarantees payment to the seller if the seller conforms to its requirements, but there is no such guarantee with documentary drafts. An unscrupulous buyer can refuse to pay the drafts when presented and then attempt to bargain with the seller for a lower price. The seller must then acquiesce, try to find another buyer, pay a large freight bill to bring back the goods, or abandon them. If the seller chooses the last alternative, customs will auction off the goods, and the chances are that the original buyer will be able to acquire them at a bargain price. The seller, of course, receives nothing.

Compensatory Trade

A form of payment that has become increasingly popular is *compensatory trade*—any transaction that involves asset transfers as a condition of purchase, including local content requirements, licensing, and other performance requirements as well as the traditional forms of countertrade, which are described in detail in Chapter 18. For example, the government of a nation importing railway cars might insist that they be assembled locally as a condition of the pur-

Figure 16-4
Draft Specimen

MOBILE, ALA., July 6, 19____

PAY TO THE ORDER OF

_____ DOLLARS

$ 2,500.00

Sight D/P

Clayton Motor Company

Two Thousand Five Hundred

VALUE RECEIVED AND CHARGE SAME TO ACCOUNT OF

CLAYTON MOTOR COMPANY

To First National Bank of Mobile

P. O. Box 1467

Mobile, Alabama 36621

BY John P. Clayton, President

FIRST NATIONAL BANK
MOBILE ALABAMA

chase, or a construction company building roads might be asked to put up some low-cost housing as part of the deal.

Barter-type arrangements, which are estimated to comprise 5 percent of world trade ($100 billion), are occurring because (1) Third World and communist nations lack convertible currency and (2) these nations wish to exploit the marketing networks in the industrialized nations. However, even Australia is demanding offsets (a portion of the work on a project or product to be performed in that country) or a counterpurchase (the seller agrees to purchase goods in Australia equivalent in value to a minimum of 30 percent of the cost of goods sold).

Compensatory trade has become so important that a number of MNEs, such as General Motors and Volkswagen, have wholly owned subsidiaries to handle such transactions. Smaller firms can contract with independent barter-switch companies, which will do the work for them. Figure 16–5 illustrates a countertrade operation by means of which Chrysler automobiles were exchanged for Jamaican bauxite.

Export Financing

Although exporters would prefer to sell on the almost riskless letter of credit terms, increased foreign competition and the universally tight money situation are forcing them to offer credit. To do so, they must be familiar with the available sources and kinds of export financing, both private and public

Private Source

Commercial banks have always been a source of export financing through loans for working capital and the discounting of time drafts, but in recent years new types of financing have been developed.[6] One of these is factoring.

Factoring. This financing technique permits the exporter to be more competitive by selling on open account rather than by means of the more costly letter of credit method. Long used in the United States, factoring is now being employed in international trade.

Factoring is essentially discounting *without* recourse because it is the sale of export accounts receivable to a third party, which assumes the credit risk. A factor may be a factoring house or a special department in a commercial bank.

Under the export factoring arrangement, the seller passes its order to the factor for approval of the credit risk. Once the order has been approved, the exporter has complete protection against bad debts and political risk. The customer pays the factor, which, in effect, acts as the exporter's credit and collection department. The period of settlement generally does not exceed 180 days.

Forfaiting. Forfaiting denotes the purchase of obligations that arise from the sale of goods and services and fall due at some date beyond the 90–180 days that are customary for factoring. These receivables are usually in the form of trade drafts or promissory notes with maturities ranging from six months to five years.

Figure 16-5

Jamaican Countertrade

Countertrade made simple: If you think it's tough selling cars and trucks in the United States, this is what Chrysler went through to sell several hundred vehicles to credit-starved Jamaica. The American and Canadian mining companies (far left), which dig Jamaica's bauxite and refine it into alumina, hand over some 50,000 tons of alumina to the government's Bauxite & Alumina Trading Co. The trading company, in turn, gives the alumina to Metallgesellschaft, a German metals company. MG sells the alumina to a refiner, which converts it to aluminum. The money MG gets for the alumina goes to the European American Bank, Chrysler's adviser, EAB sends part of the money back to the Bauxite & Alumina Trading Co., which pays the mining companies. The balance goes to finance a letter of credit made out to Chrysler, which then ships trucks to Jamaica. Title is taken by another government firm, the Jamaican Commodity Trading Co., which sells the vehicles to Motors Sales & Services Co., Chrysler's local distributor. The dealer sells them to the public. The part you don't see—and the parties want to keep hidden—is what makes the convoluted deal click. Jamaica probably is shaving price to unload bauxite, while Chrysler is absorbing extra costs to make the sale.

Source: "The Explosion of International Barter," *Fortune*, February 7, 1983, pp. 88–89.

Because it is sold without recourse, forfaited debt is nearly always accompanied by bank security in the form of a guarantee or aval. While the guarantee is a separate document, the aval is a promise to pay written directly in the document ("per aval" and the signature).

The forfaiter purchases the bill and discounts it for the entire credit period. Thus, the exporter, through forfaiting, has converted its credit-based sale into a cash transaction.

Although banks have traditionally concentrated on short-term financing, they have become involved in medium- and even long-term financing because numerous government and government-assisted organizations are offering export credit guarantees and insurance against commercial and political risks.

Government and Government-Assisted Organizations

The Export-Import Bank (Eximbank) is a government institution that not only offers direct loans for large projects and equipment sales requiring long-term financing (over five years), such as commercial aircraft and power plants, but also provides medium-term (181 days to five years) and long-term credit guarantees for commercial bank financing. Most industrialized nations have similar institutions for granting export credit.

In 1970, PEFCO (Private Export Funding Corporation), a corporation owned by 54 commercial banks, 7 large manufacturers, and an investment bank, was established to be a supplemental lender. PEFCO makes financing available only in cases where other private sector lenders will not provide sufficient financing on competitive terms. Although PEFCO's loans are mostly medium term (average seven years), some are made for as long as 20 years. All of its loans must be covered by an unconditional guarantee of the Eximbank.

Until October 1983, the Foreign Credit Insurance Association (FCIA), consisting of 50 private insurance companies, had insured exporters against political and commercial risks of nonpayment in short- and medium-term export credit sales. However, because of heavy commercial losses, especially in Mexico, 41 of the original members withdrew from the association. The Eximbank is now covering the political and commercial risks, leaving FCIA to operate as its marketing and service agent.

Larger exporters with below-average losses can now obtain commercial risk insurance from two major private insurers, AIG Political Risk, Inc. and AFIA. Private insurers are appealing because of their advantages over FCIA-Eximbank:

1. They are not constrained by U.S. foreign policy restrictions on coverage of exports to South Africa.
2. Coverage can be obtained faster.
3. They can insure barter and countertrade operations.
4. They cover sales in other currencies in addition to U.S. dollars.

With three sources to choose from, exporters should definitely shop for the best terms.[7]

Other Government Incentives

There are other government incentives for trade, which, although not strictly a part of export financing, are certainly closely related to it. These are the Overseas Private Investment Corporation (OPIC), the Foreign Sales Corporation (FSC), and the foreign trade zone (FTZ).

OPIC. OPIC is a government corporation that was formed to stimulate private investment in developing nations. It offers investors insurance against expropriation, currency inconvertibility, and damage from wars or revolutions. OPIC also guarantees private loans and equity investments. Its connection with exports stems from the fact that exports of capital equipment and semiprocessed raw materials generally follow these investments.

Foreign Sales Corporation. The **Foreign Sales Corporation (FSC)** is a new entity authorized by the Tax Reform Act of 1984. It replaces the domestic international sales corporation (DISC), which was the object of complaints by U.S. trading partners that DISCs violated the General Agreement on Tariffs and Trade.

Unlike its DISC predecessor, an FSC must be located either in a U.S. possession other than Puerto Rico or in a foreign country that has an information exchange agreement with the United States. The FSC's shareholders' and directors' meetings must be held outside the United States, and its principal bank account must be maintained outside the United States.

The portion of the FSC's income that is exempt from U.S. corporate taxation is 32 percent if the FSC buys from independent suppliers or uses the section 482 arm's-length pricing rule with related suppliers.[8]*

Foreign Trade Zones. For centuries, various forms of duty-free areas have existed in many parts of the world to facilitate trade by lessening the effect of customs restrictions. These customs-privileged areas may be free ports, transit zones, free perimeters, or free trade zones. In each instance, a specific and limited area is involved, into which imported goods may be brought without the payment of import duties. At present, there are nearly 350 such areas located in 72 countries. Of the four types, the free trade zone is the most common.

The *free trade zone* is an enclosed area that is considered to be outside the customs territory of the country in which it is located. Goods of foreign origin may be brought into the zone pending eventual transshipment, reexportation,

---

*See Chapter 15, for details on Section 482.

or importation into the country. While the goods are in the zone, no import duties need to be paid.

The American version, called the **foreign trade zone (FTZ),** has been growing in popularity, and there are now more than 240 of these zones in operation.* Many are situated at seaports, but some are located at inland distribution points.

Goods brought into the FTZ may be stored, inspected, repackaged, or combined with American components. Because of differences in the import tariff schedule, the finished product often pays less duty than what would be charged for the disassembled parts. Volkswagen pays only 2.9 percent duty on the Rabbit, which it assembles in the New Stanton, Pennsylvania, FTZ, rather than the 6 percent that would be charged on imported parts. Importers of machinery improve their cash flow by storing spare parts in an FTZ, because duty is not paid until they are withdrawn.

Although the advantages of the FTZ to importers are well known, its benefits to exporters appear to have been overlooked. Foreign trade zones can provide accelerated export status for purposes of excise tax rebates and customs drawbacks. Manufacturers of such items as tires, trucks, and tobacco products are required to pay federal excise taxes when these items are produced, but the taxes are rebated if the items are exported. Firms including imported parts in their finished product must pay duty on the imports, but this duty is returned when the product is exported (customs drawback). The recovery of this money takes time, however, and meanwhile the exporter can have considerable capital tied up in excise taxes and import duties. Because a product is considered to be exported as soon as it enters an FTZ, the exporter can immediately apply for a rebate or a drawback while waiting to make an export sale. If assembly or manufacturing is done in the FTZ using imported components, no duties need ever be paid when the finished product is exported.

Export Procedures

When nonexporters complain about the complexity of export procedures, they are generally referring to documentation. Instead of the two documents, the freight bill and the bill of lading, to which they are accustomed when shipping domestically, they are suddenly confronted by five to six times as many documents for a foreign shipment. According to an OECD study, the average overseas transaction needs 35 documents with a total of 360 copies. The study states that the "paper costs" of international trade come to between 1.4 percent and 5.7 percent of the value of the trade. "Exports move on a sea of documents" is a popular saying in the industry. Although the extra burden may be handled by the traffic department, many firms give all or at least part of the work to a foreign freight forwarder.

*Includes subzones for individual plants.

Foreign Freight Forwarders

Foreign freight forwarders act as agents for exporters. They prepare documents, book space with a carrier, and in general act as the firm's export traffic department. If asked, they will offer advice about markets, import and export regulations, the best mode of transport, and export packing and will supply cargo insurance.

Export Documents

Correct documentation is vital to the success of any export shipment. For discussion purposes, we shall divide export documents into two categories: (1) shipping documents and (2) collection documents.

Shipping Documents

Shipping documents are prepared by exporters or their freight forwarders so that the shipment may pass through U.S. Customs, be loaded on the carrier, and sent to its destination. They include the domestic bill of lading, export packing list, export licenses, export bill of lading, and insurance certificate. Inasmuch as the first two documents are nearly the same as those used in domestic traffic, we shall limit our discussion to the export licenses, the insurance certificate, and the export bill of lading.[9]

Export Licenses. All exported goods with the exception of those going to U.S. possessions or Canada (with a few exceptions) require **export licenses**—either a *General License* or a *Validated Export License.*

Most products can be exported under the General License, for which no special authorization is necessary. The correct General License symbol, which is obtainable from the Department of Commerce district office, is merely written in the *Shipper's Export Declaration.* This document, which must be filed with U.S. Customs, indicates that there is an authorization to export and also provides the statistical information for the *FT410.* For strategic materials and all shipments to communist countries, a Validated Export License is mandatory. This is a special authorization for a specific shipment and is issued only upon formal application to the Department of Commerce's Office of Export Administration for scarce materials, strategic goods, and technology or to the Department of State for war materials.

Exporters selling strategic and high-tech products overseas must be aware that the Department of Commerce checks very thoroughly license applications for these products, as do all member governments of COCOM (Coordinating Committee on Multilateral Export Controls), a voluntary group comprising all NATO countries except Spain and Iceland plus Japan. COCOM nations administer a common set of export controls intended to prevent the transfer of advanced technology to Soviet-bloc countries. Particular attention is given to dual-use items—those that have both commercial and military applications. To enforce controls in this country, the Department of Commerce has an Office of Export Enforcement with armed agents in field offices located near high-tech production centers and in U.S. embassies in Vienna and Stockholm. Violators of diversion laws and export controls can be fined and imprisoned.

> In December 1986, an exporter in Reno, Nevada, was sentenced to 1½ years' imprisonment for violating the Export Administration Act. He was guilty of unlawfully exporting semiconductor manufacturing equipment valued at $220,000 to the United Kingdom, knowing that the goods were ultimately destined for East Germany.[10]

Export Bill of Lading. The export **bill of lading (B/L)** serves a dual purpose. First, it is a contract for carriage between the shipper and the carrier, and second, it is evidence of title to the merchandise. Bills of lading are generally called *air waybills* (air shipments) or *ocean bills of lading* (steamships).

Ocean bills of lading may be either "straight" or "to order."[11] A straight bill of lading is nonnegotiable, and only the person stipulated in it may obtain the merchandise upon arrival. An order bill of lading, however, is negotiable. It can be endorsed like a check or left blank. In this case, the holder of the original bill of lading is the owner of the merchandise. Sight draft or letter of credit shipments require "to order" bills marked "Clean on Board" by the steamship company, which means that there is no apparent damage to the shipment and that it has actually been loaded onto the vessel.

Insurance Certificate. The insurance certificate is evidence that insurance coverage has been obtained to protect the shipment from loss or damage while it is in transit. Unlike domestic carriers, oceangoing steamship companies assume no responsibility for the merchandise they carry unless the loss is caused by their negligence.

Marine insurance on an international transaction may be arranged by either the exporter or the importer, depending on the terms of sale. The laws of a country often require the importer to buy such insurance, in order to protect the local insurance industry and save foreign exchange. If the exporter has sold on sight draft terms, it is at risk while the goods are in transit. In this case, the firm should buy contingent interest insurance to protect it in the event that the shipment is lost or damaged and it is unable to collect from the buyer.[12]

Broadly speaking, there are three kinds of marine insurance policies: (1) basic named perils, (2) broad named perils, and (3) all risks.

1. *Basic named perils* includes perils of the sea, fires, jettisons, explosions, and hurricanes.

2. *Broad named perils* includes theft, pilferage, nondelivery, breakage, and leakage in addition to the basic perils. Both of these policies contain a clause that determines the extent to which losses caused by an insured peril will be paid. The purchaser of the insurance may request either (1)

free of particular average (excluding partial loss) or (2) with particular average (covering partial loss). Obviously, the rates differ.

3. *All risks* covers all physical loss or damage from any external cause and is more expensive than the policies previously mentioned.

4. War risks are covered under a separate contract.

For the sake of convenience, the occasional exporter will ask the forwarder to arrange for insurance, but when shipments begin on a regular basis, the shipper can economize by going directly to a marine insurance broker. The broker, acting as the shipper's agent, will draw up a contract to fit the shipper's needs by choosing appropriate clauses from among the hundreds that are available. Because neither the policies nor the premiums are standard, it is highly recommended that the exporter obtain various quotations.[13]

Collection Documents

These are the documents that the seller is required to provide the buyer in order to receive payment. For a letter of credit transaction, the collection documents must be submitted to a bank, but to collect against documentary drafts, anyone may be designated to act on the seller's behalf. A few exporters send their drafts overseas to a representative or bank for collection, but it is preferable to have a bank in the exporter's country forward them to its correspondent bank in the city of destination.

First of all, the collection costs are usually less, because the correspondent bank charges the exporter's bank less than it would charge the exporter. Second, because of the correspondent relationship between the banks, the foreign bank will generally exert a greater effort to collect the money on time. Should the exporter wish to change instructions to the foreign bank, the private cable codes and tests of banks permit new instructions to be authenticated and acted on quickly, whereas a cable from the exporter to a foreign bank would probably be ignored until it had been confirmed by a letter with a signature that could be checked for authenticity.

The documents required for collection vary among countries and among customers, but some of the most common are: (1) commercial invoices, (2) consular invoices, (3) certificates of origin, and (4) inspection certificates.

Commercial Invoices. Commercial invoices for export orders are similar to domestic invoices but include additional information, such as the origin of the goods, export packing marks, and a clause stating that the goods will not be diverted to another country. Invoices for letter of credit sales will name the bank and the credit numbers. Some importing countries require the commercial invoice to be in their language and to be visaed by their local consul.

Consular Invoices. A few countries require both the commercial invoice and a special form called the consular invoice. These forms are purchased from the consul, prepared in the language of the country, and then visaed by the consul.

Certificates of Origin. Despite the fact that the commercial invoice carries a statement regarding the origin of the merchandise, a number of foreign governments require a separate *certificate of origin*. This document is commonly issued by the local chamber of commerce and visaed by the consul.

Inspection Certificates. Inspection certificates are frequently required by buyers of grain, foodstuffs, and live animals. These are issued by the Department of Agriculture in the United States. Purchasers of machinery or products containing a specified combination of ingredients may insist that an American engineering firm or laboratory inspect and certify that the merchandise is exactly as ordered.

Export Shipments

All too often, newcomers to exporting are so preoccupied with the flow of documents that they fail to concern themselves with the physical movement of their goods. As long as the carrier delivers their shipments in good condition at a reasonable cost, they are satisfied. However, tremendous advances in materials-handling techniques over the past two decades, such as containerization, RO-RO, and LASH, offer opportunities for cost savings and also enable exporters to reach markets that they previously could not serve.

Containerization

Containers are large boxes 8 × 8 feet in cross section by either 10, 20, or 40 feet that the seller fills with the shipment in its own warehouse.[14] These containers are then sealed and opened only when the goods arrive at their final destination. Over the long voyage, the containers, but not the goods, will be handled several times. A container will be picked up by a tractor-trailer or a railroad for delivery to shipside, where huge cranes will load it aboard ship. From the port of entry, railroads or trucks will deliver the container, often unopened even for customs inspection, to the buyer's warehouse, where customs officials will go to examine the shipment. This not only reduces handling time but also minimizes the risks of damage and theft. Both air and water carriers encourage the use of containers by charging lower rates for containerized shipments.

Ocean Shipping

RO-RO
Another innovation in cargo handling is the **RO-RO** (Roll On–Roll Off) ship, which permits loaded trailers and any equipment on wheels to be driven onto

Figure 16-6

Courtesy California Photo Service

RO-RO Vessel

this specially designed vessel (see Figure 16–6). RO-RO service has brought the benefits of containerization to ports that have been unable to invest in the expensive lifting equipment required for containers.

LASH

Similar to RO-RO is the **LASH** (Lighter Aboard Ship) vessel, which gives customers located on shallow inland waterways access to ocean freight service (see Figure 16–7). Sixty-foot-long barges are towed to inland ports, loaded, and towed back to deep water, where they are loaded aboard the anchored LASH vessel. LASH service has been especially useful where adequate port facilities are lacking, because the vessel carrying the barges is able to load and unload offshore.

Figure 16-7
LASH Vessel

Courtesy Aeromarine Fotos Limited

Air Shipments

Airfreight has had a profound effect on international business because it permits shipments that once required 30 days to arrive in one day. Huge freight planes carry payloads of 200,000 pounds, most of which goes either in containers or on pallets. Airlines guarantee overnight delivery from New York to many European airports and claim that their planes can be completely loaded or unloaded within 45 minutes.

Although airfreight rates are higher than ocean freight rates, when the total costs of the two modes are compared, it frequently turns out that shipping by air is less expensive. Components of the total cost that may be lower for airfreight than for ocean freight are: (1) insurance rates, (2) customs duties when they are calculated on gross weights, (3) packing, and (4) inventory costs. In addition, the necessity for warehousing at the destination is often eliminated. Table 16-2 illustrates how the total cost of airfreight may be lower.

Table 16-2

Sea-Air Total Cost Comparison (shipment of spare part)

	Ocean Freight (with warehousing)	Air Freight (no warehousing)
Warehouse administrative costs	$ 850	—
Warehouse rent	1,400	—
Inventory costs		
Taxes and insurance	630	$ 330
Inventory financing	240	160
Inventory obsolescence	1,500	850
Seller's warehouse and handling costs	1,550	950
Transportation	350	2,000
Packaging and handling	250	100
Cargo insurance	60	30
Customs duties	110	107
Total	$6,940	$4,527

Figure 16-8

Courtesy Lufthansa

A transport van brings lower deck containers to a Lufthansa Boeing 747 for loading.

Figure 16-9

Courtesy Lufthansa

Two 10-foot "bungalows" and an outsized piece of cargo that is even longer than its pallet move to their loading positions on the main deck of Lufthansa's Boeing 747F.

Even when the total costs based on these items are higher for airfreight, it may still be advantageous to ship by air when factors other than the conventional expense, inventory, and capital are considered:

1. *Production and opportunity costs,* although somewhat more difficult to calculate, are properly a part of the total cost. Getting the product to the buyer more quickly results in faster payment, which speeds up the return on investment and improves cash flow. The firm's capital is released more quickly and can be invested in other profit-making ventures or can be used to repay borrowed capital, thus reducing interest payments. Production equipment may be assembled and sent by air so that it may go into production sooner without the transit and setup delays associated with ocean shipments.

2. *The firm may be air dependent;* that is, export business may be possible only because of airfreight. Suppliers of perishable food products to Europe, Japan, and the Middle East are in this category, as are suppliers of live animals (newly hatched poultry and prize bulls). Without airfreight, these firms would be out of business.

3. *The products may be air dependent* when the market itself is perishable. Consumer products with extremely short life cycles (high-fashion and fad items) are examples, but many industrial products also fit into this category. A computer, for example, is perishable to the extent that the time it loses between the final assembly and the installation at the customer's location is time in which it is not earning income (the leasing fee).

4. The sales argument that spare parts and factory technical personnel are available within a few hours is a strong one for the exporting firm that has to compete with overseas manufacturers.

Total Systems Concept

The **total systems approach** goes beyond the total cost approach to consider in addition to costs the possible effect that a physical distribution decision may have on the other functional areas of the firm. Furthermore, this approach takes into account the impact of such a decision on the channel members and the final customer. The application of this concept to exporting is creating new marketing opportunities.

Summary

Exporting is a vital part of international business even for the multinational firm that possesses overseas production facilities. In spite of the fact that both large and small firms find exporting to be profitable, there are thousands of American firms producing exportable products that do not sell internationally. The many reasons for not exporting may be classified in three problem areas: (1) locating foreign markets, (2) payment and financing procedures, and (3) export procedures.

Market screening as described in Chapter 14 will enable the firm to locate foreign markets, and various Department of Commerce programs are also helpful. When preparing the export marketing mix, special attention must be given to export pricing and the preparation of sales agreements for overseas representatives.

The terms of payment offered in the export market are: (1) cash in advance, (2) open account, (3) consignment, (4) letters of credit, and (5) documentary drafts. Although exporters would prefer to sell on letter of credit terms, the competitive situation in world markets forces them to offer credit. A number of sources and kinds of export financing, both private and public, are available. Government incentives to export trade include OPIC, Foreign Sales Corporations and foreign trade zones.

Export procedures are considered a problem by newcomers because of the multiplicity of the documents required. Foreign freight forwarders are available to act as agents in the preparation of documents and in the booking of space on carriers. In addition to the documents required for domestic shipments, goods for export usually require export licenses and export bills of lading. Inasmuch as oceangoing steamship companies assume no responsibility for the merchandise they carry, the shipper must buy marine insurance. The documents required for collection vary among customers and destinations, but they commonly include (1) commercial invoices, (2) consular invoices, (3) certificates of origin, and (4) inspection certificates.

Innovations in transportation and materials handling such as containerization, RO-RO, and LASH as well as the application of the total systems concept to exporting are enabling exporters to reach new markets.

Questions

1. *Define the following terms and explain their significance to exporting: (a) Agent/Distributor Service, (b) customs drawback, (c) export licenses, (d) foreign freight forwarder, (e)* Overseas Business Reports.

2. *Exporting is only for small firms that cannot afford to set up plants overseas. True or false? Please explain.*

3. *What are the major problem areas that nonexporting firms cite as reasons for not exporting?*

4. *What are the common terms of sale quoted by exporters? For each, explain to what point the seller must pay all transportation and delivery costs. Where does the responsibility for loss or damage pass to the buyer?*

5. *What two parts of a sales agreement with a foreign representative deserve special attention?*

6. *a. Explain the various export payment terms that are available. b. Which two offer the most protection to the seller?*

7. *What is the procedure for a letter of credit transaction?*

8. *What are the government and government-assisted organizations that offer assistance in export financing?*

9. *The manager of the international department of the Modesto Bank learns on the way to work that the ship on which a local exporter shipped some goods has sunk. The manager has received all of the documents required in the letter of credit and is ready to pay the exporter for the shipment. In view of the news about the ship, the manager now knows that the foreign customer will never receive the goods. Should the manager pay the exporter, or should he withhold payment and notify the overseas customer?*

10. *What is a foreign trade zone? Check with a customhouse broker or a U.S. Customs official or do some research in the library to find out the advantages of a foreign trade zone over a bonded warehouse.*

11. *What is the purpose of an export bill of lading?*
12. *Air shipments can lower inventory costs in at least three ways. What are they?*
13. *What three innovations in cargo handling are significant in export trade? Describe each one.*

Minicase

16–1 State Manufacturing

Export Sales Price

State Manufacturing Company, a producer of farm equipment, had just received an inquiry from a large distributor in Italy. The quantity on which the distributor wanted a price was sufficiently large that Jim Mason, the sales manager, felt he had to respond. He knew that the inquiry was genuine, because he had called two of the companies that the distributor said he represented, and both had assured him that the Italian firm was a serious one. It paid its bills regularly with no problems. Both companies were selling the firm on open account terms.

Mason's problem was that he had never quoted on a sale for export before. His first impulse was to take the regular FOB factory price and add the cost of the extraheavy export packing plus the inland freight cost to the nearest U.S. port. This price should enable the company to make money if he quoted the price FAS port of exit.

However, the terms of sale were bothering him. The traffic manager had called a foreign freight forwarder to learn about the frequency of sailings to Italy, and during the conversation she had suggested to the traffic manager that she might be able to help Mason. When Mason called her, he learned that because of competition, many firms like State Manufacturing were quoting CIF foreign port as a convenience to the importer. She asked him what payment terms he would quote, and he replied that his credit manager had suggested an irrevocable, confirmed letter of credit so as to be sure of receiving payment for the sale. He admitted that the distributor, however, had asked for payment against a 90-day time draft.

The foreign freight forwarder urged Mason to consider quoting CIF port of entry in Italy with payment as requested by the distributor in order to be more competitive. She informed him that he could get insurance to protect the company against commercial risk. To help him calculate a CIF price, she offered to give him the various charges if he would tell her the weight and value of his shipment FOB factory. He replied that the total price was $21,500 and that the gross weight, including the container, was 3,629 kilos.

Two hours later, she called to give him the following charges:

Containerization	$ 200.00
Inland freight less handling	798.00
Forwarding and documentation	90.00
Ocean freight	2,633.00
Commercial risk insurance	105.00
Marine insurance—total of items 1–5	167.15
$\times$ 1.1 = $27,858.60 at 60¢/$100*	

*Total coverage of marine insurance is commonly calculated on the basis of the total price + 10 percent.

During that time, Mason had been thinking about the competition. Could he lower the FOB price for an export sale? He looked at the cost figures. Sales expense amounted to 20 percent of the sales price. Couldn't this be deducted on a foreign order? Research and development amounted to 10 percent. Should this be charged? Advertising and promotional expense amounted to another 10 percent. What about that? Because this was an unsolicited inquiry, there was no selling expense for this sale except for his and the secretary's time. Mason felt that it wasn't worth calculating this time.

If you were Jim Mason, how would you calculate the CIF port of entry price?

Minicase

16–2 Morgan Guaranty Trust

Company Letter of Credit

MORGAN GUARANTY TRUST COMPANY
OF NEW YORK
INTERNATIONAL BANKING DIVISION
23 WALL STREET, NEW YORK, N. Y. 10015   March 5, 19*

Smith Tool Co. Inc.
29 Bleecker Street
New York, N.Y. 10012

On all communications please refer to

NUMBER **IC** - 152647

Dear Sirs:
        We are instructed to advise you of the establishment by
. Bank of South America, Puerto Cabello, Venezuela . . . .
of their IRREVOCABLE Credit No. 19845 . . . .
in your favor, for the account of John Doe, Puerto Cabello, Venezuela . . . .
for U. S. $3,000.00 (THREE THOUSAND U. S. DOLLARS) . . . .
available upon presentation to us of your drafts at sight on us, accompanied by:

Commercial Invoice in triplicate, describing the merchandise as indicated below

Consular Invoice in triplicate, all signed and stamped by the Consul of Venezuela

Negotiable Insurance Policy and/or Underwriter's Certificate, endorsed in blank, covering
marine and war risks

Full set of straight ocean steamer Bills of Lading, showing consignment to the Bank of
South America, Puerto Cabello, stamped by Venezuelan Consul and marked "Freight Prepaid",

evidencing shipment of UNA MAQUINA DE SELLAR LATAS, C.I.F. Puerto Cabello, from United
States Port to Puerto Cabello, Venezuela

Page 6
Advice of irrevocable letter of credit issued by
a foreign bank in favor of a U.S. exporter and
confirmed by Morgan Guaranty, which is
obliged to honor drafts drawn under credit.

Except as otherwise expressly stated herein, this credit is subject to the Uniform Customs and Practice
for Documentary Credits (1974 revision), International Chamber of Commerce Publication No. 290.

    The above bank engages with you that all drafts drawn under and in compliance with
the terms of this advice will be duly honored if presented to our Commercial Credits
Department, 15 Broad Street, New York, N. Y. 10015, on or before March 31, 19*
on which date this credit expires.
    We confirm the foregoing and undertake that all drafts drawn and presented in
accordance with its terms will be duly honored.

                Yours very truly,

                Authorized Signature

Immediately upon receipt, please examine this instrument and if its terms are not clear to
you or if you need any assistance in respect to your availment of it, we would welcome your
communicating with us. Documents should be presented promptly and not later than 3 P.M.

1. Who issued the letter of credit?

2. Is it irrevocable?

3. Has it been confirmed?

4. If so, by whom?

5. Who is the buyer?

6. Who is the seller?

7. What kind of draft is to be presented?

8. What documents are required?

9. What are the terms of sale?

10. When does the letter of credit expire?

11. Where does the seller go for payment?

12. Who pays the freight?

13. Who pays the marine insurance?

14. Must the steamship company attest that the merchandise has been loaded on ship?

15. What is the reason for your answer to 14?

Supplementary Readings

A Basic Guide to Exporting. Washington, D.C.: U.S. Department of Commerce, 1986.

"Export Enforcement Secures America's Technology." *Business America,* March 2, 1987, pp. 17–18.

Exportise. Boston; Small Business Foundation of America, 1983.

Fitzpatrick, Peter. *Essentials of Export Marketing.* New York: American Management Association, 1985.

Forfaiting. Zurich: Crédit Suisse, 1983.

Guide to Cargo Insurance. New York: American Institute of Marine Underwriters, no date.

"Harmonized Codification Promises to Benefit Exporters and Importers." *Business International,* March 16, 1987, pp. 82–83.

Introduction to the Export Administration Regulations. Washington, D.C.: U.S. Department of Commerce, 1985.

Investment Finance Handbook. Overseas Private Investment Corporation, no date.

Investment Insurance Handbook. Overseas Private Investment Corporation, no date.

Overview of the Export Administration Program. Washington, D.C.: U.S. Department of Commerce, 1985.

A Summary of U.S. Export Administration Regulations. Washington D.C.: U.S. Department of Commerce, 1985.

"Trade Promoting Activities of the International Trade Administration." *Business America,* May 26, 1986, pp. 6–8.

"What's New at Eximbank and Why US Exporters Should Take Another Look." *Business International.* March 1987, pp. 98–99.

Endnotes

1. Numerous surveys have been made and the answers, as one would expect, are always the same. One such survey is *Export Strategy: Go Global, Georgia,* written by C. G. Alex-

andrides and published by the Georgia Department of Community Development in 1974. See also "Expanding Small Business Exports," *Business America*, April 29, 1985, pp. 5-6.

2. These and other terms have been codified in *INCOTERMS, 1980* by the International Chamber of Commerce and in *Revised American Foreign Trade Definition—1941*, which has been adopted by the U.S. Chamber of Commerce, the National Council of American Exporters, and the National Foreign Trade Council. The point at which title and risk pass from the seller to the buyer is specified, as are the duties of each party.

3. These include wharf storage charges, handling charges, freight forwarder's fees, and consular fees.

4. To be absolutely safe, the firm should register all patents and trademarks. Policing them may be left to the representative if management so chooses.

5. The presiding judge will have the pertinent parts of the law translated or will call upon witnesses who are known experts in the area of law involved.

6. A bank may discount an export time draft, pay the seller and keep it until maturity, or, if it is the bank on which the draft is drawn, "accept" it. By accepting a time draft, a bank assumes the responsibility for making payment at maturity of the draft. The accepting bank may or may not purchase (at a discount) the draft. If it does not, the exporter can sell a bank acceptance readily in the open market.

7. "Protecting Major Exporters," *Business International*, October 14, 1983, pp. 321-22.

8. *A Basic Guide to Exporting* (Washington, D.C.: U.S. Department of Commerce, September 1986), p. 56.

9. A domestic bill of lading for goods to be exported must contain a statement by the seller that these goods will not be diverted to another destination. Export package marks and the latest allowable arrival date in the port of export should be noted. The export packing list differs from the domestic list in that it is much more detailed with respect to the weights and measurements of each package. The material in each package must be itemized.

10. "Export Enforcement Secures America's Technology," *Business America*, March 2, 1987, pp. 17-18.

11. Air waybills are always "straight."

12. We believe that the exporter selling on C&F terms (the buyer purchases the insurance) should buy contingent interest insurance to protect itself in case the buyer's insurance does not cover all risks. The premiums are low because damages are paid only on what is not covered by the buyer's policy.

13. The premiums charged depend on a number of factors, among which are the goods insured, the destination, the age of the ship, whether the goods are stowed on deck or under deck, the volume of business (there are volume discounts), how the goods are packed, and the number of claims that the shipper has filed. Brokers will sometimes admit that in the long run it is preferable not to file numerous small claims, even if these are justified, because the higher premiums charged for future shipments will be greater than the money recovered.

14. The sizes listed are the standard sizes for ocean freight, though there are still some odd sizes in use. Airlines carry these sizes also, but in addition they provide smaller containers with rounded cross sections for a better fit in the fuselage.

CHAPTER 17

EAST-WEST TRADE

"Some of our merchants believe that because of our recession, we should rely more on China for trade and economic cooperation. They have misunderstood the opportunities China offers. Even after 10–15 years, our economic links with China will be less important than those with either America, Japan or Europe, all of whom have higher technology and much greater GNP than China."

Lee Kuan Yew, Singapore prime minister, in 1986 annual budget address

"They fight by shuffling papers;
  they have bright, dead alien eyes;
they look at our labour and laughter
  as a tired man looks at flies."

C. K. Chesterton

622

Learning Objectives

After you study this chapter, you should know:

1. What countries are meant when you read or hear "East-West trade."
2. The difference between a market economy and a centrally planned economy.
3. Why the People's Republic of China (PRC), with its huge population, has never become a large consumer market.
4. Why the United States and the PRC began to trade in the 1970s and recognized each other in 1979.
5. What the East wants most from the West.
6. Why the East cannot afford to pay for all it wants.
7. How the PRC went from a deficit to a surplus in its trade with the United States.
8. The bureaucratic labyrinth through which you must find your way in order to sell to the East.
9. Some departures by the PRC from the usual practices of the East in its dealings with the West.
10. How the East has paid and is trying to pay for imports from the West.
11. What is meant by the Third World.
12. Common objections in the West to goods and services from the East.
13. Why some of those objections can probably be overcome and why that process may make the other objections stronger and more forceful.
14. Some differences between the East and the West in their concepts of costs in determining how to price a product.

Key Words and Concepts

East-West trade
Market economy
Centrally planned economy
Countertrade
Compensation
Barter
Switch trade

Joint venture
Coproduction
Specialization
Subcontracting
Licensing
Turnkey project
Unfair import competition

623

Business Incident

Foreigners doing business in communist countries are subject to certain political as well as personal risks not usually encountered in other countries. An example was the incident in Moscow in the summer of 1978 when Francis Crawford, an International Harvester executive, was accosted by Soviet police when his car was stopped at a traffic light. The police dragged Crawford from the car and took him away. He was later charged with currency speculation. After negotiations between the United States and Soviet governments, Crawford was released in exchange for the release by the United States of two Soviets who were on trial for espionage in the United States.

The Wall Street Journal, March 29, 1979, p. 17.

"*E*ast is east and west is west and never the twain shall meet" was not accurate when Rudyard Kipling wrote it, and it is even less correct today. Of course, *collide* may be a better verb than *meet* because the economic and political systems of the two groups are so different. One of the collisions is illustrated by our business incident.

We shall identify the countries of the West and the East and look very briefly at the background of their relationships. East Germany and the People's Republic of China are being treated differently by West Germany and the United States, and we shall show how.

Dumping by the East on markets of the West is not easily proved. We shall see why. Other East-West problems involve the competition of products from the East with products from LDCs with which West countries have historic relationships. Moreover, overhanging the entire subject of East-West trade are East-West political relations, which fluctuate between areas and times of detente to areas and times of shooting wars.

The East Countries

"East," as used in this chapter, includes the centrally planned economies of the Union of Soviet Socialist Republics (USSR), its East European satellites (Poland, East Germany, Czechoslovakia, Hungary, Romania, and Bulgaria), and its other satellites, such as Cuba and Vietnam. It also includes Yugoslavia and the People's Republic of China (PRC), which occupies mainland China and is to be differentiated from the Republic of China, which occupies Taiwan.

In the preceding paragraph, we spoke of **centrally planned economies.** In countries with such economies, the central, national government decides how much of what product will be made during each year or other planning period, such as a five-year plan. Yugoslavia and, to a growing extent, the PRC have delegated some decision making to some factories or industries. In most centrally planned economies, all major factors of production are owned or controlled by the government, though the PRC has begun to permit foreign companies to own parts of joint ventures and its own people to buy shares of Chinese companies previously wholly owned by the government. The labor factor is controlled, as the unions are essentially government agencies and workers must obtain government approval to move from one area or job to another.

The West Countries

"West," as used here, includes the industrial countries of Western Europe and North America plus Japan and such other countries as Australia and New Zealand. For practical purposes, the Western countries are those that are members of the Organization for Economic Cooperation and Development (OECD).

East-West Economic
Relations

Prior to World War I and again in the 1920s and 30s, many American companies played important roles in the economic development of the USSR. During World War II (WWII), hundreds of American suppliers provided billions of dollars worth of goods and services to the USSR.[1]

Following WWII, the hostilities of the Cold War succeeded the WWII alliance, and **East-West trade** dropped sharply. Even though it revived considerably in the 1960s and 70s, it has still not achieved the percentages of pre-WWII 1938. Then East-West trade accounted for 74 percent of the total trade of Eastern countries and for 9.5 percent of that of Western countries. In 1986, 48 years later, Eastern countries' trade with the West was only 30 percent of their total trade and Western countries' trade with the East was less than 3 percent of their total trade.

Tables 17–1 and 17–2 show the growth of trade between OECD countries and those with centrally planned economies between 1976 and 1985.

East Germany as a Special Case

Even though East Germany is one of the economically strongest countries in Eastern Europe, you will observe that its trade figures in Tables 17–1 and 17–2 are relatively small. This results from the fact that its major Western trading

Table 17-1

OECD Exports to Centrally Planned Economies (US$ millions)

	1976	1977	1978	1979	1980	1981	1982	1983	1984	1985
USSR	$ 4,582	$ 4,515	$ 5,316	$ 6,399	$2,066	$2,025	$1,899	$1,871	$1,825	$1,748
East Germany	435	527	514	799	175	182	143	165	149	123
Poland	1,843	1,285	1,952	2,022	466	300	270	241	246	260
Czechoslovakia	694	685	806	922	267	227	179	162	158	181
Hungary	607	774	1,037	996	234	207	239	216	210	235
Romania	672	779	1,049	1,262	288	295	139	108	116	119
Bulgaria	314	301	386	413	82	71	129	130	122	153
China (PRC)	1,251	1,372	2,529	3,362	732	890	894	978	1,288	2,050
Total	$10,398	$10,248	$13,589	$16,175	$4,310	$4,197	$3,892	$3,871	$4,114	$4,869

Source: *Foreign Trade Monthly Bulletin* (Paris: Organizations for Economic Cooperation and Development), October 1980, October 1982, and July 1986.

Table 17-2
OECD Imports from Centrally Planned Economies (US$ millions)

	1976	1977	1978	1979	1980	1981	1982	1983	1984	1985
USSR	$3,624	$4,087	$ 4,853	$ 6,681	$1,800	$1,853	$2,175	$2,079	$2,161	$1,922
East Germany	359	375	485	545	208	207	198	202	194	193
Poland	1,202	1,302	1,489	1,705	542	381	278	275	332	327
Czechoslovakia	566	625	752	920	247	198	222	218	226	220
Hungary	480	555	655	1,767	273	266	188	194	212	217
Romania	659	637	808	1,084	326	246	215	231	309	288
Bulgaria	163	168	188	307	134	155	87	61	62	59
China (PRC)	963	1,043	1,383	2,013	1,107	1,065	1,898	875	1,041	1,195
Total	$8,017	$8,790	$10,613	$15,022	$4,371	$4,371	$4,261	$4,135	$4,537	$4,421

Sources: *Foreign Trade Monthly Bulletin* (Paris: Organizations for Economic Cooperation and Development), October 1980, October 1982, and July 1986.

Table 17-3

U.S.-PRC Trade (US$ millions)

Year	Amount	Year	Amount
1971	.4.9	1980	4,800
1972	95.9	1981	5,500
1973	803.6	1982	5,300
1974	935.2	1983	4,650
1978	1,100	1984	6,383
1979	2,300	1985	8,180

Sources: *U.S.-China Business Review,* March–April 1975, p. 9; *International Letter,* Federal Reserve Bank of Chicago, February 15, 1980, pp. 2–3; *Los Angeles Times,* March 1, 1982, part 4, p. 1; *International Letter,* Federal Reserve Bank of Chicago, January 28, 1983, p. 3 and *Direction of Trade Statistics Yearbook,* October 1986, p. 133.

partner is West Germany, which considers trade with East Germany to be domestic, not foreign, trade and therefore does not report the large amounts involved as exports and imports.

China as a Special Case

China (PRC) is also a special case. Often images of trade with the PRC do not represent reality. The myth of the China market has persisted despite the fact that consumer demand has never approached Western expectations. China, an agrarian nation, has always been desperately poor, surviving on a subsistence level except for a tiny wealthy elite. The Confucian class has now been replaced by the elitist Communist party.

After the communist armies forced the Nationalist forces off the mainland to Taiwan in 1949, American contacts with the mainland were almost nonexistent until 1970. By then the PRC leadership had apparently embarked on a fundamental reappraisal of policies that included a new perception of the military threat posed by the USSR.

China and the United States

During the early 1970s, the United States was winding down its Vietnam involvement while observing the USSR's growing military might. Both the PRC and the United States perceived each other as counterweights against the USSR, and they began political and trade relations based on mutual political advantage. The growth of Sino-American trade is shown in Table 17–3.

PRC Deficits Turn to Surplus and Back to Deficit

In most years, the PRC has run a deficit in its trade with the United States, the cumulative deficit for the years 1973 through 1978 being some $1,964,000,000.

In 1980 alone, it grew to $2,691,000,000. Then the PRC began producing more of two commodities that it imported in large quantities from the United States—cotton and soy beans. At the same time, the PRC became annoyed with the United States about American arms sales to the Republic of China and about American restrictions on imports of Chinese textiles and apparel. For these reasons, the PRC cut back on its purchases from the United States and the American trade surplus fell to $1.7 billion in 1981. The surplus fell to $700 million in 1982, and the PRC ran a surplus in its trade with the United States in 1983 and 1984. During 1985, trade position of the PRC deteriorated and it fell back into deficit which grew in 1986.

U.S. Trade with the East Other than the PRC

For a number of reasons, primarily political reasons, the United States lagged behind Canada, Japan, and Western Europe in trade with the East. Despite a late start, however, U.S. trade with the East grew through 1979, as shown in Table 17–4.

Large consumer product sales to the East are unlikely, but the East is anxious to acquire Western technology and capital goods. Politics and bureaucracies permitting, these product areas represent huge market opportunities.

Political Tensions Reduce U.S.-Soviet Trade

After a decade of rapid growth, U.S. exports of nonfarm goods to the Soviet Union hit a peak of $749 million in 1979, and agricultural shipments reached $2.9 billion. After the Afghanistan assault in December 1979 and the tensions over unrest in Poland and Nicaragua, the U.S. government revoked and denied export licenses to Russia. In 1980, nonfarm exports slid to $363 million and grain and other farm sales totaled only $1.1 billion. Even though the American embargo on sales to the Soviet Union was lifted in 1981, it appears unlikely that U.S.-Soviet trade will soon again reach the 1979 levels.

Political Tensions Did Not Dampen European-Soviet Trade

In 1980, West Germany's exports to the Soviet Union rose 20 percent, to the equivalent of $3.71 billion. French industry scored the biggest percentage advance as its exports to the USSR increased 23 percent, to $2.43 billion. In 1980, British exports to the Soviet Union totaled $1.1 billion an 8.5 percent rise over 1979.

The European countries did not go as far as the United States in voicing disapproval of Russian conduct but pledged that they would not step into projects dropped by American firms. As the above figures indicate, those pledges were perhaps being ignored.

East-West trade faltered in 1985. While the volume of world trade grew 6 percent in 1985, the trade of the West with the Comecon (council for Mutual

Table 17-4

U.S. Trade with Communist Countries Excluding China (PRC)

Country	1975	1976	1977	1978	1979	1980	1981	1982	1983	1984
U.S. exports	$2,787	$3,504	$2,544	$3,679	$5,684	$3,860	$4,338	$3,610	$2,891	$3,796
Albania	1	1	2	5	10	7	6	22	3	10
Bulgaria	30	43	24	48	57	161	258	107	66	44
Czechoslovakia	53	149	75	106	281	185	83	84	59	58
German Democratic Republic	17	65	36	170	356	479	296	223	139	137
Hungary	76	63	81	99	78	80	78	68	111	88
Romania	191	250	260	319	501	722	504	224	186	249
USSR	1,835	2,310	1,628	2,252	3,607	1,513	2,432	2,587	2,003	3,284

Economic Assistance) countries fell 5 percent, and that drop occurred before the gentle slide in oil prices became a tumble in 1986. Fuel accounts for nearly 30 percent of Soviet exports and 25 percent of East European exports. The growth in the value of the East's oil exports disguised the lackluster performance of East-West trade during the decade 1975–85.

Even before the oil price drop, the Soviet petroleum output had begun to fall. And oil is not the only reason East-West trade is unlikely to grow. For one thing, Comecon economic growth has slowed. For another, the countries of Comecon are expanding trade with one another and Western suppliers are being squeezed out. In 1975, 46 percent of Comecon's capital goods imports came from the West; by 1983, the West's share was down to 36 percent.

How to Sell to the East

Selling to the East is not easy. The institutions, trading techniques, and behavior of the East in international trade are quite different from those of the West. This results from the centrally planned economies common to all the countries of the East. We shall look at the practices of the USSR; those of the other East countries are very similar.

Steps in East Countries' Purchasing Procedures

The decision on what to buy and whether to buy from a Western company (never if the desired items are available in the USSR or in another Comecon country) is made by the government agencies shown on Figure 17–1. If an order is generated to buy, say, petroleum production equipment from an American company, the order and payment steps are shown in Figure 17–2, where the numbered steps are: (1) The Gosplan, through the Ministry of Petroleum, consults various technical, research, and production organizations to determine specifications, requirements, and availability in the USSR or Comecon. If not available there, the equipment will be compared with other projects competing for scarce foreign convertible currency. At the same time, Gosplan and other ministries would be preparing a plan for export or other means to finance the desired import. (2) When all of that has been accomplished, the Ministry of Petroleum and Gosplan send a purchase order to the Ministry of Foreign Trade, which authorizes the foreign trade organization (FTO) specializing in petroleum-production equipment to enter the act. (3) That FTO consults with the Ministry of Petroleum on technical specifications. (4) The FTO solicits bids. (5) The American company submits a proposal. (Of course, there may be competition between two or more bidders.) (6) The FTO, in consultation with the Ministry of Petroleum, prepares a contract. (7) The FTO and an American supplier conclude a contract. (8) If a letter of credit is used, the Vneshtorgbank (Bank of Foreign Trade) opens a let-

Figure 17-1
An Order is Generated

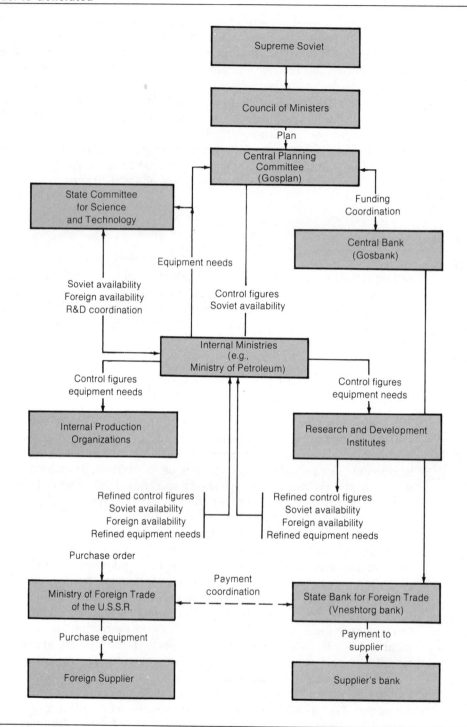

Source: John I. Hubs, "Developing Trade with the Soviet Union," *Columbia Journal of World Business,* Fall 1973, pp. 117–21.

Figure 17-2
The Soviet Union Purchasing Procedure

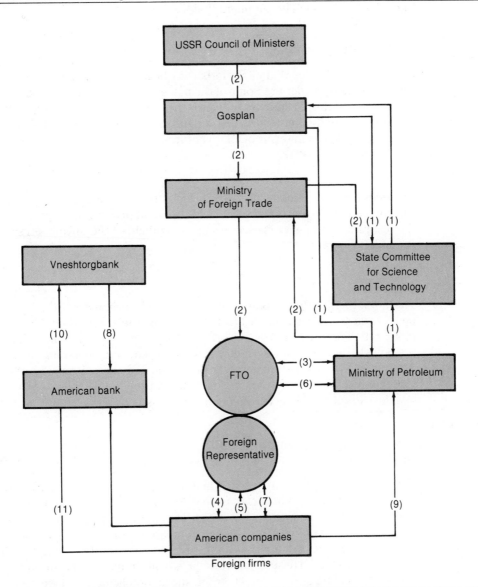

Source: "Trading with the USSR," *Overseas Business Reports,* U.S. Department of Commerce, Industrial and Trade Administration, OBR 77–78, July 1977, p. 43.

ter, usually with the supplier's bank. (9) The equipment is delivered. (10) Documents, such as bill of lading, insurance, and inspection certificates, are sent to Vneshtorgbank. (11) The supplier is paid.

Will the System Be Simplified?

In 1986, Soviet leader Mikhail S. Gorbachev began making changes in the Soviet Union's trade bureaucracy. Some of the powerful FTOs lost their rigid monopoly over Soviet trade. To spur trade, Gorbachev gave Soviet production ministers and some individual enterprises the right to deal directly with foreigners. He also began to speak in terms of joint ventures with Western companies.

Goals

Gorbachev needs to modernize Soviet industry in order to produce goods that can compete in Western markets. The drop in oil prices and oil production and the resulting loss of export earnings have highlighted the uncompetitiveness of Soviet industry.

Obstacles

The Soviet Union has a powerful, entrenched bureaucracy that can be depended on to do its best to block changes in the established system. Even though the Politburo approved Gorbachev's plans in principle in August 1986, the Soviet Union has not decided how to proceed. Hans Forsberg, president of Sandvik, a Swedish toolmaker, who has discussed the matter with the Soviet Union, says, "They really don't know what they want; they are looking for openings to get foreign investments without changing the system."[2]

How Western Companies Sell to the East

To complete the procedures listed and illustrated above is usually extremely time consuming and complex. How do Western companies sell in the East? A minority of Western companies open and maintain representative offices in Moscow or some other city.[3] Most Western companies utilize the services of companies that specialize in dealing with the East, such as Satra Corporation[4] or Tower International, Inc.[5] These companies have dealt in many sorts of products and services including chrome, steel, grain, shoes, hotels, and soybean mills. Their clients have included such major firms as IBM, Borg Warner, Caterpillar Tractor, and USX.

There are at least two other methods of selling to the East—trade fairs and personal visits.

Figure 17-3

You are in Eastern Europe and don't speak a word of the language. You have been told to go "due east at the junction." It's 4 o'clock and will soon be dark. How do you decide which way to go?

Give your trade with Eastern Europe new direction

Austria's trade links with Eastern Europe stretch back into history. Today Austria, a neutral state in a key geographical position, enjoys cultural, business and language ties with the East, and good relations with all European countries. Creditanstalt, as the country's leading international bank, offers you:

● wide experience in arranging and developing business with Eastern Europe
● specialist skills in counter-purchase, barter and buy-back transactions, services critical to success in these markets.

Call Creditanstalt, London (01) 822 2600 or Vienna (0222) 6622-2593.

CREDITANSTALT

Austria's leading international bank

Creditanstalt-Bankverein
London Branch: 29 Gresham Street, London EC2V 7AH. Telephone (01) 822 2600. Telex: 894612.
Head Office: Schottengasse 6, A-1010 Vienna. Telephone (0222) 6622-2593. Telex: 133030.
New York Branch: 717 5th Avenue, New York, NY10022. Telephone (212) 308 6400. Telex: (RCA) 239895/(ITT) 424700.

Figure 17-4

CHINA DEVELOPS 1

中國建築工程材料及設備技術交流展覽會

THE 1st INTERNATIONAL CONSTRUCTION MACHINERY & MATERIALS EXHIBITIONS & TECHNICAL EXCHANGE

at

GUANGZHOU, CHINA

from 8th July, 1980.

sponsored by

The Architectural Society of China & its Kwangtung & Guangzhou Chapter

&

Asian Consortium Exhibitions Limited

Scope of Exhibition:

- Building and Construction Machinery & Material
- New Building Methods, Systems and Knowhow
- Instrumentation for Detection and Survey
- Computer Application
- Cleansing and Maintenance and Protection Technology

Technical Exchange:

Exhibitors are required in principle to present their technology and products either on academic and commercial basis

Rental:

- Indoor from US$35.00 / sq. ft.
- Outdoor from US$10.00 / sq. ft.
- Auxiliary charge of US$20.00 / sq. ft.

For services rendered and expenses incurred by the organizers for arrangement of visa, publicity in China, customs, moving of exhibits, arrangement for translations, lighting & security etc.

Application to participate now open

Please telex or cable for application form and information:

Hongkong Office:
Telex: 73843 DORCE HX
Cable: ASIANSHOW

Asian Consortium Exhibitions Limited.
13th Floor, Stanhope House, 734, King's Road, Hong Kong.

NOTE: *To prevent crowded lines, please telex during off office hours.*

1981-1982
Our other exhibitions and technical exchange in the near future in the field of:

- Production Machinery and Light Industries
- Electronics and Appliances
- Petroleum and Exploration
- Chemicals
- Textile
- Tourism and Hotel Supplies

If you wish us to retain your name in our mailing list, please telex after 1st March, 1980 or write to us.

Source: *Los Angeles Times,* March 13, 1980, part 4, p. 7. Reproduced with permission of the publisher.

Figure 17-5

Manning a Trade Fair Stand

1. Company representatives should be knowledgeable about the company and its products, empowered to conduct business negotiations, and clear on its objectives in exhibiting.
2. Never ignore a visitor to your stand.
3. Approach visitors who seem interested in your display; do not wait for them to approach you.
4. Look interested. Do not sit about chatting with your colleagues. Do not position yourself so as to hide your products or to block access to them.
5. Start the conversation with a positive remark about your product or a question that will generate a discussion.
6. Identify as quickly as possible the visitor's business and specific interest and his importance as a prospect. Always keep your objectives in mind.
7. Answer all questions as forthrightly and factually as possible.
8. Remember to sell your company as well as your products, and relate your remarks to the visitor's interests.
9. Use the conversation to elicit information about the market and reactions to your products.
10. Carry negotiations as far forward as you are empowered to, if you are convinced the visitor represents a solid prospect.
11. Use inquiry forms and supplementary notes to record details about the visitor's company, his interests, and follow-up action to be taken.
12. Allow time after the fair closes to continue important discussions.
13. Provide promised information as soon as possible.
14. Observe fair hours, and never leave your exhibit unattended.
15. Use slack periods to make contacts at other stands, provided your own is manned.

Source: Umphon Phanachet and Zhang Huixiang, *Guidebook on Trading with the People's Republic of China,* (Trade Promotion Centre of ESCAP, 1982), p. 33.

Trade Fairs

Exhibits at fairs are important ways for Western companies to reach potential customers in both Eastern Europe and the People's Republic of China. Attendance at the Chinese fairs is by invitation only, and if you are not invited, it is unlikely that you can sell your product to the PRC. However, when a new exhibition is started, the Chinese may advertise it and offer to put your name on a mailing list. An example is the "China Develops" advertisement reproduced here, which appeared in the March 13, 1980, *Los Angeles Times* (Figure 17-4).

Common sense should probably indicate what to do and what not to do when your company has a stand at a trade fair. However, there have apparently been some unfortunate departures from common sense, so two UN officials have drawn up a checklist for "Manning a Trade Fair Stand." It is reproduced as Figure 17-5.

Personal Visits

Personal contacts are important, and when you are trying to sell products to the Soviet or East European governments, you should not rely too much on correspondence. Personal business visits to Moscow or other capitals, as appropriate, are almost always necessary if you hope to make sales. However, travel in Eastern Europe is expensive and not many sales are made, so a trip should not be made without some combination of the following conditions: (1) company personnel can meet key Soviet officials; (2) the company is contemplating a long-term sales compaign or is at a crucial negotiating point near the end of a campaign; or (3) the volume and profitability of a potential sale warrants the trip.

Similarly, dealing with the People's Republic of China calls for personal contact. The Chinese customer wants to scrutinize the Western executives personally and make assessments of their trustworthiness and goodwill. The Chinese want to feel they are dealing with a friend who will play fair and make possible a comfortable, long-term relationship.

> Hugh P. Donaghue, vice president of Control Data Corporation, visited China carrying three large boxes stuffed with product brochures and other literature which he expected to hand to his Chinese hosts at the first meeting. It didn't work that way. They first asked him about his philosophy of life and then about Control Data's business philosophy. For 10 days, they talked about all sorts of subjects except Control Data products. Finally, as Donaghue was about ready to carry the three boxes home still full, the Chinese finally asked him what he had to sell. Control Data made sales and has been doing increased business with China.

In Moscow and in Washington, the U.S. government has information for American businesses trying to sell in the USSR. It also has assistance for firms that want to enter the PRC market.

As foreign companies have sold or tried to sell to the PRC over recent years, much experience has been acquired and some checklists have been developed. One list is suggested by Ronald Wombolt, vice president and director of international operations of John Fluke Manufacturing Company, an American producer of electronic test and measurement instrumentation. Wombolt's checklist is:

> Do not always offer your most favorable price up front. The Chinese want to bargain and negotiate.
>
> Do not, without good cause, insist on selling on letter of credit terms. The Chinese are usually prompt payers.
>
> Do not make any statement you can't back up, because the Chinese record everything you say in negotiating sessions.
>
> Do not offer or accept any terms or conditions that you will not want in future transactions. Although the Chinese will constantly ask for something "this time only," it means every time.

Enjoy Coca-Cola

可口可乐, 友谊遍天下

Offer training in China and abroad.

Maintain a consistent pricing policy.

In order to follow the rules listed above, have the same group in your company deal with the Chinese over time, at least one of whom understands the language.[6]

Information from the U.S. and PRC Governments

The U.S. Commercial Office in Moscow is available to U.S. companies wishing to sell to the USSR. Interested firms can contact the Trade Promotion Division, Bureau of East-West Trade, U.S. Department of Commerce, Washington, DC 20230, or the U.S. Commercial Office, U.S. Department of State–Moscow, Washington, DC 20520.

In February 1979, shortly after the United States recognized the PRC, the U.S. Department of Commerce published the pamphlet "Doing Business with China." It can be obtained from the U.S. Government Printing Office in Washington. To give you some idea of the type of information contained in the pamphlet, its contents page is reproduced as Figure 17–6.

In recognition of the bureaucratic, linguistic, and cultural difficulties for Americans attempting to sell in the PRC market, the Chinese government set up its first U.S. trade promotion office in Los Angeles in 1986. It is called the China–U.S. Trading Corporation, and it is operated by the Foreign Enterprises Services Corporation (FESCO), a government agency.

Figure 17-6

Source: "Doing Business with China" (Washington, D.C.: U.S. Department of Commerce, February 1979).

FESCO has helped guide several American companies into the PRC market. One of these companies, Bank of America Check Corporation, the traveler's check arm of Bank of America, has opened 40 outlets in China. Another company, International Matex Tank Terminals, a New Orleans–based builder of liquid bulk tank terminals, had fallen afoul of the PRC bureaucratic maze. FESCO stepped in to help it through the maze.[7]

A Capitalist People's Republic of China?

Although the PRC bureaucratic maze is probably second to none, some developments are now under way which would have shocked Chairman Mao. The PRC is admitting foreign, private ownership of production facilities within the country, flirting with corporate stock issues, and investing abroad.

Joint Ventures

In 1979 the PRC published a **joint venture** law, and by 1983 some 100 equity joint ventures had been set up. More would probably have been launched had the law been more specific about how the ventures would work; instead, it was brief and vague. The Chinese were aware of the unease this caused foreign investors, and in September 1983 they released an implementing act for the joint venture law.[8] That should reduce uncertainty and encourage more foreign private investment, a unique development in a communist country.

Not All Successful

Although some 666 joint ventures were in place by 1986, the difficulties for foreigners operating in the PRC caused some failures, losses, and low-profit or low-quality products. As a result, the first nine months of 1986 saw a 40 percent decline in foreign investments. This so concerned the government that it began giving seminars featuring successful joint ventures. The profitable foreign venturers told others how they had done it.

Some of the keys are:

Insist on the right to hire and fire employees and to reward good workers with bonuses or otherwise.

Establish good training programs.

Choose the right location even if the costs are higher.

Obtain the support of local as well as Peking authorities.

Be prepared to invest in infrastructure such as power cables and water pipes.

Keep quality standards high.

Establish reliable foreign suppliers, because PRC sources may be unreliable.

The best technology isn't necessarily the most advanced; the technology should be easy to learn and maintain.[9]

Corporate Stock

In 1983, the PRC authorized three enterprises to raise money by selling stock to private buyers. Many residents of the country, plus overseas Chinese and others, are potential buyers, but there are obstacles to the widespread, successful use of stock sales to raise capital for Chinese companies. Diehard communist cadres have to be convinced that stock issues are just a means of raising money and do not mean that the PRC is giving up communism. Managers have to learn to report to a board of directors and be answerable to shareholders. The legal status of stock companies needs to be established in the PRC, and the mechanics of issuing and trading securities must be learned. Officials at the Bank of China's overseas branches and its 12 affiliates are probably ready to assist with the procedural problems.[10]

By mid-1986, over 1,400 PRC companies had issued bonds (mostly) or stock to the public in order to raise funds. Until September 1986, however, there was no formal, legal method to trade the securities. Then, for the first time since the communists came to power in 1949, the government authorized the establishment of a stock and bond exchange, in Shanghai. Public interest and trading are growing, but there is opposition. A number of Communist party faithful complain that a stock exchange is capitalist. The banks complain that people withdraw their deposits in order to buy securities.[11]

It must be recognized that the PRC is engaged in a unique, historic experiment. It is attempting to liberalize the economy, and even to permit private ownership and operation of farms and factories, while maintaining rigid Communist party control of the country.

The liberalization movement has been led by Deng Xiaoping, who was 82 years old in 1986, and many wonder whether his moderate, pragmatic policies will continue after his death or retirement. The American State Department feels that there are enough like-minded leaders behind Deng to prevent reversal of his policies. However, others remember the "let a thousand flowers bloom" era under Mao Tse-tung. Mao encouraged playrights, poets, and writers to speak out without fear of government reprisal. Quite a number of people took him at his word, and there was an outpouring of works that could not have been published previously. Suddenly, Mao changed his mind and his policy. The people who had spoken out were imprisoned, sent to labor gangs, or otherwise punished.

During 1986, Chinese students began to march and demonstrate for political democracy, which is anathema to a communist government. After some hesitation, the government began to suppress the students, which was not a good omen for continued liberalization of the PRC. Its action illustrates the probably irreconcilable contradiction between economic liberalization and communist political rigidity.

Investments Abroad

Since 1979, the PRC has invested in over 100 joint ventures in Southeast Asia, Hong Kong, the United States, and elsewhere. These ventures were at first in trading houses, department stores, and servicing agencies, but in 1983 the emphasis changed to focus on manufacturing companies. The PRC wants overseas stakes in iron ore, aluminum, paper pulp, fertilizer, and fisheries projects and also wants to acquire technology and management skills.

The foreign investments of the PRC demonstrate two things about the country. First, they indicate the PRC's increasingly liberal and aggressive policies in economic cooperation with foreign countries. Second, they highlight the PRC's strong financial position; at the end of 1982, the country held $11.1 billion of foreign exchange reserves. That situation continued through 1983, but in 1984 and particularly in 1985 foreign reserves declined, and so did foreign investment.

But Don't Forget the Bureaucratic Maze

For three years, British government representatives and armaments companies negotiated a major defense supplies contract with the PRC state organizations concerned. A contract was signed in November 1982, subject to ratification by the central government. Every detail had been negotiated and agreed on by the British and Chinese officials involved. The British assumed central government approval to be a mere formality. They were wrong. Ratification was not given, and the contract lapsed.

The British were particularly irked by what they considered the "simplistic" reason given for nonratification. The government "wasn't satisfied with price, technology, and delivery dates," all of which had been agreed to by the Chinese negotiators.

This case is a dramatic example of the need, when attempting sales to the PRC, to make sure of two things. First, are you talking to the right part of the PRC bureaucracy? And second, is your level of contact high enough in the hierarchy to minimize the chances that a higher authority will throw out a contract you have negotiated painstakingly over months or years?[12]

How to Get Paid for What
You Sell to the East

Getting paid for goods sold to the East is not easy. The communist nations' demand for Western goods and technology has been far greater than Western demand for Eastern exports. Therefore, the Eastern countries have not been able to pay for their imports with their exports.

The East Owes the West a Lot of Money

To finance East-West trade gaps, the Comecon countries have borrowed heavily from Western banks and suppliers. The total East European debt to the West at the end of 1984 was estimated to be well over $82 billion,[13] and Western bankers are worried about how and when they will be repaid.

In 1981, Poland's financial position was considered most perilous in the East, and then in 1982 the East European debtors were joined in the eyes of Western bankers by Mexico, Brazil, and Argentina as well as countries in Africa and Asia. However, the bankers were unwilling to define the loans to these debtors as in default, largely because of the losses that would force the banks to show in their financial statements. All of the East European countries were in debt to the West in 1984. Table 17-5 gives some amounts.

The reasons for the East's trade deficits and resulting large debts are easily stated. The manufactured products of the East European countries are not of sufficient quality to compete in markets of the West against Western products. They do not export enough raw materials to pay for the imports they desire. In lower-technology or labor-intensive products in which their quality is competitive, they encounter protectionism due to pressure from labor unions in the Western countries.

In the fields of fashion and design, Western buyers have found Eastern garments and textiles unimaginative. Emphasis on the utilitarian and failure to recognize changes in styles and consumer tastes from one year to the next make Eastern textiles difficult to market in the West. Speaking of the PRC, one buyer commented, "What can you expect from a country that still has antimacassars on all its furniture?"[14]

Nevertheless, West Trades with East

So, as we see, the East has not been able to sell enough to the West to make the money to pay for what it wants to buy from the West. Nevertheless, there has been a large volume of trade between the West and the Soviet-dominated East, with the U.S. share shrinking after 1979. As the immense debts of the Soviet bloc to the West illustrate, a lot of that trade has been financed by credits from Western banks, suppliers, and governments. One method that the East favors to

Table 17-5

Eastern-Bloc Gross Indebtedness to the West at the Beginning of 1984 (US$ billions)

Poland	$28.2
USSR	20.4
German Democratic Republic	12.2
Romania	7.1
Hungary	8.5
Czechoslovakia	3.5

Source: *Statistical Abstract of East-West Trade and Finance,* (Washington, D.C.: International Trade Administration, U.S. Department of Commerce, 1986).

obtain goods and technology is **countertrade.** There are many varieties of countertrade, all of which involve the Western seller taking all or part of its payment in Eastern goods or services rather than in money. Still another device used by Western suppliers and Eastern customers is industrial cooperation between Western companies and Eastern factories through subcontracting, joint ventures, licensing, or other schemes to minimize the need for hard-currency payments East to West.

Both countertrade and industrial cooperation are important and growing means for maintaining trade between the industrial West and countries that are short of hard, convertible currency. Such countries include not only the East but also the many noncommunist developing countries, frequently called less developed countries or LDCs.

Another term used to identify those noncommunist LDCs is *Third World countries.* This means that in addition to the Third World there are two other "worlds" of countries, and those worlds are the East and the West.

Inasmuch as countertrade and industrial cooperation are as much applicable to West-LDC trade as they are to West-East trade, we will deal with those subjects in more detail in Chapter 18. There we deal with finance, and both countertrade and industrial cooperation are used as substitutes for money.

In the West, resistance has developed to countertrade and industrial cooperation. Some of that resistance is directed particularly at the East, and so we shall discuss that here.

Opposition to Countertrade and Industrial Cooperation

Resistance to Eastern goods is sometimes based on: (1) the inferior quality of the goods and of Eastern technology, (2) damage to competing Western companies and their workers, or (3) damage to producers and their workers in friendly countries with which the West has trade agreements.

As to quality and technology, these may not be enduring problems. One need only remember the Japanese example. After WWII, Japanese products were dismissed as inferior. Within 20 years, Japan was a world leader in technology and exports. Furthermore, it has been estimated that as many as 25 percent of all the scientists in the world are now employed in the USSR.[15] There are technical areas in which the USSR leads the United States, and there has been an increase of Soviet patent registrations in the United States.[16]

Dumping

Resistance to Eastern goods being imported into Western countries is sometimes based on damage to competing Western companies and their workers. Western companies and unions have begun to complain that Eastern products are being dumped in Western markets.

Dumping was defined in Chapter 3, and you will remember that it is **unfair import** competition that involves selling abroad or in one country at lower prices than one sells at home or in other countries. The sales prices may be lower than the production costs. *Predatory dumping* is dumping whose objective is to damage or destroy competitors in the country where the goods are dumped.

EC makers of steel, cars, chemicals, shoes, textiles, clothing, and electric motors are complaining loudly about unfair Comecon competition. Some of those EC producers, and related labor unions, are already getting protection from EC antidumping action, and others want more protection.[17]

We mentioned above that the PRC exports products to the United States that are competitive with American products particularly sensitive to foreign competition. In addition to textiles, these products include footwear, watches, electronics, and glass products.[18]

Attitude of American Labor. One American labor union official said that he thought the idea of building factories for Eastern-bloc countries (industrial cooperation) was fine if production were for their home markets. But he pointed out that if an Eastern factory exported its products to the West in payment for the factory it would be difficult for noncommunist trade unionists—"who have the right to bargain collectively and to strike"—to compete with the controlled and subservient labor of the East.[19]

The labor union official was talking about the cost of the labor factor, which is one determinant of the price of goods produced. He was complaining that the East had an unfair cost advantage because it had the power to keep labor under its thumb.

Is It dumping? One aspect of deciding whether an exported product is being dumped is to determine whether the price charged by the producer covers all of its costs, including a profit and the cost of capital. In the East, the cost of labor is artificially low, compared to the West, because labor in the East is not free to bargain for higher wages and to strike for them if necessary. Other costs are differently conceived in the West than in the East. Profit is not an element in the East because production facilities in Eastern countries, unlike those in Western countries, they are not required to make profits to continue operations. The elaborate cost accounting practices of Western business are not found in the East. Thus, costs are not comparable.

For another thing, comparisons of domestic with export prices as dumping criteria are misleading because no currency of the East is convertible.[20] In addition, the Ministry of Foreign Trade can easily export at a loss by its own figures, for political purposes or to earn needed hard, convertible currencies.

Competition with Traditional Suppliers and Allies

As to damage to suppliers and workers in friendly countries, it is clear that many Comecon and PRC exports are competitive with products from other countries, particularly LDCs. For the U.S. market, there are traditional suppliers and allies such as the Philippines, South Korea, Taiwan, Hong Kong, and Central and South American countries. For the EC countries, there are ex-colonies in Africa and Asia, with which they maintain relatively close economic ties.

In the United States, it has been suggested that some of these trading partners may exert some behind-the-scenes pressures to protect their American markets. The countries mentioned above—the Philippines and so forth—all have embassies or representatives in the United States and friends in Congress and the executive branch. These can be expected to lobby and pressure to protect their U.S. markets from the competition of Eastern countries.

Fortress Comecon?

The inability of Comecon—the Soviet-dominated bloc of countries—to pay for the products and technology it wants from the West is one cause of a sweeping change in the patterns of Soviet trade that has occurred during the past few years. The Soviet Union has been cutting back on its trade with the West since 1977, a year when Soviet orders for Western machinery fell to $3.8 billion, from $6 billion the previous year. Although orders shot up to over $5 billion in 1981 because of the pipeline that would deliver Siberian natural gas to Western Europe, that was a one-shot affair. Philip Hanson, a Soviet specialist at England's University of Birmingham, expected orders to average about $2.5 billion during the 1980s.

Val Zabijaka, Soviet trade specialist at the U.S. Department of Commerce, reported that during 1981 Western trade fell to 32.2 percent of the Soviet total, from 33.6 percent in 1980. He saw continuing erosion of that percentage through the 1980s. Zabijaka said that the Soviet Union was replacing Western-made goods with goods from other communist countries. Figure 17–7 compares intra-Comecon trade with Comecon's exports to the West.

Figure 17–7

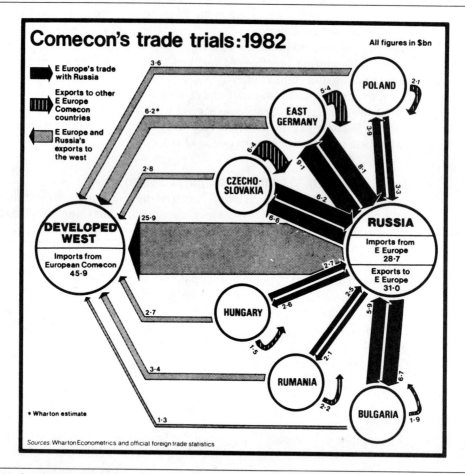

Comecon's trade trials:1982

Economist, October 15, 1983, p. 71

Why Is Comecon Turning Inward?

The shortage of hard, convertible currency is one reason, and we have spoken of that. There are other reasons. Two which have been identified are: (1) disillusionment—a feeling that Western technology can't pull up the economy of the Soviet Union, partly because it is very bad at assimilating technology, even its own; and (2) reluctance to become more dependent on Western technology.[21]

Non-Soviet East European Comecon Members

The non-Soviet East European Comecon countries are being drawn into the Soviet trading embrace with varying degrees of reluctance. The volume of their trade with the West is limited by the availability of hard currency. As it has become scarcer, they have been forced to curtail their Western imports and to turn East.

Oil constitutes almost 70 percent of Soviet exports to Comecon partners, and its price to them in 1986 was higher than the world oil price. Partly as a result of this, the partners' terms of trade with the Soviet Union have deteriorated since 1981. Thus, they have been forced to export more to the USSR, which leaves less to export to the West and draws them even more deeply into the Soviet orbit. Russia seems to be stepping up its efforts to transform Comecon into one vast planned economy, with apparatchiks in Moscow deciding where new factories should be built and what should be traded where.[22]

Détente

Because a fundamental goal of communism is the spread of its system throughout the world, communist governments—particularly the USSR—have aggressively encouraged communist takeovers of noncommunist countries. That aggressiveness has alternated with periods of relative calm, and during the calmer periods, leaders speak of détente.

Détente is defined as an easing of discord among nations. Successive American, European, and Japanese governments have had détente with the communist bloc of countries as one of their major objectives.

In large part, it is because of the desire for détente in the West that East-West trade has grown, as we have seen in this chapter. However, the USSR and its Cuban, East European, and Vietnamese allies have continued to topple governments friendly to the West (or neutral) which has alarmed a growing number of leaders in the West. The USSR used its own troops to invade Afghanistan, while the troops of its allies have occupied countries in Africa, Asia, and the Middle East.

There has always been some anticommunist feeling in the West, and the growing belligerence of the Soviet Union and its allies has reinforced that feeling. Among the results have been the embargoes placed by the U.S. president on the export of agricultural and high technology products to the USSR, which have reduced trade between that country and the United States.

It is extremely interesting to observe that at the same time that U.S. trade with the USSR has declined for political reasons, trade between the United States and the PRC has grown. The two trends are connected, as the United States and the PRC have grown closer politically—and therefore commercially—in order to counter the strength and aggressiveness of the mutually perceived danger from the USSR.

A major lesson for international business executives and students is that political forces and considerations are of paramount importance in East-West trade. As and if détente lives and prospers, so does trade.

Summary

The Comecon countries and the PRC have huge populations, landmasses, and resources. In theory, they should be excellent trading partners for the OECD countries, but translation of theory to fact is proving most difficult.

Ideological differences reinforced by armaments have made for hostilities. Hostilities have been expressed in cold wars that have frequently become hot.

There is trade, but much of it has been unnatural from the points of view of both sides. The East has been unable to earn enough money to pay for what it desires to buy from the West, and therefore the East wants the West to take payment in the form of more Eastern goods and services.

But complaints are made about many Eastern goods in Western markets. The complaints are based on the grounds that Eastern goods are of inferior quality or that they are unfairly competitive with Western or traditional suppliers and labor. It seems quite possible that the quality problems will be solved. The problem of unfair competition will be more difficult to overcome.

Concepts of costs in the East are hardly comparable to those in the West. In the East, there are no significant free markets, so that a method of establishing value or cost does not exist. There is no profit motive, and the only production factor whose cost is considered is labor. But labor in the East is not free to bargain collectively or to strike, so even that cost is not comparable between Eastern and Western countries.

Finally, the political tensions between the communist East and the socialist or capitalist West are becoming more intense. There are armed confrontations in many parts of the world—in Asia, Africa, Central America, and the Caribbean. If these continue, and particularly if they grow worse, East-West trade will surely suffer.

Questions

1. a. *When East-West trade is spoken of, what countries are included in "East"?*
   b. *"West"?*
2. *What is a centrally planned economy?*
3. *Why are the reported trade figures between East Germany and the OECD relatively small?*
4. *Why has the PRC never become a large market for consumer goods?*
5. a. *What is a major probable reason that the PRC recognized the United States in 1979 and wants to trade with the United States?*
   b. *What changes are occurring in the PRC's economic relations with foreigners?*

6. *What does the East want most from the West?*
7. *What are the major obstacles to the East getting what it wants?*
8. *How is the East getting and trying to get means to pay for imports from the West?*
9. *Why is the East having difficulties getting the West to accept its products?*
10. a. *Is the East likely to be able to improve the quality of its products?*
    b. *Why?*
11. a. *If the East succeeds in improving the quality of the products it exports to the West, will that end Western objections to imports from the East?*
    b. *Why?*
12. *What does cost have to do with determining whether an imported product is priced unfairly low, being dumped.*
13. *Identify some differences between East and West in production cost computations.*
14. a. *What trade pattern changes are now going on between Comecon and the West?*
    b. *What trade pattern changes are going on within Comecon?*

Minicase

17–1 Marketing in the
People's Republic of China

You are the CEO of a company that manufactures machine tools in American factories. Sales were low in 1981 and 1982 but began to pick up in 1983. Even with the increased order volume, your plant operations are well below capacity, and even though your technology is well advanced, import competition is tough.

You are beginning to consider export possibilities, and your marketing vice president suggests the PRC. She shows you academic studies, Department of Commerce publications, and PRC trade fair literature that convince you that the PRC market is worth a try.

What steps should your marketing vice president take to gain acceptance of your product by the PRC and to get orders? What should you and she avoid?

Minicase

17–2 Sell to Eastern Europe

You are marketing manager for an American manufacturer of machine tools. You report to the president, and he calls you to his office one day.

When you get there, he starts talking about how tough it is to get new business and about how well the company's European and Japanese competitors have been doing in the American market. He then points out that the company has never made a sale in Eastern Europe and he asks you why that is.

You reply that business has been good enough in the United States and in the several Latin American markets where the company's products are sold, so no sales efforts have been made in Eastern Europe. You can anticipate the president's next words, and they are not long in coming.

"Latin America has gone to hell in a hand basket! They are spending all their money paying back the greedy banks that lent them too much money, and they're broke when it comes to buying our stuff. We need new markets! Get out of here and see how we can get into Eastern Europe."

What steps are you going to take to try to get into that market—or those markets? To whom should you talk? Where can you turn for information? Does détente have anything to do with the likelihood of your success? Discuss. Should you make a sales trip to the area? If so, when? If not, why?

1) FSC 2) Trade Shows 3) Personal visits

Supplementary Readings

Andelman, David A. "Eastern Europe Looking Inward." *New York Times, International Economic Survey,* February 5, 1978, pp. 63, 67.

Butterfield, Fox. "China's New Dialectic: Growth." *New York Times, International Economic Survey,* February 5, 1978, p. 65.

Hanson, Philip. *Trade and Technology in Soviet-Western Relations.* New York: Columbia University Press, 1981.

Ingersoll, Robert S. "The Role of Technology Trade in the U.S. Policy of Détente." *Department of State Bulletin,* December 8, 1975, pp. 811–17.

Kanet, Roger E., ed. *Soviet Foreign Policy and East-West Relations.* New York: Pergamon Press, 1982.

Kosecki, M. M. *East-West Trade and the GATT System.* New York: St. Martin's Press for the Trade Policy Research Centre, 1979.

Nove, Alec. *East-West Trade: Problems, Prospects, Issues.* Beverly Hills, Calif.: Sage Publications, 1978.

Shipler, David K. "Moscow: Not Quite a Consumer's Paradise." *New York Times, International Economic Survey,* February 5, 1978, p. 62.

Technology and East-West Trade. Washington, D.C.: Office of Technology Assessment, Congress of the United States, 1979.

Wilczynski, Jozef. *The Economics and Politics of East-West Trade.* New York: Praeger Publishers, 1979.

Woolcock, Stephen. *Western Policies on East-West Trade.* Boston: Routledge & Kegan Paul, 1982.

Endnotes

1. Anthony C. Sutton, *Western Technology and Soviet Economic Development,* vols. 1 and 2 (Stanford, Calif.: Hoover Institution Press, 1968 and 1971).

2. Peter Galuszka and John Pearson, "Can Gorbachev Blast Open the Doors to Soviet Trade?" *Business Week*, September 29, 1986, pp. 52–53.

3. Eric Morgenthaler, "Soviet Business Climate Is Improving, but It Remains Difficult for U.S. Firms," *The Wall Street Journal*, May 29, 1979, p. 10.

4. Ray Vicker, "Trading with Russia: A Pro's View," *The Wall Street Journal*, January 22, 1973, p. 18.

5. Margaret Yao, "Difficulty of Doing Business in Communist Lands Creates Niche for Firms like Tower International," *The Wall Street Journal*, April 4, 1979, p. 40.

6. Robert McCluskey, "The Bottom Line," *International Management*, July 1986, pp. 49–50.

7. Nancy Yoshihara, "China to Open Office to Aid U.S. Firms," *Los Angeles Times*, April 13, 1986, part 4, p. 4.

8. Thomas A. Gelatt, "China Bares Its Joint Venture Policy," *The Asian Wall Street Journal*, October 17, 1983, p. 14.

9. Vigor Keung Fung, "China Flirts with a Basic Capitalist Tool: Stocks," *The Asian Wall Street Journal*, September 26, 1983, p. 14.

10. Vigor Keung Fung, "China Aims to Revive Foreign Interest," *The Asian Wall Street Journal*, December 8, 1986, p. 13; and "China, New Foreign Investment Incentives," *Standard Chartered Review*, November 1986, pp. 21–22.

11. Vigor Keung Fung, "Chinese Are Eager to Take the Plunge," *The Asian Wall Street Journal*, November 17, 1986, p. 22.

12. Sir Horace Phillips, "Braving China's Bureaucratic Maze," *The Asian Wall Street Journal*, June 20, 1983, p. 10.

13. *Statistical Abstract of East-West Trade and Finance* (Washington, D.C.: International Trade Administration, U.S. Department of Commerce, 1986), table 5, p. 29.

14. Linda Mathews, "China Peeks under the Bamboo Curtain at U.S. Market," *Los Angeles Times*, October 2, 1977, p. 11.

15. John W. Kiser III, "Technology Is Not a One-Way Street," *Foreign Policy*, Summer 1976, pp. 131–48.

16. Ibid.

17. *Economist*, August 5, 1979, pp. 38–39.

18. Jay F. Henderson, Nicholas H. Ludlow, and Eugene A. Theroux, "China and the Trade Act of 1974," *U.S.-China Business Review*, January–February 1975.

19. Benjamin A. Sharman in an interview reported in Harold W. Berkman and Ivan R. Vernon, eds., *Contemporary Perspectives in International Business* (Skokie, Ill.: Rand McNally, 1979), p. 142.

20. John S. Garland, *Financing Foreign Trade in Eastern Europe—Problems of Bilateralism and Currency Inconvertibility* (New York: Praeger Publishers, 1977).

21. "The Outlook," *The Wall Street Journal*, May 10, 1982, p. 1.

22. "Russia Is Bearish about Competition in Comecon," *Economist*, October 15, 1983, pp. 71–72.

CHAPTER 18

FINANCIAL MANAGEMENT

"*The* level of known defrauding by the international financial community is rising fast and set to take a further leap."

Analysts at Lloyd's Insurance

"In countertrading, companies sometimes let themselves get stuck with products they don't know anything about. A computer guy called me to help get rid of 30,000 tons of oranges he'd taken in a deal. I told him to squeeze them into orange juice and freeze the concentrate, or he would wind up with oranges good for nothing but penicillin."

Takis Argentinis, director, Countertrade Operations, General Electric Company

Learning Objectives

After you study this chapter, you should know:

1. That the currencies of the main trading nations change in value in terms of each other.
2. That currency value changes affect international business transactions and the reporting of profits, losses, assets, and liabilities.
3. That the importance of financial management to an international company has increased tremendously since the world's major trading currencies have begun to fluctuate in value in terms of each other.
4. That the financial management of an international company can protect the company from risks and create advantages as a result of currency value changes.
5. Financial management tools, which include various types of hedging, the timing of payments, exposure netting, price adjustments, balance sheet neutralizing, and various types of swaps.
6. That when a multinational enterprise (MNE) wishes to raise capital, its financial management is faced and presented with more problems and opportunities than is the financial management of a domestic company.
7. That international competition has forced exporters to customers in soft-currency countries to accept payment in forms other than money.
8. That a foreign investor in a soft-currency country must sometimes accept dividends, interest, or repayment in forms other than money.
9. That noncommunist less developed, and soft-currency countries are usually more open with information about their economies than are communist countries.
10. That the noncommunist less developed countries (LDCs) are more likely to get and accept financial and technological assistance from UN agencies and developed-country (DC) governments and companies.
11. International finance centers, which some MNEs have established to handle the entire intra-MNE invoicing procedure and which sometimes expand their activities to coordinate all the international financial activities of the MNE parent and its affiliated companies.

Key Words and Concepts

Multinational enterprise (MNE)
Fluctuating exchange rates
Transaction risks
Translation risks
Capital market risks
Investment risks
Hedging
Payment accelerations or delays
Exposure netting
Price adjustments
Neutralizing the balance sheet
Swap
Equity capital
Debt capital
National capital markets
International or Euro markets
Barter
Countertrade
Industrial cooperation
International finance center

Business Incident

David Edwards was born in Wichita Falls, Texas, but was intrigued by international business and finance. He worked his way up the ladder of Citibank's international operation, where he moved into a senior slot in Paris as head of *les cambistes,* as the fast-and-furious currency exchange traders are called. His boldness and quick mind equipped him well for this high-pressure operation, and he did very well for his employer and for himself. Occasionally, however, his Wichita Falls French got him in trouble. He tells of one occasion when Citibank's currency trader at the Bourse,* who was a Frenchman, phoned him and reported that the U.S. dollar bids were going down fast. Edwards shouted into the telephone, "Aw, shit!" and slammed down the receiver. A few seconds later, the trader called Edwards on another phone and reported proudly that he had bought a large block of U.S. dollars. "You did what?" Edwards yelled, to which the startled trader protested, "But you said, '*Achete*'.† That evening, Edwards walked into his boss's office and said, "I've got a funny story to tell you, but it's going to cost you a quarter of a million dollars to hear it."

Roy Rowan, *Fortune* January 10, 1983, p. 46.

*I*n Chapter 6, we spoke of some of the financial forces with which MNE management is confronted and of the financial problems that it must try to solve. In this chapter, we shall examine some of the tools and methods that financial management uses to solve those problems.

The forces or problems that we identified were fluctuating currency exchange rates, currency exchange controls, tariffs, taxes, inflation, and accounting practices. The Armco minicase at the end of this chapter is representative of a manner in which managements resolve problems caused by one of the forces, currency exchange controls.

One problem, faced by the financial management of an MNE, which can be turned into an opportunity, is in what currency to raise capital. The MNE may need or be able to use two or more currencies. If so, its financial management can shop the many financial centers around the world in order to raise the currency that it can use at the lowest cost.

A related problem results from payment for products sold internationally. If you are the seller, the buyer may pay you in your currency, which is the same as a domestic sale. But payment may be made in another currency. If it is a convertible currency, you can convert it to your currency, though there may be a

---

*Bourse is the French word for stock and currency markets.
†*Achete* means "buy" in French.

Figure 18-1

Betting on the U.S.

Europe: Magazine of the European Community (Washington, D.C.), July–August 1978

currency exchange rate risk if payment is delayed—for example, if you extend credit to the buyer.

If the buyer has too little convertible currency, the seller may accept goods or services instead of money. Financial management must convert the goods or services to money, a growing phenomenon as international competition grows keener.

Elsewhere in the book, we deal with market assessment and analysis and with production planning. Early in their assessment, analysis, and planning, marketing and production management should bring in financial management in order to coordinate capital needs with capital availability.

The financial managers must examine the alternative ways of financing the marketing and production plans. How much capital of what sorts will be needed, and when? What are the best sources, and how long can the new operations be expected to need support before they are financially self-sufficient?

Fluctuating Currency
Exchange Rates

Wherever the MNE does business, the MNE financial manager must consider **fluctuating exchange rates**—the fluctuating values of currencies in terms of each other. Also to be considered is the value of each of those currencies in terms of the currency of the MNE's home or financial and tax-reporting country.

The fluctuations create currency value risks. These may be categorized as: (1) transaction risks and (2) translation risks.

Transaction Risks

Transaction risks usually involve a receivable or a payable denominated in a foreign currency.[1] These risks arise from transactions, such as a purchase from a foreign supplier or a sale to a foreign customer. There are several methods by which the financial manager can buy protection against these risks.[2] The company can engage in various types of **hedging,*** in various ways, or if it is a buyer or a borrower, it may be able to accelerate or delay payments or provisions for payments. Within limits, price increases may be used.

Forward Hedge

This is accomplished in the foreign exchange market, and it involves a contract. The MNE contracts with another party to deliver to that other party at an agreed future date a fixed amount of one currency in return for a fixed amount of another currency. Contracts in the major trading country currencies are generally available for 30- , 60- , 90- , or 180-day deliveries. Longer-term contracts can sometimes be negotiated.

5 Norwegian krone = 1 U.S. dollar. An example could work as follows. An American MNE (exporter) sells $1 million of goods to a Norwegian importer. The rate of exchange on the date of sale is 5 Norwegian krone to 1 U.S. dollar (NK5 = US$1) and therefore involves NK5 million. The agreement is that the importer will pay the MNE NK5 million in 180 days.

The risk of any change in the US$-NK exchange rate is now on the American exporter. If the NK loses value, say to NK7 = US$1, during the 180 days, the NK5 million will buy only US$714,285.71 when received . But the American exporter's expectation was to receive US$1 million, and the exchange rate change causes a loss of more than $285,000.

---

*To hedge, in the currency exchange context, is to try to protect yourself against losses due to possible currency exchange rate changes.

Figure 18–2

Traded Currency	Ticker Code
British pound	BP
Canadian dollar	CD
Deutsche mark	DM
Dutch guilder	DG
French franc	FF
Japanese yen	JY
Mexican peso	MP
Swiss franc	SF

The Hedge Involves a Contract. The U.S. exporter could use a forward hedge to protect against such a loss by contracting at the time of sale to sell NK5 million to be delivered to the buyer (the other party to the hedge contract) in 180 days in return for US$1 million, which the other party agrees to deliver to the MNE at the same time. The actual amount received by the exporter will be less than $1 million because the other party to the hedge contract will want compensation for the risk of a drop in the value of the NK during the 180 days. Assume that the other party wants 1 percent and that the MNE agrees. One percent would be $10,000, and the other party would deliver $990,000 in exchange for NK5 million.[3]

The $10,000 can be regarded as a sort of insurance premium that the MNE pays in order to be certain how much in US$s it will receive in 180 days. Of course, it must have made the business decision that $990,000 is an acceptable amount for the goods it is selling.

As with other prices in a free market society, there is no law or regulation which mandates 1 percent, or $10,000, as the cost for a $1 million hedge. In our example, the good financial manager for the exporter will shop around among banks and will find some prices lower than others. The NK is not traded on the International Monetary Market (IMM) in Chicago. If the currency of payment were one of the eight traded there, the financial manager should also get a quote for an IMM contract. The traded currencies are shown in Figure 18–2.

The IMM Contract Is a Futures Hedge. If the financial manager uses IMM contracts, the hedge is with a futures, not a forward, contract. At the IMM, the traded currencies are treated as commodities (wheat, soybeans, sow bellies, and so forth) and traded as futures contracts. Futures contracts are traded by brokers, and the exporter must have a margin account with a broker. Futures contracts come in fixed amounts, such as BP25,000, and standardized delivery dates are used.

Currency Options. At the end of 1982, the Philadelphia Stock Exchange began dealing in options to buy or sell currencies. That offered another hedge opportunity which has been expanded since then in at least two ways. First, other ex-

Figure 18-3

Foreign currency trading is not as foreign as you think.

The potential of CME foreign currency futures, and options on futures, is easy to understand. They're volatile. They offer low margins. And they're exceptionally liquid, with average daily volume close to 100,000 contracts.

Most important, CME currency contracts trend well, year after year. And they respond to familiar, fundamental economic factors—the kind you follow every day in the news.

What's more, with CME foreign currency options, you can take advantage of opportunities in the market with limited risk.

Of course, trading foreign currency futures and options at the CME does involve risk. But if you can afford to assume it, they offer everything a speculator could want.

More bang for the buck. The mark. And the yen.

To learn more, call your futures broker. And call the CME toll-free at 1-800-331-3332, Dept. "W", for our free brochure.

CHICAGO MERCANTILE EXCHANGE®
FUTURES AND OPTIONS WORLDWIDE®
International Monetary Market   Index and Option Market

30 South Wacker Drive   Chicago, Illinois 60606   312/930-1000
67 Wall Street   New York 10005   212/363-7000
27 Throgmorton Street   London EC2N 2AN   01/920-0722

More bang for your buck!

To learn more, call our toll-free number or send this coupon to: Chicago Mercantile Exchange, Marketing Services, 30 South Wacker Drive, Chicago, Illinois 60606.

Name

Address

City   State   Zip

Telephone

10/15/86WSJ

changes have begun dealing in currency options in among other cities, London, Chicago, Amsterdam and New York. Second, there now exists an over-the-counter currency option market involving banks, MNEs, and brokers.

Intra-MNE Hedge. A rapidly growing practice is for MNEs to seek an internal hedge within their own network of parent, subsidiary, and affiliated companies. Suppose that in our NK-US$ case the financial manager found that one of the MNE companies owed about NK5 million, payable about the same time as the NK5 million was receivable under the export contract. The NK payable by one unit of the MNE could then be hedged (netted) against the NK receivable carried by the other MNE unit. Thus, two hedges are achieved at no outside cost and the bank, option, or IMM fees are avoided.

A Covered Position. Even though the MNE exporter in the above forward hedge example does not have any NKs at the time it enters the hedge contract, it does have the Norwegian importer's obligation to pay the NK5 million, which can be delivered to the other party to the hedge contract. If you either have the funds (NK5 million) when you enter the hedge contract or they are due from another business transaction on or before the due date under your hedge contract (as here), you are in a "covered" position.[4]

An Uncovered Position. A financial manager can also use the foreign exchange market to take advantage of an expected rise or fall in the relative value of a currency. There will then be created an "uncovered" long or short position. For example, if the financial manager of an American MNE believes that the NK will appreciate in value in the next few months, the procedure would be to go long on the NK at the spot rate, NK5 = US$1. This is a contract whereby the MNE buys, say, NK5 million for US$1 million, both currencies to be delivered at a future date. If the NK appreciates to NK4 = US$1, the financial manager was correct, and the NK5 million received by the MNE is worth $1,250,000. The MNE pays, as agreed, $1 million. If the financial manager believes that the NK will depreciate in the next few months, the procedure would be to short NKs at the spot rate. To short money or any other commodity is to sell it without having it either on hand or due you under another business transaction.

Using the same rate, (NK5 = US$1,) and the same amount (NK5 million), the MNE agrees to deliver NK5 million at a future date in return for US$1 million. If, in fact, the NK depreciates to NK6 = US$1, the financial manager was again correct. The MNE can buy the NK5 million for approximately $830,000. The MNE will be paid, as agreed, $1 million.

Both of the above stories had happy endings for the MNE, but it exposed itself to risk. Short-term currency value movements are extremely uncertain in both direction and amount, and those MNE stories (and perhaps the financial manager) could have had sad endings if the currencies had moved in the other directions. People who study currency markets and deal in them daily tend to be modest in their forecasts of short-term movements.

We have interviewed and talked at length with foreign exchange market officers, bank traders, and bank economists in America and Europe. Almost all of them expressed definite views, opinions, and forecasts about long-term currency value changes. Not one of them would hazard more than a guess about tomorrow's prices.

Credit or Money Market Hedge

As indicated by its name, the credit or money market hedge involves credit—borrowing money. The company desiring a hedge is the borrower. The credit or money market hedge may be illustrated by the same facts as were used above to discuss the forward exchange market hedge.

The American exporter will be paid NK5 million by the Norwegian importer for the goods in 180 days. With the money market hedge, the exporter will borrow NK5 million from an Oslo bank on the day of the sale to the Norwegian importer.* The exporter will immediately convert to US$s at the current NK5 = US$1 rate, giving the exporter the $1 million selling price, but it owes NK5 million to the Norwegian bank, due in 180 days. That will be repaid with the Norwegian importer's NK5 million payment.

The exporter has a variety of options for use of the $1 million. It can lend it, put it in certificates of deposit, use it in a swap (see below), or use it as internal operating capital. The financial manager will study all of the options to find which will be most beneficial.

Before the money market hedge is used, a comparison must be made of the interest rates in the exporter's and the importer's countries. If the interest on the exporter's borrowing in the importer's country is significantly higher than the amount that the exporter can earn on the money in its country, the cost of this type of hedge may be too great.

Other comparisons and checks should be made before borrowing the NK from an Oslo bank. Even though the NK is not one of the most widely traded currencies, the financial manager should inquire of banks in major Eurocurrency centers such as London, Paris, Zurich, and Frankfurt to ascertain whether NKs could be borrowed at a lower interest cost. And in the case of NKs, other Scandinavian financial centers—Copenhagen, Helsinki, and Stockholm—should be checked for competitive bids.

Just as in the foreign exchange market hedge situation, an MNE should check its company units to learn whether any of them have an NK balance which could be lent internally, that is, from the unit with the balance to the unit with the NK foreign exchange exposure. Thus, interest payments to banks outside the MNE could be avoided.

---

*Actually, the amount borrowed usually will be less than NK5 million. It will be an amount which, plus interest for 180 days, will total NK5 million at the end of that period. Thus, the NK5 million payment from the importer will exactly repay the loan, with no odd amounts plus or minus.

Acceleration or Delay of Payment

If you are an importer in a country whose currency is expected to depreciate in terms of the currency of your foreign supplier, you are motivated to buy the necessary foreign currency as soon as you can. This assumes that the importer must pay in the currency of the exporter, the opposite of our assumption in the hedging discussions.

Which Way Will the Exchange Rates Go? Where you have agreed to pay $1 million when the exchange rate was NK5 = US$1, your cost at that time would be NK5 million. If, before payment is due, the rate drops to NK6 = US$1, your cost will be NK6 million. You are tempted to pay early or, if possible, to make the currency exchange at once and use the foreign currency until the payment due date.

Of course, the opposite would be the case if you expect the NK to strengthen from the NK5 = US$1 rate at the time of the purchase contract. You are motivated to delay payment and to delay conversion from NKs to US$s. For example, if the rate goes to NK4 = US$1, the necessary $1 million will cost you only NK4 million. **Payment accelerations or delays** are frequently called **leads or lags.**

Unrelated Companies. While independent, unrelated companies use acceleration or delay on each other, one may be doing so at the expense of the other. Usually, however, the exporter is indifferent as to the method used by the importer to protect itself against currency risk as long as payment is received on time in the agreed currency. The MNE, on the other hand, may be able to realize enterprise-wide benefit using payment leads and lags.

Within an MNE. For purposes of examining potential payment accelerations or delays between different country operations of one MNE, we should differentiate two types of MNEs. At one extreme is the MNE which operates a coordinated, integrated worldwide business with the objective of the greatest profit for the total enterprise. At the other extreme is the independent operation of each part of the MNE as its own separate profit center.

As pointed out above, international payment leads and lags between independent companies are usually of no concern to the exporter as long as it receives payment as agreed. The same would be true of MNE units each of which operates autonomously. But an integrated, coordinated MNE can benefit the enterprise as a whole by cooperating in payment leads or lags. The overall MNE objective is to get its money out of weak currencies and into strong currencies as quickly as reasonably possible.

Thus, instead of incurring the hedging costs incurred by independent companies while awaiting the future day of payment, MNE units can make payment immediately if trading out of a weak currency or delay payment until the payment date if trading out of a strong currency. If the profit of the unit paying immediately suffers from loss of interest on the money or shortage of operating capital (manager compensation and promotion frequently depend on profit), adjustment can be made to recognize that the MNE gained as a result of the cooperation of that management's MNE unit. We shall deal with management performance measurements and compensation packages in Chapter 22.

Effects of Leads and Lags on Foreign Exchange Markets. When an importer in a weak currency country buys from an exporter in a strong currency country with payment in the future, the usual practice is to convert or hedge immediately. And by selling the currency expected to go down in value and buying the one expected to go up in value, the importer helps realize those expectations; the prophecies are self-fulfilling.

The opposite is done when the importer in a country with a strong currency buys from a country with a weak currency. Now the importer will hold onto its perceived strong currency until the last moment and not buy the weak currency till then. Again, this strengthens the perceived strong currency and weakens the other.

Purposes of Intra-MNE Payments. Payments between MNE affiliates or between them and the parent[5] are of the same kinds as any company makes. On the operations side, they may be for:

1. Services, such as management or consulting fees.
2. Rental or lease payments for land, buildings, or equipment.
3. Royalties under license agreements.
4. Receivables and payables for parts, components, or raw materials provided by one part of the MNE to another.

On the capital side, they may be for:

1. Dividends out of an affiliate's profit on stock owned by the parent.
2. Interest or principal repayment of a loan from one part of an MNE to another.
3. Investment of additional capital, usually by the parent in an affiliate.

Objectives of Intra-MNE Payments. Within the strictures of applicable laws and the minimum working capital requirements of the parent and affiliates, MNEs can maximize their currency strengths and minimize their currency weaknesses.[6] Their objectives are to:

1. Keep as much money as is reasonably possible in countries with high-interest rates. This is done to avoid borrowing at high rates or perhaps to have capital to lend at those rates.
2. Keep as much money as is reasonably possible in countries where credit is difficult to obtain. If the MNE unit in such a country needs capital, it may be able to generate it internally.

3. Maximize holdings of hard, strong currencies which may appreciate in value in terms of soft, weak currencies. Minimize, as much as is reasonably possible, holdings of the latter. You may observe that this objective may conflict with the first objective because strong currencies are usually available at lower interest rates than are weak ones. Financial management must consider all of the conditions, needs and expectations and make a balanced judgment.

4. Minimize holdings of currencies that either are subject to currency exchange controls or can be expected to be subject to them during the period in which the company will hold those currencies.

Exposure Netting

Exposure netting is the acceptance of open positions* in two or more currencies that are considered to balance one another and therefore require no further internal or external hedging. Basically, there are two ways to accomplish this: (1) currency groups and (2) a combination of a strong and a weak currency.

Currency Groups. There are groups of currencies which tend to move in close conjunction with one another even during floating rate periods.[7] For example, some LDC currencies are pegged to the currency of their most important DC trading partner; and among European DCs, the European Monetary System is an effort to coordinate movements of the participating governments' currencies vis-a-vis other currencies. In this sort of situation, exposure netting could involve the simultaneous long and short of, say, the Belgian franc and the Dutch guilder; the financial manager would have a franc receivable and a guilder payable and would feel that they cover each other.[8]

A Strong Currency and a Weak Currency. A second exposure netting possibility involves two payables (or two receivables), one in a currently strong currency, such as the deutsche mark, and the other in a weaker one, such as the Canadian dollar. The hope is that weakness in one will offset the strength of the other.[9]

An advantage of exposure netting is that it avoids the costs of hedging. It is also more risky; the currencies may not behave as expected during the periods of the open receivables or payables.

Price Adjustments

Sales management often desires to make sales in a country whose currency is expected to be devalued. In such a situation, financial management finds that

---

*An *open* position exists when you have greater assets than you have liabilities (or greater liabilities than you have assets) in one currency. A *closed,* or *covered,* position exists when your assets and liabilities in a currency are equal.

neither hedging nor exposure netting is possible or economic. Within the limitations of competition and the customer's budget, it may be possible to make **price adjustments**—to raise the selling price in the customer's currency. The hope is that the additional amount will compensate for the expected drop in value of the customer's currency.

Price Adjustments within an MNE Group. If an MNE is of the coordinated, integrated type, there is much opportunity to adjust selling prices on intraenterprise transactions between the parent and/or affiliated MNE companies.† The selling prices are raised or lowered by billing rate adjustments in attempts to anticipate currency exchange rate changes, thereby maximizing gains and minimizing losses.

Government Reactions to Intraenterprise Price Adjustments. Such intraenterprise pricing practices are often used for purposes of realizing higher profits in countries with lower tax rates and harder currencies and of decreasing import duties. Tax and customs officials have become more knowledgeable about such practices and now have the power to disregard prices that they consider unreasonably low or high. They then levy taxes or tariffs on what they determine to be reasonable profits or prices. Therefore, such practices must be used carefully and with discretion; financial management should be able to substantiate its prices with convincing cost data. Some writers do not recommend aggressive use of transfer pricing for foreign exchange management.[10]

The alternatives the financial manager for the American exporter should consider to reduce the risk of exchange losses are shown in Figure 18–4. We use the transaction discussed above, in which an American exporter sold $1 million worth of goods to a Norwegian importer. At the time of sale, the exchange rate was $1 = 5 Norwegian krone. The sales contract called for the Norwegian importer to pay the American exporter NK5 million in six months, which placed the currency exchange risk on the exporter.

Translation Risks

We have just examined the risks that an international business incurs when it buys and sells between two or more countries and agrees to either make or receive a future payment in a foreign currency. The purchase or sale is a transaction, and the currency value change risk is called a transaction risk.[11]

Financial statements of multinational enterprises must be stated in one currency, just as are the statements of any domestic business. The MNE may have businesses and assets in several currencies, such as German marks, French francs, and Japanese yen, but the financial statements would be meaningless for most people if all of those currencies were used. One must be chosen, and the values of the others must be translated to the chosen currency.

† *Transfer pricing is* a term frequently used in discussing intra-MNE transactions. See the discussion of transfer pricing in Chapter 15.

Figure 18-4

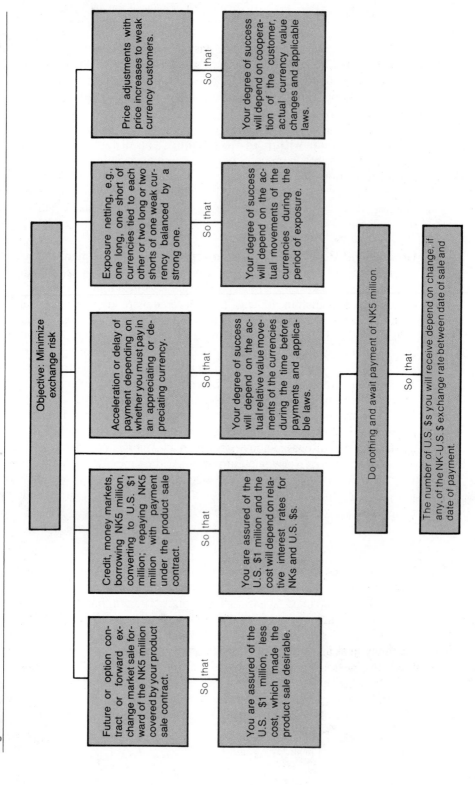

Objective: Minimize exchange risk

Future or option contract or forward exchange market sale forward of the NK5 million covered by your product sale contract.

So that

You are assured of the U.S. $1 million, less cost, which made the product sale desirable.

Credit, money markets, borrowing NK5 million, converting to U.S. $1 million; repaying NK5 million with payment under the product sale contract.

So that

You are assured of the U.S. $1 million and the cost will depend on relative interest rates for NKs and U.S. $s.

Acceleration or delay of payment depending on whether you must pay in an appreciating or depreciating currency.

So that

Your degree of success will depend on the actual relative value movements of the currencies during the time before payments and applicable laws.

Exposure netting, e.g., one long, one short of currencies tied to each other or two long or two shorts of one weak currency balanced by a strong one.

So that

Your degree of success will depend on the actual movements of the currencies during the period of exposure.

Price adjustments with price increases to weak currency customers.

So that

Your degree of success will depend on cooperation of the customer, actual currency value changes and applicable laws.

Do nothing and await payment of NK5 million.

So that

The number of U.S. $s you will receive depend on change, if any, of the NK-U.S. $ exchange rate between date of sale and date of payment.

Sooner or later, companies with international operations will have assets, liabilities, revenues, and expenses in more than one currency. The financial statements of an American MNE must translate assets and so forth from the currencies of their locations into US$s.

The **translation risks** can be illustrated by assuming that an American MNE opens a Canadian dollar (C$) bank account of C$1 million at a time when the exchange rate is C$1 = US$1. If, one year later, the exchange rate has changed to C$1.10 = US$1 and the bank balance is still C$1 million, the American MNE still has its C$1 million. However, the MNE must report financially in US$s and the Canadian bank account is now worth only about US$909,090.

FASB 8 and FASB 52

Due to significant variations in the translation methods used by American MNEs, the Financial Accounting Standards Board (FASB) issued a ruling called FASB 8 in 1975 to establish uniform translation standards.

Foreign Exchange Reserves

U.S. MNEs once established foreign exchange reserves for their foreign subsidiaries in order to compensate for financial disclosure requirements of foreign exchange gains and losses. However, FASB 8 put an end to those reserves. Accountants distrusted foreign exchange reserves because they felt that those reserves could be juggled, added to, or depleted, not so much to hedge exposure as to smooth corporate profits.

Some Did Not Like FASB 8

Some argue that foreign currency gains and losses should not be translated and reported as required by FASB 8 unless and until an actual gain or loss has been realized. They argue that unrealized gains or losses are only paper entries and that their translation and reporting distort actual business results. As reported in Chapter 6, FASB 8 requirements were relaxed in 1981 to lessen the effects of translation on MNE financial statements. FASB 52 replaced FASB 8.

Realistic Information

However, you should bear in mind that ongoing translating and reporting bring up to date the values in US$s of previously reported assets and so forth. Management must base important decisions, such as dividends, pricing, new investment, and asset location, on the consolidation of all such asset and earnings values. It is unrealistic for management to base key decisions on the assumption that exchange rates have not and will not change.

Previously used foreign exchange reserves gave management at least some cushion or leeway in making decisions regardless of changing exchange rates. Now, unable to use those reserves but being required to translate and consolidate, management is taking action to hedge its balance sheets against translation losses.

Management Fears

Managers fear that translated and reported foreign exchange losses will be regarded as speculation or, worse, bad management, by shareholders and analysts. It is difficult to explain that reported losses are irrelevant or should be ignored. Even though reserves are not permitted under FASB 52, management is attempting to insulate financial statements from foreign exchange market fluctuations by other means.[12]

Some of the means for insulating financial statements from currency value fluctuations are the same as those discussed above in connection with transaction risks. Management can hedge, accelerate or delay payment, net exposures, or adjust prices. There are other means which can also be used against transaction risks but are more often used in translation situations. Management can neutralize the company's balance sheet through the use of swaps.

Neutralizing the Balance Sheet

In **neutralizing the balance sheet,** the procedure is to endeavor to have monetary assets in a given currency approximate monetary liabilities in that currency. In that condition, a fall in the currency value of your assets will be matched by the fall in your payment obligations; thus, the translation risk is avoided.

However, before financial management neutralizes its balance sheet to avoid translation risk, it must look to the business needs of the parent and subsidiary companies. The ongoing business flow of and need for capital, the cost of capital from country to country, payrolls, payables and receivables, optimum location for new investment, and dozens of other business considerations must be factored in before an attempt is made to neutralize the balance sheets of all subsidiaries. In other words, maximizing the profit of the enterprise should be more important than avoiding translation risk where they conflict.

Swaps

Swaps may be used to protect against transaction risks, are more likely to be used against translation risks, but are most likely to be useful as MNEs raise or transfer capital. Therefore, we shall treat swaps separately and examine several types. These are (1) spot and forward market swaps, (2) back-to-back loans, and (3) bank swaps. Interest rate swaps are dealt with below in the "Capital Raising and Investing" section.

Spot and Forward Market Swaps

Suppose an American parent wants to lend Italian lira (Il) to its Italian subsidiary and to avoid currency exchange risk. The parent will buy Il in the spot market

Figure 18–5

Back-to-Back Loans by Two MNE Parent Companies (each to the subsidiary of the other)

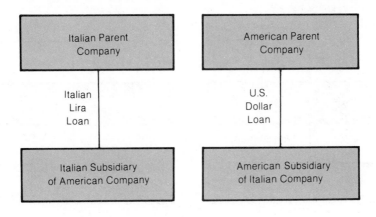

and lend them to the subsidiary. At the same time, the parent will short the same amount of Il (buying US$s for forward delivery) for the period of the loan. The short Il position is covered with the Il repaid by the subsidiary, and the parent receives the dollars. The cost will depend on the discount rate in the forward market as compared to the spot market rate.

Back-to-Back Loans

Keeping the American parent and its Italian subsidiary of the previous example, let's add an Italian parent company and its American subsidiary. Assume that each parent wants to lend to its subsidiary in the subsidiary's currency. This can be accomplished without using the foreign exchange market. The Italian parent lends the agreed amount in lira to the Italian subsidiary of the American parent. At the same time and the same loan maturity, the American parent lends the same amount (at the spot Il US$ rate) in US$s to the American subsidiary of the Italian parent. Figure 18–5 illustrates this.

As you see, each loan is made and repaid in one currency, thus avoiding foreign exchange risk. Each loan should have the right of offset, which means that if either subsidiary defaults on its repayment, the other subsidiary can withhold its repayment. This avoids the need for parent company guarantees.

This sort of back-to-back loan swap can be adapted to many circumstances and can involve more than two countries or MNE companies. If a subsidiary in a blocked currency country has a surplus of that currency in its local operation, perhaps the local subsidiary of another MNE needs capital.[13] The other MNE would like to provide that capital but would not like to convert more of its hard currency into a soft currency. The subsidiary of the first MNE lends its surplus

Figure 18-6

Back-to-Back Swap (where a soft currency is involved)

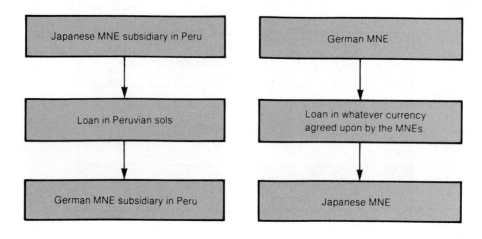

currency to the subsidiary of the second MNE. The parent company of the second MNE lends the parent company of the first MNE an equivalent amount in some other currency that it can use.[14] Figure 18-6 illustrates this.

Interest may or may not be charged on swaps. That usually depends on whether interest rates in the two countries were at similar rates or were widely different. In the latter situation, the borrower getting the higer-cost currency might pay an equivalently higher interest on repayment.

You may have observed that there has been no mention of banks in our discussion of swaps. These company-to-company loans are competition for commercial banks, but some banks will facilitate negotiations or act as a broker between MNE clients in arranging swaps. Investment banks and other money brokers sometimes facilitate or even instigate swaps as a service to clients.

Bank Swaps

Historically, swaps of this kind have been between banks (commercial or central) of two or more countries for the purpose of acquiring temporarily needed foreign exchange, but in recent years MNEs have entered the field. A typical use of a bank swap is to finance expansion of an MNE subsidiary in an LDC whose currency is soft and nonconvertible or blocked.

The mechanics are simple. Assume that a Swiss MNE wishes to expand a subsidiary's plant in Indonesia and, in doing so, to minimize foreign exchange risks and to avoid exchanging any more hard Swiss francs (Sfs) for soft Indonesian rupiahs (Irs).

The MNE may deal either with a commercial bank in Indonesia or with the Indonesian central bank. In either event, the Swiss MNE deposits Sfs in a Swiss bank to the credit of the Indonesian bank. In turn, the Indonesian bank lends Irs to the MNE's Indonesian subsidiary. At an agreed future date, the Indonesian bank repays the Sfs and the subsidiary repays the Irs.

You may have observed that in this example the Indonesian rupiahs are lent and repaid in Indonesia and the Swiss francs are lent and repaid in Switzerland, which eliminates the need to use the foreign exchange markets. Thus, exchange market costs are avoided while both parties obtain a foreign currency for which they have a use.

We have spoken of swaps as methods to lessen translation risks and raise capital. There are also more usual ways to raise capital.

Capital Raising and
Investing

When an MNE wishes to raise capital, financial management must make a number of decisions. In order to cut the costs of capital, financial managers are increasingly exploring the uses of interest rate swaps and currency swaps. As these are relatively new and growing in popularity, we shall treat them separately.

Decisions

1. The currency in which the capital will be raised.
2. Long-term estimate of the strength or weakness of that currency.
3. Whether part or all of the capital should be raised by the sale of equity instead of debt.[15]
4. Whether the money should be borrowed from (a) a commercial bank by an ordinary loan; (b) a bank as part of a swap, discussed above; (c) another company as part of a swap or otherwise; (d) another part of the MNE; or (e) a public offering in one of the world's capital markets, for example, in New York or Eurobond market.
5. If the decision is made to use one of the world's capital markets, management must then decide in which of those markets it can achieve its objectives at lowest cost. The MNE can shop among the national markets in such diverse centers as New York, London, Paris, Zurich, Bahrain, Singapore, Tokyo, and the Cayman Islands. Or it can try the international, or Eurobond, Eurocurrency-type, markets in the above-named centers and elsewhere.[16]

6. How much money the company needs and for how long. For instance, if the company is moving into a new market or product, there will probably be a period during product introduction, plant construction, or whatever when the new venture will need more capital than it can generate.

7. Whether other sources of money are available. For example, if the company is forming or expanding a joint venture operation, the joint venturer may be a good source of money. Or if the move is into a country or area which wants the MNE's technology or management or the jobs which will be created, the government may be a source of low-cost funds. Under such circumstances, the company may also be able to negotiate tax reductions or holidays.*

In order to optimize the decision results, the company needs up-to-date, accurate information. It should also have good, ongoing relationships with international bank officers and with financial management at other MNEs.

We have been dealing with external sources of capital, that is, sources outside the company's operations. Of course, a successful company generates its own capital internally, but that subject is not included here.

Interest Rate Swaps

Interest rate swaps are a product of the advent and evolution of currency swaps, which were intended as an arbitrage between currency markets. Interest rate swaps are themselves a form of arbitrage but are between the fixed-rate and the floating-rate interest markets. An interest rate swap, in its most basic form, is nothing more than an exchange by two parties of interest rate flows on borrowings made in these two markets—fixed for floating and floating for fixed. The result: each party obtains the type of liability it prefers and at a more attractive rate.

Bank-Intermediated "Plain Vanilla" Swaps

From October 1982 through February 1983 volume in so-called plain vanilla swaps approached $10 billion, and during 1985 some $100 billion in interest rate swaps were arranged. In a typical plain vanilla swap, a BBB-rated U.S. corporation is paired with an AAA-rated foreign bank. The BBB corporation wants to borrow at fixed rates but is discouraged from doing so by the high rates attached to its low rating. The company can borrow in the floating-rate market, however. The AAA foreign bank wants to borrow at floating rates, as its assets are tied to LIBOR. The bank normally pays LIBOR to obtain lendable funds. It is able to borrow at fixed rates which are better than those the corporation could get.

---

*A tax holiday is a period after an investment is made during which the government agrees not to tax the company's operations, profits, or executives.

When the swap is planned, the bank borrows at fixed rates in the Eurobond market and the BBB corporation borrows at floating rates. With this done, the two then swap rates on their respective loans. The corporation entices the bank into doing this by discounting the floating rate to the bank by LIBOR minus 0.25 percent. In return, the bank gives the BBB corporation a fixed rate that is better than the one the corporation could acquire on its own. A hypothetical numerical example is shown below.

Assume that the BBB firm can borrow fixed-rate at 12.5 percent.

1. AAA bank issues 11 percent fixed-rate debt.
2. BBB firm taps floating-rate market at LIBOR plus 0.5 percent.
3. BBB firm swaps floating-rate to bank at LIBOR minus 0.25 percent.
4. AAA bank swaps 11 percent fixed-rate to BBB firm.

Net result: the BBB firm saves 150 basis points and passes 75 of them on to the AAA bank; the bank saves 25 basis points on the normal floating rate.

There are nine basic advantages to interest rate swaps. First, swaps give the corporation the flexibility to transform floating-rate debt to fixed-rate, and vice versa. Second, there are potential rate savings, as illustrated previously. Third, swaps may be based on outstanding debt and may thus avoid increasing liabilities. Fourth, swaps provide alternative sources of financing. Fifth, swaps are private transactions. Sixth, there are no SEC reporting or registration requirements, as yet. Seventh, the swap contract is simple and straightforward. Eighth, rating agencies such as Moody's and S&P take a neutral to positive position on corporate swaps. Ninth, tax treatment on swaps is uncomplicated, as there are no withholding taxes levied on interest payments to overseas swap partners, and the interest expense of the fixed-rate payer is treated as though it were on a fixed-rate obligation.

The only drawback to swaps is the risk that one swap partner may fail to make the agreed-upon payments to the other swap partner.

The impact of swaps on financial management practices is predicted to be great. It is foreseeable that corporations will use swaps to match assets to liabilities and to protect investments in capital assets such as plant and equipment from floating-rate interest fluctuations. Financial institutions also see swaps as a way to match receivables (loans made) to liabilities (investors' deposits). For example, to match a fixed-rate loan, the financial institution would sell a floating-rate CD and then swap it for a fixed-rate liability.

Many corporations and financial institutions have engaged in swaps. The Greyhound Corporation, for example, was involved in $80 million worth of swaps with Bank of America (three times) and Goldman Sachs (once). Transamerica, ITT Financial, Great Western Financial Corporation, and Consumer Power Company have also been involved in swaps (Consumer Power did $130 million of them in 1982 and $250 million of them in 1983).

Arranging swaps is quite lucrative. Fees for arranging swaps include a 0.5 percent charge on the fixed-rate payer, 1.87 percent as the front-end Eurobond spread, and 0.125 percent as a standard Eurobond expense. Thus, total front-end fees average 2.5 percent, or $2.5 million on the average $100 million, seven-year transaction. The top investment bankers in the area of arranging swaps are First Boston Corporation, Goldman Sachs & Co., Morgan Stanley & Co., Salomon Brothers, and Lehman Brothers Kuhn Loeb. The top commercial banks in this area are Morgan Guaranty Trust, Citicorp, Bankers Trust, Manufacturers Hanover Trust, and Continental Illinois. The difference between the two groups is that investment bankers stress their Eurobond expertise and their network of corporate contacts, while commercial banks emphasize "their larger coverage of the marketplace."[17]

"Synthetic Swaps" with or without Bank Intermediation

The "synthetic swap" is created by using interest rate futures markets to fix floating rates, or vice versa. For instance, a company with floating-rate debt could fix the interest charge by selling—or, more accurately, shorting—interest rate futures contracts. Now, if interest rates go up, the company must pay more on its floating-rate debt, but it will profit on the short futures position to offset the higher interest payment.

Going the Other Direction

Suppose the company has fixed-rate debt and wants to go float. It would buy floating Euro currency or Treasury futures. In this case, if interest rates fall, the company is stuck with a fixed-rate primary loan on which interest payments remain at the same higher level. As the rates fall, however, the futures contracts would appreciate and the fixed payments would be subsidized by futures profits.

Currency Swaps

Companies use the currency swap markets when they need to raise money in a currency issued by a country in which they are not well known and must therefore pay a higher interest rate than would be available to a local or better-known borrower. For example, a medium-size American company may have need of Swiss francs (SFs), but even though it is a sound credit risk, it may be relatively unknown in Switzerland.

If it can find—if a bank or broker can pair it with—a Swiss company that wants US$s, the swap would work as follows. The American company would borrow US$s in the United States, where it is well known and can get a low interest rate. The Swiss company would borrow SFs in Switzerland for the same reason. They would then swap the currencies and service each other's loans; that is, the Swiss company would repay the US$ loan, while the American company would repay the SF loan.

The Wall Street Journal, with permission of Cartoon Features Syndicate

"We need two hundred million bucks by Friday—any ideas?"

Sales without Money

A number of countries desire goods and products for which they do not have the convertible currency to pay. That has not prevented efforts by many suppliers to sell to them anyway. Such countries are usually communist and/or less developed, and there are differences in dealings with a communist as compared to a noncommunist customer, although applicable to both are variations on the two main nonmoney trade themes—countertrade and industrial cooperation. The developed country (DC) is the seller, and the less developed or communist country (LDC/C) is the buyer.

Communist Customers Are Different

As indicated above, there are some differences between the communist and noncommunist countries in terms of nonmoney trade. The differences can be important.

The noncommunist countries tend to be more open with their production, trade, employment, education, fiscal, and monetary statistics. Such statistics are not notably reliable in LDCs, but the noncommunist ones are more likely to let in and take advice from World Bank, International Monetary Fund, or national aid experts. The statistics are improving.

The noncommunist countries are more likely to get financial aid and technology from UN agencies.[18] They are also more likely to get aid and technology from the Western developed countries, which have the most to give.

Those differences noted, it is still necessary to utilize the barter, counter-trade, compensation, coproduction, and switch devices in order to sell to the nonoil LDCs and the communist countries.[19]

Countertrade

Countertrade usually involves two or more contracts, one for the purchase of DC products or services and one or more for the purchase of LDC/C products or services. A Mitsui study speaks of six varieties of countertrade.[20] They are called (1) counterpurchase, (2) compensation, (3) barter, (4) switch, (5) offset, and (6) clearing account arrangements. All involve to a greater or lesser degree the substitution of LDC/C goods, products, or services for scarce DC money. They may be relatively simple, involving only two countries or companies, or quite complex, calling for a number of countries, companies, currencies, and contracts.[21]

Counterpurchase

In counterpurchase situations, the goods supplied by the LDC/C are not produced by or out of the goods or products imported from the DC. An example of counter-purchase is PepsiCo's arrangement with the USSR. PepsiCo sells the USSR the concentrate for the drink, which is bottled and sold in that country. In exchange, Pepsi-Co has exclusive rights to export Soviet vodka for sale in the West.

Compensation

Such transactions call for payment by the LDC/C in products produced by DC equipment. The products made in the LDC/C by the DC equipment are shipped to the DC in payment for the equipment. International Harvester has a compensation agreement with Poland for tractors. Poland is paying with components which International uses at its assembly plant in England.

Barter

Barter is an ancient form of commerce and the simplest sort of countertrade. The LDC/C sends products to the DC which are equal in value to the products delivered by the DC to the LDC/C.

Switch

Frequently the goods delivered by the LDC/C are not easily usable or salable. Then a third party is brought in to dispose of them. This process is called *switch trading.*

Offset

The offset form occurs when the importing nation requires that a portion of the materials, components or sub-assemblies of a product be procured in the local (importer's) market. The exporter may set up or cooperate in setting up a parts manufacturing and assembly facility in the importing country.

Clearing Account Arrangements

These are used to facilitate the exchange of products over a specified time period. When the period ends, any balance outstanding must be cleared by the purchase of additional goods or settled by a cash payment. The bank or broker acts as an internediary to faciliatate settlement of the clearing accouts by finding markets for counter-purchased goods or by converting goods or cash payments into products desired by the country with a surplus.

How Important Is Countertrade?

Frequently countertrade agreements and their executions are not reported publicly. Indeed, the parties often prefer privacy and confidentiality for competitive reasons and in order not to set precedents for future deals. Therefore, estimates of the extent of countertrade vary widely. The U.S. Commerce Department estimates that between 20 and 30 percent of world trade is now subject to some form of countertrade and that the proportion could reach 50 percent in 15 years.

Major U.S. firms report that transactions involving some form of countertrade increased at rates of 50 percent in 1981, 64 percent in 1982, and 117 percent in 1983. *Business Week* and General Electric each independently estimates the volume at 30 percent of world trade. By far the lowest estimate, 8 percent, was made by the General Agreement on Tariffs and Trade.

Regardless of which estimate is nearest the truth, the value of countertrade is very large. Apply any of the estimates to the approximately $2 trillion volume of world trade, and the result is big.[22]

U.S. Government's Positions on Countertrade. We say "positions" because different agencies contradict each other, and Congress contradicts itself. The Treasury Department is flatly opposed to countertrade, the Commerce Department helps companies engage in it, and the Export-Import Bank has no policy for dealing with it. In Congress, legislation has been introduced both to curtail countertrading and to encourage countertrading of U.S. surplus agricultural commodities.[23]

Other Governments' Positions on Countertrade. The governments of most LDCs either encourage or require countertrade, but so also do such industrialized countries as Australia and New Zealand. No country forbids countertrade. For information about the attitudes and laws of individual countries on the subject, see *Business International* listings such as the one in its July 14, 1986, issue, pages 220–21, which lists the positions of Asian and Pacific countries on countertrade.

Figure 18-7
Countertrade

Countertrade Transactions between World Economic Zones in 1983

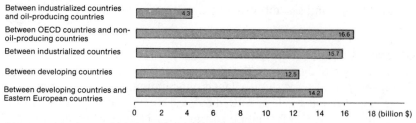

- Between industrialized countries and oil-producing countries: 4.3
- Between OECD countries and non-oil-producing countries: 16.6
- Between industrialized countries: 15.7
- Between developing countries: 12.5
- Between developing countries and Eastern European countries: 14.2

(x-axis: 0 2 4 6 8 10 12 14 16 18 (billion $))

Original source: Countertrade—Developing Country Practices, OECD, 1985

Countertrade Cases between OECD Countries and Developing Countries from 1977 to 1983

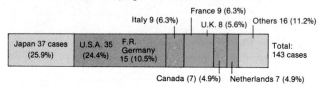

- Japan 37 cases (25.9%)
- U.S.A. 35 (24.4%)
- F.R. Germany 15 (10.5%)
- Italy 9 (6.3%)
- France 9 (6.3%)
- U.K. 8 (5.6%)
- Canada (7) (4.9%)
- Netherlands 7 (4.9%)
- Others 16 (11.2%)
- Total: 143 cases

Original source: North/South Countertrade, The Economist Intelligence Unit

Major Countertrade Products Traded from 1977 to 1983

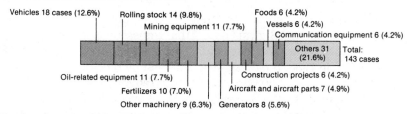

- Vehicles 18 cases (12.6%)
- Rolling stock 14 (9.8%)
- Mining equipment 11 (7.7%)
- Foods 6 (4.2%)
- Vessels 6 (4.2%)
- Communication equipment 6 (4.2%)
- Others 31 (21.6%)
- Total: 143 cases
- Oil-related equipment 11 (7.7%)
- Fertilizers 10 (7.0%)
- Other machinery 9 (6.3%)
- Generators 8 (5.6%)
- Construction projects 6 (4.2%)
- Aircraft and aircraft parts 7 (4.9%)

Original source: North/South Countertrade, The Economist Intelligence Unit

Countertrade by Type of Transaction

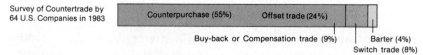

Survey of Countertrade by 64 U.S. Companies in 1983
- Counterpurchase (55%)
- Offset trade (24%)
- Buy-back or Compensation trade (9%)
- Switch trade (8%)
- Barter (4%)

Original source: Survey by Foreign Trade Council Foundation, U.S., 1983

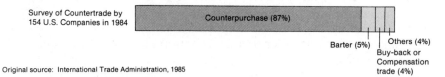

Survey of Countertrade by 154 U.S. Companies in 1984
- Counterpurchase (87%)
- Barter (5%)
- Buy-back or Compensation trade (4%)
- Others (4%)

Original source: International Trade Administration, 1985

Countertrade by U.S. Companies by Type of Transaction

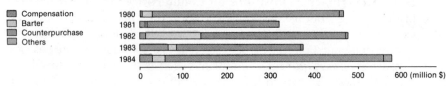

Legend:
- Compensation
- Barter
- Counterpurchase
- Others

Years: 1980, 1981, 1982, 1983, 1984

(x-axis: 0 100 200 300 400 500 600 (million $))

Original source: Assessment of the Effects of Barter and Countertrade Transaction on U.S. Industries, International Trade Administration

Industrial Cooperation

Industrial cooperation, which is favored by the LDC/C requires long-term relationships, with part or all the production being done in the LDC/C .[24] Part of the resulting products are sold in the DCs or the Third World.

One writer, Ronald E. Hayt, speaks of five industrial cooperation methods.[25]

1. *Joint venture.* Two or more companies or state agencies combine assets to form a new and distinct economic entity, and they share management, profits, and losses.

2. *Coproduction and specialization.* The factory in the LDC/C produces certain agreed components of a product, while a company in the DC produces the other components. The product is then assembled at both locations for their respective markets.

3. *Subcontracting.* The LDC/C factory manufactures a product according to specifications of the DC company and delivers the product to the DC company, which then markets it.

4. *Licensing.* The LDC/C and DC parties enter into a license agreement whereby the LDC/C enterprise uses DC technology to manufacture a product. The DC company is paid a license royalty fee in money or in product. The latter method is preferred by the LDC/C.

5. *Turnkey plants.* The DC party is responsible for building the entire plant, starting it, training LDC/C personnel, and turning over the keys to the LDC/C party. Of course, the LDC/C wants to pay in products of the new plant.

Two threads run through countertrade and industrial cooperation. The first is that the LDC/C does not have enough hard, convertible currency to buy what it wants from the DC. That leads to the second, which is the effort of the LDC/C to substitute goods for currency. The types of goods the LDC/C is sending the DC and the Third World have generated new resistance and obstacles.

International Finance Center

A number of new developments are forcing MNEs to pay more attention to their financial management. International financial management has become more and more different from domestic financial management, and in several MNEs the finance operation has become a profit center and is no longer merely a service. Some of the new developments are: (1) floating exchange rates, whose fluctuations are sometimes volatile; (2) FASB 52, which requires translation of assets liabilities, payables, and receivables from foreign currencies to the MNE's currency; (3) growth in the number of capital and foreign exchange markets where an MNE can shop for lower interest costs and better currency rates; (4) different and changing inflation rates from country to country; and (5) advances in electronic cash management systems.

Volatile, Floating Currency Exchange Rates

An international finance center can take advantage of volatile, floating currency exchange rates to make money for the MNE in several ways. It would be aware of which currencies are most susceptible to sudden weakness, avoid borrowing in undervalued currencies, and maximize short-term assets in strong currencies.[26] This is currency exposure management.

FASB 52

This rule introduced the concept of the "functional currency"—that is, the dominant currency of the economic environment of each MNE affiliate. If the functional currency is the local currency (for example, French francs for the French affiliate), FASB 52 allows translations to flow to the equity section of the parent company's balance sheet which is less visible and more desirable than putting them in the profit-and-loss statement, as was required by FASB 8. Nevertheless, it is better to minimize dramatic changes in equity, and the international finance center simplifies this in three ways.

Intraenterprise Trading

Financial dealings of this kind are funneled through the center. It can net out open positions for each of the affiliates.

Borrowing

The center quickly spots exposed assets and receivables that cannot be netted. It can borrow in the appropriate currency to cover those positions.

Hedging

Other positions that do not net out can be hedged. The center can do that quickly and efficiently.[27]

Capital and Exchange Markets

Like any company, an MNE needs to raise capital from time to time. Unlike most domestic companies, it needs to exchange currencies. Given the proliferation of capital and exchange markets, the international finance center should advise and direct the parent and affiliates where to raise and exchange money at the lowest costs.

Inflation Rates

Inflation goes up and inflation goes down, and while it's going up in one country, it's going down in another. The international finance center should be aware of all those trends and advise and direct the MNE system how to protect assets and profits from monetary erosion and other economic and political risks.

Electronic Cash Management

Currency exposure management is being simplified. New technology is permitting the creation of worldwide networks which enable firms to transfer funds electronically. The international finance center should evaluate and use the best of those developing systems. Some of them are: Electronic Funds Transfer Network, Society for Worldwide Interbank Financial Telecommunications, Clearing House Automated Payment System, and Clearing House Interbank Payments Transfer.[28]

Other Uses of the International Finance Center

Mentioned above are only a few of the possible functions of an **international finance center.** Here are some others:

Handle Internal and External Invoicing

The center can make complex decisions about financing international trade among the MNE units and between them and outside suppliers and customers. All data on imports and export can be channeled through the center, which can determine which currencies will be used and how the trades will be financed.[29]

Help Weak Currency Affiliate

An affiliate with a weak currency, could have difficulty in obtaining needed imports. By placing itself in the trade chain, the center can arrange the financing needed by such an affiliate.

Strengthen Affiliate Evaluation and Reporting Systems

The center is in a unique position to understand and interpret the performance of affiliates in countries around the world. Inherent differences are exacerbated by volatile exchange rates, different inflation rates, varying tax laws and accounting rules, transfer price policies, and a host of environmental factors. MNE decisions about transfer pricing, choosing one subsidiary over another to compete for a contract or adding capital to one subsidiary rather then another also complicate performance evaluations with which the international finance center can assist.

A Racy Convertible from Toyota

Although Toyota, Japan's biggest carmaker, was flush with cash during 1986, in that year it floated the biggest convertible yen bond that had ever been seen in Japan. In one go, it raised Y200 billion (about $1.23 billion), twice as much as any other Japanese company had ever raised in this way. Why?

As the bluest of Japanese blue chips, Toyota commanded the finest of fine terms, and those convertibles carried a coupon of only 1.7 percent. The normal interest for other companies was around 2.5 percent.

Toyota reinvested the Y200 billion in financial instruments on better terms than it paid and thus made more than it could have made from building and selling automobiles. In Japan, this practice is called *Zaiteku*, or "financial engineering," and numerous companies have been doing it.

For the 10 biggest earners from *Zaiteku*, it accounted for at least a third of their pretax profits in the first half of 1986. For Nissan, *Zaiteku* made the difference between a profit and a loss. But not all *Zaiteku* practitioners were as skilled as Nissan—some lost money at it.[30]

Summary

The importance of financial management has so increased in the last few years that some MNEs have made financial management a profit center. Financial management is no longer just a service. Foreign currency exchange gains or losses on payables, receivables, assets, and liabilities can substantially alter MNE profit-and-loss statements and balance sheets.

The chapter examined transaction and translation risks and the means used by multinational company managers to deal with these risks, such as hedges, acceleration or delay of payment, exposure netting, price adjustments, and swaps. It spoke of how FASB 8 dealt with translation risks and of how FASB 8 was replaced by FASB 52.

The chapter also dealt briefly with the raising and investing of capital and the decisions that financial management must make in connection with those activities. Other types of decisions are called for if a company wishes to do business with a customer that has little or no convertible currency.

Relatively new and of growing importance are international finance centers. These represent an extension of the increasing recognition of financial management as a potential profit center.

The objectives of this chapter have been, not to identify all the problems of financial management and all the tools and practices used to solve them, but to introduce you to the subject, to make you aware that international business presents more financial problems than purely domestic business, and to assure you that most of these problems can be overcome. In fact, not only can they be overcome, but in some instances they can be turned to the company's advantage.

Some of the big Japanese companies have such good credit ratings that they can borrow money at lower interest rates than are available to most Japanese companies. They are therefore able to borrow money and to lend the borrowed money at a profit. The Japanese call this process *Zaiteku*, which translates as "financial engineering."

Questions

1. *Why is an exporter that is to be paid in six months in a foreign currency worried about fluctuating foreign exchange rates?*
2. *Are there methods that this exporter can use to protect itself? If so, what are they?*
3. *How does the credit or money market hedge work?*
4. *Why is acceleration or delay of payments more useful to an MNE than to smaller, separate companies?*
5. *How would you accomplish exposure netting with currencies of two countries which tend to go up and down together in value?*
6. *Why is the price adjustment device more useful to an MNE than to smaller, separate companies?*
7. *Some argue that translation gains or losses are not important so long as they have not been realized and are only accounting entries. What is the other side of that argument?*
8. *Is the back-to-back loan a sort of swap? How does it work?*
9. *What advantage has an MNE over a single-country operation in raising capital?*
10. *Why would a seller make a sale to a buyer that has no money the seller can use?*
11. *In countertrade and industrial cooperation, what difference does it make whether the customer is a communist country or a noncommunist country?*
12. *How have international finance centers become valuable for MNEs?*

Minicase

18-1 Dealing with the

Transaction Risk Caused by

Fluctuations of Relative

Currency Values

You are the finance manager of an American multinational. Your company has sold US$1 million of its product to a French importer. The rate of exchange on the day of sale is US$1 = Ff5, so on that day the 1 million U.S. dollars equals 5 million French francs.

The contract calls for the French importer to pay your company Ff5 million six months from the date of sale. Therefore, your company bears the transaction risk of a change in the currency exchange rates between the US$ and the Ff.

Assume that your company has no need for French francs and will want U.S. dollars no later than the payment date. Assume further that you do not wish to carry the transaction risk. Give two methods by which you might protect your company from that risk.

Minicase

18-2 Countertrade

An American company and a Soviet foreign trade organization (FTO) have reached agreement on all the technical aspects of the product that the company wants to sell and the Soviet Union wants to buy. All export license problems have been cleared, but one obstacle remains. The Soviet Union is not willing to pay in a hard, convertible currency.

The product includes late technology, but it has some relatively simple components. The company has not sold previously to the East or to any customer for which U.S. dollar availability was a difficulty.

The company turns to you, an international business consultant with extensive experience in dealing with communist and Third World customers. What inquiries will you advise your client to make? What steps would you advise the client to take in efforts to consummate the sale and get the U.S. dollars it needs?

Minicase
18-3 Decisions of the Chief
Finance Officer's (CFO) when
the Company Has a
Temporary Surplus of Funds

You are the CFO of an MNE. The parent company has a temporary surplus of funds. You do not foresee an operating need for the money, $5 million, for about six months.

What are possible uses for that money by the parent? What uses are possible within the MNE system? What considerations will govern your decision as to how best to utilize the money? *Invest it   Buy an open contract in the forward market*

Minicase
18-4 The CFO with a
Temporary Fund Surplus Has
Decided to Use It to Make
Some Profit in Currency
Forward Markets

Assume that your decision in Minicase 18–3 was to use the $5 million to buy one or more open contracts in the currency forward markets. The first contract was long in British pounds @ 1.5138 for 30 days with your $5 million.

How many pounds and pence is your company long?

In 30 days when you cover the contract, the price is 1.5347. Did you make or lose money for your company? How much? (For purposes of these minicases, ignore commissions.) *lost money*

Minicase
18-5 Short the French Franc

Use the same facts as in Minicase 18–4. Your decision is to invest the $5 million in a contract shorting the French franc @ 8.0475 for 30 days. How many francs and cents are you short? In this instance, you cover at the end of the 30-day contract @ 7.8992. Did you make or lose money for your company? How much?

Minicase

18-6 Armco's Trapped

Pesetas

Armco, Inc. had 125 overseas subsidiary and affiliated companies, and in countries whose currencies were falling in value in US$ terms, Armco's policy was to convert the local currencies to US$s and bring the money out as fast as it could. However, some countries restrict how much cash can be taken out. At one point, Spain was one of those countries, and Armco found itself with some $2 million of "trapped" cash in Spain. It had no need for the money in its Spanish operation.

Armco's center and headquarters in Spain was in Barcelona. The business of the Armco Spanish operation had grown rapidly, and it had hired many new employees during the past two years. In that process, it quickly outgrew the original headquarters offices and began renting spaces wherever it could find them in and around Barcelona, so that its offices were scattered in some 20 locations many kilometers from one another.

The Spanish telephone system is not always reliable, so communication among the Armco offices was difficult. The company considered improving communications by using the trapped money to buy automobiles and to hire messengers who would drive them from office to office.

However, the company's senior vice president for finance visited Barcelona, looked matters over, and made a different decision. Her decision consolidated Armco's personnel and turned the trapped cash into an asset that should appreciate in value over time. What did she do?

Supplementary Readings

Aliber, Robert Z. *Exchange Risk and Corporate International Finance*. New York: Macmillan, 1978.

Argy, Victor E. *Exchange-Rate Management in Theory and Practice*. Princeton, N.J.: International Finance Section, Department of Economics, Princeton University, 1982.

Babbel, David F. "Determining the Optimum Strategy for Hedging Currency Exposure." *Journal of International Business Studies*, Spring–Summer 1983, pp. 133–39.

Bance, Nigel. "How Siemens Runs Its Treasury." *Euromoney*, April 1977, p. 71.

Batra, Raveendra N.; Shabtai Domenfeld; and Josef Hadar. "Hedging Behavior by Multinational Firms." *Journal of International Business Studies*, Winter 1982, pp. 59–70.

Battersby, Mark E. "Avoiding Risks by Parallel Lending." *Finance Magazine*, September–October 1975, pp. 56–57.

Blin, J. M.; Stuart I. Greenbaum; and Donald P. Jacobs. *Flexible Exchange Rates and International Business*. Washington, D.C.: British–North American Committee, 1981.

East-West Trade: Recent Developments in Countertrade. Paris: Organization for Economic Cooperation and Development, 1981.

Ethier, Wilfred, and Arthur I. Bloomfield. *Managing the Managed Float.* Princeton, N.J.: International Finance Section, Department of Economics, Princeton University, 1975.

Foreign Currency Translation. Stamford, Conn.: Financial Accounting Standards Board, 1981.

Frey, Karen M. "Management of Foreign Exchange Risks with Forward Contracts." In *Contemporary Perspectives in International Business,* ed. Harold W. Berkman and Ivan R. Vernon. Skokie, Ill.: Rand McNally, 1979, pp. 62–69.

George, Abraham M. *Foreign Exchange Management and the Multinational Corporation: A Manager's Guide.* New York: Praeger Publishers, 1978.

Gernon, Helen. "The Effect of Translation on Multinational Corporations' Internal Performance Evaluations." *Journal of International Business Studies,* Spring–Summer 1983, pp. 103–12.

Gull, Don A. "Composite Foreign Exchange Risk." *Columbia Journal of World Business,* Fall 1975, pp. 51–69.

Hagemann, Helmut. "Anticipate Your Long-Term Foreign Exchange Risks." *Harvard Business Review,* March–April 1977, pp. 81–88.

Herring, Richard J., ed. *Managing Foreign Exchange Risk: Essays Commissioned in Honor of the Centenary of the Wharton School, University of Pennsylvania.* New York: Cambridge University Press, 1983.

Imai, Yutaka. "Exchange Rate Risk Protection in International Business." *Journal of Financial and Quantitative Analysis,* September 1975, pp. 447–56.

Kenyon, Alfred. *Currency Risk Management.* New York: John Wiley & Sons, 1981.

Kettell, Brian. The Finance of International Business. Westport, Conn.: Quorum Books, 1981.

Kohlhagen, Steven W. "A Model of Optimal Foreign Exchange Hedging without Exchange Rate Projections." *Journal of International Business Studies,* Fall 1978, pp. 9–20.

Lessard, Donald R., ed. *International Financial Management.* Boston: Warren, Gorham & Lamont, 1979.

Levcik, Friedrich, and Jan Stankovsky. *Industrial Cooperation between East and West.* Translated by Michael Vale. White Plains, N.Y.: M. E. Sharp, 1979.

"Playing the Rate Spread between Continents." *Business Week,* January 30, 1978, p. 75.

Prindl, Andreas R. "Guidelines for MNE Money Managers." *Harvard Business Review,* January–February 1976, pp. 73–80.

Ricks, David A. *International Dimensions of Corporate Finance.* Englewood Cliffs, N.J.: Prentice-Hall, 1978.

Riehl, Heinz, and Rita M. Rodriquez. *Foreign Exchange Markets: A Guide to Foreign Currency Operations.* New York: McGraw-Hill, 1977.

Rodriquez, Rita M. *Foreign Exchange Management in U.S. Multinationals.* Lexington, Mass.: Lexington Books, 1980.

Setting Intercorporate Pricing Policies. New York: Business International Corporation 1973.

Shapiro, Alan C. "Payments Netting in International Cash Management." *Journal of International Business Studies,* Fall 1978, pp. 51–59.

Soenen, Luc A. *Foreign Exchange Exposure Management: A Portfolio Approach.* Germantown, Md.: Sijthoff and Noordhoff, 1979.

Solving International and Currency Problems. New York: Business International Corporation 1976.

Vinson, Joseph D. "Financial Planning for the Multinational Corporation with Multiple Goals." *Journal of International Business Studies*, Winter 1982. pp. 43–58.

Endnotes

1. See the first illustration and accompanying discussion in Chapter 6.
2. There is almost always some cost for protection, and an important management function is to compare the magnitude of the risk with the cost of protection against it.
3. If you were dealing in a currency more actively traded than the krone, such as the British, Canadian, French, Japanese, Swiss, or West German currency, you would use the 180-day futures quotation for that currency.
4. Covered positions are also referred to as "square" or "perfect" positions.
5. In every MNE, there is one central company at the top of the organization. That company is called the parent company. The other companies are referred to as affiliated or subsidiary companies.
6. The power of MNEs to control the timing and currencies of payment and of asset accumulation has not been ignored by governments. In furtherance of their tax and exchange control policies, most countries have legal limits on acceleration, delays, and intra-MNE netting.
7. Currencies may be fixed in value in terms of each other by international agreement; or if there are no such agreements, they are said to float.
8. The Netherlands and Belgium are both members of the European Monetary System.
9. Andreas R. Prindl, *Foreign Exchange Risk* (New York: John Wiley & Sons, 1976), p. 61.
10. Ibid., p. 65.
11. Alan C. Shapiro, *Foreign Exchange Risk Management* (New York: AMACOM, 1978), p. 12.
12. "Why a Reserve Is Cheaper," *Euromoney,* February 1979, p. 56.
13. A blocked currency situation arises either because there is no satisfactory market for the currency or because of a country's laws.
14. In such circumstances, the equivalent amount is subject to some negotiation, because a blocked, nonconvertible currency does not have a free market spot or other exchange rate, which would be used when dealing with two convertible currencies.
15. When equity securities (stock) are issued, part of the ownership is being sold. No money is being borrowed that must be repaid, as is the case when debt securities (bonds) are issued.
16. The international, or Euro-type, capital market has been created by national currencies being traded, borrowed, and lent outside their countries of origin. Thus, U.S. dollars outside the United States are Eurodollars and West German deutsche marks outside Germany are Euromarks.
17. Beth McGoldrick, "The Interest Rate Swap Comes of Age" *Institutional Investor,* August 1983, p. 83.
18. See Chapter 4.
19. Nonoil LDCs are LDCs that are net petroleum importers.
20. Mitsui Trade News, March/April, 1987, pp 1–4.

21. Edward W. Stroh, "Countertrade: Not for Everyone, but Worth a Look," *International Business and Economic Studies*, November, 1979, pp. 87–89.

22. Stephen S. Cohen and John Zysman, "Countertrade Deals Are Running Out of Control," *Los Angeles Times*, March 23, 1986, part 4, pp. 3 and 7.

23. Ibid.

24. Karen C. Taylor, *East-West Trade: Managing Encounter and Accommodation*, ed. Lawrence C. McQuade, Atlantic Council of the United States (Boulder, Colo.: Westview Press, 1977), pp. 72–79.

25. Ronald E. Hayt, "East-West Trade Growth Potential for the 1980's," *Columbia Journal of World Business*, Spring 1978, p. 63.

26. "Defending against a Strong Dollar," *Business International*, July 16, 1982, p. 226.

27. Christopher Power, "RJR's Foreign Coup," *Forbes*, September 12, 1983, p. 226.

28. "Fine Tuning Financial Management," *Business International*, January 14, 1983, p. 10.

29. For an account of one reinvoicing center, see "An Invoice Center that Juggles Currencies," *Business Week*, November 27, 1978, p. 128. For a more complete account of international finance centers and in-house banks, see "A Special Report: Global Finance and Investing." *The Asian Wall Street Journal*, October 6, 1986.

30. *Economist*, December 13, 1986, p. 84.

CHAPTER 19

PRODUCTION SYSTEM

"The manufacturing responsibility is possibly the least-discussed aspect of international operations, often shunted aside in considerations of investment site selection, financing requirements, tax considerations, and market research and strategy. But the manufacturing sphere is probably the most complex facet of operations, and the one that offers the greatest possibilities for cost reductions and customer appeal in increasingly competitive world markets."

M. Z. Brooke and H. Lee Remmers, *International Management and Business Policy* (Boston: Houghton Mifflin, 1978), p. 146

692

Learning Objectives

After you study this chapter, you should know:

1. Why multinational firms wish to standardize production processes and procedures on a worldwide basis.
2. The impediments to worldwide standardization of production processes and procedures.
3. The four principal factors involved in the efficient operation of the production system—plant location, plant layout, materials handling, and the human element.
4. The two general classes of activities, productive and supportive, that must be performed in all production systems.
5. Some of the reasons why a given production system may not perform as expected.
6. The principal supportive activities—purchasing, maintenance, and the technical function.
7. What the just-in-time production system is.

Key Words and Concepts

Labor-intensive processes
Capital-intensive processes
Backward vertical integration
Hybrid plant design
Intermediate technology
Appropriate technology
Productive activities
Supportive activities
Preventive maintenance
Rationalization
Kanban

Business Incident

In markets smaller than Iran, Gillette has flourished even while sacrificing economies of scale. When the Malaysian government quietly threatened in 1968 to exclude all foreign-made blades, Gillette put up a 60 percent–owned "mini-plant." Less automated than Gillette's standard blade factories, the mini-plant employs 35 to 50 people and has a maximum capacity of 50 million blades a year (compared to a 100 million minimum in a standard factory). Much of the packaging, which accounts for about half the cost of a blade, is done by hand, an arrangement that suits Malaysia's need for labor-intensive industries. And Gillette has found labor cheap enough to keep costs in line with those of larger installations.

The mini-plant concept proved so successful that Gillette put one in the Philippines in 1972 when the government, to protect a local manufacturer, suspended all letters of credit needed to import blades. Others have been set up in Indonesia, Jamaica, Morocco, and Kenya, countries where Gillette hopes import barriers will give it the same hammerlock on the market that they give in parts of Latin America. . . .

Reducing the lag in product introduction took a lot more than changing policies at the pinnacle. Over the years local managers had been making their own improvements in blade-manufacturing techniques and building locally such machines as tempering furnaces. Robert Britton, vice president for operations services, recalls that "as recently as five years ago, our equipment wasn't standardized around the world. So we found ourselves developing a new blade and a new production process that we couldn't transfer abroad because different countries didn't have the same equipment capabilities." Today, Britton's group, which is responsible for speeding up worldwide introduction of products, has brought all plants up to standard, and the local manager changes nothing without checking first with Boston.

Reprinted from the November 1974 issue of *Fortune* magazine
by special permission; © 1974 Time, Inc.

Gillette is typical of a growing number of MNEs that are working to standardize their production systems worldwide.[1] As with marketing and finance processes and procedures, many production processes and procedures can be transferred unchanged from the parent company to the affiliate, though they must at times, undergo modification because of environmental differences.

Reasons for Worldwide
Standardization

Multinational firms would prefer to standardize production processes and procedures on a worldwide basis in order to simplify their administration and enhance management's capabilities to form an effective organization. All of the management functions in the home office benefit from production unification, but local conditions frequently make this goal unattainable.

Organization and Staffing

Simpler and Less Costly when Standardized

The standardization of production processes and procedures simplifies the production organization at headquarters because their replication enables the work to be accomplished with a smaller staff of support personnel. Fewer labor hours in plant design are involved because each new plant is essentially a scaled-up or scaled-down version of an existing one. The permanent group of experts that multinationals maintain to give technical assistance to overseas plants can be smaller. Extra technicians who are accustomed to working with the same machinery can be borrowed from the domestic operation as needed.

Worldwide uniformity in production methods also increases headquarters' effectiveness in keeping the production specifications current. Every firm has hundreds of specifications, and these are constantly being changed because of new raw materials or manufacturing procedures. If all plants, domestic and foreign, possess the same equipment, notice of a change can be given with one indiscriminate mailing; there is no need for highly paid engineers to check each affiliate's list of equipment to see which ones are affected.[2] Companies whose production processes are not unified have found the task of maintaining current a separate set of specifications for each of 15 or 20 affiliates to be both more costly (larger staff) and also more error prone.

Logistics of Supply

Multinationals have become increasingly aware of the increased profits that may be obtained by organizing all of their production facilities into one logistical supply system that includes all of the activities required to move raw materials, parts, and finished inventory from vendors, between enterprise facilities, and to customers.[3] The standardization of processes and machinery provides a reasonable guarantee that parts manufactured in the firm's various plants will be interchangeable. It is this assurance of interchangeability that enables management to divide the production of components among a number of subsidiaries in order to achieve greater economies of scale and to take advantage of the lower production costs in some countries.

Rationalization

Production **rationalization,** as this production strategy is called, involves a change from manufacturing by a subsidiary only for its own national market to producing a limited number of components for use by all subsidiaries. The Ford Escort car, for example, is sourced from a number of Ford factories. Figure 19–1 illustrates that the global car receives components from fifteen nations.

SKF, a major bearing manufacturer with headquarters in Sweden, was able to reduce the types of ball bearings produced in five major overseas subsidiaries from 50,000 to 20,000. Of the 20,000 remaining types, 7,000 have been rationalized among the five plants and the other 13,000 are produced solely by one or another subsidiary for its local customers.[4]

These examples illustrate that for production rationalization to be possible, the product mix must first be rationalized; that is, the firm must elect to produce products that are identical worldwide or regionwide. Once this has been done, each subsidiary can be assigned to produce certain components for other foreign plants, thus attaining a higher volume with a lower production cost than would be possible if it manufactured the complete product for its national market only. Obviously, this strategy is not viable when consumers' tastes and preferences differ markedly among markets. For less differentiated products, however, production rationalization permits economies of scale in production and engineering that would otherwise be impossible. Nissan Motors is able to employ the most modern methods, including CAM* in its Mexican motor plant because of the high output it obtains through exports (80 percent of the total) to Tennessee, Japan, and Latin America.[5]

Purchasing. When foreign subsidiaries are unable to purchase raw materials and machinery locally, they generally look for assistance from the purchasing department at headquarters. Because unified processes require the same materials everywhere, buyers can handle foreign requirements by simply increasing their regular orders to their usual suppliers and passing on the volume discounts to the subsidiaries. However, when special materials are required, purchasing agents must search out new vendors and place smaller orders, often at higher prices.

Control

All the advantages of the worldwide standardization of production cited thus far also pertain to the other functions of management. Three aspects of control—quality, output, and maintenance—merit additional discussion, however.

---

*CAM—computer-assisted manufacturing—generally includes automated materials handling and programmable robots.

Figure 19-1

Global Manufacturing: The Component Network for the Ford Escort in Europe

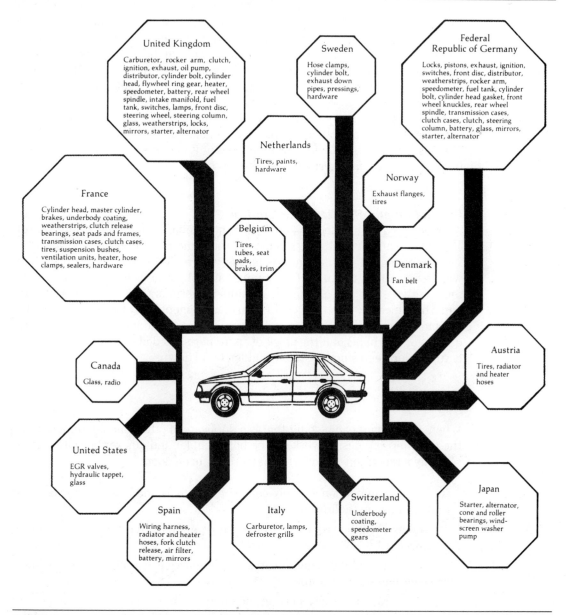

Note: Final assembly takes place in Halewood (United Kingdom) and Saarlouis (Federal Republic of Germany).
Source: P. Dicken, *Global Shift: Industrial Change in a Turbulant World* (London: Harper & Row, 1986), Fig. 9.9, p. 304. Updated information from John Emmert, Public Affairs, Ford International, August 3, 1987.

Quality Control

When production equipment is similar, home office control of quality in foreign affiliates is less difficult because in this situation management can expect all plants to adhere to the same standard. The periodic reports that all affiliates submit can be compared, and deviations from the norm that require remedial action, such as a large number of product rejects, can be quickly spotted. Separate standards for each plant because of equipment differences are unnecessary.

Incidentally, a product rejection rate that is lower than normal must also be investigated because such a rate may indicate that either (1) quality inspectors are not adhering to the standards or (2) the affiliate, especially if it is located in an area of low wage rates, is repairing a considerable amount of faulty output. There is nothing wrong with this practice; but it may keep central management from perceiving that a serious production problem exists.

Production and Maintenance Control

A single standard also lessens the task of maintenance and production control. The same machinery should produce at the same rate of output and have the same frequency of maintenance no matter where it is located. In practice, there will be deviations because of the human and physical factors (dust, humidity, temperature), but at least similar machinery permits the establishing of standards by which the effectiveness of local managements may be determined. Furthermore, the maintenance experience of other production units as to the frequency of overhauls and the stock of spare parts needed will help plants avoid costly, unforeseen stoppages from sudden breakdowns.

Planning

When a new plant can be built that is a duplicate of others already functioning, the planning and design work will be both simpler and quicker because it is essentially a repetition of work that has already been done:

1. Design engineers need only copy the drawings and lists of materials that they have in their files.
2. Vendors will be requested to furnish equipment that they have supplied previously.
3. The technical department can send the current manufacturing specifications without alteration.
4. Labor trainers experienced in the operation of the machinery can be sent to the new location without undergoing special training on new equipment.
5. Reasonably accurate forecasts of plant erection time and output can be made based on the experience with existing facilities.

In other words, the duplication of existing plants greatly reduces the engineering time required in planning and designing the new facilities and eliminates many of the start-up difficulties inherent in any new operation. To be sure, a newly designed plant causes problems when it is erected domestically, but those problems are greater when the plant is located in a different environment at a great distance from headquarters. Just how important the savings from plant duplication are was emphasized in a study which showed that in the chemical and refining industries, the cost of technology transfer was lowered by 34 and 19 percent for the second and third start-ups.[6]

Since the case for international standardization of production is so strong, why do differences among plants in the same company persist?

Impediments to Worldwide Standardization

Environmental Forces

The fact that units of a multiplant operation are diverse with respect to size, machinery, and procedures stems from the intervention of the foreign environmental forces, especially the economic, cultural, and political forces,

Economic Forces

The most important element of the economic forces that impede production standardization is the wide range of market sizes, which we examined in Chapter 14.[7] To cope with the great variety of production requirements, the designer generally has the option of selecting either a **capital-intensive process** incorporating automated, high-output machinery or a **labor-intensive process** employing more people and semimanual general-purpose equipment with lower productive capacity. The automated machinery is severely limited with respect to flexibility (variety of products and range of sizes), but once set up, it will turn out in a few days what may be a year's supply for some markets.[8] For many processes, this problem may be resolved by installing one machine of the type used by the hundreds in the larger home plant. However, sometimes this option is not available because for some processes, only one or two large machines are used even in production facilities with large output. Until recently, when the option was not available, plant designers had to choose between the high-output specialized machinery and the lower-output general-purpose machines mentioned earlier.

However a third alternative is becoming available, though its high cost and high technological content have limited its application to manufacturers in industrialized nations. Computerized integrated manufacturing systems (CIM) enable a machine to make one part as easily as another in random order on an instruction from a bar code reader of the kind used in supermarkets. This reduces to one the economic batch quantity—the minimum number of a part that can be made economically by a factory. For example, a GE plant in New Hampshire can be programmed to make up to 2,000 variations of the 40 basic models of an electric meter. There is a limit, nevertheless, to the variety of shapes, sizes, and materials that can be accommodated.[9]

Another economic factor that influences the designer's selection of processes is the *cost of production*. Automation tends to increase the productivity per worker because with automation less labor is used and output per machine is higher. But, if the desired output requires that the machines be operated only a fraction of the time, the high capital costs of automated equipment may result in higher production costs even though labor costs are low. In situations where production costs favor semimanual equipment, the designer may be compelled to install high-capacity machines instead because of a lack of floor space. This is because, generally, the space occupied by a few high-capacity machines is less than that required for the greater number of semimanual machines to produce the same output. On the other hand, because the correct type and quality of process materials are indispensable for specialized machinery, the engineers could not recommend this equipment if such materials are unobtainable either locally or through importation. Occasionally, management will bypass this obstacle by **backward vertical integration;** that is, manufacturing capacity to produce essential inputs will be included in the plant design even though it would be preferable from an economic standpoint to purchase these materials from outside vendors. For example, a textile factory might include a facility for producing nylon fibers.

The economic forces that we have described are fundamental considerations in plant design, yet elements of the cultural and political forces may be sufficiently significant to override decisions based on purely economic reasoning.

Cultural Forces

When a factory is to be built in an industrialized nation where there is a sizable market and high labor costs, capital-intensive processes will undoubtedly be employed. However, such processes may also be employed in developing countries, which commonly lack skilled workers in spite of having an abundant supply of labor. This situation favors the use of specialized machines because, although a few highly skilled persons are needed for maintenance and setup, the job of *attending* these machines (starting, feeding stock) can be performed by unskilled workers after a short training period. In contrast, general-purpose machinery requires many more skilled operators.[10]

These operators could be trained in technical schools, but the low prestige of such employment, a cultural characteristic, affects both the demand for and the supply of vocational education. Students do not demand it, and the traditional elitist attitude of the educational administrators in many LDCs causes resources to be directed to professional education instead of to the trades where they are needed.

Firms that attempt to reduce their requirements for skilled workers by installing automatic machinery, are, of course, left vulnerable to another cultural characteristic of the less developed countries—absenteeism. If the setup and maintenance crews fail to report to work, the entire production line may be shut down. Some managers resolve this difficulty by training a few extra people as backups. Having extra personnel is viewed as production insurance necessary to keep the plant in operation. This extra expense may be far less than the expense of handling the greater number of labor-management problems resulting from the larger work force in a nonautomated factory of similar capacity.

These economic and cultural variables, important as they are, are not the only considerations of management; the requirements of the host government must be met if the proposed plant is to become a reality.

Political Forces

When planning a new production facility in a developing country, the multinational is frequently confronted by an intriguing paradox. Although the country desperately needs new job creation, which favors labor-intensive processes, government officials often insist on the most modern equipment. Local pride may be the cause, or the cause may be that these officials, wishing to see the new firm export, believe that only a factory with advanced technology can compete in world markets. They not only may be reluctant to take chances on "inferior" or untried alternatives, but they may also feel that low-productivity technology will keep the country dependent on the industrialized countries. In some developing countries, this fear has been formalized by laws prohibiting the importation of used machinery.

Some Design Solutions

Hybrid Design

More often than not, the resultant plant design will be a hybrid of capital-intensive processes when they are considered essential to ensure product quality and labor-intensive methods. As an example, machine welding rather than hand welding may be required while the painting, packaging, and materials handling are performed with semimanual equipment.

Intermediate Technology

In recent years, the press of a growing population and the rise in capital costs have forced LDC governments to search for something less than highly automated processes. They are becoming convinced that there should be something midway between the capital- and labor-intensive processes that will create more jobs, require less capital, but still produce the desired product quality. Governments are urging investors to consider an **intermediate technology,** which unfortunately is not readily available in the industrialized nations. This means that the multinationals cannot transfer the technology with which they are familiar but must develop new and different manufacturing methods. It is also possible that the savings in reduced capital costs of the intermediate technology may be nullified by higher start-up costs and the greater expense of its transfer.

Appropriate Technology

One multinational, Philips in the Netherlands has worked systematically to match a country's markets with its resources and ability to produce certain components in order to obtain an optimal technological mix. A pilot plant devises commercially viable production patterns based on the factors which enable foreign subsidiaries to manufacture small volumes with processes that are less automated than those of the home plant.[11]

Rather than search for an intermediate technology, the emphasis of Philips and others is on employing the **appropriate technology,** which can range from the most advanced to the most primitive, depending on the economic, sociocultural, and political variables. For some products, the superiority in productivity and product quality of the modern process is so marked that it makes the labor-intensive method totally inappropriate. Compare resource mapping by satellites with geologists on horseback, for example. Yet in the case of sugar refining, it was found in India that for the same amount of capital, either a large plant capable of producing 12,000 tons of sugar annually with 900 employees or 47 small plants with an output of 30,000 tons employing 10,000 workers could be built.[12]

Does this mean that the government should urge a company to adopt the second alternative? It may be that the cost per unit produced is higher with the less capital-intensive process. In this case, government administration must choose between (1) the use of the less capital-intensive technology to save scarce capital and create more jobs and (2) the more capital-intensive processes that will provide a less expensive product for its citizens. The choice obviously depends on government priorities.

These examples help to substantiate a growing belief that there is no universally appropriate technology. In fact, proponents of this concept state that what may be suitable for the cultural, political, and economic situation in one region is not necessarily applicable even in another area of the same country. Its effect on attempts to standardize production worldwide is obvious.

The Local Production
System

Basis for Organization

The local production organization is commonly a scaled-down version of that found in the parent company. If at home the firm is organized by product companies or divisions (tires, industrial products, chemicals), the subsidiary will be divided into product departments. Manufacturing firms that use process organizations (departmentalized according to production processes) in the domestic operation will set up a similar structure in their foreign affiliates. In a paper-box factory, separate departments will cut the logs, produce the paper, and assemble the boxes. The only noticeable difference between the foreign and domestic operations is that in the foreign plant all of these processes are more likely to be at one location because of the smaller size of each department.

Horizontal and Vertical Integration

The local production organization is rarely integrated either vertically or horizontally to the extent that the parent is. Some vertical integration is traditional, as in the case of the paper-box factory, and some will occur if it is necessary to assure a supply of raw materials. However, the additional investment is a deterrent to vertical integration, as are the extra profits gained by supplying inputs to these captive customers from the home plants. In some countries, vertical integration is prohibited by law for certain industries. Mexico, for example, will not allow automobile manufacturers to own parts suppliers.

Horizontal integration is much less prevalent in the foreign subsidiaries, although restaurant chains, banks, food-processing plants, and other industries characterized by small production units will, of course, integrate horizontally in the manner of the domestic company. Overseas affiliates themselves become conglomerates when the parent acquires a multinational.

> European ITT affiliates found themselves in hotels (Sheraton), car rental (Avis), and electrical connectors (Cannon Electric) when these multinationals were bought by the parent. The affiliates themselves have acquired insurance companies, schools, and manufacturers of auto parts, cosmetics, and food products. When considered as a separate company, ITT Europe ranks 25th in sales among European firms.

Design of the Production System

A *production system* is essentially a functionally related group of activities for creating value. Although the production system as described below is basically one for producing tangible goods, nearly everything that is said applies equally to the production of services. Factors involved in the efficient operation of a production system are:

1. Plant location.
2. Plant layout.
3. Materials handling.
4. Human element.

Plant Location

Plant location is significant because of its effect on both production and distribution costs, which are frequently in conflict. The gain in government incentives and in the lower land and labor costs obtained by locating away from major cities may be offset by the increased expense of warehousing and transportation to serve these markets.* Management will, after ascertaining that adequate labor, raw materials, water, and power are available, seek the least cost location, which is the one for which the sum of production and transfer costs is minimized. Management's first choice may then be modified by market requirements, the influence of competitors' locations, employee preference (climate, recreational facilities), and conditions imposed by the local authorities.

Governments that are anxious to limit the congestion of large urban areas may either prohibit firms from locating in the major cities or offer them important financial inducement to locate elsewhere.

> Businesses that establish plants in the Mezzogiorno (southern Italy) can obtain soft loans, tax exemptions, and outright grants of up to 40 percent of the fixed investment. Nearly all of the European nations and some nations in Latin America offer similar advantages.

Plant Layout

Modern practice dictates that the arrangement of machinery, personnel, and service facilities should be made prior to the erection of the building. In this way, the building is accommodated to the layout that is judged to be most capable of obtaining a smoothly functioning production system.

The designer must attempt to obtain the maximum utility from costly building space while simultaneously providing room for the future expansion of each department. Space can become critical very quickly if forecasts, especially for new products, prove to have been unduly pessimistic. Managements of plants located in developing countries may attempt to stint on space for employees' facilities, reasoning that the workers' standard of living in these countries is lower and that they will accept less just to have employment. Often, however, foreign labor laws are more demanding than those of the home country.

Materials Handling

Considerable savings in production costs can be effected by a careful planning of materials handling, which often constitutes as much as three fourths of the total production expense. Nevertheless, in areas where an abundance of labor dictates the use of labor-intensive methods, this fact may be overlooked. What management fails to perceive is that inefficient handling of materials may cause excessive inventories of partly finished parts to accumulate at some stations,

---

*Governments will often offer incentives (the UK offers 22 percent of the cost of new machinery and buildings) to persuade firms to locate in special development areas away from major cities.

while at others, expensive machinery is idle for lack of work. Marketers are concerned because poor materials handling can result in late deliveries and damaged products, which, in turn, lead to order cancellation and a loss of customers.

Whether materials handling is highly automated or largely labor intensive, certain basic principles hold: (1) the materials should be moved the shortest distance possible; (2) partial loads should be avoided; (3) equipment should carry loads in both directions; (4) gravity should be used to move materials whenever possible; and (5) the periods during which the equipment is stationary should be minimized.

Human Element

The effectiveness of the production system depends on people who are, in turn, affected by the system. Productivity suffers when there is extreme heat or cold, excessive noise, or faulty illumination. Colors also influence human behavior—pale colors are restful and unobtrusive, whereas bright colors attract attention. Plant designers take advantage of this fact by painting the walls of the working areas pale blue and green but mark exits with a bright yellow and paint safety equipment red. This practice is accepted nearly everywhere, although as we have indicated in the sociocultural chapter, color connotations vary among cultures.

For reasons of safety and ease of operation, controls of imported machinery must frequently be altered to accommodate the smaller worker. Extra lifting devices, unnecessary in the home county, may be required. Where illiteracy is a problem, safety signs must include pictures. For example, a picture of a burning cigarette with a red line through it may substitute for a "No Smoking" sign. Plants in multilingual nations and plants that employ large numbers of foreign workers will require warnings to be in more than one language.

Because of the prohibitive cost of automobiles in many LDCs, employees ride bicycles to work, so bicycle stands must be provided in the parking lots. Special dietary kitchens are necessary when workers from more than one culture work together. These and other special conditions caused by environmental differences must be reckoned with in the design of the production system.

Operation of the Production System

Once the production system has been put into operation, two general classes of activities—*productive activities* and *supportive activities*—must be performed.

Productive Activities

After the initial trial period during which the workers become familiar with the production processes, management will expect the system to produce at a rate sufficient to satisfy market demand. It is the function of the line organization from production manager to foreman to work with labor, raw materials, and machinery in order to produce on time the required amount of product with the desired quality at the budgeted cost.

Obstacles to Meeting Production Standards

Management must be prepared to deal with any obstacle to meeting the production standards. Among these obstacles are: (1) low output, (2) inferior quality, and (3) excessive manufacturing costs.

Low Output. Any number of factors may be responsible for the system's failure to meet the design standards for output.

1. Raw materials suppliers may fail to meet delivery dates or may furnish material out of specification. This is a common occurrence in the sellers' markets of developing countries, but it is also occasionally a problem in the industrialized countries. The purchasing department must attempt to educate the vendor as to the importance of delivery dates and specifications, although the effectiveness of this strategy is limited when, as is often the case in LDCs, there is only one supplier. Increasing the price paid and sending technicians to assist the vendor generally improve this situation.[13]

2. Poor coordination of production scheduling slows the delivery of finished products when, for example, completely assembled automobiles wait for bumpers. Scheduling personnel may require additional training or closer supervision. Often scheduling personnel, or any production workers for that matter, are unaware of the importance of their jobs—they have not been shown "the big picture." Firms that teach employees why they do what they do, as well as how, find that this pays off in creating a better attitude that results in higher productivity.

Another aspect of production scheduling that is responsible for low output is the failure to recognize the economies of scale that result from long production runs. With large back orders, many short runs are made to fill orders according to their dates, and the situation is perpetuated. The aversion to longer-range planning and the desire to please everybody that are prevalent in some cultures prevent production personnel from neglecting back orders and going to longer production runs for greater output. In other word, the production personnel are reluctant to incur the wrath of the marketing department for failing to deliver according to order date while they build up inventories with the increased production that the longer runs make possible.

> An American-owned company in Mexico fell far behind in the production of conveyor belting but the production department continued to produce against orders of 30- and 40-foot lengths, each of which required a special machine setup. Finally, it was suggested that it cease filling firm orders for a few weeks and begin to produce 200-foot rolls of the popular sizes. Output increased by more than 50 percent, and soon 90 percent of the back orders were eliminated without having added a single new worker.

3. *Absenteeism,* always a problem for production managers, is an especially significant obstacle to meeting production standards in developing countries.

Whole departments may be idled while workers are home helping with the harvest. When poor transportation systems make getting to work difficult, managements frequently provide transportation. To counteract absences because of illness and injury, firms subsidize workers' lunches prepared by trained nutritionists and provide special shoes and protective clothing without charge. Employees are told that they can report safety hazards without fear of recrimination.

Low morale conducive to high absenteeism will result if foreign managers, accustomed to a participative leadership style, fail to assume the role of *patron* that workers in most LDCs expect. When employees have personal problems, they presume that the boss, not the personnel office, will find a solution. Personal debts, marital problems, and difficulties with the police are all part of manager-employee relations.

All too often, expatriate managers accept high absenteeism and low productivity as the norm instead of attempting to correct them. Yet those who apply all of the corrective means used at home, making adjustments for the foreign environment when necessary, do achieve notable success. One corrective measure, the discharge of unsatisfactory workers, is frequently impossible to apply because of legal constraints; but a consistent, energetic program of employee training, good union and labor relations, and the use of such morale builders as employee recognition, company reunions, sponsorship of team sports, and even suggestion boxes with rewards can be as successful in a foreign location as in the domestic operation.

Inferior Product Quality. Good quality is relative. What passes for good quality in the industrialized nations may actually be poor quality where a lack of maintenance and operating skills requires looser bearing fits and strong but more unwieldy parts. If the product or service satisfies the purpose for which it is purchased, then the buyer considers it to be of good quality.

> In World War II, the American military found that the Japanese submachine gun, poorly finished except at the working surfaces, killed as many of the enemy as did the Thompson, which was finely finished all over. A gun collector would consider the American weapon to be of higher quality, but was it of higher quality from the Japanese standpoint?

Production quality standards are not set arbitrarily. It is the responsibility of the marketers, after studying their target market, to choose the price-quality combination that they believe is most apt to satisfy that market. On the basis of this information, the quality standards for incoming materials, in-process items, and finished products should be established.

When headquarters insists that all foreign subsidiaries maintain the high-quality standards of the domestic plants, a number of problems can occur. Production may have to accept inputs of poorer quality when there is no alternative source of supply and then rework them. As we have pointed out, quality tolerances are especially tight for automated machinery. Finished-product standards

Figure 19-2

Courtesy: R. J. Reynolds

Export-quality cigarettes

set by a home office concerned about maintaining its global reputation can cause a product to be too costly for the local market. Many multinationals resolve this problem by permitting the subsidiary to manufacture products of lower quality under different brand names. If they wish the local plant to be part of a worldwide logistic system, they may require that a special quality be produced for export. In some areas, "export quality" still denotes a superior product. Quality control, by the way, is not left exclusively in the hands of the subsidiary. Most multinationals require their foreign plants to submit samples of the finished product for testing on a regular basis.

Excessive Manufacturing Costs. Any manufacturing cost that exceeds the budgeted cost is excessive and naturally is of concern to the marketing and financial manager as well as to production personnel. Low output for any of the reasons we have discussed may be the cause, but the fault may also lie with the assumptions underlying the budget. Overoptimistic sales forecasts, the failure of suppliers to meet delivery dates, the failure of the government to issue import permits for essential raw materials in time, and unforeseen water or power failure are a few of the reasons why output may be lower than expected.

Inventory control of raw materials, spare parts, and finished products is difficult under the best of conditions, but when there is an uncertainty of supply, as in most developing nations, stocks of these items can quickly get out of hand. Production tends to overstock inputs to avoid the expense of changing production schedules when a given raw material has been exhausted. Maintenance personnel lay in an excessive stock of spare parts because they worry about not having something when they need it. Marketers, fearful of the frequent delays in production, overreact by building up finished-goods inventories to avoid lost sales. When sales decrease, production may continue to produce finished products rather than lay off workers, because the labor laws in many countries, unlike American labor laws, make employee layoffs both difficult and costly. In countries where skilled workers are in short supply, management does not dare to lay them off even if the law permits, because these people will obtain employment elsewhere. The only alternative in the short run is to keep the factory running.

Finance, the one headquarters department that would ordinarily act to limit inventory building, will not move aggressively to stop this practice in countries afflicted with hyperinflation (most LDCs). It knows that under this condition, sizable profits can be made by being short in cash and long in inventory. Nevertheless, where inflation is under reasonable control and the shipment of supplies is regular, it is still prudent financial management to minimize inventories in relation to safe stock sizes and economic order quantities.

Management's concern about inventory size, always present, was heightened by the sharp rise in interest rates, which greatly increased inventory carrying costs. At about the same time, American businesspeople and management experts were returning from Japan with reports on the almost total absence of inventory in Japanese factories. Toyota, especially, became known for its *kanban* (just-in-time) system for handling inventory.

Just in Time. The just-in-time system requires that materials and parts arrive at the plant when they are needed and not before. At Toyota, for example, seats are delivered every few hours by a supplier's truck and are loaded directly on a conveyor. Because the supplier knows what Toyota's production schedule is, it can deliver brown seats for automobiles being assembled with brown exteriors for example. This means that there can be little flexibility in Toyota's production schedule. Also, the manufacturer offers far fewer product options than do American companies.

The benefits of the just-in-time system are appreciable. A former Chrysler executive who has studied the system estimates that it permits Japanese automakers to carry only $150 in work-in-process inventory per car built as compared to an American average of $775. The reduction in inventory also reduces the requirements for plant and warehouse space. An American assembly plant will need at least 2 million square feet for a daily capacity of 1,000 cars, but in Japan the same output can be handled in an area of just 1.5 million square feet. The Japanese plant is less expensive to build, heat, and maintain.

Figure 19-3

Courtesy of Fruehauf

Gull-wing type trailer sold to GM by Fruehauf for JIT delivery

Why do U.S. plants have such large work-in-process inventories? A principal reason is that they produce in "economic lots," which attempt to balance inventory costs against the setup charges that occur when the production line switches from one product to another. Toyota, on the other hand, believing that inventory per se is bad, has sought to reduce setup costs thereby eliminating the need to produce in economic lots. As an example of its success, Toyota's changeover time for dies in its presses is 12 minutes. A similar changeover in an American auto company takes six hours.[14]

Are American companies adopting the just-in-time concept? Not surprisingly, much of the interest in just in time is being shown by firms in industries threatened by Japanese competition. Ford, for example, has reduced its in-process inventory from 40 days in some plants to just 2 or 3 days and has saved hundreds of millions of dollars by doing it. Ford also eliminates twice a year the options ordered by less than 2 percent of its customers.[15]

General Motors has invested $40 billion in Buick City, an industrial complex where suppliers' plants are just minutes from GM assembly lines. By eliminating much of GM's inventory, said to amount to $9 billion, GM is saving $3 billion annually on storage handling and freight charges.[16] Harley-Davidson, General Electric, and Westinghouse are other large multinationals that have implemented a **kanban** program.

Interestingly, in 1921, Ford's Highland Park plant was unloading 100 freight cars of material daily, which flowed through fabrication, subassembly, final assembly, and back on to freight cars in about four days—and that included processing ore into steel in the steel mill Ford had built there. That equals the record of the best Japanese JIT auto manufacturing plants in operation today. Of course, it was easier for Ford, whose marketing policy at that time was, "They can have it any color they want, so long as it's black."[17]

Because of the difficulties discussed previously, the just-in-time system stands little chance of being implemented in most LDCs.

Supportive Activities

Every production system requires staff units to provide the **supportive activities** that are essential to its operation. Two of these, quality control and inventory control, were examined in the previous section. Let us look now at the purchasing, maintenance, and technical functions.

Purchasing. Production depends on the purchasing department to procure the raw materials, component parts, supplies, and machinery it requires to produce the finished product. The inability to obtain these materials when needed can result in costly shutdowns and lost sales. If the buyers agree to prices that are higher than what competitors are paying, the firm must either sell the finished product at higher prices or price competitively and earn less profit. The quality of the finished product may suffer if the quality of the purchased materials is inadequate.

Even in the industrialized countries, purchasing agents rarely can satisfy all of their companies needs by waiting for the suppliers' representatives to come to them. They must seek out and develop suppliers by visiting their plants and arranging for their companies' production and technical personnel to discuss materiel problems with the vendors' counterparts. In the developing countries, where many suppliers do not retain a sales force because they can sell everything they produce, supplier development assumes greater importance. The ability to locate vendors can easily compensate for a lack of other skills that management would require of a buyer at home.

When the firm depends heavily on imported materials, the prime criterion for hiring will be the purchasing agents' knowledge of import procedures and their connections with key government officials. The purchasing agents must constantly monitor government actions that can affect the availability of foreign exchange. They will often buy as much as possible of regularly consumed materials because they know that they can always sell the excess to others, possibly at a profit.

Whether to fill the critical position of purchasing agent with a local citizen or with someone from the home office is often the subject of considerable debate at headquarters. A native has the advantage of being better acquainted with the local supply sources and government officials, but there is a chance that he or she suffers from such cultural disadvantages as a tendency to favor members of the extended family or to accept as a normal business practice the giving (scarce supply) or receiving (plentiful supply) of bribes. The employee from the home office, on the other hand, will be experienced in company purchasing procedures and should be free of these cultural disadvantages.[18]

Maintenance. A second function supporting production is the maintenance of buildings and equipment. The aim of the maintenance department is to prevent the occurrence of unscheduled work stoppages caused by equipment failures. Because of difficulty in obtaining imported spare parts and machinery, the machine shops of many maintenance departments actually manufacture these items.

> General Tire–Spain began building tire molds for its own use but became so proficient that it was soon selling them to other affiliates. General Motors subsidiaries are regularly supplied with tools and dies made by GM in Mexico.

It is common practice in the industrialized countries to establish **preventive maintenance** programs in which machinery is shut down according to plan and worn parts are replaced. The production department with advance notice of a shutdown can schedule around the machine. By working the machine overtime, inventories can be built up, permitting the rest of the production process to continue during its overhaul.

This concept is not well developed in LDCs, where firms seem to take a fatalistic attitude toward equipment: "If it breaks down, we'll repair it." Furthermore, in a seller's market, maintenance personnel are pressured by production and marketing managers to keep machinery running. This short-term view allows no time for scheduled shutdowns. The subsidiaries that do practice preventive maintenance with overhaul periods based on headquarters standards frequently find these standards to be inadequate because of local operating conditions (humidity, dust, and temperature) and the manner in which the operators handle the machinery. When the amount of spare parts ordered with the machinery is based on domestic experience, it is often insufficient.

In one sense, proper maintenance is more critical than 100 percent attendance of workers. The absence of one worker from a group of six usually will not halt production, but if a key machine suddenly breaks down, the entire plant can be idled.

Technical Function. The function of the technical department is to provide production with manufacturing specifications. Usually technical personnel are also responsible for checking the quality of inputs and the finished product. The task of the technical department in a foreign subsidiary is not simply one of maintaining a file of specifications sent by the home office, because difficulty in obtaining the same kinds of raw materials as those used by the home plants may require substitutions that necessitate the complete rewriting of specifications.

When a synthetic rubber plant was established in Mexico to produce some kinds of synthetic rubber, the government banned imports of all synthetic rubbers. Technical departments worked day and night to produce specifications that enabled the tire companies to substitute the few types available locally for the many kinds formerly imported.

The affiliate's technical manager is a key figure in the maintenance of product quality and thus is extremely influential in selecting sources of supply. Multinationals go to great lengths in persuading host governments and joint venture partners of the need to place one of their people in this position. In this way, the multinationals are certain to keep the affiliate as a captive customer purchasing all of the inputs that the more highly integrated parent manufactures.

Summary

Parent company production managers, like marketing and financial managers, are concerned with global standardization, the functions of management, and the influence of environmental forces. Although many of the production processes and procedures employed by the parent can be transferred overseas, some must be altered or discarded because of environmental differences. Central managements' preference for worldwide standardization is based on the fact that unified methods simplify the execution of the management functions and are usually less costly.

LDC governments, preoccupied with high unemployment and rising capital costs, are urging investors to consider an *intermediate technology* rather than the highly automated processes of the industrialized nations. The multinationals' response, in some instances, has been to search for an *appropriate technology*, which matches a country's market with its resources. Under this concept, the production processes used may vary from the most advanced to the most primitive, depending on the influence of the economic, sociocultural, and political variables.

A production system is essentially a functionally related group of activities for creating value. Factors included in the system's operations are: (1) plant location, (2) plant layout, (3) materials handling, and (4) the human element. After the system is operable, two general classes of activities, productive and supportive, must be performed. Among the important supportive activities are purchasing, maintenance, and the technical function. The primary aim of both types of activities is to assure that the system produces on time the required amount of product of the desired quality at the budgeted cost.

Questions

1. a. *What is the connection between Japanese manufacturers' insistence on receiving component parts with as close to zero defects as possible and the* kanban *system?*

   b. *Why, in introducing the* kanban *system, are U.S. manufacturers such as GM insisting that suppliers locate very close to their assembly plants?*

2. *What are the advantages to the multinational firm of worldwide production standardization?*

3. *What is the relationship between the standardization of production systems and the logistics of supply?*

4. *Discuss the influence of the environmental forces on worldwide standardization.*

5. *What effect will the LDCs' insistence on the use of intermediate and appropriate technology have on the design of production systems?*

6. *Why are plant location and materials handling important factors in the design of the production system?*

7. *What are some of the reasons for low production output?*

8. *Why might production costs be excessive?*

9. *Who should be appointed as manager of the purchasing department, a local citizen or someone from the home office? Why?*

10. *Why might it be difficult to establish a preventive maintenance program in a foreign plant?*

Minicase

19–1 Site Selection: Johnson Machine Tool Manufacturing (Europa)

A site selection committee was named by the president of a small company, Johnson Machine Tool Manufacturing (annual sales—$21 million), to recommend the location of Johnson's first plant in Europa. A subcommittee consisting of the managers of finance, marketing, and production has just returned from a two-week visit. Its members are in agreement that two locations in Europa are preferable to all others:

1. Carlsburg, the capital and largest city (2,300,000 population).

2. Andein (180,000 population).

Carlsburg, also a manufacturing center for the country, is located almost equidistant from the borders. Andein, on the other hand, occupies the southeastern corner of the nation, almost 350 kilometers away. There are some light manufacturing plants in Andein.

To reduce the time required to gather the information needed to choose a plant site, the subcommittee divided the work as follows:

1. Marketing manager:
   a. Confirmed desk study concerning the marketing analysis.
   b. Checked on the availability of freight carriers, especially carriers of motor freight, and on freight rates.
   c. Investigated the availability and rent of warehouse space in Carlsburg.

2. Production manager:
   a. Obtained information concerning wages and the cost of fringe benefits for various skill levels in Carlsburg and Andein. Checked both markets for labor supply.
   b. Obtained cost estimates for plant construction in Carlsburg and Andein.
   c. Visited the utility companies to learn about the supply and rates in both cities.
   d. Checked the availability and cost of housing in both cities.
   e. Inquired about cultural and recreational activities and schools in both cities.

3. Finance manager:
   a. Inquired about taxes in both cities—property, state income, and payroll taxes.
   b. Visited the national development office to confirm the amount and kinds of assistance to be obtained from the national government for establishing a manufacturing plant in Europa.
   c. Obtained prices on tracts of lands in Carlsburg and Andein.

The results of the investigation are as follows:

1. Monthly rent of warehouse and office space in Carlsburg—$1,500. This is necessary if the plant is set up in Andein. Warehousing and offices will be at the plant site if the company locates at Carlsburg.

2. Annual transportation costs for incoming raw materials and component parts should average $160,000 if the plant is located in Carlsburg and $270,000 if it is established in Andein. Transportation costs for finished goods will be $270,000 for the Carlsburg location and $390,000 if the plant is set up in Andein. Service is adequate to both locations.

3. Labor costs are somewhat higher in the capital. With fringe benefits included, the cost should be $1,100,000 for Carlsburg and $970,000 for Andein. The supply of labor is adequate at both locations.

4. Annual depreciation of building and equipment will amount to $160,000 in Carlsburg and $100,000 in Andein. It is planned to use straight-line depreciation over a 10-year period.

5. To include differences in land costs, the treasurer has recommended that 10 percent of the value of the land purchase be included under the heading of Implied Interest. This amounts annually to $90,000 for Carlsburg and $50,000 for Andein.

6. Power and heat are expected to cost $76,000 annually in both Carlsburg and Andein because the same power company supplies both areas. The power supply is adequate at both locations.

7. Water will cost $15,000 annually in Carlsburg and $12,000 in Andein. The supply is adequate in both cities.

8. Insurance is slightly higher in Andein—$39,000 annually versus $36,000 for Carlsburg.

9. Property values are lower in Andein, as are the tax rates. Property taxes are expected to be $27,000 in Carlsburg and $14,000 in Andein.

10. State income taxes are also lower in Andein—$14,000 versus $27,000 in Carlsburg.

11. Although the payroll tax is a federal tax with the same rate in all parts of the country, Andein's lower wage rates cause its payroll to be lower than that of Carlsburg. Payroll taxes are $15,400 in Carlsburg and $13,600 in Andein.

12. The federal government is urging companies to locate away from the capital and offers a 10-year tax exemption equal to 50 percent of federal income taxes to those that do. The financial manager estimates that by the second year, the subsidiary should have taxable earnings of approximately $750,000. The tax rate is 40 percent.

13. There are state parks within an hour's drive from each city. Carlsburg has an opera company, a symphony orchestra, and various golf courses and tennis courts. The major university of the nation is located in Carlsburg. There is also an English-speaking school with grades K through 12.

14. Andein is near two lakes and a forest. Fishing and hunting are permitted. A regional university is in the city. Although there is no English-speaking school for grades K through 12 in Andein, the U.S. Army base 15 miles away does have such a school for army dependents, some of whom live in Andein. There is a daily bus service from Andein to the school on the base, and American children who are not army dependents are permitted to attend if they pay an $80 monthly tuition.

In light of these results:

1. Which city do you recommend as a plant site?

2. Show all of your calculations.

3. In addition to costs, what other factors are you considering?

Minicase

19-2 Stockless Production

Management: More than

Inventory Control*

Stockless production (S.P.), also called just-in-time production (*kanban* in Japanese), has attracted the attention of American managers as being the secret of Japan's industrial miracle.

Ideally, stockless production keeps all material moving. None is in inventory to generate carrying charges. Materials arrive in time to be turned into fabricated parts, which, in turn, arrive at the precise moment to go into subassemblies. Similarly, subassemblies reach the final assembly area just in time to be assembled into finished products, which are being delivered just in time to be sold.

Setup versus Carrying Costs

It is apparent that S.P. requires the manufacturer to produce only enough at each stage to be used up by the end of the day in the finished product. This necessitates small runs, which can require a worker to move from one machine to another—a "generalist" rather than the specialist more common in U.S. industry. However, smaller runs require more machine setups than do longer ones. When it takes six hours of skilled labor to set up a large press to form automobile hoods, shouldn't the plant produce them for several days before changing to another size that will require another six-hour work stoppage for a new setup? Is there a point at which the setup charges equal the cost of carrying the parts inventory? There is such a point. It is called the economic order quantity, and it is the basis of American inventory management.

Other Costs

However, carrying and setup costs are only part of the total costs related to manufacturing lot size. Also involved are scrap, quality, productivity, and employee motivation. Furthermore, even setup times are not fixed. In 1971 an hour was required in the Toyota plant to change an 800-ton press, but after a five-year campaign for improvement the setup time was lowered to 12 minutes. Toyota is still working to get the time below 10 minutes (versus six hours in the United States).

*Sources: From "Can Kanban Ban Inventory Blues?" *Industry Week*, July 26, 1982; Richard J. Shonberger, "Why the Japanese Produce Just in Time," *Industry Week*, November 29, 1982; "Japanese Productivity—The Three-Pronged Attack," *The Chronicle*, Arthur Andersen, & Co. 1981; and "High Tech to the Rescue," *Business Week*, June 16, 1986, pp. 100–108.

To obtain these greatly reduced setup times, a machine must frequently be altered. However, as management experts point out, once altered, the machine's resale value may be reduced considerably—a somewhat strange argument. Because commercial machine tools are designed for a number of industries, they are frequently not the best for a given process. To overcome this difficulty, the Japanese often replace them with single-purpose machines made in the company's own machine shop. No setup time is required for a single-purpose machine. Since the machine does only one job, there is never any need to set it up for another product or operation.

The reason that scrap is reduced by S.P. is that the part that one worker makes is immediately passed to the next instead of being thrown into a barrel where it remains for days, with thousands of other similar parts made by various workers, until the next operation begins. When the next worker receives from the first worker a defective part that does not fit what is being assembled, the first worker will be told immediately that his or her part is no good. This is a blow to the first worker's pride, but it also increases awareness of the need to do it correctly and provides immediate feedback so that a correction can be made. Workers become extremely conscious of the importance of quality and are motivated to improve their workmanship. In fact, Japanese workers' concern for quality and slowdowns for any reason is so great that they meet in peer groups voluntarily to discuss these problems (quality circles). Under these conditions, quality control can be given to the worker, thereby greatly reducing the cost of maintaining a large group of quality control inspectors.

Suppliers Need S.P.

In order to lower the size of the inventory of products furnished by suppliers, the manufacturer must provide suppliers with a production schedule that will remain unchanged for a certain length of time. In Japan, this is commonly a month. Depending on the product, a supplier may be required to make daily deliveries. To accomplish this, it must either institute S.P. or depend on costly inventories. It must also be as conscious of quality as the first worker we mentioned previously. Naturally, the supplier's suppliers need S.P., and so on.

Japanese Miracle

This then, is, the Japanese miracle—a constant cycle of inventory reductions that force improvements in quality and productivity. The result is an ever better and less expensive product.

American Experience

Why haven't American firms instituted S.P.? Some have. A shock absorber manufacturer signed a contract requiring delivery every two to four days to Nissan's new plant in Tennessee. To do so, this manufacturer also had to adopt the S.P. system.

Some managers, forgetting that Japan has no natural resources and must bring them long distances, claim that S.P. functions better in Japan because suppliers are within a 50-mile radius of their customers. The problem in the United States, they say, is that many suppliers are thousands of miles away from their customers. However, some suppliers have traditionally erected plants close to their customers in this country. Can manufacturers have built plants next to breweries and food processors. Tire companies have located factories near Detroit.

In a move to emulate the *kanban* system, General Motors has invested $40 billion in Buick City, an industrial complex where suppliers' plants are just minutes away from GM assembly lines. The company has eliminated much of its $9 billion parts inventory.

1. American firms have been using the economic order quantity model for years. This model regards ordering costs, holding costs, daily demand, and order lead time as important variables. Does the S.P. production method neglect these variables? Don't the Japanese have to strike a balance between setup costs and inventory carrying costs as American firms do?

2. Why do some experts state that American managers should forget their EOQ training?

3. What other benefits does S.P. provide in addition to lower inventory costs?

Supplementary Readings

"Factories That Turn Nuts into Bolts." *U.S. News & World Report*, July 14, 1986, pp. 44–45.

"Factory Automation Takes the Slow Road."*Standard Chartered Review,* September 1986, pp. 2–6.

"French Quality Circles Multiply, but with a Difference." *International Management*, December 1986, pp. 30–32.

"Harley-Davidson Takes Lessons from Arch-Rivals' Handbook." *International Management*, February 1985, pp. 26–30.

"Having a Hard Time with Just-in-Time." *Fortune*, June 9, 1986, pp. 64–65.

Improving Productivity in Less-Developed Countries. Research Bulletin 107 (New York: Conference Board, 1982).

"Just-in-Time: The Corporate View." *Industrial Distribution*, May 1985, pp. 83–84.

Medford, Robert N. "Determinants of Productivity Differences in International Manufacturing." *Journal of International Business Studies*, Spring 1986, pp. 63–82.

"Texas Instruments Now Has Japan's Praise." *The Wall Street Journal*, October 3, 1986, p. 28.

"The Vital Elements of World-Class Manufacturing." *International Management*, May 1986, pp. 76–78.

Wells, Nancy. "The Growing Dilemma of Locating Internationally." *Institutional Investor,* May 1982, pp. 231–40.

Endnotes

1. Production as defined here is referred to as operations by those who consider production to be the manufacturing of tangible goods only.

2. We know of firms that mail specification changes to all plants regardless of whether all are affected. This merely transfers the work of deciding whether these changes are relevant from the home office to the technical manager in each affiliate.

3. Donald J. Bowersox, *Logistical Management* (New York: Macmillan, 1974), p. 1.

4. Yves L. Doz, "Managing Manufacturing Rationalization within Multinational Companies," *Columbia Journal of World Business,* Fall 1978, pp. 82–93.

5. Jane Bussey, "Gearing Up to Export Three Million Engines to Auto Plants Abroad," *R & D Mexico,* February 1982, pp. 20–23.

6. D. J. Teece, "Technology Transfer by Multinational Firms," *Economic Journal,* June 1977, pp. 242–61.

7. A number of studies confirmed by personal experience have shown that the foremost criterion for plant design is the output desired. Once this is known, the engineering department of a multiplant operation will check to see whether a factory already built has a capacity similar to the output specified. If so, this facility will serve as a design standard for the new plant, though modifications may be made to eliminate problems encountered in the original design. Many large multiplant firms actually have standard designs for large, medium, and small production outputs.

8. A highly automated machine might make only one or two sizes or types of a product, whereas a general-purpose machine may be capable of producing not only all sizes of a product but other products as well. Its output, however, may be as little as 1 percent of that of the specialized machine.

9. "Factories That Turn Nuts into Bolts," *U.S. News & World Report,* July 14, 1986, pp. 44–55; and "Factory Automation Takes the Slow Road," *Standard Chartered Review,* November 1986, pp. 2–6.

10. The skill level required of general-purpose machine operators is much higher than that required of operators attending automated machinery but is lower than that needed to set up and maintain this equipment.

11. "Efficient Use of Resources to Create Employment," *Employment and Development of Small Enterprises* (Washington, D.C.: World Bank, February 1978), p. 15.

12. This does not mean that unit production costs are lower in the small plants, and certainly the coordination of their activities will be formidable. The example does illustrate the extreme range of possibilities when capital costs are a primary consideration. From Colin Norman, *Soft Technology, Hard Choice* (Washington, D.C.: Worldwatch Institute, June 1978), p. 14.

13. When the automobile plants in Mexico were required to incorporate locally made parts into the product, they not only provided their own technical assistance to vendors but also arranged for licensing agreements from U.S. suppliers and even guaranteed bank loans enabling the vendors to buy production machinery. This tremendous assistance program, literally dumped in the laps of small local manufacturers, was a leading factor in creating the Mexican parts industry.

14. Robert H. Hayes, "Why Japanese Factories Work," *McKinsey Quarterly,* Autumn 1982, pp. 32–48.
15. Charles G. Burck, "Can Detroit Catch Up?" *Fortune,* February 8, 1982, pp. 34–39.
16. "High Tech to the Rescue," *Business Week,* June 16, 1986, pp. 100–108.
17. "The Vital Elements of World-Class Manufacturing," *International Management,* May 1986, pp. 76–78.
18. Managers are not so naive as to believe that belonging to a certain culture guarantees that an individual will or will not engage in unethical activities. However, the tendency to commit these acts will be greater where there are no cultural constraints.

CHAPTER 20

LABOR RELATIONS POLICIES AND MANAGEMENT

"*The* task of the union is to secure as much in pay and benefits as possible. The task of the employer negotiators is to keep the pay and benefits as low as possible."

Journal of Business Ethics, August 1985, p. 283

"When all else fails, one is forced to do the sensible."

An old adage

"Labor cannot make progress at the expense of the rest of the community. Labor can only make progress as the rest of the community makes progress."

Walter Reuther (1963), quoted in the *Economist,* March 2, 1985, p. 31

From Eugene Losijn, "European Patterns in Working Time," *Personnel Management,* September 1985, pp. 33–34.

Learning Objectives

After you study this chapter, you should know:

1. The importance of a thorough analysis of the available labor force before a company makes an investment which will require workers in a foreign country.
2. Methods of recruiting and selecting employees, which may vary depending on whether the host country is in a developed or a developing state.
3. The necessity and methods of training new employees and upgrading training for existing employees.
4. Some precautions managers from industrialized countries should observe when they begin recruiting, selecting, and training employees in nonindustrialized countries.
5. That although money is a necessary factor in the motivation of employees, it is by no means the only motivating factor.
6. Some possible ways to enrich employees' jobs, making them more interesting and less boring.
7. Types of benefits that employees frequently receive in addition to money wages.
8. Labor unions, which may be parts of an industry's disciplinary system and which negotiate all sorts of other matters, such as wages and working conditions, with employers.
9. Laws that mandate working conditions and other labor matters such as severance pay when workers are fired.
10. Codetermination, which puts worker representatives on company boards of directors.
11. Quality circles and why they might or might not work.
12. The difference between the human relations school of employee relations and Taylorism.
13. Robotics.
14. How faster, cheaper computers together with robotics are creating the factories of the future.
15. The importance for an MNE of coordinating labor relations among the parent, subsidiary, and affiliated companies.

Key Words and Concepts

Fringe benefits
Skilled and unskilled labor
Employee facilities
Labor recruitment sources
In-house training programs
On-the-job-training
Apprenticeship programs
Off-premises training
Employee motivation
Job enrichment
Compensation
Performance incentives
Employee discipline
Labor unions
Collective bargaining
Codetermination
Termination of employment
Quality circles
Company-wide quality control (CWQC)
Human relations school
Taylorism
Robotics

Business (Labor) Incidents

Since 1982 the normal workweek in Italy has been 40 hours on average, although in the most important collective labor agreements, working hours are limited not by week but by year. The labor unions are currently exerting pressure to reduce the average workweek to 35 hours without loss of pay and to reduce the working hours in the form of days off rather than shorter workdays. Employers are resisting, but it is expected that the outcome will be a reduction from an average 40 hours to 38 by a gradual reduction of one hour per week per year, with provision for seasonal flexibility where necessary.

The standard workweek in Finland has been 40 hours for the past three years, but under the terms of a collective labor agreement signed in 1984 the hours worked per week began to be reduced in 1986 gradually until the workweek will be only 32 hours. This will be accomplished without loss of earnings. Because of the great seasonal differences in Finland, both employees and employers agree that flexibility of working hours is required. How such flexible hours are scheduled is the subject of ongoing labor union–employer negotiations.

From Eugene Losijn, "European Patterns in Working Time,"
Personnel Management, September 1985, pp. 33–34.

*I*n Chapter 11, we saw some of the labor forces with which international business management is faced from country to country. Are there enough bodies present? Do the persons in the bodies possess the skills your operation needs? Even if there are sufficient bodies and skills, will they work for your operation? If there are insufficient bodies, skills, or willingness to work, can you find and train other labor?

In this chapter, we shall not concern ourselves with the problems of executive-level personnel, which are dealt with in Chapter 22. The problems of lower-level management and the workers are the ones we shall attempt to solve here.

The effectiveness of every organization depends to a great extent on how well its human resources are utilized. Their effective use is dependent on management's policies and practices. Management of a company's human resources is shared responsibility. The day-to-day supervision of people on the job is the duty of the operating managers who must integrate the human, financial, and physical resources into an efficient production system. However, the formulation of policies and procedures for (1) estimation of work force needs, (2) recruitment and selection, (3) training and development, (4) motivation, (5) compensation, (6) discipline, (7) relations with employee associations, and (8) employment termination are generally the responsibility of personnel managers working in cooperation with executives from marketing, production, and finance as well as the firm's lawyers.

The St. Gobain minicase at the end of the chapter is an example of lack or failure of cooperation—and perhaps communication—between financial and personnel management. The personnel people should have been able to warn of the possible adverse labor relations results caused by sudden revelations of previously secret financial information.

Personnel Needs, Availability, and Labor Laws[1]

Analysis of the Labor Force

Because of the labor force's influence on the choice of plant site, factory design, and production processes, data on the available labor force must be gathered prior to making final decisions in these areas. Labor laws, going wage rates, and the characteristics of workers, such as their skills, work attitudes, and prejudices about sex and caste, as well as their propensity to join labor organizations and to strike, all weigh heavily in these decisions. All too often, failures to obtain such information result in costly mistakes. Managements, attracted by low wage rates, have set up plants only to learn later that the labor costs are considerably higher than expected because of the existence of **fringe benefits,** * which are usually government requirements. Such errors could have been avoided by consulting local experts.

A simple reading of the labor laws by a layman, and particularly a foreign layman, will almost never give a complete or accurate understanding of their exact meaning nor of how they are applied and enforced by the authorities. Sometimes laws are enforced very stringently and in surprising ways, but often they are ignored. In addition, firms frequently pay and give more than the legally required minimums. A study by the American Chamber of Commerce in Mexico showed that 19 percent of the 121 companies surveyed gave punctuality and attendance bonuses averaging 20 percent of monthly wages. Death benefits paid by the firms averaged 15 months' wages for natural deaths and 26 months' wages for accidental deaths. One company gave a 100-minute coffee break. In all, more than two dozen types of benefits were offered that were not required by law.

Another costly omission is the failure to ascertain the availability of **skilled labor** or of **unskilled labor** willing to work on an assembly line. Establishing a

---

*Fringe benefits are benefits for employees over and above base wages. They may include bonuses, sick or education leaves, termination payments, medical or dental payments, or additional holidays, to name a few.

plant solely because of an abundance of low-cost labor can be a big mistake if the cost and time required to train for necessary skills have not been factored into the cost analyses and start-up plans.

Of course, the multinational (MNE) may try to bring from abroad the skilled personnel who are unavailable locally, but that effort usually meets with host country government hostility and resistance; the host country wants its own people hired and trained. Less host country resistance may be encountered if a labor shortage is due to its people's unwillingness to work on an assembly line.

> When General Tire in the Netherlands was unable to fill the assembly lines with Dutch workers, management called on the Spanish affiliate for assistance. The Spanish company's personnel department located dozens of workers who were willing to emigrate to the Netherlands and work there. Quite evidently, the Dutch aversion to assembly line work had not spread to Spain.

This is another example of the guest worker phenomenon, which we discussed in Chapter 11. In the Netherlands, as in France, Germany, and other countries in northern Europe, the growing and stubborn unemployment of the 1980s has caused resentment of the foreigners who have jobs that the Dutch now want back or who are on relief at the cost of the native taxpayers.

Employee Facilities

Another element of personnel planning is that of **employee facilities** on and off the job. For example, will a first-aid dispensary be sufficient, or must a hospital and dental clinic be provided either because the law demands it or because there are no satisfactory facilities nearby? If an appreciable number of foreign workers will be employed, special dietary kitchens and recreation equipment may be needed. When women are employed, provision must be made to care for children, and the firm may build a nursery (required by law in some countries) or contract private nurseries to provide the services. In Germany, a number of firms subsidize privately operated day nurseries in exchange for guaranteed numbers of places for their employees' children. Local authorities in Italy provide nurseries financed by part of the employer's social security payments.

In situations where the plant is located some distance from the nearest city, the firm may construct a "company town." However, in extended family-type societies, this may be a trap for the well-intentioned employer. Employee dissatisfaction and unrest may develop as the employee's extended family moves into housing designed for only the immediate family, causing overcrowding and shortages of water, sewage facilities, medical facilities, or schools. Alternatives to the company town are for the employer to provide or subsidize transportation to and from the nearest communities or to subsidize local government housing. Using these alternatives, the workers are less likely to blame their employers for problems that arise with their living quarters.

Recruitment and Selection

Recruitment

Once it has been determined how many of what types of employees will be needed, the personnel department can begin to recruit. Various kinds of **labor recruitment sources** are available. Suitable candidates may be found within the company if it is already in operation or within other units of the enterprise of an MNE or from the outside.

Internal Sources

The use of internal sources, the company's present employees, can be an effective recruitment method. The cost is relatively low, morale benefits from inside promotions, and each applicant is already known to the employer. In some cases where labor is organized, the company-union contract may require that members be given the first opportunities to apply for vacant positions.

Employees as Recruiters—Advantages. The use of a firm's present workers to locate new employees can be efficient and low cost. Such practices can build morale.

Employees as Recruiters—Disadvantages. It is human nature that the employees will try to help family and friends. Thus, considerations of family, similar social status, caste, geographic origin, culture, or language are usually more important than qualifications for the vacant position. Such considerations exist in any country, but they are especially prevalent in less developed countries, where an employed member of the extended family is under pressure to help the other members find work. More than one foreign managing director has been shocked to find that the local personnel director has filled the plant with relatives or people from the same hometown. Such a work force can be expected to be more loyal to the personnel director than to the firm.

External Sources

Overseas, MNEs tend to employ the same kinds of external recruiting methods and sources as are used in their home countries. These may include: (1) newspaper advertising, (2) trade schools, (3) radio advertising, (4) labor unions, and (5) employment agencies. However, there are important differences between their use in the industrialized countries and their use in the developing countries.

Unskilled Workers. Because of high unemployment in most LDCs, the MNE subsidiaries there generally have no difficulties in filling jobs calling for little or no skill. Furthermore, such companies usually have a recruiting advantage over indigenous concerns because of the MNEs' reputations for on-the-job training plus higher wages and other benefits.

Skilled Workers. The recruitment of skilled workers is more difficult because they are generally in short supply in developing countries. Some walk in, attracted by the knowledge that advancement may be more rapid in foreign-owned firms than in locally owned ones, but managements will try to utilize other methods and sources as well. Newspaper advertisements will not have the effectiveness to which foreign managers are accustomed, because in the LDCs many workers who learned their skills on the job can neither read nor write. A solution to this difficulty is to announce the jobs on radio.

Employment agencies are much less utilized in the LDCs than in the industrialized countries. The job applicants frequently cannot afford to pay the agency's fee even if that were legal, which it often is not. In cases where the companies pay the fee, it is not unusual for the agencies to connive with the applicant to split the payment. The applicant takes the job, and the company pays the agency's fee, which it splits with the hired applicant, who then quits. The agency and the applicant can repeat this as many times as they can get away with it.

Selection

By means of the selection processes, management chooses from among the applicants those whose qualifications seem most nearly to match the job requirements.

Industrialized Countries

Most companies in the industrialized countries follow rather standard procedures of requesting personal information, including work experience, to be given on an application form and during interviews. In some countries, the worker carries an identification book, which must be presented when seeking employment. The book entries constitute a record of employment, including jobs, wages, and employer comments. If the worker has a prison record, the book will include information about that. The MNE may give prospective employees a physical examination and aptitude or psychological tests.

Developing Countries

In LDCs, the hiring process is usually less formal. Less testing is done, and when it is done, the results are likely to be used somewhat superficially. As has been mentioned before, family ties, social status, caste, language, and common origin are more likely to be elements of hiring decisions in LDCs than in other countries.

Recruiting and selecting employees are steps in building an effective work force. Once the workers have been hired, they must undergo training and development.

Training and Development

Most new employees need to be trained and developed in order to fit into the employer firm's specific operations. In addition, because of technological or market changes, employees sometimes need to have their skills upgraded or need to be taught new ones. The preparation and supervision of training and development programs, both in-house and off-premises, are normally the responsibility of the personnel department after it ascertains operating department needs.

In-House Programs

Several kinds of **in-house training programs** are offered by firms in both the developed and developing nations. Among these programs are on-the-job training, apprenticeship training, classroom sessions, conferences, and simulation. The programs frequently overlap.

On-the-Job Training

On-the-job training methods make either a supervisor or an experienced operator responsible for training new or promoted employees. Probably the most significant difference between the developed and developing countries as to on-the-job training is the utilization in the former of more training aids. The use of audiovisual equipment and simulation training on identical equipment set up in an area away from the actual production space enable the learning workers to master the job more quickly than they could on the production line. Because of the high cost of many training aids and shortages of experienced trainers, these methods have been slow to appear in the less developed nations. However, this is changing as many multinationals are transferring the methods to their LDC subsidiaries with excellent results.

One of those results is the recruiting edge that good training gives the MNE subsidiaries in attracting needed employees. This works both ways, however, as the locally owned firms regularly hire away workers who have been trained by foreign-owned companies—one of the benefits that LDCs derive from multinational operations within their borders.

> Managers of MNE subsidiaries in Mexico have been heard to complain that "they must be training half the machinists in Mexico."

Labor trainers in developing nations have found that the people learn industrial skills rapidly. What is more difficult is to teach new workers who come from farms and villages how to adjust socially and psychologically to factory life. Some of these workers must be taught not only job skills but also the concept of time. They are not accustomed to reporting to work at the same time and place each workday or to meeting production schedules.

They must be introduced to the factory sort of teamwork and to an industrial hierarchy. Frequently the company must compromise and not attempt to change customary farm and village practices too quickly and completely.

A Spanish company opened a factory in Guatemala, hired local people, and tried to operate as if it were in Europe. The Spanish management installed work hours and production routines and schedules that had worked efficiently in Spain. They were nearly disastrous at that stage of development in Guatemala.

Reactions. The people refused to work and became hostile. Guatemalan troops were necessary to protect the factory. Management at last considered local needs and compromised, and mutually satisfactory solutions were found.

Solutions. The solutions included four-hour breaks between two daily work periods. During the breaks, the male employees took care of their farms and gardens and the female employees attended to household needs and cared for their children. As another part of the solution, the employees were willing to work Saturdays to make up production lost during the breaks.[2]

Through compromise and patience, European management, operating in a preindustrial setting, was able to achieve satisfactory production. It studied, negotiated, and adapted to local needs. The alternatives were low production or perhaps even a destroyed factory.

Apprenticeship Programs

Apprenticeship programs are a special kind of on-the-job training for skilled tradespeople, such as plumbers, electricians, and toolmakers, that has existed for many years. Young workers called apprentices assist experienced craftsmen for periods of two to five years, until the apprentices are capable of doing the job without supervision.

In the more developed nations, the majority of the trades require the apprentices to pass examinations before they are certified as skilled craftspeople. Europe's apprenticeship training is especially good. It is a highly formalized part of a nation's educational system, and it includes classroom instruction as well as on-the-job training.

The combination of classroom and on-the-job training is utilized in the United States by some firms, but the practice has not been incorporated into the national educational system to the extent that it has in Europe. Some vocational schools and community colleges do offer cooperative programs with industry which approach the European system, and many community and city colleges and high schools have a wide variety of vocational and trade courses which workers can take on their own.

Managers coming from countries with formal training programs to a developing nation must be careful when they hire persons claiming to have a skilled trade; the types of training programs with which the manager is familiar are extremely rare in the LDCs. Even if the applicant is truly skilled, the skill may be narrowly limited to what was learned on the job.

Off-Premises Training and Development

Sending workers and supervisors off the company's premises has become an accepted practice in the United States and other developed nations. Personnel managers have learned that training and development by skilled educators working in an educational setting are often less costly and more effective than training and development done in-house with company employees. France has a particularly innovative law which permits workers to apply for a one year's leave of absence to enroll in an approved training program if they have been employed for at least two years. The French government and the employers share the expenses, which include the employees' salaries while they are in training.[3]

Off-premises training is far less common in the developing nations, but beginnings are being made as multinationals' subsidiaries in LDCs are cooperating with the host governments and inaugurating such programs. In addition, schools and universities in the LDCs, aided by their counterparts from the industrialized countries, are offering training and development programs to local industry.

Motivation

Regardless of how well employees are selected and trained, they will not perform satisfactorily unless they are properly motivated. Effective personnel management requires an understanding of the motivational processes, including human needs. Without an understanding of those needs, managers cannot determine the kinds of **employee motivation** that are needed to induce employees to work toward the organization's goals. Considerable insight into the needs and wants of employees and into the incentives that motivate them is provided by two models: (1) Maslow's needs hierarchy and (2) Herzberg's two-factor theory.

Maslow's Needs Hierarchy

Maslow, a psychologist, classified human needs into a hierarchy of five categories, which he arranged, as illustrated in Figure 20–1, from the most fundamental at the bottom of the hierarchy to the most subtle at the top.[4]

It is apparent that there is some overlap in these needs and that two or more may be satisfied by one factor. For example, pay will satisfy the physiological needs by permitting the employee to buy food and so forth; the security need by permitting saving; the social need by making possible a more expensive

Figure 20-1

Maslow's Needs Hierarchy on the Job

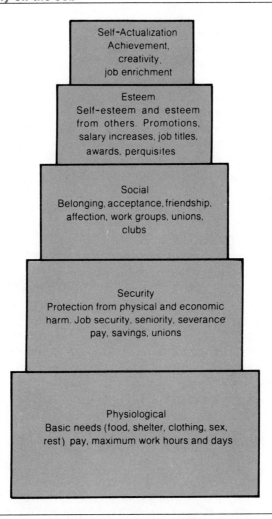

From *The Wall Street Journal,* with permission of Cartoon Features Syndicate.

home and more club memberships; and the esteem need as salaries increase along with promotions, better job titles, awards, and so forth.

Physiological, Security, Social, and Esteem Needs

These needs are relatively easily understood, at least in concept. Of course, the person going into personnel management should study them in depth together with the factors and methods that are economically available to the employer

Reading

The Shinjinrui of Japan

The emergence of the shinjinrui *is one development that seems to indicate a weakening of loyalty to employers in Japan. A growing sector of Japan's young people are doing the minimum amount of work necessary to keep from being demoted or fired. They are unwilling to work overtime, and they prefer to socialize with their friends rather than make the expected after-hours rounds of bars with bosses and coworkers. They are called "shinjinrui" (pronounced sheen jeen roo ee), which, literally translated, means "new human species."*

Traditional Japanese are contemptuous of the shinjinrui, *saying, for example, "These Japanese are not Japanese. They all want to live in California. You know, roller skating and surfing" or "Go to hell shinjinrui." One commentator, Tetsuya Chikushi of the Asahi Journal urged something be done to discipline the new breed before they bring about the ruin of Japan. Chikushi unflatteringly compared Japan's* shinjinrui *with Americans whom he described as lazy and unwilling to work.*

and feasible for motivating its employees by meeting their needs. In this text, we shall not dwell further on those subjects except to mention a potentially important change at the security level in Japan.

Job security had never been a problem in Japan until 1973. The so-called lifetime jobs were commonplace, and many employees could expect to work for the same employer all of their working lives. This caused a sense of company or employer loyalty on the part of the employees and prevented labor unions from becoming as powerful as they were in other industrial countries. Then in the 1970s, the recession caused by the quadrupling of imported oil prices forced firms to lay off workers despite many efforts to avoid layoffs or soften the blows. Japanese executives are now concerned that employees, threatened with a loss of job security, will become job oriented rather than company oriented and that the loyalty of employees to their employers will weaken.[5]

Self-Actualization Needs

Satisfying the worker's needs for self-actualization is difficult when all the individual does is drill a hole or tighten a bolt. Personnel managers have devised a number of programs to meet these needs. Classes in the language of the home office have proven popular because (1) the employees feel a sense of accomplishment at learning another language and (2) fluency in it may bring a promotion. Drama clubs, company-sponsored sport teams, and continuing education classes all give the participant a sense of achievement. Attempts to relieve the boredom of the hole drillers and bolt tighteners are made through job enrichment measures, dealt with later in this chapter.

Evaluation

One thing to which Maslow's hierarchy of needs points is that financial incentives do not always result in greater productivity. Managers from industrialized nations have been surprised to find that the financial incentives which worked so well at home fail to obtain the same results in other cultures. Higher wages, for example, may increase absenteeism if the workers can earn enough to satisfy their physiological and security needs in three days instead of five. All too frequently, foreign managers conclude that the workers are lazy and have no ambition, but the managers may be incorrect. With the first two levels of needs satisfied, workers could be at home with their families and friends to satisfy their social needs. Instead of concentrating on financial incentives, the managers should be concentrating on ways to satisfy the needs at the top of Maslow's hierarchy.

Herzberg's Two-Factor Theory

Herzberg's two-factor theory of motivation is an extension of the Maslow model.[6] Herzberg emphasizes the importance of job content factors, which has resulted in increased attention being given to job enrichment.

Job Enrichment

Efforts to make industrial jobs less boring and more interesting are being made in numerous countries. These **job enrichment** efforts include minimization of production line monotony, flexitime, and shop floor committees. These committees are similar to quality circles, but quality circles have purposes beyond job enrichment and will be dealt with as a separate subject later in this chapter.

Minimize the Production Line. One type of job enrichment effort is the substitution of group or module assembly for production line methods. Each group is assigned production goals, but each group sets its own tempo and divides the tasks among its members.[7] The tasks can be rotated as another boredom retardant, and thus each worker learns more than one job, possibly even that of the group supervisor.[8] Renault, France's largest industrial employer, has introduced some varieties of group or modular job enrichment programs and reports a 20 percent productivity improvement plus higher worker morale. Volvo and Saab, both Swedish companies, have adopted modular concepts.

Flexitime. Another job enrichment effort, called flexitime, permits flexible working hours. Within some necessary limits, the individual workers or groups determine their own daily and weekly work schedules.[9]

Shop Floor Committees. One American company that has successfully applied a variety of job enrichment efforts is Harman International Industries. Shop floor committees of its workers make decisions about everything from redesigning assembly lines and schedules to painting the walls. Defects have been reduced and savings realized. Bids for new sales contracts are worked out with the involvement of the affected committees, and the company has become more competitive.[10]

Job Enrichment Efforts Do Not Always Work

As would be expected, not every job enrichment effort achieves the desired results. Some have floundered because the company's middle management was not consulted, and others because only part of the workers were involved.[11] At least one writer has concluded that job enrichment programs attract only a minority of workers.[12]

Even proponents of job enrichment admit that changing people's behavior and work patterns is a slow process requiring at least two years to implement. As one expert remarked, "It takes six months to get workers even talking about it."[13]

Communication and Sensitivity

During the 1920s, Elton Mayo spoke and wrote in favor of opening lines of communication between supervisors and workers. He urged managers to be sensitive to workers' needs and desires. This came to be called the **human relations school** of management, and it was expanded upon by A. V. Feigenbaum, W. Edwards Deming, and Joseph Juran, among others. It was the human relations school of thought that had a particularly strong impact on the Japanese during the immediate post–World War II period, and this may help account for the vaunted labor harmony in Japan.

Taylorism

Mayo and the other writers named in the preceding paragraph are Americans, but their school of thought about management has only recently been given much of a try in America. Meanwhile, the ideas of Frederick Taylor have reigned in the United States. Taylor advocated rewards to workers for performing in accordance with certain standards; those were the carrots. On the stick side, Taylor urged managers to ensure that workers met the standards by "cracking the whip over them with an occasional touch of the lash." **Taylorism** squeezed out some additional productivity, but at the cost of alienating workers. Nevertheless, as late as 1970 Henry Ford II said, "The average worker wants a job in which he does not have to put much physical effort. Above all, he wants a job in which he does not have to think." Even later, in 1976, the labor leader William Winpisinger opined, "If you want to enrich the job, enrich the paycheck." Clearly, these two are not devotees of the human relations school. (See also the quotation from the *Journal of Business Ethics* at the beginning of this chapter.)

Human Relations Now Being Tried

A number of companies—as diverse as General Motors, Moose Creek Restoration, Vermont Asbestos, and Gaines Dog Food, to name only a few—have tried or are trying human relations management. The results have been mixed; improvements have been achieved in worker morale, productivity, and profitability. In some instances, however, the new systems were brought in too rapidly and without sufficient preparation of all levels of management to achieve long-term cooperation. Sometimes expectations were too high and results were expected too quickly. At Gaines Dog Food, for example, all kinds of reforms aimed at increasing worker participation were tried and the process was covered by the press and television. Productivity improved sharply, but then came the slump. The workers found that after all of the media people had left, they were still dealing with dog food. Moreover, they discovered that management, not they, was deciding the ingredients, the amounts, and the customers.

Most authors agree that there is no single best system to organize work, and each company and its workers must seek the system best for them. However, two authors have found that "people are beginning to recognize the psychological and economic importance of self-esteem and dignity for the individual."[14]

Human Relations Management Works in Government Too

Many, if not most, government agency heads establish rules for nearly everything their bureaucrats do, following Taylor's philosophy. The rules are to prevent the bureaucrats from doing it wrong; unfortunately, they also prevent the bureaucrats from doing their jobs better. At least a couple of recent agency heads have approached their people differently. They are Drew Lewis at the Department of Transportation and Jerry Carmen at the General Services Administration. Both consulted, trusted, and relied on their bureaucrats and got good results.

The Reagan administration proposed expanding merit pay systems to reward civil servants for better performance, and a study by the Public Agenda Foundation found that opportunity for advancement affects employee productivity even more than incentive pay. The study also demonstrated that nonmonetary recognition for good work is as important as performance-linked pay.[15]

Quality Circles (QCs)

Quality circles are treated apart from the subject of employee motivation because although motivation is one objective of quality circles, there are others. As the name indicates, one of these objectives is improving product quality. Others are: productivity, employee involvement, communications improvement, team building, professional and personal growth opportunities, and better company profits.

"Quality circles are a raging disease in America and in many other countries," said Dr. W. Edwards Deming in a keynote lecture to the 1982 International Convention on Quality Circles in Seoul, Korea. A recent New York Stock Exchange survey bears him out; it found that 75 percent of manufacturing companies with over 10,000 employees had begun QCs. However, Dr. Deming feels that management in non-Japanese companies expects quick fixes from employee QCs but is not doing its part to permit these QCs to be successful. He says that mangement must research and experiment with engineers, designers, and production people and must listen to and act on QC suggestions.

At the same convention, Dr. Kaoru Ishikawa said of American management that it had "long experience and high pride, so it doesn't listen to others." Dr. Ishikawa became a leader in the Japanese QC movements after learning a great deal about the subject from Dr. Deming.[16]

The Idea behind Quality Circles

The idea behind quality circles is that it is cheaper to prevent rejects than to cure them. Quality control has a big effect on costs; in too many companies, it is the task of a few managers isolated from the shop floor. Dr. Deming taught, and his Japanese students learned, that workers ought to be made responsible for meeting quality targets. This helps motivate the workers and permits problems to be tackled early in production.

Close Partnership with Suppliers

Another principle that Deming advanced and his Japanese clients adopted, was the establishment of close, long-term relationships with a company's suppliers. Such relationships result in trust and understanding between the company and its suppliers, and they improve the quality of the materials received by the company. This practice, now very prevalent in Japan, is attacked by would-be exporters to Japan as a nontariff barrier to trade.[17]

QCs in America: Comparisons with Japan

Jill H. King* suggests the outline of a QC as shown in Figure 20–2. She has identified a number of problems and issues in the QC movement. A few of them are middle-management resistance, unclear goals, little or no union involvement, and inadequate training. Another problem she identified is lack of top-management commitment, which brings us to the subject of company-wide quality control.

*King is manager, personnel training and development, Human Resources, Radar Systems Group, Hughes Aircraft Company.

Figure 20-2

Quality Circle

Definition:
A small group of people from the same work area who meet together on a regular basis to identify, analyze, and solve product quality and other problems in their area.

Participants:
Leader—train, maintain records, motivate, lead, resource.
Facilitator (part- or full-time)—train, resource, group dynamics.
Member—identify problems, contribute ideas, develop solutions, implement solutions when feasible.
Management—obtain ownership support, furnish prompt responses, deal with issues and problems that surface, share information, provide resources.

Company-Wide Quality Control (CWQC)

Company-wide quality control (CWQC) is not a new system or scheme. According to one writer, it is a holistic approach to achieving objectives more effectively for an entire company.[18]

Company-Wide

With CWQC, quality control begins with the product design in the production process and, equally important, applies to every job in the company. In Japan, all the employees in every aspect of their jobs are thought of as being components of CWQC. In the United States, by contrast, quality control grew out of inspecting the end product to ascertain whether it met engineering specification. In many American companies, that is still all it means.

Quality

In Japan, quality means user satisfaction. The Japanese feel that the American definition of quality as meaning conformance with engineering specifications is too narrow. For the Japanese, the user may be the ultimate customer, but in a multiple—procedure manufacturing process, the user is the next department of the company, and the work done at each production stage must satisfy each succeeding stage. Some American departments regard the next department as a "policeman" or even as an "enemy."

A good comparison between the American and Japanese approaches to quality control can be seen in Figure 20-3, which illustrates the several more stages employed in Japan. Control is approached from more points of view in Japan than in the United States.

Figure 20–3

The Buildup of Quality in Seven Stages

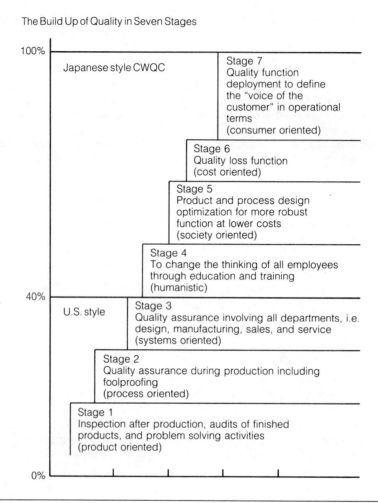

The Build Up of Quality in Seven Stages

Source: *Quality Progress,* May 1986, p. 78.

Figure 20–4 shows that Japanese manufacturers involve their suppliers in the production process at the product development and design phases. That is much sooner than is the usual American practice, and the American suppliers are much more likely to be involved in later problem solving than are their Japanese counterparts.

Figure 20-4
Quality Effort by Activity

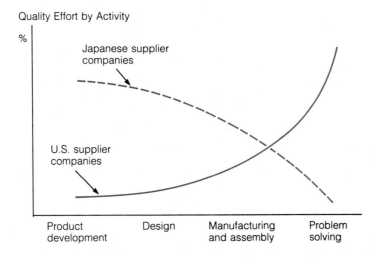

Source: *Quality Progress,* May 1986, p. 78.

Control

For most Americans, control has the connotation of someone in charge of someone else. In the Japanese language, there are at least two characters to write the word *control.* One pictures a person looking into a basin of water and "seeing yourself." The other symbolizes penetration of the rings in a bamboo stick and connotes "achieving your objective." Thus, control for the Japanese comes from within each person to achievement. They illustrate this idea with the "Deming Wheel," referred to as PDCA—Plan, Do, Check, Action.

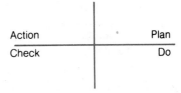

        With the American management, using Taylorism, the wheel would sometimes look like this.[19]

Fight	Plan
Check	Do

"Today we'll be talking about some new approaches."

CWQC and Quality Circles

We are brought back to the idea expressed earlier that management—from top to bottom—must be involved for QCs to be truly and lastingly effective. QCs must be only one part of company-wide quality control activities.

To envision the top-to-bottom and bottom-to-top nature of CWQC, see Figure 20–5. It illustrates that quality control must be the concern of everyone in the company, from the CEO down, with ideas and suggestions for improvement originating at every level.

Figure 20–5

Old Image	New Image
Low quality is caused by low performance of people. Automation is the key to higher quality.	Low quality is caused by poor management of people. Respect for people is the key to higher quality.
Loss of work ethic causes poor quality in the United States. The Japanese maintain a quality edge due to their ethical and cultural values.	American workers, when properly managed, are as good as or better than any others, particularly in their commitment to jobs.
Some defects are acceptable. Lots are accepted if they meet minimum quality standards on average.	Zero defects is the goal. There is not a minimum average acceptable quality. All units should be free of defects.
Inspect for product problems regularly, then rework. Rework is done at a later and separate stage.	Inspect for process problems; and fix problems so that they do not recur. Any repair work is done on the line with no delay.

Figure 20-5

Continued

Old Image	New Image
Higher quality means higher costs and therefore lower profits. Quality is expensive and a burden for manufacturing.	Higher quality is a means to higher profits. Quality is the goal; it is not a burden for manufacturing.
Quality is inspected into the product. Nonconforming units are continuously discovered, reworked, or scrapped.	Quality is designed and built into the product. A nonconformance is a means for resolving the problems permanently.
A quality control organization, as a separate department, inspects the output of manufacturing and evaluates the quality of production.	Quality is everyone's job. Total quality control includes all functions and individuals and all stages of manufacturing.
Quality is secondary to profits. To maximize profits, the sum of prevention, inspection, and failure costs is minimized.	Initial investment in quality is key to long-term profits. The book value of nonconformances is not simply deducted from profits.
Catch mistakes and fix them. Units are routed to manufacturing and inspection several times to pass the requirements.	Do it right the first time. Quality at the source is the key. Do not make mistakes. Quality is free if produced the first time.
Suppliers are adversaries and thus suspect. All products must have at least a second source. Order as needed and expedite.	Suppliers are trusted members of our team. Work with a primary source to ensure reliability and quality.
Buy from the lowest bidder. Competition among the suppliers will reduce the total cost.	Buy for quality and reliability. Information and profits may be shared with suppliers.
Quality is a function of manufacturing. The products have high quality if they are manufactured properly.	High quality depends on all stages from design to shipping and is reached only if all functions work properly together.
Errors will be caught by the inspectors. Keep the production line moving by keeping a safety stock.	Do not pass on nonconformances. Stop the line if there is a quality problem. A safety stock of work in progress is a waste.
Produce as many units as possible in the shortest possible time to increase efficiency and utilization.	Produce effectively only what is needed and only when it is needed for the quality requirement of the internal or external customers.
Use specialized workers on operations to reduce the time needed for training. Produce units on an assembly line with highly specialized, single-operation-type workers. Do not rotate workers; rotation may reduce efficiency.	Train workers for diversified jobs and high flexibility. Promote cross-training and job sharing among workers.

Figure 20-5
(concluded)

Old Image	New Image
The quality department is responsible for quality. Problems need not be communicated to and from manufacturing.	Quality consciousness is the responsibility of everyone involved. Suggestions and discussions are particularly welcomed.
Management must discern quality problems and delegate responsibility for improvement. Employes should carry out the plans.	Management depends on employees to identify and solve problems. Management works closely with employees to resolve problems permanently.
The worker is responsible for most quality problems. He should be disciplined and trained to perform properly.	Management systems are the cause of most quality problems. Workers should be allowed to participate in management.
Statistics is an exotic tool for quality engineers. Control charts are used to highlight the problems.	Every employee should have an understanding of statistical quality control, which is used to highlight areas for improvement.
Additional inventory is maintained to keep workers utilized. The workers' idle time is a waste.	Inventory is a waste. The workers may spend their nonproduction time in other productive functions.
Large lot sizes are produced to increase quality and to reduce production cost and average setup time.	Setup should be reduced to allow for lot sizes of one. Lower lot size means lower lead time, higher flexibility, and less rework.

Source: Mehran Sepehri, "Quality Control Circles: A vehicle for just-in-time implementation," *Quality Progress,* July 1985, p. 23.

Robotics

Robotics is the industry of machines that work with human-like skill. Robots are substitutes for human workers, and American management has concluded that it must use many more robots in order to improve productivity. As in other areas, the competition that is forcing American management to this conclusion is coming from Japan; Europe is behind both Japan and the United States in robotics. As between Japan and the United States, however, the comparison is very unfavorable to the United States.

At the end of 1984, there were the following number of industrial robots in:

Japan	67,300
United States	14,500
West Germany	6,600
France	3,380
Italy	2,700
Britain	2,623
Sweden	2,400
Belgium	859
Canada	700
Spain	516

Steel-Collar Migrant Workers

As members of management have been termed white-collar workers and members of the labor force have been termed blue-collar workers, some writers refer to robots as steel-collar workers, and these workers are migrating. Japan sold over 50 billion yen worth of robots to the world in 1985, and in 1986 the export value of Japanese robots rose to almost 60 billion yen. The United States was the biggest market, followed by West Germany.

However, neither the Japanese nor the American robot manufacturers made much profit in 1985 or 1986. The Westinghouse subsidiary, Unimation, was a loser in the robotics field, as was General Electric. Cincinnati Milacron and Sweden's ASEA made small profits, and the most profitable robot manufacturer was GMF Robotics, a joint venture between General Motors and the Japanese robot company Fanuc. Two thirds of GMF Robotics' 1985 sales were to GM, which slowed its robot purchase program in 1986.

The reason for the losses or low profits of robot manufacturers is that you cannot simply wind up a robot in the morning and send it out to do a person's work. Robots require complex software to do even the simplest tasks, and they must be taught to communicate with the other machines working beside them on the shop floor. Great expense is involved in creating the necessary software and communication links, not to mention training and paying the people needed to service and maintain the entire complex. However, the software is being created and the people are being trained.

Factories of the Future

As computers become more powerful and less expensive, they are reshaping the factory. Computer-aided design, robotic tools, sensors, and improved telecommunications techniques are forging the factory of the future.

Using computers instead of people costs 8,000 times less today than in 1950. Electronic transactions can be made 80 million times faster now than then. Errors occur in modern computers at a rate of 1 in 3 million, compared with 1 in 30 when humans do similar calculations.[20]

New Future Directions

Businesses adopting computer-aided management methods may find themselves heading in a variety of new directions. These directions include:

Production Disbursement. Production is moving into ever smaller manufacturing units.

Labor Costs Less Important. As computer-controlled robots become less expensive and more efficient, labor costs will shrink as a percentage of total costs. MNEs may become less attracted to low-wage countries.

Engineering Centralized. Characteristic of high-tech engineering is centralized design. Product blueprints are likely to be transmitted from the head office via long-distance telephone lines to computer-aided manufacturing plants in the company's principal market regions and countries.

Manufacturing Flexibility. A wider variety of products can be produced at no greater costs. The plants could break even at 30–35 percent of capacity, compared to 65–70 percent in conventional operations.

Plug-In Repairs. Product faults can usually be diagnosed by plugging the product into a computer. General Motors plans to use computerized diagnostics in its U.S. repair shops.

Economies of Scale. The conventional, assembly line economies of scale will be diminished. That could be counteracted by economies in such areas as marketing or research and development.

Consultants and Contractors. Small businesses with the latest computer-aided designs and techniques are beginning to sell services to the bigger companies. Some of those companies may decide to subcontract production.[21]

Fears

Many managers are hesitant to adopt computerized manufacturing systems. Their concerns include potential misuse, reliability, security, difficult maintenance, and cost. Perhaps kicking and screaming, they will probably be forced to go along by competition.[22]

Compensation

We have seen that financial **compensation** is not the only motivator, but it is a pervasive one which affects people at every economic level. In addition to satisfying basic wants, money satisfies social and esteem needs, and personnel managers must formulate compensation plans that combine employee needs satisfaction with incentives which result in satisfactory work performance for the employer.

Wages and Salaries

Employees are paid on the basis of productivity, time spent on the job, or a combination of the two unless labor union contracts or government laws specify otherwise. In the industrialized countries, the time unit for which pay is established is generally the hour, whereas a daily rate is most common in developing countries. The piece rate* pay method is quite common. In some countries, of which Japan is a good example, seniority is an important element in determining employees' pay rates.

When the subsidiaries of multinationals commence operations in a foreign country, they usually set their pay scales at or slightly higher than the prevailing wages paid by indigenous companies. The foreign-owned subsidiary does not want to be accused of exploiting the local workers. Although it might seem that paying wages higher than the going rate would be welcomed by the host government, usually the opposite is true. Local firms are quick to complain that such wages will cause unrest and disruption in the labor force. The foreign manager—even in developed countries—is repeatedly counseled by local managers, "Don't spoil our people."

Benefits

The types and sizes of the supplementary benefits† that workers receive vary considerably among nations and are frequently higher as a percentage of wages than the U.S. average of 35 percent. A study conducted a few years ago revealed such benefit percentages to be: Belgium, 55 percent; France, 70 percent; Germany, 45 percent; Italy, 92 percent; Luxembourg, 41 percent; and the Netherlands, 50 percent. The benefit percentages tend to increase as labor unions negotiate new contracts or as governments legislate more and higher benefits.

Benefits: Contractual or Legislated

In the United States, many—but by no means all—benefits result from labor contracts. The opposite is true of many other countries, where most benefits are legislated and ordered by the governments. In France, for example, the following are mandated by law: (1) profit sharing, (2) year-end bonuses, (3) paid holidays, (4) paid vacations of two days for each month worked, (5) three days' leave for the father when his child is born, (6) severance pay, (7) 70 to 90 percent of medical and dental expenses, (8) disability benefits, (9) retirement insurance,

---

*Piece rate is payment per unit produced; for example, $1 per basket woven or 25 cents per button sewn on.
†Frequently called fringe benefits.

and (10) payments to relatives upon the employee's death. In addition, the law requires allowances for maternity, housing, moving, and children. Similar benefits and allowances are required by the laws of all European countries.

Europe is not alone in such requirements. Brazilian law includes most of the benefits listed for Europe, plus an extra one—a grant paid to the dependents of a worker who has been sent to prison. An unusual benefit called for in Mexican law is up to three scholarships for workers or their children.

Additional Voluntary Benefits

Some employers grant benefits greater than those required by laws. Japanese firms are notable in this regard and typically pay such things as commuting expenses and housing allowances as well as providing resort housing for employee vacation use. Some American banks make low-interest loans to employees to purchase housing or an automobile.

Performance Incentives

Unlike wages and benefits, whose purposes are to attract and retain employees, **performance incentives** are given only for above-average performance. The principal kinds of incentive plans are (1) piece rates, (2) bonuses for exceeding quotas, (3) awards for cost-reducing or productivity-increasing suggestions, (4) profit sharing, and (5) sales contests.

For incentive plans to be successful in increasing productivity and reducing costs, they must be reviewed and updated constantly. Allowance must be made for any factor change that can affect the standards.

> A government-owned oil organization instituted an incentive system for typists. They were expected to type a given number of pages for their regular salary, and if they exceeded that amount, they could earn a bonus of up to 10 percent of the salary.
>
> After a time, management noticed that the typists were sitting idly at their desks for most of the afternoons, yet were turning in at the end of each day the number of pages necessary to earn the maximum bonus. An investigation disclosed that although the typists had recently been provided new, faster machines, no one had thought to change the bonus standards.

Discipline

Although an effective personnel program of selection, training, motivation, and compensation is essential for the attainment of the organization's goals, there always will be occasions that require **employee discipline**. Employees' job performance may be poor, or safety, time, or other rules may be broken. Such rules can be especially difficult to enforce if the employees are unaccustomed to working in an industrial organization.

Less Developed Countries (LDCs)

When managers from industrialized nations start factory operations in developing countries, they frequently encounter different practices, attitudes, and cultures. If the safety shoes hurt the workers' feet, the workers take them off just as they did on the farm, and if the workers are tired, they rest when they want to and not when the rules permit. Usually it is not that they set out to break the rules deliberately; they just fail to understand or see any sense in them. This is why, as we have mentioned previously, workers without industrial experience must be taught not only how to do the job but also how to work in an industrial setting.

The extended family encountered in some LDCs can cause discipline problems. Loyalty tends to be more to one another than to the employer, and the supervisor member of the family may hesitate to discipline other members who are workers. Companies have tried to avoid situations of this kind by bringing in young, nonfamily, technical graduates as supervisors. The workers will generally accept the authority of such supervisors unless they regard the new supervisor as belonging to a lower caste or having a lower social status than their own. As we have indicated, such problems exist in certain developing countries.

One other cultural difference which can lead to disciplinary difficulties in some LDCs is leadership style. Managers from Europe or North America, especially those who practice participative leadership, may view the local supervisor's authoritarian approach as too tough or cruel. However, those managers should change the local supervisor's approach slowly and cautiously and maybe not at all. In cultures accustomed to a strong father figure, the workers regard a supervisor who attempts participative leadership as weak and indecisive.

With the growth of industry in LDCs and perhaps with a second generation of workers in the factories, the attitudes of workers, including those toward authority, change, and management, must be sufficiently flexible to adapt to these changes. In addition, the managers will be working to effect change. Concepts and methods of supervisory training and practices developed in industrialized nations are exportable and should be utilized.[23]

Developed Countries

In industrialized nations, the rules and expected performance must be communicated to employees, but unlike the situation in some LDCs, the reasons for them will be understood and accepted by the employees. When they are not, management must take corrective steps, such as (1) clearer explanation of the rules, (2) docking of some pay, (3) demotion, or (4) discharging the worker.

In nonunion plants, management selects the corrective steps, subject to the constraints that it wants a productive, efficient work force and must select, train, motivate, and compensate well enough to achieve that.

In industrialized nations, however, management is quite likely to encounter labor unions. They have great impact on the whys, hows, and whens of discipline but are sufficiently important to be treated separately.

Union Relationships

Labor unions can be a force for discipline because (1) they should require their worker members to adhere to rules agreed on and (2) they establish with management a set of disciplinary procedures through collective bargaining.

Collective Bargaining

Of course, disciplinary procedures are not the only subjects of bargaining between labor and management. In the United States, some other subjects of **collective bargaining** are wages, retirement plans, union shop, work rules, and management rights. Elsewhere, as has been pointed out, in both developed and developing countries, many of those subjects and others are legislated or decreed by the government.

Labor's Political Influence

Labor has considerable political influence in the United States, as the large unions have powerful lobbying operations in Washington and the state capitals and support friendly candidates in their political campaigns. However, labor in European and other countries is sometimes even more powerful politically, and it sometimes merges with a major political party. One of the two largest political parties in Britain is called the Labour party, and the Histadrut, the general trade union in Israel, has a powerful influence in the formation of Israeli governments.[24]

Even when collective bargaining takes place, the governments in some countries are deeply involved. Their involvement often stems from the fact that large parts of industry are nationalized. For example, in Renault, the French government-owned automobile manufacturer, unions make use of political pressures in their bargaining with managers who are essentially government employees. The resulting agreement terms then set the standards for other firms.

A number of developing nations require that a government official be present during the bargaining process because they fear that the generally weak unions with relatively uneducated leaders will lack the capacity to bargain with the skilled management representatives. In addition to government help, union negotiators in LDCs sometimes get help from the union that organized the employees of the parent company in its home country.

Home Country Assistance

American labor unions which have organized the parent company occasionally send their negotiators abroad to bargain with its subsidiaries. They may do this both to help the local unions and to help themselves. A more costly contract will increase the subsidiary's labor expense and thus may impede the transfer of production from the American plant to overseas facilities. This sometimes produces an odd situation, such as the one that occurred at an American subsidiary in the Caribbean. Company negotiators from the home office were surprised to find themselves face-to-face with the same union officials who had negotiated the union's contract with the parent company in the United States.

Localize Labor Relations

Until subsidiary management becomes skilled in labor contract negotiation and union relationships, the MNE headquarters should send negotiators and consultants from the home country. However, recognizing the fact that each country presents a unique set of labor conditions, types of unions, attitudes, and laws, most multinational enterprises hold local management of foreign subsidiaries responsible for labor relations in their own country.

In the first place, this is done because the subsidiary's management should be much better informed about conditions and trends in its country than parent company management would be.[25] Second, it will be the subsidiary's management that will have to live with its labor agreement, so it should have the authority to negotiate and agree with labor. Without such authority, the prestige of the subsidiary's management would be lowered, and it would have much more difficulty in developing and implementing the long-term personnel policies necessary for the subsidiary's successful operation.[26]

Before the MNE headquarters would entrust subsidiary management with the scope of authority suggested above, headquarters would want to be satisfied that the subsidiary managers are thoroughly trained and capable. The MNE should also exercise some coordination.

Coordination of Labor Relations

Coordination of labor relations can be important because labor contracts made in one country might provide precedent and example in other countries. This will be more and more the case as unions develop international cooperation.*[27]

If MNE headquarters is to carry out its coordinating duties intelligently, it must require a continuing flow of labor relations information from each subsidiary. This provides MNE management with the facts needed to use labor conditions as one important component in investment or reinvestment decisions. Such facts are also necessary to permit management evaluations among the subsidiaries.

Not only has union activity become international, thus requiring MNE management to coordinate labor policy worldwide, but labor has also entered

---

*Remember the examples given in Chapter 11 of the European unions' international actions against ITT and of the Coca-Cola boycotts in Europe and elsewhere because of alleged antilabor practices in Guatemala.

the boardroom and become a part of management. One name for this process is codetermination.

Labor in Management: Codetermination

Like it or not (most managements do not), there is a growing movement toward granting workers some voice in management. Participatory management is required by law in various countries; companies must comply if they wish to do business there. In other countries, worker participation is being brought about voluntarily by management. As was mentioned in Chapter 11, in 1980 Chrysler Corporation elected the president of the United Automobile Workers to its board of directors.

The oldest legal requirement for **codetermination** was the 1951 German law calling for a 50–50 management-labor membership on the board of directors of the iron, coal, and steel industries. In 1951, the Germans passed another law calling for a one-third representation for labor on the boards of other German industries of certain sizes. In 1976, the labor representation was increased to 50 percent. Other European countries and Japan have similar legislation.[28]

Much of management has objected and resisted. At least one German firm, Volkswagen, has had difficulties with new investment decisions because of codetermination.[29] On the other hand, some reporters find more labor peace in countries with labor participation in management (sometimes referred to as "industrial democracy") than in those without it.[30]

Some students of MNE operations foresee possibilities that intraenterprise cooperative projects* could become difficult or impossible because of codetermination. If labor board members of an important subsidiary in Europe believe a parent-ordered project not to be in the best interest of the subsidiary's labor force, they can block it. The possibility has been referred to as "mutiny on the multinational."[31]

Management is learning to live with codetermination, industrial democracy, or whatever it is called because, in most cases, it must. Among the measures that management has adopted for this purpose have been opening and improving lines of communication and improving relationships between labor and management board members. There has also been some inclination to lessen dependence on a subsidiary which might "mutiny" against the MNE. One management function that has been complicated by codetermination is the firing of workers.

---

*A true MNE operation will take advantage of relative strengths and efficiencies among its subsidiaries to specialize and cooperate on an enterprise-wide basis.

Employment Termination

As we have mentioned, Volkswagen and other firms have faced delays in decisions to invest in new plants in other countries because of labor fears of job losses in the home country. When labor is represented on a company's board of directors, it has the power to delay or even prevent actions that it feels will cause layoffs among the work force. In addition, labor has the power to strike, and labor unions negotiate labor contracts with employers.

Labor Contracts

One subject that is probably covered in every labor contract is the **termination of employment.** Standards of work performance are established, and when managers feel that a worker is not performing up to the standards, management must consult with union representatives before firing the worker. The union representatives may agree that the worker is not performing adequately and should be discharged, or they may suggest a transfer to a different job. If management and the union disagree, the contract contains a provision for grievance procedures or arbitration to resolve their differences. In most countries, many aspects of labor relations, including worker discharge, are covered by laws and government regulations.

Labor Laws

A number of countries have laws which oblige firms to give severance pay to terminated employees who have obtained permanent status, usually after a 60- to 90-day trial period. In Mexico, workers who have been employed for even one day after the trial period must be paid three months' wages if they are discharged. That amount is increased by 20 days' wages for each additional year of employment.

Because of laws requiring that sizable sums be paid to permanent workers upon discharge, some companies have striven to keep a large part of their work force as temporary workers by firing them one day before the temporary period expires and then rehiring them. Many governments have amended their laws to prevent that sort of practice.

A number of multinationals and other employers have complained of the excessive labor costs imposed by labor laws, and some countries have changed their laws to make employee discharge easier. Peru now requires a worker to be employed for three years instead of 90 days before becoming a permanent employee. Chile has eliminated the requirement that allowed permanent workers to be fired solely for legally recognized causes. Now the firm need give only 30 days' notice or 30 days' severance pay.[32]

Other Termination Conditions

Of course, not all employees are union members, not all companies are organized by unions, and not all countries have laws dealing with employment termination. Under such circumstances, the discharge of employees is at the discretion of the employers subject to any agreements between the employees as individuals and their employers. The employees' skills and the availability of replacements would affect the relative bargaining positions of the employees and the employers.

Summary

When planning investments that will require employees in foreign countries, a company's executives must be particularly careful to learn the composition of the work force available there. Is labor abundant or in short supply; what skills are available; and what attitudes do the people have about work, social status, women working, and labor organizations? The would-be investors should also examine the labor laws of the intended host country as well as the labor unions and their history of strike action.

If the needed labor or skills are not available in the host nation, the multinational may consider bringing in foreigners. In that connection, however, the company must first ascertain whether work permits are required and whether the government will grant them. The host governments typically want their own people hired and trained.

Another part of preplanning an investment is to determine what employee facilities must be provided. These might include such facilities as housing, schools, recreation, nurseries, and hospitals.

New employees may be sought through advertising or through employment agencies, and they may come from within the multinational enterprise or from elsewhere. Labor unions and trade schools are also potential sources of new employees.

The company will want to learn some things about prospective new employees such as job skills and experience, and it may want applicants to take physical examinations. The hiring process is usually less formal in developing countries than in industrialized countries.

New employees frequently need training and development, and present employees sometimes require more training if new technology or methods are adopted. There are various kinds of training, including on-the-job training, apprenticeship, classroom training, conferences, and simulation.

A reputation for good training sometimes gives MNE subsidiaries in less developed countries recruiting advantages over local companies. However, the foreign-owned firm should be cautious about introducing the production methods of industrialized countries too rapidly in LDCs; the available workers may not be able to adapt, and the results can be poor production and hostility.

In the developed countries, management has learned that training and development of employees are often less costly and more effective when they are done off company premises by skilled educators than when they are done inhouse. Those methods are being exported with good results to developing countries.

After being hired and trained, employees must be motivated to perform well. Motivation demands insights into human needs and the formulation of programs to meet those needs. The hierarchy of needs, from the bottom up, comprises physiological, security, social, esteem, and self-actualization needs.

Job enrichment programs are parts of motivation, and these programs include minimizing production lines, flexitime, and shop floor committees. Job enrichment programs have been quite successful in some places, reducing absenteeism, improving morale, improving productivity, and cutting costs. In other attempts, they have failed, sometimes because only a few of the workers were involved or because the programs were not adequately planned or explained.

The human relations school of employee relations and quality circles were developed by Americans but have been more widely adopted in Japan than in the United States. Both are now being tried by many American companies. A uniquely Japanese extension of quality circles is the practice of company-wide quality control.

Robotics is the industry of machines that work with human-like skill. Robots are substitutes for human workers, and American management has concluded that it must use many more robots to improve productivity. As in other areas, the competition is Japanese. Faster and cheaper computers combined with robotics are creating new production environments. One result of these developments may be to lessen the importance of low wage costs in determining where to locate factories.

Money, of course, is an important motivator, and employees are paid on the basis of productivity, time spent on the job, or a combination of the two. Another determinant of pay rates in some countries is the employee's seniority with the company.

Besides money, employees get other benefits and rights by law, contract, or voluntarily granted by employers. In addition, some employers make incentive payments for above-average performance.

Discipline is necessary for the efficient functioning of any organization. Rules must be explained to and understood by the employees, and they must be enforced. Working in different nations, managers encounter cultural differences which they must understand if they expect to discipline effectively.

Labor organizations such as unions are one possible source of worker discipline, and worker discipline is one subject of collective bargaining between companies and labor unions. Other subjects can include wages, benefits, vacations, work conditions, and many more. Particularly in the developed countries, labor is a political force, and in some countries it is part of a political party. In many nations, most labor conditions are not bargained between labor unions and companies but are legislated by the governments.

Government representatives sometimes help local unions when they bargain with foreign-owned companies, and those unions may also get help from the union that negotiated the contracts with the parents of the foreign-owned companies. The multinational companies frequently help their subsidiaries abroad with labor relations, but labor relations should be localized to the greatest extent possible. While delegating labor matters to subsidiary management, the MNE headquarters should coordinate labor policy throughout the enterprise because settlements or problems in one country can set precedents for or cause troubles in other countries.

A recent development in labor-management relations is codetermination, under which labor representatives serve on company boards of directors. This is required by law in some countries, but it is done by mutual agreement in others.

Employment termination is a subject of probably every labor contract, so when a contract exists, the union must be consulted before a member is fired. The laws of a number of nations deal with worker discharges, and those laws may not permit such discharges or may require severance payments to the persons let go. In the absence of labor contracts and laws, worker discharge is at the employer's discretion unless the individual worker has an agreement with the employer.

Questions

1. *Before making an investment that will involve hiring employees in a foreign country, what are some questions concerning labor in that country to which management should get answers?*
2. *What are some advantages and disadvantages of using present employees to recruit new employees?*
3. *Why have many firms begun to utilize off-premises training and development programs?*
4. a. *Discuss Maslow's needs hierarchy.*
   b. *Does money satisfy every level of needs? Discuss.*
5. a. *How does the human relations school of employee relations differ from Taylorism?*
   b. *What are quality circles, and how do they relate to company-wide quality control?*
6. *What are some of the more common fringe benefits?*
7. *Discuss the changes in the types of factories and production being brought about by faster, cheaper computers and more efficient robots.*
8. *What is collective bargaining?*
9. *Why is it important for a multinational to coordinate labor relations?*
10. *What is codetermination? What are some contrasting attitudes toward it?*

Minicase

20-1 Your Salary in

Philippine Pesos

The company for which you work manufactures a product that is sold in the home market and exported. The manufacturing process calls for semiskilled and skilled labor.

In order to assure itself of a production facility within the ASEAN market, which your company forecasts will grow and raise trade barriers to outside products, the company has decided to invest in the Philippines. Research and negotiations by your representatives in Manila and elsewhere in the country have led to decisions not to build the plant in Manila but in a rural area on an island near Luzon, where Manila is located.

The chosen area is depressed economically, with high unemployment and low literacy. Most of its people have few industrial skills.

The Philippine government induced the company to locate there by offering an array of enticements. There will be a 10-year tax holiday for the company and for the foreign management and technical personnel it employs. The government will donate the land site chosen by your company for its plant. The government will improve the ferry and air transport and the telephone and telegraph service between the island and Luzon.

The government has other funds available to help your company set up and get into successful operation.

You are the personnel manager for the new Philippine operations. What problems should you anticipate? What solutions should you consider? The government has asked your suggestions as to how it can best spend the funds it has available for helping your company—Philippine pesos only—to assist you in solving personnel problems you foresee. How will you suggest that the pesos be spent?

Minicase

20-2 Japanese Competition

You are a management consultant in the United States, and one of your clients is suffering from intense competition from Japanese imports. Your client's difficulties are with productivity and quality.

The client's executives are experienced American businesspeople. They have tried all the devices they know to improve productivity and to reduce quality problems. They have reorganized production lines; they have issued detailed instructions for every step of the production process; they have disciplined employees found not to be following instructions; and they have paid bonuses to employees who were punctual and followed instructions.

There has been some improvement, but the Japanese competitive product is still a little less expensive and there are fewer customer complaints about its quality. Your client calls you in.

What would you suggest the client try? How should it go about implementing your recommendations? In other words, what should it try to do first, second, and so forth?

Minicase

20-3 Keep It Top Secret*

Management of the French multinational enterprise St. Gobain opposed the efforts of another company to acquire control of St. Gobain. As part of its opposition campaign, the management appealed to St. Gobain's stockholders not to sell their stock and revealed to them much of the previously secret financial data about the company. Its profitability (larger than had been publicly admitted previously) and its use of a Swiss holding company to reduce taxes were told to stockholders to induce them to hold their shares.

At that time, St. Gobain also had labor relations difficulties with unions in France, Italy, the United States, and West Germany. Of course, the unions got their hands on the previously confidential information.

The unions coordinated their collective bargaining in all four countries. St. Gobain was hit by strikes and finally made large concessions to settle. As a result, St. Gobain made little profit during the late 1960s.

1. Would you have handled this situation in the same way that St. Gobain's management did? Discuss.

2. Now that the damage has been done, what labor relations steps should St. Gobain take? Explain.

3. What is your guess as to why management made the revelations?

Supplementary Readings

Albano, Debbie. "British Miners Strike—Seek World Support." *Labor Today,* January 1985, p. 1.

Bhatt, Bhal J., and Edwin L. Miller. "Industrial Relations in Foreign and Local Firms in Asia." *Management International Review,* Summer 1984, pp. 62–73.

Busch, G. K. *The Political Role of International Trade Unions.* London: Macmillan, 1983.

Dreyer, Peter H. "European Unions on the Defense." *Journal of Commerce,* March 12, 1986, p. 4A.

*Source David A. Ricks, M. Fu, Jeffrey S. Arpan, *International Business Blunders* (Columbus, Ohio: Grid, 1974), pp. 59–60.

Ebrahimpour, Malig. "An Examination of Quality Management in Japan: Implications for Management in the United States." *Journal of Operations Management*, August 1986, pp. 4–9.

Enderwick, Peter. "Ownership Nationality and Industrial Relations Practices in British Non-Manufacturing Industries." *Industrial Relations Journal*, January 1986, pp. 50–62.

Gordon, William I. "Gaining Employee Commitment to Quality." *Supervisory Management*, November 1985, pp. 30–38.

Harnett, Donald C., and L. L. Cummings. *Bargaining Behavior: An International Study.* Houston: Dame Publications, 1980.

Hutchins, Dave. "Quality Is Everybody's Business." *Management Decision*, Winter 1986, pp. 3–10.

Jacoby, S. M. "The Future of Industrial Relations in the United States." *California Management Review,* Summer 1984, pp. 90–94.

Jones, Sam L. "Quality Circles Can Enhance Firm's Communication." *American Metal Market,* September 7, 1984, pp. 6–11.

Kaha, Helen. "Cooperation Is Focus of Labor Study." *Automotive News*, June 23, 1986, p. 1.

Landon, David N., and Steve Moulton. "Quality Circles: What's in Them for Employees?" *Personnel Journal*, June 1986, pp. 23–29.

Matsuura, Nanthi. "Japanese Management and Labor Relations in U.S. Subsidiaries." *Industrial Relations Journal*, Winter 1984, pp. 38–44.

Poole, Michael. "Industrial Relations in the Future." *Journal of General Management*, August 1985, pp. 38–48.

Reitsperger, Wolf D. "Japanese Management: Coping with British Industrial Relations." *Journal of Management Studies*, January 1986, pp. 72–86.

Siberman, David. "Labor Law Turned Upside Down." *American Federationist*, July 6, 1985, pp. 5–11.

Trever, Malcolm. "Quality Control—Learning from the Japanese." *Long Range Planning*, October 1986, pp. 46–54.

Weinberg, Paul. *European Labor and Multinationals.* New York: Praeger Publishers, 1978.

Zahasin, Gretchan. "Quality Control: It's Money in the Bank." *ABA Banking Journal*, December 1986, pp. 22–27.

Endnotes

1. Some experts refer to the subject we shall cover here as human resources planning. However, that appears to us to include all the functions numbered in the introduction, and we wish to limit the material in this section to the analyses of the company's personnel needs, the availability of the needed personnel, and applicable labor laws.

2. Manning Nash, "The Interplay of Culture and Management in a Guatemalan Textile Plant," in *Culture and Management,* ed. Ross A. Webber (Homewood, Ill.: Richard D. Irwin, 1969), pp. 317–24.

3. Denis Debost, *Summary of French Labor and Social Security Laws* (Paris: French Industrial Development Agency, 1972), p. 7.

4. A. H. Maslow, *Motivation and Personality*, 2nd ed. (New York: Harper & Row, 1970). There are also at least two published doctoral theses on the implications of Maslow's needs hierarchy.

5. "Japan, the End of Lifetime Jobs," *Business Week*, July 17, 1978, pp. 82–83.

6. Frederick Herzberg, *The Managerial Choice: To Be Efficient and to Be Human* (Homewood, Ill,: Dow Jones-Irwin, 1976).

7. *European Business*, Winter 1973, p. 13.

8. *Business International*, December 19, 1975, p. 406.

9. "Lifelong Allocation of Time," *OECD Observer*, May–June 1976, pp. 25–26.

10. Bruce Stokes, "For Many Workers, Productivity and Participation Go Hand in Hand," *Los Angeles Times*, April 22, 1979, part 4, pp. 1, 3.

11. Ibid.

12. Mitchell Fein, "Job Enrichment: A Re-evaluation," *Sloan Management Review*, Winter 1974, p. 77.

13. "Job Enrichment: No Real Future in Sight," *Vision*, November 1973, pp. 79–83.

14. John Simmons and William Mares, *Working Together* (New York: Alfred A. Knopf, 1983).

15. Clayton C. Christensen, " 'Bureaucrat' Need Not Be a Dirty Word," *The Wall Street Journal*, September 1, 1983, p. 24.

16. Davida M. Amsden and Robert T. Amsden, "ICQCC Seoul '82," *Quality Circle Journal*, September 1983, pp. 12–14.

17. *Economist*, November 23, 1985, p. 81.

18. Wayne S. Rieker, "QC Circles and Company-Wide Quality Control," *Quality Progress*, October 1983, pp. 14–17.

19. Ibid.

20. M. E. Porter and V. E. Millar, "How Information Gives You Competitive Advantage," *Harvard Business Review*, July–August 1985, pp. 75–83.

21. "Management in the 1990s Research Program," Organizational Reform Workshop, Sloan School of Management, January 1986.

22. Porter and Millar, "How Information Gives You Competitive Advantage," p. 77.

23. W. Skinner, *American Industry in Developing Economies* (New York: John Wiley & Sons, 1968), p. 65.

24. *Trade and Investment in Israel* (Tel Aviv: Bank Leumi Le Israel, 1978), p. 67.

25. B. J. Widick, "The New Look in Labor Relations," *Columbia Journal of World Business*, July–August 1971, pp. 63–67.

26. Malcolm L. Denise, "Industrial Relations and the Multinational Corporations: The Ford Experience," in *Bargaining without Boundaries*, ed. Robert J. Flanagan and Arnold R. Weber (Chicago: University of Chicago Press, 1974), p. 140.

27. David C. Hershfield, *The Multinational Union Challenges the Multinational Corporation* (New York: Conference Board, 1975).

28. Robert J. Kuhne, "Co-determination: A Statutory Restructuring of the Organization," *Columbia Journal of World Business*, Summer 1976, pp. 17–25.

29. Alfred J. Thimm, "Decision Making at Volkswagen, 1973–1975," *Columbia Journal of World Business*, Spring 1976, pp. 94–103.

30. *Business International*, May 28, 1976, p. 172.

31. Robert J. Kuhne, "Statutory Co-determination: Mutiny on the Multinational?" Paper presented at the annual national meeting of the Academy of International Business, Orlando, Florida, August 1977.

32. "Labor Trends in Latin America," *Business Latin America*, August 23, 1978, p. 266.

CHAPTER 21

PLANNING AND ORGANIZING

"*R*unning a business without planning can be compared to driving a car while looking only at the rear view mirror. You can tell where you've been, but heaven help the occupants during a trip on winding or congested roads."

From Arthur Andersen & Co.'s *Strategic Planning,* quoted in *Industrial Distribution,* June 1986, p. 37

However

"At the very mention of strategic planning, heads nod, yawns are stifled, and eyes glaze over. Yet this little-understood aspect of business management accounts for more successes—and failures—than any other."

R. Smith, vice chairman of Bell Atlantic, from *Bell Atlantic Quarterly,* Winter 1986, pp. 57–63

762

Learning Objectives

After you study this chapter, you should know:

1. The steps involved in the planning process.
2. Ways to monitor the political forces.
3. Strategic planning methods.
4. The reasons why more multinationals are adopting global planning.
5. The bases for organizing.
6. The reasons why hybrid organizations exist.
7. Some new organizational forms.

Key Words and Concepts

Watch lists
Strategic planning
Top-down planning
Bottom-up planning
Tactical planning
Global planning
International division
Global corporation
Hybrid organizations
Matrix organization
Scenarios
Contingency planning
Strategic business units (SBUs)

Business Incident

In a portfolio of businesses as diverse and complex as those within RJR, there has to be a two-way flow to the strategic planning process. From the bottom up, it is quite regular and formal. Planning is highly decentralized at the early stages, with subsidiary company strategies devised at the operating levels. Operating company management rather than company planners are best equipped to make the plans at the early stages. At later stages, subsidiary company plans are consolidated, reviewed, and measured against corporate standards and goals.

The other part of the two-way flow is from the top down. It's much less formal and structured. It's where the CEO sits down with a few knowledgeable and forward thinkers, closes the door, and puts the butcher paper on the wall and opens up the blackboard. It's a time to question everything and put it to the test.

In the fall of 1983, we held one of those small meetings of key officers of RJR to look at strategic direction. Out of this meeting came a significant refinement of that direction. We examined and restated the company mission. We defined what we wanted to be, established corporate goals for each of the businesses, and defined the measures by which we would chart progress. What emerged was a detailed strategy for growth and a vision of RJR's future. . . .

Planning is no panacea. Nor is it necessary to overcomplicate the process, making up those elaborate flow charts with circles and squares and arrows going in every direction, which was so evident in the 1970s. But good planning is something we simply cannot do without. Planning in business is not a virtue: it is a necessity. As such, it's the real mother of invention.

J. Tylee Wilson, chairman and chief executive officer, "Strategic Planning at R. J. Reynolds Industries," *Journal of Business Strategy,* Fall 1985, pp. 22–28. Reprinted with permission from Journal of Business Strategy, Fall 1985. Copyright © 1985, Warren, Gorham & Lamont, Inc., 210 South Street, Boston, MA 02111. All rights reserved.

*F*ormal planning in the manner of R. J. Reynolds is relatively new, having attained importance in industry only after World War II. In fact, it was the successful experience of governments in organizing scarce resources for the war effort that brought home to managements the benefits of careful forward planning. They came to realize that the planning function provides an orderly process for gathering relevant data and examining the expected consequences of available alternatives. Formal corporate planning also requires executives to concern themselves with the broader aspects of company-wide activities rather than merely the operations of the departments or regions under their direct control. While working on the plan, key managers are brought together to exchange information and agree on corporate goals. Long-time relationships and methods of doing business are questioned and often changed to improve the company's operations. Once the plan is in effect, top management has a quick and accurate means of spotting performance variations by comparing actual results with the plan's targets.

Strategic Planning

Planning, the primary function of management, is the process of setting objectives and establishing a course of action to attain them. In other words, it is the process that addresses the fundamental questions of a firm's identity—who are we, where do we want to go, and how do we get there? The steps in the planning process include: (1) defining the firm's business and mission; (2) formulating the firm's objectives; (3) quantifying the objectives; (4) analyzing the uncontrollable foreign, international, and domestic environmental forces; (5) analyzing the controllable forces; (6) determining the strategies necessary to reach the objectives; and (7) preparing tactical plans.

Planning Steps

Defining the Firm's Business and Mission

To set meaningful objectives, management must first define (1) the business the firm is in and (2) the firm's mission. The Rorer Group ($845 million sales), for example, states that its business is "developing, manufacturing, and marketing prescription and over-the-counter pharmaceuticals worldwide." Its mission is "to be a world-class health care company in every respect, able to compete effectively in selected therapeutic areas in the major markets of the world."[1] General Motors states that its business is building transportation to serve people.[2] The company's mission reads as follows: "The fundamental purpose of General Motors is to provide products and services of such quality that our customers will receive superior value, our employees and business partners will share in our success, and our stockholders will receive a sustained, superior return on their investment."[3] Figure 21-1 shows the pocket card of General Motors' mission statement that GM executives carry in their pockets.

Formulating the Firm's Objectives

Objectives direct the firm's course of action, maintain the firm within the boundaries of the stated mission, and ensure its continuing existence. Thus,

Figure 21-1

General Motors' Mission Statement

GENERAL MOTORS MISSION

The fundamental purpose of General Motors is to provide products and services of such quality that our customers will receive superior value, our employes and business partners will share in our success, and our stockholders will receive a sustained, superior return on their investment.

Understanding General Motors mission...and guided by our principles of operation...every General Motors unit can better define its objectives and develop strategies to meet them.

Similarly, every GM man and woman...with our mission and principles in mind...can identify with his or her unit's goals and plans...and better understand and manage his or her job.

Working together and sharing knowledge of our purpose, we will accomplish our mission.

Chairman

GENERAL MOTORS GUIDING PRINCIPLES

1. We will establish and maintain a Corporate-wide commitment to excellence in all elements of our product and business activities. This commitment will be central to all that we do.

2. We will place top priority on understanding and meeting our customers' needs and expectations.

3. General Motors is its people. We recognize that GM's success will depend on our involvement and individual commitment and performance. Each employe will have the opportunity, environment, and incentives to promote maximum participation in meeting our collective goals.

4. We recognize that our dealers, suppliers, and all our employes are partners in our business and their success is vital to our own success.

5. We recognize that a total dedication to quality leadership in our products, processes, and workplaces is of paramount importance to our success.

6. We are committed to sustained growth which will enable us to play a leading role in the world-wide economy.

7. We will continue to focus our efforts on transportation products and services, both personal and commercial, but will aggressively seek new opportunities to utilize our resources in business ventures that match our skills and capabilities.

8. We will offer a full range of products in the North American market and participate with appropriate products in other markets on a world-wide basis.

9. We will maintain strong manufacturing resources at the highest levels of technology and be cost competitive with each manufacturing unit.

10. We will operate with clearly articulated centralized policies with decentralized operational responsibilities to keep decisions as close to the operations as possible.

11. We will participate in all societies in which we do business as a responsible and ethical citizen, dedicated to continuing social and economic progress.

there are objectives with respect to profits, employee relations, market position, company maintenance, and social responsibility. GM expresses these objectives for its worldwide operation:

1. To remain profitable and competitive by supplying customers with products of superior quality.

2. To compete vigorously in the growing world market for vehicles.

3. To provide opportunities for employment regardless of age, race, color, sex, national origin, religion, or handicap.

4. To continually find new ways to cut costs.

5. To scrutinize every GM program closely to see that its benefits justify the firm's investment of facilities, personnel, and money.[4]

Quantifying the Objectives

To the extent that they can be quantified, objectives should be converted into quantitative goals. ITT, for example, stated in an annual report that its primary objective was a "substantial improvement in profitability." But how much is "substantial"? How will management know whether this objective has been achieved? ITT continues, "Specifically, we intend to reach at least a 15 percent return on stockholders' equity in the early 1980s."[5] Pfizer, the pharmaceutical giant, has as one of its primary objectives a growth in net income. But how much? Management states in its 1986 *Annual Report* that "the growth in our net income was within the 10 to 15 percent range that is the corporate objective."[6]

In spite of the strong preference of most top managers for verifiable objectives, objectives do frequently include nonquantitative or directional goals. For example, R. J. Reynolds included the following among its long-range objectives: (1) protecting and enhancing the corporation's competitive position in the food and beverage industry, (2) securing new sources of business growth, and (3) achieving an expanded international presence.[7] In synthesis, the firm was seeking to acquire a food and beverage company with international operations. Its merger with Nabisco in 1985 created the second-largest consumer products company in the world, and as its board chairman, J. Tylee Wilson, said, "The opportunity for such a merger arose sooner than had been anticipated. Because RJR had done its planning homework, the company was able to hold meaningful discussions with Nabisco."[8]

Up to this point, only *what, how much,* and *when* have been stipulated. *How* these objectives are to be achieved will be determined in the strategic planning step. To be able to develop strategies, however, managements of international businesses must first have an analysis and forecast of the domestic, international, and foreign environmental forces (uncontrollable) and a clear idea of the present company position (analysis of the controllable forces). After receiving the results of these analyses, managements frequently alter the original goals and also add new ones.

Analyzing the Foreign, International, and Domestic Environmental Forces

Precisely because the firm has little opportunity to control these forces, it is essential that its managers know not only what the present values of the forces are but also where the forces appear to be headed. Commonly, prognoses of these variables for periods of from one to five years are obtained from company personnel and from specialized external sources.

> Exxon requires regional and operating organizations to submit an annual report on political, social, and economic developments in their areas. The report is expected to contain a forecast discussing the key economic, social, and political

forces prevailing in the region, with emphasis on their implications for the corporation. During the development of this report, there are discussions between regional and operating organizations and headquarters units.

If a high degree of uncertainty exists, the regional organization is requested to try and indicate the degree of confidence in the outlook which is presented and to attempt to identify principal alternatives and their implications to Exxon.

In the political and social area, the analyses may consider, among other factors, general social goals in a society, the goals of specific key groups in a society, and the likelihood that these goals will receive serious governmental attention. An effort is made to cover both the short and long term: that is, the period of the next few years and then the period of the next decade or two.

We believe that the affiliates, while in many cases having smaller staffs than corporate headquarters, can generally come up with the most realistic appraisal of a situation because of their continuing exposure to local developments. Through the review process at the regional and corporate headquarters' levels, it is possible to raise questions about these forecasts and also to take into account the activities of intergovernmental organizations such as the Organization for Economic Cooperation and Development and the United Nations.[9]

Notice the attention paid by Exxon to the political forces, which we believe are among the most significant. Political actions can be both sudden and drastic and can result in huge financial losses. Yet insufficient emphasis is given to this important subject in many enterprises. An example of inattention that caused huge losses for some MNEs was the sudden halving of the Mexican peso's value, which caught many financial officers with large peso deposits. Had management paid only minimal attention to the signs of a pending devaluation—(1) a rapidly increasing inflation rate, which was ruining the tourist industry and the competitiveness of Mexican exporters; (2) a massive conversion of pesos to dollars by Mexican citizens (well known in the banks of Laredo, Texas, and other border cities); and (3) a falling off of foreign investment—it would not have heeded the assurances of Mexican government officials that the peso's value would continue unchanged. Given these very obvious warnings, there was no reason for the translation losses that many large multinationals suffered.

Because of the significance and pervasiveness of political affairs in the conduct of international business, we believe that executives must expend considerable effort to be current on them. This includes reading business periodicals such as *Business Week*, the *Economist*, and *Financial Times* and subscribing to services that specialize in political risk assessment. Most multinationals subscribe to these: (1) Haner's *Business Environment Risk Index*, (2) Business International's *Country Ratings*, and (3) Frost & Sullivan's *World Summary* and *60 Country Reports*.[10]

Other environmental developments must also be monitored. The use of **watch lists** containing specific items of interest is common among many firms. A petroleum refiner, for example, would want to follow the progress being made in extracting crude oil from the Canadian tar sands. To learn where dams and roads are to be built, construction firms study the lists of loans made by the World Bank and other international lending agencies. An outstanding example of the effort expended on environmental analysis by multinationals is a study prepared by Philips to forecast future developments in labor relations.

New forms of labor contracts—part-time work, work at two jobs, and temporary project-related employment—will blur the concept of the "employee" and will reduce the need for identification with an organization such as a union. Despite these problems, the unions will continue to fulfill a role in society, the report concludes.

In the field of incomes, the forecast group foresees a move to a more bureaucratic salary structure under the influence of increased government involvement in investment, profit distribution, and wages.

The unions and the works councils will gain a bigger say in setting individual incomes. The unions are naturally in favor of a more formalized income structure since this will give them a greater control of wage levels, but this trend will be opposed by senior staff. . . .

How do companies like Philips, which has 391,500 employees worldwide and is the largest private sector employer outside the United States, go about looking into the future? And why the need to add its own crystal gazing to that carried out by the many private and government forecasting institutes?

The aim is to see "if the forecasting was sufficiently tangible to make a real contribution to decisions on the company's social policies," the forecast group says. Philips, like many other companies, usually restricts itself to a four-year review. This survey, which was completed in May 1978, looks 13 years ahead to 1991—not too close and not too far into the future.

More than 50 written sources of material are listed. They include government studies, reports by specialist government advisory groups, studies by the unions and the employers' organizations, as well as academic texts. . . .

The survey begins with a list of assumptions about the future, drawn from the written sources and based on Philips' own experience in social matters. These assumptions are then worked out in more detail in several areas, including income, personnel, and company structures. In the final section of the 65-page report a number of points raised are checked to see if they could form the basis for policy decisions.*

Analyzing the Controllable Forces

The analysis of the forces controlled by the firm will include both a situational analysis and a forecast. Where are we now, and where are we headed if we maintain the same course? What are our strengths and weaknesses? What are

*Reprinted from page 25 of the February 12, 1979, issue of *Financial Times World Business Weekly*, 135 West 50th Street, New York, NY 10020.

our human and financial resources? Where are we with respect to our objectives? What are our market opportunities? How effective have our present strategies been in achieving our objectives? Have we uncovered any facts in this or the uncontrollable forces analysis that require goals to be deleted or modified? Should new goals be added? After this internal audit has been completed, management is ready to begin strategic planning.

Such an analysis, which included supply and demand forecasts for basic chemical and plastics, led Dow Chemical management in 1978 to establish a diversification objective. The quantitative goal was "to generate consistently 50 percent of the Company's earnings from value-added products and services by the late 1980s."[11]

Strategic Planning

Based on the corporate objectives, the environmental analysis, and the internal audit, managers must now formulate alternative strategies or action plans to take advantage of the opportunities offered by the three environments and to cope with perceived threats. These plans will attempt to maximize the company's internal strengths and correct its weaknesses.[12]

The Stanford Research Institute states that six questions must be answered:

1. Why is some kind of action necessary?
2. What action should be taken?
3. With what resources?
4. What will the action accomplish?
5. When?
6. What conditions must be met to assure that expectations will be achieved?[13]

Strategic Plan Features. Two prominent features of the strategic plan are *sales forecasts* and *budgets*. The sales forecast not only provides management with an estimate of the revenue to be received and the units to be sold but also serves as the basis for planning in the other functional areas. Without this information, the production, financial, and procurement plans cannot be formulated. Budgets, like sales forecasts, are both a planning and a control technique. During planning, they coordinate all of the functions within the firm and provide management with a detailed statement of future operating results.

Kinds of Strategic Plans. Although strategic plans may be classified as short, medium, or long term, there is little agreement as to the length of these periods. For some, long-range planning may be for a five-year period, whereas for others, this would be the length of a medium-term plan. Their long range might cover 15 years or more. Short-term plans are usually for from one to three years, but a plan for conducting a special sale might cover just one month.

Some multinationals require a three-year plan from their subsidiaries, whereas the headquarters plan covers five to seven years. The rationale of these multinationals is that although the subsidiaries are in a position to know what is expected to occur in their own markets over this shorter period of time, they do not have access to global plans that govern longer periods.

The *business function* is another basis for classification. There are marketing, production, personnel, purchasing, and financial plans, with additional breakdowns within each function. For instance, the personnel department may have special plans for hiring minorities, training employees, and recruiting college graduates. Marketing will certainly prepare plans for sales, advertising, and sales promotion.

Methods of Planning. For purposes of discussion, we can consider two methods of planning, *top-down planning* and *bottom-up planning* (sometimes called centralized and decentralized planning).

In **top-down planning,** corporate headquarters develops and provides guidelines that include the definition of the business, the mission statement, company objectives, financial assumptions, the content of the plan, and special issues. If there is an international division, its management may be told that this division is expected to contribute $5 million in profits, for example. The division, in turn, would break this total down among the affiliates under its control. The managing director in Germany would be informed that the German operation is expected to contribute $1 million; Brazil, $300,000; and so on.

Disadvantages of top-down planning are that it restricts initiative at the lower levels and shows some insensitivity to local conditions. Furthermore, especially in a multinational firm, there are so many interrelationships that consultation is necessary. Can top management, for example, decide on rationalization of production without obtaining the opinions of the local units as to its feasibility?

The advantage of top-down planning is that the home office with its global perspective should be able to formulate plans that assure the optimal corporate-wide use of the firm's scarce resources.

Bottom-up planning operates in the opposite manner. The lowest operating levels inform top management of what they expect to do, and the total becomes the firm's goals. The advantage of bottom-up planning is that the people responsible for attaining the goals are formulating them. Who knows better than the subsidiaries' directors what and how much the subsidiaries can sell? Since the subsidiaries' directors set the goals with no coercion from top management, they feel obligated to make their word good. However, there is also a disadvantage. Since each affiliate is free to some extent to pursue the goals it wishes to pursue, there is no guarantee that the sum total of all the affiliates' goals coincides with those of headquarters. When discrepancies occur, extra time must be taken at headquarters to eliminate them.[14]

In actual practice, a combination of top-down and bottom-up planning is generally employed. Headquarters may set some tentative overall goals and allow the management of each subsidiary to submit its goals.

These goals are compared, and changes are made at both locations until they coincide. On the other hand, top management may elect to require the subsidiaries to submit their own goals first, with no indication of corporate intentions. The goals are then compared at headquarters, where corporate and/or subsidiary goals may be altered.

Tactical Planning

Because strategic plans are fairly broad, tactical (also called operational) plans are a requisite for spelling out in detail how the objectives will be reached. In other words, very specific, short-term means for achieving the goals are the object of **tactical planning**. For instance, if the British subsidiary of an American producer of prepared foods has as a quantitative goal a 20 percent increase in sales, its strategy might be to sell 30 percent more to institutional users. The tactical plan could include such points as hiring three new specialized sales representatives, attending four trade shows, and advertising in two industry periodicals every other month. This is the kind of specificity that is found in the tactical plan.

Scenarios. Because of the rapidity and unpredictability of environmental changes, a number of companies have become dissatisfied with a single forecast and have turned to **scenarios,** descriptions of possible alternative futures. The use of the most likely, worst, and best cases is fairly common.

Scenarios assist managers in becoming aware of the critical elements of the external forces. Strategies formulated to handle these elements can be tested quickly by means of computer runs. Frequently they are the basis for **contingency planning** (or standby planning).

Contingency Planning. Although contingency plans are drawn up for the best and worst case scenarios in some firms, other firms have them ready for a few critical events that, should they occur, would have a severe impact on their financial and strategic goals. A contingency plan to combat an attempted unfriendly takeover is an example.

A poll taken of 94 leading firms in 1985 found that 66 percent of them either have crisis response plans or are preparing them. The Union Carbide Bhopal incident prompted many of them to take action, the pollsters claim.[15]

Summary of the Planning Process

A flowchart of the planning process appears in Figure 21–2. Note that the information obtained from the analysis of the environments and controllable variables may necessitate a change of, or possibly an addition to, the objectives and quantitative goals.

Figure 21-2

The Multinational Corporate Planning Process

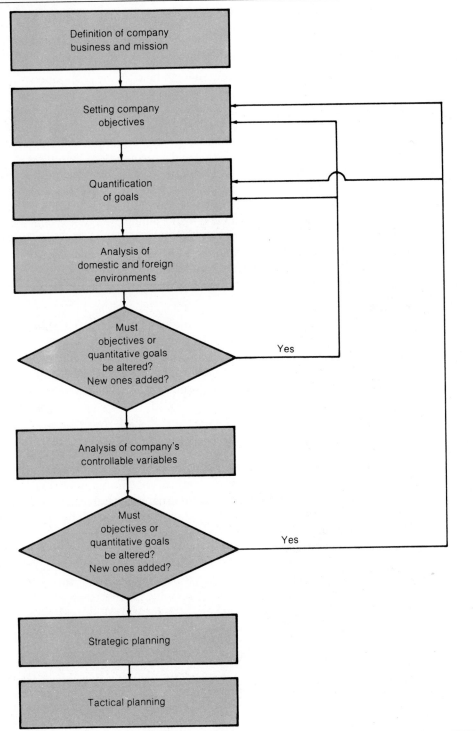

Plan Implementation Facilitators[16]

Once the plan has been prepared, it must be implemented. Two of the most important plan implementation facilitators that management employs are policies and procedures.

Policies

Policies are broad guidelines issued by upper management for the purpose of assisting lower-level managers in handling recurring problems. Since policies are broad, they permit discretionary action and interpretation. The object of a policy is to economize managerial time and promote consistency among the various operating units. If the distribution policy states that the firm's policy is to sell through wholesalers, marketing managers throughout the world know that they should normally use wholesalers and avoid selling directly to retailers. The disclosure of the widespread occurrence of bribery prompted company presidents to issue policy statements condemning this practice. Managers were put on notice by these statements that they were not to offer bribes.

Procedures

Procedures prescribe how certain activities will be carried out, thereby assuring uniform action on the part of all corporate members. For instance, most corporate headquarters issue a procedure for their subsidiaries to follow in preparing the annual budget. This procedure assures corporate management that all budgets will be prepared using the same format, which will facilitate their comparison.

Global Planning

According to various surveys, managements of 80 to 90 percent of large firms say that they engage in corporate planning. But in many of them, corporate planning is an extended form of budgeting that deals only with the financial aspects of future policies, and there is neither formulation of objectives nor an environmental analysis.[17]

However, according to a Conference Board study of 213 firms with a median sales volume of nearly $2 billion, 72 percent had established a prescribed format for planning and 55 percent had instituted a planning calendar during the past five years. This is an indication that a formal planning process had been put in place recently. Interestingly, though, far fewer (22 percent) had introduced planning for international units, and there are no data that indicate how these firms incorporated international planning into corporate planning.[18]

The analysis of dozens of MNE annual reports leads us to believe that many firms are recognizing the need for corporate planning that integrates both the international and domestic operations. As international companies develop into MNEs that source from, finance in, and market to subsidiaries worldwide, it seems logical that the trend to **global planning** will continue. Let us look at some other reasons for global planning.

Reasons for Global Planning

A number of reasons lie behind the growing realization of MNE managements that corporate planning must be global in nature:

1. *The scope of the multinational management task.* Multinational firms have so grown in size and complexity that management is virtually impossible without a coordinated plan of action detailing what is expected of whom during a given time period. Without such a plan, the common practice of management by exception* is impossible.

2. *Increased internationalization of the firm.* There are three aspects of international business that make global planning necessary, all of which have been discussed at great length in this book. They are: (1) differences among the environmental forces, (2) greater distances, and (3) the interrelationships of international operations.

3. *Information explosion.* Estimates have been made to the effect that the world's stock of knowledge is doubling every 10 years. Without the aid of a formal plan, it is no longer possible for executives to know all that they must know to solve the complex problems they face. The analyses we mentioned previously and, indeed, the entire planning process provide an ordered procedure for assembling, analyzing, and distilling the information required to make sound decisions.

4. *Increased competition.* We pointed out in Chapter 12 that because international competition is increasing at a rapid rate, firms must constantly adjust to changing conditions or lose markets to competitors. Increased competition also spurs managements to search for greater efficiency and economy, as one of the General Motors objectives stated. In Chapters 15 and 19, we examined the increased tendency to standardize worldwide both marketing and production methods as a means of lowering costs to improve the firm's competitiveness.

5. *Rapid development of technology.* We have also noted that the rapid development of technology has contributed greatly to the shortening of product life cycles. Managers must plan in an organized manner to ensure that new products will be available to replace those that are moving into the maturity stage, with fewer sales and declining profits. Planning gives management greater control of all aspects of new product introduction.

6. *Planning breeds managerial confidence.* The manager who has a plan for reaching an objective is similar to a motorist with a road map. Both know where they are going. The plan breeds confidence because every step along the way is spelled out and the responsibility for performing every task is delineated. The plan simplifies the job.

---

*Managers receive comparative reports that include the especially good and the especially bad exceptions.

New Directions in Planning

Planning during the 60s and early 70s commonly consisted of a company's CEO and the head of planning getting together to devise a corporate plan, which would then be handed to the operating people for execution. Changes in the business environment, however, caused changes to be made in three areas: (1) who does the planning, (2) how it is done, and (3) the contents of the plan.[19]

Who Does It

By the mid–70s, strategic planners had become dominant figures in their companies. They were accustomed to writing a blueprint for each subsidiary, which they would then present to the management of each operating unit. The planners' power grew and the operating managers' influence waned, and of course there was hostility between the two groups. Roger Smith, chairman of GM, says, "We got those great plans together, put them on a shelf, and marched off to do what we would be doing anyway."[20]

But a number of factors were acting to upset this pattern. It became clear that world uncertainty made long-range planning in detail impossible, so corporate plans had to be short and simple. With huge, detailed plans no longer as useful as they had been, there was less need for professional planners. Stronger competition required as essential input to strategic planning a practical knowledge of the company and the industry. This brought senior operating managers into the planning process, enabling firms to change the role and reduce the size of their planning staffs. General Electric, for example, reduced its corporate planning group from 58 to 33, and GM decreed that "planning is the responsibility of every line manager. The role of the planner is to be the catalyst for change—not to do the planning for each business unit."[21]

The way strategic planning is done now varies among companies and depends primarily on the wishes of the chief executive. Various reports and studies indicate that it is common for CEOs and their senior management teams to set some guidelines, which are transmitted to operating managers who formulate plans for their units. These plans are then reviewed by the senior management teams and discussed with the managers in conferences, during which the plans may be accepted or altered to conform better to the guidelines. The R. J. Reynolds Business Incident is an example.

How It Is Done

By the 1960s, firms were using computer models and sophisticated forecasting methods to help produce the voluminous plans we mentioned above. These plans were not only huge but also very detailed. As a Texas Instruments executive put it, "The company let its management system, which can track the eye of every sparrow, creep into the planning process, so we were making more and more detailed plans. It became a morale problem because managers knew they couldn't project numbers out five years to two decimal points."[22]

The heavy emphasis on these methods tended to result in a concentration on factors that could be quantified easily. However, it was the less quantifiable factors relating to sociopolitical developments that were becoming increasingly important. Also, the rapid rise in the levels of uncertainty made it clear to top managers that there was no point in using advanced techniques to make detailed five-year forecasts when various crises were exposing the nonsense of many previous forecasts. (Prior to 1973, for example, there had been a great discussion as to whether the price of crude oil would ever go above $2 per barrel).[23]

Because of these problems, there has been a decided move among many firms toward a less structured format and a much shorter document. General Electric chairman J. F. Welch says, "A strategy can be summarized in a page or two."[24]

Contents of the Plan

The contents of the plan are also different. According to the Conference Board study cited earlier, the managements of most companies say that they are much more concerned now with issues, strategies, and implementation. The planning director of Shell Oil, the British-Dutch multinational, says that "the Shell approach has swung increasingly away from a mechanistic methodology and centrally set forecasts towards a more conceptual or qualitative analysis of the forces and pressures impinging on the industry. What Shell planners try to do is identify the key elements pertaining to a particular area of decision making—the different competitive, political, economic, social, and technical forces that are likely to have the greatest influence on the overall situation. In a multinational organization, the higher level of management is likely to be most interested in global scenarios—looking at worldwide developments—while the focus becomes narrower as one proceeds into the more specialized functions, divisions, and business sectors of individual companies."[25]

Summary of the Planning Process

Perhaps a good way to summarize the new direction in planning is to quote Frederick W. Gluck, a director of the multinational management consulting firm McKinsey & Co., and a principal architect of its strategic management practice. Gluck says that if major corporations are to develop the flexibility to compete, they must make the following major changes in the way they plan:

1. Top management must assume a more explicit strategic decision-making role, dedicating a large amount of time to deciding how things ought to be instead of listening to analyses of how they are.

2. The nature of planning must undergo a fundamental change from an exercise in forecasting to an exercise in creativity.

3. Planning processes and tools that assume a future much like the past must be replaced by a mind-set that is obsessed with being first to recognize change and turn it into competitive advantage.

4. The role of the planner must change from being a purveyor of incrementalism to that of a crusader for action and an alter ego to line management.

5. Strategic planning must be restored to the core of line management responsibilities.[26]

Organizing

If the firm is to reach the goals set out in the corporate plan, its people need to be organized to perform specific tasks according to well-defined authority-responsibility relationships. In fact, planning and organizing are so closely connected that normally the structure of the organization is treated by management as an integral part of the planning process. Strategic changes regarding products, customers, or markets generally necessitate changes in the organization. In addition, the planning process itself, since it encompasses an analysis of all the firm's activities, often discloses the need to alter the organization.

In designing the organizational structure, management is faced with two concerns: (1) finding the most effective way to departmentalize in order to take advantage of the efficiencies gained from the specialization of labor and (2) coordinating the firm's activities to enable it to meet its overall objectives. As all managers know, these two concerns run counter to each other; that is, the gain from the increased specialization of labor may sometimes be nullified by the increased costs of greater coordination. It is the constant search for an optimum balance between them that causes the organizational structure to change continually. Several executives interviewed by the Conference Board were reluctant to furnish organization charts because "they would be superseded before the results were published" or because "the organization was in a state of transition."[27]

International Division or Global Corporation?

The attempt to achieve balance is evidenced by the manner in which management locates the responsibility for directing the firm's nondomestic activities. In some organizations, these activities are centralized in a separate international division, whereas in others, no organizational distinction between home country and non–home country business is noted. In effect, the firm is a world or global company. Interestingly, although we commonly associate large size with global firms, it is not a prerequisite for this type of organization. A company's foreign business may be too small to support a separate organization, or its product lines may be so diversified that an international unit could not possibly assemble the necessary experts to handle all of them.

As foreign business increases, management may create a separate international unit, only to revert to the global corporation organization when the international division becomes too large and unwieldy for effective control. We want to emphasize that either type of organization is perfectly consonant with any of the three management philosophies characterized as *ethnocentric* (home country oriented), *polycentric* (the host country does it better), or *geocentric* (worldwide approach in which management favors neither the home country nor the host country viewpoint).[28] In fact, the change from the world corporation to the international division, or vice versa, may be made because the corporation is increasing its emphasis on international business and, concomitantly, is altering its philosophy.

International Division

The **international division,** which in larger firms may be a separate company with its own president domiciled at headquarters, or even in another country, centralizes in one location all of the responsibility for directing the non–home country activities.

Why an International Division? Top managements that prefer a separate international division evidently believe that, because of the differences between the domestic and foreign environmental forces, a special kind of expertise is required of the employees in all functions. They also believe that if there is no one separate entity to represent the foreign aspects of the business, they themselves may find it difficult to maintain a proper perspective because of their closeness to the domestic operation. Firms that have been organized globally on a product basis sometimes find that the product managers lack the interest or the ability to promote international sales. Creating an international division in which the responsibility for handling all products is posited eliminates this difficulty.

> Bristol-Myers operated as a global corporation in which each product division, such as Clairol, Bristol Laboratories, and Mead Johnson, was responsible for its own international marketing. As the 1974 Bristol-Myers *Annual Report* states, "In every case, business outside the United States was secondary to the domestic effort." In 1967, the Bristol-Myers Company International was formed as a single entity responsible for marketing all company products sold outside the United States. Every year since its inception, the division has shown substantial increases.[29]

Obviously, the managements of Bristol-Myers, IBM, Du Pont, and other large multinationals that utilize an international division believe that the primary basis for specialization is not product knowledge but a knowledge of the environments. How, in this type of organization, are the domestic and international activities coordinated?

Coordination of Domestic and International Activities. Generally, the chief executive will be assisted by an executive committee on which both the domestic and international activities are represented, and/or there may be a single staff to serve both divisions, as in the case of Xerox (see Figure 21–3). Moreover, although the organization charts do not show it, lower-level meetings between domestic and international personnel are common. International staff members and overseas operating personnel frequently visit the domestic division for special training or a discussion of common problems.

The planning process is always a means of coordination in either the international division or the global firm organization. Xerox ($9.8 billion sales), for example, requires the local companies and regional headquarters to become thoroughly involved in the establishment of corporate, regional, and country goals. In certain specified areas that are of worldwide importance, such as pricing and product planning, local and area managements are required to submit plans to be approved by headquarters. Before doing so, they are encouraged to communicate directly with the corresponding domestic departments. Top management believes that this improves communication among managers throughout the company.

Global Corporation

The only alternative to the international division at the highest level in the organization is the **global corporation.** In this structure, there is no dichotomy of we (domestic) and they (the rest of the world) *at the top level.* Instead, the organization is divided most commonly by (1) product or (2) geographic region. Two other dimensions, function (production, finance, personnel, marketing) and customer classes, are much less common, although Caterpillar ($7.3 billion sales) and Lockheed ($10.3 billion sales) use the functional dimension and a number of multinational service companies and financial institutions are organized at the primary level by customer classes. At secondary, tertiary, and still lower levels, these four dimensions plus three more—(1) process, (2) national subsidiary, and (3) international or domestic—will provide the basis for subdivisions. The international operations of Xerox, for example, are organized by geographic regions and one national affiliate.

Product. During the 1970s, a considerable number of large multinational firms that had had international divisions changed to a global product structure in which the organization was departmentalized by product lines and each department was given worldwide responsibility for the marketing and production of its products. The expectation of three key benefits prompted this change.

Figure 21-3
International Division—Xerox Corporation

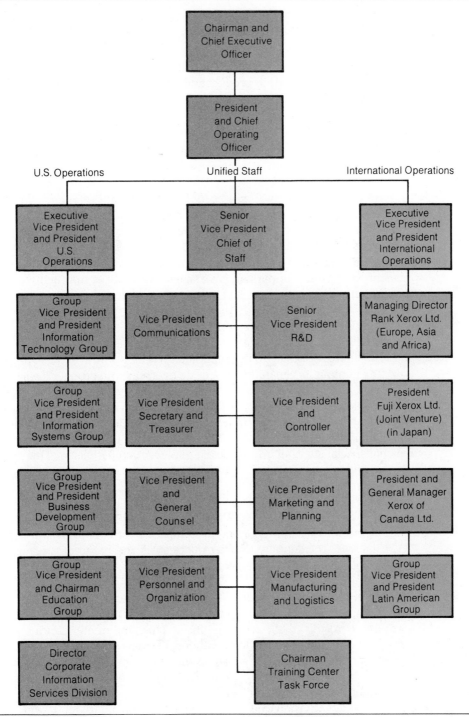

Source: Reprinted from page 68 of *Organization and Control of International Operations* with the permission of the publisher, The Conference Board.

1. The new organization would be more capable of developing a competitive strategy to confront the new global competition that was developing, as we discussed in Chapter 12.

2. A global product organization would obtain lower production costs by promoting the worldwide product standardization and rationalization of production that we examined in Chapter 19.

3. Managements felt that the centralized production management and planning resulting from the new structure would enhance technology transfer (sending information on new products, processes, and production inputs) and the allocation of company resources.

However, studies by *Business International* and Professors Davidson and Haspeslagh presented evidence that this reorganization actually *reduced* the international commitment of many firms because there was no longer an international division to speak for nondomestic business. Technology transfer was actually retarded, and there was a trend toward licensing rather than direct foreign investment.[30] This is understandable when one realizes that many of those in charge of the product divisions had little or no overseas experience and thus opted for licensing, which is "safer" in that it requires a commitment of fewer company resources. Also, domestic business would get more of the managers' attention when most of their profits were coming from domestic sales. Bristol-Myers, as you saw, changed back to an international division because of these problems.

To maintain its capability to operate overseas, the product form of the global corporation will generally have regional experts working at a lower level. Thus, while product divisions avoid the duplication of product specialists, they create another duplication of area experts. Occasionally, to eliminate the placing of regional specialists in each product division, a company will have a group of regional specialists similar to those of an international division. This group, unlike the regional specialists in an international division, serves in an advisory, not an operational, capacity.

Rockwell International ($12 billion sales) (see Figure 21–4) is an example of a firm organized by products. With the exception of the North American Aerospace Operations, each product group comprises both domestic and nondomestic businesses. Incidentally, North American is the name of a company that Rockwell acquired and does not connote a geographic area.

Geographic Regions. Firms in which geographic regions are the primary basis for division put the responsibility for all activities under area managers who report directly to the chief executive officer. This kind of organization simplifies the task of directing worldwide operations, because every country in the world is clearly under the control of someone who is in contact with headquarters. Occasionally, the management of a multinational will change to a regional organization to emphasize the firm's global nature, but as we have already pointed out, the product division that has worldwide responsibility for a product line or

Figure 21-4
Global Corporation Organized by Product—Rockwell International

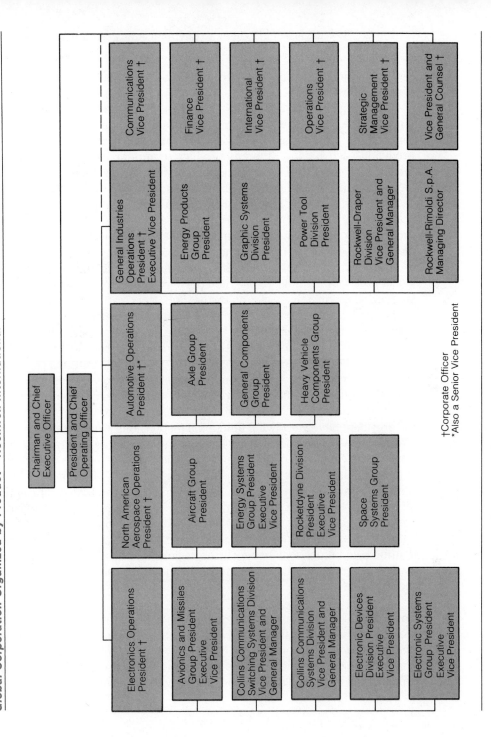

Chairman and Chief Executive Officer

President and Chief Operating Officer

Electronics Operations President †
- Avionics and Missiles Group President Executive Vice President
- Collins Communications Switching Systems Division Vice President and General Manager
- Collins Communications Systems Division Vice President and General Manager
- Electronic Devices Division President Executive Vice President
- Electronic Systems Group President Executive Vice President

North American Aerospace Operations President †
- Aircraft Group President
- Energy Systems Group President Executive Vice President
- Rocketdyne Division President Executive Vice President
- Space Systems Group President

Automotive Operations President †*
- Axle Group President
- General Components Group President
- Heavy Vehicle Components Group President

General Industries Operations President † Executive Vice President
- Energy Products Group President
- Graphic Systems Division President
- Power Tool Division President
- Rockwell-Draper Division Vice President and General Manager
- Rockwell-Rimoldi S.p.A. Managing Director

- Communications Vice President †
- Finance Vice President †
- International Vice President †
- Operations Vice President †
- Strategic Management Vice President †
- Vice President and General Counsel †

†Corporate Officer
*Also a Senior Vice President

the international division form of organization are equally well suited to the geocentric philosophy.

The regionalized organization appears to be popular with companies that manufacture products with a rather low or, at least, stable technological content that require strong marketing ability. It is also favored by firms with diverse products, each having different product requirements, competitive environments, and political risks. Producers of consumer products such as prepared foods, pharmaceuticals, and household products employ this type of organization.[31] The disadvantage of an organization divided into geographic regions is that each region must have its own product and functional specialists so that although the duplication of area specialists found in product divisions is eliminated, a duplication of product and functional specialists is necessary.

Product coordination across regions presents difficult problems, as does global product planning. To alleviate these problems, managements often place specialized product managers on the headquarters staff. Although these managers have no line authority, they do provide input to corporate decisions concerning products. CPC International ($4.5 billion sales; see Figure 21–5) is a regionally organized firm. Note that within each region except for the United States, there is a subdivision according to the kinds of products, industrial or consumer, and a further subdivision based on functions. Worldwide coordination is accomplished through the office of the president, which assists the president in long-range and strategic planning. Two of the senior vice presidents in the office of the president have worldwide functional responsibility and divide their time between domestic and foreign activities. The Corporate Operations Advisory Committee, composed of the president's office, the president, and five divisional presidents,* reviews operations and makes policy. The committee also takes recommendations from the Consumer Council and the Industrial Council, reviews them, and makes its recommendations to the president. The two councils are composed of the top staff executives from the domestic and regional companies and represent industrial or consumer products, as their names indicate. Routine communications between the regions and headquarters are facilitated by liaison personnel who are located at headquarters but work for and report to the regional managers.

Function. Few firms are organized by function at the upper level. Those that are obviously believe that worldwide functional expertise is more important than product or area knowledge. The commonality among the users of the functional form is a narrow and highly integrated product mix such as exists at Caterpillar, Lockheed, and some of the mining and petroleum companies.

---

*These are the heads of the U.S. Industrial, U.S. Consumer, Europe, Latin America, and Asia divisions.

Figure 21-5
Regional Organization—CP

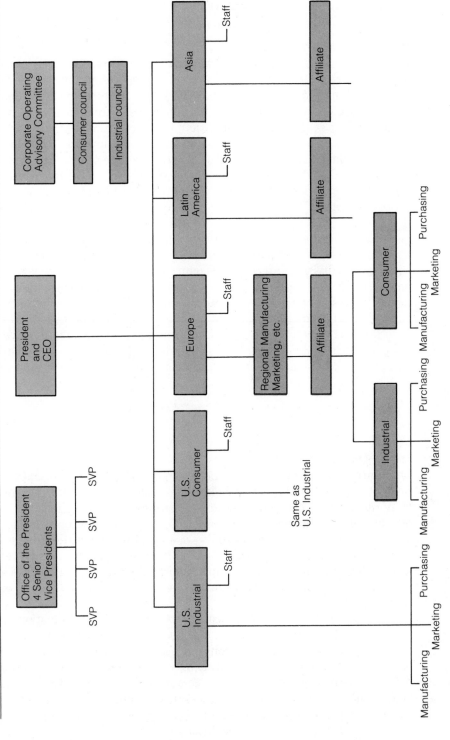

Source: Reprinted from page 99 of *Designing the International Corporate Structure* with the permission of the publisher, Business International Corporation (New York).

Hybrid Organizations

Most firms establish **hybrid organizations.** In such organizations, a mixture of the organizational dimensions for the various operating levels may be used, such as an initial division by product lines that are further subdivided by regions, or vice versa, and frequently the subdivisions are mixed. CPC, which we mentioned as a regionalized organization, is somewhat of a hybrid because it divides the United States by products and the rest of the world by areas. Such a mixture of dimensions at the primary level is extremely common. Dow Chemical, for example, has divided line responsibility for all products except one among five regional managers. The sixth division is a product division with global responsibility. A Worldwide Headquarters Group coordinates the six divisions.[32]

Such combinations are often the result of having introduced a new and different product line that management believes can best be handled by a worldwide product division. An acquired company with distinct products and a functioning marketing network may be incorporated as a product division even though the rest of the firm is organized on a regional basis. Later, after corporate management becomes familiar with the operation, it may be regionalized.

A mixed structure may also result from the firm's selling to a sizable, homogeneous class of customers. Special divisions for handling sales to the military or to original equipment manufacturers are often established at the same level as regional or product divisions.

Matrix Organizations

The **matrix organization** has evolved from management's attempt to mesh product, regional, and functional expertise while still maintaining clear lines of authority. It is called a matrix because it superimposes an organization based on one dimension on an organization based on another dimension.[33] In such an organization, both the area and product managers will be at the same level and their responsibilities will overlap. An individual manager, say a marketing manager in Germany, will have a multiple reporting relationship, being responsible to the area manager and, in some instances, to an international marketing manager at headquarters.

Ciba-Geigy, the Swiss chemical and pharmaceutical multinational, has an organizational structure based on a matrix of three dimensions: (1) product, (2) functions, and (3) geographic regions (see Figure 21–6). Lines of communication flow both horizontally and vertically across these main dimensions. However, final authority rests with the executive committee, which is the highest executive body in the parent company. The task of this committee is to maintain two-way communication between the home office and the lower units. Committee members are not supermanagers of the divisions.[34]

Figure 21-6
Matrix Organization—Ciba-Geigy Limited

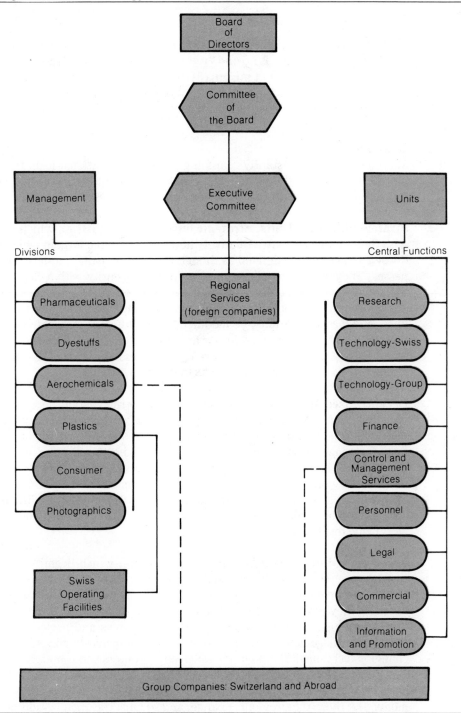

The "Right" Organizational Form

Four facts concerning organizational forms should have become evident from our discussion: (1) there is no one "right" way to organize; (2) generally, organizations are not "pure," but mixed; (3) the greater the specialization of the organization's units, the more difficult it is to coordinate their activities; and (4) organizational structures are never permanent.

Changing Forms

Managements are constantly searching for an organizational form that will be more responsive to the firm's needs. Not only have they mixed the standard forms, but they have conceived some entirely new ones.

Strategic Business Units. Strategic business units (SBUs), which originated with General Electric, are a relatively new organizational form in which product divisions have been redefined as though they were distinct, independent businesses. They are commonly defined as a business entity with a clearly defined market, specific competitors, the ability to carry out its business mission, and a size appropriate for control by a single manager. Most SBUs are based on product lines, and if a product must be modified to suit different markets, a worldwide product SBU may be divided into a few product/market SBUs serving various countries or groups of countries. Strategic business units do not determine how a company as a whole will organize its internal operations.[35]

Decentralized Matrix. Companies that are concerned about the volatile conditions in regional markets and are organized in a worldwide product and global matrix managed from the home office are expected to shift to a regional-product matrix managed from several locations. A subsidiary in France, for example, would report simultaneously to regional and product managers located in the European regional office in Brussels. This new organizational form should permit swifter reaction to changes in regional and local conditions. A slimmer home office would be responsible for major strategic decisions and the monitoring of worldwide results.

Free-Form Management Design. This structure, which began in the 1960s, may become popular again, especially for conglomerates or holding companies, because it encourages entrepreneurship. Local managers are free to do almost anything they wish as long as they meet profit or ROI requirements set at headquarters, which offers assistance through task forces and project teams. The free-form management design is also useful for companies involved with rapidly changing technological innovations such as computers and robots.[36]

Much of the choice of form depends on the managerial philosophy of the chief executive officers and on what they perceive to be their firms' requirements. But these requirements change, and so must the organization. Increased foreign production, a growing appreciation of national differences, the formation of regional markets, especially the European Community, and the rising importance of international business have all motivated corporate reorganization.

Managerial Talent

The managerial talent available to the corporation has been and will continue to be extremely significant both in the choice of organizational form and in the transition from one form to another. Evidently, the lack of global orientation on the part of product managers was a strong factor in Bristol-Myers' decision to revert to an international division.

The importance of capable managers cannot be underestimated. They can make a less than optimum organization function well. There is less need for a matrix organization, for example, if area managers work well with managers having global responsibility for products. By their personal capabilities, these managers can overcome the problem of other organizational forms in getting the needed cooperation and coordination, which is usually achieved through a matrix. Product managers who are able to generate support and enthusiasm for their product lines do not require a dotted line to be drawn on a chart. In fact, such actions are often formalized by management after observing what actually takes place.

Characteristics of the "Right" Organization

Regardless of the form, the right organization should, according to Peter Drucker, have the following characteristics:

1. *Clarity,* as opposed to simplicity (the Gothic cathedral is not a simple design, but your position in it is clear; you know where to stand and where to go. A modern office building is exceedingly simple in design, but it is very easy to get lost in one; it is not clear).

2. *Economy* of effort to maintain control and minimize friction.

3. *Direction* of vision toward the product rather than the process—the result rather than the effort.

4. *Understanding* by each individual of his own task as well as that of the organization as a whole.

5. *Decision making* that focuses on the right issues, is action oriented, and is carried out at the lowest possible level of management.

6. *Stability,* as opposed to rigidity, to survive turmoil, and *adaptability* to learn from it.

7. *Perpetuation* and *self-renewal,* which require that an organization be able to produce tomorrow's leaders from within, helping each person develop continuously; the structure must also be open to new ideas.[37]

Corporate Survival in the 1990s

Top managements in the 1980s are recognizing that an outstanding determinant of an MNE's survival and growth is its ability to fully utilize its human potential. *Business International's* researchers find that MNE executives are implementing or considering many structural reforms to reduce bureaucratization while retaining the advantages of global economies of scale for the 1990s:

1. Reorganization of the company into freestanding enterprises.
2. Implementing systems to track true financial accountability.
3. Restructuring managerial jobs to attain a close link between business performance and compensation.
4. Eliminating the jobs that focus on "control" or "coordination," both of which stimulate bureaucratic growth.
5. Revising performance appraisal systems so that they are based on business content and reflect actual business performance.
6. Refocusing top management's attention on the firm's strategic priorities.[38]

Summary

Planning, the primary function of management, is the process of setting objectives and establishing a course of action to attain them. The steps in planning are: (1) defining the firm's business and mission, (2) setting the firm's objectives, (3) quantifying the objectives, (4) analyzing foreign and domestic environmental forces, (5) analyzing controllable forces, (6) planning strategies, and (7) planning tactics. Changes in the business environment have caused changes in (1) who does the planning, (2) how it is done, and (3) the contents of the plan. Policies and procedures are established to provide direction for the plan's implementation.

The forces responsible for global planning are: (1) the increased scope of the multinational management task, (2) the increased internationalization of business, (3) the information explosion, (4) increased competition, (5) the rapid development of technology, and (6) the confidence created by planning.

To reach the goals set in the planning process, an organization of people must be created to perform specific tasks according to well-defined authority—responsibility relationships. Companies are organized to handle international business either in an international division or in the entire firm (global corporation), which is divided by one of the four basic dimensions of product, geographic area, function, or type of customer. Mixed (hybrid) organizations based on two or more dimensions are common. To improve coordination while still maintaining specialization, some managements have turned to newer organizational forms such as the matrix.

Four facts concerning corporate organizational forms are: (1) there is no one right way to organize; (2) generally, organizations are mixed, not pure; (3) the greater the specialization of the organization's units, the more difficult it is to coordinate their activities; and (4) organizational structures are never permanent.

Questions

1. *Why is constant monitoring of the political force so essential to a multinational business manager?*
2. *Choose a firm with overseas production facilities and prepare a watch list.*
3. *Why are MNE managements finding global planning to be necessary?*
4. *Why are planning and organizing so closely related?*
5. *Describe the two basic organizations for a firm that markets both domestically and overseas.*
6. *Why might management use a mixed organization at the primary level?*
7. *Is the fact that a firm has an international division or is organized as a global corporation any indication as to whether management has an ethnocentric, polycentric, or geocentric management philosophy? Why or why not?*
8. *How can management coordinate product planning in an organization divided according to geographical regions?*
9. *What are some of the factors that require changes to be made in an organization's structure?*
10. *Describe some of the newer organizational forms.*
11. *What are scenarios and what is their purpose?*
12. *What reforms are corporate executives making to ensure corporate survival in the 1990s?*

Minicase

21-1 The Westinghouse

Reorganization*

After meeting still another Westinghouse salesman, the Saudi Arabian businessman reached into his desk drawer, pulled out the business cards of 24 other

*Based on Hugh D. Menzies, "Westinghouse Takes Aim at the World," *Fortune*, January 14, 1980, pp. 48–53.

Westinghouse salesmen, and asked exasperatedly, "Who speaks for Westinghouse?"

This was typical of the complaints that Douglas Danforth, newly appointed CEO, was receiving from customers as he traveled abroad in 1978. The company, he found, was gaining a reputation for being disorganized and slow to act. In short, it was difficult to do business with Westinghouse.

In 1975, the 125 divisions based on product lines had been combined to form 37 operating groups known as business units. They were given considerable autonomy to operate both domestically and abroad much in the manner of General Electric's strategic business units. Each business unit was a business entity with a clearly defined market and specific competitors. Each had control of technology, pricing, and capital budgets.

When the units went abroad, the lack of communication and coordination among them cost them sales. In Saudi Arabia, for example, although the equipment for a power substation was made by Westinghouse, a trio of European firms obtained the contract because Westinghouse could not put all the products handled by its various business units into one package.

Besides losing business, the business unit was costly. Each had a complete set of support services—legal, accounting, financial, and so forth—in each country. It was possible for one Westinghouse subsidiary to have surplus funds while another Westinghouse subsidiary in the same country was borrowing at high rates.

Although foreign sales accounted for almost 25 percent of the company's $6.7 billion sales and $311 million net operating profit in 1978, Danforth felt that the results could be better. He ordered a study to be made and appointed a veteran senior executive to head the study team.

Forty-five executives representing all 37 business units worked for 90 days to investigate the international activities of the 37 business units. They found, for example, that it was impossible to know what the profit was on $600 million in exports because the business units did not separate export business from domestic business. Overheads were sometimes charged against domestic sales only so that a foreign sale would not appear as a loss. The team also confirmed that the lack of communication and coordination frequently confused the company's clients.

Although Westinghouse had a few regional vice presidents overseas, they had little power at corporate headquarters. In fact, the impression at the home office was that those in overseas operations were second-rate people who could not make it domestically.

The team perceived the need for a way to force product managers in the business units to interact with geographic specialists in overseas markets.

Here is the plan that was presented to Danforth and his management committee. Assume that you and two of your classmates are the committee.

1. Design two alternative organizations that will eliminate most of the problems that Westinghouse international operations have now. Which do you favor?

2. What are the advantages and disadvantages of each of your organizational designs?

3. How should strategic planning be carried out in each of these designs?

Minicase

21-2 World Product Structure
May Not Be a Panacea*

As overseas operations have increased in importance to multinational firms, many have chosen a worldwide product structure. The rationale behind this move is that if all product managers concentrate on their respective product lines in overseas as well as domestic markets, then *all* products will receive global attention. Prior to the change, there were many complaints that the international division headed by geographic specialists had not promoted the sale of all products in their areas. Top management also expected that when product managers had global responsibility, there would be increased cost efficiency through global production rationalization and the centralization of planning and that technology transfer from the domestic product divisions and the international operations would be improved.

However, both *Business International* researchers and Professors Davidson and Haspeslagh found that frequently the change to a worldwide product organization actually *reduces* the firm's international commitment.† Instead of investing in overseas production facilities, a number of companies have turned to licensing. Apparently, product division managers, the majority of whom have come from domestic operations, tend to be overly cautious with respect to overseas business, with which they are less familiar. Furthermore, they usually focus their attention on the segment that provides the greatest share of the company's income, which in most instances is domestic business. Under the product division organization, there is no international division head to discuss this part of the company's business directly with top management, nor is there a special-

*"New Study Finds World Product Structure Hurts Worldwide Performance," *Business International*, August 6, 1982, pp. 249–50.
†"New Directions in Multinational Corporate Organization," New York: *Business International*, 1981; and W. H. Davidson and Philippe Haspeslagh, "Shaping a Global Product Organization," *Harvard Business Review*, July–August 1982, pp. 125–32.

ized international support staff to plan and execute international business strategy.

Assume that you are the company president. You are aware of these difficulties that seem to be the reasons why your company is not doing as well in overseas markets as you believe it should. What changes in the organizational structure should you make to turn this situation around?

Supplementary Readings

Bartlett, Christopher A. "MNCs: Get Off the Reorganization Merry-Go-Round." *Harvard Business Review*, March–April 1983, pp. 138–46.

Berkman, Harold W., and Ivan R. Vernon. *Contemporary Perspectives in International Business*. Skokie, Ill.: Rand McNally, 1979.

Brooke, Michael Z., and Mark van Beusekom. *International Corporate Planning*. London: Pitman Publishing, 1979.

Competitive Strategies for Europe. Geneva: Business International, 1983.

Davidson, William H. *Global Strategic Management*. New York: Ronald Press, 1982.

Davis, Stanley M. *Managing and Organizing Multinational Corporations*. New York: Pergamon Press, 1979.

Fayerweather, John. *International Business Strategy and Administration*. Cambridge, Mass.: Ballinger Publishing, 1978.

Galbraith, Jay R., and Robert K. Kazanjian. *Strategy Implementation: Structure, Systems, and Process*. St. Paul, Minn.: West Publishing, 1986.

Grub, Phillip D.; Fariborz Ghada; and Dara Khambata, eds. *The Multinational Enterprise in Transition*. 2nd ed. Princeton, N.J.: Darwin Press, 1984.

Henzler, Herbert, and Wilhelm Rall. "Facing Up to the Global Challenge." *McKinsey Quarterly*, Winter 1986, pp. 52–68.

Leontiades, James C. *Multinational Corporate Strategy*. Lexington, Mass.: Lexington Books, 1985.

O'Connor, Rochelle. *Facing Strategic Issues: New Planning Guides and Practices*. New York: Conference Board, 1985.

Ohmae, Kenichi. "Why Companies Must Organize in the Age of Global Products." *International Management*, September 1985, p. 117.

Pitts, Robert A., and John D. Daniels. "Aftermath of the Matrix Mania." *Columbia Journal of World Business*, Summer 1984, pp. 48–54.

Roman, Daniel D., and Joseph F. Puett, Jr. *International Business and Technological Innovation*. New York: Elsevier Science Publishing, 1983.

Schooler, Robert D. *An Introduction to International Business*. Columbia, Mo.: Lucas Brothers, 1979.

Vernon, Raymond, and Louis T. Wells, Jr. *Manager in the International Economy*. 4th ed. Englewood Cliffs, N.J.: Prentice-Hall, 1981.

Endnotes

1. Rorer Group, 1985 *Annual Report*, p. 2.
2. *General Motors Public Interest Report, 1979*, pp. 2–4.
3. "Roger Smith's Campaign to Change the GM Culture," *Business Week*, April 7, 1986, p. 85.
4. *General Motors Public Interest Report*, 1979, pp. 2–4.
5. ITT, 1978 *Annual Report*, p. 3.
6. Pfizer, 1986 *Annual Report*, p. 1. Note that although this is a quantitative goal, Pfizer calls it an objective. In practice, these terms are often used interchangeably, as are the terms *mission* and *purpose*.
7. R. J. Reynolds, 1985 *Annual Report*, p. 2.
8. J. Tylee Wilson, "Strategic Planning at R. J. Reynolds Industries," *Journal of Business Strategy*, Spring 1985, p. 28.
9. Remarks by D. L. Guertin, senior planning advisor, Exxon Corporation, at Houston, Texas, October 4, 1977.
10. *The Business Environment Risk Index* in Long Beach, California, maintains a permanent panel of experts who periodically rate nations according to 15 factors, including political stability, attitude toward foreign investment, and currency convertibility. Business International's *Country Ratings* rate 57 countries on 34 factors divided into the four categories of (1) political, legal, and social factors; (2) economic criteria; (3) monetary and financial factors; and (4) energy vulnerability. The *New World Political Risk Forecasts* from Frost & Sullivan in New York follow political events in 60 countries and estimate the probability that a major loss will be sustained where new or continued investment is contemplated. The forecasts also provide probability estimates for (1) regime change, (2) political turmoil, (3) expropriation, and (4) restrictions on the repatriation of capital and dividends.
11. Dow Chemical *Annual Report*, 1978, p. 2.
12. Kenichi Ohmae, "Foresight in Strategic Planning," *The McKinsey Quarterly*, Autumn 1982, p. 18.
13. *Planning for Profits* (New York: Business International, 1967), p. 15.
14. Bottom-up planning is the almost invariable method used by Japanese managements because they strive for a consensus at every level.
15. "Would You Make a Drama out of a Crisis?" *International Management*, June 1985, p. 8.
16. R. L. Trewatha and M. Gene Newport, *Management Functions and Behavior* (Plano, Tex.: Business Publications, 1979), p. 139.
17. *"Corporate Planning, " Weekly Bulletin* (Brussels: Kredietbank), June 18, 1982, p. 3.
18. Rochelle O'Connor, *Facing Strategic Issues: New Planning Guides and Practices* (New York: The Conference Board, 1985), p. 5.
19. John Argenti, "How to Survive Your Corporate Plan," *International Management*, June 1982, p. 35.
20. "The New Breed of Strategic Planner," *Business Week*, September 17, 1984, p. 62.
21. Ibid. p. 62.
22. Ibid. p. 64.
23. P. W. Beck, "Corporate Planning for an Uncertain Future," *Long Range Planning*, August 1982, p. 14.
24. "New Breed of Strategic Planner," p. 66.
25. Beck, "Corporate Planning for an Uncertain Future," p. 17.

26. Frederick W. Gluck, "A Fresh Look at Strategic Management," *Journal of Business Strategy,* Fall 1985, p. 6.

27. M. G. Duerr and J. M. Roach, *Organization and Control of International Operations* (New York: Conference Board, 1973), p. 39. Several MNEs gave us the same reason when we contacted them in preparation for this edition in 1987.

28. Howard V. Permutter, "Social Architectural Problems of the Multinational Firm," *Quarterly Journal of AISEC International,* August 1967, pp. 33–34.

29. Bristol-Myers, 1974 *Annual Report,* pp. 26–29.

30. *New Directions in Multinational Corporate Organizations* (New York: Business International, 1981); and William H. Davidson and Philippe Haspeslagh, "Shaping a Global Product Organization," *Harvard Business Review,* July–August 1982, pp. 125–32.

31. "Management Techniques in a Changing Environment," *Business International,* January 14, 1983, pp. 9–10.

32. *Designing the International Corporate Organization* (New York: Business International, 1976), pp. 52–55.

33. J. M. Ivancevich, J. H. Donnelly, Jr., and J. L. Gibson, *Managing for Performance* (Plano, Tex.: Business Publications, 1980), p. 163.

34. Duerr and Roach, *Organization and Control of International Operations,* pp. 93–94.

35. "Using SBUs Globally," *Business International,* August 21, 1981, pp. 265–67.

36. "Corporate Organization: Where in the World Is It Going?" *Business International,* August 15, 1980, p. 257–58.

37. P. F. Drucker, "New Templates for Today's Organization," *Harvard Business Review,* January-February 1974, p. 51.

38. "The Human Dimension in the March toward Globalism," *Business International,* January 13, 1986, p. 12.

CHAPTER 22

CONTROL AND STAFFING

"There's no great difference in managing a small or large company. In both cases, it's simply a matter of having more money at the end of the day than when you started in the morning."

Rune Andresson, managing director of Trelleborg A.B., quoted in *Sydsvenska Dagbladet*

"How does it work out when there is a woman manager in the family? There is no solution because there is no problem in Japan. Management is for men only."

William A. Cohen in a review of Mitsuyuki Masatsugu, *The Modern Samurai Society*

"As I saw it, here was a sector of the economy crying out for the application of good management skills."

Sydney Biddle Barrows, descendant of the *Mayflower* pilgrims, describing her decision to create and manage a profitable New York call girl network, quoted in the *London Standard*

798

"As a general matter, we [Americans] pride ourselves on our pioneering traditions. But outside the publicly funded defense area, we underinvest in research and development. Some high-priced managers seem to spend less time developing R&D budgets than they spend reviewing golf scores."

Richard G. Darman, deputy secretary of the U.S. Treasury, commenting on American management in a speech to the Japan Society of New York

Learning Objectives

After you study this chapter, you should know:

1. The reasons companies use controls.

2. Where decisions are made in a multinational—which may be at the headquarters of the multinational, at the subsidiaries' offices, or cooperatively by the parent and subsidiary companies—and some reasons why certain decisions are made where they are.

3. The methods used to try to control subsidiary companies less than 100 percent owned and joint venture partners when they are entirely independent organizations.

4. The importance of timely, accurate, and complete reports from subsidiaries and joint venture partners on a variety of subjects.

5. The danger that too many reports can result in an information glut and confusion unless they are organized, coded, and computerized.

6. The difficulties of finding qualified executives for multinational companies.

7. Comparisons of home country, host country, and third-country nationals as employees.

8. Advances in international business training at American business schools thanks to efforts by the Academy of International Business and the American Assembly of Collegiate Schools of Business.

799

9. Some of the complications of creating compensation packages for expatriate employees which permit them and their families to maintain their living standards abroad and reimburse them for hardships and inconveniences without overcompensating them.

Key Words and Concepts

Subsidiary detriment for the greater benefit of the MNE
Reporting (by subsidiaries and joint venture partners)
Information glut
Base salary plus percentages
Allowances such as housing, cost of living or tax differentials, schooling and moving
Bonuses such as overseas premium, home leave and contract termination payments
International status
Expatriate

Business Incident

One American company invested large amounts of money in Brazilian production facilities during the mid-1960s. That was after the 1959 formation of the 11-country Latin American Free Trade Association (LAFTA), of which Brazil was a member, and enthusiasm was high as LAFTA made promising early strides, such as the formulation of a common customs code. It appeared to the company's headquarters management that the already promising Brazilian market would now be enlarged to include the approximately 300 million people in all 11 countries from the southern tip of South America north to the Mexico-U.S. border.

The investments were completed before the 1974 petroleum price increases imposed by OPEC. Brazil, which was reducing its inflation rate, was required by those price increases to pay much more for its energy because Brazil was a large petroleum importer, and inflation turned back up as the higher energy costs flowed through production into prices. The Brazilian cruzeiro weakened against the U.S. dollar, and the Brazilian government limited repatriation of profits, royalties, and other payments to foreigners.

An excellent management team had been sent from the United States to Brazil to oversee the investment and the resulting product production and sales. Their compensation packages and management performance criteria were established before the executives left the United States and were based on the optimistic events and forecasts existing during the mid-1960s.

What actually happened was that LAFTA accomplished so little that it expired in 1980. The immense new markets for the Brazilian plants did not materialize. The promising drop in the Brazilian inflation rate, which would have made Brazilian products more competitive in export, was reversed.

None of these events was the fault of the American management team. In the minds of most outside observers, the members of this team did very good jobs of coping with the circumstances they encountered, which differed radically from those expected by them or by the home company managers who recruited them into the Brazilian jobs. Nevertheless, their compensation and their performance standards were not changed, and they suffered in terms of living standards—Brazilian inflation was much worse than anticipated—and performance evaluations. Their evaluations were compared with the evaluations of managers in countries for which headquarters' forecasts were more accurate, and their performance looked bad by comparison.

Fortunately for these managers, observers at other companies recognized their abilities. They all left the company with which they came to Brazil and took positions with other companies.

Personal conversations with authors.

*T*he planning that is the necessary foundation for all aspects of any successful business was dealt with in the preceding chapter. The control activities of which we shall speak here are the efforts to (1) put the plans in effect, (2) learn whether the plans are working as intended (they rarely do), and (3) make whatever corrections seem called for and practicable.

In Chapter 20, we discussed labor relations policies and practices of a multinational enterprise (MNE) with regard to the workers and their supervisors in the operation. In order to complete the picture, we must examine MNE policies and practices covering executive and technical personnel.

The Business Incident illustrates some problems with those policies and practices. The American parent company made forecasts based on the best information available at the time—the planning process—and based compensation and measurement standards on those forecasts. The forecasts proved incorrect through no fault of the company or the executives it sent to Brazil, but the company failed to alter its plans and standards in the face of the new realities. As a result, the executives got lower performance evaluations than they deserved and less compensation than they expected and the company lost some good managers.

Those unfortunate results could have been avoided if the parent company had utilized an effective set of controls.

Control

Every successful company uses controls to put its plans into effect, to evaluate their effectiveness, to make desirable corrections, and to evaluate and reward or correct executive performance. Matters are more complicated for an MNE than for a one-country operation. In earlier chapters, we have brought out the complicating causes. They include different languages, cultures, and attitudes; different taxes and accounting methods; different currencies, labor costs, and market sizes; different degrees of political stability and security for personnel and property; and many more. For these reasons, multinational companies need controls even more than do domestic ones.

Subsidiaries; 100 Percent Owned

The words *subsidiaries* and *affiliates* are used interchangeably, and we shall examine first the control of those in which the parent has 100 percent ownership. This avoids for now the additional complications of joint ventures or subsidiaries in which the parent has less than 100 percent ownership. We shall deal with them later in the chapter.

Where Are Decisions Made?

There are three possibilities. Two of them are that all decisions are made at either the MNE headquarters or at the subsidiary level. Theoretically, all decisions could be made at one or the other location. As common sense would indicate, they are not; instead, some decisions are made at one place, some are made at the other place, and some are made cooperatively.[1] There are many variables to determine which decision is made where. Some of the more significant variables are: (1) product and equipment, (2) the competence of subsidiary management and reliance on that management by the multinational headquarters, (3) the size of the MNE and how long it has been an MNE, (4) the detriment of a subsidiary for the benefit of the enterprise, and (5) subsidiary frustration.

Product and Equipment

As to decision location, questions of standardization of product and equipment and second markets can be important.

Standardize? An easily made argument is that the product and the equipment with which to make it should be tailored to fit each national market. The other side is that overall enterprise gains from worldwide uniformity may more than compensate for individual country losses. Standardization of equipment may result in lower purchasing costs of the equipment as well as savings in equipment operation training, maintenance, and spare parts.[2]

As to the product, uniformity gives greater flexibility in its sourcing. For example, if the product is made in two or more countries and difficulties such as strikes, natural disasters, political upheavals, or currency problems affect one country, the product can be delivered from the other.

In determining whether equipment and product should be standardized worldwide or tailored to different national markets, a multinational should gather opinion from each affected subsidiary. If any subsidiary can demonstrate that the profit potential that can be realized from tailoring to its own market is greater than the profit potential that the enterprise will realize from standardization, the subsidiary should be permitted to proceed. Elements of profit potential would include the size of the subsidiary's market, the competition there, and the possibilities for exporting to areas with similar characteristics. Of course, the decision in such a case is cooperative in that the parent has the power to veto or override its subsidiary's decisions.

Second Markets. A product may be introduced by the MNE in its largest market, and by the time that product is offered in smaller markets, it may have been adapted to eliminate "bugs" or improve performance. The MNE would want to assure that the mistakes already discovered and corrected would not be repeated in later markets.[3] Even though some subsidiaries may wish to alter the product, second-market situations would indicate MNE central decision making. Such decision making would be necessary to assure uniformity of quality and performance as well as market timing and product improvement.

Competence of Subsidiary Management and Reliance on Subsidiary Management by MNE Headquarters

Reliance on subsidiary management can depend on how well the executives know one another and how well they know company policies, on whether headquarters management feels that it understands host country conditions, on the distances between the home country and the host countries, and on how big and old the parent company is.

Move the Executives Around. Some MNEs have a policy of transferring promising-looking management personnel between MNE headquarters and subsidiaries and among subsidiaries. Thus, the manager learns firsthand the policies of headquarters and the problems of putting those policies into effect at subsidiary levels.[4]

A result of such transfers, which is difficult to measure but is nevertheless important, is a network of intra-MNE personal relationships. This tends to increase the confidence of executives in one another and to make communication among executives easier and less subject to error.[5]

Another development is that some MNEs have moved their regional executives into headquarters. The reasons are to improve communications and reduce cost.[6]

Does MNE Headquarters Understand Host Country Conditions? One element in the degree of headquarters reliance on subsidiary management is the familiarity of headquarters with conditions in the subsidiary's host country. The less familiar, the more different conditions in the host country are perceived to be, the more likely headquarters is to rely on subsidiary management.

How Far Away Is the Host Country? Another element in the degree of headquarters reliance on subsidiary management is the distance of the host country from MNE headquarters. Thus, an American parent is likely to place more reliance on the management of an Indonesian subsidiary than on the management of a Canadian subsidiary. This would be for both reasons. Management conditions in Canada would be perceived by American management as more easily understood than conditions in Indonesia, and Indonesia is much farther from the United States than Canada is.[7]

Size of the MNE and How Long It Has Been One

As a rule, a large company can afford to hire more specialists, experts, and experienced executives than can a smaller one. The longer a company has been an MNE, the more likely it is to have a number of experienced executives who know company policies and who have worked at headquarters and in the field. Successful experience builds confidence.

In most MNEs, the top positions are at headquarters, and the ablest and most persistent executives get there in time. Thus, over time, headquarters of a successful multinational is run by experienced executives who are confident of their knowledge of the business in the home and host countries and in combinations thereof.

It follows that in the larger, older MNEs more decisions are made at headquarters and fewer are delegated to subsidiaries. The smaller company, in business for a shorter period of time, tends to be able to afford fewer internationally experienced executives and will not have had time to develop them internally. The smaller, newer company has no choice but to delegate decisions to subsidiary management.[8]

The generality that the larger, older MNEs delegate fewer decisions is subject to exceptions, and there seems to come a point in growth where the centralization trend reverses. Studies by Robbins and Stobaugh show that as MNEs become very large and complex, a tendency to decentralize appears. There come to be too many decisions for headquarters to deal with each one. At that point, the companies develop policies and guidelines for the subsidiaries. Headquarters reserves decision authority only for the most important matters and establishes processes to monitor the others.[9]

Decisions That May Benefit the Enterprise to the Detriment of a Subsidiary

An MNE has opportunities to source raw materials and components, locate factories, allocate orders, and govern intraenterprise pricing that are not available to a non-MNE. Such activities may be beneficial to the enterprise yet result in **subsidiary detriments.**

Move Production Factors. For any number of reasons, an MNE may decide to move factors of production from one country to another or to expand in one country in preference to another. Tax, labor, market, currency, or political stability are a few possible reasons.

The subsidiary from which factors are being taken would be unenthusiastic. Its management would be slow, at best, to cut the company's capacity. Such decisions would be made by headquarters.

Which Subsidiary Gets the Order? Similarly, if an order, say from an Argentine customer, could be filled from a subsidiary in France or another in South Africa or a third in Brazil, MNE headquarters might decide which subsidiary gets the business. Among the considerations in the decision would be transportation costs, production costs, comparative tariff rates, customer's currency restrictions, comparative order backlogs, and taxes. One reason for having such a decision made by MNE headquarters is that this would avoid price competition among members of the same multinational.

Multicountry Production. Frequently, the size of the market in a single country is too small to permit economies of scale in manufacturing an entire industrial product for that one market. An example is Ford's production of a light vehicle for the Asian market.

In that situation, Ford negotiated with several countries to the end that one country would make one component of the vehicle for all of the countries involved. Thus, one country makes the engine, a second country has the body stamping plant, a third country makes the transmission, and so forth. In this fashion, each operation achieves the efficiency and cost savings of economies of scale.[10] Of course, this kind of multinational production demands a high degree of MNE headquarters control and coordination.

Which Subsidiary Books the Profit? In certain circumstances, a multinational may have some choice of two or more countries in which to declare profits. Such circumstances may arise where two or more units of the MNE cooperate in supplying components or services under a contract with a customer unrelated to any part of the multinational. Under these conditions, there may be opportunities to allocate higher prices to one unit or subsidiary and lower prices to another within the global price to the customer.

If the host country of one of the subsidiaries has lower taxes than the other host countries, it would be natural to try and maximize profits in the lower-tax country and minimize them in the higher-tax country. Other differences between host countries could dictate the allocation of profit to or from the subsidiaries located there. Such differences could include currency controls, labor relations, political climate, or social unrest, and it is sensible to direct or allocate as much profit as reasonably possible to subsidiaries in countries with the least currency controls, the best labor relations and political climate, and the least social unrest.

The intraenterprise transaction may also give a company choices of profit location. Pricing between members of the same enterprise is referred to as transfer pricing, and while MNE headquarters could permit undirected, arm's-length negotiations between itself and its subsidiaries, that might not yield the most advantageous results for the enterprise as a whole.[11]

Price and profit allocation decisions such as these are usually best made at parent company headquarters, which is supposed to maintain the overall view, looking out for the best interests of the enterprise.[12] Naturally, decisions to accept lower profits are not ones gladly made by subsidiary management, largely because its evaluation may suffer. We shall discuss managment evaluation further on in this chapter.

An illustration of how the enterprise might profit even though one subsidiary makes less is given in the following two tables. Assume a cooperative contract by which two subsidiaries of an MNE are selling an outside customer products and services for a contract price of $100 million. The host country of MNE Alpha levies company income taxes at the rate of 50 percent, whereas MNE Beta's host country taxes its income at 20 percent. The customer is in a third country, has agreed to pay $100 million, and is indifferent how Alpha and Beta share the money. The first table below shows the multinational's after-tax income if Alpha is paid $60 million and Beta $40 million.

	Receives (in $ millions)	Tax (in $ millions)	After Tax (in $ millions)
Alpha	$60	$30	$30
Beta	40	8	32
			$62

Thus, after tax, the enterprise realizes $62 million.

The second table shows the multinational's after-tax income if Alpha is paid $40 million and Beta $60 million.

	Receives (in $ millions)	Tax (in $ millions)	After Tax (in $ millions)
Alpha	$40	$20	$20
Beta	60	12	48
			$68

Thus, after tax, the enterprise realizes $68 million.

These simple examples illustrate that the MNE would be $6 million better off if it could shift $20 million of the payment from Alpha to Beta, while the customer is no worse off, as it pays $100 million in either case. Alpha, having received $20 million less payment is $10 million worse off after taxes, but Beta is $16 million better off and the enterprise is $6 million ahead on the same contract. Given the number of countries and tax laws in the world, there are countless combinations of how such savings can be accomplished. Financial management awareness and control are the keys.

We do not mean to leave the impression that the host or home governments are unaware of or indifferent to transfer pricing and profit allocating by MNEs operating within their borders. The MNE must expect questioning by host and home governments and must be prepared to demonstrate that prices or allocations are "reasonable." This may be done by showing that other companies charge comparable prices for the same or similar items or, if there are no similar items, by showing that costs plus profit have been used reasonably to arrive at the price. As to allocation of profits, the MNE in our example would try to prove that the volume or importance of the work done by MNE Beta or the responsibilities assumed by Beta, such as financing, after-sales service, or warranty obligations, justify the higher amount being paid to Beta. Of course, the questioning in this instance would come from the host government of MNE Alpha if it got wind of the possibility of more taxable income for MNE Beta and less for itself.

Subsidiary Frustration

An extremely important consideration for MNE management is that the management of its subsidiaries be motivated and loyal. If all the big decisions are made, or are perceived to be made, at the MNE headquarters, the managers of subsidiaries will lose incentive and will lose prestige or face with their employees and the community.[13] They may grow hostile and disloyal.

Therefore, even though there may be reasons for headquarters to make decisions, it should delegate as much as reasonably possible. Management of each subsidiary should be kept thoroughly informed and should be consulted seriously about decisions, negotiations, and developments in its geographic area.

Joint Ventures and Subsidiaries Less than 100 Percent Owned

A joint venture may be, as defined in Chapter 2, a corporate entity between an MNE and local owners or a corporate entity between two or more MNEs that are foreign to the area where the joint venture is located, or it may involve one company working on a project of limited duration (constructing a dam, for example) in cooperation with one or more other companies. The other companies may be subsidiaries or affiliates, but they may also be entirely independent entities.

All the reasons for making decisions at MNE headquarters or at subsidiary headquarters or cooperatively apply equally in joint venture situations. However, headquarters will almost never have as much freedom of action and flexibility in a joint venture as it has with subsidiaries that are 100 percent owned.

Loss of Freedom and Flexibility

The reasons for that loss of freedom and flexibility are easy to see. If shareholders outside the multinational own control of the affiliate, they can block efforts of MNE headquarters to move production factors away, to fill an export order from another affiliate or subsidiary, and so forth. Even if outside shareholders are a minority and cannot directly control the affiliate, they can bring legal or political pressures on the MNE to prevent it from diminishing the affiliate's profitability for the enterprise's benefit. Likewise, the local partner in a joint venture is highly unlikely to agree with measures that penalize the joint venture for the MNE's benefit.

How the Japanese Do It

Japanese companies used the joint venture method abroad earlier and more extensively than did American or European companies. In attempting to control their joint ventures, the Japanese companies use several devices.

The Japanese partner provides and controls the technology and the management expertise. It furnishes key components and parts for the finished product. It tries to put its Japanese personnel into the important executive positions of the joint venture.[14]

As might be expected, the Japanese have encountered resistance to putting Japanese in the important executive positions from their joint venture partners or from host governments. The natural desire of these partners and governments is that their own nationals have at least equality in the important positions and that they get training and experience in the technology and management.[15]

Reporting

For controls to be effective, all operating units of an MNE must provide headquarters with timely, accurate, and complete reports. There are many uses for the information reported. Among the types of **reporting** required are: (1) financial, (2) technological, (3) market opportunity, and (4) political and economic.

Financial

A surplus of funds in one subsidiary should perhaps be retained there for investment or contingencies. On the other hand, such a surplus might be more useful at the parent company, in which case payment of a dividend is indicated. Or perhaps another subsidiary or affiliate needs capital, and the surplus could be lent or invested there. Obviously, MNE headquarters must know of the existence and size of a surplus in order to determine its best use.

Technological

New technology should be reported. New technology is constantly being developed in different countries, and the subsidiary or affiliated company operating in such a country is likely to learn about it before MNE headquarters hundreds or thousands of miles away. If headquarters finds the new technology potentially valuable, it could gain competitive advantage by being the first to contact the developer for a license to use it.

One study indicates that most reports emphasize financial and market data. Technological information was in third place.[16]

Market Opportunities

The affiliates in various countries may spot new or growing markets for some product of the multinational. This could be profitable all around, as the MNE sells more of the product, while the affiliate earns sales commissions. Of course, if the new market is sufficiently large, the affiliate may begin to assemble or produce the product under license from the parent company or from another affiliate.

Other market-related information which should be reported to MNE headquarters includes competitors' activities, price developments, and new products of potential interest to the MNE group. Also of importance is information on the subsidiary's market share and whether it is growing or shrinking, together with explanations.

Political and Economic

Interestingly, reports on political and economic conditions have not been found to be frequent.[17] This is probably changing as a result of the revolutions, terrorism, coups, and other political unrest of the 1970s and 1980s. For example, the American bank, Citibank, had a representative office in Tehran, Iran, during the 1970s. Even though some government intelligence services were said to be surprised when the Ayatollah Khomeini threw out the shah of Iran in 1979, the Citibank Tehran office had become aware of potential danger as early as the summer of 1978. The office first lowered the ceiling on Iranian loans and then froze any new business, even to existing customers, in the autumn of 1978.[18]

Management Evaluation

One important use of reports is to evaluate and compare management performance in every unit of the multinational. The raw financial figures are not adequate for this, nor do they give a fair, comparative evaluation.

MNE headquarters decisions may have awarded an export order to one subsidiary in preference to a second even though the second might have gotten the order if competition had been permitted. Through no skill or fault of theirs, management of the first subsidiary looks good in comparison with management of the second.

Or in an intraenterprise transaction, a larger profit may be left in a low-tax country and a smaller profit in a high-tax country. This is done for the benefit of the enterprise, and management in the high-tax country should not be penalized in its comparative evaluation because it has been done.[19]

Efforts should be made to factor out of management evaluations conditions that are beyond management control. These conditions include price controls, currency controls, inflation, political upheaval, terrorism, and changes in currency exchange values. The Business Incident at the beginning of this chapter illustrates some of these.

Information Glut

A large multinational, with many, far-flung operating units, could find itself overwhelmed by reports. The solutions suggested for such an **information glut** have included centralized data banks at information centers. Information can be coded as to type and be available on call to management at MNE headquarters and at the subsidiaries.[20]

Staffing

Finding the right people to manage an organization can be difficult under any circumstances, but it is especially difficult to find good managers of overseas operations. In a survey taken of 166 senior-level international executives, more than one third mentioned the shortage of qualified management personnel as an important problem. A computer manufacturer put it this way, "The shortage is so serious that more than anything else, this may slow our expansion in key markets."[21]

The difficulties in finding the right people for foreign management positions stem from the fact that such positions require more and different skills than do purely domestic executive jobs. The right persons need to be bicultural, with knowledge of the business practices in the MNE's home country plus understanding of business practices and customs in the host country. The successful manager of a foreign affiliate must be able to operate efficiently in one culture and to explain operations in that culture to executives in another culture. Such managers exist, and they may be found in (1) the home country, (2) the host country, or (3) a third country.

Sources of Managers

Home Country

Most multinationals utilize citizens of their own countries in many foreign management and technical positions even though at first such personnel are usually not knowledgeable about the host country culture and language. Many such expatriates have adapted, learned the language, and become thoroughly accepted in the host country. Of course, it would not be necessary for a host country citizen to undergo all of that adapting, but for a variety of reasons MNE headquarters frequently needs or wants its own nationals in executive or technical positions abroad.

Host Country Nationals Unavailable. A foreign subsidiary often cannot find suitable host country personnel for management jobs, and in such instances MNE headquarters will send out its people to manage until local personnel can be found and trained. Those are full-time jobs, but there are also circumstances that call for temporary help from headquarters. Labor negotiators, mentioned in Chapter 20, and other specialists may be sent to troubleshoot such problems as product warranty, international contracts, taxes, accounting, or reporting. Teams may be sent from the home country to assist with new plant start-up, and they would probably stay until subsidiary personnel were trained to run and maintain the new facilities.

Training for Headquarters. Another reason for using home country citizens abroad is to broaden their experience in preparation for becoming high-level managers at headquarters. Firms with large parts of their earnings from international sources require top executives who have a worldwide perspective, business and political.[22] It is difficult to impossible to acquire that sort of perspective without living and working abroad for a substantial time.

Headquarters Representatives. There are firms which, although their policy is to employ host country nationals in most positions, want at least one or two home country managers (commonly the general manager or the finance officer) in their foreign subsidiaries. If new technology for the subsidiary is involved, the parent company will probably station at least one of its technologically qualified experts at the subsidiary until its local personnel learn the technology. In this way, the home office can be confident that someone is immediately available to explain headquarters policies and procedures, see that they are observed, and interpret what is happening locally to the MNE management. Positions that an MNE must take or demands that it must make are sometimes not popular with a host government. It can seem unpatriotic for a host country national to do such things, whereas the host government can understand—and sometimes accept— such positions or demands from a foreigner who is a citizen of the parent company's home country.

> One of the authors remembers the relief expressed by the Argentinean executives of an Argentine subsidiary of an American MNE because an American manager was present to press the Argentine government for what seemed to be unusually extensive payment guarantees by the Argentine government. The contract was for a product partly manufactured and assembled in Argentina but mostly manufactured in the United States and imported into Argentina from the United States.

Host Country

When host country nationals are employed, there is no problem of their being unfamiliar with local customs, culture, and language. Furthermore, the first costs of employing them are generally lower (as compared to the costs of employing home country nationals), although considerable training costs are sometimes necessary. If there is a strong feeling of nationalism in the host country, having nationals as managers can make the subsidiary seem less foreign.

The government development plans and laws of some countries demand that employment in all sectors and at all levels reflect the racial composition of the society. In other words, more skilled and managerial slots must be given to the local people. If foreign-owned firms in Indonesia fail to hire enough pribumi (indigenous Indonesians), the firms are likely to encounter difficulties with reentry permits for foreign employees as well as with other government licenses and permits that the firms need. Bribery requests have been known to increase until more pribumi were hired and promoted. Malaysia threatens to revoke the operating licenses of foreign-owned firms that fail to have a satisfactory number of bumiputra (indigenous Malays) in sufficiently elevated jobs.[23]

A disadvantage of hiring local managers is that they are often unfamiliar with the home country of the MNE and with the MNE's policies and practices. Differences in attitudes and values, as discussed in Chapter 8, can cause them to act in ways that surprise or displease headquarters. Also, local managers may create their own upward immobility if, because of strong cultural or family ties, they are reluctant to accept promotions which would require them to leave the country to work at MNE headquarters or at another subsidiary.

A new problem has developed for foreign-owned companies which hire and train local, host country people. The best of these people may be pirated away by local firms or other MNE subsidiaries, as local executive recruiters are constantly on the lookout to make raids.[24]

Finally, there can be a conflict of loyalty between the host country and the employer. For example, the host country national may give preference to a local supplier even though imported products may be less expensive or of better quality. Local managers might oppose headquarters requests to set low transfer prices in order to lower taxes payable to the host government.

Third Country

The disadvantages that are often encountered when using employees from the home or host countries can sometimes be avoided by sending nationals from a third country to fill management posts. A Chilean going to Argentina would have little cultural or language difficulty, but MNE headquarters should be careful not to rely too heavily on similarities in language as a guide to similarities in other aspects of the cultures. Mexicans, for example, would have to make considerable adjustments if they were transferred to Argentina, and they would find a move to Spain even more difficult. This is because the Mexican culture is far less European than that of either Argentina or Chile. While the latter two cultures are certainly not identical, they do have many similarities. A fair generalization is that after an executive has adapted once to a new culture and language, a second or succeeding adaptation is easier.

An MNE should not count on cost savings in using third-country nationals. Although they may come from countries where salary scales are lower, in such countries as Brazil and most of the nations of northwestern Europe, salaries may be higher than American companies are paying at comparable position levels. Furthermore, many multinationals give international status* to both home country nationals and third-country nationals, who then receive the same perquisites and compensation packages for the same job.

---

*International status is discussed later in this chapter.

Selection and Training

The selection and training of managers varies somewhat depending on whether the candidate is from the home country, the host country, or a third country.

Home Country

Relatively few recent college graduates are hired for the express purpose of being sent overseas. Usually they spend a number of years in the domestic (parent) company, and they may get into the company's international operations either by design and persistence or by luck or frequently by a combination. Those who make it into the international side may be assigned to the firm's international division, where they handle problems submitted by foreign affiliates and meet overseas personnel who are visiting MNE headquarters.

If it seems likely to the company that it will be sending home country employees abroad, the company frequently encourages those employees to study the language and culture of the country to which it expects to send them.[25] Such employees will probably be sent on short trips abroad to handle special assignments and to be exposed to foreign surroundings. Newly hired home country nationals with prior overseas experience may undergo similar but shorter training periods.

It is increasingly possible for American MNEs to supplement their in-house training for overseas work with courses in American business schools. In recognition of the growing importance of international business, those schools are expanding the number and scope of international business courses. The business schools have been urged in this direction by their accrediting organization, the American Assembly of Collegiate Schools of Business, and great credit is due to the Academy of International Business for its efforts and those of its members in this movement. In addition, a number of university-level business schools are now operating in other countries.[26]

One large problem which has plagued MNEs is caused by the families of executives transferred overseas. Even though the employee may adapt to and enjoy the foreign experience, the family may not, and an unhappy family may sour the employee on the job and split up the marriage. In either event, the company may have to ship the family back home at great expense—seldom less than $25,000. Consequently, many companies try to assess whether the executive's family can adapt to the foreign ambience before the executive is assigned abroad.

Host Country

The same general criteria for selecting home country employees apply to host country nationals. Usually, however, the training of host country nationals will differ from that of home country nationals as host country nationals generally lack knowledge of advanced business techniques and of the company.

Host Country Nationals Hired in the Home Country. Many multinationals try to solve the business technique problem by hiring host country students upon their graduation from home country business schools. After they have been hired, these new employees are usually sent to MNE headquarters to receive indoctrination in the firm's policies and procedures as well as on-the-job training in a specific function, such as finance, marketing, or production.

Host Country Nationals Hired in the Host Country. Because the number of host country citizens being graduated from home country universities is limited, multinationals must also recruit locally for their management positions. To impart knowledge of business technique, the MNE may do one or more things. It may set up in-house training programs in the host country subsidiary, or it may utilize business courses in the host country's universities.The MNE may also send new employees to home country business schools or to parent company training programs. In addition, employees who show promise will be sent repeatedly to the parent company headquarters and divisions and to other subsidiaries in order to observe the various enterprise operations and to meet personally the other executives with whom they will be communicating during their careers. Such visits are also learning experiences for the home office and the other subsidiaries.

Third Country

Often there are advantages in hiring personnel who are citizens of neither the home country nor the host country. Third-country nationals may accept lower wages and benefits than will employees from the home country, and they may come from a culture similar to that of the host country. In addition, they may have worked for another unit of the MNE and thus be familiar with its policies, procedures, and people.

The use of third-country nationals has become particularly prevalent in the LDCs because of shortages of literate, not to mention skilled, locals. It can be an advantage to get someone already residing in the country inasmuch as such an individual already has necessary work permits as well as knowledge of local languages and customs.

Host Country Attitudes. If the host government is emphasizing employment of its own citizens, third-country nationals will be no more welcome than home country people. Actually, third-country nationals could face an additional obstacle in obtaining necessary work permits; the host government can understand that the parent company of, say, a German MNE would want some German executives to look after its interests in the host country. It may be harder to convince the government that a third-country native is any better for the parent than a local executive would be.

Generalizations Difficult. We must be careful with generalizations about third-country personnel, partly because people achieve that status in different ways. They may be foreigners hired in the home country and sent to a host country subsidiary either because they have had previous experience there or because that country's culture is similar to their own. Third-country nationals may have originally been home country personnel who were sent abroad and became dissatisfied with the job but not with the host country. After leaving the MNE that sent them abroad, they take positions with subsidiaries of multinationals from different home countries. For example, some of the American executives in Brazil who are the subjects of the Business Incident at the beginning of this chapter left the American MNE that sent them to Brazil and went to work for the Brazilian subsidiary of a German company. They became third-country nationals. Another way in which third-country nationals can be created is by promotion within an MNE. For instance, if a Spanish executive of the Spanish subsidiary of an Italian multinational is promoted to be general manager of the Italian firm's Colombian subsidiary, the Spanish executive is then a third-country national.

As multinationals increasingly take the geocentric view toward promoting according to ability and not nationality, we can be certain to see greater use of third-country nationals. This development will be accelerated as more and more executives of all nationalities gain experience outside their native lands. Another, and growing, source for third-country nationals is the heterogeneous body of international agencies. As indicated in Chapter 4, these agencies deal with virtually every field of human endeavor, and all member countries send their nationals as representatives to the headquarters and branch office cities all over the world. Many of those people become available to or can be hired away by multinational companies.

Selection Do's and Don'ts

Executives who should know better sometimes assume that all nationalities work within a framework of common cultures and business practices. Instant communication of information, supersonic travel and the emergence of international financial institutions have created a global economy.

Yet, this economic interdependence does not translate into a common "business culture." Business standards and practices reflect the cultures in which they are rooted. Their nuances vary widely by continent, by country, and even by region.

An executive with no cross-cultural experience can, regardless of other professional credentials, unwittingly wreak havoc with corporate plans abroad. The ability of a company to succeed in another country rests heavily on the managers' abilities to function in that country's culture. An executive search firm has drawn up a checklist of do's and don'ts in selecting executives for foreign operations.

Do promote from within. All other things being equal, selecting a known employee reduces risk. The employee knows the company, and the company knows the employee's strengths and weaknesses. The weaknesses of a new person may not be evident at first.

Don't promote an insider if the outsider is clearly better qualified. "John's been doing a good job in New York, and he's always liked London" is not good enough. It can be a costly approach.

Don't be blinded by language fluency. Just because a candidate is fluent in the host country's language does not mean that's the best person for the job. Unless your business is the local Berlitz franchise, the candidate must have the requisite technical and managerial skills.

Do assess the total person. Functional skills, language proficiency, and knowledge of the international business environment are all important. With regard to international business savvy, third-country nationals are sometimes better qualified than people born in the host country who have not lived and worked abroad. It has been noted that Scandinavians, Dutch, and Swiss are disproportionately represented in international business management positions. They come from small countries with limited markets, so their education and business experience have been geared to the outside world. As a group, these executives have an outlook that is more cosmopolitan than nationalistic.[27]

Resumes Can Mislead

The résumés of most job applicants are probably reasonably accurate, although people are taught how to put their best foot forward and present themselves in the best light. Sometimes that light distorts reality.

The case of Friedrich von Braun was reported by the press in 1986. He was the managing director of Commodity Fundsters, a British company that was in financial difficulty.

Von Braun said that his claim to be the third son of a German baron was based on tales his mother had told him. He could not explain why he was brought up in Warrington, England, and was known to the locals as Fred.

His claims to have been educated at Eton were based on a one-day trip to Windsor in the summer of 1955; he said that he had learned a lot about history at that time. He did spend two weeks at Oxford—in a squat on the Iffley Road.

As for his listed hobbies (opera and observing art), he admitted that his work had allowed him no time for either in the past 18 years.

He worked, not for the famous banking firm Morgan Stanley, as listed in his résumé, but for Stanley Morgan, a Welsh farmer. His "brilliant" banking career was not with the American bank First Interstate but with a Panamanian financial company known to its liquidators as First Into Straits.

Von Braun said that his career details were misleading because of some "insignificant" typographical errors. He maintained that the mistakes were irrelevant to his ability to look after the interests of "wise" investors who entrusted their money to him.

People's Republic of China Different

An American banker sitting in his cramped hotel office in Peking said, "Foreigners coming to China had better be prepared for the bleakness of Chinese life." China is an especially tough assignment for Western managers; for one thing, Western-style housing is unavailable, so most Western managers must spend their entire stays in a hotel room.

A study was made of the assets that a Westerner needed to succeed in China. Knowledge of Chinese business customs, negotiating style, and social practices was ranked as most important but not much more so than Chinese language, politics, and culture.

One manager quoted in the study remarked on "a general sense of uncertainty" in his business dealings. He noted the "vagueness of the Chinese system. You think something will be a problem, and it's not, and vice versa." Another stressed that Westerners in China should understand that despite the recent economic reforms, "communism and the bureaucratic system are number one."[28]

Compensation

Establishing a compensation plan which is equitable, consistent, and yet does not overcompensate the overseas executive is a challenging, complex task. The method favored by the majority of American multinationals has been to pay a base salary equal to that paid to a domestic counterpart and then, in the belief that no one should be worse off for accepting foreign employment, to add a variety of allowances and bonuses.

Salaries

The practice of paying home country nationals the same salaries as their domestic counterparts are paid permits worldwide consistency for this part of the compensation package. Because of the increasing use of third-country nationals, those personnel are generally treated in the same way.

Some firms carry the equal pay for equal work concept one step further and pay the same base salaries to host-country nationals. In countries that legislate yearly bonuses and family allowances for their citizens, a local national may receive what appears to be a higher salary than is paid the expatriate, although companies usually make extra payments to prevent expatriates from falling behind in this regard. In Great Britain, it is the practice to pay executives relatively lower salaries and to provide them with expensive perquisites such as chauffeured automobiles, housing, or club memberships. A number of American MNEs follow British practices in compensating their executives working in Britain.

Allowances

Allowances are extra payments made to compensate expatriates for the extra overseas costs that they must incur in order to live as well abroad as they did in

Table 22–1

Housing Costs in Several Cities That House Large Numbers of Expatriates (monthly rent for a midrange, five- or six-room unfurnished apartment in a good residential area)

New York	$2,800
Tokyo	3,600
Hong Kong	2,500
Singapore	1,100
Jeddah	3,300
Lagos	2,600
Abu Dhabi	1,200
Buenos Aires	2,000
Rio de Janeiro	1,000
Paris	1,400
London	1,300
Frankfurt	800
Brussels	500

Source: *Executive Living Costs in Major Cities Worldwide* (New York: Business International), as reported by *Business International,* May 12, 1986, p. 151.

the home country. The most common allowances are housing, cost-of-living, tax differentials, education, and moving.

Housing Allowances. Housing allowances are designed to permit executives to live in houses as good as those they had at home. Typically, the firm will pay all of the rent that is in excess of 15 percent of the executive's salary. (See Table 22–1.)

Cost-of-Living Allowances. Cost-of-living allowances are based on the differences in the prices paid for food, utilities, transportation, entertainment, clothing, personal services, and medical expenses overseas as compared to the prices paid for these items in the headquarters city. Many MNEs use the U.S. Department of State index, which is based on the cost of these items in Washington, D.C., but have found that it is not altogether satisfactory. For one thing, critics claim that this index is not adjusted often enough to account for either the rapid inflation in some countries or the changes in relative currency values. Another objection is that the index does not include many cities in which the firm operates. As a result, many companies take their own surveys or use data from the United Nations, the World Bank, the International Monetary Fund, or private consulting firms. Figures and comparisons on costs of living, prices, and wages can also be found in private publications. (See Table 22–2.)

Allowances for Tax Differentials. MNEs pay tax differentials when the host country taxes are higher than the taxes that the expatriates would pay on the same base salary at home. The objective is to assure that expatriates will not have less after-tax take-home pay in the host country than they would at home. This can create a considerable extra financial burden on an American parent company because, among other things, the U.S. Internal Revenue Code treats tax allowances as additional taxable income. There are other tax disincentives for Americans to work abroad.*

Education Allowances. Expatriates are naturally concerned that their children receive educations at least equal to those they would get in their home countries, and many want their children taught in their native language. Primary and secondary schools with teachers from most industrialized home countries are available in many cities around the world, but these are private schools and therefore charge tuition. Multinationals either pay the tuition or, if there are enough expatriate children, will operate their own schools. For decades, petroleum companies in the Mideast and in Venezuela have maintained schools for their employees' children.

Moving and Orientation Allowances. Companies generally pay the total costs of transferring their employees overseas. These include transportation for the family, moving household effects, and maintaining the family in a hotel on a full expense account until the household effects arrive. Some firms find it less expensive to send the household effects by air rather than by ship because the reduction in hotel expenses more than compensates for the higher cost of airfreight. It has also been found that moving into a house sooner raises the employee's morale.

Companies may also pay for some orientation of the employees and their families. Companies frequently pay for language instruction, and some will provide the family with guidance on the intricacies of everyday living, such as shopping, hiring domestic help, and sending children to school.

Bonuses

Bonuses (or premiums), unlike allowances, are paid in recognition by the firm that expatriates and their families undergo some hardships and inconveniences and make sacrifices while living abroad. Bonuses include overseas premiums, contract termination payments, and home leave reimbursement.

Overseas Premiums. Overseas premiums are additional payments to the expatriates and are generally established as a percentage of the base salary. They range from 10 to 25 percent. If the living conditions are extremely disagreeable, the company may pay larger premiums for hardship posts.

---

*For more on this subject and other effects of U.S. tax laws on American MNEs, see the taxation section of Chapter 10.

Table 22-2

Prices and Wages (percent change at annual rate)

	Consumer Prices*		Wholesale Prices*		Wages/Earnings‡	
	Three months	One year	Three Months†	One year	Three months†	One year
Australia	+ 6.8	+ 8.4 (5)	+ 3.0	+ 4.6 (4)	+ 2.7	+ 6.5 (5)
Belgium	+ 0.3	+ 0.8 (8)	− 5.7	− 7.2 (7)	nil	+ 3.0 (3)*
Canada	+ 4.5	+ 4.3 (8)	− 4.5	+ 0.3 (7)	− 1.2	+ 3.0 (6)*
France	+ 2.9	+ 2.0 (8)	− 5.2	− 3.2 (6)	+ 3.9	+ 4.8 (4)
West Germany	− 1.3	− 0.4 (8)	− 5.8	− 3.4 (7)	+ 5.5	+ 4.1 (7)
Holland	− 3.5	− 0.5 (8)	− 7.3	− 7.3 (6)	+ 0.3	+ 2.0 (7)
Italy	+ 3.9	+ 5.9 (7)	− 7.0	− 1.8 (6)	+ 2.9	+ 5.0 (5)*
Japan	+ 0.1	+ 0.1 (7)	− 10.7	− 10.3 (8)	+ 2.8	+ 3.9 (7)
Spain	+ 8.0	+ 9.5 (8)	+ 0.6	+ 1.3 (6)	+ 10.3	+ 10.6 (6)
Sweden	+ 1.3	+ 4.0 (8)	+ 0.3	+ 1.6 (7)	+ 5.0	+ 4.3 (6)*
Switzerland	− 2.0	+ 0.7 (8)	− 4.9	− 3.8 (8)	+ 18.9	+ 3.8 (3)
United Kingdom	+ 1.2	+ 2.4 (8)	+ 2.3	+ 4.3 (8)	+ 3.7	+ 7.5 (7)
United States	+ 2.9	+ 1.6 (8)	+ 0.8	− 1.7 (8)	+ 1.2	+ 2.2 (8)

Note: American consumer prices rose 1.6 percent in the year to August, while wages went up 2.2 percent. In August, consumer prices in Switzerland were 0.7 percent higher than a year before; in Spain, they were 9.5 percent higher. Japan's wholesale prices fell 10.3 percent in the year to August. In Britain, wages rose 7.5 percent in the 12 months to July; in 20 of the previous 22 months, the year-on-year rise had also been 7.5 percent.

*Not seasonally adjusted.

†Average of latest 3 months compared with average of previous 3 months at annual rate. Small figures in brackets denote month of indication.

‡Hourly wage rates in manufacturing except Australia, weekly earnings; Japan, and Switzerland, monthly earnings; Belgium, Canada, Sweden, and United States, hourly earnings; United Kingdom, monthly earnings for all employees.

Contract Termination Payments. These payments are made as inducements for employees to stay on their jobs and work out the periods of their overseas contracts. The payments are made at the end of the contract periods only if the employees have worked out their contracts. Such bonuses are used in the construction and petroleum industries or by other firms that have contracts requiring work abroad for a specific period of time or for a specific project. They may also be used if the foreign post is a hardship or not a particularly desirable one.

Home Leave.[29] Multinationals which post home country—and sometimes third-country—nationals in foreign countries make it a practice to pay for periodic trips back to the home country made by such employees and their families. The reasons for this are twofold. One reason is that the companies do not want the employees and their families to lose touch with the home country and its culture. The other reason is that the companies want to have the employees spend at least a few days at MNE headquarters to renew relationships with headquarters personnel and to catch up with new company policies and practices.

Some firms grant three-month home leaves after an employee has been abroad about three years, but it is probably a more common practice to give two to four weeks' leave each year. All transportation costs are paid to and from the executive's hometown, and all expenses are paid during the executive's stay at company headquarters.

Compensation Packages Can Be Complicated

One might think from the discussion to this point that compensation packages, while costly—the "extras" may total 50 percent or more of the base salary—are fairly straightforward in their calculation. Nothing could be further from the truth.

What Percentage? All allowances and a percentage of the base salary are usually paid in the host country currency. What should this percentage be? In practice, it varies from 65 to 75 percent, with the remainder being banked wherever the employee wishes. One reason for these practices is to decrease the local portion of the salary, thereby lowering host country income taxes and giving the appearance to government authorities and local employees that there is less difference between the salaries of local and foreign employees than is actually the case. Another reason is that expatriate employees have various expenses which must be paid in home country currency. Such expenses include professional society memberships, purchases during home leave, or tuition and other costs for children in home country universities.

What Exchange Rate? Inasmuch as most of the expatriate's compensation is usually denominated in the host country currency but is usually established in terms of the home country currency in order to achieve comparable compensation throughout the enterprise, a currency exchange rate must be chosen. In countries whose currencies are freely convertible into other currencies, this presents no serious problem, although the experienced expatriate will argue that an exchange rate covers only international transactions and may not present a true purchasing power parity between the local and home country currencies. For instance, such items as bread and milk are rarely traded internationally, and living costs as well as inflation rates may be much higher in the host country than in the home country. Multinationals attempt to compensate for such differences in the cost-of-living allowances.

More difficult problems must be solved in countries that have exchange controls and nonconvertible currencies. Without exception, those currencies are overvalued at the official rate, and if the firm uses that rate, the expatriate employees are certain to be shortchanged. Reference may be made to the free market rate for the host country currency in free currency markets in, for example, the United States or Switzerland or to the black market rate in the host country, but these do not give the final answers. In the end, all companies must pay their expatriate employees enough to enable them to live as well as others who have similar positions in other firms, regardless of how the amount is calculated.

Compensation of Third-Country Nationals

Although some companies have different compensation plans for third-country nationals, there is a trend toward treating third-country nationals the same as home country expatriates. In either event, there are areas in which problems can arise. One of these areas is the calculation of income tax differentials when an American expatriate is compared with an expatriate from another country. This results from the unique American government practices of taxing U.S. citizens even though they live and work abroad and of treating tax differential payments made to those citizens as additional taxable income. No other major country taxes its nationals in those ways.

Another possible problem area is the home leave bonus. The two purposes of home leave are to prevent expatriates from losing touch with their native cultures and to have them visit MNE headquarters. A third-country national must visit two countries instead of only one to achieve both purposes, and the additional costs can be substantial. Compare the cost of sending an Australian employee home from Mexico with that required to send an American from Mexico to Dallas.

International Status

In all of this discussion, we have been describing compensation for expatriates who have been granted **international status** in the MNE. Merely being from another country does not automatically qualify an employee for all of the benefits we have mentioned. A subsidiary may hire home country nationals or third-country nationals and pay them the same as it pays host country employees. However, managements have found that although an American, for example, may agree initially to take a job and be paid on the local scale, sooner or later bad

Figure 22-1

We offer executives

a much better position.

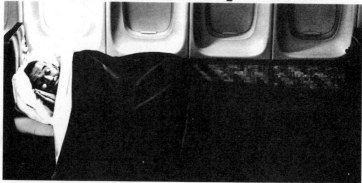

After those other airlines' San Francisco-to-Tokyo flights, you can be left feeling so bent out of shape that you half expect to be dumped off on the baggage carousel!

Not when you fly Philippine Airlines' new nonstops to Tokyo. Beginning August 2.

We offer First Class passengers the only beds between San Francisco and Tokyo. Honest-to-goodness, full-length beds! 14 of them. Tucked quietly upstairs on our 747's where no one will disturb you — even during take-offs and landings.

So catch our new nonstops to Tokyo; catch our First Class, 5-star service from your seat downstairs; then catch all the sleep you need in your very own Skybed upstairs.

And arrive in Tokyo feeling like a million. Not like excess baggage.

Philippine Airlines now to Tokyo.

Courtesy Dailey & Associates

Table 22-3

Executive Pay

Focus: White-Collar pay—The chart compares the wages of middle managers in 18 countries. The benchmark is a salary of $31,000 in Britain. According to a survey by Employment Conditions Abroad, the same job would command more than $80,000 in Switzerland, and around $65,000 in the United States and West Germany. Allowing for taxes and for differences in the cost of living, the survey ranks Britain's executives 12th in order of purchasing power. That is lower than the ranking of managers in the United States, West Germany and France. Surprisingly, it is also lower than the ranking of managers in Italy and Spain. Swiss managers top the ranking; hefty gross salaries more than make up for their high living costs.

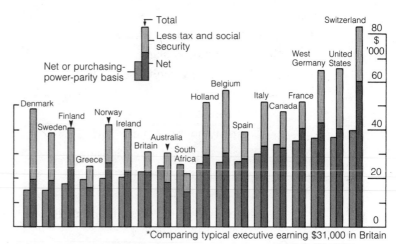

*Comparing typical executive earning $31,000 in Britain

Source: Employment Conditions Abroad Ltd.

Source: *Economist*, September 27, 1986, p. 111; based on information from Employment Conditions Abroad, Ltd.

feeling and friction will develop as that person sees fellow Americans enjoying international status perquisites to which he or she is not entitled.

Another use for international status is to promote host country employees to that status even without transferring them abroad. This is a means of rewarding valuable people and of preventing them from leaving the company for better jobs elsewhere.

So international status means being paid some or all the allowances and bonuses we have discussed, and there can be other sorts of payments as individual circumstances and people's imaginations combine to create them. Of the two men in the Philippine Airlines ad, the one in the bottom picture is clearly the one with international status (see Figure 22-1). The executives' compensation package is a subject that is sufficiently important and complicated to have become a specialization in the personnel management field; at one firm, the title is "International Employee Benefits Consultant."[30]

There is beginning to be help available from outside the MNE. For one example, Ernst & Whinney publish an International Series, and in that series are pamphlets advising about transfer to specific countries.[31] Some comparisons of white-collar pay in various countries can be seen in Table 22-3.

Perks

These originated in the perquisites of the medieval lords of the manor, whose workers paid parts of their profits or produce to the lords in order to be allowed to continue working. Today perks are symbols of rank in the corporate hierarchy and are used to compensate executives while minimizing taxes. Among the most common perks are:

Cars, which higher up the organization ladder come with chauffeurs.

Private pension plan.

Retirement payment.

Life insurance.

Health insurance.

Company house or apartment.

Directorship of a foreign subsidiary.

Seminar holiday travel.

Club memberships.

Hidden slush fund. (Such funds are illegal, but it is said that some corporations have them.)

Women

The subject of staffing the executive offices of modern American companies is not completely covered without a look at the growing role of women. In American business schools, women now comprise about half the students; they have moved into the managements of banks, businesses, and government agencies and have been at least as successful as their male counterparts. Old-girl networks are now in place alongside the old-boy networks, providing role models and helping younger female managers.

Most observers agree that these are positive developments for American management. They are developments, however, which cannot be transferred intact out of the United States to every other country of the world. As was indicated in Chapter 11, attitudes toward and treatment of women differ vastly from one culture or religion to another. A review of material in Chapter 11 could be helpful at this point.

What's Important to You?

While working abroad as an executive of an American MNE, one of the authors had a colleague who was an American expatriate married to a French woman. They had raised a family in several countries where they had been assigned by the MNE. Together with some other cosmopolites, they devised a table of items deemed important to at least one of them in choosing a city for location of a company facility which employs foreigners.

The list included the usual items, such as cost of living, safety of personnel, medical facilities, housing, and schools. It also included such other items as

THE WALL STREET JOURNAL

From *The Wall Street Journal,* with permission of Cartoon Features Syndicate.

"It's for the executive woman."

availability of good wine at reasonable prices, quality of theater and whether it was live or cinema, number and type of one-star or better (Michelin Guide)* restaurants, type and accessibility of sports facilities for both participants and viewers, and shopping facilities for fashionable clothes.

The table of items was circulated informally throughout the MNE's many locations, and many cities in its network were graded as to each item on a 1 to 10 scale. When the MNE's New York headquarters saw the table, there was much mirth and merriment; suggestions—perhaps not all of them serious—were made as to additional items about which they would like information when they visited the cities.

However, the mirth and merriment subsided as more and more executives being assigned or reassigned abroad used the table to demand better compensation packages. Some even refused transfers because of the ratings given a city.

An article in the *Economist* carried this process even further. The article is entitled "Nirvana by Numbers." Tables 22-4, 22-5, 22-6, 22-7, 22-8 are from that article.[32]

*The Michelin Guide rates restaurants and hotels in France and neighboring countries.

Figure 22-2

Every success story starts
with a kid who hated to lose.

From *Fortune* magazine. Reprinted by permission of Time, Inc.

Compensation and Benefits
Do's and Don'ts

The same executive search firm whose employee selection do's and don'ts were reported above offers some advice about compensation, benefits, and employment contracts. Expectations and practices in the United States are different from those in Europe and Japan.

Do compromise. In the United States, executive employment contracts are rare, and two weeks' notices of resignation or firing are not uncommon. In Europe, most executives have contracts, and these usually specify six months' notice. European companies hiring Americans should find out how knowledgeable the applicant is about European practices before giving benefits away to a new American manager. Six weeks' vacation may be standard in Europe, but the American may be satisfied with two or three weeks, the U.S. norm. Similarly, to many Americans a company car is a luxury, not the necessity it is considered on the continent.

Don't literally translate pay scales. The relative and changing values of currencies must be taken into account, as must differing inflation rates. Living costs and inflation rates are extremely different from place to place.

Do be flexible concerning benefits and other perks. Performance and other benefits reflect differing expectations and practices in Europe, Japan, and America. In the United States, bonuses and other nonsalary compensation are usually based on the executive's ability to meet short-term, often quarterly, performance standards. In Europe and Japan, executives are accustomed to working with much longer-term goals.

Stock options are popular in America, but this practice does not travel well to Europe or Japan, partly because the stock market is still bigger and more active in the United States than it has yet become elsewhere. More Americans have been more involved in the securities markets for longer periods than is the case for most residents of other countries.

Do maintain your corporate culture. Don't ignore that element in your hiring decision. Pay attention to personal chemistry. A company with a well-defined corporate structure should not hire a freewheeling entrepreneur, and vice versa.[33]

Narcotics: A New Control Problem

Estimates put U.S. corporate losses from drug abuse through lower productivity and health care premiums at $100 billion a year. Drug abuse and its attendant losses are now spreading in Europe.

Companies, health officials, and governments in Britain, France, Germany, the Netherlands, and most other European countries are awakening to the menace. There is general agreement that the available statistics, such as they are, grossly underrecord drug addiction. Drug abuse clinics, advisers, and hospitals are seeing a growing percentage of working people; Turning Point, a British research and treatment organization, reports that up to 50 percent of the patients at its 34 centers are employed, compared with only 5 percent a decade ago.

Why should companies be concerned? There are first the personal welfare considerations which spill over into the destructive effects of drugs on staff morale and productivity. Some experts cite the ethical compromises that addicts are often forced to make to pay for their addiction. Addicts will probably associate with criminals, and addicts in sensitive positions will be vulnerable to blackmail. The disasters that can result when such addicts are engaged in activities demanding cool judgment, such as foreign exchange dealings, or are responsible for the safety of others scarcely need elaboration.[34]

Table 22–4

Economic Indicators

	GDP per Capita ($) 1984	GDP Growth: Average Annual Rate (percent) 1977–82*	Inflation: Average Annual Rate (percent) 1977–82†	Unemployment: Percent of Total Labor Force 1982*
United States	12,220	1.6%	9.8%	9.5%
Japan	10,000	4.4	4.6	2.4
West Germany	13,450	1.6	4.7	6.2
France	12,190	2.0	11.7	8.0
Britain	9,110	0.5	12.0	12.5
Italy	6,960	2.2	16.8	8.9
Canada	11,400	1.0	10.3	10.9
Australia	11,080	2.4	9.6	7.1
Sweden	14,870	1.3	10.3	3.1
Spain	5,640	0.9	16.0	15.9
Switzerland	17,430	1.5	4.2	0.4
Saudi Arabia	12,600	6.4	1.2	0.0§
Israel	5,160	3.6	97.0	5.1
Kenya	420	5.4	14.1	15.0§
Soviet Union	5,860	2.2	0.0§	0.0§
Hungary	2,100	2.5	6.8	1.0
Mexico	2,250	6.6	29.0	4.2
Brazil	2,220	3.9§	73.6	6.9
Bahamas	3,620	3.5§	8.8	14.3
Singapore	5,240	9.6	5.8	6.7
India	260	3.4	8.2	18.3
China	300	5.5||	0.0§	2.1
Sri Lanka	300	6.1	15.4	15.3

*Or latest available year.
†For a production manager in a large manufacturing company.
‡For UN officials.
§Sometimes guesstimates, sometimes official lies.
||1970–81.
Sources: World Bank, IMF, OECO, ILO, Asian Development Bank, UN, Union Bank of Switzerland, national sources.

Cost of Living (New York City; December 1985 = 100)‡	Private Consumption per Capita ($) 1982*	Income Tax and Social Security Payments as Percent of Gross Income† 1980–1981	Number of Cars per 1,000 People 1982	Number of Telephones per 1,000 People 1984*
$100	$8,479	30.1%	550	791
127	5,263	22.3	217	495
106	6,013	24.6	385	510
92	6,847	15.0	370	542
91	5,155	29.9	286	517
85	3,847	12.6	345	382
76	6,831	31.0	435	671
85	6,444	32.2	417	520
124	6,366	52.1	357	855
93	3,465	9.9	222	350
115	9,260	18.0	385	770
125§	3,257	0.0	125	80
110§	3,554	21.0	125	321
79	246	25.0§	8	13
100§	3,650§	35.0§	36	89
61	1,306	35.0§	103	118
71	2,053	15.9	65	76
84	1,513	20.0	70	63
110	2,942	0.0	200	260
98	2,994	15.1	80	265
80	175	50.0§	1	4
68	192	35.0§	0.5	8
76	249	25.0§	9	5

Table 22-5

Social Indicators

	Number Enrolled in Primary School as Percent of Population* 6–11 Years 1980	Number Enrolled in Higher Education as Percent of Population 20–24 Years 1979	Average Number of Hours Worked per Week, Non-agricultural 1982†	Number of People per Square Mile 1982	Proportion of Population Living in Four Largest Cities (percent) 1981†	Population Growth: Average Annual Rate (percent) 1970–1982†	Proportion of Marriages Ending in Divorce (percent) 1979†	Suicide and Self-Inflicted Injury per 100,000 People 1980†
United States	98%	55%	34.8	64	12%	1.0%	50%	12
Japan	101	30	40.2	825	16	1.0	18	18
West Germany	112‡	26	40.7	643	9	0.1	9	21
France	112	25	39.8	256	22	0.5	22	17
Britain	104	20	43.0	595	20	0.1	36	9
Italy	102	27	38.8	493	12	0.5	4	6
Canada	100	36	38.2	6	31	1.1	32	15
Australia	110	26	35.0	5	54	1.4	44	11
Sweden	97	37	35.6	48	35	0.3	53	19
Spain	109	22	43.3	195	17	1.0	0§	4
Switzerland	86	17	44.1‡	398	27	0.1	31	25
Saudi Arabia	64	7	43.0‖	11	28	4.5	0§	2‡
Israel	96	26	35.4	472	56	2.6	14	6
Kenya	108	1	45.0‡	79	9	3.8	1‡	2‡
Soviet Union	106	21	40.0‡	31	6	0.9	33	45‡
Hungary	97	13	40.0‡	299	25	0.3	32	45
Mexico	120	15	45.0‡	94	29	2.9	5	2
Brazil	93	12	45.0‡	39	22	2.4	0§	2‡
Bahamas	135	3‡	48.0	44	99	2.2	7	1
Singapore	107	8	48.8	10,549	100	1.5	1‡	11
India	76	9	50.0‡	570	3	2.2	1‡	3‡
China	117	1	50.0‡	289	3	1.5	0§	3‡
Sri Lanka	100	3	53.1	610	9	1.8	1	3‡

*Figures over 100% denotes earlier age start or later finishing.
†Or latest available year.
‡Guesstimate
§No provision for divorce.
‖Excluding Ramadan.
Sources: World Bank, ILO, U.S. Department of Commerce.

Table 22-6

Cultural Indicators

	Adult Literacy Rate (percent) 1985	Number of Television Sets per 1,000 People 1980	Number of Newspapers Sold Daily per 1,000 People 1983	Number of Cinemas per million People 1979	Number of Nobel Prizes per 10 Million of 1982 Population 1901–1982	Number of Foreign Visitors as Percent of Population 1979	Number of Pints of Pure Alcohol Consumed per Person 1981
United States	99%	624	370	52	6.9	8.8%	14.6
Japan	99	539	569	22	0.3	1.0	9.9
West Germany	99	337*	423	50	9.5	14.6	22.0
France	99	354	209	105	0.7	52.4	24.1
Britain	99	404	407	27	13.9	22.4	12.5
Italy	98	386	124	223	1.9	31.1	19.2
Canada	99	471	215	52	1.3	51.8	16.0
Australia	100	378	406	44	2.7	4.4	17.6
Sweden	99	381*	578	153	32.4	21.5	9.5
Spain	98†	252	128	148	0.3	104.6	22.9
Switzerland	100	314*	395	81	21.6	117.5	19.4
Saudi Arabia	25	251	23	2†	0	65.7	0.0
Israel	90†	150*	205	66	2.5	26.7	12.0†
Kenya	47	4	13	4	0	2.4	5.0†
Soviet Union	100†	303	314	572	0.6	1.7	10.9
Hungary	99	258*	265	337	2.7	93.0	20.4
Mexico	83	104	130	40	0.1	5.2	4.2
Brazil	76	122	44	31	0	0.6	15.0†
Bahamas	93	135	163	45	0	762.1	14.0†
Singapore	85	166*	249	31	0	86.0	10.0†
India	36	2*	21	9	0.03	0.1	5.0†
China	75	5	74	2†	0.02	0.1	5.0†
Sri Lanka	85	2	42	9†	0	1.3	5.0†

*Licenses

† Guesstimate or official claim

Sources: OECD, U.S. Department of Commerce, World Bank, UN, *Whitaker's Almanack*, Brewers Society.

Table 22-7

Health Indicators

	Life Expectancy at Birth, Years 1985	Infant Mortality per 1,000 Live Births 1984	Number of Deaths per 1,000 People 1983	Number of Doctors per 100,000 People 1980	Average Daily Calorie Supply as Percent of Minimum* Calorie Requirement 1980	Deaths from Heart Disease per 100,000 People 1980†‡	Homicide and Serious Assault per 100,000 People 1980‡
United States	74	10.6	8.6	192	139%	435	9
Japan	75	6.2	6.8	128	124	266	1
West Germany	70	13.5	11.7	222	133	584	1
France	77	8.9	7.1	172	134	380	1
Britain	73	13.3	9.5	154	132	579	1
Italy	74	12.3	7	294	150	466	1
Canada	72	15	7.3	182	127	343	2
Australia	74	9.9	10.9	179	117	391	2
Sweden	76	6.8	9.3	204	119	603	1
Spain	74	10	8	217	135	361	1
Switzerland	73	9	9	244	133	448	1
Saudi Arabia	55	111	13	61	120	320§	2§
Israel	73	14.1	7	270	118	320	2§
Kenya	56	83	13	9	88	70§	2§
Soviet Union	72	20	10	357	132	500	3§
Hungary	71	20.6	12.5	250	134	718	3
Mexico	66	53	7	79§	121	109	16
Brazil	64	75	8	59	109	110§	16§
Bahamas	67	20.2	5	66	130§	72	1§
Singapore	71	10.1	5.3	87	134	179	2
India	52	121	13	27	87	175§	5§
China	68	71	7.1	52	107	250§	1§
Sri Lanka	69	43	6	14	102	175§	5§

*FAO recommended.
†Includes other diseases of the circulatory system.
‡Or latest available year.
§Guesstimate
Sources: World Bank, WHO, UN.

Table 22-8

Climatic Indicators

	Mean Average Monthly Temperature F°	Temperature Range* F°	Annual Rainfall, Inches
United States	57	43	41.9
Japan	58	41	61.6
West Germany	51	34	26.6
France	53	29	24.4
Britain	50	24	23.3
Italy	61	31	29.3
Canada	42	57	34.3
Australia	56	26	23.0
Sweden	44	38	21.8
Spain	57	34	17.5
Switzerland	50	35	42.9
Saudi Arabia	77	35	3.2
Israel	63	28	20.8
Kenya	65	6	37.7
Soviet Union	40	55	24.6
Hungary	52	35	24.2
Mexico	61	12	29.4
Brazil	73	10	42.6
Bahamas	77	12	52.8
Singapore	81	3	94.9
India	77	35	25.2
China	61	42	44.7
Sri Lanka	81	4	93.1

*Difference between average hottest and average coldest month. Day temperatures only.
Source: United Kingdom Meteorological Office.

Table 22-9

Cost of Living for Executives in Selected Cities (New York = 100)

	City Ranking	Local Inflation Index (percent)
North America		
Chicago	103	3.0
San Francisco	103	3.5
Houston	98	3.0
Toronto	78	4.0
Latin America		
Bogota	67	28.0
Lima	67	180.0
Buenos Aires	66	416.0
Santiago	53	31.0
Mexico City	46	55.0
Rio de Janeiro	46	323.0
Caracas	41	9.5
Middle East/Africa		
Lagos	140	21.0
Jeddah	91	1.0
Tel Aviv	86	193.0
Cairo	85	24.0
Johannesburg	52	24.0
Europe		
Oslo	112	5.5
Geneva	100	3.0
Vienna	96	4.5
Paris	93	5.0
Stockholm	89	6.5
Frankfurt	87	2.0
Rome	85	8.0
London	83	5.0
Brussels	82	5.0
Athens	67	23.0
Asia/Pacific		
Tokyo	155	2.5
Singapore	98	1.5
Hong Kong	85	5.0
Melbourne	78	7.5
Bangkok	70	6.5
Bombay	56	8.5
Beijing	53	12.0

Note: The inflation indicator is based *solely* on the price movements, January 1985–January 1986, of items included in the *Business International* cost-of-living index and should be considered "inflation for executives," since it takes their purchasing habits into account.
Source: *Executive Living Costs in Major Cities Worldwide* (New York: Business International).

Summary

Intraenterprise controls must be effective if an MNE is to maximize success and minimize problems. Such controls include guidelines as to where decisions will be made, which may be at the parent company level, at the subsidiary company level, or cooperatively at both levels. Among the factors that affect intraenterprise controls are product and equipment introduction, improvement, and standardization; the competence of subsidiary management; the distance of the host country from the home country and the differences in their cultures; and the size of the MNE and how long it has operated multinationally. Guidelines as to where decisions will be made are affected by circumstances in which some detriment to a subsidiary will result in greater benefit for the enterprise as a whole. Such detriment/benefit situations arise in intraenterprise transactions wherein profit can be maximized in lower-tax countries and minimized in higher-tax countries or tariffs can be minimized by intraenterprise transfer price decisions. Also, where a customer order can be filled by more than one unit of an MNE, having the parent decide which unit gets the order can avoid intraenterprise competition and can ensure that such considerations as order backlogs, labor problems, and comparative tariffs are taken into account.

It is easier for a parent company to exercise control over a subsidiary if it owns 100 percent of the subsidiary than if it owns less than 100 percent. And control of a joint venture with a separate entity in which the parent company has no ownership is more difficult than control of a subsidiary in which it has less than 100 percent ownership. In such instances, control is sought through control of the capital and technology as well as by holding strategic joint venture executive positions.

For controls to work, all operating MNE units must provide headquarters with timely, accurate, and complete reports. These reports should cover such subjects as finance, technology, market opportunities, new products, competitor activities, price changes, market share, and political and economic information.

A very important use of reports is as a means for evaluating and comparing management performance. For this purpose, the raw figures are inadequate and may be misleading. The parent company must factor in such elements as decisions it made that penalized one subsidiary while benefiting another and conditions beyond the subsidiary management's control, such as inflation or political instability.

It is difficult to locate effective executives for multinational operations. Two or more cultures are involved, and usually two or more languages. The MNE may find employees in its home country, the host country, or elsewhere, and the nationalities of those employees may be home country, host country, or third country. The types of training that MNE employees should receive and the adaptation that they should undergo depend on their nationality and previous experience. The home country national needs to learn about the host country culture and language, while the opposite is true of the host country national. Frequently, third-country nationals are hired because they have experience with both—and sometimes other—cultures and languages.

MNE headquarters often sends specialists to assist foreign subsidiaries with problems that have multinational ramifications, such as taxes, labor, or product sales contracts. In addition, headquarters usually likes to have one or two of its nationals in such key positions as general manager or financial manager.

Moving employees from country to country among subsidiaries and the MNE home operations can develop and mature those employees and provide learning experiences for the subsidiaries and home operations. Such moves can be for temporary duty or longer-term assignments. One result desired from such moves is the formation of personal relationships among MNE personnel which will facilitate intraenterprise communication and understanding.

Company loyalties and nationalistic attitudes must be taken into account. Host country employees may place host country interests above those of the company and may be reluctant to press their governments for unpopular concessions even though the company would benefit. However, all countries have rules and limitations on the number of foreign employees who can be brought in.

Most executives sent from their home countries take families, and the difficulties of cultural and linguistic adaptations may be more severe for the families than for the executives. Most companies now make efforts to evaluate whether the families can and will adapt before sending executives abroad. Failure to adapt causes broken families, poor employee morale, and expensive relocation of families back to the home countries.

Expatriate employees are generally paid the same basic salary as their domestic counterparts. However, additional expenses and hardships are frequently encountered abroad, and the expatriates receive additional payments in the forms of allowances and bonuses or premiums. Among the allowances commonly given are those for housing, cost of living, tax differentials, schooling, moving, and orientation. The bonuses include overseas premiums and contract termination payments, which are used if living conditions are difficult or if a specific term or project must be completed. Another bonus is home leave for employees and families, whose purposes are to prevent expatriates from losing touch with their native cultures and to permit expatriates to visit MNE headquarters at least periodically.

Compensation packages for expatriates are complicated because there are so many variables to consider. In addition to home country salary levels, the types and levels of compensation of equivalent executives in the host country must be considered. Comparative taxes, costs of living, and inflation rates must be factored in, as must difficulties of living conditions. An additional set of complications can arise from the currencies utilized, because some currencies are freely convertible, while most are not, and currencies fluctuate in value in terms of each other.

The expatriate who is paid some or all the bonuses and allowances we have discussed is said to be on international status. From time to time, firms will promote subsidiary host country nationals to international status. Their motives for doing so may be to reward such employees for meritorious service or to keep them from leaving to work for a competitor.

A new sort of employee control problem has arisen. This is the problem of dealing with the growing number of employees who are addicted to narcotics, which has resulted in huge losses in productivity and huge increases in health costs. From the viewpoints of the employers and the consuming public, the most worrying aspects of such drug addiction are possible failures of judgment of employees who are responsible for the safety of others and possible blackmail of addicted employees who possess or have access to company or national secrets.

Questions

1. *In determining where decisions are to be made as between the parent company and subsidiaries, what are the considerations when equipment and products are standardized worldwide rather than tailored to individual national circumstances and markets?*

2. a. *In an MNE, what are some decisions that could result in detriment for a subsidiary but greater benefit for the enterprise?*

   b. *In such circumstances, where will the decision be made—at MNE headquarters or at the affected subsidiary?*

3. *What measures can be utilized to control subsidiaries that are less than 100 percent owned by the firm or joint venture partners in which the firm has no ownership?*

4. *What are the roles of reporting in multinational controls?*

5. a. *When subsidiaries report net profits, must parent management look behind the reported numbers in order to evaluate subsidiary managements fairly?*

   b. *Why?*

6. *When staffing a multinational organization for service outside the MNE home country, what are some advantages and disadvantages of hiring home country personnel?*

7. *Why has there been an increasing use of third-country nationals in the foreign operations of MNEs?*

8. *Why are expatriate employees frequently paid more than their colleagues at equivalent job levels in the home office?*

9. *Why are compensation packages for expatriates more complicated than those for domestic employees?*

10. *What is international status? Who gets it? Why?*

11. *Why should employers and the public be concerned about the growth in drug addiction among employees?*

Minicase

22-1 Female Executives in

International Business

For a number of reasons, women are being hired and promoted as executives by American business. The United States is almost alone in this development. Some West European countries are moving slowly toward more female executive development, but elsewhere in the world, notably Latin America, Africa, Asia, and Eastern Europe, women are given very few executive opportunities.

Suppose you are the chief executive officer (CEO) of an American multinational. On your staff and in the U.S. operating divisions of your company are several bright, able, dedicated female executives. They are also ambitious, and in your company international experience is a must before an executive can hope to get into top management.

An opening comes up for the position of executive vice president in the company's Mexican subsidiary. One of the women on your staff applies for the position, and she is well qualified for the job, better than anyone else in the company. Would you give her the position? What are the arguments pro and con?

Another position becomes available, this one as treasurer of the Japanese subsidiary. The chief financial officer of the company's California division applies for this job. She has performed to everyone's satisfaction, and she seems thoroughly qualified to become the treasurer in Japan. In addition, she speaks and writes Japanese. She is the daughter of a Japanese mother and an American father, and they encouraged her to become fluent in both English and Japanese.

Would you give her the job? Why or why not?

Supplementary Readings

Adler, Nancy J. "A Typology of Management Studies Involving Culture." *Journal of International Business Studies*, Fall 1983, pp. 29–48.

Bacchus, I. William. "Staffing for Foreign Affairs: A Personnel System." *Public Personnel Management*, Fall 1985, pp. 315–30.

Bass, Bernard M., and Philip C. Burger in collaboration with Robert Doktor and Gerald V. Barrett. *Assessment of Managers: An International Comparison.* New York: Free Press, 1979.

Dymsza, William A., and Anant R. Negandhi. "Introduction to Cross-Cultural Management Issue." *Journal of International Business Studies*, Fall 1983, pp. 15–16.

England, George W.; Bernhard Wilpert; and Arant R. Negandhi, eds. *Organizational Functioning in a Cross-Cultural Perspective.* Kent, Ohio: Comparative Administration Institute, Kent State University, 1979.

Fowler, D. J. "Transfer Prices and Profit Maximization in Multinational Enterprise Operations." *Journal of International Business Studies*, Winter 1978, pp. 2–26.

Freeman, Orville L. "Communication: Key to Corporate Survival." In *Contemporary Perspectives in International Business*, ed. Harold W. Berkman and Ivan R. Vernon. Skokie, Ill.: Rand McNally, 1979. pp. 144–50.

Gates, Stephen R., and William G. Egelhoff. "Centralization in Headquarters-Subsidiary Relationships." *Journal of International Business Studies*, Summer 1986, pp. 71–92.

Gray, S. J. "Managerial Forecasts and European Multinational Company Reporting." *Journal of International Business Studies*, Fall 1978, pp. 21–32.

Harvey, Michael C. "The Other Side of Foreign Assignments: Dealing with the Repatriation Dilemma." *Columbia Journal of World Business*, Spring 1982, pp. 53–59.

Hill, Ray. "Women-Owned Companies Finally Start Making Their Mark." *International Management*, May 1986, p. 66.

Jeannet, Jean-Pierre, and Bertil Liander. "Some Patterns within Multinational Corporations." *Journal of International Business Studies*, Winter 1978, pp. 108–18.

Murray, Robin, ed. *Multinationals beyond the Market: Intra-firm Trade and the Control of Transfer Pricing.* New York: John Wiley & Sons, 1981.

Packard P., and J. Slater. "Staff Appraisal: A First Step to Effective Leaders." *Journal of Occupational Psychology*, September 1985, p. 261.

Plasschaert, Sylvain. *Transfer Pricing and Multinational Corporations: An Overview of Concepts, Mechanisms, and Regulations.* Farnborough, England: Saxon House, 1979.

Tang, Roger Y. W. *Transfer Pricing in the United States and Japan.* New York: Praeger Publishers, 1979.

Tomoda, Shizna. "Measuring Female Labor Activities in Asian Developing Countries: A Time Allocation Approach." *International Labor Review*, November–December 1985, p. 661.

Turbeyz, Peggy. "International Organization Helps Women Overcome Barriers to Obtaining Credit." *American Banker*, September 6, 1985, p. 16.

Verlage, H. C. *Transfer Pricing for Multinational Enterprises: Some Remarks on Its Economic, Fiscal, and Organizational Aspects.* Rotterdam: Rotterdam University Press, 1975.

Young, Donald L. "Promises and Pitfalls: The Challenge of Filling Overseas Management Positions." *The International Essays for Business Decision Makers.* Vol. 4. New York: AMACOM for the Center for International Business, 1979. pp. 270–76.

Endnotes

1. David P. Rutenberg, "Organizational Archetypes of a Multinational Company," *Management Science*, February 1970, pp. B337–49.
2. Richard N. Farmer and Barry M. Richman, *International Business*, 3rd ed. (Bloomington, Ind.: Cedarwood Press, 1980), chap. 12.
3. Warren J. Keegan, "Multinational Marketing Control," *Journal of International Business Studies*, Fall 1972, pp. 34–47.
4. Ulrich Weichmann, "Integrating Multinational Marketing Activities," *Columbia Journal of World Business*, Winter 1974, pp. 13–14.
5. William K. Brandt and James M. Hulbert, "Patterns of Communications in the Multinational Corporation: An Empirical Study," *Journal of International Business Studies*, Spring 1976, pp. 17–30.

6. *Business International,* July 30, 1976, p. 247.
7. Jacques Picard, "How European Companies Control Marketing Decisions Abroad," *Columbia Journal of World Business,* Summer 1977, pp. 113–21.
8. R. J. Aylmer, "Who Makes Marketing Decisions in the Multinational Firm?" *Journal of Marketing,* October 1970, pp. 27–29.
9. Sidney M. Robbins and Robert B. Stobaugh, *Money in the Multinational Enterprise* (New York: Basic Books, 1973). pp. 140–51.
10. Farmer and Richman, *International Business,* pp. 285–86.
11. James M. Fremgren, "Transfer Pricing and Management Goals," *Management Accounting,* December 1970, pp. 25–31.
12. Itzhak Sharov, "Transfer Pricing: Diversity of Goals and Practice," *Journal of Accountancy,* April 1974, pp. 56–62.
13. James Shulman, "When the Price is Wrong—by Design," *Columbia Journal of World Business,* May–June 1967, p. 74.
14. Stefan W. Robock, Kenneth Simmonds, and Jack Zwick, *International Business and Multinational Enterprises,* rev. ed. (Homewood, Ill.: Richard D. Irwin, 1977), pp. 526–28.
15. Wendell H. McCulloch, Jr., "Japan's Trade and Investment with the Less-Developed Countries," *The Wall Street Journal,* October 3, 1980, p. 19.
16. Hans Schollhammer, "Organization Structures of Multinational Corporations," *Academy of Management Journal,* September 1971, pp. 360–63.
17. Millard H. Pryor, Jr., "Planning in a Worldwide Business," *Harvard Business Review,* January–February 1965, pp. 131–32.
18. Richard F. Janssen, "U.S. Lenders Taking New Looks at Risks from Political, Social Upheavals Abroad," *The Wall Street Journal,* March 13, 1979, p. 7.
19. V. Mauriel, "Evaluation and Control of Overseas Operations," *Management Accounting,* May 1969, pp. 35–39.
20. Leland M. Wooton, "The Emergence of Multinational Information Centers," *Management International Review,* Winter 1977, pp. 21–23.
21. Michael G. Duerr and James Greene, *The Problems Facing International Management* (New York: Conference Board, 1968), p. 25.
22. Farmer and Richman, *International Business,* chap. 10.
23. *Business International,* July 2, 1983, pp. 209, 211.
24. Ibid., July 22, 1983, pp. 228–29.
25. One study of U.S.-based MNEs showed that about one half required some language training. Burton W. Teague, *Selecting and Orienting Staff for Service Overseas* (New York: Conference Board, 1976), p. 16.
26. Nancy G. McNulty, *Training Managers: The International Guide* (New York: Harper & Row, 1969), pp. 7–17.
27. Fortunat F. Mueller-Maerkl, "Do's and Don'ts in Selecting Managers for Foreign Operations," in *U.S.-German Economic Survey* (New York: German/American Chamber of Commerce, 1984), pp. 123–25.
28. John Frankenstein, "Training Experts to Manage in China," *The Asian Wall Street Journal,* August 26, 1985, p. 17.
29. Some writers regard paid home leave as an allowance, but our experience convinces us that it is a premium, because MNEs consistently give more frequent or longer home leaves to employees working in less desirable assignments.
30. G. W. Hallmark and Charles W. Rogers III, "The Challenge of Providing Benefit and Compensation Programs for Third Country Nationals," in *The International Essays for Busi-*

ness Decision Makers, vol. 3, ed. Mark W. Winchester (New York: AMACOM for the Center for International Business, 1978).

31. *Handbook for Employees Transferring to France,* Ernst & Whinney, International Series, March 1980; *to the United States,* March 1980; *to Belgium,* April 1980; *to the United Kingdom,* April 1980; *to Italy,* June 1980; *to Hong Kong,* October 1980; *to Luxembourg,* October 1980; *to Denmark,* October 1980; *Abroad,* November 1980; and more.

32. "Nirvana by Numbers," *Economist,* December 24, 1983, pp 53–57, updated from various sources.

33. Mueller-Maerkl, "Do's and Dont's in Selecting Managers for Foreign Operations."

34. Jules Arbose, "European Managers Wake Up to the Menace of Drugs," *International Management,* January 1987, pp. 34–36.

CHAPTER 23

THE MULTINATIONAL, THE GLOBAL

*"T*he old model of the multinational enterprise has become obsolete."

Kenichi Ohmae, director, McKinsey & Co., Tokyo office

"To attract the people of talent it needs, the multinational . . . increasingly will have to open its management jobs everywhere to wherever the talent can be found, regardless of passport. Also it will have to expose prominent young people early and often to the whole system rather than have them spend their careers in their own native countries and in the subsidiaries located there."

Peter F. Drucker, Clarke professor of social sciences, Claremont Graduate School

844

Learning Objectives

After you study this chapter, you should know:

1. The home country and size of many MNEs and globals.
2. MNE and global relations with and choice of host countries.
3. About changing EC policy toward MNEs and globals.
4. About continuing UN hostility toward MNEs and globals.
5. About opportunities for MNEs and globals to make sales financed by World Bank or other multilateral lending institutions.
6. The importance of MNEs and globals in international trade.
7. How MNEs and globals are being victimized by and are combating industrial espionage.
8. The differences between the MNE and the global.
9. Why the trend from MNE to global is probably irreversible for most internationally operating companies.
10. Why the Japanese lead the move to globalization.

Key Words and Concepts

Home country
Host country
Transnational consortia (in the EC)
UN hostility to MNEs and globals
Multilateral lending institutions
Industrial espionage
Global
Multinational enterprise (MNE)
Joint ventures

845

Business Incident

West European Communist parties held a secret meeting to concert their attack on multinational companies. The meeting was held on 10–11 December 1986, in the Dusseldorf headquarters of the West German Communist party. The Communist parties of Austria, Denmark, West Germany (and West Berlin), France, Greece, Italy, Luxembourg, Portugal, Sweden, and Turkey were represented.

So was the Soviet Communist party, which dispatched D. M. Motshalin section chief in the party's international department. Motshalin worked closely with V. V. Zagladin, who had been one of the Soviet delegates at the June 1986 Berlin summit meeting of European communists.

Motshalin was camouflaged as a special correspondent to the Novosti news agency. He was well known to the West German police and had been on their list of wanted people for many years, because when the West German Communist party was banned in Germany, he had been sent to supervise its clandestine activities in collusion with Kurt Bachmann, the present leader of the West German Communist party. Another of his jobs at that time had been to arrange the financing of illegal communist propaganda in West Germany.

At the Düsseldorf meeting, it was agreed to set up an "international information office" to collect details about the financial structure, technology, and business operations of multinational companies in Western Europe. The information acquired was to be disseminated to West European Communist parties, which would set up special committees to deal with the multinationals. As a further step, it was planned to establish an all-European committee for the same purpose.

The international information office was to work in tandem with the existing multinationals committee of the Soviet-controlled World Federation of Trade Unions (WFTU) and was to plan coordinated strike activities throughout Western Europe.

"Foreign Report," published by the *Economist Newspaper*, January 26, 1987, p 37.

When a group of American radicals disguised as Indians dumped chests of tea into Boston Harbor in 1773, they were attacking a multinational company. The tea that went into the sea belonged to the British East India Company, chartered by Queen Elizabeth I, which had been granted a monopoly on trade in Asia, Africa, and America.

The Dutch also had an East India company, a multinational that operated from 1602 until 1795 throughout the Far East and paid annual dividends of 12 to 63 percent in its fat days. The Dutch East India Company boasted a fleet of 40 warships and an army of 10,000 soldiers. Today's multinationals have armies of managers and workers, but no warships of which we are aware.

Throughout this book, we have referred to MNEs. How could it be otherwise? The title of the book is *International Business,* and most international business is done by MNEs. We believe that by now the reader should have a pretty good idea of what a **multinational enterprise (MNE)** is. However, adopters and reviewers have suggested that it would be appropriate to close the book with a brief look at the MNE as a distinct subject and in this chapter we shall act on that suggestion. But before we proceed to do so, let us bring to your attention that some authors use different words and initials to designate what we mean by MNEs. Some call them multinational corporations (MNCs), some call them multinational firms (MNFs); and in UN terminology they are transnational corporations.

Under perfect conditions, the MNE would be able to source its raw materials wherever in the world it found them most easily accessible at lowest cost, to produce and manufacture wherever in the world it was able to do so most efficiently at lowest cost, and to market its products and services wherever in the world it could most profitably do so. It would hire people based on their abilities and experience without regard to their nationality. Perfection for the MNE would be a global, one-world operation without political or racial boundaries.

Of course, the actual conditions do not permit such perfection. The world is splintered politically into nearly 200 separate, sovereign countries, each with its own taxes, laws, courts, and boundary regulations, and nationality is frequently a factor in the MNE hiring process.

American MNEs

The United States got a head start with foreign investments that resulted in MNEs, and most MNEs—but a diminishing percentage of the total number—are still American owned, (that is, the United States is the home country of the parent company). Table 23–1 identifies the 100 largest U.S. multinationals and gives some information about them.

MNEs of Industrial Countries
Other than the United States

Money, technology, and managerial skills are required to create and operate a successful MNE. Therefore, it should come as no surprise to learn that most MNEs whose home country is not the United States have another industrial country as their base. Most of the world's capital, advanced technology, and managerial skills are found in the developed, industrial countries.

Although Canadian, West European, and Japanese firms started substantial overseas investing later than their American counterparts, they have gone

Table 23-1

The 100 Largest U.S. Multinationals

1985 Rank	Company	Foreign Revenue ($ millions)	Total Revenue ($ millions)	Foreign Revenue as Percent of Total
1	Exxon	$59,067	$86,673	68.1%
2	Mobil	32,678^2	57,111^2	57.2
3	Texaco	21,864	46,297	47.2
4	IBM	21,545	50,056	43.0
5	General Motors	16,167	96,372	16.8
6	Ford Motor	15,995	52,774	30.3
7	Salomon	15,100	27,896	54.1
8	Chevron	12,722	41,742	30.5
9	Citicorp	10,600^5	22,504	47.1
10	E. I. du Pont de Nemours	10,551^7	29,239^7	36.1
11	ITT^8	7,754	20,007	38.8
12	Dow Chemical	6,326	11,537	54.8
13	Amoco	5,984^{2,5}	27,258^2	22.0
14	BankAmerica	5,144	13,390	38.4
15	Chase Manhattan	5,024	9,733	51.6
16	Safeway Stores	4,261	19,651	21.7
17	J. P. Morgan	3,684	6,575	56.0
18	Procter & Gamble	3,625	13,552	26.7
19	Occidental Petroleum	3,619^2	15,644^2	23.1
20	RJR Nabisco	3,262^5	13,533	24.1
21	Eastman Kodak	3,239	10,631	30.5
22	Xerox^8	3,187	11,736	27.2
23	Goodyear	3,148	9,585	32.8
24	Phillips Petroleum	3,125	15,636	20.0
25	General Electric	3,112^2	29,272^2	10.6
26	Coca-Cola	2,996	7,904	37.9
27	United Technologies	2,996	14,992	20.0
28	Sears Roebuck	2,905	40,715	7.1
29	Hewlett-Packard	2,809^{10}	6,505	43.2
30	Manufacturers Hanover	2,808	8,385	33.5
31	American Express	2,749	11,850	23.2
32	Tenneco	2,665	15,270	17.5
33	Union Carbide	2,632	9,003	29.2
34	Dart & Kraft	2,625	9,942	26.4
35	Digital Equipment	2,608	6,686	39.0
36	Minnesota Mining & Manufacturing	2,594	7,846	33.1
37	Pan Am	2,591	3,484	74.4
38	Bankers Trust New York	2,551	4,699	54.3
39	Sun Co	2,534^2	14,410^2	17.6

Foreign Operating Profit ($ millions)	Total Operating Profit ($ millions)	Foreign Operating Profits as Percent of Total	Foreign Assets ($ millions)	Foreign Total Assets ($ millions)	Assets as Percent of Total
$3,530[1]	$5,604[1]	63.0%	$30,049	$ 69,160	43.4%
1,317[3]	1,040[3]	126.6	18,867	41,752	45.2
874[4]	1,864[4]	46.9	11,142	37,703	29.6
3,084[3]	6,555[3]	47.0	21,733	52,634	41.3
419[3]	3,999[3]	10.5	13,570	63,643	21.3
527[3]	2,515[3]	21.0	15,725	31,366	50.1
286[3]	557[3]	51.3	7,800	88,601	8.8
765[3]	1,547[3]	49.5	9,165	38,899	23.6
545[3]	998[3]	54.6	78,259[6]	160,505[6]	48.8
356[4]	1,574[4]	22.6	7,546	25,140	30.0
164[3]	294[3]	55.8	11,743	37,849	31.0
382	637	60.0	5,509	11,830	46.6
785[3]	1,953[3]	40.2	6,520	25,198	25.9
− 420[3]	− 337[3]	124.6	41,882[6]	118,974[6]	35.2
194[3]	565[3]	34.3	40,830	87,685	46.6
113[3]	231[3]	48.9	1,110	4,841	22.9
335[3]	705[3]	47.5	32,476	69,375	46.8
96[3]	635[3]	15.1	1,946	9,683	20.1
132[3]	455[3]	29.0	2,667	11,586	23.0
398	2,246	17.7	4,347	16,930	25.7
167	561	29.8	3,262	12,135	26.9
152[9]	381[9]	39.9	3,926	17,163	22.9
177	640	27.7	2,320	6,954	33.4
1,339	2,729	49.1	2,687	14,045	19.1
101[3]	2,336[3]	4.3	3,809	26,432	14.4
611	1,045	58.5	1,727	6,898	25.0
116[3]	313[3]	37.1	2,780	10,528	26.4
25[3]	1,303[3]	1.9	1,917	66,417	2.9
331[11]	758[11]	43.7	1,797	5,680	31.6
124[3]	407[3]	30.5	27,361	76,526	35.8
316	1,427	22.1	18,295	74,777	24.5
202	1,496	13.5	3,387	20,437	16.6
272	826	32.9	3,054	10,581	28.9
289	998	29.0	1,416	5,502	25.7
305	450	67.8	2,254	6,369	35.4
332	1,150	28.9	1,874	6,593	28.4
50	− 182	P-D	M.A.	2,448	M.A.
167[3]	371[3]	45.0	28,428	50,581	56.2
19[12]	644[12]	3.0	3,052	12,923	23.6

Table 23–1

(continued)

1985 Rank	Company	Foreign Revenue ($ millions)	Total Revenue ($ millions)	Foreign Revenue as Percent of Total
40	Chrysler	2,488	21,256	11.7
41	CPC International	2,445	4,210	58.1
42	Johnson & Johnson	2,431	6,421	37.9
43	Colgate-Palmolive	2,354	4,524	52.0
44	F. W. Woolworth	2,310	5,958	38.8
45	American International Group	2,253[13]	5,782	39.0
46	Burroughs	2,203	5,038	43.7
47	GTE	2,169	15,732	13.8
48	Atlantic Richfield	2,138	21,723	9.8
49	Allied Signal	2,047	9,115	22.5
50	American Brands[8]	2,007	5,616	35.7
51	NCR	1,965	4,317	45.5
52	Monsanto	1,923	6,747	28.5
53	K mart[8]	1,886	23,421	8.1
54	Chemical New York	1,872	5,651	33.1
55	Motorola	1,818	5,443	33.4
56	Unocal	1,781[2]	11,059[2]	16.1
57	Philip Morris	1,779	12,149	14.6
58	Sperry	1,698	5,741	29.6
59	Pfizer	1,682	4,025	41.8
60	Honeywell	1,647	6,625	24.9
61	Trans World Airlines	1,610	3,725	43.2
62	Merck	1,589	3,548	44.8
63	Sara Lee	1,510	8,117	18.6
64	Cigna	1,506	16,197	9.3
65	Bank of Boston	1,500[5]	3,436	43.7
66	Scott Paper[8]	1,454	4,068	35.7
67	Caterpillar	1,445	6,725	21.5
68	Texas Instruments	1,418	4,924	28.8
69	Halliburton	1,400	4,781	29.3
70	H. J. Heinz	1,386	4,048	34.2
71	Gillette	1,375	2,400	57.3
72	First Chicago	1,346	4,370	30.8
73	W. R. Grace	1,320	5,193	25.4
74	Bristol-Myers	1,315	4,444	29.6
75	TRW	1,260	5,917	21.3
76	Aluminum Company of America[8]	1,223	5,805	21.1
77	Deere	1,219	4,061	30.0

Foreign Operating Profit ($ millions)	Total Operating Profit ($ millions)	Foreign Operating Profits as Percent of Total	Foreign Assets ($ millions)	Foreign Total Assets ($ millions)	Assets as Percent of Total
257^{11}	$2,370^{11}$	10.8	2,062	12,582	16.4
199	359	55.4	1,735	3,017	57.5
237^{3}	614^{3}	38.6	1,968	5,095	38.6
133	329	40.4	1,008	2,814	35.8
126	409	30.8	981	2,535	38.7
364^{13}	391	93.1	$5,948^{13}$	15,571	38.2
273	601	45.4	1,799	4,556	39.5
101^{3}	-161^{3}	P-D	3,405	26,558	12.8
96^{9}	333^{9}	28.8	1,815	20,279	9.0
129^{9}	-279^{9}	P-D	1,694	13,271	12.8
173	898	19.3	1,672	8,371	20.0
278	599	46.4	1,328	3,940	33.7
216	351	61.5	1,670	8,877	18.8
40^{9}	471^{9}	8.5	706	10,102	7.0
116^{3}	390^{3}	29.7	18,619	56,990	32.7
76	200	38.0	1,046	4,370	23.9
80^{3}	325^{3}	24.6	1,585	10,797	14.7
146	2,686	5.4	2,752	17,429	15.8
286	542	52.8	1,320	5,890	22.4
298	929	32.1	1,763	4,463	39.5
101^{3}	282^{3}	35.8	1,736	5,034	34.5
-19^{11}	-217^{11}	8.8	1,206	2,769	43.6
214	853	25.1	1,791	4,902	36.5
109^{11}	348^{11}	31.3	1,143	3,216	35.5
-44	-855	5.1	5,087	44,736	11.4
3^{3}	174^{3}	1.7	$7,314^{6}$	$23,814^{6}$	30.7
47^{3}	201^{3}	23.4	1,324	4,245	31.2
-16	513	D-P	1,273	6,016	21.2
-4^{11}	-115^{11}	3.5	949	3,076	30.9
59	89	66.3	1,156	4,662	24.8
155	491	31.6	883	2,474	35.7
233	380	61.3	1,182	2,425	48.7
-85^{3}	169^{3}	D-P	11,888	38,893	30.6
188	401	46.9	890	5,421	16.4
213	890	23.9	1,020	3,721	27.4
137	480	28.5	993	3,735	26.6
52^{14}	21^{14}	247.6	2,403	7,409	32.4
50	93	53.8	920	5,462	16.8

Table 23-1

(concluded)

1985 Rank	Company	Foreign Revenue ($ millions)	Total Revenue ($ millions)	Foreign Revenue as Percent of Total
78	Control Data	1,209	4,810	25.1
79	Warner-Lambert	1,162	3,200	36.3
80	Enron	1,142	10,253	11.1
81	Kimberly-Clark	1,135	4,073	27.9
82	Amerada Hess	1,128	7,653	14.7
83	Dresser Industries	1,080	4,111	26.3
84	Firestone	1,063	3,836	27.7
85	Continental Illinois	1,062	2,880	36.9
86	SmithKline Beckman	1,055	3,257	32.4
87	American Home Products	1,048	4,685	22.4
88	American Cyanamid	1,047	3,536	29.6
89	Security Pacific	1,045	5,537	18.9
90	Eli Lilly	1,039	3,271	31.8
91	Hercules[8]	1,035	3,146	32.9
92	Continental	1,031	5,092	20.2
93	Rockwell International	957	11,338	8.4
94	PepsiCo	952	8,057	11.8
95	Abbott Laboratories	950	3,360	28.3
96	PPG Industries	934	4,346	21.5
97	American Standard	930	2,912	31.9
98	Quaker Oats	927	3,520	26.3
99	Irving Bank	906	2,028	44.7
100	Westinghouse Electric	904	10,700	8.4

General note: 1986 data were used for those February and March companies that reported before press time.
1. Net income before special items.
2. Includes other imcome.
3. Net income.
4. Operating income after taxes.
5. Estimate.
6. Average assets.
7. Includes foreign excise taxes.
8. Includes proportionate interest in unconsolidated subsidiaries or investments.

about it vigorously. American companies have been losing their dominance in several business and finance sectors, as illustrated by Tables 23–2, 23–3, 23–4, and 23–5. These tables show the largest firms in the world by several measurements. For all companies, (Table 23–2) the rankings are by market value; earnings, sales, worldwide employment, and percentage employed outside the

Foreign Operating Profit ($ millions)	Total Operating Profit ($ millions)	Foreign Operating Profits as Percent of Total	Foreign Assets ($ millions)	Foreign Total Assets ($ millions)	Assets as Percent of Total
50	−124	P-D	1,732	8,565	20.2
286	559	51.2	819	2,358	34.7
85	620	13.7	810	9,893	8.2
67^3	267^3	25.1	1,053	3,504	30.1
119^3	-260^3	P-D	1,639	6,219	26.4
88	−95	P-D	890	3,225	27.6
91	145	62.8	772	2,528	30.5
7^3	134^3	5.2	$10,100^6$	$28,300^6$	35.7
174	740	23.5	1,035	3,733	27.7
209	1,211	17.3	673	3,395	19.8
78^3	129^3	60.5	744	3,405	21.9
68^3	323^3	21.1	11,851	53,503	22.2
204^{11}	797^{11}	25.6	1,097	3,954	27.7
121	201	60.2	1,023	2,937	34.8
1	−259	P-D	2,656	11,495	23.1
122	1,178	10.4	985	7,333	13.4
67	859	7.8	1,054	5,861	18.0
151	754	20.0	734	3,468	21.2
54	617	8.8	967	4,084	23.7
119	235	50.6	649	2,269	28.6
77	376	20.5	449	1,842	24.4
64^3	116^3	55.2	$9,310^5$	21,651	43.0
67	742	9.0	684	9,682	7.1

9. Income from continuing operations.
10. Includes U.S. exports.
11. Pretax income.
12. Profit before interest and taxes.
13. Excludes Canada.
14. Profit before equity in net income of unconsolidated subsidiaries.
D-P—deficit over profit.
P-D—profit over deficit.
—not available.
Source: Reprinted by permission of Forbes Magazine, July 28, 1986. © Forbes, Inc. 1986.

home country are also indicated. Table 23–3 ranks banks by assets and then shows capital, net income, fiscal year, worldwide employment, and percentage employed outside the home country. The rankings and other information for insurers (Table 23–4) and for securities and financial services firms (Table 23–5) are similar to those for banks.

Table 23-2

The World's 100 Largest Public Companies (by market value on June 30, 1986, converted into U.S. dollars at exchange rate for that date)

	Company Name	Headquarters	Market Value (in millions)
1	IBM	Armonk, N.Y.	$87,697
2	Exxon	New York	44,015
3	General Electric	Fairfield, Conn.	36,820
4	Tokyo Electric	Tokyo	32,421
5	AT&T	New York	27,138
6	Sumitomo Bank	Osaka, Japan	25,962
7	Toyota Motor	Toyota City, Japan	25,197
8	General Motors	Detroit	24,751
9	Dai-Ichi Kangyo Bank	Tokyo	23,729
10	Nomura Securities	Tokyo	23,151
11	Royal Dutch Petroleum	The Hague, Netherlands	21,592
12	Mitsubishi Bank	Tokyo	21,461
13	Fuji Bank	Tokyo	21,460
14	Daimler-Benz	Stuttgart, West Germany	20,874
15	British Telecom	London	20,430
16	Du Pont	Wilmington, Del.	20,093
17	BellSouth	Atlanta	19,246
18	Industrial Bank of Japan	Tokyo	19,092
19	Sanwa Bank	Osaka, Japan	18,346
20	Philip Morris	New York	17,813
21	Sears Roebuck	Chicago	17,659
22	British Petroleum	London	16,651
23	Matsushita Electri Industrial	Osaka, Japan	16,210
24	Coca-Cola	Atlanta	16,147
25	Amoco	Chicago	15,588
26	Mitsubishi Estate	Tokyo	15,112
27	Hitachi	Tokyo	14,923
28	Merek	Rahway, N.J.	14,666
29	Wal-Mart Stores	Bentonville, Ark.	14,579
30	Ford Motor	Dearborn, Mich.	14,313
31	Kansai Electric Power	Osaka, Japan	14,232
32	Bell Atlantic	Philadelphia	13,882
33	American Express	New York	13,881
34	Nynex	New York	13,649
35	American Home Products	New York	13,620
36	Shell Transport & Trading	London	13,488
37	Siemens	Munich, West Germany	13,469
38	Seibu Railway	Toshimaku, Japan	13,448
39	Procter & Gamble	Cincinnati, Ohio	13,415
40	Johnson & Johnson	New Brunswick, N.J.	13,280
41	Eastman Kodak	Rochester, N.Y.	13,243
42	RJR Nabisco	Winston-Salem, N.C.	13,218

Earnings		Sales		Worldwide Employment (000s)	Percent Employee Outside Home Country
1985	1984	1985	1984		
(in millions of home currency)		(in millions of home currency)			
6,560	6,580	50,100	45,900	405	40%
4,870	5,530	92,000	96,000	146	54
2,340	2,280	28,300	27,900	300	20
113,000	122,000	3,915,000	3,712,000	39	*
1,560	1,370	34,900	33,200	350	2
77,200	80,400	31,034†	26,442†	17	21
406,000	295,000	6,770,000	5,909,000	80	20
4,000	4,520	96,400	83,900	890	40
||	57,100	35,863†	27,587†	20	4
111,000	73,000	2,178†	1,542†	10	2
3,030	3,650	73,100	73,800	142‡	60‡
62,100	60,100	26,772†	25,315†	16	5
60,700	63,100	30,653†	25,567§	15	2
1,630	1,063	52,409	43,505	311	19
904	1,088	7,653	6,876	234	1
11,120	1,430	29,500	30,600	140	21
1,418	1,257	10,664	9,631	96	*
44,800	44,100	21,447†	18,170†	5	||
58,700	55,900	27,384†	22,287§	20	25
1,260	890	16,000	13,800	114	38
1,300	1,450	40,700	38,800	466	12
1,600	1,400	41,000	37,900	129	77
247,000	238,000	5,053,000	4,721,000	150	3
678	622	7,904	7,152	39	56
1,950	2,180	28,900	29,000	50	19
20,500	18,400	192,000	186,000	2	1
210,000	167,000	5,013,000	4,367,000	165	18
540	493	3,547	3,560	31	53
271	196	6,401	4,667	120	*
2,520	2,910	52,800	52,400	369	53
70,600	64,700	2,101,000	2,031,000	25	*
1,093	973	9,084	8,090	79	8
810	610	75†	62†	71	27
1,100	990	10,300	9,600	90	*
717	656	4,685	4,485	47	43
3,030	3,650	73,100	73,800	142†	69‡
1,502	1,049	54,616	45,819	357	32
4,620	3,050	345,000	326,000	5	0
635	90	13,552	12,946	73	39
614	515	6,421	6,125	70	57
630	920	10,600	10,600	129	31
1,001	843	16,595	12,974	147	55

Table 23–2

(continued)

Company Name		Headquarters	Market Value (in millions)
43	Ameritech	Chicago	13,184
44	Sumitomo Trust & Banking	Osaka, Japan	13,153
45	Chevren	San Francisco	13,043
46	3M	St. Paul, Minn.	13,033
47	Mobil	New York	12,965
48	Allianz	Munich, West Germany	12,861
49	Abbott Laboratories	Chicago	12,857
50	NEC	Tokyo	12,769
51	Bristol-Myers	New York	12,276
52	Pacific Telesis	San Francisco	12,050
53	Mitsubishi Trust & Bankign	Tokyo	12,012
54	Pfizer	New York	11,715
55	Glaxo Holdings	London	11,494
56	GTE	Stamford, Conn.	11,466
57	Eli Lilly	Indianapolis	11,282
58	Deutsche Bank	Franfurt, West Germany	11,240
59	Daiwa Securities	Tokyo	11,144
60	Dow Chemical	Midland, Mich	10,910
61	Southwestern Bell	St. Louis	10,908
62	Long-Term Credit Bank of Japan	Tokyo	10,890
63	Tokio Marine & Fire Insurance	Tokyo	10,863
64	Mitsui Bank	Tokyo	10,823
65	Chubu Electric Power	Nagoya, Japan	10,784
66	US West	Englewood, Colo.	10,620
67	Standard Oil Ohio	Cleveland	10,584
68	Hewlett-Packard	Palo Alto, Calif.	10,501
69	Flat	Torino, Italy	10,280
70	Assicurazion: Generali	Trieste, Italy	10,202
71	American International Group	New York	10,202
72	Digital Equipment	Maynard, Mass.	10,162
73	Schulumber	New York	10,137
74	Imperial Chemical	London	9,908
75	Tokai Bank	Nagoya, Japan	9,860
76	Boeing	Seattle	9,777
77	Nikko Securities	Tokyo	9,439
78	McDonald's	Oak Brook, Ill.	9,391
79	Atlantic Richfield	Los Angeles	9,346
80	Fujitsu	Tokyo	9,246
81	BAT Industries	London	9,236
82	Dart & Kraft	Northbrook, Ill.	9,147
83	General Electric	London	9,102
84	Union Bank of Switzerland	Zurich, Switzerland	9,060
85	Mitsui Trust & Banking	Tokyo	9,009

Earnings		Sales		Worldwide Employment (000s)	Percent Employee Outside Home Country
1985	1984	1985	1984		
(in millions of home currency)		(in millions of home currency)			
1,078	991	9,021	8,347	77	*
18,960	15,100	8,415†	6,077†	6	4
1,550	1,530	45,300	47,400	61	16
664	733	7,846	7,705	85	42
1,040	1,270	59,500	59,500	164	n.a.
n.a.	290	n.a.	9,003	25	18
465	403	3,360	3,104	36	35
67,100	44,600	2,258,000	1,762,000	128	9
531	472	4,444	4,189	36	42
929	829	8,499	7,824	75	*
18,800	14,700	8,922†	6,682‖	6	1
580	511	4,025	3,876	39	59
280	169	1,412	1,200	26	48
842	1,080	15,732	14,547	183	23
518	490	3,271	3,109	29	36
1,085	662	236†	231†	49	8
57,200	38,800	1,398†	1,026†	11	9
58	524	11,537	11,418	50	45
996	883	7,930	7,191	70	*
28,300	28,100	16,772†	14,655†	3	10
25,000	23,000	639,000	596,000	15	14
35,100	33,000	19,919†	18,576†	11	2
69,500	73,100	1,780,000	1,696,000	20	*
926	887	7,813	7,280	67	0
1,380	1,540	13,800	12,300	42	15
489	547	6,505	6,044	84	33
1,326,000	593,000	27,101,000	23,813,000	226	18
n.a.	220,000	n.a.	6,101,000	18	56
420	302	4,289	2,513	25	60
447	329	6,686	5,584	95	37
860	1,180	1,560	6,370	65	n.a.
552	605	10,725	9,909	61	52
40,300	38,000	20,358†	19,219†	13	4
566	390	13,636	10,354	112	1
51,500	38,300	1,253†	1,405†	11	5
433	389	3,761	3,415	540#	22#
1,480	1,370	22,500	24,600	29	1
89,000	66,700	1,562,000	1,210,000	n.a.	n.a.
674	784	12,696	14,426	185	86
466	456	9,942	9,759	73	40
407	390	5,976	5,600	165	21
688	579	140†	131†	19	5
14,900	12,100	8,247†	5,794†	16	4

Table 23-2
(concluded)

Company Name	Headquarters	Market Value (in millions)
86 Dun & Bradstreet	New York	9,008
87 SmithKline Beckman	Philadephia	8,991
88 PepsiCo	Purchase, N.Y.	8,880
89 Japan Air Lines	Tokyo	8,698
90 Bank of Tokyo	Tokyo	8,691
91 Texco USA	White Plains, N.Y.	8,675
92 Ito-Yokado	Tokyo	8,377
93 Marks & Spencer	London	8,277
94 Tokyo Gas	Tokyo	8,261
95 Westinghouse	Pittsburgh	8,247
96 BTR	London	8,190
97 Citicorp	New York	8,159
98 Kirin Brewery	Tokyo	8,129
99 Asahl Glass	Tokyo	8,074
100 Nissan Motor	Tokyo	8,044

*Less than 1 percent.
†Assets are used instead of sales for banking companies.
‡Combines Thill Transport & Tending over noyal inter petroleum.
§1983 assets.
||1982 assets
#Estimated to include franchise employees.

Table 23-3
The World's 50 Largest Banking Concerns (ranked by assets; converted to U.S. dollars at end of company's fiscal year 1985)

Company Name	Headquarters	Assets (in US$ millions)
1 Citicorp	New York	$173,597
2 Banque Nationale de Paris (BNP)	Paris	123,074
3 Dai-Ichi Kangyo Bank	Tokyo	122,895
4 Credit Agricole	Paris	122,884
5 Fuji Bank	Tokyo	121,384
6 Bank America	San Francisco	118,541
7 Sumitomo Bank	Osaka, Japan	113,985
8 Credit Lyonnais	Paris	111,452
9 Mitsubishi Bank	Tokyo	105,819

Earnings		Sales		Worldwide Employment (000s)	Percent Employee Outside Home Country
1985	1984	1985	1984		
(in millions of home currency)		(in millions of home currency)			
295	253	2,772	2,397	58	41
514	500	3,257	2,949	33	33
420	275	8,057	7,451	185	25
10,800	−3,400	923,000	830,000	21	15
33,700	32,900	17,442†	16,051†	14	64
1230	1070	47,500	47,900	55	38
31,800	25,600	1,201,000	1,057,000	12	*
181	166	3,194	2,855	63	11
32,300	25,500	782,000	760,000	13	*
605	536	10,700	10,265	116	15
261	168	3,881	3,150	85	47
998	890	174†	151†	81	48
25,400	20,100	1,226,000	1,141,000	8	6
30,500	29,200	818,000	722,000	22	31
82,000	74,000	4,626,000	4,308,000	n.a.	n.a.

Capital (in US$ millions)	Net Income (in US$ millions)	Fiscal Year Ended	Worldwide Employment (000s)	Percent Employee Outside Home Country
$26,020	$ 998	December	81	48%
10,117	263	December	51	8
4,170	244	March	20	4
18,347	146	December	74	*
9,195	240	March	15	2
9,935	−337	December	78	19
5,860	306	March	17	21
8,314	135	December	46	6
14,651	246	March	16	5

Table 23–3

(concluded)

	Company Name	Headquarters	Assets (in US$ millions)
10	National Westminster Bank	London	104,677
11	Sanwa Bank	Osaka, Japan	102,731
12	Societe Generale	Paris	97,621
13	Deutsche Bank	Frankfurt, West Germany	96,383
14	Barclays	London	94,169
15	Chase Manhattan	New York	87,685
16	Mitsubishi Trust & Banking	Tokyo	86,668†
17	Norinchukin Bank	Tokyo	85,199
18	Industrial Bank of Japan	Tokyo	84,932
19	Midland Bank	London	83,860
20	Sumitomo Trust & Banking	Osaka, Japan	80,813†
21	Tokai Bank	Nagoya, Japan	77,669
22	Dresdner Bank	Frankfurt, West Germany	76,652
23	Manufacturers Hanover	New York	76,526
24	Mitsui Trust & Banking	Tokyo	75,982†
25	Yasuda Trust & Banking	Tokyo	75,028†
26	Mitsui Bank	Tokyo	73,177
27	Groupe Paribas	Paris	72,897
28	J. P. Morgan	New York	69,375
29	Bank of Tokyo	Tokyo	69,072
30	Daiwa Bank	Osaka, Japan	68,888†
31	Hongkong & Shanghai Bankign	Hong Kong	68,848
32	Royal Bank of Canada	Montreal	67,237
33	Union Bank of Siwtzerland	Zurich, Switzerland	67,155
34	Long-Term Credit Bank of Japan	Tokyo	66,418
35	Lloyds Bank	London	63,279
36	Swiss Bank	Basel, Switzerland	61,607
37	Taiyo Kobe Bank	Kobe, Japan	61,196
38	Westdeutsche Landesbank Girozentrale	Dusseldorf, West Germany	57,737
39	Banco de Brasil	Brasilia, Brazil	57,176
40	Chemical New York	New York	56,990
41	Toyo Trust & Banking	Tokyo	56,161†
42	Commerzbank	Frankfurt, West Germany	55,753
43	Bayerische Vereinsbank	Munich, West Germany	53,792
44	Security Pacific	Los Angeles	53,503
45	Bank of Montreal	Montreal	53,333
46	Canadian Imperial Bank of Commerce	Toronto	52,429
47	Algemene Bank Nederland	Amsterdam	51,343
48	Bankers Trust New York	New York	50,581
49	First Interstate	Los Angeles	48,991
50	Banca Nazionale Delavoro (BNL)	Rome	48,640

*Less than 1%.
†Including trust accounts.
Note: Assets calculated without contingent liabilities.

Capital (in US$ millions)	Net Income (in US$ millions)	Fiscal Year Ended	Worldwide Employment (000s)	Percent Employee Outside Home Country
8,223	638	December	92	11
7,432	232	March	20	25
6,558	123	December	44	22
32,246	447	December	49	8
7,839	650	December	106	27
7,265	565	December	48	39
8,158	74	March	6	1
15,515	97	March	3	*
3,973	174	March	5	n.a.
6,125	176	December	67	4
978	75	March	6	4
2,370	160	March	13	4
26,910	176	December	35	n.a.
11,414	407	December	32	11
930	59	March	6	4
1,101	41	March	5	1
5,178	139	March	11	2
7,686	179	December	28	20
5,792	705	December	14	32
16,237	133	March	14	64
1,788	64	March	9	*
5,280	348	December	46	76
4,336	357	October	42	13
6,030	333	December	19	5
40,739	112	March	3	10
5,675	592	December	71	30
9,731	291	December	15	12
1,785	76	March	14	3
26,772	14	December	7	4
9,652	858	December	120	2
4,442	390	December	20	6
564	39	March	n.a.	n.a.
16,875	140	December	24	n.a.
32,089	71	December	13	2
5,948	323	December	31	5
3,371	248	October	33	20
3,412	264	October	34	8
2,328	172	December	29	32
4,133	371	December	11	18
5,505	313	December	35	2
2,494	144	December	25	n.a.

Table 23–4

The World's 25 Largest Insurers (ranked by assets; converted to U.S. dollars at end of company's fiscal year 1985)

Company	Headquarters	Assets (in US$ millions)
1 Prudential Insurance	Newark, N.J.	$91,706
2 Metropolitan Life	New York	76,494
3 Aetna Life	Hartford, Conn.	58,294
4 Equitable Life Assurance	New York	51,211
5 Cigna	Philadelphia	44,736
6 Nippon Life	Osaka, Japan	42,494
7 Travelers	Hartford, Conn.	41,642
8 New York Life	New York	31,740
9 Prudential	London	28,893
10 Dai-Ichi Mutual Life	Tokyo	27,904
11 John Hancock Mutual	Boston	26,594
12 Nationale-Nederlanden	The Hague, Netherlands	24,163
13 Teachers Insurance & Annuity	Net York	23,159
14 Sumitomo Life	Osaka, Japan	23,127
15 American General	Houston	20,668
16 Allianz Lebensversicherungs	Munich, West Germany	19,595
17 Northwestern Mutual	Milwaukee	18,087
18 Massachusetts Mutual	Springfield, Mass.	15,579
19 American International	New York	15,571
20 Meiji Mutual Life	Tokyo	15,312
21 Principal Financial	Des Moines, Iowa	14,927
22 Legal & Generl Group	London	14,871
23 Standard Life Assurance	Edinburgh, Scotland	14,572
24 CNA Financial	Chicago	14,146
25 Asahi Mutual Life	Tokyo	13,791

*For mutuals, net income equals net change in surplus
Sources: Worldscope (Wright Investors' Service and Center for International Financial Analysis & Research); additional employment figures by *The Wall Street Journal,* 1986.

Capital (in US$ millions)	Net Income* (in US$ millions)	Fiscal Year Ended	Worldwide Employment (000s)
$2,429	$ 69	December	80
2,691	110	December	35
5,353	872	December	41
1,246	24	December	30
4,747	− 733	December	49
2,459	2,250	March	91
4,012	375	December	32
1,568	32	December	9
5,475	110	December	23
1,718	1,491	March	64
958	− 87	December	30
3,823	218	December	21
773	139	December	3
1,317	1,183	March	11
4,605	506	December	16
161	27	December	n.a.
1,210	207	December	3
749	− 24	December	4
3,959	420	December	26
898	792	March	n.a.
553	76	December	7
3,583	54	December	6
48	1,248	November	3
2,290	305	December	13
790	706	March	36

Table 23-5

The 25 Largest Securities and Financial Services Firms (ranked by assets; converted to U.S. dollars at end of company's fiscal year 1985)

Company Name	Headquarters	Assets (in US$ millions)
1 Salomon	New York	$88,601
2 American Express	New York	74,777
3 Merrill Lynch	New York	48,117
4 First Boston	New York	45,531
5 Bear Stearns	New York	24,155
6 E. F. Hutton	New York	21,749
7 Compagnie Bancaire	Paris	15,860
8 Morgan Stanley	New York	15,794
9 PaineWebber	New York	13,589
10 Nippon Shinpan	Tokyo	12,824
11 Orient Finance	Tokyo	11,637
12 Trilon Financial	Toronto	10,831
13 Nomura Securities	Tokyo	10,040
14 Japan Securities Finance	Tokyo	9,588
15 Orient Leasing	Tokyo	8,765
16 Beneficial	Wilmington, Del.	8,718
17 Daiwa Securities	Tokyo	8,511
18 Kleinwort, Benson, Lonsdale	London	8,132
19 Nikko Securities	Tokyo	6,479
20 Yamaichi Securities	Tokyo	5,911
21 Morgan Grenfell	London	5,817
22 Gerrard & National	London	5,209
23 Union Discount Company of London	London	4,017
24 Hill Samuel	London	3,932
25 Schroeders	London	3,122

Sources: Worldscope (Wright Investors' Service and Center for International Financial Analysis & Research); additional employment figures by *The Wall Street Journal,* 1986.

Capital (in US$ millions)	Net Income (in US$ millions)	Fiscal Year Ended	Worldwide Employment (000s)
$ 7,193	$557	December	6
10,768	801	December	71
6,063	224	December	44
1,042	130	December	3
514	83	April	4
1,143	12	December	17
3,875	77	December	7
486	106	December	4
727	29	September	11
2,353	36	March	6
2,337	46	March	n.a.
1,676	69	December	n.a.
4,233	511	September	10
957	10	March	n.a.
3,828	41	September	2
4,963	83	December	8
2,008	264	September	7
675	88	December	2
1,901	218	September	11
1,556	198	September	7
389	47	December	1
75	6	March	n.a.
96	2	December	n.a.
404	41	March	7
335	42	December	n.a.

Other MNEs

Companies based in a number of developing or communist countries have ventured overseas. Six very big ones are Hyundai of South Korea, Walsin Lihwa of the Republic of China, and the state oil companies of Brazil, Kuwait, Mexico, and Venezuela, which have become multinationals with factories and holdings abroad.

As mentioned in Chapter 17, the People's Republic of China is investing in several foreign countries. Many Indian companies operate multinationally, as do companies based in Hong Kong and Singapore. Other companies call Indonesia, the Philippines, Malaysia, Argentina, and Thailand their home country.

One author finds that the motives of MNEs based in nonindustrial countries differ somewhat from the motives of MNEs based in industrial countries. MNEs from advanced countries speak of exploiting experience with high-technology production and using marketing expertise. MNEs from other countries stress diversification of risk, high local return, exploiting experience with labor-intensive production, relatives or countrymen business associates in the host country, and small home markets.[1] There are also similarities; both groups are abroad primarily to get and defend markets.

The growth of non-American MNEs is illustrated by the following figures. The United States accounted for 65 percent of all direct investment abroad in 1965–69; in 1980–81, its share was down to 28 percent. Japan increased its share of outflows from less than 2 percent to 7½ percent, and this growth has continued. The single largest magnet for companies investing abroad has been America. The United States and Canada between them were host to 25 percent of foreign investment in 1980, almost as much as all the developing countries.[2]

Regardless of the MNE's home country, it must deal with a variety of entities other than the home government. Among them are host countries, the European Community, the United Nations, and the World Bank.

MNEs and Host Countries

However large and powerful an MNE may be, it must observe the laws and regulations of its **host country** and its **home country** and be sensitive to the differences in their cultures. That said, it remains true that in deciding where to make new investments or to expand existing investments, the MNE can pick and choose among potential host countries, and the patterns of investment seem to be changing.

There seems to be a shift from the poor countries with low labor costs to the developed countries with the high incomes that create good markets. Remember that in a recent period, Canada and the United States received about as much foreign investment as did all the developing countries. The reasons for this are several.

In Chapter 20, we discussed the factory of the future. In that factory, faster and cheaper computers combined with efficiently programmed robots perform more and more of the production processes and reduce labor costs as a percentage of total costs. In many industries, labor costs have dropped to less than 10 percent of total manufacturing costs and no longer offset the costs of transporting components and products to and from low-wage countries. In such industries, the factory of the future either is not very distant or is already here.

At the same time, a number of host governments have grown increasingly inhospitable—imposing tariffs, local content laws, and local ownership requirements on foreign firms. Some important host countries that have done one or more of these things are Brazil, India, Indonesia, Mexico, Nigeria, and Saudi Arabia. The policymakers in many developing countries have no business experience and have difficulty understanding the realities of today's fiercely competitive and yet interdependent international marketplace.[3]

MNEs and the European Community (EC)

In a major shift from its traditional trust-busting role, the EC Commission is quietly being transformed into a promoter of high-tech **transnational consortia.** It is creating unprecedented opportunities for companies to influence the policies and participate in the activities of the EC.

In contrast to the recent past, when social and legal regulation seemed to be the EC hallmark, the EC is now moving to free enterprises from legal obstacles to transnational activity. The pressures that have wrought this shift are competition from America and Japan and the need for technological renewal in Europe. In research and development venture capital, manufacturing, and many other fields, many cross-border projects are now being encouraged in Europe by the EC.[4]

MNEs and the United Nations

The attitude of the EC Commission has changed in recent months from hostility to and regulation of business to one of cooperation with and assistance to private companies. No such change has taken place at the United Nations.

The UN arm primarily responsible for coordinating the UN's economic and social work is the UN Economic and Social Council (ECOSOC). ECOSOC's regulatory agenda has included:

A code of conduct for MNEs under the auspices of its Commission on Transnational Corporations.

Guidelines for consumer protection.

A model tax treaty to combat international tax evasion.

Hearings on the employment practices of MNEs and on the "sociocultural impact" of MNEs in South Africa.

Study of transborder data flow.

ECOSOC and other UN agencies could deal with these and many other matters in a fashion beneficial to consumers, trade, and business. However, the attitudes of these agencies have been and continue to be hostile to free trade and to MNEs.

As one example, *Development Forum*, a UN Department of Public Information, university-directed publication, contained an article that stated, "the unprecedented transnational corporation penetration of the world economy has become a leading catalyst in the global crisis of mounting unemployment, inflation, and stagnation."[5] No balancing language from the UN points out, for example, that in many places MNE investments have created new jobs, introduced new technology, and produced new products for export and better products for domestic consumption.[6]

Observers of the UN comment that its resolutions affecting business are "vague," leave "key phrases undefined, thus making compliance difficult," and create "new barriers to trade in several product markets."[7]

MNEs and the World Bank and Other Multilateral Lending Institutions

The World Bank, the Inter-American Development Bank (IDB), and other **multilateral lending institutions** lend billions of dollars each year, and much of that is contracted to businesses from member countries.

Finding out about bank-sponsored projects already in the pipeline is easy, but to maximize its chances of getting a contract, the MNE should be involved much earlier. To the maximum extent possible, it should be in at the planning stage in order to assure that it can meet the specifications decided on. Indeed, at the planning stage it can help write the specifications.

Thus, any MNE that hopes to do much bank-sponsored business must cultivate broad contacts within both the borrowing government and the sponsoring bank. It should also maintain contacts with country representatives to the bank, with the commercial staff at the borrower's embassy, and with bank officers in the country in which the project is to be undertaken.

An MNE that wants to sell consulting services should deposit an up-to-date firm profile with the World Bank's Data on Consulting Firms (DACON) and with the IDB's Office of Professional Service Firms. DACON is also used by the UN Development Program, the Asian Development Bank, and the IDB.

Announcements of projects appear in the World Bank's Monthly Operational Summary and the IDB's Monthly Operations Summary, both of which are referred to as MOS. Once a loan has been approved, notices of required goods and services are distributed as Technical Data Sheets by the World Bank.[8]

MNEs and International Trade

As a recent United Nations report noted, "Unfortunately, comprehensive data on the foreign trade of transnational corporations exist only for the United States." We shall look at a few facts and figures about the shares of American exports and imports accounted for by MNEs, but those figures cannot be extrapolated to other countries for various reasons. For one thing, each country's market for imports is unique (America's is the largest). And, of course, each country has different import duties and other taxes and different import and export regulations.

MNEs are very important for U.S. trade. They account for the majority of U.S. exports and imports. In 1982 (the year of the Commerce Department's latest survey of the subject), American-based MNEs were responsible for 72 percent of total U.S. exports, of which a bit under one third went to their foreign affiliates (intraenterprise trade). In the same year, MNEs took 46 percent of U.S. imports slightly over one third of which was shipped by their overseas affiliates.

The international orientation of American MNEs is confirmed by the fact that their 1982 share of total exports (72 percent) was considerably larger than their share of U.S. business, which accounted for only 25 percent of total nonbank employment. This probably reflected their concentration in goods-producing sectors and their greater ability to adapt their production rapidly to the needs of their foreign customers. It also reflected their close links with their foreign operations, since over half of the U.S. parents' shipments to majority-owned foreign affiliates was intended for further manufacture.

The above data concern only American MNEs and their affiliates. When the U.S. affiliates of foreign MNEs are included, the share of American trade generated by all MNEs is even more impressive. They accounted for 94 percent of U.S. foreign trade, which was split approximately two thirds/one third between U.S. MNEs and American affiliates of foreign MNEs.[9]

Industrial Espionage

The Business Incident speaks of the Soviet Union's interest in stealing the latest Western technology, much of it developed by MNEs. A book by Professors Eells and Nehemkis says, "Japanese firms are as much a threat as the Soviets."[10]

Industrial espionage or its equivalent is not new. Foreign devils purloined imperial China's secrets of silk and porcelain manufacture. Secrets of steelmaking were stolen from Britain by the German Alfred Krupp. Many competitors pirated Charles Goodyear's basic patent for vulcanization and Rudolf Diesel's car engine.

At present, the rewards of commercial spying so outweigh the risks that the unscrupulous can rationalize such activities as the most cost-effective form of R&D. The secrets are often worth millions, yet even if an employee spy is caught, it is unlikely punishment will be worse than firing. Companies are loath to expose themselves to the public embarrassment of a court case.

Some companies are trying to protect themselves against industrial espionage. IBM has a counterespionage operation, and in 1982 its work in cooperation with the FBI resulted in the arrest of Hitachi and Mitsubishi employees on

Copyright 1987, Cartoonists & Writers Syndicate.

"Excuse me, sir . . . . Want to sue a multinational?"

charges of buying secret data stolen from IBM. Some companies are taking former employees to court to prevent them from exposing company secrets to competitors. Most companies now require employees to sign agreements to keep confidential any knowledge gained on the job. Eells and Nehemkis say that the golden rule of trade secrets is, "Don't let your employees do to you what you did to your former boss."

The Global

One of the quotations at the beginning of this chapter stated, "The old model of the multinational has become obsolete." So what's new?

Most multinationals are structured and run pretty much the way the American and German inventors of the species designed them some 125 years ago. A parent company has subsidiaries in other countries around the world, and while the parent makes major decisions and does research and development, the subsidiaries have wide autonomy in manufacturing, marketing, finance, and personnel. The subsidiaries are usually managed by host country nationals, and a main objective of subsidiaries is to be a "good citizen" of the host country.

But most of those structural features are becoming inappropriate or even counterproductive. Economies of manufacturing scale are in conflict with the traditional design, which has each subsidiary manufacturing as much as possible of the final product for its country's market. Increasingly, however, a market as big as France, Germany, or even the United States is becoming too small for efficient production of every component. The cheaper, faster, better-programmed computers and robots we discussed in Chapter 20 call for centralization—manufacturing all of one component in one subsidiary, all of another in a second, and so forth.

Similar pressures to establish a **global corporation,** which diminishes the autonomy of subsidiaries, are building in marketing. In some products and services, the market has become global; in others, markets are segmented, but by lifestyles, not by geography. And some products are best marketed by emphasizing their foreignness. Increasingly, marketing decisions have become global systems decisions rather than separate decisions for each subsidiary.

In the finance area, it is even more important to go global. Now that fluctuating exchange rates—subject to sudden, wide swings—have become commonplace, separate, subsidiary financial management has become a prescription for disaster for any system operating internationally.

We discussed in Chapter 18 the system-wide international finance centers that are being used by more and more companies. In this, the Japanese are ahead of Western-based MNEs because they have historically treated foreign units as branches, not as separate subsidiaries. This enables the Japanese to take earnings out of any one unit (e.g., American, German, or Japanese) and to invest them in developing tomorrow's growth markets, such as India or Brazil. If the subsidiaries of Western MNEs control their own finances, the local management will resist loss of control of funds.

The Western MNEs will have to move more rapidly toward globalization or see the Japanese monopolize the new markets. If the Western MNEs fail to adjust, they will become inefficient and unable to compete.[11]

Not every MNE should globalize. For example, consumer product companies still need to tailor goods to local tastes and are unlikely to abandon their worldwide subsidiaries. Moreover, many governments are requiring foreign companies to manufacture minimum percentages of products locally in order to create or save jobs and to minimize component import costs.

In many companies, though, the trend toward globalization seems irreversible, and many of these companies are globalizing by engaging in **joint ventures** rather than by centralizing power away from subsidiaries or making independent, new investments abroad. One large example of the joint venture approach is that between AT&T and Olivetti. AT&T wanted an immediate presence in the personal computer market, and Olivetti wanted a piece of the American market. Olivetti had an excellent personal computer, ready to go. So the two firms agreed in 1986 that AT&T would market Olivetti's personal computer in the United States and that Olivetti would sell AT&T products in Europe.

Other American companies that signed joint venture agreements with European companies in 1986 were Du Pont and Digital Equipment. Both American and European automakers have entered into joint ventures with Japanese companies.[12]

Summary

Multinationals have been around for centuries, and they are now responsible for most of the world's international business. Tables in this chapter show their home countries and sizes.

MNEs/globals must obey host and home country laws, but can wield influence as they can choose among host countries in deciding where to invest or increase investment. Investment trends seem to be toward industrialized countries and away from poorer countries with low-cost labor, and there are two main reasons for this. New production technology has reduced labor costs to 10 percent or less of total costs even in high-wage countries, and a number of host countries are making it more difficult for foreign countries to operate profitably within their borders.

While the EC Commission is encouraging MNE/global cooperation within the EC, the UN retains its hostile stance toward MNEs/globals. Huge loans are made by multinational lending institutions, and MNEs/globals that utilize proper procedures can earn much of that money through contracts for sale of goods and services.

MNEs/globals are extremely important in world trade. Most American imports and exports are attributable to them.

The Soviet Union, Japanese firms, and many others practice industrial espionage. Companies are using counterespionage, court actions, and employee agreements in efforts to protect themselves.

As national markets—even that of the United States—become too small to support the economies of scale needed with new production technology, MNEs are shifting to global operations. Pressures to globalize come from marketing and financial developments, particularly the latter, because of global products and the wildly fluctuating foreign exchange markets. When an MNE has operated through autonomous subsidiaries, globalization results in centralization of power at the parent company at the expense of subsidiary management. Companies that have not been MNEs may globalize through joint venture agreements with companies in other countries.

Questions

1. *For the successful MNE or global of the future, what personnel policy changes does Peter Drucker find necessary?*
2. *a. Why are the communists interested in MNEs/globals?*
   b. Who else has similar interests?
3. *What are some differences between MNEs/globals based in industrialized countries and those based in developing countries?*
4. *There has been a change in the direction of the investments made by MNE/globals—in their choice of host countries. What is the change, and what are some of the reasons for it?*
5. *There has been a change in the policies of the EC Commission toward MNEs/globals. What is the change, and what are some of the reasons for it?*
6. *Is the UN moving in the same direction as the EC? Why do you think that is the case?*
7. *What should MNEs/globals do to maximize business from countries receiving loans from multilateral lending agencies?*
8. *How are companies trying to defend themselves against industrial espionage?*
9. *What is the historic and typical structure of an MNE?*
10. *How does the global differ from the MNE, and what are the advantages that the global enjoys over the MNE?*
11. *Are there any products for which the MNE structure may be better than the global structure? Explain.*
12. *Under what circumstances would a company utilize joint ventures to globalize?*

Minicase

23-1 Competition within the

Multinational

MC is an MNE with subsidiary manufacturing plants in several countries around the world. MC has just won a very large contract to supply locomotives to Paraguay, which is modernizing its entire railway system with financing from the World Bank.

MC's home country is the United States, and it could manufacture parts or all of the locomotives in its U.S. plants. MC subsidiary companies in Spain, Mexico, and Australia could also manufacture parts or all of the locomotives. The managers of all those subsidiaries know about the big new contract, and each is eager to get the work involved in performing it.

A meeting of the subsidiary chief executive officers (CEOs) is called at MC's headquarters in New York to discuss which plant or plants will get the work. The manager of the American locomotive plant is also at the meeting, and she makes a strong case for giving her plant the work. It has laid off 1,000 workers, and this big job would permit it to recall them. In addition, the American plant has all of the latest technology, some of which has not been supplied to the subsidiary companies.

The subsidiary CEOs each argue that there is unemployment in their countries too, and that as responsible citizens they must hire more local people. Each CEO also points out that hiring local people would reduce hostility to the subsidiary in the host country and give it defenses against left-wing attacks on foreign-owned companies. One CEO suggests that each plant enter competitive bids and let Paraguayan Railways make the decision.

You are the CEO of MC, and you have the authority and responsibility to allocate parts or all of the work to one or more of the plants. List and explain the considerations that will govern your decisions.

Supplementary Reading

Bergsten, C. Fred; Thomas Horst; and Theodore H. Moran. *American Multinationals and American Interests*. Washington, D.C.: Brookings Institution, 1978.

Blank, Stephen. *Assessing the Political Environment: An Emerging Function in International Companies*. New York: Conference Board, 1980.

Blin, J. M.; Stuart I. Greenbaum; and Donald P. Jacobs. *Flexible Exchange Rates and International Business*, Washington, D.C.: British–North American Committee, 1981.

Bussing, Rezu. *Power vs. Profit: Multinational Corporation–Nation State Interaction*. New York: Arno Press, 1980.

Byrne, A. John, and G. David Wallace. "For More and More Foreign Companies, America Isn't Paved with Gold." *Business Week*, February 3, 1986, p. 84.

Casson, Mark. *Multinational and World Trade Vertical Integration and the Division of Labor in World Industries*, London: Allen & Unwin, 1986.

Caves, Richard E. *Multinational Enterprise: Economic Analysis.* New York: Cambridge University Press, 1982.

Davidson, W. H., and D. G. McFetridge. "Recent Directions in International Strategies: Production Rationalization or Portfolio Adjustment?" *Columbia Journal of World Business*, Summer 1984, pp. 95–101.

Eaker, R. Mark, and Loan Lenowitz. "Multinational Borrowing Decisions and the Empirical Exchange Rate Evidence." *Management International Review*, Winter 1986, pp. 24–35.

Eiteman, David K., and Arthur I. Stonehill. *Multinational Business Finance.* 4th ed. Reading, Mass: Addison-Wesley Publishing, 1986.

Erdilek, Asim. "Multinationals in Mutual Invaders: Intra-Industry Direct Foreign Investment." *Journal of International Business Studies*, Summer 1986, pp. 182–91.

Fisher, Bart S., and Jeff Turner, eds. *Regulating the Multinational Enterprise: National and International.* New York: Praeger Publishers, 1983.

Flamn, Kenneth. *The Global Factory: Foreign Assembly in International Trade.* Washington, D.C.: Brookings Institution, 1985.

Gamwall, C. C. "Maximizing Cash Flow in Multinational Benefit Plans." *Risk Management*, October 1984, pp. 50–66.

Ghosh, Pradip K., ed. *Multinational Cooperation and Third World Development.* Westport, Conn.: Greenwood Press, 1984.

Grosse, Robert. "Financial Transfer in the MNE: The Latin American Case." *Management International Review*, Winter 1986, pp. 33–42.

Hall, R. Quane. *Overseas Acquisitions and Mergers: Combining for Profits Abroad.* New York: Praeger Publishers, 1986.

Hennast, Jean. *A Theory of Multinational Enterprise.* Ann Arbor: University of Michigan Press, 1982.

Hladik, Karen F. *International Joint Ventures: An Economic Analysis of U.S.–Foreign Business Partnerships.* Lexington, Mass.: Lexington Books, 1985.

Kester, Carl, and Timothy A. Luehrman. "Why Dollar Bashing Doesn't Work: Effect of Cheapening Currency on Manufacturers." *Fortune*, October 27, 1986, pp. 137–39.

Kettell, Brian. *The Finance of International Business.* Westport, Conn.: Quorum Books, 1981.

Kim, Suk H. *International Business Finance.* Richmond, Va.: R. F. Dame, 1983.

Kong, Leo Edwin. *The International Transfer of Commercial Technology: The Role of Multinational Corporations.* New York: Arno Press, 1980.

Lachenmayer, Hubert. "The Effect of Currency Exchange Risks on the Cost of Equity Capital of the International and Multinational Firm." *Management International Review*, Spring 1984, pp. 28–36.

Linsberry, Gary. "American Insurance Companies Help Overseas Corporate Subsidiaries to Comply with Pension Legislation." *Barron's*, November 3, 1986, p. 50.

Pratten, Cliff. "The Importance of Giant Companies," *Lloyds Bank Review*, January 1986, p. 33.

Rahman, M. Zubaidus, and Robert W. Scapins. "Transfer Pricing by Multinationals: Some Evidence from Bangladesh." *Journal of Business Finance and Accounting*, August 1986, pp. 383–90.

Sesit, R. Michael. "Dollar's Drop Helps Most Multinational Firms: Currency Approach to Decline Varies Widely." *The Wall Street Journal,* September 3, 1986, p. 6.

Shapiro, Alan C. *Multinational Financial Management.* 2nd ed. Boston: Allyn & Bacon, 1986.

Sprinivasan, Venkat, and Yong H. Kim. "Payments Netting in International Cash Management: A Network Optimization Approach." *Journal of International Business Studies,* Summer 1986, pp. 1–11.

Swanson, E. Peggy. "Portfolio Diversification by Currency Denomination: An Approach to International Cash Management with Implications for Foreign Exchange Markets." *Quarterly Review of Economics and Business,* Spring 1986, pp. 95–106.

Szala, Ginger. "How Multinational Firms Use Futures and Options: Currency Trading One Way to Curb Risk." *Futures,* September 1985, pp. 54–61.

Willson, Elizabeth. "The Impact of the Dollar on High-Tech Multinationals." *Electronic Business,* May 15, 1985, pp. 59–66.

Endnotes

1. Louis T. Well, Jr., *Third World Multinationals: The Risk of Foreign Investment from Developing Countries* (Cambridge, Mass.: MIT Press, 1983).
2. *Economist,* November 17, 1984, p. 107.
3. Kenichi Ohmae, "Rethinking Global Corporate Strategy," *The Wall Street Journal,* September 18, 1985, p. 18.
4. John Robinson, "The European Commission: A New-Found Friend of Business," *International Management,* September 1986, pp. 70–74.
5. "The Ever-Grasping Drive," *Development Forum,* November 1982, p. 3.
6. "A Third World Bias at the U.N.," *Business Week,* July 20, 1981, p. 156.
7. Mary A. Fejfar, *Regulation of Business by International Agencies* (St. Louis, Mo.: Center for the Study of American Business, Washington University, November 1983), p. 35.
8. "World Bank, IDB Projects Offer Major Market for Washington MNC Reps," *Business International,* November 11, 1983, pp. 353–57.
9. John Hein, "The Intracompany Trade of U.S. Multinationals," *World Economic Monitor,* Conference Board, Fall 1986, pp. 71–90.
10. Richard Eells and Peter Nehemkis, *Corporate Intelligence and Espionage: A Blueprint for Executive Decision Making,* (New York: Macmillan, 1986), p. 89.
11. Peter F. Drucker, "The Changing Multinational," *The Wall Street Journal,* January 15, 1986, p. 30.
12. Bill Powell, Ronald Henkoff, and Madlyn Resenner, "Rebuilding Corporate Empires," *Newsweek,* April 14, 1986, p. 40.

SECTION V THREE AUTOMOBILE INDUSTRY CASES

After an overview of the world automobile industry and the automobile industry in Africa, three cases deal with three companies in Kenya, an African developing country. These cases are adapted from David Marshall Hunt and Peter Gufwoli, Strategic Management: Kenya, a Book of Cases *(Bristol, IN: Wyndham Hall Press, 1986), and are used by permission of the authors.*

Strategic Alternatives and Choices: An Overview of the Auto Industry and a Focus on the Industry in Africa, Particularly Kenya

A Brief Synopsis of the World Auto Industry

Throughout the world, transport plays a significant role in the economic lives of people. Whether by air, sea, or land, vehicles and other modes of transport have been used to move people and their goods from place to place. As recently as the 1984 drought and famine in Ethiopia and other African nations, thousands of tons of medical and foodstuff aid were transported by air, sea, and land along with other materials and personnel to bring a measure of aid to stricken areas. Such is the capability of modern transport systems in times of crisis, but when it comes to getting around locally, the automobile (e.g., car or small truck/van) has become one of the major purchases of people all over the world, especially in developed nations, and even in developing ones where camels, donkeys, and walking people now compete with autos for road space.

Whether for taking crops to market or transporting children to school, for going to the market to shop, or just off to work or to a neighbor's for a social gathering, autos are increasingly becoming the major local method of transport in many nations. The citizens of the United States own the most cars per capita, at a rate of 1.9 persons per car, according to 1983 statistics. The average rate for Western Europe is about 3 persons per car; for Japan, 4.5; Brazil, 15.0; Russia, 26.0; South Korea, 104.9; Nigeria, 125.0; and for China, there is one car for every 10,000 people.

American, Japanese, and European auto manufacturers dominate world auto markets, as the following exhibits make clear. Japanese car exports alone totaled an estimated 4 million units in 1984 versus 1.7 million units 10 years earlier. Not only are the major manufacturers from Europe, Japan, and America; the mature markets of these developed nations are also the primary sales tar-

Table 1

The World Auto Industry, 1984

Major Auto Manufacturers	Number of Cars Manufactured (millions)
General Motors (United States)	6.33
Ford (United States)	3.62
Toyota (Japan)	2.49
Nissan (Japan)	2.05
Volkswagen-Audi (West Germany)	1.88
Renault (France)	1.55
Peugeot (France)	1.46
Fiat (Italy)	1.39
Chrysler (United States)	1.27
Honda (Japan)	1.02
Mazda (Japan)	0.77
Mitsubishi (Japan)	0.59
Daimler-Benz (West Germany)	0.48
Austin Rover (Britain)	0.40

Sources: DRI Europe; *Economist,* March 2, 1985.

gets. For example, nearly half of Japan's 4 million exported cars went to North America in 1984, and only 90,000 units went to Africa, either in assembled or kits-for-assembly form. And, in fact, total Japanese exports to Africa showed a decline in recent years from 101,000 units in 1974 (see Figure 1A).

The DRI International Automotive Group forecast world sales growth of 1.5 percent for 1985, versus the 5 percent figure for 1984. Sales have reportedly peaked in the U.S. market, and the issues of import quotas between Japan and the United States are causing considerable difficulties, not the least of which are U.S. congressional calls for protectionist measures against the Japanese in numerous industries. In short, much of the future of the world auto industry is limited to the U.S. marketplace, and to the world's two largest auto manufacturers (i.e., GM and Ford) (see Figure 1B).

However, it is the Japanese auto manufacturers that have succeeded through "cost leadership" in world, and especially U.S., markets. The issue of new technology is also a vital one to all these auto manufacturers. In 1982 alone, Detroit (the big three U.S. auto firms—GM, Ford, and Chrysler) spent over US$4 billion on research and development. Computers, automated assembly lines, and robotics are all now part of the modern technologies of auto manufacturers in the United States, Japan, and Europe and in the emerging auto-manufacturing nations South Korea and Brazil. In short, the competition for world markets is fierce and

Figure 1

A. Japanese auto exports

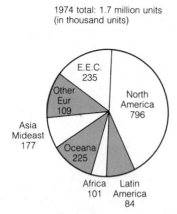

1974 total: 1.7 million units
(in thousand units)

E.E.C. 235
Other Eur 109
North America 796
Asia Mideast 177
Oceana 225
Africa 101
Latin America 84

1984 total: 4 million units
(in thousand units)

E.E.C. 790
North America 1,990
240
450
230
90
210

Sources: SMMT; DRI Europe; *Economist*, March 2, 1985.

B. Car production and trade, 1984 estimate, for the four largest markets

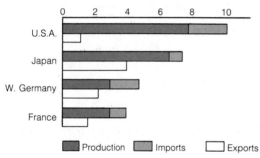

	0	2	4	6	8	10
U.S.A.						
Japan						
W. Germany						
France						

■ Production ▨ Imports ▢ Exports

Sources: DRI Europe; *Economist*, March 2, 1985.

D. Japanese domestic market shares in 1973
(in percentage of unit sales, all classes)

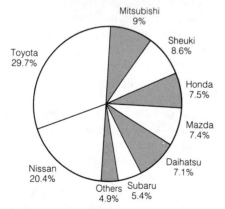

Mitsubishi 9%
Sheuki 8.6%
Toyota 29.7%
Honda 7.5%
Mazda 7.4%
Daihatsu 7.1%
Subaru 5.4%
Others 4.9%
Nissan 20.4%

Sources: W. I. Carr (Overseas) Ltd., *Economist*, March 2, 1985.

C. European auto market shares in 1984

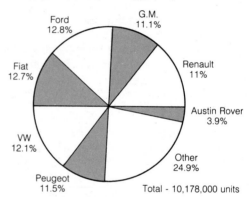

Ford 12.8%
G.M. 11.1%
Renault 11%
Austin Rover 3.9%
Other 24.9%
Peugeot 11.5%
VW 12.1%
Fiat 12.7%

Total - 10,178,000 units

Source: DRI Europe.

E. The World Auto Industry—1984 Figures

MAJOR AUTO MANUFACTURERS	NUMBER OF CARS MANUFACTURED
General Motors Corporation (U.S.A.)	6.33 million
Ford (U.S.A.)	3.62 million
Toyota (Japan)	2.49 million
Nissan (Japan)	2.05 million
Volkswagen-Audi (West Germany)	1.88 million
Renault (France)	1.55 million
Peugeot (France)	1.46 million
Fiat (Italy)	1.39 million
Chrysler (U.S.A.)	1.27 million

Sources: DRI Europe; *Economist*, March 2, 1985.

Exhibit 1

Press Releases about Recent Joint Ventures between Auto Manufacturers

"Motor Giants Set to Merge"   Johannesburg, Thursday

Ford, South Africa's second-largest motor vehicle manufacturer, and AMCAR, the third-largest producer, are to merge in an attempt to stem the operating losses of both companies. The merged company, to be known as South Africa Motor Corporation (SAMCOR), will be approximately 40 percent owned by Ford Canada, and 60 percent owned by companies in the Anglo American Group, (AFP).

Source: *Daily Nation* (Kenya), February 1, 1985.

"UK Deal for Honda"   London, Monday

Honda plans to produce engines, and later automobiles, in Britain in order to gain unrestricted access to the European Economic Community, the *Financial Times* reported today. Honda has a cooperation agreement with British Leyland to launch a new upmarket car late this year. Nissan is building a plant in Britain for an initial output of 24,000 cars, increasing to 100,000 by 1990.

Source: *Daily Nation* (Kenya), February 12, 1985.

"India Wins Truck Deal"   Tokyo, Tuesday

Japan's Nissan Motors is to become the first foreign automaker to produce trucks in India when its joint venture firm starts production of the Atlas pickup truck in March, a Nissan spokesman said yesterday. The spokesman said the Indian government was expected to approve soon a Nissan application of 15 percent equity in the Indian truck maker, Alwn Nissan Ltd. in Hyderabad, which is to produce the three-ton Atlas.

Source: *Daily Nation* (Kenya), April 15, 1985.

complex. And not the least complex issues are the interrelationships and merger/joint ventures of these auto manufacturers. There are so many "strategic and production and marketing arrangements" between auto manufacturers that it becomes difficult to know who the principals are. For example, see Exhibit 1 for recent press releases involving joint arrangements between Japanese, U.S., UK, Indian, and South African auto producers, and these are but the tip of the iceberg when viewed next to the giant Fremont, California, auto plant joint venture between Toyota and General Motors.

One small share of this complex and dynamic "world auto production/distribution situation" involves the African auto industry, to which we now turn our focus.

The African Auto Industry:
An Overview

Assembly/Production

Faced with the growing need for foreign exchange earnings, most of the sub-Saharan nations of Africa are troubled by the possibility of increasing local demand for largely imported (foreign exchange outflow) autos. Local manufacturing operations have existed in Africa for nearly 15 years (e.g., Nigeria's Peugeot plant at Kaduna). Nigeria also has plants assembling vehicles for VW, British Leyland, and Daimler. These local operations are primarily assemblers of completely knocked-down (CKD) kits of parts, or semi-knocked-down (SKD) operations (the latter usually being truck or van chassis/cab units to be fitted with locally manufactured bodies). Pure CKD operations have provided fewer jobs locally than anticipated, and therefore many African governments have required that a specified portion of the parts and components of autos be manufactured domestically (e.g., mufflers, tires, glass parts, and brake linings). Frequently, it has been further required that this percentage of locally made parts be increased over time.

The bottom line on these African auto assembly operations seems to involve the issue of mass production versus batch production technologies. Large-scale Japanese, U.S., and European auto firms utilize mass production assembly technologies with automated assembly lines, robotics, and highly computerized systems. These high-tech systems are designed to produce large runs of identical autos and trucks for a mass market. Yet demand in Africa is smaller. For example, Nigerians own one car per every 125 people, whereas every 2 Americans own one car. Most production lines in Africa are set up to assemble autos, trucks, or vans on a batch basis, and not just one type of vehicle.

Spare Parts

Another problem facing both African auto assemblers and the distributing agents for finished imports involves spare parts shortages. One estimate is that over the average life of a car (e.g., 160,000 kilometers), one fourth of the new car price will be spent on spare and replacement parts to keep the vehicle running.

Tires, brake linings, clutch assemblies, shock absorbers, and so forth need replacement, and rusted bodies need repairs. And in many African nations road conditions leave much to be desired, with the possible exception of Kenya, which has a well-developed network of tarmac roads between the major ports and inland cities. Stocks of spare parts are not always available in outlying areas. In the major cities, however, most auto dealers keep some inventories of parts, at least for their most popular models.

Dealers

Dealers who are licensed to sell the finished cars of major exporters and/or the assembled kits are another major segment of the auto industry, representing the marketing and maintenance functions. Leading finished-car exporters to Africa include British Leyland, Peugeot, Renault, Daimler-Benz, and Volkswagen. In terms of cars and light trucks/vans, several Japanese firms (e.g., Nissan, Toyota, Mazda, and Honda) now market nearly 30 percent of light vehicles in Africa.

Kenya's Auto Industry

There is one car per every 27 people in Kenya. Kenya is one of the largest African auto vehicle markets, with an estimated 250,000 vehicles on the road in 1983. In the 1970s, three major assembly facilities began operations in Thika, Mombasa, and Nairobi. Leyland (Kenya) opened in 1976 at Thika; Associated Vehicle Assemblers (AVA) then started up in Mombasa; and General Motors (Kenya), in Nairobi. Truck assembly plants were also opened by Fiat and Mack.

As in other African nations, Kenya has foreign exchange shortages. Thus, the local content rule (in Kenya up to 30 percent has been local content) is an important component of Kenyan auto assembly operations. Initially, Kenya's auto/truck assembly industry was expected to meet market growth and demands for commercial vehicles for small-scale business and farmers, as well as cars for city-dwelling citizens and tourism. In brief, Kenyan auto producers needed to be flexible to meet a multitude of small-vehicle demands. Light panel vans and trucks are one form of versatile vehicles that have sold well in the Kenyan markets. Yet the "Benz" remains the primary status symbol, and this saloon car is exported to Kenya in finished form at prices few Kenyans can afford. Even used saloon-sized cars (this is British terminology for larger, noneconomy cars) were imported to meet rising demand in recent times.

In brief, over 60 percent of the light vehicles (pickups, small buses, and vans) in operation in Kenya have been locally assembled over the past 10 years. And local content has risen to about 30 percent, but not to the targeted 45 percent. Labor and trim, fittings, and other parts comprise most of this local content. Jobs have, however, been created by the industry as a whole, and at least some foreign exchange has been saved by local assembling operations.

Many of these jobs are in the auto/vehicle spare parts segment. And there is a potential for more spare parts to be made locally, and thus even more jobs as vehicle demand increases. Champion Auto Spark Plugs and Car & General have a factory in Nairobi. Car & General is also in the brake linings, welding alloys, and retread tires business in Kenya.

Let's turn now from these three descriptions of the world, African, and Kenyan auto industries to some specific cases of auto/truck manufacturing, distribution, and maintenance within contemporary Kenya.

Exhibit 2

From March 1984 to March 1985, auto sales in Kenya were as follows:

Type of Car	Number of Cars Sold
Toyota	1,632
Nissan	1,616
Isuzu	1,200
Peugeot	1,024

Note: In addition to GM/Isuzu's locally assembled Uhuru, other auto firms are gearing up to assemble passenger cars locally, the most recent being Fiat's Uno, with Nissan and Toyota still in the planning phase, but close behind.
Source: *Daily Nation,* May 17, 1985.

Kenya's Major Auto Assemblers

Between 1976 and 1977, the Kenyan government authorized the startup of three motor vehicle assembly plants, with the government having a substantial shareholding of each (e.g., 51 percent of AVA).

Leyland (Kenya) Ltd. opened an assembly factory in Thika in 1976. Leyland, Cooper Motor Corporation (CMC), and the Kenyan government were the majority shareholders. Models assembled at Thika were as follows: first, Leyland trucks and buses; Land Rovers; Range Rovers; and VW Kombis. Later additions were the Mitsubishi Canter, the Suzuki minijeep, and the Mazda 322 panel vans.

By mid-1977, Associated Vehicle Assemblers (AVA) (51 percent government owned and 49 percent divided between the Inchape and Lonrho groups), started operations located strategically near Mombasa's port and the main road and rail routes to Nairobi. Larger than the Thika operation, AVA produced vehicles for many local distributors and has flexibility to focus operations on the best-selling vehicles at any one point in time. D. T. Dobie (franchise holder for Nissan-Datsun and Mercedes-Benz) and Marshalls (Peugeot and Volvo), Marshariki Motors (Hino trucks), Bruce Ltd. (Isuzu trucks), and the VW Golf van all were utilizers of the Mombasa plant.

Late in 1977, General Motors (Kenya) Ltd. started plant operations in Nairobi. This was the most extensive and costly auto plant to date in Kenya. Tight control over the operation from assembly to sales was held by the minority shareholders, GM of America. Isuzu light trucks and the Trooper sold well. A deal with Jeep for the assembly of CJ7 and Cherokee four-wheel-drive vehicles was not successful. And most recently, GM Kenya has beaten its competitors to the punch with the locally produced Uhuru small passenger car, publicly unveiled early in 1985 (see Exhibit 2).

A final note: As the local content seems to be reaching a maximum and as local demand matures, these three assemblers may consider exporting Kenyan-assembled vehicles to neighboring markets in the Preferential Trade Area (PTA) nations. If the PTA restrictions regarding no foreign ownership of firms subject to the agreement are lifted or modified in the near future, all three auto assemblers may start exporting.

Westlands Motors Ltd. recently (January 1985) exported three locally assembled Toyota (Hi-lux 4 × 4s) to Tanzania and has advance orders for five more units to be delivered to Mogadishu.

In sum, even though Kenya's economic climate has been a complex one in recent years, both GM Kenya Ltd. and AVA have produced operating profits, while Leyland Kenya Ltd. has been in the red. Some critics are beginning to ask whether Kenya needs three auto assembly facilities, touching off the argument of nationalization of Kenya's auto-assembling industry.

Sources

African Business, March 1985, pp. 45–50.

African Technical Review, November 1984, pp. 39–49.

Daily Nation, "Kenyan Company Exports Vehicles," January 26, 1985, and "Goods Quality Stressed," February 22, 1985.

New African, November 1984, pp. 33–37.

Newsweek, February 25, 1985, pp. 36–38.

"A Survey of the World's Motor Industry," *Economist*, March 2, 1985.

Weekly Review, January 4, 1985, pp. 26–27.

Case 1

Vizuri Auto

Late in 1974, Capital Motors was taken over by two African entrepreneurs and renamed Vizuri Auto. Vizuri is the first African dealership in all of Kenya. Vizuri had experienced its poorest performance during the previous three-year ownership. In the opinion of the present managing director, Mr. Leo, the previous management had held too many diverse interests, such as car rentals, an advertising agency, and rally car racing. This led to a breakdown in the managerial control system. There were duplication of bills, poor supervision, and unexplained losses in spare parts inventory.

The past owner of what is now Vizuri had been a wealthy man with little time to pay attention to careful control and marketing of his automobile dealership. Books were sloppily kept, and accounts were so confused that it was difficult to tell just where the unprofitable parts of the operation were. Total losses for the year 1973 were estimated at 200,000 shillings, the Kenyan currency, for all the activities related to the dealership. The break-even point for new car sales was about 20 per month, but Vizuri averaged 15 per month in 1973, and both new and used car inventory grew dangerously heavy with slow-moving, high-priced cars. In the months immediately before the takeover of the new managers, new car sales dropped to 13 per month, and service volume also fell as wary customers fled to seek a more stable place to buy and service their cars. Another unfortunate event during this period was that many of the skilled mechanics and salesmen were hired away by other dealerships, which were always in great need of trained personnel.

New Management

Against this background the new management took over. Losses continued at the rate of about 15,000 shillings per month for the first two months under their leadership. The management was concerned about the present level of overhead expenses. The dealership is very well equipped, well kept, and rather plush by general standards. As a result, overhead is very high.

Vizuri Auto is located in the city of Nairobi. It does not strike the casual observer as being very different from any other dealership in the area. It is located on a busily traveled main road. About 75 percent of the employees are Asian. Out of seven salesmen, two are African. The receptionist and other people with "high visibility" are Asians. The managers of the departments (used cars, new cars, office, service, and used car preparation) are Asians. The managing director commented that there had been no personnel problems since the takeover. The expected tension between the older Asian salesmen and the new management had not materialized to date. He went on to mention that since the takeover, many mechanics who had left during the past year had come back to the company, hoping to work for the new management. Discussions seemed very cordial, and the managers seemed to be highly motivated. On one occasion, the service manager was elated because his department was so busy for a change. He thought it would be the busiest day since the takeover.

The New Owners

The two new owners of Vizuri are the chairman, Mr. Kesho, and the managing director, Mr. Leo. Both are African. Mr. Leo worked under the old management and was the sales manager when the takeover was effected. He is a well-known and respected member of the community. Mr. Kesho received an advanced degree in engineering and then went on to take some courses in management training at Howard University in Washington, D.C.

Mr. Kesho spoke freely about why he had become involved in Vizuri and about what his plans were for the future. The most important element in defining his policy and his actions was the fact that Mr. Kesho saw African society as classist and racist. He felt that the wealthy Africans and Asians would not be able to cope with a society where all lived and worked together as equals, and that this might also be true of the Europeans. The wealthy Africans and Asians were presently in control. They ran politics, owned all property, and managed all resources. Mr. Kesho saw the possibility of wealthy folk feeling more and more threatened, and therefore furthering their own position of dominance by oppressing certain 'tribes' and the ordinary people. He continued by saying that in order for the ordinary man to be less vulnerable, they must own their own property or at least own property collectively. Ordinary people must join hands and develop a united property base in order to be less susceptible to oppression.

Mr. Kesho thought that the managerial skills he possessed might be able to help Vizuri Auto become a viable enterprise and thereby work toward his goal of some reduction in race and class distinction. While both Mr. Kesho and Mr. Leo were motivated by a desire to contribute something toward this end, they also felt the squeeze of an economic situation which demanded that they pay immediate attention to avoiding bankruptcy. They realized that to succeed in their plans, they must quickly find a way to stay in business by selling more vehicles.

The managing director thought that people would be inclined to come from outside Nairobi simply to avail themselves of Vizuri's superior servicing. Recent advertising campaigns of all manufacturers had stressed choosing the right dealer and servicing. Vizuri was very well equipped for servicing. They had an electronic test track device and other modern equipment. The managing director thought servicing to be the company's distinctive strength. High use of servicing facilities was very desirable in order to pay overhead and also because the average margin on spare parts was 37 percent. Management was busy trying to compile marketing information on the frequency of repeat sales and services in order to gain a better knowledge of the market. All were agreed that Vizuri could not concentrate its efforts on one segment of the market.

One of Mr. Kesho's chief goals was to gain a dominant share of the Nairobi market. Within Nairobi there were several dealerships. In considering his competition, however, Mr. Kesho commented that he thought many people would travel from all over the country to purchase or be serviced by an outstanding business. He also felt that it might be of some use to begin to stress in their advertising that they were the first African dealership in the nation. He felt that since they were already 'leaders' in the area, so to speak, they had a duty to push the interests of the wananchi (this Kiswahili word means the common people, the laborers, or the poor) and demonstrate to the nation that Africans could be very successful businessmen in an area that had just been opened to them.

Mr. Leo reminded him that it would be senseless to do anything that would damage the good relations that had been established with the previous European, wealthy African, and Asian customers. He said that whatever goal had to be attained, it could not be attained in an aggressive, competitive setting if they themselves were not also aggressive and competitive, even cutthroat "like the rest of them" if they had to be.

Mr. Kesho disagreed. He felt that principle was principle, that the goal would be to set an example for the nation by showing how a business could be run successfully and be beneficial to the community at large without using exploitative selling tactics and trying to take every shilling possible from the already poor and nearly destitute wananchi. He wanted to stop catering to the rich, bourgeois clientele and start making deals that would make it possible for more ordinary people to purchase their services and parts, if not their new vehicles. "If we continue to run this place the way it was run before, then where is the change, and what was it for? I say we must cater to our own and forget those partners in exploitation. We may have it difficult for a while, but are we headed for whatever was referred to as 'African socialism,' or are we going to join the mule train and exploit the surplus? I say we aim at the ordinary people in every policy way. Then, if we get the old-style business as well, it is all right. But, I tell you, my brother Leo, today is where we start."

Mr. Leo still felt that was incorrect. Earlier, he had considered a two-phased approach, wherein which they might differentiate their appeal to the two classes of markets. But the cost was prohibitive. If Kesho was correct, that would mean changing our image drastically. It would mean that we could only hope to recoup an 'attractive' image by moving beyond the European, Asian, African argument. But if the society was like this, how could we expect to survive?

Discussion Questions

1. *From a corporate strategy position, give an action plan to resolve the policy issues in this case.*
2. *Identify the problems facing Vizuri Auto's current management. Which problems (s) is/are most critical? Discuss why.*
3. *Examine the control system at Vizuri Auto, and suggest ways to improve the system. Discuss the costs/benefits of implementing your recommended improvements.*
4. *How will the change in ownership influence future operations? If you were the new owners, what strategies/alternatives would you consider? Examine both of the strategies suggested in the case and others that you can devise.*
5. *How might Mr. Kesho's views and attitudes affect operations and personnel? Examine and discuss Mr. Kesho's management style, goals, and so on. Compare Mr. Kesho's and Mr. Leo's management styles, goals, and so on.*
6. *Compare and contrast the goals and strategies of Vizuri Auto with those of General Motors (Kenya) and D. T. Dobie—the auto firms discussed in Cases 2 and 3.*

Case 2

General Motors (Kenya) Ltd.

An Introduction

America's and the world's largest producer of motor vehicles, the American-owned and -based General Motors Corporation has been operating a vehicle assembly plant in Nairobi since negotiations were completed with the Kenyan government in 1977. Fifty-one percent of the shares in GM (Kenya) Ltd. are held by the Kenyan government, with GMC of the United States holding the minority shares (49 percent).

The management of GM's (Kenya) assembly operations has recently undergone a change in leadership. Mr. R. R. Johnson was the managing director assigned by the U.S. parent company to get the operation started in 1977. And during his tenure, GM (Kenya) developed its local staff and expanded its assembly operation to a wide range of vehicles. However, the "plum in the pie" of the Kenyan auto industry, the local production of a passenger car, will now be the focus of attention for his successor, Mr. Maury F. Dieterich.

There has long been an acknowledged market potential for passenger cars that are locally assembled, but until March 1985, when GM (Kenya)'s Uhuru model passenger car was unveiled, government restrictions had kept this possible market from being realized. The AVA, GM Kenya, and Leyland assembly plants have all been interested in the local assembling of passenger cars, but GM Kenya appears now to have taken the lead with its Uhuru model.

The New Managing Director

In November of 1984, Mr. Maury F. Dieterich was appointed the new managing director of GM Kenya. Mr. Dieterich had been the financial director for three years prior to this, and he was therefore already well known by the local staff. Mr. Dieterich, as managing director, is a member of the board of GM Kenya, which is presently chaired by Mr. Bernard Hinga. Mr. Hinga and most directors are Kenyans.

Company Objectives

Discussing the production capacity of GM Kenya, Mr. Dieterich recently reported that the Nairobi plant was operating with only one shift (it has a three-shift potential) and forecast production of 2,300 units—approximately 60 percent of the capacity of one shift (e.g., 800 medium-duty trucks, 600 light-duty trucks, 500 pickups, 300 utility vehicles, and 100 buses). This is reportedly a 50 percent increase over last year's levels of production. Utilizing a greater proportion of the production capacity would help GM Kenya to fulfill a national goal of providing more jobs.

Mr. Dieterich also stated that GM Kenya had a responsibility to its customers and to the public to continually improve on the quality and safety of its products, to meet both strict international and GMC parent company standards, and to maintain high levels of service. In short, he stated that it is service and quality that really sell products.

Finally, Mr. Dieterich said that he would follow his predecessor's example of an "open-door policy" and encourage workers to present their ideas and give their opinions on work-related issues.

Keeping shareholders happy and making a profit were two other goals noted by Mr. Dieterich. And the passenger car market (e.g., the new Uhuru model) may both increase profits (and therefore dividends to shareholders) and save the government foreign exchange now spent on imports of passenger cars.

Another objective of GM Kenya that focuses on the national shortage of foreign exchange involves the exporting of assembly tools made by GM in its local plants. For example, in April 1985, it reported sending one of its engineers to Egypt to install and commission vehicle assembly equipment made in Kenya and exported to Egypt. The tools exported to Egypt were reportedly designed in Kenya and were designed as labor intensive. Other exports of assembly tools have been made to Nigeria, Zambia, Tunisia, and Latin America, and Egypt has placed a 3 million Kenya shillings order for future delivery. Many local engineers feel that Kenya's ability to manufacture for export is only in the infancy stage and has considerable future regional market potential.

Another area of export interest to GM Kenya directly involves the assembly of vehicles, and perhaps the new passenger car model. The first hurdle was cleared when the company announced that the Kenyan government and President Moi had given endorsement to go ahead with the production of Kenya's first locally assembled passenger car, the Uhuru, at a March 1985 public unveiling ceremony. The Uhuru model is powered by an 1800-cc engine and has a high content of locally made components and parts. Tires, batteries, paint, and windscreens are all to come from local manufacturing, and a prototype of the Uhuru was tested and on view at the ceremony.

The local market is the stated primary focus of GM Kenya; however, with the advent of the Preferential Trade Area (PTA), regional areas in Tanzania, Uganda, Sudan, and Zanzibar have become potential markets for automotive vehicles assembled in Kenya. In total, GM Kenya has reported exporting 10 percent of its total production during each of the past two years, but with volume increasing.

Some of the problems and strategies being considered by GM Kenya for penetrating regional markets are listed below:

First, Uganda, Tanzania, and other African nations have severe foreign exchange shortages themselves. To counter this, GM Kenya is considering barter trade arrangements as a strategy.

Second, the PTA restricts its most favorable trade terms to locally owned firms in its member countries. GM Kenya is 49 percent owned by GMC of the United States.

Third, to date the PTA is having trouble getting started, and communication, rail, air, and road transportation links between member nations are themselves a major obstacle to interregional trade. For example, Kenya has nearly completed its share of the Trans-Africa Highway across Kenya from the Tanzanian border to the Sudan to the north, but it has had to pick up the cost of a portion of the road construction that was to be paid by these neighboring nations. And meanwhile, efforts to reunite and/or reopen Kenyan and Tanzanian rail connections have been at best frustrating.

Discussion Questions

1. *How might a change in leadership affect the strategies, structure, and relationships in a firm such as GM Kenya? How would you cope with such a change? Examine the advantages and disadvantages.*
2. *Identify all of the interest groups in the case, then list their demands, and, finally, prioritize the list of demands. For example, the government wants to earn foreign exchange; is this a primary or a secondary demand placed on GM Kenya? And how do the other demands of other interest groups rank in terms of each other?*
3. *Examine the threats and opportunities in the case, and then analyze GM Kenya's past strategies and its possible future strategies. Make other recommendations of your own, and defend them with facts and sound arguments.*

Case 3

D. T. Dobie & Co. (Kenya) Ltd.

and Nissan-Datsun

Case Background

Mrs. D. T. Dobie, widow of the late Colonel David Dobie, D.S.O., has been the executive chairperson of the D. T. Dobie group of companies for 15 years. She is an

Figure 1

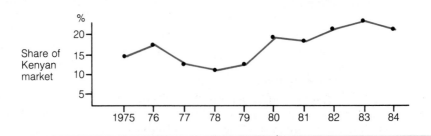

active wildlife conservationist, and many developments have occurred at D. T. Dobie during her tenure, beginning with the 1972 opening of its extensive service center, a 17,000 square-foot facility located in Nairobi on Lusaka Road. In 1973, it started operating a technical training school, also in Nairobi. The company's history with Nissan-Datsun of Japan dates back to 1966, when it became the franchised Datsun dealer for Kenya to complement the saloon car market-leading Mercedes-Benz franchise it had been operating since the founding of the firm by Colonel Dobie.

D. T. Dobie's Nissan-Datsun

Operations

This case focuses primarily on D. T. Dobie's Nissan-Datsun operations. There are estimated to be over 20,000 Nissan-Datsun vehicles in Kenya, and D. T. Dobie forecast sales of 8,500 vehicles in 1985. With current estimates ranging from just under to over 20 different makes of vehicle to choose from, Kenyan customers have been buying Nissan-Datsuns at a rate of approximately one in every five vehicle purchases since 1981. D. T. Dobie and Nissan-Datsun have been the overall vehicles sales leaders for ten straight years (1975–1985). (See Figure 1.)

Nissan-Datsun captured 15.7 percent of the Kenyan market in 1974, and it has never fallen below a 12.25 percent share (1978), with market share peaking at 22.8 percent in 1983. In terms of sales volume, however, 1980 was Nissan-Datsun's top year, with 17,200 units, versus 7,900 new vehicles sold in 1984. (See Figure 2.)

Product Mix

D. T. Dobie's Nissan-Datsun small cars and light trucks have long been complemented by its larger Mercedes-Benz luxury saloon cars. But in the small-vehicle

Figure 2

Vehicle Sales in Kenya, 1984: Some Notes, Facts, and Figures

1. 1984 new sales increases 27% over 1983:
   Sales volume, 1984—7,900
   Sales volume, 1980—17,200
   D. T. Dobie sales, 1984—1,600 (20%)
2. Notes on breakdown of sales:
   a. Light utility vehicles (38.4% of total vehicle of market)
      (1) Datsun 1200-cc pickup
      (2) Toyota panel van
   b. One-ton pickups (a very competitive market segment)
      (1) Peugeot—estimated 50%
      (2) Toyota—350 units
      (3) Nissan-Datsun (declined 2% but sold more units)
   c. Four-wheel drives (all terrain)
      (1) Land Rover (again)
      (2) Isuzu Trooper
      (3) Datsun Double Cab (4 × 4) } close to a tie
      (4) Toyota Land Cruiser (declining sales)
      Note: Suzuki Jeep is first in small four-wheelers
   d. Buses (this market grew by 50% due to tourism)
      (1) Nissan-Datsun E23 Minibus
      (2) Mitsubishi (Colts)
      (3) VW Kombi (a distant third)
   e. Matatus
      (1) One-ton pickups
      (2) Secondhand Nissan-Datsun E23s
      (3) Mitsubishi Canter, 3 tons
      (4) Nissan Cabstar, 3 tons (due in 1985–86)
   f. Heavy trucks (30% decline in new vehicle market of over 15 tons)
      (1) Leyland
      (2) Mercedes-Benz
   g. Future: Locally assembled passenger saloon or estate car?

markets of Kenya, its leadership has extended from the time of the imported Datsun Sunny, Violet, and Bluebird models to today's locally assembled pickups, double cabs, minivan buses, and four-wheel-drive vehicles. For example, D. T. Dobie records show sales of over 3,000 Datsun 1200 pickups (550 in 1984 alone), thus making it Kenya's all-time most popular vehicle.

More recently, the versatile 720 series of one-ton pickups has been selling well. This vehicle comes with a number of changes or options (e.g., petrol or diesel engines, two- or four-wheel drive, single or double cabs). In fact, D. T. Dobie instigated the popular four-wheel-drive, double-cab pickup in Kenya, and it enjoys a clear market edge with these versatile pickups.

Production

Since 1977, when Associated Vehicle Assemblers (AVA) (see Industry Study) began auto assembly operations at its Mombasa facility, more than 10,000 Nissan-Datsuns have been assembled locally. Beginning with the Datsun 620 one-ton pickups, local assembly has continued to the 720 models. In 1984, approximately 2,000 Nissan vehicles were assembled by AVA, an increase of 1,900 vehicles since AVA's first partial year of operations (1977).

Production is based largely on CKDs, with kits being imported from Nissan-Datsun of Japan for assembly in Mombasa. In 1977, CKD kits consisted of almost 100 percent imported parts and were in essence purely imported vehicles, requiring only local labor for assembly. Today's CKD kits include imported body parts, engines, and gear boxes—and not much more. And the amount of local content in locally assembled Nissan-Datsuns has increased over time to an estimated 40 percent of vehicle value. Some of an increasing list of locally supplied parts and materials are as follows: tires, batteries, brake linings, springs, paint, glass, seats, trim, upholstery, radiators, and exhausts.

The local producers/suppliers of these parts include Firestone (tires), Auto-Spring Manufacturers Ltd., R. B. Shaw (Africa) Ltd. (Don brand brake linings), and Chloride Exide (Kenya) Ltd. (batteries), to name just a few firms in Kenya's growing auto parts industry.

Most of the worldwide auto giants (e.g., General Motors, Ford, Toyota, and Nissan-Datsun) require strict adherence to company product quality standards. The Nissan Motor Company maintains a tight control on assembly and on the quality of Nissan-Datsun vehicles coming off the AVA assembly lines. Japanese technicians supervise and provide quality control checks to ensure that product standards are met. Often, these product standards are tougher than national and international vehicle quality and safety standards.

In sum, D. T. Dobie likes to say that the locally produced vehicles are better suited to local markets than even the Japanese-built equivalent. The next step that D. T. Dobie hopes for is the assembling of passenger cars, and it feels that Nissan-Datsun, AVA, and its own research and development activities are ready for such a move. But General Motors (Kenya) has beaten them to the punch and introduced the Uhuru model, which will be Kenya's first locally produced passenger car. Having been a leader in several innovations in Kenya's auto industry, D. T. Dobie and Nissan-Datsun are now behind the competition in at least this one category.

The Competition

D. T. Dobie, Kenya's Nissan-Datsun dealer, has made a commercial success of its one-ton pickup by offering it in a variety of forms. Single- or double-cab versions are available in two- or four-wheel drive, and an option of petrol or diesel engines exists. Westlands Motors (Toyota's hi-lux pickup) was quick to copy Dobie's success in this manner. Other pickup competition comes from GM's Isuzu (Chevy luv), Mitsubishi, and Mazda.

Peugeot (sold by Marshalls) may well have the best-suited multipurpose front end. The Peugeot 504 (formerly the market-leading 404 series), pickup, 504 saloon, and 504 station wagon all utilize the same front end. This versatility makes a whole family of Peugeot vehicles possible with a limited number of many common parts. However, until the government recently authorized GM Kenya to assemble locally the first Kenyan passenger car, these competitors were severely restricted.

Since 1976–77, the three Kenyan assembly plants have only been permitted to assemble commercial and utility vehicles from CKD kits. However, GM Kenya appears to have opened the door to greater expectations.

Preceded by a maze of confusing and changing restrictions on the import of both new and used passenger cars and by lesser restrictions on the import of saloon cars (e.g., the very popular, but expensive, "Benz"), because of heavy outflows of foreign exchange needed for local socioeconomic development, the GM Uhuru may be an opportunity or a threat to such competition as D. T. Dobie, Marshalls, and Westlands Motors.

Discussion Questions

1. *Compare this case and the GM Kenya case, especially the goals of each firm. How is social responsiveness reflected in each case?*
2. *What strategies are pursued by D. T. Dobie and GM Kenya to achieve social responsibility objectives? Would you suggest other social responsibility goals and strategies?*
3. *What roles do former colonial and present foreign ownership play in the goals and strategies of GM Kenya and D. T. Dobie? In their present business operations?*
4. *What is the foreign company's role in D. T. Dobie's operations?*

APPENDIX A

SOURCES OF ECONOMIC AND FINANCIAL INFORMATION

I. World

A. *Abecor Country Reports*—Barclays Bank, 54 Lombard Street, London EC3P 3AH.

B. *Business International*—Business International, One Dag Hammarskjold Plaza, New York 10017.

C. *Country Studies*—Union Bank of Switzerland, 8021 Zurich.

D. *Development Forum*—United Nations, New York 10017.

E. *Economic Review*—Public Information Dept., Federal Reserve Bank of San Francisco, P.O. Box 7702, San Francisco, California 94120.

F. *Ernst and Whinney International Series*—Ernst and Whinney, 153 East 53rd Street, New York 10022.

G. *Eximbank Record*—Exim Bank, Washington, D.C. 20571.

H. *Extebank*—Banco Exterior de España; Carrera de San Jeronimo, Madrid.

I. *Finance and Development*—International Monetary Fund, Washington, D.C. 20431.

J. *Foreign Exchange Review*—Manufacturers Hanover Trust Company, New York 10022.

K. *IMF Survey*—IMF, Washington, D.C. 20431.

L. *International Economic Conditions*—Research and Public Information, Federal Reserve Bank of St. Louis, P.O. Box 442, St. Louis, Missouri 63166.

M. *International Finance*—The Chase Manhattan Bank, New York.

N. *OPEC Bulletin*—Public Information Department, Organization of the Petroleum Exporting Countries, Obere Donaustrasse 93, 1020 Vienna, Austria.

O. *Overseas Business Reports*—U.S. Department of Commerce, Washington, D.C.

P. *Prospects*—Swiss Bank Corporation, CH-4002, Basel.

A

Q. *U.N. Statistical Yearbook*—United Nations.
R. *UNU Newsletter*—1911 Kenbar Court, McLean, Virginia 22101.
S. *World Development Report* (annual)—Publications, The World Bank, 1818 H Street, N.W., Washington, D.C. 20433; $12.95. This is an invaluable data source.
T. *World Statistics in Brief*—United Nations.
U. *Yearbook of Labor Statistics*—International Labor Organization.

II. Africa

A. Region
Business Europe—Business International, see above.
B. South Africa
South African Digest—Department of Information, Private Bag X152, Pretoria 0001.
C. Tunisia
Tunisia Industrial News—Tunisia Investment Promotion Agency, 630 Fifth Avenue, Suite 862, New York 10020.

III. Asia

A. Region
1. *ABD Quarterly Review*—Asian Development Bank, P.O. Box 789, Manila, The Philippines
2. *Business Asia*—Business International, see above.
3. *Pacific Basin Economic Indicators*—Federal Reserve Bank of San Francisco, P.O. Box 7702, San Francisco 94120.
4. *Standard Chartered Review*—see above.
B. India
United Commercial Bank Review—United Commercial Bank, 10 Brabourne Road, Calcutta.
C. Indonesia
Indonesia Development News—National Development Information Office, Hill and Knowlton, Inc., 633 Third Avenue, New York 10017.
D. Japan
1. *Japan Banking Briefs*—Fuji Bank, C.P.O. Box 148, Tokyo.
2. *Japan Report, Consulate General of Japan*—280 Park Avenue, New York 10017.
3. *Jetro Business Information Series*—Japanese Trade Organization, 1221 Avenue of the Americas, New York.
4. *Sell in Japan*—U.S. Department of Commerce, Washington, D.C. 20230.
5. *Sumitomo Bank Review, Economic Survey*—Sumitomo Bank, 3-2, 1-Chome, Marunouchi, Chiyoda-ku, Tokyo.
6. *The Wheel Extended*—Toyota Motor Sales, Public Relations Department 2-3-18, Kudan-Minami, Chiyodo-ku, Tokyo 102.

7. *Japan Periodicals 1985*—This is a listing of 225 business periodicals in Japan, some of which are free. Write Keizai Koho Center, 6-1, Otemachi 1-Chome, Chiyoda-ku, Tokyo 100. Tell them you are a professor of international business.
8. *Speaking of Japan*—Same address as 7.
9. *Economic Eye*—Same address as 7.

E. Korea
1. *Monthly Bulletin*—The Bank of Korea, Seoul.
2. *Monthly Economic Statistics*—The Bank of Korea.
3. *Quarterly Economic Review*—The Bank of Korea.

F. Middle East
Middle East Executive Reports (monthly)—Middle East Executive Reports, 1115 Massachusetts Avenue, N.W., Washington, D.C. 20005. $300 annually ($145 to universities).

G. Taiwan
1. *Economic Review*—International Commerical Bank of China, Taipai, Taiwan.
2. *Taiwan Industrial Panorama*—Industrial Development and Investment Center, Taipai, Taiwan.
3. *Monthly Economic Survey*—The International Commercial Bank of China, Head Office, Taipai, Taiwan.

H. Thailand
Monthly Review—Public Relations Dept., Bankok Bank, 23 Surawong Road, Bankok.

I. Turkey
1. *Bulletin Mensuel*—Banque Centrale de la Republique de Turquie, Ankara.
2. *Turkey, An Economic Survey* (annual)—Turkish Industrialists and Businessmen's Association, Cumhuriyet Cadessi, Dortler Apt. 18/2 Elmadag, Istanbul.
3. YAPI ve KREDI BANKASI, Economics Department, P.O. Box 250, 250 Beyoglu, Istanbul.

IV. Europe

A. Region
1. *Bulletin*—Credit Suisse, 8021 Zurich, 8 Paradeplatz, Switzerland.
2. *Business Europe*—Business International One Dag Hammarskjold Plaza, New York 10017.
3. *Business Facts and Figures*—Union Bank of Switzerland, Zurich.
4. *EFTA Bulletin*—EFTA, 9-11 rue de Varembé CH-1211, Geneva 20.
5. *Europe*—European Community, 2100 M Street, N.W., Washington, D.C. 20037.
6. *OECD Economic Indicators* (annual)—OECD.
7. *OECD Economy Surveys*—OECD.

8. *OECD Observer*—OECD, 1750 Pennsylvania Avenue N.W., Washington, D.C. 20006.
9. *Prospects*—Swiss Bank Corporation, Aeschenvorstadt 1, Basel.

B. Austria

Landerbank Report, Landerbank, A-1010 Vienna, Am Hof 2, Austria.

C. Belgium

Weekly Bulletin—Kredietbank, Opzichterstraat 41, B-1020, Brussels.

D. Denmark
1. *Main Features of the Danish Economy*—Den Danske Bank, AF 1871 Aktieselskab, Holmens Kanal, Dk-1092 Copenhagen K.
2. *Quarterly Review*—Copenhagen Handelsbank, 2, Holmens Kanal, Dk-1091 Copenhagen K.

E. Finland
1. *Economic Review*—Kansallis—Osake—Pankki, Box 10, SF-00101, Helsinki 10.
2. *Monthly Bulletin*—Bank of Finland, Helsinki.

F. Germany East

GDR Economics Service, Chamber of Foreign Trade of the GDR, DDR-108 Berlin, Schadowstrasse 1.

G. Germany West
1. *German-American Trade News*—German American Chamber of Commerce, 666 Fifth Avenue, New York 10019.
2. *Monthly Report*—Deutsche Bundesbank, P.O. Box 2633, D6000, Frankfurt am Main 1.
3. *Deutsche Bank Bulletin*, Deutsche Bank, Frankfurt (Main).

H. Great Britain
1. *Economic Progress Report*—H.M. Treasury, Parliament Street, London SW1P3AG.
2. *Quarterly Bulletin*—Bank of England, London, EC2R8AH.
3. *Lloyds Bank Review*—The Editor, Lloyds Bank Review, 71 Lombard Street, London EC3P 3BS.
4. *Quarterly Review*—National Westminster Bank Limited, 41 Lothbury, London EC2P 2BP.
5. *Midland Bank Review*—Midland Bank plc, P.O. Box 2, Griffin House, Silver Street Head, Sheffield, S1 3GG.

I. Italy
1. *Italian Trends*—Banca Nazionale del Lavoro, Via Veneto 119, Rome.
2. *Review of the Economic Condition in Italy*—Banco di Roma, Via del Corso, 207, 00186 Rome.
3. *The Italian Economy*—Economic Research Dept., Banca Commerciale Italiana, Milan.

J. Netherlands
1. *Bank Mees and Hope NV*, P.O. Box 95, 3000 AB Rotterdam.
2. *Economic Review*—ABN Bank, 32 Vijzelstraat, Amsterdam.

3. *Holland Info*—Economic Information Service, The Hague.
K. Norway
   1. *DNC Monthly Survey*—Den Norske Creditbank, Oslo.
   2. *Economic Bulletin*—Norges Bank, P.O. Box 336, Sentrum, Oslo 1.
   3. *Economic News*—Bergen Bank, Oslo.
   4. *Financial Review*—Norwegian Bankers' Association, P.O. Box 1489, Vika, Oslo.
   5. *Norway Information*—Norwegian Information Service, 825 Third Avenue, New York 10022.
L. Spain
   Noticiario Economico—Banco de Vizcaya, Gran Via, 1, Bilbao.
M. Sweden
   Newsletter from Sweden—Swedish-International Press Bureau, Skeppargatan 37, S-11452, Stockholm.
N. Switzerland
   SwissBusiness (bimonthly)—Swiss Office for Development of Trade, Case Postal 1128, CH-1001, Lausanne.

V. Western Hemisphere

A. Region
   1. *Andean Group*—Junta de Cartagena, Casilla 3237, Lima, Peru (official organ of the Andean Group).
   2. *BOLSA Review*—Bank of London and South America, 40-66 Queen Victoria Street, London EC4P 4EL.
   3. *Business Latin America*—Business International, One Dag Hammarskjold Plaza, New York 10017.
   4. *Caribbean Basin Economic Survey*—Federal Reserve Bank of Atlanta 30303.
   5. *Carta Informativa*—SIECA, 4a Av. 10-25, Zona 14, Guatemala, Guatemala (official organ of CACM).
   6. *Comercio Exterior*—Banco Nacional de Comercio Exterior, Avenue Chapultapec, 230; Mexico 7, D.F., Mexico.
   7. *IDB News*—Inter-American Development Bank, 303 17th Street, N.W., Washington D.C. 20577.
   8. *Lateinamerkia*—Deutsche Bank, Frankfurt (Main), Germany.
   9. *Notas Sobre la Economia y el Desarrollo de America Latina*—Cepal, Casilla 179 D. Santiago, Chile.
B. Argentina
   Economic Information on Argentina—Ministerio de Economia (prensa), Hipolita Yrigoyen 250, piso 6, oficina 625, Buenos Aires.
C. Brazil
   1. *ML Monthly Letter*—Banco do Brasil, 550 Fifth Ave., New York, N.Y. 10036.

2. *Newsletter Brazil*—the First National Bank of Boston—see Argentina.
3. *Trends and Perspectives of the Brazilian Economy*—quarterly from Banco Lar Brasileiro, caixa Postal, 221-Zc-00, 20,000, Rio de Janeiro, R.J. Brazil.
4. *Brasil*—Comercio e Industria, SIG, Q4-No. 217, 70.610-Brasilia, D.F., Brazil.

D. Canada
1. *Business Review*—Bank of Montreal, P.O. Box 6002, Montreal, P.O., H3C 3B1.
2. *Monthly Review*—The Bank of Nova Scotia, 44 King Street, W., Toronto, Canada M5H 1H1.

E. Caricom
Caricom Perspective—The Caricom Secretariat, Bank of Guyana Building, P.O. Box 10827, Georgetown, Guyana, S.A.

F. Chile
Economic News—Corfo, One World Trade Center, Suite 1551, New York 10048.

G. Colombia
Colombia Today—Colombia Information Service, 144 E. 57th Street, New York 10022.

H. Costa Rica
Información Economica Semanal—Banco Central de Costa Rica, San Jose, Costa Rica.

I. Mexico
1. *El Mercado de Valores*—Nacional Financiera, see 6 below.
2. *Mexican American Review*—Camara de Comercio Americano, Lucerna 78, Mexico 6, D.F.
3. *Mexico Statistical Data*—Banco Nacional de Mexico; Isabel la Catolica, 44; Mexico 1, D.F.; Mexico.
4. *Panorama Economico*—Bancomer, S.A., V. Carranza 44, Mexico 1, D.F.
5. *Review of the Economic Situation in Mexico*—Banco Nacional de Mexico.
6. *Statistics on the Mexican Economy*—Nacional Financiera, Isabel la Catolica, 51; Mexico 1, D.F.; Mexico.

VI. Oceania

A. Australia
1. *ANZ Bank Business Indicators*—Australia and New Zealand Banking Group Limited, 55 Collins Street, Melbourne, 3000, Australia.
2. *Australian Investment and Economic Newsletter*—The National Bank of Australasia, Ltd., P.O. Box 84A, Melbourne, Victoria 3001.

3. *Monthly Summary*—National Australia Bank Limited, 500 Bourke Street (P.O. Box 84A), Melbourne, Victoria 3001.
B. New Zealand
    1. *Bulletin*—Reserve Bank of New Zealand, Wellington.
    2. *New Zealand News Review*—Reserve Bank of New Zealand, Wellington.

VII. Eastern Bloc

A. Region
    1. *Business Eastern Europe*—Business International, One Dag Hammarskjold Plaza, New York 10017.
    2. *Newsletter*—East-West Trade Expansion Committee, 600 New Hampshire Ave., N.W., Washington, D.C. 20037.
B. Bulgaria
    Bulgarian Foreign Trade—Bulgarreklama Agency, 42 Parchevich Street, Sofia.
C. Hungary
    1. *Hungarian Foreign Trade* (quarterly)—Hungarian Chamber of Commerce, Kultura, P.O. Box 149, H 1389 Budapest.
    2. *Marketing in Hungary* (quarterly)—same as above.
    3. *The Hungarian Economy* (quarterly)—same as above.
D. Romania
    Publications of the Chamber of Commerce of the Socialist Republic of Romania, 22, N. Balcescu Boulevard, Bucharest.
E. Russia
    Soviet Business and Economic Report—Porter International, 1776 K Street, N.W., Washington, D.C. 20006.
F. Yugoslavia
    Statistical Pocket Book of Yugoslavia—Federal Institute for Statistics, Beograd, Kenza Milosa 20, Yugoslavia.

APPENDIX

B

Alphabetical list of the names, acronyms, or initials by which some of the more-important international organizations are known:

ACM Andean Common Market

ADELA Adela Group

AID Agency for International Development

ASEAN Association of South-East Asian Nations

BMSE Baltic Mercantile and Shipping Exchange

BIS Bank for International Settlements

CACM Central American Common Market

CCM Caribbean Common Market, Caribbean Community

COMECON Council for Mutual Economic Assistance

EEC European Economic Community, generally referred to as the Common Market and frequently as EC for European Community

ECOWAS Economic Community of West African States

EFTA European Free Trade Association

ESA Department of Economic and Social Affairs

FAO Food and Agriculture Organization

GATT General Agreement on Tariffs and Trade

IAEA International Atomic Energy Agency

IBRD International Bank for Reconstruction and Development, commonly called World Bank

ICAO International Civil Aviation Organization

IDA International Development Association

IFAD International Fund for Agricultural Development

IFC International Finance Corporation

ILO International Labor Organization

IMCO Inter-Governmental Maritime Consultative Organization

IMF International Monetary Fund

ITU International Telecommunication Union

LAAD Latin American Agribusiness Development Corporation

LAAI Latin American Association for Integration

NAFTA New Zealand–Australia Free Trade Agreement

OECD Organization for Economic Cooperation and Development

OPEC Organization of Petroleum Exporting Countries

PICA Private Investment Company for Asia

SIFIDA Societé Internationale Financiere pour les Investissements et Developpement en Afrique S.A.

UN United Nations

UNCITRAL UN Conference on International Trade Law

UNCTAD UN Conference on Trade and Development

UNDP UN Development Program

UNESCO UN Educational, Scientific and Cultural Organization

UNICEF UN Children's Fund (formerly UN International Children's Emergency Fund)

UNIDO UN Industrial Development Organization

UNITAR UN Institute for Training and Research

UPU Universal Postal Union

WFP World Food Program

WHO World Health Organization

WMO World Meteorological Organization

GLOSSARY

absolute advantage The advantage enjoyed by a country because it can produce a product at a lower cost than can other countries.

accounting exposure The total net of accounting statement items on which loss could occur because of currency exchange rate changes.

adjustment assistance Financial and technical assistance to workers, firms, and communities to help them adjust to import competition.

ad valorem tariff or duty Literally "according to the value." A method in which customs duties or tariffs are established and charged as a percentage of the value of imported goods.

advising bank The bank which notifies the beneficiary of the opening of a letter of credit. The advising bank makes no payment commitment.

affiliated company May be a subsidiary or a company in which an MNE has less than 100 percent ownership.

A.G. Aktien-Gesellschaft. A joint stock company in Germany.

agency office An office of a foreign bank in the United States which cannot accept domestic deposits. It seeks business for the bank when U.S. companies operate internationally.

air waybill For goods shipped by air, performs the functions of a bill of lading in land surface transport or of a marine bill of lading in water transport.

American depository receipt (ADR) Stock of a foreign corporation is deposited at an American bank. The bank issues an ADR, not the corporation's stock certificate, to an American investor who buys shares of that corporation. The stock certificate is kept at the bank.

antiboycott law An American law against complying with the Arab countries' boycott of Israel.

antitrust laws Laws to prevent business from engaging in such practices as price-fixing or market sharing.

appreciation An increase in the value of one currency in terms of another currency.

arbitrage The simultaneous purchase and sale of something in two (or more) markets at a time when it is selling (being bought) at different prices in the markets. Profit is the price differential minus the costs.

arbitration The settlement of a dispute between parties by a third, presumably unbiased, party.

arm's-length transaction   A transaction between two or more unrelated parties. A transaction between two subsidiaries of an MNE would not be an arm's-length transaction.

back-to-back letter of credit (L/C)   A paying bank which will pay the exporter opens a back-to-back L/C based on the underlying L/C. Under the back-to-back L/C, the exporter's supplier (a manufacturer, for example,) may be paid.

back-to-back loans   A unit of one MNE lends to a unit of a second MNE; and at the same time and in equivalent amounts, another unit of the second MNE lends to another unit of the first.

balance of payments (BOP)   A financial statement that compares all reported payments by residents of one country to residents of other countries with payments to domestic residents by foreign residents. If more money has been paid out than received, the BOP is in deficit. If the opposite condition exists, the BOP is in surplus.

banker's acceptance   A draft drawn, for example, by an exporter on an importer's bank. If the bank accepts the draft, the bank has agreed to pay in accordance with its terms.

bank swaps   To avoid currency exchange problems, a bank in a soft-currency country will lend to an MNE subsidiary there. The MNE or its bank will make hard currency available to the lending bank outside the soft-currency country.

barter   The exchange of goods or services for goods or services. No money is used.

bill of exchange (draft)   An unconditional written order calling on the party to whom it is addressed to pay on demand or at a future date a sum of money to the order of a named party or to the bearer. Examples are acceptances or the commercial bank check.

bill of lading (B/L)   A receipt given by a carrier of goods received and a contract for their delivery. Usually a B/L is made to the order of someone and is negotiable. The B/L is also a document of title with which the holder may claim the goods from the carrier.

blocked account   Financial assets that cannot be transferred into another currency or out of the country without the government's permission.

branch office   An office or department of a company at a location away from headquarters. It is a part of the company and not a separate legal entity, as is a subsidiary, an affiliate, or a joint venture.

Bretton Woods   A resort in New Hampshire at which bank and treasury officials of the major Allied powers met near the end of World War II. There they established the international monetary system that, in some parts, still endures. It is known as the Bretton Woods system.

buffer stock   A supply of a commodity that the executive of a commodity agreement tries to accumulate and hold so that when the price of the commodity begins to rise above desirable levels, sales can be made from that stock to dampen the price rise.

capital intensive Describes processes that require a high concentration of capital relative to labor per unit of output and products produced by such processes. The opposite is labor intensive.

cartel An organization of suppliers which controls the supply and price of a commodity. To be successful, a cartel should have relatively few members who control most of the export supply of the commodity, the members must observe the cartel rules, and the commodity must be a necessity with a price-inelastic demand.

central banks Government institutions with authority over the size and growth of the national monetary stock. Central banks frequently regulate commercial banks and usually act as the government's fiscal agent.

centrally planned markets Markets in which there is almost no free market activity and the government owns all major factors of production, controls labor, and tries to plan all activity.

chaebols The large South Korean business conglomerates that have succeeded worldwide in such fields as computers, construction, shipbuilding, textiles, and steel.

CIF (cost, insurance, and freight) A term used in the delivery of goods from one party to another. The price includes the costs of the goods, the maritime or other appropriate transportation, the insurance premium, and the freight charges to the destination.

codetermination A system in which representatives of labor participate in the management of a company.

commodity agreement An agreement between the producers and consumers of a commodity (for example, tin, cocoa, or rubber) to regulate the production, price, and trade of the commodity.

common external tariff Under an agreement reached by a group of nations such as the EC, the same level of tariffs is imposed by these nations on all goods imported from other nations.

comparative advantage Unless a country has the same absolute advantage in producing all goods and services, there would be some goods and services in which it had less relative advantage. It would gain by importing those and exporting the ones in which it had an absolute advantage, or the greatest relative advantage.

compensation A form of countertrade involving payment in goods and cash.

compensatory financing A program to assist countries in financial difficulties due to drops in export earnings because of natural causes such as drought or because of international market price decreases. The IMF and the EC have compensatory financing programs.

confirmed letter of credit (L/C) An L/C confirmed by a bank other than the opening bank. Thus, it is an obligation of more than one bank.

confiscation Seizure by a government of foreign-owned assets which is not followed by prompt, effective, and adequate compensation.

contract manufacturing Manufacturing of a product or component by one company for another company. The two companies may or may not be related by stock ownership, common parent, or otherwise.

convertible currencies Currencies that may be changed for or converted into other currencies, at least for current account payments, without government permission.

coproduction A form of industrial cooperation in which two or more factories produce components for a final product.

cottage industry Production away from a central factory, typically in the worker's own home or cottage. Workers are paid on a piece rate basis, so much for each unit produced.

countertrade A transaction in which goods are exchanged for goods. Payment by a Comecon or LDC purchaser entirely or partially in goods instead of hard currencies for products or technology from developed countries.

countervailing duty An additional amount of tariff levied on an import that is found to have benefited from an export subsidy.

covered investment or interest arbitrage Investment in a second currency which is "covered" by a forward sale of that currency to protect against exchange rate fluctuations. Profit depends on interest rate differentials minus the discount or plus the premium on a forward sale.

covering Buying or selling foreign currencies in amounts equivalent to future payments to be made or received. A means of protection against loss due to currency exchange rate fluctations.

credit or money market hedge Hedging by borrowing the currency of risk, converting it immediately to the ultimately desired currency, and repaying the loan when payment is received.

cross rate The exchange rate between two currencies, which is determined by means of the U.S. dollar although neither of these currencies is the U.S. dollar. For example, if someone wants to sell Japanese yen and buy Swiss francs, the procedure is to buy dollars with the yen and then to buy Swiss francs with the dollars.

currency area The group of countries whose currencies are pegged to any one DC currency. Many LDCs peg the value of their currency to that of their major DC trading partner.

currency exchange controls A government's controls over how much foreign currency its residents or visitors can have and how much they must pay for it.

currency swap The exchange of one currency into another at an agreed rate and a reversal of that exchange at the same rate at the end of the swap contract period.

customs union An arrangement between two or more countries whereby they eliminate tariffs and other import restrictions on one another's goods and establish a common tariff on the goods from all other countries.

depreciation of a currency A decline in the value of a currency in terms of another currency or in terms of gold. "Depreciation" and "devaluation" are used interchangeably.

devaluation Depreciation of a currency by official government action.

development banks Banks that aid less developed countries (LDCs) in economic development. They may lend or invest money and encourage local ownership. They may be worldwide, regional, or national.

direct investment Sufficient investment to obtain significant management control. The U.S. government considers 10 percent or more equity in a foreign company to be significant.

dirty float A currency that floats in value in terms of other currencies but is not free of government intervention. Governments intervene to "smooth" or "manage" fluctuations.

documentary drafts Drafts accompanied by such documents as invoices, bills of lading, inspection certificates and insurance papers.

domestication Term used to indicate process in which a host government brings pressure to force a foreign owner to turn over partial ownership to the host country government or host country citizens.

domestic international sales corporation (DISC) A subsidiary corporation of a U.S. company that is incorporated in a state of the United States for the purpose of exporting from the United States. DISCs are given certain tax advantages. Generally, they have been superseded by foreign sales corporations.

drafts (bills of exchange) Orders drawn by a drawer which order a second party, the drawee, to pay a sum of money to a payee. The payee may be the same party as the drawer.

drawback The reimbursement of the tariff paid in an imported component that is later exported. When a component is imported into the United States, a tariff is levied on it and paid by the importer. If that component is later exported, the exporter is entitled to get 99 percent of the tariff amount from U.S. Customs.

drawee See *drafts.*

drawer See *drafts.*

dumping Selling abroad at prices lower than are charged in the home or other markets.

duties (tariffs) Amounts charged when goods are imported into a country. If such duties are based on the values of the goods, they are called ad valorem. If they are based on the number of items imported, they are called specific.

earned income   Income derived from efforts, labor, sales, or active participation in business. Salaries, wages, bonuses, and commissions are examples. Unearned income is a return on investment of money or time. Examples are interest, dividends, and royalties. The distinction is important for purposes of U.S. taxation of American residents abroad.

East-West trade   Trade between the centrally planned economies of the communist bloc (East) and the more market-oriented economies of the OECD nations (West).

Edge Act corporation   A subsidiary of a U.S. commercial bank that operates in a foreign country. The Edge subsidiary, operating abroad, is free of restraints of U.S. law and may perform whatever services and functions are legal in the countries where it operates.

equity-related bonds   Bonds that are convertible at the option of the holder into other securities of the issuer, usually common stock–type equity. Called convertibles in the United States.

escape clause   A legal provision concerning products whose tariffs have been reduced. If, thereafter, imports increase and threaten the domestic producers of those products, the escape clause permits the tariffs to be put back up.

Eurobonds   Bonds that are issued outside the restrictions applying to domestic offerings and are syndicated and traded mostly from London. Most of these bonds are denominated in U.S. dollars (about 71 percent in 1985), and some pay interest in one currency but are redeemable in another.

Eurocurrency   A currency that is being used or traded outside the country that issued it.

Eurodollar   The U.S. dollar is the most widely used Eurocurrency.

European Currency Unit (ECU)   A currency unit established by the European Monetary System. Its value is determined by reference to the value of a "basket" of currencies. The currencies in the basket are those of the system's member countries.

European Monetary Cooperation Fund (EMCF)   Lends assistance to EMS member countries that have difficulties in keeping their currencies within the agreed value relationships.

European Monetary System (EMS)   A system, established in 1979, under which West European countries agreed to keep their currency values within an established range in relation to one another.

exchange rate risk   In activities involving two or more currencies, the risk that losses can occur as a result of changes in their relative value.

Export-Import Bank (Eximbank)   A U.S. government agency that makes loans to foreign customers to facilitate exports of U.S. goods. It can also give loan or investment guarantees.

export management company   A company that acts as the export department for other companies. It performs all export-related services for its customers except supplying the product.

exposure netting   An open position in two or more currencies whose strengths and weaknesses are thought to balance one another.

expropriation   Seizure by a government of foreign-owned assets. Such seizure is not contrary to international law if it is followed by prompt, adequate, and effective compensation. If not, it is called confiscation.

extraterritorial application of laws   Attempts by a government to apply its laws outside its territorial borders.

fixed exchange rates   A system under which the values of currencies in terms of other currencies are fixed by intergovernmental agreement and by governmental intervention in the currency exchange markets.

fixed interest rate   This is an interest rate which is set when a loan is made and which remains the same for the life of the loan regardless of whether other interest rates rise or fall.

floating exchange rates   A system in which the values of currencies in terms of other currencies are determined by the supply of and demand for the currencies in currency markets. If governments do not intervene in the markets, the float is said to be "clean." If they do intervene, the float is said to be "dirty."

floating interest rates   A loan situation in which the interest rate set when a loan is made, may rise or fall as the interest rates of some reference such as LIBOR or the prime rate vary. Sometimes called variable rates.

floating-rate notes or bonds   Debt instruments with floating or variable interest rates. The interest rates are pegged to a fluctuating interest rate such as the six-month LIBOR rate.

fluctuating exchange rates   See *floating exchange rates.*

Foreign Corrupt Practices Act of 1977   An American law against making questionable payments when American companies do business abroad.

foreign exchange   The exchange of the currency of one country for that of another country.

foreign exchange rates   Prices of one currency in terms of other currencies.

foreign exchange reserves   Gold, SDRs, U.S. dollars, and other convertible currencies.

foreign financing   Occurs when a foreign company or other borrower comes to a nation's capital market and borrows in the local currency—for example, when an Italian company borrows U.S. dollars in New York or French francs in Paris.

foreign sales corporation (FSC)   A new corporation provided for in the Tax Reform Act of 1984. The FSC replaces the domestic international sales corporation (DISC) as a tax incentive for exporters.

foreign tax credit   The credit that an American taxpayer may take against American income tax for tax on income by a foreign government.

foreign trade organization (FTO)   An organization involved in procurement from foreign suppliers. The USSR and other communist countries have a number of FTOs, each specializing in an industry.

foreign trade zone (FTZ) American version of a free trade zone. In an FTZ, goods may be imported and manufactured or handled and changed in any way. No tariff need be paid unless and until the goods are removed from the FTZ into the country where the FTZ is located.

forfaiting Has the same purposes and procedures as factoring, which is the sale by an exporter of its accounts receivable for immediate cash. However, there are two important differences: (1) factoring involves credit terms of no more than 180 days, while forfaiting may involve years; (2) factoring does not usually cover political and transfer risks, while forfaiting does.

forward contract A contract to exchange one currency for another currency at an agreed exchange at a future date, usually 30, 60, or 90 days. May be used to hedge. See *forward rate.*

forward rate The cost today for a commitment by one party to deliver to or take from another party an agreed amount of a currency at a fixed or future date. This rate is established by the forward contract. See *forward contract; spot rate.*

Fourth World The poorest of the world's countries.

friendship, commerce, and navigation (FCN) treaties The basic agreements between nations about such matters as treatment of each others' citizens or companies.

general trading companies Exist in many countries, including the United States, though the Japanese versions of these companies, called sogo shosha in Japanese, are the best known. For many years, the sogo shosha have imported and distributed commodities and products for use by Japanese industries and consumers, sought foreign customers for Japanese companies, and exported to other countries.

gilts Technically, British and Irish government securities, though the term also includes issues of local British authorities.

global corporation A company that markets a standardized product worldwide and allows only minimum adaptations to local conditions and tastes from country to country. Its financial, marketing and advertising strategies are global with little differentiation among countries or areas as to product.

GmbH *Gesellschaft mit beschrankter Haftung* (organization with limited liability). A German form of business organization.

gold exchange standard The system established at Bretton Woods whereby the value of one currency (the U.S. dollar) was set in terms of gold. The United States held gold and agreed that when another country accumulated U.S. dollars, it could exchange them for gold at the set value.

gold standard A system under which currency values are set in terms of gold and each country agrees that if a second country accumulates more of a first country's currency than it wants for other purposes, the second country can exchange the first country's currency for that amount of the first country's gold.

gold tranche   The amount of gold paid by a country as its contributed capital in the International Monetary Fund.

gold window   At the New York Federal Reserve Bank. Under the gold exchange standard, when foreign countries accumulated U.S. dollars, they could trade them for gold at $35 per ounce. The New York Fed office where they did that was called the gold window.

Gosbank   Central planning agency for the USSR.

gross domestic product (GDP)   The market value of a country's output attributable to factors of production located in the country's territory. It differs from GNP by the exclusion of net factor income payments such as interest and dividends received from, or paid to, the rest of the world. See *gross national product (GNP)*.

gross national product (GNP)   The market value of all the final goods and services produced by a national economy over a period of time, usually a year.

Group of 5   The term used for meetings of the finance ministers and central bank governors of France, the Federal Republic of Germany, Japan, the United Kingdom, and the United States.

Group of 7   The Group of 5 plus Canada and Italy.

Group of 10   The Group of 7 plus Belgium, the Netherlands, and Sweden.

Goup of 77   Had its origins in the caucus of 75 developing countries that met in 1964 to prepare for UNCTAD. After the first UNCTAD meeting, the caucus grew to 77.

guest workers   Foreign workers who are brought into a country by legal means to perform needed labor.

hard currency   A currency that is freely convertible into other currencies.

hedging   Selling forward currency exchange, borrowing, or using other means to protect against losses from possible currency exchange rate changes that affect the values of assets and liabilities.

hierarchy   A system in which there are several layers of authority between the lowest rank (say, the peasants or untouchables) to the highest rank (say, king, commissar, or brahmin.)

host country   The country in which foreign investment is made.

INCOTERMS   A publication of the International Chamber of Commerce setting forth recommended standard definitions for the major trade terms used in international trade.

indexing   Taking into account the effects of inflation on assets and liabilities and adjusting the amounts of these items in order to preserve their original relationships.

industrial cooperation   A long-term relationship in which a Comecon country or an LDC produces products for its own market and/or export to the West.

industrial espionage Stealing trade, process, customer, pricing, or technology secrets from a business.

infrastructure The fundamental underpinnings of an economy—roads, railroads, communications, water supplies, energy supplies, and so forth.

interest arbitrage Lending in another country to take advantage of higher interest rates. Such arbitrage tends to equalize interest rates.

Interest Equalization Tax (IET) From 1963 to 1974, a tax that U.S. residents were required to pay on the purchase of foreign securities. The IET was a device to combat U.S. BOP deficits.

international financing Occurs when a borrower raises capital in the Euro-currency or Eurobond markets, outside the restrictions that are applied to domestic or foreign offerings. See *foreign financing.*

international law A body of principles and practices that have been generally accepted by countries in their relations with other countries and with citizens of other countries.

international monetary system The agreements, practices, laws, customs, and institutions that deal with money (debts, payments, investments) internationally.

intervention currency A currency bought or sold by a country (not necessarily the one issued by it) to influence the value of its own currency.

intraenterprise transaction A transaction between two or more units of the same MNE.

irrevocable letter of credit (L/C) An L/C that the issuing bank agrees not to revoke before the payment date.

J curve A curve illustrating the theory that immediately after a country devalues its currency, its imports become more expensive and its exports cheaper, thus worsening a BOP deficit. As the country's exports increase, it earns more money and the deficit bottoms out and becomes a surplus up the right side of the *J.*

joint venture May be (1) a corporate entity between an MNE and local owners, (2) a corporate entity between two or more MNEs that are foreign to the area where the joint venture is located, or (3) a cooperative undertaking between two or more firms of a limited-duration project.

key currencies Those held extensively as foreign exchange reserves.

labor intensive Describes products whose production requires a relatively large amount of labor and a relatively small amount of capital. Also describes the manufacturing process.

less developed countries (LDCs) Countries with low per capita income, low levels of industrialization, high illiteracy, and usually political instability.

letter of credit (L/C) A letter issued by a bank which indicates that the bank will accept drafts (make payments) under specified circumstances.

licensing A contractual arrangement in which one firm, the licensor, grants access to its patents, trademarks, or technology to another firm, the licensee, for a fee, usually called a royalty.

linkage In international marketing, the creation of demand in a second national market by movement of the product and/or the customer into that market.

Lombard rate The interest rate that a central bank charges other banks on loans secured by government and other selected securities.

London Interbank Offered Rate (LIBOR) The interest rate the most creditworthy banks charge one another for loans of Eurodollars overnight in the London market. LIBOR is a cornerstone in the pricing of money market issues and other short-term debt issues by both government and business borrowers. Interest is often stated to be LIBOR plus a fraction.

long position The position taken when a party buys something for future delivery. This may be done in the expectation that the item bought will increase in value. It may also be done to hedge a currency risk.

managed float See *floating exchange rates*. "Managed" is a more decorous word than "dirty."

market economies Economies that are characterized by a relatively large, free (nongovernmental) market sector. There is no such thing as a totally free market; all governments regulate, tax, and intervene in various ways.

Marshall Plan The U.S. aid program that assisted European countries to reconstruct after World War II. Cooperation among the European countries was a forerunner of the EC.

mercantilism The economic philosophy that equates the possession of gold or other international monetary assets with wealth. It also holds that trade activities should be directed or controlled by the government.

merchant banks Combine long- and short-term financing with the underwriting and distributing of securities.

Mitbestimmung German for "codetermination." The Germans pioneered codetermination, and their word for it is frequently used.

most-favored nation (MFN) The policy of nondiscrimination in international commercial policy; extending to all nations the same customs and tariff treatment as are extended to the most-favored nation.

multinational enterprise (MNE) An organization that produces in, markets in, and obtains the factors of production from multiple countries for the purpose of furthering overall enterprise benefit.

nationalization Government takeover of private property.

national tax jurisdiction Taxation on the basis of nationality regardless of where in the world the taxpayer's income is earned or the activities of the taxpayer take place.

neutralizing the balance sheet   Having the assets in a given currency approximate the liabilities in that currency.

nonrecourse financing   Financing in which the factor assumes the full responsibility and all the risk of collecting from a third party. See *forfaiting*.

note issuance facility (NIF)   Medium-term arrangements that enable borrowers to issue paper, typically of three or six months' maturity, in their own names. A group of underwriting banks guarantees the availability of funds to the borrower by purchasing any unsold notes or by providing standby credit.

offshore banking   The use of banks located in other countries, particularly tax havens such as the Caymans and the Bahamas.

offshore funds   Investment funds whose shares are usually denominated in U.S. dollars but which are located and sell their shares outside the United States. There are tax and securities registration reasons for such funds.

opening bank   The bank that opens a letter of credit (L/C). This bank will honor (pay) drafts drawn under the L/C if specified conditions are met.

orderly marketing agreements (OMAs)   Compacts negotiated between two or more nations under whose terms the exporting nation or nations agree to limit exports of specified goods to the importing nation.

Overseas Private Insurance Corporation (OPIC)   A U.S. government agency which insures against risks of expropriation, war, or currency nonconvertibility.

overvalued currency   A currency whose value government action keeps higher than it would be in a free market.

paper gold   See *special drawing rights (SDRs)*.

parallel importing   The importing of a product by an independent operator that is not part of the manufacturer's channel of distribution. The parallel importer may compete with the authorized importer or with a subsidiary of the foreign manufacturer that produces the product in the local market.

parent company   A company which owns subsidiary companies.

par value   The value that a government, by agreement or regulation, sets on its currency in terms of other currencies. At Bretton Woods, other currencies were assigned par values in terms of the U.S. dollar.

paternalism   A system in which a chief, sheik, or other authority figure cares for all the people as if he were their father.

pegged exchange rate   An exchange rate in which a country's currency is fixed in terms of another country's currency. Frequently the other country is a major trading partner or a country with which there was a colonial relationship.

peril point   In U.S. law, a point below which a tariff cannot be lowered without causing or threatening serious injury to U.S. producers of competitive products.

political risks   The risks to a business and its employees that stem from political unrest in an area. As a result of such unrest, the markets or supplies of the business may be disrupted or the business may be nationalized and its employees may lose their jobs or be kidnapped, injured, or even killed.

preindustrial societies   A designation that can signify anything from traditional societies up through societies in the early stages of agricultural and industrial organization.

purchasing power parity   The relative ability of one unit of two country's currencies to purchase similar goods. From this relative ability, an indication of what the market exchange rate between the two currencies should be derived.

questionable or dubious payments   Bribes.

quota   (1) A limitation on imports by number or by weight; for example, only so many of a given item or only so many pounds or kilos may be imported. (2) At the IMF, each member nation has a quota which determines the amount of its subscription and how much it can borrow.

reinvoicing   Centralizing all international invoicing by an MNE. The reinvoicing center decides which currencies should be used and where, how, and when.

repatriation   The transfer home of assets held abroad.

representative office.   The office of an out-of-state or foreign bank which is not permitted to conduct direct banking functions. The purpose of such an office is to solicit business for its parent bank where it can conduct such functions.

reserve assets   Assets such as gold or convertible foreign currencies held by a country's central bank. These assets can be used to intervene in the currency exchange markets.

restrictive trade practices legislation   The European versions of American antitrust laws.

revaluation of a currency   An increase in a currency's value in terms of other currencies. See *devaluation*.

revocable letters of credit (L/Cs)   L/Cs that the opening bank may revoke at any time without notice to the beneficiary.

S.A.   Societe Anonyme, Sociedad Anonima, or Societa Anonima. Joint-stock companies in French, Spanish, and Italian, respectively.

S.A.R.L.   Société a`Responsibilité Limitée.

short position   The position of a party when it has sold something it does not own and to which it has no contractual right. This is usually done for future delivery in the expectation that the item sold will decrease in price. It is also done to hedge a currency risk.

sight draft   A bill of exchange which is payable immediately upon presentation or demand. A bank check is a sight draft.

Smithsonian agreement New agreements on currency par values, the value of gold, and tariffs reached by the major trading countries at the Smithsonian Institution in Washington, D.C., in December 1981. When the United States closed the "gold window" in August 1971, the world currency exchanges were thrown into turmoil and such agreements became necessary.

snake During the 1970s, several West European countries agreed to keep the values of their currencies within established ranges in terms of one another. The currencies would all float in value in terms of other currencies, for example, the U.S. dollar and the Japanese yen.

soft currency A currency that is not freely convertible into other currencies. Such a currency is usually subject to national currency controls.

soft loans Loans such as those granted by the IDA. These loans may have grace periods during which no payments need be made; they may bear low or no interest; and they may be repayable in a soft currency.

sogo shosha The Japanese term for general trading companies.

sovereign immunity The immunity of a government from lawsuits in the courts of its own country or other countries unless it submits voluntarily. Such immunity is particularly likely to exist if the government limits itself to "governmental" functions as opposed to economic ones.

sovereignty The power of each national government over the land within its borders and over the people and organizations within those borders.

special drawing rights (SDRs) Accounting entries at the IMF. SDRs are treated as reserve assets and are credited or debited to member countries' accounts. Sometimes called paper gold, they permit liquidity to be created by agreement at the IMF rather than having it depend on the U.S. BOP deficit.

specific tariff or duty A method of measuring customs duties or tariffs by number or weight instead of by value. Thus, the amount of the tariff or duty is based on how many units or how many pounds or kilos are imported, regardless of their value. See *ad valorem tariff or duty.*

spot rate or spot quotation The rate of exchange between two currencies for immediate delivery, one for the other. See *forward rate.*

straight bonds or notes Issues with a fixed (not floating) coupon or interest rate.

subcontracting A prime manufacturer's purchase of components from other suppliers. Used in industrial cooperation.

subsidiaries Companies owned by another company, which is referred to as the parent company.

subsidies, export Financial encouragement to export. Such subsidies can take the form of lower taxes, tax rebates, or direct payments.

swaps Are of two basic kinds: interest rate swaps and currency swaps. Interest rate swaps typically exchange floating-rate payments for fixed-rate payments. Currency swaps are accords to deliver one currency against another currency at certain intervals.

swing In a bilateral trade agreement, the leeway provided for mutual extension of credit.

switch trade Utilized when a country lacks sufficient hard currency to pay for its imports. When it can acquire from a third country products desired by its creditor country, it switches shipment of those products to the creditor country. Its debt to the creditor country is thereby paid. A type of countertrade.

takeoff A phase in the development of an LDC when its infrastructure has been sufficiently developed, enough interacting industries have been established, and domestic capital formation exceeds consumption, so that the country's own momentum carries the development process onward.

tariff quota A tariff that has a lower rate until the end of a specified period or until a specified amount of the commodity has been imported. At that point, the rate increases.

tariffs See *duties*.

tax haven A country that has low or no taxes on income from foreign sources or capital gains.

tax incentives The tax holidays that LDCs sometimes give companies and their management if they will invest in the country or that DCs sometimes give them to induce investment in an area of high unemployment.

tax treaty A treaty between two countries in which each country usually lowers certain taxes on residents who are nationals of the other and the countries agree to cooperate in tax matters such as enforcement.

terms of trade The real quantities of exports that are required to pay for a given amount of imports.

territorial tax jurisdiction The levying of tax on taxpayers while living and working in the territory of the taxing government. Income earned while living and working elsewhere is not taxed or is taxed at a lower rate.

third window A World Bank lending facility that provides loans at interest rates midway between IDA (no interest) and regular World Bank terms (full market rates).

Third World The Eastern-bloc countries dominated by the USSR are considered one world. The countries of the West, primarily the OECD countries, are considered another world. All other countries are sometimes referred to as Third World countries.

tied loans or grants Loans or grants that the borrower or recipient must spend in the country that made them.

time draft A bill of exchange that is payable at an established future date or a given number of days after sight.

trade acceptance A draft similar to a banker's acceptance, the difference being that no bank is involved. The exporter presents the draft to the importer for its acceptance to pay the amount stated at a fixed future date.

trade bloc A group of countries with special trading rules among them, such as the EC or Comecon.

trade (deficit) surplus A trade deficit is an excess of merchandise imports over exports. A trade surplus is the opposite.

traditional economy An area in a most rudimentary state. In such an economy, the people are typically nomadic, agriculture is at a bare subsistence level, and industry is virtually nonexistent.

transaction risk The risk run in international trade that changes in relative currency values will cause losses.

transfer price The price charged by one unit of an MNE for goods or services that it sells to another unit of the same MNE.

translation risk The apparent losses or gains that can result from the restatement of values from one currency into another, even if there are no transactions, when the currencies change in value relative to each other. Translation risks are common with long-term foreign investments as foreign currency values are translated to the investor's financial statements in its home currency.

Treaty of Rome Established the EC.

turnkey project A project in which the seller does all the planning, construction, manufacturing, and installation, trains the buyer's personnel, and starts up the operation, after which the buyer takes over.

undervalued currency A currency that has been oversold because of emotional selling or a currency whose value a government tries to keep below market in order to make its country's exports less expensive and more competitive.

untouchables Lowest-caste Indians. Mahatma Gandhi called them harijans, the children of God.

value-added tax (VAT) A tax levied at each stage in the production of a product. The tax is on the value added to the product by that stage.

vehicle currency A currency used in international transactions to make quotes and payments. The U.S. dollar is the currency most used.

venture capital Money invested, usually in equity, in a new, relatively high-risk undertaking.

vertical mobility An individual's opportunities to move upward in a society to a higher caste or a higher social status.

Vneshtorgbank USSR state bank for foreign trade.

Webb-Pomerene Act Exempts from U.S. antitrust laws associations among business competitors engaged in export trade. They must not restrain trade within the United States or the trade of any other U.S. competitors.

zaibatsu Centralized, family-dominated, monopolistic economic groups which dominated the Japanese economy until the end of World War II, at which time they were broken up. As time passed, however, the units of the old zaibatsu drifted back together, and they now cooperate within the group much as they did before their dissolution.

zero-coupon bonds Bonds that are issued at a heavy discount and pay no interest but are redeemable at par at a future date.

INDEX

Foreign Sovereign Immunities Act (U.S.), 351
Foreign trade organizations (FTOs), 631
Foreign Trade Report (FT 410), 512, 592
  sources of information for, 606
Foreign trade zones (FTZs), 604–5
Foremost, 534
Forfaiting, 601, 603
Forsberg, Hans, 634
Forward hedging, 659–60
Forward market swaps, 670–71
France
  accounting practices in, 212
  competition in, 425–26
  fringe benefits in, 747–48
  frozen food in, 573
  government ownership of business in, 317–18
  industrial targeting in, 435
  labor unions in, 750
  language in, 291–92
  mercantilism in modern, 73
  product liability in, 355
  protectionism in, 354
  retailers in, 455
  television in, 560
  worker training in, 732
Franchising, 62
Fraser, Douglas, 414
Free float, 171
Free-form management design, 788
Free market rate, 200
Free trade areas, 143; *see also* European Free Trade Association (EFTA)
Free trade zones, 604–5
French solution, 320
Friendship Bridge, 239
Fringe benefits, 726, 747–48
  and international wage rates, 81
  and labor costs, 356, 483
Frozen food, 573
FT 410, see Foreign Trade Report (FT 410)
Fuji Bank, 194
Fujioka, Masao, 134
Fujitsu, 58–59, 430
Function-based organization structure, 784
Futures contracts
  on crude oil, 139
  to hedge exchange risk, 659–60
  on interest rates, 676

G

Gaines Dog Food, 737
Gandhi, Mahatma, 397

Gasoline, and climate, 545
Gautama, Prince, 276
General Agreement on Tariffs and Trade (GATT), 136–37, 329
  and value-added tax, 347–48
General American Convention for Trademark and Commercial Protection, 361
General Electric, planning at, 508
General Foods, 424
Generalized System of Preferences (GSP), 429
General License, 606
General Motors
  inexpensive product substitutes of, 544
  in-process inventory of, 711
  international sales of, 330
  in joint ventures, 883
  mission of, 765–66
  objectives of, 766
  and robotics, 745
  size of, 8–9
General Motors of Canada Ltd., 226
General Motors (Kenya) Ltd., 885–86, 891–93
General purchasing power-adjusted (GPP) accounting, 213
General Tire, 48
  licensing agreements of, 61
  logo of, 549
Geocentric management, 779
  and promotion of managers, 816
Geography
  diversification based on, 54
  organization structure based on, 782, 784
  specialized, 226–27
German Federal Cartel Office, 349
Germany, hyperinflation in, 161; *see also* East Germany *and* West Germany
Gifts, 294–95
Gillette, 694
Global-company organization, 778–85, 871–72
Global quotas, 85
Gluck, Federick W., 777
GNP, 471
GNP/capita, 45, 471
  growth of, and market expansion, 485
  and income distribution, 93–94
  and level of economic devleopment, 91–93
  and level of technology, 281
Godeaux, Jean, 136
Gold
  IMF sales of, 130

Gold—*Cont.*
  and inflation, 160–61
  and international trade, 73
  price of, 159
  as reserve asset, 160
Gold bloc, 162
Gold exchange standard, 168–70
Gold standard, 159–61
  attempts to revive, 161–62
  and Depression, 162
Gold window, 170
Goods or merchandise account, 164
Gorbachev, Mikhail S., 634
Gosplan, 631
Governments; *see also* Taxation
  birth rate control efforts of, 486
  under capitalism, 312
  as capital sources, 674
  control of advertising media by, 551, 553–54
  and countertrade, 679–80
  economic involvement of, 494–95; *see also* Privatization
  economists' influence on, 72
  European versus American, 371
  export financing by, 603–4
  human relations management in, 737
  and importation of skilled labor, 727
  inducements to new investment, 49
  industrial targeting by, 435
  inhospitable, 867
  and labor unions, 750
  level of technology sought by, 701–2
  measures to stimulate exports, 435
  MNE relations of, 8–9, 330–31
  and multinational profit allocation, 807–8
  ownership of business by, 73–74, 311–18, *see also* Privatization
  as parties to contracts, 357–59
  and plant location, 704
  protection of local industry by, 45, 53, 320–24
  regulation of business by, 312
  restrictions on wholly owned subsidiaries, 56–57
  stability of, 310, 324–27, 516
  technology contolled by, 282
  terrorism sponsored by, 323
  and third-country nationals as managers, 815
Grace, W. R., 447
Graham, E. M., 100
Grease, 367; *see also* Bribery

Production—*Cont.*
　operation of, 705–13
　standardization of; *see*
　　Rationalization of production
Productivity
　and automation, 700
　and drug abuse, 829
　human element of, 705
　influence on, 396–97
　and labor costs, 483
　and labor force composition, 391
　and motivation, 737
　and performance incentives, 748
　and robots, 742
　and strikes, 412
　and terrorism, 321–22
　in United States, 395
Product liability, 354–55
Product life cycle; *see* International
　product life cycle (IPLC)
Product managers, 779
　in regional organization structure,
　　784
Product mix
　and climate, 241–42
　and market size, 545
Profit-and-loss statement, and FASB
　52, 681
Profits
　allocation among subsidiaries,
　　806–7
　in communist countries, 647
　and performance evaluation, 810
Pro forma invoice, 598
Promotion, 546–49
　versus advertising, 535
　sales; *see* Sales promotion
　of third-country nationals to
　　management, 816
　from within, 816–17
Protectionism, 80–83; *see also*
　Tariffs
　in France, 354
　in Japan, 352, 354
　as legal force, 352
　and nationalism, 320
Protestant Ethic, 274
Publications
　of Dept. of Commerce, 592
　economic data from, 470
　of GATT, 137
　of IMF, 132
　on legal and political forces, 517
　of OECD, 147
　of UN, 120
　of World Bank, 125
Public relations, 565–67
Punitive damages, 356

Purchasing, 711–12
　commission earnings from, 61
　frequency of, 543
　and indirect exporting, 450
　and rationalized production, 696
　in Soviet Union, 631, 634
　UN influence on, 118
　World Bank influence on, 125
Purchasing power
　and GNP/capita, 471
　indexes of, 512–13
　parity, and exchange rates, 173–
　　76
　and GNP estimates, 93
　and manager compensation, 823

Q

Quality
　company-wide control of; *see*
　　Company-wide quality
　　control (CWQC)
　and price, 567
　standards for, 707
　as user satisfaction, 739
Quality circles (QCs), 737–38
Quality control
　in automobile industry, 896
　and rationalized production, 698
Questionable payments, 295–96,
　366–67
Quotas
　GATT reductions of, 137
　on imports, 85–86
　as legal forces, 352

R

Race relations
　and guest workers, 389
　and refugees, 387
　and social status, 400–401
Radial tires, 442
Radio
　in Europe, 551, 553
　worker recruiting ads in, 729
Radio-Television Luxembourg (RTL),
　553
Railroads, 248–49
　French, 435
　government ownership of, 316
　versus water transportation, 235
Rain forests, 234–35
Ramadan, 278–79
Ransom; *see* Kidnapping
Rationalization of production, 695–99
　and appropriate technology, 702
　environmental impediments to,
　　699–701

Rationalization of
　production—*Cont.*
　and product-based organization
　　structure, 782
　at subsidiaries, 803
Raw materials
　foreign expansion to obtain, 53–54
　inventory control for, 709
　Japanese imports of, 30
　and output level, 706
　purchasing agent for, 711
　and vertical integration, 703
Raytheon, 329
Reagan, Ronald, 14–15, 30, 247,
　364, 448, 737
Recruitment of workers, 728–29
　and training programs, 730
Refugees, 385, 387
　and labor force composition, 390
Regional Cooperation for
　Development (RCD), 145
Regional development banks, 133–34
Regional dualism, 94
　in Pakistan, 498–99
Regional marketing groups; *see*
　Multinational economic unions
Regional organization structure, 782,
　784
Regression analysis, in market
　screening, 515
Rejection rates, 698
Religions
　and achievement motivation, 272
　Asian, 275–77
　as component of culture, 274
Renault, 266, 540, 735
　and labor unions, 750
　nationalization of, 318
Repatriation of earnings
　restrictions on, 516
　and transfer prices, 569
Replacement cost, 211, 394
Replenishment, 127
Research and development (R&D),
　394
Reserve assets
　accounting for, 166
　gold as, 160
　SDRs as, 177–78
　U.S. dollars as, 169
Resumes, 817
Retailers, 455–56
　difference among countries, 571
　as direct importers, 451
　in Japan, 455
　relations with, 535
　wholesaling taken over by, 452
Reverse engineering, 439

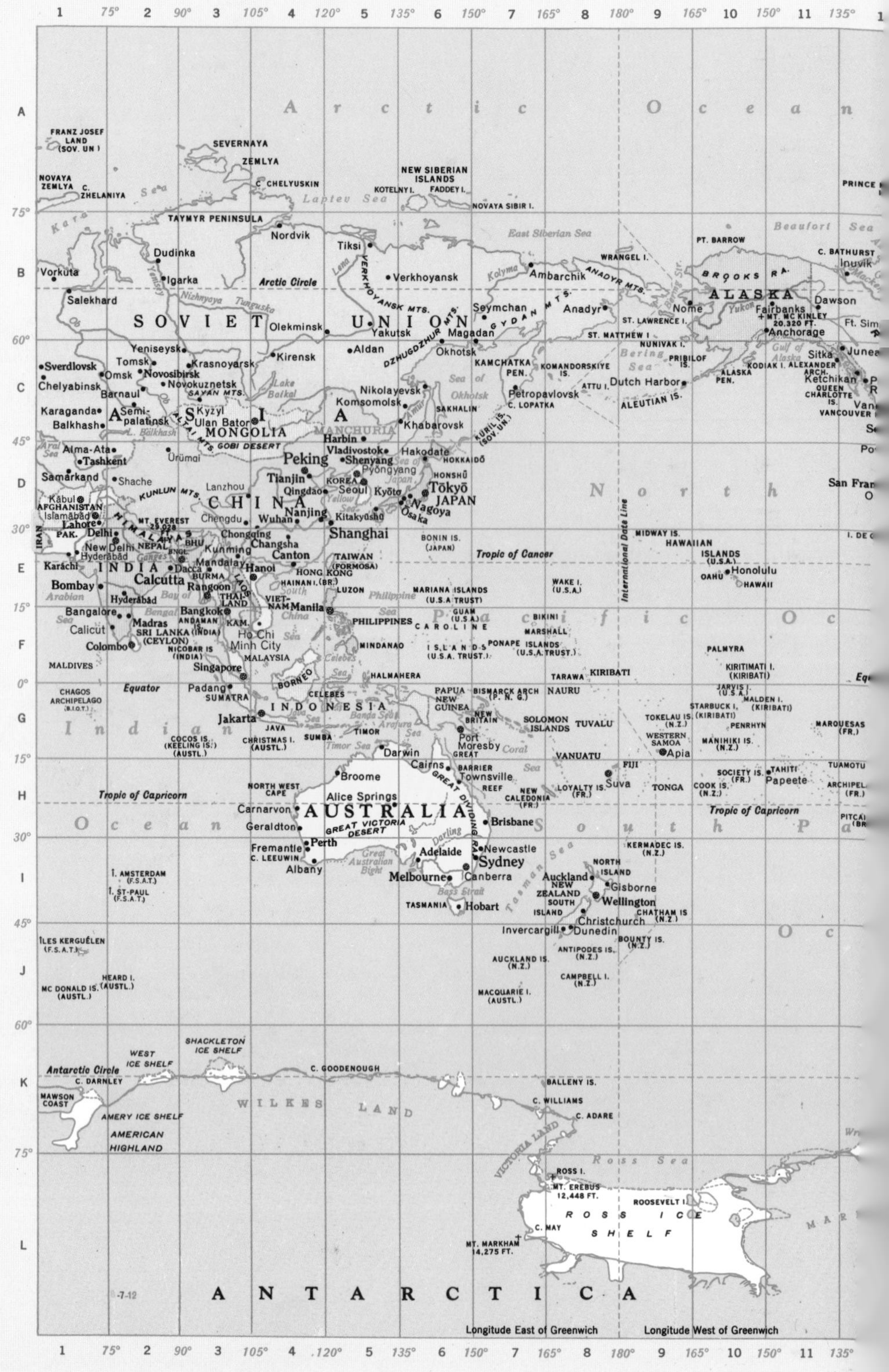

1 75° 2 90° 3 105° 4 120° 5 135° 6 150° 7 165° 8 180° 9 165° 10 150° 11 135°
A
B
C
D
E
F
G
H
I
J
K
L
75°
60°
45°
30°
15°
0°
15°
30°
45°
60°
75°
Arctic Ocean
FRANZ JOSEF LAND (SOV. UN.)
SEVERNAYA ZEMLYA
NOVAYA ZEMLYA
C. ZHELANIYA
Kara Sea
C. CHELYUSKIN
Laptev Sea
NEW SIBERIAN ISLANDS
KOTELNYI I.
FADDEY I.
NOVAYA SIBIR I.
TAYMYR PENINSULA
Nordvik
Tiksi
East Siberian Sea
Beaufort Sea
PT. BARROW
C. BATHURST
Inuvik
PRINCE
Dudinka
Vorkuta
Igarka
Arctic Circle
VERKHOYANSK MTS.
Verkhoyansk
Kolyma
Ambarchik
WRANGEL I.
ANADYR MTS.
BROOKS RA.
ALASKA
Salekhard
Nizhnyaya Tunguska
SOVIET UNION
Olekminsk
Yakutsk
Seymchan
GYDAN MTS.
Anadyr
Nome
Fairbanks
MT. MC KINLEY 20,320 FT.
Dawson
ST. LAWRENCE I.
Yukon
Ft. Sim
Magadan
Anchorage
Yeniseysk
Aldan
DZHUGDZHUR MTS.
Okhotsk
ST. MATTHEW I.
NUNIVAK I.
Gulf of Alaska
Sverdlovsk
Tomsk
Krasnoyarsk
Kirensk
KAMCHATKA PEN.
KOMANDORSKIYE IS.
PRIBILOF IS.
Bering Sea
ALASKA PEN.
KODIAK I.
Sitka
Juneau
ALEXANDER ARCH.
Omsk
Novosibirsk
Novokuznetsk
Chelyabinsk
Barnaul
SAYAN MTS.
Lake Baikal
Sea of Okhotsk
Nikolayevsk
Petropavlovsk
ATTU I.
Dutch Harbor
Ketchikan
QUEEN CHARLOTTE IS.
Karaganda
Semipalatinsk
Kyzyl
Ulan Bator
ASIA
ALTAI MTS.
Komsomolsk
SAKHALIN
C. LOPATKA
ALEUTIAN IS.
VANCOUVER I.
Balkhash
L. Balkhash
MONGOLIA
Khabarovsk
KURIL IS. (SOV. UN.)
MANCHURIA
Aral Sea
Alma-Ata
GOBI DESERT
Harbin
Tashkent
Ürümqi
Vladivostok
Hakodate
HOKKAIDŌ
Peking
Shenyang
Sea of Japan
Samarkand
Shache
Tianjin
Pyongyang
HONSHŪ
North
San Fran
Lanzhou
KOREA
KUNLUN MTS.
Qingdao
Seoul
Kyōto
Tōkyō
Kābul
AFGHANISTAN
Islamabad
CHINA
Yellow Sea
JAPAN
Nagoya
Ōsaka
Lahore
HIMALAYAS
MT. EVEREST 29,028 FT.
Chengdu
Wuhan
Nanjing
Kitakyūshū
IRAN
PAK.
Delhi
New Delhi
NEPAL
BHU
Chongqing
Changsha
Shanghai
BONIN IS. (JAPAN)
MIDWAY IS.
HAWAIIAN ISLANDS (U.S.A.)
I. DE G
Hyderābād
Ganges
BNGL.
Kunming
Tropic of Cancer
Karāchi
INDIA
Dacca
Mandalay
Hanoi
Canton
TAIWAN (FORMOSA)
International Date Line
Calcutta
BURMA
HONG KONG
WAKE I. (U.S.A.)
OAHU
Honolulu
HAWAII
Bombay
Rangoon
LAOS
HAINAN I. (BR.)
LUZON
Hyderābād
Bay of Bengal
THAILAND
VIET-NAM
South China Sea
Philippine Sea
MARIANA ISLANDS (U.S.A. TRUST)
Arabian Sea
Manila
Bangalore
ANDAMAN IS. (INDIA)
Bangkok
KAM.
PHILIPPINES
GUAM (U.S.A.)
BIKINI
Pacific Oc
Madras
Calicut
SRI LANKA (CEYLON)
Ho Chi Minh City
CAROLINE ISLANDS (U.S.A. TRUST)
MARSHALL ISLANDS (U.S.A. TRUST)
PONAPE
Colombo
NICOBAR IS. (INDIA)
MINDANAO
PALMYRA
MALDIVES
MALAYSIA
Celebes Sea
Singapore
KIRIBATI
KIRIMATI I. (KIRIBATI)
BORNEO
HALMAHERA
TARAWA
Equator
Padang
CELEBES
NAURU
JARVIS I. (U.S.A.)
CHAGOS ARCHIPELAGO (B.I.O.T.)
SUMATRA
PAPUA NEW GUINEA
BISMARCK ARCH. (P. N. G.)
MALDEN I. (KIRIBATI)
STARBUCK I. (KIRIBATI)
INDONESIA
Java Sea
Banda Sea
NEW BRITAIN
SOLOMON ISLANDS
TUVALU
TOKELAU IS. (N.Z.)
PENRHYN
MARQUESAS (FR.)
Indian
Jakarta
JAVA
Arafura Sea
Port Moresby
WESTERN SAMOA
MANIHIKI IS. (N.Z.)
COCOS IS. (KEELING IS.) (AUSTL.)
CHRISTMAS I. (AUSTL.)
SUMBA
TIMOR
Timor Sea
Coral Sea
Apia
Darwin
VANUATU
GREAT BARRIER REEF
FIJI
TUAMOTU
Cairns
Townsville
Suva
SOCIETY IS. (FR.)
TAHITI
Papeete
Broome
NORTH WEST CAPE
NEW CALEDONIA (FR.)
LOYALTY IS. (FR.)
TONGA
COOK IS. (N.Z.)
ARCHIPELA (FR.)
Tropic of Capricorn
Alice Springs
Carnarvon
AUSTRALIA
GREAT DIVIDING RA.
Brisbane
Tropic of Capricorn
Geraldton
GREAT VICTORIA DESERT
South Pa
PITCA (BR.)
Ocean
Darling
Fremantle
Perth
Newcastle
KERMADEC IS. (N.Z.)
C. LEEUWIN
Adelaide
Sydney
Tasman Sea
NORTH ISLAND
Albany
Great Australian Bight
Canberra
Auckland
I. AMSTERDAM (F.S.A.T.)
Melbourne
Gisborne
I. ST-PAUL (F.S.A.T.)
Bass Strait
NEW ZEALAND
Wellington
TASMANIA
Hobart
SOUTH ISLAND
CHATHAM IS. (N.Z.)
Christchurch
Invercargill
Dunedin
Oc
ILES KERGUÉLEN (F.S.A.T.)
BOUNTY IS. (N.Z.)
ANTIPODES IS. (N.Z.)
AUCKLAND IS. (N.Z.)
HEARD I. (AUSTL.)
CAMPBELL I. (N.Z.)
MC DONALD IS. (AUSTL.)
MACQUARIE I. (AUSTL.)
SHACKLETON ICE SHELF
WEST ICE SHELF
Antarctic Circle
C. GOODENOUGH
C. DARNLEY
BALLENY IS.
MAWSON COAST
WILKES LAND
C. WILLIAMS
C. ADARE
AMERY ICE SHELF
AMERICAN HIGHLAND
VICTORIA LAND
Ross Sea
ROSS I.
MT. EREBUS 12,448 FT.
ROOSEVELT I.
ROSS ICE SHELF
C. MAY
MT. MARKHAM 14,275 FT.
ANTARCTICA
Longitude East of Greenwich
Longitude West of Greenwich
1 75° 2 90° 3 105° 4 120° 5 135° 6 150° 7 165° 8 180° 9 165° 10 150° 11 135°